ENCYCLOPEDIA OF WORLD LITERATURE
in the 20th Century

ENCYCLOPEDIA OF

in the

General Editor

IN THREE VOLUMES

An enlarged and updated edition of the

WORLD LITERATURE

20th Century

Wolfgang Bernard Fleischmann

Professor of Comparative Literature
University of Massachusetts, Amherst

VOLUME 2
G - N

Herder *Lexikon der Weltliteratur im 20. Jahrhundert*

FREDERICK UNGAR PUBLISHING CO.
NEW YORK

Board of Advisers

Contributors to Volume 2

Friedrich Abendroth
Herzmanovsky-Orlando

Claude K. Abraham
Marcel

Ralph M. Aderman
Mencken

Douglas Alden
Lacretelle

Fernando Alegría
Icaza, J.
Mallea
Mistral
Neruda

Ernst Alker
Krusenstjerna
Malmberg

Antonio Soares Amóra
Machado de Assis

David D. Anderson
Iqbal

James Osler Bailey
Hardy

Max Baym
Literary Aesthetics

Pierre Bellaunay
Mac Orlan
Morand

Helmut Bender
Gheorghiu
Just

Bruno Berger
Kaschnitz
Kessel
Maurois
Mehring

Konrad Bieber
Goes
Guéhenno
Guilloux
Martin du Gard

Bharati Mukherjee Blaise
Indian Literature

Anton Böhm
Miller, H.

Joseph E. Bourgeois
Handel-Mazzetti

Carlos Bousoño
Lyric Poetry: Spain

CONTRIBUTORS TO VOLUME 2

Helmut M. Braem
Jens
Lowry

Wilhelm Braun
Musil

Jacques Brenner
Nouveau

Niels C. Brögger
Hoel
Ibsen

Allen B. Brown
Maugham

Calvin S. Brown
Lampedusa

Douglas Brown
Myers

Lee A. Burgess, Jr.
Jones

Colin Campbell
Macleish

Louis Chaigne
Genevoix
Jaloux

R. F. Christian
Korolenko

P. Christophorov
Javorov

Alí Chumacero
Gonzáles Martínez

Arthur B. Coffin
Jeffers

Gustavo Correa
Gallegos
Güiraldes

Patrick Cruttwell
Kipling

Allan Danzig
Nabokov

Donald Davie
Lyric Poetry: England and America

Ann Demaitre
Hungarian Literature

O. Deschartes
Ivanov, V. I.

Anton Dieterich
Gironella

Giorgio Dolfini
Gozzano
Moretti

Wolfgang Drews
Kerr

Richard M. Eastman
Ionesco

Lilo Ebel
Italian Literature

Mauritz Edström
Högberg

Stefan Einarsson
Icelandic Literature

Reidar Ekner
Karlfeldt

Claude Elsen
Malraux

Donald Emerson
Marquand

CONTRIBUTORS TO VOLUME 2

Michel Euvrard
Jammes
Michaux

Richard Exner
Goll

Robert Faesi
Inglin

Zoltan L. Farkas
József

W. B. F. (W. B. Fleischmann)
Ginsberg
Miller, A.

W. B. F. and Jack A. Posin
Gladkov

Nick Aaron Ford
Hughes, L.

Emil Frederiksen
Hansen
Jørgensen
Knudsen
Michaelis, K.
Michaelis, S.
Munk

Herbert Frenzel
Meyrink
Montale

Melvin J. Friedman
Irish Literature
James

Erhard Friedrichsmeyer
Grass
Johnson, U.

Gerhard Fritsch
Koeppen
Kramer

Josef Fuchs
Miegel

Albert S. Gérard
Hausa Literature
Malagasy Literature

Helmut E. Gerber
Moore, G. A.

Bernard Gicovate
Lugones

Ulrich K. Goldsmith
Kommerell

Sheldon Norman Grebstein
Lewis, S.

Wilhelm Grenzmann
Molo

Hans Grossrieder
Hochwälder
Miłosz, O.

Eugen Gürster
Heym

Marius François Guyard
Gracq

Stanislaus Hafner
Nušić

Lois Hartley
Masters

Erich Heller
Mann, T.

Helmut Henning
Krolow

Jost Hermand
Mombert

ix

Hellmuth Himmel
> *Grotesque in Literature, The*
> *Irony*
> *Morgenstern*

Gerald Hinteregger
> *Mackenzie*

Hans Hinterhäuser
> *Levi*

Charles G. Hoffmann
> *Huxley*

Frederick J. Hoffman
> *Moore, M.*
> *Murdoch*

Johannes Holthusen
> *Jastrun*
> *Kuzmin*
> *Lyric Poetry: Russia*

Alfred Holzinger
> *Jünger, F.*

André Honoré
> *Giraudoux*

Eberhard Horst
> *Kolmar*

Johannes Hösle
> *Gadda*

Virgil Ierunca
> *Goga*
> *Iorga*
> *Istrati*
> *Minulescu*
> *Noailles*

Paul Ilie
> *Jarnés*

Astrid Ivask
> *Latvian Literature*

George Ivask
> *Ivanov, G.*

Ivar Ivask
> *Guillén, J.*
> *Gütersloh*

Janheinz Jahn
> *Guillén, N.*

Oscar Jancke
> *Hesse*

Horst Jarka
> *Lewis, A.*

Bruce Johnson
> *Green, H.*

John H. Johnston
> *Gascoyne*

Joseph Jones
> *New Zealand Literature*

Brigitte Kahr
> *Loti*

Andrée Kail
> *Gary*

Carl Keilhau
> *Grieg*
> *Hamsun*
> *Heiberg*

Hugh Kenner
> *Joyce*

Elizabeth M. Kerr
> *Interior Monologue*

Lilyan Kesteloot-Lagneau and Emile Snyder
> *Neo-African Literature*

Kay H. Kim
> *Korean Literature*

x

Fritz Knöller
Gaiser

Heinrich Krämer
Hjortø

Magnus Jan Krynski
Hłasko

Helmut Kuhn
Lewis, C. S.

Heinrich Kunstmann
Hašek

Eugen Kuri
Henry
Kerouac

Kai Laitinen
Hellaakoski

Betty Rita Gomez Lance
López Albújar

Richard H. Lawson
Kafka

Marie T. Lehn
Hofmannsthal

Diana E. Lestourgeon
Lehmann

Robert W. Lewis, Jr.
Hemingway

Gerhard Loose
Jünger, E.

George Luckyi
Katayev

Antanas Maceina
Maironis
Mykolaitis

Charles A. Madison
Hirschbein
Leivick

Hans Albert Maier
George

Lina Mainiero
Móricz

Paul A. Mankin
Jouvet

Otto Mann
Halbe

Sister Maria Humiliata, I.S.M.
Mauriac, F.

Vladimir Markov
Khlebnikov
Mandelstamm
Mayakovski

Eudo C. Mason
Kassner
Masefield

Sigrid V. Massenbach
Maurras

Herbert McArthur
Menen

Edwin McClellan
Natsume

E. Allen McCormick
Keyserling

Frederick P. W. McDowell
Glasgow

Ulrich Melzer
Kasack

Margaret Kober Merzbach
Kaiser
Le Fort

John Michalski
Gombrowicz

xi

CONTRIBUTORS TO VOLUME 2

Charles Moeller
Gide

Emir Rodríguez Monegal
Ibarbourou

Marcel Moussy
North African Literature: French Language

David J. Niederauer
Loüys
Maeterlinck

Elisabeth Nonnenmacher
Hviezdoslav
Jesenský
Kukučín

Otto Oberholzer
Norwegian Literature

Helmut Olles
Gascar

Kurt Opitz
Jahnn

Ants Oras
Hindrey

Harold Orel
Lindsay
Millay

Sergio Pacifici
Moravia

Karl O. Paetel
Koestler
Lawrence, T. E.

Marian Pehowski
Kawabata

Jean Perrette
Jouhandeau

xii

Carol Petersen
Mann, K.

Fran Petré
Gradnik

Donald Sanford Petrey, Jr.
Mauriac, C.

Spire Pitou
Lesort

Jack A. Posin and W. B. F.
Gladkov

Eva Preiß
Holz
Klepper

Cecil Price
Hughes, R.

Peter Prochnik
Nossack

Gregory Rabassa
Meireles

Bernhard Rang
Linde

Walter A. Reichart
Hauptmann, G.

Herbert Reichert
Nietzsche

Karel Reijnders
Heijermans
Marsman

Henry H. H. Remak
Novella

Joseph Reményi
Karinthy
Kassák
Kosztolányi

Justin Replogle
Macneice

Guenther C. Rimbach
Hartlaub

Fred C. Robinson
Linguistics and Literature

Peter P. Rohde
Gjellerup
Herdal
Jensen
Kirk
Klitgaard
Kristensen

Isidora Rosenthal-Kamarinea
Greek Literature
Myrivilis

Anton M. Rothbauer
Gálvez
González Prada
Icaza, F. A. de

Earl Rovit
Hawkes
Malamud

Horst Rüdiger
Marotta

Raymond S. Sayers
Morales, R.
Morales, T.

George D. Schade
Herrera y Reissig

Georges Schlocker
Jouve

Paul Schlueter
McCarthy

Franz K. Schneider
Naturalism

Albert Arnold Scholl
Lyric Poetry: Germany

Gertrude Schwebell
Greene
Jarrell
Kazantzakis
Laxness
Lowell
Mailer
Molnár

Frank Sedwick
Madariaga

Ingo Seidler
Hauptmann, C.
Huelsenbeck
Klabund
Münchhausen

Jules Paul Seigel
Housman

R. Baird Shuman
Green, P. E.

Rimvydas Silbajoris
Lithuanian Literature

Grover Smith
Isherwood

Emile Snyder and Lilyan Kesteloot-Lagneau
Neo-African Literature

J. P. L. Snyman
Millin

Gonzalo Sobejano
García Lorca
Gómez de la Serna
Hernández
Hidalgo
Jiménez
Machado y Ruiz, A.
Machado y Ruiz, M.
Miró

CONTRIBUTORS TO VOLUME 2

xiv

John B. Vickery
Graves

Robert B. Voitle
Nin

Werner Vordtriede
Macaulay

Ernst Waldinger
Herrmann-Neisse

Florence L. Walzl
Nash

Howard W. Webb, Jr.
Lardner

Harvey Curtis Webster
Hartley

Irwin Weil
Gorki

Kurt Weinberg
Gourmont
Huysmans
Jacob
Jarry
Lyric Poetry: France
Mirbeau

René Wellek
Literary Criticism

John C. Weston
Maccaig
MacDiarmid

Franz Weyergans
Ghéon
Giono

Kenneth S. White
Lenormand
Neveux

Per Wieselgren
Heidenstam

Paul Wimmer
Ghelderode
Guareschi
Kokoschka
Kubin
Kurz
Mansfield
Meersch
Mell
Neumann

Johanna Wolf
Machar
Medek

Friedrich W. Wollenberg
Huch, R.
Kästner, Erhart

Günther Wytrzens
Halas
Holeček
Hora
Ivanov, V. V.
Khodasevich

Peter Yershov
Klychkov
Kuprin

Theodore Ziolkowski
German Literature

Leon M. Zolbrod
Ishikawa
Japanese Literature

Abbreviations for Periodicals, Volume 2

AALIAM	Arcadia, Accademia Letteraria Italiana. Atti e Memorie	*DramS*	Drama Survey (Minneapolis)
AL	American Literature	*DRs*	Deutsche Rundschau
APh	Acta Philologica (Roma: Societas Academica Dacoromana)	*DS*	Danske Studier
		DubR	Dublin Review (London)
AQ	American Quarterly	*DVLG*	Deutsche Vierteljahrsschrift für Literaturwissenschaft und Geistesgeschichte
ArL	Archivum Linguisticum		
ArQ	Arizona Quarterly		
AUC	Anales de la Universidad de Chile	*EA*	Études Anglaises
		EG	Études Germaniques
BA	Books Abroad	*EIC*	Essays in Criticism (Oxford)
BB	Bulletin of Bibliography	*EJ*	English Journal
BHS	Bulletin of Hispanic Studies		
		FdL	Forum der Letteren
		FH	Frankfurter Hefte
CathW	Catholic World	*FL*	Figaro Littéraire
CCa	Civiltà Cattolica	*FLe*	Fiera Letteraria
CE	College English	*FR*	French Review
CHA	Cuadernos Hispanoamericanos (Madrid)	*FS*	French Studies
ChC	Chinese Culture	*GaR*	Georgia Review
ChiR	Chicago Review	*Gids*	De Gids
CL	Comparative Literature	*GL&L*	German Life and Letters
CLAJ	College Language Association Journal (Morgan State Coll., Baltimore)	*GQ*	German Quarterly
		GR	Germanic Review
		GRM	Germanisch-romanische Monatsschrift, Neue Folge
CMLR	Canadian Modern Language Review		
CPe	Castrum Peregrini	*HSS*	Harvard Slavic Studies
Crit	Critique: Studies in Modern Fiction	*HudR*	Hudson Review
CritQ	Critical Quarterly	*ICS*	L'Italia che Scrive
CS	Cahiers du Sud	*ILA*	International Literary Annual (London)
DA	Dissertation Abstracts	*IQ*	Italian Quarterly
DR	Dalhousie Review	*ISS*	Indiana Slavic Studies

JAAC	Journal of Aesthetics and Art Criticism		*RI*	Revista Iberoamericana
JGE	Journal of General Education		*RLI*	Rassegna della Letteratura Italiana
JGG	Jahrbuch der Grillparzer-Gesellschaft		*RLM*	La Revue des Lettres Modernes
JHI	Journal of the History of Ideas		*RMS*	Renaissance and Modern Studies (Univ. of Nottingham)
KR	Kenyon Review		*RomN*	Romance Notes (Univ. of North Carolina)
MD	Modern Drama		*RUL*	Revue de l'Université d'Ottawa
MdF	Mercure de France		*SatR*	Saturday Review
MFS	Modern Fiction Studies		*SCB*	The South Central Bulletin (Tulsa, Okla., Studies by Members of the South Central MLA)
MinnR	Minnesota Review			
ML	Modern Languages (London)			
MLJ	Modern Language Journal			
MLN	Modern Language Notes		*SEEJ*	Slavic and East European Journal
MLQ	Modern Language Quarterly		*SEER*	Slavonic and East European Review
MLR	Modern Language Review			
			SI	Svizzera Italiana
NDH	Neue Deutsche Hefte		*SlavR*	Slavic Review (Seattle)
NDQ	North Dakota Quarterly		*SLT*	Svensk Litteraturtidskrift
NL	Nouvelles Littéraires		*SoR*	Southern Review (Louisiana State Univ.)
NM	Neuphilologische Mitteilungen			
NRF	Nouvelle Revue Française		*SP*	Studies in Philology
NSammlung	Neue Sammlung		*SR*	Sewanee Review
NTg	De Nieuwe Taalgids		*SRo*	Studi Romani
NVT	Nieuw Vlaams Tijdschrift		*SS*	Scandinavian Studies
NY	New Yorker		*SSL*	Studies in Scottish Literature (Texas Technological Coll., Lubbock)
PBA	Proceedings of the British Academy			
PMLA	Publications of the Modern Language Association of America		*TamR*	Tamarack Review (Toronto)
			TCL	Twentieth Century Literature
PolR	Polish Review (New York)		*TDR*	Tulane Drama Review
PR	Partisan Review		*TLS*	Times Literary Supplement (London)
PSA	Papeles de Son Armadans (Mallorca)			
			TM	Temps Modernes
			TR	La Table Ronde
RCB	Revista de Cultura Brasileña		*TSLL*	Studies in Literature and Language (Univ. of Texas)
RealM	Realtà del Mezzogiorno			
RESl	Revue des Études Slaves			
RFE	Revista de Filología Española		*UKCR*	University of Kansas City Review
RGB	Revue Générale Belge		*UTQ*	University of Toronto Quarterly
RHL	Revue d'Histoire Littéraire de la France			
			VQR	Virginia Quarterly Review
RHM	Revista Hispánica Moderna		*WHR*	Western Humanities Review

xviii

WPQ	Western Political Quarterly (Univ. of Utah)		*YCGL*	Yearbook of Comparative and General Literature (Indiana Univ.)
WSCL	Wisconsin Studies in Contemporary Literature		*YFS*	Yale French Studies
WuWahr	Wort und Wahrheit		*YR*	Yale Review
WZ	Wort in der Zeit (Vienna)			
WZUB	Wissenschaftliche Zeitschrift der Humboldt-Universität zu Berlin. Gesellschafts-und Sprachwissenschaftliche Reihe			

Illustrations

ILLUSTRATIONS

Acknowledgments

RÓMULO GALLEGOS	OAS Photos, Washington, D. C.
JOHN GALSWORTHY	Bildarchiv Herder, Freiburg im Breisgau
FEDERICO GARCÍA LORCA	Bildarchiv Herder, Freiburg im Breisgau
DAVID GARNETT	Lucilla Sherrard and The Viking Press, Inc., N. Y.
JEAN GENET	Jerry Bauer and Grove Press, Inc., N. Y.
STEFAN GEORGE	Bildarchiv Herder, Freiburg im Breisgau
ANDRÉ GIDE	Süddeutscher Verlag, Munich
MARNIX GIJSEN	Bildarchiv Herder, Freiburg im Breisgau
MAURICE GILLIAMS	Bildarchiv Herder, Freiburg im Breisgau
JEAN GIRAUDOUX	Verlag Ullstein, Berlin
KARL ADOLPH GJELLERUP	Royal Danish Ministry for Foreign Affairs, Copenhagen
MAKSIM GORKI	Historia-Foto, Berlin
GÜNTER GRASS	German Information Center, N. Y.
ROBERT GRAVES	Doubleday & Company, Inc., N. Y.
JULIEN GREEN	French Cultural Services, N. Y.
GRAHAM GREENE	Islay Lyons and The Viking Press, Inc., N. Y.
GIOVANNINO GUARESCHI	Istituto Italiano di Cultura, N. Y.
KRISTMANN GUÐMUNDSSON	Consulate General of Iceland, N. Y.
JORGE GUILLÉN	Dr. Ivar Ivask
GUNNAR GUNNARSSON	Consulate General of Iceland, N. Y.
GUÐMUNDUR HAGALÍN	Consulate General of Iceland, N. Y.
PER HALLSTRÖM	Swedish Information Service, N. Y.
KNUT HAMSUN	Süddeutscher Verlag, Munich
MARTIN HANSEN	Royal Danish Ministry for Foreign Affairs, Copenhagen
THOMAS HARDY	The Bettmann Archive, N. Y.
JAROSLAV HAŠEK	Line drawing by Mr. Francis Reisz, from a photograph
GERHART HAUPTMANN	Verlag Ullstein, Berlin
ERNEST HEMINGWAY	Süddeutscher Verlag, Munich
HERMANN HESSE	Martin Hesse SWB., Bern
MAREK HŁASKO	E. P. Dutton & Co., Inc., N. Y.
HUGO VON HOFMANNSTHAL	Bildarchiv Herder, Freiburg im Breisgau
RICARDA HUCH	Fritz Eschen, Berlin
LANGSTON HUGHES	John Taylor and Alfred A. Knopf, Inc., N. Y.
ALDOUS HUXLEY	Bildarchiv Herder, Freiburg im Breisgau
EUGÈNE IONESCO	Jerry Bauer and Grove Press, Inc., N. Y.
MOHAMMAD IQBAL	Line drawing by Mr. Francis Reisz, from a photograph
HENRY JAMES	United States Information Service, Bad Godesberg
FRANCIS JAMMES	Verlag Ullstein, Berlin
JOHANNES JENSEN	Royal Danish Ministry for Foreign Affairs, Copenhagen
JUAN RAMÓN JIMÉNEZ	Verlag Ullstein, Berlin
EYVIND JOHNSON	Swedish Information Service, N. Y.
JOHANNES JØRGENSEN	Royal Danish Ministry for Foreign Affairs, Copenhagen
JAMES JOYCE	Ulrike Friedrich-Schreiber, Starnberg
ERNST JÜNGER	Neske-Verlag, Pfullingen
FRANZ KAFKA	Bildarchiv Herder, Freiburg im Breisgau
GEORG KAISER	Line drawing by Mr. Francis Reisz, from a photograph

ACKNOWLEDGMENTS

GUÐMUNDUR KAMBAN	Consulate General of Iceland, N. Y.
KAWABATA YASUNARI	Harold Strauss and Alfred A. Knopf, Inc., N. Y.
VOLTER KILPI	Consulate General of Finland, N. Y.
RUDYARD KIPLING	The Bettmann Archive, N. Y.
ARTHUR KOESTLER	Horst Tappe and Camera Press-Pix, N. Y.
KARL KRAUS	Verlag Otto Müller, Salzburg
TOM KRISTENSEN	Royal Danish Ministry for Foreign Affairs, Copenhagen
PÄR LAGERKVIST	Bildarchiv Herder, Freiburg im Breisgau
SELMA LAGERLÖF	Verlag Ullstein, Berlin
GIUSEPPE DI LAMPEDUSA	Pantheon Books, Inc., N. Y.
ELISABETH LANGGÄSSER	Käthe Augenstein, Bonn
RING LARDNER	Charles Scribner's Sons, N. Y.
D. H. LAWRENCE	The Viking Press, Inc., N. Y.
HALLDÓR LAXNESS	Suhrkamp Verlag, Frankfurt am Main
GERTRUD LE FORT	Th. Ruminy, Oberstdorf-Reute
CARLO LEVI	Mondadori Press, Milan
PIERRE LOTI	French Cultural Services, N. Y.
ROBERT LOWELL	The New York Times, N. Y.
JOAQUIM MACHADO DE ASSIS	OAS Photos, Washington, D. C.
ARCHIBALD MACLEISH	Antony Di Gesú and Houghton Mifflin Company, Boston
SALVADOR DE MADARIAGA	Frederick A. Praeger, Inc., N. Y.
MAURICE MAETERLINCK	Süddeutscher Verlag, Munich
NORMAN MAILER	The New York Times, N. Y.
BERNARD MALAMUD	Paul De Vries-Pix, N. Y.
ANDRÉ MALRAUX	Wilfried Göpel, Berlin
HEINRICH MANN	Verlag Ullstein, Berlin
THOMAS MANN	Fritz Eschen, Berlin
W. SOMERSET MAUGHAM	Editta Sherman and Doubleday & Company, Inc., N. Y.
FRANÇOIS MAURIAC	French Cultural Services, N. Y.
ANDRÉ MAUROIS	French Cultural Services, N. Y.
MARY McCARTHY	Horst Tappe and Camera Press-Pix
H. L. MENCKEN	The Bettmann Archive, N. Y.
HENRI MICHAUX	Gisèle Freund, Paris
EDNA ST. VINCENT MILLAY	The Bettmann Archive, N. Y.
HENRY MILLER	Cedric Wright and Grove Press, Inc., N. Y.
GABRIELA MISTRAL	Bildarchiv Herder, Freiburg im Breisgau
CARL MOBERG	Swedish Information Service, N. Y.
HENRY DE MONTHERLANT	Verlag Kiepenheuer & Witsch, Cologne
MARIANNE MOORE	The Viking Press, Inc., N. Y.
ALBERTO MORAVIA	Istituto Italiano di Cultura, N. Y.
KAI MUNK	Royal Danish Ministry for Foreign Affairs, Copenhagen
IRIS MURDOCH	The Viking Press, Inc., N. Y.
ROBERT MUSIL	Bildarchiv Herder, Freiburg im Breisgau
VLADIMIR NABOKOV	Horst Tappe and Pix, Inc., N. Y.
OGDEN NASH	Kay Bell and Little, Brown and Company, Boston
PABLO NERUDA	Bertil Dahlgren and Camera Press-Pix, Inc., N. Y.

ENCYCLOPEDIA OF WORLD LITERATURE
in the 20th Century

G

GADDA, Carlo Emilio
Italian novelist, b. 14 Nov. 1893, Milan

G. volunteered for military service in World War I and in 1918 was a prisoner of war in Germany. From 1920 to 1935 he worked as an engineer in various countries, including the Argentine, France, and Germany.

G.'s literary work is marked by avoidance of emotionalism and rhetoric; his feelings are veiled by a caustic irony. His metaphors, often taken from the field of technology, counterbalance the spontaneity of his perceptions. Even in his first vast work, the novel *La Madonna dei filosofi* (1931), G. was already mercilessly analyzing the daily lives of his characters, while avoiding all facile effects. He enriched his vocabulary by drawing upon colloquial and dialect forms. The war novel *Il castello di Udine* (1934) presents a prototype of the masculine attitude toward the inevitable. The virtuosity of his humorous sketches of Milan collected in *L'Adalgisa* (1944) recalls baroque forms. Here G. shows an impressive familiarity with all fields of knowledge.

G.'s *Novelle dal ducato in fiamme* (1953) received a literary award. In his novel *Quel pasticciaccio brutto di via Merulana* (1957; That Awful Mess on the Via Merulana, 1965), G. produced a panoramic picture of fascist Italy. It reveals a virtuosity nurtured on the Milanese *scapigliatura* (bohemianism), the Spanish baroque, and Jean Paul (1763-1825).

FURTHER WORKS: *Gagliardi* (1932); *Le meraviglie d'Italia* (1939); *Gli anni* (1943); *Il primo libro delle favole* (1952); *Giornale di guerra e di prigionia* (1955); *I sogni e la folgore* (1955); *I viaggi la morte* (1958); *Verso*

la Certosa (1961); *La cognizione del dolore* (1963; Acquainted with Grief, 1969); *I racconti: accoppiamenti giudiziosi, 1924-58* (1963); *I Luigi di Francia* (1964); *Il guerriero* (1967)

BIBLIOGRAPHY: Fusio, M., "L'oeuvre de G.," in *Critique* (Paris), XIX (1963), 21-32; on *That Awful Mess on the Via Merulana—The New York Times* (29 Aug. 1965), p. 5; *Nation* (1 Nov. 1965), p. 306

JOHANNES HÖSLE

GAISER, Gerd
German novelist and art critic, b. 15 Sept. 1908, Oberriexingen, Enz Valley

G., a descendant of Swabian pastors, left the theological seminary in Urach to become a painter. He traveled in Spain, served as an air force officer during World War II, worked as a lumberjack after Germany's collapse, and finally became a drawing teacher at the Reutlinger *Gymnasium*.

Politically disillusioned by the war like many of his generation, G. sought an inner certainty to cling to and found it in man's ability to stand the test. Accordingly he loves the man who, heart-stricken at the evil of the world, fights fearlessly and remains true to himself. In *Die sterbende Jagd* (1953; The Last Squadron, 1956), an air force squadron, knowing itself betrayed by the regime, nevertheless maintains decency and dignity in its desperate situation. In *Eine Stimme hebt an* (1950) a returning soldier, finding his country devastated and its inhabitants morally bankrupt, sets an example by laying the foundation for a new life of integrity. The geological epic, *Das Schiff im Berg* (1955), shows how

3

man, representing a higher level of creation, holds his own amid the ceaseless conflict of the elements. G.'s novel *Schlußball* (1958; The Final Ball, 1960) depicts the activity of a small town from the widely differing viewpoints of the various characters. This kaleidoscopic picture symbolizes the soulless, technically advanced world laid bare by G., the champion of a true life.

G.'s volumes of novellas, *Zwischenland* (1949) and *Einmal und oft* (1956), make it poignantly clear that man is at the mercy of the higher powers of fate and of omnipresent death. *Sizilianische Notizen* (1959) fuses myth and man to produce a portrait of the ancient Mediterranean land of Sicily.

FURTHER WORKS: *Reiter am Himmel* (1941); *Revanche* (1956; 2nd revised ed., 1961); *Gianna aus dem Schatten* (1957); *Aniela* (1958); *Damals in Promischur* (1959); *Gib acht in Domokosch* (1959); *Am Paß Nascondo* (1960); *Alte Meister der modernen Malerei* (1963); *Tempel Siziliens* (1963); *Gazelle, Grün* (1965); *Die schönsten Städte Baden-Würtembergs* (1966); *Vergeblicher Gang* (1967)

BIBLIOGRAPHY: on "The Final Ball," *NYT* (14 Feb. 1960), p. 4; Hohoff, C., *G.G.: Werk und Gestalt* (1962); Reich-Ranicki, M., "Der Fall G.G.," in *Monat*, XV (1963), 68–84
FRITZ KNÖLLER

GAŁCZYŃSKI, Konstanty Ildefons
Polish dramatist and poet, b. 23 Jan. 1906, Warsaw; d. 6 Dec. 1953, Warsaw

G.'s work consists mainly of plays with a fantastic element which bears witness to an amazing imagination. His world is one of magic, legerdemain, and perpetual metamorphosis. His writing is a mixture of poetry, satire, and cabaret-type songs. It is perhaps comprehensible only to those familiar with the specific Polish mentality, with its tendency to romantic pathos counterbalanced by self-irony and macabre humor. His work includes "one minute plays," published between 1946 and 1948 in the Cracow weekly *Przekrój* under the running title "Zielona Geś."

G. was greatly esteemed for his influence as an avant-gardist and for his literary culture.

WORKS: *Porfirion Osielek* (1929); *Koniec świata* (1930); *Zabawa ludowa* (1934); *Utwory poetyckie* (1937); *Wiersze wybrane* (1938);

Zaczarowana dorozka (1948); *Niobe* (1953); *Wybór wierszy* (1954); *Wiersze* (1956); *Satyra, groteska, zart liryczny* (expanded, 1957); *Liryka, 1926–1953* (1962)

BIBLIOGRAPHY: Blónski, J., *G.* (1955)

* * *

GALLEGOS, Rómulo
Venezuelan novelist, b. 2 Aug. 1884, Caracas, Venezuela; d. there, 4 April 1969

G. studied in the city of his birth, and for a long time was a teacher in secondary schools. He played an active part in the political life of his country, becoming a senator in 1929 and Minister of Education in 1936. From 1941 to 1948 he served as President of the Republic. The period 1931–36 he spent in voluntary exile in Spain, where he published several of his novels. Like the rest of his work, these describe the landscape and people of Venezuela.

G. began his literary career with short stories. His first novel, *El último Solar* (1920; in later eds. entitled *Reinaldo Solar*), depicts social conditions in the interior of Venezuela. Its unstable hero, incapable of any effective effort, symbolizes the inner confusion of the equally immature country, *La trepadora* (1925) describes the clash between the plebeians and the old aristocracy and the attempt to shape a new society in an environment dominated by rural tradition. *Doña Bárbara* (1929), which is considered G.'s major work, describes the conflict between civilization and barbarism, but is also an epico-lyric hymn in praise of the Venezuelan lowlands. The poetry of the country is brought out again in *Cantaclaro* (1931), which depicts the adventurous life of a traveling magician. In *Canaima* (1935) the primeval forest takes on an almost demonic aspect. *Pobre Negro* (1937) deals with the life of the rural proletariat in the hot Tuy Valley.

FURTHER WORKS: *Los aventureros* (1913); *El forastero* (1945); *Sobre la misma tierra* (1947); *Novelas escogidas* (2 vols., 1951); *La brizna de paja en el viento* (1952); *Obras completas* (1958)

BIBLIOGRAPHY: Damboriena, A., *R.G. y la problemática venezolana* (1960); anon., "Search for a Country's Soul" [revised article on R.G.], in *TLS* (10 Feb. 1961), p. 88; Bellini, G., *Il romanzo di R.G.* (1962); Allen,

RÓMULO GALLEGOS

JOHN GALSWORTHY

R.F., "Social and Political Thought in the Early Narrative of R.G.," in *DA*, XXV (1964), 1901; Consalvi, S.A., *R.G., el hombre y su escenario* (1964); Hyde, J. E., "The Function of Symbol in the Novels of R.G.," in *DA*, XXV (1965), 3573–74

GUSTAVO CORREA

GALSWORTHY, John

(pseuds.: *John Sinjohn, A.R.P.–M.*), English novelist, dramatist, and critic, b. 14 Aug. 1867, Kingston Hill, Surrey; d. 31 Jan. 1933, London

G. was born to wealth; his father was a successful London solicitor and director of companies. G. was educated at Harrow School and at Oxford, where he dutifully read law (although called to the bar, his interest in law was slight), lived the life of a wealthy young man in London, and traveled extensively. A crisis occurred when in 1895 he and Ada, his cousin's wife, became lovers. With her encouragement (after her divorce, G. and Ada married in 1905) he decided to become a writer.

Influenced by Turgenev, Maupassant, and Tolstoi (q.v.), he spent the years 1897–1901 learning his craft, and in the process produced two volumes of short stories and two novels. His third novel, *The Island Pharisees* (1904), was, despite weaknesses, his first important literary achievement. *The Man of Property* (1906) was his first full-length treatment of the Forsytes and is an acknowledged masterpiece. In 1906 G. also began his career as a dramatist with *The Silver Box.*

G. established himself as a leading novelist and playwright, and world fame came with the publication of *The Forsyte Saga*, a trilogy consisting of three satiric novels (*The Man of Property*, 1906; *In Chancery*, 1920; *To Let*, 1921) and two connecting lyric interludes (*Indian Summer of a Forsyte*, 1918; *Awakening*, 1920). He continued his study of the Forsytes in a second trilogy, *A Modern Comedy*, comprising *The White Monkey* (1924), *The Silver Spoon* (1926), and *Swan Song* (1928), and two further interludes (*A Silent Wooing* and *Passers By*), both published in 1927. His last major work was a trilogy devoted to the Charwell family, *End of the Chapter* (*Maid in Waiting*, 1931; *Flowering Wilderness*, 1932; *Over the River* [Am., One More River], 1933). Although G. refused a knighthood in 1918 for his literary achievements, he accepted the Order of Merit in 1929 and the Nobel Prize for Literature in 1932.

Of his non-Forsyte writings *Fraternity* (1909) is one of his finest novels, and of his plays *Strife* (produced 1909), *Justice* (produced 1910), and *Loyalties* (produced 1922), are three of his most compelling.

By the 1920's G. had the reputation of a literary giant, but much of his fame rested on the mistaken belief that he was a sociological writer whose satiric analyses of man and society were photographically lifelike. Although this belief still prevails, present-day critical evaluation of his work poses a very different viewpoint: since the society he chronicled and the causes he espoused are now past history, G. is dismissed as an out-of-date social historian. However, if the emphasis on the sociological aspect of his writings is a mistaken one, it is evident that G.'s work should be examined anew and on its own terms as literature. G.'s achievement is clearly greater than his present reputation would allow; indeed, he may justly be considered the last great Victorian novelist.

An important statement of G.'s artistic creed is "A Novelist's Allegory" (1909). The allegory tells of an old man, Cethru, who as a nightwatchman aids passers-by as they traverse dark streets. Because the light from his lantern shone on some unpleasant scenes, Cethru is accused of criminal intent. In his defense the point is made that the lantern impartially reveals both good and evil and shows the true proportion of things to one another. In G.'s view the artist is important because he is the discoverer of truth or spiritual proportion. Beauty and art (profound embodiments of the spiritual, the humane, and the civilizing) are the cornerstones of his humanitarianism. G. thought the phrase "spiritual realist" fairly accurately characterized his work, and although he used immediate and specific details to give his writings the solidity of reality, his ultimate concern was to evoke spiritual reality and human insight.

FURTHER WORKS: *From the Four Winds* (1897); *Jocelyn* (1898); *Villa Rubein* (1900); *A Man of Devon* (1901); *Caravan* (1905; 2nd ed., 1925); *Joy* (1907); *The Country House* (1907); *A Commentary* (1908); *A Justification of the Censorship of Plays* (1909); *Plays* (1909); *A Motley* (1910); *The Spirit of Punishment* (1910); *The Little Dream: An*

Allegory (1911); *The Patrician* (1911); *The Eldest Son* (1912); *The Pigeon* (1912); *The Inn of Tranquillity* (1912); *Moods, Songs and Doggerels* (1912); *For the Love of Beasts* (1912); *The Slaughter of Animals for Food* (1913); *The Dark Flower* (1913); *The Fugitive* (1913); *The Mob* (1914); *The Army Veterinary Corps* (1915); *The Freelands* (1915); *A Bit O' Love* ([suppressed 1st ed., *The Full Moon*], 1915); *The Little Man and Other Satires* (1916); *A Sheaf* (1916); *Your Christmas Dinner Is Served* (1916); *Five Tales* (1918); *The Apple Tree* (1918); *The Children's Jewel Fund* (1918); *The Land: A Plea* (1918); *Five Poems* (1919); *Saint's Progress* (1919); *Addresses in America* (1919); *Another Sheaf* (1919); *The Burning Spear* (1919); *Awakening* (1920); *The Foundations* (1920); *The Skin Game* (1920); *Tatterdemalion* (1920); *The Bells of Peace* (1921); *Six Short Plays* (1921); *A Family Man* (1922); *Windows* (1922); *Works* (25 vols., 1922-29); *Captures* (1923); *International Thought* (1923); *Memorable Days* (1924); *On Expression* (1924); *Abracadabra and Other Satires* (1924); *The Forest* (1924); *Old English* (1924); *Is England Done For?* (1925); *The Show* (1925); *Escape* (1926); *Verses New and Old* (1926); *A Talk on Playing the Game with Animals and Birds* (1926); *The Way to Prepare Peace* (1927); *Castles in Spain and Other Screeds* (1927); *Mr. G.'s Appeal for the Miners* (1928); *Exiled* (1929); *The Roof* (1929); *A Rambling Discourse* (1929); *On Forsyte Change* (1930); *Two Essays on Conrad* (1930); *The Creation of Character in Literature* (1931); *Literature and Life* (1931); *Candelabra* (1932); *Autobiographical Letters of J.G.: A Correspondence with Frank Harris* (1933); *Author and Critic* (1933); *Letters from J.G. 1900-1932* (Garnett, C., ed., 1934); *The Winter Garden* (1935); *Forsyte, Pendycars and Others* (1935); *Selected Short Stories* (1935); *Glimpses and Reflections* (1937)

BIBLIOGRAPHY: Chevrillon, A., *Three Studies in English Literature: Kipling, G., Shakespeare* (1923); Marrot, H. V., *The Life and Letters of J.G.* (1935); Dupont, V., *J.G.: The Dramatic Artist* (1942); Mottram, R. H., *For Some We Loved: An Intimate Portrait of Ada and J.G.* (1956); Ross, W. O., "J.G.: Aspects of an Attitude," in *Studies in Honor of John Wilcox* (Wallace, A. D., and Ross, W. O., eds., 1958); Stevens, E. E., "J. G.: An Annotated Bibliography of Writings About Him," *ELT*, I (1958), iii, 7-29, and VII (1964),

ii, 93-110; Choudhuri, A. D., *G.'s Plays* (1962); Barker, D., *The Man of Principle: A Biography of J. G.* (1969)

EARL E. STEVENS

GÁLVEZ, Manuel

Argentinian narrative writer, b. 18 July 1882, Paraná; d. 14 Nov. 1962, Buenos Aires

In 1903 G. was editor of the literary magazine *Ideas*. He became known throughout the Spanish-speaking world with *El solar de la raza* (1911), a literary account of his travels in Spain. His novels *La maestra normal* (1914) and *Nacha Regules* (1920) stand squarely in the realistic-naturalistic tradition. A better work from the literary point of view is *Historia del arrabal* (1922, 1956), a description of life in a dock district whose characters are given poetic depth. The setting of *El mal metafísico* (1916) is the milieu of the Buenos Aires literati.

Within the specifically Argentinian novel G., breaking away from the gaucho theme in favor of historical subjects, perhaps did for Argentina what Pérez Galdós (q.v.) did for Spain with his *Episodios Nacionales*. The war waged by the Argentine, Brazil, and Uruguay against the Paraguayan dictator Francisco Solana López from 1864 to 1870 is depicted in great detail, right up to its shocking culmination in the ruin of a nation, in the trilogy *Escenas de la guerra del Paraguay* (1928-29). G.'s handling of this powerful subject is a triumph of novelistic technique. The novel triology *Escenas de la época de Rosas* (1931-33) is a similar treatment of Argentinian history centered on the dictator Rosas and the country's internal struggles in the 1850's and 1860's.

FURTHER WORKS: *La sombra del convento* (1917); *Luna de miel y otras narraciones* (1920); *La tragedia de un hombre fuerte* (1922); *El cántico espiritual* (1923); *La pampa y su pasión* (1926); *Una mujer muy moderna* (1927); *Miércoles Santo* (1930); *Hombres en soledad* (1938); *La cuidad pintada de rojo* (1947); *La vida perfecta de Ceferino Namuncura* (1949); *Obras escogidas* (1949); *Tránsito Guzmán* (1956); *La noche toca a su fin* (1956); *Los caminos de la muerte* (1957); *Poemas para la recién llegada 1954-1956* (1957); *Vida de Aparicio Saravia* (1957); *Perdido en su noche* (1958); *Humanitá* (1959); *Jornadas de agonia* (1959); *Recuerdos de la vida literaria* (1961); *La tragedia de un hombre fuerte* (1961); *Me mataron entre todos* (1962); *Vida del fray Mamerto Esquiú* (1962); *Las dos vidas del pobre Napoleón* (1963); *José Hernández* (1964)

BIBLIOGRAPHY: Lichtblau, M. I., "The Recent Novels of M. G.," in *Hispania,* XLII (1959), 502-5; Turner, E., "Hispanism in the Life of M. G.," in *DA,* XIX (1959), 3311; Stevens, L. E., "Feminine Protagonists in M. G.'s Novels," in *DA,* XXVI (1965), 1050-51

ANTON M. ROTHBAUER

GARCÍA CALDERÓN, Ventura

Peruvian short story writer, poet, critic, journalist, and essayist (French and Spanish languages), b. 23 Feb. 1886, Paris; d. 28 Oct. 1959, Paris

In his youth G. lived in Paris and was associated with the modernist movement. There he edited the *Revista de América,* which reported on literary and intellectual events in Latin America; later he edited several Latin American periodicals. In his volumes of letters, *Frívolamente* (1908), *En la verbena de Madrid* (1920), and *Sonrisas de Paris* (1926) he brought the contemporary poets and writers of Spain and France to the attention of Peru. He later served as Peru's ambassador to Belgium (1935) and to Switzerland (1940).

G. is one of the most important writers of fiction and criticism in Latin America. In his novellas, *La venganza del cóndor* (1924), and his collection of lyric prose pieces, *Cantilenas* (1920), there are overtones of both romanticism and Peruvian folklore; his fictions about Peru are short, realistic, and dramatic, though at times the country is transformed into an exotic imaginary place of romance. G.'s style is always elegant, and his work is noted for its harmonious structures.

FURTHER WORKS: *Del romanticismo al modernismo en el Perú* (1910); *Literatura peruana 1535-1914* (1914); *Dolorosa y desnuda realidad* (1914); *Literatura uruguaya 1757-1917* (1917); *El nuevo idioma castellano* (1920); *Semblanza de América* (1920); *Danger de mort* (1926); *Holofernes* (1931); *Couleur de sang* (1931); *Le Sang plus vite* (1936); *Páginas escogidas* (1947); *La Perichole* (1959); *Cuentos peruanos* (1961)

BIBLIOGRAPHY: Barbagelata, H. D., "Ventura G. C.," in *RNM,* IV (1959), 584-86; Salazar Bondy, S., "G. C.: Distancia y soledad," in *RNC,* XXIV (1962), 44-47

* * *

GARCÍA LORCA, Federico

Spanish poet, b. 5 June 1898, Fuentevaqueros, Granada; d. 19 Aug. 1936, Viznar, Granada

G. L. is considered Spain's most important 20th c. poet. After attending school in Almería and Granada he studied literature and law in Granada, becoming imbued with its atmosphere; there he also learned to play the guitar and piano and published his first works. In 1919 he went to Madrid, where he became friendly with the foremost poets of the time, including Jiménez and Alberti (qq.v.), who shared his urge to proclaim Andalusian themes and his popular poetic style, and also Aleixandre, Cernuda, and the Chilean poet Neruda (qq.v.). For a time they all upheld the ideals of surrealism (q.v.).

G. L. became known as an original, restless graphic artist and as the author of several very novel dramatic works, but his interest lay primarily in poetry, to which he almost totally devoted himself in the years 1920 to 1930. The collection *Romancero gitano* in particular established his reputation. After its publication in 1928 success never turned its back on him. Bonds of brotherly friendship linked him with the poets of his own generation, with the composer Manuel de Falla, and with the painter Salvador Dali; together they brought about a heyday of the arts in Spain.

In 1929 G. L. studied at Columbia University in New York. The following year he returned to Spain by way of Cuba, but soon left again for a triumphal visit to South America. As head of the Spanish traveling student theater "La Barraca" he visited many parts of Spain. Shortly after the outbreak of the Civil War, when his genius and his fame were both at their height, G. L. was assassinated by unidentified nationalists.

His first significant lyrical work, *Libro de poemas* (1921), mirrors his childhood and adolescence against the background of the Granada landscape. Although his personality was already emerging, the poet did not yet diverge from the style of modernism or the spirit of his direct models, Jiménez and Antonio Machado (qq.v.). What is new in this work is primarily the lively sensuality, the fresh, down-to-earth approach, the liking for themes drawn from the world of childhood, and the boldness of some of the images. In the subsequent *Poema del Cante Jondo*, written between 1921 and 1922 and published in 1931, the elemental, tragic voice of Andalusia is condensed into images and symbols of an admirable economy of expression. The characteristic melancholy tinge of Andalusian emotions, the spell of the Andalusian earth and the Andalusian soul as they are captured in the music of de Falla, find in G. L. a highly sensitive sounding board. Thus, what was originally no more than the special nature of a Spanish landscape pervaded by oriental beauty and yearning is raised into a universal category of emotion. In G. L.'s next works, *Primeras canciones*, written in 1922 and published in 1936, and *Canciones*, written between 1921 and 1924 and published in 1927, all these characteristics of his poetry are consolidated to reveal a fully matured personality.

One single work, however, insured the immortality of G. L.'s particular genius—a genius which stemmed on the one hand from a very bold imagination and on the other from his completely reliable sense of the popular in its essential form. This was *Romancero gitano* (Gypsy Ballads, 1953), written between 1924 and 1927 and published in 1928, perfect in form, strongly realistic, and appealing directly to a broad spectrum of readers. Although many of the ballads have nothing to do with the gypsy theme, most of them reflect the grace, beauty, pride, and unhappiness of this mercurial race. Their superlative quality lies, however, not in their content but in the brilliant newness of their style, with its concentrated density of expression and its extraordinary imaginative power deriving from a mixture of popular and cultural elements, which radically renews the ancient Castilian "romance" form. Here we find the most sophisticated modernist synesthesia, the powerful imagery of ultraism, the expressive condensation used by Góngora, and the innate Andalusian gracefulness of vision and communication—all combined in a completely modern but nonetheless traditional poetry.

Both in content and form this book, which for the general public established G. L. for all time as the "gypsy poet" and the modern Andalusian minstrel, is very different from the collection of poems which immediately followed it, *Poeta en Nueva York* (Poet in New York, 1957). These poems, first published privately in 1940, are the fruit of the year G. L. spent in New York. Here the poet—who was always drawn to the abysses of surrealistic experimentation—focuses his attention on a chaotic, repulsive world of machines, human wasteland, and civilized putrefaction. In free form showing a strong tendency toward expressionism (q.v.), he sings of the animals, the diseases, the Negroes, the streets, and the anonymous crowds driven to despair by anger, disgust, and remorse.

Returning to Spain, G. L. resumed the writing of plays, which he had abandoned in favor of poetry. He wrote *Bodas de sangre* (1933; Blood Wedding, 1941, 1959), *Yerma* (1934; Eng., 1941, 1959) and *Doña Rosita la soltera o El lenguaje de las flores* (1935), which were given their first, very successful performances between 1933 and 1935. *La casa de Bernarda Alba* (Bernarda Alba, 1941, 1959); written in 1936, was not performed until 1945. These plays, on Andalusian yet universal themes and written in a new, largely expressionist form, are masterpieces of elemental, naked dramatic art; the intensity of their passion and their poetic force approach that of Greek tragedy. In all of them a woman is the leading character. *Bodas de sangre* presents the eternal conflict between two men who kill each other out of love for the same woman. Sterility is the tragic theme of *Yerma*; the woman despairs because she cannot bear a child. *Doña Rosita*, perhaps the tenderest and best constructed of all G. L.'s plays, deals with the lack of fulfillment, the shattered hopes, and the constant lonely fear of a young girl eating her heart out as she gradually grows older in a provincial milieu, waiting in vain for love and happiness. *La casa de Bernarda Alba* is set in an isolated rural region of Andalusia. The characters, all women, are sisters thirsty for freedom and love, tyrannized by a grasping, domineering mother who is concerned only with keeping up appearances. These plays, which have been performed all over the world, place G. L. among the great contemporary dramatists.

In 1935 G. L. published his most important lyrical work, *Llanto por Ignacio Sánchez Mejías* (Lament for the Death of a Bullfighter, 1937). A masterpiece of construction and dramatic impact, this poem represents the quintessence of G. L.'s poetic genius transformed into verses of gripping rhythm and heart-rending pathos. In 1936 he wrote still another series of poems, "El diván del Tamarit," first published in Vol. VI of his *Obras completas* (1940). Here, in poems which in

FEDERICO GARCÍA LORCA

DAVID GARNETT

the Arabic manner he called *gacelas* and *casidas*, he merged memories of love and premonitions of death in a form partly traditional partly surrealistic, and at the same time characterized by a new pure, limpid, self-contained style. This form apparently indicated the new course he was embarking upon.

G. L.'s work aroused the unanimous admiration of a world-wide public as well as the intense interest of literary critics. His poems and plays have been translated into all major languages; his translators include Spender and Éluard (qq.v.). G.L.'s popular, cultivated, and revolutionary statement represents an authentic poetic expression of universal passions, deep restlessness, and human suffering. His work also stands as a perfect embodiment of the Spanish character.

FURTHER WORKS: *Impresiones y paisajes* (1918); *Mariana Pineda* (1928); *La Zapatera prodigiosa* (1930; The Miraculous Shoemaker's Wife, n.d.) *Así que pasen cinco años* (1931); *Retablillo de Don Cristobal* (1931; The Puppet Play of Don Cristobal, 1957); *Amor de Don Perlimplín con Belisa en su jardín* (1933; The Lass, the Sailor, and the Student, 1957); *Obras completas* (8 vols., 1949; 3 vols., 1957; 8 vols., 1960). **Selected English trans.:** *Poems* (1939); *Selected Poems of F. G. L.* (1943): *Lorca* (1961)

BIBLIOGRAPHY: Honig, E., *G. L.* (1944); Eich, C., *F. G. L., poeta de la intensidad* (1958); Cobelli, E., *G. L.* (1959); Guillén, J., ed., *Federico in persona* (1960); Fulbeck, J. F., "A Comparative Study of Poetic Elements in Selected Plays by John Millington Synge and by F. G. L.," *DA*, XXI (1961), 1564-65; Cano, J. L., *G. L.* (1962); Durán, M., *L.: A Collection of Critical Essays* (1962); Torre, G. de, *La aventura estética de nuestra edad* (1962); Lima, R., *The Theatre of G. L.* (1963); Young, H. T., *The Victorious Expression: A Study of Four Contemporary Spanish Poets* (among whom L., 1964); Zardoya, C., "Reflexiones en torno a una antología crítica sobre F. G. L.," *Hispano*, N. 24 (1965), 55-59 (review article)
GONZALO SOBEJANO

His art was no mere department of his life; it filled and inspired everything that he did. His sensibility was so vivid that he was able to reveal to others much that they would otherwise not have noticed, to find undiscovered characteristics in trivial things, and to cast over all his irresistible gift of melody. He had no message to give; he followed his instincts and wrote about anything that excited his insight or his fancy. All this made him the poet for which his generation was looking. Though speculations meant nothing to him and he always denied that he had any theory of art, his practice realized many hopes and justified many beliefs. His poetry was really poetry and nothing else; his imagery was of an enthralling brilliance and originality; his vision was actual and contemporary in that it centered round his Andalusian homeland and on the varied life which he found in it.

Bowra, C., *The Creative Experiment* (1949), p. 192

L.'s poetry—and his plays are poetry too—has the tangy freshness of a beginning as well as the formal poise, the well-schooled sureness of rhythmic gesture, which a poet can derive so effortlessly only from tradition. . . . With the certainty and self-assurance of one who has roots and knows himself to be sustained by them, he stands firm against the modern laboratory-world, yet without closing himself to it. He absorbs and envelops and grows beyond it; he endows it with the shadows in which the spirits of oldtime, undestroyed life still dwell. . . .

Blöcker, G., *Die neuen Wirklichkeiten* (1957), pp. 215 ff.

In contemporary poets, poetry is born from an abstract idea or out of certain subtle vibrations before a general reality—light, spring, sea. In L. poetry was born from the experience of the perceived material, material observed in its concrete forms and its most minute details. From these, reality disappears completely; the emotions become purified and lose their allusive significance. In L. the sight of the concrete and the emotions it invokes are expanded until they produce a kind of cosmic sound. . . .

His spontaneous emotion, which his inspiration reveals to be direct and vital, is translated into a dynamic and dramatic lyricism, the ultimate motivation of which is to deliver us into the presence of death. In it we recognize the grand theme of L.'s poetry, his constant obsession, even when the delicate grace of the rhythm and the image or the irony make us forget it. . . .

It appears, like in the baroque, in the very flesh, with actual presence, and is accompanied by the whole retinue of blood, crime, violence, foreboding, and loneliness.

del Rio, A., *Vida y obras de F. G. L.* (1952), pp. 162, 164 ff.

Both L.'s suffering and his capacity for suffering were very great. He did not suffer morbidly, but as a true poet should, by trying to turn his suffering into poetry, and he did this better than most other contemporary poets. . . .

In the end it is clear that L. is not deliberately inflicting pain on the reader, in order to shock or annoy him; but that he feels so poignantly that he has to share this feeling with others. This is the motive underlying his insistence on themes of cruelty. We know that in his life he was cheerful, full of fun, a radiant and kindly personality, and that considering the extent and nature of what he had to suffer, there was not much perversity in his make-up, as modern poets go.

Campbell, R., *L.* (1952), pp. 31, 37

Down to the last detail of his stage settings, L.'s vision remains a poetic one. His plays, concentrating on a few themes that he was continually intensifying, created a language dominated by symbols, each theme inventing its own symbols, each emotion inventing a few images heavy with obsessional meaning. . . .

This obsession—the cold man, too old to love a young woman or too timid to satisfy a passionate one—recurs throughout L.'s work. . . . In these plays of death, life is always bursting forth.

Nourissier, F., *F. G. L.* (1955), p. 127 f.

L.'s drama as a whole is an act of social criticism as well as a document of unresolved personal dilemma.

Honig, E., *G. L.* (1944), p. 194

GARNETT, David
English novelist, b. 9 March 1892, Brighton

G. is the son of Edward Garnett, friend and backer of Conrad, D. H. Lawrence (qq.v.), and other writers. Although he grew up in a literary environment, he first studied botany. His career as a writer began with the great success of his early short novel *Lady Into Fox* (1922). The effectiveness of this story of the metamorphosis of an animal lies in G.'s skill in giving the fantastic element a semblance of reality. In his novels G. shows a liking for outsiders and bizarre characters. Nature, the animal world, and flying are the themes of the novel *The Grasshoppers Come* (1931) and of the essays in *A Rabbit in the Air* (1932) and *The War in the Air* (1941). G.'s autobiographical works, *The Golden Echo* (1953) and *The Flowers of the Forest* (1955), are important as commentaries on the English literary scene during World War I and the 1920's, and for their striking portraits of many writers, particularly those of the Bloomsbury group (see English Literature) and those associated with D. H. Lawrence. G.'s style is concise and simple.

FURTHER WORKS: *Dope Darling* (1919); *A Man in the Zoo* (1924); *The Sailor's Re-*

turn (1925); *Go She Must* (1927); *The Old Dovecote* (1928); *No Love* (1929); *The Appreciation of Voltaire's "Zadig"* (1929); *Never be a Bookseller* (1929); *A Terrible Day* (1932); *Pocahontas* (1933); *Beany-eye* (1935); *Aspects of Love* (1955); *A Shot in the Dark* (1958); *A Net for Venus* (1959); *The Familiar Faces* (1962); *Two by Two* (1963)

BIBLIOGRAPHY: Heilbrun, C. G., "The G. Family," *DA*, XX (1959), 1024-25

FRANZ STANZEL

GARY, Romain
(pseud. of *Roman Kassef*), French novelist and diplomat, b. 8 May 1914, Vilno

G. is the son of a Georgian diplomat and a French mother. He served as a French Air Force officer in World War II, and was a member of the French diplomatic service until 1961.

His first work, published in English as *Forest of Anger* (1944), established G. as a writer of the war and postwar era. The novel depicts the life of the underground in a Polish forest, and to his description of the miseries brought about by war and man's inhumanity to man G. adds a message of hope for a better world without which man cannot survive. In *Le grand vestiaire* (1948; Company of Men, 1950) G. uses postwar Paris as a setting for a bitter diatribe against the selfishness and greed of cowardly men who have accepted life on its own humiliating terms. But his next work shows that he has not lost hope: Morel, the hero of *Les Racines du Ciel* (1956; The Roots of Heaven, 1958), embarks on a crusade to rekindle among men of good will everywhere the traditional beacons of humanism—justice, liberty, and love. The book, while a proof of its author's unshakeable confidence in man and a reflection of his own energetic personality, is marred by improbable dreams of an "improved" law of the universe and of man's nature. However, while keeping his faith in the ultimate betterment of this world through men, G. seems to have gone back to a more realistic, if more pessimistic, view of the human condition in his later works, in which irony scarcely conceals the anguish of men aware of their absurd situation.

FURTHER WORKS: *Tulipe* (1946); *Les Couleurs du jour* (1952; Colors of the Day, 1953); *La Promesse de l'aube* (1959; Promise at Dawn, 1961); *Lady L ...* (1959; Eng., 1959); *Trois histoires pour rire d'un diplomate* (1960); *Johnie Cœur* (1961; The Ski Bum, 1965); *Gloire à nos illustres pionniers* (1962; Hissing Tales, 1964); *Pour Sganarelle* (1965); *Les Mangeurs d'étoiles* (1966; The Talent Scout, 1961); *La Danse de Gengis Cohn* (1967; The Dance of Genghis Cohn, 1968)

BIBLIOGRAPHY: Abbé, D. van, "A Margin of Humanity," *Meanjin*, XVII (1958), 172-74; on *The Roots of Heaven*, cf. *The New Yorker* (1 Feb. 1958), p. 86; on *Lady L ...*, cf. *ibid.* (4 Apr. 1959), p. 161; on *The Ski Bum*, cf. *Book Week* (28 Feb. 1965), p. 4

ANDRÉE KAIL

GASCAR, Pierre

(pseud. of *Pierre Fournier*), French narrative writer, b. 13 March 1916, Paris

After World War II, during which he was a German prisoner of war, G. took up journalism and soon began writing fiction as well. In the volume of novellas *Les Bêtes* (1953; Beasts and Men, 1956) he tries to present a new image of the relationship between man and animal, dominated by close kinship and mutual hatred. These stories, with their emphasis on cruelty, also symbolize the aggressiveness of contemporary life and its general climate of hostility.

In 1953 G. was awarded the Prix Goncourt for *Les Bêtes* and for the novella *Le Temps des morts* (1953; in Beasts and Men, 1956). The latter, an account of events of his prisoner-of-war days in the Rawa-Ruska camp, is intended to be a "story of death"; behind the deceptively idyllic surface lies the reality of the persecution and slaughter of Jews in Poland. According to G.'s pessimistic view, and suggested through an original use of metaphor, the world is a place of perdition and despair. In the two novels *La Graine* (1955; The Seed, 1959) and *L'Herbe des rues* (1956), which show autobiographical traits and deal with childhood, youth, and the prewar period, he uses a simpler style.

FURTHER WORKS: *Les Meubles* (1949); *Le Visage clos* (1951); *Les Femmes* (1955; Women and the Sun, 1964); *Chine ouverte* (1955); *Les Pas perdus* (1957); *Voyage chez les vivants* (1958); *La Barre de corail* (1958; The Coral Barrier, 1961); *Soleils* (1960); *Le Fugitif* (1960; The Fugitive, 1964); *Le Feu mal éteint* (1961); *Camille Hilaire* (1961);

Chambord (1962; Eng., 1964); *Vertiges du présent* (1962); *Les Moutons de feu* (1963; Lambs of Fire, 1965); *Le Meilleur de la vie* (1964; The Best Years, 1967); *Les Charmes* (1965); *Histoire de la captivité des Français en Allemagne* (1967)

BIBLIOGRAPHY: Borbas, L., "Man and Beast in G.'s Tales," *Kentucky Foreign Language Quarterly*, VI (1959), 1-5; Obuchowski, C. W., "The Concentrationary World of P. G.," *FR*, XXXIV (1961), 327-35; Radke, J. L., "The Metamorphoses of Animals and Men in G.'s *Les Bêtes*," *FR*, XXXIX (1965), 85-91; on *Women and the Sun* (in the context of a revised article), *The New York Times Book Review* (13 Jan. 1965), p. 5

HELMUT OLLES

GASCOYNE, David Emery

English poet, critic, translator, b. 1916, Salisbury, Wiltshire

At first strongly characterized by the techniques of Surrealism (q.v.), G.'s poetry deals with contemporary man's loneliness and suffering in a world deprived of spiritual values.

G. was educated at the Cathedral Choir School in Salisbury and began to publish very early. His first volume, *Roman Balcony and Other Poems* (1932), appeared when he was fifteen. *Opening Day* (1933) is a novel of adolescence which combines a strain of aestheticism with the themes and modes of James Joyce and Virginia Woolf (qq.v.). In France he met, among others, Paul Éluard and Pierre Jean Jouve (qq.v.), some of whose lyrics he has translated. Also translated by him were prose works by Salvador Dali (*Conquest of the Irrational*, 1935) and Breton (q.v.; *What Is Surrealism?*, 1936). At various times he has published translations of poems by Benjamin Péret, Georges Hugnet, René Char (q.v.), Luis Buñuel, and Jules Supervielle (q.v.). In 1935 he published *A Short Survey of Surrealism*, the first well-documented account of that movement to appear in England. *Man's Life Is This Meat* (1935) is an attempt at "automatic" or involuntary poetry similar to that produced by Breton and Éluard. Translations (or "adaptations") from Hölderlin plus original lyrics make up the volume entitled *Hölderlin's Madness* (1938). G.'s concern with the moral rather than the external aspects of the social revolution of the 'thirties may be seen in *Poems, 1937-1942* (1943). In this first

11

collection the poet returns to traditional romantic modes of expression, presenting directly an agonized struggle for meaning amid the demoralizing effects of war, suffering, and guilt. In *A Vagrant and Other Poems* (1950) he attained a charity and compassion rare in modern verse and emerged as "a poet with a vision of human society, its corruption and its possibilities of redemption, passionately concerned with the true nature and conditions of human liberty." In 1952 he published a study entitled *Thomas Carlyle,* and in 1956 a play for radio entitled *Night Thoughts.*

FURTHER WORKS: *Collected Poems* (Skelton, R., ed., 1965)

BIBLIOGRAPHY: Atkinson, A., "D. G.: A Check-List," *Twentieth Century Literature,* VI (1961), 180-92; Stanford, D., "D. G. and the Unacademics," *Meanjin,* XXIII (1964), 70-79; Anon., "The Orphic Voice (revised art. on G.)," *TLS,* 12 Aug. 1965, p. 696

JOHN H. JOHNSTON

GENET, Jean

French novelist, dramatist, and poet, b. 19 Dec. 1910, Paris

An illegitimate child who was abandoned soon after birth, G. was reared by peasants in central France. At fifteen he was accused of stealing a small sum of money and sentenced to the famous reformatory at Mettray. He escaped and subsequently joined the Foreign Legion. After deserting from the Legion, he wandered as a tramp for many years through much of North Africa and most of the countries of Europe, earning a living chiefly by black-marketeering, smuggling, and theft. He has spent many terms in various prisons; today he lives as a bookseller in Paris.

G. began to write poetry and fiction during one of his many prison terms. His novels and poems, drenched with autobiographical elements, but so imaginatively transformed as often to enter the realm of fantasy, describe landscapes of prisons and reformatories, gathering places and living quarters of criminals and perverts, and the waste areas inhabited by the homeless, the hopeless, the beggar.

G. has felt himself betrayed by the world and alienated from its free and open society; but seeking some form of deeply needed spiritual integration with the world, he has embraced those people cast out and those values rejected by society at large: as ordinary society understands salvation to be progress toward an ideal of goodness, as it values kindness, truth, loyalty, etc., so G. has arbitrarily chosen supreme evil as the ideal goal of living, so he sings of sexual perversion, criminality, cruelty, and betrayal. As society at large sets up its great leaders as heroes, so G. has heroized the sexually unnatural brute who is guilty—or at least capable—of the most monstrous crimes; minutely examining this personality type, G. has found the core of his evil to consist of cowardice, betrayal, and utter self-interest.

In his first novel, *Nôtre-Dame-des-fleurs* (1942; Our Lady of the Flowers, 1949), all these themes are introduced along with a structure that recurs in G.'s other novels: the wilful submission of a feminine male to a ruthlessly egocentric masculine male who is always a petty criminal but never a really major breaker of the law, never one of those criminal heroes guilty of heinous actions that shock the public and galvanize the dreams of the feminine male, who is consciously unworthy of such perfection in evil.

Nôtre-Dame-des-fleurs also contains G.'s real theme, the one that dominates in all his works, especially the plays: the quest for identity and an examination of the meaning of identity. So obsessed is G. with this burning question that all his other "themes"—his subject matters—are in actuality merely modes of thought and reference points in a continuing discussion of his main preoccupation. G., the foundling and social outcast, conceives of identity—almost objectively—as a complex that is external to the actual being of a person. Deliberately created by an individual out of dream, fantasy, wish, experience, and unavoidable circumstances, it is assumed or put away at will and convenience, much as a mask, a suit of clothes, or an actor's part in a play is put on or off.

In G.'s works the relation of identity and being is discussed at its most metaphysical near the beginning of *Journal du voleur* (1949; Thief's Journal, 1954), where in an extraordinary metaphor a pervert, being harassed by the police as they jail him, achieves a spiritual identification with a tube of petroleum jelly found on his person, which event G. equates to a religious achieving spiritual union with the godhead through a crucifix; the relation is presented at its most concrete in the play *Le Balcon* (1956; The Balcony, 1957;

revised ed., 1966), in which clients of a brothel who act out fantasies of themselves as bishop, judge, and general do actually become such real officials during a revolution. In the same play G. makes his clearest statement of a further aspect of identity: a greater or lesser union, or congruence, occurs between this created artifice "identity" and the actual being of the individual; and when this union is complete, it means essential death, whether or not physical death actually occurs then.

This basic problem of identity can be traced in all of G.'s works, but notably in the play *Les Nègres* (1958; The Blacks, 1960), where it is studied in terms of the concept of race. The examination has two aspects: the individual's sense of the pertinence of race to himself and to groups, both those to which he belongs and those to which he does not belong; and the question of the validity of the group's sense of itself as a race.

G. is recognized as one of the most significant contemporary writers. One of the "black poets" of France, in the line from Villon to Baudelaire and Verlaine, his style is marked by rich language filled with argot, by a baroque fullness of metaphor and exotic imagery, and by firm control of the writing per se. His novels, lyrical in tone like all his work, disdain well-made plots and psychologically coherent characters in order that G. may pursue the more unrestrainedly, the more relentlessly, his discussion of identity and the ethics of evil. His dramaturgy shows influences of Pirandello (q.v.); but although the conflict between reality and illusion and the blurring of the boundaries between them is a favorite theme of modern drama, especially of French drama, G.'s plays, oddly enough, do not treat this idea as a central subject matter; rather reality and illusion are manipulated as a theatrical device in presenting the truth of whatever the central subject matter might be. It is merely another device of stylization, a persistent quality of G.'s work seen in such things as the free, nonchronological treatment of time and the juxtaposition of unconnected fragments and episodes in his novels, and in such elements as the masks, fantastic props and costumes, and even cothurni (the thick-soled boots of the ancient Greek theater), which he uses in his plays.

G. is a profound moralist, and his works, in a way his own created "identity" and objectification of his experience, force us to examine the very foundation of self and society.

FURTHER WORKS: *Le Miracle de la rose* (1943; The Gutter in the Sky, 1955; Miracle of the Rose, 1966); *Chants secrets* (1944); *Pompes funèbres* (1947); *Querelle de Brest* (1947); *Les Bonnes* (1948, 1954; The Maids, 1954); *Poèmes* (1948); *Haute Surveillance* (1948; Deathwatch, 1954); *L'Enfant criminel* (1949); *Les Beaux Gars* (1951); *Le Condamné à mort* (1951); *Oeuvres complètes* (3 vols., 1952-53); *Le Pêcheur du Suquet* (1953); *L'Atelier d'Alberto Giacometti* (1958; 2nd ed., 1962); *Théâtre* (1958); *Les Paravents* (1961; The Screens, 1963); *Les Bonnes et comment jouer les bonnes* (1963)

BIBLIOGRAPHY: Sartre, J.-P., *Saint G., comédien et martyr* (1952; Saint G., Actor and Martyr, 1963); Bataille, G., *La Littérature et le mal* (1957); Esslin, M., *The Theatre of the Absurd* (1961); Guicharnaud, J., *Modern French Theatre* (1961); Grossvogel, D., *Four Playwrights and a Postscript* (1962); Pronko, L. C., *Avant-garde: The Experimental Theater in France* (1962); McMahon, J. H., *The Imagination of J. G.* (1963); Kostelanetz, R., and Colt. J., "J. G." *On Contemporary Literature*, XIV (1965), 347-65

* * *

GENEVOIX, Maurice
French novelist, b. 29 Nov. 1890, Decize, Nièvre

G. made his reputation with documentary stories of World War I, *Sous Verdun* (1916; 'Neath Verdun, 1916). In 1925 he received the Prix Goncourt for his novel *Raboliot* (The Last Hunt, 1940), whose leading character is a poacher from G.'s native province of Sologne. This was followed by other novels of a distinctly regional character: *Cyrille* (1928), the story of a taciturn peasant, and *Rroû* (1931; Eng., 1932), the life of a cat. The novel *Eva Charlebois* (1944) resulted from a visit to Canada. In 1946 G. published *Sanglar,* the portrait of a bandit leader in the district of Rouergue. He has also written a book of memoirs about the Loire country, *La Boîte à pêche* (1926).

In powerful language, rich in imagery, G. succeeds in exposing elemental forces and the subtleties of the heart. He has been a member of the French Academy since 1946.

13

FURTHER WORKS: *Nuits de guerre* (1917); *Rémi des Rauches* (1922); *Les Éparges* (1923); *La Joie* (1924); *Les Mains vides* (1928); *Forêt voisine* (1931); *Gai l'amour* (1932); *Marcheloupe* (1934); *Tête baissée* (1935); *Un Homme et sa vie* (3 vols., 1934-37); *La Dernière harde* (1938); *Bernard* (1938); *L'Hirondelle qui fit le printemps* (1941); *La Framboise et Belle-Humeur* (1942); *Canada* (1945); *L'Écureuil du Bois-Bourru* (1947); *Afrique blanche, Afrique noire* (1949); *Chevalet de champagne* (1950); *L'Eau, l'arbre, la bête et quelques hommes* (1950); *Ceux de 14* (1950); *L'Aventure est en nous* (1952); *Fatou Cisse* (1954); *Orléannais* (1956); *Le Petit chat* (1957); *Mon Ami écureuil* (1957); *Le Roman de Renard* (1958; The Story of Renard, 1959); *Routes de l'aventure* (1958); *Marcheloup* (1959); *Le Jardin dans l'île* (1959); *Au Cadran de mon clocher* (1960); *Vaincre à Olympic* (1960); *La Loire* (1962); *Derrière les collines* (1963); *Destination Saint-Pierre* (1963); *Pages choisies* (1964); *Christian` Caillard* (1965); *Beau-François* (1965)

BIBLIOGRAPHY: Berger, M., *Quatre études de "Style au microscope"* (1948); Timbaldis Abruzzese, E., *Il romanzo rurale di M. G.* (1956); Saint-Phalle, T de, "Derrière les collines de l'Académie," *Revue de Paris*, LXXI (1964), 144-47; Bourdet, D., "M. G.," *ibid.*, LXXII (1965), 120-24

LOUIS CHAIGNE

GEORGE, Stefan (Anton)

German poet, b. 12 July 1868, Büdesheim, Hesse; d. 4 Dec. 1933, Minusio, Switzerland

G. was the son of an innkeeper and wine merchant whose father—after French military service under Charles X—in 1833 had moved to Büdesheim from Lorraine. G. grew up at Bingen and Darmstadt (*Gymnasium,* 1881-88). Samples of his early poetry were published in 1901 in *Die Fibel.*

G. acquired a wide knowledge of foreign languages and contemporary literatures by travel and independent study. During his first stay in Paris (1889) he attended Mallarmé's *Cénacle.* Mallarmé and Verlaine became his early models; however, his own clear and harsh style resembled more the style of the Parnassians. Because of his admiration for Mallarmé and his early technique of mood evocation by poetic suggestion, G. was considered a symbolist (see symbolism).

G. translated Baudelaire (1891), Mallarmé, Verlaine, Rimbaud, Verhaeren (q.v.), and English, Danish, Dutch, Italian, and Polish poets (*Zeitgenössische Dichter*, 2 vols., 1905). From 1892 to 1919 he published a periodical, *Blätter für die Kunst.* Up to 1898 G.'s works were printed privately: *Hymnen* (1890; Odes, 1949), *Pilgerfahrten* (1891; Pilgrimages, 1949), *Algabal* (1892), *Die Bücher der Hirten- und Preisgedichte, der Sagen und Sänge und der hängenden Gärten* (1895; The Books of Eclogues and Eulogies, of Legends and Lays, and of the Hanging Gardens, 1949), *Das Jahr der Seele* (1897; The Year of the Soul, 1949).

Since young G. was mostly interested in mastery of the language, the subject matter of his early poetry is varied and relatively unimportant: the poet and his muse, the temptations of love, art (preferably pre-Raphael), landscapes, portraits of friends. The first highly characteristic work is *Algabal.* A very young priest-emperor (=Heliogabalus) creates an artificial subterranean palace where he lives in divine dignity and isolation, and any disturbance is punished by mercifully immediate death. Other works occasionally contain features which later became typical: beautiful athletes, young knights and their older friends, Oriental potentates. *Das Jahr der Seele* contains G.'s most popular (although least typical) poems. The main theme is the poet's love for a young woman who is unable to respond adequately to his needs (the woman who was G.'s model later became the wife of Dehmel [q.v.] and therewith the model for the lady in the latter's *Zwei Menschen,* where her sexual-erotic proclivities seem to be more than adequate). Most of these poems are set in parkscapes; natural phenomena suggest moods of the human soul.

In 1898 public editions of G.'s early works appeared. In 1899 *Der Teppich des Lebens und die Lieder von Traum und Tod, mit einem Vorspiel* (Prelude, The Tapestry of Life, The Songs of Dream and Death, 1949) was privately printed (public ed., 1901). This is G.'s most artful and most rigid work. Each part consists of twenty-four poems of sixteen lines each. The prelude contains the poet's conversation with an angel, the poet's alter ego. The poet has to create in dignified but painful isolation, responsible only to his own law. In the tapestry of life G. shows positive and negative types of cultural history. Artistically *Der Teppich* represents the highest point G. reached as a poet.

JEAN GENET

STEFAN GEORGE

As a human being he passed a severe crisis after *Der Teppich* was completed. There appeared a most important new element in his life when, in 1899, G. found the first young man—Friedrich Gundelfinger (1880-1931)—who was willing to recognize the poet as an absolute master. Renamed Gundolf by G., he (under that name) became a literary historian, famous during the second and third decade of this c.

The section "Gezeiten" of G.'s next work—*Der siebente Ring* (1907; The Seventh Ring, 1949)—contains G.'s poems written about 1900 for Gundolf and—some five years later—for Robert Boehringer. They are the most beautiful and warmly human love poems G. wrote for young men and—coincidentally—the best homosexual love poems in the German language. Nowhere else do G.'s verses flow as easily and harmoniously as in these poems.

Although his association with Gundolf lasted some twenty years, several of his poems present the new partner as an insufficient one. The ideal partner appeared in a boy whom G. called Maximin after the latter had died in 1904 at the age of sixteen (his poems and diary notes concerning G. were privately printed in 1937: *Maximilian Kronberger Nachlaß*). G. himself published several Kronberger poems in *Maximin—Ein Gedenkbuch* (1906). G.'s own poems written for young Kronberger during the latter's lifetime are few and hardly impressive; obviously the boy gained full significance for the poet through his early death at the moment of adolescent bloom (although the photos—G. published one in *Maximin*—show the youth as being far from beautiful). For the end of G.'s life Maximin became the center of the poet's new personal religion. *Der siebente Ring*, in whose central (fourth) part the new god is presented, is G.'s richest, most voluminous, most ambitious, but also most uneven work.

After G. became a master and leader (i.e., since 1899), he abandoned his former attitude of disdainful indifference toward the secular contemporary world. In the section "Zeitgedichte" of *Der siebente Ring* he began to attack the follies of his own age and to praise its last remaining great human figures. For a time G. participated in the orgiastic life of a Munich group rediscovering primitivism and matriarchy (Ludwig Klages and Wolfskehl [q.v.] being the most fruitful spirits of this frenzied coterie). Thus there are orgiastic poems in *Der siebente Ring*, the like of which cannot be found in G.'s earlier or later works. For the last time G. made use of his original symbolistic technique, e.g., he suggested his suffering caused by Maximin's death by showing young trees cut by noisy axe blows. In the poems celebrating the life, the death, and the subsequent deification of Maximin, G. often descended below his previous high literary level. There are many allusions to Christ's childhood story, and the tone often becomes bigoted and sanctimonious. After *Der siebente Ring* was published, many of G.'s old admirers refused to go along with G., the prophet of a new god. At the same time there formed around the poet a circle of disciples (the George group) accepting him as an absolute authority.

G.'s two remaining original works are of far less artistic interest than his previous ones, but from sociological and political viewpoints they are most significant. *Der Stern des Bundes* (1914; The Star of the Covenant, 1949), reveals the character of the new god and the laws governing the lives of the poet and his disciples. Many of the 100 short poems were originally written for individual disciples. For pedagogic reasons G. strove after the greatest clarity, avoiding all possible ambiguity. Because of this intended simplicity these poems sound disappointingly flat today. Immediately after their publication they served as a gospel, not only to G.'s followers, but also to the *Wandervogel* (a pre-Hitler youth movement) and to young German soldiers of World War I.

Several poems concerning that war and its young victims were published independently. In 1928 they were incorporated in G.'s last original work *Das neue Reich* (The Kingdom Come, 1949), a shapeless collection of poems written during the two previous decades. Stylistically nothing new was achieved. One new type —originally rejected by G. as being unpoetic— was added, however: the long didactic poem. *Das neue Reich* contains obnoxious ideas of expansionistic German nationalism and predictions of a desirable cultural collapse followed by barbaric rule of former criminals. Many of G.'s striking coinages were taken over by Hitler and his propagandists. G., although partly rejecting Nazism, uttered satisfaction about his work's effect outside his own circle (see Edith Landmann, *Gespräche mit S. G.*, p. 209).

During the second half of his life G. was more a platonic teacher and schemer than a productive poet. He aimed at creating an elite that would infiltrate the institutions of higher learning and central administration in Germany and finally take over the government. When the members of G.'s small conventicle spoke and corresponded about "the State," it often sounded ludicrous. When, eleven years after G.'s death, one of his former young followers—Claus von Stauffenberg—tried to interfere with history (he placed the bomb in the famous attempt on Hitler's life on July 20, 1944), he and his brother had to pay with their lives for their failure.

As a poet G. is one of the most influential figures in German literary history. His language often has a monumental quality which never before had been achieved in German and could not even have been considered possible before G. He is most successful in the coining of forceful, sloganlike single lines. A certain hardening of the German language may be considered a negative effect of G.'s works. His literary and linguistic importance does not rest in his influence on his own circle (which produced merely university professors but no important poet besides G.) but rather in his influence on all serious young writers about 1900 (and far beyond that date) and on the contemporary German language (even though after 1945 his dictatorial attitude was considered repelling).

FURTHER WORKS: *Tage und Taten* (1900); *Shakespeare, Sonnette* (adaptation, 1909); *Dante, Die göttliche Komödie Übertragungen* (1912); *Gesamt-Ausgabe der Werke* (18 vols., 1927-34); *Briefwechsel zwischen G. und Hofmannsthal,* ed. R. Boehringer (1938; 2d enlarged ed., 1953); *S. G.-Friedrich Gundolf Briefwechsel,* ed. R. Boehringer and G. P. Landmann (1962). **Selected English trans.:** *The Works of S. G.* (1949)

BIBLIOGRAPHY: Gundolf, F., *G.* (1920; 3rd enlarged ed., 1930); Wolters, F., *S. G. und die Blätter für die Kunst* (1930); Duthie, E. L., *L'Influence du symbolisme français dans le renouveau poétique de l'Allemagne* (1933); Koch, W., *S. G., Weltbild, Naturbild, Menschenbild* (1933); Lachmann, E., *Die ersten Bücher S. G.s* (1933); Morwitz, E., *Die Dichtung S. G.s* (1934); Verwey, A., *Mijn Verhouding tot S. G.* (1934); Butler, E. M., *The Tyranny of Greece over Germany* (1935); Benrath, H., *S. G.* (1936); Salin, E., *Um S. G.* (1948; 2d enlarged ed., 1954); David, C., *S. G., son œuvre poétique* (1952); Boehringer, R., *Mein Bild von S. G.* (1951); Landmann, G. P.,

S. G. und sein Kreis. Eine Bibliographie (1960); Morwitz, E., *Kommentar zu dem Werk S. G.s* (1960); Landmann, E., *Gespräche mit S. G.* (1963); Nijland-Verwey, M., *Albert Verwey en S. G.* (1965); Schultz, H. S., *Studien zur Dichtung S. G.s* (1967)

HANS ALBERT MAIER

GERMAN LITERATURE

German literature from 1900 to 1945—which is understood here in a broad sense, embracing both Austrian (q.v.) and German-language Swiss literature—is essentially a literature of irrationalism, stemming from a reaction against the positivism and materialism of the later 19th c. This is not to say that rationalism died out completely during that period; but the impulse that united almost all the movements was nonrational and at times even antirational. It is this spirit that lends coherence to an era otherwise chaotic in its literary currents. The labels of form or political and philosophical allegiance are less relevant. The so-called *Neue Sachlichkeit* (new factualism) of Ernst Jünger and Musil (qq.v.) or the neoclassicism of Wilhelm von Scholz (b. 1879) and Schröder can be used just as effectively as the stylistic excesses of expressionism and Dadaism (qq.v.) as a basis for irrational doctrines. The writers of the conservative revolution and of emergent Nazism shared the same distrust of reason and progress as the authors of the Christian Renaissance. Poets as different as Rilke and George (qq.v.), novelists as far apart as Hesse and Broch (qq.v.), are united in their rejection of rationalism and in their belief in an ideal that transcends contemporary reality.

The revolt against positivism in philosophy was paralleled by a turning away from realism in form. Despite the immense variety of literary forms oscillating between the extremes of neoclassicism and Dadaism, the basic impulse of the period from 1900 to 1945 was one of rebellion and thrust for liberation, manifested by three transformative waves. Lyric poetry was the first genre to free itself from the traditions of the past. Most of the major poets of the c. had found their voices by World War I: Rilke, George, Hofmannsthal, Benn, Trakl, Heym (qq.v.), Schröder, Loerke, among others. What followed is based almost completely upon literary experiments of these years.

The next wave affected drama (*see* Drama and Theater). Until 1911 German drama was essentially realistic, whether this realism took the form of Gerhart Hauptmann's (q.v.) naturalism (q.v.), Schnitzler's (q.v.) impressionism, or Paul Ernst's (q.v.) neoclassicism. Expressionistic drama of the period 1911 to 1924 moved away from realism and created a totally new conception of theater.

The novel of the first quarter c. had followed, with few exceptions, 19th c. traditions. The early works of Hesse, Mann (q.v.), and Musil, though they contain hints of future developments, were primarily realistic or impressionistic. But during the twenties the novel underwent a radical transformation, freeing itself from the strictures of realism and becoming a vehicle for the expression of a wholly new conception of reality.

These stylistic and thematic changes, which precipitated the three waves of literary reform, shape the profile of the first half of the c. Within this development there were many trends, genres, forms, and movements as well as political, philosophical, and religious currents. But the basic thrust of the period remained remarkably constant.

1890-1910: The Rise of Irrationalism

Literature before 1900 was by no means uniformly rationalistic and realistic. Impressionism was not a reaction against realism, but merely a different application of its principles: the aim was still to capture external reality, but reality as it appears to the filtering consciousness of the viewer. Intellectual history, however, recognizes a turning point around 1890, after which the voices of irrationalism become ever stronger until, by 1910, they were heard full force in the new literature of expressionism (q.v.)—the first movement of the c. to combine an irrationalistic view of man with experimentation in literary style. The development was heralded in Germany by such eccentric documents of social protest as Paul de Lagarde's (1827-91) *Deutsche Schriften* (1875-81) and Julius Langbehn's (1851-1907) *Rembrandt als Erzieher* (1890), immensely successful popular books in which rationalism and urban industrial civilization in general were attacked in favor of a return to a mystique of primal Germanic virtues.

These so-called "prophets" of a "politics of cultural despair" (Fritz Stern) were paralleled by a "reconstruction of social thought" in the writings of scholars like Sigmund Freud (1865-1939), C. G. Jung (1875-1961), Wilhelm Dilthey (1833-1911), Max Weber (1864-1920), Ernst Troeltsch (1865-1923), and Friedrich Meinecke (1862-1954), who turned away from positivism and Marxism to unmask the unconscious in psychology and to recapture idealism in history and politics. The two great literary heroes of this new direction, whose writings now became meaningful to the public, were Nietzsche (q.v.) and Dostoyevski, both of whom proclaimed a mystical ideal.

These developments were not without counterparts in literature. Realists like Wilhelm Raabe (1831-1910) and Theodor Fontane (1819-98) had already exercised considerable criticism of late 19th c. German society and its rationalistic optimism. Gerhart Hauptmann (q.v.), along with his early naturalistic works (*Vor Sonnenaufgang*, 1889 [Before Dawn, 1909]; *Die Weber*, 1892 [The Weavers, 1899]), wrote a series of dramas in which transcendent elements are important (*Hanneles Himmelfahrt*, 1894 [Hannele, 1894]; *Die versunkene Glocke*, 1897 [The Sunken Bell, 1898]). The poet Arno Holz (q.v.), whose theory of "thoroughgoing naturalism" (in *Die Kunst, ihr Wesen und ihre Gesetze*, 1891-92) had been misread to mean no more than the photographic rendition of life in a superficially naturalistic manner, wrote a special supplement (1892) to prove that his theory had, in fact, taken the irrational into account. In *Meister Oelze* (1892), often regarded as the high point of naturalistic drama, Johannes Schlaf (1862-1941) employed poetic symbolism (q.v.). Impressionists such as Schnitzler, Wedekind, and Dehmel (qq.v.) addressed themselves to the literary expression of problems in depth psychology, which positivistic theories of behaviorism had either overlooked or ignored.

This growth of irrationalism was punctuated by a remarkable document. A literary period comes of age only when its means of expression catch up with its intellectual and emotional substance. The naturalism (q.v.) and impressionism of the nineties, even when they ventured into areas outside of positivism, had continued to draw upon realistic language. Hofmannsthal's (q.v.) *Der Brief des Lord Chandos* (1902; The Letter of Lord Chandos, 1952) is significant in German literary history because it marks the first programmatic rejection of 19th c. forms. The fictitious author of the letter claims that it is impossible to

17

write poetry because the words at his command no longer correspond to the objects and ideas that he wishes to express. Hofmannsthal, like his Lord Chandos, is a symbolic figure because he eschewed lyric poetry after 1902 out of protest against a ravaged language incapable of true expression and communication. German literature enters the decade of the "crisis of language" (*Sprachkrise*), a struggle to find commensurate modes of expression that cut across all differences of genre and philosophical commitment.

While the decade of the nineties was characterized more by its incipient nonrationalism, the first decade of the new c. was avowedly antirational, a tendency that shows up especially in poetry, since prose and drama were slower to free themselves from the traditions of realism. The poets characteristic of these years poised between impressionism and expressionism—the period sometimes designated collectively as *Jugendstil*—are flamboyant figures such as Else Lasker-Schüler (1876-1945), who rejected reality for the sake of a fantasy world of the Orient, which she projected in her poems (*Styx*, 1902; *Hebräische Balladen*, 1913) and dithyrambic prose (*Die Nächte der Tino von Bagdad*, 1907).

Among the many other writers of these years who found in the Orient a symbol of their revolt against Western rationalism were: Rilke ([q.v.], *Das Stundenbuch*, 1905 [Book of Hours, 1961, first complete translation]); Döblin ([q.v.], *Die drei Sprünge des Wang-Lun*, 1915); Hesse ([q.v.], *Aus Indien*, 1913); and Hermann Keyserling ([q.v.], *Reisetagebuch eines Philosophen*, 1918 [Travel Journal of a Philosopher, 1925]). Close to Else Lasker-Schüler in their visionary works were the so-called "ecstatic" poets, Alfred Mombert, *Der himmlische Zecher*, 1909), Däubler ([q.v.], *Das Nordlicht*, 1910), and Dauthendey (q.v.), who developed in lyrical works of epic scope a private cosmic myth of the spirit. Another related figure is Barlach (q.v.), whose Russian-inspired vision is reflected not only in his brooding sculptures but also in his later writings.

Other figures typical of the time were the poet-philosophers of the club (and journal) *Charon* (1904 ff.), who sought to create a universal unity of thought and literature: Otto zur Linde ([q.v.], *Die Kugel: Eine Philosophie in Versen*, 1909), Pannwitz (q.v.), Karl Röttger (1877-1942), and Rudolf Paulsen (b. 1883).

A similar mystical goal was pursued by the "Cosmic Circle" of Wolfskehl (q.v.), Alfred Schuler (1865-1923), and Ludwig Klages (1872-1956), who indicted "intellect as the adversary of the soul" and turned back to ancient mystery cults and to the mystical anthropology of J. J. Bachofen (1815-87), thus paving the way for the investigations of Jung into the nature of the matriarchal and archetypal myths. As part of their rebellion the writers of this period rejected the idols of German classicism in favor of newly rediscovered writers like Hölderlin (1770-1843), Jean Paul (1763-1825), and Kleist (1777-1811) whose timeliness became apparent to a literary generation groping for new forms.

During these years the patterns of lyric poetry for the c. were established. Side by side with the symbolic formalism of Stefan George (q.v.), stemming from Mallarmé, there came into being the new poetry of ecstasy; and along with Rilke's sinuous lyrics of introspection came a new cult of the ballad, which extended from Lulu von Strauss und Torney (1873-1956), Börries von Münchhausen (q.v.), and Agnes Miegel (q.v.) down to Ina Seidel and Brecht (qq.v.) in the twenties. All of these forms, however, reflect a view of the world—at once irrationalistic and idealistic—common to the times. This is true even of the often irreverent satire of Morgenstern (q.v.), behind whose *Galgenlieder* (1905; C. M.'s Galgenlieder: A Selection, 1964) lurked an essentially mystical temperament that later revealed itself in religious poetry.

1910-1920: The Expressionist Impulse

Out of the chaos of that decade there emerged the violent literary explosion known loosely as expressionism (q.v.). It is necessary to distinguish between expressionism as form and expressionism as content. The writers who can be called true expressionists are marked by a merging of experimentation in form and an irrationalistic world view. Most of the major writers of the c. (e.g., Mann, Hesse, Rilke, Hofmannsthal, Hauptmann, Musil [qq.v.], and Schröder) were not directly engaged in the stylistic revolt of expressionism. But few Germans were unaffected by the messianic feeling of a better future to come and by the rebellion against the general cultural stagnation of the Wilhelmine empire that informed the works of this young generation in revolt.

Although there were many articulate and passionate pacifists in these prewar years (Werfel [q.v.], Hesse), the great majority of writers, like the population in general, regarded the war as a necessary moral catharsis that would clear the air and open the way to a new and better world. Poets saw the war as a savior (Becher [q.v.]) or as the voice of God (Heinrich Lersch); the young hero marching off to battle with a volume of Nietzsche (q.v.) in his knapsack became one of the clichés of the era. Countless documents have captured the euphoria of those August days of 1914 (Mann, *Der Zauberberg,* 1924 [The Magic Mountain, 1927]; Joseph Roth [q.v.], *Radetzkymarsch,* 1932 [Radetzsky March, 1933]; Hesse, *Demian,* 1919 [Eng., 1923]—especially remarkable because it was the work of a pronounced pacifist).

This whole feeling of revolt against the past, which alone explains the enthusiastic greeting of the war by men otherwise pacifistically inclined, is symbolized in many expressionist works through the father-son conflict, most vehemently in Hasenclever's (q.v.) play *Der Sohn* (1914) and Hanns Johst's (b. 1890) *Der junge Mensch* (1916).

The first wave of expressionism, carried along by the momentum of the "ecstatic poets," was essentially lyrical—a fantastically rich but brief flurry of poetry that had ended by 1915, when many of the finest poets were already dead (Trakl, Heym [qq.v.], Alfred Lichtenstein (1889-1914), E. W. Lotz (1890-1914), Ernst Stadler (1883-1914), Stramm [q.v.]). It is difficult to characterize the twenty-three poets of Kurt Pinthus's (b. 1886) standard anthology *Menschheitsdämmerung* (1920). The poems are just as ambivalent as the title, which can mean either the "Twilight of Man" or the "Dawning of Humanity." Stylistically they have little in common beyond the rejection of rationalistic expression. This rejection extends from the poetry of Trakl, written in a lyrical, deceptively simple language that employs a logic of metaphor rather than any logic of ideas, to the ejaculatory poetry of Stramm, which often consists of strings of exclamations with no syntactical connections whatever.

These poets sought to express their own inner visions rather than to convey the impressions made upon them by external reality. Their common concerns are suggested by the title of Pinthus's anthology: humanitarianism and messianic belief in the dawning of a new humanity. Often their thinking was blurred and without clear-cut goals; the parodistic

label *"O-Mensch! poetry"* is not without justification. It was, as a matter of fact, precisely this inner diffuseness of expressionism, its unfocused enthusiasm, that caused adverse critical reaction after the war. Yet its finest poets, like Trakl, attained new heights of lyrical expression and belong to the major writers of the c.

Among the many organs of expressionism, which featured such titles as *Revolution* and *Das neue Pathos,* the two most characteristic ones were Herwarth Walden's (1878-1941) *Der Sturm* (1910 ff.) and Franz Pfemfert's (1879-1959) *Die Aktion* (1911 ff.), which reflect the dualism of revolt noted earlier. *Der Sturm* was essentially the aesthetic center of the movement; it is significant that during those years Walden was married to Else Lasker-Schüler, thus constituting a living link between the young poets of expressionism and the high priestess of the earlier cult of irrationalism. In the pages of *Der Sturm* the art historian Worringer first introduced the term "expressionism" in a discussion of contemporary painting; its contributors included artists like Kokoschka (q.v.), Marc, Klee, and Feininger. It also attracted the most radical linguistic experimenters of the generation (Stramm, Wilhelm Runge (1894-1918), Kurt Heynicke [b. 1891]).

From *Der Sturm* a direct line of descent leads to the poetic excesses of dadaism (q.v.) as it was developed in Zurich (1916, in the Cabaret Voltaire) by Arp, Ball, Tzara (qq.v.), and others; and to the sublime nonsense of the *Simultangedicht* (simultaneous poem) of Huelsenbeck (q.v.). *Die Aktion* was, by contrast, the center for those writers whose revolt was more sociopolitical than literary (Stadler, Carl Einstein [1885-1940], Karl Otten [1889-1963], Ludwig Rubiner [1881-1920]). It was the home of the "activist group" within expressionism, who propagandized for political reform; after 1918 it was transformed smoothly and naturally into a Communist organ with contributors such as Rudolf Leonhard (1889-1953) and Becher (q.v.), who became, after 1945, the official head of the East German Academy of Letters.

Expressionist drama is sometimes said to have begun with Kokoschka's one-act playlet *Mörder, Hoffnung der Frauen* (1907), but the first significant effort is Reinhard Sorge's (1892-1916) *Der Bettler* (1911). The new dramatists (Toller, Kaiser [qq.v.], Reinhard Goering (1887-1936), Sternheim [q.v.], Fritz von Unruh (b. 1885), Goll [q.v.], Rolf Lauckner

(1887-1954), Csokor [q.v.], Paul Kornfeld (1889-1942), et al.) derived their inspiration from Büchner (1813-37), Strindberg (q.v.), and Wedekind (q.v.) rather than from the naturalism (q.v.) of Henrik Ibsen (q.v.), Hauptmann, and Zola. Many of their plays dealt with the poet-prophets of the past, in whose works they sensed their spiritual ancestors: Christian Dietrich Grabbe ([1801-1836] in Hanns Johst's *Der Einsame*, 1917), Büchner (in Csokor's *Gesellschaft der Menschenrechte*, 1929), and Rimbaud (in Paul Zech's [q.v.] *Der schwarze Baal*, 1917). Concerned as they were with the inner life of the individual rather than the conflicts between men (the traditional realm of drama), their works tended to be epic and narrative, even lyrical, rather than dramatic. Some of their techniques anticipated the contemporary "theater of the absurd," for the tendency to objectify the subjective elements of the human psyche and to project them onto the stage leads to the concretization of metaphor and visualized idiom of the sort found in the plays of Ionesco and Beckett (qq.v.).

To this extent there is a consistency between the drama and poetry of expressionism; the logic of rational thought is replaced by a logic of subconscious association and metaphor. The conflict is between aspects of the personality (as in Sorge's *Der Bettler*), a tendency that leads to the generalization of character with idealized or stylized figures instead of individualized people. Because such dramas cannot be sustained at length, they tend to dwindle to one-act efforts or are developed as a series of loosely related scenes rather than integrated actions. Expressionist drama was largely abortive and self-defeating. Because of its divorce from reality it easily became lifeless stylization. It is revealing that the two finest dramatists emerging from the movement (Kaiser and Brecht [q.v.]) turned away from the highly abstract drama of typical expressionism and imbued their works with realism and life.

As a whole, expressionist drama is more memorable for its ambition than for its achievement; its principal merits are to be found in its side-effects. First, expressionism provided the background from which emerged dramatists like Brecht and, by derivation, contemporaries like Frisch and Dürrenmatt (qq.v.), whose works are incomparably better as theater, yet unthinkable without the experimentation of expressionism. Innovations in the

theater between 1910 and 1920 transformed subsequent drama not only in Germany but also abroad (Ionesco, Beckett, Wilder [qq.v.]). A second result was the spectacular upsurge of stagecraft and acting. The lifeless stylization of many dramas had to be counterbalanced by other effects: gesture, lighting, color symbolism. It is no accident that great directors arose from that turmoil: Max Reinhardt with his theater in the round; Leopold Jessner with his *Spieltreppe* and multiple stage; Erwin Piscator and his anti-Stanislavski techniques. The more viable elements of expressionism were appropriated by the nascent film industry in such early masterpieces as *The Cabinet of Dr. Caligari* (1919) and gradually became standard techniques, still evident in the films of Ingmar Bergman and the French *nouvelle vague*.

Expressionist prose is almost a contradiction in terms. Poetry can exist in exclamation and metaphor; drama has at its disposal various techniques of the theater by which to supplement irrational speech. But narrative prose requires more continuity than expressionist language normally provides. Noteworthy as curiosities are the shorter pieces by writers such as Edschmid ([q.v.] *Die sechs Mündungen*, 1915), Klabund ([q.v.] *Karussell*, 1914), and Heym (*Der Dieb*, 1913), as well as the early prose efforts of Döblin ([q.v.] *Die Ermordung einer Butterblume*, 1913) and Gottfried Benn ([q.v.] *Gehirne*, 1916). But most writers soon abandoned the ecstatic cry of expressionism in their attempts to find a new prose style. The themes of expressionism, on the other hand, are evident in many works of the period: in Leonhard Frank's (q.v) *Der Mensch ist gut* (1919) and *Die Räuberbande* (1914; The Robber Band, 1929); in the pacifistic humanitarianism of Remarque's (q.v.) *Im Westen nichts Neues* (1929; All Quiet on the Western Front, 1929); and in the pleas for a spiritual rebirth of humanity in Hesse's *Demian* (1919).

1920-1933: Pluralism

Expressionism (q.v.) was the dominant force during the decade 1910-20. Some self-styled expressionists limped along until 1925, but during the twenties the tradition of the movement was no more than one trend among many others. The euphoric enthusiasm that kindled the initial revolt was sobered by the experience of war, defeat, and postwar depression

(Ernst Gläser [b. 1902] tells this story in his best-selling novel *Jahrgang 1902* [1928]). Directionless optimism sufficed as long as the nation was moving forward, as most Germans felt that they were in the years immediately preceding the war. In the gloomy light of defeat and depression, reflected in Oswald Spengler's (1880-1936) *Der Untergang des Abendlandes* (1918-22; The Decline of the West, 1927), men required a more specific solace. The literature of the years 1920-33 is not unified as it was—even provisionally—by the central *élan* of expressionism. It breaks down, instead, into a group of parallel currents, each of which offers a more substantial ideal than expressionism had done with its vague messianic humanitarianism.

This pluralism of movements is in turn characteristic of the relativism of values that became a central theme in the literature of the twenties and thirties. In *Die Schlafwandler* (1931-32; The Sleepwalkers, 1932) Broch (q.v.) discussed the "disintegration of values" and traced the emergence of the new "valueless" or "objective" man of the postwar era, who succeeded the "romantic" and "anarchistic" types of the preceding generations. Musil's (q.v.) *Der Mann ohne Eigenschaften* (1930, 1933, 1943; The Man without Qualities, 1953) has likewise a hero caught in the dilemma of relativism; surrounded by so many conflicting value systems, he is unable to commit himself to any one of them. The education of Hans Castorp in Thomas Mann's (q.v.) *Der Zauberberg* is similarly an exercise in relativism, in which the young hero is forced to pick his way cautiously among conflicting sets of allegiances. Thus, pluralism and relativism not only constitute the historical and philosophical background of the period; they also inform the substance of most of the major literary works, which, as previously mentioned, were principally novels. It is no accident that the novel of ideas became the predominant genre of those years: the great adventure of the twenties was an intellectual one. Before the hero of the novel can act, he must create the world within which his action is possible. In view of the pluralism of views of the world, the very act of choosing becomes Herculean.

Politically the catastrophic defeat aroused two strong, opposing groups. From the humanitarian impulse and activistic side of expressionism there emerged a socialist literature that attracted writers of the caliber of Arnold Zweig, Heinrich Mann, and Leonhard Frank (qq.v.). This left-wing group gradually produced a hard core of Communist authors such as Brecht, Becher (qq.v.), Anna Seghers, Erich Mühsam (1878-1934), and Karl Otten (1889-1963), whose works in many instances set the pattern for postwar East German literature.

In opposition to this group (and harking back to Lagarde, Langbehn, and Nietzsche [q.v.]) there came into being a literature of the right that reflects the spirit often called the "Conservative Revolution." Its organ was the journal *Gewissen* (Conscience), and its spiritual mentor was Arthur Moeller van den Bruck (1876-1925), who proposes in *Das dritte Reich* (1922) a new conservative party that would reinstate the old Germanic values as an antidote to the vacuum left by the postwar collapse. In popular appeal this movement vastly outweighed any of the other allegiances of the twenties and paved the way for the rise of Nazism, which cleverly exploited certain of its convictions. It had less appeal to the writers.

Moeller van den Bruck complained in 1923 that the best writers were attracted to the left. But in its respectable form, before it degenerated into the propaganda of the Nazi period, this movement enlisted the sympathy of conservative writers like Hermann Stehr (1864-1940) and Wiechert (q.v.), who further developed the *Heimatkunst* (regional literature) of older writers like Gustav Frenssen (1863-1945) and Hermann Löns (1866-1914) in order to depict Germans against the background of their regional homes; or Joseph Ponten (1883-1940) and Hans Grimm (1875-1959), who portrayed the struggles of German colonials outside the national boundaries; or Erwin Guido Kolbenheyer (q.v.) and Hans Friedrich Blunck (1888-1961), who delved into the Germanic past to discover national glories no longer evident in the disenchantment of the Weimar Republic.

This same reaction against the debilitating influence of liberalism, industrialization, and urban culture is evident in the nature poetry (Lehmann, Loerke) that emerged during this period to become one of the happiest developments of German literature in the twenties. During World War II nature poetry provided a means of expression for writers working under conditions of strict censorship, and after 1945 many writers, in their search for values, reached back to Lehmann and Loerke for inspiration.

A third possibility of orientation during these troubled times was offered by the humanistic renaissance, which, without the political reference of the conservative revolution, likewise turned to the past—to the classical age of Goethe and the traditions of Graeco-Roman, Judaeo-Christian civilization—in order to find values for the present. Associated with this trend, and grouped around journals like the *Neue Rundschau* and *Corona*, were many of the most distinguished names of the period: Hofmannsthal, Thomas Mann, Hesse (qq.v.), R. A. Schröder, Carossa (q.v.), and others. In poetry, prose, and drama they looked back beyond the expressionistic revolt to the standards of the past. As a group they displayed more sophistication than the writers of the "Conservative Revolution," who clung almost desperately to a homely realism. Neither did they descend to the naïve mysticism of Kolbenheyer, nor did they flee from the present. They attempted instead to counterbalance the present with the ideals of the past and to come to grips with the problems of modern civilization in a traditional style modified to suit the exigencies of the age. In their essays and autobiographical writings, Hofmannsthal and Carossa provided some of the most distinguished prose of the 20th c., while Schröder and Borchardt (q.v.) brought about a virtual renaissance of classical forms in lyric poetry.

Other writers, who were disengaged politically but not satisfied with the ideals of the humanistic renaissance, turned to a new Christian literature—predominantly Catholic and analogous to the Catholic renaissance of Claudel, Bloy, Bernanos, Mauriac (qq.v.), and others in France. The South German focal points from which this literature emerged before World War I were Carl Muth's (1867-1944) periodical *Hochland* and Richard Kralik's (1852-1934) *Der Gral*. The religious impulse in expressionism had been strong but undirected. Many writers now found a direction in Catholicism: Catholics by birth like Mell, Billinger, Schneider, Elisabeth Langgässer (qq.v.); converts like Gertrud von Le Fort and Bergengruen (qq.v.); and nonconverts who were nevertheless oriented toward Catholicism, such as Werfel (q.v.). Konrad Weiß (1880-1940), one of the most brilliant lyric poets of the c., forged out of Christian imagery a thrilling combination of traditional substance and modern poetic techniques.

The satirists and social critics constituted a group unto themselves. Though they tended generally toward the left (notably Brecht), their humor and cool objectivity often restrained them from any ideological commitment. Unique among them is Karl Kraus (q.v.), who for almost forty years was the incorruptible judge of everything that was rotten in the state of Austria (the Austrian monarchy) and broadly in the whole area of German culture. His periodical *Die Fackel*, which he started in 1899 and from 1911 to his death wrote alone, was a polemical tool with which he untiringly and passionately attacked the corruption of the mind in all fields of public life. His bitterest hatred was directed against the journalism of his day, in which he saw the embodiment of intellectual prostitution. A high point of his writing is the antiwar drama *Die letzten Tage der Menschheit* (1919), a satirical tragedy that is an apolyptical warning of the world's end. The so-called *Gebrauchslyrik* ("functional poetry," analogous to the period's functional architecture, furniture, etc.) of the twenties and thirties was based on an established tradition of satire, reaching back to *fin-de-siècle* journals like *Simplizissimus* and *Die Jugend*, as well as Ernst von Wolzogen's popular cabaret *Das Überbrettl*. Their contribution ranged from the nihilistic skepticism of Brecht and Erich Kästner (q.v.) through the milder parody of Ringelnatz (q.v.) and Dr. Owlglass (pseud. of H. E. Blaich [1873-1945]) to the self-ironization of Eugen Roth (b. 1895). To these satirists none of the allegiances of the chaotic twenties was sacred.

This ideological pluralism is mirrored in the pluralism of forms rampant during those years. The drama ranged from the rigidly classical pieces of the mystic Wilhelm von Scholz (b. 1874) and the socialistically inclined Ernst (q.v.) through the realistic works of the conservative humanist Gerhart Hauptmann (q.v.) and his more satirical disciple Zuckmayer (q.v.) to epigones of expressionism such as Jahnn (q.v.) and the epic theater of Brecht.

Lyric poetry reveals a similarly wide span. By 1907 George (q.v.) had attained a peak of symbolist formalism which he maintained, without significant development, until his death in 1933. The metrical forms of classical antiquity were cultivated both by the modern humanist Schröder and the Catholic Schneider. The "Conservative Revolution" brought forth the nature poetry of Loerke and Lehmann as well as the expressionistically inspired "absolute" poetry of Benn (q.v.). Rilke (q.v.), with his epoch-making *Duineser Elegien* (1923; Duino Elegies, 1931) and *Sonette an Orpheus* (1923; Sonnets to Orpheus, 1936), occupied a lonely prominence between the *l'art pour l'art* of Benn and the introspective searchings of Loerke and Konrad Weiß.

The verse epic, which attained little public success, deserves mention because of the persistence of the genre and the number of outstanding poets who employed the form. Derleth, Spitteler, Däubler, Albrecht Schaeffer, Döblin (qq.v.), Ernst, Blunck, and Gerhart Hauptmann all produced major works in this genre. (It has been resuscitated since World War II by Rudolf Hagelstange (q.v.) in his popular *Ballade vom verschütteten Leben,* 1952; Ballad of a Buried Life, 1962).

Whereas poetry and drama began their development earlier and reached their respective peaks in the first and second decade of the c., the novel matured later. Until 1920 it had remained largely conventional in form, but under the impact of foreign novelists like Joyce, Proust, Gide, Aldous Huxley, and Dos Passos (qq.v.) the German novel was startlingly transformed. It is the beginning of the era of what has been called the *poeta doctus*, the writer sensitive to the intellectual and scientific developments of his time, who seeks to incorporate in "polyhistoric" (Broch) or "essayistic" (Musil) novels the new ideas of the day: Einstein's theory of relativity (Mann), Heisenberg's principle of indeterminacy (Broch), Bohr's theory of complementarity (Musil), Jung's archetypes, logical positivism, and symbolic logic—all make their triumphant entry into literature, not merely as content but also as structural elements.

Though it is especially in prose fiction that these influences make themselves felt, they are not absent from the poetry of intellectuals like Benn. In general, however, the poetry of the age (Rilke, George, Loerke, Weiß, Schröder) is nonintellectual and even anti-intellectual. The drama is social, and concerned with problems of a more political nature.

The intellectual achievements show up most strikingly in the cluster of brilliant novels of the twenties and thirties, in which form is transmuted by new techniques (essayism, lyricism, stream of consciousness, archetypal myth, parallel plots, montage, typological prefiguration, stereoscopic vision, epiphany, etc.) to suit the demands of new ideas (Thomas Mann, Hesse, Döblin, Musil, Broch, Jahnn, Ernst Jünger). There was, of course, a strong current of realistic literature that continued along its traditional way. This is especially conspicuous in the political and social-critical literature of the left (Arnold Zweig (q.v.), Anna Seghers) and the right (Blunck, Ernst von Salomon [b. 1903]) as well as in the best-selling writers of the day (Fallada, Remarque [qq.v.]).

Another noteworthy branch of narrative prose that flowered during this period was the popular biographical and historical novel (Stefan Zweig, Feuchtwanger, Bruno Frank, Alfred Neumann [qq.v.], Emil Ludwig [1881-1948], Walter von Molo [q.v.], and others), based largely upon the impressionistic techniques developed by earlier writers such as Ricarda Huch (q.v.).

The creative prose of the era belongs to the category that is conventionally but imprecisely called "magical realism." This describes the prose of such different writers as Kafka (q.v.), Broch, and Jünger, all of whom employed a surface realism that renders scenes vivid while at the same time pointing to the immanent symbolism (q.v.) of the objects and scenes presented. "Magical realism" is better than the term "new factualism," which is best restricted to critical or satirical works in which the transcendental or even mystical element is not so conspicuous as it is in most of the major prose writers of the generation (Zuckmayer, Brecht).

1933-1945: The Tragic Years

The magnificent interwar period, which produced a literature so rich and variegated in all genres, ended abruptly with the book burnings and censorship of National Socialism. Within Germany literature was under the control of the Nazi party; writers and publishers without the seal of approval of Goebbel's *Reichsschrifttumskammer* (headed by such men as the conservative revolutionary Hans Friedrich Blunck [1888-1961] and the former expressionist Hanns Johst [b. 1890]) were compelled to fall silent or to emigrate. There were certain writers who, because they were not so radically experimental as to deserve the label "degenerate" or who restricted themselves to politically "safe" topics (children's stories, nature poetry, biographical reminiscences), were permitted to continue publishing for a time: for example, Manfred Hausmann (b. 1898), Reinhold Schneider, Andres (qq.v.), Kurt Kluge (1886-1940), Kurt Kusenberg (b. 1904), Edzard Schaper (b. 1908), Albrecht Goes (q.v.), Gerhart Hauptmann, Kasack, (qq.v.), and Loerke. Some, such as Ernst Jünger and Benn (qq.v.) were initially sympathetic to the aims of National Socialism and apologists for the Third Reich. But both these writers became disenchanted during the late thirties: Benn was no longer permitted to publish; Jünger restricted his work to nonpolitical, "objective" literary media—diaries and essays. These writers, who were as a whole deeply committed to Germany and had no urgent personal reasons to leave the country, are sometimes called collectively "the inner emigration."

Officially, literature was represented by the approved propagandists of the *Reichsschrifttumskammer* (Will Vesper [1882-1962], Baldur von Schirach [b. 1907], Gerhart Schumann [b. 1911], Bethge [q.v.], and others whose names have virtually—and with justification—disappeared from subsequent literary histories). The works of the period fall into various types often summed up as a *Blut- und Bodenliteratur* ("blood and soil" literature): peasant novels in praise of homely Germanic virtue; politically slanted plays, festivals,. and propagandistic "hymns"; historical works that reinterpreted the past to conform to the ideals of the Nazi present. (In *Die große Fahrt* [1934] Blunck attributed the discovery of America to a German!)

The most memorable literature of the period was written in exile, in prison, or in secret. After 1933 some German and Austrian publishers carried on operations, first in Vienna and Prague, then in Stockholm and New York, while a number of firms re-established themselves in Zurich, Basel, Paris, Amsterdam, London, and New York, some of them enjoying the hospitality of established domestic publishers. Many books by emigrant German writers were published by Swiss, Scandinavian, English, and American publishers, most of them in translations.

Centers of orientation were also provided by exile journals like *Die Sammlung* (Amsterdam, 1933-36) or *Maß und Wert* (Zurich, 1937-40), more than 150 periodicals being established between 1933 and 1945 as an outlet for exiled writers. These include *Aufbau* (New York, 1934 ff.), *Die Neue Weltbühne* (Prague-Zurich-Paris, 1932-39), *Das andere Deutschland* (pub. in Buenos Aires as *La otra Alemania*, 1937-49), and *Das Wort* (Brecht and Feuchtwanger [qq.v.], eds., Moscow, 1936-39; later merged with *Internationale Literatur*, Becher [q.v.], ed., Moscow, 1931-45).

Books of great quality by Thomas Mann, Hesse, Werfel, and Brecht (qq.v.)—among many others—were published during this period. Some writers ended in concentration camps, while others were executed after the revolt of July 20, 1944. The *Moabiter Sonette* of A. Haushofer (published posthumously in 1946) and the poems in anthologies such as *De Profundis* (1946) afford a stirring testimony to some who perished. In *Der Totenwald* (1945; Forest of the Dead, 1947), Wiechert (q.v.) narrated his experiences in Buchenwald, where he was imprisoned for several months. Among the most fascinating documents of the times are the many secret journals, which helped to engender a lean, glittering prose that has made an impact on many postwar writers: Ernst Jünger's *Strahlungen* (1940); Hartlaub's (q.v.) *Im Sperrkreis* (1955); Theodor Haecker's (1879-1945) *Tag- und Nachtbücher* (1947; Journal in the Night, 1950); and Klepper's (q.v.) *Unter dem Schatten deiner Flügel* (1956).

The German public, and of course the new generation of writers—unless they were among the few privileged to read manuscripts occasionally circulated in secret—were almost completely cut off from German and world literature except for official publications. Even the literature of the past (Lessing, Schiller, Kleist) was slanted for propagandistic purposes, while the "degenerate" works of the recent past, produced by Jewish and Communist writers (Kafka [q.v.], Werfel, Brecht, Toller [q.v.], and virtually all the major expressionists) were burned. The Nazis thereby brought about an intellectual and cultural nadir just as desperate as the military collapse in 1945.

1945: The Existential Age

Into this literary vacuum there poured, in the years immediately after the war, floods of works which hitherto were virtually unknown in Germany. There was a torrent of foreign literature in translation, and now for the first time Germans became acquainted with writers who had achieved international fame in the thirties and forties. Wilder, Sartre, Camus, Claudel, Hemingway, Eliot, and Faulkner (qq.v.) were among the many who made an immediate and immense impression.

There followed a spate of documents from the prisons and concentration camps, as well as numerous biographical reports from left and right. Ernst von Salomon, for instance, in his notorious *Fragebogen* (1951; Questionnaire 1954), rationalized his participation in the violence of the "Conservative Revolution" and his antagonism toward the Allied occupation after the war; while in *Kirschen der Freiheit* (1952) Andersch (q.v.), a former Communist, justified his desertion from the German *Wehrmacht* and called for a new democratic Germany. These were paralleled by works of a documentary nature in which the events of the recent past and present were laid open for discussion—Theodor Plievier's (q.v.) novels of the Russian campaign; Ernst Schnabel's (b. 1913) brilliant radio features on postwar life —and there were documentaries on the atrocities of the Nazi period.

Among the outstanding major works that appeared in the immediate postwar years were: Broch's (q.v.) *Der Tod des Vergil* (1947; The Death of Virgil, 1945); Hesse's (q.v.) *Das Glasperlenspiel* (1943; Magister Ludi, 1949); Elisabeth Langgässer's (q.v.) *Das unauslöschliche Siegel* (1946); Kasack's (q.v.) *Die Stadt hinter dem Strom* (1947; The City Beyond the River, 1953); Thomas Mann's (q.v.) *Doktor Faustus* (1947; Eng., 1949); and Benn's (q.v.) *Statische Gedichte* (1948). Publishers, eager to replenish their catalogues, reached back into the past and, in the popular new paperback format, began reprinting works that had scarcely had a chance to make a public impact before the curtain of National Socialist censorship closed down on them (e.g., those of Kafka [q.v.]). These great works of literature, becoming accessible all at once to a generation of writers who had had no chance to assimilate them in their natural sequence of organic development, created a literary chaos during the years 1945-50, from which new voices only gradually broke free. Young German writers had to overcome a twelve-year handicap in order to catch up with the rest of the world; for this reason their early works, being dependent upon existing forms, were often highly derivative and, in the eyes of foreigners, poignantly old-fashioned. The problem was complicated by the fact that the new authors found no immediate audience, the market being flooded with the works of older, established writers.

As a first step, the younger generation of writers rejected much that struck them as outmoded and no longer relevant to the more urgent existential problems of the postwar world. This rejection was expressed by the most stirring voice of the first five postwar years, that of Borchert (q.v.), in his poems, stories and, especially, in his play *Draußen vor der Tür* (1947). Borchert expressed the emotions of a generation that felt itself alienated from the past, not only socially and politically, but also literarily. His impatience with prewar literature was echoed by many. Weyrauch (q.v.), in his anthology *Tausend Gramm* (1949), called for a "clearing in our literary thicket" (*Kahlschlag*—a word that has become a shibboleth for the postwar generation of writers). In his important essay, *Deutsche Literatur in der Entscheidung* (1948), Andersch (q.v.) demanded a new, existential literature of commitment. And Hans Werner Richter (b. 1908) spoke out against the "calligraphers" of the past and established, in protest, the now famous "Gruppe 47."

The Gruppe 47, though it has vociferous opponents among postwar writers, was by all odds the dominant force in German letters between 1945 and 1965. The great majority of writers of merit have been more or less closely associated with the group, which is avowedly of a political and social nature, inasmuch as they are committed to action and not merely to aestheticism. These young men who had had to serve in Hitler's armies felt betrayed by the past. As a result, their books have strong elements of political and social criticism: geared first to uncovering the mentality that made Hitler and his henchmen possible; and second, to preventing a similar situation arising in Germany. Thus many of these writers are deeply involved in organizations with a specific political orientation.

The Gruppe 47 had its origin in the debates of prisoners of war in Allied internment camps. The intellectuals among these were eager to create a forum in which they could express the thoughts and sentiments of their generation, which had gone unheeded during the war. Their first mouthpiece was the short-lived periodical *Der Ruf* (1946-47), stifled by the occupation authorities because they considered it too overtly political and not always in line with official policy. In protest against this postwar censorship Hans Werner Richter established informally in 1947 the core of what later became a large, although loose-knit, association of writers. They met informally once or twice a year in order to give new writers a chance to be heard and criticized by their peers. There is a remarkable coherence of theme in the works of these young writers, many of whom constitute the literary elite of postwar Germany (Böll, Schallück, Eich, Jens, Weyrauch, Andersch, Ilse Aichinger, Celan, Ingeborg Bachmann, Martin Walser,

Grass [qq.v.], and Lenz). One finds an unconditional abhorrence of war, and the classical notion of knowledge through suffering is rejected as inhuman. There is a marked turning away from the idealism of the prewar (World War II) generations in favor of human commitment and a concern with the immediate problems of existence (social, philosophical, etc.).

There is, too, a renewed concern with language, but not from a philosophical viewpoint —as was the case around 1900, when language became the object of passionate philosophical arguments. Instead, the writers are anxious, in a meaningless world, to try to redefine even the simplest concepts and words, to search for new values in place of the idealistic values of the past. In protest against the former abstract concern with ideologies, these men are essentially *engagés* (i.e., committed to the politics of the present). Their goal is a true democracy, and their alignment is uniformly somewhat to the left—certainly to the left of the Adenauer (1949-63), Erhard (1963-66), and Kiesinger (1966-) regimes. The new quality of their political attitude can be seen clearly if one compares the statements in Weyrauch's anthology *Ich lebe in der Bundesrepublik* (1960) with the more philosophical tone of the political utterances of Thomas Mann, Hesse, or Broch. Opponents of the group (Hans Egon Holthusen [b. 1913], Krämer-Badoni, Gaiser [q.v.], Kurt Ziesel [b. 1911]) are as conspicuous by their political conservatism as they are by their literary orientation to the past.

These themes and interests are expressed in a variety of literary forms. Quite in line with the often journalistic interests of the young writers, the forms to which they turned first after the war were those that promised a large reading public. The traditional *Novelle* was largely abandoned in favor of the more immediately accessible short story, often written under the influence of American writers such as Hemingway. The radio provided another convenient vehicle. The German *Hörspiel*, a distinguished literary genre, has a history reaching back to 1924. The early years, however, were largely exploratory and tentative. From 1924 until 1929 writers did not fully exploit the new medium, relying largely upon adaptations of stage dramas.

The period 1929-33 was one of radical experimentation. Bold avant-gardists such as Brecht and Döblin (qq.v.) were awake to the new potentialities afforded by radio (Brecht's *Der Flug der Lindberghs,* 1929; Döblin's radio version of *Berlin Alexanderplatz,* 1930), but their experiments are more interesting as historical documents than for any intrinsic literary merit. During the Nazi period the literary *Hörspiel* virtually died; the Nazis were interested in the radio only for propagandist purposes. After the war, however, and especially because of the possibilities revealed by the invention of magnetic tape, the genre suddenly came to life again. Borchert's *Draußen vor der Tür* (1947) made its initial impact as a radio play. Resourceful writers and directors like Ernst Schnabel and Paul Schallück exploited the vast possibilities of the documentary radio feature. Eich, especially, transformed the radio play into a unique poetic genre. Since his first postwar *Hörspiel, Träume* (1953), Eich has enriched the medium of the spoken word. He and other writers have found here a genre in which language is reduced to its essence, and for this reason the *Hörspiel* has attracted not only dramatists and narrative writers (Böll, Wolfgang Hildesheimer [b. 1916], Dürrenmatt and Jens [qq.v.]), but also those whose essential impulse is lyrical (Eich, Bachmann).

Poetry of the first five postwar years, like the short story and the radio play, was essentially sober, in reaction to the disengaged, aesthetic poetry of the twenties and thirties. The characteristic voice, again, is that of Eich, whose early works (e.g., *Abgelegene Gehöfte,* 1948) are often no more than a listing of the basic things that alone seem sure in the uncertain world of the soldier and the postwar veteran. A turning point was marked in 1951. In that year Benn delivered his famous talk, *Probleme der Lyrik,* in which he advanced the arguments for an absolute poetry harking back to expressionism (q.v.)—a poetry that is sufficient unto itself, unreliant upon the outside world. Under the impact of Benn's dicta several young poets turned to a new, hermetic poetry (Eugen Gomringer [b. 1925], Franz Mon [b. 1926], Helmut Heißenbüttel [b. 1921]). But the more characteristic reaction, which has produced the best poetry of the decade after 1951, was a synthesis of the old and the new. Poets like Celan and Bachmann combined in their works the existential concerns manifested by Eich with the stylistic achievements of *l'art pour l'art.* Others, like Krolow (q.v.), Heinz Piontek (1925-67), Walter Höllerer (b. 1922) and A. A. Scholl (b. 1926), reached back to the nature poetry of Loerke and Lehmann. Still others, like Grass and Enzensberger (q.v.), informed modern techniques with the satiric intent of Erich Kästner or Ringelnatz (qq.v.). The representative anthology of these years is Höllerer's *Transit* (1956), which stresses the experimental nature of modern poetry and its existential concerns more than Hans Egon Holthusen's conservative collection, *Ergriffenes Dasein* (1953).

A vigorous, contemporary German drama was slow to develop. The postwar stage was primarily under the domination of radically different types of work, such as Gerhart Hauptmann's (q.v.) realistic dramas with their cosmic overtones and Brecht's epic theater. The first young voices were those of the Swiss writers Frisch (q.v.) and Dürrenmatt, whose work grew out of Brecht's theater though they rejected its ideological substance. The postwar German theater did not become independent of foreign influences until the mid-fifties, and in the works of the last years one can perceive a clear attempt to forge a synthesis in dramatic style of the naturalism (q.v.) of the contemporary American theater (Arthur Miller, Tennessee Williams [qq.v.]; Reginald Rose's television drama, *Twelve Angry Men*, has been of especially great influence) and the surrealism (q.v.) of the post-Sartrean French stage (Beckett, Ionesco [qq.v.]). This tendency, which results in dramas that might be called realistic abstractions, is evident in the works of Weisenborn (q.v.), with his "placeless theater," of Lenz, Hermann Moers (b. 1930), Böll, Richard Hey (b. 1926), and Tankred Dorst (b. 1925), among others. In general these dramatists do not depart radically enough from realism to be labeled "surrealistic"; yet because of their symbolic characters and concern with existential problems they represent abstract rather than traditional naturalism. In the theater seasons 1963-66 this sense of realism produced the documentary theater of Heinar Kipphardt ([b. 1931] *Der Fall Oppenheim*, 1964), Rolf Hochhuth ([b. 1931] *Der Stellvertreter*, 1963; The Deputy, 1964), and Peter Weiss ([q.v.], *Marat/Sade*, 1964; Eng., 1965; *Die Ermittlung*, 1965; The Investigation, 1966).

Like the poets and dramatists, who experimented with various forms before evolving a natural synthesis of types suitable to their needs, the novelists also revealed a variety of literary influences that are gradually being absorbed and refined into something new. There was a pronounced Kafka vogue after the war, but with few exceptions (Kasack and Hans

Erich Nossack [q.v.]) its products were inferior. Some writers reached back to such models as Döblin (Koeppen [q.v.]), Musil (Doderer [q.v.]), Thomas Mann (Jens), Hesse (Ernst Kreuder [b. 1903]), or Jahnn (Schmidt [q.v.]). Others, like Gaiser (q.v.), seemed to lean on the steely prose of Ernst Jünger (q.v.). Böll, the best among the postwar novelists, began with fiction patterned after Hemingway, and then, developing under the influence of Faulkner, perfected a style admirable for reflecting the complexities of postwar German society.

Characteristically, the novels of this generation are mildly experimental in form: for the purpose of examining the past in the context of the present a wide variety of techniques were exploited (Schallück, *Engelbert Reineke*, 1959; Böll, *Billard um halbzehn*, 1959 [Billiards at Half-past Nine, 1961]; Gaiser, *Schlußball*, 1958 [Final Ball, 1960]; Grass, *Die Blechtrommel*, 1959 [The Tin Drum, 1962]). Their themes are not abstract, as were those of the novels of the twenties and thirties, but existential; they are concerned with the situation of man in a world without values. Their narrative impulse is consistently stronger than was generally the case with the works of the older writers.

Alongside these developments there has arisen in East Germany a literature of a much different order, much of it isolated in nature. As in the past, often it is lyric poetry that transcends political boundaries. The East German regime, like that of any totalitarian state, has produced its share of odes to Stalin and Ulbricht; East German anthologies have their fair share of traditional commemorative poems dedicated to new factories, roads, and production quotas. The better poets, however, numbering such hard-core Communists as Becher (q.v.) and Stefan Hermlin (b. 1915), forced to leave their country during the thirties, have earned a rightful place in Western anthologies. Nature poetry especially, in the manner of Lehmann and cultivated by Huchel, Bobrowski (qq.v.) and Christa Reinig (b. 1926), has flourished. But in general there has been a dearth of technical experimentation.

The drama and novel have also remained traditional. The East German theater, including its most promising young dramatist, Peter Hacks (b. 1928), has not progressed beyond Brecht at his most ideological. The prose adheres to the socialist realism exemplified, at its best, by older novelists like Arnold Zweig (q.v.) and Anna Seghers, who, like Becher and Huchel, returned to East Germany after the years of exile. Since 1960 certain young writers have come to the fore, and in their work may be seen much the same features as are found in the writings of their West German counterparts.

The variegated literary texture of postwar Germany is reflected in the criticism and literary journals of the period. The critics, like the journals, can most easily be characterized by their political slant. On the reactionary right one finds extremists like Kurt Ziesel, who reacts violently to anyone associated with the Gruppe 47. A milder view is represented by Hans Egon Holthusen, whose literary allegiances go back to the generation of Benn and Eliot, just as his political sympathies lie largely with the present conservative government; he is supported by other moderates such as Hermann Kesten (b. 1900) and Curt Hohoff (b. 1913). In the center, allied with the Gruppe 47, are its official spokesmen Jens and Walter Höllerer; while on the left one finds excellent critics like Hans Mayer (b. 1907) and Marcel Reich-Ranicki (b. 1920), who fled from the East Zone but still retain their Marxist orientation.

The weekly newspaper *Die Zeit* has been scathingly referred to as the "house organ" of the Gruppe 47. This is an exaggeration, but it contains an element of truth. Likewise, the literary journal *Akzente*, edited by Walter Höllerer and Hans Bender (b. 1919), provides a forum for the experimental writing of the younger generation. More conservative politically and aesthetically is the *Merkur*, with regular contributors like Holthusen and Karl August Horst (b. 1913). The *Neue Rundschau*, at one time (before World War I) the official publication of avant-gardism, now represents the conservative forces. The leading East German literary journal, *Sinn und Form*, was long under the direction of Johannes R. Becher and Huchel; it represented the official voice of East German literature.

The situation outlined here represents the main literary trends in Germany in the years 1945-60. It is the picture of a generation in revolt against its fathers; and like most revolts it is characterized in its early years by a groping, from which a positive direction has only recently emerged. Although many writers of the Gruppe 47 are now in their most productive years, the group itself, as a literary

phenomenon, no longer has the homogeneity it once had and can no longer be regarded as the official voice of postwar West German literature. Two of the most outstanding names of German literature since 1960 (Uwe Johnson and Grass [qq.v.]) have indeed emerged from the Gruppe 47, but being much younger than other members such as Eich, Böll, and Andersch, their experiences and concerns are radically different.

Grass has forsaken the experimental techniques of the twenties and thirties to return to the tradition of the picaresque novel represented in Germany by Winckler ([q.v.] *Der tolle Bomberg,* 1923), Kurt Kluge ([b. 1886] *Der Herr Kortüm,* 1938), Albert V. Thelen ([b. 1903] *Die Insel des zweiten Gesichts*, 1953), Krämer-Badoni (*In der großen Drift,* 1949), and Mann (*Felix Krull,* 1954 [Confessions of Felix Krull, Confidence Man, 1955]). Grass's *Blechtrommel* as well as his more recent novels are a culmination of this genre. Johnson's works (*Mutmaßungen über Jakob,* 1959 [Speculations about Jacob, 1963], etc.), on the other hand, represent an attempt to adapt the *roman nouveau* of contemporary France as a means of representing a politically divided Germany.

These developments, which are not so characteristically German as the works of the Gruppe 47, have brought the most recent German literature more into line with trends in France and America. They may well presage a new direction.

BIBLIOGRAPHY: Eloesser, A., *Modern German Literature* (1933); Bertaux, F., *Panorama of German Literature from 1871-1931* (1935); Samuel, R., and Thomas, R. H., *Expressionism in German Life, Literature and the Theater, 1910-1924* (1939); Lange, V., *Modern German Literature, 1870-1940* (1945); Friedrich, W. P., with Shelley, P. A., and Seidlin, O., *History of German Literature* (1948; 4th ed., 1959); Boeschenstein, H., *The German Novel, 1939-1944* (1949); Holthusen, H. E., *Der unbehauste Mensch* (1951); Heller, E., *The Disinherited Mind* (1952; 2nd ed., 1957); Grenzmann, W., *Deutsche Dichtung der Gegenwart* (1953); Holthusen, H. E., *Ja und Nein* (1954); Friedmann, H., and Mann, O., eds., *Deutsche Literatur im zwanzigsten Jahrhundert* (1954; 2nd ed., 1956); Friedmann, H., and Mann, O., *Christliche Dichter der Gegenwart* (1955); Friedmann, H., and Mann, O., *Expressionismus* (1956); Pascal, R., *The German Novel* (1956); Closs, A., *Medusa's Mirror* (1957); Hamburger, M., *Rea-*

son and Energy: Studies in German Literature (1957); Horst, K. A., *Die Deutsche Literatur der Gegenwart* (1957); Jens, W., *Statt einer Literaturgeschichte* (1957); Blöcker, G., *Die neuen Wirklichkeiten: Linien und Profile der modernen Literatur* (1958); Hughes, H., *Consciousness and Society: The Reorientation of European Social Thought, 1890-1930* (1958); Jens, W., *Moderne Literatur: Moderne Wirklichkeit* (1958); Bithell, J., *Modern German Literature, 1880-1950* (3rd ed., 1959); Garten, H. F., *Modern German Drama* (1959); Kayser, W., ed., *Deutsche Literatur in unserer Zeit* (1959); Lennartz, F., *Deutsche Dichter und Schriftsteller unserer Zeit* (8th ed., 1959); Sokel, W. H., *The Writer in Extremis: Expressionism in 20th Century Literature* (1959); Waidson, E. M., *The Modern German Novel* (1959); Fechter, P., *Geschichte der deutschen Literatur*, revised by Tank, K. L., and Jacobs, W., Vol. 2: *Die Literatur des zwanzigsten Jahrhunderts* (1960); Bennett, E. K., *A History of the German Novelle* (2nd ed. revised by Waidson, E. M., 1961); Geissler, R., ed., *Zur Interpretation des modernen Dramas* (1961); Heselhaus, C., *Deutsche Lyrik der Moderne* (1961); Holthusen, H. E., *Kritisches Verstehen* (1961); Jens, W., *Deutsche Literatur der Gegenwart* (1961); Soergel, A., and Hohoff, C., *Dichtung und Dichter der Zeit* (2 vols., 1961, 1963); Arntzen, H., *Der moderne deutsche Roman* (1962); Geissler, R., ed., *Möglichkeiten des modernen deutschen Romans* (1962); Richter, H. W., ed., *Almanach der Gruppe 47* (1962); Sternfeld, W., and Tiedemann, E., *Deutsche Exil-Literatur, 1933-1945; Eine Bio-Bibliographie* (1962); Nonnenmann, K., ed., *Schriftsteller der Gegenwart: Deutsche Literatur. 55 Porträts* (1963); Schwitzke, H., *Das Hörspiel: Dramaturgie und Geschichte* (1963); Reich-Ranicki, M., *Deutsche Literatur in West und Ost* (1963); Kunisch, H., and Hennecke, H., eds., *Handbuch der deutschen Gegenwartsliteratur* (1965); Wiese, B. von, ed., *Deutsche Dichter der Moderne* (1965)

THEODORE ZIOLKOWSKI

GHELDERODE,
(Adhémar-Adolphe-Louis-) Michel de

Belgian dramatist and narrative writer, b. 3 April 1898, Elsene; d. 1 April 1962, Brussels

G., a Belgian of Flemish extraction who wrote in French, was the son of an official in the Brussels national archives. Before assuming a position in this same government department he was a sailor, soldier, laborer, and journalist. His literary work is as extensive as it is diverse, and includes contributions to the fields of ethnology and Belgian history as well as short stories and plays. The latter—numbering more than fifty—established his reputation as a powerfully expressive writer.

G.'s plays contain elements of existentialist (see existentialism), mystical, and "expressive" theater. A caustic irony and an extremely keen sense of the fantastic and the ludicrous mark his style. All his plays express a most deep hatred of the commonplace and a contempt for the conventional and the bourgeois mentality. Ironical farce and mystical drama meet in his poetic work. In this his aim is not to smooth things over but to provoke; he is aware of the demonic within man and of the diabolical elements besetting him.

G. deliberately includes the coarse and the repulsive in his writing. Like the work of Pieter Brueghel the Younger and of Goya and James Ensor, to whom he felt drawn, his writing depicts the irrational side of man. As he himself said, his world was that of the Middle Ages and the early Renaissance—violent, passionate, and at the same time pervaded by a longing for purity.

FURTHER WORKS: *La Halte catholique* (1922); *L'Histoire comique de Kaizer Karel* (1923); *La Mort du Docteur Faust* (1926); *Don Juan* (1928); *Pantagleize* (1930; Eng., 1958); *Escurial*, (1930; Escorial, 1958); *Barrabas* (1933; Eng., 1958); *Arc-en-ciel* (1933); *Les Aveugles* (1933); *Sire Halewijn* (1934; Sir Halewyn, 1958); *Christophe Colomb* (1934); *La Ballade du grand macabre* (1936); *Fastes d'enfer* (1938); *Sortilèges* (1941); *Hop Signor* (1942); *Un Soir de pitiê* (1955); *Le Club des menteurs* (1955); *Les Entretiens d'Ostende* (1956); *Théâtre complet* (5 vols., 1950-57; Seven Plays, 1960); *La Flandre est un songe* (1953); *Crépusculaires* (1962). **Selected English trans.:** *The Strange Rider, and Seven Other Plays* (1964)

BIBLIOGRAPHY: Lepage, A. *M. de G.* (n.d.); Hauger, G., "Notes on the plays of M. de G.," TDR, IV (1959), 19-30; Draper, S., "Discovery of G.," *Commonweal*, LXXIII (1960), 113-15.

PAUL WIMMER

GHÉON, Henri

(pseud. of *Henri [-Léon] Vaugeon*), French dramatist, novelist, biographer, and essayist, b. 15 March 1875, Bray-sur-Seine; d. 13 June 1944, Paris

As a precursor of modern Christian drama in France, G. was primarily concerned with bringing home to his audience through the simplest possible scenic resources the crucial conflicts in the lives of the saints. His influence as a writer was by no means negligible, thanks to the spirit in which he wrote his more than sixty plays rather than to their actual texts. With his company, Les Compagnons de Nôtre-Dame, founded in 1924, G. was one of the first to go back to "acting oh the naked boards," which Jean Vilar and other directors subsequently took up with such enthusiasm.

G. intended his plays, which are oriented toward medieval mysteries, to be taken as dramatic arguments. What he was most interested in was the movement of his characters on the stage. These characters are, in fact, often no more than personified ideas: The powerful theatrical expression with which they are endowed is devised to compensate for the literary poverty of the text.

From *Le Comédien et la grâce* (1925; The Comedian, 1933) to *Judith* (1937) G.'s aim was always to reveal to the spectator the struggle of good against evil. His plays were intended to show a perpetual "seesawing between heaven and earth"; to this end, implanted in them are theatrical, fairytale magic and popular symbolism.

G. published novels too, including the very appealing *Le Saint curé d'Ars* (1928; The Secret of the Curé d'Ars, with a note on the saint by G. K. Chesterton [q.v.], 1929). He also wrote essays (*Nos Directions*, 1911) and several "lives of saints," which combine literary elegance with genuine piety.

FURTHER WORKS: *Le Consolateur* (1903); *Le Pain* (1911); *Le Pauvre sous l'escalier* (1911); *La Farce du pendu dependu* (1911); *L'Impromptu du charcutier* (1920); *L'eau de vie* (1921); *Jeux et miracles pour le peuple fidèle* (2 vols., 1922); *Sainte Maurice ou l'obéissance* (1922); *Les Trois miracles de Sainte Cécile* (1922); *Thomas d'Aquin* (1924); *Sainte Claire d'Assise* (1924); *Le Miracle des pauvres claires at de l'homme au képi brodé* (1924); *La Parade du pont au diable* (1925; The Farce of the Devil's Bridge, 1956); *Les Trois sagesses du vieux Wang* (1925); *La Merveil-leuse histoire du jeune Bernard de Menthon* (1926); *La Vie profonde de Sainte François d'Assise* (1926); *Les Jeux de l'enfer et du ciel* (3 vols., 1929); *La Vieille Dame des rues* (1930); *Sainte Anne d'Auray* (1931; St. Anne and the Gouty Rector, 1950); *La Mort de Lazare* (1931; *Promenades avec Mozart* (1932; In Search of Mozart, 1934); *Sainte Thérèse de Lisieux* (1934); *Le Mystère du Roi Saint Louis* (1935); *Le Noël sur la place* (1935; Christmas on the Village Square, 1938); *Saint Jean Bosco* (1935; The Secret of Saint John Bosco, 1936); *Les Chants de la vie et de la foi* (1936; The Mystery of the Finding of the Cross, 1956); *Le Jeu des grandes heures de Ruins* (1938); *Saint Vincent Ferrer* (1939; Eng. 1939); *Saint Martin* (1941; Saint Martin of Tours, 1946); *La Jambe noire* (1941); *L'Art du théâtre* (1944; The Art of the Theatre, 1961); *Œdipe* (1952)

BIBLIOGRAPHY: Raymond, M., *H. G.* (1939); Deléglise, M., *Le théâtre de G.* (1947); Clemente, Sister M., "H. G.," *Renascence*, XII (1960), 67-73

FRANZ WEYERGANS

GHEORGHIU, Constantin Virgil

Rumanian novelist and essayist writing in French, b. 15 Sept. 1916, Razboenie-Neamtz

Until the outbreak of World War II, G. was an assistant secretary in the Rumanian ministry of foreign affairs. Later he served on the German side as a Rumanian war correspondent. In 1946 and 1947 he spent a year and a half in prison camps at Weimar and Heidelberg. In the course of this period he collaborated with his wife on the science-fiction novel *La Vingt-cinquième heure* (1947; The Twenty-Fifth Hour, 1950), first published in Paris and a great success. G. subsequently settled in Cannes.

La Vingt-cinquième heure is a bold satire of conditions in the modern totalitarian state. Resemblances to Orwell's (q.v.) *1984*, which appeared a year later, have often been noted. G.'s novel, like Orwell's, shows man at the mercy of the anonymous forces of technology, of mechanistic ideologies and collectivism. G.'s hero, a young Rumanian peasant, is registered as a Jew through "administrative error" and from then on is shunted from one concentration camp to another. As the narrative progresses, his complete enslavement by the forces of totalitarian bureaucracy and brutal police systems is presented as an example of mid-twentieth-century man's distress. In *La Seconde Chance* (1952) G., within the framework of a similar theme, pleads for a firm Western stand against Soviet totalitarianism; his continuing work as a novelist and an essayist has been concerned with restating this argument in the context of current political events.

FURTHER WORKS: *Rumänische Märchen* (in German, 1948); *L'Homme qui voyagea seul* (1954); *Le Peuple des immortels* (1955); *Les Sacrifies du Danube* (1957); *Saint Jean Bouche d'or* (1957); *Les Mendiants de miracle* (1958); *La Cravache* (1960); *Perahim* (1961); *La maison de Petrodava* (1961); *Alibi pour Limitroff* (1962); *Vie de Mahomet* (1962); *De la vingt-cinquième heure à l'heure éternelle* (1965); *La Tunique de peau* (1967)

BIBLIOGRAPHY: On *The Twenty-Fifth Hour*—*N.Y. Herald Tribune Book Review,* 29 Oct. 1950, p. 5, *Time,* 6 Nov. 1950, p. 110; Chappey, J., *Le Communisme n'est pas seul responsable* (1951)

HELMUT BENDER

GIDE, André
French novelist and essayist, b. 22 Nov. 1869, Paris; d. there, 19 Feb. 1951

G.'s work is a confession; it provides a picture of his life as a spiritual odyssey leading from the exquisite symbolism (q.v.) of Mallarmé and a Huguenot morality to the atheism of Renan, and culminating in a serenity reminiscent of Goethe. His works have been translated into seventeen languages; he himself translated English, German, and Russian works into French. If one were to attempt to determine G.'s place in literature, one would place him somewhere near Montaigne, for he was more of a moralist than a creative artist.

On his father's side G. was descended from Huguenot peasants in the Cevennes, and on his mother's from a Norman family of court officials. His father died in 1880 and G. grew up in a strictly Protestant environment. Calvinistic morality and dogmatic liberalism (for the minister from whom he received his religious training did not believe in the divinity of Christ) were the keynotes of his Christian education. He always felt drawn to the "evangelical" Jesus, full of gentleness and joy, but later rejected "Huguenot" moralism, which he thought had been introduced into Christianity

by St. Paul. From 1897 on G. set Jesus, the "God" of love, over against God the creator, the originator of morality. In 1942 he even identified God the creator with the laws of the world and the God of love with the human striving toward the good and the beautiful. For him Jesus personified the burgeoning and progress of humanity. The influence of this extremely freethinking interpretation of the Gospels is perceptible in nearly all G.'s works.

In 1895 G. married his cousin, Madeleine Rondeaux, who was two years older than he. Tossed and torn between deviant sensuality and an excessively "desensualized" love for his wife, he was unable to consummate the marriage. This became the "secret drama" of his life. In G. pederasty (to which he succumbed after his visit to Africa in 1893, and to which he was one of the first writers to allude openly in his books) was a deep-rooted manifestation of his emotional make-up. This was never discussed between husband and wife (except for one unsuccessful attempt in 1916). In fact, until 1917, when Madeleine learned of her husband's propensity from Ghéon (q.v.)—and to a lesser extent until her death in 1938—she remained for G. "the mystical light of his life," the pole "Alissa" of his humanism (the Christian attitude of renunciation).

At the age of eighteen, under the influence of Pierre Louÿs (q.v.), G. discovered Goethe's *Faust*. Faust's monologue on his awakening to nature was a revelation to him. G. discovered that God could speak to him through the senses too. His epicurean hedonism—in *Les Nourritures terrestres* (1897; The Fruits of the Earth, 1949) or *L'Immoraliste* (1902; The Immoralist, 1930), for example—can to some extent be traced to this earliest influence of Goethe, which was more significant than the influence of Pierre Loti (q.v.), Renan, or Flaubert, whose works he also read in 1887. G. was neither a mystic nor a formal philosophical thinker, as many critics have claimed. His mind was more given to the aesthetic perception of the sensuous world than to the investigation of inner realms. He demanded constant preparedness for the moment but never let himself be overwhelmed by delight in it or by the joy of existence. He dissected and tested his sensations and toyed with them. In some years, particularly between 1902 and 1913, the conflict between the spiritual and the physical in him was very strong, but apart from this he tended toward aesthetic enjoyment of life.

From 1881 on, a strong influence of Mallarmé becomes noticeable. Louys drew G. into avant-garde literary circles and introduced him to "the Magician." Mallarmé taught him to scorn the concerns of the moment and helped him to solve psychological as well as stylistic problems. The reserved attitude toward the world of things, the aestheticism and the musicality of the sentences in G.'s first works (the prose poems of *Les Nourritures terrestres*, for instance) are the result of Mallarmé's influence. But above all Mallarmé taught G. to impose highly wrought form upon romantic feeling. This spirit inspired the literary movement that found its organ in the *Nouvelle Revue française*. For almost thirty years this review, founded in 1909 by G. in collaboration with Schlumberger (q.v.), Jacques Copeau, and Rivière (q.v.), attracted the youthful talent of Europe. During this period G.'s thinking was shaped by Nietzsche (q.v.), whom he studied while working on *L'Immoraliste*, which he consciously based on Nietzsche's *Zarathustra*. G.'s superman is one "whose moral demands are not met either by the morality of society or by the religions which society has ruined" (Albérès). Thus, according to G., "immorality" does not lie in surrendering to one's desires: " ... to follow one's inclinations is good, provided one moves upward" (*Les Faux-monnayeurs* [1925; The Counterfeiters, 1927]). G.'s concept of the "*acte gratuit*" (the motiveless act committed out of absolute freedom), the pivotal idea of his first works, also stems from Nietzsche's influence.

From 1902 to 1914 G. was an obscure writer known only to a few connoisseurs of literature such as Jammes, Valéry, Claudel (qq.v.), Larbaud, Ghéon, Rivière, and Charles Du Bos. This group's adoption of Mallarmé's concept of the absolute work of art brought it into conflict with the waning naturalism (q.v.). G.'s contact with Du Bos and Marcel (q.v.) in 1914 led him to devote himself for a time to moral and religious problems. (*Numquid et tu,* published in 1926, dates from the years 1916 and 1917.) After 1917, however, he turned to a humanism rooted in the world.

During the 1920's G.'s fame grew rapidly. The doctrines attributed to him of the alternation of the spiritual and the sensual, of passion, unrest, and "availability," and of the "*acte gratuit*," fascinated a generation that was sickened by patriotic slogans and that largely rejected religious ties. In *Les Caves du Vatican* (1914; Eng., The Vatican Swindle, 1925; Am.,

Lafcadio's Adventures, 1928) G. associated himself briefly with surrealism (q.v.). The publication of *Corydon* (1924; privately pub. in 1911; Eng., n.d.; Am., 1950) and the unabridged version of his sensational autobiographical notes *Si le Grain ne meurt* (1924; If It Die, 1935) made a vital breach in the widespread tendency of the 1920's to ban the literary discussion of sexual problems. The publication of G.'s novel *Les Faux-monnayeurs* made him one of the most widely read and most controversial writers in France and abroad, along with Claudel, Montherlant, Cocteau, and Bernanos (qq.v.).

G.'s travels in the Congo (1926-27), which led to valuable reforms in colonial administration, and his activities in legal matters (1930) made him a sort of unofficial "magistrate of the mind." As early as 1933 he protested against the arrest of Thälmann, the leader of the German Communist Party. In 1935 he admitted before the "Union pour la vérité," to which Mauriac (q.v.), Daniel Halévy, Marcel, Maulnier, and Jacques Maritain also belonged, that what had led him to communism was the concept of a basically Christian humanism which, it seemed to him, Catholicism could never achieve. The same year he presided, with Malraux (q.v.), over the first meeting of the International Congress for the Defense of Culture. During these years G. "engaged" himself on the side of the leftist intellectuals in the ideological and political fight against fascism. (His writings dating from this period were published in 1950 under the title *Littérature engagée* [The White Notebook, 1967]). In 1936 he was invited to the Soviet Union, but nonetheless soon broke with communism (*Retour de l'U.R.S.S.*, 1936 [Back from the U.S.S.R., 1937]; *Retouches à mon Retour de l'U.R.S.S.*, 1937 [Afterthoughts on the U.S.S.R., 1938]). After the death of his wife G. gradually relinquished all political activity. The events of 1939 and the postwar period estranged G. from the younger generation to a great extent. In his old age he strove more and more for the "Olympian serenity" of Goethe and the ultimately skeptical rationalism of Renan.

In 1932 G. received the Goethe Medal; in 1946 Oxford awarded him an honorary degree; in 1947 he won the Nobel Prize for Literature, and in 1949 the Goethe Plaque of the city of Frankfurt am Main. He was buried in Cuverville, the property in Normandy where his wife had lived. In 1952 his works were placed on

ANDRÉ GIDE

the Index of the Roman Catholic Church. ("The works of this writer must be condemned as much for what he affirms as for what he denies.... The high gifts he possessed, his penetrating intelligence, his rich poetic sense, make the necessity of this judgment even more painful."—*Osservatore Romano*)

G.'s first literary works were influenced by symbolism (q.v.). Between 1902 and 1926 his writing follows the line of the French "moralists"; from 1926 until his death its spirit is that of Goethe. His early work, the romantically sensitive story *Les Cahiers d'André Walter* (1891), gives evidence of the drama, moral rather than religious, that played itself out in his mind before he came to his decision, in 1893, in favor of "feeling, which is more beautiful than thinking." G. later repudiated this work, but its style makes it one of the most beautiful he ever wrote. *Le Traité du Narcisse* (1891), dedicated to Valéry, *Les Poésies d'André Walter* (1892), and *La Tentative amoureuse* (1893) leave reality even farther behind, and their musical style is even more exquisite. Here G. deliberately avoided an epic narrative style. *Le Voyage d'Urien* (1894; Urien's Voyage, 1964), the fantastic, symbolic story of a "dream journey," and *Paludes* (1895) in which G. discusses the freedom the individual must fight to attain, are written with irony and satire. *Les Nourritures terrestres* sings of desire, unrest, and "the ecstasy of the senses," in a style which imitates the gospels. This was one of G.'s most influential works among French youth after 1920. In the short story *L'Immoraliste* Nietzsche's influence is obvious in the striving for "authenticity" (G.'s translation of the German *Wahrhaftigkeit*), which is the distinguishing characteristic of the hero. Wilde's influence is documented in G.'s book (1905; Eng., Oscar Wilde: In Memoriam, 1949) on the poet. Here G. expresses his liberal, individualistic attitude toward life; it consists of complete rejection of traditional morality, unqualified acceptance of the absolute autonomy of the completely free individual, and self-observation as the essence of artistic creativity. This spirit also inspired two volumes of critical articles which G. published under the title *Prétextes* (1903; Pretexts, 1959) and *Nouveaux Prétextes* (1911). *La Porte étroite* (1903, Strait is the Gate, 1924), perhaps stylistically the most balanced work of this period, is a classical treatment of the renunciation of human bonds of love (more in the spirit of Corneille than of Christianity, more Protestant

than Catholic), in which G. implies that he considers the "religious" sacrifice senseless. In 1913 the *Nouvelle Revue française* published the ironical crime story *Les Caves du Vatican*, which G. at first intended to call a novel but later labeled a *sotie* and which he also dramatized. The ludicrous crusade of Amédée Fleurissoire satirizes fear of life and traditional moral standards. The murder—the *"acte gratuit"* of Lafcadio, the "French superman" —must be taken in its context, the particular literary climate of the *sotie*. G. now takes up man's blindness to values, the relativity of his moral and religious judgments, his disastrous emotional aberrations, as the theme of *La Symphonie pastorale* (1919; The Pastoral Symphony, 1931). While the language of this "study in the pathology of the moral sense" (Curtius, q.v.) is well-proportioned, its structure and composition occasionally seem contrived.

The scandalous work *Corydon* continued this series of radically anti-Christian and antimoral works. It consists of four dialogues discussing homosexuality from biological, moral, sociological, and historical viewpoints. The only one of his books that G. himself called a novel is *Les Faux-monnayeurs*, which, thanks largely to its original formal structure and the psychological subtlety of its characterization, is his most famous work. Events and characters are reflected by a series of "mirrors." Edouard in particular, a writer occupying a central position in the story, is a mirror, as it were, for all the other characters and for himself too. The *Journal des faux-monnayeurs* (1925; Journal of the Counterfeiters, 1951) which appeared within a few months of the novel, records the various stages of its composition. Its technique derives from the big novels of James (q.v.)—the first time this technique had been used in French literature. This story of the adventures of a group of young people is an attempt to expose the shortcomings and rich potential of the French bourgeoisie.

In the third phase of G.'s work the element of artistic "creativeness" gave way to the stronger influence of formal, speculative thought. *L'École des femmes* (1929; The School for Wives, 1950), *Robert* (1929; Eng., 1950), and *Geneviève* (1936; Eng., 1950) are dry stories serving merely as pretexts for discussing the problem of women in marriage.

G.'s talent for psychological observation, particularly for self-interpretation, found expression in his voluminous journals. These cover a period of more than fifty years and offer a documentary picture of intellectual Europe in the first half of the 20th c. (*Journal 1889-1939*, 1939; *Journal 1939-1942*, 1946; and *Journal 1942-1949*, 1950; The Journals of A. G., 1947-1951) and are imbued with the blend of lofty serenity and shuddering awe that G. loved in Goethe. The posthumously published autobiographical notes, too, are marked by a practical wisdom and Goethean devotion to the realities of this world. They lay bare G.'s tragic marriage and his wife's mental suffering (*Et nunc manet in te*, 1951 [Am., Madeleine, 1952]; *Ainsi soit-il, ou Les jeux sont faits*, 1951 [So Be It, or The Chips Are Down, 1959]). Schlumberger's book *Madeleine et A. G.* (1956), presenting a portrait of G.'s wife, is an indispensable supplement to *Et nunc manet in te*. *Thésée* (1946; Theseus, 1950), G.'s literary testament, is also to be regarded as autobiographical. In balanced prose, as economical as it is expressive, it treats of the problems of mature age.

G.'s correspondence with many of his friends and famous contemporaries also contains self-revelations of artistic and human significance. The correspondence with Claudel in particular shows G.'s struggle for traditional Christianity but also his firm insistence on remaining in the anti-Christian world (*Correspondance entre Paul Claudel et A. G., 1889-1926*, 1949).

FURTHER WORKS: *Le Promethée mal enchaîné* (1899; Eng., Prometheus Illbound, 1919; Am., Marshlands and Prometheus Misbound, 1953); *Saul; Le roi Candaules* (1904); *Isabelle* (1911); *Le Retour de l'enfant prodigue* (1912; The Return of the Prodigal, 1953); *Morceaux choisis* (1911); *Dostoïevski* (1923; Dostoevsky, 1926); *Incidences* (1924); *Voyage au Congo* (1927; in Travels in the Congo, 1929); *Retour du Tchad, Suite du voyage au Congo* (1929; also in Travels in the Congo, 1929); *Essai sur Montaigne* (1929; Eng., 1929); *L'Affaire Redureau* (1930); *M. Proust* (1930); *Œdipe* (1931; in Two Legends: Oedipus and Theseus, 1950); *Les nouvelles nourritures* (1935); *Œuvres complètes* (15 vols., 1931-39); *Interviews imaginaires* (1942); *Notes sur Chopin* (1948; Notes on Chopin, 1949); *Francis Jammes et A. G., Correspondance* (1947); *Feuillets d'automne* (1949); *C. Du Bos* (1950); *Poésie, Journal, Souvenirs* (2 vols., 1952; Recollections of A. G., abridged trans., 1953); *Rainer Maria Rilke et A. G., Correspondance* (1952); *Paul Valéry et A. G., Correspondance, 1890-1942* (1955; Self-Portraits, abridged trans., 1966); *Amyntas* (1958;

Eng., 1958); *The Correspondence of A. G. with Edmund Gosse* (1961); *A. G. - A. Suarès, Correspondance* (1963); *A. G. - A. Bennett, Correspondance* (1964)

BIBLIOGRAPHY: Du Bos, C., *Dialogue avec G.* (1929); Albérès, R. M. *L'Odyssée d'A. G.* (1951); Martin du Gard, R., *Notes sur A. G.* (1951); Curtius, E. R., *Französischer Geist im 20. Jahrhundert* (1952); Starkie, E., *A. G.* (1953); Lang, R., *A. G. et la pensée allemande* (1953); O'Brien, J., *Portrait of A. G.* (1953); Beigbeder, M., *A. G.* (1954); Delay, J., *The Youth of A. G.* (1963); Brée, G., *G.* (1963); Hytier, J., *A. G.* (1963); Ireland, G. W., *G.* (1963); Freedman, R., *The Lyrical Novel* (1963); Martin, C., *A. G. par lui-même* (1963); Brennan, J. G., *Three Philosophical Novelists: Joyce, G., Mann* (1964); Fowlie, W., *A. G.: His Life and Art* (1965); Mauriac, C., *Conversations with A. G.* (1965)

CHARLES MOELLER

A bold experimenter in the field of the novel, a born confessor and moralist, he grew in stature to great intellectual eminence as time went by, despite the problematical side of his nature, which moralists of a simpler breed felt obliged to censure. He remained true to this problematical side, which we can define more exactly only by pushing the concept of "curiosity" to its highest, most spiritualized level. Curiosity, then, is the skepticism, now transformed into a creative force, which he found in Goethe, perhaps his most beloved teacher, and which he translated as *Forschungsdrang*. What mattered to him was not peace of mind, satisfaction, psychological certainty or security; unrest, creative doubt, the never-ending advance toward truth were his lot— a lifelong wooing of truth with all the resources his intellect and his talent could muster.

Thomas Mann, *Nachlese* (1956), p. 143

This acceptance of the complexity of his own life's substance is no longer Narcissus coquettishly admiring his own reflection. It is the posture of the truly honest man . . .

Gide would see any premature simplification as a lie to himself and to the world. That is why he may feel it his duty to leave the plexus within himself tangled and unresolved . . .

What Gide means by indecisiveness is the firmness of an honest man, is faith in his inner voices— "piety."

Ernst Robert Curtius, *Französicher Geist im zwanzigsten Jahrhundert* (1952), p. 61 f.

He has remained the victim of that 19th c. individualism stigmatized by Malraux. He taught us the taste for and the joy of living, the value of beautiful language, curiosity, fervor, irony, sometimes even disinterestedness and courage, sincerity to ourselves, and the worship of truth. He taught us to juggle with ideas, to detach ourselves successively from everything we have loved. He did not teach us to live: he taught us only the worship and idolization of life.

Pierre de Boisdeffre, *Métamorphose de la littérature*, I (1953), p. 182

The impression this book [*Les Caves du Vatican* (Lafcadio's Adventures)] left on me was not disgust or contempt: it was the sort of pang one feels under the impact of something that horrifies chiefly through its atony. This book is truly sinister; all the opinions in it are somehow blighted. No plan: insignificant events come to the fore and assume a morbid importance; there are stories which never come to an end, events link up, or rather succeed one another, with the absurdity, the flaccidity and sometimes the obscenity of a nightmare.

Paul Claudel, *Correspondance entre Paul Claudel et A. G., 1899–1926* (1949), p. 233

I think a good deal of his sincerity, especially at the last, can be attributed to his urge—to use an ugly word—for exhibitionism. It seems impossible to believe that there was not a kind of exhibitionistic cynicism in the attitude he adopted, especially at the end of his life—or, if you prefer it, a kind of defiance. As for the sincerity . . . he was a man who was obviously unsure of his feelings, who was—and for Heaven's sake, this is human nature, not something unique in Gide—intensely attracted by certain ideal aspects and, on the other hand, held prisoner by a certain vice which he had made the grave mistake of allowing to degenerate into a habit.

Mémoires improvisés de Paul Claudel, ed. Jean Amrouche (1954), p. 214 f.

What remains incomprehensible to me is his influence. Artistically and intellectually Gide is nothing. His influence is one of the mysteries that surround me.

Ibid, p. 249

Gide's writing seeks to establish a compromise between the risk and the rule; in him a balance is struck between Protestant law and the homosexual's nonconformity, between the proud individualism of the *grand bourgeois* and the Puritan liking for social constraint; a certain dryness, a difficulty in communicating and a humanism of Christian origin, a keen sensuality, which would like to be innocent; here observance of the rule is combined with the quest for spontaneity. From this play of counter-

poises stems the inestimable service that Gide rendered to contemporary literature: it was he who lifted it out of the symbolist rut.

. . . in a word, he lived his ideas—especially one of them: the death of God.

Jean-Paul Sartre, "Gide vivant," *Les Temps Modernes* (1951), p. 1539 f.

. . . He serves France by writing French better than anyone else in the world. If it were dedicated to a moral end, his language would perhaps be less pure. . . .

. . . His interior disorder becomes, to be sure, the subject of his work, but that is the noblest use to which the godless man can put his misery. . . .

But any man who enlightens us as to ourselves prepares in us the ways of Grace. Gide's mission is to throw torches into our abysses, to collaborate with us in examining our conscience.

François Mauriac, "Bref plaidoyer pour André Gide," *Mes grands hommes* (1949), p. 232 ff.

Language itself is his primary concern. And in the first place it is a matter of "propriety": the propriety of the word, failing which there is no intellectual "appropriation" nor even any human pertinence. Hence that cardinal spiritual sin of "impropriety," which as a Puritan he is obliged to fight. The standard of excellence sought far beyond the word, beyond even the syntax, in the prime matter of the work and its prime movement; life reunited with the very source of artistic creation, as a pledge of the true, the real and the just.

Jean Cocteau, *Face aux lettres françaises* (1909), in *NRF*. *Hommage à André Gide* (1951), p. 75 f.

Gide demanded total accord with himself and the right not to refuse or repudiate any part of the contradictory aspirations of his profound nature. But nothing can prevent such a demand from ending in the inexpiable transposal: the claim that evil is good.

François Mauriac, "Les Catholiques autour d'André Gide," *ibid.*, p. 105

Few men have made me feel that the religious problem was present in their life as a permanent problem. Brushed aside, repressed in some; in others resolved—as they think. I do not say that it tormented Gide, except for a few crises for which we have documentation, but it remained, for him, a problem.

Gide had little religious instinct, and still less taste for metaphysics. He preferred what he considered important to what others consider profound.

Denis de Rougemont, "Un complot de protestants," *ibid.*, p. 285

GIJSEN, Marnix

(pseud. of *Jan-Albert Goris*), Flemish poet, novelist, and essayist, writing in Flemish, English, and French, b. 20 Oct. 1899, Antwerp

G. studied history, and from 1941 to 1964 was the Belgian Commissioner of Information in New York.

He began with Christian-humanitarian expressionist (see expressionism) poetry (*Loflitanie van den H. Franciscus van Assissië*, 1920; *Het huis*, 1925). Later he published chiefly criticism, anthologies, and travel books.

After World War II G. quite unexpectedly emerged as a novelist of a strongly intellectual cast, superior and ironical in tone, and clear and restrained in language. In *Het boek van Joachim van Babylon* (1948; The Book of Joachim of Babylon, 1951), written in the form of a biblical allegory, he turns away—not without cynicism—from the Christian, Flemish idealism of his youth. In *Telemachus in het dorp* (1948) and *De man van overmorgen* (1949) he continued his settlement of accounts with the past; but the overemphatic social slant and unconcealed resentment weaken these novels artistically. *Klaaglied om Agnes* (1951), largely autobiographical, is warmer in tone and tells with great directness of a tragic youthful love. *Goed en Kwaad* (1950) is G.'s bitterest novel and a profession of his belief in an agnosticism like that of Sartre (q.v.). In other novels, including *De vleespotten van Egypte* (1952) and *Er gebeurt nooit iets* (1956), G. contrasts his adopted country, America, with the classical tradition of Europe.

FURTHER WORKS: *Ontdek Amerika* (1927); *Odysseus achterna* (1930); *Ons volkskarakter* (1932); *De literatuur in Z. Nedl. Sedert 1830* (1941); *Peripatetisch Onderricht* (2 vols., 1941-42); *Belgium in Bondage* (1943); *Strangers Should Not Whisper* (1945); *Du génie flamand* (1945); *Belgian Letters* (1946); *The Growth of the Belgian Nation* (1946); *Modern Sculpture in Belgium* (1948); *Modern Belgian Wood Engravers* (1949); *Belgian Letters* (1950); *Drawings by Modern Belgian Artists* (1951); *De kat in de boom* (1953); *De lange nacht* (1954); *De oudste zoon* (1955); *Maria-Anna von Antwerpen* (1955); *Ter wille van Leentje* (1957); *De stem uit Amerika* (1957); *Mijn vriend, de moodenaar* (1958); *De school van Fontainebleau* (1959); *De herkomst van Jan van Eyck* (1959); *De Diaspora* (1961); *Allengs gelyk de spin* (1962); *The House by the Leaning Tree* (1963); *Candid Opinions on*

Sundry Subjects (1964); *Karel Jonckheere* (1964); *Zes van M. G.* (1964); *Jan van Eyck in de Kempen* (1964); *Harmágedon* (1965); *Scripta manent* (1965); *Zelfportret, gevleid, natuurlijk* (1965); *Er gebeurt nooit iets* (1965); *Kroniek der poëzie* (1966); *De parel der diplomatie* (1966)

BIBLIOGRAPHY: Poelants, M., *M. G.* (1958); Westerlinck, A., "Novellen van M. G.," *Dietsche Warande en Belfoort*, CIV (1959), 114-16; Demedts, A., "Naoogst der Expressionisten," *ibid.*, CIX (1964), 282-87; Scheer, L., "De hoofdkaraktere in het werk van M. G.," *ibid.*, XX (1965), 30-51

JORIS TAELS

GILLIAMS, Maurice

Flemish poet, narrative writer, and essayist, b. 20 July 1900, Antwerp

Like his models van de Woestijne and Rilke (qq.v.), G. sees art as a means to thorough self-knowledge. In their hermetic, aristocratically refined form the poems collected in *Het Maria-leven* (1932) and *Het verleden van Columbus* (1938) display a striking correspondence with Rilke's *Dinggedichte*.

In *Elias of het gevecht met de nachtegalen* (1936)—influenced by Rilke's *Malte Laurids Brigge* and *Le Grand Meaulnes* by Alain-Fournier (q.v.)—G. dissects, with the most sympathetic understanding, the feelings and psychic condition of a child. In *Winter te Antwerpen* (1953), too, he succeeds through his use of metaphor in creating a fantasy world of wondrous atmosphere. Here the too esoteric aestheticism that marks most of his work is deepened by a concern for human and religious problems. As an essayist G. is also one of the foremost stylists of the Netherlands.

FURTHER WORKS: *Eenzame vroegte* (1928); *De flesch in de zee* (1929); *Oefentocht in het luchtledige* (1933); *Inleidung tot de idee Henri de Braekeleer* (1941); *De man voor het venster* (1943); *Rubens- en zijn bejde vrouwen* (1947); *Het werk der leerjaren* (1947); *Een bezoek aan het Prinsengraf* (1952); *De kunst van de fuga* (1954); *Vita Brevis* (4 vols., 1956-60); *Emmanuel de Bom* (1958); *Poètes nederlandais* (1967)

BIBLIOGRAPHY: De Vree, P., *M. G.* (1947); Bernlef, J. and Schippers, K., "Gesprek met M. G." (literary interview), *Gids*, CXXVIII (1965), 59-66; Buijnsters, P. J., *"Het Maria-*

MARNIX GIJSEN

MAURICE GILLIAMS

leven van M. G.," *Spiegel der Letteren*, VIII (1965), 184-201; Haes, J. de, "G. in het Duits," *Dietsche Warande en Belfort*, CX (1965), 371-372

JORIS TAELS

GINSBERG, Allen

American poet and social critic, b. 3 June 1926, Paterson, N. J.

G. became prominent in the late 1950's as the leader of the "beat generation" in American literature. His poem "Howl" (in *Howl and Other Poems*, 1956) resumed, in long unrhymed lines reminiscent of Whitman, sentiments reflected earlier and after in the work of G.'s fellow "beat" writers Lawrence Ferlinghetti (b. 1919), Jack Kerouac (q.v.) and Gregory Corso (b. 1925): total disillusionment with the American way of life, protest against man's alienation from authentic feeling in industrialized civilizations, and glorification of mysticism and ecstasy as escapes from both.

G.'s subsequent development as a poet and social critic took a decided turn from the escapist nihilism of "Howl" toward more affirmative doctrines: *Kaddish-Poems 1958-60* (1961) revaluates the Jewish faith of G.'s childhood in a positive sense; *Reality Sandwiches* (1963) pleads for activism on behalf of peace and social justice. G.'s work, which shows decided affinities with expressionism (q.v.), has been less influential in America than it has abroad: Scandinavian, Dutch, and German poetry of the 1960's has been significantly influenced by G. Synchronizing poetry readings with jazz, a style of performance fostered and developed by G., became in the sixties a world-wide mode of presenting poetry.

FURTHER WORKS: *Howl for Carl Solomon* (1956); *Siesta in Xbalba and Return to the States* (1956); *Journals* (1960); *Empty Mirror: Early Poems* (1961); *The Yage Letters* (with William Burroughs, 1963); *The Change* (1963); *Prose Contribution to Cuban Revolution* (1966); *Wichita vortex sutra* (1966); *T. V. Baby Poems* (1968)

BIBLIOGRAPHY: Trilling, D., "The Other Night at Columbia," *PR*, XXVI (1959), 214-230; Ehrlich, J. W., ed., *Howl of the Censor* (1961); Grossman, A., "A. G.: The Jew as an American Poet," *Judaism* XI (1962), 303-8; Hunsberger, B., "Kit Smart's 'Howl'," *WSCL*, VI (1965), 34-44

W.B.F.

GIONO, Jean

French novelist, dramatist, and essayist, b. 30 March 1895, Manosque

Although G.'s plays, especially *Le Voyage en calèche* (1947), and his essays, such as *Les Vraies richesses*, are remarkable, he is first and foremost a novelist. His work falls into three categories consisting of dramatic, lyrical, and psychological stories. For G. is primarily a storyteller, an inspired bard, a singer who began to spin his stories without really knowing where these would lead him. Nevertheless his fiction always conforms to classical patterns. It clings to traditional themes that can be distilled from the adventure of human existence.

At first G. was dominated by the spirit of Homer and Virgil. His first book, *Naissance de l'Odyssée* (not pub. until 1930), is an attempt to transpose the story of the Odyssey into the present day. His first novels, the Pan trilogy *La Colline* (1929; Hill of Destiny, 1929), *Un de Beaumugnes* (1929; Lovers Are Never Losers, 1931), and *Regain* (1930; Harvest, 1931), are lyrical condensations of events in the lives of Provençal mountain peasants. These stories, whose plots are intrinsically naturalistic and interesting only for their exposition of detail, are sparked with poetry; the earth, with its animated, almost personified forces—winds, plants, and animals—is omnipresent. G.'s expansive style, his strongly individual use of metaphor, and his tendency to pantheism—all perfectly blended with the subject matter—made these three books a stimulating and original contribution to 20th c. French literature. Nevertheless, despite the poetic element, the predominant factor in G.'s early work is dramatic action.

Soon thereafter G. began to publish lyrical essays proclaiming the Pan-like joy he derived from union with nature and his rejection of the world of money and the machine (*Le Serpent d'étoiles*, 1933; *Les Vraies richesses*, 1936; *Lettre aux paysans sur la pauvreté et la paix*, 1938). This attitude is carried over into his subsequent novels, which are more loosely constructed, often suggesting prose poems. Here the action sometimes takes on an epic dimension, as, for example, in *Que ma joie demeure* (1935; Joy of Man's Desiring, 1940) and *Bataille dans la montagne* (1937). The characters are minutely described yet at the same time they are mythical figures; they declaim rather than speak. The lyrical passages now become longer and more numerous.

Now came the eventful years 1936 to 1939.

G. had become a pacifist—a position he was later to abandon. The soul-searching of the war years and the disillusionment resulting from the collapse of his Rousseauesque dreams led him to a new novel form which he called the *chronique*. His language became more compressed and colloquial; the unusual adjectives disappeared; a psychology pressed at times to the point of pitilessness is more and more emphasized. *Les Âmes fortes* (1949), *Un Roi sans divertissement* (1947), and *Le Moulin de Pologne* (1952; The Malediction, 1955) date from this period. Their themes are taken from the daily life of country people. Although G. treats these themes in his individual way and introduces a fantastic note, he no longer elevates them into Pan-like intoxication. The allusions to nature are woven into the fabric of the action, and G. seems to be concentrating more and more on economy in his narrative technique. In this period he also produced *Le Hussard sur le toit* (1951; Eng., The Hussar on the Roof, 1953; Am., The Horseman on the Roof, 1954), a book which defies classification. It is the picaresque chronicle of the hussar Angelo who roams about a Provence ravaged by cholera in the year 1835. The hero's zest for life and his natural goodness are paralleled by a merciless scrutiny of the people stricken by the disease, their fears and their selfishness. This book was the first of a trilogy, which includes *Angelo* (1958; Eng., 1960) and *Le bonheur fou* (1957; The Straw Man, 1959).

The autobiographical *chronique*, *Noé* (1947; Noé, His Chroniques, 1961) offers insights into G.'s personal world and his work.

G.'s works prove that literature devoted to the people and landscape of a single region may achieve universality provided that the writer feels philosophically at one with the essence of his native home.

FURTHER WORKS: *Accompagnés de la flûte* (1924); *Manosque-des-plateaux* (1930); *Présentation de Pan* (1930); *Le grand troupeau* (1931); *Jean le Bleu* (1932); *Solitude de la pitié* (1932); *Lanceurs de graines* (1932); *Entrée du Printemps* (1933); *Le Chant du monde* (1934; Song of the World, 1937); *Refus d'obeissance* (1937); *Le Poids du ciel* (1938); *Précisions* (1939); *Pour saluer Melville* (1941); *Le Bout de la route* (1942); *Triomphe de la vie* (1942); *La Femme du boulanger* (1942); *L'Eau vive* (1943); *Théâtre* (1943; partial trans., Three Plays, 1964); *Fragment d'un paradis* (1948); *Mort d'un personnage* (1949);

Faust au village (1951); *Les Grands chemins* (1951); *Le Voyage en Italie* (1953); *Notes sur l'affaire Dominici* (1955; The Dominici Affair, 1956); *Lundi* (1956); *Romans* (1956); *Provence* (1957); *L'Écossais, ou La Fin des héros* (1961); *Chroniques Romanesques* (1962); *Carnet du Maroc* (1963); *Le Désastre de Pavie, 24 Février 1525* (1963; The Battle of Pavia, 24th February 1525, 1965); *Deux cavaliers de l'orage* (1965; Two Riders of the Storm, 1967); *Le Bal* (1965); *Le Déserteur* (1966); *Provence perdue* (1967). **Selected English trans.:** *G. Selections* (1965)

BIBLIOGRAPHY: Michelfelder, C., *J. G. et les religions de la terre* (1938); Marion, B., *J. G.* (1947); Pugnet, J., *J. G.* (1955); Chonez, C., *G.* (1956); Clarke, K. A., "Interview with J. G.," *FR*, XXXIII (1959), 3-10; Smith, M. A. "G.'s Cycle of the Hussard Novels," *FR*, XXXXL (1962), 287-94; Boisdeffre, P. de, *G.* (1965)

FRANZ WEYERGANS

GIRAUDOUX, Jean (Hippolyte)

(pseuds.: *Andouard* [1904], *Maurice Cordelier* [1907]), French dramatist and novelist, b. 29 Oct. 1882, Bellac, Haute-Vienne; d. 31 Jan. 1944, Paris

G.'s reputation was originally that of a precious, cultivated impressionist of brilliant style and facile language. But behind the playful, captivating mastery of language his plays—and especially his last works—reveal a longing for the absolute and a deep skepticism concerning the stupidity of man and his blindness to fate.

G. came from a simple Limousin family. From 1903 to 1904 he studied German language and literature at the École Normale Supérieure in Paris and passed the *agrégation*. In 1905 he became tutor to the Sachsen-Meiningen family of Munich, patrons of the historicizing German theater. He spent the year 1906 in the United States as a lecturer at Harvard, and in 1907 became executive secretary of the Paris *Matin*, to which he contributed graceful little literary pieces (pub. in 1952 under the collective title *Les Contes d'un matin*). He traveled in literary circles, his acquaintances including Morand (q.v.), and also the publisher Bernard Grasset. In 1909 the latter published G.'s *Provinciales*, a collection of novellas admired by Gide (q.v.).

In 1901 G. entered the diplomatic service, where he got to know Claudel (q.v.). He served

JEAN GIRAUDOUX

KARL ADOLPH GJELLERUP

in World War I, recording some of his impressions and opinions about the war in *Lectures pour une ombre* (1917) and *Adorable Clio* (1920). He then embarked upon a brilliant career at the Quai d'Orsay, and at the same time began his real literary career with the youthful novel *Simon le Pathétique*. Next came *Suzanne et le Pacifique* (1921; Suzanne and the Pacific, 1923), a satire on esoteric artistic life in which G. describes the adventures of a French girl shipwrecked on a South Sea island. This was followed in 1922 by *Siegfried et le Limousin* (My Friend from the Limousin, 1923), a bitingly ironical, Faustian dialogue between France and Germany which castigates the cult of racism. *Bella* (1926; Eng., 1927), a love story set against a background of political turmoil in Paris, deals with the Briand-Poincaré controversy. *Eglantine* appeared in 1927, and *Les Aventures de Jérome Bardini* in 1930. The three last-named novels constitute a trilogy. In 1934 G. published *Combat avec l'ange* (Duel of Angels in *Plays*, 1963), and in 1938 his last novel, *La Choix des élues*. These present the major themes of life, love, war, and death to some extent playfully, like a fata morgana—and sometimes with artificiality. It has been asserted that G.'s smooth prose, full of paradoxes and of a cleverness and facility that often make it quite aggressive, bears traces, particularly in his early works, of the style of Jules Renard, as well as showing the influence of Jean Paul. G. certainly knew the poets Paul-Jean Toulet, Jacob and Apollinaire (q.v.), as well as Charles-Louis Philippe and Alain-Fournier (q.v.) The magical element in G.'s work suggests the influence of Philippe and Alain-Fournier, and the humorous element reflects the influence of Toulet, Jacob, and Apollinaire.

An event of decisive importance to G.'s dramatic work was his meeting with the actor-director Louis Jouvet, who produced *Siegfried* (1928; Eng., 1930) at the Comédie des Champs-Elysées in 1928. Literary drama as a genre, with its word-magic, graceful wit, and high-spirited action, now began to compete in popularity and esteem with the cheap, stereotyped *boulevard* theater. *Siegfried* was followed by the sarcastic comedy *Amphitryon 38* (1929; Eng., n.d.), a witty humanization of the classical story; by *Judith* (1931; Eng., 1958), an ironically modified treatment of the traditional Bible story transposed into the present day; and by the delightful comedy *Intermezzo* (1933; The Enchanted, 1950) and the enigmatic, bitter comedy *La Guerre de Troie n'aura pas lieu* (1935; Tiger at the Gates, 1956)—a prophetic look at Europe's destiny. Another theatrically very effective treatment of a classical subject is *Electre* (1937; Electra, n.d.), the tragedy of which is relieved by comically ironic characters. The imaginative play *Ondine* (1945; Eng., 1954), based on Friedrich de la Motte-Fouqué's *Undine*, was first performed in 1939.

At the outbreak of World War II G. was appointed minister of information—a function which he did not find congenial. The collection of political essays *Sans pouvoirs* (1946) dates from this period; its title is a variation on *Pleins pouvoirs*, a volume of short pieces G. had published in 1939.

After the defeat of France in 1940 G. left Paris. In 1943, despite Jouvet's absence, his play *Sodome et Gomorrhe* (1945) was performed in Paris with Edwige Feuillère. It was the bitterest thing he ever wrote about the relationship between man and woman. Next he wrote screenplays for the films *La Duchesse de Langeais* and *Les Anges du péché*, which were directed by R. Bresson. The posthumous play *La Folle de Chaillot* (1945; The Madwoman of Chaillot, 1947), which has a fairy tale quality, deals with the triumph of good over human ignobility and meanness.

G., who was possessed by "a spirit of extravagant romanesque fantasy, an irrepressible talent for distortion and an enchanting disregard for realism" (Thibaudet), wanted to rise above plain, everyday life. In his works man makes fun of his daily life. As a novelist and dramatist G. ridicules the stupidity of the mediocre, which plays into the hands of fate, provoking calamities and base deeds, so that in the end those who stand for uncompromising fairness emerge as the vanquished. Thus G.'s sparkling wit and his somewhat snobbishly precious style hide the bitterness of a pessimist and skeptic. Yet no less does his work also impart the idea of an attainable human happiness, and unfettered and wise way of life.

FURTHER WORKS: *L'École des indifférents* (1911); *Retour d'Alsace 1914* (Campaigns and Intervals, 1918); *Amica America* (1918); *Adieu à la guerre* (1919); *Elpénor* (1919; Elpenor, 1958); *La Pharmacienne* (1922); *La Prière sur la tour Eiffel* (1923); *Visite chez le Prince* (1924); *Juliette au pays des hommes* (1924); *Hélène et Touglas; ou les joies de Paris* (1925); *Premier Rêve signé* (1925); *Le Cerf* (1926); *Les Hommes tigres* (1926); *Le Sport* (1928); *Marche vers Clermont* (1928); *La*

Grande Bourgeoise; ou toute femme a la vocation (1928); *Le Signe* (1929); *Racine* (1930; Eng., 1938); *Rues et visages de Berlin* (1930); *Je présente Bellita* (1931); *Mirage des Bessines* (1931); *Fin de Siegfried* (1934); *Tessa* (1934); *Supplément au voyage de Cook* (1937; The Virtuous Island, 1956); *L'Impromptu de Paris* (1937); *Et Moi aussi, j'ai été un petit Meaulnes* (1937); *Cantique des Cantiques* (1938); *Les Cinque Tentations de La Fontaine* (1938); *Pour l'Avenir français* (1940; The France of Tomorrow, 1940); *L'Appolon de Marsac* (1942; new title, *L'Appolon de Bellac,* '1947; Apollo of Bellac, 1951); *Pour Lucrèce* (1953; Duel of Angels, 1958); *Théâtre complet* (16 vols., 1945-54); *Œuvres complètes* (1958) **Selected English trans.:** Le Sage, L., *L'Œuvre de J. G.* (I, 1956; II, 1958); *Plays* (1964)

BIBLIOGRAPHY: Brasillach, R., *Portraits* (1935); Magny, C. E., *Précieux G.* (1945); Cocteau, J., *Souvenir de G.* (1946); Sartre, J. P., *Situations I* (1947); Albérès, R. M., *Esthétique et morale chez J. G.* (1957); Le Sage, L., *J. G., His Life and Works* (1959); Durry, M.-J., *L'univers de G.* (1961); Raymond, A., *G. devant la victoire et la défaite* (1963; Eng. rev. version, J. G.: The Theatre of Victory and Defeat, 1966); Hatzfeld, H., "Conceptual and Verbal Wit in *Amphytrion 38*," in Frank, J., ed., *Horizons of a Philosopher* (1964), pp. 162-75; Cellier, L., *Études de structure* (1964)

ANDRÉ HONORÉ

The example of G. reassures us: nothing could be at once more modern than his book [*Provinciales*], younger or slower. I like to abandon myself to him without knowing exactly where he is taking me. What does it matter, since he takes me along a path where everything invites us to loiter? We dawdle along; he is continually plucking and picking this, that, or the other, chatting with everything, finding a smile for everything, and making a recreation of all creation.

Gide, A., in *NRF* (1909), p. 463

I wonder whether any writer ever had as much modesty as G. He carries it so far that when he notices that we may be about to recognize the loftiness of his judging glance he hurriedly throws over it a triple veil of fantasy.

Du Bos, C., *Journal 1921-1923* (1946), p. 348

His books are collections of samples. Socrates, questioned by Parmenides, hesitated to admit that there was an Idea of filth, an Idea of a louse. G. for his part would not hesitate. The lice he is concerned with are admirable in that they realize the perfection of the louse—all to an equal degree, though in different ways....

A romantic universe emerges, enchants us through its indefiniable charm and its air of novelty; we draw closer and discover the world of Aristotle.

Sartre, J.-P., *Situations I* (1947), pp. 86, 96

While writers such as G. or Julien Green move unhampered by the theoretical consistency of surrealism, they too are visionaries rather than storytellers. G.'s characters are poetic allegories; rather than following the inventions of a plot they follow the spontaneous prompting of the word, and this in turn is directed by the will or the grace to see the world differently, with newly awakened eyes, more freshly, more absolutely.

... G.'s forte was to make every word take away some of the weightiness of the story that was striving to get itself told and so to irradiate it with irony that the absolute bloomed out of the conventional image.

Rütsch, J., "Situation des französischen Romans," in *Trivium*, VIII/1 (1950), p. 13

No writer has demonstrated more faith in the magical property of the metaphor or abandoned himself more completely to its authority. It is the alpha and omega of his art. In the improvisation, which is his sole manner of composition, he allows himself to be led where his wit and imagination will take him ...

Barriers which human industry has erected between phenomena, between the moral and the physical, are suddenly breached. The accepted order is shattered and the elements of the world as we know it scatter and regroup anew. It is as if out of chaos the world were restored to its original order and brilliance.

Le Sage, L., "J. G., Surrealism, and the German Romantic Ideal," in *Illinois Studies in Language and Literature*, XXXVI (1952), p. 24ff

His work lacks the sense of sin, of evil, of the irreparable, the corrupt, the unsound. Even the excessively brisk tempo of his style reflects this angelism: there are times when we wish that G.'s creatures had the leaden feet and the animal heaviness that continually pulls Balzac's characters downward....

... G. wanted to deliver us from that servitude, as the German romantics did, by offering us the image of an incorruptible world. But in doing so he also suppressed the qualitative Becoming, nontemporal in its essence, which the human consciousness grasps as the reciprocal externality of the moments that make up duration. Hence, the monotony of his writing....

Magny, C.-E., *Histoire du roman français depuis 1918* (1950), p. 167

G. stands out as the poet of cosmic correspondences. He reconstructs the world according to the principle of a poetic vision for which supreme beauty is the harmony of the spheres, and instead of depicting man in relation to human society he sets him in the context of the whole universe. Yet in this evocation of the poetry of the cosmos he is discreet and restrained rather than fulminating and apocalyptic, for it is through the human detail that he suggests the mysterious liaisons that govern the universe, and in addition to a cosmological vision he supplies the poetic currency of a cosmology.

Albérès, R. M., *Esthetique et morale chez J. G.* (1957), p. 8

His approach to the theatre was always fastidiously through the ear rather than the eye. The action proceeds from within the language. . . . Like other great masters of theatrical prose—one thinks of Congreve and Shaw—he was not happy with the conventional dramatic plot in which the fuse is carefully lit in the first act and the explosion occurs in the last. No dramatist, of course, can do without suspense completely, but in Giraudoux's theatre the tension is almost wholly intellectual. All his plays find their form in the bringing together of opposites, moral, mental and, on one occasion, national. . . . On one side of it there is war, on the other peace, or it may be vice and virtue, or the individual and the married couple, or, most often, whenever in fact he invoked some immortal, the real and the unreal. His mind, like the least effect of his style, was inevitably governed by the idea of antithesis.

"Trissotin's Revenge," in *The Times Literary Supplement* (18 July 1958)

He alone has managed to transform our mores, our national, political and social lives, drab as they are and overloaded with detail like ordnance survey maps, into bright, contrast-filled colored maps. And he has managed to compose out of completely modern material pictures as boldly illuminated as the world of our old *chansons de geste.* . . .

An ideal of the Middle Ages at their best, from which only Christian hope and the rewards of an afterlife are gone, a sporting readiness to give of himself as he scorns reward—this is what has made G. the purest artist of our time.

Prevost, J., "L'Esprit de J. G.," in *NRF* (1933), p. 48

GIRONELLA, José Maria

Spanish novelist, b. 31 Dec. 1917, Darnius, Gerona

G. won the Nadal Prize in 1946 for his novel *Un hombre* (Where the Soil Was Shallow, 1957). His poem *Ha llegado el invierno y tu no estás aqui*, published in 1945, had gone unnoticed. The novel *La marea* (1949) was fol-

lowed in 1953 by *Los cipreses creen en Dios* (The Cypresses Believe in God, 1955), an account of the Civil War which M. Fernández Almagro called "the most ambitious venture in the contemporary Spanish novel." Not until 1958, after five years of morbid depression, did G. publish *Los fantasmas de mi cerebro* (Phantoms and Fugitives, 1964), most of which is a perspicuous history of his own illness and how he overcame it through writing. G. carries on the tradition of the *Episodios Nacionales* of Pérez Galdós (q.v.), but an even more decisive influence upon him has been the cinematic technique of the most recent Spanish novelists. His language has benefited from the renewal of Spanish prose achieved by the "Generation of '98" and by modernism.

FURTHER WORKS: *El novelista ante el Mundo* (1953); *Un millón de muertos* (1961; One Million Dead, 1963); *Todos somos fugitivos* (1961; in: Phantoms and Fugitives, 1964); *Mujer, levantate y anda* (1962); *Personas, ideas, mares* (1963; partial trans. as On China and Cuba, 1963); *El Japón y su duende* (1964); *China, lágrimas innumerables* (1965); *Ha estallado la paz* (1966)

BIBLIOGRAPHY: Klibbe, L. H., "G.'s *Where the Soil Was Shallow*," *Cath W*, CLXXXIII (1959), 399-402; Urbanski, E. S., "Revolutionary Novels of G. and Pasternak," *Hispania*, XLIII (1960), 191-97; Cano, J. L., "Carta de España," *Asomante*, XVII (1961), 59-61; Gramberg, E. J., "J. M. G., e novelista?," *Cuadernos del Congreso por la Libertad de la Cultura*, No. 79 (1963), 62-68

ANTON DIETERICH

GJELLERUP, Karl Adolph

Danish novelist and dramatist, b. 2 June 1857, Roholte, Seeland; d. 11 Oct. 1919, Klotzsche (near Dresden)

While G.'s major field of study was Protestant theology, he also studied aesthetics, with especial reference to Goethe and Schiller. Before finishing his courses in theology, however, and having investigated modern biblical criticism, he rejected Christianity. Soon he also broke with his Danish heritage as well as with his patron Brandes (q.v.). *Møllen* (1896), probably his most important work, combines a Zolaesque realism with a mysticism typical of the 1890's.

At the turn of the c. G.'s work underwent

another change through the influence of Schopenhauer. He turned away from individualism and the cult of the superman to pessimism and denial of the world as taught by Buddhism. Works like *Offerildene* (1903), a play dedicated to Paul Deussen, or *Den fuldendte hustru* (1907), a drama about a wife's quarrel with her perfection-seeking husband, were derived from various Indian sources. During the last decade of his life G. returned to Danish themes and settings, at the same time drawing closer to Christianity again. In 1917, not long before his death, he was awarded the Nobel Prize (jointly with his fellow countryman Pontoppidan [q.v.]) for his novel *Pilgrimmen Kamanita* (1906; The Pilgrim Kamanita, 1912).

G. was more a thinker than a writer, and viewed life through the medium of literature. Literary themes constantly recur in his individual works; all the trends of his time find expression in his writing. His handling of language was not very felicitous: he had no gift for directness or striking imagery. On the other hand he possessed a restrained passion, impressive in its manner of posing problems.

FURTHER WORKS: *En idealist* (1878); *Det unge Danmark* (1879); *Antigonos* (1880); *Rødtjørn* (1881); *Aander og tider* (1882); *Germanernes laerling* (1882); *Romulus* (1883); *G-dur* (1883); *Brynhild* (1884); *En klassisk maaned* (1884); *Vandreåret* (1885); *Saint-Just* (1886); *Hellkon* (1887); *En arkadisk legende* (1887); *Kampen med muserne* (1887); *Bryllupsgaven* (1888); *Hagbard og Signe* (1889); *Minna* (1889; Eng., 1913); *Herman Vandel* (1891); *Wuthorn* (1893); *Pastor Mors* (1894); *Fra vôr til høst* (1895); *Hs. excellence* (1895); *Ved graensen* (1897); *Verdensvandrerne* (1910); *Rudolph Stens Landpraksis* (1913); *Guds Venner* (1916); *Den gyldne Gren* (1917; own trans. into Ger., *Der goldene Zweig,* 1917); *Das heiligste Tier* (1920); *Madonna della laguna* (1920)

BIBLIOGRAPHY: Rosenberg, A., *K. G. der Dichter und Denker* (2 vols., 1921-22)

PETER P. ROHDE

GLADKOV, Fedor Vasilievich

Russian novelist, dramatist, and poet, b. 21 June 1883, Chernavka, Pensa district; d. 20 Dec. 1958, Moscow

G. was the son of a poor peasant with a large family. He was reared in the strict puritanical tradition of the Old Believers. From age twelve on, the poor financial circumstances of G.'s family forced him to become self-supporting. His schooling was limited, yet he read avidly and began writing poetry under the influence of Lermontov and Nekrasov. Having schooled his prose by the example of Dostoyevski, G. also began writing short fiction. In 1901, at age eighteen, he read the stories of Gorki (q.v.) and fell under the spell and influence of the older man. G.'s first novel, *Izgoi* (1912), is frankly imitative of Gorki's style: the work depicts the lives of political prisoners; G. himself had spent a number of years in Siberia, having been exiled for revolutionary activities in the uprisings of 1905. He had been able to enter a teacher's college in 1901 and, in the period between his return from exile and the events of 1917, was able to support himself as a teacher.

G. greeted the Bolshevik revolution of 1917 with enthusiasm. The great majority of his work was written and published thereafter. From its range the novel *Cement* (1924; Eng., 1929) is singled out most frequently as G.'s outstanding literary achievement. The hero of the book, an energetic revolutionary workingman, succeeds in reorganizing a cement factory almost single-handedly but does not know how to arrange his personal life. His relations with his wife, represented as an emancipated "new woman" of the postrevolutionary era, are notably a failure. The novel, later touted in the Stalinist era as an example of "socialist realism," thus by no means offers a blanket endorsement of life in the Soviet state, as party-line oriented imitations of the work by lesser writers and "corrected texts" of *Cement* itself, published in the thirties and forties, have led critics to believe. In essence *Cement* presents the perennial problem of which is more important, the state or the individual? While the novel's over-all statement seems to attribute the greater importance to the state, there is enough artistic honesty and integrity in the work's presentation of situations and characters to allow of a different solution. A sincerity of expression that transcends politics also characterizes G.'s autobiography, *Povest' o detstve* (1949; Restless Youth, 1955). The high favor G.'s work enjoyed in the Stalinist era was due as much to its authentic literary quality and to the circumstance of his humble origins and early struggles as a member of the revolutionary proletariat, as to G.'s undoubted dedication to the ideals of communism.

FURTHER WORKS: *Ognennyi kon'* (1923); *Staraya sekretnaya* (1926); *Pyatve solntze* (1927); *Sobraniye sochinenii* (4 vols., 1928); *Rasskazy* (1929); *Novaya zemlya* (1931); *Pyanoye solntze* (1932); *Energiya* (1932-38); *Malen'kaya trilogiya* (1932); *Gordost'* (1935); *Tragediya Lyubashi* (1935); *My pobedim!* (1942); *Opalennaya dusha* (1943); *Klyatva* (1944); *Boyetz Nazar Suslov* (1946); *Vol'nitza* (1950); *Sochineniya* (5 vols., 1950-51); *Likhaya godina* (1954); *O literature* (1955); *Sobraniye sochinenii* (8 vols., 1958); *Myatezhnaya yunost'* (1961)

BIBLIOGRAPHY: Pozner, V., *Panorama de la littérature russe contemporaine* (1929); Thorgevsky, I., *De Gorki à nos jours: la nouvelle littérature russe* (1945); Struve, G., *Soviet Russian Literature: 1917-50* (1951); Lettenbauer, W., *Kleine russische Literaturgeschichte* (2 vols., 1958)

JACK A. POSIN & W.B.F.

GLASGOW, Ellen (Anderson Gholson)

American novelist, poet, and critic, b. 22 April 1873, Richmond, Va.; d. there, 21 Nov. 1945

Ellen G. was born of the Virginia gentry, and in her fiction she cherished the traditions and satirized the inadequacies of her society. She began as a rebel against the restrictiveness and the "evasive idealism" of Southern life. Her radical literary and social values alienated her from her contemporary South but did not obliterate her sympathy with a culture that she could appreciate as a social being. By its frankness her early work offended the prejudices of genteel critics, although it was a moderate success with the reading public. Throughout her career Ellen G. was a dedicated literary artist, struggling always to secure the critical recognition that eluded her until the publication of *Barren Ground* in 1925.

Ellen G. was much affected by her deafness, the sudden death of her mother, by a tragic love affair with a married New York financier that ended with his death, by the suicide of her brother, by the untimely death of a sister from cancer, by the harshness of her father, by the unsettling effects of World War I, and by a frustrating engagement to a Richmond lawyer and politician, Henry W. Anderson, during World War I and afterward. For psychological release and personal satisfaction she turned to the writing of fiction, which in range and tone modulates from the comic to the tragic, the two realms of experience being bridged by an ironic sense of the disparities in human existence.

The Descendant (1897), with its New York setting and rebellious Nietzschean hero, was somewhat akin to the naturalistic work of Frank Norris (1870-1902) and secured for Ellen G. some recognition and notoriety. In *The Voice of the People* (1900) and *The Battle-Ground* (1902) she returned to the Virginia region she knew best. In *The Deliverance* (1904), a powerful novel, she expressed the resentment of conquered Virginia by means of the tortured hatred that Christopher Blake developed toward the dishonest overseer who had dispossessed him early in the Reconstruction era.

Seven years elapsed before Ellen G. published another important book. *The Miller of Old Church* (1911) is distinguished for its satirical comedy, its mordant analysis of the decadent rural gentry, and its insight into the psyche of the libertine Jonathan Gay. In 1913, *Virginia,* the best of her early books, was published. A strong novel, this is noteworthy for its marshaling of the new South against the old, its largeness of vision, its profound irony, and its sympathetic (albeit critical) analysis of "the feminine ideal of the ages," the Southern lady Virginia Pendleton.

Ellen G. began her major phase with *Barren Ground* (1925). In this book Dorinda Oakley's struggle for self-possession gains depth through her simultaneous efforts to master the primordial land, which is throughout an animating and symbolically pervasive presence. Two delightful excursions into social comedy appeared next. In *The Romantic Comedians* (1926), Ellen G. analyzed the absurdities and the tragic undercurrents present in a May and December marriage. In *They Stooped to Folly* (1929) she ridiculed conventional sexual standards. Milly Burden, pregnant though unmarried, refuses even to admit that she is "ruined," in contrast to Mrs. Dalrymple and Agatha Littlepage of the preceding two generations. Mrs. Dalrymple was forced to flee to Europe while Agatha Littlepage retreated to an attic room.

The sardonic note deepened in *The Sheltered Life* (1932), Ellen G.'s masterpiece. Central to the book is the sacrifice of Eva Birdsong to the conventional moral code. She is unable as a "lady" to acknowledge even the existence of her husband's habitual infidelity. Eva Birdsong is a haunting symbol of the Southern lady and the vanishing South of tradition; and she is the victim of a civilization grown decadent from artifice and hypocrisy. In the 1930's Ellen G.'s work became still more somber, although it showed less incisiveness, as she turned to the analysis of contemporary society and its ills. *Vein of Iron* (1935) chronicles the fortunes of the Fincastles in the Great Valley of Virginia and in Depression Queenborough: and *In This Our Life* (1941), on the eve of World War II, unmasks the hypocrisies of the Timberlakes, which are symbolic of American moral weaknesses.

At the start of her career Ellen G. determined to write truthfully, not sentimentally, about the late nineteenth-century South. To write a truthful social history in fiction, she found no help in the American literary tradition but turned instead to the "great realists" of France —Balzac, Maupassant, Flaubert, and Zola. For over forty years Ellen G. wrote fiction notable for its living characters, its psychological depth, its fusing of characters with scene, its witty and exact phrasing, and its structural firmness. She infused into Southern literature of the early twentieth century the "blood and irony" needed to prepare the way for Wolfe, Faulkner, Warren, Welty, Katherine Anne Porter (qq.v.), and others. In her novels she revealed love of the land, knowledge of Virginia social life and manners, feeling for the complexities of Southern history, and profound insight into the intricacies of human nature. She is a transitional figure in American literature and a major artist in her own right.

FURTHER WORKS: *Phases of an Inferior Planet* (1898); *The Freeman and Other Poems* (1902); *The Wheel of Life* (1906); *The Ancient Law* (1908); *The Romance of a Plain Man* (1909); *Life and Gabriella* (1916); *The Builders* (1919); *One Man in His Time* (1922); *The Shadowy Third and Other Stories* (1923); *The Old Dominion Edition of the Works of E. G.* (8 vols., 1929-33); *The Virginia Edition of the Works of E. G.* (12 vols., 1938); *A Certain Measure: An Interpretation of Prose Fiction* (1943); *The Woman Within* (1954); *Letters of E. G.*, ed. B. Rouse (1958); *E. G.'s Letters to Paul Revere Reynolds* (1961); *Literary Realism or Nominalism* (1962); *The Collected Stories of E. G.*, ed. R. K. Meeker (1963); *E. G.'s Letters to the Saxtons* (1963); *Beyond Defeat* (1966)

BIBLIOGRAPHY: Quinn, A. H., *American Fiction* (1936); Monroe, N. E., *The Novel and Society* (1941); Commager, H. S., *The American Mind* (1950); Hoffman, F. J., *The Modern Novel in America 1900-1950* (1951); Wagenknecht, E., *The Cavalcade of the American Novel* (1952); Geismar, M., *Rebels and Ancestors* (1953); Rubin, L. D., Jr., *No Place on Earth* (1959); McDowell, F. P. W., *E. G. and the Ironic Art of Fiction* (1960); Rouse, B., *E. G.*; Parent, M., *E. G. Romancière*; Kelly, W. W., *E. G.: A Bibliography* (1964); Auchincloss, L., *E. G.* (1964); Holman, C. H., *Three Modes of Modern Southern Fiction* (1966)

FREDERICK P. W. McDOWELL

GOES, Albrecht

German narrative writer, poet and critic, b. 22 March 1908, Langenbeutingen, Württemberg

A Lutheran minister and son and grandson of Swabian ministers, G. resigned from the ministry in 1953 to devote all his time to writing, except for a few regularly delivered sermons. He has written poetry and symbolic plays since about 1930. In World War II he served as an army chaplain. One of his prose narratives, *Unruhige Nacht* (1950, 1955; Arrow to the Heart, 1951; also published under the title Unquiet Night, 1951) is a direct echo of his wartime experience. In it G. displays great gifts for the dispassionate evocation of stark reality, coupled with compassion and a deep sense of humanity. *Das Brandopfer* (1954; The Burnt Offering, 1956) is the moving yet sparsely told legend of a German butcher's wife who feels a compulsion to atone for the Nazis' treatment of the Jews; she experiences that "love that contains the world."

G.'s interests are manifold. He is a precise and knowledgeable literary and music critic, an art lover, and an able guide to archaeological treasures. Above all, his ethics are a model of unpretentious, straightforward development of essential themes both in religion and in civic life. His role as a mediator between East and West Germany should not be underestimated. G. often expresses the voice of German conscience, of reflection, and of quiet strength in confused times. Whether he deals with Goethe's poetry, Bach's music, or with biblical parables, G. maintains a sober yet noble tone of fine, subtle, and tactful simplicity. But it is the refined simplicity of a virtuoso of word and thought, whose message is as intellectually convincing as it is gripping and enlightening.

G., who has received the Lessing Prize (1953), is a member of the German Academy for Language and Poetry and of the West Berlin Academy of the Arts. One of the most forward-looking German writers as far as supranational relations are concerned, G. is also widely acclaimed for his readings of poetry.

FURTHER WORKS: *Die Hirtin* (1934); *Der Hirte* (1934); *Heimat ist gut* (1935); *Die Roggenfuhre* (1936); *Vergebung* (1937); *Der Zaungast* (1938); *Mörike* (1938); *Über das Gespräch* (1938; rev. ed., 1957); *Leuchter und Laterne* (1939); *Der Nachbar* (1940); *Der Weg zum Stall* (1940); *Die guten Gefährten* (1942); *Schwäbische Herzensreise* (1946); *Auf der Flucht* (1946); *Die Herberge* (1947); *Der Mensch von unterwegs* (1948); *Von Mensch zu Mensch* (1949); *Die fröhliche Christtagslitanei* (1949); *Gedichte 1930-1950* (1950); *Unsere letzte Stunde* (1951); *Christtag* (1951); *Freude am Gedicht* (1952); *Vertrauen in das Wort* (1953); *Erfüllter Augenblick* (1955); *Das dreifache Ja* (1955); *Ruf und Echo* (1956); *Der Gastfreund* (1958); *Hagar am Brunnen* (1958); *Goethes Mutter* (1958); *Wagnis der Versöhnung* (1959); *Ravenna* (1960; Eng., 1963); *Krankenvisite* (1960); *Die Gabe und der Auftrag* (1962); *Gehe, leide, warte* (1962); *Die Weihnacht der Bedrängten* (1962); *Aber im Winde das Wort* (1963); *Alle unsere Tage* (1963); *Das Löffelchen* (1965); *Dichter und Gedicht* (1966)

BIBLIOGRAPHY: Trainer, J., "Two Prose Works by A. G.," *ML*, XLII (1961), 137-39

KONRAD BIEBER

GOGA, Octavian

Rumanian poet and essayist, b. 1 April 1881, Răşinari; d. 7 May 1938, Ciucea

G., the leading Transylvanian poet of the 20th c., made a decisive stand against the oppression of Rumanian minorities. His first work, *Poezii* (1905), expresses his national awareness. The poetic content of *Nĕ cheamă pământul* (1909) is more topical: the village, with its inhabitants, traditions, and customs, is the principal theme of this volume. *Din umbra zidurilor* (1913), on the other hand, reveals G. as the melancholy poet of rootless city folk. In addition to his strongly traditional poetry G. wrote remarkable memoirs (*Precursorii*, 1930), and as a journalist he played an active role in the political and social controversies of his time.

FURTHER WORKS: *Insemnările unui trecător* (1911); *Domnul Notar* (1914); *Strigăte în pustiu* (1915); *Cântece fără tară* (1916); *Poezii alese* (1924); *Mustul care fierbe* (1927); *Mesterul Manole* (1928); *Fragmente autobiografice* (1934); *O seamă de cuvinte* (1936); *Din Larg* (1939); *Poezii* (1943)

BIBLIOGRAPHY: Papadima, O., *Neam, sat şi oraş în poezia lui O.G.* (1943)

VIRGIL IERUNCA

GOLDING, William

English novelist, b. 19 Sept. 1911, St. Columb Minor, Cornwall

In 1934, while still an undergraduate at Oxford, G. published a slim volume, *Poems,* and after his graduation he did some acting, directing, and writing at a small London theater. However, in 1939 he bowed to family tradition and became a schoolmaster in Salisbury. He served five years in the Royal Navy, and it was not until 1954, with the publication of his first novel, *Lord of the Flies,* that he achieved literary fame. The novel had an enormous success, most notably among students in both England and America.

The greatest influences on G. have been Greek literature, particularly Euripides, and experiences during the war that seemed to him to confirm Euripides' vision of man's irrationality. G. considers man's greatest problem that of "learning to live fearlessly with the natural chaos of existence," and his own major task as a writer that of curing man of "his appalling ignorance of his own nature." Thus in *Lord of the Flies* he reverses Ballantyne's idyllic *Coral Island* and depicts how a small group of boys, marooned on an island during World War III, degenerate into a society of primitive savagery; and in *The Inheritors* (1955) he overturns Wells's (q.v.) view of Neanderthal man and shows how innocent and loving he is in comparison to Homo sapiens, who destroys and succeeds him. *The Inheritors* is written almost entirely from the point of view of Neanderthal man; *Pincher Martin* (1956; Am., The Two Deaths of Christopher Martin) from that of a drowned man. Through Martin's post-mortem thoughts G. reveals the unmitigated pride and greed of his subject's life.

In *The Spire* (1964) G. reveals the workings and consequences of the moral and spiritual corruption that underlies a dean's fanatical attempt to erect the spire of what strongly suggests Salisbury Cathedral. Only in *Free Fall* (1959), where for the first time G. uses a first-person narrative and creates a contemporary social situation, is a Golding hero granted some measure of recognition of his loss of innocence.

Though G.'s rejection of liberal humanism is not unfamiliar, his style suggests a consistent effort to avoid the forms that the modern novel has taken. His novels have been called fables, parables, and allegories, but he would like to think of them as myths about human nature. It has been charged that his moral concerns are too obviously reflected in his novels and that his attempts at stylistic innovations, particularly his experiments with varying points of view, result in "gimmickry." His defenders point to the poetic intensity of his language and to his uniqueness among novelists writing today.

FURTHER WORKS: "Envoy Extraordinary," in *Sometime, Never: Three Tales of Imagination* (1956); *The Brass Butterfly* (1958); *The Hot Gates* (1965); *The Pyramid* (1967); *Dick* (1967)

BIBLIOGRAPHY: Hynes, S., *W. G.* (1964); Baker, J. R., *W. G.* (1964); Oldsey, B. S., and Weintraub, S., *The Art of W. G.* (1965); Green, M., "Distaste for the Contemporary," in *The Nation*, CXC (1960), 451-54; Kinkead-Weekes, W., and Gregor, I., *W. G.: A Critical Study* (1967)

R. C. TOWNSEND

GOLL, Yvan

Alsatian poet, novelist, playwright, and essayist writing in French, German, and English, b. 29 March 1891, St.-Dié; d. 27 Feb. 1950, Paris

G. was one of the very few poets who wrote excellent verse in more than one language. He is almost equally well known for his French as for his German poetry. During his stay in New York he wrote *Fruit from Saturn* (1946). He studied in Strassburg and lived in various countries—Germany, Switzerland, the United States, and France. Together with his wife, Claire, he contributed some of the most unforgettable love lyrics to French and German literature.

G. played a role in German expressionism (q.v.) (*Der Panamakanal*, 1912; *Der Eiffelturm*, 1924), and in several short treatises and manifestoes prepared the way for the movement that became known as surrealism (q.v.). The invigorating effect which the grafting of French surrealistic techniques has had upon post-expressionistic German verse is attributable almost solely to G. *La Chanson de Jean sans Terre* (1936, 1939; Landless John, 1943, 1958) is a cycle of poems which exhibit G.'s great skill in the use of various poetic forms, and depict his never-ending concern with love, homelessness, and death. His later works, especially *Le Mythe de la roche percée* (1947), *Elégie de dhpétonga, suivi de masques de cendre* (1949), *Le Char triomphal de l'antimoine* (1949), *Les Cercles magiques* (1951), and *Traumkraut* (1951), tend to include alchemistic and cabalistic symbolism.

Conversant with and contributing to all of the literary movements important during his lifetime, G. fell victim to none. His justly famous and much admired love poetry, particularly *Poèmes d'amour* (with Claire G., 1925; Love Poems, 1947), *Chansons malaises* (1934), *Dix mille aubes* (with Claire G., 1951), *Traumkraut* (1951), and *Abendgesang* (1954), is the most widely translated part of his work.

FURTHER WORKS: *Lothringische Volkslieder* (1912); *Elégies internationales* (1915); *Requiem pour les morts de l'Europe* (1916); *Requiem für die Gefallenen von Europa* (1917); *Der Torso* (1918); *Dithyramben* (1918); *Die drei guten Geister Frankreichs* (1919); *Die Unterwelt* (1919); *Astral* (1920); *Die Chapliniade: Eine Kinodichtung* (1920); *Das Herz des Feinds* (1920); *Die Unsterblichen* (1920); *Das Lächeln Voltaires: Essai* (1921); *Methusalem oder der ewige Bürger* (1922); *Le nouvel Orphée* (1923); *Der Stall des Augias* (1924); *Germaine Berton, die rote Jungfrau* (1925); *Poèmes de jalousie* (with Claire G., 1926); *Le Microbe de l'or* (1927); *Die Eurokokke* (1928); *Der Mitropäer* (1928); *Agnus Dei* (1929); *Lucifer vieillissant* (1934); *Songs of a Malay Girl* (1942); *Atom Elegy* (1946); *Traumgras* (1948); *Les Géorgiques parisiennes* (1951); *Nouvelles petites fleurs de St. François* (with Claire G., 1952); *Melusine: pièce lyrique* (1955); *Der Mythos vom durchbrochenen Felsen* (1956); *Duo d'amour* (with Claire G., 1959); *Dichtungen: Lyrik, Prosa, Drama* (G., Claire, ed., 1960); *Four Poems of the Occult* (1962); *Théâtre* (1963)

BIBLIOGRAPHY: Raymond, M., *La Vie et l'Oeuvre d'Y. G.* (1948); Brion, M., Carmody, F., Exner, R., Romains, J., *Y. G.* in *Poètes d'aujourd'hui*, 50 (1956); Carmody, F., *The Poetry of Y. G.: A Biographical Study* (1956);

Exner, R., "Surrealist Elements in Y. G.'s Franco-German Poetry," in *Symposium,* XI (1957) 92-99; Auden, W. H., Bogan, L., Mills, C., Romains, J., and Tate, A., in *Y. G.: Jean sans Terre* (1958); Müller, J., *Y. G. im deutschen Expressionismus* (1962)

RICHARD EXNER

GOMBROWICZ, Witold

Polish-Argentinian novelist, b. 4 Aug. 1905, Maloszice-Opatow

G. first became popular in Poland with a collection of stories entitled *Pamiętnik z okresu dojrzewania* (1933). His fame became international when he wrote the novel *Ferdydurke* (1938; Eng., 1961) which was translated (1961) into German, French, Italian, English, Spanish, and Swedish. This novel depicts in a satirical style the regressive transformation of an adult man into a child. It also reveals the author's philosophy of life, namely, that a human being can exist as such only in conjunction with other human beings—as a social animal, not as an island unto himself. G. calls social living the "interhuman church."

As a guest of the National Argentine Literary Society, G. visited Buenos Aires in 1939 and, when World War II broke out, decided to remain in the Argentine permanently. He reiterated his philosophy of life in his next story, *Trans-Atlantyk* (1953), which was serialized in *Kultura,* a Polish magazine published in Paris. *Trans-Atlantyk* has been widely read in Europe and in the Americas. His play *Slub* (1953) was quickly acclaimed in Europe and abroad by writers and critics alike, among them Kuncewiczow and Wittlin. In spite of his "unrealistic style" and ironic posture toward communism, he is widely read in Poland and considered by many the most independent Polish writer alive.

FURTHER WORKS: *Dziennik 1953-56* (1957); *Bakakai* (1957); *Iwona; księzniczka Burgunda* (1958; Yvonne, Princess of Bourgogne, 1967); *Pornografia* (1960; Eng., 1966)

BIBLIOGRAPHY: Jelenski, K. A., "W. G. ou l'immaturité adulte," *Preuves* (Jan. 1959), 21-24; Bondy, F., "Polens phantastische Realisten: Zu den Büchern von Bruno Schulz and W. G.," *Forum,* IX (1962), 105-7; *idem,* "W. G. oder: Die Schattenduelle eines polnischen Landedelmannes," *Akzente,* XII (1965), 366-83

JOHN MICHALSKI

GÓMEZ DE LA SERNA, Ramón

Spanish novelist, dramatist, biographer, and essayist, b. 3 July 1888, Madrid

G.'s work comprises all genres—essay, chronicle, biography, novel, drama—and he even invented a new one, the *greguería,* a kind of parable revealing unexpected aspects of things in a brilliant, often humorous manner through passing allusions.

From his earliest youth G. was interested in journalism and literature and at the beginning was greatly encouraged by the writer Carmen de Burgos. In the Madrid *Ateneo,* under the slogan "Time to Revolt," he appealed for a new concept of literature, advocating dynamism and the creation of new forms and denouncing the static character of existing literature.

His most important works include: *Pombo,* Vol. I (1918) and Vol. II (1924), a charmingly written chronicle of a famous literary coterie; numerous volumes of *Greguerías* (1918-55; Some Greguerías, 1944, sel. translations), which best reveal his inexhaustible inventiveness; and *El Circo* (1924), a book extolling the circus. He is also notable for relatively plotless novels in which he seeks a new form (*El chalet de las rosas,* 1923; *El incongruente,* 1925; *El torero Caracho,* 1927); for humorous novels such as *Seis falsas novelas* (1926); and finally for many essays on Madrid and for lively anecdotal sketches of contemporary writers and artists, living and dead. One of his most important works is *Autormoribundia* (1948), a picture of an entire epoch in Spanish literary life presented within the framework of a gripping autobiographical story.

Known popularly as "Ramón," G. is the Quevedo of the 20th c., overflowing with ideas, though in his work he does not by any means maintain a consistently high standard. Between 1918 and 1936 he exercised a strong influence on the younger generation, but today his work appears somewhat mannered and superficial; his originality, however, remains remarkable. Since 1936 he has lived in Buenos Aires.

FURTHER WORKS: *Entrando en fuego* (1904); *Ei Rastro* (1910); *La viuda blanca y negra* (1918); *Senos* (1918); *Oscar Wilde* (1921); *El doctor inverosímil* (1921); *El Gran hotel* (1922); *El secreto del acueducto* (1922); *El novelista* (1923); *Ramonismo* (1923); *La malicia de las acacias* (1924); *Cinelandia* (1924; Movieland, 1930); *El Prado* (1925); *La quinta de Palmyra* (1925); *Gollerías* (1926); *El dueño del átomo* (1928); *El caballero del hongo gris*

(1928); *Goya* (1928); *La mujér de ámbar* (1928); *Efigies* (1929); *Ismos* (1930); *Azorín* (1930); *La nardo* (1930); *Elucidario de Madrid* (1931); *Policéfalo y señora* (1932); *Flor de Greguerías* (1933); *Los muertos, las muertas y otras fantasmagorías* (1935); *¡Rebeca!* (1936); *Retratos contemporáneos* (1942); *Lo cursi y otros ensayos* (1943); *Don Ramón María del Valle-Inclán* (1944); *Lope de Vega* (1944); *Nuevos retratos contemporáneos* (1945); *El hombre perdido* (1946); *Greguerías completas* (1953); *Total de greguerías* (1955); *Obras completas* (1956); *Biografías completas* (1959); *Greguerías del mar* (1961); *Guia del Rastro* (1961); *Retratos completos* (1961); *Ensayo sobre lo cursi* (1963)

BIBLIOGRAPHY: Larbaud, V., *Echantillons de G.* (1923); Pérez Ferrero, M., *Vida de Ramón* (1935); Del Rio, A. and Bernardete, M. J., *El concepto contemporáneo de España* (1946; p. 717 features G. bibliography); Granjel, L. S., *Retrato de Ramón* (1963); Jackson, R. L., "A New Literary Genre: the *Greguería*," *BA*, XXXIX (1965), 415-17; *idem*, "Toward a Classification of the *Greguería*," *Hispania*, XLVIII (1965), 826-32

GONZALO SOBEJANO

GONZÁLES MARTÍNEZ, Enrique

Mexican poet, b. 13 April 1871, Guadalajara; d. 19 Feb. 1952, Mexico City

G.M., along with Amado Nervo (1870-1919) and others, belonged to Mexico's most brilliant literary epoch. He was a practicing physician until 1910, when he began to devote himself entirely to journalism and literature. He became a member of the "Ateneo de la Juventud," a group that included the best writers of the time. In 1920 he began his diplomatic career, which took him to Chile, Spain, and Portugal. From 1931 until his death he again lived in Mexico.

G. M. was a great admirer of French literature and was at first strongly influenced by Lamartine, Baudelaire, Verlaine, Herédia, and Jammes (q.v.), all of whom he included in his anthology of translations of symbolist poetry *Jardines de Francia* (1915). In 1903 he published the volume of poetry *Preludios*, which gave him entrée to literary circles. In *Silenter* (1909) his poetry took on a more mysterious tone, recalling Georges Rodenbach and Maeterlinck (q.v.). From then on his verse

seemed quieter and more restrained; its nuances emerged more clearly. Love for the world and for his fellow men led G. M. to seek the hidden meaning—"the soul of things."

In *Los senderos ocultos* (1911) G. M. presented his pantheistic ideas, attributing a particular significance to silence. In contrast to the striking rhythms of the modernist schools, G. M. used delicacy and subtlety. His contemplative attitude and depth of thought supplanted mere outward beauty. Thus in his famous sonnet "Tuércele el cuello al cisne" (1915) he proclaims the triumph of wisdom (typified by the owl) over purely superficial beauty (symbolized by the swan). These two contrasting images came to stand in Spanish-American poetry for two different concepts of art. Thus G. M.'s demand for deeper meaning in poetry introduced a split in the modernist movement. While G. M. remained a friend and admirer of Darío's (q.v.), *La muerte del cisne* (1915) definitely created a turn away from the purely aestheticist imitation of French symbolism that Darío, as leader of the movement, had advocated.

FURTHER WORKS: *Lirismos* (1907); *La hora inútil* (1916); *El libro de la fuerza, de la bondad y del ensueño* (1917); *Parabolas* (1918); *Poemas de ayer y de hoy* (1918); *La palabra del viento* (1921); *El romero alucinado* (1920-22); *Las señales furtivas* (1925); *Poesía 1909-1929* (1929); *Poemas truncos* (1935); *Ausencia y canto* (1937); *El diluvio de fuego* (1938); *Poemas 1938-40* (1940); *Bajo el signo mortal* (1942); *Poesías completas* (1944); *El hombre del buho* (1944); *Segundo despertar* (1945); *Villano al viento* (1948); *Babel* (1949); *La apacible locura* (1951, part II of *El hombre del buho;* both constitute G.'s autobiography); *Narciso* (1952); *Cuentos y otras paginas* (1955)

BIBLIOGRAPHY: Reyes, A., in G. M.'s *Los senderos ocultos* (1916 ed.); Estrada, J., *Poetas nuevos de Méjico* (1916); Arrieta, R. A., "Epistolario de G. M.," *Abside*, XXIII (1959), 46-48; Bradman, H., "El sentimiento elegíaco en la poesía de E. G. M.," *DA*, XXV (1964), 1903

ALÍ CHUMACERO

GONZÁLEZ PRADA, Manuel

Peruvian poet, critic, and essayist, b. 6 Jan. 1848, Lima; d. there, 22 July 1918

The defeat suffered by Peru in the 1879-81 war with Chile led G. P. to adopt a critical attitude corresponding to that of the "Generation of '98" in Spanish literature (q.v.). One of the great renewers of Latin-American thought, he bitterly attacked the Spanish tradition, advocating a literary program of modernity and emulation of foreign poets and writers, especially German ones. G. P.'s lyrical work, which is often sarcastic in tone, is not extensive, but in its unrhymed, polyrhythmic versification with freely structured stanzas it was far ahead of its time and thus led to modernism.

FURTHER WORKS: *Páginas libres* (1894); *Minúsculas* (1901); *Horas de lucha* (1908); *Presbiterianas* (1909); *Exóticas* (1911); *Baladas peruanas* (1915); *Grafitos* (1917); *Trozos de vida* (1918); *Bajo el oprobio* (1933); *Obras* (8 vols., 1933-40); *Anarquía* (1936); *Nuevas páginas libres* (1937); *Figuras y figurones* (1938); *Libertarias* (1938); *Baladas* (1939); *Propaganda y ataque* (1939); *Antología poetica* (1940); *Prosa menuda* (1941); *El tonel de Diógenes* (1945); *Florilegio: poesía, ensayo, critica* (1948)

BIBLIOGRAPHY: Melián Lafineur, A. "G.P." in *Nosotros* (1917); Nuñez, E., "G. P. y la cultura inglese," *La Nueva Democracia* (New York), XL (1960), 73-77; Sánchez, L. A., "Las ideas y la influencia de G. P.," *Revista Interamericana de Bibliografia*, XIII (1963), 271-92

ANTON M. ROTHBAUER

GORKI, Maksim

(pseud. of *Aleksei Maksimovich Peshkov*), Russian novelist, dramatist, and essayist, b. 28 March 1868, Nizhny-Novgorod (now Gorki); d. 18 June 1936, Moscow

G. was the most prominent prerevolutionary Russian writer to identify his life's work and interest with the Communist Revolution and its literary program. He stood as a kind of bridge, first between the uneducated Russian people and its literary intellectuals, then between Soviet and prerevolutionary Russian literature. Before 1917 the Russian reading public regarded him as the literary representative of revolutionary Russia; afterward the world considered him the literary champion of the Soviet regime. In neither period did his sometimes strong internal doubts overcome his revolutionary stance and convictions.

Born into the merchant class, a much more marginal social position in Russia than in western Europe, G. experienced an extremely disorganized childhood which might have crushed a less hardy spirit: his father died of a cholera infection received from the three-year-old boy; his mother held her son "responsible" for his father's death. She ran away, remarried, returned, and died when the future writer was ten. The child received little formal education, but he developed and retained the literary earnestness necessary for the successful autodidact. G. spent much of his youth wandering about Russia, from one occupation to another, and gained wide popularity in the 1890's with a series of stories describing the milieu of the wandering barefoot Russian tramps. These figures proved novel and provocative to the Russian reading public.

G. was not completely happy with the literary success of his tramps, for he sensed condescension from the readers he most respected, those with education and taste. By the turn of the c., he was eager to undertake the genre generally admired in late 19th c. Russia, the topical novel. From 1899 until 1913 he wrote a series of novels which explored widely varying aspects of the young revolutionary's duties and problems in Czarist Russia. It was during this period, even while in political exile (1906-1913), that G. became an authoritative Russian public figure with a definite, though sometimes inconsistent, public voice on literary and political matters. He founded a publishing house, Znaniye ("Knowledge"), whose authors were mainly the Russian neorealists who argued against the Russian symbolists (see Symbolism) and decadents. While G. defended the primacy of the revolutionary political struggle as a theme for writers, he found himself attracted by his opponents' literary style and skill as well as by their highly erudite arguments for the primacy of aesthetics over any other subject, including politics, for the purpose of judging literature. His own work sometimes reflected the literary devices of the symbolists, and he found himself defending their aesthetic argument in his relations with revolutionary theorists, especially Lenin. The revolutionary leader became a very close friend, with enormous influence over the writer; Lenin excused G.'s lapses from Bolshevik orthodoxy partly on grounds of expediency, since the writer was aiding the cause, and partly because of his personal charm and sincerity. In spite of G.'s ideological convolutions, sufficient to pain any philosopher believing in consistency, Lenin never subjected his friend to the usual blasts of revolutionary polemical rhetoric.

During the extreme deprivations of the immediate postrevolutionary period (1918-21), G.

performed an outstanding service for Russian literary and intellectual life by using his friendship with Lenin to assure food and shelter and some freedom from arrest for writers and intellectuals, regardless of their political opinions. He remained somewhat critical of the early Soviet policies, and he expressed his opinions openly in the Bolshevik newspaper *Novaya Zhizn'* (New Life), which Lenin proscribed in 1918. Lenin tried to demonstrate the writer's political immaturity in a series of letters which continued during 1919 and 1920, but G. refused to move away from the orbit of dissident intellectual elements in Petrograd to the ancient city of Moscow where the Soviets had re-established the center of government. In 1921 Lenin urged him to go abroad for good medical treatment, at that time unavailable in Soviet Russia, and the writer followed this advice after the execution of Gumilev (q.v.), a rival poet whose life G. had tried to save.

The next twelve years G. spent almost entirely as an émigré, living first near Berlin and later in Sorrento. He cooperated with Soviet publishing houses, putting out the most carefully edited series of his collected works in Berlin, starting in 1923. In Sorrento he maintained a quasiliterary center, attracting Russian writers and intellectuals for short visits and maintaining contact with a wide spectrum of political and literary camps. Indeed, he became the focus of some very intense rivalries between the Soviets and the émigrés, and he seemed to vacillate in his views from one to the other. To Soviet men of letters, G. the emigrant became an increasingly uneasy topic; many critics among them made ironic reference to it. However, after several tentative visits, G. returned permanently to the Soviet Union in 1933, when the internal political situation looked most favorable to him. There was at that time the kind of jubilation among the general population, as well as among government leaders, which is peculiarly strong in Russia when national feeling becomes identical with the political climate of the day. The event has been recorded in impressive documentary films. For three years, until his death, G. added his influential voice to those Soviet critics who wanted the new generation of writers to learn from Russia's past literature and not discard it in favor of the new. He continued his never-ending advice and intercession on behalf of Soviet and émigré writers of all persuasions, even while helping to formulate a new Soviet party line in literature. Although he died

during the upswing of Stalinist tyranny and executions, his death was probably due to natural causes. Past Soviet (and émigré) sources published accusations that he had been murdered—subsequently the supposedly guilty officials were even tried and executed—but there is good evidence to the contrary. Present Soviet sources do not repeat the accusation of murder; they are silent on the subject.

Evaluations of G.'s writing vary radically, often in relation to the critics' political views. In the past, many Soviet critics have accorded him exaggerated adulation, but since 1953 they have viewed G. with much more objectivity. Many émigré critics have been extraordinarily unkind in their reactions to his return to the Soviet Union, although his death elicited some highly intelligent and sensitive appreciations from them. It is a mistake to place G. (as many do) in the highest rank of 19th c. Russian writers; he had neither the uncanny stylistic control of Pushkin, the philosophically enlivening talent of Dostoyevski, nor Tolstoi's (q.v.) breadth of characterization. Nevertheless G. had considerable ability, impressively demonstrated in his best work and apparent in all his writing. He had a piercingly sharp eye for details of scene and person, and in rendering the sounds of the Russian language when spoken by a particular social stratum his pitch was near-perfect. When G. describes Russian singing, as he often does, one can almost hear the melody without seeing the notes. His literary genius was combined with so ardent a desire for social justice that he became almost physically sick at the thought or sight of cruelty, in a country whose history and daily life were unusually saturated with oppression. He used his position as a tribune to save the lives of literally thousands of the best elements of the Russian intelligentsia. Unfortunately he also inundated some of his works with the raw feelings of the tribune. As a result many of his attempts at aphoristic writing are aesthetically unsuccessful, although they had an enormously enlightening political effect in Russia.

G. was intensely self-critical, and he tried many genres to develop the style most appropriate to his talent. His early short stories (1892-99), at their best, show the opposition of the active, lawless tramp and the passive, settled person, as in *Chelkash* (1894; Tchelkache, 1902). A few years later, however, in such stories as *Suprugi Orlovy* (1897; The Orloff Couple, 1901), his tramplike protagonists find

MAKSIM GORKI

GÜNTER GRASS

their strength and will power diminished by the actions of strong women. The men end up bitterly self-deceived, as in *Dvadtzat' shest' i odna* (1899; Twenty-Six and One, 1902), where rough bakery workers idolize an attractive, but all too fallible, girl. This story, crude in incident, is made beautiful and moving by G.'s art, especially his language.

G. was, however, dissatisfied with the limitations of his simple characters and the restricted framework of the short story. He turned to the novel, where he hoped to master more complex themes and narrative devices. From *Foma Gordeyev* (1899; Eng., 1901) to *Zhizn' Matveya Kozhemyakina* (1910; The Life of Matvei Kozhemyakin, 1959) he concentrated on the Russian political and social situation. His revolutionary protagonists suffer the tragic fate of those who wanted to change Czarist Russia. His merchant-class antagonists, ideologically obnoxious but aesthetically well drawn, seem to have inherited the strength and will power of the early tramp characters. *Mat'* (1906; Mother, 1907), later to become the paragon of Soviet novels, is the one exception: in this novel, the revolutionaries are strong and unflinching, and unafflicted by internal weakness or doubt.

G. tried to exemplify Lenin's patience with such works as *Ispoved'* (1908; A Confession, 1909), urging a synthesis between Marxism and Christianity. He also wrote a series of plays, the best known of which, *Na Dne* (1902; Down and Out, 1903 [later The Lower Depths]) explored the nature of hope and illusion in the context of a Russian flophouse; its production by the Moscow Art Theater made G. famous throughout Europe and America.

In 1913 G. started writing a series of memoirs which were to be more finished aesthetically than anything else he wrote. In a brilliant series of reminiscences, *Detstvo* (1912-13; My Childhood, 1915) and *Vlyudyakh* (1914, In the World, 1917), he brought under firm and sure control his reiterated themes of activeness versus passivity, illusion versus real achievement, Russian backwardness versus the revolutionary's zeal, sexual relations as both constructive and destructive, which had been only under intermittent control in his earlier novels and plays. It was as if the ultimately subjective genre, autobiography, allowed him to be more objective and precise than the supposedly objective genre of the novel narrated through the third person or a fictional first person. A re-examination of G.'s earlier fiction

shows how steadily his writing, at its best, was moving toward the narrative solution of autobiography. His later memoiristic portraits of fellow writers include many masterpieces, foremost among them his *Vospominaniya o L've Nikolayeviche Tolstom* (1919; Reminiscences of Lev Nikolaevich Tolstoy, 1920), the sternest yet most vivid picture we have of the giant from any of his contemporaries. It was only after the memoiristic period that G. had his narrative gift under control; his fiction from the 1920's on bears out this new-found discipline, notably his novel about three generations of a Russian merchant family, *Delo Artamonovykh* (1925; Decadence, 1927). G.'s last major work, *Zhizn' Klima Samgina* (1927-32; The Bystander, 1930; The Magnet, 1931; Other Fires; 1933, The Specter; 1938), probably represents an aesthetic decline, when it is compared with his masterpieces, although there are many Soviet and Western critics who praise it highly. His whole career is marked by the splendor, as well as by the pain, of a prophet who saw his own vision realized.

FURTHER WORKS: *Konovalov* (1897; Konovalov, 1901); *Byvshiye lyudi* (1897; Creatures That Once Were Men, 1901); *Mal'va* (1897; Eng., 1901); *Troye* (1901; Three of Them, 1902); *Meshchane* (1901; The Smug Citizen, 1906); *A. P. Chekhov* (1905; Chekhov, 1905); *Zhizn' Nenuzhnovo Cheloveka* (1907; The Spy, 1908); *Gorodok Okurov* (1909); *Po Rusi* (1915; In Old Russia, 1921); *Moi Universitety* (1922; My University Days, 1923); *L. Andreyev* (1922; Andreev, 1922); *Sobraniye Sochinenii* (1923-28); *Sobraniye Sochinenii* (1933 ff.); *Sobraniye Sochinenii* (1949-56). **Selected English trans.:** *Selected Short Stories* (1959)

BIBLIOGRAPHY: Voguë, E. de, *M. G.: l'oeuvre et l'homme* (1905); Shklovski, V., *Udachi i porazheniya Maksima Gor'kovo* (1926); Gruzdev, I., *Biografiia Gor'kovo* (1927, 1948); Kaun, A., *M. G. and His Russia* (1932); Balukhatyi, S. D., *Kritika o Gor'kom* (1934); Gorki, M., *Materialy i issledovaniya* (1934-51); Desnitski, V., *Ocherki zhizni i tvorchestva Gor'kovo* (1935, 1959); Balukhatyi, M., *Literaturnaia rabota M. Gor'kovo* (1936-38); Lunacharski, A., *Stat'i o Gor'kom* (1938); Bialik, B., *Esteticheskiye vzglyady Gor'kovo* (1938); Khodasevich, V., *Nekropol'*, "Gor'kii" (1939); Chukovski, K., *Vospominaniya* (1940); *Gorkovskiye chteniya* (1947 ff.); Holtzmann, F., *The Young M. G., 1868-1902* (1949); Gourfinkel, N., *G. par lui-même* (1954); Lenobl',

51

G., *O M. Gor'komkhudozhnike slova* (1957); Lenobl', G., *M. G. v bor'be za razvitie sovetskoi literatury* (1958); Yershov, P., *Letters of G. and Andreev* (1958); Bialik, B., and Mikhailovski, B., *Tvorchestvo Gor'kovo i voprosy sotsialisticheskovo realizma* (1958); *Letopis' zhizni i tvorchestva A. M. Gor'kovo* (1958-60); Mikhailovski, B., and Tager, E., *O khudozhestvennom masterstve M. Gor'kovo* (1960); Ovcharenko, A., *Publitzistika M. Gor'kovo* (1961); Bialik, B., *M. G., Dramaturg* (1962); Hare, R., *M. G., Romantic Realist and Conservative Revolutionary* (1962); *Literaturnoye Nasledstvo,* CXX (1963), "M. G. i sovetskie pisateli (special G. issue)"

IRWIN WEIL

GOURMONT, Rémy de

French poet, novelist, and essayist, b. 4 April 1858, Bazochesen-Oulmes; d. 27 Sept. 1915, Paris

G., a cofounder of the *Mercure de France* (1889), was employed until 1891 at the Bibliothèque Nationale.

His first work, *Le Latin mystique* (1892), reveals a deep knowledge of medieval hymnology. Although an atheist, G., like Baudelaire, combined mystical and sensualistic themes in his poetry (*Hiéroglyphes,* 1894; *Les Saintes du Paradis,* 1899; *Oraisons mauvaises,* 1900; *Simone,* 1901; *Les Divertissements,* 1912). In his short stories the antinaturalistic G. is close to Villiers de l'Isle-Adam (*Histoires magiques,* 1894; *Le Pèlerin du silence,* 1896; *D'un Pays lointain,* 1898; *Couleurs,* 1908 [Colors, 1929]; *La Patience de Griseldis,* 1921). The form of his novels is based on Mallarmé's "word aesthetics" and on Huysmans' (q.v.) *A Rebours: Sixtine* (1890; Very Woman, 1922); *Les Chevaux de Diomède* (1897; The Horses of Diomedes, 1923); *Une Nuit au Luxembourg* (1906; A Night in the Luxembourg, 1912); *Un Coeur virginal* (1907; A Virgin Heart, 1921). An unlifelike, cold, yet at the same time passionate tone pervades these novels. They are really no more than derivative, amateur trifles, although their perspicacity and undeniably good taste evidence an excellent essayist.

As an aesthetician of the language G. developed the concept of dissociation of ideas. Words are to be treated as organisms; liberated from the cliché and used in new contexts, they acquire new freshness (*L'Esthétique de la langue française,* 1899; What Is Pure French?, 1922; *La Culture des idées,* 1900; *Le Problème*

du style, 1902). *Le Livre des masques* (2 vols., 1896-98; The Book of Masks, 1921), the *Promenades littéraires* (7 vols., 1904-1927), and the *Promenades philosophiques* (3 vols., 1905-1909; Decadence and Other Essays, 1921) show G.'s love of sonorous words and of a wide range of literature. They also reveal a certain eroticism (*Physique de l'amour,* 1903 [Am., The Natural Philosophy of Love, 1922; Eng., The Physiology of Love, 1932]). Pessimist, encyclopedist, skeptic, post-symbolist, the pupil of La Rochefoucauld, Voltaire, Renan, and Mallarmé, G. shows himself to be witty, original, and eclectic as thinker, stylist and writer.

FURTHER WORKS: *Les Français au Canada et en Acadie* (1888); *Lilith* (1892; Eng., 1946); *Theodat* (1893); *Le Vieux roi* (1897); *Le Songe d'une femme* (1899); *Le Chemin de velours* (1902); *Epilogues* (1895-1910); *Muses d'aujourd'hui* (1910); *Lettres à l'Amazone* (1914; Letters to the Amazon, 1931); *Pendant l'orage* (1915); *Dans la tourmente* (1916); *Pendant la guerre* (1917); *L'Hombre d'une femme* (1923); *Dissociations* (1925); *Lettres intimes à l'Amazone* (1926)

BIBLIOGRAPHY: Coulon, M., *L'enseignement de R. de G.* (1925); Jacob, P. E., *R. de G.* (1932); Rees, G., *R. de G.* (1940); Burne, G. S., "R. de G.: A Scientific Philosophy of Art," *WHR,* XIII (1959), 71-79; Uitti, K. D., *The Symbolist Novel* (1962; on G.'s fiction)

KURT WEINBERG

GOZZANO, Guido Gustavo

Italian narrative writer and poet, b. 19 Dec. 1883, Aglié Canavese; d. there, 9 Aug. 1916

G. was tubercular from youth. Except for a journey to India (1912-13) his life was outwardly uneventful. He obtained a degree in law but did not practice this profession. His writing was at first influenced by D'Annunzio (q.v.); later he was associated with the *crepuscolari* movement (see Italian Literature). He soon dissociated himself from his first works, *Domani* (1904) and *La via del rifugio* (1907), and abandoned himself to a sentimental melancholy that stemmed from his realization that he could never undertake anything outside the limited area of his personal environment. G. yearned for the simple life; his favorite setting for his works was the mid-19th c. Biedermeier period.

Even his visit to India failed to bring G. the satisfaction he had hoped for (*Verso la cuna del mondo* [letters posthumously pub. by G. A. Borgese], 1917). Passages in *I primi e gli ultimi colloqui* (1915) indicate that toward the end of his life he found relief from inner conflict in religious faith. The unrest that characterizes G.'s work is typical of the small-town intellectual of a transitional period who through a kind of self-imposed restraint remains caught in the narrowness of provincial life. G.'s poetry owes its effectiveness less to the quality of his verse or to his poetic style, which is often unpolished, than to its musical urgency and its loving description of objects.

FURTHER WORKS: *I tre talismani* (1904); *I colloqui* (1911); *La principessa si sposa* (1917); *L'altare del passato* (1918); *L'ultima traccia* (1919); *Primavere romantiche* (1924); *Opera omnia* (1934-38); *Calcaterra* (1948); *Lettere d'amore di G. G. a Amalia Guglielminetti* (1951); *Fiabe* (1961)

BIBLIOGRAPHY: Biondolillo, F., *La poesia di G. G.* (1926); De Lisa, G., *La poesia di G. G.* (1935); Brusati, M., *Incontri con G. G.* (1951); Vaccari, W., *La vita e i pallidi amori di G. G.* (1958); Modena, I., *Ricordando G.* (1960); Presco, C., "The Crepuscularianism of G. G.," *DA*, XXI (1961), 3791; Boni, M., *A colloquio con G. G.* (1962); Circeo, E., *Ritratti di poeti: G. e Corazzini* (1963)

GIORGIO DOLFINI

GRACQ, Julien

(pseud. of *Louis Poirier*), French novelist, b. 27 July 1910, Saint-Florent-le-Vieil

After finishing his secondary education G. entered the École Normale Supérieure in 1930 and became a professor of history and geography.

His novel *Au Château d'Argol* (1938) is a "demonic version" of the Parsifal theme written under the influence of surrealism (q.v.) and falling into the category of the *roman noir*. The novel *Un Beau Ténébreux* (1945), the story of a Dorian Gray type, appears on the one hand better constructed but on the other less original. G.'s masterful talent proved itself, however, in *Rivage des Syrtes* (1951), which received the Prix Goncourt the year of its publication. Through its symbolic plot this novel, set in an imaginary landscape, suggests a nihilistic view of man's fate. The essential charac-

teristics of G.'s work are a disciplined, almost classical surrealism, a reaction against the excesses of *littérature engagée*, and a desire to restore style to its pre-eminence.

FURTHER WORKS: *Liberté grande* (1947); *Lautréamont Fougours* (1947); *André Breton* (1947); *Le Roi pêcheur* (1948); *La Littérature à l'estomac* (1950); *La Terre habitable* (1951); *Prose pour l'étrangère* (1953); *Un Balcon en forêt* (1958; Balcony in the Forest, 1959); *Le Chemin du Seigneur* (1961; Saint Paul, 1961); *Préférences* (1961)

BIBLIOGRAPHY: Hubert, R. R., "J. G., Historien du rêve," *FR*, XXXVIII (1965), 630-36; Leutrat, J.-L., "Bref essai sur l'univers humain des œuvres de J. G.," *Cahiers du Sud*, XLI (1965), 248-81

MARIUS FRANÇOIS GUYARD

GRADNIK, Alojz

Slovene poet, b. 3 Aug. 1882, Medana

G. studied in Vienna and served as a judge in various towns on the Slovenian coast. He later held high judicial offices in Yugoslavia.

G. belongs to the second generation of Slovene modernists. Part of his lyrical work consists of a warmly humane yet factual chronicle of life in Brda, a combination of social questioning and sorrowful nationalism. But G.'s personally tinged, eruptive lyric poetry, some of which has been translated into English (Selected Poems, 1964), met with greater attention. His nature is dark, instinctive, and contradictory: sensual passion runs parallel with renunciation and self-abasement, love with fear of death. His works represent the transition from naturalism (q.v.) to psychologism and are based partly on autobiographical material. Although extremely well acquainted with other literatures, G. has been less given to poetic experimentation than other Slovene modernists; for the most part he has used the sonnet form. G. has also translated romance, oriental, English, and German works into Slovene.

WORKS: *Padajoče zvezde* (1916); *Pot bolesti* (1922); *De profundis* (1926); *Svetle samote* (1932); *Večni studenci* (1938); *Zlate lestve* (1940); *Bog in umetnik* (1943); *Pesmi o Maji* (1944); *Pojoča kri* (1934); *Pesmi* (1952); *Narobe svet* (1953); *Petrarca: Soneti i Kancone* (1954); *Harfa v vetru* (1954); *Pesmi* (1962); *Eros-Tanatos* (1962); *Izbrane pesmi* (1964)

BIBLIOGRAPHY: Boršnik, M., *Pogovori s pesnikom Gradnikom* (1954); Slodnjak, A., *Geschichte der slowenischen Literatur* (1958)

FRAN PETRÉ

GRAF, Oscar Maria

German novelist and poet, b. 22 July 1894, Berg am Starnberger See, Bavaria; d. 28 June 1967, New York City

G., the son of a baker, was at first an apprentice in his father's trade. When he was seventeen, he left home and went to Munich, where he led a bohemian life, working at a number of widely varied jobs such as elevator boy and sandwich man. In World War I he was a soldier on the Russian front. After returning, he became a factory worker and then a post office helper. In January 1918 he took part in the strike of munitions workers. He joined the revolutionary group around the socialist leader Kurt Eisner (1867-1919) and participated in the November Revolution in Bavaria that deposed the Wittelsbach dynasty just before the end of World War I. After the demise of the short-lived Socialist Republic of Bavaria in spring 1919, G. became a director for the Munich Workers' Theater; later he became a writer. In 1933 he fled Germany and during the next two years lived briefly in Vienna, Moscow, and Czechoslovakia. In 1938 he fled Europe, going first to Mexico, then to the United States, where he settled in New York.

G. began his literary career as a poet, essayist, and short story writer treating themes of social revolution and protest. He then turned to autobiographical writing; the novel *Frühzeit* (1920; reissued as *Dorfbanditen*, 1932) is based on his own life, and he used autobiographical elements in many other novels. G. found particularly congenial the writing of *Kalendergeschichten*, simple folklike tales and sketches, of which he wrote many, often in Bavarian dialect, dealing with Bavarian life and customs. He also wrote many novels about Bavarian peasants marked by blunt honesty and strong naturalism (q.v.) that shrinks from nothing in treating openly and fully the chosen subject; at the same time G.'s work is tempered by a warm humor. In these works G. showed a narrative skill comparable to that of Thoma (q.v.).

A socialist and a pacifist, G. was concerned with his own times, though later he did write some novels dealing with the future. He cared greatly about the conditions of life for contemporary man, which he saw threatened by the modern world; this received notable expression in his Utopian novel *Die Eroberung der Welt* (1949; reissued as *Die Erben des Untergangs*, 1959).

FURTHER WORKS: *Die Revolutionäre* (1918); *Georg Schrimpf* (1919); *Amen und Anfang* (1919); *Ua-pua!* (1921); *Bayrische Lesebücherl* (1924); *Die Chronik von Flechtling* (1925); *Die Heimsuchung* (1925); *Finsternis* (1926); *Im Winkel des Lebens* (1927); *Wir sind Gefangene* (1927; Prisoners All, 1928); *Bayrische Kalendergeschichten* (2 vols., 1929); *Das Bayrische Dekameron* (1930); *Wunderbare Menschen* (1931); *Bolwieser* (1931; The Stationmaster, 1933); *Einer gegen alle* (1932; The Wolf, 1934); *Notizbuch des Provinzschriftstellers O. M. G.* (1932); *Der harte Handel* (1934); *Der Abgrund* (1936); *Anton Sittinger* (1937); *Der Quasterl* (1938); *Das Leben meiner Mutter* (1940; The Life of My Mother, 1940); *Unruhe um einen Friedfertigen* (1948); *Kalendergeschichten* (1957); *Mitmenschen* (1959); *Die Flucht ins Mittelmäßige* (1959); *Größtenteils schimpflich* (1962); *Altmodische Gedichte eines Dutzendmenschen* (1962); *Der große Bauernspiegel* (1962); *Er nannte sich Banscho* (1964); *Gelächter von außen* (autobiography, 1966)

BIBLIOGRAPHY: Pinthus, K., "O. M. G.: Fünf Bücher erscheinen zu seinem 65. Geburtstag," *DRs*, LXXXV (1959), 725-28; Swarowsky, H., "Probleme der Gesellschaft in der Gegenwart im Werk O. M. Gs.," *Wissenschaftliche Zeitschrift der Pädagogischen Hochschule Potsdam*, IX (1965), 93-110

* * *

GRASS, Günter

German novelist, dramatist, and poet, b. 16 Oct. 1927, Danzig (now Poland)

In 1944 G. was drafted into the German army. After the end of the war he went to the Rhineland. He enrolled as a student of painting and sculpture at the Academy of Arts in Düsseldorf. In 1952 he moved to West Berlin to continue his art studies, and in 1956 he went to Paris, where he wrote *Die Blechtrommel*, which established his fame.

Though G. originally saw his future in sculpture and painting, his initial efforts at writing date back to the late 1940's. Some of his poems received a minor prize and earned him an invitation to read before "Gruppe 47," an influential group of German writers. His performance secured a publisher for his first volume of poetry, *Die Vorzüge der Windhühner* (1956), with drawings and a dust jacket designed by the author (G. designs the covers of all of his books). Between 1956 and 1958 he wrote a number of plays and playlets. In 1958 he was awarded the coveted "Preis der Gruppe 47" for his forthcoming *Die Blechtrommel* (1959; The Tin Drum, 1962), which became an immediate commercial and critical success, receiving several important awards. In 1961 appeared the novella *Katz und Maus* (Cat and Mouse, 1963) and in 1963 the novel *Hundejahre* (Dog Years, 1965). G. received Germany's most prestigious literary award, the "Büchnerpreis," in 1965.

Although G.'s fame up till now rests almost entirely on his prose writings, he is also a poet and dramatist of stature. He feels equally at home in all three genres. An idea may present itself to him in any of the three and then may undergo a metamorphosis into any of the others. His early poetry contains numerous metaphors, images, and motifs that later appeared in his prose writings. The poem "Vogel," e.g., employs a bird motif—also prevalent in his drawings—which he later expanded considerably in *Hundejahre*. A chapter of this novel was, in turn, changed into a dramatic dialogue and staged as *Goldmäulchen* (1964). G. has a clearly circumscribed stock of highly personal metaphors and images that again and again appear in different constellations and guises.

His continued focus on his personal range of experience and background applies to locale as well. He is one of the most autochthonous writers of our time. Danzig, its workers' suburb of Langfuhr, and the region at the mouth of the Vistula are strikingly real in his writings. As Melville, whom G. admires, is able to project the world through the microcosm of a whaler in *Moby Dick*, G. succeeds in lending the habitat of his youth the dimensions of a universe. With this locale and environment, he himself has said, he "will not be through for quite some time to come." When his characters leave this area, their vitality and credibility as individuals become diminished, the props in the new environment are paler, the contours of the new locale are vague. The later chapters of *Die Blechtrommel,* when Oskar lives in the Rhineland, are a case in point.

Though the lyrics and plays reveal as much of G. the writer as do his prose works, until now they have almost entirely been ignored by both the critics and the public. The wide

success of his prose writings is in large measure due to a basic conservatism in his craft. His prose is much less elusive than his rather surrealistic plays and poetry. Time schemes in his novels are seldom confusing, and events are by and large chronological; the situations are concrete. Although numerous influences can easily be discerned in his work (Melville, Stern, Döblin (q.v.), Unamuno (q.v.), Jean-Paul)—and are readily admitted by G.—his novels are unique, owing mainly, to be sure, to the highly imaginative and potent narrative talent of the author, but also to a very personal credo.

G. refuses to see the world in terms of any specific ideology: "I have always rejected having my body, which does cast a shadow, violated by an idea, which has none." Thus G. avoids the barrenness and abstractness of the modern intellectualized novel. He does, however, have a fixed perspective; it is artistic: he believes in the pre-eminence of artistic form. Content to him is the pretext (*Vorwand*) for and obstacle (*Widerstand*) to form. Form to G. is style. His style can be intentionally cumbersome and grinding, it can be playful and flippant, it can be monstrously involved and paratactically simple—all depending on how it can best mold and sublimate the content.

Thus, for example, in a satire on Heidegger and his professional jargon he outdoes his target in his linguistic contortions. When he wants to evoke the symbolic-associative significance of the dog in *Hundejahre*, he does so with playful virtuosity by racing through what might be called the tonal scale of the color black. The dog's hair "glistened black, umbrella-black, priest-black, widow-black, SS-black, blackboard-black, Falange-black, blackbird-black, Othello-black, Ruhr-black, violet-black, tomato-black, lemon-black, flour-black, milk-black, snow-black." Though his language is vital in its virility and adaptability, G. is not a primitive. His style is at once naïve and sophisticated. The craftsman, indeed the sculptor and painter, is very obvious in his style.

Whatever exists in G.'s novels is securely grounded in the world of reality. All things, be they a clock, a dog, or a person, first and foremost "cast a shadow." This is their all-important common denominator. Things and people are, in this sense, equal. There is no fundamental difference between them in terms of an abstracted pattern by which they are classified and evaluated. In this light it becomes obvious that G.'s notorious obscenities ought not to be viewed in the context of "morality," that is to say, in terms of an "ideology." Any such framework is alien to the artistic perspectives inherent in his work. Even G.'s language has the properties that make it "cast a shadow." His style so thoroughly sublimates content that in itself it seems to acquire the substance of "things."

Language and style, therefore, assume such central importance in G.'s works that he may assert, as he does, that there are no "meanings" in his writings. Many of his symbols do in fact lead nowhere. Their function is to create stylistic tension. Yet there are "meanings," especially in terms of myth and archetype. Though G. would wish to classify these as abstractions, they are a formidably substantial substratum in his work.

By evoking vestigal and subliminal contents of human experience G. succeeds in a major accomplishment: the disarming of the "demons" in the German past. He places them on center stage and exposes them in the context of the grotesque as a crippled dwarf in *Die Blechtrommel*, as a dog in *Hundejahre*, and even as a freakish teen-ager in *Katz und Maus*. He comes to grips with the "demons" on their own ground, that of archetype and myth, and thus avoids intellectualizing, that is, rationalizing, the German past. In doing so G. has provided an efficacious, even if shocking, therapy for the German conscience. His international reputation in no small measure is due to his ability as a writer to prescribe this therapy, not merely for the Germans, but for everyone to whom the Hitler era is still an open wound. More so than any other postwar German writer G. has achieved a catharsis of attitude toward a people still suffering from the trauma of its history.

FURTHER WORKS: *Hochwasser* (1957); *Noch zehn Minuten bis Buffalo* (1957; Only Ten Minutes to Buffalo, 1967); *Stoffreste* (ballet, 1957); *Onkel, Onkel* (1957; Mister, Mister, 1967); *32 Zähne* (1958); *Die bösen Köche* (1957; The Wicked Cooks, 1967); *Fünf Köche* (ballet, 1959); *Beritten hin und zurück* (1959); *Gleisdreieck* (1960); *Die Ballerina* (1963); *Die Plebejer proben den Aufstand* (1965; The Plebeians Rehearse the Uprising: A German Tragedy, 1966); *Ausgefragt* (1967); *Über das Selbstverständliche: Reden, Aufsätze, Offene Briefe, Kommentare* (1968); *Der Fall Axel C. Springer am Beispiel Arnold Zweig: Eine Rede, ihr Anlass und die Folgen.* **Selected English trans.:** *Selected Poems* (with German

originals, 1966); *Four Plays* (1967); *New Poems* (with German originals, 1968); *Speak Out! Speeches, Open Letters, Commentaries* (1969)

BIBLIOGRAPHY: Ahl, H., "Ohne Scham—ohne Tendenz—ohne Devise: G. G.," in *Literarische Porträts* (1962), pp. 28-35; Blöcker, G., "G. G.: *Die Blechtrommel*," in *Kritisches Lesebuch* (1962); pp. 208-14; "Drum of Neutrality," in *TLS* (5 Oct. 1962), p. 776; Wagenbach, K., "G. G.," in *Deutsche Literatur der Gegenwart* (1963), pp. 118-26; Horst, K. A., "Die Vogelscheuchen des G. G.," in *Arbeiten und Berichte aus der Süddeutschen Versuchs- und Forschungsanstalt für Milchwirtschaft*, XVII (1963), 1003-8; "Dogs and the Deflation of Demons," in *TLS* (27 Sept. 1963), p. 728; Bauke, J. B., "A Talk with G. G.," in *The New York Times Book Review* (31 May 1964), p. 16; Steiner, G., "The Nerve of G. G.," in *Commentary* (May 1964), pp. 77-79; Friedrichsmeyer, E. M., "Aspects of Myth, Parody and Obscenity in G. G.'s *Die Blechtrommel* and *Katz und Maus*," in *GR*, XL (1965), 240-50; Enright, D. J., "Casting out Demons," in *New York Review of Books* (3 June 1965), pp. 8-10; "Green Years for G.," in *Life* (4 June 1965), pp. 51-56; Tank, K. L., *G. G.* (1969)

ERHARD FRIEDRICHSMEYER

Oscar Bronski-Mazerath [in *Die Blechtrommel*], the eternally three-year-old drummer, refuses to grow up into a world inhabited by his Polish-German family in Danzig and especially the larger world, made up in succession of an imperialistic bourgeoisie, *Freistadt* Danzig mercantile spirit, Nazi storm troopers, Polish lancers charging gallantly against tanks, the elusive *Endsieg*, Russian occupation, black marketeering in West Germany, *Aufbau*, and middle-class prosperity, American-style. From his unique position Oscar the drummer records with ironic detachment how stupidity, savagery, empty traditionalism, and the seven deadly sins are perpetuated from one generation to the next, abetted by political, social, and religious institutions. G.'s all-pervading ironic mood is sustained by the skilful manipulation of unconventional syntax, daring imagery and choice of vocabulary, revealing the poet beneath the prose writer. Like any great novelist, he possesses the gift to breathe life into his characters. . . .

Lewald, H. E., in *BA* (1961), p. 340

The poetry of G.G. . . . is not as well known as one might wish. . . . He combines in his verse a black humor, an awareness of human absurdity, and an almost incredibly sharp sense of linguistic fun. G. is good, and, indeed, required reading for those who think that poetry must elevate and transfigure.

Exner, R. in *BA* (1962), p. 252

When this sprawling, bad-mannered novel [*The Tin Drum*] appeared in Germany three years ago, G. instantly became the hero and spokesman for West Germany's dissident, anti-Adenauer intellectuals. . . . The question remains: at whom is G. pointing his skittish, ink-stained finger? G. has left it to his readers to decide whether he accuses them of being midgets or whether his message is that only dwarfs and children can survive the evils of this world. What really matters is that G. has created something more lasting than a political satire; . . . he has written a fully rounded portrait of the artist as a young dwarf, a genuine fantasy figure in the best tradition of some notable German folk heroes. . . . *The Tin Drum* is a work of art and power and thus a liberating event for the new German literature.

Grunfeld, F. in *The Reporter* (1963), p. 54

I don't think I have read any other postwar novel in which this diligent sense of life's interrelatedness and unity has been set down in such iron sentences or, through patient assembly of the fruits of exact examination, made so stark. . . . The book is a work of genius, no matter how cantankerous, willful, filthy, tedious, brutal, nihilistic, long-winded, importunate, self-conscious or Germany-obsessed you find it. If execution can be lyrical, then *Dog Years* is that. But the hangman is far from affable and, it is worth pointing out, this is the second time he has formally executed this body. Never has a dunghill been reported with such a consummate sense of its pageantry or the violence of racism smacked dead with so savage a hand.

West P., Review of *Dog Years*, in *The Nation*, 201 (16 Aug. 1965), p. 81

He derives pleasure from the objective realities of our world, and if his unprejudiced descriptions of them have proved shocking they merely did what the writer intended them to do.

His new poems, too, proceed from objects and observations; they center around specific events and persons; their purpose is above all to depict situations and conditions. Time and again his imagination takes fire from concrete facts and always—wherever it has taken us—returns to concrete facts. But still more than in his earlier collections, G. is here concerned with unobtrusive hues, which "between black and white, intimidated always, are grieving." He would like "to pin-point precisely the imprecise."

. . . G. has preserved his oft-extolled candor, but this is now coupled with a detached lucidity that does not, however, impair the refreshing splendor, the forceful tone, and the pungent appeal of these verses. His naiveté has become wiser, his playfulness more sophisticated.

G. G.'s new poems show that our world—in spite of everything—is still amenable to lyrical statement.

They also refute the belief that the poet cannot face the present except in irony and parodies. There are lines in the volume *Ausgefragt* in which the ephemeral achieves permanence. More cannot be expected from poetry.

Reich-Ranicki, M., in *Die Zeit* (23 May 1967), p. 11

GRAU DELGADO, Jacinto
Spanish dramatist, b. 1877, Barcelona; d. 14 Aug. 1958, Buenos Aires

Although G.'s plays are revolutionary in technique, his themes are the traditional ones of dramatic literature and the Spanish "romance" ballads. This can be seen in his drama *El conde de Alarcos* (1917). Despite its archaic language, this play was successful—though more so in France than in Spain. *El señor de Pigmalión* (1921), a play of great technical originality, was equally well received; it has features in common with the dramatic work of Cervantes and Pirandello (q.v.). *El hijo pródigo* (1918) was inspired by a biblical theme, while in *Don Juan de Carillana* (1913) G. turned back to the old theme of the *burlador* —the mocker of Seville. *El burlador que no se burla* (1930) presents an extremely personal concept of the Don Juan figure; this one, though a Don Juan so far as outward life is concerned, is nevertheless "full of inner emotion and love" and akin to Werther.

G. holds a unique place in the 20th c. Spanish theater. His original treatment of old myths revived in modern dress is particularly characteristic. G. created individual characters of psychological depth and gave expression to elemental feelings.

FURTHER WORKS: *Trasuntos* (1899); *Las bodas de Camacho* (1903); *Entre Llamas* (1905); *El tercer demonio* (1908); *En Ildaria* (1918); *Conseja galante* (1919); *Los tres locos del mundo* (1930); *Estampas* (1941); *Unamuno* (1943); *La Casa del Diablo* (1945); *Don Juan en el tiempo y en el espacio* (1953); *Teatro* (1954)

BIBLIOGRAPHY: V. Valbuena Prat, A., *Historia de la literatura española* (1946), II, 823-24; Guiliano, W., "The Last Words of J. G.," *Hispania*, XLIII (1960), 393; Schwartz, K., "J. G. and the Meaning of Existence," *Hispania*, XLIV (1961), 34-41

ALONSO ZAMORA VICENTE

GRAVES, Robert (von Ranke)

English novelist, poet, essayist, and critic, b. 26 July 1895, London

G. was one of five children born to Alfred Percival Graves and his second wife, Amalie von Ranke Graves. His education was obtained in his father's extensive library, at various preparatory schools, at Charterhouse and St. John's College, Oxford. During World War I he served as an officer in the Royal Welsh Fusiliers and was wounded in action. After receiving his degree from Oxford, he taught briefly at the University of Cairo (1926) before moving to the island of Majorca, where he has lived much of the time since. He has been married twice and has eight children.

G. began his career as a poet with the wartime publication of *Over the Brazier* (1916), *Goliath and David* (1916), and *Fairies and Fusiliers* (1917). Subsequent volumes contain either the work of specific periods or those poems he wishes to preserve. The latter are to be found in several different volumes of *Collected Poems* (1938, 1947, 1959). Throughout his literary career he has steadily refined his style so that he has achieved a distinctive poetic voice: his poems mingle the artless simplicity of ballads and nursery rhymes, the tough-minded argumentativeness of the Metaphysicals, and the mythopoeic intensity of Blake or the later Yeats (q.v.). Among his major themes are the dangerous complexities of love, the memories of childhood, the presence of ghosts and the spirit world, and the frailties, both tender and contemptible, of mankind. Of recent years his reputation has increased steadily, and he is currently considered one of the foremost poets writing in English.

As a novelist G. has been largely content to make a living rather than a reputation. His classical training and historical curiosity have resulted in a dozen or so novels whose settings range from the 13th c. B.C. onward. The first two, *I, Claudius* (1934) and *Claudius the God* (1934), vigorously narrated the power struggles of the Roman empire and the forces that transform a human being into a tyrant. For the former he received the Hawthornden and James Tait Black prizes. Other works have subjects as diverse as Byzantine history, Milton, a famous 19th c. murderer, the American Revolution, and the Golden Fleece. Two novels of particular importance are *King Jesus* (1946) and *Seven Days in New Crete* (1949), both of which draw on his original and encyclopedic researches in comparative religion.

G.'s researches have also been embodied in critical studies like *The White Goddess* (1948) and *The Nazarene Gospel Restored* (with Podoro, J., 1953), as well as in his interpretive collection *The Greek Myths* (1955). In all of these works his voracious reading, cavalier attitude toward presumptive evidence, and vigorously independent habits of mind are exhibited equally. He has also written literary criticism of a challenging, idiosyncratic temper, dating from *Poetic Unreason* (1925) to *The Crowning Privilege* (1955) and *Oxford Addresses on Poetry* (1962), the latter two consisting of essays delivered at Oxford, where he held the chair for poetry in 1961-62.

FURTHER WORKS: *Country Sentiment* (1920); *The Pier Glass* (1921); *Whipperginny* (1922); *On English Poetry* (1922); *The Meaning of Dreams* (1924); *Poems 1914-1926* (1926); *A Survey of Modernist Poetry* (with Laura Riding, 1927); *The English Ballad: A Short Critical Survey* (1927); *Lawrence and the Arabs* (1927); *Good-bye to All That* (1929); *Poems 1926-1930* (1930); *But It Still Goes On* (1931); *Poems 1930-1933* (1933); *The Real David Copperfield* (1933); *Antigua, Penny Puce* (1936); *Count Belisarius* (1938); *Sergeant Lamb of the Ninth* (1940); *The Long Week-End: A Social History of Britain, 1918-1939* (with A. Hodge, 1940); *Proceed, Sergeant Lamb* (1941); *Wife to Mr. Milton* (1943); *The Reader Over Your Shoulder* (with A. Hodge, 1943); *The Golden Fleece* (1944); *Poems 1938-1945* (1945); *The Common Asphodel* (1949); *The Isles of Unwisdom* (1949); *Poems and Satires* (1951); *Occupation: Writer* (1951); *Poems* (1953); *Homer's Daughter* (1955); *Adam's Rib* (1955); *Catacrok!* (1956); *English and Scottish Ballads* (1957); *Jesus in Rome: A Conjecture* (with Podoro, J., 1957); *They Hanged My Saintly Billy* (1957); *Steps* (1958); *More Poems* (1961); *New Poems* (1962); *The Siege and Fall of Troy* (1962); *Hebrew Myths* (with Patai, R., 1963); *The Bird of Paradise* (1963); *Man Does, Woman Is* (1964); *Collected Stories* (1964); *Collected Poems* (1965); *Collected Short Stories* (1965); *Love Respelt* (Eng., 1965; Am., 1966); *Ann at Highwood Hall* (1966); *Poems Selected by Himself* (1966); *Two Wise Children* (1966); *Love Respelt* (1966); *Colophon to Love Respelt* (1967); *The Big Green Book* (1968); *The Original Rubaiyyat of Omar Khayaam* (with Omar Ali-Shah, 1968)

BIBLIOGRAPHY: Hayman, R., "R. G.," in *EIC, V* (Jan. 1955), 32-43; Seymour-Smith, M., *R. G.* (1956); Jarrell, R., "G. and the White Goddess," in *YR*, XLV (Winter 1956), 302-314; *ibid.* (Spring 1956), 467-78; Steiner, G., "The Genius of R. G.," in *KR*, XXII (Summer 1960), 340-65; Cohen, J. M., *R. G.* (1960); Day, D. T., *Swifter than Reason: The Poetry and Criticism of R. G.* (1963); Higginson, F. H., *A Bibliography of the Works of R. G.* (1966)

JOHN B. VICKERY

GREEK LITERATURE

Greek literature, which waned to a minimum under four hundred years of Turkish domination, reemerged only when Greece was liberated and the modern state was established (1833). This was the beginning of the new era in which modern Greek literature was born. The language problem—the long-standing struggle between the older, scholarly, structured language and the spoken Greek that represented the natural development of the language—also came to a head during this period. The artificial, scholarly—and puristic—Greek language known as *katharevousa* was first designated the official language of the country and its literature, notwithstanding the literary merits of the popular poetry that had achieved remarkable vigor and aroused admiration in the West during the period of Turkish rule and the work of the first great modern Greek poet, Dionysios Solomos (1798-1857), who brought the popular language to a high pitch of literary maturity. The generation of writers who upheld the puristic language achieved no success because their work lacked the vitality of genuine artistic creativity. In 1888, however, the publication of *To taxidi* in demotic Greek by Psycharis, a scholar of linguistics as well as a writer, provided the long-awaited signal for the outbreak of the language revolution, and a whole generation of writers, led by Palamas (q.v.), espoused the popular language.

From then on the development of Greek literature parallels that of the new state. Lost ground was recovered; Greek antiquity, Byzantine-Greek tradition, the popular Greek heritage, and western European culture were the forces that enabled Greek literature to rise to the level of other European writing. Palamas, who is considered the most important modern Greek writer, had a very strong influence on his own generation, chiefly through his thematically versatile poetry but also as a prose writer and critic. All the western European movements found followers; the parnassians (Ioannis Gryparis [1871-1942]) were succeeded by the symbolists (see symbolism), and they in turn by the generation of Sikelianos (q.v.), who sought to revive Greek antiquity and tried to re-create it in his dynamic poetry. This generation included tender lyricists, such as Miltiades Malakassis (1869-1943); urbane pessimists, such as Kostas Uranis (1890-1953); masters of vital, vigorous poetry, such as Kostas Varnalis (b. 1884); the symbolist poet Tellos Agras (1899-1944); and Kostas Karyotakis (1896-1928), the lonely, embittered decadent and forerunner of contemporary poetry who depicted modern existential *angst*. Cavafy (q.v.), who lived in Alexandria, went his own way, writing narrative poetry in an original, archaic-sounding language. Papatzonis, a religious poet, also writes this narrative type of poetry in which he points up the relation between nature and intellect. Younger poets, such as I. M. Panayotopulos (q.v.), Melissanthi (b. 1910), and Rita Bumi-Papa (b. 1906), began in a traditional vein, but later their inward-looking lyricism and their poetic interpretation of experience found more relaxed forms. Musicality and feminine warmth of a hymnic imaginative quality mark the work of the women poets—Myrtiotissa (pseudonym for Theone Drakopulu, b. 1885), Maria Polyduri (1902-1930), Aemilia Daphni (1881-1941), Dialechti Zevgoli (b. 1907), and Lili Yakobidu (b. 1900).

The next generation was that of the modernists: Seferis (q.v.), the symbolist with Greek features, and Odysseas Elytis (b. 1911), in whom surrealism (q.v.) is combined with closeness to nature and luminous style. Followers of Seferis include Antoniu (b. 1906)—especially in his reminiscences—and Ghiorgis Kotsiras (b. 1921), a contemplative, lyrical symbolist. Nikephoros Vrettakos (b. 1911) writes inward-looking poetry of great forcefulness, while Iannis Ritsos (b. 1909) tends more toward the expression of subjective feeling. Other representatives of modernism are Takis Varvitsiotis (b. 1916), the sensitive recorder of life experienced as a dream; Karydis (b. 1914), who evokes a mood of rapture; Minas Domakis (b. 1917), the perpetual seeker, whose mood is one of despair; Ghiorgos Sarantaris (1909-1941), who experimented with a new kind of existential (see

59

existentialism), surrealistic poetry; Alexandros Baras (b. 1906), who writes with aloof objectivity; G. T. Vaphopulos (b. 1904), who presents his personal metaphysics in lyrical myths; and Takis Sinopulos (b. 1917), who experiences and depicts visionary things in physical terms. Others are Georg Themelis (b. 1900: fusion of the graphic with the ideal); Mitsos Lygisos (b. 1915: modern forms combined with still vital tradition); Zoe Karelli (b. 1901: existential *angst* depicted through rich imagery); Yannis Sphakianakis (b. 1908: a symbolistic, surrealistic poet who was the founder of sensualism); Yannis Skarimbas (b. 1899); and Aris Dikteos (b. 1918). Extreme surrealism is represented principally by Andreas Empirikos (b. 1901) and Nikos Engonopulos. Michael Stasinopulos (b. 1903), Theodoros Xydis (b. 1910), and Ghiorgos Geralis (b. 1917) deserve mention as poets who write in a tender, muted tone. Nikos Kavadias (b. 1910) and Orestis Laskos (b. 1908) are followers of Ringelnatz (q.v.).

In prose, Alexandros Papadiamantis (q.v.), with his genre paintings, is the acknowledged master. The novels and short stories of Psycharis were of great importance in the development of modern Greek literature, especially from the linguistic standpoint, although their literary value is by no means beyond challenge. Among the older narrative writers the following are outstanding: Andreas Karkavitsas (1866-1922: sea stories and fantastic short stories in the manner of Gogol and E. T. A. Hoffmann); Moraitidis (1851-1929: scenes of everyday life); Gheorgios Visyinos (1849-96: short stories focused on sharply delineated characters); Chantzopulos (1868-1920: a symbolist who dealt with social problems); and Demosthenes Vutyras (1872-1958: a popular symbolist with strong influence on the younger generation of fiction writers). The prose of Kazantzakis (q.v.) has a remarkable poetic quality; his books have been enthusiastically received abroad as well as in Greece. The leading members of the generation that emerged after World War I are Venesis (q.v.) whose work shows human greatness withstanding rigorous tests; Myrivilis (q.v.), the master of a dynamic pictorial style; Petsalis, an epic narrator of national themes from the Greek past; Theotokas (q.v.), who deals with social problems of bourgeois society; and Kosmas Politis (b. 1888), who writes subtly about the psychology of young people. Tersakis (q.v.) wrote formally excellent panoramic novels with a wealth of characters. Manolis Karagatsis (1908-

1960) is a neorealist of forceful, bold style and manner. Petros Charis (b. 1902) is a symbolist and mood poet. Pantelis Prevelakis (b. 1909), a Cretan and a friend of Kazantzakis, who has a liking for grandiose historical themes, is notable for his highly polished, expressive language. Other members of this generation are Kostas Sukas (b. 1899); Christos Levandas (b. 1904: descriptions of the omnipotence of the sea and the life of seamen); Alkis Yannopulos (b. 1896); and the neo-Byzantinists Kontoglu (b. 1895) and Nikos Gabriell Pentzikis (b. 1908).

Several women have achieved considerable reputations in contemporary prose. They include Tatiana Stavru (b. 1899: fiction of delicate psychological shading); Katina Papa (b. 1903), who writes of human kindness; Elli Alexiu (b. 1899); Lilika Naku (b. 1906); Galateya Kasantzaki (b. 1886: realistic treatment of social themes); and Galateya Saramti (b. 1920: inward-looking narrative technique with a tendency to surrealism). Outstanding among the younger generation of fiction writers are Menelaos Lundemis (1912-38: realistic and social themes); Michael Peranthis (b. 1917: novelistic biographies); Yannis Manglis (b. 1909: realistic stories full of humanity and a spirit of forgiveness); Renos Apostolidis (b. 1924), who writes in a hectic, willful style; Asteris Kovantzis (b. 1916); Nestoras Matsas (b. 1931); Takis Doxas (b. 1913); and Kostas Makistos (b. 1895).

After Antonios Matesis (1794-1875) prepared the way for dramatic literature, Xenopulos (q.v.), who was also well known as a narrative writer, laid its foundations with his psychologically based dramas of society. The leading personality in Greek drama is Spyros Melas (b. 1882); his existing plots, rich in conflict, proved very successful on the stage. As a writer of short stories and historical biographies, Melas is also fascinating for his expressive language and his unforced character drawing. Other dramatists are Tersakis, whose tragedies on Byzantine themes were very well received, Prevelakis, Alekos Lidorikis, Vassilis Rotas, Iakobos Kambanellis, and last but not least Kazantzakis and Sikelianos.

A number of critics and essayists have been closely connected with creative writing and the promotion of literary life. These include Yannis Apostolakis, I. M. Panayotopulos, Aemilios Churmusios, Alkis Thrylos, Kleoon Paraschos, K. D. Demaras, Herakles Apostolidis, Petros S. Spandonidis, Yannis Chantzinis,

ROBERT GRAVES

JULIEN GREEN

GRAHAM GREENE

Andreas Karantonis, and Panaiotis Kanell-opulos (b. 1902), who wrote about culture and the history of ideas.

BIBLIOGRAPHY: Baud Bovy, *Poésie de la Grèce moderne* (1946); Mirambel, A., *La Littérature grecque moderne* (1953); Sherrard, P., *The Marble Threshing Floor* (1956); Rosenthal-Kamarinea, I., ed., *Neugriechische Erzähler* (1958); Knös, B., *L'Histoire de la littérature néogrecque* (1962)

ISIDORA ROSENTHAL-KAMARINEA

GREEN, Henry

(pseud. of *Henry Vincent Yorke*), English novelist, b. 29 Oct. 1905, Tewkesbury, Gloucestershire

After Eton, two years at Oxford, and an early novel based partly on his Eton diary (*Blindness*, 1926), G., who was much disturbed by the General Strike of 1926, left Oxford to serve an apprenticeship in his father's Birmingham foundry, the managing director of which he now is.

Living (1929), delicately symbolic and hardly a proletarian novel at all, was nonetheless the result of his awakening to the realities of the workers' lives. During the ensuing ten years of economic depression, G. prepared an almost mythic comic vision of his own class, Mayfair, paralyzed and ineffectually toying with life-and-death problems of the social structure (*Party Going*, 1939). With this novel G. achieved a symbolic style dependent on those elaborately funny and minutely intimated patterns of imagery that have become his hallmark.

In *Caught* (1943), *Loving* (1945), and *Back* (1946), G. again probes the relations of his class to firemen, servants, and, in general, to the classes whose protest in 1926 had done so much to change his life. In these novels, however, the war itself is neurotically intensifying and distorting the old relationships. In *Loving*, G.'s technique begins to include elements of what has been called a "deliberately inverted fairy-tale," and this sense of fairy-tale verisimilitude is carried into *Concluding* (1948), which is an elusive satire of England's future when the all-seeing, all-comforting state will have come into existence. In *Nothing* (1950) and *Doting* (1952), the present of the 1950's seems as sterile as the future had in *Concluding*; but even the fairy-tale "floating world" of that earlier novel has degenerated into endless circles

of conversation. One reason for this is that G. had become convinced that the future of the English novel lay in virtually uninterrupted dialogue. Though these last two novels return in some ways to the critique of Mayfair offered in *Party Going*, they seem more often to be purely formal experiments in the possibility of authorial control without intrusion.

Throughout his work, however, even in his last two novels, G.'s dedication to the social awarenesses first explored in *Living* and *Party Going* is astonishingly consistent. Never a social reformer, always a pioneer in the poetic novel, G. has nonetheless seen the individual human significance of class barriers and—perhaps surprisingly—of class affinities as steadily as anyone since Jane Austen. And like Miss Austen, he has usually given class its reality through the eyes of people in love.

FURTHER WORK: *Pack My Bag* (1940)

BIBLIOGRAPHY: Stokes, E., *The Novels of H. G.* (1959); Russell, J., *H. G.: Nine Novels and an Unpacked Bag* (1960); Weatherhead, A. K., *A Reading of H. G.* (1961); Russell, J., "There It Is," *KR*, XXVI (1964); Johnson, B., "H. G.'s Comic Symbolism," *BSUF*, VI, iii (1965)

BRUCE JOHNSON

GREEN, Julien (Hartridge)

French novelist and dramatist, b. 6 Sept. 1900, Paris

G., the son of a Protestant American, was brought up in the spirit of Calvinism and Jansenism; at fifteen he was converted (with his father) to Catholicism, only to break away from it again a few years later. He served with the French forces in World War I, after which he went to the United States to study languages and literature. Returning to France in 1922, he devoted himself to literature, painting, and music. Under the influence of Gide (q.v.) he was for many years close to Buddhism, but in 1939, after reading the *Treatise on Purgatory* of St. Catherine of Genoa, he returned to the Catholic faith. He spent World War II in the United States, giving university and public lectures, and radio talks to the French people.

G. found two modes of expression for the problems and experiences that beset him: his diaries (*Journal, 1928-58*, 7 vols., 1938 ff. [selections in Personal Record, 1928-39, 1939 and in Diary, 1928-57, 1964]) and his novels.

Unlike his contemporaries, G. is not a moralist describing man in his worldly condition. Haunted by religion, he sets man in the border area between the given world and another one, which he calls "the world of truth." The sense of perdition, isolation, and death affects him metaphysically rather than in its material aspect, as it does Sartre (q.v.) or Céline (q.v.). His journal shows him to be threatened by the invisible, by night which obliterates all appearances, or stirred by great elations of the soul which are bound up with hope of eternity. In his novels he creates a world of dark-seeking tragedies where the power of evil lurks in the depths of insignificant creatures. (Since he returned to the Catholic faith this evil appears balanced by a positive moral counterforce— cf. *Varouna* and *Moïra*. However, G.'s most successful and most characteristic works were written before 1940.)

The inhabitants of G.'s world are weak-willed sleepwalkers—inhibited, frustrated characters who explosively give vent in terrible actions to the chaos and sinful desires of their hearts and passions. Love, an irrational dread, and death hang like a curse over these creatures of a tormenting, tormented imagination. However familiar to surrealism (q.v.) dreams and hallucinations may have become, G.'s treatment of them, which is inspired by Poe and emanates from his own Puritan background, is new and original in its suffocating quality and agonizing mystical obsessiveness.

Like Bernanos (q.v.), G. created a literature of evil, yet this evil is not rooted, as it was for Bernanos, in the personality as a whole but in the will—or lack of it—in the unconscious from which the forces of the perverse and the unclean break forth.

The only literary criticism Bernanos ever wrote dealt with G.'s first novel, *Mont-Cinère* (1926; Avarice House, 1929), a study of the mutual hatred of three women in a Puritan American setting which suggests Emily Brontë's *Wuthering Heights*.

With an authenticity reminiscent of Balzac's *Scènes de la vie de province* in its incisive realism, *Adrienne Mesurat* (1927; The Closed Garden, 1928) depicts a young girl gradually overtaken by madness and perishing within the narrow confines of her fate. *Leviathan* (1929; The Dark Journey, 1929) marks the emergence of a stronger element of dream and magic in G.'s poetic work. *L'Autre Sommeil* (1931), written and published at the urging of Gide, is the most autobiographical of his books. G. be-

gan *Minuit* (1936; Midnight, 1936) in 1934 but interrupted work on it to write the occult, fantastic novel *Le Visionnaire* (1934; The Dreamer, 1934), in which he admitted his obsession with death. Both works deal with the cruel fate of young people whose way leads through loneliness, rejection, and inescapable fear of life. In *Varouna* (1940; Then Shall the Dust Return, 1941) G. shows that the Cross alone offers deliverance from a fate-ordained chain of transmigrations and catastrophes: through the communion of the saints the personal love of God reaches man. In *Si j'étais vous* (1947; If I Were You, 1949) hope of grace and redemption again underlies the plot —the story of a human being caught in lust and fear of life. *Moïra* (1950; Eng., 1951) is a psychoanalytical study of a sexually repressed young student, a psychopath and moral fanatic who nevertheless yields in a moment of weakness to the temptation of a woman. He strangles her and in stupefied awareness of his lost innocence gives himself up to justice.

G.'s first play, *Sud* (1953), deals with a homosexual's fatal aberrations and his atonement in death. G. reveals the inner tragedy of themes made fashionable by Gide's *Corydon* and *Si Le Grain ne meurt*, offering also the one possible spiritual solution. In *L'Ennemi* (1954) he tries to show that good—and apparently even God Himself—may sometimes resort to sin in order to reach man.

FURTHER WORKS: *Pamphlet contre les catholiques de France* (1924); *Suite anglaise* (1927); *Le Voyageur sur la terre* (1927; The Pilgrim on the Earth, 1929); *Christine* (1927; Christine and Other Stories, 1930); *Un Puritain Homme de lettres* (1928); *Epaves* (1932; The Strange River, 1932); *Memories of Happy Days* (1942); *Oeuvres complètes* (1954 ff.; 2nd ed., 9 vols., 1957-60); *Le Malfaiteur* (1956; The Transgressor, 1957); *L'Ombre* (1956); *Le Bel Aujourd'hui* (1958); *Chaque Homme dans sa nuit* (1960; Each in His Darkness, 1961); *Théâtre 1953-56* (1960); *Partir avant le jour, mille chemins ouverts* (2 vols., 1963-64; To Leave before Dawn, 1967); *Terre lointaine* (1966)

BIBLIOGRAPHY: Stokes, S., *J. G. and the Thorn of Puritanism* (1955); Gaddis, M., "The Critical Reaction to J. G.," *DA*, XIX (1959), 1756-57; Prévost, J. L., *L'Âme engagée, J. G.* (1960); Rose, M. Gaddis., "The Production of J. G.: Microcosm of Mid-Century Writing," *FR*, XXXIV (1960), 164-69; Lago Alonso,

J., *La obra de J. G.* (1962); Rose, M. G., "J. G., Novelist as Playwright," *MD*, VI (1963) 195-203; Semolué, J., *J. G. ou l'obsession du mal* (1964); Reck, R. D., "J. G. on James Joyce," *James Joyce Quarterly*, II (1965), 138-39

* * *

GREEN, Paul Eliot

American dramatist, novelist, and screen-writer, b. 17 March 1894, Lillington, N. C.

G. is well known for his plays dealing with Southern decadence as exemplified in his Pulitzer Prize play, *In Abraham's Bosom* (1927), as well as in *The Field God* (1927), *The House of Connelly* (1931), *Shroud My Body Down* (1935), and a host of one-act plays, some of which are to be found in *Out of the South: The Life of People in Dramatic Form* (1939). He is author of a memorable pacifist play, *Johnny Johnson* (1937), and in recent years has been most acclaimed for his outdoor historical dramas, such as *The Lost Colony* (1937) and *The Common Glory* (1940). He has written two novels, *The Laughing Pioneer* (1932) and *This Body the Earth* (1935), and several collections of short stories, among them *Wide Fields* (1928), *Salvation on a String* (1946), and *The Dog on the Sun* (1949).

While G. demonstrates great social consciousness in plays such as *The House of Connelly* and *Johnny Johnson*, his most significant achievement lies in his convincing depiction of the temper of the South in such plays as *The Field God* and *In Abraham's Bosom*. His one-act plays also present vivid insights into Southern life, particularly into the lives of Southern Negroes. His symphonic dramas and outdoor plays are significant experiments in the uses of drama, and the former are much concerned with the interrelation of music and drama. G. reproduces Southern dialect with greater accuracy than any writer has achieved since the death of Joel Chandler Harris and Irwin Russell.

FURTHER WORKS: *The Lord's Will, and Other Plays* (1925); *Contemporary American Literature* (with E. L. Green, 1925); *Lonesome Road* (1926); *In the Valley, and Other Plays* (1928); *Roll, Sweet Chariot* (1934); *Fixin's*; *Hymn to the Rising Sun* (with E. Green, 1936); *The Lost Colony Songbook* (1938); *Franklin and the King* (1939); *The Enchanted Maze* (1939); *The Critical Year* (1939); *Native Son* (with

R. Wright; 1941); *The Highland Call* (1941); *The Free Company Presents...A Start in Life* (1941); *The Hawthorn Tree* (1943); *Forever Growing* (1945); *Faith of Our Fathers* (1950); *Peer Gynt* (1951); *The Common Glory Songbook* (1951); *Dramatic Heritage* (1953); *Wilderness Road* (1956); *Challenge to Citizenship* (1956); *The Founders* (1957); *Drama and the Weather* (1958); *Wings for to Fly* (1959); *The Confederacy* (1959); *The Stephen Foster Story* (1960); *Plow and Furrow* (1963); *The Sheltering Plaid* (1965); *Cross and Sword* (1966); *Texas* (1967); *Texas Song Book* (1967)

BIBLIOGRAPHY: Clark, B. H., *P. G.* (1928); Carmer, C. L., "P. G., the Making of an American Dramatist," in *Theatre Arts Monthly*, XVI (1932), 995-1006; Adams, A. B., "P. G.: Poet-Playwright," in *Carolina Quarterly*, I (1948), 51-59; Gassner, J., ed., *Five Plays of the South* (with an introduction to P. G.'s work, 1963)

R. BAIRD SHUMAN

GREENE, Graham

English novelist and dramatist, b. 2 Oct. 1904, Berkhampstead, Hertfordshire

G., son of a headmaster and great-nephew of R. L. Stevenson, studied at Oxford. He turned to writing early, working as a reporter for the London *Times* and as an editor for the *Spectator*. In 1934 he became a Roman Catholic, one with a Puritan orientation. He traveled widely, and this gave him the authentic background for his future novels. During World War II he worked for the British Foreign Office and did special duty in West Africa. After 1957 he was managing editor of the publishing house The Bodley Head in London.

A prolific, skillful writer, with great power of invention and with a passionate devotion to religion, G. has written thrillers as well as serious novels. He has made the distinction between his "entertainments," which is what he called his sinister spy-chase psychological thrillers, and his "true novels," works of somber, moral reflection with "utilization of sin by grace" (F. Mauriac). His serious novels exhibit the same narrative skill and the same high suspense that characterize his "entertainments."

In 1938, G. was assigned to report on the situation of the Roman Catholic church in Mexico. His lengthy stay there resulted in a brilliant travelogue *The Lawless Roads* (1939;

Am., *Another Mexico,* 1939) and in his most powerful and universally praised novel *The Power and the Glory* (1940). The hero is a priest who dares to oppose the communists and drinks to squelch his fear. Unrestrained in many aspects, he never loses his sense of guilt and shame or his knowledge that his priesthood is irrevocable. In spite of the tempting sum being offered by those who wish to apprehend the "whiskey priest," the people, who love him, do not betray him. Finally he knowingly walks into a trap because as a cleric he is required to bestow the last rites on a criminal who has asked for them. The power and the glory of the Catholic faith is revealed in this sinner, who remains a vessel of God's mercy.

Among his major novels are *The Heart of the Matter* (1948), set in a British colony in Nigeria, and *The End of the Affair* (1951), a psychological novel about an adulterous woman. *The Quiet American* (1955), the result of the period G. spent as a war correspondent for the London *Times* in Vietnam, is a tragic story about a young and idealistic American, employee of a large corporation, who becomes involved with the people and their civil war and fights on the side of the insurgents.

Good plot construction makes G.'s novels well suited for motion-picture adaptation, e.g., *The Third Man* (1950). In the fifties he turned playwright. *The Living Room* (1953) is a psychological study of a young girl and her bigoted hysterical aunt, who drives her to suicide. *The Potting Shed* (1953) and *The Complaisant Lover* (1959) are successful plays that criticize society.

G.'s main concern is the struggle between good and evil, and he treats the temporal and spiritual aspects of each. His religiosity is not that of the quiet, childlike trust in God. Instead, a passionate analyst of every nuance of religious feeling, he bares man's tormented soul as he experiences angst and loneliness. Devoid of illusions, G. shows evil, in often brutal, naturalistic portrayals, as a disease of body and soul, for he seems to consider sickness, poverty, and death as symbols of evil.

G. was both highly praised and strongly berated by Catholics and Protestants alike for his presentation of religion. It was said that he wrote about religion "as if religion were a drug addiction" (Mary McCarthy [q.v.]) or "a mechanical superstition" (Traversi). But his themes are of general concern—the insecurity of modern man and his failure to communicate in love.

G.'s concise language is spare and clear; the conflicts, well-motivated; the tension, sustained dramatically; the psychological aspects of his characters, well-delineated. But G.'s work is controversial because of its mixture of adventure, religion, eroticism, and abnormal psychology.

FURTHER WORKS: *Babbling April* (1925); *The Man Within* (1929); *The Name of Action* (1930); *Rumour at Nightfall* (1931); *Stamboul Train* (1932; Am., *Orient Express*); *It's a Battlefield* (1934; rev. ed., 1948); *The Basement Room* (1935); *The Bear Fell Free* (1935); *England Made Me* (1935; Am., *The Shipwrecked*); *A Gun for Sale* (1936); *Journey Without Maps* (1936); *Brighton Rock* (1938); *The Confidential Agent* (1939); *British Dramatists* (1942); *The Ministry of Fear* (1943); *Nineteen Stories* (1947); *Why Do I Write?* (1948); *The Third Man* (1950); *The Lost Childhood* (1951); *Twenty-One Stories* (1954); *Loser Takes All* (1955); *Our Man in Havana* (1958); *A Burnt-Out Case* (1961); *In Search of a Character* (1961); *A Sense of Reality* (1963); *Carving a Statue* (1964); *The Comedians* (1966); *May We Borrow Your Husband?* (1967)

BIBLIOGRAPHY: Allen W., *The Novels of G. G.* (1943); Bowen, E., *Why Do I Write? An Exchange of Views between E. Bowen, G. G. and V. S. Pritchett* (1948); Madaule, G., *G. G.* (1949); Rostienne, E., *G. G.: Témoin des temps tragiques* (1949); Allot, K., and Farris, M., *The Art of G. G.* (1951); Rischik, J., *G. G. and His Work* (1951); Mauriac, F., *Mes Grands Hommes* (1951); Atkins, J. A., *G. G.* (1957); Matthews, R., *Conversations with G.* (1957); Wyndham, F., *G. G.* (1958); McCarthy, M., *Sights and Spectacles, 1937-1958* (1959); Buonaventura, A., *Religious Ideas in the Novels of G. G.* (1960); Barry, E. F., *The Divided Soul: Theme and Technique in the Novels of G. G.* (1961); Pryce Jones, D., *G. G.* (1963); Lodge, D., *G. G.* (1966); Maurois, A., *Points of View: From Kipling to G. G.* (1968)

GERTRUDE C. SCHWEBELL

GRIEG, (Johan) Nordahl Bruun

Norwegian novelist and dramatist, b. 1 Nov. 1902, Bergen; d. 2 Dec. 1943

As a young man G. traveled all over the world as a seaman, and studied for a year at Oxford. This restlessness, like his changes of religion, stemmed from deep inner conflicts, which, however, did not prevent him from remaining faithful to certain ideas. He cherished a violent dislike of all forms of tyranny and brutality on the one hand, and of the spirit of defeatism and passive humanism on the other. His versatile talent enabled him to work in all literary genres, and he became the most temperamental 20th c. Norwegian writer as well as the most susceptible to his time and milieu.

G. scored his first striking success in 1924 with the novel *Skibet går videre* (The Ship Sails On, 1927), a critical description of life on board ship and in ports. In the late 1920's, when love of country was considered bad form in Norway, he published a collection of fervently patriotic poems, *Norge i våre hjerter* (1929).

G.'s best play is *Nederlaget* (1936; Defeat, 1944), a description of the Commune revolution in Paris in 1871. Its theme—that freedom must be won through struggle—is close to that of Sartre's (q.v.) *Les Mouches*. During a stay in Russia G. came under the influence of communism. This is particularly obvious in *Ung må verden ennu være* (1938), an artistically significant novel in which he defends the Moscow trials of 1938.

Having emigrated to England during World War II, G. read poems full of patriotic feeling and love of peace in B.B.C. broadcasts to Norway. These war poems were published posthumously in the collection *Friheten* (1945), and some were included in *Håbet* (1946). Selected English translations saw print as *War Poems of N. G.* (1944). He was shot down over Berlin in a Norwegian-British battle plane.

FURTHER WORKS: *Rundt Kap det Gode Haab* (1922); *Stene i strømmen* (1925); *Barrabas* (1927); *Kinesiske Dage* (1927); *En ung mands Kjaerlighet* (1927); *De ung døde* (1932); *Atlanterhavet* (1932); *Vår aere og vår makt* (1935); *Men imorgen* (1936); *Spansk sommer* (1937); *Dikti utvalg* (1944); *Flagget* (1945); *Veien frem* (1947); *Samlede verker* (7 vols., 1947); *Samlede dikt* (1948); *Længselen* (1957)

BIBLIOGRAPHY: Hansen, A., *N. G.* (1939); Borgen, J., *N. G.* (1945); Mjöberg, J., *N. G.* (1947); Haslund, F. J., *N. G.: En dikter og hans tid* (1962); *Wissenschaftliche Zeitschrift der Ernst-Moritz Arndt Universität Greifswals,* XII (1963, G. volume)

CARL KEILHAU

THE GROTESQUE IN LITERATURE

The grotesque, a term denoting a literary form and a literary effect, has been called (by W. Kayser) "playing with the absurd." Of Italian derivation, it originally signified ornamental patterns of human figures, animals, and plants (or parts of them) linked with one another or with inorganic things, as found in late classical painting. Toward the end of the 18th c. the grotesque, along with the arabesque, came to denote a literary medium for depicting a world beyond rational grasp, in contrast to the imitation of nature in its beauty. As an anticlassical form, the grotesque plays an important part in all maneristic movements. Classical aesthetics has falsely identified it with the crudely comic or the burlesque. In German romanticism and in Poe (*Tales of the Grotesque and Arabesque,* 1840) its keynote is the "smiling terror" (W. Kayser) that characterizes both grotesque humor (e.g., *Torrents of Spring* by Hemingway [q.v.]) and the grotesque ghost story (e.g., *The Canterville Ghost* by Wilde [q.v.]). But standing as it does on the borderline of the tragic and the comic, the grotesque may also be regarded as an element of tragicomedy. Dürrenmatt (q.v.) sees in the grotesque, as it supersedes tragedy, "the face of a faceless age." Sometimes, however, the term "grotesque" may signify no more than an exaggerated withdrawal from reality. This is true of grotesque satire (q.v.), which can still be grasped in its relation to a real situation and which remains capable, through its grotesque element, of turning into liberating humor.

The root of the grotesque per se—at least in modern art—is the subjective feeling that the world is nonhomogeneous. This feeling is, however, immediately objectivized, producing an "other" world within (or in place of) a "normal" one. While humor rises subjectively above the "nonsensicality" of the world, and irony (q.v.) exposes this "nonsensicality" as a subjective attitude, the grotesque artist is overwhelmed by the negative impact of the world. It is possible, however, to alternate grotesque and ironic treatment, as for instance in Malaparte's (q.v.) *La Pelle*. Moreover, intermittently ironic treatment of various viewpoints, as in Pirandello's (q.v.) *Così è se vi pare* (Right You Are if You Think You Are), may reveal the objective grotesqueness of a situation. Thus the grotesque may be said to objectivize the negative structure of the fantastic. As a borderline phenomenon it is an appropriate medium for depicting the "borderline situation" of modern man (e.g., Beckett's [q.v.] *En attendant Godot*).

Grotesque imagery in modern lyric poetry stems from *humeur noir,* e.g.: "That was caused by the light bulb he was carrying in his mouth" (Krolow [q.v.]). The automatism of material things, which the surrealists took over from Lautréamont, is close to the static grotesque element in painting, whereas in literature the potentialities of the grotesque are much more diverse. Its characters may, in the tradition of Victor Hugo's Quasimodo, produce a grotesque impression through the disparity between their outer form and their inner nature. This is true of *Cyrano de Bergerac* by Rostand (q.v.) and *Le Sagouin* by F. Mauriac (q.v.). They may also be monomaniacs imprisoned by a fixed idea or an instinct—as grotesque figures in a painting are imprisoned in an animal's body—or divorced from themselves by amnesia. This is the lot of characters such as Christian Maske in *Der Snob* by Sternheim (q.v.), Lennie in *Of Mice and Men* by Steinbeck (q.v.), or Efflam in *Prinz Efflam* by Salminen (q.v.). The effect they produce may lie anywhere between the extremes of the revolting and the affecting, or it may vacillate between them. The characters of Kafka, Julien Green, and Camus (qq.v.) show grotesque traits. Even Rilke (q.v.) considered inventing a grotesque character "just for the sake of making use of the sentence: 'He spent the last six or seven years buttoning a coat button that kept undoing itself again.'" The grotesque situation (Kafka's *Die Verwandlung*) or event (*La Botella* by Kurt Kusenberg, b. 1904), usually character-connected because of the objectivizing tendency of the grotesque, may result from a disturbance in normal causality or from the operation of some strange, different causality. Furthermore, fiction and drama may use the grotesque as a passing mood (the aquarium scene in *Doktor Faustus* by Thomas Mann [q.v.]) or allow it suddenly to take over (*Lady into Fox* by Garnett [q.v.]) or to build up gradually (*Der Hauptmann von Köpenick* by Zuckmayer [q.v.]). But they may also subject it to clarifying analysis or give it meaning (the "Father Brown" stories and *Four Faultless Felons* of Chesterton [q.v.]; *Gerichtet! Gerettet!* by Hans Kaltnecker (1895-1919)). The modern detective novel (q.v.), too, often amounts essentially to the creation and subsequent resolution of a grotesque state of affairs. The grotesque element in language, however, is chiefly confined to poetry.

Although attempts have been made to define

a "grotesque period" in literature succeeding naturalism (q.v.) and neoromanticism, the grotesque remains a genre that is distinct from all existing literary styles. The grotesque works of Wilhelm Busch ([1832-1908] *Eduards Traum*), O. J. Bierbaum ([1865-1910] *Die Schlangendame*), and Paul Scheerbart (1863-1915) coincide with late realism and naturalism. Symbolism (q.v.) lends the grotesque a satanic element which should not be overlooked in Meyrink ([q.v.], "Der heiße Soldat"), Kubin ([q.v.], *Die andere Seite*), and Andreyev (q.v.). In Sternheim, Ehrenstein (qq.v.), and others expressionism (q.v.) is an accompanying element in grotesque prose, while the role of the grotesque in futurism, surrealism (qq.v.), and imagism (see English literature) is undeniable. Besides the grotesque satire of Evelyn Waugh (q.v.) and others, true grotesque elements exist in short stories by Aymé, Elizabeth Bowen, Thurber (qq.v.), Kurt Kusenberg, and other writers of the present day.

In drama the grotesque is well in evidence in Wedekind (q.v.) and plays a less obvious role in Schnitzler (q.v.) and Pirandello. In Curt Goetz (1888-1960) the grotesque situation loses its sting, while Dürrenmatt heightens it to a satirical statement of the age. In expressionism the grotesque drama of Sternheim and Kaiser (q.v.) is the antipode of the hymnic style; a composite grotesque-hymnic form is therefore possible, and this serves as the point of departure for the grotesque satire of Brecht ([q.v.] *Aufstieg und Fall der Stadt Mahagonny*. Ionesco's (q.v.) form of grotesque drama derives from that of the *Sturm* group of expressionists, where the grotesque pervades even the setting and the language, and from similar experiments by the French avant-garde.

In poetry grotesque imagery and grotesque language prevail; they tend to combine, particularly in "collage" poetry, which has its counterpart in many prose passages by Joyce, Döblin, and Koeppen (qq.v.). Here the grotesque in the language becomes a dynamic element which distorts the visual grotesquerie and leads up to a new idea of the image. Morgenstern (q.v.) introduced grotesque poetry in Germany with the *Galgenlieder*; etymology as well as sound was soon subjected to grotesque treatment. The poetry of Ringelnatz (q.v.) tends more strongly toward grotesque situations; that of P. P. Althaus (b. 1892) toward grotesque language. In England grotesque poetry is represented by De la Mare and Osbert Sitwell (qq.v.) and is found sporadically in many other writers. It is undeniable that grotesque poetry reveals a language-destroying element; diversion into humor protects the language from its onslaught. When used alone, the grotesque, which often "jests with the terrible," reveals the disintegration of the bond with reality, while in combination with other creative elements it strives to restore it. Grotesque creativity can be regarded as "an attempt to evoke and exorcise the demonic element in the world" (Kayser) only insofar as supplementary elements such as humor, satire, and irony reveal this element as "the Other" —as a threatening though not invincible reverse side of the world.

BIBLIOGRAPHY: Spitzer, L., *Motiv und Wort* (1918); Hocke, G. R., *Die Welt als Labyrinth* (1957); Kayser, W., *Das Groteske. Seine Gestaltung in Malerei und Dichtung* (1957); The Grotesque in Art and Literature, 1963); Hocke, G. R., *Manierismus in der Literatur* (1959); Burke, K., *Perspectives by Incongruity* (Hyman, S. E. and Karmiller, B., eds., 1964)

HELLMUTH HIMMEL

GUARESCHI, Giovannino

Italian novelist and journalist, b. 1 May 1908, Fontanelle di Rocca Bianca, Parma; d. 23 July 1968, Cervia

In his youth G. worked first as a journalist, then as a commercial artist, a teacher, a caricaturist, and subsequently at other jobs. From 1936 to 1943 he was editor-in-chief of the weekly magazine *Bertoldo*; from 1943 to 1945 he was a prisoner of the Germans; and after 1945 he was editorial director of *Candido*.

G. has enjoyed enormous popular success in Italy, and with his novel *Don Camillo— Mondo piccolo* (1948; The Little World of Don Camillo, 1951), first published in *Candido,* he achieved world fame. Translated into many languages and also made into a motion picture, this novel was at first unsuccessful in Italy; soon, however, it was recognized both at home and abroad as a picaresque masterpiece. Politics, both of the left and of the right, are satirized in this humorous account of the running war—to gain the favor of the village populace—between the village priest, Don Camillo, and the communist mayor, Peppone. G. showed himself in all his writings to be an opponent of utilitarianism, conformism, and all forms of political pigheadedness; and against these and all of the faults, failings, and mis-

takes in public life he directed his sharp humor and telling satire.

FURTHER WORKS: *La scoperta di Milano* (1941); *Il destino si chiama Clotilde* (1942; Duncan and Clotilda, 1968); *Il marito in collegio* (1943; A Husband in Boarding School, 1967); *Favole di Natale* (1945); *Il Diario clandestino, 1943-1945* (1946; My Secret Diary, 1958); *Italia provvisoria* (1947); *Lo zibaldino* (1948); *Don Camillo e il suo gregge* (1953; Don Camillo and His Flock, 1954); *Il dilemma di Don Camillo* (1953; Don Camillo's Dilemma, 1954); *Il corrierino di famiglia* (1954; My Home, Sweet Home, 1966); *Una notte nel Cremlino* (1955); *Don Camillo prende il diavolo per la coda* (1956; Don Camillo Takes the Devil by the Tail, 1957); *Compagno Don Camillo* (1960; Comrade Don Camillo, 1964); *Vita in Famiglia* (1968; Family Life, 1969). **Selected English trans.:** *The House That Nino Built* (1953).

PAUL WIMMER

GUÐMUNDSSON, Kristmann

Icelandic novelist, b. 23 Oct. 1902, Þverfell, Borgarfjörður

After a difficult youth G. settled in Norway; from there he traveled throughout Europe. His first collection of novellas, *Islandsk Kjærlighet* (1926), written in Norwegian, was favorably received; his subsequent novel, *Brudekjolen* (1927; The Bridal Gown, 1931), notable for its powerful characterization and poetic descriptions of nature, made him famous. A long series of novels then appeared in rapid succession. Although uneven in quality, they have been translated into many languages. In 1939 G. returned to Iceland, and since then has written in his native Icelandic.

G.'s work falls into two groups. The novels of the first group are set in the present day and based for the most part on personal experience; psychological analysis plays an important part in them. *Den blå kyst* (1930), *Den förste vår* (1933), and *Hvitte netter* (1934) are all inspired by the theme of young love, secret and unfulfilled. The other group consists of family novels suggested by the old sagas telling of primitive Icelandic farmers deeply rooted in family and tradition and often divided by enmity (*Livets Morgen,* 1929 [Morning of Life, 1936]; *Jordens barn,* 1935). Among G.'s hallmarks are his skill at depicting emotions, an atmosphere of hatred and disaster, and stress on the instinctual, especially in his later novels written in Icelandic (*Náttíröllið glottir*, 1943; *Félagi kona*, 1947; *Kvöld i Reykjavik*, 1948; and *Þokan rauða*, 1950-52). Nevertheless, his attitude to life is basically optimistic.

FURTHER WORKS: *Rökkursöngvar* (1922); *Armann og Vildis* (1928); *Sigmar* (1930); *Det hellige fjell* (1932); *Lampen* (1936); *Gyðjan og uxinn* (1938; Winged Citadel, 1940); *Arma Ley* (1940); *Saga um Skáld* (1948); *Leikmanns pankar* (1949); *Ritsafn, island* (8 vols., 1952-54); *Kristmannskver* (1955); *Harmleikurinn à Austurbæ* (1955); *Heimbókmenntasaga* (2 vols., 1955-56); *Ísold hin svarta* (1959); *Aevintýri í himingeimnum* (1959); *Daegrin blá* (1960); *Völuskrín* (1961); *Loginn hvíti* (1961)

BIBLIOGRAPHY: Einarsson, S., *K. G.* (1946)

JORIS TAELS

GUÉHENNO, Jean

French nonfiction writer, educator, and editor, b. 1890, Fougères, Brittany

G., the son of a shoemaker, like Giono and Guilloux (qq.v.), worked in a factory from his fourteenth to his eighteenth year. Against overwhelming odds he passed his *baccalauréat* and started out on a brilliant academic career leading him to the very top of university honors. Venerated by his students, G. ultimately became Inspector General of all French universities.

G. also was editor of the monthly magazine *Europe* in the late nineteen twenties and of *Vendredi* in the mid-thirties. The critic is acclaimed for his studies of Michelet, Renan, and above all Rousseau. However, his fame derives substantially from other essays where scholarship is blended with human wisdom, and from autobiographical writings which constitute a unique documentation of his times. Thus *Journal d'un homme de quarante ans* (1934) marked the viewpoint of a whole generation, through war and postwar times. As G. himself stated, he was always aware that "the feeling of resemblance with others and of community with them can produce just as much fullness and satisfaction as that of being different or of uniqueness." A fundamental loyalty to his origins has helped G. find his way through stormy seas in politics where his sympathies were for a time on the extreme left. Never a renegade, G. soundly reassessed his position and was sharply attacked by communist critics.

G., who served in the French army during World War I and taught in Lille and Paris between the wars, became a leading member of the underground National Council of Writers during World War II. The Fascist Vichy government dismissed him from his position. *Journal des années noires* (1946) is one of the finest testimonies out of occupied France. In it the writer re-evaluates the spiritual forces needed to help France regain freedom and independence. Part of the book was published clandestinely as *Dans la prison* (1944) under the pen name of Cévennes. G. also was one of the most sought-after advisers to youth during and after the war, helping many of the writers of today through moral and intellectual crises.

G., who traveled extensively in Europe, North and South America, and Africa, was awarded the Prix des Ambassadeurs in 1953 and the Grand Prix de la Ville de Paris in 1955. In 1961 he was elected to the Académie Française. His stature was particularly enhanced by books that trace his intellectual itinerary, such as *La Foi difficile* (1957) and *Changer la vie* (1961), a charming and lively account of his childhood and adolescence.

FURTHER WORKS: *L'Évangile éternel* (1927); *Caliban parle* (1928); *Conversion à l'humain* (1931); *Simon Mondzain* (1931); *Jeunesse de la France* (1936); *Journal d'une "Révolution" 1937-1938* (1939); *L'Université dans la résistance et dans la France nouvelle* (1945); *La France dans le monde* (1946); *Jean-Jacques* (3 vols., 1948-52; Jean Jacques Rousseau, 1966); *La Part de la France* (1949); *Voyages, tournée Américaine, tournée Africaine* (1952); *Aventures de l'esprit* (1954); *La France et les noirs* (1954); *Sur le Chemin des hommes* (1959); *Ce que je crois* (1964)

BIBLIOGRAPHY: *Livres de France*, XII (10 Dec. 1961), special issue on J. G.; Sénart, P., "J. G. ou la foi inutile," *TR*, No. 197 (1964), 102-107

KONRAD BIEBER

GUILLÉN, Jorge

Spanish poet and critic, b. 18 Jan. 1893, Valladolid

After receiving his secondary education at the Institute of Valladolid, G. studied at the Maison Perreyve of the French Fathers of the Oratory in Fribourg, and at the universities of Madrid and Granada. In 1917 G. began at the Sorbonne a long academic career that took him to Murcia,

GIOVANNINO GUARESCHI

KRISTMANN GUÐMUNDSSON

Oxford, Seville, Middlebury College (after 1938, when he became a voluntary exile from war-torn Spain), McGill University, and finally, Wellesley (1940-57). Since 1947 he has also been a visiting professor at various universities in North and South America, having delivered the Charles Eliot Norton Lectures in Poetry at Harvard in 1957 and 1958.

On his seventy-fifth birthday, the collected poems of G. were published as *Aire Nuestro* (1968). In this volume of 1700 pages the poetry written during forty-seven years is gathered into one carefully planned composition. *Aire Nuestro* is made up of the following books published earlier: *Cántico/Fe de vida* (1928, 1936, 1945, 1st complete ed., 1950); *Clamor/Tiempo de Historia* (Vol. I., *Maremágnum*, 1957; Vol. II., . . . *Que van a dar en la mar*, 1960; Vol. III., *A la altura de las circunstancias*, 1963); and *Homenaje/Reunión de vidas* (1967).

For many years G. was known as the author of one book, *Cántico*, which grew and was perfected from one edition to another. "It has an overall architectural design like Baudelaire's *Fleurs du mal*, with a mathematically conceived order of Dantean severity" (H. Friedrich). "In Spanish poetry there is probably no creation more austere than *Cántico*, or any work more simple, dedicated to one single theme . . . . The composition of *Cántico* is that of a rose" (J. Casalduero).

"G. is the only poet of the 20th c. who has written a single volume of the scope, unity, and quality of the works of Baudelaire and Whitman" (W. Barnstone). What these critics say about *Cántico* can also be said about *Aire Nuestro*, an even more amazing achievement of organic growth and architectural planning.

If García Lorca (q.v.) is the outstanding Andalusian poet of that splendid Generation of the Twenties, then G. is its quintessential Castilian. He has inherited something of the dynamic fervor of Saint John of the Cross and the classical clarity of Fray Luis de Leon. Yet G.'s *Cántico* is dedicated to the celebration of this world and its real wonders. As a matter of fact the spiritual beyond is right here, according to "Más allá," the opening poem in *Cántico*. Air is celebrated all through these poems as the giver of life, light, happiness. Air reveals to us what is real while being the perfect symbol of spirituality, even of eternity itself. G.'s technique owes much to the French poets from Baudelaire to Valéry (q.v.), but he has infused their approach with a spirit all his own. In its *élan vital*, G.'s poetry has more affinities with

G. M. Hopkins and Pasternak (q.v.) than with the masters of French symbolism (q.v.).

Because G.'s highly concentrated style, one that is often even elliptical, forgoes nonessentials, he is never facile. Brief questions, abrupt answers, ecstatic exclamations mark his style; nouns are given preference over verbs, and the present is the preferred tense. These features of G.'s poetry have led to charges of abstraction, intellectualism, and hermeticism by critics who were unable to penetrate through the style to discover the meaning. G.'s form is as disciplined as his style. He moves with masterful assurance from *décimas* to *romances*, from sonnets to poems in free verse, and summarizes his main themes in contrapuntally built longer poems such as "Más allá," "Anillo," and "Vida extrema."

Cántico embodies G.'s vision in its most original form. It presents the reader with an "affirmation of being and living" (J. G.). Chance, chaos, evil, suffering, death are held in the background in order to voice the more effectively G.'s "jubilant existentialism" (E. Frutos), which celebrates the elemental life of childhood, youth, adulthood transfixed in an "eternal present."

Cántico exhibits a spiritual discipline that does not surrender to anxiety, despair, negation in contemplating reality in all its aspects. It strives for a vital equilibrium and hence does not overlook joy and hope as fundamentals of human existence. *Cántico* is one of the rare books of consolation in modern poetry. Yet there is nothing facile about G.'s luminous affirmation that has to be wrested again and again from the encroaching shadows of absurdity, ever present and threatening.

The emergence of *Clamor* in no way annulled the faith in life proclaimed by G.'s *Cántico*. Many of the poems in *Clamor* are continuations of poems in *Cántico*. Thus *Clamor*, subtitled "Time of History," acts as a clarification of and a complement to *Cántico*, one in which the negative aspects of life are brought to the fore. G., now older, evinces a natural gift for the elegy. The "In Memoriam" of *Clamor* moves one as strongly by its restrained but intense evocation of lost love as one is moved by the cycle "Salvación de la Primavera" in the *Cántico*, which has been described as Spanish love poetry at its most ecstatic.

Clamor in general is immersed in time and the present age through references to places, autobiographical episodes, facts, and anecdotes. Satire, epigrams, narrative and politically engaged poems ("Potencia de Pérez") are new departures in G.'s work. Almost a book within a book is formed by the many *tréboles*—the three-to-four line "cloverleaves" that distill the themes of *Clamor* with haiku-like lyricism or nail them down with epigrammatic force.

Homenaje constitutes the cornerstone of the structure *Aire Nuestro*. New facets enter into G.'s poetry while once more the main preoccupations of the previous two books are being woven together. The center of *Homenaje* is titled precisely "El centro" and contains the third great cycle of G.'s love poems, dedicated to his second wife, which reveals a Goethean ability to be renewed in love. This love poetry is so deceptively simple, yet so full of freely given love, of grace, and of human dignity.

In other poems G. looks back upon a lifetime of friendships with poets and years of reading and teaching literature. "Al margen" is made up of poems of homage (or protest) written in response to various works—from Genesis to his own *Cántico*. "Atenciones" are verse portraits of writers, among which are Juan Ruiz and G.'s friends Salinas and García Lorca (qq.v.). "Variaciones" is an anthology of translations/imitations from Tasso and Shakespeare to Valéry and Yeats.

Homenaje reflects not only G. the voracious reader; it also reflects the exile and traveler who literally made the world his home. France, Italy, Greece, Portugal, North and South America are celebrated in occasional verse. Indeed, in this volume G. proves himself to be a major writer of minor poems, one who equals the artistry and wit of a Mallarmé in this demanding genre.

Though *Aire Nuestro*, through a web of mottoes, references, and quotations, belongs at the heart of the Spanish literary tradition, it is just as aware of the great European poetry, past and present. Ingratitude does not mar G.'s generous humanism, nor does admiration for other poets handicap his originality. Perhaps only the poet who is completely assured of his own vision of the world can be so open to the achievement of others.

The richness of variations that makes up *Aire Nuestro* springs from the one fundamental intuition that sees human life as a constant impulse toward form, as an appeal to human inventiveness to create and recreate order out of absurdity. It is not any extraordinary order that G. has in mind. The *"energía de normalidad"* that enables us to perceive the "minimal miracles" in everyday living, the only one we have, will do. A secular mystic, G. has realized in his *Aire Nuestro* that *ars vivendi* for which

he praises the city of Paris, because *"Sin cesar inventándose permanece en su ser"* (Ceaselessly inventing itself inheres in its being).

FURTHER WORKS: *La poética de Bécquer* (1943); *Federico en persona* (1959); *El argumento de la obra* (1961; Eng. trans. in *Affirmation*, 1968); *Lenguaje y poesía* (1962; Language and Poetry, 1961). **Selected English trans.:** *Cántico: A Selection* (1965); *Affirmation: A Bilingual Anthology 1919-1966* (1968)

BIBLIOGRAPHY: Pleak, F. A., *The Poetry of J. G.* (1942); Casalduero, J., *J. G.: Cántico* (1946, 1953); Salinas, P., *Literatura española siglo XX* (1949); Gullón, R., and Blecua, J. M., *La poesía de J. G.* (1949); Curtius, E. R., *Kritische Essays zur europäischen Literatur* (1950); Alonso, D., *Poetas españoles contemporáneos* (1952); Valverde, J. M., *Estudios sobre la palabra poética* (1952); Trend, J. B., *J. G.* (1952); Cassou, J., "Le lyrisme ontologique de J. G.," in *CS*, XL (1953), 51–60; Lind, G. R., *J. G.'s "Cántico"* (1955); Granados, J., *J. G.: Antología* (1955); Friedrich, H., *Die Struktur der modernen Lyrik* (1956, 1967); Vivanco, L. F., *Introducción a la poesía española contemporánea* (1957); Salinas, P., *Ensayos de literatura hispánica* (1958); Darmangeat, P., *J. G. ou Le Cantique émerveillé* (1958); Biedma, J. G. de, *Cántico* (1960); Zardoya, C., *Poesía española contemporánea* (1961); Muela, J. G., *La realidad y J. G.* (1962); Vigée, C., *Révolte et louanges* (1962); Weber, R. J., "De 'Cántico' a 'Clamor,' " in *RHM*, XXIX (1963), 109–119; Couffon, C., *Dos encuentros con J. G.* (n.d.); Siebenschein, G., *Die moderne Lyrik Spaniens* (1965); Ciplijauskaite, B., *El poeta y la poesía* (1966); Paz, O., *Puertas al campo* (1966); Ivask, I., ed., "A Symposium on J. G. at 75," in *BA*, XLII (1968), 7-60; Debicki, A. P., *Estudios sobre poesía española contemporánea* (1968); Zardoya, C., *Poesía española del 98 y del 27* (1968); Ivask, I., and Marichal, J., eds., *Luminous Reality: The Poetry of J. G.* (1969)

IVAR IVASK

Every time (I read it) your clean, beautiful (that's the word) poetry penetrates me more deeply. Beautiful, filled with divine emotion, completely *conscious of itself* yet intact. . . . I protest against this excessive cerebralism that they ascribe to you. There is an extraordinary natural fragrance in your poetry that, *truly felt*, can move one to tears. I wish that I could express to you the extent of my admira-

JORGE GUILLÉN

GUNNAR GUNNARSSON

tion for you. The *only* complete admiration that I hold within the entire young literature.

> García Lorca, F., Letter to J. G., dated January 1927, in J. G., *Federico en persona* (1960), p. 158

In its radiance, swiftness, and continual "becoming" the poetry of J. G. takes us back to the poetry of two great Castilians of the sixteenth century, Luis de León and San Juan de la Cruz, both poets of an intense rapidity, full of the emotion of tremulous movement.

> Bell, A. F. G., *Castilian Literature* (1938), p. 115

It happens seldom that a poetic work of the 20th c. is nothing but a song of praise as is that of J. G. Everything happens in a major key here, everything moves and rejoices in the sun. Here are no dissonances, no neuroses, no *fleurs du mal*. The inconceivably lofty works are as glorious as on the first day. Some readers will have to adapt their eyes to these cascades of light. Here is a realm without tragic sentiment, without bitterness, without accusation. Where else do we find this in modern poetry? . . . J. G.'s affirmation of existence stands in flaming contrast to this (i.e., the negative perspective of P. Valéry). It is unique and incomparable in contemporary literature. "Poetry is ontology," Maurras once decreed. If this formula should be true, then G.'s poetry would be a striking example of it. But luckily his poetry is as independent of any philosophy as of any ephemeral intellectual fashion. "Essentialism," which is being prepared on the left bank of the Seine since existentialism has exhausted itself, will not make this any less true. The poetry of G. is self-sufficient. It does not need any philosophic commentary, yet it could well serve as a text for the meditation of philosophers.

> Curtius, E. R., *Kritische Essays zur europäischen Literatur* (1950), pp. 383, 384

G. is a great poet because of the perfection of his creations, not because of the influence he has wielded. His poems are real poems: verbal self-contained objects that are animated by a powerful impulse of feeling and intellect. This impulse is called enthusiasm. It has another name: inspiration. Yet another one: fidelity, faith in the world and in the word. The world of the word as much as the word of the world: *Cántico*. Facing the spectacle of the universe—and not that of history—he once said: "The world is well made. . . ." Before his work the only thing to do would be to repeat his words.

> Paz, O., *Puertas al campo* (1966), pp. 84-85

J. G., who is beyond dispute the greatest living Spanish poet, seems at first sight to stand definitely outside the literary tradition of Spain. He never strives after local color as so many . . . of his countrymen do; he is not self-consciously Spanish.

Gradually, one begins to realize that he harks back to a tradition that came before Gongorism or Euphuism, the Platonic tradition of Fray Luis. . . . Literature in our time is only too full of dark mazes and of harrowing involutions; the poems of J. G., though signally and splendidly modern, breathe a serenity and a tenderness that have something of the godlike about them. Precision and infinitude, as of music, are their constant gift to the reader.

> Borges, J. L., in J. G., *Affirmation* (1968)

GUILLÉN, Nicolás
Cuban poet, b. 10 July 1902, Camagüey

G. was a typesetter, clerk, and journalist and fought in the Spanish civil war. About the year 1928 the *Postmodernismo* writers Carpentier (q.v.), Ramón Guirao, and José Tallet discovered the potentialities for poetry lying in the folklore of the Cuban Negroes, and G., who is of mixed European and African descent, became a master of this "Afro-Cuban" poetry.

His exciting, popular verses, which can be recited to a drum accompaniment, combine rhythm and musicality, sensuousness and humor, closeness to nature and the Cuban Negroes' desire for freedom with the traditional forms of Spanish poetry. G. thus became a modern troubadour of the tavern, chanting his tropically glowing ballads and wryly humorous songs of freedom to a rumba rhythm. He has been widely imitated and has had a lasting influence on modern poetry thoughout Latin America.

WORKS: *Motivos del son* (1930); *Songorocosongo y otros poemas* (1930); *West Indies Ltd.* (1934); *Claudio José Domingo Brindis de Salas* (1935); *Cantos para soldados y sones para turistas* (1937); *España* (1937); *La poética de Bécquer* (1943); *El son entero* (1947; Cuba Libre: Poems, 1948); *Variaciones sobre temas de Jean Cassou* (1951); *Viviendo y otros poemas* (1958); *Sus mejoras poemas* (1959); *La Paloma de vuelo popular* (1959); *¿Puedes?* (1961); *Prosa de prisma* (1962); *Balada* (1962); *Elegía a 'Jésus Menéndez* (1962); *Poesías* (1962); *Tengo* (1964); *Buenas días, Fidel* (n.d.)

BIBLIOGRAPHY: V. Cúneo, D., *Esquemas americanos* (1942); Torre, G. de, *La aventura y el orden* (1943); Jahn, J., *Schwarzer Orpheus* (1954)

JANHEINZ JAHN

GUILLOUX, Louis

French novelist and essayist, b. 15 Jan. 1899, Saint-Brieuc, Brittany

The son of a cobbler, like Guéhenno and Giono (qq.v.), G. started out by being a journalist. His first novel, *La Maison du peuple* (1927) shows him as a keen, yet warm-hearted observer, capable of evoking human drama against the background of social struggle. A sense of mystery pervades the clipped and powerful prose of *Dossier confidentiel* (1928), the narrative of the boyhood and slow but determined self-assertion of a lonely individual. His most homogeneous work, *Le Sang noir* (1935; 2d rev. ed., 1964; Bitter Victory, 1936) is rated among the few best novels of the half-century. It is the story of a philosophy teacher, derisively called "Cripure"—from his pet subject, Kant's *Critique de la raison pure*—who has dismally failed, intellectually as well as in life. The atmosphere of a town in France during World War I with its smug, conformist society encompasses lavish glimpses of human passion, of genuine and mock devotion to causes; of monsters engendered by the hero's imagination; above all, of the pangs of a conscience clear enough to be ruthless in front of responsibilities too crushing for a single man to shoulder. The novelist has adapted the plot to a play, *Cripure* (1962), maintaining the essential preoccupation with ideals betrayed through everyday compromise, and casting the monsters in a most felicitous ballet.

Le Pain des rêves (1942) won the Prix populiste; it, too, deals with the hardship of a family poor in worldly goods but rich in perception and affection. *Le Jeu de patience* (1949) is a vast panorama of G.'s home town through the two world wars and many social upheavals. Again G. sketches a gripping indictment of social injustices, enlivened by the colorful portrayal of Frenchmen of all classes and numerous waves of refugees from all parts of Europe. *Les Batailles perdues* (1960), perhaps his most ambitious endeavor, is disappointing in its verbose and sometimes repetitive development of characters, not all of which are worthy of G.'s earlier novels. G. also distinguished himself as a translator.

FURTHER WORKS: *Compagnons* (1930); *Hyménée* (1932); *Le Lecteur écrit* (1933); *Angélina* (1934); *Histoires de brigands* (1936); *Souvenirs sur Georges Palante* (1939); *Absent de Paris* (1952); *Parpagnacco; ou la Conjura-*tion (1954); *Le Muet mélodieux* (1957); *La Confrontation* (1967)

BIBLIOGRAPHY: "The World of L. G.," in *TLS,* (26 March 1954); Brombert, V., *The Intellectual Hero: Studies in the French Novel, 1886-1955* (1961), Chapter 7.

KONRAD BIEBER

GÜIRALDES, Ricardo

Argentinian novelist and poet, b. 13 Feb. 1886, Buenos Aires; d. 8 Oct. 1927, Paris

G. came from a wealthy family and was familiar with country life. He received a careful education and traveled in Europe. In Paris he became friendly with avant-garde writers, and in his own country, too, was associated with modernist authors. Two formative factors in his intellectual development—the facts that G. is deeply rooted in the Argentinian soil and that he is also a cosmopolitan of European stamp—also left their mark on his work.

His first work, *Cuentos de muerte y de sangre* (1915, 1958, 1960), which is set in Argentina and deals with Argentine themes, already showed him to be a master of language. In the volume of poems *El cencerro de cristal* (1915) he drew away from the modernistic style and used avant-garde forms. *Raucho* (1917) is an autobiographical novel. *Xaimaca* (1923) describes a romantic journey through several countries, and their landscapes and customs.

G.'s most important work is *Don Segundo Sombra* (1926; Eng., with subtitle "Shadows on the Pampas," 1935), a novel composed of a series of autobiographical sketches. Its leading character is conceived as the prototype of the gaucho. In this work G. succeeded in giving universal validity to a national theme and essential Argentine qualities.

FURTHER WORKS: *Rosaura* (1922); *Poemas místicos* (1928); *Poemas solitarios* (1928); *Obras completas* (1930); *El sendero* (1932); *Obras completas* (1962)

BIBLIOGRAPHY: Weiss, G. H., "Technique in the Works of R. G." *Hispania,* XLIII (1960), 353-58; Predmore, M. P., "The Function and Symbolism of Water Imagery in *Don Segundo Sombra*," *Hispania,* XLIV (1961), 428-30; Ara, G., *R. G.* (1961); Kovacci, O., *La pampa a través de R. G.* (1961)

GUSTAVO CORREA

GULLBERG, Hjalmar Robert

Swedish poet and critic, b. 30 May 1898, Malmö; d. 19 July 1961, Stockholm

From 1936 to 1950 G. was literary director of the Swedish radio. A member of the Swedish Academy since 1940, he ranks with Ekelund (q.v.) as one of the most important renewers of Swedish poetry.

From the outset G.'s poetic work (*I en främmande stad*, 1927; *Sonat*, 1929; *Andliga övningar*, 1932; *Kärlek i tjugonde seklet*, 1933) was marked by a paradoxical mixture of the sublime and the mundane. Ironically grotesque effects go hand in hand with nobility and loftiness, slang and themes from popular songs with echoes of classical drama, traditional meter and rhyme with a strikingly modern choice of words and imagery. G.'s skeptical, pessimistic attitude to life is typical of the post-World War I generation—the generation of the *tjugotalet*—which was saved from cynicism and despair by faith in the authenticity of religious values. In nearly all his poetry collections, but especially in *Att övervinna världen* (1937), the religious element is important, not in the form of a positive belief in God but as a pantheistic, mystical compulsion toward union with the divine. In the later volume *Dödsmask och lustgård* (1952) the religious element has been relegated to the background.

G. also translated works from Greek, Spanish, German, and French.

FURTHER WORKS: *Ensamstående bildad herre* (1935); *Selma Lagerlöf* (1940); *Fem kornbröd och två fiskar* (1942); *Samlade dikter* (4 vols., 1948); *Själens dunkla natt, och andra tolkningar av främmande lyrik* (1956); *Terziner* (1958); *Ögon, läppar* (1959); *50 Dikter* (1961)

BIBLIOGRAPHY: Lindér, E. H., *H. G.* (1946); Gierow, K. R., *H. G.* (1961)

JORIS TAELS

GUMILEV, Nikolai Stepanovich

Russian poet, b. 22 March 1886, Kronstadt; d. 25 Aug. 1921, Petrograd

G.'s name is associated with the so-called acmeist group of poets (see Russian literature), which he led and of which he and Mandelstamm (q.v.) were the most talented members.

The son of a navy doctor, he was educated in Saint Petersburg, Tiflis, and Tzarskoye Selo, where he came under the influence of the symbolist poet Annenski (q.v.), who was at that time principal of the *Gymnasium*. A brief youthful enthusiasm led him to join a socialist group of senior students, but his reading of Nietzsche (q.v.) and of the Russian and French symbolists (see symbolism) soon alienated him from all party politics. In 1906 he went to Paris to study at the Sorbonne. His stay there had a decisive effect upon his development. Latin, Parnassian ideals took hold of him, turning him against Russian symbolism. His literary activity in Paris (and after 1908 in Saint Petersburg) was interrupted by several visits to Africa. These expeditions strengthened his conviction that life must be heroic, disciplined, and "dangerous," and his rejection of any kind of bohemianism. In 1910 G. married the Russian poet Anna Akhmatova (q.v.). After contributing for a time to symbolist journals, he founded the "Poets' Guild" together with the poet S. M. Gorodetzki and published a magazine, *The Hyperborean*, in which he defended his idea of poetry as a strictly craftsmanlike, realistic artistic exercise. G. served in the war as a volunteer in a cavalry regiment. The revolution caught him in France on his way to the Salonica front. He returned to Russia early in 1918 and resumed his literary work. Although for the time being he had no political affiliations, it was no secret to any of his friends that he privately disapproved of the new regime. In 1921 he became involved in a monarchist conspiracy and was shot on orders of the Petrograd Cheka.

G. and the acmeists supported Théophile Gautier's "art robuste seul à l'éternité" against Verlaine's "de la musique avant toute chose," which was the doctrine of the symbolists. Thus G.'s poems are full of sharply observed images and portraits abounding in reality, evoked with the most rigorous, sometimes even stark economy. A characteristic feature is the specifically modern emotional effect of their avoidance of emotion.

G. was the only Russian poet of stature to welcome the war wholeheartedly. Nevertheless the tone of his poetry, originally quite worldly, was increasingly pervaded by a virile religiosity, which sought in Christianity not consolation and reassurance but a symbol of the tragedy of historical existence pointing to that which transcends history.

73

WORKS: *Put' konkvistadorov* (1905); *Romanticheskiye tzvety* (1908); *Zhemchuga* (1910); *Chuzhoye nebo* (1912); *Kolchan* (1916); *Kostior* (1918); *Mik: Afrikanskaya poema* (1918); *Ditya Allakha: Arabskaya skazka* (1918); *Shatior: Afrikanskiye stikhi* (1921); *Ognennyi stolp* (1921); *Ten' ot pal'my* (1922); *Stikhotvoreniya* (1923); *K sinei zvezde* (1923); *Pis'ma o russkoi poezii* (1923); *Sobraniye sochinenii* (1947; 1962; 2 vols., 1964, ed. G. Struve and B. Filippov); *Neizdannyi, G.* (1952); *Otravlennaya tunika* (1952). **Selected English trans.:** *The Abinger Garland* (1945)

BIBLIOGRAPHY: Strakhovsky, L. I., *Three Poets of Modern Russia* (1949); Struve, G., *Neizdannyi G.* (1952); Demjenjuk, E., "The Literary Development of G.," *AULLA Proceedings* (1965), 161-62

HEINRICH STAMMLER

GUNNARSSON, Gunnar

Icelandic novelist, playwright, poet, and essayist, b. 18 May 1889, Valthjófsstadur, Fljótsdalur

G. came from a line of clergymen and farmers. At the age of eighteen he went to Denmark and took university extension courses in Askov. After that he lived in Aarhus and Copenhagen, where he was a member of the Icelandic bohemian colony. After many unsuccessful years, he published a volume of poems, *Digte* (1911). This was soon followed by the first volume of the four-part novel *Af Borgslaegtens Historie* (I, *Ormarr Ørlygsson*, 1912; II, *Den danske Frue paa Hof*, 1913; III, *Gaest den Enøjede*, 1913 [Guest the One-Eyed, 1922]; IV, *Den unge Ørn*, 1914), which made him famous overnight. In 1939 he returned to Iceland and settled in Skridurklaustur, quite close to his native village, and from then on he wrote in Icelandic. He has received many honors, both in Iceland and abroad.

G. has published some thirty-five books, including poems, novellas, essays, and plays, but by far the most important are his novels, which have been translated into all major languages. *Af Borgslaegtens Historie* is a panoramic family saga, distinctly romantic in spirit; its powerful epic style with frequent dramatic climaxes compensates for the still rather rudimentary psychology.

After World War I G. wrote a series of serious problem novels, partly in a naturalistic style, partly modeled on the expressionism (q.v.) of Strindberg (q.v.). These express his horror of war and his undeviating search for a new philosophy of life.

After the pessimistic novels *Livets strand* (1915) and *Varg i Veum* (1916) came *Salige er de enfoldige* (1920; Seven Days' Darkness, 1930). The psychology of this novel is more convincing and its tone more positive as a result of G.'s newly acquired faith in the vigor of his people. This new faith was most strongly expressed in the five-volume autobiographical novel *Kirken paa bjerget* (I, *Leg med Straa*, 1923; II, *Skibe paa Himlen*, 1925 [Ships in the Sky, 1938]; III, *Natten og Drømmen*, 1926 [The Night and the Dream, 1938]; IV, *Den uerfarne Rejsende* (1927); V, *Hugleik den Haardtsejlende*, 1928). Here G., looking back to his earliest childhood, creates a picture of life in remote Icelandic valleys and unforgettable character sketches of Icelandic national types.

In 1918, proceeding from this same underlying idea, G. began a series of twelve projected novels (of which only seven have so far appeared) describing the major phases of his country's history. The highlights of this series are: *Edbrødere* (1918; The Sworn Brothers, 1921), on the Vikings and early settlers; *Jord* (1933), on the foundation of the Icelandic nation; *Hvidekrist* (1934) and *Graamand* (1936), on the introduction and spread of Christianity; and, above all, *Jón Arason* (1930), the epic story of the last Catholic bishop in Iceland. These novels conclusively established G.'s position as a European writer.

FURTHER WORKS: *Moðurminning, Vorljós* (1906); *Søgur* (1912); *Smaa historier* (1916); *Drengen* (1917); *Sma Skuespil* (1917); *Ringen* (1921); *Dyret med glorien* (1922); *Den glade gaard* (1923); *Det nordiske rige* (1927); *En dag til overs* (1929); *Svartfugl* (1929; The Black Cliffs, 1967); *Raevepelsene* (1930); *Verdens Glaeder* (1931); *Vikivaki* (1932); *De blindes hus* (1933); *Saga Ø* (1935); *Advent* (1937; The Good Shepherd, 1940); *Das Rätsel um Didrik Pining* (1939); *Trylle og andet smaakram* (1939; Trylla and Other Small Fry, 1947); *Heidaharmur* (1940); *Rit* (19 vols., 1941-57); *Brandur paa Bjarg* (1942); *Arbók 45* (1945); *Arbók 46-47* (1948); *Salumessa* (1952); *Brimhenda* (1954); *Sonata ved havet* (1955); *Cladnestadir og nágrenni* (1956); *Borgaraettin* (1958); *Fjórtán sögur* (1959); *Vardagsjud* (1959); *Rysp-Svensk-Lexicon ooch Alexander de Roubetz* (1961); *Skáldverk* (18 vols., 1960-63)

BIBLIOGRAPHY: Elfelt, K., *G. G.* (1929); Arvidson, S., *G. G.* (1960); Beck, R., "G. G.: Some Observations," in *SS*, XLVI (1965), 293-301

JORIS TAELS

GÜTERSLOH, Albert Paris

(pseud. of *Albert Konrad Kiehtreiber*), Austrian novelist, poet, and painter, b. 5 Feb. 1887, Vienna

Educated for the priesthood, G. refused to take the vows; instead he studied acting and painting with G. Klimt; in 1907 he went to Berlin, where he worked with Max Reinhardt as stage designer and director. There he wrote his first novel, *Die tanzende Törin* (1911; shortened version, 1913), which is an early example of expressionist prose. In 1929 he was appointed a professor at the Vienna School for Applied Arts. After the Anschluss in 1938, he was forced to resign his professorship and to do factory and office work. Then, in 1945 he was appointed as a professor at the Vienna Academy of Fine Arts; he served as its rector from 1954 to 1955. In 1952 he was awarded the Austrian State Prize for painting; in 1961 he received the same award for literature.

Although G.'s early prose works are significant contributions to the development of expressionism (q.v.), his writing cannot be explained in terms of any particular modern school or literary movement. His art is the result of his unusual life and his diverse talents. A strong inclination toward theological-philosophical speculation is equaled by the painter's sensuous delight in surfaces and textures. By means of his humor, G. has overcome dialectically the tensions between his talents and interests, the spiritual and the sensual, the divine and the human. His writing reflects also a love of the baroque—its vitality, exaggeration, obscurity, and lucidity, its view of the world as a stage. In this preference, G. is profoundly Austrian.

G.'s most unusual autobiography, *Bekenntnisse eines modernen Malers: Quasi un'allegoria*

(1926), can serve as an introduction to his life work. *Kain und Abel* (1924) is called a legend, but *Die Vision vom Alten und vom Neuen* (1921) and *Innozenz oder Sinn und Fluch der Unschuld* (1922) are also closer to allegory and legend than to realism.

The subtitle of the last-listed—the meaning and curse of purity—characterizes well the central preoccupation of these shorter works as well as an important theme of the novels *Die tanzende Törin, Der Lügner unter Bürgern* (1922) and *Eine sagenhafte Figur* (1946). These three novels focus on the theme of the fate of spiritual purity in an impure material world. The stories of *Die Fabeln vom Eros* (1947) move actually more and more out of the realm of allegory, legend, and fable into that of realistic narrative.

G. is most accessible to the reader in his latest collection of stories *Laßt uns den Menschen machen* (1962) and the major novel *Sonne und Mond/Ein historischer Roman aus der Gegenwart* (1962; written 1935-63). It is one of the great original novels of Austrian self-interpretation along with Stifter's *Nachsommer*, Musil's (q.v.) *Der Mann ohne Eigenschaften*, and Doderer's (q.v.) *Die Strudlhofstiege*.

A selection of G.'s art criticism from 1911 to 1957 is available in the volume *Zur Situation der modernen Kunst* (1963).

FURTHER WORKS: *Egon Schiele* (1911); *Die Rede über Franz Blei oder der Schriftsteller in der Katholizität* (1922); *Der Maler Alexander Gartenberg* (1928); *Musik zu einem Lebenslauf* (1957); *Gewaltig staunt der Mensch* (1963); *Der innere Erdteil* (1966)

BIBLIOGRAPHY: Doderer, H. v., *Der Fall G./Ein Schicksal und seine Deutung* (1930); Blei, F., *Schriften in Auswahl, Nachwort von A. P. G.* (1960), pp. 288-294; *A. P. G.: Autor und Werk* (1962); Basil, O., Eisenreich, H., and Ivask, I., *Das große Erbe* (1962); Ivask, I., "Sonne und Mond," *BA*, XXXVII (Summer 1963), 304-305.

IVAR IVASK

H

HAGALÍN, Guðmundur Gislason

Icelandic novelist, poet, and playwright, b. 10 Oct. 1898, Lokinhamrar, Arnarfjörður

Descended from farmers and fishermen, H. attended secondary school in Reykjavik. He had decided early in life to become a writer, and from 1918 to 1923 he worked as a journalist in Reykjavik and Seyðisfjörður. He traveled in Norway on lecture tours from 1924 to 1927. In 1928 he returned to Iceland and became librarian at Ísafjörður, where he remained until 1946, when he became a librarian in Reykjavik.

H.'s first works in the 1920's were lyrical poems in a classical, sagalike style; but even then the influence of Hamsun (q.v.) is seen in the subjects of *Blindsker* (1921), poems about the simple, primitive farmers and fishermen of Iceland and the way they lead their lives. Like his countryman Laxness (q.v.), H. turned away from this early style and after 1930 developed an original way of writing more suited to his subject matter. In short stories and novels this new style is characterized by a rough dialect that fits the primitive types about whom he writes. His best-known works show these traits clearly: *Kristrún í Hamravík* (1933), a novel about an old woman who lives alone in a cottage on the northern coast of Iceland, poor and content with her life, fearing nothing and quite in control of her little world; and *Sturla í Vogum* (2 vols., 1938), the story of a determinedly independent farmer who develops a growing social consciousness, which he expresses in agreeing to cooperate with his fellow men in some practical matters. In both these works H. also depicts the untamed nature of his homeland and the gloomy superstition of some of its people.

FURTHER WORKS: *Brennumenn* (1927); *Virkir dagar* (2 vols., 1936, 1938; new ed., 1958); *Förunautar* (1943); *Blitt laetur veröldin* (1943); *Gróður og sandfok* (1943); *Ritsafn* (2 vols., 1948); *Konungurinn á Kalfskinni* (1945); *Moðir Ísland* (1945); *Sól á nattmálum* (1957); *Prettán sögur* (1958); *Virkir dagar* (1958); *Töfrar draumsins* (1961)

BIBLIOGRAPHY: S. Einarsson, *A History of Icelandic Literature* (1957), pp. 309-11.

* * *

HAGELSTANGE, Rudolf

German poet, novelist, and essayist, b. 14 Jan. 1912, Nordhausen

After studying German philology in Berlin from 1931 to 1933, H. traveled until 1936 in Italy, Greece, and the Balkans. In 1937 he became editor of the local newspaper in his home town. A soldier in France and Italy during World War II, he was taken prisoner by the Americans in 1945. He became a professional writer after he returned from the war, and settled first in Nordhausen, then in Hemer (Westphalia), and in 1948 in Unteruhldingen, on the Lake of Constance. In 1954 he made a trip through the United States.

H. became known immediately after the war with his sonnet cycle *Venezianisches Credo*, which he had privately printed in Verona in 1944. This book, the first voice of the new postwar generation of poets in Germany, showed H.'s rigorous formalism, an intellectual resistance to totalitarianism, and his concern with ethical ideals. These traits are present throughout H.'s subsequent work, although his poems written in Spain, *Corazón* (1963), show

GUÐMUNDUR HAGALÍN

PER HALLSTRÖM

a loosening of the tight formal structures he had earlier favored.

Writing from a humanitarian viewpoint and a sense of engagement with his world and his time, H. searches among the shocks of contemporary life for those things that point to the future and give evidence of permanence. His poetry, which shows the formal influence of Weinheber (q.v.), uses strong images and rhythms in depicting the suffering of the world and indicting the age for it; his poems also show a basically Christian attitude and a deep sense of responsibility. In *Ballade vom verschütteten Leben* (1952; Ballad of the Buried Life, 1962), which won the Critics' Prize, H. tells of the fate of six soldiers buried alive in a bunker and makes of his poem a parable of man's life in general.

In his prose works H. continues his examination and critique of his times. The novel *Spielball der Götter* (1959), subtitled "Notes of a Trojan Prince," is an invented biography of Paris and his life during the siege of Troy; but although original and charming in style and structure, it contains social criticism pointedly applicable to the present day. H. also attends to the questions and problems of his age in speeches, essays, and also, though less directly, in numerous travel books.

H.'s writing is marked by clarity of style and a complete lack of artificiality. He shows a talent for the sharp image and concise, economical delineation of character and situation; and he is particularly adept at finding and describing the comic and humorous in life, but always with his characteristic humanitarian warmth.

FURTHER WORKS: *Ich bin die Mutter Cornelias* (1939); *Strom der Zeit* (1948); *Meersburger Elegie* (1950); *Balthasar* (1951); *Es steht in unserer Macht* (1953); *Zwischen Stern und Staub* (1953); *Die Beichte des Don Juan* (1954); *Griechenland* (1957; Greece, 1957); *How Do You Like America?: Impressionen eines Zaungastes* (1957); *Verona* (1957); *Das Lied der Muschel* (1958); *Offen gesagt* (1958); *Wo bleibst du, Trost* (1958); *Ein Licht scheint in die Finsternis* (1958); *Die Nacht Mariens* (1959); *Huldigung: Droste, Eichendorff, Schiller* (1960); *Römische Brunnen* (1960); *Römisches Olympia* (1961); *Lied der Jahre* (coll. poetry, 1931-61, 1961); *Phantastische Abenteuererzählungen* (1961); *Die schwindende Spur* (1961); *Reise nach Katmandu* (1962); *Olympische Impressionen* (1963; Olympic Impres-

sions, 1963); *Die Puppen in der Puppe* (1963); *Zeit für ein Lächeln* (1966); *Der schielende Löwe* (revised version of *How Do You Like America?*, 1967)

BIBLIOGRAPHY: Pocar, E., "R. H. e la 'Ballata della vita sepolta,' " *Letteratura moderna*, XII (1962), 619-23; Kunisch, H., ed., *Handbuch der deutschen Gegenwartsliteratur* (1965), pp. 237-39

* * *

HALAS, František

Czechoslovak poet and prose writer, b. 3 Oct. 1901, Brno; d. 27 Oct. 1949, Prague

H. came from a proletarian background. In his work the self-assurance of the Communist poet extolling collectivism gradually yields to *poésie maudite*, to the painfully experienced "exitless" immanence of the modern individualist. The cult of language as a value in itself often makes H. difficult to understand. The suffering of his country, sacrificed in 1938, inspired his magnificent poem *Torso naděje*—"Torso of Hope" (1938). In 1945 H. assumed an important position in the Ministry of Information. His political testament, published in the *Figaro littéraire* of 12 Jan. 1952, outspokenly repudiated the regime and caused a sensation.

H. also produced excellent translations, particularly of Mickiewicz.

FURTHER WORKS: *Sepie* (1927); *Kohout plaší smrt* (1930); *Hořec* (1933); *Staré ženy* (1935); *Dokořán* (1936); *Časy* (1939); *Naše paní Božena Němcová* (1940); *Ladění* (1942); *V řadě* (1948); *Kemka* (1950); *Ja se tam vrátím* (1956); *A co?* (1957); *Básně* (1957); *Magická moc poesie* (1958); *Máje a prosince* (1959); *Oczekiwanie* (1959); *F. H. dětem* (1961)

BIBLIOGRAPHY: Václavek, B., *F. H.* (1934)

GÜNTHER WYTRZENS

HALBE, Max

German dramatist and narrative writer, b. 4 Oct. 1865, Güttland near Danzig; d. 30 Nov. 1944, Neuötting, Upper Bavaria

H. began in the tradition of Friedrich Hebbel (1813-63) and Otto Ludwig (1813-65) but later became the spokesman of a resolute naturalism (q.v.), which, however, he soon toned down to a regionalistic realism. His evocative rendering of young love and of the half-Slavic atmosphere of western Prussia, together with his criticism of celibacy, made his *Jugend* (1893; Youth, 1916) one of the most successful plays of its time. Later H. also wrote historical and verse drama, but was successful only with effectively constructed, realistic, regionalistic plays such as *Mutter Erde* (1897). Realism, closeness to the soil, and rich vitality also mark his short stories, particularly the village story *Frau Meseck* (1897). His most important epic work is the novel *Die Tat des Dietrich Stobäus* (1911).

H.'s autobiographical books, *Scholle und Schicksal* (1933) and *Jahrhundertwende* (1935), are significant as a key to his work and as accounts of the cultural life of his time.

FURTHER WORKS: *Ein Emporkömmling* (1889); *Freie Liebe* (1890); *Eisgang* (1892); *Jugend* (1893); *Der Amerikafahrer* (1894); *Lebenswende* (1896); *Der Eroberer* (1899); *Die Heimatlosen* (1899); *Das tausendjährige Reich* (1900); *Haus Rosenhagen* (1901; The Rosenhagens, 1910); *Der Strom* (1904); *Die Insel der Seligen* (1906); *Das wahre Gesicht* (1907); *Blaue Berge* (1909); *Der Ring des Lebens* (1909); *Der Ring des Gauklers* (1911); *Freiheit* (1913); *Jo* (1917); *Hortense Ruland* (1917); *Schloß Zeitvorbei* (1917); *Kikeriki* (1921); *Der Frühlingsgarten* (1922); *Die Auferstehungsnacht des Doktor Adalbert* (1928); *Die Traumgesichte des Adam Thor* (1929); *Ginevra oder der Ziegelstein* (1931); *Generalkonsul Stenzel und sein gefährliches Ich* (1931); *Heinrich von Plauen* (1933); *Die Elixiere des Glücks* (1936); *Erntefest* (1936); *Kaiser Friedrich II* (1940); *Gesammelte Werke* (12 vols., 1945-50)

BIBLIOGRAPHY: Weder, H., *Die Stimmungskunst in Hs. Gegenwartsdramen* (1932); Zillmann, F., "Zum Gedächtnis M. Hs.," *Ostdeutsche Monatshefte*, XXV (1959), 837-41; Ude, K., "Glanz und Elend des Literaturbetriebs um 1900: Nach Dokumenten aus M. Hs. unveröffentlichtem Nachlaß," *Welt und Wort*, XVII (1962), 271-74

OTTO MANN

HALLSTRÖM, Per August Leonard
Swedish narrative writer and poet, b. 29 Sept. 1866, Stockholm; d. there 18 Feb. 1960

H. spent several years in London and Philadelphia as an engineer, and turned to writing in 1898. After his not very felicitous first publication, the volume of poetry *Lyrik och fantasier* (1891), H. turned to the novella. His early ones are naturalistic, pessimistic (under Schopenhauer's influence), and emotional in tone, and full of sympathy for the poor and oppressed. But H. soon turned away from ugly reality and, following Selma Lagerlöf and Heidenstam (qq.v.), sought refuge in distant times and exotic climes in which he could give his imagination free play. This resulted in four novella collections: *Purpur* (1895), *Briljantsmycket* (1896), *Reseboken* (1898), and *Thanatos* (1900), which mark a climax in his work —lyrical, overrefined prose, strikingly akin to that of Jens Peter Jacobsen though with a stronger intellectual cast. The action always remains subordinate to the psychological analysis. During the same period H. also wrote several novels: the gentle, melancholic small-town idyll *En gammal historia* (1895); the kindly, ironical *En skälmroman* (1906); and his best one, *Döda fallet* (1902), set in the Arctic wastes. H.'s other works, including the novels *Våren* (1898), *Gustaf Sparverts roman* (1903), and the novella collections *De fyra elementerna* (1906), *Nya Noveller* (1912), *Händelser* (1927), and *Leonora* (1928), only intermittently attained the level of his novella masterpieces. Man and reality gradually moved to the fore, thus rendering the moralistic slant of his works more pronounced.

Among H.'s dramas *En venetiansk komedi* (1901) deserves mention, as do the legendary plays *Alkestis* and *Ahasverus* (both 1908) and especially *Erotikon* (1908), a satire on free love. The historical dramas *Greven av Antverpen* (1899), *Gustaf III* (1918), and *Karl XI* (1918) plainly show the influence of Shakespeare, whose works H. translated. Finally, H.'s essays reveal an art critic as scholarly as he was aesthetically sensitive.

FURTHER WORKS: *Hårda tider* (1891); *Vilsna fåglar* (1894); *Lille Karl* (1897); *Skepnader och tanker* (1910); *Två sagodramer* (1910); *Folkfienden* (1915); *Konst och liv* (1919); *Samlade berättelser och romaner* (12 vols., 1922 ff.); *Ryssar, engelsmän och andra* (1952); *Modernas psykologi* (1954). **Selected English trans.:** *Modern Swedish Masterpieces* (1923); Larsen, H. A., ed., *Sweden's Best Stories* (1928)

BIBLIOGRAPHY: Bergstedt, H. *Grekiska motiv i P. H.s diktning* (1917); Gullberg, H., *Berättarkonst och stil i P. H.s prosa* (1939);

Holmberg, O., "Somrer i Falsterbo," *SLT*, XXIV (1961), 172-81; Arvidsson, R., "Trä otryckte brev ur Georg Brandes och P. H.s brevvärling (Correspondence between P. H. and Georg Brandes, q.v.)," *ibid.*, XXV (1962), 175-79

JORIS TAELS

HAMSUN, Knut

(pseud. of *Knud Pedersen Hamsund*), Norwegian novelist and dramatist, b. 4 Aug. 1859, Lom, Gudbrandsdal; d. 19 Feb. 1952, Nørholm, Aust-Agder

H.'s reputation throughout Europe is that of Norway's greatest novelist; he is particularly widely read and admired in Germany. He is equally significant as a writer dealing with nature and love, a psychologist and a satirist. In 1920 he was awarded the Nobel Prize for his novel *Markens Grøde* (1917; Growth of the Soil, 1920). H. was extremely individualistic by temperament, a nonconformist with a romantic, aristocratic attitude toward life to which he held with fanatical pertinacity. Toward the end of his life he allowed his sympathies for National Socialism to outweigh his loyalty to his native country.

At the age of three he was taken to Hamarøy in Nordland, where he grew up on his father's small, rather poor farm. The landscape there left a strong impression on the boy. His youth was a struggle for existence, full of ups and downs and often hard; at one time or another he worked as a salesman, shop assistant, cobbler's apprentice, longshoreman, civil servant, schoolmaster, and road laborer. His first literary attempts, *Den Gaadefulde, Et Gjensyn,* and *Bjørger*, written between 1877 and 1878, are of little interest. Between 1882 and 1888, H. made two visits to America, where he earned his living as a streetcar conductor and a laborer. During his second visit he had some success with lectures on literary subjects; and when he returned to Norway, he took the Americans to task for their materialistic civilization in the witty, provocative book *Fra det moderne Amerikas Aandsliv* (1889).

Since the summer of 1888, H. had been working on the novel *Sult* (1890; Hunger, 1899) and had published extracts from it. When the complete work appeared in 1890, it was hailed as a literary event. It presented some ideas that he was to develop in a lecture series a year later: literature should not be a programmatic de-

scription of society bearing the stamp of Mill's utilitarianism, Comte's positivism, and Zola's (q.v.) scientific methods; instead, it should reveal the secrets of spiritual man's complex mentality, his unconscious psychic life, his daydreams and enigmatic feelings. H. felt as close to Nietzsche and Strindberg (qq.v.) as to Dostoyevski (1821-81), of whom, incidentally, he had read nothing until *Sult* was almost finished. *Sult* was something completely new in Norwegian literature (q.v.). No writer before H. had ever described in this way the psychological strength and unpredictability of an intelligent, hypersensitive, ambivalent nonconformist. Stylistically too it represented a revolution in Norwegian literature.

Although H.'s next novel, *Mysterier* (1892; Mysteries, 1927), was coolly received by his contemporaries, it is today considered one of his most interesting books. The leading character, Johan Nagel, exemplifies the spirit of Nietzsche; in him H. expressed his scorn for the doctrinaire rationalism and radicalism of his time. Yet Nagel's aristocratic ideas and self-conscious poses are in contrast to his helplessness in the face of life and love. In this respect he is typical, of a whole series of H.'s heroes who are condemned to failure with the woman they love. The most remarkable figure in this book is "the Minute," Nagel's shadow, a part of his self.

Redaktør Lynge (1893) and *Ny Jord* (1893; Shallow Soil, 1914), which are written in an impersonal, realistic novelistic style, mark an interlude in H.'s literary production. The satirizing of contemporary urban civilization and its empty craving for sensation is somewhat dry. The novel *Pan* (1894; Eng. 1920), however, was much stronger again; here H. is no longer polemical but openly admits his feelings. His romantic longing for a return to nature finds expression in the passionate, lyrical descriptions of the Nordland summer and the mysterious forests. The leading character, the gamekeeper Thomas Glahn, is torn between two women. As is always the case in H., the hero is attracted by the proud, moody woman rather than the mature, warmhearted woman who has much to give him.

In the trilogy *Ved Rigets Port* (1895), *Livets Spil* (1896), and *Aftenrøde* (1898), H. tried his hand at drama, but his proclamation of Nietzschean ideas is dramatically lifeless. With the novel *Victoria* (1898; Eng. 1923), however, his literary work reached another climax. This tragic, romantic love story is among the most beautiful works in Norwegian writing—even in world literature.

From 1898 to 1899, H. lived abroad, in Finland and Russia. In 1902 he published a verse play, *Munken Vendt,* in which his interest again focuses on the hero's love conflict with a proud woman. His own religious ideas, which depart drastically from Christianity in addressing themselves to life here and now, are put forward rather weakly. The exotic play *Dronning Tamara* (1903) and the travel book *I Æventyrland* (1903) are also less successful artistically.

The publication of H.'s collection of poetry, *Det vilde Kor,* in 1904, was, however, a great event in Norwegian poetry. These nature and love lyrics struck vigorous new notes. In the same year H. published the novel *Svermere* (Am., Dreamers, 1921; Eng., Mothwise, 1921). If the poetry collection may be called his farewell to his stormy, poetic, romantic youth, the novel introduces a new phase in his literary creativity. This work is tinged with the resignation of age. The action of *Svermere* is not so dramatically exciting; the destinies of its characters are not taken with such deadly seriousness as in H.'s youthful works; humor comes to the fore. After a book of memoirs, *Stridende Liv* (1905), which is weak in parts, H. wrote the novel *Under Høststjernen* (1906; Under the Autumn Star, in *Wanderers,* 1922), which reflects the mounting crisis of age. Its hero, Knut Pedersen, a restless, driven, homeless man of middle age, has some of H.'s own characteristics. He is half involved in the play of life, half a spectator. The novel is pervaded now by a lyrical melancholy, now by a playfully ironic wit. Its sequel, *En Vandrer spiller med sordin* (1909; With Muted Strings, in *Wanderers,* (1922), has an even stronger tone of resignation. In between the two, H. published two related novels *Benoni* (1908; Eng., 1925) and *Rosa* (1908; Eng., 1926). *Benoni* is written in an objective, realistic narrative style, but in *Rosa* the writer again portrays himself in the guise of a romantic vagabond figure. The play *Livet ivold* (1910; In the Grip of Life, 1924) concludes H.'s treatment of the theme of the hardships of growing old.

At this time H. was emerging in lectures and articles as a polemical cultural critic, issuing mocking warnings about the social and intellectual trends that had followed industrialization. Instead of trying to go along with so-called progress, man should stick to the soil. In this spirit H. now wrote a series of social novels.

Den sidste Glæde (1912; Look Back on Happiness, 1940) is a not very successful satire on the contemporary technological spirit; but *Børn av Tiden* (1913; Children of the Age, 1924) and *Segelfoss By* (1915; Segelfoss Town, 1925) are full of brilliantly witty attacks on the meaningless bustle and myopic barbarism that ensue when an aristocratic peasant society is transformed into an industrialized anthill. The capitalist figure of Tobias Holmengraa is contrasted with the aristocratic landowner Willatz Holmsen, who is destined to ruin, though his downfall has a tragic grandeur. In 1911, H. himself had become a landowner, with a farm of his own in Hamarøy in Nordland; he left there in 1918 to go to Nørholm. In 1917 he published his magnificent novel *Markens Grøde,* glorifying the tilling of the soil. Isak Sellanraa, a settler, is by no means a noble "hero," but the reverence for life that imbues him as he goes about his primitive work gives him, so to speak, a halo of earthly saintliness. ("Isaac went barefoot in Jesus' name and sowed. . . .") He personifies the most profound, inward meaning of life.

A gloomy mood of doom, broken only occasionally by a shimmer of humor, characterizes *Konene ved Vandposten* (1920; The Women at the Pump, 1928) and *Sidste Kapitel* (1923; Chapter the Last, 1929). The former depicts with psychological insight the inferiority feelings that so often play a part in H.'s work. A much lighter mood pervades the trilogy *Landstrykere* (1927; Vagabonds, 1930), *August* (1930; Eng. 1931), and *Men Livet lever* (1933; The Road Leads On, 1934). Through the brilliantly witty story of August, a fraud and adventurer, H. describes the growth of the capitalist spirit in modern Norway. August has some of the characteristics of Ibsen's (q.v.) Peer Gynt. Here H. depicts not the sound, enduring aspect of peasant life but the vagrant, the restless, drifting quality that was typical of much of his own youth.

In his last novel *Ringen sluttet* (1936; The Ring Is Closed, 1937) he again contrasts the vagabond with the man in settled circumstances. This work is insignificant in content but notable for its language.

During World War II, H. welcomed the occupying Nazis and viewed with disfavor the Norwegian patriots; his position aroused resentment in Norway. In 1949, at the age of ninety, he published his own defense, *På gjengrodde stier* (On Overgrown Paths, 1967). Untenable as his case is legally and morally, the work represents a wonderful new flowering of H.'s artistry. No other Norwegian writer has possessed his splendid, startling imagination. He is the great nonconformist who created his own world and lived in it, in both the good and the bad sense.

FURTHER WORKS: *Siesta* (1898); *Kratskog* (1903); *Dikte* (1921); *Samlede verker* (17 vols., 1936)

BIBLIOGRAPHY: Morburger, C., *K. H.* (1910); Landquist, J., *K. H.* (1917); Larsen, H. A., *K. H.* (1922); Wiehr, J., "K. H.," *Smith College Studies in Modern Languages,* III (i-ii), (1921-22); Berendsohn, W., *K. H.* (1929); Skavlan, E., *K. H.* (1929; new ed., 1934); Braatøy, T., *Livets cirkel* (1929; new ed., 1954); Gustafson, A., *Six Scandinavian Novelists* (1940); Hamsun, T., *Mein Vater* (1940); idem., *K. H.* (1952; new ed., 1959); Fechter, P., *K. H.* (1952); Mendensohn, P. de, *Der Geist in der Despotie* (1953); Hamsun, M., *Regnbuen* (1953); McFarlane, J. W., "The Whisper of the Blood," *PMLA*, LXXI:4 (1956); Thiess, F., *Das Menschenbild bei K. H.* (1957); Lowenthal, L., *Literature and the Image of Man* (1957); Sparre Nilson, S., *En ørn i uvær* (1960); Naess, H., "The Three H.'s: The Changing Attitude in Recent Criticism," *SS*, XXXII (1960), 129-39; Oysleko, O., *H.* (1964); Naess, H., "H. and America," *SS*, XXXIX (1967), 305-328

CARL KEILHAU

Hamsun takes the step that makes him the first of the great 20th c. modernists: the step into nihilism, which necessarily follows from sheer belief in life, from sheer will for life. . . . He knows that the final result of all seeking and all desire that is confined to life alone is nothingness, and that man's task, despite this realization, is still to pursue his way to the end. . . .

Paul Fechter, *K.H.* (1952), p. 8

Hamsun brought to the modern novel . . . something new and mysterious: the wasteland, and this is anything but *Blut und Boden* literature. . . .

This may be the most characteristic quality of Hamsun's work: the enchantment of pristine times in a late world.

Max von Brück, *Die Sphinx ist nicht tot* (1956), pp. 109 ff.

In our youth this giant in body and spirit, in natural talent and responsiveness of heart, was the hero we would have liked to be. He was the ideal of a man: a skeptic, contemptuous of literature and civilization, a vagabond in the cities and forests. . . .

Only now do I realize that his influence was not without its dangers: he fostered a natural proclivity to sentimentality in our youth; he encouraged us in our emotional vacillation; he gave our defiant isolation the stamp of heroism and aroused our arrogance; he made us conceited about our inarticulate babbling of moods.

Peter Suhrkamp, *K.H.*, in *Die neue Rundschau* XLV (1934), 333f.

Knut Hamsun is a name which characterizes a whole period, defines a literary era. The artistic influence of this writer of genius reaches far beyond the frontiers of his native land. With his unexcelled, profound knowledge of the human mind, magician of style, master of the pen, who can make a masterwork, a jewel of literary art, out of an insignificant, commonplace happening. . . .

Russia—and this means Soviet Russia too—is the country where Hamsun's works and incomparable art are highly prized and eulogized. Hamsun's name is a favorite one among Russian readers. . . .

The modern Russian reader glorifies power of willing, not passive endurance. Dostoyevski's spirit is hardly typical of the new activist citizen of the Soviet Union. But all over the modern world there are new moral ideals, and Hamsun, the troubador of the will, is much closer to their heart than Dostoyevski. The virtues of "good nature" and patient endurance are quite foreign to modern man. Rather brutality than "meekness." People today much prefer a naïve scoundrel like August or a strong-willed murderess like Ane Marie in *Landstrykere* to a Sonya Marmeladova or an Alyosha Karamazov.

Aleksandra Kollontay, in *K.H.*: *Festskrift til 70 aarsdagen* (1929), p. 98 ff.

. . . all Hamsun's later works constitute an entity inasmuch as they depict the infinite variations and ramifications of the basic theme of petty bourgeois ideology, impotence and, at the same time, infatuation with power. . . .

Glorification of the hero reasserts the utter insignificance of the average individual as such, while at the same time glossing it over ideologically.

Leo Löwenthal, "K.H.: Zur Vorgeschichte der autoritären Ideologie," in *Zeitschrift für Sozialforschung* VI (1937), 303 ff.

He did not betray human society because he did not belong to it, having created a cosmos of his own. He did not betray its moral principles because he had never recognized them and had never been one of their defenders. Neither did he surrender the intellect to despotism, but merely to his visionary cloudland.

Peter de Mendelssohn, *Der Geist in der Despotie* (1953), p. 120

In France too Hamsun possesses some ardent admirers, and I pride myself on being one of them. . . .

This book [*Pan*], which I greeted with enthusiasm and made all my friends read, seemed to me—and on rereading still seems—powerfully original and, furthermore, a real literary tour de force. I think it even had a fairly profound, though not clearly defined influence upon me. I found in it, very plausibly set forth, the unacknowledged relationships between our opinions, our thoughts, even our religious convictions, and the physiological state of our being, as in Dostoyevski's Raskolnikov, but perhaps with even more subtlety and in a quite unexpected, deeply personal way. . . .

André Gide, in *K.H., Festskrift til 70 aarsdagen* (1929) p. 68 f.

His work—the early one which rose above the horizon around the turn of the century—ranks among the most moving literary experiences of my youth. The culmination of his marvelous life work in *Markens Grøde* twelve years ago was for me, too, the soul-stirring event that many war-torn German hearts in those years felt that splendid work to be. . . .

And, in fact, for anyone who knows only plain unhealthiness there is something bewildering in the phenomenon of healthy sophistication and sophisticated health that Hamsun magically portrays; in the organically resolved conflict between his ripe, delicious, seasoned technique and the peasant conservatism of his attitudes, between his democratic modernity and his internationalism, the perfected progressiveness of his artistry and his aristocratic closeness to the earth and to nature, which is the source of all the antisocial, antipolitical, antiliterary, antidemocratic, and antihumane attacks and demonstrations of will that the world has had to put up with from him. He is, to put it briefly, a wonderful flowering—perhaps the final one—of that Nordic individualism which simply does not cherish in its inmost heart Schiller's line that "man has great need of man for his mighty goals." The social element is missing from his intellectual makeup—and today, when even the unwilling have come to accept the political and social element as the dominating factor in our time, this hardly makes him look like a *Führer*.

Thomas Mann, in *K.H.: Festskrift til 70 aarsdagen* (1929), p. 128 f.

HANDEL-MAZZETTI, Enrica von
Austrian narrative writer and poet, b. 10 Jan. 1871, Vienna; d. 8 April 1955, Linz

H.-M. had a background combining Austrian, Dutch, German, Hungarian, and Italian strains. From the paternal side of the family she inherited the Austrian barony and the name of an Italian great-grandfather, Milan's noted jurist Antonio Mazzetti. Her mother was the daughter of a Hungarian court counselor and a Dutch Protestant.

Introduced to German readers primarily through the Catholic intellectual periodical *Hochland*, she published, between 1900 and 1951, twenty-one volumes of novels, including five trilogies, in addition to poems, short plays, short stories, and miscellaneous prose pieces. The central theme of all her works is the triumph of the theological virtue of charity. This message, already dominant in the first novel, *Meinrad Helmpergers denkwürdiges Jahr* (1900), is conveyed to the reader practically to the exclusion of all others in the three works dealing with the counter-Reformation, *Jesse und Maria* (1906; Jesse and Maria, 1931), *Die arme Margaret* (1910), and *Stephana Schwertner* (1912-14), in which the struggle between Catholics and Protestants is depicted with consummate skill and a degree of objectivity rarely encountered in historical novels.

A predilection for the antitheses of the baroque age and of the counter-Reformation led H.-M. to excel in the portrayal of opposites in her first four novels. But later, when she turned to other times and problems, the limited scope of her artistic view became apparent. Although many of the best critics maintain that she produced the best historical novel of recent years, her position in the history of modern German literature is still open to question. On the other hand, she occupies an unchallenged place as the first writer to implement *Hochland's* program for a revival of German Catholic literature.

FURTHER WORKS: *Nicht umsonst* (1892); *Pegasus im Joch* (1895); *Der Verräter* (1902); *Erzählungen* (2 vols., 1903); *Deutsches Recht und andere Gedichte* (1908); *Acht geistliche Lieder* (1908); *Geistige Werdejahre* (2 vols., 1911-13); *Brüderlein und Schwesterlein* (1913); *Ritas Briefe* (1915-21); *Ilko Smutniak* (1917); *Der deutsche Held* (1920); *Ritas Vermächtnis* (1922); *Sand-Trilogie* (1924-26); *Johann Christian Günther* (1928); *Frau Maria* (1929-31); *Christiane Kotzebue* (1934); *Die Waxenbergerin* (1934); *Graf Reichard* (1939-50)

BIBLIOGRAPHY: Siebertz, P., *et al., E. v. H.-M.'s Persönlichkeit, Werk und Bedeutung* (1930); Hemmen, A., "The Concept of Religious Tolerance in the Novels of E. v. H.-M." (diss. Univ. of Michigan, 1945); *E. v. H.-M., Festschrift zur 75. Jahrfeier*, ed. F. Berger and K. Vancsa (1946); Bourgeois, J. E., "Ecclesiastical Characters in the Novels of E. v. H.-M." (diss. Univ. of Cincinnati, 1956); *Ein groß Ding ist die Liebe*, selections with introduction

KNUT HAMSUN

MARTIN HANSEN

by K. Vancsa (1958); Bourgeois, J. E., "E. v. H.-M.'s Tribute to Schiller," *Monatshefte*, LI (1959), 313-14

JOSEPH E. BOURGEOIS

HANSEN, Martin Alfred

Danish novelist and essayist, b. 20 Aug. 1909, Strøby, Zealand; d. 27 June 1955, Copenhagen

H. died before he could complete his great body of work, which has had a remarkable influence on modern Danish literature. He was the last Danish writer to come directly from farming stock, and he himself was a farmer for a time.

H.'s first work, the two-part novel *Nu opgiver han* (1935), dealt with the depression of the 1930's; it also contains a settlement of accounts with communism which was very meaningful to Denmark's younger generation. In the fantasy novel *Jonathans Rejse* (1941) H. contrasted ancient folk wisdom with modern intellectualism and confronted the downhearted mood of the Occupation period with vigorous humor. The historical novel *Lykkelige Kristoffer* (1945), set in the time of the Reformation, deals with the problems of a change of religion. From 1941 to 1945 H. belonged to the anti-Nazi resistance movement.

After the Liberation a disillusionment conducive to nihilism arose in Denmark. H.'s philosophy, which resisted this disillusionment, proclaims itself in the novella trilogy *Tornebusken* (1942) and particularly—as well as less problematically—in the novella collection *Agerhønen* (1947). His last, purely poetic work was the psychological novel *Løgneren* (1950; The Liar, 1954), which won him a wide audience throughout Europe. The leading character is a teacher whose nature is a mixture of dreaminess and realism. Rich in characters, this work is pervaded by a typically Danish tone of melancholy, humor, and skepticism, resignation and strength of will.

A series of essayistic writings reaches its climax in the great work on the history and philosophy of religions, *Orm og Tyr* (1952; 2nd ed., 1959).

H. was an important stylist, expert in simple, popular narrative forms, though he also experimented with new ones. The tone of ancient fairy tales pervades his novellas; his novels show a highly developed feeling for nature.

FURTHER WORKS: *Kolonien* (1937); *Aasynet* (1946); *Tanker i en skorsten* (1948); *Sankt*

Hans Aften (1949); *Dansk vejr* (1953); *Kringen* (1953); *Paradisaeblerne* (1953); *Rejse på Island* (1954); *Konkylien* (1955); *Midsommerkrans* (1956); *Efterslaet* (1959); *Mindeudgave* (10 vols., 1961)

BIBLIOGRAPHY: Bjørnvig, T., *M. A. H.* (1948); Hellern, V., *M. A. H.* (1959); Nielson, F., *M. A. H.* (1961); Bjornig, T., *Kains Alter: M. A. H.s Digtning og Taenkning* (1964); Christensen, E. M., *Ex auditorio: Kunst og ideer hos M. A. H.* (1965)

EMIL FREDERIKSEN

HANSSON, Ola

Swedish poet, narrative writer, and essayist, b. 12 Nov. 1860, Hönsinge, Skåne; d. 16 Sept. 1925, Buyukdere, near Constantinople

H., whose ancestors were farmers, studied in Lund and after 1889 lived abroad, chiefly in Germany. Some of his work was written and first published in German.

His first collections of poems, *Dikter* (1884) and *Notturno* (1885), already reveal the conflicts of his nature. His first novella collection, *Sensitiva amorosa* (1887), a series of "Studies in Psychic Anatomy," subtle analyses of subconscious and instinctive life, attracted attention. In *Materialismen i skönlitteraturen* (1892) and *Kåserier i mystik* (1897) H. showed himself to be a precursor of Freud and Bergson (q.v.) as a theoretician.

Disappointed and embittered by the lack of understanding shown by the Swedish public, H. never returned to his native land. During the next few years he wrote a number of remarkable works of prose criticism, including essays on various French writers. Most of these were written in German but some were in Danish and Norwegian; Tigerstedt called them "the first Swedish models in the art of the modern literary essay." Nietzsche (q.v.) and Julius Langbehn influenced H., and for a time he was close to Catholicism (*Resan hem*, 1894; *Vägen till livet*, 1896).

Resan hem and *Vägen till livet* and H.'s last novel, *Rustgården* (1910), as well as his many novella collections are all marred by his inability to create lifelike characters. His lyric poetry, written after 1900, is more significant, particularly the nature poems, which subtly depict nature in his beloved Skåne with a moving undertone of melancholy, yearning, and fear of life. With this poetry H. initiated the so-called *skånska diktarskolan* (Skåne school of poetry), whose major representatives were the *tiotalis-terna* (Vilhelm Ekelund [q.v.], etc.)

FURTHER WORKS: *Parias* (1890); *Tidens kvinnor* (1891); *Das junge Skandinavien* (1891); *Ung Ofegs visor* (1892); *Fru Ester Bruce* (1893); *Tolkare och siare* (1893); *Före giftermåler* (1894); *En uppfostrare* (1895); *Der Schützengel* (1896); *Det förlovade landet* (1906); *Nya visor* (1907); *På hemmets altare* (1908); *Samlade skrifter* (17 vols., 1919-22); *Psyke och hemma* (1925); *Ur minnet och dagboken* (1926); *Slättbyhistorier* (1927); *Efterlämnade skrifter i urval* (Gullberg, H., ed., 5 vols., 1928-31); *Valda dikter* (1943); *Husvill, och andra berättelser* (1960)

BIBLIOGRAPHY: Holm, J., *O. H.* (1957); Gustafson, A., *A History of Swedish Literature* (1961), pp. 281-84

JORIS TAELS

HARDY, Thomas

English poet and novelist, b. 6 June 1840, Upper Bockhampton, Dorset; d. 11 Jan. 1928, Dorchester

The roots of the H. family lay deep in rural Dorset, where H.'s father was a master mason (small contractor). H. attended Last's Academy in Dorchester until 1856, his studies including Latin and French. He learned by heart the services at Stinsford Parish Church, and at fifteen began to teach in the Sunday School. He thought of going to a university to prepare for religious orders, but the expense and his father's wishes caused him to decide to apprentice himself to an architect. Continuing his education on his own, H. learned enough Greek to be able to read the *Iliad* and the New Testament.

In 1862 he went to London, still as assistant to another architect; here he won two prizes for essays on architectural subjects. But architecture did not lead him to neglect his reading of Greek drama in translation, Shakespeare's plays, and the romantic poets. He also studied Darwin, Huxley, Spencer, and Mill, whose positivism and logic led him to accept a reluctant agnosticism. Around this time H. submitted a number of grim poems to several publishers, but they all were rejected.

In 1874, H. married Emma Gifford. In 1885, H. had his home built in Dorchester, calling it Max Gate, where he lived the rest of his life. After his wife's death in 1912, he married a friend of hers, Florence Dugdale, in 1914. At H.'s death his heart was buried in his first

wife's grave in Stinsford, and his body in the Poet's Corner, Westminster Abbey.

As novelist and poet of "Wessex" (his fictional name for southwestern England), H. set the "emotional history" of faithfully drawn rural characters "against the stupendous background of the stellar universe"—or at least of the unfeeling cosmos as seen by 19th c. scientists and philosophers. As a boy H. had thrilled to the Gothic romances of such writers as W. H. Ainsworth (1805-1882), had absorbed the folklore of Dorset, and had brooded upon historical remains in a region that included Stonehenge, a Roman Ring at Dorchester, and the burial mounds of many centuries and cultures. When he accepted the conclusions of rationalist thinkers (including Schopenhauer and Hartmann) and became an agnostic monist, he saw the world as the expression of a mysterious, unconscious "immanent will" uncaring for the individual. The blind thrusts of this indifferent universe, the impulses of the "will," and the operations of chance seemed to belong to the realm of evil.

In writing serialized stories with striking incidents in each issue. He expressed his view of life (its mistimed actions, unhappy coincidences, and hopes turned into tragedy) most tellingly through images of fate, peasant choruses based on Greek drama, the device of a Mephistophelian visitant, the tones of Hebrew prophecy, and the tools of folklore and superstition. Yet when called a pessimist, H. characterized himself an evolutionary meliorist, asserting that human beings can remedy many ills and that in the course of time they will do so.

After failing to find a publisher for his poetry, H. turned to prose with a novel of social protest, *The Poor Man and the Lady*. Rejected by one publisher, the manuscript was read by George Meredith (1828-1909) for another; Meredith advised H. to give up satire and write a story with a thrilling plot. H. followed this advice in *Desperate Remedies* (1871). Fourteen other novels, uneven in quality, had settings which treated nearly every decade of the 19th c. and every part of Wessex.

H.'s six best novels are these: *Far from the Madding Crowd* (1874) presents a pretty woman whose vanity and pride lead her to wreck two men's lives until she humbles herself before the genuine worth of her shepherd, Gabriel Oak. The novel is enriched with a rustic chorus, scenes of sheepshearing, and the prophetic tones of biblical prophecy. The setting of *The Return of the Native* (1878) is

Egdon Heath, a microcosm of the world. The heath, ruling the destinies of pleasure-loving, vain Eustacia, who hates its austerity, and the compassionate idealist Clym, frustrates each of them in different ways. The emotional power of the story is increased by H.'s use of folk-lore, superstitions, and ritual to heighten the action. But the action is in fact ruled by temperament, impulse, and natural laws. *The Woodlanders* (1887) presents the Darwinian view of nature but lets a tragedy of mismating pivot upon artificial class divisions and injustices in the marriage and divorce laws. *The Mayor of Casterbridge* (1886) develops the theme that "character is fate." With all the mischances typical in H.'s work, this novel presents a strong man determined to master destiny but ironically defeated by the impulsive egoism in which his strength lies. (The concluding chapter, in the portrait of Elizabeth-Jane, presents a fine statement of H.'s philosophy.) In *Tess of the D'Urbervilles* (1891) H. daringly made a seduced girl his heroine, showed that she was strengthened and deepened by her experience, and traced the processes by which prudery, hypocrisy, and intolerance destroyed her. *Jude the Obscure* (1896) exhibits a tragedy brought about by pruderies and legal follies in matters of sex, love, and marriage. Readers shocked by the realism and candor of this novel attacked H. so viciously that he gave up the novel and devoted himself to poetry for the rest of his life.

The first of eight volumes of poetry, *Wessex Poems* (1898), included poems H. had been writing since the 1860's. H.'s 918 poems are of many types on many subjects—tales in dialect, ironies, love lyrics, and meditations upon the cosmos. Some poems present H.'s philosophic speculations more succinctly than the novels, often depicting nature as a mindless process and life and consciousness as accidental developments. Yet, thought intellectually a determinist, H. was religious in feeling; his poetry meets tragic realization with instinctive hope. Many poems are reminiscent of H.'s life; this is especially true of the poems of lyrical magic that recall his young love in Cornwall and the early days of his first marriage.

H.'s great work, which he planned for years, is *The Dynasts*, an epic-drama of the Napoleonic wars, in three parts (1903, 1906, 1908), nineteen acts, and 130 scenes, written in a variety of poetic forms and passages of prose (for humor and realism). The Napoleonic struggle, extending from Trafalgar to Waterloo, is presented from two points of view: that of the human actors and that of Intelligences (Spirits of the Years, Pities, Ironies, the Earth, etc.), who watch and comment upon the human drama staged and manipulated by the "immanent will," or the unconscious, amoral force whose impulses urge and control the action. The theme of the drama is England's implacable opposition to Napoleon's ambition through battle after battle—at Austerlitz, in Spain, in Moscow, and at Waterloo—until Napoleon, bloated, decayed, and seeing himself in the perspective of history, is finally defeated.

FURTHER WORKS: *Under the Greenwood Tree* (1872); *A Pair of Blue Eyes* (1873); *The Hand of Ethelberta* (1876); *The Trumpet-Major* (1880); *A Laodicean* (1881); *Two on a Tower* (1882); *Wessex Tales* (1888); *A Group of Noble Dames* (1891); *Life's Little Ironies* (1894); *The Well-Beloved* (1897); *A Changed Man* (1913); *Poems of the Past and Present* (1902); *Time's Laughingstocks* (1909); *Satires of Circumstance* (1914); *Moments of Vision* (1917); *Late Lyrics and Earlier* (1922); *Human Shows* (1925); *Winter Words* (1928)

BIBLIOGRAPHY: Abercrombie, L., *T. H.: A Critical Study* (1912); Duffin, H. C., *T. H.: A Study of the Wessex Novels* (1916); Hardy, F. E., *The Early Life of T. H.* (1928) and *The Later Years of T. H.* (1930); Firor, R. A., *Folkways in T. H.* (1931); McDowall, A., *T. H.: A Critical Study* (1931); Chakravarty, A., *The Dynasts and the Post-War Age in Poetry* (1938); Rutland, W. R., *T. H.* (1938); Weber, C. J., *H. of Wessex: His Life and Literary Career* (1940); Blunden, E., *T. H.* (1942); Cecil, Lord D., *H. the Novelist: An Essay in Criticism* (1942); Southworth, J. G., *The Poetry of T. H.* (1947); Webster, H. C., *On a Darkling Plain* (1947); Guerard, A. J., *T. H.: The Novels and Stories* (1949); Hawkins, D., *T. H.* (1950); Hardy, E., *T. H.: A Critical Biography* (1954); Purdy, R. L., *T. H.: A Bibliographical Study* (1954); Bailey, J. O., *T. H. and the Cosmic Mind: A New Reading of the Dynasts* (1956); Patterson, J., *The Making of "The Return of the Native"* (1960); Brown, D., *T. H.* (1961); Hynes, S., *The Pattern of H.'s Poetry* (1961); Orel, H., *T. H.'s Epic Drama: A Study of the Dynasts* (1963); Weber, C. J., *H.'s Love Poems* (1963); Wing, G., *H.* (1963); Howe, I., *T. H.*, vol. VII of "Masters of World Literature" series, ed. L. Kronenberger (1967)

JAMES OSLER BAILEY

HARTLAUB, Felix

German narrative writer, dramatist, and essayist, b. 17 June 1913, Bremen; d. April 1945 (listed as missing in the battle of Berlin)

None of H.'s belletristic writings were published before 1950. Their posthumous fame rests almost entirely on *Im Sperrkreis*, which is closely connected with H.'s military service. Drafted in 1939, he worked as a clerk in historical archives, serving the last three years in the "War Diary" department of Hitler's headquarters. In this "eye of the hurricane," the private, who had access to the highest state secrets, composed a very unusual war journal. By interchanging realistic and detached observations with the interior monologue of an apparently machinelike collective being, he succeeded in recording the twilight of the false gods, the progressive disintegration of the organizational center of the Third Reich.

But the diary is more than *l'art pour la politique*. Transcending the limits of the eyewitness report, H.'s writings exhibit a philosophy of history, which, paradoxically, runs counter to his otherwise individualistic attitude. H. describes history as an unintelligible process governed by anonymous powers. Good and evil are illusive concepts; individual suffering is dependent upon the whims of fate. He was against Hitler, but condemned the conspirators of the July plot; he uncovered the evils of the totalitarian regime, yet considered any resistance pointless.

This rift between two conflicting convictions is visible also in H.'s short stories and literary fragments. In the latter, written shortly before his death, he attempted an artistic synthesis of fatalism and individualism, a *coincidentia oppositorum* culminating in the fragment *El Picaro. Der negative Held*. The symbol of the passive hero incarnate, it consists of a series of conceptual contradictions, and deals with an individual that because of—or in spite of—fate magically comes out on top.

H. was close to being a child prodigy, and even his very early stories—e.g., the astoundingly mature *Kinderkreuzzug* (1927)—are devoted to the theme of man and history. Others worthy of mention are *Die Reise des Tobias* (unfinished; 1932), and the novella *Parthenope* (1934).

The war diary was published under two titles: *Von unten gesehen* (1950) and *Im Sperrkreis* (1955). All H.'s extant writings are collected in *Das Gesamtwerk* (edited by Geno Hartlaub 1955), and *F. H. in seinen Briefen,* (edited by Erna Krauss et al 1958).

FURTHER WORK: *Don Juan d'Austria und die Schlacht bei Lepanto* (1940)

BIBLIOGRAPHY: Holthusen, H. E., "Der negative Held," in *Ja und Nein* (1954), 181-206; Rychner, M., "F. H.," in *Arachne* (1957), 234-48; Plard, H., "Tout seul: La Conscience de la solitude chez F. H.," in *EG*, IX (1959), 128-47

GUENTHER C. RIMBACH

HARTLEY, Leslie Poles

English novelist and critic, born 30 Dec., 1895, Peterborough, Northamptonshire

H.'s work as a novelist is unusual both in its quality and in its relatively recent acceptance as work of the first order. In a recent article in *London Magazine* he was mentioned as the best novelist of the fifties by four out of six contributors. His relative neglect is probably due to his having written only criticism and short fiction between 1925 and 1944. His work is distinguished by an unusual and subtle concern for Christian values, especially as they affect the sensitive individual whose heroism is never acted out spectacularly but is shown by his endurance in the ordinary life of an undistinguished citizen. None of his contemporaries surpasses him in sympathetic portraiture of the so-called "neurotic," and there is no better novel about the sort of trauma that might cause neurosis than *The Go-Between* (1953). H.'s most ambitious work is the trilogy collected under the title of *Eustace and Hilda* (1958), but he will certainly be remembered also for his remarkable novel about passive resistance in wartime, *The Boat* (1949), and *Facial Justice* (1960), as good a non-Utopian novel about the future as any modern novelist has written.

FURTHER WORKS: *Night Fears and Other Stories* (1924); *Simonetta Perkins* (1925); *The Killing Bottle and Other Stories* (1932); *The Shrimp and the Anemone* (1944; Am., The West Window, 1945); *The Sixth Heaven* (1946); *My Fellow Devils* (1951); *The Travelling Grave* (1951); *The White Wand* (1954); *A Perfect Woman* (1955); *The Hireling* (1957); *Two for the River* (1961); *The Brickfield* (1964); *The Betrayal* (1966); *The Novelist's Responsibility* (1967)

THOMAS HARDY

JAROSLAV HAŠEK

BIBLIOGRAPHY: Bien, P., *L. P. H.* (1963); Webster, H. C., *The Novels of L. P.* (1961)

HARVEY CURTIS WEBSTER

HARTOG, Jan de

(pseud. of *F. R. Eckmar*), Dutch novelist, essayist, and dramatist, b. 22 April 1914, Haarlem

H. left home at an early age and spent many years at sea as a cabin boy and ordinary seaman. During World War II he fled to England, and since 1946 he has lived on the Isle of Wight and in Paris. Some of his work was first published in English.

His novels and plays deal with the moral problems of modern man as seen from a Christian viewpoint. He scored his first success with a novel *Hollands Glorie* (1940). The Indonesian trilogy *Gods geuzen* (3 vols., 1947-49) reveals the inner development and fortitude under stress that man can show when forced into extreme situations. The Convoy Cantata trilogy (*Stella,* 1950; *Mary,* 1951; *Thalassa,* 1952 [Am., The Distant Shore, 1952]) deals with the war at sea.

Among H.'s dramatic work, the play *Schipper naast God* (1942; Skipper next to God, 1949) and the comedy *Het hemelbed* (1943; The Fourposter, 1952) brought him international success.

FURTHER WORKS: *Fort 99* (1931); *Het huis met de handen* (1934); *Een linkerbeen gezocht* (1935); *Ave Caesar* (1936); *Spoken te koop* (1936); *De ondergang van "De Vrijheid"* (1937); *Ratten op de trap* (1937); *Oompje Owadi* (1938); *Drie doode dwergen* (1938); *De maagd en de moordenaar* (1939); *Mist* (1940; new version, *De dood van een rat,* 1956); *De duivel en juffer Honesta* (1941); *Leven en werk van Johan C. P. Alberts* (1950); *The Lost Sea* (1951); *De kleine ark* (1953; The Little Ark, 1953); *A Sailor's Life* (1956); *The Spiral Road* (1957); *Scheepspraat* (1958); *The Key* (movie script, 1958); *De kunstenaar* (1959; The Artist, 1963); *The Inspector* (1960; Dutch version, *De inspecteur,* 1961); *Waters of the New World, Houston to Nantucket* (1961); *Omnibus* (1962); *The Hospital* (1964); *The Sailing Ship* (1964); *The Distant Shore,* in *The Call of the Sea* (1966); *The Captain* (1966)

BIBLIOGRAPHY: Gielen, J., and J. G. W., *Synthese* (1963), pp. 266 ff.; Slaughter, F. G., in *New York Times Book Review,* 15 Nov. 1964, p. 22

HELGA THOMAS

HAŠEK, Jaroslav

Czechoslovak poet and novelist, b. 24 April 1883, Prague; d. 3 Jan. 1923, Lipnice

H., the son of a secondary-school teacher in Prague, attended business school and then embarked on a writing career. He traveled in central and southern Europe, and as a prisoner of war in Russia during World War I did journalistic work for the Czech legions stationed there. He joined the Russian communist party and collaborated on communist propaganda. After his return from Russia he devoted himself exclusively to literary work.

He began with the volume of poems *Májové výkřiky* (1903). In 1912 the short story collection *Dobrý voják Švejk a jiné podivné historky* appeared. After the war the comic hero of its title, a dog trader from the dregs of Prague society, was completely reworked into the hero of the novel *Osudy dobrého vojáka Švejka za světové války* (4 vols., 1920-23; The Good Soldier Schweik, 1930). Two sequels, *Osudy dobrého vojáka Švejka v ruským zajetí* (1923-24), which obviously fall short of H.'s own style and conception, were written by the Czech writer and journalist Karel Vanek.

For many years H.'s novel, one of the outstanding satirical works in world literature, was ignored by official Czech literary criticism or rejected as "a plague spot on Czech literature." Only its enthusiastic reception abroad changed this. Schweik, the "little man" of the common people, defies Austrian military bureaucracy by relying on two devices acquired through his experience of practical life: craftiness and idiocy. Thanks to these this modern Sancho Panza escapes from the clutches of militarism. H. castigates not only conditions inside the Austrian military machine but also war itself. But the antimilitarist and pacifist tenor of this novel is only the "outward" manifestation of an individualism which borders on anarchy. In H.'s opinion, craftiness and idiocy are the only defenses against dictatorial regimentation at the disposal of a mass age. As a character delineation Schweik ranks with the great figures of world literature, such as Hamlet, Don Quixote, Don Juan, Faust, Oblomov, etc. The colloquial tone of this novel is enhanced by the special vividness it derives from the symbiosis existing between the German and the Czech languages. For this reason translations of this work can only approximate the original. It has been translated into eighteen languages and dramatized and filmed several times; the most recent German dramatization, which gave the theme a contemporary setting, was by Brecht (q.v.).

FURTHER WORKS: *Když člověk spadne v Tatrách* (1912); *Tři muži se žralokem* (1920); *Spisy* (16 vols., 1924-29; 19 vols., 1955-61)

BIBLIOGRAPHY: Longen, E. H., *J. H.* (1928); Giusti, W., "Lo Svejk primogenito," *Dialoghi*, IX (1961), 523-30; Anon., "The King of Bohemia," *TLS*, 7 Sept. 1962, 665-66; Vlach, R., "Gogol and H.: Two Masters of 'Poshlost,'" *Études Slaves et Est-Européennes* VII (1963), 239-42

HEINRICH KUNSTMANN

HASENCLEVER, Walter

German dramatist and poet, b. 8 July 1890, Aachen; d. 21 June 1940, Les Milles, Aix-en-Provence, France

After an unhappy childhood with difficult parents, H. broke with his family and went to study at the universities of Oxford (1908), Lausanne (1909), and Leipzig (1909); enrolled as a law student, he actually concentrated on literature. In Leipzig he met Kurt Pinthus and Werfel (q.v.), who introduced him into the most important circles of early expressionists. Influenced by Ibsen and Rilke (qq.v.) and experiencing an attraction for Buddhism, he wrote several early works—plays and poems—but it was only with his drama *Der Sohn* (1914) that he established himself as an important artist. This revolutionary play brought to the stage in 1916 for the first time the expressionist style and typical themes—conflict between the generations (hatred of father and son, which runs throughout the works of the whole expressionist school), the brotherhood of man, and undisciplined youth rebelling against authority that has become rigid. With tight, well-constructed scenic technique, H. used a flat, almost poster-like style of terse speech to raise a pathetic and ecstatic entreaty almost to the level of a stifled cry.

In 1914 H. volunteered for military service, and until 1916 served on the Western front and in Macedonia. These war experiences made of him a pacifist, and this new turn of mind was expressed in the dramatic poem *Der Retter* (1915) and the revolutionary poems in *Der politische Dichter* (1919). Another pacifist work, though at the same time H.'s most violent creation, is the play *Antigone* (1917),

for which he was awarded the Kleist Prize that year. The old Greek story is used for anti-militaristic arguments, and the emperor, Wilhelm II, is thinly disguised as the Greek Creon. In the later 1920's H. turned to comedy, and wrote plays, traditional in form, full of sparkling humor and witty irony.

In his last play, *Münchhausen* (1934), H. created one of his finest dramas. In this work he achieved a truly superb synthesis of tragedy and comedy: the old man Münchhausen experiences love and founders on it; through his encounter he is led to a more beautiful, happier, and resigned renunciation. In H.'s last work of all, *Die Rechtlosen*, written between 1939 and 1940 and published posthumously only in 1963, he tells of the life endured by those in French refugee camps; it is one of the most disturbing documents of that period.

In 1933 H. was deprived of his citizenship and emigrated to southern France. From there he wandered to Dubrovnik (1935), London (1935-36), Nice (1936-37), Florence and again London (1937-39), and finally to Cagnes-sur-Mer, in southern France, where he was interned twice. In June 1940, at the refugee camp in Les Milles, as the German troops approached, he killed himself.

FURTHER WORKS: *Nirwana, Eine Kritik des Lebens in Dramaform* (1908); *Städte, Nächte und Menschen, Erlebnisse* (1910); *Der Jüngling* (1913); *Das unendliche Gespräch* (1913); *Die Hochzeitsnacht* (1914); *Tod und Auferstehung* (1917); *Die Menschen* (1918); *Die Entscheidung* (1919); *Die Pest* (1920); *Jenseits* (1920); *Gedichte an Frauen* (1922); *Gobseck* (1922); *Mord* (1926); *Ein besserer Herr* (1927; The Magnificent Hugo, 1960); *Ehen werden im Himmel geschlossen* (1929); *Kulissen* (1929); *Bourgeois bleibt Bourgeois* (produced 1929); *Napoleon greift ein* (1930); *Kommt ein Vogel geflogen* (1931); *Sinnenglück und Seelenfrieden* (1932); *Ausgewählte Werke: Gedichte, Dramen, Prosa*, ed. K. Pinthus (1963)

BIBLIOGRAPHY: Diebold, B., *Anarchie im Drama* (1925); Pinthus, K., "Introduction" to H.'s *Gedichte, Dramen, Prosa* (1963)

* * *

HAUPTMANN, Carl

German dramatist and novelist, b. 11 May 1858, Obersalzbrunn, Silesia; d. 3 Feb. 1921, Schreiberhau, Silesia

H., the elder brother of Gerhart Hauptmann

(q.v.) and a philosophically oriented natural scientist, was a pupil of Ernst Haeckel but abandoned his scientific career in 1893. At first he wrote dramas in the style of naturalism (q.v.), but he soon broke away from this. His study of the Silesian mystics and of Meister Eckhart is reflected in his subsequent symbolic dramas (*Die Bergschmiede*, 1902; etc.) and in the introspective *Aus meinem Tagebuch* (1900). His fiction shows greater artistic tension; *Mathilde* (1902), a novel about women, and *Einhart der Lächler* (1907), a partly autobiographical novel about artists, are his best works. While H.'s liking for Silesian characters and settings, his frequent use of Silesian dialect, and his interest in fairytales and legends make him in the main a regionalist, the problems he poses in his works go beyond this category.

FURTHER WORKS: *Marianne* (1894); *Waldleute* (1896); *Sonnenwanderer* (1897); *Ephraims Breite* (1900; pub. as *Ephraims Tochter*, 1920); *Aus meinem Tagebuch* (1900); *Aus Hütten am Hange* (1902); *Des Königs Harfe* (1903); *Die Austreibung* (1905); *Miniaturen* (1905); *Moses* (1906); *Panspiele* (1909); *Napoleon Bonaparte* (1911); *Nächte* (1912); *Die armseligen Besenbinder* (1913); *Ismael Friedmann* (1913); *Die lange Jule* (1913); *Krieg* (1914); *Aus dem großen Kriege* (1915); *Rübezahlbuch* (1915); *Tobias Buntschuh* (1916); *Musik* (1919); *Die goldenen Straßen* (1919); *Der abtrünnige Zar* (1919); *Tantaliden* (1927); *Leben mit Freunden* (letters, 1928); *Heimstätten und Schicksale* (1958)

BIBLIOGRAPHY: Razinger, H., *C. H.* (1928); Goldstein, W., *C. H.* (1931); Milch, W., *C. H.* (1931); Duglor, T., ed., *C. H., ein schlesischer Dichter* (1958); Alker, E., " ... Studie über die Erzählprosa C. Hs.", *Zeitschrift für deutsche Philologie*, LXXVIII (1959), 129-40; Sünden, M., *"Marianne* und *Einsame Menschen," Monatshefte*, LIV (1962), 311-21

INGO SEIDLER

HAUPTMANN, Gerhart

German dramatist and novelist, b. 15 Nov. 1862, Obersalzbrunn, Silesia; d. 6 June, 1946, Agnetendorf, Silesia

H.'s ancestors had lived in Silesia since 1600, where many of them had been weavers, but his father owned a resort hotel. His school years were unhappy and unsuccessful; he spent

1878-79 working on his uncle's farm, where the pietism of his relatives heightened a natural leaning towards mysticism. He turned to sculpturing, spent two years at the Art Academy in Breslau and another year of desultory study at the University of Jena before setting up a sculptor's studio in Rome. Typhoid fever forced him to return home. At Jena he had listened to lectures on philosophy, archaeology, and literature. Through his brother, who was a student in the natural sciences, H. came under the influence of the German exponent of Darwinism, the popular lecturer, Ernst Haeckel. The scientific determinism of the age, combined with a youthful zeal for social reform, challenged the religious orthodoxy of his boyhood. This unresolved conflict helps to explain the polarity of his literary work, and caused Eloesser to characterize H. as "our most pagan, our most Christian poet."

H.'s engagement to the wealthy Marie Thienemann in 1881 and his marriage in 1885 provided the financial support that made his literary career possible. His earliest poetic efforts are now available in a facsimile printing (*Früheste Dichtungen*, 1962), but his serious concern with literature began after an unsystematic study of Greek literature, history, and philosophy and wide reading in the German classics and modern authors. After his marriage he lived first in Berlin and then in its suburb Erkner. He established contacts with the leaders of naturalism (q.v.) and formed friendships with Strauss, Holz, Schlaf (qq.v.), the brothers Heinrich (1855-1906) and Julius Hart (1859-1930), Wilhelm Bölsche (1861-1939), Bruno Wille (1860-1928), Max Kretzer (1854-1941), and others, some of whom were members of the literary club "Durch." In his diary he recorded (1897): "Then came Brandes (q.v.), the awakener of the North, and encouraged me; finally Ibsen and Tolstoi (qq.v.) put before my eyes what I believed to be attainable only in the most distant future." Performances of *Ghosts* and *The Power of Darkness* made him study the dialogue and the effectiveness of these dramas. At his own expense he published *Promethidenlos* (1885), a Byronic epic, and a collection of lyrics, *Das bunte Buch* (1888), and contributed to magazines two realistic stories, "Fasching" (1887) and "Bahnwärter Thiel" (1888; Flagman Thiel, 1933).

The success of his first drama, *Vor Sonnenaufgang* (1889; Before Dawn, 1909), signaled the beginning of a new era for the German theater. It was performed on Oct. 20 by the Freie Bühne, the German equivalent of Antoine's Théâtre Libre in Paris, where Ibsen's social dramas had already avoided official censorship. All the shocking details of the life of a dissolute peasant family, presented with grim realism, aroused the audience. Indignant protests against the revolting presentation of a sordid environment and the vicious consequences of hereditary alcoholism mingled with vociferous acclaim of the courageous young dramatist. The ponderous, epigonous style of the day was suddenly swept away and a painstakingly accurate reproduction of the speech and mannerisms of every character introduced a new technique of the drama. Serious critics recognized the importance of this performance, and Theodor Fontane wrote his daughter, "Hauptmann is really what Ibsen wanted to be . . . he presents life as it is, in its full horror; he adds nothing but he leaves out nothing either and thus attains a colossal effect."

Now followed in rapid succession *Das Friedensfest* (1890; The Coming of Peace, 1900) and *Einsame Menschen* (1891; Lonely Lives, 1898), both family tragedies, and *Die Weber* (1892; The Weavers, 1899), the masterpiece of German naturalism. The historic uprising of 1844, a protest against the mechanical looms which destroyed the simple livelihood of Silesian weavers, is vividly recreated. Five seemingly independent acts form a crescendo in dramatic action in which the numerous characters are carefully individualized but in their totality become the tragic protagonists of the suffering masses. Despite H.'s objective presentation of the misery and wretchedness that he had witnessed in visiting some areas of his province, he was accused of tendentious writing by the imperial government, which tried unsuccessfully to prevent public performances. *Der Biberpelz* (1893; The Beaver Coat, 1912), using similar dramatic techniques and realistic characterizations, is a social satire and ranks high as a comedy. *Florian Geyer* (1895; Eng. 1929), a drama of the Peasant War, attempted to present the social, cultural, and linguistic background of the 16th c. with such an abundance of characters and epic breadth that the audience was overwhelmed. A complete failure at its first performance, it won understanding and appreciation after the collapse of Germany, when the tragedy of political disunity had become meaningful, and the acting of Rudolf Rittner and Eugen Klöpfer in the title role carried the play.

A year earlier, in *Hanneles Himmelfahrt* (1894; Hannele, 1894) H. had combined the sordid atmosphere of the village poorhouse with a sensitive, psychological analysis of the bruised and tortured spirit of an adolescent girl who finds solace in a sensuous dream world of religious symbolism. The neo-romantic aspects surprised the critics who had called H. a "naturalist," but gave further proof that H.'s art transcended all labels. An almost complete surrender to romanticism is reflected in *Die versunkene Glocke* (1897; The Sunken Bell, 1898), his most popular dramatic success. Its folklore and fairy-tale elements combined with the sentimental love story of a struggling artist delighted an audience surfeited with drab realism, but its fame was meteoric.

More permanent, perhaps even the most enduring of the tragedies depicting the brutality of life that destroys the individual, are *Fuhrmann Henschel* (1899; Drayman Henschel, 1913), *Rose Bernd* (1903; Eng. 1913), and *Michael Kramer* (1900; Eng. 1914), which might be grouped together as tragedies of isolation. Henschel and Rose Bernd are simple peasant types who are goaded and hounded to death. They are guided by instinct rather than reason, and in despair become the victims of their loneliness. H.'s sympathetic understanding of these characters, whose inevitable destruction is presented with restraint and artistic veracity, is unmatched in modern drama. In *Michael Kramer* the tragedy is transferred to an artist's family, where the son possesses the divine spark but lacks moral fibre and the father has artistic integrity but limited talent. The son yearns in vain for a love that might redeem his soul and restore him to society. Despair drives him to self-destruction. *Der arme Heinrich* (1902; Henry of Auë, 1914) reveals the only solution: redemption through love. The drama contains some of H.'s finest poetry and psychologizes this miraculous legend of Middle High German literature. H. continued to return to older themes in literature, which he reinterpreted with sympathetic understanding of the demonic conflicts of the soul: *Elga* (1905; Eng. 1906), *Kaiser Karls Geisel* (1908, Charlemagne's Hostage, 1915), *Griselda* (1909; Eng., 1909), *Der Bogen des Odysseus* (1914; The Bow of Odysseus, 1917), *Winterballade* (1917; A Winter Ballad, 1924), and *Veland* (1925; Eng., 1929). Despite its realistic background, *Und Pippa tanzt!* (1906; And Pippa Dances, 1907) is perhaps the finest expression of H.'s yearning for beauty, symbolized by this fragile, exotic creature pursued by all men.

After years of marital difficulties H. was divorced in 1904 and married Margarete Marschalk, a gifted young violinist. A journey to Greece three years later yielded not mere travel impressions but a profound appreciation of the Dionysian spirit of the Hellenic world (*Griechischer Frühling*, 1908), where human sacrifice was the bloody root of tragedy. Henceforth H.'s dramatic work freed itself more and more of the artifice of the modern theater and its popular realism. He attempted to recapture the essence of what he called *das Urdrama*, the simplest and yet most dramatic conflict of the individual, split and torn asunder by antagonistic facets of his own personality.

H.'s narrative work, though secondary in importance, gives further proof of the breadth and scope of his literary genius. The novel *Der Narr in Christo Emanuel Quint* (1910; The Fool in Christ, Emanuel Quint, 1911) chronicles the life of a simple peasant who literally relives the experiences of the historical Jesus. H.'s deeply religious nature comes to grips with modern scientific skepticism and his own anticlerical leanings. The religious ecstasy of a modern mystic, combined with asceticism and naïve faith, reflect H.'s own feeling for a religious experience almost incompatible with the temper of modern society. The profound sympathy and psychological insight of the narrative are tempered with a faint irony that suggests the inadequacy of both mysticism and rationalism. Diametrically opposed in spirit is *Der Ketzer von Soana* (1918; The Heretic of Soana, 1923), a Rousseauan paean of praise to the goodness and fullness of life governed by natural instincts. The sensuous beauty of the landscape of Ticino and the pagan assertion of the senses make it a hymn to Eros. Stylistically and structurally it is H.'s most perfect narrative work.

Public recognition came soon after the first theater successes. The Imperial Academy in Vienna gave H. its highest award, the Grillparzer Prize, three times (1896, 1899, 1905) for *Hanneles Himmelfahrt, Fuhrmann Henschel,* and *Der arme Heinrich.* Only the personal antagonism of the Emperor prevented his receiving the German drama award, the Schiller Prize, for which he was repeatedly recommended. In 1905 Oxford University bestowed on him the honorary degree of doctor of letters; other honorary degrees followed from the universities of Leipzig (1909) and Prague (1921), and from Columbia University (1932). Most important of all was the international recognition that came with the Nobel Prize (1912). The Weimar Republic gave him its highest decoration, Pour le Mérite (1922), and celebrated his sixtieth birthday as a national event. The Third Reich ignored him, but his dramas continued to be performed.

After the First World War H. published the dramas *Der weiße Heiland* (1920; The White Saviour, 1924) and *Indipohdi* (1920; Eng. 1924) which had preoccupied him for some time and represent something of a flight from reality into an exotic world of fantasy. The first depicts the cruel conquest of Mexico and the tragedy of the guileless and trusting Montezuma, who falls victim to the avarice of the Christian invaders; the second reflects H.'s disillusionment and despair during the war years. Inspired and suggested by Shakespeare's *Tempest*, it was meant as H.'s farewell to the world of the drama. The epic *Till Eulenspiegel* (1928), written in hexameters, tells the adventures of a former aviator who wanders in despair through postwar Germany in the guise of the legendary prankster of German folk literature. H. not only portrays the chaotic conditions of his fatherland but takes his hero back through history in a series of visionary episodes that include a blissful existence in the realm of ancient Greece before his return to the chaotic phenomenal world, where he plunges to his death in the Swiss Alps.

After years of preoccupation with the study of Shakespeare and the "Hamlet problem" H. published a revision of the text, wrote the drama *Hamlet in Wittenberg* (1935), and a novel, *Im Wirbel der Berufung* (1936), concerned with the theater and the staging of *Hamlet. Das Buch der Leidenschaft* (1930) is a veiled confession of the emotional stress occasioned by his divorce and remarriage, *Das Abenteuer meiner Jugend* (1937) a detailed biographical account of his formative years and early literary struggles. The story "Das Meerwunder" (1934) transcends the realm of reality, and its almost surrealistic style reflects H.'s despair at man's inhumanity and betrayal of the brotherhood of man. The tortured cry "I don't want to be a part of the human race" symbolizes H.'s repugnance at the Hitler era. During the war years the epic *Der große Traum* (1942), written in the *ottava rima* of Dante's *Divine Comedy*, depicts a series of grandiose visions of the eternal conflict between the forces of darkness and light. Again H.'s speculative thinking, tinged with the philosophy of the gnostics, attempts to transcend human limitations. The tragedy of medieval witchcraft and the Inquisition, *Magnus Garbe* (1942), had its origin in H.'s interest in the age of the Reformation and the Anabaptists, and was completed by 1915; but its unmitigated gloom, "the bitterest tragedy of mankind," as the poet called it, made him postpone its publication until the end of his life. The "Atrides tetralogy," the tragedy of Agamemnon and his family, consists of the concluding drama *Iphigenie in Delphi* (1941), the opening drama *Iphigenie in Aulis* (1944), and the connecting one-act dramas *Agamemnons Tod* (1948) and *Elektra* (1947), the last two published after H.'s death. All the horror and despair that the war years had aroused find full expression in this cycle of crime, passion, and bloodshed. The curse of Tantalus and his race endangers and destroys humanity. Mankind longs helplessly for salvation. Only human sacrifice makes any sort of atonement possible.

H.'s last work, the unfinished novel *Der neue Christophorus* (1943), is again the story of suffering humanity to be redeemed by Erdmann, who represents the eternal rebirth of mankind. Shortly after the end of World War II and the occupation of Silesia by the Russians, who showed respect and friendship for the aged poet and protected him and his property against the indignities of Polish looting, H. died—at the very moment when orders were given for the mass evacuation of all Germans from that province. He, whose greatest fear at the end of his life had been the threat of deportation, virtually died with the anxious words "Am I still in my house?" on his lips.

His versatile talent in creating real human beings, his subtle exposition of milieu, and his lifelike dialogue gave his work a dominant place in German literature for fifty years after his sensational success in 1889, and made H. the representative figure of that epoch. Despite excessive adulation or temporary neglect, his work is firmly established and reflects the complexity, doubts, uncertainties, and relativism of our time. It represents the highest artistic expression of what may eventually be regarded as a transitional age. The contradictions and irrational forces of human nature are revealed sympathetically and understandingly. The appeal of H.'s artistic interpretations of the demonic forces of life have been aptly characterized by Behl as "the magic of the elemental." H. was always the naïve artist, whose keen observation, paired with visionary insights, achieved a plastic reality. The simplicity and yet the universality of his work, the sympathetic understanding of suffering humanity, have received high recognition and praise from his greatest contemporaries, Rilke and Thomas Mann (qq.v.).

FURTHER WORKS: *Schluck und Jau* (1900; Eng., 1915); *Der rote Hahn* (1901); *Das Hirtenlied* (1904; Pastoral, 1917); *Die Jungfern vom Bischofsberg* (1907; The Maidens of the Mount, 1915); *Die Ratten* (1911; The Rats, 1913); *Gabriel Schillings Flucht* (1912; Gabriel Schilling's Flight, 1915); *Atlantis* (1912; Eng., 1912); *Festspiel in deutschen Reimen* (1913; Commemoration Masque, 1917); *Lohengrin* (1913); *Parsival* (1914); *Peter Brauer* (1921); *Anna* (1921); *Phantom* (1922; Eng., 1922); *Ausblicke* (1922); *Die blaue Blume* (1924); *Die Insel der großen Mutter* (1924; The Island of the Great Mother, 1925); *Dorothea Angermann* (1926); *Wanda* (1928); *Spuk* (1930); *Um Volk und Geist: Ansprachen* (1932); *Die goldene Harfe* (1934); *Die Tochter der Kathedrale* (1939); *Ulrich von Lichtenstein* (1939); *Mignon* (1947); *Die Finsternisse* (1947); *Die großen Beichten* (1966); *Gesammelte Werke* (6 vols., 1906); *Gesammelte Werke* (6 vols., 1912); *Gesammelte Werke* (12 vols., 1922); *Gesammelte Werke: Ausgabe letzter Hand* (17 vols., 1942); *The Dramatic Works* (9 vols., 1912-29); *Sämtliche Werke in zehn Bänden* (1962 ff.; Centenar-Ausgabe, will include all published works, three volumes of unpublished works, fragments, and variants and thirty pages of critical study by H.-E. Hass)

BIBLIOGRAPHY: Ludwig, V., *G. H. Werke von ihm und über ihn 1881-1931* (1932); Requardt, W., *G. H. Bibliographie* (3 vols., 1931); Reichart, W. A., "Fifty Years of H. Study in America (1894-1944): A Bibliography," in: *Monatshefte* (1945); "H. Study in America: A Continuation Bibliography," in: *Monatshefte* (1962); Tschörtner, H. D., *G. H. Ein bibliographischer Beitrag* (1962); Reichart, W. A., Kremkus, M., and Culbertson, H., "Bibliographie der gedruckten und ungedruckten Dissertationen über G. H. und sein Werk," *Philobiblon* (1967); · Holl, K., *G. H., His Life and His Work* (1913); Fechter, P., *G. H.* (1922); Freyhan, M., *G. H.* (1922); Schlenther, P., and Eloesser, A., *G. H.* (1922); Kühnemann, E., *G. H.* (1922); Hülsen, H. v., *G. H.* (1927); Sulger-Gebing, E., Linden, W., *G. H.* (1932); Gregor, J., *G. H.* (1944); Garten,

GERHART HAUPTMANN

ERNEST HEMINGWAY

H. F., *G. H.* (1954); Behl, C. F. W., *G. H.: His Life and Work* (1956); Behl, C. F. W., and Voigt, F. A., *Chronik von G. H.'s Leben und Schaffen* (1957); Tank, K. L., *G. H.* (1959); Guthke, K. S., *G. H.* (1961); Seyppel, J., *G. H.* (1962); Zeller, B., ed., *G. H.* (1962)

SPECIAL STUDIES: Röhr, J., *G. H.'s dramatisches Schaffen* (1912); Marschan, J. H., *Das Mitleid bei G. H.* (1919); Vollmers-Schulte, F., *G. H. und die soziale Frage* (1923); Heynen, W., *Mit G. H.* (1922); Heise. W., *G. H.* (1923); Chapiro, J., *Gespräche mit G. H.* (1932); Voigt, F. A., *Antike und antikes Lebensgefühl im Werke G. H.'s* (1935); *G. H. Jahrbuch* (1936, 1937, 1948); Müller, I., *G. H. in Frankreich* (1939); Schreiber, H., *G. H. und das Irrationale* (1946); Voigt, F. A., and Reichart, W. A., *Hauptmann und Shakespeare* (1947); Behl, C. F. W., *Wege zu G. H.* (1948); ibid., *Zwiesprache mit G. H.* (1949); Muller, S., *G. H. and Goethe* (1949); Weisert, J. J., *The Dream in G. H.* (1949); Voigt, F. H., *G. H. der Schlesier* (1953); Fiedler, R., *Die späten Dramen G. H.'s* (1954); Gutknecht, H., *Studien zum Traumproblem bei G. H.* (1954); Sinden, H., *G. H. The Prose Plays* (1957); Shaw, L. R., *Witness of Deceit: G. H. as Critic of Society* (1958); Grueneberg, E., *Demon and Eros in Some Plays of Gerhart Hauptmann* (1960); Heuser, F. W., *G. H.* (1961); Berger, P., *G. H.s "Die Ratten"* (1962); Gustavs, A., *G. H. und Hiddensee* (1962); Michaelis, R., *Der schwarze Zeus* (1962); Pohl, G., *G. H. and Silesia* (1962); Machatzke, M., ed., G. H., *Die Kunst des Dramas: Über Schauspiel und Theater* (1963); Alexander, N. E., *Studien zum Stilwandel im dramatischen Werk G. H.'s* (1964); Knight, K. G., and Norman, F., eds. *H.'s Centenary Lectures* (1964); Meinert, D., *Hellenismus und Christentum in H.'s Atriden-Tetralogie* (1964); Studt, W., ed., Voigt, F. A., *G. H. und die Antike* (1965; rev. and enlarged ed. of *Antike und antikes Lebensgefühl im Werke G. H.'s* (1935)

WALTER A. REICHART

Never have I seen such an event on the stage [*Michael Kramer*], never had I anticipated such a return of the soliloquy, such power, simplicity and beauty of the word, surpassing everything spoken and sung; it is really nothing but gesture, posture, and image—the opposite of "talking about something." . . .

Rainer Maria Rilke, *Briefe 1899–1902* (1931), pp. 410 and 415

I venture to say that within our literary heritage there scarcely exists another lifework comparable in richness of characters to Gerhart Hauptmann's. . . . Yet the vital forcefulness of the vision, clamoring for communication, is . . . so direct—arising, as it were, without any intervening reflection, from the excitement of characters, plots and images perceived and immediately carried into the presentation—that one has to go back to Balzac or, better still, to Dickens to find such an exuberant, outgoing gift for communication, such open-heartedness toward the world and other people.

Rudolf Alexander Schröder, *Die Aufsätze und Reden* I (1952), pp. 903 f.

Hauptmann's soul is at bottom contemplative, not active, without inner tension and dynamism, a soul for which the world becomes transparent in images and events, not really in activity toward a goal. . . . From this passivity there stems in the end Hauptmann's much-vaunted compassion, which in him takes the place of fellow feeling in suffering.

Paul Fechter, *Gerhart Hauptmann* (1922), pp. 16 ff.

. . . Hauptman lacks an essential ingredient: an awareness of evil, of man's productive demonism. Thus he is not truly and essentially a psychologist, that is, a discoverer and portrayer of areas of the soul hitherto unexplored and often characteristic of a specific period, in the exact and decisive sense in which, for instance, Shakespeare and some of his contemporaries and, later, Stendhal and Strindberg were psychologists. He is not so much an explorer of the soul as an apologist for it. . . . In Hauptmann there is none of the splendid—so to speak, total—harmony and unity, the dialectical and contrapuntal fugal treatment of all themes, that appears in its full glory in the drama of Schiller, Kleist, and Racine. This is undoubtedly connected with the fact that this genius who makes no assumptions has absolutely no relationship to history. For him all history finally becomes happening.

Hans Hennecke, *Dichtung und Dasein* (1950), p. 129

The basic characteristic of all that is human in Gerhart Hauptmann's world is a real, indissoluble kinship with the elemental. . . . The elemental is still one with the origin of all being; it is the source of creation, still unsullied by the blessed curse of consciousness and thus immune to the tragic conflict in man's world. Therefore the elemental is for Hauptmann always that which heals, which expiates, which sanctifies.

Carl Friedrich Wilhelm Behl, *Wege zu Gerhart Hauptmann* (1948), pp. 35 f.

We have before us a lifework of tremendous scope, yet one which still fell far short of mastering and clarifying, of giving substance and form to everything this man had within him. There was in him a flood of dreams which, as we know, made him cry out in his sleep. To master and reduce this to order without failures or, indeed, awkwardness, was beyond human ability. . . . Suffering, blood, the terror of the night: and besides, emanating from these and passionately involved with them, the desire for beauty, light, for the "liberating jubilation of the suns."

Thomas Mann, *Altes und Neues. Kleine Prosa aus fünf Jahrzehnten* (1953), pp. 449 ff.

HAUSA LITERATURE

Hausa is the language generally spoken by the predominantly Muslim population of northern Nigeria. Its creative literature, both oral and written, is vast; and as is the case with most vernacular African literatures, much of it has not yet been recorded, and even less has been really studied, either historically or critically.

Like all illiterate societies, the Hausa have produced an impressive number of oral works for the composition of which no date, of course, can be assigned. They are chiefly proverbs, folk tales, and poems which were first retrieved, recorded, and published by German missionaries in the second half of the 19th c. and later by British scholars. Oral composition is still widely practiced today.

Although the Arabic script was introduced in the area in the late 11th c. under the Almoravid dynasty, there is no conclusive evidence that the vernacular language was committed to writing before the early 19th c. Hausa literati preferred to resort to the Arabic language which was used in Hausaland for literary purposes as early as the end of the 13th c.

The decisive event for the birth of creative writing in Hausa was the Holy War which began in 1804, when the Fulani inhabitants of Hausaland, led by °Uthmān dan Fodio (1754-1812), rose up in arms against the allegedly pagan Hausa kings; they were helped in this by Hausa Muslims. Scholars belonging to the new, predominantly Fulani ruling class produced their own literature in Arabic, as instanced in *Tazyīn al-waraqāt* ("The Adorning of the Manuscripts," ed. A. Braas, 1920, and M. Hiskett, 1963), a chronicle of the *Jihad* interspersed with poems by °Abdullāh b. Muhammad, brother of °Uthmān and first emir of Gwandu.

But the Fulani writers at an early stage resorted to the Hausa language, presumably for propaganda purposes. It is not known whether °Uthmān's famous song on Abdulkādir (the Fulani leader who, from 1776 to 1778, established the Islamic state of Futa Toro between the Senegal and Gambia rivers) was originally composed in Fulani or Hausa; it was later translated into Arabic by °Abdullāh. But it was in the early 19th c. that there arose a body of writing in the Hausa language couched in a variant of the Arabic script known as *ajami* (=foreign): this tradition seems to have been initiated by a contemporary of °Uthmān, Mohammadu Na Birnin Gwari, through his letters and poems; it was further spread through the poems of °Uthmān's daughter Nanna, who wrote about woman's place in Muslim society. Those early poets of the *Jihad* period wrote in the dialect of Sokoto, now regarded as the literary language of northern Nigeria.

Simultaneously with this didactic trend the *ajami* script was used to record works of purely Hausa inspiration, such as the *Wakar Bagauda* (ed. Hiskett, 1964-65), a verse chronicle of the Kano dynasty from its legendary founder, Bagauda; later generations of poets brought the story down to the reign of Abdullāhi Bayero, who ruled from 1926 to 1953.

At the time of Lugard's conquest of the northern states, much poetry was composed to celebrate Muslim resistance to the white man and to his religion, most notably by Ibrahim Nagwamatse (1857-1922), the ruthless slave-trading emir of Kontagora, and by Aliyu dan Sidi, who was emir of Zaria from 1903 to 1920. Others, such as Ibrahim Nalado, of Katsina, who introduced alliteration into Hausa prosody, continued the old trend of devotional and educational poetry which is characteristic of most islamized areas in Africa, whether along the southern border of the Sahara or on the East Coast. At the same time, vagrant scholars and court poets went on composing poetry in the folklore tradition, especially praise songs (*yābó*), but also satires (*zambó*) and love poems (*bēgé*).

After the Arabic and the *ajami* periods, colonial rule, the printing press, and Western-type education initiated a new development in Hausa literature. Vernacular writing in Roman characters spread among the educated Hausa as early as the beginning of this century. The Roman alphabet, however, was not used for creative purposes on any notable scale until 1935, when a Government Literature Bureau was set up at Zaria and started printing vernacular novelettes written for school use by local teachers. Among the first of these was *Shaihu Umar* by Abubakar Tafawa Balewa (1912-66), later to become the first prime minister of independent Nigeria; it is the sentimental story of a mother's pathetic adventures as she searches for her lost son. *Gandoki* by Muhammadu Bello Kagara (c. 1910-), now Wali of Katsina, deals with a great warrior who leaves his country in consequence of the British conquest; when he comes back, after many adventures, he is delighted with the changes that have taken place! Anecdotal and edifying, such works are of little intrinsic interest, but they were a beginning. At a later stage other pieces of prose fiction were added, including a full-length novel by Jabiru Abdullahi Mashi, *Nagari Na-Kowa* (1958); a collection of folkstories, *Magana Jari Ce*, by Abubakar Imam (b. 1911); and plays by Shu'aibu Makarfi.

As the art of composing verse has always been part of the traditional education, poets are very numerous in northern Nigeria today. Their output ranges from the devotional and moralizing verse of Aliyu Na-Magni, the blind poet from Zaria, to the intellectual tone and contemporary preoccupations of Sa'adu Zungur (d. 1958), the first northerner to attend Yaba Higher College when it was opened in 1934. Many of the younger poets, especially in Kano, write both in Hausa and in Arabic. Although a majority of them keep to *ajami*, the Roman script was introduced for poetry after World War II by a group of modernist writers, the best-known representatives being Ma'adzu Hadeja (d. 1955) and Mudi Sipikin. However, Hausa culture is exceedingly conservative; although its literary production is enormous, especially in verse, little of it ever reaches print, and what does get into print reflects the most traditional outlook to be found in the whole African literary output today.

ALBERT S. GÉRARD

HAWKES, John

American novelist, b. 17 Aug. 1925, Stamford, Conn.

One of the most original of contemporary novelists, H. has utilized the sadistic-masochistic rhythms of the unconscious as a structural and thematic principle in his work. His prime means of entry into the nightmare world of latent image and concealed desire has been the poetic evocation of an incredibly flexible prose style. Since his first novel, *The Cannibal* (1949), he

has gradually moved away from the lush extremes of surrealism to a greater reliance on the structures of traditional plot and characterization, as in *The Lime Twig* (1961).

FURTHER WORKS: *Charivari* (1949); *The Beetle Leg* (1951); *The Goose on the Grave* (1954); *Second Skin* (1964); *The Innocent Party* (1966)

BIBLIOGRAPHY: Fiedler, L., "Introduction" to New Directions ed. of H.'s *The Lime Twig* (1961); Malin, I., *New American Gothic* (1962); On *Second Skin*—see Adams, R. M., *New York Review of Books* (2 April 1964), p. 12

EARL ROVIT

HEDBERG, Carl Olof (Olle)

Swedish novelist, b. 31 May 1899, Norrköping

H.'s extensive work satirizes the wealthy Swedish bourgeoisie. His study of psychoanalysis sharpened his eye for the contrast between man's outward façade and his true self. With amazing sureness he unmasks the unconscious egoism, the ill-will, and the hypocrisy of his respectable characters. While H.'s first novels are nearly all extended novellas describing one particular episode in a human life, several of his works written after 1937 are conceived as developmental novels in more than one volume. In those, psychological analysis is often more important than action. *Bekänna färg* (1947) and *Dockan dansar, klockan slår* (1955) deal with the possibility of a religiously oriented life. All H.'s work is moral and intellectual, and shows remarkable virtuosity of form.

FURTHER WORKS: *Rymmare och fasttagare* (1930); *Skära, skära havre* (1931); *Får jag be om räkningen* (1932); *Fria på narri* (1933); *Iris och löjtnantshjärta* (1934); *Att fä tillhöra dig* (1935); *Jag är en prins av blodet* (1936); *Karsten Kirsewetter* (trilogy, 1937-39); *Ut med blondinera!* (1939); *Josefine eller säg det med blommor* (1940); *Bo Stennsson Svenningsson* (1941-45, novelistic cycle: *Vad suckar leksakslådan?*, 1941; *Sista sommarlovet*, 1942; *Vackra vita tänder*, 1943; *Slå dank*, 1944; *Den felande länken*, 1945); *Större än du nånsin tror* (1946); *Dan före dan* (1948); *Mera vild än tam* (1949); *Blenda Heurman* (tetralogy, 1948-51); *Häxan i pepparkakshuset* (1950); *Da bleknar bruden* (1951); *Drömtydning* (1952); *Foto von Blomberg* (1953); *Vänstra kinden* (1954); *Ven-*

dela Borg (trilogy, 1956-58); *Sardinens begravning* (1956); *Storken i Sevilla* (1957); *Djur i bur* (1959; Animals in Cages, 1962); *Herre var är du?* (1960); *I barnens närvaro* (1961); *Mitt liv var en dröm* (1962); *Kring Dalinminnet* (1963); *Allt vad du säjer kommer att användas emot dej* (1964); *Öppna Fågelburen!* (1967)

BIBLIOGRAPHY: Andersson, E., *O. H.* (1945); Kulling, J., *O. H. romaner* (1952); Svenringer, B., *Sprickan i universum* (1965)

JORIS TAELS

HEIBERG, Gunnar (Edvard Rode)
Norwegian dramatist and critic, b. 18 Nov. 1857, Christiania; d. there, 22 Feb. 1929

Although H. was not of Ibsen's (q.v.) stature, he was Ibsen's most important successor in Norway. He began his career as a dramatist with plays of social protest, in which he used Ibsen's retrospective technique and in which woman personifies sound moral sense (*Tante Ulrikke*, 1884). Later, under the influence of the neoromantic trends of the 1890's, he moved on to the poetic psychological drama *Balkonen* (1894; The Balcony, 1943), whose theme is the antagonism between man and woman, represented here as the conflict between idealism and erotic passion. In *Kjærlighedens tragedie* (1904; The Tragedy of Love, 1921), too, the real problem posed by the play is the nature of love.

H. also wrote witty, elegant comedies (*Gerts have*, 1894). *Jeg vil vaerge mit land* (1912) is a work of political criticism.

H.'s stylistic technique, strongly influenced by the French spirit which he had come to know during long residence in Paris, is displayed most clearly in his essays.

FURTHER WORKS: *Kong Midas* (1890); *Konstnere* (1893); *Det store lod* (1895); *Folkeraadet* (1897); *Harald Svans mor* (1899); *Pariserbreve* (1900); *Kjærlighet til naesten* (1902); *Paradesengen* (1913); *Set og hørt* (1917); *Samlede dramatiske verker* (4 vols., 1917); *Ibsen og Bjørnson på scenen* (1918); *Franske visitter* (1919); *Norsk teater* (1920); *1905* (1923); *Salt og sukker* (1924); *Novellisten Kinck* (1927)

BIBLIOGRAPHY: Bab, J., *Das Drama der Liebe* (1925); Skavlan, E., *G. H.* (1950); Rudler, R., "Holberg: Ibsens regi," *Nordisk Tidsskrift*, XXXVIII (1962), 323-42

CARL KEILHAU

HEIDENSTAM, (Carl Gustav) Verner von
Swedish poet, b. 6 July 1859, Olshammar, Närke; d. 20 May 1940, Övralid, Östergötland

H. was the first to free Swedish poetry from the fetters of the "social problem poetry" of the 1890's and of naturalism (q.v.), and thus became the leader of a new literary school which no longer regarded poetry as a tool of ideology. This group, which was gifted with unusual poetic imagination, sought a renewal of poetic form through rhythm.

Because of his poor health H. as a young man spent a number of years in the Middle East. This provided the material for his first collection of poems, *Vallfart och vandringsår* (1888). In 1892 *Hans Alienus* appeared, a broadly conceived psychological novel with dreamlike and fantastic interludes. The volume of poems *Dikter* (1895) shows H.'s imagination and his descriptive powers—which have much in common with the visual arts—at their peak. *Om svenskarnas lynne* (1896) deals with the Swedish national character. *Karolinerna* (2 vols. 1897-98) and *Folkungaträdet* (2 vols., 1905-1907) are concerned with important periods in Swedish history. While H. tried here to create an artistic, psychological likeness of Charles XII, the main stress falls on the depiction of the ordinary people of that heroic age.

Between 1900 and 1910 H. participated vigorously in national cultural affairs, wrote national-liberal campaign songs, and was an active public speaker. He became involved in a vindictive quarrel with Strindberg (q.v.) and was induced to conform politically to the rightist line, so that in 1914 he found himself in the same camp as Sven Hedin. World War I was a crushing blow to H., and caused him to abandon all political activity. In *Nya dikter* (1915) he sought the meaning of life humbly and in simple, heartfelt words. He was awarded the Nobel Prize in 1916.

FURTHER WORKS: *Från Col di Tenda till Blocksberg* (1888); *Renässans* (1889); *Endymion* (1889); *Pepitas bröllop* (with O. Levertin, 1890); *Klassicitet och germanism* (1898); *Tankar och teckningar* (1899); *Ett folk* (1899); *Sankt Göran och draken* (1900); *Heliga Brigittas pilgrimsfård* (1901); *Skogen susar* (1904); *Svenskarna och deras hövdingar* (1908-1910); *Dagar och händelser* (1909); *Samlade skrifter* (16 vols., 1909-1912); *Proletärfilosofiens upplösning* (1911); *Uppsatser, tal och fantasier* (1929); *När kastanjerna blommade* (1941); *Tankar och utkast* (1941); *Sista dikter* (1942); *Samlade verk*

(Bang, K., and Böök, F., eds., 23 vols., 1943-45); *Dikter i urval* (Aspenström, W., ed., 1959); *Fragment och aforismer* (1959); *V. v. H. och Ellen Belfrage* (Gullberg, H., ed., 1960)

BIBLIOGRAPHY: Blomberg, E., *H. och humanismen* (1940); Kamras, H., *Den unge H.* (1942); Böök, F., *V. v. H.* (2 vols, 1945-46; rev. one volume ed., 1959); Björck, S., *H. och sekelskiftets Sverige* (1946); Axberger, G., *Diktaren och elden* (1959); Björck, S., *V. v. H.* (1959); Brandell, G., *Vid sekletskällor: Studier och essäer* (1961); Stork, C. W., "H. v. H.," *American-Scandinavian Review,* XLIX (1961), 39-44

PER WIESELGREN

HEIJERMANS, Herman

(pseuds.: *Iwan Jelakowitch, Samuel Falkland, Koos Habbema,* etc.), Dutch dramatist and narrative writer, b. 3 Dec. 1864, Rotterdam; d. 22 Nov. 1924, Zandvoort

H. wrote novels and short stories, but he made his greatest reputation as a dramatist. He was an ardent champion of the proletariat and an enemy of all religiosity. He also opposed the bourgeois conception of marriage and glorified free love.

H.'s style was influenced by naturalism (q.v.), although in many works, especially in his novels about children, he tends to succumb to the romanticism of beautiful dreams. He lived in Berlin from 1907 to 1912, later returning to the Netherlands to found a theater company. Some of his work was written in German.

WORKS: *Dora Kremer* (1893); *Trinette* (1893); *Ahasverus* (1893; Eng., 1934); *Kamertjeszonde* (1897); *Schetsen* (1896-1915); *Intérieurs* (1898); *Ghetto* (1899); *Het zevende gebod* (1899); *Op hoop van zegen* (1901; The Good Hope, 1928); *Ora et Labora* (1903); *Schakels* (1903; Links, 1926); *Diamantstad* (1904); *De meid* (1905); *Allerzielen* (1905); *Uitkomst* (1907); *De opgaande zon* (1908; The Rising Sun, 1926); *Berliner Skizzenbuch* (1908); *Glück auf* (1912); *Eva Bonheur* (1917; Eng., n.d.); *De wijze kater* (1919); *De dageraad* (1921); *Van oudts "De Morgenster"* (1924)

BIBLIOGRAPHY: Hulleman, F., *H.s-herinneringen* (1925); Flaxman, S. L., *The Dramatic Work of H. H.* (1949); Spigt, P., "H. H. (1864-1924)," *De Nieuwe Stem,* XIX (1964), 267-76

KAREL REIJNDERS

HELLAAKOSKI, Aaro Antti

Finnish poet, b. 22 June 1893, Oulu; d. 23 Nov. 1952, Helsinki

H. studied natural science, which unmistakably influenced the development of his philosophy, but he was also interested in sculpture and painting.

In 1921 he published *Elegiasta oodiin*; in 1928 the collection of experimental writing *Jääpeili.* After fifteen years of silence *Uusi runo* (1943) and *Huojuvat keulat* (1946) appeared. The *Sarjoja* (1952) show spacious rhythm, plasticity, and a strong meditative element; the thematic keynote is assent—to the world, to fate, and also to his own death. H.'s restrainedly powerful meditative poetry and austere nature lyrics established him as Finland's foremost post-World War II poet.

FURTHER WORKS: *Runoja* (1916); *Nimettömiä lauluja* (1918); *Hiljaisuus* (1949); *Huomenna seestyvää* (1953); *Lumipalloja* (1955)

BIBLIOGRAPHY: Kupiainen, U., *A. H.* (1953)

KAI LAITINEN

HEMINGWAY, Ernest (Miller)

American novelist, short story writer, and journalist, b. 21 July 1899, Oak Park, Ill., near Chicago; d. 2 July 1961, Ketchum, Idaho

In his youth H. had already begun the travels that are reflected in his work and that have also shaped it to suggest an allegorical pilgrimage of a modern Odysseus. From the American youth Nick Adams of many early short stories to the Cuban Santiago of the last novel, *The Old Man and the Sea,* H.'s protagonists shared a concern with performing well under the mental and physical stresses of richly varied life. From his family's summer home in northern Michigan, where H. learned the skills of hunting and fishing from his physician father, to Paris, Spain, Italy, East Africa, and the Gulf of Mexico, where he and his heroes savored life and death, H. made both a personal and literary pilgrimage.

H. came of age at the historical watershed of World War I, when a new literature began confronting new psychological problems. At eighteen he was already a newspaper reporter for the prestigious Kansas City *Star,* and as a volunteer in a Red Cross ambulance unit in Italy he received his violent initiation to life "in our time" when he was blown up by a mortar shell and narrowly escaped death. From this traumatic event and its aftermath of painful psychic rebirth all of H.'s work departs. He and his protagonists are the wounded, sometimes sacrificed heroes, not simply of a world in crisis but of a mythic world emotionally felt by a wide-ranging audience that has crossed intellectual as well as national boundaries. Those of H.'s heroes who survive become, as he put it, "strong at the broken places," but the first reaction of the maimed body and sensibility was a withdrawal from life and then a gradual return to it as a sensitive observer of life. Like many of his heroes H. was a wanderer on the face of the earth, skeptical but enduring as long as the power of his art of writing provided the necessary articulation of his experiences that were nevertheless the common lot of mankind. After the war H. returned to journalism but also began serious writing. While he was European correspondent for the Toronto *Star*, virtually unknown and newly a husband and father, he quit his job and henceforth devoted himself entirely to his creative writing until he had achieved professional skill and status.

H.'s first two slender books, *Three Stories and Ten Poems* (1923) and *in our time* (1924), were both published in Paris in very small editions for very few readers, but his readers and counsellors were of the most influential and helpful sort, including Gertrude Stein, Sherwood Anderson, Ezra Pound, and F. Scott Fitzgerald (qq.v.). In 1925 the expanded *In Our Time* was published in the U.S. and signaled the beginning of a successful and illustrious career. As his literary reputation grew, so did his personal fame as a sportsman and *bon vivant*. Many of the stories spread about his life were apocryphal, but enough of them were true to make the man himself as widely discussed as his work. Unfortunately for the sake of accuracy, much of his fiction was read as autobiography; and unfortunately for the sake of the seriously conceived and carefully written fiction, it was often read as hard-boiled adventure and enjoyed or depreciated on this ground alone.

One of the first examples and an important instance of a confused reading was that given *The Sun Also Rises* (1926), which was commonly read as an epitomized biography of the "lost generation"—the disillusioned, vaguely suffering, yet attractive young men and women whose values and faiths, like some of their very bodies, were also blown up by World War I.

H. denied that he or his sexually incapacitated hero Jake Barnes was "lost," but many readers submerged or overlooked the traditional values like love and courage that H. championed; glamorous nihilism and toughness were more the vogue of the 1920's.

This novel and the next, *A Farewell to Arms* (1929), were written in an understated, informal, but carefully controlled and objective or closely dramatic prose style, even though both novels are first-person narrations. Along with the bulk of the short stories this early work best exemplifies the style that was of great influence in shaping modern prose fiction. The early H. distrusted abstract terms, but still this style was rich in imagery and symbolic action that suggested a tentative ethic or moral code. Certain character types suggested implicit principles: on one hand was the so-called "code hero" who denied or ignored traditional faiths or found them inadequate in coping with a meaningless world. This recurrent character type turned to self-imposed and often stringent rituals that obviated metaphysics. On the other hand were either the careless and undisciplined men with no ritual controls or men living by corrupted beliefs, such as chauvinism or romanticism, that were irrelevant to H.'s efforts to give shape to those values a violent world and careless people had mutilated. Between these extremes, both rather simplistic and naïve, stood the H. protagonist who was drawn to the admirable and controlled life of the code hero but who was also too complex and sensitive to accept the planned discipline of, for example, a matador's or professional hunter's life. By making his "separate peace" in a senseless world at mad war, Lt. Frederic Henry of *A Farewell to Arms* briefly enjoys an idyllic love affair, but inexorable fate destroys the committed and uncommitted alike; there is no escape.

The style of H.'s later work changed somewhat to a prose more loosely structured and more complex than before. This change has been variously judged by his critics. Similarly his subjects and themes evolved into socially and politically conscious contemporary problems. At the time of the swing to the political left by many writers in the U.S. during the 1930's, H. was widely applauded for his championing of the economic "have-nots" and his apparent loss of detachment in *To Have and Have Not* (1937). But this novel was one of his weakest in its stylistic achievement; its experimental techniques were not fully realized.

For Whom the Bell Tolls (1940) also aligned the wandering H. hero—this time in Civil-War Spain—with the left, but H.'s liberalism was far from orthodox. His conclusion in this novel, his most ambitious and possibly his best, was that neither political programs nor action in their behalf offered a substitute for the individual's need to obtain salvation for himself through tragedy, love and self-knowledge. The hero, Robert Jordan, fought for the Spanish loyalists against the Fascists; but this widely acclaimed novel has never been published in the Soviet Union, although H.'s other work has been given an audience there.

H. participated in World War II, first as a modern privateer on antisubmarine duty in the Gulf of Mexico and then as a war correspondent in Europe. His next novel, *Across the River and Into the Trees* (1950), had for its hero an aging U.S. Army colonel who was having an affair with a young Italian countess in Venice. The story lacked the drama of H.'s previous work, and its critical reception was generally unsympathetic. Yet it, too, was carefully written and perhaps was misunderstood because it was a shift in mood and subject of a still developing, exploring author moving into an unexpected region and upsetting some critical preconceptions.

His last novel, *The Old Man and the Sea* (1952), was even more radically different from his preceding work; but this deceptively simple, short fable of the courage, faith, love, and endurance of a poor Cuban fisherman was widely acclaimed. It both won H. a Pulitzer Prize and helped win him the Nobel Prize for Literature in 1954. Although he had conceived other ambitious projects, this novella was to be his last book published in his lifetime.

H.'s nonfiction is of widely varying quality and seriousness, but it includes some of his best work: *Death in the Afternoon* (1932), an unsurpassed book on bullfighting, also contains important statements on his aesthetics; *Green Hills of Africa* (1935) is a novelistic but factual narrative of his hunt for big game on safari in East Africa; *A Moveable Feast* (1964), his reminiscences, mainly set in Paris in the 1920's, includes sketches of Ezra Pound, Gertrude Stein and F. Scott Fitzgerald.

Along with William Faulkner (q.v.), H. is often considered the major writer of fiction in American literature of the twentieth century. Some critics reserve this praise for his short stories only, but H.'s vision of man is most completely and powerfully presented in his novels. The volume of his work was not great, but it was consistently professional, and his influence as a stylist is unquestioned. For some readers H.'s value stops at a grudging appreciation of his style and at a belief that he is anti-intellectual and even adolescent. But as the exact quality of that style comes to be better understood and is seen as an organic medium for the expression of symbolic meaning and human understanding, his reputation grows.

FURTHER WORKS: *The Torrents of Spring* (1926); *Men Without Women* (1927); *Winner Take Nothing* (1933); *The Spanish Earth* (1938); *The Fifth Column and the First Forty-nine Stories* (1938); *Complete Stories* (1954); *By-Line: E. H.* (1967)

BIBLIOGRAPHY: Warren, R. P., "E. H.," *Kenyon Review,* IX (Winter 1947), 1-28; McCaffery, J. K. M., ed., *E. H.: The Man and His Work* (1950); Baker, C., *H.: The Writer as Artist* (1952; 3d ed. 1963); Young, P., *E. H.* (1952; rev. ed., 1966); Fenton, C. A., *The Apprenticeship of E. H.: The Early Years* (1954); Baker, C., ed., *H. and His Critics: An International Anthology* (1961); Hemingway, L., *My Brother, E. H.* (1962); Lewis, R. W., Jr., *H. on Love* (1965)

ROBERT W. LEWIS, JR.

The primary intent of his writing, from first to last, has been to seize and project for the reader what he has often called "the way it was." This is a characteristically simple phrase for a concept of extraordinary complexity, and Hemingway's conception of its meaning has subtly changed several times in the course of his career—always in the direction of greater complexity.

Carlos Baker, *Hemingway: The Writer as Artist* (1952), p. 48

Hemingway uses symbolism . . . with a severe restraint that in his good work always staunchly protects his realism. So likewise does he use irony. It is the ambiguity of life itself that Hemingway has sought to render, and if irony has served him peculiarly well it is because he sees life as inescapably ironic. But if we must classify him let us do him justice: with all his skilful use of artistic ambiguity, he remains the great *realist* of twentieth-century American fiction.

E. M. Halliday, "Hemingway's Ambiguity: Symbolism and Irony," *American Literature,* XXVIII (March 1956), 22

He is, within his honestly stated limits, and despite the weaknesses and idiosyncrasies that belong to the coarser element of his mind, a writer whose subject is *l'essence de l'homme et son tragique immuable*. . . . I place Hemingway, in his own modest way, in the great and almost defunct classical tradition.

Sean O'Faolain, *The Vanishing Hero* (1956), p. 142

He has won his reputation as an artist of the first rank by operating within limits that would have stifled a lesser writer. But within and because of these limits, he has in his best work uttered a lyric cry that—although it may not resemble the full orchestra of Tolstoy or the organ tones of Melville—is nonetheless a moving and finely wrought response to our times.

Robert P. Weeks, "Introduction," *Hemingway* (1962), p. 16

Hemingway's "man" is not an ideal, not a glorified Superman type. He represents the proper, the necessary life species for a world which beats us down. . . . It is a back-to-the-wall position; no one knows whether anything remains to be gained, whether man can again move forward and come through. This is Hemingway's point of departure, the ground plan on which he constantly erects new characters and plots. There are plenty of diffident humane sidelights, but the dominant idea is that it is time to talk about a man rather than about Man. Reality's brutal enmity for man is Hemingway's "ontological" premise.

Hans Blumenberg, "Über das Werk Ernest Hemingways," in *Hochland* 48 (1955-56), 221

Hemingway is a very deliberate artist; he constructs, describes a tight circle, relates the beginning to the end. The style of understatement, the suppression of emotion, the almost indifferent handling of the extraordinary, calls for the visualization of what is unspoken, for a true appraisal and evaluation of what has not been said. Thus the subjective will may be easily recognized behind the very objectivity of his—extremely objective—reporting. Hemingway's artistry really proves itself in the significance of what is left unsaid, in the gesture of falling silent.

Wilhelm Grenzmann, *Weltdichtung der Gegenwart* (1958), p. 409

HENRY, O.

(pseud. of *William Sydney Porter*), American short story writer, b. 11 Sept. 1862, Greensboro, N. C.; d. 5 June 1910, New York

A doctor's son, H. left school at fifteen and worked for the next five years in his uncle's drug store. He then moved to Texas for his health, settling in 1884 in Austin, where he worked first as a bookkeeper and then for four years as a clerk in a land office. In 1887 he married, and about this time he began sending short sketches to newspapers. He was a teller at the First National Bank in Austin in 1891.

In 1894 H. bought a weekly newspaper, *The Iconoclast*, in which he published mainly satire, humorous pieces, and burlesques. After the financial failure of the paper H. became a columnist on the Houston *Post* in 1895. In 1896 he was indicted for embezzlement of some eleven hundred dollars from the Austin bank, and fled to South America to escape prosecution. The question of his guilt or innocence has never been satisfactorily cleared up. H. returned to Texas in 1897 to face the charges, and in 1898 was sentenced to five years in the Ohio penitentiary; after serving three years and three months, he was paroled for good behavior in 1901.

H.'s stories were first published in leading magazines while he was in jail awaiting trial; later, in prison, he worked hard at learning the craft of writing. After his release he settled in New York to earn his living with his pen. Poor at first, be became an alcoholic; but he quickly achieved fame when he started to provide the New York *World* in 1903 with one story each week at a hundred dollars per story, an unusually high fee at that time. In 1904 his first book, *Cabbages and Kings*, was published; in 1906 appeared his most famous collection, *The Four Million*, whose title is a pun on and a rebuke of the well-known description of New York's leading society as "the Four Hundred."

In 1907 H. married for the second time, and during the next three years he lived a secluded life, writing constantly. He had produced over six hundred stories when he died.

H.'s work has been hugely successful with the public, and many of his stories have been much translated. Full of warm humor and vivid imagination, they show great narrative skill only occasionally marred by traces of journalistic writing and haste. H. was fatalistic in his outlook, and he dealt often with the idea of chance in the lives of people of all social classes; but while a frequent ingredient of his stories is sad misfortune, he avoided dreariness and dismal melancholy as well as evil and squalidness in his subject matter. A devoted and accurate observer of the common life about him, H. always showed for life's unfortunates a concern and compassion which he had learned from his own bitter experiences. His style is characterized by severe understatement that leads most frequently to a "surprise" ending; thus in these respects his stories resemble certain ones by Maupassant.

The most famous stories of H. are those about New York's "four million," but probably more lasting in effect and literary value are those of the South and Southwest, which show less straining for effect and more carefully developed and subtle narration. Established in his memory, the annual O. Henry Memorial Award has been given since 1918 for the best story of the year.

FURTHER WORKS: *The Trimmed Lamp* (1907); *Heart of the West* (1907); *The Gentle Grafter* (1908); *The Voice of the City* (1908); *Roads of Destiny* (1909); *Options* (1909); *Whirligigs* (1910); *Let Me Feel Your Pulse* (1910); *The Two Women* (1910); *Strictly Business* (1910); *The Gift of the Wise Men* (1911); *Sixes and Sevens* (1911); *Rolling Stones* (1912); *Waifs and Strays* (1917); *Complete Writings* (14 vols., 1917); *O. Henryana* (1920); *Letters to Lithopolis* (1922); *Postscripts* (1923); *Collected Works* (18 vols., 1929)

BIBLIOGRAPHY: Smith, C. A., *O. H.* (1916); Jennings, A. J., *Through the Shadows with O. H.* (1921); Williams, W. W., (1936); Clarkson, P. S., (1938); Long, E. H., *O. H.: The Man and His Work* (1949); Kramer, D., *The Heart of O. H.* (1954); Langford, G., *Alias O. H., A Bibliography of William Sydney Porter* (1957)

EUGEN KURI

HERDAL, Harald
Danish poet and novelist, b. 1 July 1900, Copenhagen

H., who continues the tradition of Andersen Nexø, is one of the leading representatives of social realism. He came from a proletarian background and tried his hand at various occupations, at the same time educating himself in public libraries.

In a series of social realist and collectivist novels he described the bitter experiences of his life. These uncompromising, truthful, disillusioned books (*Man skal jo leve*, 1934; *En lidt almindelig Historie*, 1934; *Løg*, 1935) present a picture of the lower strata of contemporary Danish society. Like many of his generation, H. was associated with the Communist movement, but was expelled from the party for his critical attitude. His best work is his three-volume autobiography, *Barndom, De unge År, Læreår* (1944-46).

FURTHER WORKS: *Den første verden* (1936); *Mens vi blir voksne* (1937); *Tusmørke* (1943); *Ukuelige menneske* (1949); *Digte 1929-49* (1949); *Den Danske Sommer* (1963); *Læreår* (1963); *Udvalgte fortællinger* (1967)

BIBLIOGRAPHY: Møller Kristensen, S., *Dansk litteratur 1918-1952* (6th ed., 1962), s.v. "H."

PETER P. ROHDE

HERNÁNDEZ, Miguel
Spanish poet, b. 30 Oct. 1910, Orihuela; d. 28 March 1942, Alicante

During his childhood H. was a shepherd in his native village. Friends helped him with his education and encouraged him to write. He completely mastered classical Spanish poetry—Góngora, Quevedo, Garcilaso, and Calderón. In 1935 he went to Madrid, where he became friendly with Aleixandre, Neruda (qq.v.), and José María de Cossío (b. 1893). During the civil war he supported the republic, and in 1937 visited Moscow and Leningrad. He was arrested after the war and died in prison.

H. did not write much, but his work shows remarkable originality. His first book, *Perito en lunas* (1933), which is notable for its technical artistry in the style of Góngora, was followed by *Quien te ha visto y quien te ve* (1934), an attempt to revive the Calderónesque religious play. *El rayo que no cesa* (1936) established H. in the first rank of Spanish lyric poets. In these love sonnets, which display great technical resources and whose tone recalls the melancholy of Garcilaso and the stern stoicism and compressed style of Quevedo, H. revealed unusual strength of feeling. His next theme, taken up in *Viento del pueblo* (1936) and in the drama *El labrador de más aire* (1937), influenced by Lope de Vega, was communal life, the nation, and the war. His last poems depict with great emotional depth his love for his wife and son, and his unhappiness and loneliness as a prisoner.

H. stands at the juncture which marked the decline of the poets of the period between 1920 and 1936 and the rise of the postwar generation. As a literary phenomenon he represents a reversion to the form and style of classicism. He created a poetry of human passions, masculine yet elegiac, to which the poets of the last decade have been deeply responsive.

FURTHER WORKS: *El hombre acecha*

(1939); *El silbo vulnerado* (1949); *Cancionero y romancero de ausencias* (1958); *Obra escogida* (1952); *Obras completas* (1959)

BIBLIOGRAPHY: Guerrero Zamora, J., *M. H., poeta* (1955); Couffon, C., *Orihuela y M. H.* (1963); Gullón, R., "El rayo de Miguel," *Sur,* 294 (1965), 86-97

GONZALO SOBEJANO

HERRERA Y REISSIG, Julio
Uruguayan lyric poet, b. 1 Aug. 1875, Montevideo; d. 18 March 1910, Montevideo

H. stands out as one of the most original of the group of modernist poets flourishing in Spanish America at the beginning of the 20th c. In his ten brief years of poetic creation (1900-10) he produced a series of books (*Las pascuas del tiempo*, 1900; *Los maitines de la noche*, 1902; *Los éxtasis de la montaña*, 1904, 1910; *Los parques abandonados*, 1908; *La torre de las esfinges*, 1909; *Las clepsidras,* 1910) reflecting much of the taste and tenor of the modernist movement: a striving and straining for originality in expression; an emphasis on vivid colors, plasticity of form, and musicality of verse; voluptuous, frivolous, and hedonistic tones; and a delighted wallowing in the exotic.

The ivory-tower poet par excellence, in both his rather bohemian life and his works, H. tried frenziedly to escape from humdrum realities and a hostile bourgeois society, turning to exotic sources for most of his inspiration—the opulent, sensual world of Greco-Roman mythology; the dark, satanic spheres of French decadent and symbolist poets, etc.—always shunning the facile and obvious and seeking out the subtle and bizarre. Like a glittering dragonfly, he went skimming over the modernist garden, flashing, iridescent, dazzling at times but also elusive and dizzying to follow. He possessed an extraordinary imagination that loved to heap metaphor upon metaphor, often producing a rich kaleidoscope of images.

H. handled various metrical forms, long poems and short, with grace and ease, but he had a particular gift for the sonnet. In addition to his several well-known volumes composed entirely in that form, he translated from the French Albert Samain's collection *Aux Flancs du vase.*

FURTHER WORKS: *La vida* (1900); *Ciles alucinada* (1903); *Sonetos vascos* (1906); *Berceuse blanca* (1910); *Obras completas* (5 vols,

1911-13); *Prosas* (1918); *Poesías completas* (1941, 1951)

BIBLIOGRAPHY: Gicovate, B., *J. H. and the Symbolists* (1956); Bula Píriz, R., *H. y R. Vida y obra. Bibliografía. Antología* (1952); de Torre, G., *Estudio preliminar a Poesías completas* (1945)

GEORGE D. SCHADE

HERRMANN-NEISSE, Max
German poet, novelist and playwright, b. 23 May 1886, Neisse, Silesia; d. 8 April 1941, London

H.-N. comes from old Silesian Protestant peasant stock. His work reflected this origin throughout his life, even during the years of emigration in Switzerland and England. It represents an almost perfect blending of regionalism and expressionism and, last but not least, of matter-of-fact style in the manner of Erich Kästner (q.v.), without Kästner's mannerisms. Thomas Mann (q.v.), in the introduction to one of H.-N.'s volumes of poetry praises his lucidity and his *Gefühlsvernunft,* the harmony of reason and emotion of his verse. There are distinct traces of Protestant religiosity in this poetry, despite its secular coloring, although it lacks the old Silesian trend toward mysticism still to be found in Gerhart Hauptmann (q.v.) or Hermann Stehr (1864-1940).

H.-N. bravely overcame the resentments caused by his physical defect, and his last books show no sign of any bitter feelings aside from nostalgia and frustrations, qualities essential to the literature of exile. Being a hunchback, to be sure, does not prevent anybody from achieving greatness.

Although H.-N. wrote novels, novelettes, and plays—his comedy *Albina and Aujust* (*Josef, der Sieger*) became a hit in the performances of the Kleines Berliner Schauspielhaus in 1919 —he is foremost a lyrical poet whose work culminated in the two last collections of verse written outside his homeland.

After his studies in the universities of Munich and Breslau in German literature and art history he returned to his native city, where he worked as theater critic for the *Neisser Tageblatt.* Gerhart Hauptmann, Alfred Kerr (q.v.), and Oskar Loerke (1884-1941) sponsored him, and he contributed to well-known expressionist magazines such as *Aktion, Pan, Die weißen Blätter, Dichtung, Mistral,* etc. He moved to Berlin in 1917. In 1933, after Hitler took over the government in Germany, he left the country and did not retreat into the "inner emigration," chosen by so many other writers, because of his vehement loathing of nationalism, war, and Nazi barbarism. He went first to Switzerland, then, after a short stay in France and Holland, to London, which he disliked intensely. He always longed for his beloved Zürich, his favorite place of refuge, and even more for a cleansed and renewed Germany. It is as if the title of one of his early collections of verse, *Verbannung* ("Exile,"; 1919) had shown a presentiment of his final fate.

FURTHER WORKS: *Ein kleines Leben* (1906); *Das Buch Franziskus* (1911); *Porträte des Provinztheaters* (1913); *Sie und die Stadt* (1914); *Empörung, Andacht, Ewigkeit* (1917); *Die Laube der Seligen* (1919); *Die Preisgabe* (1919); *Cajetan Schaltermann* (1920); *Hilflose Augen* (1920); *Der Flüchtling* (1921); *Der letzte Mensch* (1922); *Im Stern des Schmerzes* (1924); *Die Begegnung* (1925); *Der Todeskandidat* (1927); *Einsame Stimme* (1927); *Abschied* (1928); *Musik der Nacht* (1932); *Um uns die Fremde* (1936, introduction by Thomas Mann); *Letzte Gedichte* (1941); *Mir bleibt mein Lied* (1941); *Heimatfern* (1945); *Erinnerung und Exil* (1946); *Lied der Einsamkeit* (1961); *Die Entstehung der berufsmäßigen Schauspielkunst im Altertum und in der Neuzeit* (1962)

BIBLIOGRAPHY: Milch, W., in *Der Oberschlesier*, XII (1932); Alker, E., "M. H.-N.," in *Neue Zürcher Nachrichten*, 290 (1946); Anon., "Der schlesische Nachfahr Eichendorffs," *Der Wächter,* 11 (1947-57); Grieger, F., *M. H.: Eine Einführung in sein Werk und eine Auswahl* (1951); Groeger, A. C., "Dem Andenken von M. H.-N.," *Schlesien*, VI (1961), 75-78.

ERNST WALDINGER

HERZMANOVSKY-ORLANDO, Fritz von

Austrian narrative writer, b. 30 April 1877, Vienna; d. 27 May 1954, Merano

H. may well be the last representative of the Austrian type which, having its habitat somewhere between the Baroque and the Grotesque, is a compound of Germanic-Slavic and Latin elements (H.'s name itself is an example); it is precisely this mixture that enables these men to take a detached, universalistic stance.

H. came from an old titled family of government officials. His preferred source of ideas and subjects was yellowing documents of the period leading to the revolution of 1848, but he also reached still further back. His major work, *Maskenspiel der Genien* (1929-31), still in manuscript form at his death, is a grandiosely designed novel about Austria's mystical mission; its setting is the dream country of "Tarokkania" (conceived long before Musil [q.v.] conceived his "Kakania"). *Gaulschreck im Rosennetz* (1928) is a brilliant, farcical variant of the long-outmoded novel of courtly intrigue. The very titles of H.'s other works, such as "Exzellenzen ausstopfen—ein Unfug" ("Taxidermy of Noble Lords Is a Misdemeanor"), "Sellawie, oder Hamlet der Osterhase" ("Sellawie or Hamlet, the Easter Bunny"), or "Tyroler Drachenspiel" ("Tyrolean Dragon Play"), suggest a writer who combines a crotchety logic and a delight in spinning fantastic tales with a penchant for the uncanny and absurd. Critics have compared H. with Jean Paul (1763-1825), Nestroy (1801-1862), and Hašek (q.v.). He was rediscovered and revived in 1957 with the first performance, at the Munich Kammerspiele, of *Kaiser Joseph und die Bahnwärterstochter*, dramatized by Torberg (q.v.), who is editor of H.'s complete works (5 vols., 1957-62).

BIBLIOGRAPHY: Akselrad, R.-M., "F. von H.-O.," *BA*, XXXVIII (1964), 376-80; Eisenreich, H., "Der Illusionist und seine Wirklichkeiten," *Merkur*, XVIII (1964), 494-96; Torberg, E., "Die Österreichische Spirale" (commemorative survey article), *WZ*, X: iv (1964), 1-6

FRIEDRICH ABENDROTH

HESSE, Hermann

German narrative writer, poet, and essayist, b. 2 July 1877, Calw, Württemberg; d. 9 Aug. 1962, Montagnola, Switzerland

H. was a lyricist and a teller of tales. The melodic language of his poetry is also that of his prose, where it was first brought to perfection. The fact that this language also gave form to problematic content drawn from H.'s own life establishes his position in 20th c. German literature as that of one who, in tune with his time yet caught in tradition, goes his own solitary way.

H. was of Baltic origin on his father's side, Swabian on his mother's. His parents first met at Calw; both were in the service of the Basel

Mission and lived in its atmosphere; both had been in India, where his mother was in fact born. In "Kindheit des Zauberers" (*Gesammelte Dichtungen*, IV) H. wrote of his childhood home: "Many worlds, many parts of the globe stretched out their arms and beamed their light to meet and mingle in our house. . . . Here there was praying and Bible-reading; here people studied and read Indian philology; here was good music-making; here Buddha and Lao-Tzu were known. . . ." From 1881 to 1886 the H. family lived in Basel, where the father took out Swiss citizenship. After their return to Germany it was decided that H. should become a theologian, and he was sent to the Latin Grammar School in Göppingen to prepare for the so-called "regional examination," which he passed in 1891. In the autumn of that year he entered the Protestant theological seminary of the Maulbronn monastery but ran away the following spring. From then on he went his own way, though at first still under the guidance of his parents. This turned out to be a detour, involving another abortive attempt to stay at school, three days as a shopkeeper's apprentice, six months as his father's assistant, then a year and a half's training in a Calw mechanic's shop and church-clock factory. He did, however, manage to complete his apprenticeship to a Tübingen bookdealer, begun in October 1895, and from then until 1903 earned his living as a bookdealer (from 1899 on in Basel). The choice of this occupation probably stemmed as much from his love of reading as from a desire to become self-supporting in order to carry out his literary plans. H. used his self-acquired professional training not only as a means of immersing himself in the world of poetry and thought but also to assure himself of his own talent. The *Romantische Lieder,* written in Tübingen between 1895 and 1898, and nine prose studies entitled *Eine Stunde hinter Mitternacht,* appeared in 1899. *Die hinterlassenen Schriften und Gedichte von Hermann Lauscher,* edited by H., was followed in 1902 by another volume of *Gedichte.* Through an introduction by the Swiss writer Paul Ilg, H. now established his momentous connection with the publishing house of S. Fischer, which in 1904 published *Peter Camenzind* (Eng., 1961) after it had been serialized in the *Neue Rundschau.* This book, H.'s first real success, enabled him to earn his living as a writer from then on. He married that year and settled first in Gaienhofen on Lake Constance, where he induced his friend Ludwig Finckh (1876-1964) to join him.

This was the beginning of H.'s "bourgeois period," of which Ball (q.v.) has written: "For better or worse the writer H. is still dominated in his whole attitude to life by the judgment of his parents and relatives. It pleases him to have proved to those at home that even the profession of writing can keep the wolf from the door, given a bright, alert talent." According to Ball, H.'s development had "reached a dead end." Only personal crises and later the war years opened a way out— though this way led also to new perils previously unsuspected even by H. himself.

In 1912 H. moved to Bern, soon after returning from a visit to India in 1911, which at the time seemed more disappointing than rewarding. As a German citizen married to a Swiss wife—H.'s father had had his son's German citizenship restored for the sake of the regional examination—he was unable to share in the 1914 war fervor or in the attitude many German writers adopted toward the war. His essay, "O Freunde, nicht diese Töne!" in the *Neue Zürcher Zeitung* provoked extremely violent political attacks on him from Germany; the aftereffects persisted until at least 1945. However, H. did valuable social work for prisoners of war during World War I, especially in connection with supplies for German prisoners. But at this time he again suffered acute inner crises, as had happened before while he was a student at Maulbronn. ("I was back at school again; again I had to unlearn my contented acceptance of myself and of the world. Only through this experience did I cross the threshold of initiation into life" [*Kurzgefaßter Lebenslauf*, 1925]). Nervous breakdown, marital trouble (divorce, 1919), psychoanalytic therapy (1916-17)—altogether the war years were a time of multiple conflicts for H.

With *Demian,* however, written in 1917 and first published under the pseudonym Emil Sinclair, he made a fresh start. This work was even awarded the Fontane Prize, though H. returned it when the book's true authorship became known. In 1919 he moved from Bern to Montagnola, above Lake Lugano in the canton of Ticino, which was henceforth to be his home. In 1923 he became a Swiss citizen. In 1946 he received the Nobel Prize and the Goethe Prize of the City of Frankfurt, and in 1955 the Peace Prize of the German bookdealers' association.

Few of H.'s contemporaries were more to him than literary acquaintances: in his early days Ludwig Finckh was among those few, and

HERMANN HESSE

in the 1920's Ball, whose last work, written in 1927, was a biography of H. which is still basic. But in the last years of his life there were hardly any famous men among H.'s friends, except perhaps Thomas Mann (q.v.), and hardly any contemporary influences. On the other hand his entire work, deeply attuned to the landscape of southern Germany, was inspired again and again by Novalis (1772-1801), Hölderlin (1770-1843), Mörike (1804-1875), and Eichendorff (1788-1857), and by the folk song.

H.'s work up to 1914, his "first period" (which extends to *Knulp* [1915]), consists of three volumes of poems and the prose works *Peter Camenzind, Unterm Rad* (1906; The Prodigy, 1957), *Gertrud* (1910; Gertrude and I, 1915), and *Roßhalde* (1914). Hugo Ball has called *Peter Camenzind* "a vehement attempt by the writer to create his dwelling place." Here pure nature holds sway. Through the Gottfried Kelleresque overtones a new language is already becoming audible—H.'s own—full of musicality and romanticism, simple and forceful. Many traits of the hero provide clues to the writer's own life; there is a constant merging of the autobiographical with the not yet realized but secretly hoped for; yet in all this indeterminate yearning there is renunciation. The school novel *Unterm Rad,* a poetic reflection of H.'s brief time at Maulbronn, is artistically inferior to *Freund Hein* by Strauss (q.v.) and *Verwirrungen des Zöglings Torleß* by Musil (q.v.), yet it was the most successful of these and related works on this favorite early 20th c. theme. The background of *Gertrud* and *Roßhalde* is much closer to the bourgeois world, despite the "artistic" milieu in which they seem to be set (music in *Gertrud,* painting in *Roßhalde*). The theme of *Gertrud* is renunciation and consolation through art; that of *Roßhalde* the collapse of an already disintegrating marriage in which the husband's devotion to art is mere window dressing, as though art were just another profession. *Knulp —Drei Geschichten aus dem Leben Knulps* is about a nonbourgeois type, a vagabond driven by an unhappy youthful love affair to an unsettled life, which he nevertheless on the whole accepts.

Knulp marks the end of H.'s "Swabian" period. His visit to India in 1911 had proved unrewarding (*Aus Indien. Aufzeichnungen einer indischen Reise,* 1913). To quote Ball: "He revived some submerged childhood images and gained insights which enabled him to see European quarrels in a larger perspective. But the journey did not set him free, was not much help to him personally."

Demian represents a manifesto of inner liberation and change. In an essay commemorating H.'s seventieth birthday, Curtius (q.v.) wrote "H.'s literary work had not reached the younger generation. But this changed as if by magic in 1922 [i.e., 1919] when *Demian* [Eng, 1923] appeared. *Demian* speaks with the voice of a writer who is no longer talking only about himself." To use the phrase of Novalis, H. had begun his "inward journey" and was taking others with him. The short stories "Kinderseele," "Klein und Wagner," and "Klingsors letzter Sommer," written in 1920, were published in 1931 together with *Siddharta* (Eng., 1951), under the title *Weg nach Innen.* "Klein und Wagner" and "Klingsors letzter Sommer" are suffused with the contemporary expressionist style in which H. was also painting at that time—simplifying the style in his painting but heightening it in his fiction. In *Siddharta* the visit to India bore fruit again, this time more maturely and conclusively than in the India book of 1913. The most important books between *Siddharta* and *Steppenwolf* (1927; Eng., 1929) were two autobiographical experiments, *Der Kurgast* (1925; originally *Psychologia Balnearia oder Glossen eines Badener Kurgastes,* 1924) and *Die Nürnberger Reise* (1927), written in a new tone which leans toward precision and humor. Their self-irony and serenity mask a dissonance which often comes through, finding stark expression later especially in *Steppenwolf.*

In the novel *Narziß und Goldmund* (1930; Death and the Lover, 1932) H. attains a new level. Here intellectual man, the thinker, is contrasted with the artist, and their differing ways of life are illustrated. Goldmund knows nothing of his true vocation when he is sent to the monastery, where Narziß, only a little older, is already a teacher (later to become a monk and abbot). Narziß makes him aware of this vocation. Goldmund runs away from the monastery and gives himself over to "life," as his temperament demands. Goldmund's very worldly life keeps the story flowing. Later the two are brought together again. Goldmund, saved by Narziß from mortal danger, ends as a woodcarver in the monastery of which Narziß is the head. In its clear composition and its discussion of the problems of the spirit versus life, of aceticism versus the sensual pleasure, which are now successfully balanced with each other, *Narziß und Goldmund* may well be the climax of H.'s work up to that time. In its maturity, however, this book belongs to his final period.

The outstanding work of this last period is *Das Glasperlenspiel* (1943; Magister Ludi, 1949), for which *Die Morgenlandfahrt* (1932; The Journey to the East, 1957) served as a kind of preliminary sketch. The eastward wayfarers to whom *Das Glasperlenspiel* was to be dedicated are those who throughout the ages, joined in secret brotherhood, have made the pilgrimage "to the East, to the abode of light" in their pursuit of self-realization. Thus H. can playfully shift time and place as he pleases. *Das Glasperlenspiel*, an attempt to depict the life of Josef Knecht, the "Magister Ludi" or Master of the Game, together with Knecht's posthumous works, occupied H. from 1931 on but did not appear until 1943 in Switzerland and 1946 in Germany. This is a retrospective survey of "the age of popular journalism" seen from about the year 2400 (to the extent that the present is needed at all to understand the story of the Game). Yet it is far from being Utopian. The theme of this Game "with all the content and values of our culture," practiced by the Castalian Order, becomes the heart of the life story of Josef Knecht, the Master of the Game: his apprenticeship, his elevation to Master, his resignation from office, and his brief remaining life in the "world." In the detached form of a chronicle and scholarly report whose sources are not easily accessible, *Das Glasperlenspiel* assembles nearly all of H.'s themes, this time treated with serene irony. The world of action is contrasted with the contemplative world, which is both a world of the spirit and a religiously spiritual world. In this confrontation the chances of the humanistic world of the spirit are no longer rated very highly. As Curtius summed it up: "In this work of the poet's old age all the earlier stages of his life have become transparent to him. He has reached the stage of second sight.... *Das Glasperlenspiel* is the outcome and testimonial of an act of self-healing—the only genuine and worthy kind of healing because it rises from the very heart of the personality. Psychoanalysis, yoga, and Chinese wisdom were footholds. 'The awakened one' no longer has need of them." In a *Rundbrief aus dem Engadin* (1953) H. writes (in connection with a rereading of *Narziß und Goldmund*): "Again what struck me most forcibly was that most of my larger stories do not establish new problems or new human images, as the real masters do and as I thought at the time I did. Instead, they repeat with variations those few problems and types that are congenial to me—though from a new vantage point in life and experience."

Aside from the teasing self-mockery of "as the real masters do," which need not be taken too seriously, this is true. It is also strikingly borne out by H.'s poetry, which accompanies his prose work as a constant reminder that his major prose work is lyrical in nature. In addition to the volumes of poetry already mentioned, others appeared under various titles until 1937. In 1942 a collected edition, *Die Gedichte*, was published (first in Switzerland)—a work which H. called "an acknowledgment of what I have lived and done, an unreserved offering of all the material with nothing retouched or suppressed, an affirmation of the whole with all its flaws and questionable aspects." This edition contains over six hundred poems.

The autobiographical element in H.'s creativity has something in common with that of Thomas Mann, but the lyrical element sets him apart from Mann and explains both his lesser intellectual impact and his appeal to "seekers" of all kinds, who find support and hope in H.'s process of growth and inner healing.

FURTHER WORKS: *Boccaccio* (1904); *Franz von Assisi* (1904); *Diesseits* (1907); *Nachbarn* (1908); *Unterwegs* (1911); *Umwege* (1912); *Aus Indien* (1913); *In der alten Sonne* (1914; In the Old Sun, 1914, in German Classics, vol. 19); *Musik der Einsamen* (1915); *Am Weg* (1915); *Brief ins Feld* (1916); *Schön ist die Jugend* (1916; Youth, Beautiful Youth, in *German Stories and Tales,* ed. Robert Pick, 1955); *Kleiner Garten* (1919); *Märchen* (1919); *Zarathustras Wiederkehr* (1919); *Gedichte des Malers* (1920); *Wanderung* (1920); *Blick ins Chaos* (1921); *Ausgewählte Gedichte* (1921); *Italien* (1923); *Sinclairs Notizbuch* (1923); *Prosa* (1925); *Piktors Verwandlungen* (1925); *Bilderbuch* (1926); *Betrachtungen* (1928); *Krisis* (1928); *Eine Bibliothek der Weltliteratur* (1929); *Trost der Nacht* (1929); *Kleine Welt* (1933); *Fabulierbuch* (1935); *Das Haus der Träume* (1936); *Stunden im Garten* (1936); *Gedenkblätter* (1937); *Neue Gedichte* (1937); *Orgelspiel* (1937); *Berthold* (1945); *Der Pfirsichbaum* (1945); *Traumfährte* (1945); *Der Europäer* (1946); *Krieg und Frieden* (1946); *Frühe Prosa* (1948); *Briefe* (1951; augmented ed., 1959);

Späte Prosa (1951); *Gesammelte Dichtungen* (6 vols., 1952); *Zwei Idyllen* (1952); *Engadiner Erlebnisse* (1953); *Beschwörungen* (1955); *Gesammelte Schriften* (7 vols., 1957); *Bericht an die Freunde* (1961); *Traktat vom Steppenwolf* (1961); *Cavaliere Huscher und andere Erzählungen* (1963); *Ein Blatt von meinem Baum* (1964); *H. H.–Thomas Mann: Briefwechsel* (ed. A. Carlson; 1968)

BIBLIOGRAPHY: Ball, H., *H. H. Sein Leben und Werk* (1927; rev. eds., 1947, 1956); Schmid, H. R., *H. H.* (1928); Goes, A., *Rede auf H. H.* (1946); Mileck, J., *H. H. and his Critics* (1958); Baumer, F., *H. H.* (1959); Beerman, H., "H. H. and the *Bhagavad-Gita*," *Midwest Quarterly,* I (1959), 27-40; Furst, L. R., "A Dead End: H.'s *Haus der Träume*," *NM,* LIX (1959), 253-43; Peppard, M. B., "Notes on H.'s Narrative Technique," *Kentucky Foreign Language Quarterly,* VI (1959), 169-78; Fickert, K. J., "The Development of the Outsider Concept in H.'s Novels," *Monatshefte* LII (1960), 171-78; Colky, T. E., "H. H.'s Attitude toward Authority," *DA,* XXI (1961), 3355; Willecke, F. H., "The Style and Form of H. H.'s *Gaienhofer Novellen*," *DA,* XXI (1961), 3463-64; Waibler, H., *H. H.: Eine Bibliographie* (1962); Freedman, R., *The Lyrical Novel: Studies in H. H., André Gide, and Virginia Woolf* (1963); Willson, A. L., "H.'s Veil of Isis," *Monatshefte,* LV (1963), 313-21; Woerner, R. F., "D. H. Lawrence and H. H.: A Comparative Study of Two Critics of Modern Culture," *DA,* XXIV (1963), 306-7; Rose, E., *Faith from the Abyss: H. H.'s Way from Romanticism to Modernity* (1965); Ziolkowski, T., *The Novels of H. H.: A Study in Theme and Structure* (1965)

OSCAR JANCKE

The more intimately H. is bound to nature the less he can find his way in, or accommodate himself to, the disjointed formal world of contemporary civilization. The alien quality of the world which oppresses him so grievously is not only metaphysical but also temporal: "We are travelling in a carriage over an abyss, and the horses have taken fright. We are facing destruction, we must die, all of us, we must be born again, we have arrived at the great turning point."

Maurer, K. W., *Universitas* (1962), pp. 44-45

Demian is Hesse's portrait of the artist as a young man. . . . When all the reservations have been made, *Demian* stands as a classic document of the revolt against the unreflected life. Despite the fanciful touches, Hesse is not a traditional teller of tales but a novelist of ideas and a moralist of a high order. . . . The autobiographical undercurrent gives *Demian* an existentialist intensity and a depth of understanding that is rare in contemporary fiction.

Bauke, J., *Saturday Review* (19 June 1965), p. 38

The secret of H.'s work lies in the creative power of his poetic similes, in the "magic theater" of the panoramas of the soul that he conjures up before the eyes and ears of the world. It lies in the identity of idea and appearance that, to be sure, his work— like any work of human hands—can do no more than suggest. But in H.'s work the asymptotic approximation reaches a point that few beside him can claim to have reached. In suggesting this identity H. H. becomes the mediator of what cannot be said, the prophet of what remains silent, and time and again his creative spontaneity vanquishes the arbitrariness of existence through his "ability to live by the strength of a faith."

Ball, H., *H. H.* (1947), p. 271

His struggle with the basic problems of his life, with the dichotomy of mind and soul, thus leads the poet toward a biocentric world view instead of the logocentrism that has dominated the attitudes of modern European man since the time of the Renaissance.

In the narrative *Die Morgenlandfahrt* . . . there is evidence of an impending change in H.'s attitudes, and in the poem "Besinnung" that change is first given a conceptually clear formulation. Meditation becomes H. H.'s major concern. It assures him the harmonious style of the life of reason imbued with a vital warmth, whose major stress, however, undergoes in *Glasperlenspiel* a progressively apparent shift from the element of warmth to that of reason. The world view of the aging poet, whose power of imagination revolves around the central harmony, becomes progressively logocentric. The Castalian harmony is not—as Goethe's was—an organic growth. It is the fruit of self-discipline, forced into being by a strict monastic code, by meditation, by ascetic self-control exercised under the rules and regulations of sober vigilance, and by the most meticulous exclusion of all external influences from the inner core of the soul. This Castalian harmony is a mask that conceals the face of the wolf of the steppe.

The romanticist H. has thus a classicist H. as his next-door neighbor, and the more the poet approaches the classical ideal of harmony, the more logocentric his world view becomes.

Schmid, M., *H. H.* (1947), p. 223

H. has always believed, together with the eminent Dr. Radhakrishnan . . . that this world can only survive if "we strive for a philosophy which will combine the best of European humanism and

Asiatic religion, a philosophy profounder and more loving than either, endowed with greater spiritual and ethical force, which will conquer the hearts of men and compel peoples to acknowledge its sway" (Radhakrishnan, p. 636).

Beerman, H., Midwest Quarterly
(Autumn 1959), pp. 38–39

The urge to find the "secret" about one's self and the hidden corners of life, curiosity in the widest and most dangerous sense, is the driving force behind H.'s work. It is a ruthless curiosity, shameless and without mercy, and it will not rest until the last veil is drawn back. For this reason then, and not for the sake of psychological subtleties, H. has delved again and again into the minds of vagrants and adolescents, since for them everything is unknown and without name before they have "found out." They are all spies, tracking themselves down, excited by the scent of the Unknown, hankering after secrets.

Seidlin, O., Symposium (1950), p. 328

HEYM, Georg

German poet, b. 30 Oct. 1887, Hirschberg, Silesia; d. 16 Jan. 1912, Berlin

H. was a lyric poet; his position in 20th c. German poetry is unique in that two years before World War I he anticipated the catastrophes and destruction that were to ravage Europe. He was particularly fascinated and horrified by the phenomenon of the modern metropolis, which he saw as a "mechanized jungle." In some respects his visions of destruction and his hatred of the big city recall his model, the Belgian poet Verhaeren (q.v.). H. developed an individual, pessimistic, evocative mode of expression appropriate to his visions of catastrophe. Through his liking for harsh colors and the aggressiveness of his style he rendered in literature what the artists of the "Brücke" school (Otto Mueller, Erich Hekkel, Karl Schmidt-Rottluff, and E. L. Kirchner) were trying to express in painting: the break-up of the bourgeois world. Those elements that in expressionism (q.v.) often developed into tendentiousness and social criticism were heightened in H. to true poetic form. He tended to personify the demonic forces he saw at work in the modern world of the cities. Thus he describes "the God of the city" in these words: "Upon a city block he sprawls/The winds settle black about his brow." While ice-skating on the Havel River in one of Berlin's parks, he fell through the ice and drowned.

Although his somber descriptions of fever hospitals, cemeteries, decaying suburbs, and mortuaries might suggest that H. was a poet committed to nihilism, his poems unmistakably voice a desire for a purer, simpler life. Occasionally his visions take on a gigantic dimension: the landscape joins in the inner movement that has stirred him. Many of his poems ("Der Blinde," for instance) have a symbolic impact equalled perhaps by certain paintings by Emil Nolde or sculpture by Barlach, but by hardly any other German poet of the last few decades.

WORKS: Der Athener Ausfahrt (1907); Der ewige Tag (1911); Atalanta (1911); Umbra vitae (1912); Der Dieb (1913); Marathon (1914; augmented ed. by Schneider, K. L., 1956); Pinthus, K. and Loewensohn, E., eds., Dichtungen (1922); Seelig, C., ed., Gesammelte Gedichte (1947); Schneider, K. L., ed., Dichtungen und Schriften (4 vols., 1960-65)

BIBLIOGRAPHY: Schneider, K. L., Der bildhafte Ausdruck in den Dichtungen G. H.s, G. Trakls und E. Stadlers (1954); Krispyn, E., "Sources and Subject Matter in Two Short Stories of G. H.," Journal of the Australasian Modern Language Association, XII (1960), 52-57; Mahlendorf, U. R., "The Myth of Evil: The Reevaluation of the Judaic Christian Tradition in the Work of G. H.," GR, XXXVI (1961), 180-94; Mautz, K., Mythologie und Gesellschaft im Expressionismus: Die Dichtung G. H.s (1961); Loewenson, E., G. H. oder vom Geist des Schicksals (1962); Schwartz, G., G. H. (1963); Mahlendorf, U. R. "G. H.'s Development as a Dramatist and Poet," Journal of English and Germanic Philology, LXIII (1964), 58-71; Vortriede, W., "The Expressionism of G. H.," WSCL, IV (1963), 284-97

EUGEN GÜRSTER

HIDALGO, José Luis

Spanish poet, b. 10 Oct. 1919, Torres, Santander; d. 3 Feb. 1947, Madrid

H. wrote, painted, and drew from early youth. After the Spanish Civil War he studied art in Valencia.

His first books, Raíz (1944) and Los animales (1945), which are uneven artistically, show the influence of Alberti, García Lorca, and especially Aleixandre (qq.v.), while revealing a gloominess and depth that are all his own. The inner tension of his posthumous Los muertos

(1947) marks H. as an important postwar poet. In monologues full of sadness this religious-minded yet never devout poet turns to a God who appears to him now as problematical or imaginary, now as a cruel, malevolent destroyer of His creatures. Here H. creates, with heart-rending sincerity, a metaphysical landscape of death and negation.

BIBLIOGRAPHY: Rodríguez Alcalde, L., *J. L. H.* (1950); Fernández, A. R. and Susinos Ruiz, F. "J. L. H.: La vivencia poética de J. L. H.," *Archivum* (Oviedo), XI (1961), 231-322; Romano Colengeli, M., *J. L. H., poeta della morte* (1962)

GONZALO SOBEJANO

HINDREY, Karl August
Estonian narrative writer, b. 3 Aug. 1875, Abja; d. 1947

The son of a brewer, H. grew up on a large estate, and studied art in St. Petersburg, Munich, and Paris. He first achieved popularity as a cartoonist and as a writer of witty feuilletons and children's books. In the thirties he started producing serious fiction, beginning with short stories ("Välkvalgus" (1932); "Armastuskiri" (1933); "Sigtuna häving" (1937); "Südamed" (1938); "Hukatus Mälaril" (1939)), most of which keenly analyze, from a conservative point of view, the mentality of the higher Estonian bourgeoisie. His novels (*Sündmusteta suvi*; 1937; *Ja ilma ja inimesi ma tundsin viimati ka,* 1939) share these characteristics. H. successfully revived the historical novel (*Urmas ja Merike,* 1935-36). His stories about animals, interspersed among his other short stories, are remarkable for sympathetic insight and narrative brilliance.

FURTHER WORKS: *Minu elukroonika* (1929); *Murrang* (1930); *Tõnissoni juures* (1931); *Suremise eod* (1935); *Loojak* (1938); *Nõiel* (1948); *Lembitu* (1949); *Kogutud novellid* (1962)

BIBLIOGRAPHY: Harris, E. H., *Estonian Literature* (1947); Oras, A., *Laiemasse ringi* (1961)

ANTS ORAS

HIRSCHBEIN, Peretz
Yiddish playwright and novelist, b. 7 Nov. 1880, government of Grodno, Poland; d. 16 Aug. 1948, Los Angeles

H. received the traditional Hebrew education that prepares for the rabbinate, but his interest was early diverted to literature and writing. His first dramatic efforts, influenced by Russian and Scandinavian writers, were steeped in abject poverty, but were generally artistically unsuccessful. In 1908 he organized a theatrical troupe and toured the cities of Eastern Europe with various Yiddish plays. In 1910 he returned to writing and soon began to work on plays that have a pristine setting and that treat Jewish rustic life with simple but sympathetic humor. Four of them are of high merit: *Di Puste Kretchme* (1912; The Haunted Inn, 1921), *A Farvorfen Winkel* (1912), *Dem Shmidt's Tekhter* (1918), and *Grinne Felder* (1918). Sparkling with pastoral humor, they were performed successfully in New York and other American cities as well as in Europe.

H. was a world traveler, and his books of travel contain concrete and shrewd observation as well as keen understanding of people and events. Perhaps his best writing appears in *Meine Kinder Yoren* (1932), the sensitive and idyllic recollections of his childhood and adolescence. Toward the end of his life he completed another volume of memoirs, *In Gang fun Leben* (1948). He also wrote two long but not wholly successful novels: *Roite Felder* (1935) and *Bovel* (1942). A good part of his writing was translated into several European languages and into English.

FURTHER WORKS: *Gezamelte Drames* (5 vols., 1916); *Lyber America* (1918); *Arum der Welt* (1927); *Alle Werk* (7 vols., 1929-30)

BIBLIOGRAPHY: *Yubiley-bukh P. H.* (1940); *Lexicon fun der Neier Yiddisher Literatur,* ed. S. Niger, J. Shatsky, et al., 1956-68; Glatstein, J., *In Tokh Genumen,* 1960; Madison, C., *Yiddish Literature: Its Scope and Major Writers* (1968)

CHARLES A. MADISON

HJORTØ, Knud
Danish narrative writer, b. 4 Jan. 1869, Kirke Vaerløse; d. 2 Nov. 1931, Frederiksberg

H., who came from a Zealand farm family, studied philology. A year in Paris from 1896 to

109

1897 provided a formative artistic stimulus. He later became a secondary-school teacher.

H. had a speculative mind with a bent for caustic satire, and depicted the cleavage between rural and city culture at the turn of the c. But the principal features of his short stories and novels are his philosophical observations and paradox-prone psychological studies, in which the influence of Stendhal (1783-1842) is clearly discernible. H. also wrote treatises on language.

WORKS: *Syner* (1899); *Folk* (1903); trilogy: *Støv og sterner* (1905); *To verdener* (1905); *Hans Raaskov* (1906); *Grøn ungdom og graa sjaele* (1911); *Aeventyret* (1915); *Fra ordenes samfund* (1918); *Den gule krønike* (1923); *Hans Heilums sidste nat* (1924); *Sprogets luner* (1927); *Svundne somre og gamle vintre* (1931); *Under livets trae* (1932); *Skrift og tale* (1936)

BIBLIOGRAPHY: Friis, O. and Johansen, F., *K. H. Karakteristik og Bibliografi* (1924); Nathansen, H., "K. H.," in *Portrætstudier* (1930)

HEINRICH KRÄMER

HŁASKO, Marek

Polish novelist and short story writer, b. 14 Jan. 1934, Warsaw

H.'s first stories, published in 1955, coincided with the beginnings of the Polish postwar "thaw." By 1957 he had achieved immense popularity as the spokesman for the disenchanted younger generation. He ran afoul of the censorship and defected in 1958 while traveling in Western Europe, moving first to Israel and then, in 1960, to West Germany.

H.'s favorite motif is that of love destroyed by the shabbiness of physical surroundings and by the cynicism and brutality of the world. It is most brilliantly developed in the novel *Ósmy dzień tygodnia* (1956; The Eighth Day of the Week, 1958), which deals with the plight of a young couple who cannot consummate their love because of lack of privacy in war-ravaged Warsaw. In the novel *Cmentarze* (1958; The Graveyard, 1959), published in Paris after his defection, H. depicts the corruption of ideals and human relationships in Stalinist Poland, skillfully combining nightmarish and humorous elements in a brilliant example of sustained grotesque which is perhaps his finest artistic achievement. *Cmentarze* shows the influence of Kafka (q.v.); elsewhere, however, Hemingway's (q.v.) example is supreme: H. cultivates an

extreme economy of style and infuses his stark naturalism with a strain of lyricism.

FURTHER WORKS: *Pierwszy krok w chmurach* (1956); *Next Stop—Paradise* (1960); *Opowiadania* (1963); *Wszyscy byli odwróceni. Brudne e zyny* (1964); *Nawrócony w Jaffie. Opowiem wam o Esther* (1966)

BIBLIOGRAPHY: Anon., "Notes about the Author," in *East Europe*, II (Sept. 1957), 11; Iur'eva, Z., "Marek Hłasko. Cmentarze. Następny do raju," in *Novyi zhurnal*, XVII (June 1958), 285-90; "A Letter from M. H.," *East Europe*, VII: ix (1958), 32-33; Kryński, M. J., "Marek Hłasko—the Lyrical Naturalist," in *PolR*, IV (Autumn 1961), 11-21

MAGNUS JAN KRYŃSKI

HOCHWÄLDER, Fritz

Austrian dramatist, b. 28 May 1911, Vienna

H. was originally a craftsman; his first attempts at playwriting date from about 1930. In 1938 he emigrated to Switzerland and has since lived in Zurich as a journalist. In 1944 he met Kaiser (q.v.). But H.'s strongest creative stimulus came in his youth from the tradition of the Viennese popular theater.

The play *Das heilige Experiment* (1943), which deals with the decline of the Jesuit empire in Paraguay, was performed all over the German-speaking world as well as in Paris, New York, Rome, London and other major cities. It presents the conflict between power and humanity, obedience and conscience. Other plays of H. also treat contemporary problems in historical guise. Thus *Meier Helmbrecht* (1946) takes up the question of the responsibility of the individual and the nation for a wrong done to the community as a whole; out of weakness and acquiescence Helmbrecht allows his son to become an overlord who "devours his country." In *Donadieu* (1953), the subject of which is taken from Conrad Ferdinand Meyer's poem "Die Füße im Feuer," the Huguenot Donadieu's vengeful feelings are transformed into submission to the will of God. In *Der öffentliche Ankläger* (1954) Fouquier-Tinville (of the French Revolution), in the course of passing judgment, condemns himself and the whole absolutist system. In the legendary play *Die Herberge* (1956) the characters are involved in personal decisions about property and life, hidden and patent guilt, self-seeking and justice.

MAREK HŁASKO

HUGO VON HOFMANNSTHAL

FURTHER WORKS: *Jehr* (1932); *Liebe in Florenz* (1936); *Esther* (1940); *Die verschleierte Frau* (1946); *Der Flüchtling* (1948; rev. ed., 1955); *Der Unschuldige* (1949; rev. ed., 1956); *Virginia* (1951); *Hôtel du Commerce* (1954); *Donnerstag* (1959); *Dramen* (1959); *Der Himbeerpflücker* (1965)

BIBLIOGRAPHY: Hochwälder, F., "Über mein Theater," *GL&L*, XII (1959), 102-14; Fontans, O. M., "F. H. zum 50. Geburtstag," *WZ*, VII: v (1961), 10-14; Wellworth, G. E., "F. H.: The Drama within the Self," *Quarterly Journal of Speech*, XLIX (1963), 274-81; Loram, I. C., "F. H.," *Monatshefte*, LVII (1965), 8-16

HANS GROSSRIEDER

HOEL, Sigurd

Norwegian novelist, b. 14 Dec. 1890, Nord-Odal; d. 14 Oct. 1960, Oslo

H. studied natural science at the University of Oslo. He was a teacher from 1912 to 1918 and secretary of the Oslo Academy of Science (*Videnskapsakademiet*) from 1919 to 1924; he then became a literary critic and editor of foreign novels.

In 1922 H. published a novella collection—*Veien vi går.* The novel *Syvstjernen* (1924) is a satire on the Europe of the Treaty of Versailles. So far as the critics and the public were concerned, his breakthrough came with the charming, serene novel *Syndere i Sommersol* (1927). *En dag i Oktober* (1931) is a satirical novel set in Oslo; *Veien til verdens ende* (1934) is a story of Norwegian farm children; and *Fjorten dager før frostnettene* (1935), an erotic novel which is also concerned with fear of life. *Sesam, Sesam* (1938) is an Oslo satire which pays particular attention to the dilemma of the intellectual in the years immediately preceding World War II.

From 1943 to 1945 H. was a refugee in Sweden. *Møte ved Milepelen* (1947) is an account of the psychological problems "that the occupation years made so pressing." *Ved foten av Babels tårn* (1956) describes a generation that does not thrive in the modern welfare state.

H. is among the Norwegian writers who have been most deeply influenced by psychoanalysis; he has always been a sincere admirer and disciple of Freud. As a novelist he relies particularly on the potentialities of satire.

FURTHER WORKS: *Ingenting* (1929); *Mot muren* (1930); *Don Juan* (1930); *Prinsessen på glassberget* (1939); *Arvestålet* (1941); *Tanker i mørketid* (1945); *Tanker fra mange tider* (1948); *Samlede romaner og fortellinger* (8 vols., 1950); *Jeg er blitt glad i en annen* (1951); *Tanker mellom barken og veden* (1952); *Stevnemøte med glemte år* (1954); *Trollringen* (1958); *Essays i utvalg ved Nils Lie* (1962)

BIBLIOGRAPHY: Stai, A., *S. H.* (1950); Krog, H., "Profilen i S.H.," *Vinduet*, XIV (1960), 248-52; Ytreberg, S., "Om pessimisme og optimisme hos S. H.," *Edda*, LII (1965), 315-24

NIELS C. BRÖGGER

HOFMANNSTHAL, Hugo von

Austrian poet, dramatist, essayist, novelist, b. 1 Feb. 1874, Vienna; d. 15 July 1929, Rodaun

H. lived all his life, except for occasional travels in Europe, in or near Vienna. While still a schoolboy, he published poems and essays under the pseudonyms Loris Melikow, Loris, and Theophil Morren. At the University of Vienna he studied first law and then Romance philology, earning his doctorate in 1898. In 1901 he submitted a habilitation thesis, *Studie über die Entwicklung des Dichters Victor Hugo*, with the intention of entering upon an academic career, but withdrew the application a short time later. After his marriage in 1901 he lived in Rodaun, near Vienna, until his sudden death at the age of fifty-five in 1929.

H.'s *oeuvre* contains an astounding richness of all literary forms. Beginning with poetry, short lyrical dramas or playlets, and early, brief essays the poet turned in his later period toward the drama, the libretto, and the mystery play as his main form of expression, while his essayistic work continued throughout his lifetime. In *Ad me ipsum* (1930), notes about himself, the poet states about his early period: "The beginning is pure magic: pre-existence." The concept of pre-existence is for H., in retrospect, a form of existence in which exterior and interior experiences mystically flow together, a consciousness of all things, experienced and even creatively formed before they have been rationally absorbed. In this "state of heightened consciousness" the poet is able to achieve complete identification with other forms of existence, to step out of himself and into the figures he creates. Unity of vision, combined with a richness and splendor of poetic language rarely or perhaps never before found in one so young, put H. on the literary scene already in the early 1890's. He was at that time identified with the neoromantic movement, the turning away from naturalism, impressionism (qq.v.), and the *art pour l'art* tendencies of his older contemporaries.

H., his own severest critic, selected and retained only twenty-six poems when he prepared the last edition of his works published in his lifetime. Almost all of these poems were written between his seventeenth and twenty-third year, the period of pre-existence, which he described as the "loneliest" of his life. Such poems as "Terzinen über die Vergänglichkeit," "Ballade des äußeren Lebens," "Ein Traum von großer Magie," "Reiselied," "Der Schiffskoch, ein Gefangener, singt" (*Gedichte und Lyrische Dramen. Werke in Einzelausgaben*, 1946; Poems and Verse Plays, 1961) belong to the highest achievements in European lyric poetry.

After his first lyrical dramatic work *Gestern* (1891) was published, the attention of the critics turned to only one aspect of H.'s poetic production: the esoteric, impressionistic, self-investigating, precocious preciosity of the very young genius. But other verse dramas of that time, while continuing to display the rich flow of lyrical language, show in their content an increasing concern with human existence in the framework of social responsibility. In fact, all of H.'s lyrical dramas written in the decade which established his fame contain in one form or another, not the message of withdrawal from human experience, but rather a reaching out toward other human beings, a desire to step across a threshold from the isolation of pre-existence into the world of human contacts. Despite a profound understanding of the literary problems of the *fin de siècle*, H. was already critical of it and realized early that his own youthful lyrical productions were the fulfillment, indeed the expression, of just that period. This insight doubtless contributed to the poet's constant striving toward new creative goals.

Proof for this change of attitude can be found in the themes of the early one-act plays. Whereas *Der Tod des Tizian* (1892; The Death of Titian, 1913) deals almost exclusively with the concerns of the artist who is cut off from the problems of the world, much as Titian's garden is protected by a wall from the threat of the city, *Der Tor und der Tod* (1893; Death

and the Fool, 1913) already sees a form of guilt in egocentric withdrawal from life. *Der weiße Fächer* (1897; The White Fan, n.d.) goes further in its condemnation of world denial and aesthetic isolation, while *Die Frau im Fenster* (1897; Madonna Dianora, 1961) deals with the tragic death of a disloyal wife. *Alkestis* (1894, published 1911) is a retelling of Euripides' story about the noble wife who saves her husband through self-sacrifice and is restored to her family. The theme of marriage, parenthood, and children as the basic concerns of human existence are here dealt with by H. In the later dramas and especially the comedies these themes are taken up again (*Die Frau ohne Schatten*, 1919; *Der Schwierige*, 1921; to name only two). Sobeide, in *Die Hochzeit der Sobeide* (1899; The Marriage of Sobeide, 1899) must perish, for she is unable to face the reality of life. In *Der Kaiser und die Hexe* (1897) the theme is again loyalty and necessity for action, whereas in *Das Bergwerk zu Falun* (1899) the fatal attraction of the realm of "pre-existence" and the attempt to return to it, thus rejecting the responsibilities of life, shows precisely by its negative outcome the direction which H.'s commitment as a poet was taking.

In *Der Brief des Lord Chandos* (1902; The Letter of Lord Chandos, 1952), a fictitious letter written by Lord Chandos to Francis Bacon, the problems which led to a crisis in H.'s artistic production are clearly expressed. At the turn of the century the seemingly effortless flow of poetic language had come to a stop. Language itself had become suspect and a doubtful means of expression. The problem of language, particularly words which were used too glibly, appears often in H.'s writings at that time (the Mitterwurzer essay, 1894; *Poesie und Leben*, 1896). In part the crisis in H.'s poetic creativity was precipitated by the controversy with George (q.v.), whose attempt to draw the young poet into his circle and thus commit him to his aesthetic gospel had failed. H., in contrast to George, turned toward the challenge of the stage and thus away from symbolist poetry.

The first decade of the new century shows H.'s firm establishment of dramatic production. *Elektra* (1903; Electra, 1908), *Oedipus und die Sphinx* (1906), and *Das gerettete Venedig* (1904-5; Venice Preserved, 1915; an adaptation of Otway's play of that title [1682]) are followed by comedies: *Cristinas Heimreise* (1910; Christina's Journey Home, 1917), *Der Rosenkavalier* (1911; The Rose Bearer, 1912), and *Ariadne auf Naxos* (1912; Ariadne on Naxos, 1913). This decade also saw the beginning of a collaboration with Richard Strauss that was to continue uninterruptedly until the poet's death. The operas *Elektra* (1909; Eng., 1966), *Der Rosenkavalier, Ariadne auf Naxos, Der Bürger als Edelmann* (1918; adaptation from Molière), *Die Frau ohne Schatten* (1919), *Die Ägyptische Helena* (1928), and *Arabella* (posth. 1933) are brilliant proof of a combined artistic endeavor which is unique in its scope. With the exception of *Elektra*, which was initially written as a drama and later used as libretto by Strauss, the librettos were created with the demands of the opera stage constantly in mind. In many ways opera served to solve the problem of the inadequacy of language as expression of the complexity of human existence. "All the open secrets of life, all the secrets which we cannot bring closer than close to ourselves with words: through sound they can be drawn into our hearts, and it is to do just this that poetry calls in music." In order to achieve the perfect combination of words and music, the poet and the composer have to work not just "with each other" but literally "inside each other."

The Strauss-Hofmannsthal collaboration extended also to works other than opera, such as *Kantate* (1914), *Josephslegende* (1914, in collaboration with Count Harry Kessler), and *Die Ruinen von Athen* (1924). The correspondence between the two artists, in itself a work of art, reflects their exchange of ideas over a period of twenty-five years.

The great mystery plays *Jedermann* (1911; The Play of Everyman, 1917; after the medieval English morality play) and *Das Salzburger große Welttheater* (1922; after Calderón) are traditional in form but deal in content with the universal themes of man's condition. The dramatic figures are stylized and the play of the "dying of the rich man" carries the message of the mutability of worldly existence. Whereas in *Jedermann* H. was fascinated by the universality of the old morality play, he intended in *Das Salzburger große Welttheater* to present a parable for modern times. The beggar is a representative of the disinherited of the world and his metamorphosis a hopeful message for mankind. H., together with Max Reinhardt, was the driving force behind the founding of the Salzburg festival, which has become an expression of the living tradition of the theater in Germany and Austria, a tradition of which H. was always most conscious.

Der Turm, first conceived (1902) as a translation of Calderón's *La vida es sueño*, then reworked in various versions (1923, 1925, 1927; The Tower, 1966), remained in many respects a fragment. Dramatic form is sacrificed to depth of philosophical ideas and symbolism. H.'s untimely death precluded a final version which might have been a more satisfactory stage play.

H.'s narrative prose is a relatively small but nevertheless highly polished part of the *oeuvre*. There are three novellas—*Reitergeschichte* (1908), *Erlebnis des Marschalls von Bassompierre* (1900; An Episode in the Life of the Marshal de Bassompierre, 1952), and *Lucidor* (1910)—and four stories, or perhaps fairy tales, of which two, *Das Märchen der 672: Nacht* and the prose version of *Die Frau ohne Schatten,* were completed. The project of a psychological novel, *Andreas oder die Vereinigten* (1932; Andreas, 1936), remained a fragment. The idea of a novel in the tradition of Goethe's *Wilhelm Meister* had occupied H. since 1910, and revision of the first chapters was done in 1913 under the titles *Die Dame mit dem Hündchen* and *Die wunderbare Freundin.* The subject of the novel is, as H. stated in a letter to R. Strauss, "how a young Viennese reaches manhood," the process of maturing, or, as H. wrote in a brief note: "first to become capable of love, then to learn that body and spirit are one." This, in essence, is the theme of all of H.'s creative work.

Four volumes of the *Gesammelte Werke in Einzelausgaben* contain H.'s essays, literary criticism, lectures, fictitious letters and dialogues, and other prose. The essays reflect the multiplicity of the poet's concerns: not only purely literary problems or criticism but observations on art, the dance, music, the theater in all its forms, and again and again the problem of language. Such essays as "Der Dichter und diese Zeit" (1907), "Augenblicke in Griechenland" (1924), "Das Spiel vor der Menge," "Das Schrifttum als geistiger Raum der Nation" (1927), "Wert und Ehre deutscher Sprache," to name only a few of the most significant ones, belong without question among the treasures of European thought. Although cosmopolitan in heritage and outlook, H. showed a special sensitivity and the sure touch of good taste in selections he made from German and Austrian writings for anthologies such as *Das deutsche Lesebuch* (1922-23), *Deutsche Erzähler* (1912), and the last one, named after the essay *Wert und Ehre deutscher Sprache* (1927).

FURTHER WORKS: *Der Abenteurer und die Sängerin* (1899; The Adventurer and the Singer, 1917); *Der Schüler* (1903); *Ausgewählte Gedichte* (1903); *Das kleine Welttheater* (1903); *Unterhaltung über literarische Gegenstände* (1904); *Kleine Dramen* (1906); *Vorspiele* (1908); *Reden und Aufsätze* (1921); *Die Salzburger Festspiele* (1921); *Florindo* (1923, 1963); *Der Unbestechliche* (1923); *Gesammelte Werke* (6 vols., 1924); *Früheste Prosastücke* (1926); *Loris* (1930); *Berührung der Sphären* (1931); *Nachlese der Gedichte* (1934); *Gesammelte Werke in Einzelausgaben,* Steiner, H., ed. (15 vols., 1951-63); *Ausgewahlte Werke* (2 vols., 1957). **Correspondence:** *H. v. H. Briefe 1890-1901* (1935); *Briefwechsel H.–Wildgans* (2nd ed., 1935); *H. v. H. Brief 1900-1909* (1937); *Briefwechsel George–H.* (1938, 1953); *Richard Strauss–H. v. H. Briefwechsel* (1952); *H. v. H.–Eberhard v. Bodenhausen. Briefe der Freundschaft* (1953); *H. v. H.–Rudolf Borchardt. Briefwechsel* (1954); *H. v. H.–Carl Burckhardt. Briefwechsel* (1956); *H. v. H. Briefwechsel mit Josef Redlich* (1956); *A Working Friendship, Correspondence between Richard Strauss and H. v. H.* (1961); *Briefwechsel H. v. H.–Arthur Schnitzler* (1964); *Briefwechsel mit Helene v. Nostitz* (1965); *H. v. H.–Edgar Karl von Bebenburg. Briefwechsel* (1966). **Selected English trans.:** *Selected Writings, Prose* (1952, with an introduction by H. Broch); *Selected Writings, Poems and Verse Plays* (1961, with an introduction by T. S. Eliot and Michael Hamburger); *Selected Plays and Libretti* (1963); *Three Plays* (ed. E. Schwarz, 1966)

BIBLIOGRAPHY: Borchardt, R., *Rede über H.* (1905); Kommerell, M., *H. v. H.* (1930); Schaeder, G., *H. v. H. Die Gestalten* (1933); Krüger, K. J., *H. v. H. und R. Strauss* (1935); Perl, W., *Das lyrische Jugendwerk H. v. H.'s* (1936); Jacoby, K., *H. v. H. Bibliographie* (1936); Butler, E. M., "Alcestis in Modern Dress," *Journal of the Warburg Institute* (1937); Naef, K. J., *H. v. H.'s Wesen und Werk* (1938); Burckhardt, C. J., *Erinnerungen an H. und Briefe des Dichters* (1943); Schaeder, G., *H. v. H. und Goethe* (1947); Cohn, H., "Loris, die frühen Essays des jungen H.", *PMLA,* LXIII:4 (1948); Schaeder, G., "H. v. H.'s Weg zur Tragödie," *DVJS* II:3 (1949); Heuschele, O., *H. v. H.* (1949, 2nd ed. 1965); Rey, W. H., "Tragik und Verklärung des Geistes in H.'s 'Turm,'" *Euphorion,* XLVII:2 (1953); *idem,* "Die Drohung der Zeit in H's Frühwerk," *Euphorion,* XLVIII, (1954); Wyss, H., *Die Frau in der Dichtung H.'s* (1954); David, C., "Le dernier homme de lettres," *Critiques,* XI (1955); Jens, W., *H. und die Griechen* (1955); Rey, W., "Dichter und Abenteurer bei H. v. H.," *Euphorion,* XLIX: 1 (1955); Broch, H., "H. und seine Zeit," in *Essays* (1955); Metzler, W., *Ursprung und Krise von H's. Mystik* (1956); Rey, W. H., "Eros und Ethos in H's. Lustspielen," *DVJS,* XXX: 4 (1956); *idem,* " 'Gebet Zeugnis, ich war da!' Die Gestalt H.'s in Bericht und Forschung," *Euphorion,* L (1956); Fahrner, R., *Dichterische Visionen menschlicher Urbilder in H's. Werk* (1956); Pulver, E., *H's. Schriften zur Literatur* (1956); Steingruber, E., *H. v. H.'s sophokleische Dramen* (1956); Hammelmann, H. Z., *H. v. H.* (1957); Pestalozzi, K., *Sprachskepsis und Sprachmagie im Werk des jungen H.* (1958); Alewyn, R. *Über H. v. H.* (1958); Weischedel, H., "Hofmannsthal Forschung 1945-1958," *DVJS,* XXXIII (1959); Derungs, W., *Form und Weltbild der Gedichte H. v. H.'s in ihrer Entwicklung* (1960); Mauser, W., *Bild und Gebärde in der Sprache H.'s* (1961); Rey, W. H., *Weltentzweiung und Weltversöhnung in H.'s griechischen Dramen* (1962); Schwarz, E., *H. und Calderón* (1962); E. Rösch, *Komödien H.'s* (1963); R. Exner, *H. v. H.'s "Lebenslied"* (1964); Haas, W., *H. v. H.* (1964); Hamburger, M., *H. v. H.* (1964); Szondi, P., *Satz und Gegensatz* (1964)

MARIE T. LEHN

HÖGBERG, Olof

Swedish novelist, b. 27 Sept. 1855, Högsjö, Ångermanland; d. 12 Oct. 1932, Njurunda

H. was the first important author from northern Sweden. As a storyteller of harsh peculiarity, he combined in fictitious chronicles his attempt, inspired by local patriotism, to write the history and heroic epic of the northern provinces of Sweden with sharp criticism of the times and visionary description of an ideal society of a rural, conservative type.

H. came from an old farming family, studied natural sciences and mathematics at Uppsala, and later became a teacher and journalist. Contact with 19th c. liberalism and his interest in folklore and provincial Swedish history inspired him to rework the saga themes—his heritage from the environment of his youth.

Den stora vreden (3 vols., 1906), his first and most important book, contains myth and saga as well as descriptions of popular life. In the same way his later—artistically inferior—

novels fuse exuberant richness of detail with an apocalyptic view of events.

FURTHER WORKS: *Fribytare* (2 vols., 1910); *Baggbölingar* (2 vols., 1911); *Utbölingar* (2 vols., 1912); *Fågelskytten* (1912); *Storfursten av Lappland* (1915); *Lambertska milliarder* (1916); *Boltzius och andra gubbar* (1920)

BIBLIOGRAPHY: Bromé, J., *O. H.* (1955)

MAURITZ EDSTRÖM

HOLEČEK, Josef

Czechoslovak novelist, b. 27 Feb. 1853, Stožice near Vodňany, Bohemia; d. 6 March 1929, Prague

After completing his studies H. turned to journalism and traveled in the Slavic countries of southern Europe and later in Russia. He became an enthusiastic supporter of the ideals of the Montenegrin patriarchal system, the theories of the Czech reformers, Tolstoi (q.v.), and the Russian Slavophiles. To him the unspoiled national characteristics of the peasants represented the most precious moral and cultural value; for this reason he opposed the cosmopolitanism prevalent in Czech literature of the time and purely literary writing in general. H. summed up his life and thinking in the twelve-volume novel cycle *Naši* (1898-1931), a grandiosely conceived, unfinished chronicle of peasant life in southern Bohemia between the years 1840 and 1866. The Bohemian aristocracy he painted in the darkest colors.

H.'s translations and adaptations (*Sokolivič*, 1922) were invaluable in making Serbo-Croatian and Finnish folk poetry more widely known.

FURTHER WORKS. *Černohorské povídky* (2 vols., 1880-81); *Junácké kresby černohorské* (3 vols., 1884-89); *Sebrané spisy* (22 vols., 1909-23); *Pero* (4 vols., 1922-25); *Má svépomoc* (1931)

BIBLIOGRAPHY: Chalupný, E., *Dílo J. H.* (1926)

GÜNTHER WYTRZENS

HOLZ, Arno

German poet, b. 26 April 1863, Rastenburg, East Prussia; d. 26 Oct. 1929, Berlin

H. was a reformer of German poetry and drama and became widely known mostly as the theoretical founder of "thoroughgoing naturalism" (*see* naturalism).

In 1875 his father moved from Rastenburg to Berlin, where H. attended a *Gymnasium* and later studied literature. Except for brief trips H. lived until his death in Berlin. A freelance writer, he was often in financially precarious circumstances. His songbook *Klinginsherz* (1883) and his first attempts at lyric poetry, *Deutsche Weisen* (1884), written in collaboration with Oskar Jerschke (1862-1918), still show the influence of Emanuel Geibel (1815-1884), whom H. profoundly admired. But already with *Das Buch der Zeit* (1885; rev. eds., 1905, 1924) H. was shaking off the pseudo-classical style of Geibel. His experience of hardship, both his own and other people's, aroused his social conscience.

As an adherent of naturalism (q.v.) H. discovered a completely new subject for poetry in the modern metropolis. The "Phantasus" poems contained in the volume of that name tell of the ruin of a starving poet who holds on to his belief in beauty even in the utmost misery. H. was concerned with this theme throughout his life. In *Phantasusgedichte*, which appeared between 1898 and 1924, he creates an unrhymed, nonstanzaic poetry entirely sustained by rhythm and characterized by its "central axis." In some ways this may be regarded as a successful step forward from naturalism to impressionism. H. carried out his epic and dramatic innovations in collaboration with his friend Johannes Schlaf (q.v.). In 1889 their novella-like series of sketches *Papa Hamlet* appeared, signed—to the confusion of the critics—with the name B. P. Holmsen. In the drama *Die Familie Selicke* (1891, in collaboration with Schlaf) H. adopted the new *Sekundenstil* (*Die Kunst, ihr Wesen und ihre Gesetze*, 2 vols., 1891-92), which regards nothing as irrelevant and which seemed particularly well suited to the naturalistic description of poverty. H.'s later works (*Der geschundene Pegasus*, 1892; *Die Blechschmiede*, 1901; etc.) offered nothing really new.

FURTHER WORKS: *Neue Gleise* (with J. Schlaf, 1892); *Sozialaristokraten* (1896); *Revolution der Lyrik* (1899); *Lieder auf einer alten Laute* (1903; rev. ed. as *Dafnis*, 1904; aug. ed., 1924); *Traumulus* (with O. Jerschke, 1904); *Frei* (with O. Jerschke, 1907); *Sonnenfinsternis* (1908); *Ignorabimus* (1913); *Kindheitsparadies* (1924); *Das Werk von A. H.* (10 vols., 1924-26; 12 vols., 1926); *Briefe* (Wagner, A. and M., eds., 1949); *Werke* (6 vols., 1962-64)

BIBLIOGRAPHY: Milch, W., *A. H.* (1933); Döblin, A., *A. H. Die Revolution der Lyrik* (1951); Emrich, W., *Protest und Verheißung* (1961), "A. H.: Sein dichterisches Experiment," *NDH*, XCIV (1963), 43-58

EVA PREISS

HORA, Josef

Czechoslovak poet, b. 8 July 1891, Dobřín, near Roudnice on the Elbe; d. 21 June 1945, Prague

H. is considered one of the most talented representatives of the poetistic movement which dominated Czechoslovakian writing after World War I and which combined an intellectual Communist attitude with meticulous attention to poetic form (*Pracující den,* 1920; *Bouřlivé jaro,* 1923). In the late 1920's he turned away from Communism to an inward-looking, meditative, metaphysical form of "absolute" poetry whose central theme was time and space. After the tragic events of 1938 he became again a society-oriented, nationally conscious regional poet.

H. has also made a reputation as a translator of lyric poetry (Pushkin, Lermontov, Yesenin, and Pasternak from the Russian; Goethe and Lenau from the German).

FURTHER WORKS: *Strom v květu* (1920); *Srdce a vřava světa* (1922); *Hliněný Babylon* (1922); *Italie* (1925); *Probuzení* (1925); *Hladový rok* (1926); *Struny ve větru* (1927); *Deset let* (1929); *Tvůj hlas* (1931); *Tonoucí stíny* (1933); *Dvě minuty ticha* (1934); *Máchovské variace* (1936); *Domov* (1938); *Dech na skále* (1938); *Jan houlista* (1939); *Zahrada Popelčina* (1940); *Dílo* (14 vols., 1946-54; rev. ed., 1957); *Spisy* (1957 ff.)

BIBLIOGRAPHY: Václavek, B., *H.* (1925); Pekárek, V. *et al., H.* (1949)

GÜNTHER WYTRZENS

HORVÁTH, Ödön von

Austrian novelist and playwright, b. 9 Dec. 1901, Fiume; d. 1 June 1938, Paris

The son of an Austro-Hungarian diplomat descended from the minor Hungarian nobility, H. grew up in Belgrade, Budapest, Munich, Pressburg, and Vienna. After studying at the University of Munich, he lived in different cities before settling in Vienna and then Henndorf, near Salzburg. In 1931 he was awarded the Kleist Prize. In 1938 he fled Austria and wandered through Hungary, Czechoslovakia, Yugoslavia, and Italy, until he at last took up residence in Switzerland. He was killed when hit by a falling limb as he walked along the Champs-Elysées in Paris.

After his first book was published, H. bought up the edition and destroyed it. He began his career as a dramatist with popular plays such as *Revolte auf Côte 3018* (1927; reissued as *Die Bergbahn,* 1929), about the building of a mountain railway, and *Geschichten aus dem Wienerwald* (1931), which deals with the ossified conventions of petty bourgeois life, especially as revealed in language reduced by meaningless repetition to little more than hollow phrases. Painfully acute in observation of life, H.'s plays are set in suburbs, amusement parks, and such places of the common people, whose accent he catches and imitates very accurately as he shows the hopelessness of each man's struggle in a godless world.

Shortly before his death H. completed two remarkable novels that treat the theme of indifference and coldness as guilt. *Jugend ohne Gott* (1938; Youth Without God, 1939) and *Ein Kind unserer Zeit* (1938; A Child of Our Time, 1939) give a frightening vision of the inner nature of dictatorship as they show man's guilt and the workings of the hand of God. Both appeared under the collective title *The Age of the Fish* in an American translation in 1939; they were published together under this same title, *Zeitalter der Fische,* in German in 1953.

One of the most talked-of playwrights of his generation before 1933, H. fell into oblivion in the German-speaking world after that date; and for the past three decades he has been unjustly forgotten by the rest of the world as well. Today, however, his plays and novels are being rediscovered and again appreciated as more than just social criticism. As H. himself said, he meant them to help man win, through self-knowledge, the serenity that will make the battle of life and death easier for him.

FURTHER WORKS: *Sladek, der schwarze Reichswehrmann* (1930); *Der ewige Spießer* (1930); *Italienische Nacht* (1931); *Glaube, Liebe, Hoffnung* (1932); *Hin und Her* (1933); *Eine Unbekannte aus der Seine* (1933); *Der jüngste Tag* (1955); *Figaro läßt sich scheiden* (1959); *Stücke* (Krischke, T., ed., 1961)

BIBLIOGRAPHY: Weisstein, U., "Ö. v. H.: A Child of Our Time," *Monatshefte,* LII

(1960), 343-52; Kuschke, T., "Der Dramatiker Ö. v. H.: Versuch einer Darstellung," *Akzente,* IX (1962), 157-64; Strelka, J., *Brecht—H.— Dürrenmatt: Wege und Abwege des modernen Dramas* (1962)

* * *

HOSTOVSKÝ, Egon
Czechoslovak novelist, b. 23 April 1908, Hronov

H., an official in a government ministry in Prague, emigrated to the U.S.A. in 1938.

He began to publish short stories in 1926, and in most of his novels the influence of Dostoyevski is obvious. In the novel *Ztracený stín* (1931) the doubleganger theme is slanted toward social problems. The problems of the degraded and the humiliated are taken up in the novel *Černá tlupa* (1933), which deals with the homeless young people who ran wild during World War I. H. constantly harks back to the theme of the spiritual ghetto from which his half-assimilated Jewish fellowmen can never break free (see the short story "Ghetto v nich" [1928] and the novels *Případ profesora Körnera* [1932] and *Dům bez pána* [1937]). *Úkryt* (1943; The Hideout, 1945), *Listy z vyhnanství* (1941; Letters from Exile, 1942), and *Cizinec hledá byt* (1947; Seven Times the Leading Man, 1945), the last of which appeared first in English, recount the life stories of refugees.

FURTHER WORKS: *Stezka podél cesty* (1928); *Žhár* (1935); *Tři stárci* (1938); *Missing* (1952); *The Midnight Patient* (1954); *The Charity Ball* (1957); *The Plot* (1961); *Tři noci* (1964; Three Nights, 1964)

BIBLIOGRAPHY: Merrigi, B., *Storia della letteratura ceca e slovaca* (1958)

OTTO TUREČEK

HOUSMAN, A. E.
English poet and classical scholar, b. 26 March 1859, Fockbury, Worcestershire; d. 30 April 1936, Cambridge

From his birthplace H. could see to the northwest the hills of Shropshire for which the title of his celebrated book of sixty lyrics, *A Shropshire Lad* (1896), is named. H.'s poetic output was meager, and his reputation rests on this thin volume and two other small books of poetry (*Last Poems* [1922] and *More Poems* [1936]). His reputation as an excellent classical scholar is well established in his editions and criticisms of Manilius, Juvenal, Propertius, and others.

The eldest son of a Victorian middle-class family, H. was fondly devoted to his mother, whose death on his twelfth birthday had a considerable effect on his sensitive and retiring nature. After attending Bromsgrove School and supposedly, as he tells us, becoming attached to paganism by reading Lemprière's *Classical Dictionary,* he matriculated in 1877 at St. John's College, Oxford, where he met Alfred W. Pollard and Moses J. Jackson. H. allegedly had a strong attraction for Jackson, and there is good reason to believe that this abnormal affection was instrumental in H.'s failure in the Greats at Oxford.

In 1881 H. went from Oxford to an uncongenial and menial clerkship in the Patents Office in London. He spent his free evenings during the next ten years in the British Museum preparing scholarly papers on Aeschylus, Sophocles, Propertius, and Ovid; this scholarship in part led to an appointment as Latin professor at University College, London, in 1892.

It was during these London years that H. experienced his "continuous excitement" which ended in the lyrical beauty of *A Shropshire Lad.* Meanwhile his papers and reviews on Manilius and Juvenal began to appear, and in 1911 he was appointed Kennedy Professor of Latin at Cambridge and held the position until his death.

For H. poetry was catharsis: his poetry, while revealing his personal frustrations, disappointments, and doubts, is likewise microcosmic of late Victorian fatigue and weariness. In many ways his stoic despair, his preoccupation with death, his fatalistic view of the cosmos, his melancholic longing, and his sardonic disillusionment—his lads and lasses loving and dying against the beautiful background of the counties of Shropshire—are typical of *fin de siècle* poetry, a poetry which foreshadows the modern consciousness.

In mirroring his dark fatalism H. was greatly indebted to the classics and often to the traditional structures of English poetry. He owes as much to the traditional English ballad as he does to Heinrich Heine for his verse cadences. His clipped, colloquial speech patterns and his simplicity and felicity of phrasing sometime obscure to cursory readers the contrived simplicity and the elegance of his polished and graceful poetry.

117

His prose criticisms and prefaces are as carefully developed as his poetry and are very often balanced and classically rhetorical. His criticisms of scholars who violated the exacting and demanding disciplines of meticulous scholarship are barbed and frequently savage.

H's muse was ironic. His poetry, almost always fatalistic, unfortunately lacked the range and depth of a major poet.

FURTHER WORKS: *The Name and Nature of Poetry* (1933); *The Collected Poems of A. E. H.* (1934; rev. eds., 1953, 1956); *Manuscript Poems* (Heber, T. B., ed., 1955); *Thirty Letters to Witter Bynner* (1957); *Complete Poems* (1960); *A. E. Housman: Selected Prose* (Carter, C., ed., 1961)

BIBLIOGRAPHY: Gow, A. S. F., *A. E. H. A Sketch* (1936); Housman, L., *My Brother, A. E. H.* (1938); Wilson, E., *The Triple Thinkers* (1938); Richards, G., *H., 1897-1936* (1942); Stallman, R. W., comp., "Annotated Bibliography of A. E. H.," *PMLA*, LX (1945), 463-502; Watson, G. L., *A. E. H.: A Divided Life* (1957); Marlow, N., *A. E. H.: Scholar and Poet* (1958)

JULES PAUL SEIGEL

HUCH, Friedrich
German novelist, b. 19 June 1873, Brunswick; d. 12 May 1913, Munich

Son of a notary, H. was a cousin of Ricarda Huch (q.v.) and a grandson of the novelist Friedrich Gerstäcker (1816-72). After studying philology and philosophy during the 1890's in Munich, Berlin, and Paris, H. was a tutor for several years in Hamburg and later near Lodz, Poland. In 1903 he set himself up as a writer in Munich, where he was associated with Thomas Mann, George (qq.v.), and Ludwig Klages (1872-1956).

Working in the tradition of Goethe and Adalbert Stifter (1805-68), and showing traces of impressionism in his psychological narrative style, H. cannot simply be labeled a "neoclassicist," which evades the problem his work presents. His novels, combining elements of realism and neoromanticism, open the questions of (1) the philosophical attitude that may require a revival of the traditional style of the novel and (2) the possibility of classically stylizing the novel, a genre usually considered the most suitable for realism. H.'s works provide eminently successful answers to both questions.

One of H.'s main preoccupations was the analysis of the decadent characters of a dying *bourgeoisie,* whose overrefined souls he sometimes attacked with grotesque comedy, at other times handled with delicately ironic satire. In *Peter Michel* (1901) the hero grows from a simple rural type to a petty bourgeois snugly and smugly fitted in his milieu. However, during the course of this development he achieves transcendence of his own character and shares in the ageless and the universal through his yearning for a short time to be a better person and lead a more worthwhile life. H. brilliantly realized this story through severely controlled diction and classically simplified plot, two characteristics which were to remain true of all his subsequent work.

H. was always concerned with his contemporary world and with the problems common to mankind. In *Die Geschwister* (1903) he examined borderline psychological states in a modern version of Goethe's Elective Affinities; while in *Pitt und Fox* (1909), where irony and satire are again dominant as they were in *Peter Michel,* H. shows how genuine love evolves slowly out of a complex of baser passions. *Mao* (1907), the story of an inordinately delicate boy, and *Enzio* (1911), his most significant "musical novel" about a failed artist, show H.'s deep interest in morbid psychology and skill at dissecting such decadent character types. But both these novels also demonstrate H.'s method of treating the complexity of today's world within the terms of simple, straightforward plots.

FURTHER WORKS: *Träume* (1904); *Wandlungen* (1905); *Drei groteske Komödien* (1911); *Erzählungen* (1914); *Gesammelte Werke* (introduction by Thomas Mann, 4 vols., 1925)

BIBLIOGRAPHY: Hartung, H., *H.s epischer Stil* (1929); Denecke, R., *F. H. und die Problematik der bürgerlichen Welt* (1937); Kaderschafka, M., *Der Träumer F. H.* (1948)

* * *

HUCH, Ricarda
(occasional pseud. in early works: *Richard Hugo*), German poet, narrative writer, essayist, and historian, b. 18 Aug. 1864, Brunswick; d. 17 Nov. 1947, Frankfurt am Main

H. is one of the most outstanding women in German literature. In her early poetry she was the neoromantic prophet of Dionysian glori-

RICARDA HUCH

fication of life; as a historian and, later, a biographer she devoted herself to tragic or heroic figures; finally, in her late work she appealed for national self-examination in the spirit of the Protestant-Christian culture of the personality.

H. came from a merchant's family of peasant origin in Lower Saxony. Her brother Rudolf Huch (1862-1943) and her cousins Felix (1880-1952) and Friedrich Huch (q.v.) were also writers. She studied in Zurich, where she was a librarian and teacher until 1896. In 1899 she married an Italian physician, Ermanno Ceconi, with whom she lived in Trieste until 1900 and then in Munich until 1907. After her divorce from Ceconi she married her cousin Richard Huch, vainly seeking fulfillment of a long-cherished youthful love. Her divorce from him three years later (1910) resulted in the most severe crisis of her life. After this she lived in Munich, for the most part with the daughter of her first marriage, whom she followed to Berlin in 1927. The last ten years of her life were spent in Jena. H. was the first woman to be elected to the Prussian Academy of the Arts, she resigned from it in 1933 for political reasons.

The two Hanseatic novels *Erinnerungen von Ludolf Ursleu dem Jüngeren* (1892) and *Vita somnium breve* (1903, later [1913] entitled *Michael Unger*) in effect mark the limits of H.'s early neoromantic phase—her most productive one so far as spontaneous creativity was concerned. The fateful decline of the Ursleu family is brought about by strong, aristocratically inclined people giving themselves over with wholehearted passion to the beauty and richness of life. Michael Unger, however, understands the practical demands of life; while he leads his life in the same spirit, he leads it on a spiritualized level of mature resignation.

One of H.'s most important achievements is her comprehensive history of the literature and ideas of romanticism (*Romantik*, 2 vols, 1908; first published as *Blütezeit der Romantik*, 1899, and as *Ausbreitung und Verfall der Romantik*, 1902), which she wrote between the two novels. Besides being an attempt to revive the key ideas of the romantic age, this book is a statement of belief which demonstrates both congenial, intuitive understanding and critical detachment; as such it is also an artistic self-examination. This study emphasizes the polarity in the romantic character between nature and mind, the contradiction between irrationalism and heightened awareness. Most of H.'s poetry

(*Gedichte,* 1891; 1894; *Neue Gedichte,* 1907; *Gesammelte Gedichte,* 1929), among which the love poems are particularly outstanding, also falls into the early phase.

This creative, subjective period was followed by a second phase of complete absorption in history. H. developed a style of historical and biographical writing in which poetic and descriptive elements complement one another. The principal works of this period are the two trilogies *Die Geschichte von Garibaldi* (of which only two volumes appeared, 1906-7; Eng., Garibaldi and the New Italy, 1928-29) and *Der große Krieg in Deutschland* (1912-14); as *Der dreißigjährige Krieg,* 1937). The theme of the Garibaldi epic is the heroic man of action seen as the exponent of a nation's destiny in the struggle for freedom. In connection with the crisis in H.'s personal life about 1910, her moral concept of history and of man is perhaps most strikingly expressed in *Das Leben des Grafen Federigo Confalonieri* (1910), which is already leading up to the tragic view of history expressed in *Der große Krieg in Deutschland.* Here moral action stemming from idealistic motives yields to the theme of moral suffering and the imperiled position of human greatness. But *Der große Krieg in Deutschland* is the passion of a whole nation, seen "from below" and painted in bleak, frescolike scenes of suffering. It is now the anonymous forces of history, not the tragically exalted fate of the individual, that dominate the scene.

In H.'s third creative period, that of her late religious, philosophical work, the poetic statement recedes into the background. The works *Luthers Glaube* (1916), *Der Sinn der Heiligen Schrift* (1919), *Entpersönlichung* (1921), *Quellen des Lebens* (1935), and *Urphänomene* (1946) reveal a liberal, Christian concept of man unmistakably derived from the tradition of the 19th c. They testify to the creative human spirit's oneness with God and to the inwardness of a faith that consists of trust in and submission to God's will in the world. The same spirit inspired H.'s last historical works, especially the *Deutsche Geschichte* (3 vols., 1934-49), in which she appeals to the nation to be mindful of the sublime moments of its history. For her the *Römische Reich Deutscher Nation* (Vol. I, 1934)—"The Holy Roman Empire"—is the symbol of a divinely willed political order.

H.'s literary work is rooted in the romantic world view and in the sense of life of the bourgeois age. From this tradition it derives the power of its appeal to the human and political conscience, which has lost none of its effectiveness even in the face of modern problems.

FURTHER WORKS: *Evoe* (1892); *Der Mondreigen von Schlaraffis* (1896); *Erzählungen* (3 vols., 1897); *Fra Celeste* (1899); *Aus der Triumphgasse* (1902); *Gottfried Keller* (1904); *Von den Königen und der Krone* (1904); *Seifenblasen* (1905; partial trans., Eros Invincible, 1931); *Die Verteidigung Roms* (1906); *Der Kampf um Rom* (1907); *Menschen und Schicksale aus dem Risorgimento* (1908); *Der Hahn von Quakenbrück* (1910); *Der letzte Sommer* (1910); *Natur und Geist* (1914); *Wallenstein* (1915); *Der Fall Deruga* (1917; The Deruga Trial, 1929); *Michael Bakunin und die Anarchie* (1923); *Freiherr vom Stein* (1925); *Der wiederkehrende Christus* (1926); *Im alten Reich* (1927); *Alte und neue Götter* (1930; as *Die Revolution des 19. Jahrhunderts in Deutschland*, 1948); *Frühling in der Schweiz* (1938); *Weiße Nächte* (1943); *Herbstfeuer* (1944); *Der falsche Großvater* (1947); *Der lautlose Aufstand* (1953); *Briefe an die Freunde* (1960); *Gesammelte Erzählungen* (1962)

BIBLIOGRAPHY: Hoppe, E., *R. H.* (1936; rev. ed., 1951); Bäumer, G., *R. H.* (1949); Baum, M., *Leuchtende Spur* (1950); Leopold, K., *R. H.'s Der letzte Sommer: An Example of Epistolary Fiction in the Twentieth Century* (1962); Baumgarten, H., *R. H.: Von ihrem Leben und Schaffen* (1964)

FRIEDRICH W. WOLLENBERG

HUCHEL, Peter

German poet and radio dramatist, b. 3 April 1903, Berlin-Lichterfelde

H. grew up on his grandfather's country estate at Alt-Langerwisch in the Brandenburg marches; the effects of this landscape and his feeling for it and its people have permeated all his writings. After studying literature and philosophy at the universities in Berlin, Freiburg im Breisgau, and Vienna, he spent many years in France, the Balkans, and Turkey, earning a living sometimes as a translator, sometimes as a farm laborer.

A poet of nature, H.'s early work is similar to that of Eich and Langgässer (qq.v.): he was concerned with the people and situations of his home country in Brandenburg, with the peasants and their speech, and with the idyllics of village life. In the early 1930's he wrote radio pieces in which songs, verses, and dialogues were playfully mixed together. However he had to withdraw his first book of poems, *Der Knabenteich* (1933), after the Nazi take-over, and thenceforth the tone of his lyric work changed. His experiences in the following years came to dominate as themes in his work. In World War II he served on the Russian front and was taken prisoner; he returned from his Russian internment in 1945. H.'s *Gedichte* (1948) and even so late a work as *Chausseen, Chausseen* (1963) are marked by the shadowy silences of war service, of being a prisoner, and of the images of catastrophe everywhere visible in the landscape of his country.

H. has become one of the leading cultural officials of East Germany. Immediately after the war he was artistic director of the East Berlin radio; from 1949 to 1962 he was editor of *Sinn und Form*, which he made one of the important literary magazines in all of Germany and which he conceived of as a cultural bridge between East and West Germany. He was awarded the National Prize of the (East) German Democratic Republic in 1951; although forced by the Communist party to give up the editorship of *Sinn und Form* in 1962, he was still awarded the Fontane Prize in 1963.

Conservative rather than experimental in his style, H. has a sure feeling for nature and a sense for the terse, precise image and phrase. And his motifs—sometimes strange Mediterranean landscapes, sometimes cities, but most usually the bleak marches of Brandenburg—are given voice in poems sometimes songlike in their rhyming, sometimes in the freest of rhythms, but always clear and carefully shaped.

FURTHER WORKS: *Sternreise* (1928); *Dr. Faustens Teufelspakt und Höllenfahrt* (1933); *Die Magd und das Kind* (1935); *Maria am Weg* (1935); *Die Herbstkantate* (1935); *Der Bernsteinwald* (1935); *Der letzte Knecht* (1936); *Gott im Ährenlicht* (1936); *Hans Sonnenburg* (1936); *Brigg Santa Fé* (1936); *Reihe 3, Stand 10* (1937); *Zille Martha* (1938); *Die Sternenreuse* (1967)

BIBLIOGRAPHY: Zak, E., *P. H.* (1953); Wilk, W., "P. H.," *NDH*, XC (1962), 81-96; Hamm, P., "Vermächtnis des Schweigens: der Lyriker P. H.," *Merkur*, XVIII (1964), 480-88; Schonauer, F., "P. H.'s Gegenposition," *Akzente*, XII (1965), 404-14

* * *

HUELSENBECK, Richard

German novelist and poet, b. 23 April 1892, Frankenau, Hesse

H., now a psychoanalyst in New York, was one of the most controversial personalities in literature at the end of World War I and also the spokesman of dadaism (q.v.) (of which he was a cofounder) in Germany. In numerous publications and anthologies and in public demonstrations he promoted the politically engaged, extreme left-wing Berlin variant of dadaism as a "German Bolshevik affair" whose aim was the "symbolic slaughter, at a reasonable price, of everything connected with spirit, culture, and inwardness." His *Phantastische Gebete* (1916), which are notable as an experiment with language, and his early novellas were followed, after H. became a ship's doctor, by several less pretentious travel novels.

FURTHER WORKS: *Schalaben, Schalomai, Schalamezomai* (1916); *Azteken oder die Knallbude* (1918); *Verwandlungen* (1918); *En avant Dada* (1920); *Dada siegt* (1920); *Dada Almanach* (1920); *Doktor Billig am Ende* (1921); *Afrika in Sicht* (1928); *Der Sprung nach Osten* (1928); *China frißt Menschen* (1930); *Der Traum vom großen Glück* (1933); *Die New Yorker Kantaten* (1952); *Die Antwort der Tiefe* (1954); *Mit Witz, Licht und Grütze* (1957); *Dada, ein Literarisches Dokument* (1964)

BIBLIOGRAPHY: Motherwell, R. B., ed., *The Dada Painters and Poets* (1951); Schifferli, P., *Das war Dada* (1963); Richter, H., *Dada: Art and Anti-Art* (1966)

INGO SEIDLER

HUGHES, Langston

American Negro poet, novelist, short story writer, playwright, and librettist, b. 1 Feb. 1902, Joplin, Mo.; d. 22 May 1967, New York

H. received his elementary and secondary education in the schools of Kansas, Illinois, and Ohio, and earned the A.B. degree at Lincoln University, Pennsylvania. Among the awards he received for his creative achievements are Witter Bynner Undergraduate Poetry Award (1926), Harmon Gold Medal for Literature (1931), Anisfield-Wolfe Award (1953), and Spingarn Medal (1960).

H.'s first book of poems, *The Weary Blues* (1926), was followed by more than ten other volumes. His subject matter was generally chosen from the lower levels of Negro life, and his language was that of the untrained urban worker. H. was the poet of city life, its raucous discords and its pleasurable dissipations. His chief topics were night life and cabarets, primitive love-making, humorous experiences of Negro life, and the serious reaction of Negroes to social barriers.

His most popular fictional work, *Simple Speaks His Mind* (1950), is centred around a humorous Negro character named Jesse Simple, whose satirical wit is directed at the inconsistencies of Negro conduct and the naïveté of white Americans in their attitudes toward Negroes. In his three volumes of short stories, as well as his three novels, his style is delightfully simple and informal, dominated by a satirical humor that is both devastating and charming.

His philosophy of art and life is revealed succinctly in the second volume of his autobiography, *I Wonder as I Wander* (1956), where he said: "I did not want to bat out slick non-Negro short stories in competition with a thousand other commercial writers trying to make *The Saturday Evening Post*. I wanted to write seriously and as well as I know how about Negro people, and make that kind of writing earn for me a living."

Probably Hughes' greatest contribution to American literature was the daring originality of his style and subject matter, including his acceptance of the blues pattern as worthy of poetic dignity.

FURTHER WORKS: *Fine Clothes to the Jew* (1927); *Not Without Laughter* (1930); *Dear Lonely Death* (1931); *The Dream Keeper* (1932); *The Ways of White Folks* (1934); *Mulatto* (1936); *The Big Sea* (autobiography, 1941; augmented ed., 1963); *Shakespeare in Harlem* (1941); *Montage of a Dream Deferred* (1951); *Laughing to Keep From Crying* (1952); *Simple Speaks His Mind* (1953); *Tambourines to Glory* (1958); *Selected Poems* (1959); *Something in Common and Other Stories* (1963); *The Prodigal Son* (1963); *Simple's Uncle Sam* (1965); *The Panther and the Lash* (1967); *Simple's Uncle Sam* (1968)

BIBLIOGRAPHY: Presley, J., "The American Dream of L. H.," *Southwestern Review,* XLVIII (1963), 380-86; Dickenson, D. C., "A Bio-Bibliography of L. H., 1920-1960," *DA,* XXV (1965), 7282-83; Dodat, F., ed., *L. H.* (1964)

NICK AARON FORD

HUGHES, Richard Arthur Warren

Anglo-Welsh novelist and dramatist, b. 19 April 1900, Weybridge, England

H. was educated at Charterhouse and Oriel College, Oxford, and has traveled extensively. His first play, *The Sisters' Tragedy* (1922), was produced at the home of John Masefield (q.v.). It ends with a mad child leading an imaginary brother to a chair by the fire. In 1924 *A Comedy of Good and Evil* was presented at the Royal Court Theatre, London. The devil-girl, Gladys, serves as a link between this sardonic play and Mr. Hughes's best-known work —his novel *The Innocent Voyage* (1929; Am., *A High Wind in Jamaica*). The amoral children who journey on the pirate ship have a vigor and depth that are memorable. The high wind that sends them on their travels is as well described as the hurricane in the Caribbean that is the real subject of H.'s second novel, *In Hazard* (1938). His collection of short stories, *A Moment of Time* (1926), and of stories for children, *The Spider's Palace* (1931) and *Don't Blame Me* (1942), deal sometimes fantastically with flamboyant characters and the supernatural. If any influences are to be found in his work, they are perhaps those of Conrad (q.v.), Arthur Machen (1863-1947), and the Grand Guignol.

His long silence as a creative writer was broken in 1961 with *The Fox in the Attic*, the first volume of a projected trilogy to be called "The Human Predicament." Once again the macabre is intensified by setting the melodramatic in the midst of everyday happenings. Episodes are placed so starkly one against the other that they have a symbolic force. The feeling of nightmare persists in the imaginative part of the book; the documentary part, concerning the Ludendorff march on Munich, is much less significant.

FURTHER WORKS: *Gipsy Night and other Poems* (1922); *The Sisters' Tragedy and other Plays* (including *The Man Born to Be Hanged* and *Danger*; 1924); *Confessio Juvenis* (1926); *A Moment of Time* (1926); *R. H., An Omnibus* (1931); *Plays* (1928; rev. eds., 1959, 1966); *Gertrude's Child* (1966); *Rhetoric: Principles and Usage* (1967)

BIBLIOGRAPHY: Emanuel, J., *L. H.* (1967); Dickinson, D. C., *A Bio-Bibliography of L. H.* (1967)

CECIL PRICE

HUIDOBRO, Vicente

Chilean poet, b. 10 Jan. 1893, Santiago; d. there, 2 Feb. 1948

H. lived in Paris from the time he was sixteen, and at seventeen he began publishing. His first productions, *Canciones en la noche* (1913) and *La gruta del silencio* (1914), were influenced by symbolism (q.v.), but H. found his own voice in the prose poems *Las pagodas ocultas* (1915) and the poem *Adán* (1916). Editor of the periodical *Sic*, he collaborated on another, *Nord-Sud*, after 1917. While in Paris he became the friend of Apollinaire and Reverdy (qq.v.).

H. energetically championed his new poetic theories in various manifestoes, making himself a typical "avant-garde" writer. In 1917 he founded the movement *Creacionismo*, a new radicalism that sought "to create a poem as nature creates a tree" (see Spanish literature). The aesthetic premise of this movement was threefold: to humanize "things," to make the indeterminate precise, and finally to make the abstract concrete and the concrete abstract. After starting *Creacionismo* H. began to write some of his works in French. Possessing a powerful sense of fantasy and capable of inventing utterly new metaphors, H.'s bold innovations, although some were scoffed at, found acceptance in part, and he continued to influence Spanish and Spanish-American poetry up to the mid-1930's.

FURTHER WORKS: *Ecos del alma* (1910); *Espejo en el agua* (1916; Mirror of a Mage, 1931); *Horizon carré* (1917); *Ecuatorial* (1918); *Poemas árticos* (1918); *Hallali* (1918); *Tour Eiffel* (1918); *Saisons choisies* (1921); *Automne régulier* (1925); *Tout à coup* (1925); *Mío Cid Campeador* (1929; Portrait of a Paladin, 1932); *Altazor o el viaje en paracaídas* (1931); *Ver y palpar* (1941); *El ciudadano del olvido* (1941); *Ultimos poemas* (1948); *Poesía y prosas* (1957)

BIBLIOGRAPHY: Holmes, H. A., *V. H. and Creationism* (1934); Bary, D., *H. o la vocación poética* (1963); Laffranque, M., "Aux sources de la poésie espagnole contemporaine: La querelle du 'créationnisme,' " *Mélanges à Marcel Bataillon* (1964), pp. 479-89

* * *

LANGSTON HUGHES

ALDOUS HUXLEY

HUNGARIAN LITERATURE

The classic-romantic-populist movement that began with a bang in the 1840's when the reform generation burst on the literary scene, ended with a whimper amidst the placid artificiality of the *fin de siècle*. The reform generation fought for political emancipation as well as for the revitalization of Hungarian literature. At the end of the century its political and, particularly, its literary programs were hopelessly outdated. The lull caused by the gradual exhaustion of traditional literary forms was, however, of short duration. In the first years of the 20th c. the creative forces of the rising generation regained sufficient momentum to give entirely new dimensions to modern Hungarian literature.

The process of revitalization was triggered mainly by poets. This was hardly surprising since poetry, particularly lyrical poetry, was the traditional genre in which the literary genius of Hungary usually manifested itself. As in the age of enlightenment and in the reform period, poetry thus provided the most effective means through which the hopes and aspirations of the new generation were to be expressed.

The group formed around the periodical *Nyugat*, founded in 1908 by the critics Ignotus (1869-1950) and Ernö Osvát (1877-1929), did not, of course, consist entirely of poets. But although the group included fine writers such as Móricz (q.v.), Margit Kaffka (1880-1918), and Karinthy (q.v.), it was chiefly through the *Nyugat* poets, headed by Endre Ady (1877-1919), that the movement exerted the galvanizing effect that was to result within the next decade in the radical transformation of the literary scene. This was due, in addition to the traditional response to poetry, to Ady's almost demoniac ability to present in strikingly new forms the revolutionary message, which was to change—so he hoped, at least—the spiritual and political physiognomy of "the vast fallow lands of Hungary."

When *Nyugat* was founded, Ady had already published two volumes (*Uj Versek*, 1906; *Vér és Arany*, 1919) containing some of his major poems (some of these have been translated in *Poems*, 1941). The influence of the French symbolists (see symbolism)—Ady had spent some time in Paris—is evident, particularly in the early poems. Nevertheless, Ady was too individualistic and too original to be classified as the representative of any one literary school.

While he preferred to express himself by means of symbolist techniques, as shown by his famous poems *As Ös Kaján* and *A fekete zongora,* Biblical and folklore influences are also clearly discernible in the sometimes moody, sometimes apocalyptic lines in which he described the tragic search of an oversensitive but dedicated man for truth, justice, love, faith, and inner peace. His poems, abounding in an overpowering imagery, melodious resonance, and almost balladlike density, represented the quintessence of "the new songs of new times" the *Nyugat* group were writing while setting out to give new form and content to Hungarian literature.

In contrast to Ady's tumultuous individualism, Babits (q.v.), the second most influential poet of the *Nyugat* group, displayed a classic discipline that brought fully into relief the immaculate perfection of his artistry. Kosztolányi (q.v.) expressed, with the self-assurance—and often with the audacity—of the virtuoso, the changing moods of his generation. Erudition, refinement, and an impressive faculty to translate into poetical terms the sensitivities of a lonely soul were the hallmarks of Árpád Tóth's (1886-1928) poetry. Regardless of their allegiance to the various schools, ranging from Parnassianism to symbolism, from pre-Raphaelitism to early futurism (q.v.), all the poets of the *Nyugat* group, such as Gyula Juhász (1883-1937), Oszkár Gellért (b. 1882), Milán Füst (b. 1888), Simon Kemény (1883-1945), Anna Lesznai (b. 1885), and Ernö Szép (1884-1953), united originality of expression with astounding versatility in their search for new poetical forms and techniques.

One of the great accomplishments of the group was the widening of literary horizons through closer contacts with Western literature. Most poets gathering around *Nyugat,* particularly Babits, Kosztolányi, Tóth, and later Lörinc Szabó (1900-1957), were exceptionally gifted translators whose masterly renderings of Wilde, Yeats, Jammes, Verhaeren, Rilke, and George (qq.v.), Byron, Keats, Shelley, Rossetti, Baudelaire, Verlaine, Rimbaud, Mallarmé, Poe, and Whitman contributed considerably to refining literary tastes and adding further momentum to the great literary renaissance.

Social protest, so strongly expressed in Ady's revolutionary poetry as well as in the lyrical output of less robust poets such as Tóth and Juhász, provided the main theme for the novelists who appeared on the literary scene in the decade preceding World War I. The social, economic, and psychological plight of the peasantry was described with forceful realism by Móricz, considered the most significant Hungarian prose writer of the 20th c. While village life (*Sárarany*, 1911; "Hét krajcár," 1909), the Hungarian past (*Tündérkert*, 1922), and the eccentricities of the country squires "Úri muri" provided the raw material for Móricz's penetrating sociopsychological analyses, the drab monotony of *petit bourgeois* existence, and the sullen hopelessness of the proletariat inspired the caustic protests voiced in the novels and short stories of Lajos Nagy (1883-1954). In Karinthy's imaginary travels (*Capillaria*, 1921; *Utazás Faremidóba*, 1916) the fantastic, interwoven with the absurd, became the vehicle for witty social satire, while his parodies (*Igy irtok ti*, 1912) concealed highly spirited literary criticism under a façade of whimsical playfulness.

Although sweeping generalizations should have no place in literary history, it is fairly safe to say that the *Nyugat* group represented, in both a political and a literary sense, leftist-radical tendencies (radicalism in the European rather than in the American sense). To the right of the radical opposition stood the proponents of 19th c. liberalism such as the poet József Kiss (1843-1921), the novelist and playwright Sándor Bródy (1863-1924), and the highly versatile Jenö Heltai (1871-1957). Kiss, whose literary weekly, *A Hét* had paved the way for the *Nyugat*, showed great skill and sincerity in broadening the poetical scope of classic-romantic traditions. Bródy contributed considerably to the development of a new literary idiom marked by strong naturalistic tendencies (*A tanitónő*, 1903). Heltai, who began his career as the author of chansonlike poems and amusing novelettes, acquired, after World War II, solid literary stature with his psychological novel *Álmokháza* (1929) and the play *A néma levente* (1936). Géza Gárdonyi's (1863-1922) impressive historical frescos (*Isten rabjai*, 1908; *Egri csillagok*, 1901) were highly appreciated by critics as well as the public.

The increasing activities of the literary avantgarde did not fail to call forth a vigorous reaction from conservative nationalists, headed by the influential Jenö Rákosi (1842-1929). The polemics between defenders of literary orthodoxy and their progressive opponents, such as the critics Ambrus (q.v.), Aladár Schöpflin (1872-1950), and Georg Lukács (b. 1883), created an exceptionally tense literary atmosphere in which the clash of ideological and particularly aesthetic currents added further

stimulus to the creative processes (1908-1918). In the conservative camp the leading literary figure was Ferenc Herczeg (1863-1954), a novelist (*Pogányok*, 1902), and playwright (*Bizánc*, 1904) whose psychological insight, stylistic skill, and highly developed sense for both humor and drama commanded the respect even of his most resolute opponents.

Curiously the playwright who succeeded about this time in putting Budapest on the theatrical map of the world took little or no part in the momentous debates. The reason for this was that essentially they had no program to defend, no ideology to propagate, no message to deliver. Dezsö Szomory (1869-1944), from a literary point of view perhaps the most interesting figure in this group, dedicated all his talents to the search for artistic perfection, which he sought to attain by projecting the opaque elements of the subconscious through the medium of a highly colored, impressionistic imagery (*II. József*, 1918). Molnár (q.v.) was at his best when describing the secret tragedies of metropolitan life (*A Pál uīcai fiuk*, 1907); *Széntolvajok*, 1918; *Liliom*, 1909). Sincere, moving, and abounding in poetical tenderness, these masterly reconstructions of the world of children, vagabonds, and thieves provide a far better evidence of Molnár's exceptional literary talents than his technically flawless comedies (*Játék a kastélyban*, 1926; *Az ördög*, 1907). A very similar technical virtuosity and dramatic flair contributed to making Menyhért Lengyel's (b. 1880) *Tajfun* (1907) a world success.

By the early 1920's the literary revolution triggered by the *Nyugat* group had run its course. But while humanistic-cosmopolitan ideas propagated by the periodical have lost much of their significance as a result of the social and intellectual upheavals that followed World War I, the revolutionary-populist content of Ady's and Móricz's writings provided a rich source of inspiration for newer poets and writers. The most original representative of the revolutionary-populist mystique was Dezsö Szabó (1879-1945), whose torrential style and polemical zest added an entirely new and powerful note to Hungarian prose (*Az elsodort falu*, 1919; *Segitség*, 1925). The tendency to consider the peasantry as the main source of national regeneration was clearly reflected in the novels of János Kodolányi (b. 1899), József Darvas (b. 1912), and Pál Szabó (b. 1893). The leading figure in this group was Illyés (q.v.), who succeeded in lending both persuasiveness and originality to all genres—poetry, drama, novel, and reportage—to whose cultivation he dedicated his impressive talents.

While the interest of writers gathering around the so-called village sociographers (*falukutatók*) remained focused on rural life, particularly on the plight of the agrarian proletariat, other novelists chose different terrains for their psychological and social explorations. Gyula Krúdy (1878-1933), who belonged to the first *Nyugat* generation, used almost surrealist techniques in evoking with nostalgic tenderness the moods of the past and in recalling dreamlike episodes in the lives of strange, lonely men and women (*A vörös postakocsi*, 1919). In contrast to Krúdy's delicately emotional approach, Sándor Márai (b. 1900) followed an intellectual method of Proustian rigor in his brilliant analyses of the bourgeoisie (*Idegen emberek*, 1931; *Vendégjáték Bolzanoban*, 1940). Mihály Földi (1894-1943), a physician by profession, used Freudian techniques in trying to solve intricate psychological problems (*Sötétség*, 1918; *Szahara*, 1920). Ferenc Móra's (1894-1934) tender and amusing character sketches revealed great literary skill joined with a genuinely humanistic outlook (*Ének a búzamezökröl*, 1927). Treating mainly Transylvanian themes, Áron Tamási (b. 1897) and Jözsef Nyirö (1889-1953) showed considerable ingenuity in molding into new forms romantic and populist traditions. Irén P. Gulácsy (1894-1945) breathed new life into the writing of historical novels (*Fekete völegények*, 1927), a genre that seemed to decline after reaching an exceptionally high point of development in Gárdonyi's, Herczeg's, and Móricz's reconstructions of the Hungarian past. Zilahy's (q.v.) well-constructed plays (*Süt a nap*, 1924) and novels (*A két fogoly*, 1927; *Ararát*, 1947) reflected an intense awareness of the social and psychological developments that preceded the moral and political disintegration of central and eastern Europe. The remarkable autobiography of Kassák (q.v.), the first authentic worker-poet and the first Hungarian poet of stature to experiment with futurist and expressionist (see expressionism) techniques, provided in highly articulate literary terms a valuable human document on the corrosive processes that were threatening 20th c. Hungarian society. Critic, novelist, and playwright, László Németh (b. 1901) demonstrated successfully that even the most confused ideas can be presented in an attractive literary form.

The same extraordinary diversity that distinguished Hungarian poetry in the beginning of the century remained the characteristic feature of the new literary era. Illyés, József Erdélyi (b. 1896), and Ferenc Juhász (b. 1928) represented the populist trend; Lörincz Szabó (b. 1900), Miklós Radnóti (1909-1944), and Sándor Vörös (b. 1913) followed in the footsteps of the first *Nyugat* generation by seeking to broaden in a highly individualistic manner the classic-romantic forms of poetical expression. Catholic poets such as László Mécs (b. 1895) and Sándor Sik (1889-1963) translated successfully into lyrical terms their spiritual yearnings and experiences. Unconnected with any group or literary school, József (q.v.) emerged as the greatest poet of this period. Uniting a moving, almost naive sensitivity and an inexhaustible artistic imagination with a melodious flexibility of expression and a passionate commitment to human dignity and justice, József succeeded in expressing with equal ease and credibility moods and attitudes ranging from serene introspection and quiet nostalgia to indignant social protests.

Social criticism, which had been one of the leitmotivs of 20th c. Hungarian literature, was turned into parodistic farce by the party hacks who dominated literature in the years following the establishment of the communist regime in Hungary. Curiously enough, the intellectual terror that lasted almost ten years provided the best evidence of the resilience of Hungarian poets and writers, who succeeded in preserving the traditional vigor of their creative powers even in the literary sahara of the *zhdanovchina*, the era of compulsory "socialist realism" (so called after Soviet chief ideologist Andrei Zhdanov). In fact, both poets and writers had a lion's share in preparing the intellectual climate for the uprising of 1956. Several writers and poets of this period, such as Déry (q.v.), Tamás Aczél (b. 1921), Gyula Háy (b. 1900), Zoltán Zelk (b. 1906), György Faludy (b. 1910), and László Benjámin (b. 1915), produced works of considerable literary value.

In the more relaxed atmosphere of the 1960's the leading literary figures of the prewar period as well as the writers of the new generation could engage once again in literary experimentation and produce imaginative works reflecting genuine aspirations and sensitivities. Literary debates on important subjects, such as the nature of realism or socialist aesthetics, were resumed and greatly stimulated by the publication of several literary periodicals of outstanding quality (*Kortárs, Nagyvilág, Alföld, and Jelenkor*).

BIBLIOGRAPHY: Várkonyi, N., *A modern magyar irodalom* (1928); Pinter, J., *Magyar irodalomtörténete* (8 vols., 1930-41); Helfe, L., ed., *Hungaria: A Hungarian Anthology* (1935); Schöpflin, A., *A magyar irodalom története a XX, században* (1937); Várkonyi, N., *Az újabb magyar irodalom 1880-1940* (1942); Tabori, P., ed., *Hungarian Anthology* (1943); Szerb, A., *Magyar irodalomtörténet* (1947); Sivirsky, A., *Die ungarische Literatur der Gegenwart* (1962); Reményi, J., *Hungarian Writers and Literature* (1964); Klaniczay, T., Szabolcsi, M., and Szaunder, J., *History of Hungarian Literature* (1964); Budapest Institute of World Literature, *Landmark: An Anthology Published on the Occasion of the Twentieth Anniversary of Hungary's Liberation in 1945* (1965)

ANN DEMAITRE

HUXLEY, Aldous Leonard

English novelist, essayist, and critic, b. 26 July 1894, Godalming, Surrey; d. 22 Nov. 1963, Los Angeles, Calif.

H. was born into an eminent British family of letters and science. His grandfather was the renowned biologist Thomas Henry Huxley, who popularized Darwinism; his granduncle was the poet-essayist Matthew Arnold, and his grandaunt was the novelist Mrs. H. Ward; his father, Leonard, was an essayist and the editor of *Cornhill* magazine; his brother, Sir Julian, is a noted biologist; and his half brother, Andrew Huxley, won the Nobel Prize for physiology in 1963. H. maintained an interest in science throughout his life, and indeed he first decided on a career in medicine, but a serious eye affliction that nearly blinded him forced him to abandon his medical studies and instead turn to the study of literature. He published his first two books of poetry, *The Burning Wheel* (1916) and *The Defeat of Youth* (1918), while still a student at Oxford. It was during this time that he met D. H. Lawrence, with whom he had a lifelong friendship and who influenced his early philosophy. He married Maria Nys in 1919 while on the editorial staff of *The Athenaeum*, and in 1920 published a volume of short stories, *Limbo*, and a third volume of poetry, *Leda*. In 1921 he published his first novel, *Crome Yellow*, and his literary career was well launched.

H. has written numerous volumes of nonfiction, ranging from the early travel book, *Jesting Pilate* (1926), in which he examines the cultures of the East, to biographies such as *Grey Eminence* (1941), a study of Cardinal Richelieu's assistant François Leclerc in which H. indicates his dissatisfaction with orthodox Christianity, and *The Devils of Loudon* (1952), in which he explores the psychological and spiritual implications of nuns seemingly possessed by devils; and to philosophical essays such as *Ends and Means* (1937), in which he views the inadequacies of modern Western civilization, and *The Perennial Philosophy* (1945), in which he suggests personal mysticism as the means of salvation for modern man, and *The Doors of Perception* (1954) and *Heaven and Hell* (1956), which analyze his experiences under the influence of mescalin (he believed that the heightened perceptions induced by this hallucinatory drug lead to visionary revelations, either mystical or artistic). Yet H.'s literary reputation is mainly that of a novelist. However, there is a continuity and an interrelationship between H.'s fiction and his nonfiction in the development of his philosophy and his art.

H. once described himself as an essayist who sometimes wrote novels; there is an essential truth in this remark made somewhat facetiously late in his career when he was writing more nonfiction than fiction: all of H.'s novels are novels of ideas, a genre that derives its form in part from the dramatic essay in which a symposium of ideas is presented; thus, for example, ideas and attitudes on politics, religion, and education expressed in the essays in *Proper Studies* (1927) are dramatized in the novel *Point Counter Point* (1928). H., through his character Philip Quarles, defines the novel of ideas also in relation to allegory: "The character of each personage must be implied, as far as possible, in the ideas of which he is the mouthpiece. Insofar as theories are rationalizations of sentiments, instincts, dispositions of soul, this is feasible." In his early novels (through *Brave New World,* 1932) H. maintains a philosophical skepticism about the differing ideas and attitudes, and he achieves the necessary artistic balance through satire, using the technique of counterpoint to play one idea or attitude against another. In his later novels (beginning with *Eyeless in Gaza,* 1936) H. is no longer skeptical, and characters such as Miller and Beavis in *Eyeless in Gaza,* Propter in *After Many a Summer Dies the Swan* (1939), and Barnack and Rontini in *Time Must Have a Stop* (1944) become mouthpieces for H.'s mysticism.

Crome Yellow (1921), *Antic Hay* (1923), and *Those Barren Leaves* (1925), his first three novels, of which *Antic Hay* is the best, form a continuity of characterization, ideas, and situations found in *Point Counter Point*; together they are a satiric portrait of the 1920's with that decade's skepticism, hedonism, and clash of ideas and values. Gumbril, Jr., and Mrs. Viveash in *Antic Hay* are the earlier counterparts of Walter Bidlake and Lucy Tantamount in *Point Counter Point* sophisticated young men and women of the 1920's, hedonistic, certain that the old values of the prewar generation died in the war but uncertain of anything else beyond pleasure-seeking and personal freedom; Coleman the cynic and Shearwater the scientist but incomplete man are prototypes of Spandrell and Lord Edward Tantamount. The changing patterns of the characters' relationships, suggested by the title (a rustic dance in which the partners weave in and out), is the same technique of counterpoint used to dramatize the conflict of ideas or the instability of human relationships in a world where intellectual values themselves are unstable. In *Point Counter Point* H. provides a norm (the artist Mark Rampion) against which the lives and ideas of the other characters are counterpointed, whereas in *Antic Hay* no single viewpoint dominates. Rampion, who expounds Lawrentian ideas in *Point Counter Point*, is happily married, the only character in the novel who has a satisfactory love relationship; thus his naturalistic philosophy of life and his criticism of modern science and industrialism and of orthodox Christianity for creating incompleteness and disharmony in modern life and human relationships are given added credence. Burlap represents the perversion of spirituality in the modern world, and Illidge and Webley represent the perversion of political action; even Philip Quarles, who essentially agrees with Rampion, is satirized for his overintellectualism. Yet in the end H. withholds from Rampion in his debate with Spandrell the ultimate answer to the meaning of life. Thus H. remains sufficiently detached from even the Lawrentian philosophy of life, which he obviously admired at this time, by not presenting it as a final solution and means of human salvation; for while it may work as a practical solution to the problem of living in the modern world, it does deny the soul. Inherent in the inadequacy of Rampion's philosophy of life to explain the soul is the clue to H.'s later adoption of mysticism as a way out of the modern wasteland.

Brave New World (1932), an antiutopian novel, is the last of H.'s novels in which his philosophical skepticism balances opposing ways of life; Mustapha Mond's controlled society with its modern technological advances utilized solely for the purpose of achieving material happiness and John Savage's "primitive" belief in the tragic condition of man are both equally untenable ways of life. Though the former eliminates war, disease, and suffering, it creates a monstrously hedonistic society devoid of humanistic and spiritual values; it is the direction in which modern society is moving, provided mankind does not annihilate itself in atomic warfare, H. indicates in the foreword he wrote to the 1946 American edition of the novel, a theme he expands upon in the volume of essays *Brave New World Revisited* (1958). Though John Savage's world of traditional values, the world of Shakespeare's plays from which the ironic title of this novel is taken, has its poetry, spiritual visions, and deeper human relationships, it also has its wars, poverty, suffering, and unhappiness because the artistic and spiritual vision and the significant human relationship are dependent on man's acceptance of his tragic condition. Nowhere is H.'s changed philosophical viewpoint better illustrated than in his fictional "brave new world revisited," *The Island* (1962), a utopian novel in which an isolated island of sanity exists in this still wasteland world, an island where the people devote their lives to the contemplative life, utilizing such scientific knowledge as necessary to the good life, such as hallucinatory drugs to induce or intensify spiritual and creative visions.

In 1932 H. met the English theologian and mystic Gerald Heard, who had an important influence on his acceptance of mysticism, but H. was not suddenly converted to mysticism by his association with Heard; the whole direction and development of his thought, as it was for T. S. Eliot (q.v.), was a quest for certainty, and behind the urbane, sophisticated mask of intellectual wit and satire was the moralistic indignation of an Old Testament prophet. All of Huxley's later novels, from *Eyeless in Gaza* to *The Island*, are dramatic essays expounding his own personal philosophy; H. is no longer the detached, skeptical novelist but an explicit philosopher, a partisan rather than an observer in the drama of ideas. Thus H.'s later novels are less satisfactory artistically because in writing them H. the philosophic essayist overshadows H. the satiric novelist.

H.'s mystical philosophy as developed in these later novels and in his volumes of essays, particularly *The Perennial Philosophy*, is a search for what Heard called "the eternal gospel," the essential truths that are found in all great religions. As Anthony Beavis in *Eyeless in Gaza* states, everything that causes separation and division is evil, whether it be of the body, mind, or soul; everything that creates unity and harmony is good. Since the human condition of modern man is divisive and separatist in all aspects of human endeavor—social, political, religious, and psychological—the individual must seek to achieve inner peace by transcending time through the contemplative life. Time, which is associated with the ego, must have a stop. This is the realization Sebastian Barnack comes to in *Time Must Have a Stop*. "It is axiomatic," H. states explicitly the following year in *The Perennial Philosophy*, "that the end of human life is contemplation, or the direct and intuitive awareness of God." Modern man, however, beset by a confusion of moral standards, by a standardization of material life, and by social and political regimentation, is lost in the wasteland of technology, totalitarianism, and militant religious orthodoxy. He follows the ape of bodily passions, not the essence of being, which is the spirit, H. shows in *Ape and Essence* (1948); he worships the genius of science, not the goddess of love, H. suggests as his allegorical theme in *The Genius and the Goddess* (1955). It is the mission of what Heard calls "men of the margin," modern prophets, to act as voices in the wilderness pointing the way to the promised land of spiritual fulfillment and happiness, "the island" of inner peace. Thus in his later novels H., through his characters who act as spokesmen for his philosophy, assumes the role of such a prophet.

FURTHER WORKS: (w. T. S. Eliot), *Chapbook* (1920); *Mortal Coils* (1922); *On the Margin* (1923); *Little Mexican* (1924); *The Gioconda Smile, A Play* (1924); *Along the Road* (1925); *Selected Poems* (1925); *Two or Three Graces* (1926); *Essays, New and Old* (1926); *Arabia Infelix* (1929); *Do What You Will* (1929); *Holy Face* (1929); *Vulgarity in Literature* (1930); *Brief Candles* (1930); *The Cicadas* (1931); *Music at Night* (1931); *The World of Light* (1931); *Texts and Pretexts* (1932); *Beyond the Mexique Bay* (1934); *The Olive Tree* (1936); *Stories, Essays, and Poems* (1937); *The Art of Seeing* (1942); *Verses and Comedy*

(1946); *Science, Liberty, and Peace* (1946); *Collected Edition* (1947); *Themes and Variations* (1950); *Joyce, the Artificer* (1952); *Adonis and the Alphabet* (1956); *Collected Short Stories* (1957); *Collected Essays* (1959); *On Art and Artists* (1960); *Literature and Science* (1963); *The Crows of Pearblossom* (1968)

BIBLIOGRAPHY: Henderson, A., *A. H.* (1935); Daiches, D., "A. H.," in *The Novel and the Modern World* (1939); Savage, D. S., *Mysticism and A. H.* (1947); Tindall, W. Y., "Hunt for a Father," in *Forces in Modern British Literature* (1947); Hoffman, F. J., "A. H. and the Novel of Ideas," in W. J. O'Connor, ed., *Forms of Modern Fiction* (1948); Brooke, J., *A. H.* (1954); Atkins, J. A., *A. H., A Literary Study* (1956); Eschelbach, C. J., and Shober, J. L., *A. H., A Bibliography* (1961); Hoffmann, C. G., "The Change in H.'s Approach to the Novel of Ideas," *The Personalist*, XLII (Winter 1961), 85-90; Ghose, S., *A. H.: A Cynical Salvationist* (1962); Huxley, J., ed., *A. H., 1894-1963* (1965)

CHARLES G. HOFFMANN

HUYSMANS, Joris-Karl (Charles-Marie-Georges)

French novelist and critic, 5 Feb. 1848, Paris; d. there, 12 May 1907

From 1866 to 1898 H. was connected with the French Ministry of the Interior. He lived a secluded life but participated actively in literary movements of his time. In 1880 he became associated with Zola and contributed the novella *Sac au dos* to the naturalistic anthology *Les Soirées de Médan* (1881). Stylistically, however, he took Gautier, Flaubert, Villiers de l'Isle-Adam, and later Barbey d'Aurevilly as his models. In 1882 he was close to Mallarmé, and about 1890 he influenced the young Valéry (q.v.). H. was among the first ten members of the Académie Goncourt chosen by Edmond de Goncourt.

His early works—*Le drageoir aux épices* (1874; A Dish of Spices, 1927), *Marthe, histoire d'une fille* (1876; Marthe, 1957), *Les soeurs Vatard* (1879; Four Fallen Women, 1953), and *En ménage* (1881)—already show him to be a sophisticated stylist who combined a sense of color with a sharp ear for syntactical irony. *À vau-l'eau* (1882) deals with the gastronomical vagaries of a bachelor who suffers from a stomach ailment; *En rade* (1887;

Downstream, 1927), with the disappointments of a holiday trip. H. castigates the petty suffering of the "outsider," the nonconformist, who is bored by the dullness of life. He was Baudelaire's equal as a connoisseur of art and discovered Renoir, Whistler, and Degas (*L'Art moderne*, 1883; partial trans., Critical Papers, 1927; *Certains*, 1889). *À Rebours* (1884; Against the Grain, 1922; Against Nature, 1959) describes the inner poverty of an overstimulated aristocratic nature. Its hero, Des Esseintes, disgusted with himself and his time, becomes an aesthete-hermit, trying in vain to titillate his surfeited senses and ascend to the supranatural realm of the "artificial." Playful experiments with synesthesia alternate with perceptive observations on Latin literature of decadence and contemporary writers.

Taken to task by Zola, H. became a contributor to the symbolist *Revue Indépendante*; Mallarmé wrote the "Prose pour Des Esseintes" in his honor; but for all that H. remained a naturalist. *Là-Bas* (1891; Down There, 1924) prepared the way for his Catholic novels. Demonology, magic rites, and the black mass, treated historically but also as practiced in the Paris and Lyons of his own time, are the theme of this novel, whose unbelieving hero, Durtal, becomes the biographer of Gilles de Rais, the 15th c. Bluebeard. *En route* (1895; Eng., 1908) describes Durtal's—and thus H.'s own—reconversion to Catholicism. *La cathédrale* (1898; The Cathedral, 1898), *L'Oblat* (1903; The Oblate, 1924), and *Les foules de Lourdes* (1906; The Crowds of Lourdes, 1925) complete the Catholic tetralogy. As a novelist as well as in his *Croquis parisiens* (1880; Parisian Sketches, 1962) H. remained all his life an inveterate Parisian, a dandy in the Baudelairean sense, and a gripping, ironic portrayer of certain seamy sides of modern city life. From 1899 until shortly before his death he lived as a lay brother in the Benedictine monastery of Ligugé ("Val des Saints" in *L'Oblat*).

FURTHER WORKS: *La Bièvre et Saint Séverin* (1898); *Trois églises et trois primitifs* (1908; partial trans., Saint Lydwine of Schiedam, 1923); *Oeuvres complètes* (Descaves, L., ed., 23 vols., 1928-34); *Lettres inédites à E. Zola* (1953)

BIBLIOGRAPHY: Thérive, A., *J. H., son oeuvre* (1924); Bachelin, H., *J. H., Du Naturalisme littéraire au naturalisme mystique* (1926); Valéry, P., "Souvenir de J. H." in *Variété II* (1929); Trudgian, H., *L'esthétique de H.* (1934); Cogny, P., *J. H. à la recherche de l'unité* (1953); Gallot, H. M., *Explication de J. H.* (1954); Laver, J., *First Decadent, Being the Strange Life of J. H.* (1954); Baldick, R., *The Life of J. H.* (1955); Chastel, G., *J. H. et ses amis* (1957); Georgin, R., *Le style de H.* (1957); Baldick, R., *La vie de H.* (1958); *Cahiers de la Tour Saint-Jacques*, VIII (1963), "H. issue."

KURT WEINBERG

HVIEZDOSLAV

(pseud. of *Országh Pavol*), Slovak poet, b. 2 Feb. 1849, Vyšný Kubín; d. 8 Nov. 1921, Dolný Kubín

H.'s first mature work was the lyric-epic poem *Hájnikova žena* (1884), which contrasts the morality of the common people with the conduct of the aristocracy. *Žalmy a hymny* (1886) and *Sonety* (1886) combine deep religiosity with faith in a better future for the people. The cycle *Letorosty* (3 vols., 1885, 1886, 1895) is written in classical strophes and deals with personal and national suffering. *Ežo Vlkolinský* (1890) and *Gábor Vlkolinský* (1897), stories in verse about the life of the lower aristocracy, are examples of the descriptive epic, while *Prechádzky jarom* and *Prechádzky letom* (1898) glorify God, nature, and work. In 1909 H. wrote the drama *Herodes a Herodias* on a biblical theme. The cycle *Krvavé sonety* (1914; Bloody Sonnets, 1950), a protest against the cruelties of war, was written at the beginning of World War I. H.'s numerous translations demonstrated the maturity of the Slovak language. His literary work influenced not only his contemporaries but also later generations.

FURTHER WORKS: *Stesky* (1903); *Dozvuky* (3 vols., 1909-11); *Sobrané spisy* (15 vols., 1924-31, 1939-42); *Spisy* (12 vols., 1951-63)

BIBLIOGRAPHY: Tichý, F., *H.* (1920); Kostolný, A., *P. O. H. Život a dielo* (1949)

ELISABETH NONNENMACHER

I

IBARBOUROU, Juana (Fernández) de

(pseud. of *J. Fernández Morales*), Uruguayan poet, b. 8 March 1895, Melo

In 1929 I., who at that time had published only three volumes of poems, was crowned Juana de América by the Uruguayan Romantic Juan Zorrilla de San Martín and the Mexican poet and critic Reyes (q.v.)—an event which aroused great controversy. Her first book, *Las lenguas de diamante* (1918), gripped its readers by the directness of its poetic vision and the feminine personality discernible behind it. The poems show a tender narcissism and at the same time a bold vitality. I. celebrated youth; she sang the beauty of the female body, joy at the coming of the beloved, harmonious accord with the world of animals and plants.

Her later volumes prove her poetic talent, though genuine, to be limited to a narrow range of themes. After 1930 her influence yielded to that of the avant-garde. Between 1930 and 1949 she published only four prose works, which, with *Chico Carlo* (1944) excepted, are of no significance. A deep inner crisis led her to new themes: anxiety in the face of life, of the evanescence of beauty and love, and of death. *Perdida* (1950) is her most profound, if not her best, book.

FURTHER WORKS: *Ejemplario: Libro de lectura* (n.d.); *El cántaro fresco* (1920); *Raíz salvaje* (1922); *La rosa de los vientos* (1930); *J. de I.: Sus mejores poemas* (1930); *Los loores de Nuestra Señora* (1934); *Estampas de la Biblia* (1934); *San Franciso de Asís* (with J. N. Quagliotti; 1935); *Los más bellos versos* (ed. F. Santelso, 1936); *Antología poética* (1940); *Poemas* (1942); *Los sueños de Natacha* (1945); *Autobiografía* (1950); *Obras completas*

(1953); *Azor* (1953); *Romances del destino* (1955); *Los mejores versos de J. de I.* (1956); *Oro y tormenta, sonetos* (1956); *Angor Dei* (1962; Spanish and English); *Tiempo* (1963); *El dulce milagro* (ed. D. I. Russell, 1964)

BIBLIOGRAPHY: Bollo, S., *La poesía de J. de I.* (1935); Russell, D. I., *J. de I.* (1951); Suiffet, N., *Tres poetas uruguayos: I. de I., Sara de Ibáñez, Hugo Petraglia Ajuirro; ensayos* (1955); Queiroz, Maria José de, *Á poesía de J. de I.* (1961)

EMIR RODRÍGUEZ MONEGAL

IBSEN, Henrik (Johan)

Norwegian playwright, lyrical poet, and essayist, b. 20 March 1828, Skien; d. 23 May 1906, Oslo

I.'s father was a wealthy businessman who lost his money when the boy was eight years old. What this meant to I., then and later on, is clearly apparent in his dramatic characters John Gabriel Borkman (in the play with that name as its title), Daniel Hejre (in *The Young Men's League*), and old Jon Gynt (in *Peer Gynt*). For a while I. planned to be a painter but was apprenticed to the apothecary at Grimstad, where he held out for six years without great enthusiasm. During his leisure hours he wrote poems, some of which expressed radical political tendencies. The February revolution in France in 1848 affected him deeply and has left its traces in I.'s first significant dramatic work, *Catalina* (1850; revised, 1875; Catiline, 1921), which was also influenced by his studies for his secondary school examinations and his personal status as a "*déclassé* aristocrat."

In the spring of 1850, I. went to Oslo in order to take his examination, intending to study medicine. At the university he came to know Aasmund Olafsen Vinje (1818-70) and Bjørnstjerne Bjørnson (1832-1910) and came in contact with radical circles. In 1850, the year of publication of *Catalina,* I.'s play *Kjæmpehøien* (The Warrior's Barrow, 1921) was performed at the Christiania theater. The following year I. was appointed theatrical adviser to the new Norwegian Theater in Bergen. In 1852 he received a modest travel grant that allowed him to go to Copenhagen and Dresden to study stagecraft. After his return he resumed his work in Bergen, this time working as stage director.

The Bergen years (1851-57) were of decisive significance in I.'s development. At the theater in Bergen he took an active part in the staging of his first plays, thereby acquiring a practical experience that was to prove invaluable for him as a playwright. He was as yet under the spell of Scandinavian national romanticism and the corresponding heroic style—*Fru Inger til Østråt* (1855; Lady Inger of Ostrat, 1909); *Sankthansnatten* (1853); *Gildet på Solhaug* (1856; The Feast at Solhoug, 1909); *Olaf Liljekrans* (1857; Eng., 1921)—but he was beginning to emancipate himself from these influences. With the play *Hærmændene på Helgeland* (1858; The Vikings of Helgeland, 1909), in which he still used the grandiloquent style of the sagas, he took leave of the glorious days of yore and its hero worship. From 1857 to 1864 he held the post of artistic adviser at the Norwegian Theater in Christiania. This institution, however, which rested on a weak financial foundation, went bankrupt in 1862.

This coincided with a crisis in I.'s personal life. He was given to understand that he had not lived up to his early promise as a playwright and that he was regarded as an insignificant author. During the years 1858 to 1863 he wrote the historical play *Kongsemnerne* (1864; The Pretenders, 1907) in which the portrayal of the principal characters indicated that I. for the first time was drawing on the tenets of modern psychology. The première in 1864 was a great success, the greatest thus far in I.'s career. The following year he went abroad and stayed away from his homeland for twenty-seven years, returning only briefly in 1874, 1885, and 1890.

In Italy he wrote *Brand* (1866; Eng., 1899). In this dramatic poem, the ethical ideology of which reveals parallels to Kierkegaard's world of thought, I. strove to formulate on a symbolic level the idea of the individual's being "chosen and called," which was to remain a leitmotiv of most of I.'s dramas of society. Next came a portrayal of Pastor Brand's polar opposite in *Peer Gynt* (1867; Eng., 1907), a work teeming with energy, sparkling with wit and irony, and abounding in sarcastic (but in no sense heartless) derision for the Norwegian national character with its self-satisfied complacency. Peer Gynt has been called the Faust of the North. In Act V in particular he "turns out to be, in full, Man in the sense of the old medieval mystery plays" (H. Schneider).

Brand and *Peer Gynt* established I. as the best-known but also the most controversial Scandinavian author. After the publication of the first of those two works, the Norwegian parliament granted I. a poet's pension. In 1868 he moved to Germany, living first in Dresden then (from 1875 on) in Munich. His comedy, *De unges forbund* (1869; The Young Men's League, 1900) was followed in 1873 by a ten-act tragedy on Julian the Apostate (*Kejser og Galilæer* (The Emperor and the Galilean, 1876), on which I. had been at work for nine years. The work bears witness to the deep impressions I. had received through his encounter with classical art in Rome, but it also reflects the conflicts of the present, *i.e.,* of I.'s own time (such as the Franco-Prussian war and the Commune of Paris). Yet this drama was bound to fall short of becoming a lasting and lastingly valid world tragedy, for I. "had not as yet found himself."

In the course of the next six years, I. published *Samfundets støtter* (1877; The Pillars of Society, 1888) and *Et dukkehjem* (1879; A Doll's House, 1889). In these works I. used for the first time modern natural dialogue. The latter of the two dramas mentioned, in particular, established I. as a world celebrity. Nora, the central figure in *A Doll's House,* was looked upon as the embodiment of the emancipation of women. Its performances throughout the civilized world were a succession of triumphs. The family drama *Gjengangere* (1881; Ghosts, 1923) was greeted with a sense of shock and also of indignation. It is a psychological masterpiece—technically an analytical drama like numerous other works of I.—in which the principal part is really played by fate. During the Victorian era it was regarded as a scandal, the more so since venereal disease and delicate problems of heredity were frankly discussed in it. No theater in Scandinavia would produce it. In righteous indignation at the reception of

Ghosts, I. wrote the play *En Folkefiende* (1882; An Enemy of the People, 1923), in which he expressed his contempt for the voice of the masses and hence for the principles of democracy, proclaiming simultaneously an "aristocratic radicalism."

While I. has come to be regarded as a radical critic of society, it must not be overlooked that he always upheld the rights of the individual. It was always the individual, the solitary, the elect who were the real concern of his works. It has been said—aptly, in a sense —that all I.'s social dramas are anti-society. He fought for the right of the individual to be himself. The work generally regarded as the high point in I.'s dramatic career appeared in 1884; this was *Vildanden* (The Wild Duck, 1897), a partly symbolic, partly realistic play in which I., the critic of men, coined the concept of the life-sustaining lie. In *Rosmersholm* (1886; Eng., 1900) I. achieved a further triumph through his ability to compress personal conflicts within the drama to lucid and stylistically flawless dramatic subentities. In *Hedda Gabler* (1890; Eng., 1891) I. presented a penetrating study of a frigid woman. In *Lille Eyolf* (1894; Little Eyolf, 1894) he dealt with the "law of change," the autumnal happiness of renunciation that appears after the ebbing or the sublimation of basic human drives. The motif of the erotic in brother-sister relationships—a motif with which I. was often preoccupied— also appears in this play. Hedvig bears the name of his sister. In *Bygmester Solness* (1892; The Master Builder, 1893) and *John Gabriel Borkman* (1896; Eng., 1897)—both of which paint the tragic solitude of the genius—we find a significant religious element. Solness and Borkman spend their lives wrestling with God as Jacob did, but God remains hidden. This same motif was used by I. for the last time in the "dramatic epilogue" *Når vi døde vagner* (1899; When We Dead Awaken, 1900).

FURTHER WORKS: *Kjærlighedens Komedie* (1862; Love's Comedy); *Terje Vigen* (1862; Eng., 1917); *Digte* (1871-75; Lyrics and Poems from Ibsen, 1912); *Fruen fra Havet* (1888); *Samlede Verker* (10 vols., 1898-1902); *Breve* (2 vols., 1904); *Episke Brand* (1907); *Efterladte Skrifter* (3 vols., 1909); *Samlede digterverker* (7 vols., 1918); *Samlede Verker* (20 vols., 1928 ff.). **Selected English trans.:** *The Correspondence of H. I.* (1905); *The Collected Works of H. I.* (12 vols., 1906-1912)

BIBLIOGRAPHY. Shaw, G. B., *The Quin-*

tessence of Ibsenism (1891); Brandes, G., *H. I.* (1906); Gosse, E., *I.* (1907); Bradbrook, M. C., *I. the Norwegian* (1946; 2nd ed., 1966); Northam, J., *I.'s Dramatic Method* (1952); McFarlane, H. W., *I. and the Temper of Norwegian Literature* (1960); Brustein, R., "I. and Revolt," in *TDR,* VII (1962), i, 113-54; Tedford, I., *I. Bibliography 1928-57* (1962); Haakonsen, D., ed., *I. Yearbook, VIII: Contemporary Approaches to I.* (1966)

NIELS C. BRÖGGER

I.'s plays do not depend for their interest on the action, or on the incidents. Even the characters, faultlessly drawn though they be, are not the first thing in his plays. But the naked drama—either the perception of a great truth, or the opening up of a great question, or a great conflict which is almost independent of the conflicting actors, and has been and is of far-reaching importance, this is what primarily rivets our attention. I. has chosen average lives in their uncompromising truth for the groundwork of all his later plays.

Joyce, J. "Ibsen's New Drama," in *The Fortnightly Review* (April 1900), p. 586

Yes, I. is ugly, common, hard, prosaic, bottomlessly bourgeois—and with his distinction so far in, as it were, so behind doors and beyond vestibules, that one is excusable for not pushing one's way to it. And yet of his art he's a master—and I feel in him, to the pitch of almost intolerable boredom, the presence and the insistence of life. On the other hand, his mastery, so bare and lean as it is, wouldn't count nearly as much in any medium in which the genius was otherwise represented.

James, H., (1893), in Peacock, R., *The Poet in the Theatre* (1946), p. 65

There were in I. from his earliest period two very powerful forces, one an overriding passion for Truth, or perhaps rather Truthfulness, and the other an exceptional sense of dramatic situation based on the interplay of character.

By temperament he was an idealist, but an idealist with only one ideal. If others evade facts and become romantics of illusion, I. faced them and became a romantic of Truthfulness.

Peacock, R., *The Poet in the Theatre* (1946), p. 66

His social plays, like Gotthelf's short stories, are sermons, in which the Old Testament god of retribution is proclaimed in the profane language of contemporary common speech. In these plays Ibsen passes judgment on his time and on himself.

Muschg, W., *Tragische Literaturgeschichte* (1953), p. 159

In him, as in Nietzsche, contemporary culture breakes the grip of positivism and soothing morality and acquires a spiritual dimension. . . . I. is not only a great artist but a moralist and reformer too. . . . His basic theme is the clash of dream and reality, creation and life. . . .

Berdyaeff, N., *H. I.*, in *Neue Schweizer Rundschau*, XXI (1928), p. 743

I. gives free play to ideas: in its metallic coldness the idea expertly straightens out the tangled yarn of feelings. What he loses in action, he gains in analysis. The mechanism of the mind has found its master. His heroes are skeletons who bespeak a powerful and gloomy humanity: they bear the names of very great passions, which they do not serve. I. is not willing to admit that he prefers ideas to living beings. And he is truthful: life is indeed his subject, as it naturally is for every artist; it is also true that he gives life to ideas rather than endowing life with ideas. His heroes argue before they act. They do worse: they discern all their actions intellectually. They have more consciousness than passion, and more principles even than acts to perform.

Suarès, A., *Trois hommes* (1935), p. 117

I. [merely] continued the struggle of his predecessors and stood at the end of a long succession in which the opponents of romanticism were united. The fatal blow which he struck at the enemy consisted in his exposure of the tragi-comedy of romantic idealism. It is true that there had been nothing absolutely new about that since the appearance of *Don Quixote*, but Cervantes had still treated his hero with a good deal of sympathy and forbearance, whereas Ibsen completely destroys his Brand, Peer Gynt, and Gregers Werle. The "ideal demands" of his romantics are revealed as pure egoism, the harshness of which is scarcely mitigated by the artlessness of the egoists themselves.

Hauser, A., *Sozialgeschichte der Kunst und Literatur*, Vol. II (1953), p. 467 ff.

He relies upon the form that became typical in the works of Lessing and of more modern French writers—not upon the form of Gerhart Hauptmann. He simply sets up the elements essential to the action. Episodes as an end in themselves are nonexistent. And his mastery of the mathematics of drama is more complete than that of Lessing or of the French writers; he is probably the most exact dramatic technician in the literature of any age.

Kerr, A., *Die Welt im Drama* (1954), p. 13 f.

Only in the Attic drama did the past exact its tribute so inexorably from the present. On I.'s stage, time sometimes seems to stand still. For the characters immerse themselves in the past far too passionately to have any breath or interest left for the present. Yet to resurrect the present from the past takes the most intense focusing of all the dramatic creativity with which H. I. was endowed.

Jacobs, M., *Ibsens Bühnentechnik* (1920), p. 47

This nagging quality, this habitual bitterness— they are essential in his greatness, because they beckon to the poetry in him, and carry it with them under the ground. . . .

Forster, E. M., *Abinger Harvest* (1953), p. 101

ICAZA, Francisco A. de

Mexican poet and essayist, b. 2 Feb. 1863, Mexico City; d. 27 May 1925, Madrid

I. was a diplomat and spent many years in Spain and some time in Germany. Despite his attempts to emulate 17th c. Spanish lyrics, his characteristic quality as a poet is the so-called "soft tone" of the Mexican. His essayistic works include several books on Cervantes and studies of *Hebbel* (1919) and *Nietzsche* (1922). His *Lope de Vega* (1923; rev. ed., 1962) received a Spanish Academy prize. More wedded intellectually to the 17th than to the 20th c., I. was an inspired gentleman amateur of letters in the manner of Montaigne or John Evelyn. His detachment from the professional concerns of his writing contemporaries, coupled with the excellence of his critical work, helped secure I. the highest esteem in Madrid's literary circles.

FURTHER WORKS: *Efímeras* (1892); *Lejanías* (1899); *Las "novelas ejemplares" de Cervantes; sus críticos, sus modelos literarios, sus modelos vivos, y su influencia en el arte* (1901; rev. ed., 1915); *La canción del camino* (1905); *La universidad alemana; su idea; su función; su objeto, y sus relaciones con la cultura general* (1915); *De cómo y porqué La trá fingida no es de Cervantes, y otros nuevos estudios cervánticos* (1916); *Supercherías y errores cervantinos puestos en claro* (1917); *El "Quijote" durante tres siglos* (1918); *Cancionero de la vida honda y de la emoción fugitiva* (1922); *Conquistadores y pobladores de Nueva España; diccionario autobiográfico sacado de los textos originales* (2 vols., 1923); *Obras completas* (4 vols., 1928); *Estudios cervantinos* (selected by de A. Henestrosa, 1947); *Obras escogidas* (with Introduction by F. C. Sáinz de Robles, 1951); *Páginas escogidas* (1958)

BIBLIOGRAPHY: *CHA*, LIII (1963), 485-500, contains short commemorative pieces on I. by A. V. Zamora, L. Rosales, A. de la Serna, and others; Abreu Gómez, E., "Centenario de don F. A. de I.," *Cuadernos Americanos,* XXXVIII (1963), 193-209

ANTON M. ROTHBAUER

ICAZA, Jorge
Ecuadorian writer, b. 10 July 1902, Quito

I., who was also a diplomat, became the leader of the neorealistic movement in Ecuador. His novel *Huasipungo* (1934; rev. ed., 1951; Huasipungo: The Villagers [trans. of 1951 version], 1964), which has been translated into many languages, presents the drama of the oppressed, exploited Indians of Ecuador. It was sharply criticized for its realism and even its literary significance was questioned. Nevertheless the novel is not merely a social document: it is also notable for its directness and powerful language.

FURTHER WORKS: *Sin sentido* (1927); *El intruso* (1928); *"Como ellos quieren" ¿Cuál es?* (1931); *Como ellas quieran* (1932); *El otro* (1933); *Barro de la Sierra* (1933); *En las calles* (1934); *Flagelo* (1936); *Cholos* (1937); *Media vida deslumbrados* (1942); *Huairapamuchas* (1948); *Seis relatos* (1952); *El chulla Romero y Flórez* (1958); *Viejos cuentos* (1960); *Obras escogidas* (1961)

BIBLIOGRAPHY: Ferrándiz Alborz, F., *El novelista hispano-americano J. I.* (1961); Ojeda, E., *Cuatro obras de J. I.* (1961); Mata, G., *Humberto Memoria para J. I.* (1964)

FERNANDO ALEGRIA

ICELANDIC LITERATURE

Icelandic nationalism, which had been passive for centuries, was reborn under the impact of 19th-c. romanticism. Dual in nature, one aspect of it was characterized by the striving for national independence in accord with the spirit of the times. Its other aspect was characterized by a deep admiration of the saga literature and the saga age, which, not without reason, is looked upon as a golden age by the present leaders. Fortunately, there was an unbroken tradition of poetry, religious and secular, from the earliest times. The secular poetry was in form and diction directly descended from skaldic poetry, while its matter and spirit was that of the chivalric and metrical romances (*rímur*), sometimes approaching the heroic spirit of the sagas.

The modern romantic poetry of Jónas Hallgrímsson (1801-1845) is formed in deliberate reaction against the ornate and unnatural *rímur* style, hence it is almost classical in its simplicity. The scholar Konráð Gíslason (1808-1891) wrote and formulated rules for the modern puristic style, based partly on the saga style, partly on the modern rural style of Icelandic folktales. These men were followed by Jón Thoroddsen (1818-68), father of the modern novel, and Benedikt Gröndal (1826-1907), splendid poet and humorous prosaist. Following Hallgrímsson, the romantic heroic poetry of Grímur Thomsen (1820-96), Steingrímur Thorsteinsson (1831-1913), and Matthías Jochumsson (1835-1920) drew its vitality from Icelandic nature and Icelandic cultural traditions, especially the heroic spirit of the sagas. Jochumsson was for half a c. considered the greatest poet of Iceland. Two autodidacts, Sigurður Breiðfjörð (1798-1846) and Hjálmar Jónssonfrá Bólu (1796-1875), were fine representatives of the *rímur* poetry, despised by Hallgrímsson because of its ornate, baroque style, but still very popular in Iceland. Jochumsson wrote the first Icelandic romantic play (1864); he was followed by Einarsson (q.v.), who also wrote mostly romantic, but also realistic plays.

It is to the credit of Brandes (q.v.), who did so much to introduce modern European thinking into Scandinavia, that contemporary European thought—and indirectly realism—began to make its way in Iceland. The dates of the periodicals *Verðandi* (1882) and *Heimdallur* (1884-85) can be cited as the birth of realism in Iceland. Important among the realists was Gestur Pálsson (1852-91), a novelist of social satire. But the lyric poet and political leader Hannes Hafstein (1861-1922) and the novelist Einar Hjörleifsson Kvaran (1859-1938) soon turned from realism to a new, national, progressive romanticism, the gospel of progress. Realists, too, were the social-democratic poet Erlingsson (q.v.), the autodidact novelist Þorgils Gjallandi (1851-1915; pseud. of Jón Stefánsson), and the Canadian farmer-poet Stephansson (q.v.).

Benediktsson (q.v.) was chief poet of the neoromantic school as well as the most eloquent apostle of progress, both material and spiritual, in Iceland. He was joined by Friðjónsson as well as Trausti (qq.v.). Both started as realists, both became ardent progressives as well as admirers of rural culture, and both became anti-socialistic. The world-famous priest Jón Svensson (1856-1944) was an exile and a Catholic convert, hence inordinately fond of the Iceland of his youth. He imparted this love to all the youngsters of Europe, America, and Japan through his *Nonni* books.

About the turn of the century the lyric took a turn from realism to neoromanticism under the influence of the French decadents and Nietzsche. This group was represented by Benediktsson, the poet Guðmundur Guðmundsson (1874-1919), the poet and novelist Hulda (1881-1946; pseud. of Unnur Benedikstdóttir Bjarklind), and the poets Sigurjón Friðjónsson (1867-1950) and Sigurður Sigurðsson frá Arnarholti (1879-1939), both closely connected with Scandinavian neoromantics and symbolists. Two poets of a more realistic turn were Jakob Thorarensson (b. 1886) and Örn Arnarsson (1884-1942; pseud. of Magnús Stefánsson). Apart from Benediktsson, the neoromantic poets took little interest in politics, probably the chief interest of their romantic and realistic forebears. Another current of neoromanticism came from England and America: spiritualism and theosophy, the Oriental philosophy. Converts to this group were the realist Kvaran and the poet Jakob Jóhannesson Smári (b. 1889).

A Scandinavian bohemian coterie in Copenhagen drew a new group of writers who took no interest in politics. They chose to leave Iceland primarily because they could not make a living by writing in Icelandic. But though they wrote in Danish to gain an audience, they cherished their Icelandic memories, folktales, sagas, and modern life. Jóhann Sigurjónsson (1880-1919) gained at once Scandinavian, and even European, fame as a playwright, but he was short-lived. Kamban (q.v.) was also a fine playwright and novelist, while Gunnarsson (q.v.) was also a prolific novelist of great popularity in Scandinavia, Europe, and America. Jónas Guðlaugsson (1887-1916), who died before thirty, was a fine poet. Another novelist, Friðrik Ásmundsson Brekkan (1888-1958), and the playwright Tryggvi Sveinbjörnsson (1891-1964) also wrote in Danish.

World War I had practically no influence on Icelandic literature, except in Gunnarsson's problem novels. The neoromantic movement continued during and after the war, stressing individual emotion, imagination, and beautiful verse forms as well as natural diction. Its greatest representatives were Stefán Sigurðsson fá Hvítadal (1887-1933), later a Catholic convert, and David Stefánsson (1895-1964), a most prolific poet. They influenced their contempo-

raries and followers such as Jón Magnússon (1896-1944), Jóhann Jónsson (1896-1932), and Magnús Ásgeirsson (1901-1955), greatest translator of his time in Iceland. But Jón Helgason (b. 1899), a satirist and a professor of Old Norse at the University of Copenhagen, and Tómas Guðmundsson (b. 1901), a humorist, were both fine poets, and each had a tone of his own.

Most important of the neoromantic prose writers was Sigurður Nordal (b. 1886), professor of Icelandic literature at the University of Iceland. He wrote prose poetry, but was most important as a critic. He was editor-in-chief of the great edition of the sagas (1933 ff.) and wrote the epoch-making *Íslenzk Menning* (1942), a study of Icelandic culture. Stefánsson was also a novelist and playwright, and one of his plays is already a classic. Guðmundur G. Hagalín (q.v.) is a prolific novelist, short story writer, autobiographer, and essayist. Some of his novels are written in a primitive style, and he is anticommunist. So is K. Guðmundsson (q.v.), also a prolific novelist, short story writer, and autobiographer, who wrote his works in Norwegian. His works, like those of Jón Svensson (and unlike those of Hagalín), have been translated into many languages.

Guðmundur Daníelsson (b. 1910) is another prolific novelist and author of travel books. Jón Björnsson (b. 1907) wrote novels in Danish, some historical.

Four playwrights wrote symbolic, even expressionistic, plays: Sigurður Pétursson Eggerz (1875-1945), the Canadian-Icelanders Guttormur J. Guttormsson (b. 1878) and Jakobina Johnson (b. 1883), and Jóhannes P. Pálsson (b. 1881). (After Stephansson, Johnson is the finest of the Canadian-Icelandic poets.)

Part of the generation maturing during World War I and after it, under the influence of German expressionism, French surrealism, and Marxistic socialism, revolted against the form and spirit of the old national romanticism and its puristic style. A milestone in this development was Þórbergur Þórðarson's (q.v.) *Bréf til Láru* (1924). It is a fiery protest against capitalism, church, and clergy and an equally passionate eulogy of socialism. At the same time the book is full of autobiographical anecdotes and droll humor, and it contains as well a few things to shock the bourgeoisie. Even more shocking in form and ideas was *Vefarinn mikli frá Kasmír* (1927) by Laxness (q.v.), written in a monastery with the abandon of the French surrealists and teeming with postwar ideas, a true record of the mind of the author, a Catholic convert. His next book, *Al Þýðubókin* (1929), written in California, marked his conversion to communism, afterward his guiding philosophy. From this point of view he wrote five important novels before he won the Nobel Prize for Literature in 1955.

During the depression of the 1930's most writers became socialists: the poets Einarsson (q.v.), Jóhannes Jónasson úr Kötlum (b. 1899), Guðmunder Böðvarsson (b. 1904), Snorri Hjartarson (b. 1906), Steinn Steinarr (1908-1958), and Jón Jónsson úr Vör (b. 1917). Now all turned to the leftist periodical *Rauðir Pennar* (1935-38), published by Kristinn E. Andrésson (b. 1901). Later Andrésson joined with others to found a society, Mál og Menning, to publish good books and translations (which did not necessarily have to be leftist). Among their publications was Sigurður Nordal's *Islenzk Menning* (1942).

During World War II, Iceland was occupied by the British (1940) and Americans (1941-44). In 1942 Iceland cut the last ties with Denmark and became an independent republic. The war changed Iceland from an austere, poor country into a newly rich one with a chronic inflation. The story that Laxness tells in *Atómstöðin* (1948) of the occupation and the country joining NATO is not a flattering one, but one must not forget that it is written from a communistic and nationalistic point of view. Vying with Mál og Menning, another new society was formed by the Co-operative party headed by Jónas Jónsson frá Hriflu; it was called Menningarsjóður ("The Culture Fund") and Þjóðvinafélagið. Another society to publish cheap and good books was Almenna Bóka-félagið, founded in 1955 by conservatives and anticommunists. Of publishers the maecenas Ragnar Jónsson (b. 1904), of Helgafell, was most important; he published a periodical (1942 ff.). The periodical *Birtingur* (1957 ff.) was published by modernistic artists and writers.

Snorri Hjartarsson experimented with end-rhymes; his poetry is an apostrophe to Icelandic independence. Steinn Steinarr and Jón úr Vör both were pessimists, Steinn Steinarr more deeply so. His poetry grew to be quite modernistic, even abstract, though he mostly preserved the time-honored rhyme and alliteration. This was given up by Jón úr Vör, and some of the modernists of the fifties: he, like them, was mostly influenced by the *förtitalistar* of Sweden. The best of the modern poets was Hannes Pétursson (b. 1931), but he was comparatively conventional. Even more conventional in the neoromantic style was Þóroddur Guðmundsson (b. 1904), son of Guðmundur Friðjónsson á Sandi. But the most interesting representative of the traditional poetry of Iceland was Sveinbjörn Beinteinsson (b. 1924), author of a collection of *rímur* which made him at once the chief *rímur* poet of his time. He also wrote a description of *rímur* meters, which was better and more comprehensive than the older works on the subject. Finally he published a collection of the *rímur* of other poets, most of whom were contemporary. What was astounding was to see the *rímur* poetry flourishing side by side with the modernist poetry, the so-called "atom poetry," and practiced even by some of the same authors. While that is the case, one should not despair about the old rhyme-alliterative poetry.

Of prose writers Elías Mar (b. 1924) has written one good novelette, *Vögguvísa* (1950); Indriði G. Þorsteinsson (b. 1926), *79 af stöðinni* (1955), a very popular novel (later filmed); and Björn Björnsson (b. 1922), *Virkisvetur* (1959), a prize novel. Some recent playwrights are: the father and son Jakob Jónsson (b. 1904) and Jökull Jakobsson (b. 1933), who wrote one successful play, *Hart í bak* (1962); Agnar Þórðarson (b. 1917), who has had many successes; and the brothers Jón (b. 1921) and Jónas (b. 1923) Árnason, who wrote one musical comedy, a successful farce. Of the leftist critics and poets Hannes Sigfûsson (b. 1922) and Sigfús Daðason (b. 1928) may be mentioned; of the rightist, Sigurður A. Magnússon (b. 1928) and Mattías Johannessen (b. 1930) are most promising.

BIBLIOGRAPHY: Nordal, S., *Udsigt over Islands Litteratur i det 19. og 20. aarhundrede* (1927); Blanker, F., *The History of Scandinavian Literatures* (1938); Dzulko, R., *Studien zur isländischen Lyrik der Gegenwart* (1941); Einarsson, S., *History of Icelandic Prose Writers 1800-1940* (1948); Gislason, B. M., *Islands Litteratur efter Sagatiden ca. 1400-1948* (1949); Beck, R., *History of Icelandic Poets 1800-1940* (1950); Andrésson, K. E., *Det moderna Islands Litteratur 1918 bis 1948* (1955); Einarsson, S., *History of Icelandic Literature* (1957), *Islensk Bókmenntasaga 874-1960* (1960); Bjarnason, L., ed., *Anthology of Modern Icelandic Literature* (1962)

STEFAN EINARSSON

IKOR, Roger

French writer, b. 28 May 1912, Paris

I., whose parents emigrated from Russia to France, spent his childhood in Paris, studied philology, and became a high-school teacher.

Les Fils d'Avram (1955; The Sons of Avrom, 1958) was awarded the Prix Goncourt in 1955. This novel, about Jewish immigrants in France in the first half of the 20th c., vividly describes the fortunes and sufferings of a Jewish family. L's work, which never succumbs to a hatred that would be understandable in the light of recent Jewish history, is an appeal to mankind to turn away from contemporary errors and get back to the path of pure humanity.

FURTHER WORKS: *A Travers nos déserts* (1950); *Les Grands Moyens* (1951); *Mise au net* (1957); *Ciel ouvert* (1959); *Alma Mater* (in *Les oeuvres libres*, 1960); *Le Semeur de vent* (1960); *La Carte du tendre* (in *Les Oeuvres libres*, 1960); *Un Grand Garçon*, (in *Les Oeuvres libres*, 1961); *Les Murmures de la guerre* (1961); *La Pluie sur la mer* (1962); *Ronge-temps* (in *Les Oeuvres libres*, 1963); *La Ceinture de ciel* (1964); *Gloucq, ou La Toison d'or* (1965); *Les Poulains* (1966)

BIBLIOGRAPHY: Rose, M. G., "I.'s Moral Metaphor," *FR,* XXXIX (1965), 220-29

* * *

ILLYÉS, Gyula

Hungarian poet, fiction writer, essayist, and dramatist, b. 2 Nov. 1902, Rácegres-puszta

I. was on his way to getting a fine education despite the fact that he was born into a poor peasant family. But in 1919 he broke off his studies to join the Hungarian Red Army. After the fall of the Hungarian Republic in 1919, he emigrated to Paris, where he came into contact with the working-class movement as well as with surrealistic circles (see surrealism). When he returned to Hungary, he was assistant editor to Babits (q.v.) on the periodical *Nyugat.* After Babits died, I. continued to publish the literary magazine until 1944 under the title *Magyar Csillag.* I. lived in Tihany, on Lake Balaton.

A socialist, I.'s aesthetics and Marxian ideals place him in the tradition of János Arany (1817-82) and Sándor Petöfi (1823-49). Strongly influenced by modern French writing, I. is nevertheless closely bound to his home district,

the Puszta. He is the spokesman and champion of its small farmers and rural laborers. Having fought as a revolutionary when a young man, I. became a zealous advocate of agrarian reform; with the novel *Puszták népe* (1936; People of the Puszta, 1967) he was counted among the most respected writers of the nationalistic school. I. is original in his language and shows a deep sense of humor coupled with an ability to render objective judgment of his chosen subject matter—the characteristic qualities of the trans-Danube peasant.

FURTHER WORKS: *Nehéz föld* (1928); *Sarjúrendek* (1930); *Oroszország* (1934); *Szálló egek alatt* (1935); *Petöfi* (1936); *Rend a romokban* (1937); *Magyarok* (1938); *Külön világban* (1939); *Összegyüjtött versei* (3 vols., 1940); *Csizma az asztalon* (1941); *Kora tavasz* (1941); *Mint a darvak* (1942); *Hunok Párisban, regény* (1946); *Összes versei* (3 vols., 1947); *Franciaországi változatok* (1947); *Lélekbúvár* (1948); *Petöfi: 4. át dolgozott Kiadás* (1950); *Két férfi* (1950); *Két kéz* (1950); *I.G. válogatott versei* (1952); *Ozorai példa Színmü három felvonásban* (1952); *Válogatott Költemények* (1953); *Fáklyaláng; dráma két felvonásban, utójátékkal* (1953); *György Dózsa* (1954); *A csudafurulyás juhász: verses mesék és müfordítások* (1954); *Kézfogások* (1956); *Hetvenhét Magyar népmese; Szántó Piroska rajzaival* (1956); *Kinai szelence* (1958); *Új versek* (1961); *Ebéd a Kastélyban: egy électregény fejezetei* (1962); *Nem volt elég; válogatott versek* (1962); *Petöfi Sándor* (1963); *Másokért, egyedül. Két dráma* (1963); *Ingyen lakoma; tanulmányok, vallomásak* (2 vols., 1964); *Tüz vagyok: Petöfi élete* (1964); *Hetvenhét Magyar Népmese* (1964; Once Upon a Time: Forty Hungarian Folktales, 1964); *Ki a Magyar* (1965)

BIBLIOGRAPHY: Csicsery-Rónay, I., "G. I.: Grand Prix for Poetry," *BA,* XL (1966), 156-57

* * *

INDIAN LITERATURE

Indian literature in the 20th c. encompasses literary activity in the fourteen major languages of India. These vernacular literatures developed autonomously after the disintegration of the classical unity of Vedic India. Though there is no uniform development, there are certain thematic, aesthetic, and formal similarities between these separate literatures. In addition the present century has seen the emergence of a significant body of Indian writing in English.

The literature of the early decades witnessed a determined search for a new national identity. The close association between the artist and the patriot resulted in writing that was both nationalistic and mystical, for emphasis on the Vedanta (a monistic philosophy derived from the Vedas) was equated with rejection of the West. Following Independence in 1947, fervent nationalism gave way to cultural introspection and a reappraisal of traditions that had been held sacrosanct for centuries.

Some modern Indian writers have tried to reconcile present social and historic dislocations with traditional Hindu values in terms of the conservative *chayavada* hero. Others have sought resolution through the *pragativada* hero, a common man of the working classes conscious of strength of labor unions and strikes. Though the approaches are diverse the emphasis is on the hero and on the necessity of recovering human dignity.

In Bengal, the traditional seat of culture in India, the patriotic pre-Independence *swadeshi* and *satyagraha* movements found literary expression in political balladeering. This atmosphere of nationalism forged the early sensibilities of Rabindranath Tagore (q.v.).

Rabindranath (1861-1941) is the most outstanding literary figure of modern India. *Gitanjali* (1912) won him world recognition and the Nobel Prize in 1913. The poems in the collection dramatize man's search for God in the changing masks of nature. A prolific artist, Rabindranath also wrote several novels including *Chokker Bali* (1901-1902), *Noukadubi* (1903-1905), *Gora* (1909), *Chaturanga* (1916), and *Jogajog* (1929). The early novels expose a tension between Vedic orthodoxy and modern individualism; the later novels, however, reveal his break with traditional society. Compassion for the individual is also apparent in *Hungry Stones and Other Stories* (1916). The same spirit of humanism informs his plays, especially *Pryaschitta* (1909), *Rakta Karabi* (1926), and *Tapati* (1929). His philosophy is articulated in the essays "Personality" (1921), "Nationalism" (1921), "Manusher Dharma" (1933), and "Kalantar" (1937). The final impression of Rabindranath is that of an artist who rose above narrow nationalism and who regarded art as a means of self-knowledge.

Among the followers of Rabindranath was Sarat Chandra Chatterjee (1876-1938). Sarat

Chandra rejected the romantic milieu of the aristocratic land-owning *zamindar,* and drew his characters instead from the urban middle classes. For this he was labeled a "social realist" by some critics and severely attacked by the orthodox.

While Sarat Chandra explored the urban crises of his people Bibhuti Bhusan Banerjee (1899-1950) restricted his vision to rural Bengal. In the novel *Pather Panchali* (1930), he describes the dwindling fortunes of a Brahmin family until its dissolution as a unit. Pathos, though a dominant element in this novel, is balanced by humor and irony.

The majority of novelists and short-story writers—among whom are Tarashankar Bandopadhya (b. 1898), Annada Sankar Ray (b. 1904), and Narayan Ganguli (b. 1918)—are continuing the traditions of 19th c. Bengali prose. Bandopadhya's novels *Kalindi* (1940), *Hansuli Bamker Upakatha* (1947), *Arogya Niketan* (1952), and *Bicharak* (1956), Ray's *Satyasatya* (6 vols., 1930-42) and *Ratna o Shrimati* (1955-56), and Ganguli's *Upanivesh* (1943), *Shilalipi* (1949), and *Pada Sanchar* (1955) are connected by theme and execution to the preceding century.

The most prominent novelist in the small group of innovators is Manik Bandopadhya (1908-1956), whose work is characterized by a compassionate social realism and the creation of non-traditional types: the cheat, the destitute, the sexually frustrated.

In poetry the need to break with past traditions was evident as early as 1925. In the decade 1925-35, there emerged a group of young men—Premendra Mitra (b. 1905), Jibanananda Das (1899-1954), Buddhadeva Bose (b. 1908), and Achintyakumar Sengupta (b. 1903) —who rejected the cult of Tagoresque imitations. The magazine *Kavita,* edited by one of the group, became their chief outlet. In collections of poems such as Mitra's *Prathama* (1933), Das's *Jhara Palak* (1926), and Sengupta's *Amavasya* (1929), one notices the younger poets' search for new themes and new idioms, often influenced by Jung and Freud. Perhaps the most important of the group was Das, who injected a necessary, at times even savage, note of irony and sensuous metaphysics into contemporary Bengali poetry.

More disciplined and intellectual is the poetry of Sudhindranath Dutta (1901-1960), who termed himself a "nihilist." He was a nihilist in a special sense; faith in democracy, in revolutions, appeared suspect to him, and in his poetry he advocated an independent inquiry into values. His most significant work is a long lyric poem, *Samvarta* (1943). He also turned his attention to translating Shakespeare, Valéry, and Mallarmé.

Hindi, the official national language, did not mature as a literary vehicle until the turn of this c. The Hindi writer, like his Bengali counterpart, found sufficient inspiration in patriotic sentiments. Once sovereignty was assured, the writer turned his attentions inward, exploring the themes of authenticity and identity. Sambhunath Singh (b. 1917), Kedarnath Singh (b. 1934), Kedarnath Agarwal (b. 1912), and Trilochan Shastri (b. 1917), have sought to discover integrity in the village culture that survived waves of foreign invasion. Works such as S. Singh's *Chhayalok* (1945) and *Divalok* (1953), K. Singh's *Abhi* and *Bilkul Abhi* (1959), Agarwal's *Yug ki Ganga* (1947), and Shastri's *Dharati* (1945) reveal these poets' desire to revitalize folk and regional literatures.

The search for authenticity has also led to experimentation. In a time of social upheaval the Hindi poet often sees himself as an *anastha,* an orphan, who has been abandoned by (or who himself has abandoned) the orthodox values of tradition-loving India. The *anastha* poet has to create new meanings and new areas of reverence that are in keeping with the contemporary world of steel foundries, dams, locomotives, slums, unemployment, hunger, and the black market. He also has to discover new forms, methods, and vocabulary to communicate this contemporary Indian sensibility.

The experimentalism of the Hindi poets manifests itself in a variety of approaches. Shyamsher Bahadur Singh (b. 1911) is a self-conscious and esoteric writer who uses personal imagery and unusual syntax. Bhawaniprasad Misra (b. 1914), on the other hand, approximates the rhythms of everyday speech in order to communicate directly with the masses.

Contemporary Punjabi literature appears to be inspired by the main socio-political movements of the region: Singh Sabha, Akali, and Marxism.

The best-known of the earlier generation of writers was Bhai Vir Singh (1872-1957). His popular novels, such as *Sundari* (1898), extol the chivalric courage of the Sikhs. His main contribution was a much-needed rejuvenation of the Punjabi language.

Mohan Singh of the following generation,

an editor of *Punj Darya*, can be considered a progressive poet. His early poetry—*Savey Pattar* (1936), *Kasumbaara* (1939), *Adhvate* (1943) and *Asia da Chanan* (1944)—were very well received. His later work—*Kuch Sach* (1950), *Avazan* (1954), and *Vedda Vela* (1958)—is written from a Marxist position.

Amrita Pritam (b. 1919), one of the few successful women poets of this generation, enjoys popularity in both East and West Punjab (Pakistan). Her poetry, especially *Lamian vatan* (1948), *Sune Hure* (1955), and *Ashoka Chetti* (1957), is remarkable for its spontaneity and musicality. She has also written novels, among which are *Pinjar* (1950) and *Ahalna* (1952), and short stories (*Akhari Khat*, 1956).

In the state of Gujarat the novel has been at the center of literary activity. An implicit dissatisfaction with contemporary society has led to a thematic rebirth of nationalism and to the revitalization of the historical novel. The setting is generally the last decades of the British raj. The naive patriotism of the first wave of nationalist literature in India is in this case replaced by romance and a certain glorification of the cultural genius.

One of the most significant Gujarati novelists is Pannalal Nanalal Patel (b. 1912). In *Malela Jiv* (1942) and *Manvi ni Bhavai* (1947), he presents peasant characters displaying a wide range of folk emotions. His short-story publications include *Sukh Dukh-nan Sathi* (1940), *Orata* (1954), and *Dil-ni Vat* (1956).

Drama, though not a traditional art form in Gujarat, has developed rapidly in the last fifty years. Initially, the plays fell into one of two categories, the literary (for reading) and the professional (for staging). No attempt was made to fuse the two elements into a single play. Current theatrical taste, both of the dramatist and of the audience, discourages the development of the purely literary play, and the last such drama of merit was published as long ago as 1914. The first decade of the present century saw partially successful attempts to modernize the provincial stage through the introduction of female players, experimentation with lighting techniques, musical accompaniments, and a revision of the repertory itself. Since World War I the amateur stage has matured remarkably in Ahmedabad, Baroda, Rajkot, and Surat. The most promising playwright in this area is Umashankar Jethalal Joshi (b. 1911). In *Sapna Bhara* (1934), a collection of one-act plays, he attacks social hypocrisy in a village setting. He has also written the verse play *Prachina* (1944).

The major languages of southern India are Tamil, Telegu, Malayalam, and Kannada. These languages, and the cultures they reflect, are in many ways wholly different from those of northern India.

The 19th c. witnessed an increase in foreign missionary activity throughout the country, but especially in the province of Madras. The most immediate effect was the popularizing of the English language in a predominantly Tamil-speaking area, and the subsequent introduction of Western ideas. The 20th c. Tamil writer retains an admiration for Western modes of inquiry but is intensely regional in choice of themes.

Patriotism, which found diverse expression in the 20th c. Indian imagination, was refined to mysticism by Subramanian Bharati (1882-1921). His most important contribution was his thematic and formal modernization of the vernacular literature. In his prose poems he often incorporated Western ideas and techniques. But he was also a scholar of the traditional Hindu epics and reinterpreted the *Mahabharata* for the modern Tamil reader.

Contemporary Tamil prose reflects the impulse for glorification of the past, and the historical novel, with its documentation of the Pallava and Chola dynasties, appears to dominate the scene.

More interesting and more symptomatic of contemporary conditions in Tamilnad is the problem of literary criticism. Because the modern reader in Tamilnad often finds himself socially and spiritually dislocated from Vedic and medieval India, he has created a need for the revision of Tamil prose and the reinterpretations of the vernacular classics. This has led to the establishment of the critical essay as a powerful form.

Contemporary Kannada literature is inspired by a conscious spirit of renascence. This renascent impulse has urged the Kannarese artist to question the values of his society, to renew interest in local mythology and temple carvings, and to reevaluate Hindu epics. The rehabilitation of traditional values has been undertaken by a small group that consists largely of swamis. The most significant achievement of traditionalists like Raghavendracharya Swamirayacharya Panchmukhi (b. 1898) has been in the area of textual criticism.

Disillusionment of the artist has enriched Kannarese satire. Vishnu Govind Bhat (b.

1923) ridicules social, political, and religious institutions in his poetry—*Raktangali* (1946), *Kavya Vedane* (1951), *Tutana Padagalu* (1951) —and in his short stories and sketches—*Sahyadri* (1947) and *Divya Kathegalu* (1949). His methods are generally those of realism, but his resolutions sometimes allow faith in the inherent goodness of man to triumph over skepticism.

The poetry of Dattatreya Ramachandra Bendre (b. 1896) is motivated by social criticism. However, unlike Bhat, Bendre resolves the issues in terms of socialist philosophies. His best-known collections are *Krishna Kumari* (1922), *Gari* (1930), and *Aralu-Maralu* (1957). His literary theories are stated in *Sahitya Mattu Vimarsha* (1935) and *Sahitya Samsodhan* (1941).

At the beginning of the 20th c., Malayali literature was dominated by Sanskritic traditions: by *sringara* (classical convention) and *nayaikas* (Sanskrit love conventions). Vallathol and Uloor Parmeswara are considered the founders of modern literature in Malayalam.

Vallathol Narayana Menon (1879-1958) began his career by translating the *Ramayana, sloka* by *sloka*. His early poetry—*Ritu Vilasam* (1899), *Badhira Vilapam* (1909), and *Anirudhan* (1913)—was influenced by classical discipline. *Oru Chitram,* in 1915, marked his departure from Sanskrit traditions. His later work *Sahitya Manjari* (8 vols., 1917-50), *Vishukkani* (1944), and *Bapuji* (1950) displayed a difficult balance between formal discipline and contemporary thematic preoccupations. His later work also revealed a fascination with the mythology of the major religions of the world, especially with that of Islam and Christianity.

The most remarkable feature of post-1936 Malayali poetry was the emergence of the Purogamana Vadam movement. The theorists for this movement shaped not only a literature that experienced no conflict between life and art, but they also influenced the later genius of Vallathol himself.

Recent Malayali fiction has developed in the direction of the sociological and historical novel. The historical novel that explored moments of romance and grandeur in Kerala's past was extremely popular in the 1920's and 1930's. Contemporary literary taste, however, demands a more thorough exploration of society. Among the younger novelists, T. S. Pillai describes the lives of landless farmers and local fishermen. His strength lies in his ability to picture universal tragedy in a small village and to create convincing and sympathetic characters.

The English language came into India as the native speech of a minority of foreign rulers, but in the course of the long British raj it transformed itself into a living Indian vernacular. For the purposes of this article it is necessary to limit Indian writing in English to that literature produced by Indians living in India but using English to explore or recapture specifically Indian themes and moods. It therefore excludes discussion of expatriate Indian writers like Dom Moraes, Raja Rao, Aubrey Menen (q.v.), or Shanta Rama Rao.

In the years immediately after Independence the Indian writer in English, carefully educated in a foreign language, went out of his way to reassert his Indianness by reviving Hindu legends or by recounting Hindu occult experience.

Dilip Kumar Roy (q.v.) is the most representative of his group. In *The Eyes of Light* (1945), Roy used the Prahlad story, familiar from the *Bhagavata,* and his verse has the overall effect of a yogic revelation. *The Upward Spiral* (1949) also uses yogic methods of discussion and insight in its attempt to analyse the natures of and the relationship between aspiration and fulfillment.

One of the most germinal works of Indian writing in English is *All About Mr. Hatter* (1949) by Govindas Vishnudas Desani (b. 1909). Desani used experimental techniques reminiscent of Joyce to describe the India of Holy Rivers and *sadhus.*

R. K. Narayan (b. 1906), is perhaps the best known Indian writer in English. His novels such as *Swami and Friends* (1935), *The Dark Room* (1938), *Waiting for the Mahatma* (1955), *The Guide* (1958), and *The Man-Eater of Malgudi* (1961), are characterized by their successful use of regionalism and remain intensely Indian despite the foreign medium.

Mulk Raj Anand (b. 1905) focuses attention on the poor and destitute hero. A vital concern for social injustice and his compassion for the suffering lower classes is evident in such novels as *Untouchable* (1935), *Coolie* (1936), *Two Leaves and a Bud* (1937), *The Big Heart* (1945), and *Seven Summers* (1951).

The majority of Indian writers in English, however, especially of the 1950's and 1960's, are alienated from the emotional, mythical, and intellectual currents of Indian literature; and they are doubly alienated from the Indian people. They manage a certain validity as social

critics and satirists, but thus far they have not overcome the influence of their Western models.

It should be emphasized that the designation Indian is a term of political convenience, which is extremely deceptive when applied to the literature of the entire subcontinent. Most Indians, perforce, remain ignorant of literatures outside of their regions. The government itself, in sponsoring the Sahitya Akademi, has recognized this problem and is engaged in massive projects of translation and literary conferences.

BIBLIOGRAPHY: Kumarappa, B., ed. *The Indian Literatures of Today: A Symposium* (1947); Sadig, M., *Twentieth Century Urdu Literature* (1947); Bose, B., *An Acre of Green Grass: A Review of Modern Bengali Literature* (1948); Divedi, R. A., *Hindi Literature* (1953); *Contemporary Indian Literature: A Symposium* (Sahitya Akademi, 1957); Lal, P., and Rao, Raghavendra, eds. *Modern Indo-Anglian Poetry* (1958); Sen, S., *History of Bengali Literature* (1960); Chakravarty, A., ed., *A Tagore Reader* (1961); Ahluwalia, J. S., *Tradition and Experiment in Modern Punjabi Poetry* (n.d.)

BHARATI MUKHERJEE BLAISE

INGLIN, Meinrad
Swiss novelist, b. 28 July 1893, Schwyz

In both subject matter and spirit I.'s fiction is a candid, comprehensive rendering of the Swiss character; from this it derives its unity and coherence. I. began in 1922 with the novel *Die Welt in Ingoldau,* a realistic critical portrait of small-town life in Switzerland. *Werner Amberg* (1949), a story of youth, has an autobiographical basis. *Die graue March* (1935) and the novella collection *Güldramont* (1943) are set in the still virgin mountain wilderness. With the accuracy of a chronicle, *Ehrenhafter Untergang* (1952) depicts the fall of the old Swiss confederacy after the invasion by the French Revolutionary army in 1799. With *Der Schweizerspiegel* (1938) I. achieved the representative documentary work in artistic form on the new confederation in World War I. Like *Der Schweizerspiegel*, I.'s novellas (*Die Lawine,* 1947) also display the expert realistic technique with which he brings up to date and continues the best tradition of Swiss fiction.

FURTHER WORKS: *Über den Wassern* (1925); *Wendel von Euw* (1925); *Grand Hotel Excelsior* (1928); *Lob der Heimat* (1928);

Jugend eines Volkes (1933); *Urwang* (1954); *Verhexte Welt* (1958); *Besuch aus dem Jenseits* (1961); *Erlenbüel* (1965)

BIBLIOGRAPHY: Wilhelm, E., *M. I., Weite und Begrenzung. Roman und Novelle im Werk des Schwyzer Dichters* (1957)

ROBERT FAESI

INTERIOR MONOLOGUE

Interior or inner monologue (*monologue intérieur, Innerer Monolog, erlebte Rede*), is a fictional technique that represents a character's verbalized but unspoken thoughts under circumstances conducive to introspection or heightened awareness. Used most extensively in stream-of-consciousness or psychological novels, it may also be used in conventional novels to reveal mental processes and unexpressed motives. It differs from psychological analysis in wholly or largely excluding author interpretation. In the first person, the interior monologue recalls the Shakespearian soliloquy and the dramatic monologue of Tennyson and Browning, but it differs from them in being "unspoken." It may resemble the intimate journal, as illustrated in Joyce's (q.v.) *Portrait of the Artist as a Young Man,* or fiction narrated by the hero in the first person, but it differs from them in being "unwritten."

"Interior" connotes what is unvoiced and unwritten; "monologue" connotes what is verbalized, with some selection and control. The content of the interior monologue is on the preconscious or conscious level; it does not plumb the depths of the stream of consciousness. In interior monologue the mind is active, responding to sense impressions by ideas, not merely by registering images. The monologue may range from active free association of ideas to controlled patterns of rationalization or self-dramatization. Except as the content of the conscious mind may suggest the unconscious, interior monologue does not involve Freudian psychology.

"Interior monologue," used in its present sense, first appeared in an essay by Nikolai Chernyshevski on Tolstoi's (q.v.) *Childhood and Boyhood* and *War Stories* in *Sovremennik,* VIII (1856). Gleb Struve quotes the passage from Tolstoi and Chernyshevski's comment, in "Monologue Intérieur: The Origins of the Formula and the First Statement of its Possibilities," *PMLA,* LXIX (1954). Used as an occasional device, the interior monologue or its psychological equivalent may be found in other 19th c. writers such as Dostoyevski (1821-81), Stendhal (1783-1842), and Flaubert (1821-80). Edouard Dujardin (1861-1949) first used it extensively, but not exclusively, in *Les Lauriers sont coupés* (1887; We'll to the Woods No More, 1938). Following Dujardin, George Moore (q.v.) used interior monologue in *Mike Fletcher* (1889) and *Celibates* (1895) and Schnitzler (q.v.) in *Leutnant Gustl* (1901), before Joyce's spectacular success with the technique.

After Joyce, influenced by Dujardin, popularized the technique in *Ulysses* (1922), Dujardin explained the theory in *Le Monologue intérieur* (1931). Lawrence Bowling points out that Dujardin errs in assuming that "the whole of the consciousness can be presented in the form of interior monologue" ("What Is the Stream of Consciousness Technique?" *PMLA,* LXV [1950]).

In *Ulysses* the interior monologues include Leopold Bloom's monologues on domestic life, Dublin streets, the funeral of Paddy Dignam, and the charms of the self-dramatizing Gerty MacDowell, Stephen Dedalus's meditation at the seashore on "the ineluctable modality of the visible," and Molly Bloom's unbroken nocturnal monologue at the end. All of these monologues show the fluidity of time, swirling from past to future in the current of the present. Sense impressions stimulate Stephen and Leopold to translate them into words and to recall past experiences.

Persons and situations characteristic of interior monologue are well illustrated in *Ulysses:* individuals who are articulate and self-conscious, often inclined to self-dramatization, are presented in situations that encourage self-examination and reminiscence and that either stimulate reactions or permit uninterrupted meditation. A keen sense of duality or of multiple selves is likely to distinguish such people: the use of "I," "you," and "we" by Eliot's (q.v.) J. Alfred Prufrock reveals that his love song is an interior monologue between his public and his private selves, his ego and his id. The mystery of multiple selves—"who am I who *calls* me 'you'?"—is the subject of a short story by Robert Henderson, "The Storeroom" (*NY,* 7 Sept. 1963). The theme of self-criticism and the conflict between impulse and will is developed in *The Man Within* (1929) by Graham Greene (q.v.): interior monologues are inserted into conventional narrative at critical junctures in the hero's life. In addition to inner conflict, common mental states or activities in interior monologue include reminiscence and anticipation, self-analysis, rationalization, self-justification, and self-dramatization, which often includes imagined dialogue within the monologue.

The interior monologue is used with a wide range of techniques, from the traditional to the highly experimental. The direct monologue is usually in the first person, as in Molly's at the end of *Ulysses* or Robert Jordan's at the end of Hemingway's (q.v.) *For Whom the Bell Tolls* (1940). Jordan's use of "you" and the imperative shows the conflict between the dying body and the will to live. Butor (q.v.) uses "you" in the interior monologue as "an intermediary form between the first person and the third," to "describe the situation of the character and the way in which language is born in him" (quoted by Peter Brooks, "The Laboratory of the Novel," *Dedalus*, XCII [1963]). Butor's *La Modification* (1957; A Change of Heart, 1959) is devoted to Leon's inner debate, in the second person, and his new resolution on a night trip from Paris to Rome. Leon's reminiscence of other journeys on the same route is well motivated. Shifts from "I" to "he" or "one" may show an objective view of self or, as in Darl's monologue at the end of Faulkner's (q.v.) *As I Lay Dying,* complete dissociation. The indirect interior monologue in the third person is marked by "he thought," "he wondered," "he told himself"; it usually combines direct quotation, often with quotation marks, with indirect discourse. Author comment may be excluded or may be interjected, as in Huxley's (q.v.) *Point Counter Point* (1928). The expression may range from a realistic "transcription" of thought and idiom, like Bloom's elliptical "utterances," to the highly stylized and poetic monologues of the six characters that make up Virginia Woolf's (q.v.) *The Waves* (1931) or the elaborate, poetic, symbolic expression and structure of Broch's (q.v.) *Der Tod des Vergil* (1947; The Death of Virgil, 1945). The dying Virgil's interior monologue encompasses external action and dialogue.

The high point of the interior monologue was reached in the 1920's, with Joyce's *Ulysses* and such novels as Schnitzler's *Fräulein Else* (1924; Eng., 1925), Larbaud's *Amants, heureux amants* (1924), Virginia Woolf's *Mrs. Dalloway* (1925) and *To the Lighthouse* (1927), Daniel-Rops' (q.v.) *Le Vent dans la nuit* (1927;

Two Men in Me, 1931), and Faulkner's *The Sound and the Fury* (1929) and *As I Lay Dying* (1930). Faulkner's use of the interior monologue, continued in later novels, shows much more variety than is usually recognized. In *The Sound and the Fury,* Benjy's section is not interior monologue but sensory impressions, without time distinctions; Quentin's section ranges from first-person objective narrative broken by memories to complete reliving of the past, with pure interior monologue at the end; Jason's section is completely verbal, logical, and colloquial, like a soliloquy or dramatic monologue. In *As I Lay Dying* the "monologues" include: "reporting" of sense impressions and action; true inner monologues, such as Darl's, Dewey Dell's, and Vardaman's; and monologues that suggest an audience, such as those of the Tulls and other neighbors. Variations on interior monologue, with a central intelligence, are used in "The Bear" (*Go Down, Moses,* 1942), the passages on Mink Snopes (*The Mansion,* 1959), and *Intruder in the Dust* (1948), in which Charles Mallison's consciousness most fully reveals the Bergsonian sense of duration and of coexistence of past and present. (Faulknerian interior monologue of a single character fills most of Claude Simon's (b. 1913) *L'Herbe* (1958; The Grass, 1960).

Less well known than Joyce, Woolf, or Faulkner but significant as an original experimenter with interior monologue is Dorothy Richardson (q.v.), whose twelve-novel *Pilgrimage* (1915-38) presents the consciousness of an articulate, introspective heroine who engages in innumerable meditative, reminiscent, self-analytical interior monologues. Ford's (q.v.) tetralogy, *Parade's End* (1924-28), uses interior monologue with distinction, most notably to present the effect of war on the mind of a highly civilized gentleman. Aiken's (q.v.) *Blue Voyage* (1927), a psychoanalytical novel, is complemented by his third-person autobiography, *Ushant* (1952), in which he comments on the Joycean "long soliloquy" in *Blue Voyage.* Henry Handel Richardson ([q.v.], pseud. of Ethel Richardson, 1870-1946) used interior monologue to reveal the mental deterioration of the hero throughout her trilogy, *The Fortunes of Richard Mahony* (1917-31).

Use of interior monologue by other major novelists than those noted for it shows its scope and its continued vitality as a subsidiary device or one controlling content and structure: Gide (q.v.) in *Les Faux-monnayeurs,* (1925; The

Counterfeiters, 1927) and Malraux (q.v.) in *La Condition humaine*, (1933; Man's Fate, 1934) used it in multiple-view, experimental technique; Huxley in *After Many a Summer Dies the Swan* (1939) used it for satire; Farrell (q.v.) in *Studs Lonigan* (1932-35) and the Danny O'Neill tetralogy, for sociological realism; Sartre (q.v.) used it existentially in *Les Chemins de la Liberté* (1945-49; Roads to Freedom, 1947-50). Lowry (q.v.) in *Under the Volcano* (1947) and Hemingway in *Across the River and into the Trees* (1950) used it as the dominant method for multiple and single points of view respectively; Styron (q.v.) used it climactically once, at the end of *Lie Down in Darkness* (1951), for the single direct presentation of the heroine. It pervades the detective novel, presenting the tensions and inner conflicts of criminals, victims, and detectives. The interior monologue is a versatile technique for exploring the conscious inner life and mental processes of characters who strive to escape "the pale cast of thought," or who seek to resolve inner conflicts, or who rationalize or ratiocinate, or who find in the life of the mind the true reality.

BIBLIOGRAPHY: Daniel-Rops, H., "Une Technique nouvelle: le monologue intérieur," *Le Correspondant*, 326 (1931); Walzel, W., "Von 'erlebter Rede,'" *Das Wortkunstwerk* (1926); Blanchot, M., "Le Monologue intérieur," *Faux pas* (1943); Hoffman, F. J., *Freudianism and the Literary Mind* (1945); Pouillon, J., *Temps et roman* (1946); Tindall, W. Y., *Forces in Modern British Literature* (1947); Isaacs, J., *An Assessment of Twentieth Century Literature* (1951); Humphrey, R., *Stream of Consciousness in the Modern Novel* (1954); Edel, L., *The Psychological Novel* (1955); Meyer, K. R., *Zur erlebten Rede im englischen Roman des 20. Jahrhunderts* (1957)

ELIZABETH M. KERR

IONESCO, Eugène
French dramatist, b. 13 Nov. 1912, Slatina, Rumania

A prominent author in the "theater of the absurd," I. is often linked with such Parisian playwrights as Genet, Beckett, Adamov (qq.v.). Although he was born in Rumania, French is his first language; his mother was French, and his parents, soon after his birth, moved to Paris. At thirteen he returned to Rumania, where he attended the University of Bucharest and be-

came a teacher of French and a literary critic. He came back to settle in France in 1938 and later found work with a Paris publishing house.

I.'s first play was *La Cantatrice chauve* (1953; Eng., The Bald Prima-Donna, 1958; Am., The Bald Soprano, 1958), first produced in 1950. This one-act "antiplay," a savagely comic exhibition of the futility of language, folded after a lame run. It was followed by other short plays, all generally neglected by the public until 1954, when, with the production of his first full-length play, *Amédée ou comment s'en débarrasser* (1954; Amedée or How to Get Rid of It, 1958), I. began to find a strongly interested public. It now became possible to revive older plays that had failed with the public as well as produce early plays that had never been staged. His work after this time included both short plays and longer ones such as *Tueur sans gages* (1958; The Killer, 1960), *Le Rhinocéros* (1959; Rhinoceros, 1960), *Le Roi se meurt*, performed in 1962, and *Le Piéton de l'air*, performed in 1963. He has also written short stories (from which his plays often germinate), a ballet scenario, and numerous short theoretical essays on drama and theater. I. has been translated and produced for highly curious audiences on the continent, in England, and in America.

Vehemently opposed to formal intellectualizing, I. has created a blatantly surrealistic drama that pointedly avoids the plot design and the intelligibility of conventional theater. It expresses with bizarre impact certain major themes, such as the breakdown of bourgeois culture, the absurdity and isolation of the self, the affirmation of childlike wonder. I. is especially fertile in theatrical experiment. His fluid, miraculous spectacles, his effects with nonreferential language, his systematic exploitation of the irrational—all have wide application beyond his own humanistic concerns.

FURTHER WORKS: *La Leçon* (1953; The Lesson, 1958); Les Chaises (1954; The Chairs, 1958); collected plays in *Théâtre*, Vols. I and II, and *Le Rhinocéros* (1954, 1958, 1959); *Le Photo du colonel* (1962; The Colonel's Photograph, 1967); *Notes et contre-notes* (1962; Notes and Counter-Notes, 1962); *La Faim et la Soif* (performed 1966); *Délire à Deux* (1966); *Journal en Miettes* (1967; Fragment of a Journal, 1968). **Selected English trans.:** *Plays* (4 vols., 1958-60); *Four Plays* (1958); *Three Plays* (1958); *The Killer and Other Plays* (1960); *Rhinoceros and Other Plays* (1960)

EUGÈNE IONESCO

MOHAMMAD IQBAL

BIBLIOGRAPHY: Doubrovsky, J. S., "I. and the Comic of Absurdity," *YFS*, XXIII (1959), 3-10; Pronko, L., "The Anti-Spiritual Victory in the Theatre of I.," *MD*, II (1959), 29-35; Coe, R. N., *I.* (1961, with bibliography); Esslin, M., *The Theatre of the Absurd* (1961; ch. 3 deals with I.); Grossvogel, D., *Four Playwrights and a Postscript* (1962); Sénart, P., *I.* (1964); Pronko, L., *I.* (1965); Benmussa, S., *I.* (1966); Bonnefoy, C., *Entretiens avec I.* (1966)

RICHARD M. EASTMAN

IORGA, Nicolae

Rumanian historian, essayist, poet, and dramatist, b. 5 June 1871, Botosani; d. 28 Nov. 1940, Bucharest

I., whom the critic G. Călinescu called "a Rumanian Voltaire," was an extremely prolific writer and one of the most controversial personalities of his time and country. He studied in Paris and Leipzig and later became a historian and politician; from 1931 to 1932 he was prime minister. As a historian, he occupied himself with Rumanian and world history but was also interested in the history of literature, art, and the church. He wrote poems, memoirs, and over seventy plays (the latter of no great significance). Though no philosopher—not for anything would he have relinquished his active role in current events—he built up an ethical code of action and enthusiasm that he set forth most clearly in his *Cugetări* (1911). The objects of this enthusiasm are the past, Rumania's national life, and everything native to Rumania. I.'s studies in ancient and literary history such as the *Istoria literaturii romîne în secolul al XVIII*[lea] (1901) show good taste and a capacity for unbiased evaluation, which, however, is lacking in his studies of his own times. Aside from his too traditional aesthetics and his dogmatism, I. was the great memorialist, journalist, and spiritual awakener who gave to a whole epoch its sense of pathos. During the disorders of 1940 he was assassinated.

FURTHER WORKS: *Notes et extraits pour servir à l'histoire des croisades au XV*[e] *siècle* (3 vols., 1899-1902); *L'histoire de la vie byzantine* (1906; The Byzantine Empire, 1907); *Istoria literaturii românești in veacul al XIX*[lea]*, dela 1821 înainte* (3 vols., 1907-1909); *Histoire de l'église roumaine* (2 vols., 1908); *Geschichte des osmanischen Reiches* (5 vols., 1908-1913); *Histoire des états balkaniques à l'époque moderne* (1914); *Histoire des Rela-tions angloroumaines* (1917; A History of Anglo-Roumanian Relations, 1931); *O luptă literară* (2 vols., 1914-16); *Istoria literaturilor romanice în desvoltarea și legăturile lor* (3 vols., 1919 f.); *Histoire des Roumains et de leur civilisation* (1920; A History of Roumania, 1925); *Tudor Vladimirescu* (1921); *Histoire de l'art roumain ancien* (1922); *Moartea lui Dante Molière se ràzbunà* (1923); *Isus* (1925); *Istoria literaturii românești* (2 vols., 1925-28); *Essai de synthèse de l'histoire de l'humanité* (4 vols., 1926-28); *Cleopatra* (1927); *Art et littérature des Roumains* (1929); *America și Românii din America note de drum și conferințe de N. I.* (1930; My American Lectures, 1932); *Istoria literaturii române contemporane* (2 vols., 1934); *Oameni care an fost* (1934-39); *O viată de om: Așa cum a fost* (3 vols., 1934); *Istoria Românilor* (10 vols., 1936-39); *Memorii* (7 vols., 1939); *Sfaturi pe intuneric* (1940); *Ramon Muntaner i l'Imperi bizanti* (1961)

BIBLIOGRAPHY: Iancoulesco, V., ed., *Mélanges offerts à N. I.* (1933); Domanovszky, S., *La méthode historique de N. I.* (1938)

VIRGIL IERUNCA

IQBAL, Mohammad

Indian Muslim poet and philosopher, b. 22 Feb. 1873, Sialkot; d. 21 April 1938, Lahore

Born into a deeply and traditionally religious middle-class Indian Muslim family that was nevertheless aware of the demands of a rapidly changing world, I. was educated in a manner that combined the best of East and West. He studied in India, at the Scotch Mission College, and at the University of the Punjab; in England, at Cambridge and Lincoln's Inn; in Germany, at the University of Munich. He returned to India in 1908. In Lahore he became a professor of philosophy and English literature at Government College, but he soon turned to law, which he practiced until ill health forced his retirement in 1934.

I. promptly won recognition as a poet-philosopher as he labored to revitalize the Urdu vernacular, to introduce innovations in traditional Urdu and Persian poetic forms, and to redirect Islamic literary philosophy from its traditional emphasis upon personal mystic experiences to revolutionary socially active doctrines. His ultimate poetic vision was that of a mystic yet tangible pan-Islamic force that would be a fusion of Eastern and Western social and humanistic values. Islam was to become a dynamic, liberal religious and social force firmly rooted in contemporary reality, rather than in a myth-ridden past and otherworldly future; it was to assimilate into itself the remarkable non-Islamic cultural and intellectual advances of the modern age.

Although I.'s early poetry had been primarily lyrical and mystic in content and had followed the traditional *ghazal* in form and content, he became known as a major poetic innovator at the publication of two works (in Persian): *Asrar-i-Khudi* (1915; The Secrets of the Self, 1920) and *Rumuz-i-Bekhudi* (1918; Mysteries of Selflessness, 1953). In these two works, he formulated a comprehensive statement of the relationship between the individual (whose personality development is treated in *Asrar-i-Khudi*) and the greater Islamic community (the definition of which dominates *Rumuz-i-Bekhudi*).

In his poems, I. defines the basis of his philosophy. Life, he asserts, is a "forward, assimilative movement"; the individual grows and advances by means of assimilation of that which it encounters. The self moves through three stages: "obedience to the law of life"; "self-control"; and, finally, "divine viceregency." At that point the self becomes complete; thought and action, instinct and reason, are united within him, and he is prepared to live the dynamic Islamic life. The self thus becomes a collective rather than individual entity, and the society that such individuals develop is that defined in *Rumuz-i-Bekhudi*. I. reinforces these philosophic pronouncements in numerous other poems and essays, perhaps the most important of which are the seven essays in *The Reconstruction of Religious Thought in Islam* (1934).

That Urdu is the flexible, viable literary language that it is today is to the credit of I., who, building upon the accomplishments of Sayed Ahmed Khan (1817-98) and Shamsul Ulama Altaf Hussain Hali (1837-1914), was largely responsible for this development. As for the content of Urdu literature, he rejected subjective experience and deemphasized art for art's sake; in place of these, he emphasized a dynamic social ethic. He gave the *ghazal* new life by introducing to it a wide range of new subjects and by revising its traditional classic form (it had hitherto depended for its effect upon carefully controlled end-rhyme assonance). And he gave power and emphasis to the new, free form of the *nazm*.

The central figure in the development of a modern Indian Muslim literary approach (which was accepted by the nation of Pakistan after independence and partition in 1947), I. contributed much of the substance to a resurgence of Indian Muslim poetry, which was based upon Islamic philosophical principles, a revitalized Urdu vernacular, and a continued traditional stylized Persian. But his literary and philosophical contributions are in danger of becoming obscured by a nationalistic myth that threatens to become a cult surrounding his memory. As presiding officer of the Muslim League meeting at Allahabad in 1930, he envisioned a separate Muslim state in northwest India, a vision that ultimately led to the creation of Pakistan. Since then he has been hailed as the founder of the Pakistani ideal, just as Mohammed Ali Jinnah (1876-1948) has been called the Quaid-i-Azam, the father of the political reality.

FURTHER WORKS: *The Development of Metaphysics in Persia* (1908, in English); *Bang-i-Dara* (1924, in Urdu); *Javid-Namah* (1932, in Persian); *Bal-i-Jibrail* (1935, in Urdu); *Pas Chai Bayad Kard* (1936, in Persian); *Zarb-i-Kalim* (1937, in Urdu). **Selected English trans.:** *Complaint and Answer* (1943); *Poems from I.* (1947); *Persian Psalms* (1943)

BIBLIOGRAPHY: Ali, S. A., *I.: His Poetry and Message* (1932); Khana, Q. K., *Aspects of I.* (1938); Enver, I. H., *Metaphysics of I.* (1944); Krishna, R. *I.* (1945); Sinha, S., *I.: The Poet and his Message* (1946); Vahid, S. A., *Introduction to I.* (ca. 1960)

DAVID D. ANDERSON

IRISH LITERATURE

The "Irish renaissance," which began in the 1890's and continued through the early years of the 20th c., was an attempt to develop a national literature. Certain enthusiasts referred to it fondly as the "Gaelic revival" because of their belief in the inevitability of Gaelic as the spoken and written language of the Irish people. But they were clearly in the minority and had little success reintroducing Gaelic into the literature. Most of the writers favored the position of Yeats (q.v.), who questioned, "Can we not build up ... a national literature which shall be none the less Irish in spirit from being English in language?" Within a decade this resurgence of Irish literature was felt almost everywhere: Yeats turned Irish legends into successful poems and plays; George Moore (q.v.) returned from the continent to write novels and to act as historian for the new movement with the publication of his three-volume autobiography *Hail and Farewell* (1911-14); Lady Augusta Gregory (1852-1932) contributed to the revival by translating Gaelic texts into English and by reworking Irish stories into plays.

The 20th c. felt acutely the need to rid itself of the accustomed 19th c. "stage Irishism" of such writers as Charles Lever (1806-1872) and Samuel Lover (1797-1868). In a series of rapid and decisive gestures *Poems and Ballads of Young Ireland* was published in 1888; the Irish Literary Society was set up in London and the Irish National Literary Society in Dublin (both in 1892).

The genuine beginning of the Irish renaissance, however, probably dates from the formation of the Irish National Theatre Society in 1902, which developed into the celebrated Abbey Theatre in 1904. This experiment is important in the history of European drama and it has already been compared to France's *théâtre libre* and to Germany's *Freie Bühne*. Indeed it is in the theater that the new movement was officially launched.

It has often been suggested that any plays written by Irishmen before this period properly belong to English rather than to Irish literature. It is probably only with Yeats's first play, *The Countess Cathleen* (1892), that Ireland finally had its own playwright. From then on there is no paucity of dramatic talent. Under the stimulus of Yeats and Lady Gregory, the Irish National Dramatic Company gave its first performance on April 2, 1902; the plays produced were A. E.'s (Russell, q.v.) *Deirdre* and Yeats's *Cathleen Ni Houlihan*. In the following year Synge's (q.v.) *In the Shadow of the Glen* and Colum's (q.v.) *Broken Soil* were offered.

The meeting between Yeats and Lady Gregory in 1898 has become a permanent part of Irish literary history. (The importance of the encounter to Yeats's development can only be compared to his first trip to Paris in 1894, which brought him into touch with the French symbolists.) Their friendship was the occasion for collaboration on a series of plays and the eventual establishment of the Abbey Players. Lady Gregory's own plays are probably less important than her influence on the development of a peculiarly Irish conception of the theater. Yet the series of comedies beginning with *Spreading the News* (1904) and carrying through *The Rising of the Moon* (1907) deserve a per-

manent place in Irish drama. No less important are her translations from the Gaelic of Douglas Hyde (*The Marriage* and *The Twisting of the Rope,* both 1910) and her *kiltartan* dialect works including her Molière translations.

Yeats turned to the theater after writing Pre-Raphaelite and Romantic poetry and fairy-tale prose pieces. He wrote a group of plays, including *The Shadowy Waters* (1900) and *The King's Threshold* (1904), which attempted to turn Irish "epic" material into dramatic verse. His folk plays include *The Pot of Broth* (1902), *Cathleen Ni Houlihan* (1902), and *The Hour Glass* (1903). Yeats even tried out new stage techniques, mainly under the influence of the Japanese theater, in such later works (characterized by Ernest Boyd as "the Anglo-Irish Noh plays") as *Four Plays for Dancers* (1920).

Acting on a suggestion made by Yeats, Synge returned to Ireland from the continent and devoted his attention to a clinical study of what he believed to be the "real Irishman." He lived among the peasants of the Aran Islands, studied their customs, and emerged with a series of plays beginning with *In the Shadow of the Glen* (1903) and ending with the unfinished *Deirdre of the Sorrows* (1909). Synge's talents were directed toward enriching the Anglo-Irish idiom, giving it positive dramatic form, and raising peasant drama to the position of literature.

O'Casey (q.v.) gave social awareness to the Abbey Theatre. He was more aware of political problems than the earlier generation. *Juno and the Paycock* (1924) and *The Plough and the Stars* (1926) have as their setting the Dublin of the World War I period, heightened by the suspenseful events growing out of the Easter Rebellion of 1916. While Yeats and Lady Gregory searched for subject matter in Irish mythology, O'Casey found his in contemporary Ireland. His theater is as distinctively Irish as theirs and is equally colored by a poetic energy so much a part of the Irish renaissance.

All during this period of intense creativity in the Irish theater Shaw (q.v.) wrote plays quite outside its orbit. *John Bull's Other Island,* written by Shaw in 1904 at Yeats's request, occupies an insignificant position in the Shaw canon and is indeed his only acknowledgement of the literary revival in his native Ireland. His expatriation and rejection of things Irish make him less a part of Irish literature than James and Eliot (qq.v.) are of American literature.

Lady Gregory's *Journals,* edited by the Irish writer Robinson (q.v.), was published in 1947. It explains a great deal about the development of the Abbey Theatre and acts as a companion piece to the other storehouse of Gaelic-revival reminiscences, George Moore's *Hail and Farewell.* The Abbey Theatre group doubtless shaped the development of Irish drama in the 20th c. so that it could assume a deserved place next to the theater of Periclean Athens, Elizabethan England, and 17th c. France and Spain. It was not, however, the only venture of its sort in contemporary Ireland. The Dublin Gate Theatre, founded in 1928 for the production of a group of experimental plays, was another indication of increasing dramatic awareness.

One of the curiosities of 20th c. Irish literature is that many of the playwrights were also successful poets. The intense literary feeling that pervaded Ireland at the turn of the c. was contagious to the point that a writer was rarely content to deal in a single genre. Yeats, for example, despite his Herculean role in reviving interest in the theater, is clearly more important as poet than as playwright. With the protean aspect of a Picasso, he went through many stages of development.

His early poetry reflected a mysticism that grows out of his association with the so-called Hermetic Society. There was also the pervasive and stifling quality of the "Celtic Twilight," which surrounded his youthful offerings. (Yeats published a volume called *The Celtic Twilight* in 1893 and enlarged it in 1902; this was intended as a testimony of the period.) Upon Yeats's return from Paris in the late 1890's, he was able, under the influence of French symbolism, to turn from his Pre-Raphaelite period to more mature work. He finally developed to the point at which he could reject the abuses of the 19th c. French and German symbolists and create new poetic forms such as he did with "The Tower" (1926), "Sailing to Byzantium" (1927), and "Among School Children" (1928). A lasting tribute to his accomplishments was the award in 1924 of the Nobel Prize.

A. E. has similar poetic origins. Like Yeats, he was nurtured on mysticism and symbolism, and together they were referred to as "the Dublin mystics." His contribution to the literary revival, however, is more in the way of personal than of poetic influence. The Sunday-evening gatherings held at A. E.'s house on Rathgar Avenue were a meetingplace for the young poets of Dublin. (These literary seances

are comparable to the *mardis* held at Mallarmé's house in the rue de Rome in Paris.) A. E. also exerted influence on the poetic developments of the period by editing *The Irish Statesman,* a literary review.

In 1911, Colum, with the help of Stephens (q.v.) and Thomas MacDonagh (1878-1916), founded the *Irish Review.* Colum himself, one of the most productive writers of the period, figured prominently in the poetic aspect of the revival. He and his wife, Mary, (1887?-1957) left Ireland in 1914 to settle permanently in the United States and in some measure to carry the spirit of the Irish renaissance to another continent. (America has been hospitable to Irish men of letters. Oliver St. John Gogarty [1878-1957], the doctor-litterateur who was the model for Buck Mulligan in Joyce's [q.v.] *Ulysses,* and who was himself the author of *As I Was Going Down Sackville Street* [1937] and other Irish reminiscences, died in New York. The Colums both taught at Columbia University until Mary's death. O'Faolain [q.v.] gave a series of six lectures at Princeton University in the spring of 1953, which have since appeared in volume form as *The Vanishing Hero* [1956].)

O'Connor (q.v.) and Austin Clarke (b. 1896) started their careers as poets deeply imbued with Irish folklore. Clarke continues to be an active poet and a commentator on modern poetry, while O'Connor turned to the short story. Ireland also boasts a distinguished contemporary poet, known widely outside his own country, in Patrick Kavanagh (b. 1905).

The novel in Ireland has a curiously lyrical quality. This is probably not accidental, as it is a form often used by poets. Stephens's *The Crock of Gold* (1912) mixes unlikely Irish ingredients in a hybrid that is a compromise between poetry and prose. In his version of *Deirdre* (1923), we have an example of what Blanche M. Kelly has aptly called "the English prose of a Gaelic-speaking Irishman."

In Joyce we have another novelist who began as a poet. His *Chamber Music* (1907) marked a return to an Elizabethan lyrical convention. Then Joyce turned to prose, and after a series of heated controversies with unsympathetic publishers, he brought out *Dubliners* in 1914, *A Portrait of the Artist as a Young Man* in 1916, *Ulysses* in 1922, and *Finnegans Wake* in 1939. His prose style became increasingly complicated, as did his application of the stream-of-consciousness technique.

Joyce's instinctive impulse was to turn his

back on the Irish renaissance and reject it, to seek support outside of his immediate literary heritage. The large part of his life was spent away from his native Dublin in a restless movement among Paris, Trieste, and Zurich. The themes of his later work are close to continental literature: the mythical parallels of *Ulysses* and *Finnegans Wake*. But in the end Joyce is much less an expatriate than Shaw, and his work genuinely belongs to the Ireland that he once characterized as "the sow that eats her farrow."

Stanislaus Joyce (1884-1955) revealed new facets of his brother's achievement and, more important, established himself as a new literary talent in the posthumously published *My Brother's Keeper* (1958) and *Dublin Diary* (1962). Eliot (q.v.) suggested in his preface to *My Brother's Keeper* that it "is worthy to occupy a permanent place on the bookshelf beside the works of his brother."

Austin Clarke is another poet who wrote novels: *The Bright Temptation* (1932) and *The Singing Men at Cashel* (1936). A developed lyrical quality also runs through the novels of Kate O'Brien (b. 1897). O'Flaherty (q.v.), one of the race of Aran peasants that Synge studied so diligently, is the first of his cultural group to contribute significantly to the novel. *The Informer* (1925), *Famine* (1937), and *Insurrection* (1950) all have timely political overtones and have profoundly influenced the direction of Irish fiction.

O'Connor and O'Faolain, both of whom have had rare success with the short story, are popular on both sides of the Atlantic. O'Connor's *Domestic Relations* (1957) rounds out an impressive production that gives his work a place in the history of the Irish short story next to Joyce's *Dubliners*. His *The Lonely Voice: A Study of the Short Story* (1963) is a defense of short fiction and its important place in a literary world dominated by the novel.

This resurgence of Irish literature is, on a small scale, parallel to the *risorgimento* that occurred in Spain and France in the 16th c., and in Italy in the 14th c. Literature even entered other phases of public life when one of the sages of the revival, Douglas Hyde, was elected first president of Ireland in 1938.

There are certain universal aspects of the movement that make it an essential part of the history of literature. The Deirdre myth—treated by Yeats, Synge, A. E., and Stephens—is comparable to various of the Greek legends. It has been said by at least one commentator

that Deirdre was to the Irish dramatist what Iphigenia was to the Greek playwright.

It is interesting to note that most of the important figures of the revival spent time on the continent before they returned to reform the literature of their native Ireland. Moore, Yeats, Synge, and Joyce sopped up European culture before they systematically launched their own writing careers. The French symbolists had an important influence on each. Ibsen (q.v.) made a special appeal to the young Joyce, who wrote of "Ibsen's New Drama," and to the more mature Joyce, who wrote a single play, *Exiles* (1918). Two plays by Edward Martyn (1859-1923)—*The Heather Field* (1899) and *Maeve* (1900)—are strongly Ibsenian. Even Shaw admits his debt in a long essay, *The Quintessence of Ibsenism* (1891).

Among the most recent generation of Irishmen, Behan (q.v.) enjoyed the most cosmopolitan reputation. His two plays *The Quare Fellow* (1954) and *The Hostage* (1958) have been widely and frequently performed. His autobiographical *Borstal Boy* (1958) enjoyed an international *succès de scandale*.

And so Irish literature genuinely comes into its own in the 20th c. It is strongly nationalistic and at the same time exerts an impelling universal appeal.

BIBLIOGRAPHY: Malye, J., *La Littérature irlandaise contemporaine* (1913); Boyd, E. A., *The Contemporary Drama of Ireland* (1917); Morris, L. A., *The Celtic Dawn; A Survey of the Renascence in Ireland, 1889-1916* (1917); Boyd, E. A., *Ireland's Literary Renaissance* (1922); O'Connor, N. J., *Changing Ireland; Literary Backgrounds of the Irish Free State, 1889-1922* (1924); Téry, S., *L'Île des bardes, "Notes sur la littérature irlandaise contemporaine"* (1925); Colum, P., *The Road Round Ireland* (1926); Law, H. A., *Anglo-Irish Literature* (1926); Brugsma, R. P. C. B., *The Beginnings of the Irish Revival* (1933); Gwynn, S., *Irish Literature and Drama* (1936); Alspach, R. K., *A Consideration of the Poets of the Literary Revival in Ireland, 1889-1929* (1942); O'Sullivan, T. F., *The Young Irelanders* (1945); Clarke, A., *Poetry in Modern Ireland* (1951); Kelly, B. M., *The Voice of the Irish* (1952); Ussher, A., *Three Great Irishmen—Shaw, Yeats, Joyce* (1953); Ellis-Fermor, U. M., *The Irish Dramatic Movement* (2nd ed., 1954); Taylor, E. R., *The Modern Irish Writers* (1954); Howarth, H., *The Irish Writers, 1880-1940* (1958); Kain, R. M., *Dublin in the Age of*

William Butler Yeats and James Joyce (1962); Mercier, V., *The Irish Comic Tradition* (1963); Browne, R. B., Roscelli, J. W., and Loftus, R., eds., *The Celtic Cross: Studies in Irish Culture and Literature* (1964); Loftus, R. J., *Nationalism in modern Anglo-Irish Poetry* (1964); Thompson, W. I., *The Imagination of an Insurrection, Dublin, Easter, 1916: A Study of an Ideological Movement* (1967)

MELVIN J. FRIEDMAN

IRONY

While the fiction writer can depict his hero, as it were, from outside, the dramatist is per se an ironist in that in every word he writes he must express the viewpoint of the character who speaks it. In addition, dramatic speech can itself be ironical from the viewpoint of the character speaking. Friedrich Schlegel's definition of irony as "alternation between self-creation and self-destruction" postulates irony as a state of suspension that prevents the poet and writer from being completely submerged in his work.

Kierkegaard devoted his dissertation (1841) to the problem of irony and came to the conclusion that irony represents subjectivity self-contained, i.e., a subjectivity that is conscious of its own self. Irony, he says, is critical in its essence, but fails in the task of achieving criticism. Kierkegaard considers Socrates' critical irony toward persons justified. For Nietzsche (q.v.), however, it is "vulgar vindictiveness"; he recognizes irony as the relation between the artist and his work and even lays claim to it for himself as a philosopher. The subject was not fully treated again until the 20th c., when irony begins to play an important role in literature. In any event irony remains one of the most controversial concepts in aesthetics.

Irony as a figure of speech that, when used extensively, produces the "ironical style" says something different from what it means, and would thus appear to be related to the stylistic devices of euphemism, understatement, litotes, and hyperbole. It posits the opposite of the concept that is really meant and counts upon the listener's or reader's recognizing the inversion of meaning through his own knowledge or through details given to him. The other figures of speech mentioned above may also have an ironic effect if they "are carried too far," but in that case it is not the fact itself but the accompanying emotion that is ironized—often

in the form of self-irony. Schlegel already recognized the connection between irony and paradox, in which each part of a statement ironizes the other (Oscar Wilde [q.v.]: "Life is far too important a thing ever to talk seriously about.") Characteristically Wilde sees paradox precisely as a path to truth, which thus resides not in the objective validity of a statement but in its capacity to be experienced. In the same way many writers (Aldous Huxley, Thomas Mann, Musil, Gide [qq.v.]) use irony as a style, the function of which is not to describe reality but to communicate it through keeping possibility in a state of suspension, in Kierkegaard's sense.

In polemics to refer to one's opponent in his own terms (mimesis) creates an impression of involuntary self-exposure on his part ("polemical irony"). Shaw (q.v.) and his opponent Chesterton (q.v.) were both virtuosos in the use of this technique. Parody uses it too; in fact, it is the most important technique of modern satire (q.v.). Through this form of irony Erich Kästner (q.v.) exposes the hollowness of patriotic bourgeois phraseology; Kraus (q.v.) goes even further, printing newspaper articles verbatim, sometimes even without any commentary at all. Expressionism (q.v.), on the other hand, tends in its satire to sharpen irony to the point of sarcasm. Sarcasm expresses a subjective compulsiveness, so that the intellectual detachment characteristic of irony—the pathos of detachment—is lost. This is the case, for instance, in the comedies of Carl Sternheim (q.v.).

While "polemical irony" remains bound to the artist's vision of the world, irony as the relation of the artist to his work needs only conscious subjectivity in order to unfold. This category of "subjective irony" includes travesties in which classical subjects are transposed into the present day (plays by O'Neill, Anouilh, Csokor [qq.v.]). In the ironic suspension between the original and its contemporary reflection, the story is to prove its truth. Deliberate anachronisms (as in *Der heilige Crispin* by Ernst [q.v.]) show the same tendency, as it were, in miniature. Analogous to this is the description of human—or even divine—happenings from the viewpoint of an animal (Woolf and Supervielle [qq.v.]). Once the artist has established this sort of ironical attitude toward his own work ("romantic irony"), he does not want just to destroy the illusions of his readers or audience; instead he enters into a game with them in which the freedom of the creator plays against that of the listener. The nonreality of what happens in the work is made known, but by being made known it becomes the problem of the reader or audience. Priestley, Pirandello, and Jens (qq.v.) exemplify this.

"Aesthetic irony" carries the ironical attitude toward the work of art a step further in that it sees life, too, as merely a noncommittal game, since reality is mirrored differently in different subjects. In the modern connection between art and life, art is a part of deceptive reality and can no longer be exposed as a mere façade by "romantic irony" because reality as its opposite no longer exists. This "game-playing" attitude to life may be exemplified by the hero of the work, as in *Der Tor und der Tod* by Hoffmannsthal (q.v.), *Paracelsus* by Schnitzler, (q.v.) or *Le vergini delle rocce* by D'Annunzio (q.v.); he may experience it as liberation from the tragedy of life (*Alexis Zorbas* by Kazantzakis [q.v.]; or as a tragic shock (*Il giuoco* by Coccioli [q.v.]).

If the alienation from reality does not stop short of the self, the writer is deprived of the last being he can grasp, and we may speak of "ontic irony." A variant of this is "tragic irony," which in its classical concept shows the hero at the height of success while, unknown to him, his downfall is already being prepared. The result of "ontic irony" may be either utter skepticism or recognition of the pervading insecurity of life and of man's imperfection. Thus the believer and the skeptic use ontic irony in literature for opposite purposes: to demonstrate man's need of God (Mauriac [q.v.]) or to prove the nonexistence of divine guidance (Sartre [q.v.]). As a result, however, it may happen that in a particular work it is no longer possible to determine which effect the author was aiming at. Such works are then left in a state of ironical suspense between hope and despair. Yet this very ambivalence may constitute the strongest appeal to the reader's capacity for self-realization (Aldington, Auden, Waugh, Beckett, Buzzati [qq.v.]).

Since irony expresses itself in such a diversity of relationships, it is understandable that each writer should use a characteristic combination of its specific forms. The popularity of irony in modern writing, in which it plays an essential role, stems from widespread alienation from reality, mistrust of the "spell" cast by art, and doubt in the existence of universally valid insights. Moreover, step-by-step exposure of the ironic slant also creates additional elements of tension. At the same time, of course, the more subtle the irony, the greater the risk of its being completely misinterpreted, and the more inaccessible the work becomes to the naive reader.

BIBLIOGRAPHY: Chevalier, H. M., *The Ironic Temper: Anatole France and His Time* (1932); Allemann, Beda, *Ironie und Dichtung* (1956); Sharpe, R. B., *Irony in the Drama; an Essay on Impersonation, Shock, and Catharsis* (1959); McDowell, F. P., *Ellen Glasgow and the Ironic Art of Fiction* (1960); Paiva, M. H. de N., *Contribuição para uma estilística da ironia* (1961); Dyson, A., *The Crazy Fabric: Essays in Irony* (1965)

HELLMUTH HIMMEL

ISHERWOOD, Christopher

English novelist and playwright (American citizen since 1946), b. 26 Aug. 1904, High Lane, Cheshire

I. attended Corpus Christi, Cambridge, where as an undergraduate he wrote or plotted various satiric romances. Leaving in 1925 without a degree, he worked as a secretary and as a tutor. In this period he renewed his acquaintance with Auden (q.v.), whom he had met at Repton, their preparatory school. His first published novel was *All the Conspirators* (1928). After briefly studying medicine, he joined Auden in Berlin and taught English there (1930-33). *The Memorial* (1932) was followed by two Berlin novels, *Mr. Norris Changes Trains* (1935; Am., *The Last of Mr. Norris*) and *Goodbye to Berlin* (1939). The last-named was adapted by John van Druten into a play and film, *I Am a Camera* (1951). I. collaborated with Auden on three plays, *The Dog Beneath the Skin* (1935), *The Ascent of F.6* (1937), and *On the Frontier* (1938), and on a journalistic record of experiences in China, *Journey to a War* (1939). His novels, largely autobiographical, form what in his memoir *Lions and Shadows* (1938) he called "an epic in an album of snapshots." The literary technique of presenting character on the discrete time strata of its development is most conspicuous in *Down There on a Visit* (1962).

I. traveled widely, and in 1940 he came to the United States as a film writer. Attracted to Vedanta, he edited *Vedanta and the West* (1943). In 1959 he joined the faculties of Los Angeles State College and the University of California, Santa Barbara.

I. has translated Brecht (q.v.; Eng., *A Penny for the Poor*, 1937; Am., *The Threepenny Novel*, 1958) and, with Swami Prabhavananda, also *Bhagavad-Gita* (1944), *Shankara's Crest-Jewel of Discrimination* (1947), and *How to Know God: the Yoga Aphorisms of Patanjali* (1953).

FURTHER WORKS: *Prater Violet* (1945); *The Condor and the Cows* (1949); *Vedanta for Modern Man* (1951); *The World in the Evening* (1952); *A Single Man* (1964); *Rama Krishna and his Disciples* (1965); *Exhumations* (1966); *A Meeting by the River* (1967)

BIBLIOGRAPHY: Gerstenberger, D., "Poetry and Politics: The Verse Drama of Auden and I.," *MD*, V (1962), 123-32; Hazard, F. E., "The Auden Group and the Group Theatre," *DA*, XXV (1964), 1913-14; Wickes, G., "An Interview with C. I.," *Shenandoah*, XVI: iii (1965), 23-52

GROVER SMITH

ISHIKAWA Takuboku

Japanese poet, critic, and diarist, b. 20 Feb. 1886, Hinoto Village, Iwate Prefecture; d. 13 April 1912, Tokyo

I., one of the first modern voices in Japanese poetry, is best remembered for his *waka* (thirty-one syllable verses), the classical form of prosody. From his student days on, I. engaged in literary activity, dropping out of school in 1902 in order to go to Tokyo to become a writer. His first verses were published in the influential periodical, *Myôjô* ("Morning Star"), and I. benefited from the tutelage of the editor, Yosano Tekkan (1873-1935), and his wife, the poet Yosano Akiko (1878-1942).

In February 1903, I. became ill and was forced to return to his home in northern Japan. From this time until his death of tuberculosis, he struggled against abject poverty, and failing health. His first collection of verse, *Akogare* (1905; "Yearnings"), demonstrated a strong romantic bent, but thereafter I.'s poetry developed in an independent direction. With *Ichiaku no suna* (1910; A Handful of Sand, 1934) he established himself as a leading writer of *waka,* to which he imparted a new romantic tone. He endeavored to write "poems that are down to earth, poems with feelings unremoved from real life," and he abhorred all traces of imitativeness. The 551 verses of *Ichiaku no suna* were integrated to form a unified sequence, imparting

an organic structure to the collection and giving somewhat the effect of an autobiography in verse. Through *Ichiaku no suna* and his last book of verse, *Kanashiki gangu* (1912; "A Sad Toy"), I. infused a powerful new current of life into the old tradition of *waka*.

In the last years of his life, after the trial behind closed doors and execution (which followed immediately) of the Japanese anarchist philosopher, Kōtoku Shūsui (1871-1911), I. was increasingly moved by socialist ideals, as verses such as the following reveal: "Still quite far away/I believed it all to be;/But the terrorists'/Plaintive and heart-rending cry/Day by day now draws nearer." (*Yaya tōki/mono ni omoishi/teroristo no/kanashiki kokoro mo/ chikazuku hi no ari/*.) In 1910-12, in association with Toki Zemmaro (b. 1885), *waka* poet, essayist, and scholar of Japanese literature, I. attempted to publish a socialist literary magazine. The venture failed, but their friendship, ardor for socialism, and efforts to establish a proletarian *waka* group continued undiminished. One week before I.'s death, Zemmaro delivered the manuscript for *A Sad Toy* to the publisher and used the twenty-yen advance to buy medicine to comfort his dying friend.

I.'s diaries and miscellaneous writings, as well as his verse, are admired for the stark revelation of his search for love and his struggle against poverty, despair, and death. His *Romaji nikki* (1948-49, The Romaji Diary, excerpts pub. in *Modern Japanese Literature,* 1956), the especially noteworthy journal that I. kept in the spring of 1909, stands out as one of the memorable works of 20th c. Japan. It reveals a completely modern three-dimensional man, capable of introspection and espousing fierce, self-destructive honesty.

I.'s work is sometimes contrasted with that of Kitahara Hakushū (1885-1942). Whereas Hakushū is remembered as an early symbolist poet, I.'s chief claim to fame lies in the way he utilized the old *waka* form to articulate new problems of modern life. I.'s writings reveal not a world of soft rain sounds and delicate relations but rather the shrill outcry of a tortured young soul, pouring forth a red-hot stream of uncontrollable passion.

FURTHER WORKS: *Yobiko to kuchibue* (1913; "Whistles and Flutes"); *"Jidai heisoku no genjō"* (1913; "Sclerosis of Society Today"); *T. ikō* (1913; "T.'s Posthumous Manuscripts"); *I. T. nikki* (1948-49; "I. T.'s Diaries"); *T.*

zenshū (1952-53; "T.'s Complete Works"); *Shin-hen I. T. senshū* (1960; "Selected Works of I. T.: Newly Edited"). **Selected English Trans.:** *The Poetry of I. T.* (1959); *Poems to Eat* (1966)

BIBLIOGRAPHY: Iwaki, Y., *I. T.* (1961); Takamine, H., *A Sad Toy* (1962); Iwaki, Y. "*I. T.,*" *Gendai Nihon bungaku daijiten* (1965; "Encyclopedia of Modern Japanese Literature")

LEON M. ZOLBROD

ISTRATI, Panait

Rumanian novelist and short story writer (in French), b. 11 Aug. 1884, Bràila; d. 14 April 1935, Bucharest

At the age of twelve I., the son of a smuggler, embarked upon a wandering life through Turkey, Syria, and Egypt, later reaching France. Rolland (q.v.) called him "a Balkan Gorki." With a few exceptions he wrote all his works in French, translating them into Rumanian himself.

I.'s work reflects his eventful life. It falls into two groups, the first of which includes *Les Récits d'Adrien Zograffi: Kyra Kyralina* (1924; Eng., 1926), *L'Oncle Anghel* (1925; Uncle Anghel, 1927), *Présentation des Haidoucs* (1925; The Bandits, 1929), *Domnitza de Snagov* (1926), *Codine* (1926), and *Mikhail* (1927). In these novels I. describes with the vividness of a wandering minstrel a primitive, oriental Rumania.

The second autobiographical cycle, *La Vie d'Adrien Zograffi,* includes *La Maison Thüringer* (1933), *Le Bureau de placement* (1934) and *Méditerranée*: Part I, *Lever du soleil* (1935) and Part II, *Coucher du soleil* (1935). In addition to picturesque local color these short stories contain an element of human pathos. *La Famille Perlmutter* (1927) and especially *Les Chardons du Baragan* (1928: The Thistles of the Baragan, 1930) belong to neither series; here I. describes the famous Rumanian peasants' revolt of 1907. After spending sixteen months in the Soviet Union in 1927, I. became an opponent of the Communist regime —earlier than other revolutionary writers did. *Vers l'Autre Flamme* (1929) is a violent indictment of this "naked Russia" (*La Russie nue,* 1929; Russia Unveiled, 1931).

After thirty years of neglect, I., in 1968, was "rediscovered," and is now being read in Europe with much pleasure. He has won the admiration of his new readers by his charm and humor, by his conviction that the betterment of man's lot has got to be achieved, by his commitment to social change, and, especially, by his devotion to man.

FURTHER WORKS: *Trecut şi viitor* (1925); *Kir Nicolas* (1926); *Isaac le tresseur de fil de fer* (1927); *In Lumea Mediteranei* (2 vols., 1927); *Nerrantsoula* (1927); *Le Refrain de la fosse* (1927; The Bitter Orange Tree, 1931); *Adolescence d'Adrien Zograffi* (1928); *Mes Départs* (1928); *Après Seize Mois en U.R.S.S.* (3 vols., 1929); *Enfance d'Adrien Zografii Codine* (18th ed., 1929); *Pour avoir aimé la terre* (1930); *Le Pêcheur d'éponges* (1930); *En Egypte* (1931); *Tsatsa Minka* (1931); *La Vie d'Adrien Zograffi* (4 vols., 1933-35); *Ma Croisade ou notre croisade* (1941); *Pusztai bogáncsok* (1961); *Chira chiralina Mos Anghel Ciulinii Bărăganului* (1962)

BIBLIOGRAPHY: On *Kyra Kyralina,* see *New York Times Book Review,* 10 Oct. 1926, p. 10; on *Uncle Anghel,* see *ibid.,* 25 Sept. 1927, p. 4; on *The Thistles of the Baragan,* see *ibid.,* 23 March 1930, p. 6; On *The Bitter Orange Tree,* see *ibid.,* 15 March 1931, p. 7

VIRGIL IERUNCA

ITALIAN LITERATURE

Modern Italian literature may be said—not too arbitrarily—to have begun when, after long struggles, Italy finally achieved national independence and unity. The occupation of Rome in 1870 completed the establishment of the kingdom; for the first time in centuries Italy was free of foreign domination, and rigorous centralization, copied from the French, replaced the particularistic system of small separate states.

This new state of affairs soon produced repercussions in cultural life. In the first place it had an important effect upon language. The Italian that was the official language and the language of literature was not the language of the people, who understood only the various dialects, which often diverged drastically from what was officially accepted as Italian. (This situation was additionally complicated by the long struggle between the purists, who wanted to recognize only pure Tuscan, and the advocates of a more liberal policy.) Moreover, in northern and central Italy, Italian was not even the language of the educated classes, who generally used French. After the unification of Italy, however, thanks to the standardization of administration, the universal educational system, and compulsory military service, official Italian became the vernacular. The language itself benefited from this: expanding beyond the confines of pure Tuscan it became richer, more comprehensive, more flexible.

Besides consolidation of the language, political unification had a second important consequence: Italy was again brought into contact with the ideas of the rest of Europe. In the first decades of the 19th c., Italian literature had participated in European romanticism and with Alessandro Manzoni (1785-1873) had achieved European stature. In addition it had played a leading role in the political upheaval —it had in fact instigated it. But after this creative upsurge it had subsisted for more than twenty years on the ideas and forms of romanticism without any fresh inspiration and had become provincial.

Aided by the abolition of censorship, Italy now proceeded to absorb ideas from abroad as readily as a vacuum. Two main trends emerged, contradictory but parallel: on the one hand, positivism, the religion of natural science and of facts, with its accompanying agnosticism; on the other hand, the philosophy of Hegel and his pupils. Positivism penetrated all the Italian universities; its influence spread beyond philosophy to other fields such as natural science, law, and medicine. Hegelianism established itself primarily in Naples; it outlived positivism and has maintained its leading position up to the present day. Both trends, however, were somewhat modified in Italy, positivism becoming more idealized and Hegelianism more mechanized.

This juxtaposition of native Italian late romanticism and of still unassimilated ideas from abroad at first produced resistance and reaction in Italian literature. Between 1860 and 1870 the so-called Scapigliati ("the tousleheads") came together in Milan under the leadership of Giuseppe Rovani (1818-74) and Emilio Praga (1839-75). Following the French example, particularly that of Baudelaire, they wanted to overthrow native Italian late romanticism in art and life: in art with a mixture of decadence and realism, in life with a tempestuous, exhibitionistic Bohemianism. Other members of this group were Arrigo Boito (1842-1918), better known today as a composer and opera librettist than as a writer, and the professor of

literature Arturo Graf (1848-1913), with his postromantic poems (*Medusa,* 1880; *Le Danaidi,* 1897), which deal with the dark side of life.

Far more important than this reaction (which is essentially still romantic) is the classical one led by "the first poet of the new Italy," Giosuè Carducci (1835-1907). A Tuscan by birth and for many years a professor of Italian literature at the University of Bologna, Carducci was for decades the Italians' national poet and their artistic and political oracle. Whatever befell the nation, it turned to him for advice and guidance, believing, in those early years of national unity, that he spoke with the voice of national feeling, as the prophet of Italian nationalism. The early Carducci preached a return to "Romanness"—to classical paganism, classical meters, and rigorous form in general —as well as war on Christianity (which he thought negated the national virtues and made men soft) and of romanticism (believing its loosening of form and fondness for the Middle Ages to be contrary to the best Italian tradition).

One must never forget how strong the classical tradition in Italian literature had always been, how conscious this country was of being the daughter and heir of ancient Rome, how long Latin poetry and rhetoric had maintained their vitality. There was also the Italian attachment to the classics of their own literature—a literature that had not risen gradually to greatness but had begun at the topmost peak with Dante, Petrarch, and Boccaccio. To achieve a style independent of this double heritage took laborious, conscious effort. The first successful break was the one into romanticism. Now came another setback.

In his fight against the church, Carducci voiced a widespread feeling, just as he did in his fight against romanticism. However, what he was voicing, primarily, was anticlericalism, rather than a pagan sense of life in the Nietzschean sense (see Nietzsche). The centuries-old intermixing of religious and worldly interests in papal politics, which had often proved so fateful for Italy, had left the Italians' relationship to the pope and the Vatican heavily tinged with resentment.

In time Carducci himself went far beyond mere patriotic passion and his exaggerated, polemical emphasis on classical and pagan values. His final period in particular revealed his ever-broadening European culture and the maturing of his poetic forcefulness. Especially when he spoke in elegy and idyl form he broke new ground for Italian poetry. Thus the reversion to classicism became a new departure.

In the meantime, in the 1870's a completely different tendency began to emerge in the novel. Under the influence of positivism and in the tradition of Balzac (1799-1850), Flaubert (1821-80), Zola (q.v.), and Maupassant (1850-93), attempts toward some kind of "experimental novel" began in Italy too. The first representatives of this new realism were Luigi Capuana (1839-1915), the theoretician of the new trend, and Alfredo Oriani (1852-1909). Their novels of society based on French models, however, often fall back into a theatrical late romanticism in which the naturalistic elements become melodramatic effects. One reason for this may be that bourgeois society in the European sense scarcely existed in Italy, the country having lived too long in unnatural political circumstances; it was a poor country, almost without industry and without any trade to speak of, and its social structure was completely antiquated. Literary realism became fruitful only when it merged with another trend, namely, regionalism.

Despite political centralization, the various centers of culture in Italy had kept their vitality. Rome, quite unlike Paris, has never yet played an important part in literature. Milan, Florence, Naples, and Venice, as well as smaller centers were—and still are—the important ones. Moreover, interest was now arising in the country's various landscapes, their inhabitants and dialects. Thus it was not bourgeois society but the people of the various regions—peasants, fishermen, poor city people—that provided the leading characters of novels.

The most important representative of this naturalism (q.v.), which in Italy was called *verismo*, was Verga (q.v.). He too had begun in Milan and Florence with novels of society, but it was his native Sicily that led him to his own style. Verga is the first in a long line of poets and writers who made southern Italy the symbol of a new tragedy. This region (which includes Sicily and the other islands as well as the southern portion of the mainland) is racially a mixture including everything from Normans to Arabs. Politically it has from time immemorial been subject to foreign domination and cut off from central and northern Italy; economically it is centuries behind; sociologically it is split into a very sparse property-owning class and the dispossessed masses who live in utterly primitive conditions. From the

intellectual and human point of view, it is a world very difficult for the outsider to comprehend; only gradually is it catching up with the development of the rest of Italy. Verga was the first to create a valid artistic rendering of all this. Though his major works are not written in dialect, their cadence and syntax have a Sicilian ring. They describe in unsurpassable concentration the destinies of the Sicilians, their hardships and their fatalistic, atavistic sense of life. The language never degenerates into mere rhetoric; the action never lags; the characters confront their fates with the inevitability great art demands. Sensual passion and social conditions are interwoven in such a way that they cannot be viewed as separate and distinct consequences or causes of individual destinies. No explanations are sought, no charges made, no solutions proposed. This fatalism on the part of the writer and his characters, for which no motivation is provided, leads in Verga's novellas to a ruthless simplicity, in his novels to inextricable entanglement.

Grazia Deledda (q.v.) and Matilde Serao (1856-1927) are pessimistic like Verga but much more intuitive, much weaker artistically, and much more indebted to French naturalism, Deledda's novels and novellas, usually set in Sardinia, are full of violent, often operatic highlights, while Serao describes the proletariat and petty bourgeoisie of Naples in Zolaesque frescos.

Inside Italy the poetry of Ada Negri (1870-1945) and the prose of Edmondo De Amicis (1846-1908), one of the most widely read writers of his time, achieved great popularity. Both were close to *verismo*; both were concerned with social problems (De Amicis as an educator promoting a bourgeois social attitude); both pushed sentimentality to its limits. Here a group of regionalists who use a more humorous style should be mentioned: Renato Fucini (1843-1921), with his descriptions of Tuscan peasants and his sonnets in Pisan dialect; and the dialect poets Pascarella and Di Giacomo (qq.v.), the former a Roman and the latter a Neapolitan. Di Giacomo, the only great modern dialect poet, went beyond the mere humorous portrayal of popular life to achieve a truly poetic, guardedly melancholic impressionism.

In addition to Carducci's soaring idealism and the positivistic problematic themes of *verismo,* a very specific element of the Italian romantic heritage recurred in the last quarter of the 19th c.—liberal Catholicism. In his masterwork *Piccolo mondo antico* (1895; The Patriot, 1906), the Lombard Antonio Fogazzaro (1842-1911), philosophically and stylistically a successor of Manzoni and a follower of the theories of the philosopher Antonio Rosmini (1797-1855), depicted the struggle for freedom of the years 1850 to 1860. Against the background of the fight against Austria, he described the psychological evolution of his heroes, especially their religious and moral entanglements and decisions. So far as external plot is concerned, this novel belongs somewhere between late romanticism and sentimental, bourgeois belletristic writing, but it ranks as a significant work by virtue of its perceptive rendering of complex personnages whose clashes culminate in dramatic climaxes, its fervent yet disciplined love of country, its genuine religious passion, and its sense of an ever-changing nature interwoven with man's destiny—and by virtue of the happy balance of all these elements and Fogazzaro's relaxed mastery of his material. Another of Manzoni's heirs is Emilio De Marchi (1851-1901), with his moralistic novels *Il cappello del prete* (1888) and *Demetrio Pianelli* (1890).

In poetry Pascoli (q.v.) bridged the gap between Carducci, whom he succeeded to the chair of literature at the University of Bologna, and the younger Italian poets. Though still a controversial figure in Italian criticism, Pascoli undoubtedly introduced a new tone to Italian poetry—an ear for the voice of things in themselves and an effort to capture that which is unique, characteristic—the specific mood, the passing moment, the fleeting quality of a sound, a fragrance. or a color. For him poetry consists in "finding in things their laughter and their tears"; the poet is the child looking around himself in wonderment at life, he is one who works at "reducing the scale of things in order to see them and magnifying them in order to marvel at them." Pascoli therefore confines himself, with a sometimes intentional, affected childlikeness, to poetry of small things, to simple life and the simple emotions. He uses traditional forms but loosens their interior structure into a fragmentary, often arbitrary series of images and words that are linked in gentle, melancholic fluidity.

The first writer to restore Italian literature to European stature was D'Annunzio (q.v.), who himself represents a sort of synthesis of all European tendencies—a poetic virtuoso of sensualism who in poetry, novellas, novels, and plays glorified beauty and delight. A genius in

assimilation and imitation, he borrowed elements in his work and his philosophy chiefly from the French poets, from Verlaine (1844-96) and Rimbaud (1854-91) down to Barrès (1862-1923) and Claudel (q.v.), from the Italian philosophers, from the Romantics and Nietzsche down to Ludwig Feuerbach (1804-1872) and Max Stirner (1806-1856), without overlooking the pseudo-Christian ecstaticism of Wagner's *Parsifal*.

Yet these diverse elements all serve one single aim: a hedonism revealing the artist, exempt from moral, bourgeois, and religious law, as the true superman and creating a new myth—the naturalistic myth of naked life. This myth, which made use of all contemporary trends and influences from abroad, was in fact a development of tendencies already existing in Italian literature. Its turbulent themes stem from the robust sensuality of Verga, its formal sophistication from the recent achievements of Carducci and Pascoli. In addition to his brilliant technique, which caused him to be frequently written off as a mere spellbinder and syncretistic imitator, D'Annunzio also possessed an unfailing creative sensitivity and a real mastery of poetic language. The diversity of his meters, his richness of vocabulary and imagery, his gift for the vivid statement and exposition of a theme, his power to express the elemental wildness of nature in exquisite words and concepts, prove him to be a great poet. In D'Annunzio's poetry sensualism splits into two completely divergent streams: strong and vigorous in the *Alcyone,* sick and weary in the *Poema paradisiaco*. Both streams had a lasting influence on later Italian poetry.

As Carducci's influence had dominated many decades, several more were held under D'Annunzio's spell. The dominant chord of Carducci's poetry rang out again triumphantly when D'Annunzio too finally became a patriot. The singer of joy in beauty and the senses became the singer of joy in action, especially action in the service of the fatherland. The hedonistic man of letters and hero of many public love affairs was transformed into the hero of World War I, the romantic conqueror of Fiume.

But in the prewar years, when D'Annunzio's influence and glory were at their height, other forces too were at work in Italy—some similar in nature, some quite different. The period from 1900 to 1914 was dominated on the one hand by striving for political and economic expansion, on the other by cultural unrest. In the general jockeying for power in Europe, Italy attempted a balance-of-power policy. While she did in fact become a major European power, many external and internal problems remained unsolved, many needs unmet.

In Italian literature the so-called futurists (see futurism) made themselves the spokesmen of a generation striving for a new, modern Italy. They rejected "Carducci's rhetorical, professorial, Greco-Roman and medieval Italy, Pascoli's georgic, tearful, wistful Italy, the bigoted Italy of the dwarf Fogazzaro, and D'Annunzio's erotic Italy of shopkeepers." This nation of museumpieces and professors was to become a nation of large-scale trade and factories. The artists, too, were to refrain from all sentimentality ("today we can admire nothing but the ghastly symphonies of shrapnel and the crazy sculpture our inspired artillery carves out of enemy masses"). But leaving aside these exaggerations and this one-sidedness, futurism is a valid link in the chain of Italian and European poetry. In his *Manifesto* (1912), Filipo Marinetti (1876-1944) proclaimed the overthrow of traditional rhetoric, classical form, poetic circumscription, and conventional imagery, and demanding the loosening of syntax, the "liberation of words," the direct juxtaposition of associations without logical connection, the recognition of technology, the glorification of matter, the suspension of space and time. Futurism, which already existed in the visual arts and which later led to dadaism, expressionism (qq.v.), cubism, and surrealism (q.v.), became a European movement. Marinetti wrote much of his poetry in French, achieved sensational success in France, and was admired by poets such as Apollinaire and Claudel (qq.v.). Although essentially the breakthrough to a free poetry had long been accomplished, the futurist experiment was obviously necessary in Italy in order that poetry might be freed once and for all from its old fetters. Most members of the futurist group, such as Ardengo Soffici (b. 1879) and Corrado Govoni (b. 1884), were associated with it only briefly and soon went their own ways.

Two journals published in Florence had a formative effect on the intellectual life of this period: *Leonardo,* founded in 1903, and *La Voce,* founded in 1908, both of which were directed by Giovanni Papini (q.v.) and Giuseppe Prezzolini (b. 1882).

Giovanni Papini was one of the most restless spirits in modern Italian literature. His life was a series of crises, and he had a talent for being always the center of an important group of artists, writers, and poets. For a time he belonged to the futurist school and with Soffici edited the journal *Lacerba,* in which he made vigorous propaganda for Italy's entry into the war. He also wrote a series of critical treatises questioning the reputations of some of the most distinguished names in world literature. After World War I he returned to Catholicism and wrote the sensational *Storia di Cristo* (1921; Eng., Life of Christ, 1923; Am., The Story of Christ, 1924); he achieved considerable notoriety again after World War II with his *Lettere agli uomini del papa Celestino VI* (1946; Eng., 1948) and *Il Diavolo* (1953; The Devil, 1948).

In *Leonardo* and *La Voce,* Papini and especially Prezzolini carried on a crusade for the renewal of Italian culture. Nationalistic in politics and in cultural affairs, they opposed the predominant positivism of the first decade of the 20th c., worked toward a new concept of art, and introduced foreign cultural movements, including American pragmatism and American writers, to Italy. In their leaning toward the unconventional, both these journals contributed, with futurism, to the transformation of Italian prose style.

While the struggle for renewal in the modernist spirit was going on in Florence, in Naples, the city that had always been Italy's most important philosophical center, a revival of speculative interests occurred. Out of German idealism the philosopher Giovanni Gentile (1875-1944) developed "actualism," which proclaimed the coincidence of divine and human life in history. The cultural philosopher Croce (q.v.), who collaborated with Gentile for many years but eventually broke with him because of political differences, concerned himself principally with aesthetics and the science of history. In his treatises on aesthetics, which were internationally read and acclaimed, he replaced classicistic categories (see literary criticism) with idealistic and romantic ones. Here art is conceived as a phenomenon distinct from all mental activities.

In his science of history Croce denied that history had a metaphysical goal but conceived the course of history as the area in which human freedom painfully yet surely realizes itself. Above all, in the journal *La Critica,* which he founded in 1903 and which continued to appear until his death, Croce served as cultural arbitrator to two generations right up to the period following World War II. Almost every work of any significance that appeared in Germany, France, England, or elsewhere was reviewed in this journal. Whether Croce approved or rejected it, he invariably gave an objective account of the work in question. This made *La Critica* an inexhaustible source of information for the Italian intelligentsia.

Croce was also the originator of the collection *Gli Scrittori d'Italia,* in which the most important documents of Italian literature from its beginnings appeared in critical editions and which shed new light on many a forgotten author and neglected period. Politically Croce was a liberal who never made the least concession to demagogy and vigorously opposed all totalitarian hocuspocus. In all these areas he established a trend. Many of his pupils became professors at Italian universities, while his influence can be clearly seen in widely differing tendencies in the critical works of Borgese (q.v.), Attilio Momigliano (1883-1952), Francesco Flora (b. 1891), and others.

Before the outbreak of World War I a wide variety of intellectual movements flourished in Italy. On the one hand there were D'Annunzio's aesthetic sensualism and rhetorical patriotism, the futurists' modernism and nationalism, and the political, philosophical, and literary endeavors of the Florentine circle; on the other hand there were Croce's and Gentile's movements. In addition there was the group of poets nicknamed the Crepuscolari ("twilight poets"), which included Gozzano (q.v.), Govoni, Sergio Corazzini (1887-1907), and Palazzeschi (q.v.). As their name implies, they rejected both D'Annunzio's spirited brilliance and the explosions of the futurists, stressing instead—not without clever detachment and slight irony— a taste for the eccentric. They developed a melancholic mannerism in which marionettes and barrel organs, bells and monastery gardens —along with life's failures, prostitutes, and the mortally ill—became symbols of quiet despair. Thematically and stylistically, this poetry of decadence derives from Pascoli, from those poems of D'Annunzio that tend toward a tired, as it were, convalescent, sensualism, and last but not least from French symbolism (q.v.)

The years of disillusionment and confusion after 1918 did not mean stagnation for Italian literature. The structural loosening of prose style, deeper psychological insights, new potentialities in the playful treatment of reality, and a new soberness continued to be discussed and pursued.

In the journal *La Ronda,* founded in 1919,

the poet and writer Cardarelli (q.v.) and the writers and critics Cecchi (q.v.) and Baldini (q.v.) opposed the fragmentation of language preached by futurism and demanded a return to syntax and to the careful polishing of style. Cecchi in particular achieved far-reaching influence through his wide cultural range and tireless vigilance, his familarity with other countries and their literatures, his versatility and dexterity. While following the contemporary tendency toward the fragmentary in subject matter, stylistically he made a great contribution to the creation of a prose style in which modern sensitivity, however erratic, nervous, or surrealistic, can express itself in an exquisite, balanced Italian. Thus modern Italian style achieved a synthesis between old constraints and new freedom.

The work of the novelist and dramatist Pirandello (q.v.) is both an outcome of this synthesis and an essential contribution to it. Born in 1867, Pirandello was not recognized until after 1918, but during the 1920's his comedies dominated the European stage. He was awarded the Nobel Prize in 1934.

Until the turn of the century the Italian theater was a mixture of late romanticism and out-and-out naturalism (q.v.). Giuseppe Giacosa (1874-1906) was typical; he began with sentimental historical plays in the romantic style, and then under the influence of Ibsen and of French naturalism he turned to social and psychological drama. His works include the naturalistic librettos of Puccini's *La Bohème* and *Tosca.* Pietro Cossa (1830-81) and Paolo Ferrari (1822-89) developed in a similar way. *Verismo* appeared in opera librettos such as *Cavalleria Rusticana* (after a peasant novella by Verga) and Leoncavallo's *I Pagliacci* and in plays by Girolamo Rovetta (1851-1910), Giannino Antona Traversi (1857-1934), and Roberto Bracco (1862-1943). The dramatic work of D'Annunzio, who besides writing tragedies revived the old genre of the pastoral play, is predominantly poetic and overloaded with symbolism. Sem Benelli (1877-1949), one of his successors, wrote bombastic historical dramas. Luigi Chiarelli (b. 1886) and Rosso di San Secondo (q.v.) indulged in fantasy and paradox, while *Scampolo* (1916), a comedy by Dario Niccodemi (1874-1934) abounded in sentimentality.

Pirandello was the first to strike a new note and introduce new subjects in Italian—and European—drama. A friend of Luigi Capuana (1839-1915) and of Verga, he is close to *verismo* in his almost exclusive interest in daily life, cramped circumstances, and simple people —peasants and farm laborers, the petty bourgeoisie, and minor intellectuals—and above all in his pessimism. Pirandello, like Verga, was born in Sicily; his earliest emotional experience was the misery, harshness, and hopelessness of this world, which became for him a symbol of life itself. But contrary to *verismo,* he sees this life as a mixture of truth and mirage, in which reality becomes fantasy, fantasy reality, in which faces turn into masks and masks into faces, in which tragedies become ironical and jokes become tragic, all actions appear ambiguous, individual personalities become blurred, in which the poet's characters are more real than the characters of so-called reality. On the stage this led to the shattering of all conventions and to a loose surrealistic form that influenced the whole subsequent development of the theater.

Pirandello's best known comedy *Sei personaggi in cerca d'autore* (1921; Six Characters in Search of an Author, 1922) shows nonreality, so to speak, "raised to the second power." Into the make-believe world of the play within the play, the characters of a drama not yet written step out of nowhere. They act out their roles for the actors, only to see their own existences and natures immediately betrayed by them. Similar themes form the background for Pirandello's novellas (*Novelle per un anno,* 1922-37), which often serve as sketches for his plays and novels. Pirandello's world, described now poetically, now dialectically, now tragically, now humorously, is always enigmatic—a metaphysical comedy in which all the laughter is tinged with deep sorrow and bitterness. It is hard to say whether his own summation—"I never tried to destroy anything except illusions" —adequately defines his work.

With his pessimism, his conviction of the insubstantiality of existence, Pirandello, like Verga, struck a note that is very clearly echoed in contemporary Italian writers. Melancholy, disillusionment, repudiation not only of paltry excuses but also of solutions, had always existed in Italian literature to a degree astonishing to foreigners. Now this tendency is intensified by a sense of the nothingness of all happenings. Wherever the metaphysical world—which here means Catholicism—has collapsed, usually nothing is left but skepticism, smiling resignation, or else a bitter irony that often goes hand in hand with a certain voluptuous enjoyment of the darker sides of life. Optimism toward

the world is practically nonexistent; faith alone offers consolation—to such writers as still possess it. The novels of Borgese are pessimistic, those of Svevo (q.v.) pessimistically ironical. The latter contain the long psychological analyses and criticisms of contemporary life so common in modern European literature, for which the Italians generally have little affinity. The world of Tozzi (q.v.), who died at an early age, is a pessimistic one; his best novel, *Tre Croci* (1920; Three Crosses, 1921), describes the disconsolateness of a small town in which history becomes a grave and the characters die out one by one.

A more robust outlook and more humor are found in Panzini (q.v.), author of more than sixty volumes of novels, novellas, diaries, and critical works, who was a pupil of Carducci, a connoisseur of the Greek and Roman classics, and a humanist who regards the modern world with a sometimes friendly, sometimes ironical, sometimes skeptical smile, but at last becomes increasingly perturbed by it. By stringing together terse, characteristic episodes, he describes and comments on the course of the early 20th c. and on World War I and the moral and social changes it produced.

The most momentous change at the time— fascism—did not actually interrupt the development of Italian literature. To be sure, pressure was applied, and there was no longer absolutely free choice of themes. The ideological and social problems arising out of the existence of fascism either were treated by writers in exile —notably by the novelist Silone (q.v.)—or were not tackled until after the fall of the regime. At best they appeared in veiled satires such as those of the Roman dialect poet Trilussa (q.v.). Yet Mussolini, once a journalist himself, was favorably disposed toward stylistic experiments. He nominated the futurist Marinetti to the newly founded Accademia d'Italia, and his attitude toward formal boldness was friendly rather than hostile. Considerable latitude was also granted in choice of themes. Thus a wide range of literary works, some of them significant, came to be not only written but also printed in fascist Italy.

In his journal *Novecento,* founded in 1926, Bontempelli, writer of novellas, novels, and comedies, opposed regionalism and advocated cosmopolitanism in art and transformed the present day into a magic world of unreal myths. Other citizens of a realm of nonreality are Giovan Battista Angioletti (b. 1896), with his fantastic short stories and the surrealistic fantasy *Donata* (1941), Fabio Tombari (b. 1899), with his imaginary small town Frusaglia (*Tutta Frusaglia*, 1929), and finally one of the most interesting of contemporary Italian writers, Buzzati (q.v.), whose books have been translated into many languages. While the influence of Kafka (q.v.) is obvious, Buzzati's technique is a characteristic mixture of reality and symbol. Characters and action, sometimes even place and time, are depicted with remarkable originality, accuracy, and realism; yet for all that they take on an unreal, transparent quality, like figures in a nightmare.

A similar sense of life pervades modern Italian poetry. Here the anticlassical and antirhetorical tendencies prevailing not just in Italy but all over Europe were pushed to the extreme by the so-called Hermeticists. The leader of this most recent group is Ungaretti (q.v.), who tries to heighten poetic intensity to its very limit. His poems, which often consist of only a few words, dispense, so far as form goes, with rhyme, meter, punctuation, and often even with syntax; so far as content goes, with all decoration, elaboration, and explanation. In a kind of mystical austerity the word itself is made absolute to become the sole expression of material things and the direct vehicle of inner experience. This is essentially individualism carried to its highest pitch, where language is no longer communication but self-revelation, so that it does not matter whether it is comprehensible to others or not. It stands to reason that such a form should lend itself above all to the expression of man's loneliness, the enigma of life, the hardships of existence, and the darkness of death. The same themes dominate the poetry of Quasimodo (q.v.), who also strived to make the word the germ of poetry, and of Montale (q.v.), who has been called "the poet of despair." Less extreme and one-sided in his forms than Ungaretti, Montale's richer powers of expression and his more open attentiveness make him the most important of the Hermeticists. Umberto Saba (1883-1957) is more strongly tied to older models, especially to Pascoli, whose underlying tone of gentle melancholy he shares. The impressionistic poetry of Diego Valeri (b. 1887) recalls the Crepuscolari most of all.

Since the 1930's, Palazzeschi, a one-time futurist poet and Crepuscolare, has devoted himself chiefly to prose. His world is in the main a bitter one, depicted with caustic irony. The world of Piovene (q.v.) is also bitter, ambiguous, unscrupulous, passionate, and confused, as

is that of the novelist Moravia (q.v.), who attained his greatest success abroad after World War II. Modern in style and taking depth psychology as his point of departure, Moravia seeks to transcend traditional, erotic *verismo*. His rootless characters, however, are almost without exception entangled in sexual problems. His tendency to introduce morbid elements and situations into literature has influenced a wide range of younger writers.

After the preference for fragmentary style and fantastic, surrealist, or ironically critical subjects, the classical concept of the novel reestablished itself. And here we find a whole series of works in which the certitude of faith glimmers through the uncertainties of the world, lending some meaning to existence and a moral foothold to the protagonists, even though life itself remains perplexing, good seems impotent, and the basic tone is still melancholy. The outstanding writers to be mentioned here are Chiesa (q.v.), Bruno Cicognani (b. 1879), Marino Moretti, and Bacchelli (qq.v.). Bacchelli is the author of one of the most important Italian novels of all time: the three-volume *Il mulino del Po* (1938-40), which tells the story of three generations of millers from 1812 to 1915. Despite the historical background, which only occasionally becomes too prominent, the novel's main theme is the continuity of human life with its struggles for self-assertion and self-protection and also its generous dedication to altruistic ideals. The style, which recalls Manzoni, though not in an imitative way, reflects the vastness of Bacchelli's human experience and artistic maturity.

The versatile Malaparte (q.v.), always polemical and aggressive, always brilliant and sensational, also writes about events of the war and postwar period. The baroque brutality of his descriptions is often unbearable.

The most important literary characteristic of the postwar period may well be the revival of realism and regionalism, which became known abroad largely through the success of neorealistic Italian films. Even the problems of fascism, the war, and the postwar years are generally treated in a faithfully described regional cultural setting. Thus Pratolini (q.v.) describes Florence under fascism (*Cronache di poveri amanti*, 1946); Bartolini (q.v.), postwar Rome (*Ladri di biciclette*, 1944); Marotta (q.v.), the common people of Naples (*L'oro di Napoli*, 1947); Pavese (q.v.), his native Piedmont (*La luna e il falò*, 1950); and Enrico Pea (1881-1958), Lucca, the city of churches, with its ancient spirituality ("Lisetta" in *Peccati in piazza*, 1956).

Giuseppe Berto (b. 1914) is not so closely tied to regionalism. His novel *Il cielo è rosso* (1947) describes the communal life of four young people during air raids and during Italy's collapse, while the account of the events of a single night in his short story "Le opere di Dio" (1948) amounts virtually to a symbolic summary of World War II.

Again southern Italy plays the leading role in the new regionalism. In the 1930's Alvaro (q.v.) was already pursuing the tradition of Verga—and to a certain extent of D'Annunzio —in his novellas *Gente in Aspromonte* (1930), though his sharp social criticism took him beyond both his models. A whole series of novelists followed his lead—more soberly and sometimes with more humor; these include Francesco Jovine (q.v.), the moralistic, melancholy humorist Brancati (q.v.), and finally Vittorini (q.v.), whose short stories reveal a primarily lyrical bent and who in a syncopated style, modeled on modern American literature, makes Sicily the symbol of a world that "is big and beautiful, but sick, very sick."

Southern Italy is also the theme of one of the best-known Italian books of the postwar period, *Cristo si è fermato a Eboli* (1946; Christ Stopped at Eboli, 1947), in which Levi (q.v.), a Turin doctor, painter, and writer, depicts with the curiosity and wonder of the bystander this region that is so foreign to him, this "closed world, wrapped in black veils, bloody and earthy, which one can never penetrate without the key of magic."

These names by no means complete the roll of contemporary Italian writers. It has come to include several outstanding women, among others Anna Banti (pseudonym of Lucia Lo Presti) and Alba de Cèspedes (b. 1911).

A novel written in 1958 deserves special mention: the masterfully written *Il Gattopardo* (The Leopard, 1959) by the Sicilian nobleman Giuseppe di Lampedusa (q.v.). It deals with the incorporation of Sicily into a united Italy and its effects on the Sicilian nobility, which was forced to come to terms with the liberal bourgeoise. Events are mirrored chiefly in the passionate, sensitive, conservative, skeptical Prince Salina, who, seeing his familiar world crumbling, strives in vain to master the new situation inwardly. *Il Gattopardo* is one more chapter in Sicilian regionalism and one more example of the predominant pessimism of contemporary Italian literature.

BIBLIOGRAPHY: Falqui, E., ed., *Prosatori e narratori del Novecento italiano* (1950); Livingston, A., *Essays on Modern Italian Literature* (1950); Girardi, E. N., *Il mito di Pavese, ed altri saggi* (1960); Veltori, V., *La nostra civiltà letteraria dal futurismo al secondo Novecento* (1960); Falqui, E., *Novecento letterario. Serie seconda* (1960); Salinari, C., *Miti e coscienza del decadentismo italiano: D'Annunzio, Pascoli, Fogazzaro, e Pirandello* (1960); Debenedetti, G., *Saggi critici: terza serie* (1961); Triggiani, D., *Dizionario degli scrittori; scrittori, poeti, critici, autori drammatici, giornalisti, e pubblicisti* (1961); Bàrberi Squarotti, G., *Poesia e narrativa del secondo novecento* (1961); Luti, G., *Italo Svevo ed altri studi sulla letteratura italiana del primo Novecento* (1961); Camerino, A. (comp.), *Le più belle pagine del 1961 scelte nei quotidiani italiani* (1962); Robertis, G. de, *Altro Novecento* (1962); Grana, G., *Profili e letture di contemporanei* (1962); Pacifici, S., *A Guide to Contemporary Italian Literature, from Futurism to Neorealism* (1962); Solmi, S., *Scrittori negli anni: saggi e note sulla letteratura italiana del 1900* (1963); Heiney, D. W., *America in Modern Italian Literature* (1965); Monelli, Paoto, *Ombre cinesi; scrittori al girarrosto* (1965); Scrivano, R., *Riviste, scrittori e critici del Novecento* (1965)

LILO EBEL

IVANOV, Georgyi Vladimirovich

Russian poet and novelist, b. 29 Oct. 1894, province of Kovno; d. Aug. 1958, Hyères, France

I. came to France as a refugee in the early 1920's. His first poems show the subtle stylization typical of Kuzmin and Loüys (qq.v.), but after the Russian revolution he developed his own style and philosophy modeled on the symbolism of Blok (q.v.). His poetry shows a disillusioned romantic irony, sometimes even a nihilism, which, however, is combined in a quite remarkable way with a poetic belief in music.

I. is regarded as the last poet of the St. Petersburg period of Russian culture. The language of his melodic poems is simple and precise. In his last poems he tried to tone down his *poésie pure* by introducing certain prosaic expressions into his vocabulary. His novel *Treti Rim* (published in fragmentary form in a magazine in 1929) remained unfinished.

FURTHER WORKS: *Otplytiye na ostrov Tziteru* (1912); *Veresk* (1916); *Sady* (1921); *Peterburgskiya zimy* (1928); *Leonid Kannegiser* (1928); *Rozy* (1931); *Raspad atoma* (1938); *Stikhi* (1953); *Stikhi, 1943-1958* (1958)

BIBLIOGRAPHY: Tschiżewski, D., "Unbekannte Epigramme I.'s," *Die Welt der Slawen,* V (1960), 415-17; Pascal, P., "Trois poètes russes au début du XXe siècle (I., Blok, Gumilev)," in *Venezia nelle letterature moderne* (1962), 219-29

GEORGES IVASK

IVANOV, Vsevolod Vyacheslavovich

Russian novelist, b. 24 Feb. 1895, Lebyazh'ye, Kirghiz Steppe; d. 15 Aug. 1963, Moscow

After a youth packed with adventures that took him through all of Siberia—he was a sailor, a printer, a clown, among other things —I. fought in the Red army and came to Leningrad in 1920. There, sponsored by Gorki (q.v.), he joined the Serapion Brothers.

Man as driven by his instincts is the topic of his writing. Therefore the Russian Civil War, whose epic poet I. became, is described more as a terrible yet awesome eruption of the elemental force of the people, especially of the peasant, than as an act of conscious class warfare.

I. became famous for his novel *Bronepoyezd 14-69* (1920; Armoured Train 14-69, 1933), which was also a great success as a play. His autobiographical adventure novel, *Pokhozhdeniya fakira* (1935; The Adventures of a Fakir, 1935), leads the average Russian reader into a world totally unknown to him. Again and again I. was censored by Marxist criticism for the anarchistic-individualistic character of his heroes and for his own pessimistic fundamental ideas. I. finally came around and accepted the socialist realism that the party decreed; the result was his novel *Parkhomenko* (1937) and the play *Glavnyi inzhener* (1947), whose subject is the five-year plan. Alongside Pilnyak, Babel, the early Leonov (qq.v.), and others, I. remains important because of his style and his subject matter, and especially because of his contribution as the epic poet of the Russian Civil War.

FURTHER WORKS: *Partizany* (1921-23); *Tzvetnyye vetra* (1922); *Golubyye peski* (1923); *Vozvrasheniye Buddy* (1923); *Tainoye tainykh* (1927); *Puteshestviye v stranu kotoroi*

yeshche net (1931); *Povesti brigadira Sintzyna* (1931); *Vstrechi s Maksimom Gorkim* (1947); *P'yesy* (1954); *Lomonosov* (1956); *Voyennyye rasskazy i ocherki* (1960); *Khmel'; sibirskiye rasskazy* (1963); *Rasskazy* (1963); *Edesskaya svyatynya* (1965)

BIBLIOGRAPHY: Janovsky, N. N., *V. V. I.* (1956); Muchnic, H., "Literature of the NEP Period," in Hayward, M., and Labedz, L., eds., *Literature and Revolution in Soviet Russia, 1917-62* (1963), pp. 28-43; Reeve, F. D., *The Russian Novel* (1966)

GÜNTHER WYTRZENS

IVANOV, Vyacheslav Ivanovich

Russian writer, philologist, and philosopher, b. 16 Feb. 1866, Moscow; d. 16 July 1949, Rome

At the age of twenty, I. left Moscow for Berlin and became a student of Mommsen in 1886. His study of Nietzsche (q.v.) conveyed to him an understanding of the Dionysiac. Long journeys followed, which took him through Europe, Palestine, and Egypt. His tower apartment in Saint Petersburg, where he and his wife, the writer Lidiya Zinov'yeva-Annibal, had a *jour fixe* for Russian writers and artists every Wednesday, became famous as a gathering point. I. was celebrated as a *"maître"* and "arbiter" by poets of modern trends.

The years 1912 and 1913 were again spent abroad, but he remained in Moscow and Baku as a professor of classical philosophy during World War I and the revolution. In 1924 he succeeded in emigrating to Italy, where his creative powers flourished once more. In 1926 he became a Catholic. I. died in Rome in 1949, leaving a novel—which he claimed as his most important work—and a collection of poems.

Together with Blok and Belyi (qq.v.) I. was one of the leaders of the religious "realistic" symbolism (q.v.) in Russia in contrast to the ornamental "idealistic" symbolism of Bryusov and Bal'mont (qq.v.). In a poem to Blok, I. declared: "Forever we remain brothers since Solov'iov secretly gave us in marriage to the One." But to I. the "One"—the Greek Orthodox Saint Sophia—was not Blok's "fair lady"; instead she was the intrinsic wisdom of God. His books of poetry—*Kormchiya zviozdy* (1903) and *Prozrachnost'* (1904)—bear witness to this.

They also point to the right way—ecstasy. Dionysus, the dying and resurrected god of the Greeks, was for I. the mythological expression of this ecstasy. "The Hellenistic religion of the suffering God" (*Ellinskaya religiya stradayushchavo boga,* 1904) was supposed to prove, in contradiction to Nietzsche, that the Dionysiac cult represented a step toward Christianity, as if it were a kind of Old Testament of the pagan world.

I.'s profusely ornamental style, reminiscent of a Byzantine gown, reached its culmination in the poetry of *Cor ardens* (2 vols., 1909-1911). Here he writes of death vanquished by love and of the awakening of the soul in a transfigured body. The contents of his songs are theoretically interpreted by I. himself in his books of essays 1909-1918, and in *Perepiska iz dvukh uglov* (1920). I. considered spiritual culture to be the continuous result of an innate memory. Nonexistence manifests itself directly as a consequence of no-recall. Thus memory testifies as to existence. A poet stirs memory and herewith reveals existence to the senses. Then he meets beauty. "The 'Exchange of Letters' is the most important thing that has been said about Humanism since Nietzsche" (E. R. Curtius).

From 1915 to 1919 I. worked on a group of heartfelt poems in diverse styles (which were published as *Chelovek* in 1939), in which he expressed his original theories about cognition and expounded his philosophy. True cognition can be reached only by transcending oneself by the act of love. *All-Einheit*—transcendental unity—was for I. a gnostic and an eschatological principle at the same time.

FURTHER WORKS: *Tantal* (1905); *Po zviozdam* (1909); *Nezhnaya taina* (1912); *Goethe na rubezhe dvukh stoletii* (1912); *Borozdy i mezhi* (1916); *Rodnoye i vselenskoye* (1917); *Mladenchestvo* (1918); *Krizis gumanizma, Kruchi* (1918); *Prometei* (1919); *Zimniye sonety* (1919); *De Profundis Amavi* (1920); *Dostoyevski* (1920; Freedom and the Tragic Life: A Study in Dostoevsky, 1952); *Rimskiye sonety* (1925); *Svet vechernii* (1960)

BIBLIOGRAPHY: Poggioli, R., *The Poets of Russia 1890-1930* (1960); Struve, G., "The Transition from Russian to Soviet Literature," in Hayward, M., and Labedz, L., eds., *Literature and Revolution in Soviet Russia, 1917-62* (1963), pp. 1-27; Pascal, P., "Trois poètes russes à Venise," in Pellegrini, C., ed., *Venezia nelle letterature moderne* (1961)

O. DESCHARTES

IWASZKIEWICZ, Jarosłav

(pseud.: *Eleuter*), Polish poet and narrative writer, b. 20 Feb. 1894, Kalnik, Ukraine

Western literature—George, Valéry, and Gide (qq.v.)—exercised an unmistakable influence on I.'s poetry, which possesses great suggestivity of color and tone (*Kasijdij,* 1925; *Wiersze wybrane,* 1938). His best prose works include the short stories in the volume *Panny z Wilka* (1933), with their erotic atmosphere and feeling of transitoriness, and the novels *Księżyc wschodzi* (1925) and *Czerwone tarcze* (1934), a poetic novel about 13th c. Europe with allusions to Poland's impotence during the years 1918 to 1939. I. wrote two plays set in artists' milieus, *Lato w Nohant* (1936) and *Maskarada* (1938). After 1945 he was a newspaper editor and president of many organizations in Warsaw.

FURTHER WORKS: *Oktostychy* (1919); *Zenobia Palmura* (1920); *Hilari syn buchaltera* (1923); *Siedem bogatych miast nieśmiertelnego Kościeja* (1924); *Księżyk wschodi* (1925); *Kochankowie z Weromy* (1928); *Fryderyk Szopen* (1928; new ed. as *Chopin,* 1966); *Ksiega dnia i księga nocy* (1929); *Zmowa mężczyzn* (1930); *Powrót do Europy* (1931); *Lato* (1932); *Pasje blędomierskie* (1938); *Kongres w Florencij* (1941); *Wzlot* (1956); *Sława i chwała* (1956-59); *Powieści* (2 vols., 1958); *Proza poetycka* (1958); *Wiersze* (1958); *Dziela* (4 vols., 1958-64); *Tatarak* (1960); *Wesele Pana Baltaka* (1960); *Jan Sebastian Bach* (1963); *Opowiadania wybrane* (1964); *Heydenreich* (1964)

BIBLIOGRAPHY: Kridl, M., *A Survey of Polish Literature and Culture* (1956)

* * *

J

JACOB, (Cyprien-) Max

French poet and painter, b. 11 July 1876, Quimper; d. 5 March 1944, in the German concentration camp at Drancy

J.'s reflections on the avant-garde cubist Rue de Ravignan group, of which he, Salmon, Apollinaire (qq.v.), and Picasso were members, were published in 1937 in *Feux de Paris* under the title "Le tiers transporté." After the two visions he experienced in 1909 and 1914 led him to Catholicism in 1915, he retired to the monastery at Saint-Benoît-sur-Loire. The poems and the prose texts of the *Défense de Tartuffe* (1919) and the novel *Saint Matorel* (1909) hark back to his religious experience. With ironical compassion, *Saint Matorel* tells the story of a Parisian petty bourgeois who, following his vocation, becomes abbot of the monastery of St. Teresa in Barcelona. He returns to earth after his death and leads a vagabond's life but is finally canonized. *Les Oeuvres mystiques et burlesques de Frère Matorel* (1911) deals with the saint's experiences. *Le siège de Jérusalem* (1912-14) presents the dramatic conclusion of the trilogy: after his glorious death Matorel must prove himself worthy of his sainthood in the next world.

Matorel, the innocent tempted by his own intelligence, reflects J.'s dual nature, which combines Jewish skepticism, humor, and bitterness with the mystical naiveté and imagination of the Breton. Faith, love, and art are treated in a burlesque manner yet with tenderness. Irony, satanism, and sanctity mask a tragic seriousness, which Gide misjudged. Gide compared J. with Heine, though Gide does acknowledge that J.'s work has that stylistic "density" that J.'s *Art poétique* (1922) praises as a literary virtue. Here J. sets off the new poetry

against symbolism (q.v.). The new poetry is self-sufficient and omits explanations but is bound by the perennial laws of beauty, by which the innovator is also bound, though each in his own individual way. The writer of the new poetry transposes commonplace things to exotic settings, prefers either excessively rich rhyme or none at all, has a liking for the dreamlike, for unexpected associations of words and ideas, for the poetic for its own sake. Its meaning is not to be found in its thought content. According to J., the modern poet strives toward the "objective epic." In simple clear language J.'s prose poems (*Le cornet à dés*, 1906) imply that poetry results from the spontaneity of free and direct expression. J.'s "unperformable" plays, opera librettos, religious meditations, verse portraits, poems of hallucination, and imaginary conversations show his indifference toward mere content and the picturesque, as well as his versatile creative talent and power to "perform miracles" through the magic of words and syntax, to renew language from within, and to "create a celestial climate on earth"—as he had set out to do.

FURTHER WORKS: *La Côte* (1911); *Le Phanérogame* (1918); *Le Laboratoire central* (1921); *Dos d'Harlequin* (1912); *Ne Coupez-pas, mademoiselle* (1921); *Le Roi de Béotie* (1921); *Le Cabinet noir* (1922; rev. ed., 1928); *Filibuth ou la montre en or* (1923); *Isabelle et Pantalon* (1923); *Le Terrain Bouchaballe* (1923); *Visions infernales* (1924); *Les Pénitents en maillot rose* (1925); *L'Homme de chair et l'homme de reflect* (1925); *Le Sacrifice impérial* (1928); *Cinématoma* (1929); *Tableau de la bourgeoisie* (1929); *Rivage* (1931); *Le Bal masqué* (1932); *Morceaux choisis* (1936); *Ballades* (1938); *Méditations réligieuses* (1945);

Derniers poèmes (1945); *L'Homme de cristal* (1946); *Correspondance* (2 vols., 1953-56). **Selected English trans.:** in Oxenhandler, N., *M. J. and Les Feux de Paris*, (1964)

BIBLIOGRAPHY: Andreu, P., *M. J.* (1962); Kamber, G., "M. J. et Charles Baudelaire: Une Étude de sources," *MLN, LXXVIII* (1963), 252-60

KURT WEINBERG

JAHNN, Hans Henny
German writer and musician, b. 17 Dec. 1894, Hamburg-Stellingen, Germany; d. 29 Nov. 1959, Hamburg-Blankenese

Son of a shipbuilder, J. divided his interest among writing, musical theory, and organ-making. Opposed to war, he spent the years 1915-18 in Norway. After 1933 he emigrated to Sweden, where he lived with his family as a farmer and biologist. He returned finally to Hamburg in 1950.

Like his literary next-of-kin Döblin and Nossack (qq.v.), J. was a novelist to the extent to which a novel can be regarded as an allegory of human life. Maintaining in his works the precarious utopian balance between art and propaganda so characteristic of Expressionism (q.v.), metaphysical anxiety shaped his message to man, fixed in a system with the coordinates *poverty, wealth, man,* and *beast* (later the title of his most significant drama). Let mankind be saved by compassionate love—the river unbound uniting all disparate life in deep sympathy (in biologic and spiritual symbiosis)—to recapture the lost mythic state of nature.

The earliest examples of this concern are found together with faint narcissistic overtones in the play *Der Arzt, sein Weib, sein Sohn* (1922) and the long novel *Perrudja* (1929). The latter is a work of cascading images and words that articulate the cosmologic pathos of an exile from the conventions of society, who is searching, in the Norwegian wilderness, complete harmony of existence. This cannot be achieved without its measure of evil, as shown in J.'s magnum opus, *Fluß ohne Ufer*, a trilogy consisting of *Das Holzschiff* (1949), *Die Niederschrift des Gustav Anias Horn* (1949-50), *Epilog* (1961). This novel of suspense, concerned at first sight with murder and mutiny during a mysterious voyage ending in shipwreck, develops into a retrospective account that analyzes motives and meaning in the life of two central characters. This is finally ex-

panded to proportions of universal principle through the technique of cyclic repetition—another murder is committed, another murderer assumes his share of guilt, which is but transmuted love.

Reflecting the expressionist urge for direct communication, J.'s plays are, for the most part, built on the thesis that man's despair, the curse of evanescent youth, results from his loss of animal innocence, and that this sanctuary can be recovered only partially through an archetypal love, of which the goddess in *Medea* (1926) becomes a symbol. This theme, first expressed in *Der Arzt, sein Weib, sein Sohn,* persists through the posthumously published *Die Trümmer des Gewissens* (1961), which tries to assess the consequences of man's fall from innocence in a vision of atomic holocaust as proof of scientific and political vanity. Becoming more and more convinced in his last years that the "league of the weak" (men of good faith) had to assume political action, and possibly to sacrifice themselves to save mankind from pointless destruction, J. was working on another drama of protest entitled *Die andere Seite greift ein* on the eve of his death.

His creed he had stated long ago: "We have witnessed too much; ignorance no longer becomes us. It is not our misfortune but our hope that man's soul has been found inconstant. Let us rebuild it and strengthen it against the tide of rational catastrophes, to reunite it to the harmonious structure of being" ("Aufgabe des Dichters in dieser Zeit," 1932).

FURTHER WORKS: *Pastor Ephraim Magnus* (1919); *Die Krönung Richards III* (1921); *Hans Heinrich* (1922); *Der gestohlene Gott* (1924); *Neuer Lübecker Totentanz* (1931); *Straßenecke. Ein Ort, eine Handlung* (1931); *Armut, Reichtum, Mensch und Tier* (1948); *Spur des dunklen Engels* (1952); *Thomas Chatterton* (1955); *Die Nacht aus Blei* (1956); *Aufzeichnungen eines Einzelgängers* (1959); *Auswahl* (Muschg, W., ed., 1959); *Dramen* (1963); *13 nicht geheure Geschichten* (1963); *Über den Anlaß und andere Essays* (1964)

BIBLIOGRAPHY: *H. H. J.* (Symposium, 1954); Lohner, E., "H. H. J.," in *Expressionismus—Gestalten einer literarischen Bewegung* (1956); Helwig, W., *Briefe um ein Werk* (1959); Nossack, H. E., "Nachruf auf H. H. J.," *Jahrbuch 1960 der Akademie der Wissenschaften und der Literatur*; Baader, P., "Schriftenverzeichnis," *Jahrbuch 1960 der Akademie der Wissenschaften und der Lit.*; Fritz, W., "Der

Einzelgänger: Hinweise auf Texte von und über H. H. J.," *WuW* XV (1960); Muschg, W., *Von Trakl zu Brecht: Dichter des Expressionismus* (1961); Marr, W. M., "Compassion and the Outsider: H. H. J.'s *Die Nacht aus Blei*," *GR,* XXXIX (1964), 201-210; Meyer, J., *Verzeichnis der Schriften von und über H. H. J.* (1967)

KURT OPITZ

JAIMES FREYRE, Ricardo

Bolivian poet, historian, and critic, b. 12 May 1868, Tacna-Tucumán; d. there 24 April 1933

From 1907 to 1917 J. F. was a historian at the University of Tucumán in Argentina. Later he entered the diplomatic service. A contemporary of Darío and Lugones (qq.v.), modernists who lived in Buenos Aires at the turn of the century, he is Bolivia's leading modernist. With Darío he founded the *Revista de América* in 1894; Lugones wrote the preface to his volume of poetry *Castalia bárbara* (1899).

Using a new expressive technique, J. F. created a fantastic world. The neoromantic element in him reveals itself in his liking for Germanic and Scandinavian mythology. In the volumes of poetry *Los sueños son vida* (1917) and *País de sueño, país de sombra* (1918), the tone becomes somewhat more reserved, although it does not depart from the modernistic tendency. J. F.'s *Poesías completas* were published only in 1944 (with an introductory study by E. J. Colombres). His theory of Spanish versification, *Leyes de la versificación castellana* (1912) is a work of the greatest distinction.

FURTHER WORKS: *La hija de Jephté* (1899); *La lectura correcta y expresiva* (1908); *Anadiomena* (1917); *Las víctimas* (1917); *Los conquistadores* (1928)

BIBLIOGRAPHY: Cerilla, E., *R. J. F.* (1965)

* * *

JALOUX, Edmond

French critic, novelist and short story writer, b. 19 June 1878, Marseilles; d. 22 Aug. 1949, Lutry near Lausanne

J. made his reputation primarily as an author of imaginative and poetic novels, which also contain acute psychological analysis (*Le reste est silence . . . ,* 1909; *L'éventail de crêpe,* 1911; *La Grenade mordue,* 1933; *L'égarée,* 1938).

He became a member of the Académie Française in 1936. His last short stories—*Le Vent souffle sur la flamme* (1941), *Le Pays des fantômes* (1948), and *Le Dernier acte* (1950)—go even further in the use of psychological and transcendental themes. J. wrote works of even greater significance in the field of criticism (*L'Esprit des livres,* 7 vols., 1922ff).

FURTHER WORKS: *L'agonie de l'amour* (1898); *Fumées dans la campagne* (1918); *Les Profondeurs de la mer* (1922); *Figures étrangères* (1925); *L'alcyone* (1925); *La Fugitive* (1926); *O toi que j'eusse aimée* (1926); *R. M. Rilke* (1927); *Du Rêve à la réalité* (1932); *Vie de Goethe* (1933); *La Grenade mordue* (1933); *Le Pouvoir des choses* (1941); *Essences* (1944); *D'Eschyle à Giraudoux* (1946); *Introduction à l'histoire de la littérature française* (2 vols., 1948); *La Constellation* (1950); *Les Saisons littéraires* (2 vols., 1950)

BIBLIOGRAPHY: Kolbert, J., "E. J. as a Popularizer of English literature," *FR,* XXXIV (1961), 432-39; Kolbert, J., *E. J. et sa critique littéraire* (1962); Maurois, A., "E. J. ou l'instinct de l'éternel," *NL,* 14 June 1962, p. 3

LOUIS CHAIGNE

JAMES, Henry

American novelist, short story writer, playwright, and essayist, who spent most of his literary career in England, b. 15 April 1843, New York City; d. 28 Feb. 1916, London

J.'s life has been characterized many times as being almost entirely cerebral. His crowded literary output left little time for domestic occupations in the usual sense—despite the formidable intellectual qualities of his own family. His father, Henry J., Sr., was a friend of the litterateurs of his day, a devotee of Swedenborg, and an occasional essayist. His brother, William, was to become an important philosopher and a forerunner of introspective psychology. J. was educated in the United States and in Europe. His life is divided unequally between the two, Europe clearly having the advantage.

He went to Europe in 1869 and returned twice during the following six years. By 1876 he had established himself permanently in London, and he continued to live there and in Sussex for the rest of his life. He revisited America in 1881 and 1904 and returned again in 1910 with his dying brother, William. He also took frequent trips to the continent.

HENRY JAMES

The notion of two cultures, of two continents, was consistently a part of J. Europe could perhaps be described as the element of Turgenev in him; America represented the Hawthorne in him. (J. admitted these debts in his essay on Turgenev, first printed in the *North American Review* of April 1874, and in his long study of Hawthorne, published in 1879.)

J.'s friendship with Turgenev was, according to F. W. Dupee, "the great human event" of his year in Paris (1875-76). Turgenev introduced J. to Flaubert and helped him gain access to an important circle of French contemporaries. J. managed to ingratiate himself with them, mainly because of his conversational skills, which were believed to rival Mallarmé's.

J. left Paris for London in 1876 and settled down to what critics have called his "early prime." In that year *Roderick Hudson*, the novel which usually signifies the end of his apprenticeship, was brought out in book form. *Roderick Hudson* marks the first extensive treatment of the American in Europe, a theme which consistently runs through the Jamesian novel. This work deals with a young American sculptor who is corrupted by life in Italy and finally dies by falling over a precipice in the Alps. This is the culmination of an unrequited love and a series of artistic failures.

The American appeared the following year without offering any change in J.'s conception of the novel. It is the story of an American businessman, Christopher Newman (the name is of some symbolic importance), who is introduced into an aristocratic Parisian setting for which he is totally unprepared. He is finally betrayed by the Bellegarde family, in whom he trusts implicitly through most of the novel.

The Portrait of a Lady (1881) is probably J.'s most convincing treatment of what he referred to as the "international situation." Isabel Archer is another in the long line of Jamesian characters who have been victimized by a European setting. Her escape from Gardencourt and its pastoral simplicity ends in an unfortunate marriage and the gradual heightening of Isabel's capacity to suffer. *The Portrait of a Lady* is a stylistic refinement on all his previous work. For some critics it is the happiest balance in the Jamesian style.

Much closer perhaps to his full maturity is *The Princess Casamassima* (1886). This is the first occasion on which J. touches on the political problems of the day. (He comes very close to certain moments in Dostoyevski's *The Possessed* and Turgenev's *Fathers and Sons*.)

Hyacinth Robinson turns revolutionary in adolescence as a reaction to the poverty of his childhood. He attracts the wealthy and beautiful Princess Casamassima to the cause, falls in love with her, and resorts finally to suicide when she apparently rejects him. "Hyacinth Robinson is J.'s sensibility cast for a time among thieves but instructed to come home at last, immaculate as ever although with a bullet through its head" (Dupee, *H. J.*, p. 156).

The final novel of this period (just before J. abandoned the novel temporarily for the theater) is *The Tragic Muse* (1890). Its protagonists are a young politician who sacrifices everything to paint and an actress who immerses herself in her art. This concern with the artist and his problems is the subject of so many of J.'s shorter works of this period. In "The Lesson of the Master" (1892) he considers the case of the artist and marriage; in "The Middle Years" (1893) he deals with the frustrations of a writer who has dedicated too much of his life to art; in "The Death of the Lion" (1894) we have the artist who tires of being a showpiece and demands integrity from his audience.

The artist story par excellence is "The Beast in the Jungle" (1903). John Marcher, the protagonist, feels that he is reserved for something special, something unprecedented. His life assumes strange proportions as he waits around for something to happen. He finally comes to realize before the grave of May Bartram that he is destined to accomplish nothing. Here J. gives us the ultimate rejection of the artist type.

During the period that J. developed the artist story to this point of perfection, he turned to the theater. The stage had tempted him for some time, as can be seen from his 1882 play version of "Daisy Miller." He turned *The American* into a play in 1891. However, only two of J.'s dramas were performed at this time: *The American* and *Guy Domville*. The unfortunate reception of the latter temporarily put a halt to his playwriting ambitions.

But the period as dramatist had one important effect on J. Sensitive critics from Joseph Warren Beach on have seen definite symptoms of the attempt at playwriting in the novels written after 1896. They are almost all constructed as a series of situations "scenically" (to use a favorite expression of the critical prefaces), as if J. had started by drafting a scenario in the manner of the dramatist. *The Spoils of Poynton* (1897) is almost completely told from the "point of view" of Fleda Vetch.

Mrs. Gereth opposes the marriage of her son to a certain Mona Brigstock. She gradually draws Fleda Vetch into the intrigue and destines her, finally, for her son and the inheritance of the "spoils" of Poynton. Fleda is the casual observer who becomes so involved in the action that the outcome would seem to affect her more than any of the participants. The development of the plot, as one critic has 'suggested, is less essential than the "screening" of Fleda's consciousness—an increasing concern of J.'s later fiction.

J. wrote what has often been called a technical tour de force in *What Maisie Knew* (1897). This is the story of a child who witnesses the most intimate affairs in the relationship between her capricious stepparents. Divorce, with all its sordid detail, stifles Maisie, the naive little girl, hopelessly involved in what she only instinctively understands.

The Ambassadors (1903) is often thought of as the high point of J.'s method. Lambert Strether is a would-be man of letters who is financed by a certain Mrs. Newsome to eavesdrop on her son, Chad, and to bring him back from Paris. Not only does he fail in his mission but decides finally to settle down himself in Paris and reject entirely the world of Woollett, Massachusetts, and the Newsomes— although he does eventually return to America. Almost all of the novel is seen through the eyes of Strether, who is another in the long line of Jamesian heroes who passes from disinterested observer to active participant.

The second of the two-volume novels to be written in this period, published a year before *The Ambassadors,* is *The Wings of the Dove* (1902). The situation centers entirely about Milly Theale, who is the unfortunate victim of a plot by Merton Densher and Kate Croy to seize control of her money. Milly is fated to die from the earliest moments of the novel. Milly's death has a symbolically reassuring effect on the participants in the tragedy. Both Merton and Kate cannot help resolving her in emblematic terms: Merton sees her as the "tortured sensibility," the dove with the broken wings; Kate cannot avoid the association between Milly's death and the biblical image of the dove extending its wings to embrace all humankind.

In *The Golden Bowl* (1904) all the principal characters conceive of one another in symbolic terms. It represents a splendid example of the French symbolist notion of poetry fusing with prose. The central metaphor of the novel, the golden bowl, determines all the human relationships. The Prince's marriage to Maggie is the excuse offered Charlotte to marry Adam Verver. Charlotte continues to deceive her husband with Amerigo until Maggie becomes aware of the situation and finally regains her husband's fidelity. The imagery in the novel is clearly as important as the characters. Several critics connect the pagoda and the caravan with Maggie's growing awareness of the situation. The golden bowl itself is probably the most elaborate poetic figure in all of J. This is his equivalent of the Wagnerian usages of Thomas Mann (q.v.) and the mythical cycles of Joyce (q.v.).

J.'s writing reaches a kind of apogee with *The Golden Bowl.* His occasional autobiographical writings, his critical prefaces for the New York edition of his works (1907-1917), his renewed attempts at playwriting, and his two unfinished novels, *The Ivory Tower* (1917) and *The Sense of the Past* (1917) occupy the last decade of his life.

J. has often been said to have contributed a new structural element to the novel. His insistence on "the scenic method" has become an important entree into modern fiction. The positing of what J. variously referred to as a "post of observation" or "large lucid reflector" prepares for the monologuists of the so-called "Bergsonian novel." The Jamesian method turns up in much of the fiction written during and after World War I. When Joyce and Virginia Woolf (qq.v.) use it, we frequently call it "stream of consciousness" (an expression coined by William J.). This caused one critic to say: "H. J., rather than anyone else, may be said to have introduced the method [stream of consciousness] in English fiction" (K. F. Gerould, "Stream of Consciousness," *Saturday Review of Literature,* 4 [1927], 233).

The novels of the mature period, then, prepare for a new kind of fiction. J. first offered it a theoretical basis in "The Art of Fiction" (1884). The artistic credo set down here received a kind of fruition in the novels written after 1896 and in the novella form, which reached a high point in 1898 with *The Turn of the Screw.* But there is always felt in this vast production the avoidance of anything genuinely real and timely. The ideologies of his time rarely affected him; they do have a certain weight in his two "social" novels, *The Princess Casamassima* and *The Bostonians* (1886) but rarely in the later novels. Eliot (q.v.), in one of the most celebrated remarks made about J., spoke of his as being "a mind so fine that no idea could violate it."

This "mind" was characteristically misunderstood, and J.'s work suffered serious neglect for a considerable time after his death. The converging interest of F. W. Dupee, F. O. Matthiessen, and Leon Edel, during a crucially arid period, has fostered J.'s reappraisal and "revival." Dupee's pioneering contribution to The American Men of Letters Series, H. J. (1951; 2d ed., 1956) was followed in 1953 by the first volume of Leon Edel's monumental biography, H. J.: The Untried Years. Edel has since added two more volumes, The Conquest of London (1962) and The Middle Years (1962), which combined to win both the National Book Award and the Pulitzer in 1963. Edel's untiring and inspired editing of J. has resulted in The Complete Plays of H. J. and The Complete Tales of H. J.

To support the renewed interest in J.'s achievement Charles Scribner's Sons, of New York, started bringing out the New York Edition of The Novels and Tales of H. J. in a new printing in 1961. The number of books and articles devoted to J., appearing regularly on both sides of the Atlantic, further attest to the serious interest in his work and his new critical popularity.

FURTHER WORKS: *A Passionate Pilgrim and Other Tales* (1875); *Transatlantic Sketches* (1875); *Watch and Ward* (1878); *French Poets and Novelists* (1878); *The Europeans* (1878); *An International Episode* (1879); *The Madonna of the Future and Other Tales* (1879); *Confidence* (1879); *Washington Square* (1880); *Portraits of Places* (1883); *The Siege of London* (1883); *Tales of Three Cities* (1884); *A Little Tour in France* (1884); *Stories Revived* (1885); *Partial Portraits* (1888); *The Aspern Papers* (1888); *The Reverberator* (1888); *A London Life* (1889); *The Real Thing and Other Tales* (1893); *The Private Life* (1893); *The Wheel of Time* (1893); *Theatricals* (1894-95); *Terminations* (1895); *Embarrassments* (1896); *The Other House* (1896); *In the Cage* (1898); *The Two Magics* (1898); *The Awkward Age* (1899); *The Soft Side* (1900); *The Sacred Fount* (1901); *The Better Sort* (1903); *William Wetmore Story and His Friends* (1903); *English Hours* (1905); *The Question of Our Speech, and The Lesson of Balzac* (1905); *The American Scene* (1907); *Views and Reviews* (1908); *Italian Hours* (1909); *The Finer Grain* (1910); *The Outcry* (1911); *A Small Boy and Others* (1913); *Notes of a Son and Brother* (1914); *Notes on Novelists* (1914); *The Middle Years* (1917); *Within the Rim and Other Essays* (1919); *Notes and Reviews* (1921); *The Art of the Novel*, ed. R. P. Blackmur (1934); *The Notebooks of H. J.*, ed. F. O. Matthiessen and K. B. Murdock (1947); *H. J. and Robert Louis Stevenson*, ed. J. A. Smith (1948); *The Selected Letters of H. J.*, ed. Leon Edel (1955); *H. J.: Autobiography*, ed. F. W. Dupee (1956); *H. J. and H. G. Wells*, ed. L. Edel and G. N. Ray (1958)

BIBLIOGRAPHY: Ford, F. M., *H. J., A Critical Study* (1915); West, R., *H. J.* (1916); Beach, J. W., *The Method of H. J.* (1918); Brooks, V. W., *The Pilgrimage of H. J.* (1925); Kelley, C. P., *The Early Development of H. J.* (1930); Edel, L., *H. J., les Années dramatiques* (1931); Matthiessen, F. O., *H. J., the Major Phase* (1944); Dupee, F. W. (ed.), *The Question of H. J.* (1947); Matthiessen, F. O., *The J. Family* (1947); Leavis, F. R., *The Great Tradition: George Eliot, H. J., Joseph Conrad* (1948); Swan, M., *H. J.* (1950); Dupee, F. W., *H. J.* (1951; 2d ed. 1956); Bewley, M., *The Complex Fate* (1952); Bowden, E. T., *The Themes of H. J.* (1956); Levy, L. B., *Versions of Melodrama: A Study of the Fiction and Drama of H. J., 1865-1897* (1957); Anderson, Q., *The American H. J.* (1957); Hoffmann, C. G., *The Short Novels of H. J.* (1957); Crews, F .C., *The Tragedy of Manners: Moral Drama in the Later Novels of H. J.* (1957); Wegelin, C., *The Image of Europe in H. J.* (1958); Poirier, R., *The Comic Sense of H. J.* (1960); Edel, L., *H. J.* (University of Minnesota Pamphlets on American Writers, No. 4, 1960); Cargill, O., *The Novels of H. J.* (1961); Ward, J. A., *The Imagination of Disaster: Evil in the Fiction of H. J.* (1961); Edel, L., and Laurence D. H., *A Bibliography of H. J.* (2d rev. ed. 1961); Stallman, R. W., *The Houses That J. Built* (1961); Krook, D., *The Ordeal of Consciousness in H. J.* (1962); Wright, W. F., *The Madness of Art, A Study of H. J.* (1962); Geismar, M., *H. J. and the Jacobites* (1963); Edel, L. (ed.), *H. J.: A Collection of Critical Essays* (1963); Holland, L. B., *The Expense of Vision: Essays on the Craft of H. J.* (1964); Stone, E., *The Battle and the Books: Some Aspects of H. J.* (1964); Vaid, K. H., *Technique in the Tales of H. J.* (1964); Lebowitz, N., *The Imagination of Loving: H. J.'s Legacy to the Novel* (1965); Putt, S. G., *H. J.: A Reader's Guide* (1966); Ward,

J. A., *The Search for Form: Studies in the Structure of J.'s Fiction* (1967); Isle, W., *Experiments in Form: H. J.'s Novels, 1896-1901* (1967)

MELVIN J. FRIEDMAN

J.'s critical genius comes out most tellingly in his mastery over his baffling escape from ideas; a mastery and an escape which are perhaps the last test of a superior intelligence. He had a mind so fine that no idea could violate it.

Eliot, T. S., "H. J.," in *The Shock of Recognition*, ed. Edmund Wilson (1947), p. 856

. . . It seems that as his artistic rigor evolves and increases, he tends more and more to see the essence of his great subjects as studies of the relationships existing between certain beings whom he visualizes not so much in themselves as exclusively in terms of these relationships. . . .

It is as if J., in preparation for each of the admirable themes he wishes to treat, first emptied out several fine, spacious places, taking care to remove every speck of dust, every possibility of contamination. The novel or novella then develops like a piece of chamber music, safe from all intrusion.

Du Bos, C., *Journal, 1921–1923* (1946), p. 258 ff

Never in a single line of his novels or short stories is H. J. an ideologist. He placed his whole knowledge of man and life and the world at the disposal of his extremely precise poetic imagination. Taking his work as a whole, one may say that H. J. sought to maintain his formulation of thematic problems creatively suspended in the fertile indecisiveness of his formative imagination. This is his great achievement and—when this is looked at more closely—his unique achievement in the history of the Western novel.

Hennecke, H. *Nachwort zu H. J.*, in *Die sündigen Engel* (1954), p. 198

J. is not a spiritual writer in the sense that Hawthorne and Dostoevsky are. What fascinated and often bewildered the friends of his latest years was how the most casual question could set into motion all his mental resources, as though he felt it his obligation to examine what the mind of H. J. was in relation to every stimulus, no matter how accidental or trivial. He never lost his boyhood curiosity about the otherness of the outside world. He was, to the end, the absorbed spectator. . . .

Matthiessen, F. O., *H. J., The Major Phase* (1944), p. 149

His religion was always a mirror of his experience. Experience taught him to believe in supernatural evil, but not in supernatural good. . . .

He was a puritan with a nose for the Pit, as religious as Bunyan and as violent as Shakespeare.

Greene, Graham, *The Lost Childhood and Other Essays* (1951), p. 38 f.

. . . Two things I do claim . . . : First, that there was emotional greatness in H. J.'s hatred of tyranny; secondly, that there was titanic volume, weight, in the masses he sets in opposition within his work, . . . in these novels, the essential qualities which make up the national qualities, are found and set working, the fundamental oppositions made clear. This is no contemptible labor. No other writer had so assayed three great nations or even thought of attempting it.

Pound, Ezra, *Literary Essays* (1954), p. 297 f.

The artist does not describe life, he creates it. . . . This concept of art places J. close to Proust, even though—for all his delight in experimentation—he unmistakably belongs to the previous generation. What definitely distinguishes him from Proust, and still more from Joyce, is the fact that he never took the final, extreme step leading to autonomous portrayal of consciousness. Like a sophisticated criminal investigator of the mind, he developed a technique by means of which man's inner being reveals itself step by step. Yet he never abandoned himself to the current of this invisible stream.

Blöcker, G., *Die neuen Wirklichkeiten* (1957), p. 63 ff.

. . . It is to the personal aspect of Puritanism that H. J. clings desperately; so desperately that his most moving creations are embodiments of a fine moral integrity, of conscience in all its infinite reaches and delicate adjustments. Wherever H. J. takes this integrity of character as his theme, there he creates his most enduring impressions. And these impressions are enduring precisely because they have gained in delicate extension, in infinite spiritual ramifications and crystallizations, what they have lost—not lost, but expended—in mere brute force and physical capacity. . . .

Read, Herbert, *The Nature of Literature* (1956), p. 361 f.

The form, being neither truly dramatic nor purely epic, has a quality that may be called lyrical insofar as the abiding impression is not one of conflict or any other action, but primarily a mood, an atmosphere, or, better still, an image composed of countless extremely subtle relationships in which the total effect overwhelmingly dominates any single detail. . . .

Lüdeke, H., *Geschichte der amerikanischen Literatur* (1952), p. 328

A tedious novelist—perhaps the first great novelist in the history of the novel to be frankly tedious. . . .

J. relies on the broken ascending and descending line of the dialogue to introduce order into his fictional world. . . .

Obviously the very source of momentum in his dialogue, the thing that enables it perpetually to get going again, is misunderstanding and restatement—misunderstanding on the part of the interlocutor, who constantly forces his partner into a precision that leads to new misunderstanding. . . . Ambiguity is essential if words are to dance, to come to life again out of their misunderstandings, if they are to wander about like this on the lookout for who knows what.

Picon, G., *Lecture d'Henry James*, in *NRF* (June 1954), p. 1080 ff.

JAMMES, Francis

French poet, b. 2 Dec. 1868, Tournay, Hautes-Pyrénées; d. 1 Nov. 1938, Hasparren

At a time when a decadent symbolism (q.v.) was predominant in Paris, J. cultivated a simple, blithe, yet sensuous, forgiving, and slyly humorous poetry, which he continued to write without change until his death. Hardly an echo of the war or of social or political crises is perceptible in J.'s work.

He lived in tranquil privacy with his wife, his children, and his Catholic faith.

A contemporary of Claudel and Gide (qq.v.), he spent his whole life in the provinces, in the little town of Orthez, which his poetry so often extolls. A journey to Algiers with Gide, another to Amsterdam, a few visits to Paris, his conversion to Catholicism in 1905, his marriage in 1908—these are the major events of this somewhat anachronistic life. His special ties with the Antilles (his father had been born on the island of Guadeloupe) and his reading of the works of Bernardin de Saint-Pierres inspired the young poet to exotic reveries. The study of the plants in the Bordeaux Botanical Gardens and his reading of Rousseau developed his talent for observation and his love of nature.

J.'s first attempts at poetry aroused the interest of Régnier (q.v.) and Gide. His first important volume, *De l'Angélus de l'aube a l'angélus du soir*, containing heartfelt religious poetry of daily life, was published in 1898. From then on, volumes of naive, unstudied verses, notable for their slightly halting rhythm and extremely clever lack of cleverness, alternated with novels as charmingly old-fashioned as the names of their heroines—*Clara d'Ellébeuse* (1899), *Almaïde d'Étremont* (1901), *Pomme d'Anis* (1904). J. gives plants and donkeys the power of speech ("Prière pour aller au paradis avec les ânes"), and in his lyrical prose masterpiece *Le Roman du lièvre* (1903; Romance of the Rabbit, 1920) created a deeply symbolical animal story that takes in the whole cosmos. Only in the poetry written after 1905 did he curb his somewhat pagan sensualism. He wrote the legend of a Franciscan poet, enriching its structure, like Lamartine before him, with the magic of poetry. In his songs of human life *Les Géorgiques chrétiennes* (1911-12), he mingled the bucolic and the Catholic sources of his inspiration.

J.'s friendships with Gide and Claudel brought him to the *Nouvelle Revue française* as early as 1909, but after his rigorous Catholicism alienated him from Gide and his circle, most of his work appeared in religious journals. J. kept aloof from all literary fashion and polemicism, which found little echo in his work. Nevertheless, his striving for a restrained, simple yet poetic language contributed to the renewal of French poetic art.

FURTHER WORKS: *Le Deuil des primevères* (1901); *Le Triomphe de la vie* (1902); *Clairières dans le ciel* (1906); *L'Église habillée de feuilles* (1906); *Rayons de miel* (1908); *Ma fille Bernadette* (1910); *Le Rosaire au soleil* (1916); *Monsieur le curé d'Ozeron* (1918); *Le Poète rustique* (1920); *Le Bon Dieu chez les enfants* (1921); *Mémoires* (3 vols., 1921-23); *De l'Âge divin à l'âge ingrat* (1921); *Premier (Deuxième, Troisième, Quatrième) Livre des Quatrains* (4 vols. 1923-25); *Cloches pour deux mariages* (1923); *Ma France poétique* (1926); *Champêtrières et méditations* (1930); *L'Antigyde, ou Élie de Nacre* (1932); *De tout temps à jamais* (1935); *Le Patriarche et son troupeau* (1948); *Oeuvres* (5 vols., 1913-26); *Elegies et autres vers* (1946); *Poèmes choisis* (1947). Correspondence with Colette (1945), A. Samain (1946), Gide (1948); Claudel (1952), A. Fontaine (1959), Vielé-Griffin (1966). **Selected English trans.** *Homer Had a Dog* (1946); *The Early White Narcissi* (1953)

BIBLIOGRAPHY: Marie-Margarita, Sr., *La Métrique de F. J.* (1959); Mallet, R., *F. J., sa vie, son oeuvre* (1961); Mauriac, F., "Le Destin de F. J.," *FL* (16 Sept. 1961), p. 1; Van der Burght, R. and L., *F. J., Le Jeune chrétien* (1961); Caron, Br. Ariston, "F. J., Novelist," *DA*, XXIII (1963), 3368

MICHEL EUVRARD

JAPANESE LITERATURE

A new era in Japanese literature following the Russo-Japanese war (1904-1905) brought fame and popularity to many young writers. As the Meiji era (1868-1912) neared its end, 20th c. world literature, with all its complexity, found root in Japan. Writers, several of whom remained active into the 1940's and 1950's, felt a surge of inspiration and confidence after Japan forced Russia to sue for peace.

By 1906 Japanese naturalism (q.v.) began supplanting romanticism. Innovations by an intense group of young writers in their thirties completed the break with tradition. The naturalistic novel was established by Kunikida Doppo (1871-1908), with his *Ummei* (1906; "Fate"); Shimazaki Tōson's (1872-1943) *Hakai* (1906; The Broken Commandment, 1956, 1 chapter), and *Ie* (1910; "The House"); Tayama Katai's (1871-1930) *Futon* (1907; "Coverlets"); Iwano Hōmei's (1873-1919) *Hōrō* (1910; "Wanderer"); and Tokuda Shūsei's (1871-1943) *Kabi* (1911; "Mildew"). Their work led to the chief Japanese contribution to 20th c. literature, the *shishōsetsu,* or "ego novel," a type of autobiographical confessional in which the hero and writer are identified. Younger authors, such as Masamune Hakuchō (1879-1963), Mayama Seika (1878-1948), and Nagai Kafū (1879-1959), also gained fame as naturalists. Still, the movement soon lost support, and by 1910 it had already passed its peak.

In their effort to oppose naturalism, Natsume Soseki (q.v.) and Mori Ōgai (1862-1922), both several years senior to the above writers, rose to prominence. Ōgai and Soseki continue to hold a firm place in the Japanese reader's affections. Soseki's crisp conversational style has particularly influenced young writers. Soseki, in *Kusamakura* (1906; Unhuman Tour, 1927; Three Cornered World, 1965), taught that the leisurely moments one devotes to art and letters offer the sole relief from the unavoidable suffering of existence. In *Kokoro* (1914; Eng., 1941, 1957), written toward the end of his life, he granted man only three equally dreary choices—death, madness, or religion. Soseki's thought therefore combined "art for art's sake" and pronounced Buddhist tenets.

Ōgai, who began as a romantic, turned to historical fiction and to belief in stoic self-discipline. A prodigious worker, Ōgai combined a medical and military career with authorship in the novel, drama, poetry, criticism, trans-

lation, scholarship, and philosophy. One edition of his complete works fills fifty-three volumes. *Maihime* (1892; The Girl Who Danced, 1964), *Gan* (1912-13; The Wild Geese, 1959), and a historical biography of Shibue Chūsai (1805-1858), a Confucian scholar and physician, are representative.

Toward the end of Meiji and into the Taishō era (1912-26), a group of writers who shared disgust at the excesses of the naturalists published a periodical called *Shirakaba* (1910-23; "White Birch"). Humanitarian in outlook and aristocratic in background and temperament, the group's noteworthy members included Shiga Naoya (b. 1883), Arishima Takeo (1878-1923), Mushakoji Saneatsu (b. 1885), and Satomi Ton (b. 1888). Meanwhile, the novels of Chikamatsu Shūkō (1876-1944), who achieved fame with his naturalistic *Wakaretaru Tsuma ni Okuru Tegami* (1910; "Letter to My Divorced Wife"), betrayed the vagueness of the boundary between naturalist and antinaturalist. As vague as such distinctions may be, they at least show how modern writers in Japan have tended to band into small independent groups.

One of the leading writers who first published prior to 1912 is Tanizaki Junichiro (q.v.). His death marked the passing of an era. Beginning with such short stories as "Shisei" (1910; Tattoo, 1914), with its strange, impelling beauty, continuing with his treatment of an unhappy marriage in *Tade Kuu Mushi* (1928-29; Some Prefer Nettles, 1955), and reaching a peak with *Sasameyuki* (1943-48; The Makioka Sisters, 1958), Tanizaki has explored broad areas of life with daring, sensitivity, and psychological acumen. His novel *Kagi* (1956; The Key, 1960), for example, abounds in profound comments on the nature of love. Tanizaki's writing appeals readily to Western readers. He rates as one of the eminent literary figures of the 20th c.

Taishō literature usually includes several years of Meiji and the early leftist literature of the Shōwa era (1926 to the present). Many Japanese commentators criticize Taishō literature for failing to transcend traditional, feudal, or nationalistic concepts. Nevertheless, the authors of the 1910's and 1920's produced delicately wrought detail and displayed acute perception. Some writers, it remains true, refused social responsibility and feigned moral decadence. Western readers, however, may easily discover untranslated authors who are original and yet part of the 20th c. world in talent and temperament. In the 1910's Rudolf C. Eucken

(1846-1926), Bergson, Tagore, Tolstoi (qq.v.), Dostoyevski (1821-81), and Maeterlinck (q.v.) became known in Japan. The art of Cezanne and Van Gogh received rave notices, and the aestheticism of Poe (1809-1849), Wilde (q.v.), and Baudelaire (1821-67) found numerous emulators.

During and after World War I, Rolland, Barbusse, and Blasco-Ibáñez (qq.v.) became widely read in Japan. Satō Haruo (1892-1964) and Kikuchi Kan (1888-1948) emerged as part of an avant-garde group that declared that only in society can man achieve individuality. Although the group traced their intellectual origins to Europe, the members never completely abandoned traditional style and sensibility. Satō Haruo ("Supein-ken no Ie," [1917; The House of a Spanish Dog, 1961]), in particular, began his career as a love poet. And from 1923 to the present Kikuchi Kan (*Okujō no Kyōjin* [1916; The Madman on the Roof, 1932]) has worked as iron-handed editor of *Bungei Shunjū* ("Literary Season"), the leading Japanese literary monthly.

Other writers, such as Akutagawa Ryūnosuke (1892-1927, also associated with Soseki), —author of *Rashōmon* (1917; Eng., 1930), *Jigokuhen* (1918; Hell Screen, 1948), and *Kappa* (1927; Eng., 1947)—and Yamamoto Yūzō (b. 1887) and Kume Masao (1891-1952) made their debuts in private periodicals. One of these periodicals, *Shin Shichō,* started at Tokyo Imperial University. In 1923, Kawabata Yasunari (q.v.), who wrote *Yukiguni* (1937-47; Snow Country, 1956) and *Sembazuru* (1949-51; Thousand Cranes, 1959), revived this periodical. Together with Yokomitsu Riichi (1898-1947) and their followers in 1924, he published yet another periodical, *Bungei Jidai* ("Literary Age") which advanced such European causes as futurism, expressionism, and dadaism (qq.v.). Yasunari's short-lived group, however intuitive, subjective, sensual, and faintly decadent, owed as much to medieval Japanese drama as to modern European "isms." Kawabata is the first Japanese writer to win the Nobel Prize for Literature.

In early Shōwa for a time it appeared that leftist literature would overshadow the efforts of these avant-garde writers and modernists. Government authorities, however, repressed the leftists, despite the support of many established writers. Two noteworthy leftist authors who failed to survive World War II are Hayama Yoshiki (1894-1945), author of *Umi ni Ikuru Hitobito* (1926; "Men Who Live on the Sea"),

"Semento-daru no naka no Tegami" (1926; Letter Found in a Cement-barrel, 1961), and Kobayashi Takiji (1903-1933), author of *Kani Kōsen* (1929; The Cannery Boat, 1933). Among leftist writers who survived government repression and the hardships of war, the following have been particularly active: Nakano Shigeharu (b. 1902), author of *Muragimo* (1954; "Nerve"), Miyamoto Yuriko (1899-1951), Hirabayashi Taiko (b. 1905), Miyamoto Kenji (b. 1908), and Hayashi Fumiko (1904-1951), author of *Hōrōki* (1929; "A Roving Record"), *Bangiku* (1948; "The Late Chrysanthemum"), and *Ukigumo* (1951; "Drifting Clouds").

Nonleftist writers active during the 1930's included Ibuse Masuji (b. 1898) and Hori Tatsuo (1904-1953). Dazai Osamu (1909-1948) best typified the immediate postwar period, a time of excruciating self-examination and extreme nihilism. His *Viyon no Tsuma* (1947; Villon's Wife, 1955), *Shayō* (1948; The Setting Sun, 1956), and *Ningen Shikkaku* (1948; No Longer Human, 1958) in some respects anticipated "beat literature." Many other noteworthy writers emerged after World War II. Notably these are: Mishima Yukio (b. 1925), author of *Kamen no Kokuhaku* (1949; The Confession of a Mask, 1958), *Kinkakuji* (1956; The Temple of the Golden Pavilion, 1958); Ōoka Shōhei (b. 1909), author of *Nobi* (1951; Fire on the Plain, 1957); Inoue Yasushi (b. 1907), who wrote *Ryòjū* (1949; The Hunting Gun, 1961); Takeda Taijun (b. 1912); and Noma Hiroshi, author of *Shinkū Chitai* (1952; Zone of Emptiness, 1956).

In the 1960's new writers continued to emerge and certain established authors extended their reputation. The work of Abe Kōbō (b. 1924)— which includes *Suna no onna* (1962; The Woman in the Dunes, 1966) and *Tanin no Kao* (1964; The Face of Another, 1965)—combines a scrupulous attention to the individual's emotional state, which characterizes much of the best traditional literature, with a deft appreciation of the present human predicament. Ōe Kenzaburō (b. 1935), active as author, editor, and critic, has probed into modern youth's confrontation with sex and society. Among older authors, Ibuse Masuji (b. 1898), who wrote *Sanshō uo* (1923; The Salamander in the Brook, 1964), also published *Kuroi ame* (1967; Black Rain, 1967), the best novel available about the atomic bombing of Hiroshima.

Developments in poetry in Japan during the 20th c. have roughly corresponded to the pattern set by fiction. An incipient romantic movement in the 1890's gave way to symbolism (q.v.) in the early 1900's. Subsequently Japanese poets have generally followed developments in modern poetry. Yet older forms of verse survive, despite the charge that they are hardly poetry. The dynamic, young nationalistic *haiku* poet Masaoka Shiki (1867-1902), single-handedly began a revolution in *haiku* by insisting that seventeen-syllable *haiku* must stand as independent verses. Hitherto all *haiku* were theoretically written for linked verse (*renku*). The thirty-one-syllable *waka*, prevalent for over twelve hundred years, has retained its supporters. During World War II, for example, militarists and extreme nationalists urged the exclusion of "decadent" Western poetry in favor of *waka*. Ishikawa Takuboku (q.v.), one of the first modern voices in Japanese poetry, is best remembered for his *waka*.

Although in fiction new and old have merged to replace premodern forms, in poetry, perhaps because of the closeness to religion, tradition persists alongside modern verse. The same holds true in the drama. Some theatergoers may prefer modern plays to the *nō*, *kabuki*, or *jōruri*, but not so much that they withhold patronage. Despite the fame of certain poets and playwrights, fiction writers have made Japan's greatest contribution to world literature in the 20th c. Modern Japanese fiction commands increasing attention from Western students not because of its supposedly exotic quality but because of genuine reflection on problems common to modern existence.

If some readers may complain of lack of power, others will surely find meaningful comment on human life, death, and love. Nowhere on earth can one find a more world-minded literary atmosphere.

The theme that dominates much modern Japanese literature is the search for the self in society. Toward the end of the Tokugawa era (1603-1867) and in early Meiji, traditional society collapsed. Old morals, religion, and loyalties proved inadequate. Modern authors have continually groped for some solution. At times some have accepted without question Western ideology, religion, or literary forms, but the best writers have sought original answers to the questions of life, literature, and art.

Perhaps the quest of the writers for independent answers to these questions may help to explain why so many Japanese authors in 1941 supported the war. After the war, however, the search for identity of the self in society continued unabated. Young authors still seek a

place for the individual in mass society. They search, so far without success, to find a substitute for the accepted system of duties and obligations that gave structure to traditional society.

BIBLIOGRAPHY: Shinkōkai, K. B., *Introduction to Contemporary Japanese Literature* (1939); Bonneau, G., *Histoire de la littérature japonaise contemporaine* (1940); Keene, D., *Modern Japanese Literature* (1956); Satō, S., and Urdang, C., "Contemporary Poetry in Japan," *Poetry*, LXXXVIII (1957), ii, 63-124; Keene, D., "Literary and Intellectual Currents in Postwar Japan and Their International Implications," in *Japan between East and West*, ed. H. Borton (1957); Kōno, I., and Fukuda, R., *An Anthology of Modern Japanese Poetry* (1957); McKinnon, R. N., *The Heart Is Alone* (1957); Ninomiya, T., and Enright, D. J., *The Poetry of Living Japan* (1957); Shinkōkai, K. B., *Introduction to Contemporary Japanese Literature*, Part 2: 1936-55 (1959); Yamagiwa, J. K., *Japanese Literature of the Shōwa Period* (1959); Japan P.E.N. Club, *Japanese Literature in European Languages* (1961); Japan Quarterly Editorial Board, *Modern Japanese Short Stories* (1961); Morris, I., *Modern Japanese Stories* (1962); Ito, S., *Nihon No Bungaku* (1963)

LEON M. ZOLBROD

JARNÉS, Benjamín

Spanish novelist and critic, b. 7 Oct. 1888, Codo, Zaragoza, Spain; d. 11 Aug. 1949, Madrid

A ranking writer of fiction, J. belonged to the cosmopolitan group gathered around Ortega's (q.v.) *Revista de Occidente* in the 1920's. His brilliant style, search for new forms, and hyperintellectualized treatment of existence exemplified the values of the vanguard. He opposed literary schools and doctrines, although his works typified contemporary movements by their formalism, experimentation, and stylization of life. His techniques, however, were not aesthetic ends in themselves; they were the means for resolving the problem that the artist could not be committed to his reality when his work represented an evasion of this reality.

Thus J.'s novels were a forum and workshop for speculating on questions such as human destiny, novelistic technique, and the relationship between realism and myth, legend, and fantasy. Other dominant themes include the search for identity in a depersonalized world, freedom and self-realization, and the critique of beauty as intellectual voluptuousness. Above all J. is noted for his irony, wit, and mathematical objectivism. The use of cold, aphoristic descriptions, cubist metaphors, abstract dialogues, and narratives wherein the author appears among his characters, made his works seem self-conscious and dehumanized. Yet despite the novels' static quality, they are interesting for their aesthetic stereognosis, in which the surface properties of reality are emphasized by sensorial and geometrical imagery.

WORKS: *El profesor inútil* (1926); *Ejercicios* (1927); *El convidado de papel* (1928); *Vida de San Alejo* (1928); *Sor Patrocinio* (1929); *Locura y muerte de nadie* (1929); *Paula y Paulita* (1929); *Teoría del zumbel* (1930); *Viviana y Merlín* (1930); *Escenas junto a la muerte* (1931); *Zumala cárregui* (1931); *Lo rojo y lo azul* (1932); *Faua contemporánea* (1933); *Castelar* (1935); *Libro de Esther* (1935); *Doble agonía de Bécquer* (1936); *Manuel Acuña* (1942); *Venus dinámici* (1943); *Españoles en América* (1943)

BIBLIOGRAPHY: Putnam, S., "B. J. y la deshumanización del arte," *RHM*, II (1935), 17-21; Ilie, P., "B. J.: Aspects of the Dehumanized Novel," *PMLA*, LXXVI (1961), 247-253; Zuleta, E. de, "Revisión de B. J. en su obra crítica," *PSA* XLII (1966), 125-136

PAUL ILIE

JARRELL, Randall

American poet and critic, b. 6 June 1914, Nashville, Tenn.; d. 14 Oct. 1965, Greensboro, N.C.

J. studied at Vanderbilt University. In World War II he served in the air force. After the war he became a professor of English, finally settling at the Women's College of the University of North Carolina. For two years he was Poetry Consultant of the Library of Congress. He also became Chancellor of the Academy of American Poets.

J. published poetry, a novel, and essays. He was recognized first as a poet for his compassionate, bitter dramatic story-poems about war, *Little Friend, Little Friend* (1945).

His most common themes are war, art, and our daily world from a child's fairy-tale-view— "monstrously knowing and monstrously innocent" (Lowell [q.v.]). He observed sharply the American way of life in stinging and satirical poems, such as *The Woman at the Washington Zoo* (1960).

His natural, idiomatic poetry was written to be listened to. He was a gifted prosodist, handling both free and traditional verse with ease, and he wrote meaningful modern versions of forms, such as the sestina. His unusually concrete poems are imaginatively and dramatically forceful, and his outstanding portraits of people have an immediate reality about them.

J.'s one novel, *Pictures from an Institution* (1954), satirizes a progressive college and its faculty in a shrewd and immensely funny way. The epigrammatic characterization is devastating.

J.'s lucid, witty essays, some of which are collected in *Poetry and the Age: History and Criticism of the Twentieth Century* (1953), reveal his perceptive understanding of modern poetry. He reviewed poetry for *The Nation, Partisan Review, Yale Review, Kenyon Review,* and other literary periodicals. In his quiet way he was an influential man of great integrity —" a man of letters in the European sense, with real verve, imagination, and uniqueness." (Lowell).

He translated Rilke (q.v.), E. Mörike, Tristan Corbière, and was working on a translation of Goethe's *Faust* at the end of his life. J. also wrote highly successful children's books, among which are *The Bat Poet* (1964) and *The Animal Family* (1965).

FURTHER WORKS: *Blood for a Stranger* (1942); *Losses* (1948); *Ghetto and the Jews of Rome* (trans. of Ferdinand Gregorovius; 1948); *The Seven-League Crutches* (1951); *Selected Poems* (1955); *Uncollected Poems* (1958); *A Sad Heart at the Supermarket* (1962); *The Lost World* (1965); *The Complete Poems* (1969)

BIBLIOGRAPHY: Adams, C. M., *R. J., A Bibliography* (1958); Lowell, R., Taylor, P., and Warren, R. P., *R. J., 1914-1965: A Collection of Critical Essays and Memories* (1967); Shapiro, K., "R. J., 1914-1965," in *SatR* (2 Sept. 1967); Moore, M., "R. J.," in *Harper's* (Sept. 1967)

GERTRUDE C. SCHWEBELL

JARRY, Alfred

French humorist, dramatist, and novelist, b. 8 Sept. 1873, Laval, Brittany; d. 1 Nov. 1907, Paris

J. identified himself with his own creation, the puppet king Ubu, whose piping mechanical voice, jerky delivery, and robotlike gestures he gradually adopted. Gide (q.v.) depicted J. thus in *Les Faux-monnayeurs* (III, 8). In this poet obsessed by his own creation, whose hallucinations became actual experience, the surrealists (see surrealism) recognized a predecessor.

J. came from a family of peasants and craftsmen established in Brittany since the 17th c. Brought up in Rennes and Paris, he first published prose works and poems in progressive journals; these were collected in 1894 under the title *Les Minutes de sable mémorial.* With Gourmont (q.v.) he founded a short-lived quarterly, *Ymagier.* His *César Antéchrist* (1895) was followed in 1896 by the *succès de scandale, Ubu roi* (pub. 1897; Am., King Turd, 1953; Eng., Ubu Roi, 1961). This satirical drama, now reworked and expanded into the myth of the brutal opportunist, originated as a puppet play written by J. and, allegedly, his fellow students at the Lycée de Rennes, making fun of a pompous mathematics teacher by the name of Hébert. With a musical accompaniment by Claude Terrasse, the play was performed on 10 Dec. 1894 on the stage of the experimental Théatre de l'Oeuvre with masked actors using staccato delivery, falsetto voices, and stylized gestures. J.'s gross language and sharp social criticism precipitated tumultuous scenes. In style and in the harshness of its grotesque humor *Ubu roi,* is a counterpart of Grabbe's *Scherz, Satire, Ironie und tiefere Bedeutung* (1827), which, incidentally, J. adapted under the title *Les Silènes* (posth., 1926). *Ubu en-chaîné* (1900; first performed in 1937; Ubu in Chains, 1965) is a continuation of the Ubu theme which is less coarse in its humor.

J.'s novels show the same mixture of poetry and tragic humor as his plays, the same neologisms and confident handling of unusual expressions and verbal acrobatics. Thus his "novel of the new science," *Gestes et opinions du Docteur Faustroll, pataphysicien* (1911; Doctor Faustroll, 1965), paying no heed to reality, carries observations on geometry, physics, and philosophy to the extreme. *L'Amour absolu* (1899) remains hermetically impenetrable; *Messaline* (1901; Messalina, 1965) is an unusually methodically documented novel of Roman antiquity. *Le surmâle* (1902; The Garden of Priapus, 1936) recounts the conquest of an American-invented love machine by an erotic hero endowed with incredible strength; the machine falls in love with the hero, and its energy constantly renews his ardor until it breaks down and they perish together. This novel is a sym-

bolic résumé of the compulsive self-destructiveness of the author himself, who identified himself with his own characters and tried in vain to drown the prophetic import of his vision in alcoholic excesses, finally dying of tuberculosis in a Paris charity hospital.

FURTHER WORKS: *Les Jours et les nuits, roman d'un déserteur* (1897); *L'Amour en visites* (1898); *Par la taille* (1906); *Le Moutardier du pape* (1907); *Albert Samain* (1907); *La Papesse Jeanne* (1908; Pope Joan, 1965); *Spéculations* (1911); *La Dragonne* (1943); *Choix de textes* (1946); *L'Autre Alceste* (1947); *Oeuvres complètes* (8 vols., 1948); *La Revanche de la nuit* (1949); *Album de l'antium* (*ou pompe à merdre*) (1965). **Selected English trans.:** *Selected Works: Poetry and Prose* (1966)

BIBLIOGRAPHY: Chassé, C., *Sous le masque de J.?: Les sources d'Ubu Roi* (1921); Breton, A., *Les Pas Perdus* (1924); Lot, F., *A. J.* (1934); Levesque, J. H., *A. J.* (1950); Lebois, A., *A. J.* (1951); Giedion-Welcker, C., *A. J.* (1960); Wellwarth, G. E., "A. J.: The Seed of the Avant Garde Drama," *Criticism,* IV (1962), 108-119; Le Clézio, J. M., "J. et le livre absolu," *FL,* 10-16 (Dec. 1964), 30; Perche, L., *A. J.* (1965)

KURT WEINBERG

JASTRUN, Mieczysław

(pseud. of *Mieczysław Agatstein*), Polish novelist and poet, b. 29 Oct. 1903, Korolówka

J., whose volumes of poems, *Dzieje nieostygłe* (1937) and *Strumień i milczenie* (1938), aroused early attention, was originally close to the Vitalist "Skamander" group. After World War II, undeterred by the course of events, he established a reputation as the guardian of the best European traditions in Polish poetry. His rich formal range proves its worth in the symbolic interpretation of individual destiny and in generalizing reflections on existential and contemporary historical problems. Polish tradition appears particularly strongly in his identification of poetry and truth in the cycle *Poezja i prawda* (1955) and in his affirmation of the artist's personal moral engagement. Yet a classical and Christian tradition, too, as well as themes from Virgil, Shakespeare, Goethe, and Adam Mickiewicz (1795-1855), are inextricably interwoven with his contemporary themes.

From 1945 to 1949 J. was co-editor of the journal *Kuźnica*; since 1956 he has been active in the literary life of Poland, to some extent in an official capacity. His essays are esteemed, as are his biographical novels on J. Kochanowski (*Gorący popioł*, 1956), J. Słowacki (1951), and, above all, *Adam Mickiewicz* (1949; Adam Mickiewicz, 1795-1855, 1963). Also his translations of German, French, and Russian poetry are important.

FURTHER WORKS: *Spotkanie w czasie* (1929); *Godzina strzezona* (1945); *Rzecz ludzka* (1946); *Poezje wybrane* (1948); *Poezje 1944-54* (1954); *Genezy* (1959); *Intonacje* (1962); *Mit Śródziemnomorski* (1962); *Strefa owoców* (1964); *Poezja i rzeczywistóść* (1965). **Selected English trans.**: in Gillon, A., "Five Poems of the Ghetto," *Literature East and West*, IX (1965), 122-28; in Milosz, C., *Postwar Polish Poetry: An Anthology* (1965); in Gillon, A., and Krzyżanowski, L., *Introduction to Modern Polish Literature: An Anthology of Fiction and Poetry* (1964)

BIBLIOGRAPHY: Trznadel, J., *O poezji M. J.* (1954); Herman, M., *Histoire de la littérature polonaise* (1963); Gillon, A., and Krzyżanowski, L., *Introduction to Modern Polish Literature: An Anthology of Fiction and Poetry* (1964); Milosz, C., *Postwar Polish Poetry* (1965)

JOHANNES HOLTHUSEN

JAVOROV, Pejo

(actually *Kračolov*) Bulgarian poet, b. 1 Jan. 1878, Čirpan; d. 29 Nov. 1914, Sofia

J. was originally a provincial postal employee (1894-1900). His first poems attracted the attention of the editors of the journal *Misăl.* He played an active part in the liberation of Macedonia. During a stay in France (1906) he became acquainted with symbolism (q.v.).

J.'s first collection of poems, *Stichotvorenija* (1901), suggests already the suffering and nobility that were to be characteristic of his brief life. Drawing on his experiences as a Macedonian *komitaji,* he told the life story of a great revolutionary leader in *Goce Delčev* (1904) and wrote the impressive diary *Hajduški kopnenija* (1909). *Bezsănici* (1907) and *Podir senkite na oblacite* (1910) reveal J.'s unhappiness and express the suffering he endured from psychic conflicts, the result of a sensitive imagination that tended toward bitterness. His life ended in suicide.

J.'s poetic technique and his description of mental states not hitherto analyzed in Bulgarian poetry mark a turning point in the poetry of his country.

FURTHER WORKS: *V politě na vitoša* (1911); *Kogato grŭm udari* (1912); *Săčinenija* (1934-36); *Paskalev* (3 vols., 1940)

BIBLIOGRAPHY: Manning, C. A., and Smal-Stocki, R., *The History of Modern Bulgarian Literature* (1960); Nejdenova-Stoilova, J., *J.* (1962)

P. CHRISTOPHOROV

JEFFERS, Robinson

American poet and dramatist, b. 10 Jan. 1887, Pittsburgh, Pa.; d. 20 Jan. 1962, Carmel, Calif.

Once ranked with Eliot (q.v.) as a major American poet, J.'s pessimism and unorthodox views are apparently responsible for his now diminished reputation at home. His work, however, is being read again in Europe, where his works are being translated into several Slavic languages. J., whose father was a Presbyterian minister and professor of Old Testament literature, attended European and American schools and studied widely in classical and modern languages, literature, medicine, and forestry. His first two volumes of poems contained traditional lyrics, but the publication of *Tamar and Other Poems* (1924) marked the beginning of his major work, for which he won international recognition.

J. believed that "poetry is bound to concern itself chiefly with permanent things and the permanent aspects of life." His several long, highly charged narrative poems are explorations of this belief, and his many, often delightful, lyrics are celebrations of permanent things, usually the beauty of nature. Together the narratives form a poetry of ideas that moved toward defining what J. called "inhumanism." J. explains it as "a shifting of emphasis and significance from man to not-man; the rejection of human solipsism and recognition of the transhuman magnificence. . . . It offers a reasonable detachment as rule of conduct, instead of love, hate, and envy." To develop "inhumanism," J. took what he could use from Nietzsche's philosophy, followed classical themes and models, drew from the historicism of Vico and Spengler and from the theories of Flinders Petrie about the periodicity of civilizations, and adapted a modified materialism from Lucretius' *De Rerum natura.*

Most of J.'s narratives are lively tales of violence, adultery, and incest, with settings in the Carmel-Big Sur region of California. Characteristically, they describe the conflict of a young rebellious figure, usually a female who cunningly uses sex to win her objectives, and an older patriarchal figure, who is either sternly orthodox or hypocritical. With few exceptions, these conflicts move from the isolated and abortive rebellion in "Tamar" of an individual against the conditions of her life to those of "Cawdor" (1928), "Thurso's Landing" (1932), and "Give Your Heart to the Hawks" (1933), in which the individual's rebellion is related with increasing attention to the values of society.

Like "Margrave" (1932), "Such Counsels You Gave Me" (1937) introduces into the theme of rebellion a hero modeled after Dostoyevski's Raskolnikov, and in "Hungerfield" (1954) the hero discovers the gross impropriety of his fantastic struggle with death. In many of these poems, J. apparently tested various principles of Nietzsche's philosophy and rejected those that proved untenable. Because of his explorations of Nietzscheanism, and his restatements of the lesson from Greek tragedy that to learn is to suffer, critics have erroneously charged J. with nihilism.

These critics believe that J.'s "Roan Stallion" (1925), *The Women at Point Sur* (1927), "Dear Judas" (1929), and "The Double Axe" (1948) support their opinions, but in these poems the Nietzschean principles of revaluation of values and of the antichrist operate to clear the way for J.'s "inhumanism," which challenges institutionalized Christianity but reaffirms God the creator. It also holds that "Man is no measure of anything," that "The beauty of things is . . . absolute," and that "Old violence is not too old to beget new values."

In 1947, J.'s very successful *Medea* (1946), a free adaptation from Euripides, was produced in New York. "Solstice" (1935) was a modernized, nondramatic version of *Medea*, and "The Cretan Woman" (1954) was modeled after Euripides' *Hippolytus*, which also provided a theme in "Cawdor." "The Tower Beyond Tragedy" (1925), an adaptation of the *Oresteia* of Aeschylus, has also been dramatized. In each instance, J. reshaped the classical source to conform to his own ideology.

J.'s troublesome and inferior "political" poems approve of World War II and the Korean War as methods of eliminating undeserving human beings who have violated the holy beauty of things with their civilizations. He regarded Hitler, Mussolini, Stalin, and Franklin Roosevelt as helpless but necessary victims of circumstances. Accordingly, metropolitan life is seen as vicious and corrupting, life in the mountains as desirable, clean, and lonely. Borrowing from Lucretius, J. believed that the truly worthy and passionate individual might transcend the flaming world walls of his being to attain direct access to the "transhuman magnificence" of things, and that, best of all, he might be comforted by the thought that in death his atoms would mingle again with those of nature.

FURTHER WORKS: *Flagons and Apples* (1912); *Californians* (1916); *Descent to the Dead* (1931); *The Selected Poetry of R. J.* (1938); *Be Angry at the Sun* (1941); *Poetry, Gongorism and a Thousand Years* (1948); *Themes in My Poems* (1956); *The Beginning and the End* (1963); *The Selected Letters of R. J., 1897-1962* (1968), ed. A. Ridgeway

BIBLIOGRAPHY: Alberts, S. S., *A Bibliography of the Works of R. J.* (1933); Gilbert, R., *Shine, Perishing Republic* (1936); Powell, L. C., *R. J., the Man and His Work* (1940); Gregory, H., and Zaturenska, M. A., "R. J. and The Birth of Tragedy," in *History of American Poetry, 1900-1940* (1946), pp. 398-412; Waggoner, H. H., "R. J.: Here is Reality," in *The Heel of Elohim* (1950), pp. 105-32; Squires, R., *The Loyalties of R. J.* (1956); Carpenter, F. I., *R. J.* (1962); Bennett, M. B., *The Stone Mason of Tor House* (1966); Carpenter, F. I., "R. J. and the Torches of Violence," in *The Twenties* (1966), ed. R. E. Langford and W. E. Taylor, pp. 14-17

ARTHUR B. COFFIN

JENS, Walter

German novelist, essayist, and critic, b. 8 March 1923, Hamburg

J. studied in Hamburg and Freiburg im Breisgau; since 1949 he has taught classical philology at the University of Tübingen.

Apart from his first work, the novella *Das weiße Taschentuch*, published in 1948 under the pseudonym "Walter Freiburger," all the novels and short stories J. has so far published show the influence of Kafka (q.v.). It is particularly apparent in the novel *Nein—die Welt der Angeklagten* (1950). In this work, often compared to Orwell's (q.v.) *1984*, the catastrophe of the "last individualist" illuminates the individual's position in a mass society. In the novels *Vergessene Gesichter* (1952) on the one hand and *Der Mann, der nicht alt werden wollte* (1955) on the other, J. deals with the problem of time experience, which is also the subject of his literary criticism, *Statt einer Literaturgeschichte* (1957). J.'s prose avoids poetic arabesques of all kinds.

He has also written several radio and television plays, including *Der Besuch des Fremden* (1952) and *Alte Frau im Grandhotel* (1953), as well as scholarly publications.

FURTHER WORKS: *Der Blinde* (1951); *Hofmannsthal und die Griechen* (1955); *Das Testament des Odysseus* (1957); *Die Götter sind sterblich* (1959); *Deutsche Literatur der Gegenwart* (1961; 2nd ed., 1964); *Zueignungen* (1962); *Herr Meister* (1963); *Literatur und Politik* (1963); *Melancholie und Moral* (1963); *Euripides-Büchner* (1964)

BIBLIOGRAPHY: Just, G., ed., *W. J.: Eine Einführung in sein Werk* (1965)

HELMUT M. BRAEM

JENSEN, Johannes Vilhelm

Danish poet, writer, philosopher and critic, b. 20 Jan. 1873, Farsø, Jutland; d. 25 Nov. 1950, Copenhagen

During J.'s childhood and youth the rugged landscape of Jutland had a formative effect upon him. In the late 1890's he published his first books, which show an uncommon literary talent, although in content they remain close to the style of decadent symbolism (q.v.). J. later repudiated these works, and they were never reissued. After a visit to America just before the turn of the century, he made a completely new departure, laying the foundation of modern Danish literature (q.v.). After the novel *Kongens Fald* (3 vols., 1901; The Fall of the King, 1933) his entire work is pervaded by the overwhelming realization that this world is the only reality and that the sole truth is that which is sensually perceptible. The *Himmerlandshistorier* (3 vols., 1898-1910) describe his native Jutland, while the poetically written detective novels *Madame d'Ora* (1904) and *Hjulet* (1905) present a vivid picture of modern America. His six-volume novel cycle *Den lange rejse* (1908-1922; I *Bræen* [1908; Fire and Ice, 1923]; II *Skibet* [1912]; III *Det tabte land* [1919]; IV *Norne-Gæst* [1919]; V *Cim-*

brernes tog [1922; The Cimbrians, 1923]; and VI *Christoffer Columbus* [1922; Christopher Columbus, 1924]) was an attempt to write an epic of the Germanic people and to depict their yearning for the South, in which J. saw an incentive to human progress. Here he developed a theory of the "Gothic Renaissance" (*Den gotiske Renaissance* 1901) that was later attacked by the National Socialists. Finally in his first collection of poems, *Digte* (1906), J. introduced modernism into Danish literature (q.v.)—to some extent under the influence of Walt Whitman (1819-92).

All these books appeared within a decade and even before World War I made J. the most controversial Danish writer of his time, as well as the most admired and imitated. After the war J. devoted himself mainly to philosophy and scientific studies. He concerned himself especially with evolutionary theories (*Dyrenes forvandling*, 1927; *Åndens stadier*, 1928), which sometimes became the subject of his poetry. Philosophical concerns again play a major role in the short stories and novellas that he called "myths" (*Myter og Jagter*, 9 vols., 1907-1944). J.'s was an original talent, although it harbored many external influences. His greatest gift, however, was his capacity for sensual perception and its expression in significant form. Here he opened new potentialities to the Danish language. His philosophical efforts, on the other hand, are those of a dilettante. The interwar generation in Denmark owes its feeling for language and to some extent its *Weltanschauung* to J. He was awarded the Nobel Prize in 1944.

FURTHER WORKS: *Danskere* (1896); *Einar Elkjaer* (1898); *Intermezzo* (1899); *Skovene* (1904); *Eksotiske noveller* (3 vols., 1907-1915); *Den nye verden* (1907; The Waving Rye, 1958); *Introduktion til vol tilsalder* (1915); *Aestetik og udvikling* (1923); *Årstiderne* (1923); *Hamlet* (1924); *Evolution og moral* (1925); *Årets højtider* (1925); *Verdens lys* (1926); *Den jyske blaest* (1931); *Dr. Renaults fristelser* (1935); *Påskebadet* (1937); *Vor oprindelse* (1941); *Digte 1901-1943* (1943; rev. ed., 1948); *Mytens ring* (1951)

BIBLIOGRAPHY: Johansen, F., and Marcus, A., *J. V. J.* (2 vols., 1933-51); Gelsted, O., *J. V. J.* (1938); Henriques, A., *J. V. J.* (1938); Nedergaard, L., *J. V. J.* (1943); Anon., *Denmark's J. V. J.* (1955); Damberg, N. B., *J. V. J.* (1961)

PETER P. ROHDE

JESENSKÝ, Janko

Slovak poet and novelist, b. 30 Dec. 1874, Turčiansky Svätý Martin; d. 27 Dec. 1945, Bratislava

J., a student of Russian and Western European literature, edited the journal *Slovenské smery.* The collection *Verše* published in 1905 contains subjective, reflective poetry. As a prose writer J. was a realist with a preference for small-town themes, as in *Malomestké rozprávky* (1913). In the poetry collection *Zo zajatia* (1919) and the prose *Cestou k slobode* (1933), he recorded his impressions of World War I when he was a legionnaire in Russia. The novel *Demokrati* (2 vols., 1934 and 1937; The Democrats, 1961) satirizes life in government service in the first Czechoslovak Republic. In 1945, J. published three volumes of occasional poems: *Proti noci; Čierne dni; Na zlobu dňa.*

FURTHER WORKS: *Po búrkach* (1932); *Sobrané spisy* (21 vols., 1944-48)

BIBLIOGRAPHY: Anon., *J. J. v kritike a spomienkach* (1955); Rechcigl, M., ed., *The Czechoslovak Contribution to World Culture* (1964), pp. 44-50; Kirschbaum, J. M., "Slovak Literary History in Marxist and Western Interpretations," *Canadian Slavonic Papers,* VI (1964), 117-34

ELISABETH NONNENMACHER

JIMÉNEZ, Juan Ramón

Spanish poet, b. 24 Dec. 1881, Moguer, Huelva; d. 29 May 1958, San Juan, Puerto Rico

J. spent his childhood in Moguer. He studied under the Jesuits at Puerto de Santa Maria in Cadiz and at the University of Seville. His first reading was the old Spanish *romanceros,* Luis de Góngora y Argote (1561-1627), Gustavo Bécquer (1836-70), and the French and German romantics. Later, at the turn of the c., he developed a strong affinity for the French symbolists (see symbolism).

His friendship with Darío (q.v.) was of formative importance and led him to identify himself completely with modernism. J. was one of the originators, with Valle-Inclán, the Machado brothers, Villaespesa (qq.v.), and other modernist poets, of *Helios,* the periodical of the modernist movement in poetry, and his books and poems soon won him a leading place among the adherents of this movement. He

now read, with great profit, Shelley, Browning, Goethe, and Hölderlin, though by no means abandoning his beloved symbolists—Verlaine, Albert Samain (1858-1900), and Jammes (q.v.).

The years between 1905 and 1916 were a productive period which J. spent partly in Moguer, partly in the Sierra Guadarrama and southwest France, and partly in Madrid, where he published continuously. His withdrawn, melancholic life was interspersed with long spells of neurasthenia and pessimism, but, far from hampering his creativity, these drove him to loftier, more ambitious achievements. In New York in 1916 he married Zenobia Camprubi, the Spanish translator of the Indian poet Tagore (q.v.), of whom he soon became a great admirer.

In the years between 1916 and 1927, while broadening and purifying his own work, he devoted substantial effort to training the younger literary generation and edited several poetry journals including *Indice, Si,* and *Ley,* which were of great significance in this period. Between 1927 and 1930 he became disappointed in the young poets, whom he now saw as bombastic and fickle. Shortly after the outbreak of the civil war, J. went to Puerto Rico, then to Cuba, and later spent a few years in the U.S.A. He finally returned to Puerto Rico, where he died. He was awarded the Nobel Prize in 1956.

While his first books hewed to the line of modernism, his fondness for certain forms (including that of the "romance") and the distinctly melancholy, dreamy, idyllic tone that pervaded his outlook were deeply personal and individual. The romances—*Arias tristes* (1903), *Jardines lejanos* (1904), and *Pastorales* (1905)— are notable for their tender, touching simplicity. Possessing an exquisite sensitivity to music and color, this poet wove delicate impressions of landscape and subtle emotional moods into a new romantic bucolic poetry.

J. gave the French formalism introduced by Darío a stronger yet more flexible musicality, as in the *Elegías puras* (1908), *Elegías intermedias* (1909), and *Elegías lamentables* (1910), in the *Poemas mágicos y dolientes* (1911) or in *Melancolía* (1912). Moreover, J. successfully blended the artistry that stems from intensive effort to render the most subtle reactions of the consciousness with his liking for a popular note; this combination is particularly successful in his *Baladas de primavera* (1910).

In prose, in addition to many theoretical and critical works, he wrote the delightful *Platero*

FRANCIS JAMMES

JOHANNES JENSEN

JUAN RAMÓN JIMÉNEZ

y yo (1917; Platero and I, 1946). The poet and his little donkey wander through their native Andalusia, marveling at the beauties and tribulations of life. This work, which achieves the purity of St. Francis's spirit, marks a peak in Spanish poetic prose. Another excellent work of this first period is *Sonetos espirituales* (1917); the sonnet in his hands was a new form, one that was free from stiffness and artificiality, one that involved an organic confluence of emotions.

The *Diario de un poeta recién casado* (1917) opens J.'s second phase, which is marked by the search for a pure poetry, a poetry that would be free of any anecdotal element and would limit itself to essentials, and that, at the same time, would be more thoughtful than emotional. While his goal had always been that of an aesthetic and esoteric poetry, his tendency to eclectic refinement became increasingly apparent after 1917, when the *Diario* appeared. The short, as it were naked, yet still abstract poems in *Eternidades* (1917) and *Piedra y cielo* (1919) express a longing for purity and eternity that reveals J.'s ideal of classicism as a living force that, after long striving to perfect itself, springs forth in all its natural spontaneity. In his last book, *Animal del fondo* (1949), J., who was increasingly absorbed in a mystical pantheistic religiosity unattached to any absolute faith, continued this refining process.

For the first thirty years of the 20th c., J. was the *pontifex maximus* of poetry in Spain. Almost all of Spain's and Latin America's great contemporary poets owe something—or a great deal—to him. "He is the teacher of poets, not the teacher of students" (A. Valbuena). Although his "universal Andalusian work" with its absolute worship of beauty bears the stamp of a timeless and vitally living classic, the ethical, social, and realistic trend of contemporary literature has to some extent diminished his earlier appeal. Nevertheless, J. will live on in Spanish literature, to the practitioners of which he set a supreme example of a life devoted with passionate tenacity to the poetic vocation.

FURTHER WORKS: *Almas de violeta* (1900); *Ninfeas* (1900); *Rimas* (1902); *La soledad sonora* (1911); *Laberinto* (1913); *Estio* (1916); *Segunda antología poética, 1898-1918* (1922); *Canción* (1936); *Españoles de tres mundos* (1942); *La estación total* (1946); *Romances de Coral Gables* (1948); *Tercera antología poética, 1898-1953* (1957); *Libros de poesía* (1957); *Moguer* (1958); *Libros de prosa* (1959). **Selected**

English trans.: *Three Hundred Poems of J. R. J.* (1962); *Forty Poems of J. R. J.* (1968)

BIBLIOGRAPHY: Bo., C., *J.* (1941); Díez Canedo, E., *J.* (1944); Gicovate, B., *La poesía de J. R. J.* (1959); Gullón, R., *Estudios sobre J. R. J.* (1960); Schonberg, J.-L., *J. R. J. ou le chant d'Orphée* (1961); Torre, G. de, *El fiel de le balanza* (1961); Sánchez Barbudo, A., *La segunda época de J. R. J.* (1962); Kemmerer, C. R., "The Creative Process of J. R. J.," in *DA*, XXIII (1963), 4359; Young, H. T., *The Victorious Expression* (1964); Predmore, M. P., "The Prose of J. R. J.," in *DA*, XXV (1965), 5939; Olson, P. R., *Circle of a Paradox: Time and Essence in the Poetry of J. R. J.* (1967)

GONZALO SOBEJANO

JOHNSON, Eyvind (Olof Verner)
Swedish novelist, b. 29 July 1900, Överluleå

J. was a student and newspaper correspondent in Germany from 1921 to 1923 and spent the years between 1925 and 1930 in France. After World War II he was a member of the Swedish UNESCO delegation in Switzerland, England, Germany, and other countries.

After some early works with a socialist, world-reforming tendency, J., taking Hamsun (q.v.) as his model, described the hunger and hardships of an unknown Swedish writer in Paris (*Stad i ljus*, 1928, first published in French as *Lettre recommandée*, 1927). In *Stad i mörker* (1927) and *Minnas* (1928), he satirized small-town life, and in *Kommentar till ett stjärnfall* (1929), *Avsked till Hamlet* (1930), and *Bobinack* (1932), Stockholm's bourgeoisie. To some extent these works show the influence of Sigmund Freud (1856-1939), whom J. had studied intensely, and of Joyce (q.v.), whose interior monologue (q.v.) he introduced in Sweden and subsequently imitated systematically. His next two novels, *Natten är här* (1932) and *Regn i gryningen* (1933), glorify primitivism and sexual freedom.

J.'s talent did not realize its potential until he wrote his volume of novellas (*Än en gång, Kapten!*, 1934) and his autobiographical novel series (*Nu var det 1914*, 1934; *Här har du ditt liv*, 1935; *Se dig inte om*, 1936; and *Slutspel i ungdomen*, 1937). This tetralogy was published in 1945 under the title *Romanen om Olof*. Its publication was followed by *Romantisk berättelse* (1953) and *Tidens gång* (1955), and, later, *Vinterresa i Norrbotten*

(1955). The core of these skillfully constructed and exquisitely stylized novels, which depict Swedish society from before World War I to after World War II, is psychological analysis and problematical intellectual questions.

In another series of novels, J. moved into the area of *littérature engagée*. Thus *Grupp Krilon* (1941), *Krilons resa* (1942), and *Krilon själv* (1943) are largely a plea for the freedom of the individual and an indictment of dictatorial coercion. (All three were published together in 1948 as *Krilon: En roman om det sannolika*.) A similar humanistic outlook is presented in the following books: *Strändernas svall* (1946; Return to Ithaca, 1952), in which the story of Odysseus is retold; *Drömmar om rosor och eld* (1949), on the notorious trial of the witches of Loudun; *Lägg undan solen* (1951); and *Molnen över Metapontion* (1957).

FURTHER WORKS: *De fyra främlingarna* (1924); *Timmans och rättfärdigheten* (1925); *Nattovning* (1938); *Den trygga världen* (1940); *Soldatens återkomst* (1940); *Sju liv* (1944); *Pan mot Sparta* (1946); *Dagbok från Schweiz* (1949); *Ett vårtal* (1951); *Stunder* (1951); *Tutidens gång* (1955); *Hans nådes tid* (1960); *Spår förbi Kolonos* (1961); *Livsdagen lång* (1964)

BIBLIOGRAPHY: Lindberger, Ö., "E. J.," in *Den andre internasjonale studiekonferense om nordisk litteratur* (1958), 1-9; Huveröd, S. H., "E. J. i Lawrensk belysning," in *Ord och Bild*, LXIX, (1960), 46-50; Lindberger, Ö., "E. J.'s möte med Proust och Joyce," in *Bonniers Litterära Magasin*, XXIX (1960), 554-63; Göransson, S., "Berättartekniken i E. J.'s roman *Molnen över Metapontion*," in *Samlaren*, LXXXIII (1962), 67-91

JORIS TAELS

JOHNSON, Uwe
German novelist, b. 20 July 1934, Cammin, Pomerania

J. attended the universities of Rostock and Leipzig. In 1959 he left the German Democratic Republic (East Germany) to live in West Berlin, where he became affiliated with the famous Gruppe 47. J.'s first published work, *Mutmassungen über Jakob* (1959; Speculations about Jakob, 1963), immediately established him as a prestigious writer. The novel was an avantgarde effort in postwar Germany. Time schemes are arbitrary. The characters, often unidentified, tend to think in random associ-

ation. Information about people and events is lacking in factual certainty. The outline of the plot emerges only if the reader makes a concentrated effort to perceive it. The novel's hero, Jakob Abs, a railroad dispatcher in East Germany, has died in mysterious circumstances. The characters in the novel, as well as the reader, conjecture about the occurrences preceding his death. The investigation of his life merely produces bits of information, which in themselves are quite inconsequential. But by their very insignificance and inconclusiveness, they magnify the enigma of the man Jakob and the contours of his personality. He, it becomes clear, cannot be contained by any scheme, category, or ideology that those conjecturing about him attempt to impose upon him. The factual incertitude regarding the hero is offset by an overwhelming certainty concerning the physical properties of things and processes: "therefore, lower your heel before the dead point at the top and push the pedal forward with the tip of your foot rather than straight down, whereas, at the low dead point, you lift your heel and press the pedal backward with your toes and pull it back up, while the other foot. . . ." Such extensive descriptions are not an indulgence in a favorite device of modern literature. They are structurally significant. Someone actually riding a bicycle, we realize upon reading this passage, is something quite different from what J. presents here as an abstracted pattern.

All of J.'s novels so far—*Das dritte Buch über Achim* (1961; The Third Book about Achim, 1967), *Zwei Ansichten* (1965; Two Views, 1966)—show the same principle. J. fixates detail *ad finitum* to demonstrate the discrepancy between the object and its objectification. Thus the elusiveness of physical things and processes is analogous to the subjectivity of the human being. J.'s descriptiveness, excessive by design, is a pointer to the inadequacy of categories, systems, and ideologies.

In *Das dritte Buch über Achim*, the hero, a bicycle racer, idol of the people, functionary of the (East) German Democratic Republic and repentant participant in the 1953 Berlin uprising, again is a person who insists on keeping a part of himself free of the molds others wish to force on him. To his West German biographer, he is an opportunist. The state holds him to be an item of property, existing only by virtue of its grace. Achim does not think of himself as a mere tool of the state. He considers himself a person of unimpaired integrity be-

EYVIND JOHNSON

JOHANNES JØRGENSEN

cause he believes that his image among the people came about by his own consent.

In *Zwei Ansichten* an affair between an East German girl and her West German lover is terminated mainly because both come to feel that in large part their marriage would be based on a cliché. They go through the motions of "love conquers all" with increasing reluctance. In the end the girl realizes that the city of Berlin is more important to her than her lover. On his way to meet the girl who has come to West Berlin, the lover has thoughts of driving into a bridge pillar with his new sports car, on which he has spent all his money that might have gone into a household. He has himself run down by a bus, though from his hospital bed he still inanely insists that he wants to marry the girl.

All three of J.'s books pit the West German situation against the East German situation. They establish clearly the ever-increasing separateness of the two Germanys. In view of J.'s insistence on the autonomy of the individual and his domain, the concept that the two Germanys are one, despite their political differences, seems ever more invalid. At present, East and West Germany appear to belong together no more than do the lovers in *Zwei Ansichten*.

The obscurity of J.'s style in his first two novels (nonconventional use of punctuation; inverted, though paratactic, sentences; non-chronological presentation of the plot) has given way to formal conservatism. Yet his hand is clearly discernible: his style is austere and unemotional; his metaphors, precise; his symbols, sparse and unostentatious. However, for all its reticence there is in his style an intensity that elicits from the reader a compassionate though also analytical affinity with the world J. creates. His primary nexus with other contemporary German and Western writers is an article of faith characteristic of the 1950's and early 1960's: it asks that the individual be socially engaged but insists that such involvement remain free from ideological adulteration.

FURTHER WORKS: *Karsch und andere Prosa* (1964)

BIBLIOGRAPHY: Blöcker, G., "U. J.," *Kritisches Lesebuch* (1962), pp. 191-99; Wunberg, G., "Struktur und Symbolik in U. J.'s Roman *Mutmaßungen über Jakob*," *Neue Sammlung,* II (1962), 440-49; Kolb, H., "Rückfall in die Parataxe," *NDH*, XCVI (1963), 42-74; Reich-Ranicki, M., "Registrator Johnson," *Deutsche Literatur in Ost und West* (1963), pp. 231-46; Schonauer, F., "U. J.," *Schriftsteller der Gegenwart,* ed. K. Nonnenmann (1963), pp. 182-88; Detweiler, R., "*Speculations about Jakob:* The Truth of Ambiguity," *Monatshefte,* LVIII (1966), 25-32; Friedrichsmeyer, E., "Quest by Supposition: J.'s *Mutmaßungen über Jakob,*" *GR,* XLII (1967), 215-26

ERHARD FRIEDRICHSMEYER

JONES, James

American novelist, b. 6 Nov. 1921, Robinson, Ill.

Because of the Depression, J.'s education ended with high school. Joining the army, he was at Pearl Harbor when the Japanese attacked; he was injured in combat on Guadalcanal, and discharged in 1944.

From Here to Eternity (1951) won the National Book Award and became an immediate bestseller. It has been described as "the definite novel of the American peacetime army" by Geismar, and with J.'s other works has been translated into thirteen languages. It is a detailed account of the life of an enlisted man in the pre-World War II army. In the tradition of naturalism ([q.v.] second only to *An American Tragedy* as a 20th c. American naturalistic novel, according to F. L. Gwynn), the book set new limits in realistic description of soldiers' language and sexual behavior. As R. P. Adams showed, it is in the Thoreau-Whitman tradition, with its presentation of the self-reliant individual struggling against dehumanizing institutions. The novel taps the emotional power of the archetypal American folk-hero to give the enlisted man tragic stature.

The Thin Red Line (1962), an account of an infantry company on Guadalcanal, demonstrates J.'s narrative power, his ability to create many individualized characters, and to document his material. The episode of the decaying corpse of the Japanese soldier, dragged out of a mass grave, is both realistic and suggestive.

By J.'s standards, his works are antiwar. An accurate report of war must show "the regimentation of souls, the systematized reduction of men to animal level, the horror of pointless death, the exhaustion of living in constant fear." A true antiwar work must show "that modern war destroys human character." Moreover J. intimates in his fiction that the dehumanizing institutions of war symbolize the tendency of all contemporary institutions.

FURTHER WORKS: *Some Came Running* (1958); *The Pistol* (1959); *Go to the Widow-Maker* (1967)

BIBLIOGRAPHY: Fiedler, L., "J. J.: Dead-End Young Werther: The Bum as American Culture Hero," *Commentary,* XII (Sept. 1951), 252-55; Adams, R. P., "A Second Look at *From Here to Eternity,*" *CE,* XVIII (Jan. 1956), 205-10; Griffith, B. W., "Rear Rank Robin Hood: James Jones' Folk Hero," *GaR,* X (Spring 1956), 41-46; Geismar, M., *American Moderns,* (1958); Geismar, M., "*The Thin Red Line:* A Review," *New York Times Book Review,* 9 Sept., 1962

LEE A. BURGESS, JR.

JØRGENSEN, Johannes

Danish poet, novella writer, critic, and essayist, b. 6 Nov. 1866, Svendborg, Fünen Island; d. there 29 May 1956

J. ranks as Scandinavia's first major Catholic poet since the Reformation. Though influenced at first by the freethinking ideas of Brandes (q.v.), he was converted in 1896, left his family in Denmark, and settled in Siena and later in Assisi. In 1953 he returned to Svendborg.

After some early novellas and volumes of poems, the poetry collection *Bekendelse* (1894) revealed J.'s spiritual and artistic evolution from the naturalism (q.v.) of his youth up to his conversion. As a critic he attracted a small group of symbolist poets and artists whose center was the journal *Taarnet* (1893-95). After his conversion he shocked his supporters by a series of violently polemical writings attacking his old friends, particularly *Livsløgn og livssandhed* (1896). In his poetry he achieved a new, simplified style influenced by the language of the liturgy (*Digte,* 1898). In 1907 his biography of St. Francis, *Den hellige Frans af Assisi* (St. Francis of Assisi, 1912) appeared, depicting the saint as a simple nature poet. His best volume of poems, *Blomster og frugter,* was also published in 1907. This was followed by the profoundly melancholy poetry of the volume *Af det dybe* (1909). Among J.'s travel books on Germany, western Europe, Italy, and the Balkans, *Goethe-Bogen* (1913) is particularly impressive. The hagiographical *Den hellige Katerina af Siena* (1915) and *Den hellige Birgitta af Vadstena* (1941-43) have no scholarly significance. In Assisi, J. also wrote his prose

masterwork, *Mit livs legende* (7 vols., 1916-28; Jørgensen, an Autobiography, 2 vols., 1928-29). This was conceived as a self-indictment and self-defense in which J. sees his life as the consequence of his submission to God's providence. This work, inspired by the French painter Andrée Carof, is also interesting as an account of J.'s religious crisis and second, definitive conversion.

J. continued to write until his old age—travel books, legends and parables, essays and memoirs, biographies of modern saints (*Don Bosco,* 1929; *Charles de Foucauld,* 1936), and finally a series of small poetry collections. He published his last poems—love poems to his second wife, the Viennese Helena Klein—at the age of eighty. His literary influence in Denmark was small, but he was highly esteemed as a master of language and as a unique personality. The number of his works translated into German, Italian, and French is unusual for a Scandinavian writer, while his biography of St. Francis is, after Andersen's fairy tales and the works of Kierkegaard, the most widely read work of Danish literature.

FURTHER WORKS: *Vers* (1887); *Forårssagn* (1888); *En fremmed* (1890); *Sommer* (1892); *Stemninger* (1892); *Hjemve* (1894); *Rejsebogen* (1895); *Den yderste dag* (1897); *Lignelser* (1898); *Vor Frue af Danmark* (1900); *Eva* (1901); *Romersk mosaik* (1901); *Romerske helgenbilleder* (1902); *Den hellige ild* (1902); *Pilgrimsbogen* (1903; Pilgrim Walks in Franciscan Italy, 1908); *Rejsebilleder fra nord og syd* (1905); *Den yndigste rose* (1907); *I det høje* (1908); *Fra Vesuv til Skagen* (1909); *Indtryk og stemninger* (1911); *Klokke Roland* (1915; False Witnesses, 1916); *Udvalgte værker* (7 vols., 1915); *Der er en brønd, som rinder* (1920); *Jorsalafaerd* (1923); *Brig "Marie" af Svendborg* (1925); *Isblomster* (1926); *Dante-stemninger* (1928); *Vers fra Vadstena* (1941); *Digte i Danmark* (1943); *Udvalgte digte* (1944)

BIBLIOGRAPHY: Walden, A., *Der Dichter-philosoph J. J.* (1904); Topsøe-Jensen, H. C., *Scandinavian Literature from Brandes to our Day* (1929), pp. 126-30; Frederiksen, E., *J. J.'s Ungdom* (1946); Nugent, R., "J.'s Devotional Verse: A Contemporary Act of Faith," *Renascence,* XV (1963), 79-81; Jones, W. G., "The Early Novels of J.," *SS,* XXXVI (1964), 103-17

EMIL FREDERIKSEN

JOUHANDEAU, Marcel

(pseud. of *Marcel Provence*), French novelist and short story writer, b. 26 July 1888, La Clayette

J. is a writer of great originality who can be ascribed to no school or movement. The world he created has a mystical, unreal character but draws its images from sensorily perceptible reality.

J. comes from a modest background. His father, a butcher in Guéret, had little sympathy for so unrobust a son, but he and his mother were drawn together by the intense sensitivity they possessed in common. His account of modest provincial life in the imaginary town of *Chaminadour* (1934-41), which recurs throughout his novels, stems from a wealth of personal memories of Guéret and its inhabitants. As a result of his success at the Collège of Guéret, J. was sent to the Lycée Henri IV in Paris in 1907. After completing his studies, he renounced an academic career so that he could devote himself to his writing, thus incurring the displeasure of his father, who withdrew all financial support. J. then took a teaching position at the Internat de Passy, remaining there until 1949. Nothing could rouse him from his self-chosen withdrawal and scorn for the world until his marriage, in 1929, to a former dancer, the model for Elise, who was one of the main characters in his novel *Elise* (1933).

J.'s works contain above all a rich vein of personal observations and memories. *La Jeunesse de Théophile* (1921) is an account of a youth spent in an atmosphere of religiosity, while *Prudence Hautechaume* (1927), *Les Miens* (1942), and *L'Oncle Henri* (1943) recall faces and figures from his own youth. In *Chroniques maritales* (1938) and *Nouvelles chroniques maritales* (1943), J. reveals the cruelty of his marriage—"a prison which one can neither remain in without being a coward nor escape from." Not content with merely describing real life, J. offers the reader his personal mythology that contains the truth he has gleaned from patient meditation. All these works are "a mixture of reality and myth, waking and dreaming, irony and metaphysics."

His first short stories were written even before World War I ("Vieille Françoise"; "La Chambre sans fenêtre"; "Le Crucifix de porcelaine"; "Les Pincengrain," first published by his friend Jacques Rivière (1886-1925) in the *Nouvelle Revue française*, 1924). Here J. appears for the first time wearing the mask of his alter ego, Monsieur Godeau, tortured by his violent craving for freedom and unshakably convinced of his immortality. The struggle between good and evil is here subordinated to the striving for greatness in good as in evil. J. returned to this theme again in *Monsieur Godeau intime* (1926) and *Monsieur Godeau marié* (1932).

This transformation of realistic characters into visionary figures with diabolical or angelic features is used even more effectively in short stories, novels, and essays such as *Manhattan* (1927), *Ximenès Malinjoude* (1927), *Astaroth* (1929), or *Eloge de l'imprudence* (1931). The erotic experiences J. discusses in *De l'abjection* (1939) or *Les Carnets de Don Juan* (1947) are not to be taken as an expression of complacent viciousness but as an attempt to transcend vice. This withdrawal into a world beyond the sensual one, together with the inexhaustible richness of J.'s inner life, transform his solitude into a defense against the danger of pessimism and enable him to experience direct happiness.

J.'s egocentricity understandably met with little approval in literary—and other—circles. He was, however, in contact with other great French writers of the 1930's. Gide (q.v.) was generous with admiration for his "terrifying mysticism, this rapture of the soul." Rivière best characterized J.'s originality and eccentricity when he wrote to him in 1922: "You are original in a terrifying way."

FURTHER WORKS: *Les Térébinthe* (1926); *Brigitte ou La belle au bois dormant* (1927); *Opales* (1929); *Le parricide imaginaire* (1930); *Le journal du coiffeur* (1931); *Tite-le-long* (1932); *Véronicana* (1933); *Binche-Ana* (1933); *Algèbre des valeurs morales* (1936); *Le saladier* (1936); *Le jardin de Cordoue ou Endymion endormi* (1938); *Triptyque* (1942); *Animaux familiers* (1947); *Essai sur moi-même* (1947); *Ménagerie domestique* (1948); *Mémorial* (6 vols., 1948); *La faute plutôt que le scandale* (1949); *Un monde* (1950); *Portraits de famille* (1951); *De la grandeur* (1952); *Éloge de la volupté* (1952); *Dernières années et mort de Véronique* (1953); *Confidences* (1954); *Ana de Madame Apremont* (1954); *Contes d'enfer* (1955); *Du pur amour* (1955); *Jaunisse; Elisæana* (1956); *Reflexions sur la vieillesse et la mort* (1956); *Nouvelles images de Paris: Remarques sur les visages* (1956); *Théâtre sans spectacle* (1957); *Carnets de l'écrivain* (1957); *Les Argonautes* (1959); *Chemeris et châteaux du Grand Meaulnes* (1961); *Journaliers, 1957-*

1959 (1961-62); *Trois crimes rituels* (1962); *Descente aux enfers* (1963); *Jean Cocteau: l'amitié faite homme* (1963); *Que tout n'est qu'allusion* (1963); *Monsieur Godeau intime* (1963); *Le Bien du mal* (1964); *Chronique d'une passion* (1964); *Être inimitable* (1964); *Divertissements: Mes préfs* (1965); *Je suis le notaire de la vie* (1965); *Riposte à Roger Perfide* (1965); *Que la vie est une fête* (1966)

BIBLIOGRAPHY: Gaulmier, J., *L'Univers de M. J.* (1959); Epling, K., "M. J.," in *WuWahr*, XV (1960), 689-97; Aberached, R., "Un Débutant célèbre: M. J.," in *Études*, CCCXV (1963), 241-44; Bàccolo, L., "L'Ultimo J.," in *Ponte*, XIX (1963), 656-62; Ganne, G., "La Minute de vérité de M. J.," in *NL* (2 Jan. 1964), p. 7

JEAN PERRETTE

JOUVE, Pierre-Jean

French poet and novelist, b. 11 Oct. 1887, Arras

J.'s shock at the horror of World War I was voiced in his humanitarian poems. In his youth he was close to *unanimisme* and for a time edited its journal, *Les Bandeaux d'or*. He never belonged to the surrealist movement, although his intellectual course ran parallel to it, yet it was surrealism (q.v.) that led him to the central theme of his poetry—the unconscious and its interpretation through psychoanalysis. Catholicism, to which he was converted in 1924, represents the opposite pole of his thinking—the transcendence of the soul ("To find a religious perspective in the act of creation—the only answer to contemporary nothingness" [*En miroir*, 1954]). Thus J.'s poetry is not determined by form but by the wish to clarify the problems of existence through the creative word.

After a period of strong psychoanalytic influence (*Tragiques*, 1922), his poetry, which has always been dominated by apocalyptic visions of terror, widened out and became clarified. *Sueur de Sang*, a great poetic work that was published in 1934, reflects the catastrophe-laden yet ecstatic spiritual complexion of his work. The function of a poem is to help and to free; this it can do only if the poet himself has experienced and suffered what he summons into words. This explains not only the demonic element in his poetry, the guilt feelings, the sense of being condemned to the unclean, the exhibition of sinful voluptuousness but also the

search for symbols having the power to exorcise the devil. The problem confronting J. as a poet is to prevent language from stifling in the troubled, bloody miasma he stirs up.

In his later volumes of poems (*Diadème*, 1949; *Ode*, 1951), the jerky, choking language of his poetry becomes calmer; the tense, painfully distorted apparitions give way to a released elation of the soul expressed in spiritual song. J. is now a eulogist who finds the right tone whether he is writing of his ascents into a luminous transcendence or on the glory of his country (during the German occupation)—*La Louange* (1945) and *Hymne* (1947). Yet his verse always preserves its reticence; his vocabulary is sparse, his forms blocklike and austere.

FURTHER WORKS: *Vous êtes des hommes* (1915); *La danse des morts* (1917); *Paulina 1880* (1925); *Le monde désert* (1927); *Hécate* (1928); *La symphonie à Dieu* (1930); *Vagadu* (1931); *Noces* (1931); *Histoires sanglantes* (1932); *La scène capitale* (1935); *Matière céleste* (1937); *Kyrie* (1938); *Porche à la nuit des saints* (1941); *La vierge de Paris* (1945); *Génie* (1947); *Inventions* (1958); *Moires* (1962); *Adventure de Catherine Grachat* (1963); *Wozzeck d'Alban Berg* (1964); *Ténèbre* (1965)

BIBLIOGRAPHY: Starobinski, J., Alexandre, P., and Eigeldinger, M., *P. J. J. poète et romancier* (1946); Micha, R., *P. J. J.* (1956); Callander, M., *The Poetry of P. J. J.* (1965); *Liberté*, IX (Jan.-Feb. 1967), *P. J. J. Special Issue*

GEORGES SCHLOCKER

JOUVET, Louis (Jules Eugène Louis)

French actor, theater critic, and director, b. 24 Dec. 1887, Crozon, Finistère; d. 16 Aug. 1951, Paris

More than anyone else, J. was responsible for the renaissance of the French theater during the *entre deux guerres* period. After a youth spent in the provinces, J. settled in Paris in 1906, ostensibly to study pharmacy. While studying at the Conservatoire, he joined the Action d'Art company and acted in a variety of roles in dramas that ranged from those of Molière to those of Ibsen (q.v.). When an attempt to become the director of the Théâtre d'Eau failed, J., in 1913, joined the newly formed Théâtre du Vieux Colombier, under the direction of the brilliant innovator Jacques Copeau. In 1917, after being discharged after three years of military service during World War I, J. went to the Garrick Theater in New York, with the troupe of the Vieux Colombier, at which he staged most of the productions and acted in seventeen widely diverse plays.

Following the reopening of the Vieux Colombier in Paris (February 1920), J. contributed seven new productions. In 1922 he went to the Théâtre des Champs Elysées, at which he was to assume the technical direction of the plays as well as to act in them. His greatest personal triumph there was in *Knock* by Romains (q.v.) in 1923; this role he performed 1,440 times during his life. (He also played the role in the two film versions of 1933 and 1951). In 1927, J., with Baty, Dullin, and Pitoëff, formed the famous *cartel,* a loose federation the members of which shared an ideology pledged to a rare noncommercial spirit.

In 1928 J. began what may have been the most felicitous episode of his theatrical career —the collaboration with Giraudoux (q.v.). Until the outbreak of World War II, J. staged and played in eleven of Giraudoux's plays, and worked with two more of them after the war. As an actor his outstanding successes were Hector in *La Guerre de Troie n'aura pas lieu* (1935) and Hans in *Ondine* (1939). In 1934, J. left the Théâtre des Champs Elysées to assume the direction of the Théâtre de l'Athénée, where he remained (with the exception of the war years, which he spent in Switzerland and in South America) until his death in 1951.

As a writer, J.'s volumes of *témoignages* show a polished professional who played and staged more by instinct ("*La vraie situation du théâtre est à l'intérieur même de l'acte dramatique*") than by reasoned analysis. Known chiefly as an actor and as a director, as one who was forever searching for new interpretations (his *Don Juan, L'École des Femmes,* and *Tartuffe* are milestones among Molière productions), J. was for two generations, both before and after World War II, the "patron" of French theater, a tireless worker who brought lasting excellence to an ephemeral world. To quote Louis Joxe, J. was truly the "*ambassadeur du génie français.*" His writings on the theater are fundamental to an understanding of 20th c. French drama.

FURTHER WORKS: *Réflexions du comédien* (1938); *Prestiges et perspectives du théâtre français—quatre ans de tournée en Amérique latine, 1941-45* (1945); *Témoignages sur le théâtre* (1952); *Ecoute, mon ami* (1952); *Le comédien désincarné* (1954)

BIBLIOGRAPHY: Cézan, C., *L. J. et le théâtre d'aujourd'hui* (1938); Hort, J., *Les Théâtres du Cartel et leurs animateurs: Pitoëff, Baty, J. et Dullin* (1944); Lipnitzki, H., *Images de L. J.* (1952); Marquetty, V., *Mon ami J.* (1952); Knapp, B., *L. J., Man of the Theatre* (1957); Bibliothèque Nationale, *Exposition organisée pour le 10e anniversaire de sa mort* (1961); Kérien, W., *L. J., notre patron* (1963)

PAUL A. MANKIN

JOVINE, Francesco
Italian novelist, b. 9 Oct. 1902, Guardialfiera, Campobasso; d. 30 April 1950, Venice

J. was a neorealist with socialist tendencies. Anecdotes and legends from the province of Molise furnish the material for his *Il Ladro di galline* (1940) and *Signora Ava* (1942). *Il pastore sepolto* (1945) is a short story pervaded by imagination and history, make-believe and reality. *L'impero in provincia* (1945; Seeds in the Wind, 1946), is a politically satirical treatment of fascism. Shortly before his death J. wrote the novel *Le terre del Sacramento* (1950; The Estate in Abruzzi, 1952), upholding the relief of the disfranchised by a just society.

FURTHER WORKS: *Un uomo provvisiorio* (1934); *Tutti i mei peccati* (1948); *Racconti* (1960)

BIBLIOGRAPHY: De Tommaso, P., "F. J." *Belfagor,* XV (1960), 284-99; Mauro, W., *F. J., Carlo Bernari, Vasco Pratolini* (1963)

* * *

JOYCE, James (Augustine Aloysius)
Anglo-Irish novelist, short story writer, and poet, b. 2 Feb. 1882, Dublin; d. 13 Jan. 1941, Zurich

As the author of *Ulysses* (1922), J. became the creator of a new prose style and of a new novel form. According to T. S. Eliot (q.v.), he was the greatest master of English since Milton.

J. was educated by Jesuit fathers. This may account for the scholastic precision manifest in the aesthetic theories that J. formulated at the age of twenty. In them he analyzed the modern novel in Aristotelian and Thomistic terms. A strong influence was exerted on J. by his father, whom he characterized in the figure of Simon Dedalus in the novel *A Portrait of the Artist as a Young Man* (1916) and in that of H. C. E. in *Finnegans Wake* (1939). While still in college J. became familiar with the plays of Ibsen (q.v.). He studied Norwegian in order to be able to read Ibsen in the original and addressed a letter of homage to the Norwegian playwright, then in his seventy-third year. (It would seem from unpublished translations of *Vor Sonnenaufgang* and *Michael Kramer* that J. saw in G. Hauptmann [q.v.] a successor to Ibsen.)

The first product of J.'s pen to attract attention outside of Dublin was an essay on Ibsen's last play (in *Fortnightly Review,* April 1900). In this essay and another, "The Day of the Rabblement" (1901), J. dissociated himself from Irish nationalism as represented in particular by Yeats (q.v.), who was J.'s elder by seventeen years. He explained that a people that had not even been able to produce a miracle play could not possibly offer literary models to its writers, who must therefore go abroad in their quest for things to emulate. He characterized the theatergoing public of Dublin as a bunch of philistines who ruled arbitrarily from the boxes and galleries.

Combining themes from Elizabethan songbooks with the versifying technique that he had learned from Paul Verlaine (1844-96), J. thus managed in the thirty-six poems of *Chamber Music* (1907) to impart to the emotional content of the Dublin love songs of the time of his father a technical precision that was bound to impress his Dublin readers as strange and unwonted. This combination of a commonplace content with formal austerity is characteristic of everything J. ever wrote. His method consisted of rendering so concretely the world of Dublin everyday life that the spirit of other ages also could be seen.

Meanwhile, J. had left Ireland, taking Nora Barnacle with him, to make his home in Trieste. Later he lived in Pola and Rome, then returned again to Trieste. It was here that J.'s children Giorgio and Lucia were born, that he made a living as a language instructor, and that he worked on an autobiographical novel while looking for a publisher for his short stories. J. had written most of these stories in Dublin by 1904. The last story, "The Dead," was completed in 1907 in Trieste. This collection of fifteen stories, which was published in 1914 as *Dubliners,* describe childhood, adolescence, maturity, and public life as they existed in Dublin. These stories, which indicate that J.

was influenced by Ibsen and by the Flaubert of *Trois Contes,* are the work not of a promising beginner but that of a master.

Shortly before the outbreak of World War I, J. came to the attention of Pound (q.v.), who included a poem from *Chamber Music* in his anthology *Des Imagistes* (1914) and continued throughout the following years to take an active interest in J. It was through Pound's good offices that *A Portrait of the Artist as a Young Man* was printed in the periodical *Egoist* and that *Ulysses* appeared in *The Little Review* (1918-20). In addition, Pound induced J. to go to live in Paris, where he introduced him to Sylvia Beach (who published *Ulysses* in 1922). And it was Pound who got for J. the subsidy from Harriet Shaw that rescued him from poverty. Most of *Ulysses,* which had been begun in Trieste, was written in Zurich (where J. and his family, fleeing from World War I, lived from 1914 to 1918) and completed in Paris (to which he returned in 1920).

Having won the acclaim of the Parisian postwar expatriates, J. now labored for seventeen years on a "Work in Progress," which first appeared in *transition* (a periodical published under the direction of Eugène Jolas) and then came out in book form in 1939 under the title of *Finnegans Wake.* The creation of this work was accompanied by considerable literary polemics. J. was claimed in the name of surrealism (q.v.) and various other avant-gard causes, both aesthetic and political. He himself, meanwhile, led the entirely unsensational life of the middle-class husband and father. The dreamlike texture of *Finnegans Wake* remains as closely associated with the atmosphere of J.'s native city as the naturalism of *Dubliners.* J. never attempted to emancipate himself from this ambience either in the products of his imagination or in his style of life.

In 1940 he and his family fled from Paris to Zurich, where he died after a grave illness. He was buried at the Fluntern cemetery.

The essential features of J.'s style can be discerned in the early *Chamber Music.* The presentation moves on two planes; every sentence projects simultaneously the orderliness of the past and the amorphous indeterminateness of the present. J.'s approach evolved not from the arbitrary decision of the author, but from a sort of fidelity to the material offered by Dublin. Here, "among the most backward people of Europe," the common usage of the spoken idiom carries an echo of the forms of language and of life of the past. Since romanticism had not intervened to sear these traces away, they had simply wilted and dried up. The style reflects the theme. That was J.'s artistic creed. And his theme was Dublin's dead and petrified style.

Though *Dubliners* is a collection of individual stories, it should be thought of as a whole. The first story tells of a paralyzed priest whose needs are taken care of by two elderly women; the last, of two old women who year after year arrange a Christmas party. J. is saying here that in this paralyzed city under the sway of priests, all of life—tradition, present culture, everything—stands under their guardianship. To be sure, the young may dream of escaping from these narrow confines, but since even their phantasies of getting away are shaped in the prevailing reality, the result is that they are caught in the ambience, whether it be in bitter resignation or smoldering rebelliousness. *Exiles* (1914), a drama written in the wake of Ibsen, crystallizes these ideas.

A Portrait of the Artist as a Young Man presents an uncommonly gifted young man who is formed by the world in which he lives and who sets about defending himself against it. For a while his effort to break away seems to be succeeding, but then he becomes enmeshed in out-dated romantic clichés that are new nowhere but in Dublin. Molded by the world he rejects, he is after all the negative impression of it. Carrying the name of St. Stephen, the first Christian martyr (the deacon of the church at Jerusalem who was stoned to death because of his visions), and the name of a Greek hero, Stephen Dedalus is very much (as the title of the book suggests) a self-portrait of J. in his younger years. He is, in fact, a humorless stereotype of the rebel that J. himself barely escaped becoming. Toward the end of the novel, now ready to fly, he spreads his wings.

But in the opening pages of *Ulysses,* Stephen is back in Dublin. His flight took him no farther than Paris and the Left Bank of the Seine. In the course of the day in which the action of *Ulysses* takes place, he meets, while wandering about his native city, in a mysterious predestined way, his spiritual father. But the man cast for that role is neither his effervescent real father nor the artful legendary hero Daedalus of his mythological dreams but an unsuspecting Jewish advertising agent, the *homme moyen sensuel* of the democratic age. Telemachus has found his Ulysses, and the progenitor of the Promethean rebel (of the stamp of a Byron or a Rimbaud) turns out to be the apotheosis of

precisely the sordidly uninspiring philistinism from which he thought he had escaped in horrified revulsion. The advertising agent Leopold Bloom spends eighteen hours wandering about a grotesque, danger-studded Dublin—the ever-restive eternal Jew unknowingly playing the part of a reincarnation of the Greek hero of the seas. With every new episode the style of the work undergoes fundamental changes, while scene after scene of modern civilization appears before us. At the close of the book Stephen disappears in the darkness of night while the Blooms are about to go to sleep.

It seems then consistent that *Finnegans Wake* should be a night book written in a dream language which owes something to the word inventions in Lewis Carroll's *Through the Looking Glass* and to Sigmund Freud's findings relative to the verbal distortions caused by the subconscious. The only reality of Dublin, its language, takes on a ghostly life, while everything else is submerged in sleep. The dreamer, an innkeeper, is characterized with many traits reminiscent of J.'s father. In him is embodied the entire past of Dublin, which the new order represented by De Valera's free state is about to replace. It is a radical process of transformation similar to the one which around 1920 effected in Ireland an abrupt substitution of the 19th c. for the 18th. In the dream, transformed into myths, are motifs from everyday life that owe their existence exclusively to accidental word sounds and word associations. This is the author's final evaluation of his native city. If the place itself is the dreamer, the river Liffey taking away the refuse is his or its wife. The book closes in the melancholy murmur of a flowing monologue while the turning earth carries the speakers toward a multifariously ambiguous and indefinite twilight.

J. had at his command a tremendous technical equipment to which all those coming after him are deeply indebted. The procedure of simultaneities, the transposing of things not said, the leitmotif-like use of specific key words and phrases, syncopes of language suggestive of interruptions in the stream of consciousness—all that has been often imitated (see interior monologue). This technique, a surface phenomenon, is neither essential nor decisive but it has obscured, or, at least, relegated to the background, what J. actually had to teach. This is the lesson of the painstakingly precise rendition of the structure of a given theme. For J. the theme was Dublin, but it was not in Dublin that J. sought to establish a reputation for himself. He addressed himself to being recognized by world literature about which, prior to J., no one in Ireland had seen fit to bother. In Ireland, J. is considered an author of the self-evident and trivial. Elsewhere he is the victim of a misunderstanding that makes him the mouthpiece of a rebellion the vanity of which he in particular saw with unequaled clarity. The difficulties that J.'s work puts in the way of the average reader have kept a generation of critics busy. All these efforts, however, have to a large extent been concerned with externals and unessentials. Among the great figures of contemporary literature J. ranks easily as the least understood and most misunderstood. Honored but neither recognized nor grasped, he may well be called the greatest enigma in the literature of the 20th c.

FURTHER WORKS: *Ibsen's New Drama* (1900); *The Holy Office* (1904); *Gas from a Burner* (1912); *Pomes Penyeach* (1927); *Anna Livia Plurabelle* (1928, fragment of "Work in Progress," *i.e., Finnegans Wake*); *Tales Told of Shem and Shawn* (1929, fragments of "Work in Progress," *i.e., Finnegans Wake*); *Collected Poems* (1937); *Stephen Hero* (1944, fragment of the first draft of *A Portrait of the Artist as a Young Man*); *Letters* (1957); *The Cat and the Devil* (1964)

BIBLIOGRAPHY: Gorman, H. *J. J.: His First Forty Years* (1924); Smith, J., *A Key to the Ulysses of J. J.* (1927); Curtius, E. R., *J. J. und sein "Ulysses"* (1930); Dujardin, E., *Le monologue intérieur* (1931); Golding, L., *J. J.* (1933); Broch, H., *J. J. und die Gegenwart* (1936); Beckett, S., *et al., Our Exagmination Round His Factification for Incamination of "Work in Progress"* (1936); Gorman, H., *J. J.* (1940); Levin, H., *J. J.* (1941; rev. ed., 1960); Soupault, P., *Souvenirs de J. J.* (1943); Campbell, J., and Robinson, H. M., *A Skeleton Key to Finnegans Wake* (1944); Edel, L., *J. J.: The Last Journey* (1947); Kain, R. M., *Fabulous Voyager* (1947); Tindall, W. Y., *J. J., His Way of Interpreting the Modern World* (1950); Slocum, J. J., and Cahoon, H., *A Bibliography of the Writings of J. J.* (1953); Wilson, E., *Axel's Castle* (1953); Kenner, H., *Dublin's J.* (1956); Magalaner, M., and Kain, R. M., *J., The Man, the Work, the Reputation* (1956); Noon, W., *J. and Aquinas* (1957); Schutte, W. M., *J. and Shakespeare* (1957); Joyce, S., *My Brother's Keeper* (1958); Ellmann, R., *J. J.* (1959); Tindall, W. Y., *Reader's Guide to J. J.* (1959); Hodgart, M., and Worthington, M. P.,

Song in the Works of J. J. (1959); Mason, E., and Ellmann, R., eds., *The Critical Writings of J. J.* (1959); Beach, S., *Shakespeare and Company* (1959); Atherton, J., *The Books of the Wake* (1960); Litz, A. W., *The Art of J. J.* (1961); Adams, R. M., *Surface and Symbol* (1962); Hart, C., *Structure and Motif in "Finnegan's Wake"* (1962); Magalaner, M., ed., *A J. J. Miscellany* (1962); Hayman, D., ed. *A First-Draft Version of "Finnegan's Wake"* (1963); Hart, C., *A Concordance to "Finnegan's Wake"* (1963); Staley, T. F., ed., *J. J. Today: Essays on the Major Works* (1966)

HUGH KENNER

I hold this book [*Ulysses*] to be the most important expression which the present age has found. . . . .

J.'s parallel use of the *Odyssey* has the importance of a scientific discovery. No one else has built a novel upon such a foundation before. . . .

In using the myth, in manipulating a continuous parallel contemporaneity and antiquity, J. is pursuing a method which others must pursue after him.

It is simply a way of controlling, of ordering, of giving a shape and a significance to the immense panorama of futility and anarchy which is contemporary history.

Eliot, T. S., "Order and Myth," in *The Dial*, 75 (1923), pp. 480 ff.

It now seems to me that all that is negative, cold-blooded, bizarre and trivial, grotesquely infernal, represent positive virtues of J.'s works for which they should be praised. The terrible tedium and horrifying monotony of an unspeakably rich, a millionfold faceted, language of tapeworm-long creeping paragraphs is epically grandiose, a true mahabharata of the inadequacies of a human nook-and-cranny world and its substrata of folly and deviltry.

O Ulysses, you are a true book of prayers for the object-trusting, object-cursed, white-skinned race. You are a workbook of exercises, an ascetic experience, a torturous ritual, a magic manual of procedure, a series of eighteen circuited alchemical retorts, in which acids, poisonous vapors, cold, and heat will distill the homunculus of a new world consciousness.

Jung, C., *Wirklichkeit der Seele* (1934), pp. 164 ff.

The theme of birth may be regarded as the geometric locus, the focus of convergence of all the basic motifs of *Ulysses*, indeed, of the entire world of thought of J.

It is from this point that the complex of the father-son problem unfolds. But the problem of sexual polarity, the relationship between the male and the female principles, is likewise variously intertwined with it.

JAMES JOYCE

ERNST JÜNGER

In what literary genre should we class *Ulysses*? The book is a chronicle; it is a novel, drama, epic, satire, parody, *summa*. It is a new *Inferno* and a new *Comédie humaine*. In Chapter 15 the temptation of St. Anthony and the apocalypse and a Walpurgisnacht interact on each other. The work in its entirety is structurally related to the *Odyssey*, but it reminds us simultaneously of Rabelais and the Elizabethans. Its symbolism and its scholasticism establish its affinity with the Middle Ages. It is the all-related and yet completely unique, the grandiose, cruel, exalting, and depressing, work of a lonely, proud man.

Curtius, E. R., *Kritische Essays zur europäischen Literatur* (1950), pp. 307, 314

The illusion of an associative concatenation is maintained in J. throughout the length of gigantic works, with I functioning as a brooding or chattering agency of reception of the phenomenal world. As a result it appears that the author speaks not to his reader or listener but to himself and the figures that he himself has created.

Hohoff, C., *Geist und Ursprung* (1954), p. 46

To consider anything as falling outside the realm of what could be said or to suppress anything for reasons other than aesthetic would have meant violation of the law under which J. set out. Both the motive and the content in his writing stem from his irrepressible need—on a biological, historical, philosophical, theological plane—to establish mastery of the world in its timeless totality and to express it through artistic modalities.

Blöcker, G., *Die neuen Wirklichkeiten* (1957), p. 67.

The radical conventionality of outlook implied throughout *Ulysses*, and exhibited in the treatment of characters, isolated from their technical wrapping, has the following bearing upon what I have said elsewhere. This conventionality is the sign that we are in the presence of a craftsman rather than a creator. That sort of effect is invariably the sign of the simple craftsman—an absence of meaning, an emptiness of philosophic content, a poverty of new and disturbing observation.

In *Ulysses* you have a deliberate display, on the grand scale, of technical virtuosity and literary scholarship. What is underneath this overcharged surface, few people, so far, have seriously inquired. In reality it is rather an apological than a real landscape; and the two main characters, Bloom and Dedalus, are lay-figures (the latter a sadly ill-chosen one) on which such a mass of dead stuff is hung, that if ever they had any organic life of their own, it would speedily have been overwhelmed in this torrent of matter, of *nature-morte*.

This torrent of matter is the einsteinian flux. Or (equally well) it is the duration-flux of Bergson—that is its philosophic character, at all events. (How the specifically "organic" and mental doctrine of the time-philosophy can result in a mechanism that is more mechanical than any other, I shall be considering later.) The method of doctrinaire naturalism, interpreted in that way, results in such a flux as you have in *Ulysses*, fatally.

Lewis, Wyndham, *Time and Western Man* (1927), pp. 119 f.

Finnegans Wake carries even farther the kind of insight into such human relations which was already carried far in *Ulysses*; and it advances with an astounding stride the attempt to find the universally human in ordinary specialized experience which was implied in the earlier book by the Odyssean parallel. J. will now try to build up inductively the whole of human history and myth from the impulses, conscious and dormant, the unrealized potentialities, of a single human being, who is to be a man even more obscure and even less well endowed, even less civilized and aspiring, than was Leopold Bloom in *Ulysses*. . . .

Instead of the myths' growing out of Earwicker, Earwicker seems swamped in the myths . . . he is not so convincing as Bloom was: there has been too much literature poured into him. . . . And not merely has he to carry this load of myths; he has also been all wound round by what seems J.'s growing self-indulgence in an impulse to pure verbal play.

Wilson, E. *The Wound and the Bow* (1947), pp. 254, 259

It also seems that J. (and how could it have been otherwise when the man's reason was as wakeful as it was?) meant to take a stand relative to the question of the possibility of providing a representation of the world, to the question of the possibility of the literary art as such, as though he wanted to prove (. . . through the complexity of his devices of representation, through the virtually rational esoteric approach on both the conceptual and verbal levels, . . . through this immense superstructure piled up by him over the underlying poetic immediacy that is still there) that what is represented through the success achieved in such a gigantic attempt, through the representation of the world thus successfully accomplished, is precisely the world's refusal to submit to representation, that what is expressed by the hypertrophic hyperexpressivity imposing itself as a necessity on the writer is precisely the inability to express of a world condemned to remain mute, and it is as though, shaken to the quick by these realizations, J. wanted to intone a superdimensional swan song.

Broch, H., *Dichten und Erkennen* (1955), p. 188

191

JÓZSEF, Attila

Hungarian poet, b. 11 April 1905, Budapest; d. 3 Dec. 1937, Balatonszárszó

When J. was three years old, his father deserted the family, which was living in the slums of Budapest, and left the country. J. published his first book of poems in 1922. In 1924 he was expelled from Szeged University, which he was attending on scholarship, as a result of the controversy aroused by the publication of his revolutionary poem *Tiszta Szivvel*. Throughout his life he was plagued by poverty and an acutely neurotic personality.

J.'s poetry was shaped by surrealist (see surrealism) and expressionist (see expressionism) influences, but the tone of his work as a whole was inspired by the Magyar literary idiom. In form and rhythm many of his poems resemble Magyar folksongs. In these often naive cadences, Marxian and Freudian concepts are intertwined with vivid descriptions of the miseries of the working class, images from his harsh childhood, and ambiguous verbalizations of his pathological obsessions.

Although, after 1934, his mental condition deteriorated, and with it his capacity for overcoming the conditions of his chronic poverty and the increasingly chaotic atmosphere of his time, his poetry became ever more brilliant. The poems written during the three years preceding his suicide are intensely subjective and painfully revealing soliloquies of his suffering. It is by virtue of these poems, and his earlier, proletarian poems, that J.'s place among the great Hungarian poets is assured.

J. published seven volumes of poetry during his lifetime, but general recognition of his genius did not come until after World War II.

FURTHER WORKS: *A szépség koldusa* (1922); *Nem én kiáltok* (1925); *Nincsen apám, se anyám* (1929); *Döntsd a tőkét ne sinránkozz* (1931); *Külvárosi éj* (1932); *Medvetánc* (1934); *Nagyon fáj* (1936); *J. A. összes versei* (1948), *Poems* (1960)

BIBLIOGRAPHY: József, J., *J. A. élete* (1940); *Homage à A. J. par les poètes français* (1955); Rousselot, J., *A. J., sa vie, son oeuvre* (1958)

ZOLTAN L. FARKAS

JÜNGER, Ernst

German novelist and essayist, b. 29 March 1895, Heidelberg

Already as a boy, J. found himself at odds with middle-class life and, generally, the age into which he was born. He joined the rebellious youth movement and even made an abortive attempt to join the French Foreign Legion. When World War I broke out, he immediately enlisted and greatly distinguished himself at the western front. From 1919 to 1923 he served in the army of the Weimar Republic.

J. began his career as a writer by setting down his unusual war experiences. *In Stahlgewittern* (1920; Storm of Steel, 1929) is the gripping account of the heroic exploits of an infantry soldier and leader of shock troops; it also expounds the conviction that World War I was but the first encounter in a planetary conflagration of ever-broadening scope and ever-increasing violence. Though not J.'s best book, *In Stahlgewittern* has been most widely read. He elaborated on his war experiences in *Der Kampf als inneres Erlebnis* (1922), *Das Wäldchen 125* (1925; Copse 125, 1930), and *Feuer und Blut* (1925).

From 1923 to 1925, J. studied zoology and philosophy at the University of Leipzig. Although not concluding his studies, he developed an abiding and scientifically productive interest in entomology. His concern with the ultimate issues also endured and deepened in time. As a result, J.'s writings (whatever their themes) constitute an original and provocative blend of keen observation and truly probing speculation.

After moving to Berlin in 1927, J. became active in radically nationalistic organizations, serving their journals as contributor and editor. During that time he developed his political philosophy, which he designated as *heroischer Realismus* and which may be characterized as "militant nihilism" or "aggressive totalitarianism." Convinced that the world was engulfed in a fundamental crisis, the ideas and ideals of democratic humanism having lost their cohesive force and motivating power, and that the ultimate struggle for power and world domination was imminent, he called for "total mobilization" (*Die totale Mobilmachung*, 1930). In *Der Arbeiter* (1932) J. describes the emergence of a new type of man who, by virtue of his technical skill and military prowess, is destined to conquer and reorganize a chaotic, strife-torn world. *Der Arbeiter* is J.'s most significant political treatise; it is the only radical, honest, and comprehensive exposition of totalitarianism written in Germany.

When Hitler came to power in 1933, J. soon convinced himself that a philosophy of agressive totalitarianism had been achieved by a plebeian and criminal group of men. He declined the overtures by the new regime (it wanted to exploit the reputation of a war hero and radical nationalist) and withdrew from the political scene. He wrote of his short-lived adventure in the French Foreign Legion (*Afrikanische Spiele,* 1936 [African Diversions, 1954]) and radically revised *Das abenteuerliche Herz* (1938; first edition, 1929), finding a chiseled style and a trim form for his highly original and illuminating essays. *Sgraffiti* (1960) is a sequel to this collection of *"Figuren und Capriccios."*

In 1939 J. showed that he had joined the "inner emigration," those men and women who, while opposed to the National Socialist regime, had not gone into exile: *Auf den Marmorklippen* (1939; On the Marble Cliffs, 1947) is an allegory of the heinous practices of totalitarianism (it was sufficiently veiled to escape the censor). This novel constitutes the most significant turning point in J.'s career, for here he arrived, beyond a scathing criticism of the prevailing conditions, at a reaffirmation of the ideas and values of the humanistic tradition.

Upon the outbreak of World War II, J. was called back into the army. At first he served as company commander behind the lines; later he was attached to the staff of the commander-in-chief of the German forces occupying France. *Gärten und Straßen* (1942) and *Strahlungen* (1949) are the diaries setting down experiences totally different from his life in World War I. While stationed in Paris, J. was in close contact with those officers who were militantly opposed to the Hitler regime. Also he did not actively participate in the (disastrously abortive) putsch of July 20, 1944; he made his contribution by dint of his pen. *Der Friede* (1941-43, published in 1945; The Peace, 1948), while recognizing Germany's responsibility and guilt, is a plea for a constructive world peace and was intended as a foreign-policy statement of the anti-Hitler resistance. *Der Friede* marks also J.'s closest approach to the world and values of Christianity.

After the war J. was for a time forbidden to publish in Germany because of his erstwhile identification with totalitarianism. In 1949 *Heliopolis* appeared; it is an antiutopian novel dealing with the unresolved conflict between freedom and tyranny, between the humanistic tradition and nihilism. *Heliopolis* is also significant as a comprehensive recapitulation of

J.'s ideas as they evolved in the course of thirty years.

Since *Heliopolis* J.'s preferred mode of expression has been the essay. He has tried to show that nihilism can effectively be dealt with, that it can be overcome, not through political arrangements and social changes, but through the endeavor of the individual who reaffirms his powers. This belief in the autonomous individual and his creative forces is closely akin to the basic concept of existentialism, but J.'s ideas cannot be identified with either its secular or religious variety. He cannot embrace Christianity, although he recognizes its enduring values; on the other hand, he does affirm an objective spiritual reality. The myth is the matrix from which the individual derives the meaning of existence and his creative strength. Such convictions are expounded in *Über die Linie* (1950), *Der Waldgang* (1951), and *Der gordische Knoten* (1953). J. ponders the problem of time in *Das Sanduhrbuch* (1954), one of his most engaging and convincing essayistic accomplishments. Time in relation to history is the concern of *An der Zeitmauer* (1959). This essay is one of J.'s most ambitious undertakings: he tries to show that mankind and, indeed, the cosmos are about to enter into a new age.

The universal political prospects are the theme of *Der Weltstaat* (1960). J. does not consider the conflict between East and West as irreconcilable. On the contrary, he is satisfied that the adversaries are the unwitting agents of historic forces aiming at an ultimately constructive and peaceful reorganization of the planet. *Der Weltstaat* is not only complementary to *Der Arbeiter* (as J. rightly insists) but also to *Der Friede.*

In addition to being a novelist and an essayist, J. is also a writer of travelogues. *Dalmatinischer Aufenthalt* (1934) describes a sojourn on the Adriatic. In *Myrdun* (1943) J. relates in epistolary form a journey to Norway. A trip to Brazil is recorded in *Atlantische Fahrt* (1947). We then hear of the Mediterranean, which has exerted an enduring fascination on J.: *Ein Inselfrühling* (1948) tells of Rhodes and *Aus der goldenen Muschel* (1948) of Sicily. To Sardinia, J. returns regularly: *Am Sarazenenturm* (1955), *Serpentara* and *San Pietro* (1957). These travelogues are doubtless among J.'s finest accomplishments: a keen yet loving power of observation, a deep understanding of nature, history, and mythology, a capacity for suggesting the creative force that manifests itself in the phenomenon, a terse yet plastic style, and compact presentation enter into almost perfect combination.

One of J.'s major achievements has thus been described. To it we add the accounts of the heroic soldier of World War I asserting himself against machine and material (*In Stahlgewittern*), the unflinching analysis of the forces of nihilism as they are unfettered by the crisis of our age (*Der Arbeiter*), the exemplary document of the "inner emigration" (*Auf den Marmorklippen*), a convincing realization of the possibilities of "magic realism" (*Das abenteuerliche Herz*), and a far-reaching view of the resolution of the conflict engulfing the planet (*Der Weltstaat*).

J. exerted a wide influence in the 1920's and early 1930's. During the Hitler regime he was mainly known as the author of a surprising and amazing critique of totalitarianism. When, after World War II, the discussion of Germany's recent history began, the baffling writings of J.'s protean mind were subjected to broad comment and heated controversy. However, the discussion of J.'s work has waned in recent years. Although much of it has been translated into a variety of foreign languages, it has found but scant recognition in the English-speaking countries.

FURTHER WORKS: *Blätter und Steine* (1934); *Sprache und Körperbau* (1947); *Besuch auf Godenholm* (1952); *Rivarol* (1956); *Gläserne Bienen* (1957; The Glass Bees, 1961); *Jahre der Okkupation* (1958); *Werke* (10 vols., 1961-65); *Das spanische Mondhorn* (1962); *Geheimnisse der Sprache* (1963); *Typus, Name, und Gestalt* (1963); *Subtile Jagden* (1967)

BIBLIOGRAPHY: Block, E., *Das Weltbild E. Js.* (1945); Martin, A. v., *Der heroische Nihilismus und seine Überwindung. E. Js. Weg durch die Krise* (1948); Paetel, K. O., *E. J. Weg und Wirkung* (1949); Becher, H., *E. J.*; Nebel, G., *E. J.* (1949); Müller-Schwefe, H. R., *E. J.* (1951); Stern, J. P., *E. J.: A Writer of Our Time* (1953); Paetel, K. O., *E. J. Eine Bibliographie* (1953); Mohler, A., ed., *Die Schleife. Dokument zu ... E. J.* (1955); Loose, G., *E. J. Gestalt und Werk* (1957); Paetel, K. O., *E. J. in Selbstzeugnissen und Bilddokumenten* (1962); Schwarz. H.-P., *Der konservative Anarchist* (1962); Shaw, M., "The Continuity of E. J.," *TSLL*, VI (1965), 472-85; Arnold, H. L., ed., *Wandlung und Wiederkehr* (*Festschrift* for E. J.'s 70th birthday, 1965)

GERHARD LOOSE

JÜNGER, Friedrich Georg

German poet, essayist, and fiction writer, b. 1 Sept. 1898, Hanover

An "early liking for animals and plants" (J.'s autobiography *Grüne Zweige,* 1951) links J. with his brother, Ernst (q.v.). Like his brother he served in World War I and was severely wounded in Flanders. He studied law in Leipzig after the war, worked in the government judiciary service, and thereafter practiced law. Later, in Berlin, he took up writing as a profession and was active with his brother in political journalism. In 1937 he moved to Überlingen on the Lake of Constance.

J. began as a poet in the tradition of Klopstock and Hölderlin, to whom he is linked by his strict meters and his closeness to classical antiquity. He recognizes the essence of the latter in the glorification of the elemental, especially water and light, in the heroic, and in the bucolic. He began a series of essays devoted to aesthetics, criticism of the times, and cultural philosophy in 1936 with the study *Über das Komische*. His contemporary orientation is reflected in *Die Perfektion der Technik* (1946) and its sequel *Maschine und Eigentum* (1949). J. condemns technology as being morally corrupting. His negative attitude to the modern trend is counterbalanced by his love of the world of the Greek myths; he sees the gods and Titans as eternally valid symbolic figures (*Die Titanen,* 1944; *Griechische Mythen,* 1947). In the poetry he has written since 1945, the lighter, more graceful trochee predominates, with shorter lines. Aristocratically reserved yet taking a polemical attitude to his time, J. immerses himself in the beauties of nature and tries in the Nietzschean tradition (see Nietzsche) to combine the Apollonian and the Dionysian, clarity and rapture.

Since 1950, J. has written chiefly fiction (*Dalmatinische Nacht,* 1950; *Die Pfauen,* 1952; *Zwei Schwestern,* 1956). *Der erste Gang* (1954) has no consecutive plot and is set mainly among Austrian soldiers during World War I. Its diagnostic acuteness and verbal beauty—the prime characteristics of J.'s work—justify this "novel," which is actually no more than a compositional experiment.

FURTHER WORKS: *Gedichte* (1934); *Der Taurus* (1937); *Der Missouri* (1940); *Griechische Götter* (1943); *Der Westwind* (1946); *Die Perlenschnur* (1947); *Die Silberdistelklause* (1947); *Das Weinberghaus* (1947); *Orient und Okzident* (1948; 2d rev. ed., 1966); *Gedanken und Merkzeichen* (2 vols., 1949-54); *Gedichte* (1949); *Nietzsche* (1949); *Iris im Wind* (1952); *Rhythmus und Sprache im deutschen Gedicht* (1952); *Die Spiele* (1953); *Ring der Jahre* (1954); *Schwarzer Fluß und windweißer Wald* (1955); *Spiegel der Jahre* (1958); *Kreuzwege* (1960); *Major Doboa und andere Erzählungen* (1965); *Wiederkehr* (1965); *Rythmus und Sprache im Deutschen Gedicht* (1966); *Die Pfauen und Andere Erzählungen* (1967); *Gesammelte Erzählungen* (1967)

BIBLIOGRAPHY: Podewils, S. D., *F. G. J.* (1947); Von Wiese, B., and Mohler, A., eds., *F. G. J. zum 60. Geburtstag* (1958); Condres, H. P., "F. G. J. Bibliographie," *Philobiblon*, VII (1963), 160-82

ALFRED HOLZINGER

JUST, Béla

Hungarian writer, b. 15 Jan. 1906, Budapest; d. 7 July 1954, Palma de Mallorca

After spending a year in Paris, J. became assistant at the Budapest Romanistic Seminar and was later a lecturer in Hungarian language and literature in Lyons and Grenoble.

His novels and short stories—the early ones written in Hungarian, the later ones in French—deal with contemporary problems, particularly the problem of freedom. *Les illuminés* (1936) is an account of a priest's attempt to reform church rites in terms of medieval Benedictine rules. The partly documentary novel *Allegro barbaro* (1951) describes the siege of Budapest and the communist victory; the central character of this work is a Jesuit priest who suffers a fate similar to that of Cardinal Mindszenty. In *Pêcheur de lune* (1951) J. tells a utopian love story, while *Mission à Paris* (1953) and *La potence et la croix* (1954) are novels about priests. With fine irony J. recounts the struggle of individuals against the unfair prejudices of society and its absurdities, most of which are unthinkingly accepted.

BIBLIOGRAPHY: Reményi, J., *Hungarian Writers and Literature* (1964)

HELMUT BENDER

K

KADEN-BANDROWSKI, Juliusz

Polish novelist, b. 24 Feb. 1885, Rzeszów; d. 6 Aug. 1944, Warsaw

K. had a leading position in Polish literary life and became general secretary of the Literary Academy of Poland. He was killed in the Warsaw revolt of 1944 against the Nazi invaders.

K. devoted himself mainly to an objective study of the mechanics of government and the political power game. In one of his major novels, *Generał Barcz* (1923), he analyzes the decline of the character of a fundamentally well-meaning dictator. In *Czarne skrzydła* (2 vols., 1928), he depicts class conflict in a Silesian mine, showing the compromising duplicity of the socialist party workers and union organizers.

K.'s style is baroque and rugged, and he presents well-rounded characters. Since he spared neither the left nor the right in his novels, critical reaction reflected political reactions. Nonetheless, K.'s *oeuvre* remains one of the most illuminating descriptions of 20th c. Polish society.

FURTHER WORKS: *Pilsudczycy* (1915); *Łuk* (1919); *Wyprawa wilenska* (1919); *Wiosna* (1920); *Podpulk Leopold Lis kula* (1920); *Rubicon* (1921; The Great Battle on the Vistula, 1921); *Przymierze serc* (1924); *Miasto mojej matki* (1925); *W cieniu zapomnianej olszyny* (1926; Call to the Cuckoo, 1948); *Nad brzegiem wielkiej rzeki* (1927); *Mateusz Bigda* (1933); *Życie Chopina* (1938)

BIBLIOGRAPHY: Guttry, A. v., "J. K.," in *Unbekannte Literatur* (1931); Czachowski, K., *Obraz wpólczesnej literatury polskiej*, III (1936), 51-98, 686-90; Kridl, M., *A Survey of Polish Literature and Culture* (1956); Krejči, K., *Geschichte der polnischen Literatur* (1958); Herman, M., *Histoire de la littérature polonaise* (1963)

* * *

KAFKA, Franz

Austrian narrative writer, b. 3 July 1883, Prague; d. 3 June 1924, Kierling, Austria

K. was the son of a well-to-do merchant. The young K.'s family friendships and sympathies were with his mother's relatives, a leading family in the German-speaking, German-cultured Jewish circles of Prague. His hatred for his father found expression, in 1919, in the unsent *Brief an den Vater* (1953; Letter to My Father, 1954). K.'s attitude toward the paternal authority, that is, his unresolved hatred and love, is usually regarded as one of the bases of his literary works.

K. attended the German *Gymnasium* in Prague. He was a competent student, despite his own later disavowals of this fact, and was well regarded by his instructors as well as by his schoolmates. In 1901 he began studying at the German University in Prague. Here he met Brod (q.v.), who became his lifelong friend and eventually his literary executor. Despite early plans for, and brief indulgence in, other fields —chemistry, Germanic studies, and art—K. acceded to pressure, probably socio-economic as well as paternal, and took up the study of law, receiving his doctorate in 1906.

In 1908, K. was appointed to a quasi-governmental insurance company. The work required no great exertion, but it held little interest for K., who came to regard it as a nerve-wracking threat to the calmness and solitude he required for his increasing literary activity. His social conscience, always considerable, was apparently heightened by his contacts with working-class people in connection with his duties for the insurance company.

K. was tormented not only by the disharmony between his civil career and his literary pursuits but also by his own indecisiveness about marriage, and by generally poor health. In 1917 his incipient tuberculosis first manifested itself. Despite his initial opposition, he agreed to undergo treatment, eventually relinquishing his civil position. The few remaining years of his life were spent in various sanatoriums, interspersed with short periods of residence in Prague, Berlin, and Vienna. In his last years K. studied Hebrew and in general deepened his connection with the religious, historical, and cultural aspects of Judaism. His disease meanwhile ran its fatal course. After almost seven years of struggle, he died in Kierling Sanatorium near Vienna.

The first literary influences on K. were those authors esteemed in the consciously German-cultured K. household and in the German *Gymnasium*. Goethe was esteemed by K. throughout his life, though one cannot speak of a continuing influence. In this category the most important name is Heinrich von Kleist (1777-1811). Gustave Flaubert's (1821-80) influence is almost equally important. Also of significance are Robert Walser, Hofmannsthal (qq.v.), Charles Dickens (1812-70) Adalbert Stifter (1805-1868), and Johann Peter Hebel (1760-1826). The presumed considerable influence on K. of the Danish philosopher Søren Kierkegaard (1813-55) lacks credibility. K. was not acquainted with the main body of Kierkegaard's work until 1917, by which time K. had already written (despite later publication dates) the major portion of his own *oeuvre*.

Although K.'s writings were published from 1909 on, he was always dissatisfied with his efforts, and he instructed Brod to destroy all his yet unpublished writing after his death. Instead, Brod edited the considerable material and published it. Critics have taken Brod to task for what they feel is his arbitrariness—though he is also occasionally accused of outright errors—in arranging and editing K.'s manuscripts. It has been asserted that Brod rearranged K.'s writings to suit his, Brod's, essentially religious, messianic interpretation, a charge against which Brod defends himself rather convincingly.

Religious, messianic, and eschatological interpretation of K.'s works has attracted a host of supporters since Brod; some, remarkably, find in K.'s works an orientation that is more Christian than Jewish. A second group of critics prefers a psychoanalytical approach. K., as a matter of fact, did have some acquaintance with Sigmund Freud's (1856-1939) early doctrine, and he was undoubtedly influenced by Freud's investigation of dreams. K.'s writings are to some extent, but often imperfectly, subject to Freudian exegesis. A more recent development in K. criticism in effect combines the religious and the psychoanalytic. The existentialists, at opposite poles from the religious interpreters, mistakenly point to K.'s late concern with Kierkegaard as evidence that Kafka was a sort of pre-existentialist. The sociologically oriented critics point to K. and his works as the end product of the particular German-Jewish situation in Czech Prague.

An older idea, that K.'s works are a development of the expressionistic movement, or at least of the ambiance that nurtured expressionism (q.v.), has gained some support once more. It is true that K.'s formative years were spent in association, though not very close association, with such stalwarts of expressionism as Werfel (q.v.). On the other hand, to state at least one obvious objection, K.'s precise, thorough descriptive style has little in common with expressionism, and much in common with naturalism (q.v.). But K. cannot easily be classified as a naturalist because his personal sympathy with the oppressed classes finds scant militantly programmatic reflection in his works.

Actually, little is to be gained by forcing K.'s works into this or that *ism*. He is almost completely *sui generis*. He surrounds his autobiographical protagonists with a meticulously described reality that nonetheless seems unreal. The resultant paradoxes, which perhaps are concretized, rationalized intensifications of the paradoxes of our essentially irrational life, have supplied ample material for the various schools of interpretation, which by and large reflect the critics' previous commitments to their own several philosophies.

Kafka's first published works were, in the journal *Hyperion,* the short dialogues "Gespräch mit dem Beter" (1909; Conversation with the Supplicant, 1948) and "Gespräch mit dem Betrunkenen" (1909), and in the Prague daily

Bohemia, the descriptive "Aeroplan in Brescia" (1909; The Aeroplanes at Brescia, 1946). The first two were written in 1904-1905, or by some accounts as early as 1902-1903, and comprise a portion of *Beschreibung eines Kampfes* (1936; Description of a Struggle, 1958). Some portions of *Beschreibung eines Kampfes,* together with other sketches, appeared under the title *Betrachtung* (1913; Meditation, 1940). The first published story of greater length was *Das Urteil* (1913; The Judgment, 1945). Even more than the earlier sketches, it gave an indication of the intensely autobiographical orientation that K.'s later works would have. The "judgment" in question is that of the father on the son, who thereupon commits suicide. In *Die Verwandlung* (1915; The Metamorphosis 1937), the son awakens to find himself changed into a monstrous bug that the father harries to death so that the family respectability, under the father's dominance, may be regained.

Ein Landarzt (1919; The Country Doctor, 1940) is a collection of fourteen tales. The theme of the title story is the disruption of an orderly but imperceptive existence by an irrational and oblivious world. *In der Strafkolonie* (1919; In the Penal Colony, 1941) again presents the K. father figure, this time as the old commander of the penal colony, devoted to the use of a horrible execution machine.

K.'s last story-length narratives were collected in a group published under the title *Ein Hungerkünstler* (1924; Hunger-Artist, 1938). The hero of the title story (which had been published separately in 1922) has chosen his odd —and in the course of the story it becomes obsolescent—profession because he cannot adapt himself to the world. The contrast figure is a healthy, hungry black leopard, who is admirably adapted, even in his world of captivity.

K.'s first novel, *Amerika* (1927; America, 1938), was written between 1911 (or 1912) and 1914 as *Der Verschollene.* The first chapter, *Der Heizer* (1913), had been published separately soon after its composition. Kafka's other two novels, which, like the first, were never completed, are *Der Prozeß,* begun around 1914 (1925; The Trial, 1937), and *Das Schloß* begun before 1922 (1926; The Castle, 1930). Brod's editions of all three novels have been criticized; it has been suggested that Kafka had in mind for *Amerika* and *Der Prozeß* a quite different sequence of chapters than the one that emerged from Brod's hands.

The novels are perhaps even more intensely autobiographical than the shorter works. All three expose a young man to the machinations of an ostensibly real, but nonetheless strange and inscrutable milieu. In *Amerika* the environmental counterforce is the country and its people. It is exceptional among the novels in that the environment is not consistently hostile to the hero. In *Der Prozeß* the antagonist is a court of law, the minions of which persistently and illogically bedevil the hero. In *Das Schloß* it is a mysterious officialdom that continually attracts, repels, bemuses. Each of the novels either ends, or was probably meant to end, in the death of the tortured hero.

The *Tagebücher 1910-23* (1951; The Diaries of Franz Kafka, 1948-49) offer a revealing confirmation of the personally hopeless situation behind Kafka's fiction. The style is typically disciplined and literal, a poignant contrast to the self-known tragedy of personal insufficiency that it often depicts. *Briefe an Milena* (1952; Letters to Milena, 1953) give a painfully detailed analysis of Kafka's love affair with the Czech girl Milena Jesenská. Kafka hoped to save himself by marriage, but his attitude toward getting married fluctuated considerably. Earlier, he had been engaged three times without getting married. Now once again a relationship, this time with Milena, already married, and non-Jewish, was not to lead to marriage. In his last invalid years K. did find a measure of happiness with his companion Dora Dymant.

Many of K.'s other letters, from 1902 until his death in 1924 (some of which, along with sketches and diary extracts, appeared in *Tagebücher und Briefe* [1937]) have been more recently collected and edited by Brod in *Briefe* (1958). Most of the letters are to Brod himself, but many others are included.

K., hardly known beyond a rather narrow circle of friends and enthusiasts during his lifetime, has now attained a belated international fame. His works, some of which waited decades for publication in the original German, and were only occasionally translated into Czech, have been published extensively in English, French, and Spanish translations. His works have also been translated, though less extensively, into such languages as Italian, Hebrew, and Norwegian.

FURTHER WORKS: *Das Urteil* (1913; The Judgment, 1948); *Beim Bau der chinesischen Mauer* (1931; The Great Wall of China, 1933); *Gesamtausgabe,* ed. Max Brod (6 vols., 1935-

FRANZ KAFKA

37); *Gesammelte Werke,* ed. Max Brod et al. (9 vols., 1950-58); *Hochzeitsvorbereitungen auf dem Lande* (1953; Wedding Preparations in the Country, 1954) *Briefe an Felice Bauer,* ed. E. Heller and J. Born (1967)

BIBLIOGRAPHY: Blei, F., *Zeitgenössische Bildnisse* (1940); Camus, A., *Le mythe de Sisyphe* (1942); Hoffmann, F. J., *Freudianism and the Literary Mind,* pp. 181-192 (1945); Flores, A., ed., *The K. Problem* (1946); Slochower, H., ed., *A F. K. Miscellany,* 2d ed. (1946); Brod, M., *F. K.: A Biography* (1947); Goodman, P., *K.'s Prayer* (1947); Brod, M., *F. K.'s Glauben und Lehre* (1948); Neider, C., *The Frozen Sea* (1948); Tauber, H., *F. K.: An Interpretation of His Works* (1948); Eisner, P., *F. K. and Prague* (1950); Brod, M., *F. K. als wegweisende Gestalt* (1951); Beißner, F., *Der Erzähler F. K.* (1952); Bense, M., *Die Theorie K.'s* (1952); Heller, E., *The Disinherited Mind: Essays in Modern German Literature and Thought,* pp. 157-181 (1952); Demetz, P., *René Rilkes Prager Jahre,* p. 107 ff. (1953); Janouch, G., *Conversations with K.* (1953); Goth, M., *F. K. et les lettres françaises* (1956); Reiß, H., *F. K.: Eine Betrachtung seines Werkes* (1956); Uyttersprot, H., *Eine neue Ordnung der Werke K.'s? Zur Struktur von "Der Prozeß" und "Amerika"* (1957); Weltsch, F., *Religion und Humor im Leben und Werk F. K.'s* (1957); Beißner, F., *K. der Dichter* (1958); Benson, A. T., "F. K.: An American Bibliography," *Bulletin of Bibliography,* XXII (1958), 112-14; Flores, A., and Swander, H., eds., *F. K. Today* (1958); Hemmerle, R., *F. K.: Eine Bibliographie* (1958); Wagenbach, K., *F. K.: Eine Biographie seiner Jugend* (1958); Brod, M., *Verzweiflung und Erlösung im Werk F. K.'s* (1959); Strelka, J., *K., Musil, Broch und die Entwicklung des modernen Romans,* pp. 5-35 (1959); Anders, G., *F. K.* (1960); Borchardt, A., *K.'s zweites Gesicht: Der Unbekannte* (1960); Hermsdorf, K., *K.-Weltbild und Roman* (1960); Järv, H., *Die K.-Literatur: Eine Bibliographie* (1961); Gray, R., ed., *K.: A Collection of Critical Essays* (1962); Politzer, H., *F. K.: Parable and Paradox* (1962); Richter, H., *F. K.: Werk und Entwurf* (1962); Sokel, W. H., *F. K.* (1966); Emrich, W., *F. K. A Critical Study of His Writings* (1968); Urzidil, J., *There Goes K.* (1968)

RICHARD H. LAWSON

While I lay special worth on the hopeful side of K.'s work, which rejoices in activity, that is to say in the fundamental recognition of the fact that man, with his spark of reason, will, and ethical perception is not altogether the plaything of super-mighty powers, who judge according to other laws than his, which he does not understand and never can understand, faced with which he is lost, and only thrown unconditionally on God's mercy—the old problem of Job—while underlining then the position of human freedom in the case of K., I do not of course wish to forget that this attitude of K.'s is only an occasional flash, and that passages which describe man as powerless, crowd in on the reader in an overwhelming majority. But the propositions of freedom and hope *are there, too*!

Brod, M., *F. K.: A Biography* (1947), p. 171

In K. we have before us the modern mind, seemingly self-sufficient, intelligent, sceptical, ironical, splendidly trained for the great game of pretending that the world it comprehends in sterilized sobriety is the only and ultimate reality there is—yet a mind living in sin with the soul of Abraham. Thus he knows two things at once, and both with equal assurance: that there *is* no God, and that there *must* be God. It is the perspective of the curse: the intellect dreaming its dream of absolute freedom, and the soul knowing of its terrible bondage. The conviction of damnation is all that is left of faith, standing out like a rock in a landscape the softer soil of which has been eroded by the critical intellect.

Heller, E., *The Disinherited Mind: Essays in Modern German Literature and Thought* (1952), p. 162

As soon as we recognize K.'s work to be a work of symbolic imagery, many apparent problems and contradictions resolve themselves. Indeed, the most diverse interpretations of the images (castle, trial, etc.) can be entertained as possible, conceivable, even tenable, provided none of them claims to be the only true one or to offer the objectively correct reading of the symbolism, and provided also that they confine themselves to ascribing a specific, possible meaning to the nonspecific parable. This is not to say that some interpretations of the symbolism will not prove more apposite and therefore more productive than others, while others again will disqualify themselves as completely inadequate and hence impossible. Ultimately, only the parable itself, with its symbolic multiplicity of meaning, is true.

Strelka, J., *K., Musil, Broch und die Entwicklung des modernen Romans* (1959), p. 11

There is not one self-explanatory word in a typical K. narrative. His mature prose shows nothing but a surface spread over happenings that remain profoundly impenetrable. Paradoxically this enables K., the visionary, to furnish his stories amply with realistic detail. Since even the inanimate objects he describes point to an undefined and mysterious background, they no longer relate to one another according to the customs and conventions of reality.

Clefts, cracks, and crevices open, revealing the depth behind the realistic detail. The same is true of the figures acting on a stage thus prepared. Ostensibly most of them are well gounded in reality, even in the reality of K.'s own life.

Politzer, H., *F. K.: Parable and Paradox* (1962), p. 17

K. denies that his God has moral grandeur, presence, goodwill, or coherent meaning, but he does this so that he may better embrace him. The absurd is recognized and accepted, man resigns himself to it, and from that moment on, we know that he is no longer absurd.

Camus, A., *Le Mythe de Sisyphe* (1942), p. 186

K. was well acquainted with the theory of psychoanalysis, as was the circle of young intellectuals which surrounded him, and a number of his stories such as "The Dog," "The Giant Mole," and "The Burrow" are more or less mechanical attempts to make a literary formula out of the symbolic system which Freud had detected in dreams.

West, R., "K. and the Mystery of Bureaucracy," *YR* (Autumn 1957), p. 14

It is in some such way as this that K. needs to be read—with a delicate and exact regard for his ability to portray his dreamlike inner life—the ability which, by his own confession, made it possible for him to write creatively. The reader will then see also, from this unitary point of view, the impressive coherence of the great novels, in which characters other than the main one also appear. But if the reader of *The Castle* takes the account of the landlady of the Bridge Inn doing this or that as implying that the land surveyor K. sees or learns that she does it, or the account of Olga saying this or that as implying that the land surveyor K. hears her say it, he will have gained a good deal in artistic understanding. Nothing happens without K.; nothing happens that has not some relationship to him, and nothing happens in his absence. Everything that happens, happens to him. And everything is told as clearly and as unclearly, as distortedly and as precisely, as he himself perceives it in his disappointment, his vexation, and his weariness. The "writer" does not stand beside him, explaining, teaching, and reflecting.

Beißner, F., "K. the Artist" in *K.: A Collection of Critical Essays*, ed. R. Gray (1962), p. 26

This is, as I said, where K. starts from. This sense of wanting to go with the rest of the people in the way they are going, and of not being able to, for too deep an awareness of futility: this is his most usual mood. And because he is by nature and upbringing so compelled to see insincerity, falsity, or sheer evil in himself and most things around him, the relentless pressure builds up into these long sentences, or even into the labyrinthine construction of a whole novel. Just as a neurotic will spin on and on with the

200

exploration of his own motives, explaining one by another, and that by another, so K.'s compulsive need drives him to these ramified constructions, both in the individual parts and in the wholes of his works. This was his nature; he had to be true to this if he was to be a writer, and if the result is often oppressive, it also exerts a fascination simply because it is so ruthlessly faithful to K.'s experience as it came to him.

Gray, R., "K. the Writer," in *K.: A Collection of Critical Essays*, ed. R. Gray (1962), p. 67

In this, too, K. has described the situation of "modern" man with precision: he has fallen completely into the clutches of the "earthly" world. The crucial element, however, in this story ["Der Jäger Gracchus"] as well as in all of K.'s stories—the element, too, that characteristically distinguishes K. from his contemporaries—is the fact that the hunter who moves in this earthly world is a "dead" person who does not belong to this earthly world at all, whom no one understands, and who, by the same token, does not understand any living person.

This "dead" person who is "in a certain sense alive, too," embraces in the midst of the earthly world the duality of death and life. Only now can one understand why this story represents the universal in its universal significance, the totality of all that is, the All-encompassing that has crossed the borders between life and death, that is found both *above* and *within* all that is. In him the mystery of all that is has awakened: everything that all human beings, mountains, and stars, from the beginning of time to the present, have told one another and continue to call out to one another.

A twofold aspect results from this: on the one hand, this dead and, at the same time, living man possesses total perspective, universal knowledge of all that has been and is; he "could be an interpreter between the people of today and their ancestors" and also has broken through all boundaries of space: "Good gracious, a man from Hamburg, and here in the South you know that he died today?" On the other hand, by reason of this intermediate position of his between life and death, he no longer fits into any fixed earthly or spiritual classification; he sails "without a rudder," completely disoriented upon the earthly waters, and is, therefore, able to reach and comprehend neither the limited world of ideas of the much-occupied living, nor the "gate" of the Hereafter that "shines on high."

Emrich, W., *F. K.: A Critical Study of His Writings* (1968), p. 10

His book [*Der Prozeß*] evades all rational explanation; the realism of its descriptions constantly crosses over into the imaginary, and I hardly know which I admire more: the "naturalistic" notation of a fantastic universe (which nevertheless seems real to our eyes, thanks to the minute exactitude of the descriptions) or the sure-handed boldness of the excursions into the strange . . . .

The *angst* that pervades this book is at times almost unbearable, for how can you avoid saying to yourself: this hounded creature is I?

Gide, A., *Pages de Journal* (1945), p. 93

He [K.] is like a man skiing on loose stones; by his somersaults and bruises he wants to prove to those who pretend the stones are snow that they are nothing but stones.

Like a man sitting before an empty plate and obstinately scooping up mouthfuls with his spoon in order to show those who think the plate is full that it is in fact empty.

Like a man who translates the cracks in slate-rocks as if they were hieroglyphics; by the very absurdity of his translation he wants to prove to those who always talk about the meaning of rock-formations that the cracks are really nothing but cracks.

Anders, G., *F. K.* (1960), p. 96

KAISER, Georg

German dramatist and novelist, b. 25 Nov. 1878, Magdeburg; d. 4 June 1945, Ascona, Switzerland

Between 1917 and 1933 K. was the most frequently performed dramatist in Germany. The performance of *Die Bürger von Calais* in 1917 was considered a landmark in the history of German drama; the production of *From Morn to Midnight* in New York City in 1922 started a new trend in modern American theater.

K., after completing his secondary education and commercial apprenticeship in Magdeburg, spent three years in Italy, Spain, and South America as a businessman. He contracted malaria on a journey into the interior of Argentina and returned to Germany a semi-invalid. From then on, he devoted all his time to writing. His health improved and he married in 1908. His literary output increased considerably though he did not publish anything before 1911. Beginning in 1917, he earned large sums of royalties, yet, he was never financially secure.

In 1933, his work was officially suppressed in Germany by the Nazis. In 1936 he fled from Grünheide near Berlin, where he had been living since 1921, via Holland to Switzerland. There he lived as an indigent refugee to his death in 1965. He continued writing and reached the height of his artistic accomplishments in the verse dramas of his last years. They did not, however, gain the attention of the public.

K.'s unpublished works have been assembled by the Georg-Kaiser-Archive in Berlin.

K.'s earliest play, *Schellenkönig* (unpublished manuscript 1895-96), an impressionistic verse drama, reveals the poet's sensibility to the conflict that inherently exists between true humanity and conventional formalism, between harsh reality and aesthetic illusion, and shows the dialectic trend that is apparent throughout his whole work. The influence of Hofmannsthal, Holz, and Gerhart Hauptmann (qq.v.) was replaced by that of Wedekind (q.v.) when in 1903, K. wrote *Rektor Kleist* (1918). He called it "a tragedy of illness and yearning." It is a tragicomedy on a schoolboy's suicide caused by the conflict between a deformed intellectual principal and an energetic athletic teacher. It is a bitter satire on the weakness and the stupidity of adults. The educator is only one representative of the numerous figures of middle-class society whose dullness and dishonesty, greed and insipidity, are the subjects of acid comedies that K. wrote before 1911, later revising and publishing them. The unaired livingroom of the bourgeois is the sphere of K.'s witty caricatures of his contemporaries.

The heroic-mythological world of the Old Testament, of medieval romance, and of Greek legends is the magical background for pagan eroticism in a voluptuous comedy, *Die jüdische Witwe* (1911), tense tragedy *König Hahnrei* (1913), and a vibrating dance play, *Europa* (1915). The vitalism of Nietzsche's (q.v.) *Zarathustra* is set against life-sapping intellect and conventional values, against impotence of body and heart, and against hyperaestheticism. To the theater audience of 1920, beautiful Europa's choice of the snorting bull seemed to symbolize contemporary Europe's recent involvement in war. K. himself, however, had not decided for the warrior against the cultivated artisan or the thinker.

Against traditional shallow patriotism that destroys rather than preserves human accomplishments, against the impulsive action of emotionalism that returns to selfishness when the spark of excitement is extinguished, K. shows—in his powerful masterpiece *Die Bürger von Calais* (1914)—the true hero who sacrifices himself for the common good and for new ideals of nonviolence and peace. Based on the medieval story of the French chronicler Jean Froissart (ca. 1333-1400) and inspired by Auguste Rodin's statues of the burghers of Calais, the drama transmits the poet's message of the New Man in an eloquent language that is contrasted to the silent action at important moments. The suicide of the burgher Eustache

201

de Saint Pierre confirms the regeneration of man.

Unlike this, the crucifixion and the rasping sigh, *ecce homo,* of the dying cashier in the earlier play *Von Morgens bis Mitternachts* (1916; From Morn to Midnight, 1920) indicates only the escape of a "man" from humdrum reality. A passion play, it is structured after the pattern of Strindberg's (q.v.) *Road to Damascus.* Nameless figures identified only by their occupations (cashier, clerk), their social roles, or their family functions (mother, wife) also remind one of Strindberg. Minor figures are named solely by their attributes (gentleman in evening dress).

Von Morgens bis Mitternachts is the first of a long line of K.'s expressionistic social dramas that point not only to new forms of existence, to the vision of a new man or a new society, but also to new methods and techniques and a new language. The plot is repeated in numerous variations: a man breaks away from conventions or the boredom of his everyday existence to search for a fuller meaning of life, of his own self, of society, or of his relation to society. The places of action are not localized; a bank, a factory, an office, a sports arena, a nightclub, stand for all banks, factories, etc. The billionaire or the petit bourgeois, the worker or the scientist-engineer, all of them stand for contemporary man. The vision of the New Man is overshadowed by doubt.

The *Gas* trilogy consisting of *Die Koralle* (1917; The Coral, 1929), *Gas* I (1918; Eng., 1924); *Gas II* (1920; Eng., 1931) shows that only spiritual renewal, and not social or economic reforms, can bring about salvation. It ends with a horrible preview of an entirely mechanized world and its final self-annihilation: "The Kingdom is not of this world."

Only one of K.'s plays promises redemption of mankind in this world: *Hölle, Weg, Erde* (1919). Hell is the present society indulging in exploitation and selfish greed; Road is the birth of social responsibility; Earth is the goal that is man guided by love for his fellow man. Earth resounds because man himself creates paradise when his soul sings the song of love. In *Nebeneinander* (1923), a new technique exceeding the method of the passion play was utilized to underline the meaning of the play, i.e., the isolation of man in an indifferent, selfish, competitive society. Three plots develop side by side in three sections of the stage.

The vision of the New Man appears in a different form in the dramas dealing with love between man and woman. The sexual desire that the characters of the early comedies experience—which still had a part as a symbol of true passion against the pretenses of convention in his first social dramas—has given way to true compassion. References to the present are strictly avoided, and historical settings force the attention to the inner action. Sometimes sensational and pretentious appeals to the instincts of a theater audience place these plays in an inferior class. Woman, through her self-sacrifice, makes man understand and experience true love: *Juana* (1918), the countess in *Das Frauenopfer* (1918), Sylvette in *Der Brand im Opernhaus* (1919; Fire in the Opera House, 1927).

During these years a variety of topics and settings, the virtuosity and facility of a furiously working artist, a mixture of dialectics and experimentation, of ecstasy and irony appeared both admirable and confusing. His essays answer this confusion. In them K. wrote of the "one vision" of the regeneration of man ("Vision und Figur," *Das Junge Deutschland,* 1918). He also wrote about the dignity of the dramatist who expresses his thoughts in yes and no, in thesis and antithesis, as Plato did through the figures of his dialogues. He described the thinker who transmutes intellectual perception into dramatic figures in order to perceive more deeply. Finally, he pronounced that writing a drama is equal to bringing a thought to its conclusions, that drama is only transition, and that it is the duty of the creative writer to turn his back on his work and to go into the desert in order to return with new treasures.

Socrates and Alcibiades, as they appear in Plato's *Symposium* and in one of Friedrich Hölderlin's (1770-1843) odes, are the figures representing ideas in *Der gerettete Alkibiades* (1920), a masterpiece of dramatic architecture that unites the clarity of cubism and the trichotomy of Gothic art. It could be called a profound comedy or a sparkling tragedy. The preceding dramatic themes return in unison: dialectic opposition of life and thought, regeneration of man, and self-sacrificing love. A thorn in his foot makes Socrates stop the flow of pulsating life around him, brings him to point to the futility of the "game with arms and legs," and also causes him to realize that the body is master so long as there is life. He welcomes death that frees him from a painful illness—life. Yet, he declares that he must die

GEORG KAISER

GUÐMUNDUR KAMBAN

to save the image of Alcibiades, which embodies the beauty and gaiety of Greece, of life itself. He exhorts Xantippe to do her duty as midwife and to help new human beings into life. The old generation that condemned the thinker will disappear—life is with the young. Among them is Plato, and they are with Socrates in his last hour. In *Die Flucht nach Venedig* (1923), it is not thought but the word (literature) that kills life. The vampirism of the writer is personified in George Sand, who assembles material for future tales from the agonies of those who love her.

The same exclusiveness that seems to be a prerogative of art in several works of K. becomes even more striking in his dramas of love. Love as an esoteric experience that strives for a final "mystical union" beyond this world, forces Marrien to the side of Catherine in her struggle against brutal reality in *Oktobertag* (1928; The Phantom Lover, 1928). He must slay the butcher Leguerche, the physical father of Catherine's child, so that the mystical marriage can take place. As in Heinrich von Kleist's (1777-1813) dramas, nothing can stop K.'s characters from an unconditional surrender to a mysterious passion.

This absoluteness assumes rather grotesque forms in *Rosamunde Floris* (1940), the heroine of which becomes a triple murderess to keep her love secret and untainted. In *Alain und Elise* (1940) the woman criminally and cruelly ruins the man, a promising young painter. When because of her false accusations, he is at the point of being deported, both of them know that in spite of physical separation their love will live to the end of creation. In *Der Gärtner von Toulouse* (1938) the protagonist demands the same absoluteness in his quest for purity as Elise does in her quest for love. To the gardener, love is without value if his companion is not immaculate. Yet, in *Die Lederköpfe* (1928), it is through love that the king's daughter changes the general, who once mutilated himself for the cause of war, into an antimilitaristic rebel. During the revolt and the slaying of the tyrannical king, the general himself is killed, after which the king's daughter leads the soldiers in order to build a new world. The story of the two lovers had grown into a passionate condemnation of war.

After the outbreak of World War II, K. pointed again to the inhumanity of militarism and war. The novel *Villa Aurea* (1940; A Villa in Sicily, 1939) is a poignant disclosure of false ideals and values. A Russian officer of World War I exchanges his identity with a dead common soldier. Many years later, before a final atonement, in obscurity, he writes to his wife who believes that he has fallen in war and who still loves his heroic image; but she does not recognize her husband when he stands before her.

K. blamed Georg Büchner's (1813-37) Woyzek because he let himself be crushed by evil without a fight. His own *Soldat Tanaka* (1940) is about a Woyzek figure; Tanaka is a soldier son of a poor rice farmer, who grows into the status of the New Man because he revolts in action and words against evil. When the judge tries to save him from execution under the condition that he ask the emperor's pardon, Tanaka makes the court visualize the emperor asking his—Tanaka's—forgiveness for all misery —war, exploitation, and suppression. Tanaka is executed.

Griechische Dramen (*Zweimal Amphitryon; Pygmalion, Bellerophon,* 1948), three classical dramas of five acts in blank verse, were written in 1943-44 and published posthumously. K. developed his own plots, using only the names and the bare outlines of Greek mythology, and disregarded former dramatic adaptations. In rapturous words, he expressed his love for the beauty of the world that divinity had created; and he unleashed his loathing and his rage against men who destroyed it. He says in *Zweimal Amphitryon* that divinity loaned the holy fire of creative force to mankind, and that corrupted species suffocated it in the holocaust and murder of war. Zeus is ready to throw his lighting to annihilate man. But the voice of human love rises up to him from Alkmene's mouth, and as the god of creation is also the god of grace, he allows the sinner Amphitryon to sacrifice and to atone. As a patient goatherd, he will guard the flocks until the birth of the son of Zeus calls him home to be the foster father of the New Man.

In *Pygmalion* the sculptor must learn through suffering that lovely innocence is safe when hidden in stone, but that when a graceful girl comes to life out of it, she is exposed to the multishaped, muddy monster—greediness of the senses, covetousness, and stupid pride. Man has lowered himself into the mire and is overdue for perdition. For the sake of the artist, the gods will grant a respite. Purple roses, new works, will burst into bloom from the bleeding wounds; but "life and dream shall not be one."

Apollo has granted *Bellerophon* time on earth to find a girl companion as pure and lovely as he. Then Anteia (evil voluptuousness), Proitos (dull avidity and uninhibited lust of a tyrant), and Iobates (helpless tool of an evil man) sink into nothingness. K. repeated what he had said in Villa Aurea: violated and violators are doomed. Those who must obey are desecrated and damned as are the tyrants. Pegasus carries Bellerophon, the artist, the favorite of the gods, and his bride away from men into the blue starry night.

FURTHER WORKS: Die Sorina (1917); Konstantin Strobel (other title: Der Zentaur, 1916); Die Versuchung (1917); Claudius, Friedrich und Anna, Juana (1918); David und Goliath (1921; other title: Großbürger Möller); Kanzlist Krehler (1922); Der Protagonist (1922; The Protagonist, 1960); Noli me tangere (1922); Der Geist der Antike (1923); Gilles und Jean (1923); Kolportage (1924); Gats (1925); Der mutige Seefahrer (1926); Zweimal Oliver (1926; Two Olivers, 1932); Papiermühle (1927); Der Präsident (1927; other title: Der Kongreß); Der Zar läßt sich photographieren (1927); Gesammelte Werke (2 vols., 1928); Hellseherei (1929); Zwei Krawatten (1929); Mississipppi (1930); Es ist genug (1932); Der Silbersee (1933); Adrienne Ambrossat (1935); Der Schuß in die Öffentlichkeit (1939); Der englische Sender (1940); Napoleon in New Orleans (1941); Die Spieldose (1942); Das Los des Ossian Balvesen (1947); Agnete (1948); Das Floß der Medusa (1948; Medusa's Raft, 1951); Klawitter (1948); Pferdewechsel (1954); Vincent verkauft ein Bild (1954)

BIBLIOGRAPHY: Diebold, B., Der Denkspieler G. K. (1924); Freyhan, M., G. K.'s Werke (1925); Koenigsgarten, H. F., G. K. (1928); Diebold, B., Anarchie im Drama (1938); Fivian, E. A., G. K. (1947); Schütz, A., G. K.'s Nachlaß (1951); Kenworthy, B. J., G. K. (1957); Behrsing, K., G. K. (1958); Paulsen, W., G. K. (1960); Elbe, A., Technische und soziale Probleme in der Dramenstruktur G. K.'s (1961); Shaw, L. R., "G. K.: A Bio-Bibliographical Report,' in TSLL, III (1961), 399-408; Kauf, R., "G. K.'s Social Tetralogy and the Social Ideas of Walter Rathenau," PMLA, LXXVII (1962), 311-17; Garten, H. F., "G. K.," in German Men of Letters (1964), II, 157-72; Jones, R. A., "German Drama on the American Stage: The Case of G. K.," in GQ, XXXVII (1964), 17-25; Reichert, H., "Nietzsche and G. K.," in SP, LXI (1964), 85-108; Last, R. W., "Symbol and Struggle in G. K.'s Die Bürger von Calais," in GL & L, XIX (1966), 201-209; Wirth, A., "G. K. und Witkiewicz," in Aspekte des Expressionismus (1968), ed. W. Paulsen

MARGARET KOBER MERZBACH

KAMBAN, Guðmundur

(pseud. of Jansson Hallgrimson), Icelandic dramatist and novelist, b. 8 June 1888, Litli-Baer (near Reykjavik); d. 5 May 1945, Copenhagen

K. became a journalist at an early age and for a time was influenced by Einar Kvaran (1859-1938) and by spiritualism. In 1910 he studied literature and philosophy at the University of Copenhagen. He scored his first great success on the Copenhagen stage with Hadda-Padda (1914; Eng., 1917), written under the influence of the romantic symbolism (q.v.) of Jóhann Sigurjónsson (1880-1919).

His play Marmor (1918) and his first novel, Ragnar Finnsson (1922), expressed the disillusionment occasioned by his first visit to America. K.'s most performed play, Vi Mordere (1920)—like his lighter satirical comedies De Arabiske Telte (1921; rev. version, Derfor skilles vi, 1939) and Ørkenens stjerner (1925) —criticizes traditional morality. It is Sendiherrann frá Júpiter (1927), however, that synthesizes his social criticism. K. later wrote the great historical novel Skálholt (4 vols., 1930-32; The Virgin of Skalholt, 1935; adapted for the stage, 1934).

Though always strongly linked with Icelandic tradition, K. was a cosmopolitan, a critic of society, and an individualist whose sole guide as to good and evil was his own conscience. Erroneously taken for a collaborationist, K. was shot by members of the Danish resistance in 1945.

FURTHER WORKS: Kongeglimen (1915); Det sovende hus (1925); 30. Generation ('933); Jeg ser et stort skønt land (1936; I See a Wondrous Land, 1938); Komplekser (1938); Tidløse Dragter (1939); Grandezza (1941); Kvalitetsmennesket (1941)

BIBLIOGRAPHY: Schneider, H., Geschichte der norwegischen und isländischen Literatur (2nd ed., 1949)

JORIS TAELS

KARINTHY, Frigyes

Hungarian short story writer, playwright, poet, and essayist, b. 25 June 1887, Budapest; d. 29 Aug. 1938, Siófok

K. maintained an ironic attitude toward the inanity of many of man's beliefs and actions. He was an extremely popular parodist. He derived many of his ideas and inspirations from Freud, as is evident in his short stories, which deal with dreams, the irrational, and madness.

There are suggestions of Jonathan Swift (1667-1745) and Voltaire (1694-1778) in K.'s work, while his "fantastic" plays, which were influenced by modern science and technology, recall Wells (q.v.). One of his most interesting works is a "confession" in which he describes a brain operation he underwent (*Utazàs a koponyám körül*, 1937; Journey Round My Skull, 1939). It was translated into several languages.

FURTHER WORKS: *Esik a hó* (1912); *Igy irtok ti* (1912); *Görbe tükör, Humoreszkek* (1912); *Ballada a néma férfiakról* (1912); *Irások irókról* (1914); *Két hajó* (1915); *Tanár ur kérem* (1916); *Holnap reggel* (1916); *Utazás Faremidóba* (1916; Voyage to Faremido, 1965); *Krisztus vagy Barabás* (1918); *Gyilkosok* (1919); *Ne bántsuk egymást* (1921); *Capillaria* (1921); *Kötéltánc* (1923); *Harun al Rasid* (1924); *Színház* (1927); *Összegyüjtött munkái* (10 vols., 1927); *Nem mondhatom el senkinek* (1930); *Hasmütét* (1932); *Még mindig igy irtok ti, Karikaturák* (1933); *Száz új humoreszk* (1934); *Üzenet a palackban* (1939)

BIBLIOGRAPHY: Reményi, J., *Hungarian Writers and Literature* (1964)

JOSEPH REMÉNYI

KARLFELDT, Erik Axel

Swedish poet, b. 20 July 1864, Karlbo, Dalecarlia; d. 8 April 1931, Stockholm

K. was elected to the Swedish Academy as early as 1904 and was its secretary from 1912 until his death. He was posthumously awarded the Nobel Prize for Literature in 1931.

In his first collection of poems *Vildmarks— och kärleksvisor* (1895), the influence of Gustav Fröding (1860-1911) and Johan Ludvig Runeberg (1804-1877) is evident. Like *Fridolins visor* (1898), this collection contains powerful though often elegiac love and nature poems. K. was increasingly influenced by the peasant tradition, folk religion, and magic of his homeland,

especially as expressed in proverbs, and also by 14th and 15th c. Swedish literature.

His next volume *Fridolins lustgård* (1901) closes with "paintings in rhyme from Dalecarlia"—poems that often treat biblical themes in a strikingly humorous manner. The series of poems entitled *Flora och Pomona* (1906) is more somber in tone; K.'s greater maturity endows it with a grandeur and intensity equaled only by *Hösthorn*, his last book. The heart of *Flora och Bellona* (1918) is a set of wartime poems. In his last poems, collected under the title *Hösthorn* (1927), K. returns to peasant themes and the past. A reconciled resignation to both life and death pervades the subject matter and the mood of *Hösthorn*.

The religious cast of K.'s poetry stems from his having been raised in a traditionally devout Lutheran family. Despite his often difficult themes, archaic climate of ideas, and pithy language, K. became one of Sweden's most widely read poets. In part, this was because of the songlike character of his romantic early poetry and because of his sure-footed musical rhythm and the sterling quality of his work.

FURTHER WORKS: *C. F. Dahlgren* (1923); *Tankar och tal* (1932); *Minnesupplagar* (5 vols., 1932); *Dikter* (1939)

BIBLIOGRAPHY: Fogelqvist, T., *E. A. K.* (1940); Wennerberg, K., *Vårgiga och hösthorn* (1944); Hallberg, P., *Natursymboler i svensk lyrik* (1951); Hildeman, K.-I., "The Evolution of *Längtan heter min arvedel*," in *SS* XXXI (1959), 47-64

REIDAR EKNER

KASACK, Hermann

German poet, dramatist, and narrative writer, b. 24 July 1896, Potsdam

K. was a reader for leading German publishers and later became a writer and radio playwright. In 1933 he was banned from lecturing by the Nazis. From 1941 to 1949 he was a reader for the publishing house of Suhrkamp, succeeding his friend Oskar Loerke (1884-1941) whose literary estate he administered and published. In 1953 he became president of the Deutsche Akademie für Sprache und Dichtung (German Academy for Language and Literature).

Das ewige Dasein (1943)—"Poems Collected over 25 Years"—whose far-ranging themes comprise basic observations on the destiny of man

205

and the essence of art, as well as the values of Western culture and Oriental wisdom, is notable for the crystalline clarity of its graphic, unemotional language and images and for its classical balance of form and rhythm.

In K.'s prose works, despite the immediacy of his realistic technique, he uses a symbolic language that enables the essential content, the universal and the typical, to shine through the subject matter. In his novel *Die Stadt hinter dem Strom* (1947; The City beyond the River, 1953), begun in 1942, K. is more concerned with expressing his thoughts than with form. He makes use of concepts of existentialism (q.v.), Buddhism, and Schopenhauer's philosophy to create, under the impact of World War II, a ghastly vision of a no-man's-land, where those who have departed this life lead a senseless, purposeless existence while awaiting their final deliverance through nothingness. The stifling atmosphere in this ghostly city of desolation, with its shadowy, anonymous inhabitants, grows into a symbol of the sinister power of the soulless totalitarian state, of human impotence and lostness.

In the utopian parable *Der Webstuhl* (1949), K. uses a purely narrative, epic treatment, which dispenses with individual characters that reveal themselves through action and dialogue, to satirize a government apparatus paralyzed by its own weight and a nation agonizing under soulless mechanical labor and an autonomous hierarchic bureaucracy. The novel *Das große Netz* (1952), too, is a grotesquely satirical critique of the age. Against the setting of a utopian small town, K. exposes the ominous activity of a collective organization that exerts the sovereign right to intervene in human life.

FURTHER WORKS: *Der Mensch* (1918); *Das schöne Fräulein* (1918); *Die Heimsuchung* (1919); *Die Insel* (1920); *Die tragische Sendung* (1920); *Die Schwestern* (1920); *Stadium* (1921); *Vincent Van Gogh* (1924); *Echo* (1933); *Tull, der Meisterspringer* (1935); *Oskar Loerke* (1951); *Fälschungen* (1953); *Chinesisches Bilderbuch* (1955); *Mosaiksteine* (1956)

BIBLIOGRAPHY: Boussert, M., "La crise européenne au travers des oeuvres d'après-guerre de H. K.," in *Revue des Langues Vivantes*, XXX (1964), 221-34; Anderle, M., "Mensch und Architektur im Werk H. K.'s," *GQ*, XXXVIII (1965), 20-29; Mainland, W. F., "H. K." in *Essays on Contemporary German Literature*, ed. B. Keith-Smith (1966), 39-59

ULRICH MELZER

KASCHNITZ (-WEINBERG), Marie-Luise von

German poet, essayist, narrative writer, and radio playwright, b. 31 Jan. 1901, Karlsruhe, Baden

After publishing a collection entitled *Griechische Mythen* (1946), Marie K. dealt with the war and the postwar period in *Menschen und Dinge 1945* (12 essays, 1946). The first volume of her *Gedichte* (1947), still traditional in form though passionate in expression, reinterprets feminine experience. In *Totentanz und Gedichte zur Zeit* (1947), *Zukunftsmusik* (1950), and *Ewige Stadt* (1952), Marie K. adopted a cyclic form. All her poems seek new hope amid the anxieties of the times, trying to conquer fear by giving meaning to elemental feeling. Her Roman essays *Engelsbrücke* (1955) and *Haus der Kindheit* (1956) are equally noted for their acceptance of life and sympathetic kindness.

FURTHER WORKS: *Liebe beginnt* (1933); *Elissa* (1937); *Gustave Courbet. Roman eines Malerlebens* (1949); *Das dicke Kind* (1952); *Neue Gedichte* (1957); *Lange Schatten* (1960); *Hörspiele* (1962); *Dein Schweigen meine Stimme* (1962); *Wohin denn ich* (1963); *Ein Wort weiter* (1965); *Beschreibung eines Dorfes* (1966); *Ferngespräche* (1966); *Die Wahrheit, nicht der Traum* (1967); *Tage, Tage, Jahre* (1968)

BIBLIOGRAPHY: Plant, R., "The Strange Poetic World of M. L. K.," in *American-German Review*, XXXII (1966), iv, 15-16; Merck, G., "Der Schriftsteller in dieser Zeit: Ingeborg Bachmann und M. L. K.," in *N Sammlung* VII (1967), 347-58

BRUNO BERGER

KASPROWICZ, Jan

Polish poet, playwright, and translator, b. 12 Dec. 1860, Szymborze; d. 2 Aug. 1926, Harenda

K. was the leading representative of the pre-1914 literary movement *młoda Polska* (*see* Polish Literature).

The son of a peasant from near Posen, he obtained an education by working his way through German universities. Persecuted by the Prussian authorities for his revolutionary activities, he moved to Lemberg, where he became professor of comparative literature.

In his work, social problems overlap with religious ones; he originally struggled with these from an atheistic outlook, later from a Catholic point of view. His early books of poems realistically describe village poverty; later ones, especially *Ginącemu światu* (1901), are mostly made up of Promethean-religious paeans that contain reminiscences of religious peasant song. The root element in his work is the metaphysical problem of evil, which he solves in the spirit of Christian humility in the volume of poems *Księga ubogich* (1918). K. also wrote several plays and translated works of Shakespeare, Goethe, Keats, Shelley, and Coleridge into Polish.

FURTHER WORKS: *Poezje* (1889); *Chrystus* (1891); *Swiat sie konczy* (1891); *Z chlopskiego zagonu* (1891); *Anima lachrymans* (1894); *Miłość* (1895); *Na wzgórzu śmierci* (1897); *Krzak dzikiej rózy* (1898); *Bunt Napierskiego* (1899); *Uczta Herodiacy* (1905); *O bohaterskim koniu i walacym sie domu* (1906); *Balada o sloneczniku* (1908); *Chwile* (1911); *Marchołt* (1920; *Hymny* (1921); *Mój świat* (1926); *Dzieła* (22 vols., 1930); *Dzieła wybrane* (5 vols., 1914)

BIBLIOGRAPHY: Zaleski, Z., *J. K.* (1928); Berger, J. *Przeklady K.* (1948); Hesztyński, S., *J. K.* (1954); Walter, H., ed., *J. K., 1926-1966* (1966)

* * *

KASSÁK, Lajos
Hungarian poet and narrative writer, b. 21 Mar. 1887, Érsekújvár

In his poems, short stories, novels, and articles and in the avant-garde periodicals he edited, K., who had been a worker himself, proclaimed his Marxist beliefs. For a time he was influenced by expressionism (q.v.). His realistic short stories and novels are sometimes weak in form and language. Nevertheless K. is more than a "proletarian curiosity," for as poet and fiction-writer, editor and journalist, he greatly widened the social horizons of Hungarian literature. In this achievement, his autobiography *Egy ember élete* (8 vols., 1927-35) was especially effective.

FURTHER WORKS: *Misilló királysága* (1916); *Angyalföld* (1929); *Földem, virágom* (1935); *Akik eltévedtek* (1936); *Költemények, rajzok* (1958); *Marika, enekelj* (1961); *Munkanélküliek* (1962)

BIBLIOGRAPHY: Radnóti, M., *L. K. költészete* (1939); Somlyok, G., "A Short Introduction to Hungarian Poetry" and "Sixteen Contemporary Poets," in *The New Hungarian Quarterly,* No. 23 (1966), 108-138; Bori, I., and Körner, E., *K.* (1967); *Kortárs* XI (1967), "K. issue"

JOSEPH REMÉNYI

KASSNER, Rudolf
Austrian essayist, philosopher, and narrative writer, b. 11 Sept. 1873, Gross-Pavlovitz; d. 1 Apr. 1959, Siders, Switzerland

K., the son of a factory- and estate-owner, was afflicted with crippling poliomyelitis at the age of nine months. Everything he created, everything he experienced, was achieved in defiance of appalling physical handicaps—his excellent command of some eight languages, of world literature in general, and of the most diverse branches of knowledge ranging from philosophy and history to mathematics and natural science; his extensive travels, which took him to the more inaccessible countries of the Far East; his active social life, which kept him in rewarding contact with the intellectual elite of Europe between 1895 and 1955; his literary productivity; and the serenity and firmness of character that he displayed in all these fields. Only at the age of eighty did he agree to give up his crutches for a wheelchair.

After a childhood, which in spite of his physical condition was happy, K. studied philology, history, and philosophy in Vienna and Berlin. In his youth he was under the influence of Nietzsche (q.v.), though he early turned definitively away from him.

Externally K.'s life was uneventful. His memorable friendship with Rilke (q.v.), began in 1907. His ambitious travels ended with World War I, during which he, like Rilke, lived mainly in Munich. From then until 1946 he lived in Vienna, suffering some difficulties through his negative attitude toward the Third Reich. During World War II he again published nothing. In 1946 the generous Maecenas Werner Reinhart became his benefactor, making it possible for K. to move to Switzerland. While the numerous books of this last period, in which his concept of physiognomics no longer plays the dominant role, unquestionably tend at times to recapitulate earlier works, there is no question of any failing of his powers. Some of these last works—*Die Geburt Christi* (1951), for instance—rank among his most valuable.

For all his philosophical and poetic talent, K. cannot be called either a philosopher or a poet, except in the sense that Plato (whom he so admired) was both. His physiognomical, mystical vision of the world is set down in essays, aphorism cycles, parables, dialogues, symbol-laden character sketches, short stories, personal memoirs, observations on the history of civilization, and extensive treatises on physiognomics. The charge of impenetrable obscurity often brought against K. can be upheld, if at all, only in these treatises, of which *Zahl und Gesicht* (1919) is the most important. His syntax is always orderly, his language, for all its solipsism, lively and direct, while humor, wit, and irony pervade all. K. is a master of the gnomic statement, comparable in this respect to Novalis (1772-1801) or Goethe, and at the same time an excellent storyteller, as is evidenced especially in his three great books of memoirs—*Buch der Erinnerung* (1938; 2nd ed., 1954), *Die zweite Fahrt* (1946), and *Umgang der Jahre* (1949). The difficulty of his writing stems chiefly from his often puzzling terminology—which, however, can never be called jargon—and from his confusingly abrupt transitions, or rather leaps, from one thought to another.

Beginning his literary career as a critic under the spell of neoromantic aestheticism, he wrote, after a long stay in England, *Die Mystik, die Künstler und das Leben* (1900), a volume of essays on English romantics and pre-Raphaelites. Throughout his life K. was to retain this cordial affinity with the language, culture, and people of England that henceforth would become intensified. Later it was only with certain reservations that he allowed this first work— and the similarly oriented *Der Tod und die Maske* (1902)—to remain in his *oeuvre*.

A decisive factor in K.'s discovery of his own nature was his encounter with Kierkegaard (1813-55) and with Indian scriptures. *Der indische Idealismus* (1903) was the first work that was truly characteristic of him.

Not until his old age, however, did he become reconciled to the term mysticism, appropriate as it is to his cast of mind.

Among the works he published before the outbreak of World War I, *Von den Elementen der menschlichen Größe* (1911) and *Die Chimäre* (1914) deserve to be singled out. Here, as in all his later works, K. is attempting an interpretive synopsis of all manifestations of the spirit—in nations, classes, and individuals; in all stages, transitional phases, and crises of culture; in history; in myths, religions, philosophical ideas, and systems; in poetry and other works of art; in science of all kinds; in dreams; even in numbers; and in the whole physical world as perceived in its symbolic configuration. In all these things K., who hardly differentiates between thought and ocular sensory perception, perceives spiritual and intellectual relationships and processes that need explaining. To explain them, he uses primarily pairs of contrasting concepts, such as space and time, eye and ear, the world of the father and the world of the son, number and vision.

The meaning revealed to K. by a world looked at and interpreted in this way differs essentially from, say, the meaning that would emerge from a scientific examination of all things according to a category of causality, which he does not recognize. It also differs essentially from the meaning that is often sought behind appearances, beneath the surface. For K. the surface, rightly seen—the "skin" of things—is actually their true essence. To denote this intellectual-sensual relationship to the world peculiar to himself, K. in 1919 coined the expression physiognomics. This term dominates his work throughout the interwar period; among other elements it includes a protest against psychoanalysis, which K. detested.

K.'s physiognomical interpretation of the world becomes considerably clearer when one recognizes that everything he wrote is essentially concerned with an analysis of Christianity. The salient factor in his work is his ruthless criticism of the modern spirit and antispirit, not only for its atheistic materialism but precisely for its metaphysical strivings. It would seem self-evident that this defender of the Christian tradition against all the anti-Christian tendencies of the modern world (who has so much in common with Pascal [1623-62] and Kierkegaard) must himself be a devout Christian, especially since his interpretation of the world is concerned with such apparently Christian ideas as "turning" (conversion), "sacrifice," "the holy," and "the god-man" (incarnation). Yet K. himself says that his thinking evolved out of a certain "rancor" against Christianity, and in his old age he was still rejecting belief in a personal God and in the Christ of the church. As to K.'s strained relationship to Christianity, it should in the first place be noted that he regarded his own resistance to the Christian as something entirely different from the anti-Christian attitude of the typical modern man, which he so sharply castigated. He himself called it "the pagan in me," the pagan being for him perhaps even more definitely opposed to the modern spirit than to the Christian spirit. In a sense, the pagan is concerned with the pre-Christian, the modern spirit with the post-Christian.

K. often spoke quite openly of a dualism between the Christian and the pagan in his own nature. In 1931, for instance, he wrote to Spoerri that "the pagan and the Christian never completely coincide in my nature. But I tell myself that if they did coincide I could perhaps not live." K. recognized in the most diverse phenomena a mixture of the Christian and the pagan that was particularly appealing to him— in the personality of Goethe, in ancient Indian mysticism, and in Catholicism.

The major preoccupation of K.'s physiognomics is nothing other than a synthesis of the Christian and the pagan (which, however, cannot coincide). The most extreme form this synthesis takes is that of an "esoteric Christianity"—a Christianity lacking an absolute personal God-the-Father, a Christianity concerned not with redeeming man from sin but with redeeming God "from man's incarnate heathenness," a Christianity in which "imagination" replaces "belief." For the sake of this esoteric Christianity, K. transposed Jesus from his Old Testament Jewish background to a setting of Greek culture and philosophy as the realization of the presentiments of Plato and the dreams of Socrates. Or he ranked Jesus with the Indian saints who need no god. What K. was attempting here is comparable in many respects to the aspirations of some of the great heretical mystics—and he did sometimes feel a spiritual kinship with Meister Eckart (ca. 1260-1327) or Jakob Boehme (1575-1624). But we may well ask whether in fact he was not even closer to the specifically modern spirit that he elsewhere so violently repudiated. K.'s great argument with Christianity, which in his work remained unresolved to the very end, was, however, resolved in his life. One year before his death he was formally reconciled with the church.

FURTHER WORKS: *Moral der Musik* (1903); *Motive* (1906); *Melancholia* (1908); *Der indische Gedanke* (1913); *Die Grundlagen der Physiognomik* (1922); *Die Verwandlung* (1925); *Die Mythen der Seele* (1927); *Narziss oder Mythos und Einbildungskraft* (1928); *Das physiognomische Weltbild* (1930); *Physiognomik* (1932); *Das Buch der Gleichnisse* (1934); *Von der Eingildungskraft* (1936); *Der Gottmensch* (1938); *Transfiguration* (1946); *Das neunzehnte Jahrhundert* (1947); *Das inwendige Reich* (1953); *Der Zauberer* (1955); *Der goldene Drachen* (1957); *Der Gottmensch und die Weltseele* (1960); *Gespräche mit Rudolf Kassner* (1960); *Die Blinde schaut* (1963)

BIBLIOGRAPHY: Usinger, F., *Geist und Gestalt* (1941); Wieser, T., *Die Einbildungskraft bei R. K.* (1949); Kensik, A. C., and Bodmer, D., eds., *Gedenkbuch zu R. K.'s 80. Geburtstag* (1953); Kensik, A. C., *Gespräche mit K.* (1960); Spoerri, T., "Das Vermächtnis R. K.'s," in *Schweizer Monatshefte*, XLI (1961), 55-62; Usinger, F., *Tellurium* (1966)

EUDO C. MASON

KÄSTNER, Erhart

German essayist and narrative writer, b. 13 March 1904, Augsburg

K. is the author of diarylike essays on Greece and Africa. He was Gerhart Hauptmann's (q.v.) secretary at one time and became a librarian in Wolfenbüttel after World War II.

Griechenland. Ein Buch aus dem Kriege (1943; reissued as *Ölberge, Weinberge*, 1953) derives its force from the clash between contemporary problems and traditional thinking that has been shaped by the heritage from classical antiquity. The same is true of *Kreta* (1946). *Zeltbuch von Tumilad* (1949) describes prisoner-of-war experiences in Africa again from a classical point of view. *Stundentrommel vom Berg Athos* (1956; Mount Athos: The Call from Sleep, 1961) depicts simply and clearly the world of the Greek hermits.

FURTHER WORKS: *Die Lerchenschule* (1964)

BIBLIOGRAPHY: Schonauer, F., *Deutsche Literatur im Dritten Reich* (1961), pp. 135-37

FRIEDRICH W. WOLLENBERG

KÄSTNER, Erich

German narrative writer, poet, author of juveniles, dramatist and radio playwright, b. 23 Feb. 1899, Dresden

K. attended a teachers' college. In 1917 he was called to active service in World War I, during which he acquired a serious heart ailment. While studying German literature, he worked as a bank clerk, then as an editor. In 1927 he went to Berlin to take up writing as a career and published his first book of poems, *Herz auf Taille*. In 1933 his books were banned by the Nazis. From 1945 to 1948, K. was an editor in Munich and one of the leading participants in the Munich cabaret Die Schaubude, which was continued after 1951 as the Kleine Freiheit.

K. has won literary recognition mainly for his poetry. *Herz auf Taille*, *Lärm im Spiegel* (1928), *Ein Mann gibt Auskunft* (1930), and *Gesang zwischen den Stühlen* (1932) are his major achievements; in them he mounted a satirical attack on the insincerity of bourgeois morality, on militarism, and on fascism. Here K. created a new variety of German poetry in which expressive devices and topics first introduced by expressionism (q.v.) are combined with conservative versification and a moralizing rationalism. His poems could serve as models for the poetry of the *neue Sachlichkeit*. The novel *Fabian* (1931; Fabian: The Story of a Moralist, 1932) is very close to them in both language and content.

In K.'s post-1933 novels his narrative vigor helps offset a certain banality of subject matter, the adoption of which may have been influenced by K.'s position as a "refugee inside Germany."

K. has achieved a considerable reputation as an author of children's books. They are moral tales in which, as in the rest of his work, he often attacks distorted, vacuous hero-worship and the glorification of war (*Der 35. Mai* [1931; The 35th of May, or, Conrad's Ride to the South Seas, 1933]; *Das fliegende Klassenzimmer* [1933; The Flying Classroom, 1934]; *Die Konferenz der Tiere* [1949; The Animal's Conference, 1949]) and in which unselfish motherly devotion often plays an important role (*Emil und die Detektive*, 1928; Emil and the Detectives, 1930).

In 1948 he published a collection of epigrams *Kurz und bündig*. In the two collections *Der tägliche Kram* (1949) and *Die kleine Freiheit* (1952) K. spoke in a new and timely voice and produced poetry that quite measures up to his early work. At the same time, under the post-1945 stimulus of the political cabaret, he became increasingly interested in the stage, for which he wrote little sketches and comedies (*Die Schule der Diktatoren*, 1949, and *Zu treuen Händen*, 1950).

FURTHER WORKS: *Pünktchen und Anton* (1931; Annaluise and Anton, 1932); *Drei Männer im Schnee* (1934; Three Men in the Snow, 1935); *Lyrische Hausapotheke* (1935); *Die verschwundene Miniatur* (1935; The Missing Miniature, or, The Adventures of a Sensitive Butcher, 1937); *Bei Durchsicht meiner Bücher* (1946); *Das doppelte Lottchen* (1949; Eng., Lottie and Lisa, 1950; Am., Lisa and Lottie, 1951); *Der kleine Grenzverkehr oder Georg und die Zwischenfälle* (1949; A Salzburg Comedy, 1957); *Emil und die drei Zwillinge* (1949; Emil and the Three Twins, 1961); *Don Quichote* (1956; Don Quixote, 1957); *Als ich noch ein kleiner Junge war* (1957; Am., When I Was a Boy, 1961; Eng., When I Was a Little Boy, 1959); *Till Eulenspiegel* (1957; Till Eulenspiegel, The Clown, 1957); *Gullivers Reisen* (1961); *K. in Probepackung* (1962); *Von Damen und anderen Weibern* (1963); *Der kleine Mann* (1963; Little Man, 1966). **Selected English trans.:** *Let's Face It: Selected Poems* (1963)

BIBLIOGRAPHY: Winkelman, J., *The Poetic Style of E. K.* (1957); Enderle, L., *K., eine Bildbiographie* (1960)

JOSEF STRELKA

KATAYEV, Valentin Petrovich
Russian novelist, b. 28 Jan. 1897, Odessa

In 1914 K., who began writing before the revolution, was a follower of Bunin (q.v.). After the revolution he settled in Moscow, where his short story "Otetz" attracted attention. His *Rastratchiki* (1926; The Embezzlers, 1929) is a satirical novel about Soviet bank employees who enjoy themselves with the money they have embezzled. His early work was criticized for concentrating on personal instead of social problems. After writing the comedy *Kvadratura kruga* (1928; Squaring the Circle, 1936) K. tried to bring his writing into line with official party demands. During the first five-year plan he wrote *Vremya vperiod* (1932; Time Forward, 1933), a novel imbued with enthusiasm for construction and technology. Perhaps his most attractive work is *Beleyet parus odinokii* (1936; Peace Is Where the Tempests Blow, 1937), the story of two young boys in Odessa during the 1905 revolution. Three other novels—much weaker artistically—in the same cycle (all four were published together as *Volny Chernovo morya*, 1961) are *Khutorok v stepi* (1950; The

Cottage in the Steppe, 1957), *Zimnii veter* (1960), and *Za vlast' sovetov* (1949). The last novel, dealing with the defense of Odessa during World War II, was severely criticized and was subsequently rewritten (1951).

FURTHER WORKS: *Vyderzhal* (1928; He Passed, 1937); *Sobraniye sochinenii* (2 vols., 1928); *Million terzanii* (1931; The Last of the Equipage, or, A Million Torments, 1934); *Doroga tzvetov* (1934; The Path of Flowers, 1936); *Komedii* (1934); *Ya syn trudovovo naroda* (1937); *Semen Kotko* (1941); *Flag* (1942); *Elektricheskaya mashina* (1943); *Zhena* (1943; The Wife, 1946; republished as *Nino-chka*, 1946); *Syn polka* (1945); *Povesti i rasskazy* (2 vols., 1947-49); *P'yesy* (1955); *Sobraniye sochinenii* (5 vols., 1956-57); *Povesti* (1957); *Pochti dnevnik* (1962); *Gorokh v stenku* (1963); *Malen'kaya zheleznaya dver' v stene* (1965)

BIBLIOGRAPHY: Brezhnina, B., *V. K.* (1960)

GEORGE LUCKYI

KAVERIN, Veniamin

(pseud. of *Veniamin A. Zilberg*), Russian novelist and short story writer, b. 19 April 1902, Pleskov

K., a musician's son, studied the violin until he was fifteen. In 1921 he became a member of the Serapion Society (see Russian literature); he and Lev Natanovich Lunc (1901-1924) represent this movement's western wing. K. took a course of Oriental studies, but gave up scholarship after a few years.

His early stories (*Mastera i podmaster'ja*, 1923) show the influence of E. T. A. Hoffmann and Edgar Allan Poe. The story collection *Bubnovaja mast'* (1927) contains elements of the grotesque realism of Gogol. The novel *Skandalist, ili Vechera na Vasil' evskom Ostrove* (1928) satirically describes a group dedicated to formalism in art with which K. was once connected. Formalistic influences, present in K. himself, are to be seen in *Chudožnik neizvesten* (1931), a short novel, rich in romantic irony, about the problem of the place of art in communist society. Its hero, a nonconformist artist, is pictured as a modern Don Quixote. This novel was severely criticized by the communists.

In *Ispolnenie zhelanir* (1935) and *Dva kapitana* (1945), K. turned to more innocuous themes and methods; these novels, which reveal

his liking for thrilling action, are ideologically irreproachable socialist realism. Nevertheless, K.'s postwar novel *Otkrytaya kniga* (1949), dealing with the career of a Russian woman bacteriologist, was again criticized for certain "unorthodox" opinions and had to be rewritten.

FURTHER WORKS: *Konetz Khazy* (1925); *Devyat' desyatykh sud'by* (1926); *Bol'shaya igra* (1926); *Vorob'inaya noch'* (1927); *Prolog* (1931); *Chernovik cheloveka* (1931); *Ukroshcheniye Robinzona, ili Poteryannyi rai* (1934); *Rasskazy* (1942); *Doktor Tatyana Vlasenkova* (1953); *Poiski i nadezhdy,* (3 vols., 1956), *Khudozhnik neizvesten* (1961)

BIBLIOGRAPHY: Ulanov, H., "K.'s *Khudozhnik neizvesten:* Structure and Motivation," *SEEJ*, X (1966), 389-99; Piper, D. G., *V. A. K.* (1967)

GLEB STRUVE

KAWABATA Yasunari
Japanese novelist, b. 11 June 1899, Osaka

Japan's first winner of the Nobel Prize for Literature (1968) and the second Asian so honored, K. is better known at home than abroad, despite the international critical acclaim that has been accorded to his *Yukiguni* (1937-47; Snow Country, 1956) and *Sembazuru* (1949-51; Thousand Cranes, 1959).

Novelist, short story writer and literary critic, K., according to his Nobel citation, exhibits "narrative mastership that with great sensibility expresses the essence of the Japanese mind." Out of a half century of Japan's often short-lived chaotic literary movements, K. early evolved, and in time refined, a highly personal impressionism characterized by simple language, startling imagery, and emphasis on the sensual aspects of his major themes—love and deprivation.

Orphaned by the age of three, K. spent a lonely childhood in school after school. In 1924 he received a degree in Japanese literature from Tokyo Imperial University, and the following year wrote his popular *Izu no Odoriko* (1926; excerpts translated as "The Izu Dancer," in *The Atlantic,* Jan. 1955). That account of an innocent encounter between a young dancer and a student on a walking tour was K.'s major contribution to *shinkankaku undō* (new sensualism or neo-impressionism), a short-lived but influential literary movement he initiated with Yokomitsu Riichi (1898-1947) and others.

211

Later claimed by the modernists, K. defies ready categorizing.

Popularly considered antiproletarian, even anti-Marxist, since his affiliation with the *Jūsannin Kurabu* (thirteen-men club) in 1929, K. actually shows little inclination for political or social didacticism. After World War II, however, he announced, "I will write only about the defeated nation." His painstakingly written fiction investigates personal relationships: a Tokyo snob and a rural geisha in *Yukiguni;* a guilt-ridden family in *Sembazuru.* A sense of history and reiteration of man's dependence on the natural world pervade K.'s works.

As a critic, and after 1948 as president of the Japanese center of the P.E.N. club, K. has consistently encouraged young writers of various literary persuasions, among them Yukio Mishima.

In 1952, K. won the Japanese Academy of Arts prize and in 1954 the Noma Literary Prize. Abroad, K. won the French Prix de Meilleur Livre Étranger in 1961. A pensioner of the Japanese Order of Cultural Merit, K. lives in semiseclusion at his Kamakura home and in a mountain retreat at Karuizawa.

FURTHER WORKS: *Jūrokusai no Nikki* (1914); *Shōkonsai* (1921); *Yugashima Onsen* (1925); *Kanjo Shushoku* (1926); *Asakusa Kurenaidan* (1929); *Kinju* (1933); *Matsugo no Me* (1933); *Bungaku Teki* (1934); *Jojōka* (1938); *Yama no Oto* (1949); *Meijin no Shogai* (1952); *Saikonsha* (1953); *Tōkyō no Hito* (1955); *Mizumi* (1955); *Nemureru Bijo* (1960); *Kyōto* (1962)

BIBLIOGRAPHY: Shinkōkai, Kokusai Bunka, *Introduction to Contemporary Japanese Literature* (1939) pp. 343 ff.; Bowers, F., "A Lonely World," in *SatR* (5 Jan. 1957) p. 14; Rexroth, K., "Ceremonial Violence in Kamakura," in *SatR* (21 Feb. 1959), p. 27; Dunlea, W., "Symbolistic Tale," in *Commonweal* (6 May 1959), p. 603

MARIAN PEHOWSKI

KAZANTZAKIS, Nikos

Greek poet, novelist, essayist, playwright, b. 2 Feb. 1882, Herakleion, Crete; d. 26 Oct. 1957, Freiburg, Germany

The son of a small farmer, K. came to know well the world of peasantry and the revolutionary ardor and heroism of the Cretan people, which exploded into an uprising against the Turks in 1897. Young K., evacuated to Naxos, was placed in a school run by Franciscan monks, in which he was introduced to an entirely different world. He learned French and Italian and became acquainted with Western philosophies and, more important, with the ascetic and untiring search of the followers of Christ for the final truth.

K. studied law at the University of Athens, where he took his degree in 1906, and then went to Paris to study philosophy with Bergson (q.v.), whose teachings of the supremacy of the mind over the body influenced him greatly. Bergson and Nietzsche (q.v.) became his principal mentors, but his restless mind caused him to pursue much of the philosophical and political thinking of his time. Later he was to renounce Nietzsche for Buddha, then Buddha for Lenin, and finally to return to Christ.

In 1919, K. became director-general of the Greek Ministry of Welfare, which brought back, under his guidance, 150,000 Greeks from south Russia and the Caucasus to be resettled in western Thrace. He widened his already immense knowledge by traveling in France, Egypt, Spain, Germany, Russia, China, and Japan. His extraordinary travelogues won wide acclaim, but his spiritual home remained his native Crete. He called himself "a mariner of Odysseus with a heart of fire, mind ruthless and clear."

From 1922 to 1924 he lived in a Germany prostrate and starving in the aftermath of World War I, and here he came under the influence of Marxism. In Berlin he wrote the programmatic essays on Marxism that were to be published as *Salvatores Dei* (1928; The Saviors of God: Spiritual Exercises, 1960). Four times K., intrigued by the communist attempt to create a new world, went to Russia. But by the early thirties, tired of the communists' propaganda and "their big ideas," K. concluded that they were unfit to satisfy the spiritual need of man.

In 1938 K. published his monumental poem *Odysseia* (The Odyssey: A Modern Sequel, 1960), an epic of 33,000 verses in which Odysseus, in spite of his fondness for his son, his reverence for his father, and his love for Penelope, sets out from Ithaca once more to gain more experience of the world. K. had worked on this epic poem for thirteen years and had rewritten it seven times. During this period he also wrote lyrical poetry, a novel *Toda Raba* (1934; Toda-Raba, 1964), philosophical essays, dramas, and comedies. He translated into

KAWABATA YASUNARI

VOLTER KILPI

modern Greek Maeterlinck, García Lorca (qq.v.), Homer, Plato, Dante, Goethe, Nietzsche, Bergson, Darwin, Rimbaud, and others. His capacity for work was inexhaustible, his grasp of languages, magnificent.

After World War II and the Greek Civil War during which, serving for a short time as Minister of Education, he tried in vain to reconcile the opposing forces, he decided that he could not live with the political and religious situation in Greece. At the age of sixty-five, in the mid-forties, he settled in Antibes. Here, during the last nine years of his life, he wrote the novels that were translated into thirty languages and won him worldwide fame.

K.'s descriptive talent is impressive, and the tangible original language which he used in his novels, and also in his epic *Odysseia*, lends great fascination to his style. He used demotic Greek, the peasant's Greek, in contrast to Atticistic Greek, which was adopted as the literary language of modern Greece. In demotic Greek, which is richly metaphoric, the concrete is preferred over the abstract. In this way K. achieved the fiery and tender language of great audacity that so admirably suited the subject of his writing—the conflict between flesh and spirit, which was the fundamental problem of his own life.

This conflict is the central theme in *Ho Christo xanastauronetai* (1951; The Greek Passion, 1954). This Homeric tale is about a Greek village, under the tyrannical rule of a Turkish aga, which is preparing to stage a passion play when a large band of starving Greek fugitives descends on it. The peasantry has no compassion, but Manolios, a shepherd who plays the role of Christ, tries to persuade the villagers to give up one tenth of their rich harvest to the starving men. The village is polarized into two camps: the prosperous, who are consumed with greed and hatred, and the followers of Manolios, who identify themselves with Christ's apostles. The red-haired harness-maker Pangiotaros (Judas in the play) becomes a traitor and denounces Manolios and his group as anarchists to the Turks. The fear of the Turks brings panic to the village, and Manolios is murdered in the church. This stark and simple tale, which reveals the passions of ordinary people driven by love, self-sacrifice, and hatred, is written without pathos in K.'s compelling language.

In *Alexis Zorbas* (1946; Zorba the Greek, 1952) K. projects the two aspects of himself in the two main characters. One is the seeker for truth, the brooder, the ascetic who withdraws from the world, a "paper-devouring mouse." He is contrasted to Zorba, the Greek-Macedonian, sixty-five years old—the unspoiled great soul, the man of exuberant vitality and unflagging strength, the adventurer and the vagabond.

K. valued freedom above all other blessings, but, believing it can never be achieved, he praised the passionate often tragic search for freedom as the greatest virtue. This is the theme of *Ho teleutaios peirasmos* (1955; The Last Temptation of Christ, 1960), a surrealistic biography of Christ, who as the prototype of the free man achieves victory over evil and fear by his constant struggle with temptation. K. depicts Christ as a man who feels the attractiveness of evil and even succumbs to it, for if 20th c. man could identify with Christ's conflict and victory he could gain a new understanding of Christ. K.'s intention was not to reform the church. What he set out to do was to create a picture of Christ, independent of the teachings of the Christian churches, an image of a warrior engaged in the incessant merciless battle between spirit and flesh that is common to man. This was heresy, in the eyes of the Greek Orthodox church.

A great furor arose in Greece. After thirty years of nonrecognition, K. now experienced the bitterness of complete misrepresentation of his aims. The Greek Orthodox Church attacked him violently as a heretic and threatened him with excommunication. The newspapers branded him as one who had betrayed his own people, for in his novel *Ho Kapetan Michales* (1954; Freedom or Death, 1956), K. had, rather than romanticizing the peasant, showed the virtues and the evil of Greek heroism. The intellectuals condemned him for failing to respect pure Greek and for using demotic Greek. The advocates of demotic Greek claimed that he went too far in his overuse of coarse and obscure words. But by now K. had gained the recognition of the world as one of the great writers of the 20th c.

In 1957, though suffering from leukemia, he accepted an invitation to visit China. Becoming gravely ill in Canton, he was taken to Freiburg in Germany, where he died. The Greeks, by now convinced of his greatness, arranged for his body to be brought to Athens, but the archbishop refused to follow the traditional practice of allowing the body of a famous man to lie in state in the church or to celebrate the mass for the dead for him. His friends took him to Crete, where he was given a Christian burial.

FURTHER WORKS: *Ophis Kai Krino* (1906); *Xemeronei* (1906); *Monoprakto* (1909); *Ho Protomastoras* (1910); *Asketike* (1927); *Nikephoros Phokas* (1927); *Taxideuontas* (1927); *Christos* (1928); *Odysseas* (1928, translation); *Ti eida ste Russia* (1928); *Iaponia-Kina* (1938; Japan, China, 1963); *Anglia* (1941; England: A Travel Journal, 1966); *He Trilogia tu Promethea* (1941-43); *Julianos* (1945); *Kapodistrias* (1946); *Kuros* (1955); *Melissa* (1955); *Konstantinos Palaialogos* (1956); *Sodoma kai Gomorrha* (1956); *Ho pektochules tu theu* (1956; Saint Francis, 1962); *Le Jardin des Roches* (1959; The Rock Garden, 1963) *Amphora sto Greco* (1961; Report to Greece, 1966)

BIBLIOGRAPHY: Prebelakes, P., *Ho poietes kai to poiema tes Odysseias* (1958); Kerenyi, K., *Streifzüge eines Humanisten* (1960); Prebelakes, P., *"N. K. and His Odyssey, A Study of the Poet and His Poetry"* (1961); Kazantzakis, H., *Nikos Kazantzakis: A Biography Based on His Letters*

GERTRUDE C. SCHWEBELL

KEROUAC, Jack

American narrative writer and poet, b. 12 March 1922, Lowell, Mass.

K., a son of a printer and of French Canadian descent on his mother's side, entered Columbia University at eighteen. He was, however, incurably restless and soon left New York City to hitchhike throughout the United States and Mexico until 1950. During those roaming years he supported himself by casual labor.

His first novel, *The Town and the City*, appeared in 1950 and was well received. The story of his youth in Lowell, it showed an enthusiasm for detail and a delight in coarseness. K. first became known outside the United States with *On the Road* (1959). This novel, written very rapidly in 1951, consists of a loose series of sketches depicting the adventures of K. and his friends, most of them penniless, on their trips across the continent. The so-called beat generation saw in it the glorification of their revolt against bourgeois society and of their eagerness to heighten feeling, by means of alcohol, drugs, jazz, sex, and amorality, to the point of intoxication.

Along with *Howl* (1956), the ecstatic, obscene

poem by K.'s friend Ginsberg (q.v.), *On the Road* became one of the sacred texts—though its significance was more sociological than literary—of the beat generation, which also includes the San Francisco school of poetry stimulated by Rexroth (q.v.).

K.'s novel *The Subterraneans* (beatniks), published in 1958, presents characters and values similar to those described in *On the Road*. It is an account of a love affair between a white boy and a mulatto girl, written in an uninhibited, spontaneous style and laden with often barely understandable jazz slang. *Mexico City Blues* (1959) consists of 242 highly rhythmic "choral songs for jazz."

FURTHER WORKS: *The Dharma Bums* (1958); *Dr. Sax* (1959); *Maggie Cassidy* (1959); *Tristessa* (1960); *Visions of Cody* (1960); *Lonesome Traveler* (1960); *The Scripture of the Golden Eternity* (1960); *Rimbaud* (1960); *Book of Dreams* (1961); *Big Sur* (1962); *Visions of Gerard* (1963); *Desolation Angels* (1965); *Satori in Paris* (1967); *Vanity of Duluoz* (1968)

BIBLIOGRAPHY: Feldman, G., and Gartenberg, M., *The Beat Generation* (1958); Webb, H. W., Jr., "The Singular Worlds of J. K.," in *Contemporary American Novelists* (1964), 120-33; Fried, F., *No Pie in the Sky: The Hobo as American Cultural Hero in the Works of Jack London, John Dos Passos, and J. K.* (1964); Charters, A., *A Bibliography of Works by J. K.* (1967); Holmes, J. C., *Nothing More to Declare* (1967)

EUGEN KURI

KERR, Alfred

(originally, Alfred Kempner), German essayist and drama critic, b. 25 Dec. 1867, Breslau; d. 12 Oct. 1948, Hamburg

K.'s criticism began in the romantic tradition; he shared the romantics' aesthetic theories and acceptance of life. He raised criticism to a fourth literary genre, equal to epic and lyric poetry and drama. As a highly individualistic socialist and progressivist, he acknowledged his debt to the artistic theories of Wilde (q.v.) and the ethos of G. B. Shaw (q.v.). He championed the "new drama" (H. Ibsen and Gerhardt Hauptmann [qq.v.]) with his penetrating analyses and wrote the most precise and succinct critiques to appear in the German language.

The influence of his critical viewpoint and

original style is obvious; his significance in the history of the theater is hard to overestimate. K. was the dominating figure of the great era of the Berlin theater—almost its symbol. His gift of expression, power of analysis, and ability to make his point in brief sketches are un- equaled. His historical approach to literature now seems dated as do many of his judgements on classical works and post-World War I drama, his indifference to myth, his sentimentality, and a certain pretentious captiousness.

K.'s enthusiastic acceptance of life—"the glory of living" that meant more to him than art of any kind—is reflected in his vivid travel books. In his verse, inspired by both hate and love, Heinrich Heine's (1797-1856) rhythm is discernible.

With the advent of Hitler, K. was forced to leave Germany in 1933, going to Switzerland, and later to France and England.

FURTHER WORKS: *Herr Sudermann, der D . . . Di . . . Dichter* (1903); *Schauspielkunst* (1904); *Das neue Drama* (1905); *Die Welt im Drama* (5 vols., 1917; abridged 1954); *Die Harfe* (1917); *Die Welt im Licht* (2 vols., 1920); *New York und London* (1923); *O Spanien* (1924); *Yankeeland* (1925); *Caprichos* (1926); *Es sei wie es wolle . . .* (1928); *Die Diktatur des Hausknechts* (1924); *Melodien* (1938)

BIBLIOGRAPHY: Chapiro, J., *A. K.* (1928); Huder, W., "A. K.'s literarischer Nachlass," in *Welt und Wort*, XVII (1962), 207-208; Hirsch- bach, F. D., "A. K. als Lieder- und Opern- komponist," in *Wirkendes Wort*, XVII (1967), 165-85, and "A. K. und der Expressionismus," in *GQ*, XL (1967), 204-211

WOLFGANG DREWS

KESSEL, Joseph

French novelist, b. 10 Feb. 1898, Clara, Argentina

K., whose parents were Russian, grew up in South America and France, studied at the Sorbonne, and became a French newspaper correspondent in bolshevik Russia. *La Steppe rouge* (1927) was the result of this experience. In addition to novels of society and travel books on Palestine, America, and Indonesia, he wrote several novels about military and civilian aviation—*L'équipage*, 1923; *Vent de sable*, 1929; and *Mermoz*, 1938. He was awarded the Grand Prix du Roman of the Académie Fran- çaise in 1927. In his other novels and the novel-

cycle *Le Tour du malheur* (1950), K. traces in a tragic way the destinies of families between the two wars.

FURTHER WORKS: *Les Rois aveugles* (1925; Blinded Kings, 1926); *Mary de Cork* (1925); *Les Captifs* (1926); *Nuit de princes* (1927; Princes of the Night, 1928); *Les Coeurs purs* (1927; The Pure in Heart, 1928); *Terre d'amour* (1927); *Les Nuits de Sibérie* (1928); *Dames de Californie* (1929); *Reine et serre* (1929); *Belle de jour* (1929; Eng., 1962); *Le Rage au ventre* (1930); *Le Coup de grâce* (1931; Sirocco, 1947); *Fortune carrée* (1932; Crossroads, 1932); *Nuits de Montmartre* (1932); *Bas fonds* (1932); *Wagon-lit* (1932); *Marchés d'esclaves* (1933); *Les Enfants de la chance* (1934); *Stavisky, l'homme que j'ai connu* (1934); *Une Balle perdue* (1935); *La Passante de Sans-Souci* (1936); *Hollywood, ville mirage* (1937); *La Rose de java* (1937); *L'Armée des ombres* (1943; Army of Shadows, 1944); *L'Embarquement pour Gibraltar* (1945); *Les Maudru* (1945); *Le Bataillon du ciel* (1947); *La Premier Amour de l'aspirant Dalleau* (1949); *La Fontaine Medicis* (1950; The Medici Fountain, 1963); *La Nagaïka, trois récits* (1951); *Au grand socco* (1952); *La Piste fauve* (1954); *Les Amants du Tage* (1954); *La Vallée des rubis* (1955; The Valley of Rubies, 1960); *Témoin parmi les hommes* (3 vols., 1956); *Les Jours de l'aventure* (1956); *Le Procès des enfants perdu* (1957); *Le Lion* (1958; The Lion, 1959); *Avec les Alcooliques Anonymes* (1960; Eng., The Enemy in the Mouth, 1961; Am., The Road Back, 1961); *Inde, péninsule des dieux* (1960); *Les Mains du miracle* (1960; Eng., The Magic Touch, 1961; Am., The Man with the Miraculous Hands, 1961); *En Tangier, zona internacional* (1962); *Tous n'étaient pas des anges* (1963; They Weren't All Angels, 1965); *Pour l'honneur* (1964); *Romans* (1964); *Les cavaliers* (1967; The Horsemen, 1968)

BIBLIOGRAPHY: Boussard, L., "J. K. à l'Académie Française," *Revue des Deux Mondes* (7 March 1964), 111-15; Marly, P., "Sous la Coupole," *Revue de Paris*, LXXI (1964), 140-42.

BRUNO BERGER

KEYSERLING, Eduard von

German narrative writer, b. 15 May 1855, Pelss-Paddermin (Courland); d. 29 Sept. 1918, Munich

After law studies at the University of Dorpat

and a brief residence in Vienna, K. returned to his home in Courland to manage the family estates. He later lived and traveled extensively in Italy, and from 1899 until his death he made Munich his home. Long troubled by failing eyesight, K. became totally blind in 1907. His final years were marked by extreme loneliness and despair at seeing his family dispossessed of their lands.

Although best known as a sensitive and sympathetic portrayer of the Baltic-German nobility, K.'s greatest achievement lies in his contribution to the flowering of impressionistic prose fiction in Germany. Sometimes called the German counterpart to the Danish writer Bang (q.v.), K. traces with infinite subtlety and delicacy the inner lives of his overrefined, melancholy, and erotically inclined characters.

In a series of novels, novellas, and tales— beginning with *Beate und Mareile* (1903; The Curse of the Tarniffs, 1928) and ending with *Im stillen Winkel* (1918)—the now vanished world of the Baltic or Prussian castle, with its aristocratic owners, the numerous uncles and cousins, the tutor, the pastor, and an array of servants, is described. With few exceptions the stories develop a common theme: isolated, bored, yet tied to their world by inborn passivity and rigid convention, the characters protest briefly, then sink back into resignation and recollection. Love, which is more convention than passion, usually opens the conflict; a duel ends it. All this is communicated in a language notable for objectivity, economy of verbs, careful and precise use of adjectives, and markedly short sentences.

Two early novels—*Rosa Herz* (1883) and *Die dritte Stiege* (1890)—and four dramas, written in the years from 1899 to 1905, are of interest mainly as illustrations of K.'s development away from naturalism (q.v.) toward impressionism and a complete mastery of the art of the novel. T. Mann (q.v.) said that ideally the novel should be characterized by "sublimation, transference, spiritualization, aristocratic style of life, aristocratic elegance and responsibility, aristocratic restraint, bearing, purity, grace, and sense of form."

FURTHER WORKS: *Schwüle Tage* (1906; Father and Son, 1928); *Dumala* (1909); *Wellen* (1911); *Abendliche Häuser* (1914; Twilight, 1927); *Harmonie* (1914; Harmony, 1927); *Am Südhang* (1916); *Fürstinnen* (1917); *Gesammelte Erzählungen*, ed. E. Heilborn (4 vols., 1922)

BIBLIOGRAPHY: Knoop, K., *Die Erzäh-*

lungen E. von K. (1929); Hewitt, T. B., "The Novels of E. von K.," in *GQ*, IV (1931); Muhr, A., "E. Graf K. als Dramatiker," in *Neues Wiener Tagblatt*, No. 80 (1943); Wonderley, W., "Dramatic Symbolism in E. von K.'s Abendliche Häuser," in *GQ*, XXV (1952); Wonderley, W., "Zu E. von K.'s 'Psychologie des Komforts,'" in *GQ*, XXVIII (1955); Haug, G., "Ein Fontane in Moll: Zum Schaffen E. von K.'s," in *Welt und Wort*, XIII (1959); Wonderley, W., *A Study of the Works of E. v. K.* (1959); Pusey, W., "E. v. K. as Essayist and Literary Critic," in *Kentucky Foreign Language Quarterly*, VII (1960), 134-46; McCormick, E. A., "Utopia and Point of View: Narrative Method in Morante's L'Isola di Arturo and K.'s Schwüle Tage," in *Symposium*, XV (1961)

E. ALLEN MCCORMICK

KHLEBNIKOV, Velimír

(pseud. of *Viktor Vladimirovich Khlebnikov*), Russian poet, b. 9 Nov. 1885, Tundutovo, Astrakhan; d. 28 June, 1922, Korostetz, Novgorod

K., who was born into a teacher's family, pursued mathematics at the University of Kazan and biology and Slavic studies at the University of Petersburg. His early literary acquaintances included Ivanov and Kuzmin (qq.v.), but K., who was to become the chief exponent of futurism (q.v.), soon met the futurists and participated in their first joint publication, *Sadok sudei* (1909). He became famous at the publication of his poem *Zaklyatiye Smekhom* (1910), which was built on one word root. In 1912 he signed the manifesto "Poshchiochina obshchestvennomu vkusu," which launched cubofuturism in Russia.

Soon K. became a penniless wanderer (Moscow, Petersburg, Volga, Ukraine), occupying himself with calculating "laws of time" and with devising unrealistic projects for reforming many aspects of human life. In 1916 he served as a private in a reserve battalion. During the revolution and the civil war, K., who was trying to found the utopian "society of globe presidents," continued his wandering. In 1920 he lived in extreme poverty in Kharkov, after which he moved to Baku. In 1921 he visited Persia with the communist troops. As a result of malnutrition he became gravely ill, and after an unsuccessful trip to Moscow to publish his writings, he died.

K.'s long urbanistic *Zhuravl'* (1910) is a surrealistic poem (see surrealism). The mystical poem *I i Ye* (1912) has a Stone Age background. In his epic, *Deti vydry*, K. tried to show the Asiatic connections of Slavic civilization. The long poem *Khadzhi Tarkhan* (1913) is based on the history and legends of his native Astrakhan. *Ka* (1916), a surrealistic prose work, takes place in the Egypt of 1378 B.C. In the symbolic (see symbolism) poem *Poet* (1919), K. discusses the problems of a poet in a scientific age. The poet is presented as an alien in the modern world, who is inspired both by paganism and Christianity. *Ladomir* (1920) is a long utopian poem that depicts a universally harmonious future.

Nasha osnova (1920), K.'s most important theoretical essay, treats the creation of new words out of existing roots, explains his theory of *zaum* (trans-rational language), and expounds his theory of the mathematical foundation of history. *Truba Gul' mully* (1921) is K.'s poetic diary of Persia. In the poem *Nochnoi objsk* (1921), K. presented the Russian Revolution as tragic retribution. *Zangezi* (1922), which is a collection of imaginary conversations between a philosopher and the people, is K.'s testament and encyclopedia of all his principal verbal and poetic experiments.

Declared a genius by some and dismissed as a madman by others, K. has been one of the strongest influences in modern Russian poetry, an influence that was especially strong in the twenties.

FURTHER WORKS: *Sobraniye proizvedenii V. Khlebnikova* (5 vols., 1928-33)

BIBLIOGRAPHY: Yakobson, R., *Noveishaya russkaya poeziya, nabrosok pervyi* (1921); Gofman, V., *Yazykovoye novatorstvo Khlebnikova* (1936); Stepanov, N., "K. V. V., biograficheski acherk," in *K.'s Izbrannyye stikhotvorenya* (1936); Tynyanov, Y., "V. K.," in *Arkhaisty i novatory* (1936); Markov, V., *The Longer Poems of K.* (1962); Hausmann, R., "Introduction à une histoire du poème phonétique," in *GL&L*, XX (1965), 19-25

VLADIMIR MARKOV

KHODASEVICH, Vladislav (Felitziyanovich)

Russian poet and critic, b. 29 May 1886, Moscow; d. 14 June 1939, Biancourt (near Paris)

K.'s father belonged to a noble Polish family and his mother was of Jewish descent; through education and social background he became completely Russian. After graduating from Moscow University he began his writing career. In 1922 he emigrated via Berlin to Paris, where until 1925 he served as a critic on refugee journals and tried to rally the younger generation of émigrés around himself.

K.'s early poems, which were published from 1905 on in Russian symbolist (see symbolism) journals, were strongly influenced by Bryusov and Belyi (qq.v.). It took the impact of the October Revolution to mature him into a great poet whose work perpetuated the great traditions of Russian poetry. *Putem zerna* (1920), *Tyazhelaye lira* (1923), and *Yevropeiskiye nochi* (1927) reveal his mastery at its peak. In these collections up-to-date, stirring themes (Russia's catastrophe, regrets for Europe's threatened way of life, the sufferings of the refugees) are handled by K. in verse of classical austerity and utmost perfection of form. Thus, everyday scenes take on a symbolic character. K.'s poetic work, although small in volume, ranks among the supreme achievements of 20th c. Russian lyric poetry. His later work includes extensive criticism and scholarly works, as well as a volume of memoirs, *Nekropol'* (1939), in which he brings to life the last great flowering of Russian culture and literature at the beginning of this century.

K. is among the few Russian émigrés who, besides continuing the same genres and trends they had practiced at home, tried to provide in their works an answer to the catastrophe that had befallen the Russian intelligentsia.

FURTHER WORKS: *Moloaost'* (1908); *Shchastlivyi domik* (1914); *Stat'i o russkoi poezii* (1922); *Zagadki* (1922); *Poeticheskoye Khozyaistvo Pushkina* (1924); *Sobraniye stikhov* (1927); *Derzharin* (1931); *O Pushkine* (1937); *Literaturnyye stat'i; vospominaniya* (1954)

BIBLIOGRAPHY: Vejdle, V. (Weidle'), "Poeziya K.," in *Sovremennyye Zapiski* 34 (1928); Struve, G., in *Literature and Revolution in Soviet Russia, 1917-62—A Symposium* (ed. M. Hayward and L. Labedz; 1963), pp. 1-27

GÜNTHER WYTRZENS

KILPI, Volter Adalbert

Finnish novelist, b. 12 Dec. 1874, Kustavi; d. 13 June 1939, Turku

K. was influenced chiefly by the English pre-

Raphaelites, German romanticism and the philosophy of Nietzsche (q.v.). His late works —the trilogy made up of *Alastalon salissa* (1933), *Pitäjän pienempiä* (1934) and *Kirkolle* (1937)—are the most valuable. Here K. continues the tradition of the contemporary European novelists (Proust and Joyce [qq.v.]). In vivid, original language and a rich, compressed style, he describes his own bailiwick, a west-Finnish island community, its people and its way of life. Past and present merge in a colorful overall picture that is pervaded by warm humor.

FURTHER WORKS: *Parsifal* (1902); *Antinous* (1903); *Kansallista itsetukistelua* (1917); *Tulevaisuuden edessä* (1918); *Suljetuilla porteilla* (1938); *Gulliverin matka Pantomimian mantereelle* (1944)

BIBLIOGRAPHY: Suomi, V., *Nuori V. K.* (1952); *Suomen Kirjallisuus V* (1965); Lappalainen, P., *Die Ideen der realistischen Hauptströmung und ihre Kontinuität in der Literatur von Finnland* (1967)

VILHO SUOMI

KIPLING, (Joseph) Rudyard

English novelist, short story writer, and poet; b. 30 Dec. 1865, Bombay; d. 18 Jan. 1936, Sussex

One of the most widely-read authors of his time, K. won the Nobel Prize for Literature in 1907. His very varied work has always aroused violent and conflicting reactions, often for political reasons, since he was regarded as a "prophet of British imperialism." But his real genius was that of an imaginative storyteller, in prose and verse.

The main influences in his early life were separation in childhood from his parents and some years of great unhappiness in England (described in *Baa Baa Black Sheep*), education at a school that specialized in training boys to be army officers (described in *Stalky & Co.*), and living in India (from the age of seventeen to that of twenty-four) as a journalist. These years in India gave him the material for his poems and stories about India, with which he achieved, while still young, sudden and sensational fame. In 1892 he came to America, where he lived for four years. This episode was ended by a family quarrel and lawsuit, an experience that greatly intensified an inborn passion for privacy. He then returned to England and settled in rural Sussex, where he lived for the rest of his life.

About this time K.'s work began increasingly to be based on English material, especially the English past, while it was becoming more thoughtful and almost mystical. Correspondingly, he withdrew gradually into a self-made and unhappy isolation, a personality change that resulted, in part, from family tragedy (the death of a daughter in 1890, and the death of his only son in World War I in 1915) and from his hatred of modern developments in democracy and anticolonialism.

Though K. had few connections with other writers and with literary movements, his verse does owe something to Browning and Swinburne (though more to ballads, hymns, and music-hall songs) just as his stories owe something to Bret Harte and Maupassant.

The first of the Indian books were *Plain Tales from the Hills* (1888) and *Soldiers Three* (1888)—both of which were collections of short stories—and *Barrack Room Ballads* (1892). These describe the life led by the English— civilians and soldiers—in India. Readable, clever, cynical, and vigorous as these stories and poems are, most of them have little depth. The two *Jungle Books* (1894 and 1895) and *Kim* (1901), together with some of the short stories in *Life's Handicap* (1891) and *The Day's Work* (1898), contain the best of his writing about India.

Kim, usually considered K.'s masterpiece, is more concerned with the Indians than with the English in India. Its reader, as T. S. Eliot says, can really "smell India." K. loved and understood traditional India, the un-Westernized India of priests, soldiers, rajahs, and peasants; he hated and did not understand the new India, which was learning Western education and beginning to feel the passion of nationalism.

K.'s works with an English setting include the stories in *Puck of Pook's Hill* (1906) and *Rewards and Fairies* (1910), which were written for children. Like most of K.'s children's works, however, they are read with pleasure by adults. These stories, which are imaginative re-creations of historical episodes in the English past, show a deep sense of tradition and continuity. K. can be faulted, however, for allowing himself to create characters in these stories that are very much like the people he had known in India in the past. The young Roman army officer, for example, is very much like the British army officer of K.'s India.

Of K.'s books for children, the two *Jungle*

Books and the *Just So Stories* (1902) are the best. K. had a remarkable talent, very rare in the 20th c., for inventing what seem like genuine myths. By presenting simplified characters and animals who talk in the fable tradition, and by utilizing ritual repetition of phrases, he achieved an art that, though actually very sophisticated and individual, has the air of something primitive and anonymous. The French critic André Chevrillon has aptly called him a "great primitive."

The stories and poems of K.'s later life, such as those in *Debits and Credits* (1926) and *Limits and Renewals* (1932), are much more difficult than any of those he had written earlier. Many of them show an obsession with physical pain and with the supernatural and mystical. They are far less popular, and deservedly so, than his earlier work.

K. was at his best in the short story, in popular verse (a small proportion of which is genuine poetry), and in writing (prose and verse) for children. It seems likely that some of his work will survive, though he failed to create great writing. His work is flawed by an insensitivity to ideas, a streak of brutality, a quality of childishness that he never outgrew, and by a pseudo-Biblical diction (in serious passages) that does not ring true. But he remains a writer of great power, originality, and interest.

FURTHER WORKS: *Departmental Ditties* (1886); *The Phantom Rickshaw* (1888); *In Black and White* (1888); *Plain Tales from the Hills* (1888); *The Story of the Gadsbys* (1888); *Under the Deodars* (1888); *Wee Willie Winkie* (1888); *The Day's Work* (1889); *The Light that Failed* (1890); *Life's Handicap* (1891); *Many Invention* (1893); *The Seven Seas* (1896); *Recessional* (1897); *The Slaves of the Lamp* (1897); *Captains Courageous* (1897); *Ballad of East and West* (1899); *The White Man's Burden* (1899); *Collected Verse* (1907); *Actions and Reactions* (1909); *The Female of the Species* (1912); *For All We Have and Are* (1914); *Rudyard Kipling's Verse, Inclusive Edition, 1885-1918* (1919); *The Years Between* (1919); *Letters of Travel 1892-1913* (1920); *The Irish Guards in the Great War* (1923); *A Choice of the Songs from the Verse of Rudyard Kipling* (1925); *Sea and Sussex from Rudyard Kipling's Verse* (1926); *The Art of Fiction* (1926); *Rudyard Kipling's Verse, 1885-1926* (1927); *A Book of Words, Selections from Speeches and Addresses Delivered Between 1906 and 1927* (1928); *The*

One Volume Kipling, Authorized (1928); *Poems, 1886-1929* (1930); *Rudyard Kipling's Verse, 1885-1932* (1933); *All the Mowgli Stories* (1933); *Something of Myself* (1937); *Complete Works* (35 vols., 1937-39), *Rudyard Kipling's Verse* (1940); *A Choice of Kipling's Verse* (ed. T. S. Eliot; 1941)

BIBLIOGRAPHY: Chevrillon, A., *R. K.* (1936); Shanks, E. B., *R. K., A Study in Literature and Political Ideas* (1940); Eliot, T. S., *Introduction to a Choice of K.'s Verse* (1941); Wilson, E., *The Wound and the Bow* (1941); Brown, C. H., *R. K., A New Appreciation* (1945); Carrington, C. E., *R. K., His Life and Work* (1955); Tompkins, J. M. S., *The Art of R. K.* (1959; rev. ed., 1965); Rutherford, A., ed., *K.'s Mind and Art* (1964); Cohen, M. N., ed., *R. K. to Rider Haggard: The Record of a Friendship* (1965); Stewart, J. I. M., *R. K.* (1966); Rao, K. B., *R. K.'s India* (1967)

PATRICK CRUTTWELL

KIRK, Hans Rudolf

Danish novelist, b. 11 Jan. 1898, Hadsund, Jutland

Despite his family background—his father was a country doctor—and education, K. never lost touch with the farmers and fishermen of Jutland. His novel *Fiskerne* (1928) demonstrates not only his talent but also his profound knowledge of the people of Jutland. A thesis novel, it follows the Marxist theory that culture is a superstructure dependent on economic conditions. This book had extraordinarily far-reaching effects in Denmark and to some extent throughout Scandinavia.

K. later tried to develop the same theme on a larger scale, but only the first two volumes (*Daglejerne*, 1936; *De nye Tider*, 1939) of his projected trilogy have appeared. After World War II he wrote several minor works in which he tried, not too successfully, to elevate documentary reporting to the level of an art form. In his two historical novels—*Slaven* (1948) and *Vredens søn* (1950)—K. attempts a Marxist interpretation of the life of Jesus.

FURTHER WORKS: *Borgmesteren går af* (1941); *Skyggespiel* (1950); *Djaevelens Penge* (1951); *Klitgaard og sønner* (1952)

BIBLIOGRAPHY: Hjorth, P. L., "Brugen af dialektfarve i. H. K.'s *Fiskerne*," in *Danica* (1964), 171-79

PETER P. ROHDE

KLABUND

(pseud. of *Alfred Henschke*), German poet, novelist, and playwright, b. 4 Nov. 1890, Crossen (Oder); d. 14 Aug. 1928, Davos

K. spent his childhood in Crossen and Frankfurt on Oder. At the age of eighteen he had to undergo treatment for tuberculosis. He then studied literature and philosophy in Munich, Lausanne, and Berlin, but did not graduate. In 1913 he was discovered by Kerr (q.v.), and his first poems appeared in the magazine *Pan*. The initial scandal over K.'s erotic poetry was followed by others over his morals and politics. Writing feverishly, repeatedly driven back to Switzerland and Italy by his worsening illness, K. lived mostly in Berlin. After the death of his first wife, who was also ill, he married the actress Carola Neher. He died of tuberculosis.

K.'s versatile gift for form shows in the wide variety of poems he published: the provocatively erotic early experiments; the *Soldatenlieder* (1914); the simple, folksong-like poems of *Himmelsleiter* (1917); the symbolic, expressionistic hymns (*Irene oder Die Gesinnung*, 1917); the ecstatic *Dreiklang* (1920); the deeply moving *Totenklage*, written in 1918-19 for his first wife and published in 1928; more folk ballads (*Das heiße Herz*, 1922); and, finally, the Berlin street ballads, grotesque popular songs, and rhymed critiques of the times (*Die Harfenjule*, 1927).

In prose K. created his own form—the expressionist novella. His novels fall into three groups. The "novels of longing"—*Die Krankheit* (1917), *Franziskus* (1921); and *Roman eines jungen Mannes* (1924)—and the delirium-fantasy *Spuk* (1922) treat the theme of disease and love that was so crucial to K.; they are highly autobiographical. The "novels of passion"—*Moreau* (1916), *Mohammed* (1917), *Pjotr* (1923), and *Rasputin* (written in 1929 as a film scenario)—are not so much historical studies as lyrical, passionately sensual sketches of highly stylized characters, written with occasional expressionistic condensation. His greatest achievement in prose are his two "novels of fulfillment"—*Bracke* (1918), a German-Gothic novel about Till Eulenspiegel as a symbol of "man becoming himself," and the violently sensual Renaissance novel about the Borgias *Borgia* (1928; The Incredible Borgias, 1929).

Among K.'s plays, some of which are now forgotten, his excellent free adaptation from the Chinese, *Der Kreidekreis* (1925), long had a leading place on the German stage. His folk-play, *Christoph Wagner* (1925), and his marital comedy, *XYZ* (1928), were also successful for a time.

Among K.'s best works are his numerous adaptations of German, English, and French translations from the Chinese (*Li-tai-pe*, 1916; *Lao-tse*, 1921), the Japanese (*Die Geisha O-sen*, 1918; *Das Kirschblütenfest*, 1926), and the Persian (*Der Feueranbeter*, 1919; *Das Sinngedicht des persischen Zeltmachers*, 1917). His masterly gift for language found full scope in these variations on given themes.

All K.'s hasty, restless work has been much criticized for its loose composition, careless language, superficial development, and excessive amoral fantasies. An eternally young vagrant poet, who recognized himself in Hafiz (ca. 1300-1388), Li-tai-peh (701-762), Till Eulenspiegel, and François Villon (ca. 1431-63), K. left his mark on German literature as the author of a few expressionist poems and novels, but chiefly as a translator of Oriental poetry who fully measured up to its genius.

FURTHER WORKS: *Morgenrot! Klabund! Die Tage dämmern!* (1913); *K.'s Karussell* (1914); *Der Marketenderwagen* (1915); *Dumpfe Trommel und berauschtes Gong* (1915); *Montezuma* (1919); *Der himmlische Vagant* (1919); *Die Nachtwandler* (1920); *Das Blumenschiff* (1921); *Heiligenlegenden* (1921); *Geschichte der Weltliteratur in einer Stunde* (1921); *Lesebuch* (1925); *Gedichte* (1926); *Dichtungen aus dem Osten* (3 vols., 1929); *Novellen von der Liebe* (1930); *Gesammelte Werke* (6 vols., 1930)

BIBLIOGRAPHY: Benn, G., *Totenrede für K.* (1928); Grothe, H., *K.* (1933); Ludowyk, E. F. C., "The Chalk Circle: A Legend in Four Cultures," in *CL* IX (1960), 249-56; Heinrich, E., ed., *K.: Briefe an einen Freund* (1963)

INGO SEIDLER

KLEPPER, Jochen

German poet, novelist, and essayist, b. 22 March 1903, Beuthen, Silesia; d. 11 Dec. 1942, Berlin

K. studied Protestant theology and was a journalist in Berlin. When his Jewish wife and her daughter were about to be sent to a concentration camp they all committed suicide together. K.'s prose dealt with the period of Wilhelm I—*Der Vater* (1937), *In Tormentis Pinxit* (1938), *Der Soldatenkönig und die*

RUDYARD KIPLING

ARTHUR KOESTLER

Stillen im Lande (1938). His essential aim was to present earthly events in the light of divine order. K.'s spiritual, deeply religious poetry (*Kyrie,* 1938) remains within the bounds of tradition. His posthumously published diaries are deeply moving.

FURTHER WORKS: *Der Kahn der fröhlichen Leute* (1933); *Der christliche Roman* (1940); *Die Flucht der Katharina von Bora* (1951); *Unter dem Schatten seiner Flügel* (1956); *Überwindung* (1958); *Nachspiel* (1960); *Gast und Fremdling* (1961); *Gesammelte Gedichte* (1962)

BIBLIOGRAPHY: Ihlenfeldt, K., *Freundschaft mit J. K.* (1958); Meschke, E.-J., ed., *Gast und Fremdling* (1960); Arnim, H. v., *Christliche Gestalten neuerer deutscher Dichtung* (1961); Loewy, E., *Literatur unterm Hakenkreuz* (1967)

EVA PREISS

KLITGAARD, Mogens
Danish novelist, b. 23 Aug. 1906, Valby; d. 23 Aug. 1945, Aarhus

K. is a typical representative of the social realism of the 1930's. After ten years of rootless existence, he published a novel, *Der sidder en mand i en sporvogn* (1937), which can be looked at as a variation on Fallada's (q.v.) *Little Man What Now?* K. worked actively for German refugees and was secretary of several anti-Nazi organizations. In 1940 he fled to Sweden.

As an artist, K. combined a capacity for cool judgment with a highly developed sense of form and language. His two historical novels— *De røde fjer* (1940), set in the post-1807 period (in 1807 England and Denmark were at war), and *Ballade på Nytorv* (1940)—are considered his masterpieces.

FURTHER WORKS: *Gud mildner luften for de klippede får* (1938); *Elly Petersen* (1941); *Den guddommelige Hverdag* (1942); *Brunkul* (1946)

BIBLIOGRAPHY: Neergaard, E., *M. K.* (1941); Stangerup, H., on K. in Hertel, H., ed., *Tilbageblick på 30'erne* (1967), ii, 128-33

PETER P. ROHDE

KLYCHKOV, Sergei Antonovich
Russian poet and novelist, b. 5 July 1889, Dubrovki

K. began to publish in 1909. Up to 1925 he wrote almost nothing but poetry, but later concentrated on prose. He was strongly influenced by Klyuyev (q.v.). K., who was an enemy of urban civilization, nostalgically mourned the loss of Russia's ancient patriarchal way of life. This led Soviet critics to class him contemptuously as an author of "kulak literature." In his poems and his novels (*Poslednii Lel'*, 1927; *Knyaz' mira,* 1928; others), the characters are symbolically conceived; in composition, reality and fantasy are closely interwoven. After 1935 K. was subjected to disciplinary punishment; since then nothing has been heard of him.

FURTHER WORKS: *V gostyakh u zhuravlei* (1930); *Sakharnyi nemetz* (1934); *Saraspan* (1936); *Almabet i Altynai* (free translation of the Kirghiz epic *Manas,* 1936)

BIBLIOGRAPHY: Simmons, E. J., *Russian Fiction and Soviet Ideology* (1958)

PETER YERSHOV

KLYUYEV, Nikolai Alekseyevich
Russian poet. b. 1887, Vytegra, north Russia; d. (probably) Aug. 1937, Siberia

K., who was of peasant origin, had a firsthand knowledge of the sectarian peasant world, saturated with age-old tradition, which right down to the present has retained many traits characteristic of old Russian life and poetry. He was particularly attracted by the mystically ecstatic believers who, in the spirit of the apocryphal writings, regarded life as a mere pilgrimage. In 1906 he went to Baku as a courier for illegal sectarian groups and from there to Persia, Central Asia, and probably India. The poetic theme of a mythically transfigured "white India," which subsequently recurs repeatedly in his poetry, dates back to this experience. In 1908 he began his correspondence with Blok (q.v.), which continued over many years. In 1911 his first book of poems *Sosen perezvon* appeared. The rest of K.'s life was a restless pilgrimage between the metropolitan cultural centers of Russia and the monasteries and shrines.

K. greeted the outbreak of the revolution with short-lived ecstasy, but later rejected it completely. From then on, his life, like his writing, was a long-drawn-out protest against the new form of government. He was finally exiled to Siberia.

K.'s poetry centers around the Russian landscape and village and man's way of the cross. He combines these into a vaguely prophetic version of Christian dogma that is infused with the mythical chthonian ideas and eschatological expectations of primitive sects. But these three themes are actually one; they are unified by the tone of compelling melancholy pervading even the idyllic and gently humorous poems, by the anarchically exuberant pathos of brotherly love, by constant rededication to the powers of Mother Earth and pious custom, and by a religious yearning for the sanctification and transfiguration of nature and of man's communal life. Beginning with melodic, polished verses in the folk manner, K. went on to draw upon—and to blend harmoniously—the naive, archaic linguistic elements of the folksongs, ballads, and ecstatic hymns of the sectarians, the metaphors, rhythms, and cadences of 20th c. Russian poetry, and the formal innovations of the symbolists (see symbolism), acmeists, and futurists (see futurism).

In many respects K. can be compared with V. I. Ivanov (q.v.), who knew and encouraged him. In his mythical, allegorical archaic poetry in the old Russian style, Ivanov, himself formed by Greco-Roman classicism, mysticism, and idealistic philosophy and by symbolist poetry, was attempting exactly what K. successfully achieved in poems such as *Chetviortyi Rim* (1923), *Derevnya* and *Pogorel'shehina*. They represent a poetic rebirth of the Hellenistic-Byzantine-old-Russian cosmos — perhaps its last incarnation in the Russian language.

FURTHER WORKS: *Pesnoslov* (1919); *Mednyi kit* (1919); *Pesn' solntzenostza* (1920); *Izbrannyye pesni* (1920); *L'vinyi khleb* (1922); *Mat' Subbota* (1923); *Izba i pole* (1928); *Polnoye sobraniye stichotvorenyi* (1955)

BIBLIOGRAPHY: Preface, in Filippov, B., ed., *Polnoye sobraniye stichotvorenyi* (1955)
HEINRICH STAMMLER

KNUDSEN, Jacob Christian Lindberg
Danish novelist, b. 14 Sept. 1858, Rödding, North Schleswig; d. 21 Jan. 1917, Hilleröd, Sjaelland

K., son of a pastor and distinguished leader in adult education, himself taught in the Askov University extension system and from 1890 to 1896 was a Protestant minister. He was a follower of the Danish theologian Nicolai Frederik Grundtvig (1783-1872). Not until 1898

did K. begin to publish novels, novellas, essays, and sermons. Extremely critical of humanistic liberalism, he used paradox to uphold individual liberty and an undogmatic Lutheranism based on a personal relationship with God. His limitations resulted from his rejection of all aestheticism and in his tendentious leanings.

Artistically, his most successful work is his Jutland peasant novel *Sind* (1903)—a grandiose yet simple tragedy arising out of unspoiled instinctivity, Old Testament piety, a sense of justice, and hot-tempered tenacity. In a series of programmatic problem novels (*Fremskridt*, 1907; *Laerer Urup*, 1909; for example), K. dealt with questions of marriage and education in an antimodern, uncompromisingly individualistic spirit, and energetically advocated social responsibility and freedom in all spiritual matters.

An excellent work is *Rodfaestet* (1911). In his pair of novels—*Angst* (1912) and *Mod* (1914)—he attempted a highly personal interpretation of Luther, which is legendary yet intensive. *Jyder* (2 vols., 1915-17) contains humorous novellas.

FURTHER WORKS: *Den gamle Praest* (1899); *Gaering* (1902); *Afklaring* (1902); *For livets skyld* (1905); *To slaegter* (1910); *En Ungdom* (1913); *Romaner og Fortaellinger* (5 vols., 1917); *Digte* (1938); *Sind Udgivet med efterskrift* (1964)

BIBLIOGRAPHY: Roos, C., *J. K.* (1918; rev. and expanded, 1954); Norrild, S., *J. K.* (1935); Ulrichsen, E., "E. K.'s dramatik," in *Perspektiv*, IX (1961), 43-46; Henriksen, A., "Komplekset J. K.," in *Dansk Udsyn*, XLV (1965), 259-65
EMIL FREDERIKSEN

KOEPPEN, Wolfgang
German novelist, b. 23 June 1906, Greifswald, Pomerania

After eventful years as a seaman, followed by residence in Italy, France, and the Netherlands, K. settled in Berlin. His first prose works, *Eine unglückliche Liebe* and *Die Mauer schwankt* appeared in 1934 and 1935; both were swamped in the flood of Nazi-controlled literature.

In 1951, K. published his novel *Tauben im Gras* (title from Gertrude Stein [q.v.]), which presents a cross-section of daily life in Munich immediately after World War II. Its style derives from the English-language novel, especially that of Dos Passos (q.v.). K.'s most widely discussed book, *Das Treibhaus* (The Bonn Parliament, 1953), tells the story of an opposition member of the government (the culmination is his suicide). Its intensive stream-of-consciousness technique makes much use of current slang. In *Tod in Rom* (1954) the encounter between members of a mayor's family reveals the wide range of conflicting fundamental attitudes within the German middle class. In this novel K. also explores the antithesis between the permanent and the transitory by contrasting absurdly macabre happenings against the background of the Eternal City.

FURTHER WORKS: *Nach Rußland und anderswohin: Empfindsame Reisen* (1958); *W. K.'s Amerikafahrt* (1959); *Reise nach Frankreich* (1961); *New York* (1961); *Die ernsten Griechen* (1962)

BIBLIOGRAPHY: Jens, W., "Verleihung des Georg-Büchner-Preises an W. K.," in *Deutsche Akademie für Sprache und Dichtung (Darmstadt) Jahrbuch* (1962), 93-102; Reich-Ranicki, M., "Über W. K.," in *Monat*, XV (1965), 65-75; Bance, A. F., "*Der Tod in Rom* and *Die Rote*: Two Italian Episodes," in *Forum for Modern Language Studies*, III (1967), 126-34

GERHARD FRITSCH

KOESTLER, Arthur

English novelist and political writer; b. 5 Sept. 1905, Budapest

From 1922 to 1926 K. studied at the University and the Technische Hochschule of Vienna. He then became a newspaper correspondent in the Near East, in Paris and Berlin and, during the Civil War, in Spain. After returning from Spain, he resigned from the Communist party, which he had joined in 1932. At the outbreak of World War II he was interned in France but succeeded, after his release in 1940, in fleeing via Portugal to England. He served in the British army in World War II and since the war has lived mostly in England.

In autobiography, novels, and essays, K. speaks about the experiences and insights of—and on behalf of—all those commonly lumped together as "the non-aligned left." He has been a contributor to German, Hungarian, Austrian, Palestinian, French, and English newspapers. As an ardent communist, a believer in Freudian theory, and a supporter of militant Zionism

who had lost the faith—and finally as a disillusioned renegade from almost all ideologies —K. made an appeal to the "community of pessimists" that aroused a relatively widespread response among the international intelligentsia.

In 1937, while K. was covering the Spanish Civil War from loyalist Spain, he was captured by the fascists, confined to a Franco prison, and condemned to death as a spy. For a hundred days K. expected momentarily the execution of the sentence. In concentrated, economical language, with an unemotional quality K. afterward attained only sporadically, *Ein spanisches Testament* (1937; English adaptation, Spanish Testament, 1937; English abridged edition, Dialogue with Death, 1942) reveals the individual confronted with his destiny as it emerges from K.'s account of what he had undergone before he was pardoned.

In the second volume of his autobiography, *The Invisible Writing* (1953), K. stated what he was trying to do in the books that followed *Ein spanisches Testament*: "Ethical problems had hitherto played no part in my writing; now they became its central concern. In *The Gladiators* [1939] and *Darkness at Noon* [1940] which was the next book, I tried to come to intellectual terms with the intuitive glimpses gained during the 'hours by the window.' Both novels were variations on the same theme: the problem of Ends and Means, the conflict between transcendental morality and social expediency. The next novel, *Arrival and Departure* [1943], was a rejection of the ethical neutrality of science as expressed in the psychiatrist's claim to be able to 'reduce' courage, dedication, and self-sacrifice to neurotic motives.... In *The Yogi and the Commissar* [1945] I tried once more to digest, in the form of essays this time, the meaning of the solitary dialogue of cell No. 40. This book, written in 1943, closed the cycle; it had taken five years to digest the hours by the window."

K. never stopped interpreting and analyzing this deeply felt episode. In the face of death the frailty of all ideologies had become obvious to this activist idealist. Since then K. has proclaimed his message, which calls for the substitution of question marks for all-too-prevalent exclamation points. The significance of his work lies in the almost masochistic intensity with which he ceaselessly poses questions. Stylistically only certain passages in *Darkness at Noon* and a few chapters of the autobiographies—*Arrow in the Blue* (1952) and *The Invisible Writing*—really achieve the compelling impact of *Ein spanisches Testament*.

In his most recent books K. has from time to time gone beyond pure skepticism. After the word of "the new god who is about to be born," which emerged somewhat abruptly in *Arrival and Departure*, the doubter began to doubt doubt and to seek a new religious bond —though outside any denomination. *The Age of Longing* (1951)—perhaps K.'s most interesting work—is concerned with true security in "knowing." Here K. takes his stand on Christianity and communism, and on trivial bourgeois values, and reveals man's eternal longing for an inward center.

What sets K.'s books apart from all other polemical writing for or against certain ideas is chiefly his inexorability toward himself: "There has never been an intelligentsia without a guilt complex; that is the income tax we have to pay for wanting to make other people richer. . . ."

K. is one of those who write out of a compulsion to bear witness as to what has happened to them. (The description in *Scum of the Earth* [1941] of the French internment camp for "suspect persons," in which anti-Nazis were detained after the outbreak of war, is one of the few atmospherically authentic documents of what befell the refugees who fled from Nazi Germany.) The result is, to be sure, no truly great literary achievement, but it is an authentic, important contribution to the understanding of his time. Despite the growing tendency of his most recent works to blur the dividing line between experience and knowledge through a somewhat popularizing "scientism," this contribution holds good, up to a certain point, even where autobiography gives way to history.

FURTHER WORKS: *Twilight Bar* (1945); *Thieves in the Night* (1946); *Promise and Fulfillment, Palestine 1917-1949* (1949); *The Structure of a Miracle* (1949); *Insight and Outlook: An Inquiry into the Common Foundations of Science, Art and Social Ethics* (1949); *The Trail of the Dinosaur* (1955); *Reflections on Hanging* (1956); *The Sleepwalkers: A History of Man's Changing Vision of the Universe* (1959); *The Watershed: A Biography of Johannes Kepler* (1960); *The Lotus and the Robot* (1961); *Hanged by the Neck* (with C. H. Rolph, 1961); *Reflections on the Peninsula of Europe* (1962); *The Act of Creation* (1964); *Suicide of a Nation* (1964);

The Ghost in the Machine (1967); *Drinkers of Infinity: Essays, 1955-1967* (1968)

BIBLIOGRAPHY: Nevada, J., *A. K.* (1948); Atkins, J., *A. K.* (1956); Hoffman, F. J., "*Darkness at Noon:* The Consequences of Secular Grace," in *GaR*, XIII (1959), 331-45; Beum, R., "Epigraphs for Rubashov," in *DR*, XLI (1962), 86-91; Haynes, R., "Spheres in Collision," in *Month*, XXXII (1964), 261-66; Kadt, J. de., "Arthur in Wonderland," in *Tirade*, VIII (1964), 615-41

KARL O. PAETEL

KOKOSCHKA, Oskar

Austrian dramatist, narrative writer, and painter, b. 1 March 1886, Pöchlarn

K., the son of an artistic Prague family, became a professor at the Dresden Art Academy in 1918. After living for several years in Vienna and Prague, he emigrated to England in 1938. He now lives in Switzerland.

Just as K. the painter tries to reveal the typical within the individual rather than the individual itself, K. the dramatist tries "to organize human faces into compositions in which being clashes with being." His visually rich imagination breaks the bounds of logic, and his characters experience an excess of emotion expressed in ecstatic torrents of words. K.'s short stories and essays are easier to understand; they too reveal him as an ecstatic for whom the visible is but one of the masks of truth.

WORKS: *Sphinx und Strohmann* (1907); *Mörder, Hoffnung der Frauen* (1907); *Der brennende Dornbusch* (1911); *Dramen und Bilder* (1913); *Der gefesselte Kolumbus* (1916); *4 Dramen* (1919); *Die träumenden Knaben* (1920); *Schriften, 1907-1955* (1956); *Spur im Treibsand* (1956; A Sea Ringed with Visions, 1962); *Der Expressionismus Edvard Munchs* (1956); *Erzähltes Leben, ein Selbstportrait* (1963); *Handzeichnungen 1906-1965* (1966)

BIBLIOGRAPHY: Hoffmann, E., *K., Life and Work* (1947); Lucas, W. I., "O. K.," in *German Men of Letters*, III (1964), 37-52; Schwerte, H., "Anfang des expressionistischen Dramas: O. K.," in *Zeitschrift für deutsche Philologie*, XXXXIII (1964), 171-91; Denkler, H., "Die Druckfassungen der Dramen O. K.'s," *DVLG*, XL (1966), 90-108

PAUL WIMMER

KOLB, Annette

German novelist and essayist, b. 2 Feb. 1875, Badenweiler; d. 3 Dec. 1967, Munich

Of German descent through her father and French through her mother, Annette K. was familiar from earliest childhood with the culture of both nations, which accounts for the happy synthesis of the German and the French spirit in her work. The French element is strongest in her essays, some of which she wrote in French. These writings consist of critical observations on literature and music, and of analyses of the contemporary intellectual and social climate. Written in elegant, musical language, these essays reflect a witty irony and a subtle understanding.

Annette K. felt an equal allegiance to both Germany and France, and during World War I, she worked actively for peace. Tragically, she felt within herself the clash of the warring countries. This conflict was movingly expressed in her *Dreizehn Briefe einer Deutsch-Französin* (1921). In 1933 she emigrated from Germany to France, then later to America.

Familiar from an early age with the milieu of fashionable salons, Annette K. captures in her novels the atmosphere of aristocratic society in the 1920's. The leading feminine characters are full of charm yet natural and unidealized. There is a good deal of self-analysis in their psychological treatment. She has also made a reputation as a sensitive translator—of Chesterton and Giraudoux (qq.v.) among others.

In the character Jeanette Scheurl in the novel *Doktor Faustus*, Thomas Mann (q.v.) dedicated his own memorial to her.

FURTHER WORKS: *Sieben Studien* (1906); *Das Exemplar* (1913); *Wege und Umwege* (1914); *Die Last* (1918); *Zarastro: Westliche Tage* (1922); *Spitzbögen* (1925); *Daphne Herbst* (1928); *Versuch über Briand* (1929); *Die kleine Fanfare* (1930); *Beschwerdebuch* (1932); *Die Schaukel* (1934); *Mozart* (1937); *Schubert* (1941); *Ludwig II. von Bayern und Richard Wagner* (1947); *Blätter in den Wind* (1954); *Memento* (1960); *Mozart, sein Leben* (1963); *Zeitbilder* (1964)

BIBLIOGRAPHY: Rinser, L., *Der Schwerpunkt* (1960)

HELGA THOMAS

KOLBENHEYER, Erwin Guido

German novelist and dramatist, b. 30 Dec. 1878, Budapest; d. 12 April 1962

The son of a German architect, K. studied philosophy and natural science in Vienna. After the success of his novel about Spinoza, *Amor Dei* (1908; God-Intoxicated Man, 1933), he gave up his original plan—which was to teach at a university—and became a free-lance writer. He lived in Tübingen until 1932, then in Solln near Munich, and in Woolfratshausen, Upper Bavaria.

In his philosophical-biological studies K. wanted to construct a concept of life that was antipodal to German idealism (*Die Bauhütte*, 1925). For a time, chiefly because of his thesis that the individual can survive only by total submission to the natural laws of race and nation, he supported Nazism.

K. tried to incorporate ideological elements from the German past into contemporary experience and feeling in a number of his novels —*Meister Joachim Pausewang* (1910), *Paracelsus-Trilogie: Die Kindheit des Paracelsus* (1917), *Das Gestirn des Paracelsus* (1922), *Das Dritte Reich des Paracelsus* (1926), *Das gottgelobte Herz* (1938). In other novels—*Montsalvasch* (1912) and the autobiographical *Das Lächeln der Penaten* (1927)—he dealt with contemporary problems. *Reps, die Persönlichkeit* (1932), a small-town novel, is a satire.

K. also wrote a series of passionately indignant antichurch plays—*Giordano Bruno* (1903; new version, *Heroische Leidenschaften*, 1929), *Die Brücke* (1929), *Jagt ihn—ein Mensch* (1931), *Gregor und Heinrich* (1934).

FURTHER WORKS: *Ahalibama* (1913); *Drei Legenden* (1923); *Der Dornbusch brennt* (1922); *Lyrisches Brevier* (1929); *Karlsbader Novelle* (1929); *Das Gesetz in Dir* (1931); *Weihnachtsgeschichten* (1932); *Die Begegnung auf dem Riesengebirge* (1932); *Klaas Y, der große Neutrale* (1936); *Vox humana* (1940); *Götter und Menschen* (1944); *Sebastian Karst über sein Leben und seine Zeit* (2 vols., 1957-58); *Gesammelte Werke* (8 vols., 1938-41); *Metaphysica viva* (1960)

BIBLIOGRAPHY: Koch, F., *E. G. K.* (1929; 2nd ed., 1953); Wandrey, C., *K., der Dichter und Philosoph* (1934); Wehring, H., *K.'s Verhältnis zum Drama* (1941)

* * *

225

KOLMAR, Gertrud

(pseud. of *Gertrud Chodziesner*), German poet, b. 10 Dec. 1894, Berlin; since she was deported in 1943, nothing is known of her

Gertrud K. came of a wealthy upper-bourgeois Jewish family. Although she grew up amid the literary ferment of Berlin, she remained apart from the business of literature and from all literary movements. Her human loneliness led her to develop a heartfelt kinship with the world of creatures—with animals and with nature. Other formative influences on her life and work were her study of languages and her preoccupation with history, Eastern cultures, and the French Revolution. Her commitment to Judaism and her isolation as a Jew enabled her to grow to the human stature and maturity revealed in her poems and in her few letters.

Her poetry is versatile in form and content. She has used the folksong and ballad form for some of her poems, and strictly traditional meters for other poems, and she has written superb verse in verse forms she herself devised. Her tart, "utterly sensuous" poetry, with its themes of feminine unfulfillment and yearning for a child, recalls Mistral (q.v.), the Chilean poet. The animal poems and the cycle *Weibliches Bildnis* [Portrait of a Woman] radiate a magical intuitive sympathy. The sets of historical poems, especially the mighty stanzas of her last hymnlike poems in *Welten* (1947), reveal a sense for historical-mythical analogy. Since Annette von Droste-Hülshoff (1797-1848) German poetry has rarely seen such vision, such feeling for nature, and such realism, all of which is sustained entirely by sensuous, lyrical images, timelessly and originally independently expressed.

FURTHER WORKS: *Gedichte* (1917); *Preussische Wappen* (1934); *Die Frau und die Tiere* (1938); *Welten* (1947); *Das lyrische Werk* (1955; enl. 1960)

BIBLIOGRAPHY: Keyser, R., "Das lyrische Werk von G. K.," in *GQ*, XXXIII (1960), 1-3

EBERHARD HORST

KOMMERELL, Max

German critic, essayist, dramatist, and poet, b. 25 Feb. 1902, Münsingen, Württemberg; d. 25 July 1944, Marburg on the Lahn

K. played an outstanding role in the intellectual history of the 1930's and 1940's.

The son of a doctor, K. studied German literature. At eighteen he encountered George (q.v.), whose favorite disciple and companion he was to be for almost a decade. K.'s breaking with George was a remarkably fruitful self-assertion, signifying K.'s step from youth to manhood. In 1930 K. became a lecturer at Frankfurt University—his inaugural lecture was *Hugo von Hofmannsthal* (q.v.)—and was full professor at Marburg from 1941 on.

Both *Der Dichter als Führer in der deutschen Klassik* (1928) and *Gespräche aus der Zeit der deutschen Wiedergeburt* (1929) reflect George's glorification of art and the role of the poet. In *Der Dichter als Führer in der deutschen Klassik,* "the individual poet was celebrated as the ever-present incarnation of the national destiny" (Holthusen); and Goethe, Schiller, Herder, Jean Paul, and Hölderlin as the unique and ecstatically united republic of great minds. This book also revealed K. as a terse stylist and as a scholar who had full mastery of the knowledge necessary for one who would write a history of ideas.

After becoming disenchanted with George's mythography, however, K. was to see the German poets as complete individualities in their own right. He combined unusual psychological insight with a brilliant originality of approach, developing *Geistesgeschichte* from Wilhelm Dilthey's (1838-1911) position to one in which he translated the problems of his subjects into contemporary equivalents. Seeing Schiller as a penetrating psychologist of the man of action, K. brought new light to an evaluation of Schiller's dramas (*Schiller als Gestalter des handelnden Menschen,* 1934).

K.'s greatest accomplishment may well lie in his contributions to the methodology of criticism; he is a pioneer of the so-called "pure" interpretation, and thus a cousin of the new critics. Among his important volumes in this area (which are the fruit of his broad interest in world literature) are *Gedanken über Gedichte* (1943), and *Dichterische Welterfahrung* (1952). In these pages he analyzed the works of Goethe (three of his essays are signposts in modern *Faust II* criticism), Hölderlin, Novalis (1772-1801), Nietzsche and Rilke (qq.v.), and Lady Murasaki among others.

Intensive study of the drama led to *Lessing und Aristoteles* (1940), in which K. traced the history of European Aristotelian criticism and offered an astute interpretation of Aristotle's definition of tragedy.

As a poet, K. avoided imitating the grand gesture of George, was closer to the suppleness of Hofmannsthal (to whom he paid moving tribute in "Zu Hofmannsthals Nachlese der Gedichte" [1934]) and owed much to the rhythms of Hölderlin. A selection from six slender volumes of poetry, published between 1931 and 1944, is to be found in *Rückkehr zum Anfang* (1956). His dramatic work was predominantly inspired by Calderón—*Das kaiserliche Blut: Ein Drama im barocken Stil* (1938) and *Die Gefangenen: Trauerspiel in 5 Akten* (1948). Successful performances have been accorded the *Kasperlespiele für große Leute* (1948). Finally, *Der Lampenschirm aus den drei Taschentüchern* (1940) showed K. as a master of satire.

The posthumously published *Briefe und Aufzeichnungen 1919-1944: Aus dem Nachlaß* (ed. by Inge Jens, 1967) throws light on K.'s stature as a writer of letters, on K.'s dramatic break with the George circle, and on his early rejection of National Socialism as well as his widening interest in world literature.

FURTHER WORKS: *Jean Pauls Verhältnis zu Rousseau* (1925); *Michelangelo: Dichtungen* (translation, 1931); *Leichte Lieder* (1931); *Jugend ohne Goethe* (1931); *Jean Paul* (1933); *Ein vom Blitz getroffener Jüngling erzählt Gott von der Erde* (1933); *Das letzte Lied* (1933); *Die Legende von den vier Teilen des Tages* (1934); *Dichterisches Tagebuch* (1935); *Das Volkslied und das deutsche Lied* (1936); *Mein Anteil* (1938); *Die Lebenszeiten* (1941); *Mit gleichsam chinesischem Pinsel* (1946); *Beiträge zu einem deutschen Calderon* (Vol. I: *Etwas über die Kunst Calderons*; Vol. II: German translations of *La vida es sueño* and *La hija del aire*; 1948); *Hieronyma* (1954)

BIBLIOGRAPHY: Boehringer, R., *Mein Bild von Stefan George* (1951); Schulz G., "Stefan George und M. K.," in *Das literarische Deutschland* (5 Feb. 1951); Gadamer, H. G., "Gedenkrede auf M. K. mit einem Nachwort," in *Dichterische Welterfahrung* (1952); Holthusen, H. E., "M. K. und die deutsche Klassik," in *Das Schöne und das Wahre* (1958); Thormaehlen, L., *Erinnerungen an Stefan George* (1962); Landmann, E., *Gespräche mit Stefan George* (1963)

ULRICH K. GOLDSMITH

KOREAN LITERATURE

Perhaps even more than the literature of most other nations, modern Korean literature seems a direct and immediate reaction to social and political moods and events. It seems nearly always to reflect the goals of its writers for their society at large or their despair of attaining those goals.

The modern literary movement began after 1876 in Korea—after Korea established contact with other countries and ended self-imposed isolation. Usually referred to as The Era, or Movement, of Enlightenment, it is primarily a response to and an attempt to imitate Western literary movements. English, American, French, Russian, and Scandinavian influences are apparent.

Both the fiction and the poetry of the Enlightenment had a didactic purpose—the education of the Korean people to Western social and political concepts. Ideas relevant or necessary to the establishment of a democratic, or even socialistic, industrialized society were spread through these works. Since the purpose of the writers during the Enlightenment was to enlighten as wide an audience as possible, they maintained a strong link with the literature familiar to that audience and modernized it through intellectual content rather than through experiments in form or technique. Then, too, a modernized aesthetic, by means of which changes in form could be made and justified, had not yet been devised. Korean writers in the first two decades of the 20th c. may therefore be said to have put borrowed wine into old bottles.

Propagandistic in purpose, melodramatic in plot, colloquial in language, stereotyped in characterization, moralistic in ethic, the New Novel—which was the most significant manifestation of the Enlightenment—reached and influenced a wide audience ready for its message. Yi In-jik (1862-1916)—whose *Hyŭl ŭi nu* (1906; "The Tears of Blood"), *Kwi ŭi sŏng* (1908; "The Voice of the Devil"), and *Ch'iaksan* (1908; "Ch'iak Mountain") introduced the New Novel—becomes therefore a significant figure in modern Korean literary history. His *Ŭnsegye* (1908; "Silver World") was the first New Drama in Korea. By 1910, about three hundred new novels had been written; in addition to original works, there were modernizations of old novels and adaptations of foreign novels.

Wherein lies the newness of the New Novel?

227

Primarily in the substitution of contemporary life for folk tales as subject matter, in replacing the traditional narrative style with a more descriptive one, and in adapting a colloquial style.

In 1910 the nationalistic spirit that inspired Korea's writers to preach social, economic, and political modernization took on a new dimension under Japanese occupation and repression. The period thus begun has been called the era of Independence Literature. Independence Literature is characterized by a defiance, stemming from optimism, of Japanese occupation and of Japanese repressive measures against the expression of ideas they considered threatening. From this movement emerged Ch'ŏe Nam-sŏn (1886-1957), who started to write free verse for the first time in Korea, and who worked to develop Korean nationalism. In 1908, hoping to encourage young contributors, he began to publish a monthly magazine *Sonyŏn* ("Youth"). Among those young contributors, Yi Kwang-su (1892-?) stood out sharply above the others; in influence he is the successor to Yi In-jik, but his influence is far more enduring. In fact, most critics consider Yi Kwang-su the most important Korean novelist of this century. Unfortunately, he was taken captive and brought to North Korea during the Korean War in 1950.

In his *Mujŏng* (1917; "The Heartless"), he urges independence from the Japanese and attacks traditional class barriers within Korean society. *Mujŏng* is even more important as a literary landmark than Yi In-jik's *Hyŭl ŭi nu*, for its significance is artistic as well as historical. In *Mujŏng* we have what may be called the first modern Korean novel, as a Western audience would understand the term. The theme, which emerges naturally from the plot, is more complex than the old good-vs.-evil theme, and a high level of verisimilitude and credibility of character and plot are maintained. Yi Kwang-su seemed to recognize a literary approach to truth, so that literature becomes more than just fictionalized sermonizing. Among the many novels he wrote, *Hŭlk* (1930; "The Soil"); *Sarang* (1936; "Love") and *Mujŏng* are usually considered his masterpieces.

On March 1, 1919, the Japanese crushed a Korean independence revolt, stamping out at the same time the optimism that underlay the independence literature. Nevertheless, the Japanese government felt constrained to liberalize its treatment of the Koreans and to allow for the first time Korean-language periodicals.

This liberalization made possible the publication in 1919 of *Ch'angjo* ("The Creation"), a magazine published by younger men who, though influenced by Yi Kwang-su, nevertheless disagreed with him in several important respects. The Creation Circle, as it is now known, rejected his dogmatic and programmatic purpose for literature, believing instead that literature could be used to reveal the complexities of man's existence. Many of the members of the Creation Circle are among the most highly respected Korean writers of this century, both in poetry and in the novel. Among them are Kim Tong-in (1900-1951), Chŏn Yŏng-t'aek (b. 1894), Chu Yo-han (b. 1900), and Yŏm Sangsŏp (1897-1962).

The disillusionment that followed the failure of the independence revolt expressed itself in various ways during the 1920's. The rejection of political exhortation by the Creation Circle may be related to it. So may the attraction naturalism had for many of the creation writers, for in the 1920's the French naturalistic writers of the 19th c. were highly influential on a group of Korean writers who found in their country's political experience confirmation of the pessimistic determinism of naturalism.

Other French 19th c. influences are also discernible at this point. Symbolism (q.v.) and decadence of the *fin de siècle* type appear in poetry. The translation of Walt Whitman (1819-92) by Kim Hyŏng-wŏn (b. 1900) at this time can perhaps symbolize the interest in romanticism in the early 1920's, characterized by a sense of the futility of social or political activism and of despair because of that futility.

Although it is traditional to divide the literary reaction to the failure of the independence revolt into several categories, of which romanticism is only one, one might argue that the reaction was entirely romantic, however variously expressed. Shelley's (1792-1822) "The Mask of Anarchy" and his *Prometheus Unbound,* and Byron's (1788-1824) *Manfred* are, after all, all manifestations of romanticism.

The dominant tone of this time, then, is one of sentimentality, resulting in a turn to personal rather than social themes, a mood encouraging to the development of poetic forms, especially the lyrical. In this atmosphere, Pak Chong-hwa (b. 1901), Pak Yŏng-hŭi (1901-?), Hyŏn Chin-kŏn (1900-1941) and others started publishing, in 1922, the magazine *Paekjo* ("White Tide"), in which many important poems and stories appeared.

In less than a year a reaction to the *White*

Tide group, or to the mood they represented and expressed, occurred. Kim Tong-hwan (b. 1901), writing in 1923, was one of those who scorned the personal and subjective subject matter, and who, like their predecessors a decade earlier, aimed their work at a mass audience with the purpose of unifying it. They were joined before the year was out by writers known as the Singyŏnghyang-p'a (New Trend Group). This time, however, the goal was economic and social reorganization rather than national liberation. This movement may be seen as the beginning of a proletarian and socialist literature in Korea. Interestingly enough, the two most enduring developments in reaction to the events of 1919 were those of romantic lyrical poetry and socialist proletarian literature.

The New Trend movement quickly became widely influential, affecting the work even of writers not allied to the group and attracting to itself defectors from the White Tide school, which it had set out to attack. The themes and subjects of New Trend literature are familiar to readers of modern Western literature: it views the working class as a group rather than as individuals and discusses the exploitation of the workers and their need for unity to combat their exploitation with violent counteraction. Clearly this literature is a new liberation literature, this time directed not against the occupying Japanese (though they were identified with the rejected structure of society), but against largely domestic forces within Korean society itself. It might be called Independence Literature Turned Inward. Subtlety was discarded for rhetoric, and objective analysis for angry condemnation. Like American Marxist writers and critics, the Koreans railed at colleagues who did not use their literature as a weapon in the class struggle and raised the issue of the function of literature at the time, provoking a controversy that attracted many participants.

Despite their subordination of literary values to political values, the New Trend writers were first of all literary men who saw their mission to be the use of their literature for desirable social ends. However, as the debate continued and the proletarian movement gained strength, a more frankly political group, to which literature was of secondary importance, emerged in 1925; its members produced a genuine proletarian literature of which the New Trend was a harbinger. In its lifetime, it was to produce increasingly propagandistic works governed by political rather than literary values and objec-

tives. Whereas the New Trend writers aimed at improvement without a definite program, the new movement aimed at a socialist society. It seems not unfair to say that the movement for a proletarian literature was only one aspect and one part of a larger political movement toward socialism.

For Korean literature, this period from 1923 to 1926 or so was a frenetically healthy one, for it provoked writers of all persuasions into developing a defensible analysis of the purpose of literature. The controversy stimulated the growth in interest and sophistication of Korean literary criticism.

In opposition to the socialistic writers, the more established literary men of various beliefs entered the fray to support the aesthetic claims of literature. Some placed themselves within Korean literary tradition, becoming nostalgic for the past and even reviving the Korean classical poem, the *sijo* (a three-line poem, the first two lines of which set up a relationship broken by the third line).

As the battle continued, many of the disputants professed to see an underlying unity in the conflict: despite their disagreements, all the writers party to the dispute were opponents of Japanese imperialism. Consequently, there was a basis for accord among them. This accord took the form in 1926 of the Sin'ganhoe (New Stem Association), the goal of which was to attempt to find a middle ground. But though the New Stem gathered much support, it did not quell the controversy, for the main unsettled question remained. Was the message, or content, of literature primary, or did primacy reside in the form of a literary work? Which should be subordinated? Which interest overrode the other? The attempts to settle this question, and the lively debates such attempts aroused, led to the golden age—which was a period of vigorous and exciting literature and criticism that existed between 1926 and 1934.

It can readily be seen that the Korean literary world was now in a position to study with great profit the work of American and English new criticism (q.v.). At this point Eliot (q.v.) and I. A. Richards (b. 1893) became well known in Korea. One cannot estimate with confidence the depth or range of influence of their ideas and those of other critics writing in English, but there can be little doubt that those ideas had a significant place in Korean thinking about aesthetics in the 1930's.

Those ideas found an even more receptive audience than they would have found only a few years earlier because of still another political, or military, event. Japanese involvement in Manchuria in 1931 had caused Japan to adopt more repressive measures in Korea, particularly the dissolution of all Korean nationalistic and socialistic organizations. The New Stem Association and the Korean Artists Proletarian Federation (commonly known as KAPF), the organization of the socialist writers, had been disbanded, and by 1935 the overt reign of socialist and proletarian literature had been repressed.

When the ideas of modern Western critics were introduced, it was against the background of a new interest in literature as form, as an expression of the aesthetic impulse, an interest to which contemporary Westerners were seen to have much to contribute. Moreover, individual Korean writers as well as groups were working to translate, introduce, popularize, and explain the most significant foreign writers to the Korean literary audience.

We may think of this moment in Korean literature as the first real break with didacticism in the 20th c. For the first time the most prominent literary men—e.g., the Ku'inhoe (Nine Men Association), including well-known writers like Yi T'ae-jun (b. 1904), Yi Hyosŏk (1907-1940), Yi Mu-yŏng (1908-1960), Yu Ch'i-jin (b. 1905), and Cho Yong-man (b. 1909) —were concerned about the possibilities of literature as an art form, not as a means of propaganda.

It is worth noting that by this time Korea was virtually in step with Western literature. The battles of the late 1920's and early 1930's had their Western counterparts, and such American names as Sinclair, Odets (qq.v.) and John Howard Lawson (b. 1895) spring to mind as expressions of similar literary trends.

But a necessary observation is that Korean literary trends were not always allowed to run their full course. Abrupt and arbitrary termination imposed from without was the fate of the proletarian movement; its end did not come, as it does in most Western movements, as a result of a loss of vitality within the movement itself or a loss of appeal to its audience. A similar fate was in store for a two-year interest in humanism, the expression of which was suppressed by the Japanese in 1936.

A broader interest in the range available to literature led at this time to the psychological exploration of character by Yi Sang (1910-39), Chang Man-yŏng (b. 1914), and Kim Kwanggyun (b. 1913), an analysis of the frame of

mind caused by political disillusionment. The survivors of the proletarian movement were among the most disillusioned, and a sense of futility and discouragement pervades the work they did in the early 1930's, as well as that of younger writers then making their first appearance.

In 1937 the anxiety about freedom to write proved to be fully justified in the Japanese suppression of indigenous Korean cultural activities, including even a prohibition of the use of the Korean language for public occasions and in schools. Literary reaction was either to ignore contemporary reality by looking elsewhere or to oppose it by indirection. A nostalgic praise of the past became common, and so, for a second time, modern interest in Korea's tradition was aroused.

Historical fiction became popular, as well as essays on Korean traditions and history. *Kŭmsam ŭi p'i* (1935; "Blood on the Silk Dress") by Pak Chong-hwa (b. 1901) is one of the most commendable works of this genre of historical fiction. Writers used the historical novel as a means of directing attention away from an unsavory present and of criticizing it indirectly. Similar in purposes was the "farm novel," popularized by Yi Mu-yŏng (1908-1960) in 1938. Praise of farm life carried an implied criticism of urban life, which was the aspect of Korean society most affected by Japanese domination. In addition, satire became another popular form. Like historical fiction and the farm novel, satire indirectly attacked Japanese policies, though perhaps more clearly than the other two kinds of novel. Praise of rural life and a nostalgic interest in the past are traditionally recognized as characteristics of romanticism. Once again we can see modern Koreans selecting a romantic response as most relevant to their unique environment. (Satire, however, is generally considered a. classical genre.)

Those writers who did deal with the modern scene perforce did so descriptively, making no judgment. In so doing, they developed a highly objective approach, removing themselves as much as they could from their work. Though realism as a method had been employed by the naturalists, it served for them a philosophical preconception and ultimately lacked objectivity in that the content had to be manipulated to conform to that preconception. The modern precursors of the new realists may have been the psychological explorers Yi Sang and his followers.

On this dispiriting scene burst a new generation of writers who were too young to possess the social perspective or memory of their elders and who consequently merely dealt with the reality they knew. Unburdened by memories of the "good old days" or by dreams of social reorganization, they lacked the sentimentality of their predecessors as well as their visions. Insofar as they could, they presented whatever reality they could discover, broadening the range of humanity studied by Korean literature to include the outcasts of society, whether by virtue of class or personality. Kim Tong-ni (b. 1911), Chŏng Pi-sŏk (b. 1911), and others seemed to believe that literature existed to observe and reveal the truth. Painstakingly they studied their subjects but drew no other conclusions than "This is the way it is." No suggestions about how to effect improvements were made. Indeed, there was little implication that improvements were needed.

From 1941 until the Japanese defeat in 1945, Korean literature was suspended. In 1945 came the liberation Koreans had fought for in 1919 and had dreamed of since 1910, but it did not bring the anticipated stability. For with liberation came division. A confused peace lasted only five years before war broke out between the two halves of Korea. But even during the five-year prewar peace Korea was under the influence of both the United States and the Soviet Union, and the Koreans were divided by ideology as well as by class and wealth.

Most of what literature was produced between liberation and the Korean War was published in literary periodicals, which sprang up after the liberation. Han Mu-suk (b. 1919), Son So-hi (b. 1917), Chang Yong-hak (b. 1921), and Kang Sin-jae (b. 1924) achieved popularity at this time. Poets and novelists who made their reputations before 1941 now resumed their careers, and after 1948 the Korean literary world clearly seemed to be reestablishing itself, when war broke out in 1950.

Like most of the intellectuals of the South, most Korean writers (a majority of whom apparently preferred to live in South Korea) became refugees from Seoul to Pusan. The war dominated literature as it did every other aspect of Korean life. Writing was either a fictionalized or a documentary account of combat and its effects.

After the armistice of 1953, the bitter hostility among literary factions came to life again in South Korea. Writers divided into two principal camps, each of which organized itself formally. Those who believed the purpose of literature was to disseminate socialistic ideas formed the Liberal Men of Letters, publishing in *Chayu munhak* ("Liberal Literature"); those who believed aesthetic considerations should prevail organized into the Association of Korean Men of Letters, publishing in *Hyŏndae munhak* ("Modern Literature"). But by the end of the decade, the fierceness of factionalism had diminished.

Although the rivalry continues, a welcome development has been this reduction in interest among Korean literary men in such factionalism and the placing of emphasis on literature itself. Organized activity in literature has fit in with this attitude, as the Korean Academy of Arts was set up in 1954, a Korean Chapter of P.E.N. was established in 1955 in order to promote cultural exchanges with the West, and a Korean Poet's Association and a Literary Critics' Association were formed.

Just as an earlier generation of Korean writers turned to French writers for a naturalism that seemed relevent to Korean experience, so are young contemporary writers turning to France for an existentialism (q.v.) that now seems relevant to Korean experience. Perhaps Korean literary men are in tune with a mood that seems to exist in most countries. Hemingway (q.v.) did not have to read Sartre (q.v.) to write "A Clean, Well-Lighted Place." Korean writers may merely have discovered in Camus (q.v.) and others an expression of what they themselves were already feeling.

Another view of these younger men is that they represent the latest borrowings from the West in a line that goes back almost to the beginning of the century; Yi Hae-jo's (1869-1927) *Chayujong* (1910; "The Liberty Bell"), for example, is reminiscent of H. Ibsen's (q.v.) *A Doll's House.* This view could include the observation that what is at stake is the degree to which Korea—as a nation, not merely in its literature—should remain faithful to its own traditions and the degree to which it should abandon them for Western ideas and standards.

The older generation of Korean writers has picked up the threads of the past, once again attaching themselves to literary tradition. In doing so, they represent an aspect of classicism that the younger writers are romantically rejecting.

An observation that follows inevitably from a survey of Korean literature is that its future direction depends on future political events. But it also seems clear that Korean literature has made an irreversible journey. It has become a

Western literature, ultimately adapting the major Western literary values, even methods. One can conceive of the thought of Freud or Jung, for example, becoming more influential, but one cannot imagine a return to the type of folktale that was the basis of earlier Korean literature, or to the stereotyped good-and-bad characterization and morality that was once a literary staple, or to the crude propagandizing of the early modern period.

Further, the kinds of polarization among writers that persisted even into the mid-1950's no longer seem possible, since Korean writers appear now to see themselves as literary men above all else. Literary dispute is still likely to be occurring in South Korea, of course, but it is unlikely that literature will again be subordinated to ideology.

In North Korea, literature is, as is to be expected, didactic and subject to government regulation. Yi-Ki-yŏng (b. 1896) and Han Sŏl-ya (b. 1900), who were active members of KAPF in the 1930's, now are two of the leading novelists of North Korea. Their works illustrate this tendency in North Korean literature toward propaganda, since both writers have replaced their formalism of the 1930's with sprawling novels that praise the social and economic achievements of their socialist state.

A troubled, disillusioned, questing generation now seems prominent in the literature of South Korea. If Korea continues to follow the West in its literary development, we may see Korean black comedy and a literature of the absurd. A modern literature that began by questioning and disturbing a well-established, even rigid, social order would then have reached the perhaps logical conclusion of denying the presence of any order at all in the universe. That speculation about South Korea's literary future in terms of the example of Western literature is even possible, indicates how far the modern period has taken Korean literature from where it was before that period began.

BIBLIOGRAPHY: Cho, Yŏn-hyŏn, *Han'guk hyŏndae munhak sa* (1961; "History of Korean Modern Literature"); Cho, Yŏn-hyŏn, *Han'guk hyŏndae sosŏl ŭi ihae* (1966; "Understanding of Modern Korean Novels"); Cho, Yun-je, *H'an'guk munhak sa* (1963; "History of Korean Literature"); *Korea: Its Land, People and Culture of All Ages* (1963); Lee, Peter H., *Anthology of Korean Poetry: From the Earliest Era to the Present* (1964); *Munye taesajŏn* (1962; "Dictionary of Literature"); Suh, Doo Soo,

Korean Literary Reader, with a Short History of Korean Literature (1965)

KAY H. KIM

KORNFELD, Paul

German dramatist and novelist, b. 11 Dec. 1889, Prague; d. ca. 1942 in the German concentration camp at Lodz

K.'s five-act tragedy *Die Verführung* (1916; written in 1913) is expressionist (q.v.) in outlook and style. In keeping with its programmatically important epilogue, which calls for "man with a soul—psychological man," it presents figures that share in a spiritual mentality rather than individual characters. In the tragedy *Himmel und Hölle* (1919)—"drama dissolving into a conceptual oratorio" (P. Fechter)—the tone of indignation and protest gives way to one of humility and all-conquering love. *Der ewige Traum* (1922), a comedy, reflects skepticism about man's ideas of progress. K.'s novel *Blanche oder Das Atelier im Garten* (1957) was posthumously published; his "men with a soul" and their dreams come to grief in prosaic reality.

FURTHER WORKS: *Legende* (1917); *Palme oder Der Gekränkte* (1924); *Sakuntala, Nach Kalidasa* (1925); *Kilian oder Die Gelbe Rose* (1926); *Jud Süß* (1931)

BIBLIOGRAPHY: Maren-Grisebach, M., *Weltanschauung und Kunstform im Frühwerk P. K.'s* (1960)

* * *

KOROLENKO, Vladimir Galaktionovich

Russian narrative writer, b. 27 July 1853, Zhitomir; d. 25 Dec. 1921, Poltava

As a student K., an enthusiastic supporter of the Narodnik movement, was arrested and exiled for six years to various regions of Russia and Siberia as a political suspect. In 1885 he returned to European Russia. Much of his best work was written in the 1880's. Among other things he edited the influential journal *Russkoe bogatstvo*. Soon making a name as a writer, he was often called "the conscience of the Russian people" because he denounced racial persecution, authoritarianism, and judicial corruption.

K.'s most significant works are his short stories and sketches, among which are *Son Makara* (1885; in *Makar's Dream, and Other*

Stories, 1916), other Siberian stories (*Les shumit,* 1886; in *The Murmuring Forest, and Other Stories,* 1916), and his autobiographical *Istoria moego sovremennika* (1906-1910). All of them are based on precise observation of life in the Russian provinces. K.'s most successful characters are people living in the most primitive conditions—peasants, tramps, and convicts. He was less successful in describing emotional life and specific characters (*Slepoi Muzykant,* 1887; The Blind Musician, 1890).

K. admired Dickens, Dumas, Gogol, and Tolstoi (q.v.). He did not belong to any literary school. His narrative is often interspersed with lyrical word paintings comparable to Turgenev's prose poems; this gives it "an inimitable, unique charm and, despite its great spirituality, a bright, direct, childlike quality and devotion to life" (B. Goetz).

FURTHER WORKS: *V durnom obshchestve* (1885; Bad Company, 1892); *Bez yazyka* (1895); *Polnoye sobraniye sochinenii* (9 vols., 1914); *Ptitzy nebesnyya,* 1915 (in *Birds of Heaven, and Other Stories,* 1919). **Selected English trans.:** *The Vagrant, and Other Tales* (1887)

BIBLIOGRAPHY: Hausler, E., *V. K. und sein Werk* (1930); Damiani, E., *V. K.* (1944); Votov, A. K., *V. G. K.* (1957); Lelov, V. G., *G. K.-redaktor* (1961); Morozova, T. G., et al., *V. G. K.* (1962); Mironov, G., *K.* (1962); Seleteki, N. M., "The Elements of Light in the Life and Fiction of V. G. K.," in *DA,* XXVI (1965), 2224-25

R. F. CHRISTIAN

KOSZTOLÁNYI, Dezsö

Hungarian narrative writer and poet, b. 19 March 1885, Szabadka; d. 3 Nov. 1936, Budapest

K. was the son of an educated middle-class family from southern Hungary (now Yugoslavia). He combined the idyllic, melancholy spirit of the small town with cosmopolitan ideas and a lofty conception of the Hungarian national mission. Apart from a brief, unhappy period after the first communist revolt in Hungary, he stayed out of politics. His themes are childhood memories, inevitable decay, and death.

K., an extraordinary master of verse form, was as important a prose writer as he was a poet. His talent for indirect statement and his skillful blending of sympathy and irony enabled him to write outstanding fiction. His novels and psychological novellas are characteristic of the interlude between impressionism and realism. Though not a professional philologist, K. was a purist who refined the Hungarian language. His translations were also of high merit.

FURTHER WORKS: *Négy fal között* (1907); *Boszorkányos esték* (1908); *A szegény kisgyermek panaszai* (1910); *Mágia* (1912); *Mák* (1916); *Páva* (1919); *A rossz orvos* (1921); *Nero, a véres költö* (1921; The Bloody Poet, 1927); *A bús férfi panaszai* (1924); *Pacsirta* (1924); *Arany sárkány* (1925); *Édes Anna* (1926); *Esti Kornél* (1933); *Összegyüjtött költeményei* (1935); *Tengerszem* (1936); *Szeptemberi áhitat* (1939); *Lenni vagy nem lenni* (1940); *Összegyüjtött versei* (1940)

BIBLIOGRAPHY: Horvath, H., *Neue ungarische Lyrik* (1938); Kostolányi, D., *D. K.* (1938); Baráth, F., *D. K.* (1940); Szegárdy-Csengery, J., *D. K.* (1940); Rákos, P., *Rhythm and Metre in Hungarian Verse* (1966); Sötér, I., "The Place of Hungarian Poetry in Europe," in *New Hungarian Quarterly,* XXV (1967), 34-43

JOSEPH REMÉNYI

KRAMER, Theodor

Austrian poet, b. 1 Jan. 1897, Niederhollabrunn; d. 3 April 1958, Vienna

K., son of a country doctor, was disabled while fighting in World War I. He later worked as a bookdealer, as well as at various other jobs, but became unemployed during the Depression. When Hitler invaded Austria, he had to emigrate and thereafter lived in England, where he was librarian of the Guildford school of technology.

Throughout his life K. consciously devoted his work to "the voiceless ones," the urban and rural proletariat. He did, however, succeed in writing about them without tendentiousness or social crusading, and without romanticizing the proletarian milieu or glorifying the "simple life." K. was strongly drawn to the world of feeling that existed among the inhabitants of the outskirts of Vienna and the stolid villages of northeastern Lower Austria. His poems, easy in form and consistent in construction, are permeated by this atmosphere. K.'s published poems are only a fraction of his total work. His first book of poems, *Die Gaunerzinke* (1929), was a literary sensation and brought its

233

author the Poetry Prize of the City of Vienna that same year. It was quickly followed by other books and honors until he fled from Austria. Though he was uprooted, his familiar world continued to provide him with his themes. K. was one of the few poets who succeeded in writing genuine modern folk-songs without false romanticism.

FURTHER WORKS: *Kalendarium* (1930); *Wir lagen in Wolhynien im Morast* (1931); *Mit der Ziehharmonika* (1936); *Verbannt aus Österreich* (1943); *Die untere Schenke* (1946); *Wien 38. Die grünen Kader* (1946); *Lob der Verzweiflung* (1947); *Vom schwarzen Wein* (1956)

BIBLIOGRAPHY: Zuckmayer, C., "Der Lyriker T. K.," in *Forum*, IV (1959), 272-73; Chvojka, E., "T. K.," in *Akzente*, IX (1962), 143-57

GERHARD FRITSCH

KRAUS, Karl

Austrian satirist, cultural critic, aphorist, and lyrical poet, b. 28 April 1874, Jicin, Moravia; d. 12 June 1936, Vienna

When K. was three years old, his father, who was a wealthy manufacturer, moved with his family to Vienna. K.'s school and university years coincided with the heyday of the Viennese Burgtheater and the lively literary activity so characteristic of the Austro-Hungarian capital. From both K. received decisive impressions. Though he matriculated in the law school at the university, he attended only philosophical and literary lectures without ever working toward a degree. He resisted his strong inclinations toward the stage; his dramatic gifts, however, evolved subsequently into his uncommon accomplishments as a reader of his own works and those of others.

K.'s bent for polemics and satire is manifest in his early pamphlets, *Die demolierte Literatur* (1896) and *Eine Krone für Zion* (1898). An event of decisive importance for his literary career was the founding of *Die Fackel* (1899). The early contributors to this periodical included Strindberg, Wedekind, Liliencron, Dehmel, Altenberg, Trakl, Otto Stoessl (qq.v.), Else Lasker-Schüler, and Berthold Viertel, but from 1911 on to the time of K.'s death in 1936 *Die Fackel* was written exclusively by K. himself. It was, in a sense, a spiritual diary, but it was also a militantly ethical periodical that

began before long to play a unique role in the world of German letters. As conceived by K., the concern of his fighting mission, though pursued in *Die Fackel* by purely literary means, was less with literary matters than it was with generally spiritual and ethical matters. His writing posed a constant challenge to the prevailing corruption of the spirit in all domains of public life—in politics, law and justice, literature, and art. K. came to be the irreconcilable accuser of everything that was rotten in the State of Austria. His most embittered hatred had its target in the press, which he attacked with a persistence that might suggest that he considered such activity the purpose of his life. Indeed, to unmask the press as the embodiment of intellectual prostitution, as the instrument par excellence of the trivialization and mechanization of life, as a menace to the already sorely imperiled state of peace, was to him a fate-imposed obligation.

That K. saw the press and the dangers of its enormous power as he did—the Vienna press of his age showed journalism in its ugliest form—followed inevitably from the ethical imperative that was the supreme law of his life and his every endeavor. Because he measured everything by absolute standards, condoning no compromise however trivial, he was bound to regard the journalist who works under the aegis of day-to-day contingencies rather than of ultimate principles as the embodiment of everything evil. The slightest deviation from absolute integrity signified to him man's dehumanization, which, undermining society, must finally lead to its general collapse.

K.'s polemical essays, in which he fought against the enslavement of man's natural drives by state and church, appeared in book form in the volumes *Sittlichkeit und Kriminalität* (1908) and *Die chinesische Mauer* (1910). Like all his writing, these essays were first published in *Die Fackel*.

K.'s conception of language was of central importance to him and is of similar importance in any evaluation of his work. The word and the thing, he held, were one. In language he saw the magic passkey to unlock all doors. Indeed, his feared and fearful attacks—the purpose of which was to unmask the hypocrisy and the corruption of his age by making them, through the instrumentality of his mordant wit a laughing stock for his readers—used language as a means to destroy the adversary. Purity of language was to him the measure of the writer's integrity.

KARL KRAUS

TOM KRISTENSEN

"Since he considered language a direct index of morality, he believed that to purify language would produce a corresponding salutary effect on the ethical plane. K. assigned to language the primary role in human existence and elevated it to a vital position as man's only essential concern, to which every other consideration, regardless of its merits, becomes subordinate and tangential. When language loses its meaning by losing its firm basis in life, its definite correspondence to thoughts and deeds— the situation which he felt had occurred in his time—then the entire culture, which is constructed of language and exists only in language, is endangered. His aim was to restore this relationship. . . . His uncompromisingly idealistic program aimed at restoring meaning to language, the basis of the cultural and intellectual life of a nation" (Donald D. Daviau).

K. was thus not only the merciless and uncorruptible critic of his age but also the teacher of a new and wakeful awareness of language. There are many whose ears he trained to discern the hollow ring of vacuous phrases, of puff and lie, of shamelessness and perfidy that assaulted them from the columns of the daily press, particularly in this time of war. And there are many whom he strengthened in the integrity of their conduct.

The world-war drama *Die letzten Tage der Menschheit,* which bursts all conventional dimensions, was a climax in K.'s creative career. In K.'s words, "by earthly measurements" a performance would require some ten nights on the stage. Actually a reading drama, the imagination of the reader has to provide the stage. The work was written during World War I. It appeared in special issues of *Die Fackel* and in 1922 as a book. K. never doubted that Austria's declaration of war in 1914 marked the beginning of the end of that state. This satirical tragedy evolves through the prophetic power of its creator into an apocalyptic warning of an impending world-engulfing disaster. It represents a vast fresco of events at the front as well as behind the lines and back home. A more powerful denunciation of war has never been written. The work has no single hero, though each scene, in this immense concert of scenes, has a hero of its own. There is no unity of time or of place or of action, but the unity of the idea is for that very reason only the more compelling.

Admittedly, today's general reader is not likely to follow all the details of this apocalyptic tragedy without explanatory notes. But this fact will not in any way diminish the impact on the reader; the drama remains, uncannily timely, as exemplified by the epilogue "Die letzte Nacht" [The Last Night].

K. was one of the very few who never succumbed even for a moment to the chauvinistic poison that filled the air in those years. The only writer of rank to stand firmly against the Austrians who were embracing the war en masse, he challenged with absolute courage the powers that be. In Berlin, where the tide of warlike enthusiasm was running high, he read in public his sketch *Kant und ein Kantianer,* in which he contrasted the author of *Zum ewigen Frieden* with Emperor William II, who liked to fancy himself as fashioned in the mold of Kant and as one who embodied Kant's categorical imperative, but who was here referred to as a "second-class stage hero." The hope that the war would end in a German victory was to K. absolute treason, high treason against the spirit. On the basis of *Die letzten Tage der Menschheit,* professors at the Paris Sorbonne repeatedly proposed K. for the Nobel Peace Prize.

In his satirical sketches, epigrams, and dramas, K. waged a relentless war of cultural criticism against which the press, his favorite target, had no defense but that of trying to ignore the attacker. His other victims, hopelessly discredited and held up as laughingstocks, also preferred on the whole to limit themselves to reproaching him with the negative character of his criticism, which they claimed "could only destroy but not build up." To be sure, the great satirist must have a clear conception of absolute values. His endeavor to remove the worthless must be inspired by the desire to make room for the worthwhile; and a profound faith in positive values and affirmative truths is actually the basic prerequisite for his creativity.

K. was always ready to praise excellence where he saw it. In the area of public life, he supported Liebknecht, Masaryk, and Lamasch; in the area of artistic creation, the great satirists Lichtenberg, Nestroy, and Offenbach; among his contemporaries, Strindberg, Wedekind, Altenberg, Trakl, Else Lasker-Schüler, and others. He revived interest in the great poets of the German baroque, and through his public readings of Shakespeare's plays he successfully opposed the trend of abandoning Shakespeare's works to the commercialized theater of the big city with its optical illusions and sound effects. In his *Theater der Dichtung,* standing alone at the lectern, he revealed the true power of the works of Goethe and Hauptmann, of Raimund, Nestroy, and Offenbach, and others.

In matters of form K. was no innovator. He said of himself that he was one who continued in the tradition of Shakespeare (in the Schlegel-Tieck translation) and the "lambent flame of language" of the older Goethe, both of whom exerted the strongest influence on him. In matters of content, however, his work is far removed from the poetry of the neoclassicists and neoromanticists. It bears the imprint of his age, having its roots in the past and at the same time pointing the way to the future.

Many of K.'s poems are cerebral, their content frequently identical with his militant prose. Yet among his poems there are pieces of great lyrical power in which beauty of language and emotional content merge in perfect harmony. They are to be found in K.'s nine volumes of *Worte in Versen* (1916-30). A collection of penetrating essays on questions of language, which K. was preparing for publication during the years 1933 and 1934, appeared only after his death under the title of *Die Sprache* (1937). The collected volumes *Sprüche und Widersprüche* (1909), *Pro Domo et Mundo* (1912), and *Nachts* (1918) prove K. to be one of the greatest masters of the aphorism.

K. died when Austria was facing the menace of National Socialism at its western borders—this was two years before the forced anschluss. The outbreak of barbarism in neighboring Germany may have precipitated his death. His last work, written during this time, was not published until 1952. Through an analysis of language and speech, *Die dritte Walpurgisnacht* portrays the horror of the Hitler era, his dictatorship and its literary henchmen. In this work K. provides a perceptive analysis of the diabolical nature of the Third Reich.

During his lifetime the impact of K.'s work was essentially restricted to Vienna. Since the end of World War II wider circles in the realm of German letters have begun to bear witness to his importance and have acknowledged his influence, though not as yet in full proportion to his extraordinary contribution to the artistic and intellectual life of his age. Although K.'s works condemned his time and although he foresaw prophetically the dangers inherent in modern civilization, leading to an ultimate apocalypse, his work in its totality is nevertheless a profession of faith in man and in the worth of life. It was his deep confidence that his work would endure and that through it he

would "live on when I am gone." In this, too, he has proved to be prophetic.

FURTHER WORKS: *Heine und die Folgen* (1910); *Weltgericht* (1919); *Literatur oder Man wird doch da sehn* (1921); *Untergang der Welt durch schwarze Magie* (1922); *Traumstück* (1923); *Wolkenkuckucksheim* (1923); *Traumtheater* (1924); *Epigramme* (1927); *Die Unüberwindlichen* (1928); *Literatur und Lüge* (1929); *Zeitstrophen* (1931). **Translations:** *Shakespeares Sonette* (1933); *Shakespeares Dramen* (1934-35). **Selected English trans.:** *Poems* (1930)

BIBLIOGRAPHY: Stoessl, O., "Sprüche und Widersprüche," in *Lebensform und Dichtungsform* (1914); Liegler, L., *K. K. und die Sprache* (1918); Rollet, E., "K. K." in *Deutschösterreichische Literaturgeschichte* (1934); Heller, E., "The Last Days of Mankind," in *Cambridge Journal* (1948); Heller, E., *Disinherited Mind* (1952); Kraft, W., *K. K., Eine Einführung in sein Werk und eine Auswahl* (1952); Mayer, H., *"K. K. und die Nachwelt,"* in *Sinn und Form,* IX/5 (1957); Muschg, W., "Die letzten Tage der Menschheit," in *Von Trakl zu Brecht* (1961); Kohn, C., *K. K. Le polémiste et l'écrivain defenseur des droits de l'individu* (1962); Schick, P., *K. K. in Selbstzeugnissen und Bilddokumenten* (1965)

FREDERICK UNGAR

With the outbreak of war in 1914, his art transcended itself. From being Viennese it rose to become universal, from being literary it rose to become religious. The heritage of a high Jewish spirituality, dormant in K. in his younger years, came to life. In a fully secularized form the classical tradition of Judaism—the spirit of prophecy, which is the ultimate denial of the present—arose in this liberal Jew. . . . Thus the characteristic traits of K.'s craft of writing developed the ultimate precision of which they were potentially capable; his themes expanded to monumental dimensions; the sacral foundation of his art became evident. . . . The word came to be for him a holy weapon, and the critique of the desecrators of the word, a religious profession of faith. It is against this theological background that we must evaluate and appreciate the deadly edge of his dialectically oriented wit, the abundance of ready associations in his word play, the contrapuntal structure of his sentences. K. is a spirit who acts under higher orders.

Walter Muschg

His prose reflects the confluence of the two major continuities in German style: the antithetic, associative language of the romantics' Shakespeare translation, of Jean Paul Richter, and of Ludwig Börne, merges with the deep currents of Goethe's speech. The power and warmth of the German language become manifest in a form that through its precision is reminiscent of Latin. . . . Those who knew him owe him a new conception of man. The impression that Socrates made on his contemporaries must have been like that.

Sigismund von Radecki

. . . The only great polemicist and satirist of our time, the only one standing under the aegis of ethics.
Theodor Haecker

What was unique in K.—quite apart from the fact that the man was a genius—was the perfect congruence of his life and his work. . . . He was a keeper of the realm of the spirit, zealous to the point of frenzy in attacking and driving off those he thought were contaminating the sacred realm. He wreaked his vengeance on those who debased the ideal. His love for what was great fed his hatred of what was small. He served the cause in which he believed as a faithful and tyrannical servant. Those who came near him came under the spell of the permanent high tension in which his spirit and his will were living. It was possibly for this reason that his personality was so seductive, so irresistibly conducive to hatred and to love.

Alfred Polgar

He taught us how to read. He is the greatest taskmaster of reading that has ever existed. He taught us how to appraise accurately sense and nonsense in printed words, their contradictions, their frightening recurrence. Whoever has gone through the school of the red paperbound books [of Die Fackel] has completed as it were a course in moral philology. He has learned to recognize the lie lodged not in the thoughts but in the words. He has learned of the corruption of the spirit manifest in language as corrupted by phrase-mongers.

Karel Čapek

The spiritual sickness of Europe has to such an extent become an illness of the entire world that the international and extratemporal value of this work assumes gigantic dimensions. The democratizing powers of misfortune have made K. accessible to the understanding of all. Despair will translate him, hope will read him, initiative will fulfill him.
Berthold Viertel

This work [Die letzten Tage der Menschheit] of the highest ethical and aesthetic significance stands unique in world literature.

Ernst Alker

KRISTENSEN, Tom

Danish poet, novelist, and critic, b. 4 Aug. 1893, London

Deeply influenced by the Russian Revolution

and by German expressionism (q.v.), K. tried in his early poems (1918-20) to overcome aesthetically the chaos of the time. Later he vacillated between communism and Catholicism without ever deciding between them.

K. was the central figure of postwar Danish expressionism and of a moderate communism that was averse to party politics but embraced the revolution on romantic grounds.

This is the theme of K.'s first novel Livets Arabesk (1921), which ends with a revolutionary fantasy; his disillusionment is already perceptible here. This feeling of universal emptiness and lostness comes through more strongly in his next novel, En Anden (1923), which deals with the self-alienation and isolation of an intellectual. His nihilism is most characteristically expressed in the novel Hærværk (1930; Havoc, 1930), in which K. drew a merciless portrait of himself.

K., despite his expressionist beginnings, was no innovator in form, but he did handle traditional forms masterfully. For this achievement, he deserves to be placed among the important Danish writers of his generation.

FURTHER WORKS: Mirakler (1922); En kavaler i Spanien (1926); Fribytterdrømme (1929); Mod den yderste rand (1936); Mellem Scylla og Charybdis (1943); Hvad er Heta (1946); Den syngende busk (1949); De forsvundne ansigter (1933); Mens vindrosen blomestrede (1953); Til dags dato (1953); Den sidste lygte (1954); Det skabende Øje (1956); Bøger, bøger, bøger (2 vols., 1961); Amerikanske forteaeller (1963); I min tid (1963); Aabenhjertige fortielser (1966); Kritiker eller anmelder (1966); Fra Holger Drachmann til Benny Andersen (1967)

BIBLIOGRAPHY: Hallar, S., T. K. (1926); Højberg-Pedersen, T. K. (1942); Oehlenschlager, V., T. K. (1954); Vosmar, J., ed., Modernismen i dansk litteratur (1967), see especially Larsen, F. S., "Lyrik," pp. 13-117

PETER P. ROHDE

KRLEŽA, Miroslav

Yugoslavian poet, novelist, and dramatist (writing in Croatian) b. 7 July 1893, Zagreb

K. attended military school in Pec and Budapest. During the Balkan wars he fled to Serbia to enlist. After World War I he took up writing as a career. Through the Marxist-oriented periodicals he published (Plamen,

1919; *Književna repūblika*, 1923-27; *Danas*, 1934; *Pečat*, 1939-40; *Repūblika*, 1945-46) he exerted a strong influence on the younger generation.

K.'s youthful work consists mainly of poetry (*Pan*, 1917; *Tri simfonije*, 1917; *Pjesme* 1918 f.) and plays, which he later published in a collection entitled *Legende* (1933). In these K. uses historical themes as a means of handling contemporary ideological problems. In addition, he symbolically expresses his skepticism and attacks the dehumanization caused by World War I. Technically they show some expressionist traits. His experimental play *Golgota* (1922), a drama that became famous for its crowd scenes, established his reputation as a dramatist. Some of his plays, such as *U loguru* (1924), also attack militarism.

The horror of World War I provided the subject of the novellas in *Hrvatski bog Mars* (1922). In these biting, sometimes even grotesque, satires Croatia's military-feudal ruling class is the butt.

This first phase of K.'s work gradually gave way to a controlled realism. In the dramatized small-town satire *Vučjak* (1924) and in the dramatic trilogy that is made up of *U Agoniji* (1928), *Leda* (1930), and *Gospoda Glembajevi* (1931), K. reveals the ridiculous aspects of certain kinds of people that he had observed, especially in Zagreb society. The characters, presented in sharp dramatic contrasts, are psychologically well drawn and well differentiated. K., who had formerly been influenced by Nazor, Matos, Wilde, Wedekind and Strindberg (qq.v.), now sought to emulate the approach of Ibsen (q.v.).

K.'s novels—*Povratak Filipa Latinovića* (1932; The Return of Philip Latinowitcz, 1966), *Na rubu pameti* (1938), and *Banket u Blitvi* (1939), among others—show penetrating psychological analysis.

In the dialect poems of *Balade Petrice Kerempuha* (1936), K. puts forth an original, individual view of Croatian history.

In 1969, K., who at seventy-six seems to suffer no flagging of energy or creative power, is still a dominant figure in the Yugoslavian literary world. In 1968, at a writer's conference in Ljubljana, his criticism of socialist realism and Stalinist aesthetics offered younger writers a position they embraced eagerly. "Our mission," he said, "is to open doors, to prove by our works that we have always struggled for freedom of artistic expression, for the simultaneous existence of differing schools and styles, for liberty of choice and independence of moral and political convictions."

FURTHER WORKS: *Lirika* (1919); *Tri Kavalira Gdjice Milanije* (1920); *Hrvatska rapsodija* (1922); *Novele* (1923); *Vražji Otok* (1924); *Eseji* (1932); *Knijga lirike* (1932); *Sabrana djela* (20 vols., 1932-41); *Sabrana djela* (36 vols., 1945-51); *O. M. Držiću* (1949); *O Erazmu Roterdamskom* (1953); *Davni dani* (1956); *Aretej* (1959)

BIBLIOGRAPHY: Giusti, W., "M. K.," *Rivista di letteratura slave*, III (1928), 163-175; Cronia, A., *Storia della letteratura Serbo-Croata* (1956); Kadic, A., "K.'s Tormented Visionaries," *SEER* XLV (1967), 46-64

EMIL ŠTAMPAR

KROLOW, Karl (Gustav Heinrich)

German poet and essayist, b. 11 March 1915, Hanover

Oskar Loerke (1884-1941), Spanish and French poetry, and especially Wilhelm Lehmann were formative influences in K.'s poetic development. He studied philology, philosophy, and art history and now lives in Darmstadt and devotes himself to his writing.

K. is less concerned with an escape from modern civilization than with a new experience of the earthly. The universality of his poetry goes beyond the merely idyllic to take in the present day, the dubiety of modern life—"the jerry-built house of chance." His landscape poems present vast variations on the theme of nature from its bucolic sensuous aspects to its enigmas. The basic theme of his poetry, however, is "the fear of a man ... who lacks all religious backing" (H. E. Holthusen), who only rarely attains true bliss. K.'s metaphors, which reveal a tireless delight in experimentation, correlate the concrete with the abstract; they are usually stimulated by specific words and verbal associations.

FURTHER WORKS: *Hochgelobtes gutes Leben* (1943); *Gedichte* (1948); *Nachdichtungen französischer Lyrik aus fünf Jahrhunderten* (1948); *Heimsuchung* (1948); *Auf Erden* (1949); *Die Zeichen der Welt* (1952); *Von nahen und fernen Dingen* (1953); *Wind und Zeit* (1954); *Tage und Nächte* (1956); *Verzauberung* (1956); *Die Barke Phantasie; zeitgenössische französiche Lyrik* (1957); *Gedichte* (trans. of Paul Verlaine; 1958); *Fremde Körper* (1959); *Tessin* (1959); *Schatten eines Manns* (1959); *Bestiarium* (trans. of G. Apollinaire; 1959); *Aspekte zeit-genössischer deutscher Lyrik* (1961); *Ausge-wählte Gedichte* (1962); *Die Rolle des Autors im experimentalen Gedicht* (1962); *Spanische Gedichte des XX. Jahrhunderts* (1962); *Unsicht-bare Hände* (1962); *Schattengefecht* (1964); *Corrida de toros* (1964); *Reise durch die Nacht* (1964); *Gesammelte Gedichte* (1965); *Land-schaften für mich* (1966); *Poetisches Tagebuch* (1966); *Minuten-Aufzeichnungen* (1968)

BIBLIOGRAPHY: Holthusen, H. E., *Ja und Nein* (1954); Hennecke, H., "Über Günter Eich und K. K.," in *Welt und Wort*, XIV (1959), 107-108

HELMUT HENNING

KRUSENSTJERNA, Agnes von
Swedish novelist, b. 9 Oct. 1894, Växjö; d. 10 March 1940, Stockholm

Apart from Selma Lagerlöf (q.v.), whose work is of a completely different nature, Agnes von K. is undoubtedly the most important 20th c. Swedish novelist. Despite considerable un-evenness, her work is to be admired as a phe-nomenon in the use of language as well as an achievement in the prose epic.

Agnes von K. comes from the old aristocracy. Her father was a colonel and court official; her mother, the daughter of the Landshovding (lord lieutenant) Count Hamilton. Under the influence of her husband, the journalist David Sprengel (1880-1941), Agnes von K. drew away from the circles she had grown up in. Previ-ously, as a girl, she had been influenced by Ellen Key (1849-1926), who championed woman's right to a destiny of her own—a specifically feminine one. Agnes von K.'s view of the world arose out of her strong opposition to social mores and out of her belief that the meaning of life lay in sensual fulfillment. Her life was, however, constantly overshadowed by psychic disturbances and by the polemical attacks made upon her.

Agnes von K.'s first significant work, which is also her most successful artistically, is the "Tony" cycle, an account (based partly on per-sonal experience) of the unhappy love affairs of a hypersensitive young man. The "Pahlen" series of novels, with its rich treatment of the destinies of women, was found offensive be-cause of its treatment of radically pathological sex. The attacks on this novel cycle caused Agnes von K. to flee to Spain, where she attempted suicide. Later research revealed that

approximately one-tenth of the text from Volume V on was written by David Sprengel (particularly the polemical, socially critical passages). The last volumes of this incomplete cycle show marked aesthetic deterioration.

Fattigadel (1935) also remained uncompleted, mainly because of Agnes von K.'s intermittent mental depressions. It may have been these that prompted her to write this obviously autobiographical story of a young girl of aristocratic family who nourished a fanatical hatred of her mother. Compared to her en-during achievements in the field of the novel— some of which have been translated into French and Danish—Agnes von K.'s novellas are of minor significance.

FURTHER WORKS: *Ninas dagbok* (1917); *Helenas första kärlek* (1918); *Tony växer upp* (1922); *En dagdriverskas anteckningar* (1923); *Tonys läroår* (1924); *Tonys sista läroår* (1926); *Fru Esters pensionat* (1927); *Händeller på vägen* (1929); *Den blå rullgardinen* (1930); *Kvinnogatan* (1930); *Fröknarna von Pahlen* (1930-35); *Höstens skuggor* (1931); *Porten vid Johannes* (1933); *Delat rum på Kammakare-gatan* (1933); *En ung dam far till Djurgårds-brunn* (1933); *Älskande par* (1933); *Bröllop på Ekered* (1935); *Av samma blod* (1935); *Vivi, flicka med melodi* (1936); *Nunnornas hus* (1937); *Samlade skrifter* (19 vols., 1946)

BIBLIOGRAPHY: Ahlgren, S., *K. studier* (1940); Jones, L., *K.* (1948); Lagercrantz, O., *A. v. K.* (1952; rev. ed., 1963); Holm, I., and Platen, M. v., *La Littérature suédoise* (1957); Green, A., "Om A. v. K.'s novell *Originellupp-lagen*," in *Bokvannen*, XX (1965), 171-76

ERNST ALKER

KUBIN, Alfred
Austrian narrative writer, essayist, painter, and graphic artist, b. 10 April 1877, Leitmeritz, Bohemia; d. 20 Aug. 1959, Zwickledt

K. attained international recognition, primarily as a graphic artist. His cycles of weird drawings, etchings, and other forms of graphic art evoke the demonic and are elemental, tenebrous statements by a searching magician, a "wanderer in the unconscious" (Eldersch) who is building bridges from dream to reality.

In the style and subject matter of his writing, K. at an early date anticipated expressionistic (see expressionism) tendencies. His most im-portant literary work is *Die andere Seite* (1909;

The Other Side, 1967), a novel about a dream kingdom founded as "a refuge for those who are dissatisfied with modern culture." Yet life in Perle, the capital of the dream kingdom, is subject to the laws of a bureaucratic machine. K. satirically castigates the despotism, falsity, and selfishness of a decadent society and fuses elements of reality and fantastic, grotesque apparitions in this symbolic work. K.'s later writings are valuable chiefly for their autobiographical interest and as documents in art history.

FURTHER WORKS: *Die sieben Todsünden* (1914); *Die Blätter mit dem Tod* (1918); *Kritiker* (1920); *Wilde Tiere*` (1920); *Von verschiedenen Ebenen* (1922); *Der Guckkasten* (1925); *Vom Schreibtisch eines Zeichners* (1939); *Abenteuer einer Zeichenfeder* (1941); *Schemen* (1943); *Ein neuer Totentanz* (1947); *Nüchterne Balladen* (1949); *Abendrot* (1950); *Phantasien im Böhmerwald* (1951); *Dämonen und Nachtgesichte* (1959); *Ringen mit dem Engel; Künstlerbriefe 1933-1955* (1964)

BIBLIOGRAPHY: Otte, K., and Raabe, P., eds., *A. K. Leben, Werk, Wirkung* (1957); Hewig, A., *Phantastische Wirklichkeit* (1967)

PAUL WIMMER

KUKUČÍN, Martin

(pseud. of *Matej Bencúr*), Slovakian novelist, b. 17 May 1860, Jasenová; d. 22 May 1928, Lipik, Slavonia

K., author of realistic short stories and novels, is considered the most important Slovakian narrative writer.

Under the influence of Russian realism K. wrote stories about earthy peasant types— *Rysavájalovica* (1885) and *Keď bačik z Chochoľova umrie* (1890). In Brač, where he practiced medicine, he wrote his novel *Dom v stráni* (1903-1904), in which he attempted to overcome the antagonism between nobility and peasants.

After long residence in South America, K. returned to Czechoslovakia and wrote his play *Bacúchovie dvor* (1922) and the five-volume novel *Mať volá* (1926-27), about the life of Croatian emigrants. These were followed by historical stories of the Revolution of 1848-49 and by two posthumous novels set in the period of Slovakian Romanticism, *Lukáš Blahosej Krasoň* (1929) and *Bohumil Valizlosť Zábor* (1930).

FURTHER WORKS: *Neprebudený* (1886); *Dies irae* (1893); *Sobrané spisy* (32 vols., 1931-48); *Veľkou lyžicou* (1933); *Dedinský román* (1952); *Krátké prózy* (1955)

BIBLIOGRAPHY: Potoček, M. K., "M. K., Pioneer of Slovak Realism," in *SlavR*, XXII (1944); Slávik, J., "One Hundred and Twenty Years of Slovak Literary Language," in Rechcigl, M., Jr., ed., *The Czechoslovak Contribution to World Culture* (1964), pp. 44-50

ELISABETH NONNENMACHER

KUPRIN, Aleksandr Ivanovich

Russian novelist and short story writer, b. 7 Sept. 1870, Narovkhat; d. 25 Aug. 1938, Leningrad

K.'s father was a provincial government servant; his mother came of a distinguished Tartar family. After attending cadet and military schools, K. became an army officer. In 1894 he resigned from the service and tried various occupations (including clerking, surveying, and acting).

After the great success of his story *Molokh* (1896), in which he attacked the monied classes, K. began to contribute to important periodicals. Shortly before the revolution of 1905 he also collaborated on the leftist publications of the Znanie publishing house directed by Gorki (q.v.). After Russia's defeat in the war against Japan, K. gave the first informed accounts of mismanagement in the Russian army in his well-known realistic novel *Poyedinok* (1905; The Duel, 1916). This novel was followed by short stories on similar themes. Although K. remained committed to realism, he turned, after this period of debunking, to the subjects that were so popular among the Russian modernists —the subconscious, death, problems of sexuality, and a vague mysticism. K.'s heroes are characterized by neuroses and mental instability. In his short stories, however, he presented people who enjoy risk—artists, horse thieves, fishermen. In 1908 *Sulamith* (Sulamith: A Prose Poem of Antiquity, 1923) appeared; in 1911, *Granatovyi braslet* (in *The Bracelet of Garnets, and Other Stories*, 1917), a mystical story of platonic love influenced by Hamsun's (q.v.) *Victoria*. Between 1910 and 1915 K. wrote his sensational shocker *Yama* (1910; The Pit, 1922) and also tried his hand at a science-fiction utopia (*Zhidkoye solntze*, 1913). An opponent of bolshevism, he emigrated after the October revolution. In 1937 he returned to the

Soviet Union, his health impaired by an unsettled life and alcoholic excess.

K. carried on the best traditions of the 19th c. Critics have noted the influence of Tolstoi, Chekhov (qq.v.), and Gorki, but this does not detract from his own achievement, which is to be found in his marked talent for the graphic, in his humanism, and in his feeling for nature, rather than in any originality of thought.

FURTHER WORKS: *Poslednyi Debyut* (1889); *Olesya* (1898); *Rekazhizni* (1906; in *The River of Life, and Other Stories,* 1916); *Gambrinus* (1907; in *Gambrinus and Other Stories,* 1925); *Polnoye sobraniye sochinenii* (12 vols., 1906-1916); *Koleso vremeni* (1930); *Yunkera* (1933); *Povesti i rasskazy* (1946); *Izbrannyye sochineniya* (1947); *Zabytyye i nesobraniye proizvedeniya* (1950); *Rasskazy* (1953); *Sochineniye* (3 vols., 1953). **Selected English trans.:** *A Slav Soul, and Other Stories* (1916)

BIBLIOGRAPHY: Ledré, C., *Trois romanciers russes* (1935); Kulešov, F. I., *A. I. K.* (1963)

PETER YERSHOV

KURZ, Isolde

German poet and novelist, b. 21 Dec. 1853, Stuttgart; d. 4 April 1944, Tübingen

Isolde K., daughter of the German writer Hermann Kurz (1813-73), became an exponent of poetic realism, but her work also shows symbolic, mystical, and metaphysical tendencies. Her sense of form and love for the Renaissance, which she sought to comprehend and interpret as "mankind's second youth," though without overlooking the tragic background and the fanatical vitalism of that era, identified her as a pupil of C. F. Meyer (1825-98) and Paul Heyse (1830-1914).

K. published poetry, memoirs, biographies, and aphorisms, but she is significant as a writer for her fine novellas. In her work she is constantly striving to communicate the Mediterranean spirit. From her experience of Greece and Italy—she moved to Florence in 1877 and did not return to Germany until the outbreak of World War I—she derived her outlook. In her later work, especially the autobiography *Aus meinem Jugendland* (1918), she expressed her deep attachment to her own

country. Isolde K.'s work is characterized by love of the present and a restrained, almost masculine style that was sometimes veined with the satirical. She eagerly believed that fulfillment lay in "frank, unadorned humanity" and a simple, active human existence. She also felt a longing for a metaphysical realm as expressed in her fairy tales and fantasies.

FURTHER WORKS: *Gedichte* (1889); *Florentiner Novellen* (1890); *Phantasien und Märchen* (1890); *Italienische Erzählungen* (1895); *Von dazumal* (1900); *Genesung* (1901); *Die Stadt des Lebens* (1902); *Im Zeichen des Steinbocks* (1905); *Neue Gedichte* (1905); *Hermann Kurz* (1906); *Lebensfluten* (1907); *Die Kinder der Lilith* (1908); *Florentinische Erinnerungen* (1909); *Wandertage in Hellas* (1913); *Cora* (1915); *Schwert aus der Scheide* (1916); *Im Traumland* (1919); *Legenden* (1921); *Nächte von Fondi* (1922); *Vom Strande* (1925); *Leuke* (1925); *Der Despot* (1925); *Die Liebenden und der Narr* (1925); *Der Caliban* (1926); *Meine Mutter* (1926); *Die Stunde des Unsichtbaren* (1927); *Der Ruf des Pan* (1928); *Ein Genie der Liebe* (1929); *Vanadis* (1931); *Gedichte* (1933); *Aus dem Reigen des Lebens* (1933); *Die Nacht im Teppichsaal* (1933); *Die Pilgerfahrt nach dem Unerreichlichen* (1938); *Das Haus des Atreus* (1939); *Gesammelte Werke* (8 vols., 1925-38)

BIBLIOGRAPHY: Hesse, O. E., *I. K.* (1931); Nennecke, C., *Die Frage nach dem Ich im Werk von I. K.* (1957)

PAUL WIMMER

KUZMIN, Mikhail Alekseyevich

Russian narrative writer, poet, and composer, b. 6 Oct. 1875, Yaroslavl'; d. 1936, Leningrad

K., who was born into a noble family, was educated at the Saint Petersburg conservatory and did not turn to literature until he was thirty. Bohemian groups in the big cities and the world of the religious sects of so-called old believers, with which he kept in close touch, shaped his aesthetic and religious attitudes. Just before World War I, K. won considerable fame for his poems and the musical settings he composed for them; after the October revolution, however, little more was heard of him.

Most noteworthy are his attempts to revive the Alexandrian manner (*Aleksandriiskiye pesni,* 1906) and the rococo pastoral idyll, a genre to which he was particularly attracted. The graceful irony of the 18th c., and the colorful exoticism of the east—Alexandria and Byzantium—which was reflected in contemporary ballet settings, come alive again in K.'s short stories and novellas, which were written mainly between 1907 and 1918. Departing from the symbolic style of allusions and enigmatic associations, K. demanded of prose clarity and singleness of purpose. For him, fable, intrigue, and adventure are the crux of composition, as they were in the late classical Byzantine and Italian tradition.

In his poems K. reveals a naïve, serene acceptance of life, especially in his erotic ones in which late classical themes are mixed with modern ones.

FURTHER WORKS: *Kryl'ya* (1907); *Priklyucheniya, Eme-Lebefa* (1907); *Seti* (1908); *Nezhnyi Iosif* (1909); *O prekrasnoi Yasnosti* (1910); *Podvigi Velikavo Aleksandra* (1910); *Puteshestviye sera Dzhona Firbaksa po Turtzii i drugim primechatel'nym stranam* (1910); *Kuranty lyubvi* (1911); *Osenniye ozera* (1912); *Glinyannyye golubki* (1914); *Plavayushchiye puteshestvuyushchiye* (1915); *Sochineniya* (9 vols., 1915-18); *Zelenyi solovei* (1917); *Chudesnaya zhizn' Iosifa Balzamo, grafa Kaliostro* (1919); *Paraboly* (1922); *Tikhii strazh* (1924)

BIBLIOGRAPHY: Field, A., "M. K.: Notes on a Decadent Prose," in *Russian Review*, XXII (1963), 289-300

JOHANNES HOLTHUSEN

ALEKSANDR KUPRIN

PÄR LAGERKVIST

L

LACRETELLE,
(Amaury-Gaston) Jacques de,
French novelist and short story writer, b. 14 July 1888, Cormatin, Saône-et-Loire, France

Born in the Renaissance castle of Cormatin, L. belongs to a family of liberal bourgeois tradition raised to noble rank by Louis XVIII. He is the third member of his family to be a member of the French Academy. His early years were spent in the Middle East, where his father occupied various consular posts. Shortly before his father's death in 1898, he was brought back to Paris and enrolled in the lycée Janson-de-Sailly, which he was subsequently to use as the locale for his *Silbermann*. An indifferent and rebellious student, he was dismissed from school, failed his bachelor's examination, and was henceforth the despair of his mother since he did nothing for years. In the beginning of World War I, he volunteered, served very briefly in the front lines, and was then mustered out for physical reasons.

From earliest childhood, he was keenly interested in contemporary literature and was in the habit of frequenting the literary salon of Madame Ménard-Dorian, who was one of the originals of Proust's (q.v.) Madame Verdurin. In 1914, having discovered *Du Côté de chez Swann,* he visited Proust several times. Subsequently, he wrote a subjective, semiautobiographical novel of adolescence, which, in the original unpublished version, shows strong allegiance to Proust. When, in 1920, at the age of thirty-six, he published this novel as *La Vie inquiète de Jean Hermelin,* he had already returned to an admiration for Flaubert (1821-80).

L. owes his art to Flaubert, but his inspiration to Gide (q.v.) and to Proust. Proust introduced him to Jacques Rivière, the director of the *Nouvelle Revue française,* and for years L. was closely associated with this periodical's eclectic group. It was under its imprint that his masterpiece, *Silbermann,* appeared in 1922 (Eng., 1923). Gidean because of his stylistic sobriety and the use of the *témoignage* device in narration, Gidean also because of the apparent desire to treat the moral problem of the persecution of a Jewish boy at the time of the Dreyfus affair, the novel is Flaubertian in its desire for complete objectivity and its refusal to envisage the moral problem as anything but a psychological case history.

L.'s real intentions became manifest when he published a long novel, *La Bonifas,* in 1925 (Eng., 1927). This novel is modern only because the old maid heroine is suspected of Lesbianism; otherwise, it adheres strictly to the tradition of Flaubertian realism, with long analyses and much attention to external descriptions. When this novel encountered only a *succès d'estime,* L. returned to the modern scene and began to develop a literary form intermediate between the essay and fiction. His principal works in this genre are *Aparté* (1927), *Lettres espagnoles* (1926), and *Histoire de Paola Ferrani* (1929). Although much less fictional, L.'s beautifully written *Le Demi-Dieu, ou Le Voyage de Grèce* (1930) belongs to the same inspiration. However, his best work during these years was his short stories collected in one volume in 1928 as *L'Âme cachée.*

This dispersal of effort was harmful to the major work of this period, *Le Retour de Silbermann,* which appeared serially in *Candide* in 1929. L., himself, was so displeased with the result that he sacrificed a large part of the

243

novel and published the remainder as *Amour nuptial* (1929; A Man's Life, 1931), which is a psychological study, in the Gidean manner (Gide himself compared it to his *Immoraliste*), of an intellectual (ostensibly the author of *Silbermann*) who, because of innate sensuality, revolts against his wife's puritanism. The same year L. published a rewritten part of his mutilated novel as *Le Retour de Silbermann*, a brief sequel to the original *Silbermann*. *Amour nuptial* received the Prix du Roman of the French Academy, and in 1930, L. was generally acclaimed as one of the foremost writers of his generation.

From 1930 to 1935, he devoted himself to writing the tetralogy of *Les Hauts ponts,* a family saga inspired by the history of his own family at Cormatin and written in a manner that combines personal lyricism and Flaubertian objectivity. Most critics called the first volume, *Sabine* (1932), a masterpiece, but enthusiasm for the succeeding volumes was less great. In retrospect, it seems certain that *Sabine* should rank alongside *Silbermann* as L.'s finest achievements.

In 1936, L. was elected to the French Academy. Journalism occupied much of his time for the next six years. Even during the war he continued to write (in the unoccupied zone), particularly for *Le Figaro* of which he had become a director. In 1946 his *Le Pour et le contre*—a vast autobiographical novel that is also an intellectual panorama of his times—appeared in Switzerland. Showing the influence of Huxley's (q.v.) *Point Counter Point,* but reenforced by that of Gide and Proust (and, in the distance, by Flaubert's *Éducation sentimentale*), the novel is composed of much incidental dialogue and little surface action, although there is real human drama in the background. If this renewal of L.'s method had come ten years sooner, it would have attracted considerable attention, but in the age of existentialism it went unnoticed. Since that time, L. has published little —a small novel *Deux coeurs simples* (1953) in which (as the title suggests) he is as Flaubertian as he could possibly be; a play, *Une Visite en été* (1953), which, although faithful to the dramatic unities, is unfortunately conceived in the same terms as a novel of analysis; a volume of reminiscences, *Le Tiroir secret* (1959); and a volume of criticism, *Les Maîtres et les amis* (1959).

FURTHER WORKS: *La Mort d'Hippolyte* (1923); *La Belle journée* (1925); *Colère suivi*

d'un journal (1926); *Dix jours à Ermenonville* (1926); *Mort de la jalousie* (1926); *Quatre études sur Gobineau* (1926); *Trébuchet* (1926); *Aperçus* (1927); *Le Cachemire écarlate* (1927); *Le Christ aux bras étroits* (1927); *Rêveries romantiques* (1927); *Virginie ou les manies* (1927); *Album napolitain* (1928); *D'une colline* (1928); *Études* (1928); *Quatre nouvelles italiennes* (1928); *A la rencontre de France* (1930); *Luce, ou L'Enfance d'une courtisane* (1931); *Les Fiançailles* (1933); *Les Aveux étudiés* (1934); *Années d'espérance* (1935); *La Monnaie de plomb* (1935); *L'Écrivain public* (1936); *Qui est La Rocque?* (1937); *Discours de réception . . .* (1938); *Morceaux choisis* (1938); *Croisières en eaux troublés* (1939); *Le Canada entre en guerre* (1940); *L'Heure qui change* (1941); *Libérations* (1945); *Idées dans un chapeau* (1946); *Le Voyage de Grèce* (1955); *La Galerie des amants* (1963); *L'Amour sur la place* (1964); *Face à l'événement, "le Figaro," 1826-1966* (1966)

BIBLIOGRAPHY: Le Grix, F., "La Vie inquiète de Jean Hermelin; Silbermann," in *Revue hebdomadaire* (9 Dec. 1922); Massis, H. "Histoires de collégiens," in *Revue universelle* (1 Jan. 1923); Martin du Gard, M., "J. de L., in *NL* (30 May 1925); Lefèvre, F., "Une heure avec J. de L.," in *Nouvelles littéraires* (16 June 1925); Beaunier, A., "Un romancier, J. de L.," in *Revue des deux mondes* (1 Aug. 1925); Billy, A., "Des pieds à la tête: J. de L." *Candide* (13 June 1929); Souday, P., "Un jeune psychologue: J. de L.," in *Candide* (13 June 1929); Saint-Jean, R. de, "Dialogue avec l'auteur d'Amour nuptial," in *Revue hebdomadaire* (22 Feb. 1930); Bellessort, A., "Silbermann," in *Journal des débats* (9 July 1930); Bourget-Pailleron, "La nouvelle équipe," in *Revue des deux mondes* (15 Nov. 1933); Frank, A., "Sous la lampe: J. de L.", in *Larousse mensuel* (Apr. 1938); Alden, D. W., "J. de L. for and against Proust," in *Romantic Review* (Apr. 1950); Magny, C.-E., *Histoire du roman français depuis 1918* (1950); Hubbard, L. J., *The Individual and the Group in French Literature since 1914* (1955); Alden, D. W., *J. de L.: An Intellectual Itinerary* (1958)

DOUGLAS N. ALDEN

LAGERKVIST, Pär Fabian

Swedish novelist, poet, and dramatist, b. 23 May 1891, Växjö

While still at school L. rejected his parents'

pietistic beliefs and became an adherent of the "new doctrine" of Darwinism, "which swept away God and all hope and laid life bare..." (*Gäst hos verkligheten*). For a short time he studied literature and art history at Uppsala University and contributed to radical leftist periodicals. During a stay in Paris (1913) he came into contact with contemporary trends in art. The result of this was his programmatic essay *Ordkonst och Bildkonst* (1913), in which he opposed naturalism (q.v.) and impressionism and accepted expressionism (q.v.). In his prose poems *Motiv* (1914) and his collection of novellas *Järn och människor* (1915), he tried to realize his programmatic aim of presenting profound human conflicts and simple ideas with monumental rigor.

L.'s fear of life and his despair, heightened by the war, first found adequate lyrical expression in *Ångest* (1916), the explosively expressionistic collection of poems. In the subsequent collections—*Kaos* (1919) and *Den lyckliges väg* (1921)—his pessimism gradually recedes. *Hjärtats sånger* (1926) even reveals a certain tranquillity. By now L. was glorifying love as "the all-embracing force of reconciliation."

His dramatic writing followed a similar course, beginning with his play *Sista mänskan* (1917)—which was strongly influenced by the later Strindberg (q.v.)—and three one-act plays (published in *Den svåra stunden* in 1918, together with his essay, "Teater," on the modern theater). Later he went on to *Himlens hemlighet* (1921) and *Den osynlige* (1923), both of which show the influence of the medieval mystery play and of Tagore (q.v.) and reveal L.'s new belief in life. This development culminated in the almost realistic *Han som fick leva om sitt liv* (1928).

L.'s personality and philosophy of life emerge most clearly from his prose story *Det eviga leendet* (1920), from the occasionally bitter satires *Onda sagor* (1924), and above all from the autobiographical prose work, *Gäst hos verkligheten* (1925; Guest of Reality, 1936).

In 1930 a new phase began for L. Fear of dictatorship and horror at the cult of power again depressed L.'s outlook, as can be seen from the propagandistic, satirical plays *Konungen* (1932), *Mannen utan själ* (1936), and *Seger i mörker* (1939), the short novel *Bödeln* (1933), and the prose satires *I den tiden* (1935). However, L. expressed his growing faith in a heroic, humanitarian idealism and in the power of the human spirit in

Kämpande ande (novellas, 1930), *Vid lägereld* (poems, 1932), and in the essay *Den knutna näven* (1934), in which the Acropolis becomes the symbol of humanism combating barbarism.

Speculation about the meaning of life and man's relation to God—crucial problems throughout L.'s work—becomes increasingly urgent in the collections of poems—*Genius* (1937), *Sång och strid* (1940), *Hemmet och Stjärnan* (1942), *Aftonland* (1953)—and the plays—*Midsommardröm i fattighuset* (1941; Midsummer Dream in the Poorhouse, 1952), *De vises sten* (1947), and *Lat människan leva* (1949). The same religious questions underlie L.'s three masterful novels—*Dvärgen* (1944; The Dwarf, 1945), *Barabbas* (1950; Eng., 1952), and *Sibyllan* (1956). *Barabbas* was awarded the Nobel Prize in 1951. Three times L. confronts man with religiosity: in the inhuman dwarf imprisoned in his own selfish hatred; in Barabbas, incapable of faith or love; in the sublime sibyl, who finds that her vocation makes her both chosen and damned. Yet nowhere is there a liberating solution; L. the seeker never found one.

L. has always been a discordant personality, torn by inner conflicts—by thirst for life and fear of it, by elemental passion and intellectual asceticism, by an impulse toward the supernatural and an aversion to all dogma. His work compels reflection. His images and symbols are heavy with meaning and often obscure. From the literary standpoint his work shows a constantly ascending progression. His influence upon the generations of Swedish writers since 1916, especially in venturing in new literary directions, has been unparalleled.

FURTHER WORKS: *Människor* (1912); *Två sagor om livet* (1913); *Det besegrade livet* (1927); *Skrifter* (3 vols., 1932); *Dikter* (1941); *Prosa* (5 vols., 1945); *Dramatik* (1946); *Dikter* (1950); *Ahasverus död* (1960; The Death of Ahasuerus, 1962); *Pilgrim på havet* (1962; Pilgrim at Sea, 1964). **Selected English trans.:** *The Eternal Smile, and Other Stories* (1954); *The Marriage Feast, and Other Stories* (1955); *Modern Theatre: Seven Plays and an Essay* (1966)

BIBLIOGRAPHY: Scobbie, I., "Contrasting Characters in *Barabbas*," in *SS*, XXXII (1960), 212-20; Spector, R. D., "L. and Existentialism," in *SS*, pp. 203-211; Buchman, T. R., "P. L. and the Swedish Theatre," in *TDR*, VI (1961), 60-89; Ohmann, R., "Apostle of Uncertainty," in *Commonweal*, LXXVI

(1962), 170-72; Ryberg, A., ed., *P. L. in Translation: A Bibliography* (1964); Linner, S., "P. L.'s *The Eternal Smile* and *The Sybil*," *SS*, XXXVII (1965), 160-67; Swanson, R. A., "Evil and Love in L.'s Crucifixion Cycle," in *SS*, XXXVIII (1966), 302-317

JORIS TAELS

LAGERLÖF, Selma (Ottiliana Lovisa)
Swedish novelist, b. 20 Nov. 1858, Mårbacka Farm, in Värmland; d. there 16 March 1940

Selma L. studied in Stockholm and was a teacher in Landskrona from 1885 to 1895; in 1897 she went to live at Falun. After winning the Nobel Prize in 1909 she bought back Mårbacka, where she lived until her death. Selma L. was the first woman to be elected to the Swedish Academy (1914).

The old folk tales and sagas told to her from early childhood and her wide reading stimulated her interest in writing while she was still young. For years she unsuccessfully attempted naturalistic renderings of the fantastic, romantic tales about Gösta Berling. Finally, influenced by the writing of Thomas Carlyle (1795-1881) she arrived at her own style—a lyrical, subjective, often powerfully emotional prose, rich in exclamations and direct addresses to the reader. Her novel *Gösta Berlings saga* (Gösta Berling's Saga, 1898) appeared in 1891. The hoped-for success came only after a review by Georg Brandes (q.v.) who praised its originality of content and presentation. Selma L.'s tendency to moralize is already apparent in the ending of this book, where the noblemen decide to devote their lives to moral and social ideals. Selma L.'s originally exaggerated style benefited from her reading of old Icelandic family sagas, Bjørnstjerne Bjørnson's (1832-1910) peasant novellas, and Hans Christian Andersen's (1805-1875) fairy tales. This is already evident in her collection of novellas *Osynliga länkar* (1894; Invisible Links, 1899), and in the antisocialist novel *Antikrists mirakler* (1897; The Miracles of Antichrist, 1899)—"one of the few great novels of ideas in Swedish literature" (S. Stolpe). It is especially apparent in the two-part novel *Jerusalem* (*I Dalarne*, 1901; *I det heliga Landet*, 1902; translated together as Jerusalem, 1915), the epic story of men from Dalecarlia who went to the Holy Land, her masterpiece second only to *Gösta Berling*.

Almost all of Selma L.'s extensive later writing is permeated by Värmland culture and nature and inspired by its rich store of fairy tales and legends. In her best short stories and novels—*En herrgårdsägen* (1899; The Tale of a Manor, 1922), *Herr Arnes penningar* (1904; Herr Arne's Hoard, 1923), *Körkarlen* (1912; Thy Soul Shall Bear Witness!, 1921), and *Kejsaren av Portugallien* (1914; The Emperor of Portugalia, 1916)—she combines the realms of the visible and the invisible. Among her most mellow stories are the *Kristuslegender* (1904; Christ Legends, 1908) and the unusual children's school reader *Nils Holgerssons underbara resa genom Sverige* (1906-1907; The Wonderful Adventures of Nils, 1907; Further Adventures of Nils, 1911).

At the time of World War I Selma L.'s creativity flagged somewhat; her propagandistic antiwar novel *Bannlyst* (1918; The Outcast, 1920) clearly shows this. Her later works are not free from mannerism, although she reached great heights again in her Löwensköld cycle (*Den Löwensköldska ringen*, 1925; *Charlotte Löwensköld*, 1925; *Anna Svärd*, 1928; translated together as The Ring of the Löwenskölds, 1931). Here the intense romanticism of her early work has yielded to a sober, critical assessment of man and the world.

Selma L.'s autobiographical writing deserves special attention—*Mårbacka* (1922; Eng., 1922), *Ett barns memoarer* (1930; Memories of My Childhood, 1934), *Dagbok för Selma O. Lagerlöf* (1932; The Diary of S. L., 1936), *Från skilda tider* (2 vols., 1943-45). In these she expresses her rich epic talent, her fascination with the supernatural, and her sense of harmony. Again and again she is forced "to sacrifice tangible reality in order to grasp transcendent reality" (F. S. De Vrieze).

No other Swedish author ever enjoyed the world reputation that Selma L. won. Her works appeared in huge editions, were adapted for stage and film, and were translated into more than thirty languages. Nevertheless, she was the subject of considerable critical controversy. Her naiveté, love of moralizing, oversimplified psychology, and mannered style were criticized. She did, however, possess rare narrative ability, which made her an interpreter of old folk tales for modern times and enabled her to project her inexhaustible imagination into a wide variety of periods and people. Her psychology was largely intuitive.

Selma L. underwent no substantial intellectual development, but her experience of life gradually deepened. Although she was not a practicing Christian, her ethics were basically

SELMA LAGERLÖF

GIUSEPPE DI LAMPEDUSA

Christian. She believed in a living God and in the immortality of the soul. Her life and work are testimonies to her concept of life, in which "goodness and selfless love always vanquish selfish baseness and cruelty" (Tigerstedt).

FURTHER WORKS: *Drottningar i Kungahälla* (1899; From a Swedish Homestead, 1919); *En saga om en saga och andra sagor* (1908); *Liljecronas hem* (1911; Liliencrona's Home, 1914); *Valda berättelser* (1913); *Dunungen* (1914); *Troll och människor* (1915); *Zachris Topelius* (1920); *Skrifter* (12 vols., 1928); *Höst* (1933); *Julberättelser* (1938); *Briefe* (ed. I. Bäckmann; 2 vols., 1944)

BIBLIOGRAPHY Berendsohn, W., *S. L.* (1927); Maes, L., *S. L.: Sa vie et son oeuvre* (1945); Jenssen, C., *S. L. Ein Lebensbild* (1947); De Vrieze, F. S., *Fact and Fiction in the Autobiographical Works of S. L.* (1958); Johannesson, E. O., "The Narrative Art of S. L.: Two Problems," in *SS*, XXXIII (1961), 10-17; Nelson, A. T., "The Critical Reception of S. L. in France," in *DA*, XXII (1963), 4687-88; Nelson, A. T., "S. L. Research, 1900-1964: A Survey and an Orientation," in *SS*, XXXXVII (1965), 1-30

JORIS TAELS

LAMPEDUSA, Giuseppe di

Italian novelist, b. 23 Dec. 1896, Palermo; d. 25 July 1957, Rome

Giuseppe Tomasi, Duke of Parma and Prince of Lampedusa, began to write when he was almost fifty-nine, wrote for only two years, and published nothing during his lifetime.

L. came of a family prominent in Sicily for more than three centuries, was privately educated, and had a happy, meditative, largely solitary childhood, which he celebrated in his first attempt at writing, "I luoghi della mia prima infanzia" (*Racconti*, 1961). He served in World War I, was captured, and managed, after his second escape, to make his way back to Italy deviously, disguised, and on foot.

During Mussolini's reign he spent most of his time in Paris and London, and in Latvia, where he married Baroness Alessandra von Wolff-Stormersee, a psychoanalyst. He acquired a thorough knowledge of Italian, French, German, English, and Russian literature—all of which he read in the original languages. During World War II (in which he served) his ancestral palace in Palermo was destroyed by "a bomb manufactured in Pittsburgh, Pennsylvania."

L. had been planning to write a novel since about 1930, but had never started it. After attending a literary meeting at which his cousin, the poet Lucio Piccolo, received a prize, L. began to write in the summer of 1955. Two years later he died of cancer in Rome, leaving in manuscript a novel, three short stories, a memoir of his childhood, and critical essays on Stendhal, Mérimée, and Flaubert.

The novel, *Il gattopardo* (1958; The Leopard, 1960), skyrocketed L. to international fame. In 1961 three stories and a memoir appeared as *Racconti* (partially translated as Two Stories and a Memory, 1962).

Il gattopardo is a historical novel whose protagonist is a Sicilian nobleman, Fabrizio Salina. The characterization is partly a self-portrait and partly drawn from L.'s paternal grandfather. Don Fabrizio's life is set against the background of the change in Sicily that Garibaldi's actions bring about. The novel traces the decline of the old nobility, the rise of the bolder and more ruthless element of the peasantry, and the success of those among the nobility who can adapt to the new times before such adaptation becomes the obvious manipulating for survival.

The controversy that raged over the novel as political and social history coexisted with widespread agreement that the novel was a literary achievement. L. treats his characters with sympathy, but in a calm, detached, often ironic or wryly humorous style. Underlying the story is a basically tragic sense of life. He owes much to many writers (as the critics have repeatedly showed), but the final product is unmistakably and distinctively his own.

One of the short stories, "Lighea," is a remarkable tour de force (written on a bet, his wife tells us) about the passionate love between a classical philologist and a mermaid. It is essentially a classical treatment of a romantic theme, and much of its power derives from the resulting tension between the tone and the subject.

BIBLIOGRAPHY: Colquhoun, A., "L. in Sicily: The Lair of the Leopard," in *Atlantic Monthly*, CCXI (1963), 91-110; Orlando, F., *Ricordo di L.* (1963)

CALVIN S. BROWN

LANGGÄSSER, Elisabeth

German poet, novelist, short-story writer, and essayist, b. 23 Feb. 1899, Alzey; d. 25 July 1950, Rheinzabern

Elisabeth L. was the child of cultivated parents. In 1929, after teaching school in various cities, she settled in Berlin to devote all her time to writing; two years later she received her first literary prize. She married the philosopher Wilhelm Hoffmann in 1935. The following year the Nazis forbade her to publish because she was a half Jewess. During World War II she was compelled to work in a factory. She had been elected a member of the Academy of Science and Literature in Mainz shortly before her death; the Büchner prize was awarded to her posthumously.

Elisabeth L. has written three novels (*Der Gang durch das Ried* [1936], *Das unauslöschliche Siegel* [1946], *Märkische Argonautenfahrt* [1950]), two collections of shorter fiction, a few novellas (*Proserpina* [1932], *Tryptichon des Teufels* [1932]), eighteen short stories collected under the title *Der Torso* (1948), and several small collections of lyric poetry (*Wendekreis des Lammes* [1924], *Die Tierkreisgedichte* [1935], *Der Laubmann und die Rose* [1947]. *Metamorphosen* [1951], *Kölnische Elegie* [1948]).

Elisabeth L. was one of the German writers who have made the conflict between pagan (especially Graeco-Roman) and Christian ideals their principal theme. But whereas most of these writers have championed paganism, Elisabeth L. was an impassioned and militant crusader for Christian theological values. Her intellectual world was that of Claudel, Bloy, Bernanos (qq.v.), all of whom she recognized as kindred spirits. Like them, she opposed what modern man has become since the Enlightenment; she disapproved of modern man's sense of feeling at home in this world, his indifference to matters theological, his recognition of life itself, rather than God, as the ultimate value.

Where modern man tends to worship nature and justify whatever is natural, (seeing in nature the principle of health, organic growth, measure, harmony, and beauty), Elisabeth L. roundly condemns "natural" nature as cursed, demonic, magic (in the sense of bewitched and unnatural), seductive, nihilistic—in short, pertaining to the realm of the devil. Such nature is creation that has fallen away from God and, permitted an untrammeled development, will become rank. The central theme in her writing is the need to suppress this natural Adam, which exists in the phenomenal world as wild and luxuriant vegetation, in man as greed, gluttony, concupiscence, and in man's thought as rationalism, naturism, and pagan pantheism.

But nature can be redeemed from her corruption by grafting—the gardener is God's representative on earth, a sort of priest of nature. Similarly, in the human sphere, the corruption of nature can be redeemed by the mystery and miracle of faith, with the attendant rite of baptism as an outward manifestation of faith.

Man is not totally depraved, in Elisabeth L.'s eyes. Instead, like St. Augustine (354-430), Pascal (1623-62), and Kierkegaard (1813-55) she sees man as a being who stands halfway between angel and beast. His goal in life is to throw off the hubris that modern pagan humanism and rationalism breed, and to replace the religious indifference that is the curse of post-Renaissance man by an ardent belief in the spiritual values inherent in Christianity. To attain this goal, man need not practice complete asceticism, but he must constantly struggle against the temptations that the devil puts in his path.

This great Christian apology pervades Elisabeth L.'s work from its beginning (*Proserpina*) to its end (*Märkische Argonautenfahrt*).

As an artist, Elisabeth L. presents a maze of contradictions. Her work, which is profoundly serious, brings the message of salvation in a godless world; yet there is a strong element of sharp satire in it. She is a meticulous naturalist in her presentation of the outside world and in her depiction of character, in her ability to present the sordid, the disgusting, the dirty, and the realm of decay and putrefaction with the allure of fascination. At the same time she is a lyrical romanticist in her delicate descriptions of landscape and vegetation.

But Elisabeth L. also belongs to the vanguard of modern surrealism by having deliberately abolished from her work the logic of time, space, and causality, so that she professes to care nothing for psychological analysis, which has been the backbone of fiction since the 18th c. Like so many of the moderns, she presents man as an abstraction buffeted by impersonal forces rather than as a self-willed master of his own fate. Yet her work abounds in penetrating psychological vignettes. Her writing is passionately Christian and antimodern; yet it is steeped in pagan-classical mythology. She is a consummate artist in her mastery of the tools that make the poet—rich imagery,

ELISABETH LANGGÄSSER

RING LARDNER

elaborate symbolism, concrete realization and vocabulary. Yet she frequently subjects the reader to long disquisitions and dialogues on theology and philosophy.

There is a wide range in the aesthetic levels on which Elisabeth L. worked. Her lyric poetry encompasses simple nature lyrics of deep beauty (*Frühling 1946*), the most hermetic religious poetry written in the 20th c., and popular verse that approaches doggerel. Her composition is often faultless in detail but clumsy in the large. Her work shows no consistent level of taste, either in the themes she treats or in the diction she employs, which can be lyrically romantic, severely classical, crudely realistic, even morbidly decadent or just banal. At times she is obviously striving after effect, as when she overloads a descriptive passage with mythological lore in most inappropriate situations.

But it would be well to remember that this mixture of tastes, levels, atmospheres, and techniques is characteristic of some of the best literature of our age, which is an age of ambiguity, parody, pastiche, montage. All the criticism that can be leveled against Elisabeth L.'s work does not alter the fact that she is one of the major writers of the 20th c.

FURTHER WORKS: *So viel berauschende Vergänglichkeit* (1954)

BIBLIOGRAPHY: Horst, K. A. "E. L. und der magische Nihilismus," in *Merkur* (1950), pp. 562-71; Rinser, L., "E.L.," in *Der Monat* (1950); Grenzmann, W., "Die Elemente und der Logos," in *Dichtung und Glaube* (1952); Blume, B. "Kreatur und Element: Zur Metaphorik von E.L.'s; ed. by Roman *Das unauslöschliche Siegel*," in *Euphorion* (1954), pp. 71-89; Storz, G., "E.L.", in *Christliche Dichter der Gegenwart*, ed. by Friedmann and Mann (1955); Augsberger, E., *E.L., Assoziative Reihung, Leitmotiv und Symbol in ihren Prosawerken* (1962)

HARRY STEINHAUER

LARDNER, Ring (Ringgold Wilmer)

American short-story writer and journalist, b. 6 March 1885, Niles, Michigan; d. 25 Sept. 1933, East Hampton, New York

Born and raised in privileged circumstances, L. began his career as a sportswriter on newspapers in South Bend, Chicago, St. Louis, and Boston. From 1913 to 1919 he wrote a daily sports column for the Chicago *Tribune* and published a number of stories and sketches in various magazines. During this period he also published some of these writings in book form. During the twenties, he continued to write for newspapers but was concentrating on stories and sketches. He also wrote for the theater, his only notable success being *June Moon* (1929), written with George S. Kaufman (1889-1961).

Except for his nonsense pieces and the sketches in which he spoke directly, L. wrote about figures in the worlds of professional sports and show business and about middle-class people. What he most frequently derided in these people was their self-absorption, a trait that kept them out of touch with reality and made them foolish, thoughtless, or cruel. Depending on how their behavior affected others, his ridicule was good-natured or angry. L.'s principal technique was an irony that derived largely from his individual style, a skillful rendering of what Mencken (q.v.) called "common American." By means of his style, which provided a seemingly objective presentation, L. simultaneously characterized and ridiculed his figures (e.g., in the letters of the brash, semiliterate rookie pitcher in *You Know Me, Al* [1916], in the oral narratives of a social climber in *Gullible's Travels* in the dialogue in such stories as "The Love Nest" [1926] and "A Day with Conrad Green" [1926]). L.'s style has influenced a number of writers, notably Hemingway and Salinger (qq.v.).

With the publication of his first works, L. acquired a wide reputation as a humorist, but not until the appearance of his twelfth book, *How to Write Short Stories* (1924), did he receive recognition as a serious writer. Thereafter, his work was generally well-received and widely reviewed on both levels. Since his death, Clifton Fadiman (b. 1904) and Maxwell Geismar (b. 1909) have emphasized L.'s anger and portrayed him as a bitter and pessimistic misanthrope. Recent criticism, however, has directed attention to the idealistic standards that constantly informed his comic and satiric irony.

FURTHER WORKS: *Bib Ballads* (1915); *My Four Weeks in France* (1918); *Treat 'Em Rough* (1918); *Own Your Own Home* (1919); *Regular Fellows I Have Met* (1919); *The Real Dope* (1919); *The Young Immigrants* (1920); *The Big Town* (1921); *Symptoms of Being 35* (1921); *Say It with Oil* (1923); *What of It?* (1925); *The Love Nest, and Other Stories* (1926); *The Golden Honeymoon and Haircut* (1926); *The Story of a*

Wonder Man (1927); *Round Up* (1929); *Lose with a Smile* (1933); *First and Last* (1934); *Best Stories* (collected stories plus *The Big Town*) (1938); *Shut Up, He Explained* (1962); *The Ring Lardner Reader* (1963)

BIBLIOGRAPHY: Fadiman, C., "R. L. and the Triangle of Hate," *The Nation*, CXXXVI (22 March 1933), 315-17; Fitzgerald, F. S., "Ring," *The New Republic*, LXXVI (11 Oct. 1933), 254-55; Geismar, M., "R. L.: Like Something Was Going to Happen," in *Writers in Crisis* (1942); Elder, D., *R. L., A Biography* (1956); Webb, H. W., Jr., "The Meaning of R. L.'s Fiction: A Re-evaluation," *American Literature*, XXXI (Jan. 1960), 434-45; Patrick, W. R., *R. L.* (1963); Friedrich, O., *R. L.* (1965)

HOWARD W. WEBB, JR.

LATVIAN LITERATURE

Latvian literature shares the fate of its two neighbors on the Baltic, Estonia and Lithuania, of emerging as a full-fledged written literature only in the 19th c. The ground from which Latvian letters sprang had been prepared for centuries by folklore. Tribes speaking Baltic languages had settled near the Baltic Sea already during the 2nd millennium B.C., thus establishing a continuum of civilization and language paralleled in Europe only by the Greeks. Latvian and Lithuanian are the only surviving languages of this once widespread branch of Indo-European: their folk poetry has preserved many aspects of the common Indo-European heritage.

Situated at the crossroads of East and West, Latvia has been subject to Eastern and Western influences alike. After first contacts with Christianity through Byzantium, the Baltic tribes succumbed during the 13th c. A.D., after nearly a century of resistance, to the Teutonic Knights, who were desirous of securing colonial lands under the pretext of spreading Christianity. Centuries of domination by Germans, Russians, Poles, and Swedes followed, yet Latvian folk poetry not only survived but even experienced a golden age (13th-16th c.). That this could be achieved under foreign domination remains proof of the vitality of the indigenous Baltic civilization. It also explains the absence of heroic epic poetry akin to the Finnish *Kalevala*. The Finns, although under foreign rule, were never reduced to serfdom as were the Balts.

The heroic epos *Lāčplēsis* (1888) by Andrejs Pumpurs (1841-1902), based on Latvian folk tales, has great merit as an embodiment of national pride and hopes, but it is not comparable in authenticity with the *Kalevala*. Of the Latvian folksongs that have come down to us, the bulk is short lyrical songs, composed mainly by women and evincing a submission to a *modus vivendi* imposed on them by history, yet finding creative joy in commenting on the unchanging ways of nature and the main events of human lives. It is their great artistic value as well as the ethos inspiring them that have attracted foreign scholars and poets ever since their merits were first pointed out by Hamann, Herder, and Walter Scott.

At the beginning of the 20th c. Latvian literature in the accepted sense of the word was only about half a century old. Since the appearance of the first book printed in Latvian in 1585 (*Catechismus Catholicorum*), there had developed a tradition of religious and didactic writing, the authors being mainly German clergymen, that can hardly be classed as literature. The first literary work of merit is *Dziesmiņas* (1856), a volume of poetry and translations by Juris Alunāns (1832-64). The significant movement of National Awakening (1850-80) laid foundations for all literary genres except the drama. Although it did not produce a major poet, it created a body of poetry whose orientation toward a national romanticism strengthened pride in the Latvian past and hopes for a free state. The spiritual forces released by this movement were later instrumental in creating a free Latvia (1918). A group of realistic prose writers turned out fine work during the National Awakening, in spite of moralistic overtones. The panoramic novel *Mērnieku laiki* (1879) by the brothers Reinis Kaudzītis (1839-1920) and Matīss Kaudzītis (1848-1926) has become a classic of Latvian literature.

The interest in collecting Latvian folklore was perhaps the most vital seed planted during this period. Under the inspired leadership of Krišjānis Barons (1835-1923), a group of scholars, and with them a large part of the nation, embarked upon the gigantic task of collecting the still extant cultural manifestations of the Latvian spirit during past centuries of oppression. The first edition of *Latvju dainas* appeared 1894-1915 in eight volumes. The task was continued during the time of independence by the Archives of Folklore. At the outbreak of World War II the total of folk songs collected had reached 900,000 (not to mention other folkloristic material), making the Latvian national heritage one of the richest in the world.

In 1890 a new era set in for Latvian literature, replacing the National Awakening. This development was two-pronged—the socialist movement "Jaunā strāva" (New Current) and neoromanticism. Different as these two aspects may seem, they overlap considerably, as most significant writers around the turn of the century participated in both. This proves the urgency of the sociopolitical problems that had prompted the New Current into existence. (The Russification of Latvia by the Czarist Russian regime was only one of them.)

Most prominent among writers participating in the New Current were Jānis Rainis (q.v.; pseud. of Jānis Pliekšāns) and Aspazija (1868-1943; pseud. of Elza Rozenberga-Pliekšāne). In the personality and works of Aspazija we witness the interplay of the two movements dominating Latvian literature at the turn of the century. In her early dramatic works and lyrics she attacks social injustice and displays "feminist" tendencies. Her later writing, on the other hand, reveals the true personality of a romantic. Her lasting achievement lies in her "lyrical autobiography," five volumes of verse from the years 1910 to 1933. Rainis, a many-sided and philosophically inclined writer, was conscious heir to the poetic aspirations of the National Awakening in trying to incorporate the spirit and structure of the folk songs into his work. Rainis, who wrote highly successful dramatic works, and Aspazija laid the foundations for Latvian drama.

Poruks (q.v.) and Fricis Bārda (1880-1919) had both undergone the influence of German neoromanticism. Poruks, much the more important writer of the two, is credited with introducing psychological realism into Latvian literature with his prose works. Participating neither in the New Current nor in neoromanticism, Rūdolfs Blaumanis (1863-1908) continued the traditions of realism established during the National Awakening. One of the most memorable Latvian writers, he produced during his rather short life of forty-five years a body of dramatic and prose works as well as a handful of poems that have remained exemplary. The conflict between idealism and materialism, between moral values and the will for power was an evident part of the growing pains of Latvian society in an age of transition. Yet Blaumanis shifts the center of gravity from the social plane of earlier realists to the human soul, thus giving his dramatic works and stories an ageless

quality. In his drama *Indrāni* (1904), he shows this conflict in the clash of two generations. Blaumanis has also enriched Latvian drama with several very fine comedies.

After the unsuccessful revolution of 1905, political hopes were shattered and a change of pace occurred in Latvian literature. The freeing of literature from subservience to social problems was demanded as well as the right to personal and spontaneous expression, echoing West European developments of *l'art pour l'art* and symbolism (q.v.). These two literary movements acted only as catalysts. The Latvian adaptation had little in common with either, inclining toward impressionism in vividness of images and stressing lyrical qualities in poetry as well as prose. Thus a period of lyrical impressionism followed the New Current. It counted among its adherents some of the finest poets in the Latvian language, e.g., Kārlis Skalbe (1879-1945). Skalbe is master of succinct lyrical expression and simplicity of form. The spirit and ethos of folklore seem to have been reborn in his deeply national poetry and fairy tales. Sometimes called the "Latvian Andersen," he has remained unsurpassed in this genre. Impressionism with *l'art pour l'art* tendencies is found in the sonorous rhythmic patterns of Vilis Plūdonis (pseud. of Vilis Lejenieks, 1874-1940), which impelled the Russian poet Blok (q.v.) to translate his famous "Requiem."

To the trio Aspazija, Rainis, and Blaumanis, the founders as well as highest achievers in Latvian dramatic writing, we must add the name of Anna Brigadere (q.v.). If the dramatic art of Aspazija straddles the extremes of social criticism and romantic drama, if Rainis is chiefly a symbolist and Blaumanis a realist, then Anna Brigadere has "a passion for the light, color, and symbolic verities of the folk imagination" (W. K. Matthews). Out of these elements she has created very original as well as deeply national fairy tale plays. Thus the folk tale lives on in the fairy tales of Skalbe as well as in the plays of Anna Brigadere, whose childhood reminiscences have become a classic of Latvian literature. Harking back to the individual's childhood becomes equivalent to the interest of the whole nation in its origins as mirrored in folklore. Thus the genre of childhood reminiscences has not only enjoyed great popularity but also produced outstanding works. With the surge of impressionism after 1905, this genre engaged the best creative powers of such fine writers as Jānis Jaunsudrabiņš (1877-1962), Antons Austriņš (1884-1934), and Jānis

Akurāters (1876-1937). The glorification of the Latvian farmstead as reflecting in its unchanging ways an eternal order reaches its apogee in Virza's (q.v.) novel-length prose poem *Straumēni* (1933). This gem of bucolic evocations has deservedly been translated into both French and German. Even during the exile following World War II, outstanding prose works in this genre have enriched Latvian literature, e.g., the autobiographical novels by Margarita Kovaļevska (b. 1910; residing in the U.S.A.).

Side by side with the discovery of the self and nature by impressionism, realism (often verging on naturalism [q.v.]) remains a powerful means of taking stock of the native land, its history, and people. Following in the footsteps of the brothers Kaudzītes and their great novel about the times of the land surveyors in northern Latvia, two 20th c. novelists have put the landscape and past of southwestern Latvia and the capital city, Riga, on the literary map. They are Augusts Deglavs (1862-1922), with his trilogy *Rīga* (1911-22), and Jēkabs Janševskis (1865-1931), with *Dzimtene* (1921-25), also a trilogy. Their earthy style and colorful use of regional dialects engendered a whole school of novelists, attaining prominence during the 1930's and continuing in the same manner even in exile. A few names may stand here for many: Jānis Jaunsudrabiņš, Aīda Niedra (b. 1898; in exile in the U.S.A.), Alfrēds Dziļums (1907-1966), and Jānis Klīdzējs (b. 1914; in exile in the U.S.A.).

In the wake of World War I an independent Latvian Democratic Republic was declared and a new period of literature set in, destined to last until 1940. The literary achievement of these twenty-two years is impressive if not astounding, when we stop to realize that they were the only time of free development granted this literature which was not yet a hundred years old when it sank again into subservience to a foreign power. The first decade of independence was characterized by openness to foreign influences and by an efflorescence of all the arts. French models make themselves felt in the polished prose style of Jānis Ezeriņš (1891-1924). In his short stories and novels, Kārlis Zariņš (1899-1947) achieved a psychological depth and epical poise between lyricism and realism worthy of the best work of his West European contemporaries. The impact of German expressionism (q.v.) coupled with influences from Russian imagism and futurism (q.v.) called forth the first truly modern Latvian poets. Pēteris Ērmanis (b. 1893; in exile in Germany), stands out as a Latvian expressionist, while Aleksandrs Čaks (pseud. of Aleksandrs Čadarainis, 1902-1950) is doubtlessly Latvia's greatest modern poet. A born rebel and keen innovator, Čaks shocked with his first books of poetry, *Es un šis laiks* and *Sirds uz trotuāra* (both 1928). In his early work he discarded rhyme in favor of rhythm and used daring and unexpected images. Nevertheless Čaks is a lyric poet and in his best work there is poignancy of feeling and wistfulness of mood. His best collection, *Iedomu spoguļi* (1938), is one of the finest achievements of Latvian poetry. Not only are his poetic means refreshingly new, but also his world—the Latvian capital, Riga, with its suburbs—had never thus been celebrated in poetry before. Čaks has written several longer narrative poems, among them "Life," a passionate lyrical evocation of a musician, another Orpheus who holds all of life under the sway of his art; his ballad cycle about the legendary bravery of the Latvian fusiliers of World War I, *Mūžības skartie* (1938-40), stands out among the patriotic poetry of the 1930's. Čaks succeeds here in blending brilliant lyrical passages with sharply focussed descriptions of war. A remarkable work of art results, worthy of comparison with, say, Blok's *The Twelve* or Pasternak's (qq.v.) *Lieutenant Schmidt*, yet surpassing both Russian works in scope. Čaks remained in Communist-occupied Latvia and died there at the height of his creative powers.

The *coup d'état* of 1934, which brought an authoritarian government to power, also changed the course of Latvian letters. Instead of an international modernism, a return to indigenous traditions and a glorification of the past became the order of the day. The main figure of this school of poetry was Virza, a refined poet who has, however, given his best in the prose poem *Straumēni*, already mentioned. Renewed preoccupation with folklore resulted in experiments with folk-song metre in the poetry of Jānis Medenis (1903-1961) and a reincarnation of its spirit in the subtly balanced verse of Zinaīda Lazda (1902-1957). In prose, attempts were made to recreate the legendary Latvian past and to reconstruct the ancient religion of the Balts. Jānis Veselis (1896-1962) and Ilona Leimane (b. 1905; in exile in France) have given their best in this kind of fiction, due to an original use of language. Aleksandrs Grīns (b. 1895) had pioneered the novel-legend about the Latvian fight for freedom, which found a more poetic interpretation in Čaks'

Mūžības skartie. Kārlis Zariņš lifted the historical novel onto a higher artistic plane.

The literary pattern of the 1930's is a complex one, and full justice cannot be given it here. Thus a tendency toward universalism parallels the national and traditional aspirations, finding expression in the essays of Zenta Maurina (q.v.); Mirdza Bendrupe (b. 1910), gifted short story writer and poet, was influenced by Freud and Oriental mysticism. A major poet whose work developed during the 1930's in almost direct opposition to national trends was Ēriks Ādamsons (1907-1947). Bent on introspection and refinement rather than proximity to the native earth, he occupies a lonely yet prominent place in Latvian letters. His fine sense of form and independent world view, unabashedly that of an aesthete, guarantee his originality. His output includes poetry, plays, and prose works.

The mores of urban society and the psychology of love gained momentum as literary themes toward the end of the 1930's. They were explored and carried over into exile writing in the work of Anšlavs Eglītis (b. 1906). Valdemārs Kārkliņš (1906-1964), and Knuts Lesiņš (b. 1909; *The Wine of Eternity,* 1957), who have continued to develop these themes in the United States. The only dramatist of note during the 1930's was Mārtiņš Zīverts (b. 1903; in exile in Sweden), a technical innovator and author deserving wider international attention. Although a dramatist may experience more keenly the limitations imposed upon his art by exile conditions than a poet or novelist, Zīverts has continued writing.

Among the poets who began to publish during the late 1930's, Veronika Strēlerte (pseud. of Rudīte Strēlerte-Johansone, b. 1912; in exile in Sweden) showed greatest promise. Before leaving her native country, she had published two collections of verse, establishing her as the finest artist among a host of Latvian woman poets. Her polished, pliant verse lends itself well to intellectual meditation or restrained patriotic feeling. From 1945 to 1961 she published three more volumes of poetry. Andrejs Eglītis (b. 1912; in exile in Sweden) gained great popularity with his patriotic verse during the war years and has continued as a national bard in exile, producing ten volumes of poetry in all.

Since the mid 1950's a new generation of poets has begun to dominate the literary scene. Born during the 1920's and educated in Latvian schools, they began publishing only in

exile; yet it is they who have brought about a renaissance of Latvian poetry by claiming the modernist Čaks as their ancestor and incorporating the lesson learned from Western experimental poetry into their work. The most original of them are Velta Sniķere (b. 1920; in exile in England) and three poets living presently in the U.S.A. Sniķere continues the traditional dialogue with the language of the folk songs, transposing it into a surrealist key. Linards Tauns (pseud. for *Alfrēds Bērzs,* 1922-63) and Gunars Saliņš (b. 1924) both belong to the New York group of Latvian poets, also called the "Hell's Kitchen school" after a section of Manhattan, and including such other poets as Baiba Bičole, Rita Gāle, Aina Kraujiete, and Jānis Krēsliņš. The visionary poetry of Tauns presents the highest achievement to date in Latvian poetry in exile, seconded by the strong, epically colored verse of Saliņš. The fourth in this quartet of modern Latvian poets is Olafs Stumbrs (b. 1931; in exile in California). In his poetry exile becomes a simile for the poet's fate of loneliness and alienation.

A breakthrough of modernism in prose writing began during the 1950's in the novels of Modris Zeberiņš (b. 1923) and Dzintars Sodums (b. 1922; both in the U.S.A.), and became an undeniable fact in the work of Guntis Zariņš (1926-65). Zariņš produced half a dozen novels in rapid succession, all of which evinced an existentialist's point of view and a breathless search for self-identification both as an individual and a Latvian. Ilze Šķipsna (b. 1928; in exile in the U.S.A.) and Andrejs Irbe (b. 1924; in exile in Sweden) center their interest in exploring labile psychological states and the substratum of dreams and memories in the exile's inner life, which could not be reached by realistic prose writing. The painter Margarita Kovaļevska has given in her autobiographical trilogy a remarkable prose work, reflecting both the colorful earthiness and fantasy-charged atmosphere of a fairy tale. Another painter, Tālivaldis Ķiķauka (b. 1928; in exile in Canada) leans toward surrealism in his imaginative, exhilarating prose. Thus in its twenty-fifth year Latvian literature in exile shows signs of vitality and promise for the future.

As to Soviet-occupied Latvia, literature has been subject there to the same rigorous dictatorship and demands for "socialist realism" as in the Soviet Union proper. Most of the important writers of the period of independence have fled to the West and are residing in the free world, thus depriving the country of intellectual leadership in the postwar years. There have been, however, during the 1960's stirrings of genuine poetic force among the younger generation. It is easier for poets than for prose writers or dramatists to circumnavigate the socialist postulates and to find fresh approaches to poetic form. Therefore may the names of four poets stand here for this whole modest regeneration. They have each in their own way achieved a breakthrough for their considerable poetic talent. Ojārs Vācietis (b. 1933) was one of the first to demand creative freedom for the individual artist, and he has been seconded by his coeval Imants Ziedonis (b. 1933). A woman poet of unusual force and sensitivity is Vizma Belševica (b. 1931), while to Māris Čaklais (b. 1940) belongs the most promising young talent.

BIBLIOGRAPHY: Virza, E., *La Littérature lettonne depuis l'époque du réveil national* (1926); Katzenellenbogen, U., *The Dainas: Anthology of Latvian Folk-Songs* (1935); Urch, R. O., *Latvia: Country and People* (London, 1939); Spekke, A., *History of Latvia: An Outline* (1951); Bīlmanis, A., *A History of Latvia* (1951); Johansons, A., "Latvian Literature in Exile," *SEER* XXX: 75 (1952); Andrups, J., and Kalve, V., *Latvian Literature* (1954); Matthews, W. K., *A Century of Latvian Poetry* (1957); Eckhardt-Skalberg, E., *Lettische Lyrik* (1960); *Zintis/The Seer of Wisdom*, Quarterly American Latvian Magazine for Art, Literature and Science (1961); Rubulis, A., and Lahood, M. J., eds., *Latvian Literature* (1964)

ASTRID IVASK

LAWRENCE, David Herbert

English novelist, poet, dramatist, and essayist, b. 11 Sept. 1885, Eastwood, Nottinghamshire; d. 30 March 1930, Vence, France

In the course of a twenty-year writing period, L. produced more than forty volumes of fiction, poetry, drama, criticism, philosophy, and travel writing.

In his fiction he was both poet and prophet. As inspired poet, he wrote of bird, beast, and flower with sensuous immediacy, and rendered emotional conflicts with unusual depth and power. As angry prophet he sermonized on the sterile quality of his age, upheld new modes of love and friendship, and called for political and religious solutions to contemporary problems.

The fundamental theme of his *oeuvre* is the fight against unnaturalness, the constricting effects of civilization, and the demand for free development of personality. In this he assigns a decisive role to eros and sex, which he presents with utmost frankness.

L.'s work was always based on firsthand knowledge of a disrupted world. Class warfare, for example, was the conditioning factor of his earliest years. His father was an uneducated coal-miner, while his mother came from a genteel burgher family; their frequent quarrels marred the very quality of their children's lives. One result was the disruption in L. himself, as his mother turned from her husband to find satisfaction in the achievements of her sons. In his early manhood L. married a German aristocrat. His wife, the former Frieda von Richthofen, was married and the mother of three small children when Lawrence met her, but she left her family in order to live with the promising young novelist. Their union suggests the dissolution of social barriers, along with the abandonment of outworn morality, which L. would later deal with in his fiction.

L. traveled with his wife from country to country, living for brief periods in Germany, Austria, Italy, Sicily, England, France, Australia, and America. In England he met John Middleton Murry, Katherine Mansfield (q.v.), and other British writers, who later appeared in his fiction as representatives of social decadence. In Australia he wrote *Kangaroo* (1923) fusing his vivid impressions of that continent with the political chaos he had witnessed in fascist Italy.

In dealing with his prolific output, it seems feasible to consider Lawrence solely as a novelist. His earliest major novel is *Sons and Lovers* (1913), which many critics regard as his finest work. On the surface, this book resembles the traditional 19th c. British novel, but the oedipal theme sets it off from the older novel and makes L. one of the pioneers in modern psychological fiction. The setting is the coal-mining community in which L. was raised, and the Coppard family is L.'s family. Gertrude Coppard, a refined and righteous woman from the lower middle class, can find no satisfaction in her marriage with the gay and sensuous miner, Walter Morel, who is an irresponsible husband. When she turns to her sons for happiness, she destroys or damages them, as they come to manhood, by her unyielding hold on their affections. Her second son, Paul Morel, is the leading figure in the book: he is torn between his mother and two sweethearts, one of them an intensely spiritual girl, the other a potentially sensual woman who has joined the feminist movement. Both women want to possess Paul through imprisoning personal love, whereas Paul himself is in search of deeply impersonal fulfillment through sexual love. Thus, by the time his mother dies of cancer, he has already cast off both his sweethearts. At the end of the novel he resists the deathward pull from his mother's grave and stands free, apparently in the earliest stages of maturity. By embracing and then discarding three forms of counterfeit love, Paul indicates his quest for a more valid mode of life.

In the next novel, *The Rainbow* (1915), this quest is continued by three generations of an English farming family, the Brangwens. In each generation there is a conflict between sensual vitality and spiritual aspiration, which L. wants to fuse into a single religious vision. L.'s symbol for that vision is the round arch of the rainbow. The characters in this novel seek "a new knowledge of Eternity in the flux of Time." They find it chiefly through polarity or balance in love, but they are usually unsuccessful in their quest for "passionate purpose," which is the spiritual element in L.'s scheme of things. Hence their lives lack scope and fullness: they are afraid of the unknown, they are sidetracked into Christianity, or they lapse into the "violent trance" of fecund motherhood. In the third generation, however, a young girl, Ursula Brangwen, is able to break through these traps and to arrive at the threshold of true womanhood. In *The Rainbow*, L. began to experiment with new fictional techniques. He utilized dominant symbols and developed strange ritualistic scenes in which states of soul are revealed by the relations between man and nature.

L.'s next major novel, *Women in Love* (1920), is actually a well-ordered progression of such scenes. Two lovers are judged, for example, by the brutal way in which they quell a stubborn rabbit; two others are confirmed in their love by an offering of flowers in the open countryside. Here L. showed us those who deny or exploit the life within themselves, and those who affirm their own spontaneity. He also indicated the whole disintegrative process in Western civilization through such scenes. In this sense this novel is like *The Magic Mountain* by Thomas Mann (q.v.), or *The Waste Land* by Eliot (q.v.), in which the decadence of an entire culture is presented through representative figures.

The industrialist Gerald Crich, for instance, is called "a phase of life incarnate," and the phase he embodies is termed "Northern ice-destructiveness"—which is the reduction of human beings to mere instruments in the industrial scheme. Similar reduction also occurs in love, art, education, and science. They are criticized by the prophetic hero, Rupert Birkin, who insists on the inviolate "otherness" of his fellow creatures, and who succeeds in developing a balanced relationship with his future wife, Ursula Brangwen, in which each honors the other's basic separateness of being, and thereby achieves creative rather than reductive love. Though Birken achieves creative love, he fails to establish any valid *Blutbruderschaft* with his friend Gerald Crich. Yet his attempt to do so marks the start of L.'s search for a new community.

At the end of *Aaron's Rod* (1922) a prophetic figure tells the protagonist to submit his soul to a leader, or to a soul greater than his own. In the following *Kangaroo* this form of personal submission becomes a political concept, as L. explores the possibilities of communism and paternalism.

But L. finally rejected these merely political movements for the religious state he creates in *The Plumed Serpent* (1926). The setting here is modern Mexico, where two religious leaders try to replace Christianity with a curious mixture of politics and Aztec myths. They distribute hymns and sermons on printed leaflets throughout the country; they hold ritual dances among the people and use symbols and myths to implement the new faith. After a brief revolution their organic state is established. Its purpose is to fuse man's blood and spirit into new and vital unison, so as to bring out his potential godliness. Yet the leaders make no real provision for the minds and spirits of their followers; in fact, they offer them little more than static vitalism. Kate Leslie, the modern mind-centered woman who has been drawn into the movement, remains skeptical of the religion, as the novel ends. Her doubts foreshadow L.'s own rejection of his stand, a few years later, on the ground that hero worship leads to the inhumanity of the militant ideal. After *The Plumed Serpent* L. abandoned his attempt to regenerate society through political and religious programs.

Now L. turned once more to the theme of individual regeneration through sexual love. In his last important novel, *Lady Chatterley's Lover* (1928), L.'s aim is to reveal the beauty and significance of sex. Though the novel has been the object of fierce legal pornography battles, L.'s vivid descriptions of the love act are episodes in Constance Chatterley's progression toward greater fullness of being. Constance herself has been raised as a "free" modern woman. She has lived in the exciting world of art, music, and ideas, where sex is viewed as a mere primitive anticlimax. Thus, when her husband returns from World War I, paralyzed from the hips down, she scarcely feels the blow to their married life. The paralysis of this aristocratic industrialist is, however, a symbol for his contempt of the human body, and beyond this, for his basic lack of moral and emotional independence. Because Constance is gradually drained by his parasitical nature, she turns for love and rebirth to the gamekeeper on the Chatterley estate. Her lover, Oliver Mellors, is perhaps the first Lawrencian hero to incorporate all the qualities his creator admires—robust independence, sensual vitality, a sympathetic awareness of others, creative intelligence, and the capacity for growth and change. When Constance abandons her husband to marry this man, she asserts the worth of all these qualities.

Through his championing of these revolutionary demands for a reevaluation of human life, L. has stimulated such writers as Huxley, Spender (qq.v.), and Wyndham Lewis in England, and Sherwood Anderson, Jeffers, and Tennessee Williams (qq.v.) in America. He remains unsurpassed, however, in his powerful portrayal of the passionate striving for a fully lived life.

FURTHER WORKS: *The White Peacock* (1911); *The Trespasser* (1912); *Love Poems* (1913); *The Widowing of Mrs. Holroyd* (1914); *The Prussian Officer* (1914); *Twilight in Italy* (1916); *Amores* (1916); *Look! We Have Come Through* (1917); *New Poems* (1918); *Bay* (1919); *Touch and Go* (1920); *The Lost Girl* (1920); *Movements in European History* (under pseud. of Lawrence H. Davison, 1921); *Psychoanalysis and the Unconscious* (1921); *Tortoises* (1921); *Sea and Sardinia* (1921); *Fantasia of the Unconscious* (1922); *England, My England* (1922); *The Ladybird* (1923; Am., *The Captain's Doll*, 1923); *Studies in Classic American Literature* (1923); *Birds, Beasts and Flowers* (1923); *The Boy in the Bush* (1924); *St. Mawr* (together with "The Princess"; 1925); *Reflections on the Death of a Porcupine* (1925); *David* (1926); *Sun* (1926); *Glad Ghosts* (1926); *Mornings in Mexico* (1927);

Selected Poems (1928); *Rawdon's Roof* (1928); *The Woman Who Rode Away* (1928); *Collected Poems* (1928); *Sex Locked Out* (1928); *The Paintings of D. H. Lawrence* (D. H. L.'s paintings reproduced; 1929); *Pansies* (1929); *My Skirmish with Jolly Roger* (1929); *Pornography and Obscenity* (1929); *The Life of J. Middleton Murry* (1930); *Nettles* (1930); *Assorted Articles* (1930); *The Virgin and the Gypsy* (1930); *Love among the Haystacks* (1930); *Apocalypse* (1930); *The Man Who Died* (1931); *Etruscan Places* (1932); *Letters* (ed. Aldous Huxley; 1932); *Last Poems* (ed. Richard Aldington and Giuseppe Orioli; 1932); *The Lovely Lady* (1933); *The Plays* (1934); *The Tales* (1934); *Selected Poems* (1934); *A Collier's Friday Night* (1934); *A Modern Lover* (1934); *The Spirit of Place* (ed. Richard Aldington; 1935); *Foreword to Women in Love* (1936); *Pornography and So On* (1936); *Phoenix, Posthumous Papers* (ed. Edward D. McDonald; 1936); *Poems* (coll. ed., 1939); *Stories, Essays and Poems* (coll. ed., 1940); *Fire* (1940); *Full Score* (1943); *The First Lady Chatterley* (1944); *Selected Poems* (1947); *Letters to Bertrand Russell* (ed. Harry T. Moore; 1948); *A Prelude* (1949); *Selected Essays* (1950); *Selected Letters* (ed. Richard Aldington; 1950); *Selected Poems* (ed. W. E. Williams; 1950); *Selected Poems* (ed. James Reeves; 1951); *Complete Short Stories* (1955); *Selected Literary Criticism* (ed. Anthony Beal; 1955); *Complete Poems* (3 vols., 1957); *Selected Poetry and Prose* (ed. T. R. Barnes; 1957); *Selected Letters* (ed. Diana Trilling; 1958); *The Collected Letters* (ed. Harry T. Moore; 1962); *The Symbolic Meaning: The Uncollected Versions of Studies in Classic American Literature* (ed. Armin Arnold; 1962); *The Complete Poems* (ed. Vivian de Sola Pinto and Warren Roberts; 1964); *Complete Plays* (1965)

BIBLIOGRAPHY: McDonald, E. D., *A Bibliography of the Writings of D. H. L.* (1926); Potter, S., *D. H. L.* (1930); McDonald, E. D., *The Writings of D. H. L.: 1925-1930* (1931); Murry, J. M., *Son of Woman* (1931); Malraux, A., "L.," in *Criterion,* XII (1932-33); Carswell, C., *The Savage Pilgrimage* (1932); Luhan, M. D., *Lorenzo in Taos* (1932); Murry, J. M., *Reminiscences of D. H. L.* (1933); Gregory, H., *Pilgrim of the Apocalypse* (1934); Lawrence, F., *Not I, But the Wind* (1934); Chambers, J., *D. H. L.: A Personal Record* (1935); Tedlock, E. W., *The Frieda Lawrence Collection of D. H. L. Manuscripts* (1948); Aldington, R., *D. H. L.: Portrait of a Genius, But . . .* (1950); White, W., *D. H. L.:*

A Checklist 1931-1950 (1950); Moore, H. L., *The Life and Works of D. H. L.* (1951); Tiverton, W., *D. H. L. and Human Existence* (1951); Moore, H. T., and Hoffman, F., eds., *The Achievement of D. H. L.* (1953); Moore, H. T., *The Intelligent Heart* (1954); Freeman, M., *D. H. L.: A Basic Study of His Ideas* (1955); Leavis, F. R., *D. H. L., Novelist* (1955); Spilka, M., *The Love Ethic of D. H. L.* (1955); Hough, G., *The Dark Sun* (1957); Hough, G., *D. H. L.: A Composite Biography* (2 vols., 1957, 1958); Aldington, R., *D. H. L.* (1960); Vivas, E., *D. H. L.* (1960); Beale, A., *D. H. L.* (1961); Armin, A., *D. H. L. and Germany* (1963); Goodheart, E., *The Utopian Vision of D. H. L.* (1963); Moynahan, J., *The Deed of Life* (1963); Spilka, M., *D. H. L.: A Collection of Critical Essays* (1963); Tedlock, E. W., *D. H. L.: Artist and Rebel* (1963); Draper, R. P., *D. H. L.* (1964); Lawrence, F., *Frieda Lawrence: The Memoirs and Correspondence* (1964); Nin, A., *D. H. L., An Unprofessional Study* (1964); Levy, M., ed., *Paintings of D. H. L.* (1964); Panichas, G., *Adventures in Consciousness: The Meaning of D. H. L.'s Religious Quest* (1964); Corke, H., *D. H. L.: The Croydon Years* (1965); Chambers, J., *D. H. L.* (1965); Corsani, M., *D. H. L. e l'Italia* (1965); Lawrence, A., *Young Lorenzo* (1966); Moore, H. T., *D. H. L. and His World* (1966); Sagar, K., *The Art of D. H. L.* (1966); West, A., *D. H. L.* (1966); Lerner, L., *The Truthtellers: Jane Austen, George Eliot, D. H. L.* (1967)

MARK SPILKA

LAWRENCE, Thomas Edward

English writer, b. 1 Aug. 1888, Tremadoc, Wales; d. 19 May 1935, Bovington Camp Hospital, England

Both as an author and as a man L. is one of the most controversial figures in modern English literature. Repeatedly accused of self-glorification, the falsification of history, and boundless vanity, he nevertheless held a high place in official British opinion and was admired by the intellectual elite of Europe as the "uncrowned king of Arabia." Neither the conflicting biographies and analyses of the life and work of the mysterious "Colonel L." nor comprehensive editions of his diaries and correspondence have satisfactorily explained this contradictory life. When, in 1935, *Seven Pillars of Wisdom* (privately printed, 1926; first made available to a wider public in the abridged edition *Revolt in the Desert,* 1926) appeared in its definitive form, arousing enthusiasm, discussion, and dissension, the book was first evaluated from two standpoints: literary quality and accuracy of detail.

The political triumph that this unknown, burnoose-wearing English archaeologist had achieved in the Turkish theater of war by winning the Arab insurgents over to the Allied side dramatized him as a war hero, so that little attention was paid to L. the man. The "L. case" first came to public notice when it was discovered that this national hero, under a false name, was an "unknown soldier in the R.A.F." Proliferating rumors about his activities as a secret agent in all the trouble spots of Asiatic politics made him out to be a brilliant adventurer who would obviously never disclose the truth.

L.'s letters and notes published after his death and the disclosures of his acquaintances gradually defined the L. problem. It is, of course, impossible to determine whether his actions and writings stemmed from the meaningful isolation of balanced self-sufficiency or from the loneliness of a neurotic vacillating between arrogance and masochism; a case can be made for both. L.'s fascination lies in his individuality; he was vain but fully aware of his failings; he was loyal yet cynical; he was courageous while admitting that he was afraid; he believed in the power of words yet made fun of writing; he shrunk from publicity but seemed to be always seeking it through the vehemence of his protestations. Thus the stereotyped concept of the uncomplicated "hero" had to be modified when L. was being discussed. The impressive thing about him was not the bizarre quality of his life but the capacity of this man of action to analyze himself and "bring himself to trial" in the very midst of action (*Seven Pillars of Wisdom*) or suffering (*The Mint,* 1955)—a capacity that is typical, too, of others of his generation.

As a writer, L. by no means confined himself to "self-examination." Thus in his epic of the Arab revolt, vivid sketches of landscape, animals, and people punctuate the details of guerrilla war. In *The Mint* he tried to capture the atmosphere of life in the barracks through economical, photographic character sketches of the men. L. wrote out of firsthand experience, one aspect of which was the constant shift between overweening pride and deep depression.

L.'s significance lies chiefly in the fact that for a long time, whether voluntarily or not,

257

he served as an "intellectual agent provocateur" by constantly challenging himself and thus enabling friends, opponents, and readers to share the unquietness that lay behind his life and writing. Winston Churchill called him "one of the greatest men of our time."

FURTHER WORKS: *Carchemish, Reports on the Excavations at Djerabis* (with C. L. Woolley; 1914); *The Wilderness of Zin: Archaeological Reports* (with C. L. Woolley; 1915); *The Odyssey of Homer* (1932); *Letters from T. E. Shaw to Bruce Rogers* (1933); *More Letters from T. E. Shaw to Bruce Rogers* (1936); *Crusader Castles* (1936); *The Diary of T. E. L., 1911* (1937); *Letters* (ed. David Garnett; 1938); *T. E. L. to His Biographer, Liddell Hart* (1939); *T. E. L. to His Biographer, Robert Graves* (1939); *Oriental Assembly* (ed. A. W. Lawrence; 1939); *Secret Dispatches from Arabia* (1939); *T. E. L.'s Letters to H. S. Ede, 1927-1935* (ed. T. E. Shaw; 1942); *Selected Letters* (ed. David Garnett; 1952); *The Home Letters of T. E. L. and His Brothers* (ed. M. R. Lawrence; 1954)

BIBLIOGRAPHY: Graves, R., *L. and the Arabs* (1927); Hart, L., *Colonel L.: The Man Behind the Legend* (1934); Duval, E. W., *L.: A Biography* (1937); Aldington, R., *L. of Arabia* (1955); Armitage, F., *The Desert and the Stars* (1956); Howe, I., "T. E. L.: The Problem of Heroism," in *HudR*, XV (1962), 333-64; Lawrence, A. W., ed., *Letters to T. E. L.* (1962); Stéphane, R., *Portrait de l'aventurier: T. E. L., Malraux, von Salomon* (1965); Notopoulos, J. A., "The Tragic and the Epic in T. E. L.," in *YR*, LIV (1965), 331-45; Mūsa, S., *T. E. L.* (1966); Payne, P., *L. of Arabia: A Triumph* (1966)

KARL O. PAETEL

LAXNESS, Halldór Kiljan
(pseud. of *Halldór Kiljan Gudjonsson*), Icelandic novelist, dramatist, essayist, and poet, b. 23 April 1902, Laxness, near Reykjavík

Formed by peasant and urban cultures, L. started to write at an early age. His first novel, *Barn natturunnar* (1919), was published when he was seventeen years old. The next decade he spent abroad, first in Europe, then in Canada and the U.S.A., strenuously embracing various beliefs. He steeped himself in surrealism (q.v.) in France, and in expressionism (q.v.). in Germany, where he was deeply affected by the chaotic life that followed World War I.

Sigrid Undset's (q.v.) neo-Catholicism and Thomas à Kempis's *De Imitatione Christi* led him to Catholicism. He was converted and lived for two years in a monastery in Luxemburg. He described his reasons for becoming a monk in *Undir Helgahnúk* (1924) and in *Katholsk vidhorf* (1925). His wrestling with religion also brought forth his introspective novel *Vefarinn mikli frá Kasmír* (1927), which was written in an expressionistic-surrealistic style. This novel became a milestone in Icelandic literature. In this monumental autobiographical novel, the "weaver of Kashmir," a young man torn by the conflicts of ideas, is at last able to proclaim "God above woman."

From 1927 to 1930, L. lived in Canada and California, where he came under the influence of Upton Sinclair's radical socialism and of communism. By 1929 his beliefs had undergone a major reversal, as reflected in *AlÞýðubókin* (1929), which is a collection of brilliant communistic essays in which the ideals of the Catholic church are reduced *ad absurdum*. From that time on his topic was "man in his struggle and not God in his heaven." In those years he also produced his one volume of poetry, *Kvæðakver* (1930), which contained lyrics in the manner of French surrealism.

Slowly the traveler was beginning to rediscover his native country. He returned home, married (1930), and started to write his great novels about Iceland. In these novels he was to write about the downtrodden of yesterday and today, about Iceland's history, at first in the spirit of neoromantic enthusiasm that had been sparked by Gunnarsson (q.v.), and also about the difficulties of the youthful urban population of Reykjavík, which had been cut loose from the thousand-year-old farm culture.

The first of these novels were *Þú vínviður hreini* (1931) and *Fuglinn í fjörunni* (1932; in English translation, they are published together under the title Salka Valka, 1936). The first is the story of the poor fishergirl Salka Valka; the second, that of a freeholder in his struggle with the elements and human blindness. The people, drawn on a grand scale, are heroic symbols of their class.

L. forged his own individual style in *Heimsljós* (4 vols.; I, *Ljós heimsins*, 1937; II, *Höle sumarlandsins*, 1938; III, *Hús skaldsins*, 1939; IV, *Fegurð himinsins*, 1940; World Light, 1969). He uses the tragic life story of the poet of the poor, Sigurdur Breidfjörds (1798-1846). The poet in L.'s novel is anything but a hero. A

D. H. LAWRENCE

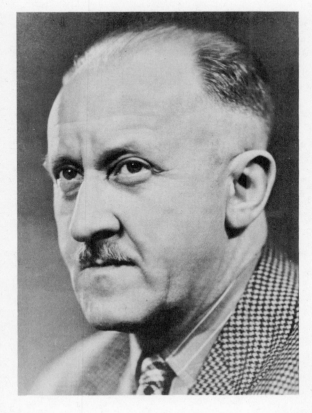

HALLDÓR LAXNESS

GERTRUD LE FORT

helpless scapegoat of a cruel world, enmeshed in his dream that he will bring light to the world, he winds up in prison for raping a schoolgirl. Fearful and humble, but idealistic to the end, he lives out his impoverished, wretched life in a world of depravity and degeneration.

The trilogy *Íslandsklukkan* (I, *Islands-klukkan*, 1943; II, *Hið ljósa man*, 1944; III, *Eldur í Kaupinhafn*, 1946) shows L. at the height of his art. At the turn of the eighteenth century, when the Danes were at their most oppressive, Iceland was going through the most bitter period in its history. Famine, a sheep disease, two devastating volcanic eruptions, and the ruthless exploitations by the Danes, had reduced the population by one fourth. Since the Danes melted down the Iceland Bell (*islandsklukkan*), a shadow hovered over the land, over the "people without honor." This is the setting of the trilogy. Árni Magnússon (1663-1730), the protagonist of these novels, is a historical figure, famous for his tireless collecting of Icelandic manuscripts, which he rescued from the harsh climate and from ignorance. A friend of the Danish king and a champion for Iceland's honor, he wavers between two loyalties, and he lives to see all his plans for Iceland miscarry. *Íslandsklukkan* is a moving and deeply pessimistic story about a once heroic people, who have been living in bondage since 1271. L.'s merciless pen uncovers the lethargy of a people without hope or honor, their inebriety, laziness, egotism, and their struggle to retain their national identity in an almost hopeless situation.

Fierce social criticism runs through all of L.'s novels and has often alienated his readers. Yet he is not a defender of so-called socialist realism but of freedom for the artist as a mouthpiece of the oppressed and the deprived. L.'s rich lyrical vein, his vigorous symbolism, his psychological insights, his naturalism, his often cynical impartiality, enable him to fuse the characters and Iceland's harsh landscape into one vast panorama of intensified reality.

The most important modern writer of Iceland, L. has received international recognition. In 1955 he was honored with the Nobel Prize.

FURTHER WORKS: *Fotatak manna* (1933); *Straumrof* (1934); *Sjálfstætt fólk* (2 vols., 1934-35; Independent People, an Epic, 1946); *Dagleið á fjöllum* (1937); *Vettvangur dagsins* (1942); *Sjálfsagðir hlutir* (1946); *Atómstöðin* (1948; The Atom Station, 1961); *Snaefridur Islandssol*

(1950); *Reisubókarkorn* (1950); *Heiman eg for* (1952); *Gerpla* (1952; The Happy Warriors, 1958); *Silfurtunglið* (1954); *Baettir* (1954); *Dagur í senn* (1955); *Brekkukotsannáll* (1957; The Fish Can Sing, 1966); *Gjörningabók* (1957); *Strompleikurinn* (1961); *Paradísarheimt* (1960; Paradise Reclaimed, 1962); *Prjónastofan Sólin* (1962); *De Islandske Sagaer og andre Essays* (1963); *Kristni hald undir jökli* (1968)

BIBLIOGRAPHY: Einarsson, S., "A Contemporary Icelandic Author," in *Life and Letters To-day*, XIV (1936), iv, 23-30; Einarsson, S., "Five Icelandic Novelists," in *BA*, XVI (1942), 254-59; Hallberg, P., *Den store vävaren* (1954); Hallberg, P., *Skaldens hus* (1956); Hallberg, P., *L. som Dramatiker* (1964); Kötz, G., *Das Problem Dichter und Gesellschaft im Werke von H. L.* (1966); Lange, W., "Über H. L.," in *GRM*, XVI (1966), 76-89

GERTRUDE C. SCHWEBELL

LE FORT (Freiin von), Gertrud
German poet and narrative writer, b. 11 Oct. 1876, Minden

Gertrud von Le F., descendant of a noble Huguenot family, spent her childhood in various garrison towns and on the family estate in Mecklenburg. She studied theology, history, philosophy in Heidelberg, Marburg, and Berlin. After the death of her professor Ernst Troeltsch, she edited his *Glaubenslehre* (1925). In 1926, she became a member of the Roman Catholic Church. The short stories and poems that she published between 1902 and 1917 were not noticed, but since 1924, her work has gained worldwide repute.

The *Hymnen an die Kirche* (1924; Hymns to the Church, 1938) are verses in free rhythm reminiscent of the Psalms. The soul locked in everlasting solitude can neither reach God nor can it escape Him, Who, speaking through the voice of the church, demands complete surrender. The holy church has embraced all religious yearnings from the days of early man; and the soul that cries out of the wilderness of the present is received into the mystical body of Christ at the end.

The *Hymnen an Deutschland* (1930) interprets the history of the German nation. By grace only, the *Reich* represented eternal order in a transient world. If Germany submits to the cross again, the downfall of the Western world is not final. The volume *Gedichte* (1949) contains poems on the role of the poet, the misery of the fatherland, the love of Christ. *Die ewige Frau* (1934; The Eternal Woman, 1954), a work in prose, views the role of woman as virgin, spouse, mother from a metaphysical position. In the self-surrender of Mary, in the answer *fiat* to the call of God, woman serves the Lord in the creation and the salvation of man.

Gertrud von Le F.'s novels and stories are dominated by three topics—church, empire, woman. In them she tells the history of Europe from the days of early Christianity (*Die Frau des Pilatus*, 1955; The Wife of Pilate, 1957) to the period after World War II (*Die Unschuldigen*, 1953). *Der Papst aus dem Ghetto* (1930; The Pope from the Ghetto, 1934) tells in legendary style of the Great Schism from which the church rose more triumphant than before. Anacletus II, the pope from a Jewish family, must learn that not justice but the cross is the heavenly award for his people.

Die Magdeburgische Hochzeit (1938), a tale full of symbolic significance, shows General Tilly (the true servant of Mary) humbly accepting the blame for the destruction of Magdeburg during the Thirty Years War and the empire, which he could not save against demonic powers and the foolishness of men striving for the splendor of the sword. *Das Schweißtuch der Veronika* (Vol. I, 1928, later subtitled *Der römische Brunnen* [The Veil of Veronica, 1932]; Vol. II, subtitled *Der Kranz der Engel*, 1946) is a fictitious autobiography. The Roman fountain symbolizes the soul longing for the sacrament of the Eucharist; the wreath of angels, a sculpture at the Heidelberg castle, stands for the sacrament of marriage. The struggle of the demonic forces of the rising ideology of National Socialism against the idealism of the declining great bourgeoisie and against the finally triumphant church is visualized against the background of the Eternal City of Rome and of romantic Heidelberg.

The novellette *Die Letzte am Schafott* (1931; The Song at the Scaffold, 1933) represents Christian existentialism pointing to the power of divine grace in the agonizing anxiety of a young girl at the time of the reign of terror in the French Revolution. In *Das Gericht des Meeres* (1943; The Judgement of the Sea, 1962) a virgin saves a child of the enemy by the strength of spiritual motherhood and dies rather than kill him. In *Die letzte Begegnung* (1959) the theme of the great novels is repeated: the Christian accepts the responsibility for the other man's sin.

FURTHER WORKS: *Das Reich des Kindes* (1933); *Die Vöglein von Theres* (1937); *Die Opferflamme* (1938); *Die Abberufung der Jungfrau von Barby* (1940); *Die Consolata* (1947); *Die Tochter Farinatas* (1950); *Plus Ultra* (1950; Eng., 1962); *Aufzeichnungen und Erinnerungen* (1951); *Die Verfemte* (1953); *Am Tor des Himmels* (1954; The Gate of Heaven, 1962); *Der Turm der Beständigkeit* (1957; The Tower of the Constant, 1962); *Die Frau und die Technik* (1959); *Das fremde Kind* (1961); *Aphorismen* (1962); *Das Schweigen* (1967)

BIBLIOGRAPHY: Eschbach, M., *Die Bedeutung G. v. L.'s in unserer Zeit* (1948); Klieneberger, H. R., "The Work of G. v. L.," *Studies*, L (1961), 436-44; Hilton, I., "G. v. L.: A Christian Writer," *GL&L*, XV (1962), 300-308; O'Boyle, I., *G. v. L.: An Introduction to the Prose Work* (1964); Hilton, I., "*Hälfte des Lebens*: G. v. L.," *GL&L*, XX (1966), 117-18; Falk, E. H., "The Leap to Faith: Two Paths to the Scaffold," *Symposium*, XXI (1967), 241-54

MARGARET KOBER MERZBACH

LEHMANN, Rosamond Nina

English novelist and short story writer, b. 13 July 1903, London, England

Member of a well-known English family (she is the sister of John Lehmann [b. 1907], poet and critic) Rosamond L. is the author of six novels, a small collection of short stories, and one play. Her first novel, *Dusty Answer* (1927), is a study of childhood and adolescence that is notable for its re-creation of the enchanted world of a sensitive and lonely girl, who gradually discovers disillusionment as she approaches the adult world. In her second novel, *A Note in Music* (1930), Rosamond L., with great artistry but emotional blandness, portrays the disillusionment of two women approaching middle age in a dull provincial town. Between these poles—youthful enchantment and adult disillusionment—her fiction swings back and forth with regularity. Her most imaginative work, *The Ballad and the Source* (1944), is a technically intricate book that explores with great power the nature of reality through the medium of consciousness of a perceptive child, who witnesses directly and indirectly a three-generation tale of tangled human emotions.

Her work is distinguished by its brilliant portraits of children and adolescents, its psychological probings of women in love, its studies of middle-class family life and conflicts between social classes, and its delicacy of style and minor experiments in technique. Her limitations are narrowness of subject matter (probably the result of a strong autobiographical element in her work), and a fatal inability to create a fully realized male character. Rosamond L. can be effectively compared to Katherine Mansfield and Elizabeth Bowen (qq.v.) both in style and thematic material, and her technique, particularly in *The Ballad and the Source,* echoes that of Henry James (q.v.).

FURTHER WORKS: *Invitation to the Waltz* (1932); *The Weather in the Streets* (1936); *No More Music* (1939); *The Gipsy's Baby and Other Stories* (1946); *The Echoing Grove* (1953); *The Swan in the Evening: Fragment of an Inner Life* (1967)

BIBLIOGRAPHY: Dangerfield, G., "R. L. and the Perilous Enchantment of Things Past," *The Bookman,* LXXVI (Feb. 1933), 172-76; Lehmann, J., *The Whispering Gallery* (1955); Gustafson, M. T., "R. L.: A Bibliography," *TCL,* IV, No. 4 (Jan. 1959), 143-47; Lestourgeon, D., *R. L.* (1965)

DIANA E. LESTOURGEON

LEIVICK, H.

(pseud. of *Leivick Halper*), Yiddish poet and dramatist, b. 1 Dec. 1888, town near Minsk; d. 23 Dec. 1962, Los Angeles

An acutely sensitive boy of very poor parents, L. was early inhibited by his father's irascibility. An idealistic rebel in adolescence, he became an activist in the *Bund,* a Jewish socialist organization. For this he was sentenced to prison and Siberian exile, where he suffered acute anguish. Both these traumatizing experiences indelibly affected his fertile and febrile imagination and characterized much of his writing. He escaped from Siberia and reached New York in 1913, where he became a paperhanger. Having already written much while in prison, he continued to compose during his free time and published his first thin volume of verse, *Intern Shloss,* in 1918.

His major poetic drama, *Der Golem* (1921; The Golem, 1928) was hailed as a masterpiece of the poetic imagination; it was produced also in Polish and Hebrew, and was the basis of an opera sung in English. L. also treated the messianic theme in *Der Moshiakh in Keyten*

(written in 1908, published in 1939) and *Die Gehule Comedie—Der Golem Kholemt* (1934).

L. wrote several prose plays in the 1920's, but they are artistically inferior to his poetic dramas. *In Keynem's Land* (1923) contains several poems about pogroms, which are weighted with the painful symbolism stemming from L.'s agonized fantasy. Even the shorter lyrics in this and subsequent volumes are poignant, dream-ridden, yet haunting in their intensity and impassioned pathos.

Stricken with tuberculosis in 1920 and again in 1932, L. spent several years in sanitariums, but his writing continued unabated. *Sodom* (1933) is a dramatic treatment of Sodom's legendary destruction. *Di Akeda* (1935) deals with the perplexing aspects of the near-sacrifice of Isaac and the subsequent relationship between Abraham and his victimized son. Isaac's plight is treated later in poems and plays. *Heloise un Abelard* (1936), a poetic drama of intense emotion and lyrical fineness, shows the love burning as a pure flame in the protagonists, both of whom are physically worn by prolonged torture. In 1937 L.'s volume of poems *Lieder fun Gan Ayden* appeared.

The Jewish experience at the hands of the Nazis opened and festered his earlier wounds. In poem after poem, collected in *In Treblinka Bin Ikh Nit Geven* (1945) and other volumes, he expressed his feelings of guilt and woe and death. He repeated the same themes in *Der Nes in Ghetto* (1944), which is concerned with the armed resistance of the Warsaw Jews, and in *Maar'am fun Rothenberg* (1945), which treats the theme of resistance in a much earlier time of woe.

In di Teg fun Eyov (1953) returns to Isaac's sacrifice and combines it with Job's "testing." Mystical, imaginative, philosophical, it probes the depths of man's suffering and achieves distinction by the emotional nature of his poetic art.

L.'s final volumes of poems—*A Blat Oifen Appelboim* (1955) and *Lieder Tzum Eiligken* (1959)—return to his earlier themes, but also contain nature lyrics of sensitive beauty.

In 1958, L. received an honorary doctorate in Jewish literature from Hebrew Union College. Later that year he suffered a paralytic stroke and remained helpless till his death four years later.

FURTHER WORKS: *Andersh* (1922); *Geklibene Werk* (1928); *Keyten* (1929); *Der Poet Is Gevoren Blind* (1936); *Wer is Wer* (1938);

Mit der Shearis Hapleto (1947); *Di Khasune in Fernwald* (1949); *Dort wu di Freiheit* (written in 1912, pub. 1952); *Oif Tzorische Katorge* (1959)

BIBLIOGRAPHY: Simon, S., *H. L.'s Golem* (1927); Gotlieb, J., *H. L.* (1939); *Lexicon fun der Neier Yiddisher Literatur*, ed. S. Niger, J. Shatsky, et al. (1956-68); Greenberg, E., *Tzentrale Problemen un Grunt-Problemen in H. L.'s Shaffen* (1961); Niger, S., *H. L., 1888-1948* (1951); Madison, C. A., *Yiddish Literature: Its Scope and Major Writers* (1968)

CHARLES A. MADISON

LENORMAND, Henri-René

French playwright, b. 3 May 1882, Paris, France; d. 16 Feb. 1951, Paris

H.-R. Lenormand was France's leading experimental dramatist from 1919 to 1927. He attempted to reestablish psychological tragedy on the French stage. After 1927, his reputation was eclipsed when Pirandello, Cocteau, and Giraudoux (qq.v.) transformed theatrical styles in Paris. Lenormand's first important drama, *Les ratés* (1918; Failures, 1923) abandoned traditional structure by acts. Fourteen tableaux trace a playwright's involuntary descent with an actress into a living inferno of decadence, betrayal, and disintegration. In *Le temps est un songe* (1919; Time Is a Dream, 1923) the protagonist commits suicide after rejecting occidental convictions that time and existence are analyzable. Catastrophic psychoanalyses (a new motif in the early 1920's) cause disillusionment and death in *Le Mangeur de rêves* (1922; The Dream Doctor, 1928), a caustic portrayal of deluded Freudianism. *L'Homme et ses fantômes* (1924; Man and his Phantoms, 1928), Lenormand's most profound play, reveals a contemporary Don Juan who is spiritually dissevered by pathological doubts and remorse.

Throughout his career, Lenormand prophetically envisioned modern ethnic calamities. Racial war, implicit in *Le Simoun* (1921), assumes terrifying proportions in *Asie* (1942) and especially in *Terre de Satan* (1942), a drama of African insurrection and massacres. *Crépuscule du théâtre* (1934; In Theatre Street, 1937) and *La Folle du ciel* (1938) show Lenormand's mastery of astringent comedy and somber fairy-tale fantasy.

Lenormand's brooding, intrinsically poetic

style, inspired in part by Baudelaire (1821-67) and Strindberg (q.v.), enhances his artistry. Although they did not revive French tragedy, his plays are significant in foreshadowing Pirandellian perspectives of ambivalent depth psychology, which infused drama in France after 1925.

FURTHER WORKS: *Les Paysages d'âme* (1905); *La Folie blanche* (1906); *Le Jardin sur la glace* (1906); *Le Réveil de l'instinct* (1908); *Au désert* (1911); *La Grande mort* (1912); *Les Possédés* (1912); *Terres chaudes* (1914); *Poussière* (1914); *Trois drames* (1918); *Le Penseur et la crétine* (1920); *La Dent rouge* (1924); *Une Vie secrète* (1924); *A l'Ombre du mal* (1925); *La lâche* (1926; The Coward, 1928); *L'Amour magicien* (1926); *L'Innocente* (1928); *Mixture* (1931); *Les Trois chambres* (1932); *Ciels de Hollande* (1934); *La Maison des Remparts* (1942); *Théâtre complet* (10 vols., 1921-42); *Les Pitoëff* (1943); *Déserts* (1944); *Les Coeurs anxieux* (1947); *Une fille est une fille* (1949; Renée, 1951); *L'Enfant des sables* (1950); *Troubles* (1951; The Rising, 1952); *Marguerite Jamois* (1950); *Les Confessions d'un auteur dramatique* (2 vols., 1949, 1953)

BIBLIOGRAPHY: Harvitt, H., "H.-R. L.," in *Representative Plays from the French Theatre of Today* (1940); Rhodes, S.A., "H.-R. L.," in *The Contemporary French Theater* (1942); Blanchart, P., *Le théâtre de H.-R. L., apocalypse d'une société* (1947); Radine, S., *Anouilh, L., Salacrou* (1951); White, K. S., "Toward a New Interpretation of L.'s Theatrical Ethos," *MD*, II, No. 4 (Feb. 1960), 334-48; White, K., "Visions of a Transfigured Humanity: Strindberg and L.," *MD*, V (1962), 323-30; Posen, R., "Aspects of the Work of ... L.," *Nottingham French Studies*, VI (1967), 30-44

KENNETH S. WHITE

LEONOV, Leonid Maksimovich

Soviet-Russian novelist, b. 31 May 1889, Moscow

L., whose father, of peasant extraction, was a self-taught poet and journalist, was educated in a Moscow gymnasium. At fifteen he published in a newspaper his first poem. He served in the Red army during the civil war period and contributed propaganda poetry to army newspapers. His first works, which were published between 1922 and 1924, revealed a great variety of influences and led critics to speak of L. as a

LEONID LEONOV

CARLO LEVI

talented *pasticheur*. The influence of E. T. A. Hoffmann (1766-1822) can be seen in "Derevyannayce koroleva"; of Hans Christian Andersen (1805-1875), in "Bubnovyi valet" and "Valina kukla"; of Oriental epic poetry, in *Tuatamur* (1924); of Aleksei Remizov (1877-1957) and Nikolai Leskov (1831-95), in "Buryga," "Petushikhinski prolom," and "Zapiski Kovyakina"; and of Dostoyevski (1821-81), in *Konetz melkovo cheloveka*. Years later, in answer to a question about the writers who had influenced him most, L. named Gogol, Dostoyevski, and Gorki (q.v.), in that order, and in 1956 he again referred to Dostoyevski as his master.

L.'s first novel, *Barsuki* (1924-25; The Badgers, 1947), was hailed by the critics as an important literary event. It depicted both pre-revolutionary merchant Moscow and Russian countryside during the revolution, against the background of a peasant rebellion. In *Vor* (1927; The Thief, 1931) the action was set in the Moscow underworld during the New Economic Policy period. Despite its obvious dependence on Dostoyevski for the characters and the problems they dealt with, it is an original and powerful work. As in *Konetz melkovo cheloveka*, L. shows here a particular interest in the underdogs of life, which stems from Dostoyevski, but there are also in *Vor* (as in *Barsuki*) some Gorkian characters and motifs. Social and ethical questions were also raised by L. in his plays written in the twenties: *Untilovsk, Provintzial'naya istoriya, Usmireniye Badadoshkina*.

His next three novels—*Sot'* (1930; Eng., 1931), *Skutarevski* (1932; Eng., 1936) and *Doroga na Okean* (1934)—were more socially oriented and dealt with problems created by the first five-year plan and the period of socialist reconstruction. In the *Doroga na Okean*, L. innovated the technique of presenting simultaneous interlocked narratives on three temporal planes—present, past, and future. All L.'s novels are characterized by an elaborate structure and a multitude of characters interrelated in a complex way, social conflicts intertwining with family and personal ones.

In the thirties, L. wrote mostly plays: *Polovchanskiye sady* (1938), *Volk* (1939), and *Metel'* (1939). In their intermingling of personal and social conflicts, the plays are reminiscent of those of Ibsen (q.v.). During World War II, L. contributed patriotic articles to newspapers, and wrote two highly dramatic plays (*Nashestviye* and *Lionushka*). He also wrote a short novel, *Vzyatiye Velikoshumska*, in which the "hero" is a Soviet tank at the front.

L.'s first postwar work, *Russkii les'* (1953; The Russian Forest, 1958), was another long and complex novel, which is set in the period between the early years of the century and the years in which Russia became engaged in war with Nazi Germany. Ostensibly its theme is the problem of deforestation of Russia, but L.'s primary interest is in human beings and life in all its many-sided and irrational complexity—life with "its acrid and coarse smell, its tart and bitter taste," as one of L.'s characters in *Vor* says. In this L. remains true to the great tradition of Russian literature.

FURTHER WORKS: *Saranchuki* (1930; published later as *Sarancha*); *Obyknovennyi chelovek* (1943); *V nashi gody* (1949)

BIBLIOGRAPHY: Struve, G., *Soviet Russian Literature: 1917-1950* (1951); Simmons, E. J., *Russian Fiction and Soviet Ideology: Introduction to Fedin, L., and Sholokhov* (1958); Rosen, N., "The Fiction of L. L.," in *DA*, XXII (1961), 1186-87; Terras, V., "L. L.'s Novel *The Russian Forest*," *SEER*, VIII (1964), 123-40, Thomson, R. B., "Bibliography of the Works of L. L.," *Oxford Slavonic Papers*, XI (1964), 137-50; Thomson, R. B., "L. L.," in *Forum for Modern Language Studies*, II (1966), 264-73

GLEB STRUVE

LESORT, Paul-André

French novelist and short story writer, b. 1915, Grandville, France

The son of a professional archivist, L. studied law, worked in a bank and wrote two unpublished novels before World War II. He was mobilized into the infantry in 1939, but he was soon captured and obliged to spend four years in a prisoner-of-war camp in Pomerania. He is presently on the editorial staff of the Du Seuil publishing house in Paris.

L.'s first novel was *Les Reins et les coeurs* (1946). The scope and power of this work prompted Marcel (q.v.) to write in 1947 that he could discern no one among the new crop of postwar novelists to whom "one can and one must give greater credit." Other critics agree that this work is one of the peaks of contemporary fiction. For L. not only displayed meticulous skill in managing the unfolding of his vast tale, but he brought new subtleties and insights to the very art of the novelist. In this first work he presented the same situations through the eyes of different characters in order to minimize the presence of the novelist creating these situations and characters. He achieved an exhaustive and convincing study in the area that French literary historians have come to describe as "the novel of the couple." In 1948, L. published a collection of seven short stories, *Les Portes de la mort,* which deal with the various aspects of war.

Having made an impressive debut with a massive novel and having sharpened his pen with the short story, L. next undertook a trilogy—*Le fil de la vie.* The first volume, *Né de la chair* (1951), relates the birth of Yves Neuville, this infant's father's experiences in World War I and his postbellum disappointments. This latter aspect of the novel recalls the theme of Arthur Miller's (q.v.) *The Death of a Salesman. Le Vent souffle où il veut* (1954), which centers around the marriage of Yves and the births of his three children, reveals L.'s preoccupation with the tenets and the spiritual concepts of the Catholic church. In 1957 L. interrupted work on this trilogy to publish *Le Fer rouge,* a long short story analyzing the position and emotions of a woman facing solitude in marriage. Nor has a later work, *G. B. K.* (1960), any connection with his trilogy; it is an incursion into the world of contemporary French writers and the problems they face in their efforts to live by their pens alone. In 1955, L. won the Grand Prix Catholique de Littérature for the sum of his creative efforts.

FURTHER WORKS: *Vie du Guillaume Périer* (1966)

BIBLIOGRAPHY: Hatzfeld, H. A., *Trends and Styles in Twentieth Century French Literature* (1957); Pitou, S., "P.-A. L., Prosateur," *Renascence,* XI (1959), 76-83; Boisdeffre, P. de, *Une Histoire vivante de la littérature d'aujourd'hui* (1959), pp. 391-95; Truc, G., *Histoire de la littérature catholique contemporaine* (1961), p. 331; Boisdeffre, P. de, *Dictionnaire de littérature contemporaine, 1900-62* (1962), pp. 423-26

SPIRE PITOU

LEVI, Carlo

Italian essayist and painter, b. 29 Nov. 1902, Turin

L.'s book *Cristo si è fermato a Eboli* (1946;

Christ Stopped at Eboli, 1948) was one of postwar Italy's most sensational successes. Exiled to Lucania from 1935 to 1936 for anti-Fascist activity, L., a practicing physician, rediscovered the world of the southern Italian peasants, a world almost untouched by government, progress, enlightenment, or prosperity, in which people vegetated in stolid passivity. In this book, in which reportage becomes literature, L. described their life "from below," not "from above," and aroused great public interest in the plight of southern Italy.

L'orologio (1950; The Watch, 1952), which is to some extent anecdotal journalism, tells the story of the Parri cabinet crisis in late autumn, 1945, which was also the crisis of the Italian resistance. He critically construes Italian history as an eternal struggle between *contadini* (peasants) and *luigini* (bureaucrats).

In recent years L. has worked chiefly as a painter.

FURTHER WORKS: *Paura della libertà* (1946); *Le parole sono pietre* (1955; Words Are Stones, 1958); *Il futuro ha un cuore antico* (1956); *La doppia notte dei tigli* (1959; Am., The Linden Tree, 1962; Eng., The Two-fold Night, 1962)

BIBLIOGRAPHY: Pacifici, S., *A Guide to Contemporary Italian Literature* (1962), pp. 114-49; Minuissi, S., "C. L.," *Terzo Programma,* No. 2 (1965), 327-334

HANS HINTERHÄUSER

LEWIS, Alun

Welsh poet and short story writer, b. 1 July 1915, Aberdare; d. 5 March 1944, Arakan, Burma

L. grew up in a Welsh mining valley and witnessed the Depression of the interwar years, though he himself enjoyed the relative security of a schoolmaster's home. The ugliness of industrialism, social and economic evils, the beauty of the Welsh countryside, and the warmth of his family life shaped his consciousness. He gained distinction as a history student at Aberystwyth and at Manchester University, but research held no fascination for him. He returned to Wales and for two years taught at Pengam Grammar School. He joined the South Wales Borderers regiment in 1940, and in 1942 was transferred to India. L. refused a staff-officer's position and insisted on going into action with his unit. He was killed in an accident while on active service.

L.'s prewar poems and stories, at their best, deal with life in Welsh mining communities. Some of the stories recall Katherine Mansfield's (q.v.) delicate lyricism. His first volume of poetry, *Raiders' Dawn* (1942), went through three printings in six months and earned L. a place in the small band of front-rank British war poets of World War II that included Keith Douglas (1920-44) and Sidney Keyes (1922-43). L.'s themes are the anonymity of the soldier, the isolation of the individual in the army, love, separation, and death. Some of the best of his poems are of a quiet strength and reveal L.'s affinity with Edward Thomas (1878-1917).

The Last Inspection (1942) is a collection of stories, which, as L. said, "are mainly concerned with the Army in England during the two years' attente since the disaster of June 1940 . . . the main motif is the rootless life of soldiers having no enemy, and always, somehow, under a shadow." Using a tone that in turn is either intimately lyrical, gently humorous, or bitterly satirical, L. analyzes the typical behavior patterns that army life brings out in his characters, and reveals their private triumphs, failures, and sufferings in times of war and separation. Here, as in his later stories, L.'s basic concern was with essentially simple people who somehow preserve their integrity and set personal loyalties against and above the impersonal forces around them.

The greatest part of *Ha! Ha! Among the Trumpets* (1945), L.'s second volume of poetry, was written after he had left England. In these "poems in transit" L. comes to terms with the new experiences of embarkation, travel, and India. In a number of songlike poems L.'s fine lyrical voice is heard as distinctly as in his first volume. In his more reflective verse, however, the youthful exuberance of the imagery displayed in *Raiders' Dawn* now gave way to simpler diction, without any loss of personal warmth; and often he let the things he observed speak for themselves. In his poems about Indian beggars, peasants, and the "landless soldier lost in war," the social consciousness and sympathy that permeate L.'s work from the beginning deepen into a universal compassion.

In India, L. wrote some of his finest short stories, and these were published posthumously with his letters in *In the Green Tree* (1948). The volume includes the haunting "Orange Grove," and "Ward 0 3(b)" which John Lehmann (b. 1907) considers "one of the most brilliant stories written by anyone during the war."

What L. wrote in India—and his letters are as revealing as his poems and stories—is the record of an "enlargement of the imagination," which he experienced in the vast spaces of India as he faced the sterility of her deserts, the strange beauty of her jungles, and the elemental life of the villagers. Through the accurately described Indian scene we discern an inner landscape that L. was exploring in his search for a "simplicity of being."

L. had no illusions about the complexity of his situation. In one of his letters he wrote: "And although I'm more and more engrossed with the single poetic theme of Life and Death, for there doesn't seem to be any question more directly relevant than this one of what survives of all the beloved, I find myself quite unable to express at once the passion of Love, the coldness of Death (Death is cold), and the fire that beats against resignation, acceptance. Acceptance seems so spiritless, protest so vain. In between the two I live."

FURTHER WORKS: *A. L.: Selected Poetry and Prose* (ed. I. Hamilton; 1966); "A. L. to Robert Graves: Three Letters," in *The Anglo-Welsh Review*, XVI, 37 (Spring 1967)

BIBLIOGRAPHY: Graves, R., foreword to *Ha! Ha! Among the Trumpets* (1945); Rowse, A. L., and Jones, G., in *In the Green Tree* (1948); Houston, R., "The Broken Arch, a Study of the Poetry of A. L.," in *The Adelphi*, 28 (Nov. 1951); Lehmann, J., "A Human Standpoint," in *The Open Night* (1952); Aykroyd, F., "Some Letters of A. L.," in *Modern Reading* (Summer 1952); Thomas, D., "Welsh Poets," in *Quite Early One Morning* (1954); Jarka, H., *A. L.—His Short Stories and Poems* (dissertation, Vienna, 1954); Currey, R. N., *Poets of the 1939-45 War* (1960); Williams, J. S., "The Poetry of A. L.," in *The Anglo-Welsh Review*, XIII, 32 (Winter 1963); Williams, J. S., "The Short Stories of A. L.," in *The Anglo-Welsh Review*, XIV, 34 (Winter 1964); Hamilton, I., "The Forties, I," in *London Magazine* (April 1964); Hamilton, I., ed., introduction to *A. L.: Selected Poetry and Prose* (1966); additional bibliography in *The Anglo-Welsh Review*, XVI, 37 (Spring 1967)

HORST JARKA

LEWIS, Clive Staples

(pseud. of *Clive Hamilton*), English novelist and essayist, b. 29 Nov. 1898, Belfast; d. 22 Nov. 1963, Oxford

L. was educated at an English public school and served in the ranks in World War I. Later he studied at Oxford and became a Fellow of Magdalen College. In 1954 he was appointed to the newly established chair of medieval and Renaissance literature at Cambridge.

L. advocates a Christian humanism very close to Roman Catholicism. His autobiographical *Surprised by Joy* (1955) describes his personal and spiritual development. He had become an unbeliever while still a schoolboy but returned to the Anglo-Catholic church after World War I; this event was to be a decisive factor in his writing. The turning point of his life was his encounter with George Macdonald's (1824-1905) *Phantastes*; L.'s *The Great Divorce* commemorates Macdonald as his master and spiritual leader. G. K. Chesterton's (q.v.) influence was also significant. Like Dorothy Sayers (q.v.), to whom he was close in spirit, L. as a religious writer adopted Chesterton's blend of common sense, witty brilliance, and Christian orthodoxy. His attitude also links him closely with the novelist and essayist Charles Williams (1886-1945).

L. has two distinct personalities: the learned scholar of English literature and the popular religious writer. The link between them is revealed most clearly in his inaugural lecture *De descriptione temporum* (1955). As a Christian apologist, L. also champions traditional ways of thought and life in opposition to worldly modernism. His critical principles, formulated in opposition to the prejudices of the biographical, psychological school of literary interpretation—the "personal heresy" —are inseparable from his philosophical and theological beliefs.

Thus in *English Literature in the 16th Century Excluding Drama* (1954) L. attacks the aftereffects of "modernist propaganda" used by the humanists to put across the notion of the Renaissance as a new dawn in the history of man. Similarly, in *A Preface to Paradise Lost* (1942), he refutes the postromantic glorification of Milton's Satan, while awarding the epic its place in literary tradition by showing it to be firmly rooted in "solemn celebration."

L. achieved national—and, before long, international—fame through his radio talks during World War II, published in 1942 under the title *The Case for Christianity*. Listeners and readers were spellbound by his unusual combination of straightforward, direct language, a rationality nourished by the study of Aristotle, and the vivid, imaginative presentation by which he brought the transcendental to life. His most successful religious work is *The Screwtape Letters* (1942), the story of a temptation and conversion told from the viewpoint of two satanic functionaries. Here it falls to the devil to reduce himself *ad absurdum* by means of impeccable theology.

L.'s trilogy—*Out of the Silent Planet* (1938); *Perelandra* (1943), and *That Hideous Strength* (1945)—occupies a special place in his work. Its action leads first to Mars, then to Venus, and finally back to earth and England. Using the medium of science fiction—of the intergalactic novel—L. presents the drama of salvation in the form of a Christianized anti-Wellsian story.

After 1950 L. wrote children's books (*The Lion, the Witch and the Wardrobe*, 1950; *Prince Caspian*, 1951; *The Voyage of the Dawn Treaders*, 1952; *The Silver Chair*, 1953; *The Horse and his Boy*, 1954; *The Magician's Nephew*, 1955). These reflect his Christian and philosophic outlook in a way that a child can understand.

FURTHER WORKS: *Spirits in Bondage: A Cycle of Lyrics* (1919); *Dymer* (1926); *The Pilgrim's Regress* (1933); *The Allegory of Love* (1936); *Rehabilitations* (1939); *The Personal Heresy* (with E. M. W. Tillyard; 1939); *The Problem of Pain* (1940); *Broadcast Talks* (1942; Am., *The Case for Christianity*); *Christian Behaviour* (1943); *The Abolition of Man* (1943); *Beyond Personality: The Christian Idea of God* (1944); *Miracles, a Preliminary Study* (1947); *Vivisection* (1948); *Transposition, and Other Addresses* (1949; Am., *The Weight of Glory*); *Till We Have Faces, a Myth Retold* (1956); *Reflections on the Psalms* (1958); *The Four Loves* (1960); *Miracles* (1960); *Studies in Words* (1960); *An Experiment in Criticism* (1961); *Screwtape Proposes a Toast* (1961); *They Asked for a Paper* (1962); *The Discarded Image, an Introduction to Medieval and Renaissance Literature* (1964); *Poems* (ed. Walter Hooper; 1964); *Letters of C. S. Lewis* (ed., with a memoir, W. H. Lewis; 1966); *Studies in Medieval and Renaissance Literature* (1966); *Of Other Worlds* (ed. Walter Hooper; 1966)

BIBLIOGRAPHY: Walsh, C., *C. S. L.: Apostle to the Skeptics* (1949); Kuhn, H., "C. S. L." in

Lob der Schöpfung und Ärgernis der Zeit (1959); Moorman, C., *Arthurian Triptych* (1960); Sale, R., "England's Parnassus: C. S. L., Charles Williams, and J. R. R. Tolkien," *HR,* XVII (1964), 203-25; Wain, J., "C. S. L.," *Encounter,* XXII (1964), v, 51-3, 56; Kilby, C., *The Christian World of C. S. L.* (1964); Gibb, J., ed., *Light on C. S. L.* (1965); Gardner, H., *C. S. L., 1898-1963* (1967)

HELMUT KUHN

LEWIS, (Harry) Sinclair

American novelist, b. 7 Feb. 1885, Sauk Centre, Minn.; d. 10 Jan. 1951, Rome, Italy

The son of a country doctor, L. studied at Yale, but subsequently led for years an unstable, roving life. At one point he worked for a time at the Helicon Home Colony, a socialist experiment of Upton Sinclair's. During these years he contributed to newspapers and periodicals until he finally took up writing as a fulltime profession. Lewis's career as a novelist covered almost forty years, from the publication in 1912 of *Hike and the Aeroplane,* a boy's adventure tale (written under the pseudonym of Tom Graham) to *World So Wide,* which appeared posthumously in 1951.

Despite flashes of the satire and realism characteristic of L.'s later and best work, his early novels largely conformed in tone and style to the standards of the day's popular fiction. Of these early books *The Job* (1917), a generally realistic account of the life of a working girl, is probably the best, although *Our Mr. Wrenn* (1914) and *The Trail of the Hawk* (1917) are of special interest to the student of L.'s career because of their autobiographical content.

With *Main Street* (1920), a bitingly satirical portrait of the American small town, Lewis gained international recognition. *Babbitt* (1922), *Arrowsmith* (1925), *Elmer Gantry* (1927), and *Dodsworth* (1929) all enjoyed huge success and strengthened L.'s position as perhaps the most widely read and controversial American writer of the decade. The extent of L.'s fame may be gauged by the fact that he became, in 1930, the first American writer to be awarded the Nobel Prize in Literature.

Unfortunately, the Nobel Prize marked the apogee of L.'s prestige and power. During the 1930's and 1940's his reputation suffered drastic decline, although in a few books, notably *It Can't Happen Here* (1935; play, 1938) and *Kingsblood Royal* (1947), he was able to cap-

ture large audiences and briefly excite interest and discussion. On the whole, however, his later work is of inferior quality, flawed by mawkish sentimentality, obvious repetition of earlier themes and techniques, and ambiguous and self-contradictory attitudes.

Almost all of L.'s novels are marked by an ambivalence toward American life and the characters that Lewis chose as representative of it, an ambivalence between negation and affirmation, realism and romance, satire and reportage. In his best work this ambivalence is balanced and controlled, producing artistically desirable tension and shading. Thus Babbitt is a more effective and remarkable character creation because L. loves him at the same time that he excoriates him, and Gopher Prairie is rendered memorable as much because of L.'s unmistakable involvement with it as because of his savage renunciation of its stultifying mode of existence. Likewise, the assault upon corrupt doctors and scientists in *Arrowsmith* is counterposed by a stirringly idealistic affirmation of the value of scientific research and man's capacity for unselfish devotion to it. A remark that L. is said to have made repeatedly during the last year of his life—"I love America . . . but I don't like it"—expresses this ambivalence and suggests its source.

L.'s enormous fame did not suffice to convince him that he was truly respected and taken seriously by his countrymen. This sense of alienation undoubtedly was rooted in his boyhood in Sauk Centre, where he felt rejected because of his literary interests, his inability to participate in the usual boyish pursuits, and his decision not to follow in the footsteps of his grandfather, uncle, father, and older brother in becoming a doctor. This personal insecurity was later intensified by a skin ailment, which made him self-conscious about his appearance, and his inner turmoil manifested itself in hypersensitivity, restlessness, and drinking. Both his marriages (the second was to Dorothy Thompson, the "first lady of journalism" and writer) ended in divorce.

But L.'s limitations were not without compensation. Neither his excesses nor his eccentricities prevented him from fully utilizing what was essentially not a major talent. Taken together, his books offer a panorama of modern American life that has not been surpassed in range and scope. His best novels are distinguished by verve, humor, an exaggerated yet authentic rendition of American idiom, and by flat yet vivid characters who at times attain

267

the stature of mythological creations. Just as we employ Swift's term "Yahoo" to describe certain kinds of people, so L.'s "Babbitt" has also been taken into the language. It is some measure of L.'s achievement.

FURTHER WORKS: *The Innocents* (1917); *Free Air* (1919); *Mantrap* (1926); *The Man Who Knew Coolidge* (1928); *Ann Vickers* (1933); *Work of Art* (1934); *Jayhawker* (1935); *Selected Short Stories* (1935); *The Prodigal Parents* (1938); *Bethel Merriday* (1940); *Gideon Planish* (1943); *Cass Timberlane* (1945); *The God-Seeker* (1949); *From Main Street to Stockholm: Letters of S. L. 1919-1930,* ed. by Harrison Smith (1952); *The Man From Main Street,* ed. by H. E. Maule and M. H. Cane (1953).

BIBLIOGRAPHY: Lewis, G. H., *With Love from Gracie* (1955); Schorer, M., *S. L.: An American Life* (1961); Grebstein, S. N., *S. L.* (1962); Schorer, M., *S. L.* (1962)

SHELDON NORMAN GREBSTEIN

LILIENCRON, Friedrich (Axel Adolf)

(pseud.: *Detlev von L.*), German poet and narrative writer, b. 3 June 1844, Kiel; d. 22 July 1909, Alt-Rahlstedt

After a withdrawn, dreamy childhood L. became a Prussian officer. Plunged into debt as the result of an unhappy love affair, he resigned his commission and came to America, where he earned his living for a year and a half as a language teacher, piano player, stable master, and house painter. Returning home, disillusioned, he taught singing in Hamburg and then became a parish commissioner in Kellingshusen. After the great success of his first volume of poetry he settled in Munich, later in Altona and Alt-Rahlstedt, and devoted himself to writing.

L.'s early novellas show the influence of Theodor Storm (1817-88) and of Turgenev (1818-83), his early poetry that of August von Platen (1796-1835), Nikolaus Lenau (1802-1850), Eduard Mörike (1804-1875), and Emanuel Geibel (1815-84). He was a close friend of Dehmel (q.v.). By the time he published *Adjutantenritte* in 1883, he had already completed the turn to naturalism (q.v.) that made him a pioneer in a new kind of down-to-earth poetry. His plays and novels, on the other hand, are of little significance today; some of his poetry and a few novellas are the only works that will have a permanent place in German literature. His *Gedichte* (1889) as well as *Der Heidegänger*

(1890) and *Neue Gedichte* (1893), later republished in *Nebel und Sonne* (1900), *Bunte Beute* (1903), and *Balladenchronik* (1906), present historical and imaginative subjects and above all experiences from every walk of life in a free and easy key and in snapshot images, though often in rigorous verse forms. This poetry typifies literary expressionism (q.v.). Yet far from being merely a hunter, a soldier, and an erotic poet, L. often attained symbolic profundity.

He rejected social democracy as strongly as he rejected feudal aristocratic theories. For a time he professed anarchism, and grim poverty drove him into a deep pessimism, which he later overcame. This is reflected in *Poggfred* (1896), a "motley epic in twelve cantos" (expanded in 1908 to twenty-nine), which describes experiences in the imaginary castle of Froschfrieden (Frogs' Haven). The autobiographical novel *Leben und Lüge* (1908) was his final stocktaking. Kai, who stands for L. himself, disappearing mysteriously, is dispersed into the elements.

FURTHER WORKS: *Knut, der Herr* (1885); *Die Rantzow und die Pogwisch* (1886); *Der Trifels und Palermo* (1886); *Eine Sommerschlacht* (1886); *Arbeit adelt* (1887); *Breide Hummelsbüttel* (1887); *Die Merowinger* (1888); *Unter flatternden Fahnen* (1888); *Krieg und Frieden* (1891); *Kriegsnovellen* (1895); *Mit dem linken Ellbogen* (1899); *Aus Marsch und Geest* (1900); *Könige und Bauern* (1900); *Roggen und Weizen* (1900); *Die Abenteuer des Majors Glöckchen* (1904); *Gute Nacht* (1909); *Letzte Ernte* (1909); *Ausgewählte Briefe* (ed. R. Dehmel; 1910); *Briefe an H. Friedrichs* (1910); *Gesammelte Werke* (ed. R. Dehmel; 1911 ff.); *Briefe* (ed. H. Spiero; 1927); *Briefe an H. von Bodenhausen* (1925); *Ausgewählte Werke* (1930)

BIBLIOGRAPHY: Böckel, F., *L. im Urteil zeitgenössischer Dichter* (1904); Bierbaum, O. J., *L.* (2nd ed., 1910); Spiero, H., *L.* (1913); Maync, H., *D. v. L.* (1920); Elema, J., *Stil und poetischer Charakter bei L.* (1937); Leip, H., *L.* (1938); Stebner, G., "Whitman-L.-W. H. Auden," in *Die neueren Sprachen* (1960), pp. 105-118; Grimm, R., "L., Dehmel, George: Seven Unpublished Letters to Karl Klammer," in *GL&L*, XIV (1961), 170-74; Laage, K., "Drei Briefe L.'s an Storm," in *Schriften der Theodor Storm Gesellschaft*, XV (1966), 33-39; Boetius, H., "L. heute," in *NDH*, CXI (1967), 125-34

JOSEF STRELKA

LINDE, Otto zur

German poet and writer, b. April 1873, Essen; d. 16 Feb. 1938, Berlin

L. studied philosophy and German language and literature, spent several years in London as a writer, and in 1904 founded the journal *Charon*. Rudolf Paulsen (b. 1883) and Karl Röttger (1877-1942) were among those associated with this magazine, which was edited by L. with Rudolf Pannwitz (b. 1881). Opposing George (q.v.), they relegated form to second place and demanded self-expression. L. called for "phonetic" rhythm appropriate to the statement.

His poetry was published between 1910 and 1925, almost sub rosa, by his own Charon press. In 1923 the Piper Verlag reissued his major work, the lyrical, thoughtful *Die Kugel* (1909), in two expanded volumes. Portions only of his late work *Die Hölle* appeared between 1920 and 1921, and he published nothing after 1925.

In L.'s poetic work an unusually lyrical, folk-song-like singing and a hearkening to the most hushed word, to the silenced sound of things, are crossed with an abstract, logical, metaphysical "thought language," which achieved its most concentrated expression in the masterwork *Die Kugel*, a "philosophy in verse." L.'s intellectual and poetic concern was to capture and depict the potential omniscience of man—of "everyman"—and to arrive at a new ethic.

FURTHER WORKS: *Gedichte, Märchen, Skizzen* (1901); *Fantoccini* (1902); *Gesammelte Werke, Thule, Traumland* (1910); *Album und Lieder der Liebe und Ehe* (1910); *Stadt und Landschaft* (1911); *Wege, Menschen und Ziele* (1913); *Charontischer Mythus* (1913); *Das Buch "Abendrot"* (1920); *Lieder des Leids* (1924); *Denken, Zeit und Zukunft* (1924); *Charon* (1952)

BIBLIOGRAPHY: Verwey, A., "Gedanken über O. z. L.," in *O. z. L., 60 Jahre* (1933); Pannwitz, R., *O. z. L.* (1933); Paulsen, R., *Blätter und Briefe von O. z. L.'s Grab* (1938); Kugel, W., *O. z. L.* (1959)

BERNHARD RANG

LINDSAY, (Nicholas) Vachel

American poet, b. 10 Nov. 1879, Springfield, Ill.; d. there 5 Dec. 1931

Lindsay considered it significant that at birth his face had been covered by a "prophet's veil," (a caul) and indeed he was destined to become a preaching poet. Born into a family of evangelical disciples, he grew up in a city permeated with memories of Lincoln. His primary interests at Hiram College (1897-1900) were oratory and art; but his odd study habits at the Art Institute of Chicago (1900-1903) and as an intermittent apprentice of Robert Henri in New York (1904-1908) lengthened the period of casting about for a career. His mother, opposed to his writing poetry, created a tension that delayed his marrying until 1925, and much of his work shows the effect of an unhealthy loneliness. On walking tours through America he sought to convince listeners of the value of beauty.

His first important poem, "General William Booth Enters into Heaven," was published in *Poetry* (1913), and launched the new poetry movement more than two decades after Whitman's death. Like many of his later poems, it was elaborately scored for musical instruments, and was set (in Lindsay's words) "to the tune that is not a tune, but a speech, a refrain used most frequently in the meetings of the [Salvation] Army on any public square to this day." He became a platform poet, disclaiming his works at universities and in small towns.

L. has written several extraordinary poems: "The Eagle That Is Forgotten," about the martyred Altgeld of Illinois; "The Congo," a memorial to a Disciple missionary in Africa, which Lindsay subtitled "A Study of the Negro Race"; "Bryan, Bryan, Bryan, Bryan," about the election campaign of 1896 as seen by an adolescent; and the sentimentally popular "Abraham Lincoln Walks at Midnight." To explain his private symbolism, he drew a map of the universe. During the 1920's he became increasingly interested in Chinese hieroglyphics, motion pictures, and Jeffersonian democracy.

The writings of Mencken and Lewis, which set the tone for the last decade of Lindsay's life, were partly responsible for the loss of reader interest in his exuberant, open poetry. Yet Lindsay himself was responsible for many of his problems. He could not evaluate his own work justly, with judgment, and wrote far too much; he was never clear in his own mind just what poetry should do, or what his message was; he remained defiantly ignorant of the technical devices whereby poetry can release meaning with power. He was, nevertheless, far more than a poet of the Jazz Age (a tag that he repudiated). His bardic powers, as well as his vision of the future (*The Golden Book of*

Springfield, 1920), confirm Yeats's judgement that this was a poet.

FURTHER WORKS: *The Tramp's Excuse and Other Poems* (1909); *Rhymes to be Traded for Bread* (1912); *General William Booth Enters into Heaven and Other Poems* (1913); *Adventures While Preaching the Gospel of Beauty* (1914); *The Congo and Other Poems* (1914); *The Art of the Moving Picture* (1915); *A Handy Guide for Beggars* (1916); *The Chinese Nightingale and Other Poems* (1917); *The Golden Whales of California, and Other Rhymes in the American Language* (1920); *The Golden Book of Springfield* (1920); *Going-to-the Sun* (1923); *Going-to-the-Stars* (1926); *The Candle in the Cabin: A Weaving Together of Script and Singing* (1926); *The Litany of Washington Street* (1929); *Every Soul Is a Circus* (1929); *Letters of N. V. L. to A. Joseph Armstrong* (1940)

BIBLIOGRAPHY: Masters, E. L., *V. L.: A Poet in America* (1935); Harris, M. *City of Discontent* (a fictionalized biography, 1952); Ruggles, E., *The West-Going Heart* (1959)

HAROLD OREL

LINGUISTICS AND LITERATURE

The union of linguistic and literary study has traditionally been accomplished through the discipline of *philology,* which is concerned with the establishment of texts and the identification of appropriate lexical and grammatical meanings of words in the texts. As such, philology remains today the most direct means of applying a knowledge of linguistic data to the elucidation of literature. In the twentieth century, however, the term *linguistics* has come to denote a new school of language analysis, one which is often felt to be indifferent or even hostile to the alliance of literary and linguistic study. Originating more or less independently in the linguistic circles of Prague, Geneva, Copenhagen, and in the American school of Bloomfield, *structural linguistics* is, in the United States especially, oriented more toward social-scientific, anthropological, or mathematical disciplines than toward the traditional sister-field, literature, an orientation that has often led linguists away from the study of meaning and that has also led to the esteeming of spoken over written language as the proper object of linguistic analysis. (This is less true,

however, of the Prague school, which states that "its true objective is the analysis of speech utterances of all kinds, both spoken and written" [*Philologica Pragensia,* I, 33] and which consequently has remained closer to literary problems; see *A Prague School Reader on Esthetics.*) On the other hand, the antagonism of some 20th c. schools of literary criticism toward the traditional alliance of linguistics and criticism under philology has aggravated the divorce. Yet, simultaneously with the divergence, there has been growing concern over it, and in recent decades numerous efforts have been made to bring the methods of the new science to the service of literary study. Although the extent of linguistics' usefulness remains in dispute, its relevance to at least some sectors of literary study has been successfully demonstrated, especially in the areas of metrics, textual explication, and stylistics.

Modern structural linguistics began with the detailed and systematic analysis of the sound system of language, and so it is not surprising that some of the earliest contacts between the linguist and the literary scholar resulted from their mutual interest in language as sound. The pioneer Russian structuralist Roman Jakobson was the first to point out the relevance of phonemics (the study of significant sound-differences) to metrical analysis, and, in fact, he explains that it was his study of the poetry of Velimir Xlebnikov, with its paronomastic play with minimal pairs, that first directed him, early in the 1920's, toward his formulation of the basic linguistic concept of the phoneme (Jakobson, *Selected Writings* [The Hague, 1962], I, 632-633). For the most part, however, linguistic and metric studies proceeded independently at first, and when American linguists in the fifties began turning to the sounds and rhythms of English verse, it was with the intention of bringing a full-blown linguistic system of phonological analysis to bear on the problem of English metrics.

Readers of conventional English verse have long been aware that the pattern of stressed and unstressed syllables which one normally uses in a prosodic description of a line does not really describe the rhythm of the line, not even when account is taken of such conventional variations as inversion or truncation. Rather these lifts and dips suggest a rough norm which the actual words of the verse approximate in various ways. The tension set up between the abstract norm and the phonological actualization of the norm in any given line is the special pleasure of English verse, and the various modes of exploiting that tension mark the difference between the rhythm of one iambic pentameter line and that of another or, cumulatively, between the iambic pentameters of, say, Shakespeare and those of Milton. So much is clear and always has been; but prosodists long found difficulty in specifying what precisely the phonological realities (as opposed to the abstract pattern) of the line were, and in stating explicitly the precise relationship between the lifts and dips of the norm and the infinitely variable speech-sounds by which the norm is variously, yet unmistakably, realized. A major difficulty was that little was known about the phonological structure of English (and, as Jakobson had shown, metrics operates on the phonemic, not merely the acoustic level of languages). But with the appearance in 1951 of G. L. Trager's and H. L. Smith's *An Outline of English Structure,* linguists were provided with a precise analysis of the suprasegmental features of English, one which identified four distinct levels of stress, four pitch levels, and four types of juncture or pause. Since this is presumably the prosodic system out of which English-speaking poets write, Harold Whitehall in 1951 suggested that the Trager-Smith analysis should be made the basis of a new system of analyzing English meter, one far more subtle than the old binary system of stressed and unstressed syllables and one which would reflect more accurately the complex relationship between the sound system of English and the poets' meters. In the first of several papers attempting to implement this suggestion, Seymour Chatman provided a detailed analysis of the meter of Robert Frost's (q.v.) "Mowing." Typical of the American linguist in his orientation toward the spoken language, Chatman's first step was to reduce the poem to sounds, making his analysis from eight recordings of oral recitations of the poem. He provided Trager-Smith notations for each reading and showed how they could be studied in conjunction with conventional scansions of the lines as a means of assessing the rhythmic tension between ideal metrical pattern and constantly deviating realizations of that pattern in performance. Subsequently, the Trager-Smith analysis has been extended into a detailed metric system by E. L. Epstein and Terence Hawkes, who categorize the conventional types of metrical feet according to the various realizations they can find in the English four-stress, four-pitch, four-juncture sound system, and even explore the relevance of such sub-phonemic features as the English speaker's tendency to give the second of two phonemically equal primary stresses more weight than the first. In addition to their tabulation of several thousand types of metrical feet, Epstein and Hawkes describe longer units such as line and strophe in structural linguistic terms.

Some poets and critics have felt that the Trager-Smith phonology is not entirely relevant to metrics or that the system of analysis is so elaborate that it confuses more than it clarifies the scansion of English verse. John Crowe Ransom (q.v.) argues that linguists fail to consider the possibility of there being an essential difference between the conventional prosodic patterns of everyday speech, such as the Trager-Smith system was designed to measure, and the rhythm of metered language. Wimsatt and Beardsley feel that the linguist, in his zeal to come to grips with the intonations of actual speech, loses sight of the normative fact of the poem's meter, which is adequately described by the conventional binary system. Some have questioned whether the linguists are dealing with metrics at all, feeling that they are in fact merely recording and analyzing individual recitations of poems, much as a linguist analyzes any corpus. In an effort to meet some of these objections, a few linguists have attempted a more precise correlation of the four Trager-Smith speech stresses with the two degrees of metrical stress, while others have clarified the distinction between performance and scansion, intonation and meter. In the most recent and comprehensive linguistic prosody, *A Theory of Meter,* Seymour Chatman abandons the Trager-Smith analysis and works from the suprasegmental system devised by Dwight Bolinger. Pointing out that metrical stress is accomplished variously and redundantly through pitch, loudness, vowel quality, length, and prosodic environment rather than through any single feature, Chatman establishes a system for deriving from numerous scansions (metrical records of individual recitations) of a poem a unified metrical analysis which is not rigid and prescriptive, but "a matrix of all meaningful scansions" (p. 104).

Chatman's study will probably remain for some time the most thorough structural linguistic exploration of the phonological properties of metrical stress and of the interplay between abstract meter and English speech rhythms. Subsequent metrical studies appear to be pushing into different areas. In Soviet Russia a group of linguists collaborating with the mathematician A. N. Kolmogorov in the Department of the Theory of Probability (Moscow State University) are now reporting important methodological innovations in metrical analysis, while Polish and West European linguists are similarly occupied in applying mathematics, communication theory, and cybernetics in their prosodic investigations.

Though not itself a metrical consideration, a noteworthy by-product of the structural linguists' metrical studies has been the frequent demonstration of the importance of intonation in guiding the interpretation of a poem. Numerous structural and lexical ambiguities which are latent in a text so long as it remains unarticulated on the printed page demand resolution when the text is read aloud or phonemicized. Thus Chatman, in his analysis of Frost's "Mowing," shows how two quite different dramatic situations are available in the poem depending upon which of two possible intonation patterns is elected for Frost's question "What was it it whispered?" in line 3. (A falling terminal contour would suggest that the poem is a soliloquy; a rising juncture would indicate a dramatic monologue.) While no one would favor substituting for the written text of any poem a phonemic record of a single recitation in which all structural ambiguities are skillfully resolved, it is useful to emphasize, both for literary-critical and for pedagogical purposes, that the reader's automatic, unconscious imposition of one or another intonational pattern on a printed line of verse selects one structural meaning and excludes others.

It is now widely conceded that linguistic methods of analyzing sound systems of languages are of at least some utility in metrical analysis. It has proved more difficult, however, to bring the methodology of linguistics to bear on literature at higher levels of analysis, although efforts to do so have not been wanting. The most direct means of effecting such an application would be to formulate step by step a set of analytical procedures for literary explication after the model of linguistic analysis, much in the way that Claude Lévi-Strauss has suggested that anthropologists should pattern their analyses of kinship problems after the linguists' system of phonemic analysis (See "Structural Analysis in Linguistics and in Anthropology," in *Structural Anthropology* [New York, 1963], pp. 31-54.) Something like this has been attempted for literary exegesis by, among others, A. A. Hill, who, in "An Analysis

of *The Windhover*: An Experiment in Structural Method," proceeds systematically from phonemic and morphemic considerations into ever larger components of the poem and ultimately into the realm of meaning. He correlates the stages of his analysis with the levels of linguistic analysis broadly defined by G. L. Trager (prelinguistic, microlinguistic, metalinguistic), and shows how certain procedures from the microlinguistic level can guide the literary critic even in metalinguistic analysis. In practice, Hill's method prescribes close attention to various types of syntactic grouping and parallelism and then urges that the structural units thus defined be allowed to guide the reader in evaluating figurative language and formulating the poem's meaning. Other linguists essaying a structural linguistic approach to literary texts are: M. A. K. Halliday, who has illustrated with a study of Yeats's (q.v.) "Leda and the Swan" how the (Edinburgh) categories of linguistic description can be re-aligned for the purposes of analyzing literary texts; Nicolas Ruwet, whose study "Sur un vers de Charles Baudelaire" attempts to demonstrate how the linguistic procedures of Louis Hjelmslev can facilitate and systematize the correlation of sound to sense in poetry; and Sumner Ives, W. N. Francis, and others who have followed more or less the pattern of Hill's approach.

These efforts at linguistically oriented exegesis have not passed unchallenged. Many non-linguists regard linguistic analyses as tour-de-force applications of a complex, scientific methodology which yield trivial results. Yet, as Hill has repeatedly stated, the primary intention of these experiments is not to reveal new meanings and insights, but rather to introduce into literary analysis the methodological rigor of linguistics and, in particular, to select and delimit "meanings" of literary works rather than multiply and expand them. (See especially his "Principles Governing Semantic Parallels.") Whatever their shortcomings, investigations of this type clearly constitute the most direct application thus far of structural linguistic methodology to the analysis and elucidation of specific literary texts.

The question of literary style has occupied several modern linguists. Most regard style as basically a pattern of linguistic choices exercised within the limitations of the author's various self-imposed restraints. The levels of restriction would include the structural constraints of the language he elects to write in, the restrictive dimensions of his chosen literary form, and, finally, within his self-imposed tonal and contextual limitations, the choices he continually makes among the various lexical, grammatical, and other options which present themselves. By describing scientifically the patterns, frequency, and distribution of the linguistic structures resulting from these choices, the style analyst can make systematic comparisons either among texts (as when the purpose is to settle questions of disputed authorship) or between a specified corpus and some norm (as when the purpose is to define the individual quality of an author's style). In this general view style often becomes a matter primarily of frequencies and probabilities, and hence stylistic study can be facilitated through the use of digital calculators, but only if these are provided with delicate and sophisticated programs. Some computer-studies of style have fallen short precisely because the programs have not been formulated with sufficient attention to the linguistic-stylistic problems of context, types of options, and the like.

A stylistic question of far-reaching significance is "How can literary language be distinguished, in general terms, from non-literary language?" The most provocative treatment of this problem is that of the East European theorists and particularly of the Prague school of structuralists, who see literary language as the result not so much of "choice" as of a deliberate violation of the norms of "standard" speech. The standard language, according to Jan Mukařovský, Bohuslav Hravánek, and others, serves purely communicative functions in a more or less inconspicuous manner, while literary discourse is marked by frequent abnormal or deviant devices which attract attention to the language of discourse itself. This process of de-automatizing speech through calculated deviation is described as "actualization" or "foregrounding," and according to Mukařovský it is the fundamental principle in differentiating literary from standard, or functional, language. The Prague school concept of literary language as "the message oriented toward itself" has gained wide attention already and will probably exert a growing influence in literary as well as linguistic circles.

The linguistic viewpoints represented thus far have all been "structuralist" in the broad sense of that term. Since the mid-1950's, however, the rival school of generative-transformational grammarians has come into prominence, and their approach is already being adopted in various areas of literary stylistic study. Unlike the structuralists, who are usually concerned with a functional, or a stratified, taxonomic analysis of a *corpus,* the new school focuses on the language-producing *mechanism* and seeks to formulate for each language the set of rules by which all and only the grammatical sentences of that language can be generated. Since these rules always proceed from the sentence unit, they govern the formation of larger linguistic structures (contrasting thereby with the more atomistic predictive statements of most structuralists) and hence can be used in quantifying stylistic differences among authors at a relatively high level of analysis. (See the discussion of transformational stylistics below.) But the new grammar also throws into sharp relief the contrast between individual literary styles and the "norm" as it is defined by the general rules. For example, an efficient generative grammar of English will automatically reject such non-sentences as "Anyone resented a how law" and "He is with up so running few songs down." Yet, just such sentences as these do occur in the poetic corpus of the language; see E. E. Cummings' (q.v.) "anyone lived in a pretty how town/with up so floating many bells down." Thus one of the signal properties of literary language would seem to be (as the "foregrounding" concept suggests) that it accords poetic status to certain, though not all, deviations from the standard or normal language structure. A theoretic rationale accommodating this phenomenon has been provided by the East German linguist Manfred Bierwisch, who suggests that poetic language presupposes a selection mechanism which ranks the output of a general grammar on a scale of poeticity and which also suspends, where necessary, conventional interdictions of the general grammar, thus permitting desirable deviations and assigning them a rank on the scale of poeticity. Bierwisch sees his linguistic model for poetic creation as potentially useful not only in stylistic studies, but also in understanding better the evolution of certain modern poetic forms, which he relates to the phenomenon of the automatizing of poetic deviants.

Another aspect of generative-transformation grammar which has proven useful in literary analysis is the concept of average sophisticated sentences as multi-layered structures deriving from one or more *kernel sentences* (basic syntactic units generated by the phrase-structure component of the grammar) restructured and organized by one or more *transformational rules* (formulations of such processes as conversion of active-voice sentences to passive voice or of positive sentences to negative). In terms of transformational grammar, then, a sentence such as James Joyce's (q.v.) "Gazing up into the darkness I saw myself as a creature driven and derided by vanity" can be regarded as deriving from a sequence of underlying simpler structures such as "I saw as a creature me," "I gazed up into the darkness," "Vanity drove the creature," etc. (Ohmann's example). Having derived, through rigorously consistent procedures for reducing transformations, the various elemental predications antecedent to Joyce's sentence, one can measure these against the finished sentence with its complex syntactical evaluation of those predications. While this contrastive device may not solve the stylistician's ancient problem of defining the indispensable, elusive form-content dichotomy, it does suggest a promising alternative way of isolating some stylistic devices. At times examination of the kernels and transformations underlying a stretch of discourse can also bring into prominence submerged preoccupations or disguised emphases which operate beneath the surface structure. Thus in Ohmann's transformational analysis of the closing sentence of Conrad's (q.v.) *The Secret Sharer* one can, by scrutinizing the deep structure, see that the syntax is actually controlled by the person described, Legget, not by the ostensible narrator, although the surface structure overlaying the deep structure artfully conceals this fact. Somewhat similar analyses, now underway, of the prose styles of Virginia Woolf, Hemingway (qq.v.), Gibbon, and others, suggest that the generative-transformational concepts offer a promising approach to style analysis, more promising, certainly, than the earlier linguistic approaches to style as dialect or as an extended idiom. All linguistic approaches will, it is true, be seriously limited as long as there is no systematic linguistic methodology for analyzing syntactic units above the rank of sentence; but the current attempts of Karl E. Heidolph and others to devise generative rules for inter-sentence units, and the earlier work of Zelig Harris in "Discourse Analysis," have made important progress in this direction, and at least one linguist (S. R. Levin) has already done exploratory work with units beyond the sentence in poetic discourse.

A summary assessment of the utility of linguistics in the study of literature would be premature when the new science itself is still developing and when the attempts to apply linguistic techniques to literary problems are still to a large extent experimental. Nevertheless, enough has been done to suggest what the general nature of linguistics' contribution to literature is likely to be. As linguists themselves often reiterate, it is a mistake to expect from linguistics revolutionary esthetic insights, the solution of major interpretational cruces, or a general formula for literary evaluation. The most arresting characteristics of linguistic science in this century have been its concern for establishing a rigorous and precise methodology and its power of revealing the system, often unsuspected, which underlies speech behavior at all levels. Hence the major contribution of linguistics to literary study is, in broadest terms, that it makes it possible to codify in overt, explicit, and systematic form the literary effects and relationships which readers and critics had previously apprehended only intuitively. This objective codification of literary perceptions can be useful in pedagogical and scholarly explication, it can cast many literary problems in a form accessible to new techniques of analysis (e.g., mathematical and computer techniques), and occasionally it can suggest further questions that are not likely to emerge from traditional procedures of inquiry.

BIBLIOGRAPHY: **Essay Collections:** "Section A: Stylistics," in *Proceedings of the Ninth International Congress of Linguists,* ed. H. G. Hunt (1964), pp. 294-330; *A Prague School Reader on Esthetics, Literary Structure and Style,* selected and translated by P. L. Garvin (1964); *Poetics—Poetyka* [Papers presented at the first International Conference of Work-in-Progress devoted to problems of poetics, Warsaw] (1961); *Style in Language,* ed. T. A. Sebeok (1960); Whitehall, H., Chatman, S., Stein, A., Ransom, J. C., "English Verse and What It Sounds Like," *Kenyon Review,* XVIII (1956), 411-477. **Individual Studies:** "An Analysis of *The Windhover*: An Experiment in Structural Method," *PMLA,* LXX (1955), 968-978; "Pippa's Song: Two Attempts at Structural Criticism," *Texas Studies in English,* XXXV (1956), 51-56; Wimsatt, W. K., and Beardsley, M. C., "The Concept of Meter: An Exercise in Abstraction," *PMLA,* LXXIV (1959), 585-598; Hill, A. A., "Principles Governing Semantic Parallels," *TSLL,* I (1959), 356-365; Epstein, E., and Hawkes, T., *Linguistics and English Prosody,* Studies in Linguistics, Occasional Papers, 7 (1959); Levin, S. R., *Linguistic Structures in Poetry* (1962); Taranovski, K., "Metrics," in *Current Trends* in Linguistics, ed. T. A. Sebeok: Vol. I: *Soviet and East European Linguistics* (1963), pp. 192-201; Francis, W. N., "Syntax and Literary Interpretation," in *Readings in Applied English Linguistics*, ed. H. B. Allen (1964), pp. 515-522; Enkvist, N., Spencer, J., and Gregory, M., *Linguistics and Style* (1964); Ohmann, R., "Generative Grammars and the Concept of Literary Style," *Word*, XX (1964), 423-439; Jakobson, R., "Der grammatische Bau des Gedichts von B. Brecht 'Wir sind sie,' " in *Beiträge zur Sprachwissenschaft ... Wolfgang Steinitz ... dargebracht* (1965), pp. 175-189; Ruwet, N., "Sur un vers de Charles Baudelaire," *Linguistics*, 17 (1965), 69-77; Thorne, J. P., "Stylistics and Generative Grammars," *Journal of Linguistics*, I (1965), 49-59; Bierwisch, M., "Poetik und Linguistik," *Sprache im technischen Zeitalter*, XV (1965), 1258-1273; Chatman, S., *A Theory of Meter* (1965); "Literature as Sentences," *College English*, XXVII (1966), 261-267; Ives, S. "Grammatical Analysis and Literary Criticism," in *Introductory Readings on Language*, ed. W. Anderson and N. Stageberg (1966), pp. 260-265; Koch, W. A., *Recurrence and a Three-Modal Approach to Poetry* (1966); Heidolph, K., "Wortstellung und Nominalgruppenstruktur," *Studia Grammatica*, VIII (1966)

FRED C. ROBINSON

LITERARY AESTHETICS

I. Definition of Literary Aesthetics: Scope and Nature

(a) INTRODUCTION: THE AESTHETIC EXPERIENCE

If we grant, with Sully Prudhomme, that the genesis of rational categories finds its poetic expression in metaphysics, then poetry (literary creation in general) becomes a fundamental statement which embraces the relationship of subject and object, and as such a *scientia universalis*. This knowledge, charged with mobility as undesirable as the motion of wind upon water, carries with it the promise of escape from ontologic banality. Rhythm and figure are the mobilia which fascinate the mind long before it can grasp the full meaning of its own experience. Literary aesthetics attempts to shed the light of analytic sophistication on the nature of that experience. The aesthetic experience involves both a hedonistic response to the thing experienced and an evaluative assessment of it.

This response may color one's view of the world. Through the reader's participation in artistic expression, which gives form and shape to experience, he is enabled to confess himself and to heal his soul (Parker, pp. 51, 50; parenthetical references are to sources listed according to date of publication in the Bibliography, section 1, at the end of this article). Hence the importance of the literary aesthetic experience as a cathartic value. The elements of feeling are of two broad kinds: (1) vague and (2) definite. In the first instance the feeling is directly linked with the sensuous medium; in the second the feeling "is mediated by ideas through which the medium is given content and meaning" (Parker, p. 60). Artistic expression embodies ideally both the evanescence and the perdurability of feeling. Within the experience in question we recognize, with Lipps (*Aesthetik*, Vol. I, ch. 3; Parker, pp. 85, 86) an "aesthetic rivalry" in which contraries (good and evil, beauty and ugliness, etc.) invoke each other. Victor Hugo's concept of the grotesque (q.v. and see below) illustrates this rivalry theoretically, while his novels illustrate it in practice. What is reflected is the dialectic nature of man's spirit and its dramatic aspect. An integral criticism which takes this into account can act as an energizing principle in the aesthetic experience. This is understandably so since every significant literary work is, in a profound sense, a criticism of life. Through expression life is not merely reported but transformed. This comes to pass through the processes of *logopoeia, phanopoeia, mythopoeia*, and *melopoeia*. The first is the use of idea and language; the second, of vision and image; the third, of history and epic; the last of music (melody and harmony). Together they compose the awesome complexity of the aesthetic experience, which is the concern of literary aesthetics.

(b) AESTHETICS AND THE DEFINITION OF BEAUTY

(1) Aesthetics, then, deals with the dramatic transformation of sensation (passivity) into perception (activity), ideation, and feeling—in general, a heightened awareness of pleasure values in expressive thought and feeling and a concomitant demand for satisfactions which are marked by a sense of having entered the domain of beauty, a form whose manifesta-

tions are myriad but whose aspect is singular and is predominantly marked by harmony and balance. Within its presence man is afforded intimations of his highest and deepest possibilities; the world is embraced as desirable. Granted that the two aesthetic senses are sight and hearing, then literature imaginatively appealing to these adds a third sense: intellectual contemplation, in which metaphysical nostalgia and pathos play an important role. It is this sense which brings into view the familial relationship between Venus (beauty), the Lost Eden (loneliness), Eros (desire and love) and Thanatos (death and annihilation).

This view is afforded us by certain works of literature which also belong in the category of philosophy (*Hamlet, Faust*) and certain works of philosophy which have literary appeal (Plato's dialogues, some of the writings of Schopenhauer, Nietzsche [q.v.], William James, and Bergson [q.v.]).

All definitions of beauty, from Plato through Schopenhauer and Santayana (q.v.), have failed to articulate the total experience subtended by the word. But one may gather from the crux points in all these definitions the following yet again tentative statement: beauty is that which wakens desire. It is a transcendental form of which each particular expression is reminiscent as shadow is of substance, as memory is of experience, and as desire itself is reminiscent of fulfillment.

(2) Hugo has underlined for us the fact that the ugly exists side by side with the beautiful, the grotesque with the sublime. The form of the grotesque is that of comedy, so that actually the grotesque is the ugly incorporated in an art form. The fertile union of the grotesque with the sublime gives birth (according to Hugo) to modern genius which, in its complexity, is opposed to the uniform simplicity of the genius of antiquity. Here we have, incidentally, the difference between classic and romantic literature. In ancient literature the grotesque occupied a recessive place. In modern thought and art, on the contrary, its role is immense. This becomes increasingly so from the days of the Elizabethans through Hugo and our contemporary literature. Sganarelle dances about Don Juan, Mephistopheles around Faust. As an element of contrast, the grotesque is (at least in Hugo's view) the richest source that nature can open to art. Thus in the drama, which, for Hugo and others, represents the summit of poetic development and of which Shakespeare is in turn the summit, the sublime

and the grotesque interlink as they do in life and in creation (Baym, "Baudelaire and Shakespeare"; Hugo, Preface to *Cromwell,* passim).

(*c*) DEFINITION OF LITERATURE AND LITERARY CRITICISM

Literature is a linguistic stylization of experience lifted from the condition of mere bodily response to stimuli, to the plane of imaginative and spiritual (psychologic) response. Accordingly, any criticism of literature is, of necessity, a criticism of the artist's ordering of experience; and any aesthetic considerations of literature are to a large extent considerations within the framework of a philosophy of experience, an ontology of expression.

(*d*) SCOPE OF LITERATURE

By common agreement, literature as an art comprehends poetry, the novel, drama, the essay, and philosophic works, when the style in which they are couched gives pleasure. Tradition has established certain literary products as prototypes of excellence. Thus Homer, Sappho, Catullus, Virgil, Dante, Ronsard, Shakespeare, Milton, Shelley, Keats, Leopardi, Heine, Rilke (q.v.), Baudelaire, Mallarmé, Valéry (q.v.) have furnished examplars in poetry; Cervantes, Rabelais, Fielding, Sterne, Hardy (q.v.), Hugo, Balzac, Stendhal, Flaubert, Proust (q.v.), Dostoyevski, Tolstoi (q.v.), and Thomas Mann (q.v.) in the novel; Euripides, Aeschylus, Sophocles, Shakespeare, Racine, Molière, Ibsen (q.v.), Strindberg (q.v.), O'Neill (q.v.) in drama; Montaigne, Francis Bacon, Samuel Johnson, Matthew Arnold, Sainte-Beuve, and Gourmont (q.v.) in the essay; Heraclitus, Plato, Pascal, Diderot, Schopenhauer, Nietzsche, William James, Santayana and Unamuno (q.v.) in certain of their philosophic works.

(*e*) LITERARY AESTHETICS: AN OPERATIONAL DEFINITION

In the light of the fact that man's "origin, his growth, his loves and beliefs are but the outcomes of accidental collocations of atoms" (Bernbaum, p. 448), it would be presumptuous to assume the posture of logic-tight certainty and unflinching authority in matters of literary aesthetics. Clearly, it takes into account a theory of perception (*aisthēsis,* Gr.=perception, sense impression, the ability to feel sensation) and susceptibility (Santayana, p. 14), as well as an awareness of the dramatic transformation of passive sensation to active perception accompanied by a sense of having entered the domain of beauty. Accordingly, the aesthetics of literature is intrinsically preoccupied with poetic essence and the extent to which that essence yields a vision of life which may be called "beauty."

Literary aesthetics is not primarily concerned with technical criticism, which, while related to aesthetics, constitutes its own domain. Rather is it preoccupied with literature as an energizing principle of contemplation whose objects are: desire, love, birth, pain, wonderment, ambition, fulfillment, frustration, hope, despair; good and evil, beauty and ugliness, the comic and the tragic, the true and the false—life and death. And all these are aspects of man's vision which when articulated in artistic form, challenge the attention and study of literary aesthetics (Lee, ch. 3, on "aspect").

If the evocation of feeling and emotion is taken to be paramount in the literary process, then literary aesthetics should unconditionally include within its definition the discrimination of literary excellence at the bar of the power of evocativeness. The means employed would be considered excellent by that test. "Our knowledge," Pater makes Marius say, "is limited to what we feel. But can we be sure that things are at all like our feeling?" Literary alchemy ambitions the power to create that identity—the universe as feeling. It is that alchemy that the literary aesthetician aims to penetrate.

The aesthetics of literature is caught at the very threshold of its domain by the possibility of a shift from the Cartesian *cogito* to the Romantic "I feel." There is a glowing tendency to suppose that the literary work of art may satisfy both claims—that of knowledge and that of feeling—that both are looking for a common metaphor whose ultimate goal would be to express a universal mathesis (Baym, "On the Relationship between Poetry and Science" and "Metaphysical Malaise"; Bronowski, pp. 48-49). Some who hold that view maintain that any sound approach to general aesthetics or to literary aesthetics in particular cannot afford to ignore the nature of brain activity which makes clear a certain homeostatic factor in the enjoyment or nonenjoyment of any experience. Vivante (*Intelligence in Expression*, p. 94) quotes James (p. 584) to this effect: "The drainage currents and discharges of the brain are not purely physical facts. They are psychophysical facts, and the spiritual quality of them seems a codeterminant of their mechanical effectiveness. If the mechanical effectiveness in a cell, as they increase, give pleasure, they seem to increase all the more readily for that fact; if they give displeasure, the displeasure seems to damp the activities." Witness that we have here, as a base for aesthetic experience, a principle of physical economy, not unrelated to Newton's laws of motion, i.e., the principles of inertia, momentum, and acceleration.

II. Ontology, Dynamics, and the Poet's Domain

(a) ONTOLOGY AND THE LITERARY WORK OF ART

For Fernandez, "the fundamental problem of aesthetics is no other than the metaphysical problem of being ... transferred to the plane of the imagination." For him, then, "aesthetics must be an imaginative ontology" (p. 7; Wheelwright, pp. 23-27). Those who see a relationship between literature and philosophy (their number is growing) and admit philosophy's concern with both the denotative and connotative aspects of reality, should also be moved to see that both through symbol and figure literature achieves an articulation of the denotative as well as the connotative. For literary aesthetics one of the pervasive problems is the integration of inner and outer experience through an imaginative grasp of total experience. This process is implicit in the activity of thought which is implemented by language. For literary aesthetics this process (the act of integration) is as serious as it is for science.

In the last analysis, they turn out to be engaged in the same dramatic enterprise: the attempt to present the resistance called "reality" in a form which makes that resistance itself a source of fascination and pleasure. In one of its aspects, that form is called art; in another, it is known as science. Haunting both is an unseen, but none the less felt, spirit called "beauty." With Bronowski, Bachelard, and others we see the interlocking of poetry and science in symbol and metaphor. Indeed, the former declares: "The symbol and the metaphor are as necessary to science as to poetry" (Bronowski, pp. 48, 49). The world stands as much to lose if it were emptied of feeling as it would if it were emptied of thought. From this point of view literary aesthetics is involved in the quest for a universal poetics (Baym, "Metaphysical Malaise," p. 199).

Wellek's position is that a work of art derives its ontologic status from a system of norms of ideal intersubjective concepts. These concepts change with the collective ideology of which they are a part. They are accessible only through individual mental experience, based on the sound structure of its sentences. He avoids the problem of value and, in general, is opposed to "the insidious psychological relativism which must always end in scepticism and finally mental anarchy" (Wellek, p. 223 and passim). But the mind being a theater of simultaneities (Wm. James's phrase), relativism in the creative process, or in any discussion of it, is a pervasive fact. This in no way makes the relativism "insidious"—except as it threatens someone's pat authoritarianism. Art may be a system of norms, but not necessarily of norms dependent on forensic strategy, no matter how shrewd.

Ransom (q.v.) would differentiate one kind of poetry from another "with respect to its ontology, or the reality of its being." The issue is drawn between the poetry of things and the poetry of ideas. Plato, of course, preferred ideas to things. The imagists—and more recently poets like Ponge (q.v.)—have presented things in their thingness. "But perhaps thing versus idea does not seem to name an opposition precisely. Then we might phrase it a little differently: image versus idea" (Ransom, *Critiques and Criticism,* p. 32). The inescapable question is, is an idea free of images? Is "red" just a color, or is it also a countless number of things associated with it? Is the idea "redness" just an abstraction, or is it, too, a countless number of things associated with it?

A poem is an orchestration of image, idea, and thing in a tonality of emotion which carries with it its own ontological validity. We know what it means for the heart to leap at the sight of a field of daffodils. Wordsworth's line communicates to us all at once the image of flower and field, the idea of surprise and promise, and the thing itself through the recovery of past sensation. The poem is an instrument which grasps for us the compenetration of past, present, and future and enables us to move, propelled by a musical principle, from the reality outside of ourselves (actuality) to the reality inside of us (ideality). Through a process of translation and transmutation, experience is musicalized. We dream, we recollect, and we

are. Plenitude supplants, if it does not annihilate, niggardliness. The landscape is unending, all things are tipped with wingedness, and we are the poem, the novel, the drama, the essay, and the philosophic system which engages us. Subject and object are melted down in one phemenologic stream of transcendence. The stuffy distinction between science and poetry falls away as does a binding element when the things it held together have become interfused and presently have no further need of an extraneous cohesive (Baym, "Metaphysical Malaise," passim).

(b) THE AESTHETICS OF POETRY AND PROSE

In poetry words yield more in sensation than in ideation; in prose the situation is reversed. The prose-poem combines the two tonalities—not always successfully. In prose the reader imagines what he knows; in poetry he knows only what he imagines. In the former the heart of the matter (so to speak) is in the brain; in the latter the brain is in the heart. Cognition and feeling are woven into both. Whereas in prose, however, the order of knowledge constitutes the horizon of feeling, in poetry the order of feeling is the horizon of knowledge. The heightened feeling of prose comes from a music of ideas, where ideas themselves create a succession of rhythms and accents. The heightened feeling of poetry comes from a music of feelings and emotions. Of course, in both cases it is a question of relative predominance. One recalls in this connection Oscar Wilde's aphorism: "If a man treats life artistically, his brain is in his heart."

In 1901 Gummere quoted from the French aesthetician Guyau these words: "Poetry will continue to be the natural language of all great and lasting emotions." For Browning poetry was the poet's "brains beat into rhythm"; for Mill, something in the nature of a soliloquy; for Verlaine, essentially music (in contradistinction to mere "literature"); and for Baumgarten, the fountainhead of modern aesthetics, it was "speech so charged with energy that it demands metrical expression" (Gummere, pp. 30, 38, 52; Guyau, pp. 89-255). For Frost (q.v.) the heart of poetry is metaphor, but so is it also for him the heart of science and philosophy (Frost, *The Constant Symbol*). For the Surrealists (*see* surrealism) it is a series of images which emerge as a result of the collision of ideas and the emotions released from a veritable logomachy in which the poet is as much an object as he is a subject of manipulation (Alquié, passim; Carrouges, passim). Recent poetics turns a highly sophisticated battery of scientific investigation on the poetic, imaginative, and emotional resonances wakened in the poet's sensorium (and in that of the re-creative reader) by the elements themselves. Here Bachelard stands at the forefront. His "psychoanalysis of the elements" and the spatiotemporal categories with which we intuit them holds intimations not only of a new poetics and literary aesthetic but of an epistemology whose roots reach down into the elements themselves (Bachelard, see works by Bachelard listed in Bibliography; see also Caws, passim).

(c) THE DYNAMICS OF A LITERARY WORK OF ART

We expect to find in art the triumph of coherence, which we too often miss in life. Its power to present the familiar in a new aspect is related to its ability to impose a monistic pattern on the heterogeneity of experience. We turn to a literary product as we turn to a musical fugue, which in itself is not a fixed form but rather a process which makes use of various forms. What we have in any ideal artistic expression is a musicalization of experience. In this process logic is discovered after the fact. The logic of the creative artist is one which brings together opposites in an equilibrium of tensions, a *dynamique musicale* (Stravinsky, *Poétique musicale,* 2ᵉ leçon).

(d) THE READER AND THE DOMAIN OF THE POET

One of the fundamental questions—how does the reader enter the domain of the poet?—has been answered variously. One answer is, of course, the process of empathy: there is something within us, both physically and psychologically, which enables us to identify ourselves with the poet's world and so to partake of his emotions. France (q.v.) maintained (*Le Jardin d'Epicure,* pp. 73, 74) that we all have in us an exemplar of each of our poets whom no one knows and who will perish forever with all his variants when we shall no longer feel anything.

Actually, the creative artist is helpless without the creative reader. Without the latter, the former runs the risk of remaining completely silent even when his work is in print. The work of art, then, is a partnership within the matrix

of creative imagination; Albert the poet takes the lead in providing the occasion for transition from passivity to activity.

III. *The Tonalities of Literary Aesthetics*

(a) CLASSICISM AND ROMANTICISM

Within the framework of Western tradition the conjugate categories of classicism and romanticism have a compelling and staying power. Among the many reasons to account for this, that offered by Gide (q.v.) and quoted by Herbert Read (q.v.) is perhaps as helpful as any: "It is important to remember that a struggle between classicism and romanticism also exists inside each mind. And it is from this very struggle that the work is born; the classic work of art relates the triumph of order and measure over an inner romanticism. And the wilder the riot to be tamed, the more beautiful your work will be" (Gide, p. 453; Read, *Reason and Romanticism,* p. 92; see Fleischmann, p. 140). Scientists, too, report a similar struggle in their reaching out for an artistic triumph over a tumult of half-conscious ideas. Poincaré speaks of sudden illumination after long periods of resistance (*Science et Méthode,* ch. 3), and Denaeyer likewise alludes to an unforeseen moment of illumination in the process of ultimate integration. Indeed, the words of Poincaré that Denaeyer quotes have the romantic overtones reminiscent of Shelley: *La pensée est un éclair dans une longue nuit.... Ah soyons tous une parcelle de cette lumière*" (Denaeyer, pp. 101-21 and passim; Baym, "On the Relationship between Poetry and Science," p. 4).

(b) UNIVERSAL ANALOGY AND SYNESTHESIA

The universal analogy of which Baudelaire spoke so tellingly, as did Emerson ("Nature is a metaphor of the mind"), derives its great sustaining support from the manifest phenomenon of synesthesia. This, in turn, points to a conspectual totality in any significant work of art. Literary aesthetics alerts the reader to the universal aspects of art. This is the secret of the abiding power of the Greek tragedians, Shakespeare, Dostoyevski, and the leading lyric poets in the various tongues. (Baudelaire, "Richard Wagner et *Tannhäuser* à Paris"; Ullmann, *Language and Style*).

(c) SYMBOLISM

To the extent that the literary artist uses language effectively, his art product will waken a multiplicity of experiences in the reader. The poem, the novel, the drama will constitute symbols of these reactions, and the experiences themselves will be their meaning (Whitehead, passim). Northrop Frye distinguishes two senses in which words are symbols: signs, or "representations of a thing outside of the pattern of words," and images, or units of a larger verbal pattern or structure. In signs the reader's mind is outward (centrifugal), toward the object represented; in images the mental movement is toward the construction of the whole pattern, i.e., centripetal. Frye adds a third sense, namely, the archetype "which regards it [the symbol] as neither image nor sign, but as the product of the two," a synthetic symbol recurring prominently in various literary works. And still a fourth conception is that of the symbol as a monad or "unit of the total poetic experience" (Frye). For Langer "signs and symbol are knotted together" in a fixed reality called "fact." Between the facts run "the threads of unrecorded reality, momentarily recognized, wherever they come to the surface, in our tacit adaptation to signs; and the bright, twisted threads of symbolic envisagement, imagination, thought—memory and reconstructed memory, belief beyond experience, dream, make-believe, hypothesis, philosophy—the whole creative process of ideation, metaphor, and abstraction that makes human life an adventure in understanding" (Langer, p. 281).

(d) LITERARY AESTHETICS AND MUSIC

Walter Pater's pronouncement with regard to the aspiration of all the arts to the condition of music is not to be taken as a vote for the confusion of the arts in the various means they employ to express beauty. The aspiration in all cases is toward the articulation of man's desires as values beyond the forces that set these desires into motion. What Langer and Gehring (whom she quotes) have to say about music, we find to be generally true for poetry or literature. She asserts that "music is our myth of the inner life," and Gehring declares that "in the case of measure, force, and tempo, music duplicates or photographs the mind; in the case of melody, it coincides with it" (Langer, p. 235; Gehring, p. 98). In the creation and in the musicalization of thought, literature

and music vie in their efforts and in their effectiveness.

IV. General Ambience and Preoccupations of Literary Aesthetics

(a) THE PREOCCUPATION WITH LITERARY AESTHETICS

The preoccupation with literary aesthetics is owing in part to the unconscious feeling or suspicion that the recognition of real value and beauty in works of literature somehow constitutes an opening wedge into the secrets of the poetic or creative process itself and into its mysterious hold both on those who originate works of art and those who appreciate them. Hence the quest for a possible science of literary aesthetics latent in one of a number of fields or in all of them combined, namely: (1) psychology, (2) the physiology of sensation, (3) linguistics, (4) semantics, (5) historical synthesis and analysis, (6) anthropology, and (7) philosophy in its various branches. The first and the second share in the endeavor to gain an understanding of the operations of the imagination and the manner in which it transforms rudimentary sensations into images and patterned articulations of feelings and ideas. The third and fourth (often with the aid of the sixth and seventh) turn the batteries of linguistics and meaning experiences upon the literary fact of which language and meaning are the factors. The fifth, preoccupied with the record, often calls upon psychology to illumine the course and destiny of literary expression. The sixth studies the literary phase of man's activity as an artifact which is highly charged with the nature of his culture and the crystallized image of that culture. The seventh explores the presuppositions, implications, and tendencies latent in the other fields.

A cynical, but none the less compelling, point of view would remind us that with all his posturings, including the aesthetic one, "man has canine teeth like the dog and the fox, and like the dog and the fox he buried them at the beginning in the flesh of his fellows. His descendants slaughtered one another with stone knives for a bit of raw fish, and the equivalent still goes on under the surface of our modern conventions" (Taine, *Graindorge*, p. 267; Babbitt, pp. 233-34). This truth and reality recognized by the head is obviously abhorrent to the heart. The instinct of the heart is to escape from such a reality into a *pays des chimères*. Taine calls this "creating for yourself an alibi." One form of the alibi is to lose yourself in aesthetic contemplation of the forms of outer nature. Another way of creating an alibi is to study history. "Through this gate," says Taine, "you enter into revery. All opium is unhealthy; it is prudent to take it only in small doses and from time to time. Since Werther and René we have taken too much of it, we are taking it in heavier doses every day; consequently the malady of the age has been aggravated, and in music, painting and politics a number of symptoms prove that the derangement of reason, imagination, sensibility, and nerves is on the increase. Among all the drugs that give us at our will factitious absence and forgetfulness, history is, I believe, the least dangerous" (*Derniers Essais*, p. 226). A third way of creating an alibi is by music. Hence the cult of Beethoven. In a word, aesthetic experience (and reflection on it) may be regarded as a romantic revery, an escape from reality through resort to an alibi.

(b) Literary Aesthetics and Speculation

Inevitably any thoroughgoing speculation on the aesthetic experience of a work of literature leads to epistemological and metaphysical inquiry into the nature of experience and the central role of language in its three stages: prelinguistic, linguistic, and metalinguistic. Lack of exact knowledge about the emergence of consciousness and self-awareness and the origin of language frustrates the study of the first stage. The second has been studied with varying degrees of success since the days of Plato, and has reached a high level of sophistication since the emergence of comparative philology and scientific linguistics. Central to this sophistication is the study of language (hence of literature) as symbol and metaphor in relation to semantics (Ullman, "Principles of Semantics," pp. 266-72 and passim; Urban, passim; Baym, "The Present State of the Study of Metaphor"). The third stage is enriched by the studies of Croce (q.v.), Freud (*see* psychology and literature), Husserl, Leone Vivante, Jean Wahl, Charles Mauron, Herbert Read, Frye, and Bachelard, among others.

These explorations lead from the level of the instinctual, where linguistic expression is but a tool for the uncovering of processes which escape linguistic articulation, to a plane in which man negotiates the universe as language and therefore as an object of aesthetic contemplation and pleasure. On this level literary aesthetics is related to a "psychoanalysis of the elements" of nature themselves (earth, fire, water, air), to the absorption of the irrational in the rational, to critique of the rational in terms of the unconscious or preconscious, and to the poetic process as a profound source of total knowledge. Valéry's (q.v.) *Cahiers* are beginning to yield a rich new harvest of knowledge in the whole of this area of speculation. To the extent that literary aesthetics is anchored in a theory of emotions and in a metaphysics of nature, it is on both counts (in its modern form) largely a product of romantic transcendentalism. In the light of this fact it is not surprising that the name of Novalis recurs through a large number of Bachelard's works.

Verbal felicity and metrical movement may account critically for a reader's response to a poem as something that creates within him a sense of beauty. Yet a deeper analysis reveals that the intensity and immediacy of response is moving to an unconscious transformation and fusion of imagery derived from a wide field of reference (Read, "The True Voice of Feeling," p. 23).

(c) Literary Aesthetics as Science and as Heuristic

As a science, literary aesthetics seeks to provide a mutual calibration for perception and sensibility and to alert the percipient to the infinite possibilities of experience provided by the imagination as articulated in a literary work of art. Heuristically, literary aesthetics may serve to lead the human mind to realize that poetry (=literature) is truly, in the words of Bachelard, the pancalist (from Greek *pankalos*, all + beautiful) activity of the will and that as such it not only expresses the desire for limited beauty but for universal beauty as well (Bachelard, *L'Air et les songes*, p. 61; see also Baldwin, on pancalism).

(d) Sincerity and Literature

To take seriously Mallarmé's alleged admonition to Degas that poetry is not written with ideas but with words (*see* Rylands, p. xi) is to agree that literature is nothing but a glorified verbal game, which has very little to do with the life process of the mind and the emotions. What comes into play here unavoidably is the role of sincerity in the means the artist uses to stir the reader's emotion. Peyre argues that, while the element of sincerity is implicit in the literary process, it is useless to insist on the degree of sincerity in the artist. Indeed, he asserts that "the stress on sincerity would be deadly to literature if it were ever to impair the freedom which must remain the privilege of creative inspiration" (Peyre, p. 339). But here Peyre himself is careful to point to those who are still on the side of Horace, who maintained that if the artist is to stir others, he must first have been stirred himself (*Ars Poetica*, I.102: *Si vis me flere, dolendum est / Primum ipsi tibi*; quoted by Peyre, p. 3).

(e) LITERARY AESTHETICS AND PSYCHOANALYSIS

Concerned with the discrimination of means and effects, literary aesthetics of necessity confronts the opposition between "inner" and "outer." Read, following Jung on the question of introversion and extroversion, cites the latter on the specific activity called "phantasy": "It is the creative activity whence issue the solutions to all unanswerable questions; it is the mother of all possibilities, in which, too, the inner and outer worlds, like all psychological antitheses, are joined in living union" (Read, *Reason and Romanticism,* p. 90; Jung, p. 69). Accordingly psychoanalysis recognized the power of art to resolve "into one uniform flow of life all that springs from the outer mechanism of actuality—doing this, not only for the artist himself, from whose own need the phantasy is born, but also by suggestion and by symbol, for all who come to participate in his imaginative work." In the artist two forces contend for balance: one in the direction of primitivism and the "disjointed fortuitous world of dreams," the other in the direction of the plastic and the architectonic. These contending forces "resolve themselves into some kind of unity" (Read, *loc. cit.,* pp. 90-92).

Literary aesthetics is normatively successful when it helps the reader to realize that a proper analysis, far from destroying the synthesis of art, helps to realize it at its fullest. At the same time it alerts the reader to the undeniable fact that vis-à-vis the materials of outer reality and of inner reality (thought and feeling) which are to be loved into artistic being, language is an embrace which often falls short of its mark. This may constitute, in part, the "lover's quarrel" that the poet has with the world.

For some aestheticians, however (like Roger Fry, for instance), it is not at all a settled matter that the work of art is a daydream in which men seek, in a verbal and symbolic manner, the fulfillment of certain desires, either repressed or denied satisfaction by the rigors of daily life. According to Fry, there is a pleasure in the recognition of order and inevitability in relations. In such a view the shift is obviously from the affective zone to the intellectual.

Fry's stance can be interpreted as a leaning toward the contemplative attitude which is shared by the scientist and poet as well as the recreative reader (see Mauron, pp. 21-28). If, according to psychoanalysis, the literary artist moves from neurosis closer to reality than he did before he became an artist, then the reader (with the normative help of literary aesthetics) should be able to follow the same route. The notion, then, that art is an escape from reality should be replaced by the idea that if art is in any sense an escape, it is from banality. Where there was flatness and mere droning, there is now plenitude and musicality.

BIBLIOGRAPHY: (1) Sources referred to in the text: Baudelaire, C., *Richard Wagner et "Tannhäuser" à Paris* (1861); Taine, H., *Vie et opinions de Thomas Graindorge* (1863-65); Guyau, J. M., *Les problèmes de l'esthétique contemporaine* (1884); James, W., *Principles of Psychology* (1891), Vol. II, ch. 26, p. 584; Taine, H., *Derniers Essais de critique et d'histoire (1866-1889)* (1894); Santayana, G., *The Sense of Beauty: Being the Outline of Aesthetic Theory* (1896); Gummere, F. B., *The Beginning of Poetry* (1901); Gehring, A., *The Basis of Musical Pleasure* (1910); Babbitt, I., *The Masters of Modern French Criticism* (1912); Lee, V., *The Beautiful: An Introduction to Psychological Aesthetics* (1913), ch. 3, "Aspects versus Things"; Lipps, T., *Ästhetik: Psychologie des Schönen und der Kunst* (2 vols., 1914-20); Baldwin, J. M., *Genetic Theory of Reality: Being the Outcome of Genetic Logic as Issuing in the Aesthetic Theory of Reality Called Pancalism, with an Extended Glossary of Terms* (1915); Parker, D. H., *The Principles of Aesthetics* (1920), esp. chs. 8, 9, 10; Gide, A., *Morceaux choisis* (1921); Jung, C. G., *Psychologische Typen* (1921; Psychological Types, 1923); Fry, R., *The Artist and Psychoanalysis* (1924); Vivante, L., *Intelligence in Expression, with an Essay, Originality of Thought and Its Physiological Conditions* (1925); Read, H., *Reason and Romanticism* (1926); Fernandez, R., *Messages* (1926; Eng., 1927); White-head, A. N., *Symbolism: Its Meaning and Effect* (1927); Rylands, G. H. W., *Words and Poetry*, with an introduction by L. Strachey (1928); Wheelwright, P. E., "Toward a Meta-physic of Literary Criticism," *The Journal of Philosophy*, XXVI: 9 (1929); Mauron, C., *Aesthetics and Psychology* (1935); Bachelard, G., *La Dialectique de la durée* (1936), ch. 7, "Les Métaphores de la durée"; Urban, W. M., *Language and Reality: The Philosophy of Language and the Principles of Symbolism* (1939); Baym, M. I., "Baudelaire and Shakespeare," *The Shakespeare Association Bulletin*, XV:3 (July 1940), 131-48 (esp. n. 4, p. 145), and XV:4 (Oct. 1940), 195-205; Langer, S. K., *Philosophy in a New Key: A Study in the Symbolism of Reason, Rite, and Art* (1942); Stravinsky, I., *Poétique musicale* (1942), ch. 2, "Du Phénomène musical"; Bachelard, G., *L'Air et les songes* (1943); *The Poems of Robert Frost* (Modern Library ed., 1946), "The Constant Symbol," p. xvi; Bachelard, G., *La Terre et les rêveries du repos* (1948), ch. 3, "L'Imagination de la qualité: Rythme—analyse et tonalisation"; Ransom, J. C., "Poetry: A Note on Ontology," in *Critiques and Essays in Criticism, 1920-1948*, ed. R. W. Stallman (1949), pp. 30-46; Wellek, R., "The Mode of Existence of a Literary Work of Art," in *Critiques and Essays in Criticism, 1920-1948*, ed. R. W. Stallman (1949), pp. 210-23; Carrouges, M., *André Breton et les données fondamentales du surréalisme* (1950); Vivante, L,. *English Poetry and Its Contribution to the Knowledge of a Creative Principle*, with a preface by T. S. Eliot (1950); Ullmann, S., *The Principles of Semantics: A Linguistic Approach to Meaning* (1951; 2nd ed., 1957); Read, H., *The True Voice of Feeling: Studies in English Romantic Poetry* (1953); Denaeyer, M. E., "Science et poésie," *Revue de l'Université de Bruxelles*, 6ᵉ année (Jan.-March 1954), No. 2, pp. 101-21; Alquié, F., *Philosophie du surréalisme* (1955); Baym, M. I., "On the Relationship between Poetry and Science," *YCGL*, V (1956), 1-5; Bronowski, J., *Science and Human Values* (1956); Bachelard, G., *La Poétique de l'espace* (1957), ch. 2, "Maison et univers," ch. 4, "Le Nid," and ch. 9, "La Dialectique du dehors et du dedans"; Frye, N., *Anatomy of Criticism: Four Essays* (1957), "Four Meanings of Symbolism"; Kayser, W., *Das Groteske. Seine Gestaltung in Malerei und Dichtung* (1957; The Grotesque in Art and Literature, 1963); Baym, M. I., "Metaphysical Malaise:

Science and the Struggle for a Universal Poetics," *Bucknell Review*, IX: 3 (1960); idem, "The Present State of the Study of Metaphor," *BA*, XXXV: 3 (1961); Peyre, H., *Literature and Sincerity* (1963); Ullmann, S., *Language and Style: Collected Papers* (1964); Baym, M. I., "Science and Poetry," in *Encyclopedia of Poetry and Poetics*, ed. A. Preminger et al. (1965); pp. 742-53; Fleischmann, W. B., "Classicism," in *Encyclopedia of Poetry and Poetics*, ed. A. Preminger et al. (1965), pp. 136-41

(2) Recommended for further reading: Elster, E., *Prinzipien der Literaturwissenschaft* (2 vols., 1897-1911); Gayley, C. M., and Scott, F. N., *An Introduction to the Methods and Materials of Literary Criticism: The Bases in Aesthetics and Poetics* (1899); Larsson, H., *Poesiens logik* (1899); Ribot, R., *Essai sur l'imagination créatrice* (1900); Scott, F. N., "The Most Fundamental Differentia of Poetry and Prose," *PMLA*, XIX (1904), 250-69; Souriau, P., *La Rêverie esthétique: Essai sur la psychologie du poète* (1906); Fauconnet, A., *L'Esthétique de Schopenhauer* (1913); Prescott, F. C., *The Poetic Mind* (1922); Cassirer, E., *Die Philosophie der symbolischen Form* (3 vols., 1923-29; The Philosophy of Symbolic Forms, 3 vols., 1953-57); Jung, C. G., "On the Relation of Analytical Psychology to Poetic Art," *British Journal of Psychology*, III:3 (1923); Baudoin, C., *Le Symbole chez Verhaeren: Essai de psychanalyse de l'art* (1924; Psychoanalysis and Aesthetics, 1924); Cazamian, L., "La Psychanalyse et la critique littéraire," *Revue de Littérature Comparée*, IV (1924), 449; Mauron, C., *The Nature of Beauty in Art and Literature* (1927); Croce, B., "Aesthetics," *Encyclopaedia Britannica* (14th ed., 1929); Ermatinger, E., *Philosophie der Literaturwissenschaft* (1930); Ingarden, R., *Das literarische Kunstwerk* (1931); Griffiths, D. C., *The Psychology of Literary Appreciation* (1932); Hammond, W., *A Bibliography of Aesthetics and the Philosophy of the Fine Arts, 1900-1932* (1933); Read, H., *Form in Modern Poetry* (1933); Bergson, H., *La Pensée et le mouvant* (1934; The Creative Mind, 1946); Rader, M., ed., *A Modern Book of Esthetics: An Anthology* (1935; 3rd ed., 1960); Iredell, J., "Art and Ontology," *Review of Metaphysics*, I (1939), 300-307; Greene, T. M., *The Arts and Art Criticism* (1940); *JAAC* (1941 ff.), annual bibliography issues; Shipley, J. J., ed., *Dictionary of World Literature* (1943); Hoffmann, F. J., *Freudianism and the Literary Mind* (1945); Auerbach, E.,

Mimesis: Dargestellte Wirklichkeit in der abendländischen Literatur (1946; *Mimesis: The Representation of Reality in Western Literature,* 1953); Elton, W., ed., *Aesthetics and Language* (1954); Wimsatt, W. K., *The Verbal Icon* (1954); Osborne, H., *Aesthetics and Criticism* (1955), ch. 7; Huisman, D., and Vergez, A., "Les Grands Courants de l'esthétique contemporaine," *Critiques,* No. 117 (1957), pp. 136-50; Marcuse, L., "Freuds Aesthetik," *PMLA,* LXXII:3 (June 1957) 446-63 (Eng. trans. in *JAAC,* XVII [1958], 1-21); Wahl, J., *Essence et phénomènes: La Poésie comme source de philosophie* (n.d. [1958]); Carritt, F., "Aesthetics," *Encyclopaedia Britannica* (1959); Weber, J.-P., *Genèse de l'oeuvre poétique* (1960); Bayer, R., *Introduction à l'esthétique contemporaine* (1961); Minguet, P., "L'Esthétique: Sémantique aux Etats Unis," *La Revue d'Esthétique,* XV (1962), 43-63; Caws, M. A., "The 'Réalisme ouvert' of Bachelard and Breton," *FR,* XXXVII:3 (1964), 302-11; Preminger, A., Warnke, F. J., and Hardison O. B., Jr., eds., *Encyclopedia of Poetry and Poetics* (1965)

MAX BAYM

LITERARY CRITICISM

Both the 18th and 19th c.s have been called "the age of criticism": surely the 20th c. deserves this title with a vengeance. Not only has a veritable spate of criticism descended upon us, but criticism has achieved a new self-consciousness, a much greater public status, and has developed, in recent decades, new methods and new evaluations. Criticism, which even in the later 19th c. was of no more than local significance outside of France and England, has made itself heard in countries that before seemed on the periphery of critical thought: in Italy since Croce (q.v.), in Russia, in Spain, and, last but not least, in the United States. Any survey of 20th c. criticism must take account of this geographical expansion and of the simultaneous revolution of methods. We need some principles of selection among the mountains of printed matter that confront us.

Obviously even today much criticism is being written that is not new in approach: we are surrounded by survivals, leftovers, throwbacks to earlier stages in the history of criticism. Day-by-day book reviewing still mediates between the author and the general public by the well-tried methods of impressionistic description and arbitrary pronouncements of taste. Historical scholarship continues to be of great importance in evaluative criticism. There will always be a place for simple comparisons between literature and life: for the judging of current novels by standards of probability and accuracy of the social situations reflected in them. In all countries there are writers, and often good writers, who practice these methods marked out by 19th c. criticism: impressionistic appreciation, historical explanation, and realistic comparison. Let us recall the charming evocative essays of Virginia Woolf (q.v.), or the nostalgic vignettes of the American past by Van Wyck Brooks (1886-1963), or the mass of social criticism of the recent American novel, and allude to the contribution which historical scholarship has been making toward a better understanding of almost all periods and authors of literary history. But at the risk of some injustice an attempt will be made to sketch out what seem to be the new trends in 20th c. criticism.

First of all, one is struck by the fact that there are certain international movements in criticism which have transcended the boundaries of any one nation, even though they may have originated in a single nation; that from a very wide perspective a large part of 20th c. criticism shows a remarkable resemblance of aim and method, even where there are no direct historical or cultural relationships. At the same time, one cannot help observing how ingrained and almost unsurmountable national characteristics seem to be: how within the very wide range of Western thought, with cross-currents from Russia to the Americas, from Spain to Scandinavia, the individual nations still tenaciously preserve their own traditions in criticism.

The new trends of criticism, of course, also have roots in the past, are not without antecedents, and are not absolutely original. Still, one can distinguish at least six general trends that have originated in this last half-c.: (1) Marxist criticism; (2) psychoanalytic criticism; (3) myth criticism appealing to the findings of cultural anthropology and the speculations of Carl Jung; (4) linguistic and stylistic criticism; (5) a new organistic formalism; and (6) what amounts to a new philosophical criticism inspired by existentialism (q.v.) and kindred world views.

Marxist Criticism

In taste and in theory Marxist criticism has grown out of the realistic criticism of the 19th c. It appeals to a few pronouncements made by Marx and Engels, but as a systematic doctrine it cannot be found before the last decade of the 19th c. In Germany Franz Mehring (1846-1919) and in Russia Georgii Plekhanov (1856-1918) were the first practitioners of Marxist criticism, but they were very unorthodox from the point of view of later Soviet dogma. Mehring combines Marx with Kant and Darwin: he believes, for instance, in a certain autonomy of art and praises Schiller (in a biography: *Schiller,* 1905) for escaping from the sordid realities of his time. In *Lessing-legende* (1893) Mehring attacks the academic conceptions of Lessing: he emphasizes his loneliness and opposition to the age of Frederick the Great and analyzes the social conditions of the time. But the method he employs is only vaguely sociological: Mehring had not yet grasped Marxist dialectics. Similarly, Plekhanov draws on Darwin to argue for an innate sense of beauty, and in his discussion of the "art for art's sake" doctrine (in *Isskustvo i obshchestvennaya zhizn',* 1912; Art and Social Life, 1953) condemns both aestheticism, as the ineffective revolt of the artist against bourgeois civilization, and purely propagandist art.

Marxist criticism as a coherent theory developed only after the victory of the revolution in Russia; Lenin is unsystematic even in his early papers, such as his attempt to make Tolstoi (q.v.) a representative Russian peasant who had not seen the significance of the proletariat. Marxist criticism crystallized into a coherent system only in the twenties; but even then, in Russia, there were still a good many vacillations, diverse shadings, and compromises allowed. Leon Trotzki (1879-1940), who in *Literatura i revolyutziya* (1924; Literature and Revolution, 1925) sharply attacked formalism, still recognized that art is "a transformation of reality, in accordance with the peculiar laws of art," and Nikolai Bukharin (1888-1938) proposed (at the All Union Congress of Soviet Writers, 1925) a compromise between Marxism and formalism which would allow formalism at least a subordinate position.

Among the strictly Marxist critics in the twenties, several groups can be distinguished: those like Vladimir Pereverzev (b. 1882), who were mainly interested in giving a social explanation for literary phenomena in genetic terms; those who saw in Marxism largely a polemical weapon with which they judged all literature according to its immediate usefulness to the Party; and finally subtler critics, such as Aleksandr Voronski (1884-1935), who thought of art largely as "thinking in images," intuitive and unconscious, which only obliquely reflects the processes of society. But by 1932 all debate was suppressed; a uniform creed was devised and imposed and all the later history of Marxist criticism in Russia is really a history of the Party line and its sinuosities.

The term "socialist realism" is the loose over-all theory which asks the writer, on the one hand, to reproduce reality correctly, accurately, to be a realist in the sense of depicting contemporary society with an insight into its structure; and on the other hand, it asks the writer to be a socialist realist, which in practice means that he is not to reproduce reality accurately, but use his art to spread socialism— that is, communism, the Party spirit, and the Party line.

Andrei Zhdanov (1892-1948) proclaimed that Soviet literature (see Russian literature) cannot be content with "reflecting" or truthfully reporting reality. It must be "instrumental in the ideological molding of the working masses in the spirit of socialism," advice which fitted Stalin's often-quoted saying that writers are "engineers of the human soul." Literature is thus frankly didactic and even idealizing, in the sense that it should show us life not as it is but as it ought to be. Good Marxist theorists understand that art operates with characters and images, actions and feelings. They focus on the concept of type as the bridge between realism and idealization. Type does not mean simply the average, the representative, but it means also the ideal type, the model, or simply the hero which the reader is supposed to imitate and follow in actual life.

Georgii Malenkov (b. 1902) proclaimed (in a speech delivered on 5 Oct. 1952) the "typical, to be the basic sphere of the manifestation of Party spirit in art. The problem of typicalness is always a political problem." The typical allows any and every manipulation of reality which serves the purposes of the Party: one can produce in Russia a simply cartoonlike art, almost in the manner of fairy tales, glorifying the Soviet man, or one can satirize the Russian bourgeoisie and its leftovers. Criticism is almost entirely criticism of the novel and the drama, criticism of characters and types. Authors (e.g., Ehrenburg or Fadeyev [qq.v.]),

285

however orthodox in their ideology, are taken to task for not depicting reality correctly—for example, for not assigning sufficient weight to the Party or for not depicting certain characters favorably enough. Soviet criticism, especially since the war, is besides highly nationalistic and provincial: no suggestion of foreign influences is tolerated and "comparative literature" was long a black-listed subject. The general level of artistic and intellectual standards in criticism is extremely low; even the insights of Marxism into social processes and economic motivation are hardly used. Criticism has become an organ of Party discipline.

Marxism spread abroad, especially in the twenties, and found adherents and followers in most nations. In the United States, F. V. Calverton (1900-1940) and Granville Hicks (b. 1901) were early adherents. Hicks made a systematic though rather innocuous reinterpretation of the history of American literature (q.v.) from a Marxist point of view (*The Great Tradition*, 1928), and Bernard Smith (b. 1906) wrote a history of American criticism (*Forces in American Criticism*, 1939). The actual Marxist movement in American literary criticism was quite short-lived, but the influence of Marxist ideas extends far beyond the strict Party line writers. It is visible in certain stages of the development of Edmund Wilson (q.v.) and Kenneth Burke (b. 1897), for instance. In England, Christopher Caudwell (pseud. of Christopher St. John Sprigg [1907-1937]) was the outstanding Marxist critic, especially with *Illusion and Reality* (1937), a book which draws also on anthropology and psychoanalysis for its weird mixture—a diagnosis of the decay of individualistic civilization and the death of false bourgeois freedom. In France there has been little distinguished Marxist criticism, but again the influence of the theory is felt widely—in Sartre (q.v.), for instance. Recently the work of Lucien Goldmann (b. 1913) on Racine, Pascal (*Le Dieu caché*, 1955), the "New Novel," the avant-garde theater, and on Malraux (q.v.) has attracted much attention. Ideologically Goldman is very close to Georg Lukács (b. 1885). In Italy, Antonio Gramsci (1891-1937), one of the founders of the Italian Communist Party who spent his last eleven years in a fascist jail, is revered as the father of Marxist criticism. He was largely a political ideologist, but his literary studies (collected in *Letteratura e vita nazionale*, 1950) manage to combine a Marxist approach with many motifs derived from the aesthetics of Croce. The strange combination of Marxism and Croceanism is his legacy to many recent Italian critics who try to preserve some of the insights of Croce while abandoning their idealistic basis for dialectical materialism. In the satellite countries Marxism has also been imposed as a general creed, though it has had of course earlier adherents: for example, Bedřich Václavek (1897-1943) in Czechoslovakia.

But by far the most outstanding Marxist critic today is Georg Lukács, not only because he has an extensive knowledge of European literatures and wrote mainly in German (though a Hungarian by birth), but because of the quality and quantity of his production. His many books, *Goethe und seine Zeit* (1947), *Essays über den Realismus* (1947; Studies in European Realism, 1950), *Der russiche Realismus in der Weltliteratur* (1948), *Deutsche Realisten des 19. Jahrhunderts* (1951), *Der historische Roman* (1955; Eng., 1962), etc., combine a thorough grasp of dialectical materialism and its sources in Hegel with a real knowledge of the main German classics and considerable argumentative skill and frequent insights into issues which are not purely political. Lukács, in his exposition of the aesthetics of Marx and Engels, manages to approximate it closely to the main tenets of German classicism, with a strong emphasis on what he calls "the great realism." Lukács tries to reinterpret German classicism as a continuation of the Enlightenment and to trace the destruction of Reason through the 19th c. The results often violate a much more complex reality, but few could deny the illuminative value of seeing Goethe and Schiller, Hölderlin and Heine through the eyes of a consistent Marxist who always looks for progressive elements and emphasizes their social implications.

The writings of Lukács preceding his return from Russia to Hungary in 1945 must be preferred: later he came under strong attack for lack of Marxist orthodoxy and for a time conformed and indulged in purely "Cold War" polemics against the West, particularly in *Die Zerstörung der Vernunft* (1954), where Nietzsche (q.v.) and even Dilthey are made out to be protofascists. In 1956 Lukács was for a short time Minister of Education in the Nagy government and, after the suppression of the Hungarian revolt, was deported to Rumania. But he was allowed to return after a few months, and, in retirement, has since written a large-scale *Aesthetik*, of which the first two volumes were published in 1963.

Lukács's influence in both East and West Germany is widespread: among his early friends Walter Benjamin (q.v.) is an extremely subtle, often obscure and precious student of literature who ranges from German baroque tragedy through romantic critical theory to Baudelaire and Kafka (q.v.). Theodor Wiesengrund Adorno (b. 1903) is primarily a sociologist and critic of music, but his literary essays (*Prismen*, 1955; *Noten zur Literatur,* 3 vols., 1958-65) show the same synthesis of Marxism, leftist Hegelianism, and a modern sensibility acutely conscious of the crisis of civilization, which constitute the appeal of Lukács and Benjamin and much of the appeal of apocalyptic writings of Marxist prophets of the doom of the West.

Psychoanalytic Criticism

Marxism is often at its best when it serves as a device to expose the latent social and ideological implications of a work of art. Psychoanalysis serves, with its very different individualistic and irrationalistic assumptions, the same general purpose: a reading of literature behind its ostensive façade; an unmasking. Freud himself suggested the leading motifs of psychoanalytical criticism (*see* Psychology and Literature). The artist is a neurotic who by his creative work keeps himself from a crack-up, yet also from any real cure. The poet is a daydreamer who publishes his fantasies and is thus strangely socially validated. These fantasies, we all know today, are to be sought in childhood experiences and complexes, and can be found symbolized in dreams, in myths and fairy tales, and even in jokes. Literature thus contains a rich storehouse of evidence for man's subconscious life and it is no accident that Freud drew the term Oedipus complex from Sophocles' play, or interpreted *Hamlet* and *The Brothers Karamazov* as allegories of incestual love and hatred.

But in Freud the literary interest is only peripheral, and he himself always recognized that psychoanalysis does not solve the problems of art. His followers, however, have applied his methods systematically to all literature: *Imago* (1912-38) was the organ devoted to these studies, and among Freud's close followers Wilhelm Stekel (1888-1942), Otto Rank (1884-1929 [see e.g., *Art and Artist,* 1932—partly based on *Der Künstler,* 1907]), Hanns Sachs (1884-1939), and others demonstrated the theories on an enormous variety of materials. Rank

was interested in the interpretation of myths and fairy tales and widened the original, purely individualistic view of literature in the study of the subconscious implications in a work of art, the subconscious drives of a fictional figure, or those to be found in the biography of an author. Also literary historians soon profited from psychoanalysis: for example, Otokar Fischer (1883-1938) analyzed the dreams of Keller's *Grüner Heinrich* (in 1908).

Freudian psychoanalysis spread slowly around the world. An English physician, Ernest Jones (1879-1958), who was later to write a comprehensive study of the master, was the first to give "The Oidipus Complex as an Explanation of Hamlet's Mystery" (in *The American Journal of Psychology,* 1910) and developed this thesis in *Essays in Applied Psychoanalysis* (1923) and again in *Hamlet and Oidipus* (1949). An American, Frederick Prescott (1871-1957)— whose articles, "Poetry and Dreams," date back to 1912—in his study, *The Poetic Mind* (1922), combined psychoanalytic insights into the nature of dreams with a highly romantic concept of the poetic process. In the United States Freudianism penetrated into strictly literary criticism after World War I. Aiken (q.v.), in *Skepticisms* (1919), was an early practitioner, and there is now a mass of psychoanalytical criticism which is not orthodox Freudian but employs the methods of psychoanalysis only occasionally and often loosely: thus Kenneth Burke, or E. Wilson (q.v.) who, in the title essay of *The Wound and the Bow* (1941), uses the Philoctetes legend as an allegory for the artist's compensation for his wound; or Joseph Wood Krutch (b. 1893) with his psychoanalytical interpretation of so obvious a subject as Edgar Allan Poe. A critic such as Lionel Trilling (b. 1905), though deeply interested in psychoanalysis, has voiced many serious reservations about this method of interpretation.

Technical medical analysts have rarely made an impression in literary circles, since they are usually insensitive to texts and artistic values. But an exception should be made in the case of Ernst Kris (1900-1957), whose *Psychoanalytic Explorations in Art* (1952) shows a subtle mind conversant both with clinical method and the aesthetics of art.

Psychoanalytical criticism is in evidence in almost all countries this side of the Iron Curtain. Charles Baudoin (b. 1883), a Swiss, in his book *Le Symbole chez Verhaeren* (1924; Psychoanalysis and Aesthetics, 1924), was an early exponent, while in France today Charles Mauron (1899-1966) is the most widely recognized adherent of the method. His recent book, *Des Métaphores obsédantes au Mythe personnel* (1963) bears the subtitle "Introduction à la psychocritique." But much of Mauron's psychoanalysis shades off into a study of myth. In England Herbert Read (q.v.), in his *In Defence of Shelley* (1936), gave an analytical interpretation of the poet's behavior, somewhat defeating his avowed apologetic intentions, however, by his frank recital of abnormalities; and John Middleton Murry (1889-1957) interpreted D. H. Lawrence (q.v.) in terms of the Oedipus complex in a biography (*Son of Woman: The Story of D. H. Lawrence,* 1931) in which he oddly vacillates between love and hate for his subject.

Myth Criticism

Out of the Freudian analysis grew the Jungian version of the subconscious as a collective subconscious which serves as a kind of reservoir of the "archetypal patterns," the primordial images of mankind. Carl Gustav Jung himself was cautious about applying his philosophy to literature: he made many reservations even when he discussed Joyce's (q.v.) *Ulysses* (1922) or Goethe's *Faust*. But, especially in the Anglo-Saxon world, his caution has been thrown to the winds and a whole group of critics have developed "myth-criticism," that is to say, they have tried to discover behind all literature the original myths of mankind: the Divine Father, the Earth mother, the descent into Hell, the purgatorial stair, the sacrificial deaths of the gods, etc. Modern anthropology, since Frazer, with its new expertise on primitive civilizations, their myths and rituals, from all over the world, and the findings of the so-called "Cambridge school" (Gilbert Murray, Jane Harrison, etc.), which has studied Greek religion and the sources of Greek drama in myth, have supplied arguments and materials for this view.

In England, Maud Bodkin (b. 1875), in *Archetypal Patterns in Poetry* (1934), studies *The Ancient Mariner* and *The Waste Land*, for instance, as poems of the rebirth pattern; Wilson Knight and Herbert Read, in their varied careers, have used Jungian concepts; Day Lewis (q.v.) explains poetic imagery (*The Poetic Image,* 1947) in terms of the survival of mythical thinking. In the United States, "myth criticism" became a great force in the fifties; it was offered as the alternative to the

"New Criticism" and will have to be discussed in its place.

These three trends—Marxism, psychoanalysis, myth criticism—are the only genuinely international ones. The resemblance between all the different movements in individual countries which, by concentrating upon textual interpretation, have reacted against 19th c. positivism, is a very general one: manifest is the preoccupation with the work of art in the modern world, its meaning and the kind of insight or knowledge it provides; and with the refinement of methods of textual analysis, whether it be focused upon details of verbal texture or upon the underlying structure of ideas. To particularize, we have to distinguish between the different national literatures and their diverse developments.

ITALY

The earliest systematic reaction against the conventions of late 19th c. criticism, its antiquarianism, its emphasis on biography, its fragmentation of the work of art, comes from an unexpected quarter—Italy. There Croce (q.v.) transformed Italian criticism and, with his *Estetica* (1902; Eng., 1909), influenced profoundly the course of criticism almost everywhere in the world. In Germany a school of brilliant scholars in the romance literatures (especially Karl Vossler) was deeply indebted to him. In England R. W. Collingwood's *Principles of Art* (1934) could be described as a Crocean aesthetics, and in the United States Joel E. Spingarn proclaimed a diluted version of Croce, *The New Criticism,* in 1911.

Croce, in an early booklet, *La Critica letteraria* (1894), had attacked the confused state of criticism and had appealed to the model of the great 19th c. historian of Italian literature (q.v.), Francesco De Sanctis, who then, as a Hegelian, was under an eclipse. But only with the founding of the review *La Critica* (since 1903) did Croce's influence on Italian criticism become decisive. Croce's position, expounded in *Estetica,* had first a negative influence on criticism: his theory of art as intuition, which completely identifies intuition with expression, radically disposed of many traditional problems. Art for Croce is not a physical fact, but purely a matter of mind; it is not pleasure; it is not morality; it is not science, nor is it philosophy. There is no special artistic genius; there is no distinction between form and content. The common view that Croce is a "formalist" or a defender of "art for art's sake" is, however, mistaken. Art does play a role in society and can even be controlled socially, though nothing can touch the artist's original act of intuition. In his practical criticism Croce pays no attention to form in the ordinary sense, but rather to what he calls the "leading sentiment." In Croce's radical monism there is no place for rhetorical categories, for style, for symbol, for genres, even for the distinctions among the arts, since every work of art is a unique, individual intuition-expression. In Croce, the creator, the work, and the auditor are identified. The true reader becomes a poet. Criticism can do little more than remove obstacles to this identification, and pronounce that the identification has been achieved, that a work is art or non-art. Croce's theory hangs together remarkably well and is not open to objections which neglect its basis in an idealistic metaphysics. If we object that Croce neglects medium, or technique, he can answer that "what is external is no longer a work of art."

In the course of his development Croce somewhat modified his position. He came to recognize the universalizing power of art, while still insisting that art does not provide any intellectual knowledge; he retracted the romantic implications of his expressionism (q.v.), which seemed to recommend emotion and passion. Rather, he endorsed "classicity," which must not be confused with rhetorical classicism. He also redefined the role of criticism in more intellectual terms: it becomes identified with aesthetics and philosophy. The aim of criticism is the characterization of an individual author, its form is the essay. There is no literary history (except external annals and compendia), as every poet is *sui generis*. Sociological and nationalistic histories of literature (Taine, Brandes [q.v.]) as well as the idea of stylistic evolution (Wölfflin) are dismissed as external.

Croce produced a stream of essays in which he tries to define the true sentiment of each writer discussed and to judge him by his, Croce's, intuitive standard. In his short work *Goethe* (1919; Eng., 1923) he completely divorces man and work from each other. Gundolf's worship of his *Gestalt* is rejected as aesthetic decadence. Problems of philosophical truth, biographical correspondence, and intentions can be dismissed. Croce can make a selection from Goethe's works and can discuss *Faust* as an album in which Goethe entered his feelings at different times of his life. There is no unity to the two parts. But this is not destructive criticism; rather, Croce argues, it removes an artificially imposed mechanism.

Similarly, in his *La poesia di Dante* (1920; The Poetry of Dante, 1922), Croce draws a sharp distinction between the "theological-political romance" and the structure as an abstract scheme, and the poetry which grows around and in it. In a later book, *La Poesia* (1936), he elaborates with great clarity his distinction between "poetry" and "literature": while "literature" is writing in its civilizing function, tied up with society, "poetry" remains unique, immediately accessible intuition-expression. In many other books of essays Croce judges Italian and foreign poets severely. In *Poesia e non poesia* (1923; European Literature in the Nineteenth Century, 1924), for instance, Schiller is labeled a philosophical rhetorician, not a poet. Kleist, on the other hand, was merely striving by will power to become a poet; but he did not succeed. Walter Scott is only a hero in a history of commerce. Croce's method is particularly well exemplified in *Ariosto, Shakespeare e Corneille* (1920; Eng., 1920). Here, the leading sentiment of Ariosto is defined as a desire for cosmic harmony, that of Corneille as the ideal of free will. In practice, his emphasis on the uniqueness of the work of art leads Croce to highly generalized and rather empty definitions.

Croce's taste is very pronounced: he despises the baroque as a form of ugliness and dislikes modern decadence (D'Annunzio [q.v.]), symbolism (q.v.), and "pure art" *à la* Valéry (q.v.). In Croce the monistic theory led increasingly to a critical paralysis; his last books are little more than anthologies of passages, with comments on contents and feelings. Croce's great historical learning came increasingly to obscure his criticism. Literary history, psychology, biography, sociology, philosophical interpretation, stylistics, genre criticism—all are ruled out in Croce's scheme. We revert to an intuitionism which, in practice, is hard to distinguish from impressionism—which isolates appealing passages, or anthologizes arbitrarily and from an unargued pronouncement of judgments.

Yet Italian criticism of the last fifty years has been almost completely dominated by Croce. Among his followers there is erudition, there is taste, there is judgment, but, on the other hand, we find no systematic analysis of texts, no *Geistesgeschichte*, no stylistics. Several critical individualities stand out, who differ often in emphasis and taste. One of these is Francesco Flora, (1891-1962) author of the five-volume *Storia della letteratura italiana* (1940-42; revised ed., 1947-49), a diffuse, florid, enthusiastic history which combines great erudition, a Crocean emphasis on intuition and individuality, with a taste very different from Croce's. Flora loves the baroque and the decadent and wrote various books (*Dal Romanticismo al Futurismo,* 1921; *D'Annunzio, I miti della parola,* 1931; *La poesia ermetica,* 1936) which reveal his sympathy for the viewpoint that sees poetry as metaphor and for the modernist trends which Croce deprecated. Flora is a colorful, sensual writer engaged in communicating the pleasure and even the voluptuousness of fine poetry, a master of evocation and description rather than a judicial critic.

Attilio Momigliano (1883-1952), though Crocean in many ways, is a sensitive psychologist and impressionistic critic, a delicate reader and interpreter of poetry, subtle, refined, even morbidly so, cautious and scrupulous. His *Storia della letteratura italiana* (1948) is a masterpiece of compression and carefully weighed characterization. Momigliano has, besides, written on Ariosto (*Saggio sull' Orlando Furioso,* 1928), and, with increasing devotion, repeatedly on Manzoni and his novel, *I promessi sposi* (1827), whose characters he has analyzed in great detail (see *L'Innominato,* 1913; *Commento ai Promessi sposi,* 1951).

Luigi Russo (1892-1962) is an ideologist, a theoretician, (e.g., *Problemi di metodo critico,* 1929; *La critica letteraria contemporanea,* 3 vols., 1942-43), a brilliant, though violent polemicist who has great social and moral concerns at heart. As a practical critic he is at his best in a book on Verga (*Giovanni Verga,* 1919) or in his *Macchiavelli* (1945) rather than with poets in a strict sense. His taste tends to the impersonal and realistic. Still, it is surprising that this orthodox Crocean should have been able to turn to Marxism in his last years.

As theorist and historian of criticism the most outstanding of the Croceans is Mario Fubini (b. 1900), who has written a long series of studies on the history of Italian criticism (e.g., *Dal Muratori al Baretti,* 1946), on Italian literature, mainly of the 18th c. and the romantic movement (on Vico, Parini, Alfieri, Foscolo, etc.), and has been working toward a solidly founded theory of criticism and literature. *Critica e poesia* (1956) shows a slow emancipation from orthodox Croceanism, especially in a learned study of the history of genre theories.

These men illustrate the enormous success Croce had in changing Italian academic scholarship: they are all literary historians, of great erudition, who still remain critics vitally concerned with the judgment of literature.

But the earliest Croceans who plunged into literary life proved unfaithful disciples. Giuseppe Borgese (q.v.) started his with a Crocean work, *Storia della critica romantica in Italia* (1905), in which he propounded the odd thesis that Italian romanticism is good classicism. More and more, however, Borgese became a declamatory apocalyptic prophet of art as the "transfiguration of man and figuration of God," absorbed in such questions as the meaning of Italian literature in general (which was and is to produce a "sacred, eternal, celestial art"). In later years Borgese (he emigrated to the United States in 1931) devoted his energies to projects for a "World Constitution." Nevertheless, his collection of essays, *Poetica dell' Unità* (1934), contains fervent polemics against Croce and his denial of a unified history of poetry, and a sketch of the history of criticism. In general, Borgese holds a romantic collectivist view of literature in the Hegelian tradition.

Alfredo Gargiulo (1876-1949), an early collaborator in Croce's *La Critica,* also moved away from his master's theories. While his book *D'Annunzio* (1912) was a Crocean attempt to distinguish between the maker of naturalistic myths and singer of lyrical landscapes and the decadent *poseur, La letteratura italiana nel novecento* (1930-33) shows Gargiulo's taste for symbolism and the Italian hermetic poets (Ungaretti [q.v.] in particular), and many papers on aesthetics (collected in *Scritti di Estetica,* 1952) argue effectively against several of Croce's central doctrines. Gargiulo developed a theory of "expressive means" which allowed him to reintroduce into aesthetics and literary theory a classification of the arts and concepts of medium and genre dismissed by Croce.

Besides the Crocean tradition, which positively or sometimes polemically at odds with the master has dominated Italian criticism, one can distinguish a second trend which is largely independent of general aesthetics and philosophy and has followed rather the tradition of French criticism: the psychological portrait, the close reading and tasting of a text.

Renato Serra (1884-1915), who was killed in World War I, has left a few essays, letters, and diaries, which are the earliest examples of what in Italy is called "criticism of the fragment." But Serra was rather a moralist, a dreamer and solitary who used criticism as self-examination (*Esame di coscienza di un letterato*, 1916) than a close student of texts. Textual, stylistic methods were developed in Italy mainly by Giuseppe de Robertis (1888-1963), who has written innumerable, often tiny essays interpreting specific passages of the poets: their sound and sense, associations and implications, which surprisingly enough lead him often to final obscurities and gestures toward mysticism (e.g., *Saggi*, 1939; *Studi*, 1944; *Saggio sul Leopardi*, 1949).

Among younger men, Gianfranco Contini (b. 1912) is the best of the close readers. He is linguistically learned and stays away from mysticism (see *Esercizi di lettura*, 1947). In subject matter his range is wide, writing as he does on the earliest Italian lyricists as well as on the latest, the most opaque, modernists.

Two other linguists who have developed new divergent methods of stylistic analysis, are Giacomo Devoto (b. 1897) and Antonio Pagliaro (b. 1898).

Somewhat apart stand three critics, all close students of American and English literature (qq.v.): Cecchi (q.v.), Mario Praz (b. 1896), and Pavese (q.v.). Cecchi began his writing career with *Storia della letteratura inglese nel secolo XIX* (1915), which never progressed beyond the first volume, devoted to the English romantics. Even here he shows his power of evocation and portraiture more in the style of Sainte-Beuve or Pater than in the Italian tradition. In his later writings he indulges in a curious sly humor and irony and in personal, often capricious judgments. *Scrittori inglesi e americani* (1946) is a collection of his many essays on English and American writers, with an emphasis on what could be called the "dark," irrational, and violent tradition in American and English literature: Melville, Faulkner (q.v.), Hemingway (q.v.), and D. H. Lawrence (q.v.). Cecchi, oddly enough, combines this taste with a penchant for witty writers such as Chesterton and Beerbohm (qq.v.). Besides, Cecchi has written also on many Italian topics (e.g., *Di giorno in giorno*, 1954) as a general essayist, the master of the "terza pagina," in the newspaper.

The starting point of Mario Praz is also English literature, of which he is an extremely erudite student. His early book, *Secentismo e marinismo in Inghilterra* (1925), devoted to Donne and Crashaw, helped to restore the two great English baroque poets to their rightful place. In many other books he has studied Italian-English relations (e.g., Macchiavelli in

England) with acumen and skill. He surveyed English literature in *Storia della letteratura inglese* (1937), which is much more than an excellent textbook. But with *La Carne, la morte e il diavolo nella letteratura romantica* (1930; The Romantic Agony, 1933) Praz went beyond his specialty to a subtle study of erotic sensibility in all 19th c. Europe, seen in terms of its sources in the Marquis de Sade and as a part of the general phenomenon of decadence. *La crisi dell' eroe nel romanzo vittoriano* (1952; The Hero in Eclipse in Victorian Fiction, 1956) shows a surprising change or broadening of Praz's taste: a sympathy for the idyllic, realistic art of the *Biedermeier*, which he traces from Dutch genre painting to the novels of Trollope, Thackeray, and George Eliot. Increasingly, in a number of essay collections (e.g., *Gusto neoclassico*, 1940; *La Casa della Fama*, 1952), Praz has tried to use the art of the essayist to define a personal taste and paint his own intellectual portrait. He studies either the psychology of the author, or the sensibility of a time, or the linkage of literature with the plastic arts. He is not so much a day-by-day critic of literature as a scholar-critic, not a theorist but a historian of sensibility and taste.

Pavese, the novelist, has as a critic introduced new motifs into Italian literature. Like Cecchi, he is an admirer of American literature (*La letteratura americana e altri saggi*, 1951), or rather of one strand in it: the mystic, the dark and violent he finds in Melville and Sherwood Anderson (q.v.). But his remarkable diary (*Il mestiere di vivere: Diario 1935-1950*, 1951; This Business of Living, 1961) has revealed a speculative critic of high order concerned with themes usually neglected in Italian criticism: with myth become figure, with time in the novel, and with pervasive imagery similar to that of Wilson Knight in England. Pavese calls his ideal "rustic classicism," which seems, finally, a primitivistic and naturalistic view in spite of all its sophistication.

But Pavese stands alone. The direction of recent Italian criticism seems unclear except for two facts: the dominance of Croce and Croceanism is waning and, at this moment, Marxist criticism seems to have found many recruits.

FRANCE

France, around 1900, was the country with the strongest critical tradition. It could look back to Sainte-Beuve and Taine, who had reestablished the leadership of France in criticism during the latter half of the 19th c. In France the divorce between scholarship and criticism never became so acute as in the other countries, and there was then a flourishing "university criticism" which combined erudition with taste, usually of a conservative kind. Ferdinand Brunetière (1849-1906), a doctrinaire upholder of 17th c. classicism who also propounded a Darwinian theory of the evolution of genres, Emile Faguet (1847-1916), an extremely versatile commentator on all periods of French literature (q.v.), and Gustave Lanson (1857-1934), the author of the most widely used *Histoire de la littérature française* (1894), were still active and influential in the early 20th c. Besides the historian-critics, the bulk of criticism was impressionist: as a theory, impressionism had been proclaimed by Jules Lemaître (1853-1914) late in the 19th c., but even he, in his later years, embraced a conservative creed which led to his sharp condemnation of Rousseau and all romanticism.

The basically rationalistic, classicist tradition of French criticism continued deep into the 20th c. and had its important revivals. Maurras (q.v.), the founder of the Action Française, had critical affiliations with the so-called École Romane (Moréas [q.v.]). He proclaimed Latinity, reason, and conservatism as its standards and condemned the Revolution and romanticism (which strangely enough were conceived as almost identical). Pierre Lasserre (1867-1930), in *Le Romantisme français* (1907), attacked romanticism and all its works as a disease due to the psychopath Jean-Jacques Rousseau, and (Baron) Ernest Seillière (1866-1955) wrote an unending series of books denouncing romanticism, Germans, and imperialism.

After World War I a purely rationalistic point of view, proclaimed to be particularly French, was restated powerfully in Julien Benda's (1867-1956) *Belphégor* (1919), and in the writings of Henri Massis (1886-1956), who had begun by attacking Lanson and academic criticism and later wrote *La Défense de l'Occident* (1925), a strident proclamation of Western, Latin values against everything Northern and Eastern. The widely read, largely journalistic critic, Paul Souday (1869-1929), can be classed with these defenders of reason, intellectualism, art as construction, and haters of everything vague, mystical, sentimental, romantic, symbolic, and irrational. Among more recent critics Ramon Fernandez (1894-1944) was nearest to the conservative classicism of the Action Française. He has on many points striking affinities

with T. S. Eliot (q.v.), sharing as he does the latter's search for objectivity and impersonality. The collection of essays, *Messages* (1926; Eng., 1927), strongly urges the claim of criticism to yield an "imaginative ontology." The metaphysical problem of being is to be solved in art, though transposed to the plane of imagination. The world of poetry is a world of quality, not a reflection of an author's psyche. Criticism should investigate the philosophical substructure of a work of art and not the biography or psychology of an author or his overt intentions. In an essay on Stendhal, Fernandez shows, for instance, how even so autobiographical an author uses private experiences only as building materials for his books. Unfortunately, Fernandez did not live up to the promise of his early work: in his last books, *Balzac* (1943) and *Proust* (1943), he pursues philosophical themes with some moralistic obtuseness: in Balzac, he argues, intuition, conception, and expression remain unfused. In Proust, there is no way from passive impression to an external world of action, no moral progress.

But clearly the classical, rationalist, and moralist point of view, though important in the Academy and in arguments on general culture, lost out to the much more powerful stream of irrationalism which has flooded French criticism in the last fifty years. One must distinguish among these irrationalisms, however, and must not obscure the strength of the classical tradition in men such as Valéry (q.v.). One must recognize different strands and chronological groupings. Symbolism (q.v.) might be considered one central critical motif, Bergsonism another, Catholicism a third, within which, however, we must distinguish between mystical thinkers and more rationalistic Neo-Thomists.

A fourth definite movement is surrealism (q.v.) and, after World War II, existentialism (q.v.). Some of these classifications are not clear-cut. A Catholic poet such as Claudel (q.v.) was a symbolist in his poetic theories; the Catholics Péguy (q.v.) and Charles Du Bos (1882-1939) felt the strong impact of Bergson (q.v.). One can speak today of a Catholic existentialism and the term Bergsonism must not always be interpreted technically: it might be combined with an interest in Freud (see Psychology and Literature) and find ways to agree with the Church. The situation is extremely fluid, the boundary lines fluctuate. The methods of French criticism of the last fifty years are mostly intuitive and often impressionistic: its form is the essay ([q.v.] so much so that many critics seem never to have written a proper book). The interest in a systematic theory is small, as criticism is conceived as an art and a means of self-expression and self-discovery rather than a body of knowledge and judgments.

Symbolism as a poetic movement was apparently on the decline since the beginning of the c., though Baudelaire, Mallarmé, and Rimbaud actually determined the course of modern French poetry and supplied also a body of poetic doctrine. Early in the c. the prolific critic de Gourmont (q.v.) can be described as a popularizer of the symbolist creed, though de Gourmont had nothing of Mallarmé's austerity and has often pronounced tones of elegant *fin de siècle* decadentism. His best books, such as *Le Problème du style* (1902), with its advocacy of bright, visual, concrete writing, and his analytical skill in the "disassociation of ideas," provided important suggestions for the imagism of Pound (q.v.) and the early criticism of T. S. Eliot.

The great poet Claudel, an intensely proselytizing Catholic, formulated a new version of symbolist poetics: image is the essence of poetry. Poetry, unlike prose, which gives us knowledge of reality, provides us with an equivalent or *species* of reality. The poet does not tell us what a thing is, but what it means, what is its place in the universe, which is a unity, linked by correspondences, surrounding us with "figures of eternity." Claudel's *L'art poétique* (1907) ranges from an immediate vision of God's universe to close prescriptions for the reform of French verse as reflecting the rhythm of the soul, rather than the mind, *anima* rather than *animus*.

A basically symbolist poetics was also formulated by Valéry in writings which in part date back to the nineties, but belong largely to the period between the wars. The five volumes of *Variété* (1924-44; Eng., 2 vols., 1929, 1938), especially, have carried his views on poetry to a wide audience, in a fragmentary fashion. But if we supplement these essays by many other pronouncements in lectures and notebooks a coherent theory of poetics emerges which is both striking and original. Valéry, more radically than anybody else, asserts a discontinuity between author, work, and reader. He stresses the importance of form divorced from emotion and takes poetry completely out of history into the realm of the absolute. For

Valéry, there is first a deep gulf between creative process and work. At times it seems as if Valéry were hardly interested in the work, but only in this process of creation. He did not publish for twenty years and seemed content to analyze the creativity of genius in general. His ideal was the universal man, a Leonardo da Vinci. Later he wrote subtle, introspective descriptions of the process of composing his poems, always citing evidence for the distance between the original idea, the germ which might be, in a word, a rhyme, a line, or a melody, and the finished product. For Valéry poetry is not inspiration, not dream, but a making with a mind wide-awake. Poetry must be impersonal to be perfect. Emotional art, art appealing to sensibility, seems to him always inferior. A poem should aim to be "pure," absolute poetry, free from factual, personal, and emotional admixtures. It cannot be paraphrased, it cannot be translated. It is a tight universe of sound and meaning, so closely interlocked that we cannot distinguish content and form. Poetry exploits the resources of language to the utmost, removing itself from ordinary speech by the use of sound and meter and all the devices of metaphorics. Poetic language is a language within language, language completely formalized. To Valéry poetry is both a calculus, an exercise, even a game, and a song, a chant, an enchantment, a charm. It is figurative and incantatory: a compromise between sound and meaning, which by its conventions, even arbitrary conventions, achieves the ideal work of art, unified, beyond time, absolute. This ideal is realized most fully in Mallarmé and in Valéry's own poetry.

The novel (q.v.), with its plot complications and irrelevancies, and tragedy, with its appeal to violent emotions, seem to Valéry inferior genres, even not quite art. The novel is historical and hence contingent, it makes claims to truth in relation to an external reality. It can be summarized and easily changed in its details, without damage, as a poem cannot.

Valéry's ideal of poetry is absolute, frozen into the grandeur of pure form. Surprisingly enough, what seems a dense objective structure is to Valéry open to many interpretations. A work of art is essentially ambiguous. "My verses have the meaning which one gives to them," is Valéry's famous paradox, which allows even for "creative misunderstanding." The door seems open for critical caprice and anarchy, but Valéry's own practical criticism— limited in scope mainly to authors such as

Mallarmé and Poe, his "pure" poets, or to universal examples of creativity like Goethe and Leonardo—preserves an admirable lucidity and balance. It defends a position which seems extreme in its austerity and vulnerable for its discontinuities. But it has been fruitful in asserting a central concern of modern poetics: the discovery of pure representation, the "unmediated vision," for which two other great poets of the c., Rilke (q.v.) and Eliot, were also searching. Valéry stands alone in splendid isolation, though the affinities of his theories with Mallarmé's are obvious. In a wide perspective, he could be seen as bringing symbolism back to the classical tradition.

Proust has also restated symbolist theory, with important modifications. Though often disguised in discussions of music and painting, Proust, especially in the last volume—*Le Temps retrouvé* (2 vols., 1927; Eng., Time Regained, 1930-31; Am., The Past Recaptured, 1932)—of his novel-cycle. *À la recherche du temps perdu* (1913-27; Remembrance of Things Past, 1922-31) expounds an aesthetics relevant to literature. The artist is concerned with a knowledge of "essences" recovered by involuntary memory: he fixes the fleeting qualitative side of the world, in his own particular singular emotion. Symbolism and Bergsonism are reconciled. Besides, Proust occasionally commented on strictly literary matters: in his introduction to his early translations from Ruskin, in curious reflections on the style of Flaubert ("À propos du style de Flaubert," in *NRF* [1920]) and in an acid attack on the biographical approach of Sainte-Beuve, which was only discovered comparatively recently (*Contre Sainte-Beuve,* 1954; On Art and Literature 1896-1919, 1958).

But the group which assembled around *Nouvelle Revue française,* founded by Gide (q.v.) in 1909, was most influential in defining the new taste of the c. The main contributors can hardly be reduced to a common denominator: but Bergson loomed in the background with his philosophy of flux, of the concrete and the immediate. Gide himself was hardly an important critic, though the *Journals* are full of literary opinions and his book *Dostoïevski* (1923; Eng., 1926) searchingly probes ethical problems on the occasion of Dostoyevski. The reigning spirit was Rivière (q.v.), who died too early to fulfill his promise. The early *Études* (1908) show him as the first sensitive expounder of Claudel and Gide. After his return from German captivity in World War I, as editor of *Nouvelle Revue française* he did much to spread the growing fame of Proust. He saw Proust rather as a classicist, that is, as a detached observer, and interpreted him also in Freudian terms. But Rivière is not sufficiently described as a psychological critic of considerable finesse and warmth: he is a figure of psychological interest himself, a man who first grappled with religion and then attempted to find himself in a theory of sincerity toward oneself. To him criticism is self-discovery, a way toward a definition of the meaning of life, best exemplified in his essays collected under the title *Nouvelles études* (1927; The Ideal Reader, 1960).

Rivière was soon eclipsed by Albert Thibaudet (1874-1936), a voluminous writer who filled the *NRF* with his essays for many years and produced, besides many monographs, an unfinished work, *Histoire de la littérature française* (1937). Thibaudet is somewhat like a modern Sainte-Beuve: he has his versatility and his aversion to clear-cut conclusions and theories. If he has a philosophical outlook, it is that of Bergsonism. He likes to surrender to the flux of impressions, to embrace a literary pantheism. He interpreted, always sympathetically, Mallarmé, Maurice Barrès (1862-1923), Valéry, and Flaubert in separate books. In his *History* he shows his skill in surveying masses: he ranges his authors in a succession of generations and manages to suggest the chain of tradition, the flow of time. Thibaudet is haunted by the vision of a literary landscape, a "Republic of Letters." He evokes the soil, the province, the place of an author. He has a strong feeling and sympathy for regionalism, which is combined with a genuine vision of European solidarity. Sympathy, even at the expense of judgment, is Thibaudet's main trait. He even imitates the style of the writer he discusses, almost compulsively. He seems like a chameleon, elusive, indistinctive. The two books, ostensibly devoted to a theory of criticism, *Physiologie de la critique* (1930) and *Réflexions sur la critique* (1939), are hardly more than random notes. Nowhere is there an attempt to define a position: it emerges largely by implication, in his admiration for Hugo and Flaubert, in his coolness to Balzac, Vigny, and Baudelaire. A final romantic vein seems to prevail.

In his psychological probing, and his impressionistic technique, Charles Du Bos was in his early stages related to Rivière. Du Bos is much more labored, earnest, groping, yet also much wider in range. In contrast to Rivière and Thibaudet, whose horizon was almost exclusively French, Du Bos knew English and German literature (q.v.) well. He wrote extensively on Wordsworth, Shelley, Keats, Browning, and Pater, and produced a full-length psychological study of Byron (*Byron et le besoin de la fatalité*, 1929; Eng., 1932). He studied Goethe in detail. In 1927 Du Bos became a convert and since then developed a concept of literature which must be described as mystical. His English book, *What Is Literature?* (1938) hinges on key-words such as "soul," "light," and "word," leading up to a "beatific vision," an ecstatic communion of the critic with the seers and sages. But this is only Du Bos's last stage: earlier he wrote much on the psychology of writers, the creative process, the concrete detail of a work of art, always with a Bergsonian fear of abstraction, a sense of life which he found also in the complexities of Henry James (q.v.) and Robert Browning. The seven volumes of *Approximations* (1922-37), which contain some of the most distinguished criticism of the time, are also typical for the course they describe: from a worship of beauty for its own sake to a glorification of God's presence, from the pleasures of sensation to the "essence" embodied in literature.

Du Bos in his concept of poetry is related to the Abbé Henri Bremond (1865-1933), the historian of religious feeling in France, who in *Poésie et Prière* (1926) and *De la poésie pure* (1926) almost identified poetry with prayer, or rather with mystical exaltation.

But within the Catholic renaissance there was a more intellectual movement, Neo-Thomism, Aristotelianism, which found a powerful spokesman in Jacques Maritain (b. 1882). He is the best known convert (in 1906), the most widely influential Catholic philosopher. Criticism is only one of his many activities. Still, *Art et scolastique* (1920; Art and Scholasticism, 1930) and *Situation de la poésie* (1938; The Situation of Poetry, 1955) did much to define a Neo-Thomist aesthetics. In his later book in English, *Creative Intuition in Art and Poetry* (1953), Maritain moved in the direction of straight mysticism. The argument is still Neo-Scholastic, but is also Neo-Platonist, even visionary. The Thomist concept of making a work of art for human needs is now combined with a belief in free creation, an inner subjectivity. Maritain, the great foe of Cartesian subjectivism, ends with a hymn to intuitive subjectivity, to revelation, even to dark unconscious creation, to

mystery and magic. Maritain admires not only English romantic poetry but also surrealism.

Surrealism is the extreme of irrationalism. It grew out of Dada (see Dadaism) and cubism, which found a rather halting theorist in Apollinaire (q.v.) just before World War I. But surrealism as a movement is largely due to the organizing and propagandizing zeal of Breton (q.v.), who composed its first manifesto in 1924. The artist is to reveal the confusion of the world; he is to contribute to the total discredit of what is usually called reality. The poetic state implies a complete renunciation of reason. Automatic writing is its technique, the dream is its model. Complete anarchy, emancipation from reason, God, morality, is proclaimed with flamboyant rhetoric and an air of assurance which suggests the circus barker.

World War II brought a reaction against all theories of pure art, all concepts which suggest the "ivory tower" or civic irresponsibility. The watchword became *la littérature engagée*, as formulated by Sartre (q.v.). But Sartre is a philosopher, the main French propounder of existentialism long before the war, and he cannot be described as a simple advocate of the social responsibility of the arts, though he has moved more and more in the direction of Marxism. *Qu'est-ce que la littérature?* (1947; What Is Literature?, 1949) is actually an impassioned plea for a metaphysical conception of art. The rights of pure poetry are recognized. The final goal of art is not very different from Schiller's dream of an aesthetic education: " . . . to recover this world by giving it to be seen as it is, but as if it had its source in human freedom."

Sartre speaks well of the varying relationship between writer and public in history and has discussed the American novelists of violence (Faulkner, Dos Passos [qq.v.]) in terms of this assertion of human freedom. But imagination is suspect to Sartre—shattered by the first contact with the absurdity and horror of real existence. The Bohemian type of artist is suspect, too. Sartre has made a cruel psychoanalytical study, *Baudelaire* (1947; Eng., 1950). In spite of all the meanness and rottenness he finds in Baudelaire, he approves his search for "being" rather than mere "existence," his defiance of destiny freely chosen. In a diffuse and turgid book, *Saint-Genet: comédien et martyr* (1952; Saint-Genet, Comedian and Martyr, 1963), a homosexual, thief, and convict is used as an example of a criticism which identifies work and author completely and wishes to convince us that good is evil and evil good. The paradoxes of Sartre's phenomenology cannot, however, succeed in making an author on the margin of literature appear a great writer.

Existentialist assumptions and motifs permeate recent French criticism, which has become increasingly philosophical, metaphysical, and often gropingly obscure as a result. Two outstanding authors—not primarily concerned with literary criticism—defined the new attitude toward art most memorably. Malraux (q.v.), in his grand survey of the plastic arts, *Les Voix du silence* (1951; The Voices of Silence, 1953), makes art appear as man's triumph over destiny. Camus (q.v.), in *L'Homme révolté* (1951; The Rebel, 1956), sees art as a tool in man's revolt against his human condition; art as conquering even death.

The attitudes, ideas, and methods of these great writers reverberate in more strictly literary and academic criticism. There they combine with suggestions which come from the writings of Gaston Bachelard (1884-1963), a somewhat fantastic philosopher of nature who calls his method psychoanalysis, but is, rather, related to Jung. He studies the elements (fire, water, air, earth) in literature and traces the distortions imposed by the imagery of poets in such books as *La Psychoanalyse de feu* (1938), *L'Eau et les rêves* (1942), *L'Air et les songes* (1933), *La Terre et les rêveries du repos* (1948), *La Poétique et l'espace* (1958). A whole group of French critics can be said to combine existentialist and "myth" interests in order to develop a special method which they call *"critique de conscience."* They aim less at analysis or judgment of works of art than at the reconstruction of the particular "consciousness" of each writer. Every writer is assumed to live in his peculiar unique world, which has certain interior structures which it is the task of the critic to discover. The emphasis on different aspects and the philosophical affiliations of these critics vary. The oldest among them, Marcel Raymond (b. 1897), in his *De Baudelaire au surréalisme* (1935; From Baudelaire to Surrealism, 1949), traces the myth of modern poetry to its sources in Baudelaire. Raymond is interested in the claim of poets such as Mallarmé and the surrealists that words are more than symbols, that they can share in the essence of being, that the absolute is somehow incarnated in their work. He is a learned literary scholar who has written well on Ronsard, the baroque, and Rousseau.

In Albert Béguin (1901-1957) the religious motivation is dominant. In his first book, *L'Âme romantique et le rêve* (1939), he studies German romanticism and the French writers who went the same way: Rousseau, Hugo, Nerval, and he ends with Baudelaire, Rimbaud, Mallarmé, and Proust. Béguin admires German romanticism because it recognized and affirmed the profound resemblance of poetic states and the revelations of a religious order. Romanticism and all poetry is a myth which leads into the dream, the unconscious, and finally into the presence of God. In later writings—in *Balzac visionnaire* (1946) and in his books on Bloy (q.v.), Péguy, Bernanos (q.v.), etc.—Béguin has become identified with a Catholic mysticism.

Georges Poulet (b. 1902) has, on the other hand, absorbed scholasticism, Descartes, and Bergson, and is primarily interested in the concept and feeling of time in writings and poets. His books, *Études sur le temps humain* (1950; Studies in Human Time, 1956), *La Distance intérieure* (1952; The Interior Distance, 1959), and *Les Metamorphoses du Cercle* (1962; The Metamorphoses of the Circle, 1967) trace a general history of French thought and feeling in terms of time with unparalleled ingenuity.

Jean-Pierre Richard (b. 1922) is related to Poulet in his method, though *Littérature et Sensation* (1954) and *Poésie et Profondeur* (1955) show his special interest in the perceptive life of the authors (Stendhal, Flaubert, Nerval, Baudelaire, Rimbaud) discussed. We are told, for example, that to Flaubert love is like drowning, or that the lover loses his bones, becomes like plastic paste. Sentences and observations, metaphors and scenes from all books and letters of an author are used indiscriminately to build up a scheme of his mental life, organized by leading motives and obsessions.

Somewhat apart from these critics stands Blanchot (q.v.), the most difficult and obscure of the group, who, in *L'espace littéraire* (1955), discusses such questions as "Whether Literature Is Possible?" or the "Space of Death," using Kafka (q.v.), Mallarmé, and Hölderlin as his favorite examples. Blanchot arrives at a strange nihilism: silence is the ultimate significance of literature, the only thing left to express.

Fortunately there are other more articulate and more rational critics in France. All share the general method and philosophical preoccupations, but remain committed to clarity. Mme. Claude-Edmonde Magny (d. 1966), in *Les Sandales d'Empédocle* (1945), expounds her philosophical method, which she then applies to Kafka, Charles Morgan, and Sartre lucidly; and Picón (q.v.), in *L'Écrivain et son ombre* (1953), has begun a systematic exposition of a theory of literature which does seem to indicate a return to aesthetic considerations. Obviously the danger of existentialist criticism is its neglect of the work as an aesthetic fact. The work is broken up or ignored in favor of the act of creation and the mind of the poet. Except for recent American attempts to emulate the French method, the gulf between French and Anglo-American criticism has become very deep indeed.

SPAIN, PORTUGAL, AND LATIN AMERICA

Spain, in the 19th c., had no great critical tradition. The dominant figure who survived into the 20th c., Marcelino Menéndez y Pelayo (1856-1912), was rather a polyhistor, an enormously productive compiler of histories of literature and ideas, than a critic. *Estudios de critica literaria* (1884-1908) are historical studies rather than criticism. His general outlook is that of Catholic romanticism.

Genuine criticism begins in Spain with the "Generation of '98," the group of brilliant writers who—after the catastrophe of the Spanish-American War—began to examine the reasons for the decay of Spain. These Spanish authors are preoccupied with the problem of nationality, a definition of *Casticismo* and *Hispanidad*, and only secondarily with strictly literary matters. Cervantes' *Don Quixote* has become a national symbol which serves as a rallying point for this intensive self-examination. In his *Vida de Don Quijote y Sancho* (1905), the philosopher Unamuno (q.v.) transforms Don Quixote into a saint: the humor of the book is ignored or forgotten. The man Don Quixote steps from the pages as a living being: art and reality are constantly, determinedly confused. Américo Castro (b. 1885) has interpreted Cervantes as a Renaissance man, a follower of Erasmus, in *El Pensamiento de Cervantes* (1925), and in *España en su historia* (1948) has tried to define the Spanish national character in terms of its racial and regional elements. Salvador de Madariaga (q.v.) has also written on Don Quixote (*Guía del lector del Quijote*, 1926) and speculated—often in essays first published in English—on Spanish creative genius (*The Genius of Spain*, 1923). The collection of essays *Shelley and Calderón* (1920) contains a remarkable essay on Wordsworth, chiding him for provinciality. Madariaga, who played a role in the League of Nations as ambassador of the Republic, and as professor of Spanish at Oxford, is a type of the new Spanish internationalist: intensely conscious of his nationality, but wide open to the world, anxious to have Spain emerge from its isolation and impotence. Madariaga is a convinced liberal. On the opposite end of the political scale, Ramiro de Maeztu (1876-1936), who served Primo da Rivera as ambassador, has also written on Don Quixote (*Don Quixote, Don Juan y la Celestina,* 1926) and has produced an antidemocratic and antiliberal work, *Defensa de la hispanidad* (1934).

These two themes, Hispanism and Don Quixote, are also the starting point of the most prominent literary critic Spain has produced: Ortega y Gasset (q.v.). Ortega is primarily a philosopher, or rather *Kulturphilosoph*, an immensely stimulating, versatile writer on all subjects of history, philosophy, art, and even science, love, pedagogy, and politics. Literary criticism is only a small part of his enormous activity. The early *Meditaciones del Quijote* (1914) is hardly literary criticism: it is an attack on the surface culture of Mediterranean man in the name of Germanic "profundity." Ortega studied philosophy with Hermann Cohen in Marburg in 1913-14, and has always preserved an intense interest not only in Kant and Kantianism, but in Simmel, Scheler, Heidegger, and especially Dilthey, from whom many motifs in his thought are derived.

Two small books by Ortega, both dating from 1925, are literary criticism in a narrow sense. *La deshumanización del arte* (The Dehumanization of Art, 1948) has a somewhat sensational title: Ortega discusses not the dehumanization of art, but rather the retreat of modern art from realism. Ortega sees the common denominator of modern art and literature in the avoidance of living, natural forms, in its ambition for being art and nothing else, with no transcendental claim, and in its essential irony. The builders of modern art are Debussy, Mallarmé, Proust (q.v.), Picasso, and Pirandello (q.v.). Though the thesis is somewhat overstated and refers particularly to the situation in the early twenties, Ortega has finely characterized the main trend of art as away from personal emotion and toward abstract form. "Poetry has become the higher algebra of metaphors" is Ortega's definition of the aim of Mallarmé and the Spanish symbolists. Quite consistently he has helped in the revival of

Góngora, the great Spanish baroque poet, with an important essay (*Góngora,* 1927) where his poetry (and implicitly all poetry) is defined as circumlocution, as the oblique naming of the taboo, the making of an X for U. An essay on Mallarmé (1923) defines poetry as a "determined escape from reality," a "keeping silent about the immediate names of things."

In *Ideas sobra la novela* (1925; Notes on the Novel, 1948) he applies substantially the same point of view to the modern novel. The novel (q.v.), with a plot and action, is exhausted as a genre and is being replaced by the "static" novel, which tends not to inspire the reader's immediate interest but requires contemplation induced by its form and structure. The classic examples are Dostoyevski, whom Ortega skillfully defends for his technique and form, and Proust, to whom he has also devoted an analytical essay, "Tiempo, distancia y forma en el arte de Proust" (1934).

The essay which created a sensation in Germany, "Pidiendo un Goethe desde dentro" (1932), is not primarily concerned with Goethe's work. It is, rather, an attempt to show that Goethe betrayed his deepest mission by going to Weimar, that classicism, and Goethe's classicism specifically, hides life, as does his optimistic biological philosophy. The real Goethe, the Goethe from within, is a problematic character, constantly fleeing from himself, a habitual deserter of his destiny.

Ortega had a commanding position in Spanish cultural life. All other critics lack his philosophical clarity and range. They are either impressionists or scholars. Azorín (q.v.) is the best sensitive literary critic of the early group. *Clásicos y modernos* (1913) and *Los valores literarios* (1913) are collections in which he tries to define the Spanish literary tradition and to trace the history of the new movement.

Among more recent critics, the sensitive essayist, Antonio Marichalar (b. 1893), is concerned largely with French and English literature (qq.v.). In *Mentira desnuda* (1933) he has collected his essays on Gide, Claudel, Joyce (qq.v.), and others. Guillermo de Torre (b. 1900) has described and criticized avant-garde European literature (*Literaturas europeas de vanguardia,* 1925) and in recent years, in exile in Argentina, has passionately defended the freedom of the writer. His *Problemática de la literatura* (1951) is deeply influenced by existentialism (q.v.) and disturbed by the problem of the engagement of the writer and the totalitarian attempt to make him serve the purpose

of the state. The crisis of the concept of literature is de Torre's main theme, which allows him to survey the present literary situation with a deep social concern which does not lose sight of the nature and freedom of art.

A new development in Spain is a highly competent cultivation of stylistics, in part suggested by German methods (Vossler, Spitzer), in part drawn from native sources of philology. Ramón Menéndez Pidal (b. 1869) was the teacher of all the younger Spanish literary scholars; a great philologist and medievalist whose *La España del Cid* (1929) is an impressive reconstruction of medieval Spanish civilization. Two younger men, of the same name though not related, stand out: Amado Alonso (1897-1952), who was primarily a philologist, but has written a model study of the Chilean poet Neruda (q.v.), *Poesía y estilo de Pablo Neruda* (1940); and Dámaso Alonso (q.v.), who started the Góngora revival with his edition of *Soledades* (1927) and his elaborate study of his poetic language, *La lengua poética de Góngora* (1935), and who has written a fine analytical book on St. John of the Cross (*La Poesía de San Juan de la Cruz,* 1942) and a large book, *Poesía española, Ensayo de métodos y límites estílisticos* (1950), which contains studies of Garcilaso, Fray Louis de León, San Juan de la Cruz, Góngora, Lope de Vega, and Quevedo. It succeeds in defining the "uniqueness of the literary object" with flexible interpretative techniques of great sensitivity and learning. Dámaso Alonso sometimes loses sight of the critical ideal and is given to speaking of the "mystery of form" or "expressive intuition." But these vague gestures toward irrationalism rarely damage the mastery of the stylistic analyst, who must surely be one of the best in contemporary criticism, and not only in Spain.

A Catalonian, Eugenio D'Ors (1882-1954), made a deep impression at first by his commentaries (*glosas*), published under the pseudonym "Xenius," consisting of ironic epigrammatic journalism on almost all subjects. His books on painters (Goya, Cézanne, Picasso, etc.) prepared the way for his well-known study of the baroque (first in French, *Du Baroque,* 1936; in Spanish, *Lo barocco,* 1944). Here baroque is conceived as a form of style which occurs in all periods of history: Góngora and Richard Wagner, Pope and Vico, Rousseau and El Greco, the Portuguese architecture of the 15th c., and recent poetry are all considered phases of the baroque. D'Ors later wrote in Spanish, became an enthusiast for *lo hispánico* and an adherent of Franco.

Guillermo Díaz-Plaja (b. 1909) is related to D'Ors: he admires him greatly, but goes his own more romantic ways. His first book on Spanish Romanticism (*Introducción al estudio del romanticismo español*, 1935) is still rather derivative, but his essays on the theory of literature (*La ventana de papel*, 1939), his book on the spirit of the baroque (*El espíritu del barocco*, 1940), and his studies of the Spanish lyric and of the prose poem in Spain established him as the most eminent of the younger Spanish literary historians who manages to combine a strongly personal, often impressionist and irrationalistic criticism, with accurate learning. As the editor of the great *Historia general de las literaturas hispánicas* (5 vols. in 6 tomes, 1949-58), he did not succeed so well as the older Ángel Valbuena Prat (b. 1900), whose *Historia de la literatura española* (3 vols., 1937) is today considered the best history of Spanish literature (q.v.). Valbuena Prat also wrote an important monograph on Calderón (*Calderón*, 1941) and a basic history of the Spanish theater (*Historia del teatro español*, 1956).

In Portugal, Fidelino de Sousa Figueiredo (b. 1888) has been the outstanding figure in literary criticism and history. He has written a series of immensely learned literary histories (*História da literatura romántica portuguesa, 1825-1870*, 1913; *História da literatura realista, 1871-1900*, 1914; and *História da literatura classica, 1502-1825*, 3 vols., 1917-24) and much, mainly psychological, criticism. He draws portraits of many Portuguese authors with great skill and understanding (e.g., *Estudos da literatura*, 5 vols., 1917-50). But Fidelino de Sousa Figueiredo has also been deeply concerned with the theory of literature and criticism (e.g., in *A luta pela expressão: Prolegómenos para una Filosofia da literatura*, 1944), with the history of criticism, and with many topics of comparative literature, such as the influence of Shakespeare in Portugal. Figueiredo describes his own outlook as that of a militant traditionalism and nationalism: but he has done much to free Portuguese intellectual life from provincialism and local complacencies.

Every Latin-American country has produced critics and criticism, mainly of the local scene. In Mexico Alfonso Reyes (q.v.) combined, like Figueiredo, wide-ranging learning with critical insight. Reyes wrote scholarly books on Greek criticism and Roman rhetoric; he early contributed to the revival of interest in Góngora (*Cuestiones gongorinas*, 1927); he has shown a fine understanding of Mallarmé (*Mallarmé entre nosostros*, 1938); and he has written a sympathetic study of Goethe (*Trayectoria de Goethe*, 1954). In a large theoretical book, *El Deslinde* (1944), he attempts extremely subtle though excessively scholastic definitions and delimitations which hardly suggest the universality and mobility of his mind. With Reyes, the Spanish culture of the New World has rediscovered its old universal Western spirit.

At the other extremity of the Latin-American world, Borges (q.v.), the eminent Argentinian novelist, is also the best critic and essayist. He ranges widely from Argentine folk literature to old Germanic epics, and judges his Argentine contemporaries with some severity. Ricardo Rojas (q.v.) is his main rival: his eight-volume work, *La literatura argentina* (1924-25), has established his reputation as an essayist.

There are of course many literary historians in the different countries, among whom Pedro Henríques Ureña (1884-1946) from Santo Domingo may be singled out due to the availability of some of his work written in English (*Literary Currents in Hispanic America*, 1945). But Henríques Ureña has written also most importantly on style and verse (*Seis ensayos en busca de nuestra expresion*, 1927) and was one of the most distinguished critics of the Spanish-American world. In every country of the New World, the critical spirit is stirring, engaged in a needed examination of local values and in the importation of ideas from all over the world.

RUSSIA (WITH REMARKS ON POLAND AND CZECHOSLOVAKIA)

Russian criticism has been dominated by Marxism since 1917. But one should realize that early in the c. very different points of view prevailed and that even after 1917 there raged a lively debate in Russia and a great diversity of doctrines were propounded. Uniformity was not imposed until about 1932. Russian literary criticism has a special appeal for the student of criticism, independent of the light it may throw on Russian literature (q.v.) itself. More sharply than anywhere in the West, Russian criticism has elaborated three irreconcilable positions: symbolism (q.v.), formalism, and Marxism.

Symbolism, which came to Russia in the 1890's, adopted there a highly metaphysical and even theological and theosophic doctrine:

poetry was thought of as a revelation of a supernatural existence, the poet became a possessor of occult knowledge. Some of the best-known symbolist poets, Bal'mont, Belyi, Bryusov (qq.v.), wrote criticism which ranges from a vague mysticism (e.g., Bal'mont's little book, *Poeziya kak volshebstvo* [Poetry as Magic], 1915) to subtle technical investigations of meter and rhyme (especially in Belyi's *Symvolizm*, 1910).

Closely related to the symbolist attitude was the cult and study of Dostoyevski, who was interpreted largely as a religious philosopher. Dmitri Merezhkovski (1865-1941) pursued, in his *Tolstoi i Dostoyevski* (1901; Tolstoy as Man and Artist, 1902), relentlessly the antithesis between Tolstoi (q.v.), "the seer of the flesh," and Dostoyevski, "the seer of the spirit," and found antithetical structures, pagan and Christian, everywhere else. Vyacheslav Ivanov (q.v.) interpreted Dostoyevski in his *Dostoyevski* (1920; Freedom and the Tragic Life: A Study in Dostoevsky, 1952) as a creator of myths, and his novels as tragedies. Berdyayev (q.v.) studied the world view of Dostoyevski (*Mirosozertzaniye Dostoyevskovo*, 1923; Dostoyevsky: An Interpretation, 1934) as a philosophy of freedom in which God's existence is justified paradoxically by the existence of evil. These were writers of Russian orthodox background, who developed their own version of religious philosophy. Two Russian Jews, Mikhail Gershenzon (1869-1925) and Leo Shestov (pseud. of Leo Schwartzmann [1868-1938]), used similar philosophical methods to interpret literature with different assumptions: Gershenzon studied the elusive skeptical wisdom of Pushkin (*Mudrost' Pushkina*; Pushkin's Wisdom, 1919), while Shestov searched for an amoral, irrational God and found nihilism everywhere: in Dostoyevski and Tolstoi, in Nietzsche (q.v.) and Chekhov (q.v.). *Apoteoz' Bezpochvennosti* (The Apotheosis of Groundlessness, 1905) is the characteristic title of one of his books. Shestov in his late writings published in exile, in French, came very near to existentialism (q.v.).

Partly in reaction to the mystique of symbolism and the growing power of social criticism, a small but lively and influential group of young scholars, linguists, and literary historians organized a "Society for the Study of Poetic Language" (*Opoyaz*) in 1916, and thus founded what came to be known as the "Formalist Movement." They flourished in the turbulent twenties, but had to conform or were suppressed in the thirties. They were a short episode in the history of Russian criticism, but their influence spread to Czechoslovakia and Poland and is beginning to be felt in the United States.

One must distinguish several stages in the development of Russian formalism: an early stage of extremism which was closely allied with the rising movement of Russian futurism ([q.v.], Khlebnikov, Mayakovski [qq.v.]); a middle period of consolidation and expansion; and a final crisis, breakup, and compromise with Marxism. One must distinguish among its members: Viktor Shklovski (b. 1893) was a firebrand, a stimulating gadfly, a crude and shrill publicist, while Boris Eichenbaum (1886-1962), Roman Jakobson (b. 1896), and Yurii Tynyanov (q.v.) brought a great fund of erudition to their bold speculations. A learned scholar such as Viktor Zhirmunski (b. 1891), on the other hand, drew ideas from his colleagues and tried to devise combinations with accepted views. Boris Tomashevski (1886-1957), with his *Teoriya literatury* (Theory of Literature, 1925), is rather the popularizer and systematizer of the group.

The formalists, like the futurists, proclaimed poetry to be free creation, its word to be independent of reality, even "beyond sense." They at first denied the social and philosophical content of art and proclaimed its complete indifference, even, to emotions and ideas. In their first stage they were interested in one problem, that of poetic language, which they conceived of as a special language, achieved by a purposeful "deformation" of ordinary language, by what they called "organized violence" committed against it. They studied mainly the sound-stratum of language: vowel-harmonies, consonant clusters, rhyme, prose-rhythm, and meter, drawing heavily on the results of modern linguistics, its concept of the "phoneme" developed by linguists such as Baudoin de Courtenay (1845-1929), (Prince) Nikolai Trubetskoi (1890-1938), and Roman Jakobson. They devised many technical methods (some even statistical) which can hardly be made comprehensible without a knowledge of Russian. Slowly they saw that they had also to study composition and meaning, and finally that no poetics is complete without aesthetics and history. Shklovski argued that the purpose of art is to shock us into an awareness of reality and that its main device to achieve this end is "making strange," making us see things from a new and surprising angle. Thus Tolstoi, in a story *Khlostomer* (1861 [sometimes called *Strider*]), makes us see the world with the eyes of a race-horse or, in *War and Peace,* looks at opera as if it were a dumbshow.

Another device of art is "putting on the brakes," forcing attention to the rocky road itself. Art is conceived even as a game of patience, or as a jigsaw puzzle. The techniques of narration, in folk tales, in the *Arabian Nights* in the mystery and detective story (see Detective Fiction) or in a novel as contrived as Sterne's *Tristram Shandy* were analyzed by Shklovski in *O teorii prozy* (On the Theory of Prose; 1923), always with the emphasis on craft, on the distinction between subject and plot. Another formalist, Boris Eichenbaum, boldly reinterpreted Gogol's *The Overcoat.* It is not a plea for our common humanity and the little man, as it was understood for a hundred years; it is, rather, a comic, grotesque story displaying the manipulation of the recital, the voice of the narrator. It has nothing to do with realism. Art is thus sharply divorced from life. Roman Jakobson asked: "Why should a poet have more responsibility for a struggle of ideas than for a battle of swords or a duel by pistols?' and formulated strikingly: "Literary scholarship should investigate what makes literature literary"—that is, its literariness, the devices which make a work of art what it is.

Thus the formalists rejected all biographical, psychological, and sociological methods as external. They ridiculed old-fashioned literary history as an *Allerleiwissenschaft* without subject matter, limits, or method. They tried to devise instead a historical poetics which would concentrate on the internal evolution of poetry. Poetic schools are considered as changing in a dialectical process of action and reaction, convention and revolt. Conventions wear out: the "automatization" of devices will need a new "actualization." The rise of new genres is seen as a revival of "low" forms, as a needed re-barbarization of literature. Thus Dostoyevski glorified the sensational French *roman-feuilleton* (see The Feuilleton) and Blok (q.v.) raised the gipsy song into the realm of art. The only criterion of value recognized by the formalists is novelty, the success of a work of art in changing the direction of literary evolution.

The parallelism between Russian formalism and similar movements in the West, such as the American "New Criticism," is striking, especially in the common preoccupation with the language of poetry. But the Russian movement seems purely indigenous: some of its forerunners were the comparatist Aleksandr Vesel-ovski (1838-1906), who attempted a historical poetics, and the linguist Aleksandr Potebnya (1835-1891). One finds only rare allusions in formalist writings to Heinrich Wölfflin, Oskar Walzel, and Ferdinand Brunetière. But the Russian formalists differ sharply from the analogous movements. They lean much more heavily on technical linguistics, especially phonemics. They disparage the role of imagery and symbolism. Their concept of the work of art as a sum of devices is mechanistic. They are positivists, with a scientific ideal of scholarship; technicians who have devised ingenious methods of analysis with great clarity. They have preserved a strong interest in literary history and historical poetics. But they do not see the crucial problem of evaluation, left as they are with the single criterion of novelty, in the blind alley of relativism.

On many points Russian formalism was greatly improved when it was exported to Poland and Czechoslovakia. In Poland Manfred Kridl (1882-1957) argued in favor of an "integral method" of literary studies, radically centered on the work of art ("ergocentric"). A philosopher, Roman Ingarden (b. 1893), applied, in *Das dichterische Kunstwerk* (1931; new ed., 1960), Husserl's phenomenology to an analysis of the different strata of the work of art and its ontological status. He thus overcame the dichotomy of content and form and grounded the theories of formalism epistemologically. In Czechoslovakia, where Roman Jakobson was settled for years, the Prague Linguistic Circle was founded (1926), partly at his instigation, and some of its members devoted themselves to literary theory. Among them Jan Mukařovský (b. 1891) was the oustanding theorist of literature. The Czechs restated Russian formalism, rechristening it "structuralism." Structure is a term like *Gestalt,* which attempts to overcome the dualism of content and form.

While the Czechs adopted the main tenets of Russian formalism, they rejected its positivism, its methods of treating literature as an art entirely determined by language and literary scholarship as almost a branch of linguistics. The Czechs had studied Hegel, Husserl, *Gestalt* psychology, and the philosophy of symbolic forms propounded by Cassirer. They saw that the meaning of a work of literature is not purely linguistic, that it projects a "world" of motifs, themes, characters, plots, and even ideas. Mukařovský has gone beyond careful stylistic and semantic analyses to a general theory of aesthetics in which key concepts like function, structure, norm, and value point to an over-all goal in a theory of semiology, of meaning in a social and historical context.

But all these promising developments were cut short by World War II and its aftereffects. In Poland and Czechoslovakia Marxism was imposed after the war: men such as Mukařovský recanted publicly. Others, such as Jakobson and Kridl, emigrated to the United States. Criticism, as an act of understanding and free judgment, is dead behind the Iron Curtain.

GERMANY

Germany, in the latter half of the 18th and early in the 19th c., produced a large body of aesthetic and critical doctrines whose influence was felt throughout the 19th c. The two brothers Schlegel, especially, carried the message of German romanticism all over the Western world. But in the later 19th c. Germany lost its leadership in criticism completely: no single German critic established, even in his own nation, a position remotely comparable to that of Sainte-Beuve or Taine in France, Arnold in England, De Sanctis in Italy, and Belinski in Russia. The cleavage between university scholarship and day-by-day reviewing was in Germany greater than elsewhere. Scholarship became purely historical, factual, "objective," and deliberately refrained from judgment and criticism, though it often assumed the standards of value developed by the great German classics. On the other hand, the reviewers became journalists who lost touch with a coherent body of doctrine: either impressionism went rampant or standards of didactic usefulness, mainly based on nationalistic ideals or political attitudes, prevailed. In either case genuine literary criticism was dead.

In the 1880's, however, the movement of naturalism (q.v.), introduced largely from France, stirred the stagnant waters and aroused violent debates (especially around Ibsen and Zola [qq.v.]). Real criticism, in the sense of a definition of a new taste, was produced, even though the theories of naturalism were derivative and often very simplist in their grasp of the nature of art.

At the dawn of the new c. the naturalist movement had run its course; its most important critics had ceased publishing—for example, Otto Brahm (1856-1912), who had fought for Ibsen and Gerhart Hauptmann (q.v.), had become a theatrical manager.

Simultaneous with the rise of German natu-

ralism another reaction had set in against the 19th c. tradition: that which loosely could be called symbolism. In Germany Stefan George (q.v.) became the leader of a group which exerted great influence on literary taste and criticism. George himself was hardly a literary critic in the strict sense of the word, but his proclamations on the prophetic mission of the artist, of the incantatory power of language, and the need of severe form and unity in a work of poetry, as well as his eulogies of Mallarmé, Verlaine, Jean Paul, and Hölderlin (collected in *Tage und Taten,* 1900), became the stimulus for the criticism systematized by his circle. Also George's anthology of German poetry (*Deutsche Dichtung,* 3 vols., 1901-1903 [ed. with Wolfskehl (q.v.)]), which, besides single volumes devoted to Goethe and Jean Paul, admitted only a very small selection from nine 19th c. poets and George's translations from Dante, Baudelaire, and many recent French and English poets, held up a new ideal of taste which sharply broke with the emotionalism and didacticism of the 19th c.

George's disciples elaborated his hints and dicta into a body of criticism which, for the first time, after a long period of relativism, historicism, and philological factualism, asserted a critical creed, proclaimed definite standards, and defined a tradition and taste. Unfortunately, the genuine insights of the school into the nature of poetry are marred by the doctrinaire tone of delivery, the aristocratic pretensions, and the often comically high-pitched, almost oracular solemnity of their pronouncements.

By far the best of George's direct followers is Friedrich Gundolf (1880-1931), while the others, whatever their merits as poets or translators, seem as critics only sectarians. Thus Friedrich Wolters (1876-1930), in his *Stefan George und die Blätter für die Kunst* (1930), asserts, at great length, George's claims not only to poetic greatness but to the leadership of the nation and to a religious revelation in George's meeting with Maximin. Other books on George by members of the circle (e.g., those by Robert Boehringer and Edgar Salin) are also written in a tone of adoration for a religious leader; they are saints' lives and acts of the apostles rather than criticism. Gundolf's *George* (1920) is no less idolatrous, but succeeds, at least, in concretely describing and analyzing George's poetic achievements.

But the book on George was preceded by Gundolf's best critical work: *Shakespeare und der deutsche Geist* (1911) and *Goethe* (1916). These are books nourished by considerable learning, in spite of Gundolf's ostentatious contempt for footnotes and acknowledgements: well-composed, finely phrased books which set, in Germany, new standards of critical judgment and analytical power. The early study of Shakespeare's influence on Germany from the English comedians of the 17th c. to the Schlegels combines criticism of the main German writers with insight into period styles. Gundolf admirably sets forth the distinction between mere borrowings and external parallels on the one hand, and deeper assimilation on the other, and penetratingly analyzes the style of translations and imitations. His harsh judgment of the naturalistic distortions of Shakespeare by the German "Storm and Stress" and of the moralism and rhetoric of Schiller are refreshingly straightforward, even though his own conception of Shakespeare divorces him too sharply from the stage. The concentration on the texts and figures, apart from biographical information and details of literary history, and the cultivated, even precious style of writing were welcome innovations after the spate of colorless books crammed with information but devoid of taste and judgment.

Gundolf's largest book, *Goethe*, shows the same qualities of insight, analytical power, organization, and finished presentation. But while the earlier book was clearly nonbiographical and antipsychological and still remained properly historical, the book on Goethe postulates some obscure synthesis of biography and criticism in a contemplation of the *Gestalt* of Goethe. In this heroically stylized figure no distinction, Gundolf argues, can be made between *Erlebnis* and work, with the result that the book again confuses life and poetry. Gundolf had studied *Das Erlebnis und die Dichtung* (1905), a collection of essays, mostly dating from the 19th c., by the great historian of ideas and feelings Wilhelm Dilthey (1833-1911), and had absorbed his philosophy: a version of *Lebensphilosophie*, which Gundolf combined with ideas derived from Bergson (q.v.). *Leben*, in Dilthey, does not mean life (*bios*), but the total *psyche*, the mental structure which fuses intellect, will, and feeling into one. The function of poetry is seen as an increase of vitality; the main criterion of judgment is emotional sincerity, engagement, personal involvement, presuming an intense *Erlebnis*. In Dilthey, this emotionalism is combined rather incongruously with a view of poetry as expressing a specific *Weltanschauung*, a popular philosophy with relativistic conclusions, as, for Dilthey, there are only three types of *Weltanschauung* (realism, dualistic idealism—what he calls *Idealismus der Freiheit*—and monistic idealism), all illustrated in literature and all ultimately equal as to their claims to truth.

Gundolf, though influenced by Dilthey, never succumbs to the psychologism and relativism of Dilthey. He saves criticism by devising a distinction between *Urerlebnis* and *Bildungserlebnis*, in which the elementary personal experience is preferred to the cultural experience, and by a somewhat parallel scale of the lyrical, symbolical, and allegorical, in which the lyrical (which is not necessarily identical with the traditional genre) precedes the other two categories. The emphasis falls on the personal lyric, but Gundolf argues that the poet experiences differently from the ordinary man, in terms anticipating his creation, forming even while living. Gundolf construes a conflict between Goethe's titanism and eroticism, between work and life, after all. The emphasis on the lyrical, on the *daimon*, which yields the fine analyses of the early poetry, and of *Werther*, does not, however, obscure his insight into the structures of Goethe's objective, "symbolic" poetry and into the relation of Goethe's works to tradition and convention. Whatever objections to individual interpretations (e.g., that of the second part of *Faust*) may be voiced, the book remains an impressive monument. Today we would feel that in spite of many fine discriminations the tone of adoration, the setting up of the pedestal, the arranging of the drapery becomes excessively monotonous. It is hard not to resent the idolatry which changes the eminently humane figure of Goethe into a demonic creator for creation's sake. Real insights are often drowned in a flood of verbiage repeating over and over again the same or similar antitheses.

Even more one-sided is Gundolf's portrait, *Heinrich von Kleist* (1922), in which Kleist is seen as "a solitary soul without nation and God," as a chaotic, even monstrous genius, great by his defiance of the time, tragic as a symbolic sacrifice. The two-volume book, *Shakespeare: Sein Wesen und Werk* (1928), is curiously neglected: it suffers from preciosity and monotony, it sees Shakespeare so completely out of the context of the time and the stage that Shakespeare's ethos is falsified. But individual observations show an insight into the poetry and its symbolism, an emphasis on what might be called the baroque in Shakespeare, which was rare at the time. Only the last essays, *Romantiker* (2 vols., 1930-31), return to more traditional methods of characterization and judgment, which, however, often are excessively unsympathetic to such volatile and elusive figures as Friedrich Schlegel.

Two other members of the George circle wrote significant literary criticism. Ernst Bertram's (q.v.) *Nietzsche* (1918) aroused much adverse comment because of its subtitle: *Versuch einer Mythologie,* and an introduction which boldly proclaimed the aim of the critic to be the creation of a legend, an "image," a myth. But the text of the book does not go all the way into subjectivism. It interprets Nietzsche (q.v.) as a lonely romantic, an ambiguous, contradictory, tortured irrationalist, an "image" which has at least as much justification as more recent attempts such as that of Walter F. Kaufmann (*Nietzsche: Philosopher, Psychologist, Antichrist,* 1950) to make Nietzsche a reasonable descendant of the Enlightenment.

Kommerell (q.v.), in *Der Dichter als Führer in der deutschen Klassik* (1928), interpreted the whole German classical group in terms of Stefan George's ideals. Klopstock is seen as a disciple of the Greeks, absorbed in antiquity and Platonic friendships, as if he had not been a Christian. Jean Paul is pressed into the Weimar company. Schiller becomes a disciple of Goethe, and Hölderlin is exalted to a national hero, a prophet of a religious regeneration of Germany as a second Greece. The deification of Hölderlin (who, in Dilthey's *Das Erlebnis und die Dichtung,* appears still as a charming, sentimental dreamer) has been stimulated by the discovery of Hölderlin's late hymns by another disciple of George's, Norbert von Hellingrath (1888-1916). He had prepared a complete new edition and written short expositions (*Hölderlin,* 2 lectures, 1921) which found greatness even in the crabbed translations from Pindar and Sophocles and the most baffling fragments from the last stage of Hölderlin's lucid life before madness beclouded his mind. But Kommerell soon broke with George, as he could not accept his intellectual dictatorship, and went his own way. We shall meet him in another context.

George, in his beginnings, attracted the Austrian poet Hofmannsthal (q.v.). They shared the opposition to naturalism, the cult of form and word, but they soon drifted apart, as Hofmannsthal would not submit to the "discipline" of the George circle and had other

ambitions in the theater and a very different concrete taste in literature. Hofmannsthal is only incidentally a critic; but his early articles written in his precocious youth under the pseudonym "Loris" (1891-97) define a taste which could roughly be called "decadent" in its love for Swinburne, Pater, and D'Annunzio (q.v.), and asserts the independence of poetry from life and its essence in form and imagery. Later, in many essays, articles, and speeches (collected in 4 vols. of *Prosa* in *Gesammelte Werke in Einzelausgaben,* 15 vols., 1951-63), Hofmannsthal has, often impressionistically and loosely, defined his preferences in literature: for the baroque and romance traditions, for Molière, Hugo, and Balzac, Calderón and the Austrians, Grillparzer and Stifter. In literary theory, Hofmannsthal has brought out the mystical, Neo-Platonic implications of his symbolist aesthetics, for example in "Gespräch über Gedichte" (1904). The bulk of his later writing on literature moves, however, in generalities of a "political" nature. Thus, in the speech "Das Schrifttum als geistiger Raum der Nation" (1927), Hofmannsthal praises tradition against romantic caprice and warns against the worn-out ideals of the *Bildungsphilister:* a "conservative revolution" is advocated, in which a high ideal of European unity is propped up by a strong consciousness of the role of old Austria as a mediator between North and South, East and West.

With Hofmannsthal two poets were associated in friendship: Borchardt (q.v.) and Schröder. Borchardt, the translator of Dante into a special archaic German, a learned student of antiquity and Italy, is a passionate, even stridently vociferous asserter of the great tradition. In a postscript to *Ewiger Vorrat deutscher Poesie* (1926), an anthology of German poetry, he makes short work of the German 19th c. and such established reputations as Heine's, and in eloquent *Reden* (collected 1955) he proclaimed his somewhat foggy ideal of a reconciliation of the German and Latin spirit, antiquity and the Middle Ages. But he is at his best in his scattered essays on Pindar and Virgil, Hartmann von Aue and Dante, Lessing, Rossetti, Hofmannsthal, and George (see, e.g., *Handlungen und Abhandlungen,* 1928). In spite of his dogmatic tone, Borchardt is full of sympathy with often very diverse minds, flexible, and even disconcertingly uncritical (e.g., his excessive enthusiasm for Edna St. Vincent Millay [q.v.]). His violent criticism of contemporary literature and its commercial aspects, his glorification of the Prussian monarchic tradition, his total condemnation of the 18th c. and the Enlightenment, his panegyric of German romanticism and historicism, his acceptance of Croce's (q.v.) aesthetics are some of the incongruous elements of his thought, fused only by his powerful temperament and brilliant eloquence.

Compared to Borchardt's violence and eccentricity, Schröder seems a modest, sensible, sober expounder of the great tradition. He is best known for his translations of Homer, Virgil, and Horace. His critical writings (collected in *Die Aufsätze und Reden,* 2 vols., 1952), in their smooth eloquence, assert persuasively the mission of the poet as the maker of language, the great comforter for the transience of our existence. The poet, in Schröder's later writings, is more and more identified with the religious leader. Schröder has made an intensive study of Protestant hymns and religious poetry, while he has clung to a defense of the classical heritage of Europe. Poets like Virgil, Horace, and Racine have found few admirers in modern Germany as sympathetic as Schröder: but Schröder seems less a critic than a scholarly expositor of the classical-Christian heritage.

Also loosely related to this group is Kassner (q.v.), who began with a book of essays, *Die Mystik, die Künstler und das Leben* (1900: revised ed., *Englische Dichter,* 1922), which combines a taste for the Pre-Raphaelites with a genuine interest in mysticism. William Blake is his early hero. The imagination, which in these essays links the poet and the mystic, becomes, in Kassner's later, mostly philosophical writings, the central concept of a pantheistic world view in which physiognomics, the interpretation of outward physical signs, plays a central role. As a literary critic Kassner remains a symbolist who has, however, developed special tastes for authors usually ignored in Germany: Laurence Sterne, whose feeling for time appeals to Kassner; Gogol; De Quincey; and even Hardy (q.v.). Shakespeare, however, remains the exemplar of the imagination. All authors and all poetry, in the later Kassner, become only specimens to substantiate a philosophy in which oriental and mystical ideas combine to support a revival of a basically romantic view of the imagination: as a "seizure of the thing by the image," a universal system of analogy, of all-in-one. A grandiose attempt is made to abolish the distinctions between sense and spirit, the concrete and the abstract, but literature as such is lost sight of.

Parallel with what could be called the Ger-

man symbolist movement, represented by Stefan George and Hofmannsthal, there arose a new classicism, or rather neoclassicism, which asserted the role of form and tradition, mainly in the drama. Paul Ernst (q.v.) found, after a youth devoted to naturalism and Marxism, a way to a new, highly intellectual classicism. In *Der Weg zur Form* (1906) Ernst pleads for necessity, for fate, for the coercion of form in the drama (see Drama and Theater) and the short story (q.v.), and disparages the novel (q.v.) and all description and psychological analysis. Drama is interpreted as an ethical conflict; tragedy as a joyous recognition of necessity even in the perdition of the hero. An absolute morality is postulated as the basis for a renewal of tragedy. The critical creed, however, remains disconcertingly abstract, and Ernst's many articles on literary figures (collected in *Völker und Zeiten im Spiegel ihrer Dichtung,* 2 vols., 1941-42) stay well within the bounds of conventional eclecticism.

In this general tradition of the defense of the cultural values of the German past, two writers might be listed who cultivated the form of the essay. Thomas Mann (q.v.) accompanied his novels and stories with a long series of articles, speeches, lectures, introductions (collected, e.g., in *Rede und Antwort,* 1922; *Bemühungen,* 1925; *Die Forderung des Tages,* 1930; *Adel des Geistes,* 1945; *Altes und Neues,* 1953 [Essays of Three Decades, 1946]), which either praise kindred spirits or circle around Mann's problem of the position of the artist in society or probe into the artist's psychology, often by means derived from Freud and Nietzsche. Mann's consciousness—whatever the changes of his political orientation—is definitely conservative, *bürgerlich,* though acutely aware of the limits of the bourgeois tradition. "Goethe als Repräsentant des bürgerlichen Zeitalters" (1932), two essays on Tolstoi (q.v.), a speech on Lessing (1929) define Mann's sympathies best. Mann's essays are too autobiographical and too monotonously engaged in developing broad antitheses to be good criticism, aside from the light they throw on Mann's art.

Another general essayist was Josef Hofmiller (1872-1933), whose *Versuche* (1909) and *Letzte Versuche* (1935) are examples of the art of portraiture in the sense of Sainte-Beuve. His outlook is Roman Catholic, his interests are widely scattered (the essays range from Emerson and Thoreau to Leskov and Fogazzaro), his tone is reasonable, his exposition skillful, but the criticism seems often colorless and imperceptive.

The change of taste, the newly acquired sense of form and tradition also influenced academic German scholarship profoundly. A group of Romance scholars, especially, combined scholarship and criticism successfully. Karl Vossler (1872-1949) traced the history of the French literary language influenced by Croce's view of language as individual creation and wrote a large study of Dante's *Divina Commedia* (*Die göttliche Komödie* 2 vols., 1907-1910; Medieval Culture, 1929), which is both learnedly historical and critical. He has written descriptive and analytical monographs on Racine, La Fontaine, Leopardi, Lope de Vega, and the Spanish poetry of solitude.

Ernst Robert Curtius (q.v.) has the most intimate relations with contemporary literature: at first as a critical importer of modern French literature (q.v.) into Germany, and then as a sensitive and often pioneering analyst of Proust, Joyce, and T. S. Eliot ([qq.v.] now collected as *Kritische Essays zur europäischen Literatur,* 1950; and *Französischer Geist im zwanzigsten Jahrhundert,* 1952). In his book *Balzac* (1923) he reinterprets the master of realism as a Swedenborgian visionary, and his last and longest book, *Europäische Literatur und lateinisches Mittelalter* (1948; European Literature and the Latin Middle Ages, 1953), weighted though it is by immense erudition, aims at a critical point in establishing the unity and continuity of European literature since classical antiquity, not only in its forms and period styles, but in its themes and commonplaces (*topoi*). In Curtius a concern for tradition, a feeling for the world of Latinity and for European unity, an admiration for George, Hofmannsthal, and Eliot, combine happily with great historical and rhetorical erudition.

Leo Spitzer (1887-1960) is more of a purely technical student of linguistics and stylistics; but in his wide-ranging studies of literature (collected in *Stilstudien,* 2 vols., 1928; *Linguistics and Literary History,* 1948; *Romanische Literaturstudien,* 1959; *Essays on English and American Literature,* 1962), he has developed a method of interpretation treating the word as a sign of mind and soul which serves genuine critical purposes. Spitzer has written much on French and Spanish literature ([q.v.] Racine, Diderot, Voltaire, Proust, Cervantes, Lope de Vega, etc.), but in recent years has also interpreted poems by Donne and Keats and a story by Poe. Spitzer works always on a small scale, with a specific text, almost micrologically, though he is inspired by a general concept of humanism.

Erich Auerbach (q.v.) also starts always with the stylistic analysis of a text, but in his *Mimesis: Dargestellte Wirklichkeit in der abendländischen Literatur* (1946; Mimesis: The Representation of Reality in Western Literature, 1953) he attempts a general history of realism from Homer to Proust. The book combines stylistic analysis of individual passages with literary, social, and intellectual history. Auerbach's concept of realism is very special: it means to him both a concrete insight into social and political reality and an existential sense of reality, understood tragically, as man in solitude facing moral decisions.

Compared to this distinguished group of scholar-critics in the romance languages, the study of German literature (q.v.) was less affected by the new understanding of form and tradition. Oskar Walzel (1864-1944) was an eniment specialist in the history of ideas, especially of the German romantic movement, before he tried to apply stylistic criteria to literature. He discovered Heinrich Wölfflin's *Kunstgeschichtliche Grundbegriffe* (1915; Principles of Art History, 1932), in which the Swiss art historian expounded a scheme for a definition of the difference between Renaissance and baroque in the plastic arts, and transferred these criteria to literature. Walzel attempted to show, for example, that Shakespeare belongs to the baroque, since his plays are not built in the symmetrical manner found by Wölfflin in pictures of the Renaissance. In a pamphlet, "Wechselseitige Erhellung der Künste" (1917), and in many later writings, Walzel defended the method of transferring criteria developed by art history to literary history and developed devices and stylistic methods of his own. But *Gestalt und Gehalt im Kunstwerk des Dichters* (1923) shows that Walzel is rather an eclectic expositor of other people's ideas and opinions than a critic, and his many very valuable, erudite books are strongest when they concern *Geistesgeschichte.* Thus *Grenzen von Poesie und Unpoesie* (1937), in spite of its deceptively Crocean title, has nothing to do with criticism: it is a historical study of German romantic aesthetics.

Fritz Strich (1882-1963) has shown that the method of Wölfflin's contraries can be applied to German classicism and romanticism. In *Deutsche Klassik und Romantik, oder Vollendung und Unendlichkeit* (1922), Strich shows that the baroque characteristics hold good of romanticism, the Renaissance of classicism. Strich interprets Wölfflin's concepts of closed and open form as analogues to the opposition between the perfect classical form and the open, unfinished, fragmentary and blurred form of romantic poetry expressive of man's longing for the infinite. In detail, Strich is full of subtle remarks and observations, but the general scheme which assumes a sharp division in the general German movement of the late 18th c. will not withstand closer criticism. With Walzel and Strich stylistic analysis clearly passes into intellectual history, which was the preoccupation of most German academic scholars. Even a book such as Paul Böckmann's *Formgeschichte der deutschen Dichtung* (1949) is only a slightly disguised *Geistesgeschichte*: neither formal nor critical, but historical and relativistic.

Some German scholars made important contributions to a formal study of literature, to a study of the evolution of a genre (e.g., Karl Viëtor, *Geschichte der deutschen Ode,* 1923; Günther Müller, *Geschichte des deutschen Liedes,* 1925; Friedrich Beissner, *Geschichte der deutschen Elegie,* 1941), and particularly to the study of imagery and the poetic symbol (Hermann Pongs, *Das Bild in der Dichtung,* 2 vols., 1927-39; Wolfgang Clemen, *Shakespeares Bilder,* 1936 [The Development of Shakespeare's Imagery, 1951]; Wilhelm Emrich, *Die Symbolik von Faust II,* 1943). But these scholars also pass back and forth to *Geistesgeschichte,* the enormously variegated impressive movement in German literary scholarship (see especially the work of R. Unger, H. Korff, W. Rehm, P. Kluckhohn, Benno von Wiese), which cannot be included in criticism even though we interpret the term very broadly.

We have traced the revival of a sense of tradition and form and the establishment of what could roughly be called the symbolist and formalist point of view up to the present time. But German literature soon after 1910 was convulsed by a very different movement: expressionism (q.v.), which corresponds to what is called "futurism" (q.v.) in Italy and Russia. Expressionism hardly produced criticism, at least in its earlier stages, but only manifestoes, declarations, polemics, often vaguely and emotionally phrased: cries, oracular dicta, or mere fancies. Still, expressionism represented an important revolution in taste. Its complete rejection of tradition, its contempt for form, coupled with a rejection of naturalism and impressionism, the proclamation of a return to metaphysics, to an inner world of expression which would not, however, be the psychological analysis of an individual but the cry of a common humanity—all these are critical motifs which were thrown out unsystematically in articles, in *Charon,* in *Der Sturm,* and other short-lived periodicals, or in small booklets like Edschmid's (q.v.) *Über den Expressionismus in der Literatur und die neue Dichtung* (1918). The versatile Austrian critic, Bahr (q.v.), who had written very early his *Die Überwindung des Naturalismus* (1891), tried, in his *Expressionismus* (1916; Expressionism, 1916), to relate the whole movement to the theory of fine arts and drew on Wilhelm Worringer's *Abstraktion und Einfühlung* (1911), a book which contrasted abstract art, imposing form on nature, with organic art, fusing with the object. Expressionism appears related to Egyptian, Byzantine, Gothic, and baroque art in its rejection of the classical human form. In writers such as Pannwitz, Lothar Schreyer (b. 1886), and Sternheim (q.v.) diverse irrationalist ideas are stressed: the vision of the artist and its power, the emancipation of the word, the role of myth in art. The relations to the past, to precursors or supposed precursors such as the rediscovered Büchner were explored only cursorily.

Among the leading expressionist poets only Benn (q.v.) can be said to have practiced criticism with any continuity and coherence. He defines expressionism largely in terms of its destruction of reality and history, of its horrifying experience of the chaos of the world and the decay of values (see introd. to *Lyrik des expressionistischen Jahrzehnts,* 1955). Benn, who even passed through a period of admiration for National Socialism, has, in recent writings, found a way to a position which is not very different (in criticism) from Eliot's or Mallarmé's. *Probleme der Lyrik* (1951) proclaims the ideal of absolute poetry, without belief, without hope, addressed to nobody, made out of words. More sharply than any other German critic Benn protests against the view that a poem is about feelings and must emanate warmth; he ridicules poems addressed to nature, full of similes starting with the word "like," full of names for colors with a seraphic tone of murmuring fountains, harps, night, and silence. Benn has become the most radical critic of the assumptions of the German romantic lyric. He believes in form and reality somehow imposed on the original chaos of the world and has ceased to be an expressionist.

307

While nothing like a coherent theory could come from the deliberately chaotic irrationalism of the expressionists proper, the general influence of expressionist attitudes and vocabulary was widely felt. In academic scholarship Herbert Cysarz (b. 1896) wrote many bombastic, tortuously phrased books which show an affinity with the baroque (*Deutsche Barockdichtung*, 1924), with all irrationalistic philosophies (*Literaturgeschichte als Geisteswissenschaft*, 1926), and ultimately with Nazism. Theatrical criticism possibly most clearly shows the expressionist mood even when the critic rejects particular expressionist plays or theories. Alfred Kerr (q.v.) in hundreds of reviews, written in an affected, clipped style, judged for years the Berlin stage. He outgrew his early naturalistic predilections more and more in the direction of expressionism: his praise of Wedekind, Sternheim, and Strindberg (qq.v.) goes with a rejection of everything classical. Kerr is constantly "bored" by Shakespeare and in his introductory pronouncements flaunts the idea (for which he looks in Heine and Wilde [q.v.] for predecessors) of criticism as art, even superior to creation, as the "eternizing of trash." Bernhard Diebold (1886-1945), in *Anarchie im Drama* (1920; expanded 4th ed., 1928), discussed Wedekind, Sternheim, Kaiser, and Strindberg (qq.v.), often very critically, and the many books by Julius Bab (1880-1955)—for example, *Der Wille zum Drama* (1919)—and those of Herbert Ihering (1888-1967) show the same taste: a dissatisfaction with naturalism as a misunderstanding of art, a turn toward experimentalism on the stage, whatever direction it may ultimately take. Though much of this theatrical criticism is necessarily ephemeral, it was the place where criticism as judgment was most alive in Germany.

In style and *Weltgefühl*, especially his bitter hatred of commercial civilization, the great Austrian satirist Karl Kraus (q.v.) is related to expressionism. The periodical he wrote single-handed for twenty-six years, *Die Fackel* (1899-1936), contains much literary criticism, mostly of a polemical sort animated by a fierce ethical pathos against all sham, written in an allusive, witty style which exploits all resources of the language. *Heine und die Folgen* (1910), an attack on the originator of German literary journalism and *Schmockerei*, and *Literatur und Lüge* (pub. outside *Die Fackel*, 1939) are some of the best-known items, but his whole work is permeated by criticism, mostly directed against contemporary Austrian literature (q.v.) and

journalism. Neither Hofmannsthal nor Bahr nor Schnitzler (q.v.) nor Werfel (q.v.) can escape the spearpoint of this harsh but salutary moralist.

The expressionist movement as a poetic trend was over by about 1920: it had been nourished by the moods of the war and its aftermath. After a few years of comparative normality, criticism was again transformed by an outside factor: the rising tide of Nazism. Nazism defined a literary theory and taste which officially prevailed for the years 1933-45. One must, however, distinguish between two kinds of Nazi criticism: one is primarily racist, biological in its ideology, vaguely realistic, provincial in its taste; the other was, rather, mystical and vaguely philosophical. The first kind wanted *Heimatskunst, Blut und Boden*; it was idyllic, or pseudoidyllic. Long before World War I Adolf Bartels (1862-1944) had produced a stream of histories and polemics which interpreted German literature from this point of view and specifically indulged in elaborate attacks on the Jews (and half- and quarter-Jews) in German literature (see *Heinrich Heine: Auch ein Denkmal*, 1906; *Geschichte der deutschen Literatur*, 3 vols., 1924-28).

A very erudite scholar, Josef Nadler (1884-1963), whose original affiliations were conservative and Catholic, has also given a biological interpretation of German literature. His *Literaturgeschichte der deutschen Stämme und Landschaften* (4 vols., 1922-28; also pub. in a Nazified ed. as *Literaturgeschichte des deutschen Volkes*, 4 vols., 1938-41) is an attempt to write literary history "from below," according to the tribes, districts, and cities, always constructing "tribal souls" of the different regions, professing to read literary traits from the ancestry of the family.

Though much of his biology seems wholly fanciful and his philosophy of German history quite fantastic (see *Die berliner Romantik*, 1921), Nadler had genuine merits: he revived interest in the submerged and neglected Catholic South, he has a fine power of racy characterization and sense of locality, which is by no means useless in the study of the frequently very local German literature. In spite of the racist assumptions (and the anti-Semitism and superpatriotism, particularly blatant in the later edition), Nadler represents the curious mixture which, in most academic Nazi scholarship, was achieved between pseudoscientific biology, old romantic conceptions of the national soul, and even categories derived from *Geistesgeschichte* and the history of artistic styles. Many other German literary historians who joined the Nazi movement and wrote Nazi literary history on a more sophisticated level (e.g., Heinz Kindermann, Franz Koch, Walter Linden) drew ideas and concepts from almost anywhere: from mysticism and romanticism, from Stefan George and Nietzsche, but capped the ramshackle structure by an overriding concept of *deutsche Art, volkhafte Kunst,* in which racist assumptions were weirdly amalgamated with philosophical and literary concepts. The special feature of this new literary criticism need hardly be described: the elimination or denigration of Jews, the contortions in fitting inconvenient but unavoidable figures such as Goethe into their pattern, the frantic search for anticipations of Nazi doctrines, the foggy, monotonous jargon, the resentful, nationalist boasting. It is a sorry chapter in the history of German scholarship, only partially excusable on grounds of political pressure.

After the end of World War II, existentialism (q.v.) began to dominate the German intellectual scene. Interpreted, as it popularly is, as a philosophy of despair, of "fear and trembling," of man's exposure in a hostile universe, the reasons for its spread are not far to seek. But the main work by Martin Heidegger (b. 1889), *Sein und Zeit* (Being and Time, 1962), dates from 1927, and existentialist ideas, in a broad sense, had been familiar to the readers of Dostoyevski and Kafka (q.v.) since the vogue of Kierkegaard in Germany, early in the twenties. Heidegger's own version of existentialism (as that of Karl Jaspers) is actually a kind of new humanism, profoundly different from the far more gloomy French school with its dominant concept of absurdity. Heidegger's contribution to literary thinking is rather that of a vocabulary and an emphasis on some new concepts, such as time and mood, than of a strictly aesthetic and critical nature. His writings on aesthetics (especially the article "Der Ursprung des Kunstwerkes," in *Holzwege,* 1950) and his interpretations of Rilke (q.v.), "Wozu Dichter?" (in the same collection), and of Hölderlin (*Erläuterungen zu Hölderlins Dichtung,* 1952), are extremely obscure and personal. Beauty is identified with truth, *"Kunst ist ein Werden und Geschehen der Wahrheit"* ("art is the becoming and happening of Truth"), *"Das Wesen der Dichtung ist Stiftung der Wahrheit"* ("the essence of poetry is the founding of Truth"), poetry is prophecy. The interpretation of Rilke

and Hölderlin are often very arbitrary: Hölderlin is celebrated for his "naming of the Holy," and Rilke is made out to be a Nietzschean. The "angel" of the *Duineser Elegien* is identified with the image of Zarathustra, the *Übermensch,* though in Rilke there is surely nothing of Nietzsche's strident voluntarism.

But more important than these later writings were Heidegger's general ideas: his justification of the neglect of psychology, his dismissal of the whole subject and object relationship which had dominated German thought. Criticism found a new reason (as it found it also in Husserl's phenomenology) to turn to the object itself, and to try to interpret and understand it as such by means which could be called intuitive rather than analytical. In Heidegger's system, moreover, the three dimensions of time —past, present, and future—assume a central importance which helped to focus attention on the concept or feeling for time in literature (q.v.).

Existentialism thus combined a rejection of the old positivistic factualism with distrust for *Geistesgeschichte,* sociology, and psychology. The newly flourishing textual interpretation in Germany is usually inspired by such philosophical motives. They are prominent in the writings of Kommerell after he had left the George circle and struck out on his own. He became adverse to easy generalizations and *Geistesgeschichte* and cultivated what in the United States would be called "close reading." In *Gedanken über Gedichte* (1943), which is mainly devoted to subtle interpretations of Goethe's lyrical poetry, the existentialist emphasis on poetry as "self-cognition" (*Selbsterkenntnis*), as the definition of a "mood" (*Stimmung*) is obvious, but it is combined, especially in Kommerell's other writings (*Geist und Buchstabe der Dichtung,* 1939; *Lessing und Aristoteles,* 1940; and *Dichterische Welterfahrung,* 1952) with a remarkable grasp of the symbolic and conventional nature of art: with a defense of French tragedy, *commedia dell'arte,* and Calderón.

Similarly, Emil Staiger (b. 1908) combines a subtle gift of sensitive interpretation with existentialist motifs. In his *Die Zeit als Einbildungskraft des Dichters* (1939) he interprets three poems by Brentano, Goethe, and Keller, in contrasts derived from Heidegger's terms—such as *"die reißende Zeit, der Augenblick,"* and *"die ruhende Zeit."* In the introduction all causal and psychological explanation, even simple description, of literature is rejected in favor of a phenomenology, of interpretation. *Grundbegriffe der Poetik* (1946) is an attempt to give the three traditional genres (lyric, epic, drama) a new meaning by linking them to the three dimensions of Heidegger's time-concept. The lyric is associated with the present; the epic, or rather the epical, with the past; the drama, or rather the dramatic, with the future. The weird scheme is based on an analysis of the German romantic lyric, of Homer, and of some tragedies (Sophocles, Schiller, and Kleist). It revives speculations suggested by Jean Paul and a little-known English 19th c. critic, E. S. Dallas, but the scheme breaks down as it has no relation to any historical meaning of the genres. Staiger has to admit that his concept of the tragic has never been purely realized in any work of poetry. In recent writings (especially *Goethe*, 3 vols., 1952-56) Staiger has found a way of combining historical and stylistic methods while still expressing the new existentialist *Weltgefühl*, and in *Die Kunst der Interpretation* (1956) he has again defended and exemplified his remarkable talent for the "close reading" of German poetry. In *Stilwandel* (1963) Staiger collected essays on changes of style, which he interprets purely in terms of the prevailing stylistic situation.

Other critics of the age reflect the turn to the text, combined with existentialist philosophizing. A collection of interpretations of thirty German poems, *Gedicht und Gedanke* (ed. Heinz Otto Burger, 1942) was a sign of the time, and even earlier Johannes Pfeiffer (b. 1902) had written a sensitive introduction to poetry (*Umgang mit Dichtung*, 1936). Pfeiffer's collection of essays (*Zwischen Dichtung und Philosophie*, 1947) also propounds the conception that poetry opens the hidden depths of existence and calls thus to decision, to *Wesenhaftigkeit*. In Hans Hennecke's essays, *Dichtung und Dasein* (1950), the existentialist motive is also apparent, but the taste is more eclectic and much effort goes into rather indiscriminating expositions of American and English authors of the recent past. While Hennecke is definitely a reviewer, a middleman, Otto Friedrich Bollnow (b. 1903) is a philosopher rather than critic. In his book *Rilke* (1951) he interprets the late poetry with great acumen in terms of existential philosophy: the *Unheimlichkeit* (uncanniness) of the world, the precariousness of human existence, the proximity of death. A later collection of essays, *Unruhe und Geborgenheit* (1953), which, besides contemporary texts, uses Novalis, E. T. A. Hoffmann, and Eichendorff, points to an escape from existentialism into a new philosophy in which man would find refuge from his anxiety.

Walter Muschg's *Tragische Literaturgeschichte* (1948; 2nd completely revised ed., 1953) is also related in mood and interests to the existentialist movement. Muschg (1898-1966) has, however, criticized Heidegger's interpretations of German poetry very severely (see his article "Zerschwatzte Dichtung," in *Die Zerstörung der deutschen Literatur*, 1956). In his large book he treats, in almost encyclopedic fashion, all the sufferings, misfortunes, and tragedies of writers and poets of all times and places, aiming not so much at a sociology of the artist as at a typology of the poet, who may have been magician, seer, singer, juggler, or priest before the modern type was established. Somewhat incongruously the book attempts, besides, a new theory of genres of the kind envisaged by Staiger: only in Muschg the first person, the poet's "I," is associated with magic, the second with mystical identification with the "Thou," the third with myth and representation. Muschg is acutely aware of what he believes to be the tragedy of German literature: the isolation and final ineffectiveness of its classics. The argument of the book is, however, weakened by its diffuseness and all-inclusive scope. All questions of poetics and literary history are drowned out by the leading theme: a solemn, monotonous dirge over the poet's cruel fate in the world.

Somewhat apart stands Hans Egon Holthusen (b. 1913). He also is deeply influenced by existentialism, but he has found his standard of judgment in Protestant Christianity. In his four books of essays, *Der unbehauste Mensch* (1951), *Ja und Nein* (1954), *Das Schöne und das Wahre* (1958), and *Kritisches Verstehen* (1961), he has proved himself a genuine critic, not only an interpreter or historian of poetry. He asserts the necessity of judging, the authority of the critic, which he feels cannot be purely aesthetic. He argues against the usual German prejudice in favor of sentiment and emphasizes the role of language in poetry. The word in poetry does not "mean" anything, but posits reality. It is a reality fraught with the need for decisions and thus eminently ethical. Holthusen, firmly anchored in his faith, has judged Rilke as a propounder of false ideas (though a great poet), has welcomed the position of the later Eliot and the passing of what he calls the "zero-point" in recent German literature: its emergence from the depth of despair. Holthusen, in his many fine essays, is not only a literary critic, but a critic of civilization deeply engaged in the present crisis of man, his loss of religion, the dangers of his predicament.

Existentialism strengthened the return to the text, but, in the long run, literary values and distinctions between poetry and philosophy tend to disappear in existentialist criticism. Heidegger proclaimed the view that all great works of art say basically the same thing. But individuality and history would disappear if this were true; discrimination and hence criticism would become impossible. Existentialism, in spite of its insights into the human condition, represents an impasse for literary theory and criticism. The structure and form of a work of art are dissolved. We are back again at the identification of art with philosophy, of art with truth, which has been the bane of German criticism since, at least, the time of Schelling and Hegel. While intuitive interpretation in this philosophical sense and *Geistesgeschichte* flourish in Germany, criticism in the sense of judgment by artistic criteria, based on a coherent literary theory, supported by textual analysis, is almost nonexistent.

ENGLAND AND THE UNITED STATES

English and American criticism in the 20th c. has to be considered together, though the conditions and developments of imaginative literature have differed widely in the two countries. But in criticism, there was not only the specially intense interchange of ideas between countries with the same language; the key figures in the renewal of criticism moved from one country to the other and influenced both profoundly. Pound and Eliot (qq.v.) were Americans who came to England in 1907 and 1914 respectively, and I. A. Richards (b. 1893), a Cambridge don, went to Harvard University in 1931. It is no exaggeration to say that all modern criticism in the English-speaking world is derived from these three critics.

But before their points of view became dominant, much time had elapsed and many various developments had taken place. As these were very different in the two countries, we must deal separately first with pre-Eliotic criticism in England.

In England, around 1900, criticism was at a low ebb. The aesthetic movement was discredited after the trial of Wilde (q.v.) and survived only in the refined, though erratic essayist Arthur Symons (1865-1945). Very little criticism

in the strict sense was produced, though academic literary scholarship with critical pretensions flourished. Several survivors from the 19th c. even wrote their most impressive books. George Saintsbury (1845-1933) wrote *A History of Criticism and Literary Taste in Europe* (3 vols., 1900-1904), a first attempt to map out the whole field from Plato to Pater, a *History of English Prosody* (3 vols., 1906-1910), and *A History of English Prose Rhythm* (1912). Saintsbury's last major work, *A History of the French Novel* (2 vols., 1917-19), shows him at his best: directly commenting on books without any need to worry about principles or theories. Saintsbury's standards are impressionistic and vaguely historical. He always celebrates *gusto*, the joy of literature, and carries his enormous reading lightly. He has great merits in boldly surveying wide fields, and he has a taste which is open to the unusual, especially the metaphysical poetry of the 17th c. But he lacks any coherent theory, despises aesthetics, and is often slipshod, jaunty, and violently prejudiced. In contrast to Saintsbury, (Sir) Edmund Gosse (1849-1928) was almost entirely a portraitist and causerist who in his later years wrote voluminously for the *Sunday Times*. His works of scholarship and biographies (e.g. *A Life of Swinburne,* 1917) are urbane, but lack Saintsbury's edge and candor.

William J. Courthope (1842-1917) was the author of a massive *History of English Poetry* (6 vols., 1895-1910), which relates poetry to political and national ideals, with a taste which can be described as neoclassical (cf. *Life in Poetry: Law in Taste,* 1901). Oliver Elton (1861-1945) wrote a monumental work, *Survey of English Literature, 1740-1880* (6 vols., 1912-28), which is always admirably well-informed, firsthand, sane, but critically rather colorless. In philosophical brainwork and subtle analysis Andrew Cecil Bradley's (1851-1935) *Shakespearean Tragedy* (1904) superseded earlier criticism of Shakespeare. His concept of Shakespeare, colored by the Hegelian theory of tragedy, and his emphasis on character almost outside and apart from the play have been sharply criticized, but must be recognized as the most coherent and penetrating of their kind. His eloquent statement on "poetry for poetry's sake" (in *Oxford Lectures on Poetry,* 1909) defines an idealistic version of the autonomy of art. W. P. Ker (1855-1923) was primarily a medievalist of wide range who, in his later years, was engaged in a study of poetics and contributed with exceptional learning to a discussion of form, style, and genres, very unusual at that time in English scholarship.

But the most characteristic figures of English academic criticism were (Sir) Walter Raleigh (1861-1922) and (Sir) Arthur Quiller-Couch (1863-1944). Raleigh, professor of English literature (q.v.) at Oxford who wrote on Milton, Shakespeare, and Dr. Johnson, always disparaged theory and criticism, and praised empire builders, voyagers, and men of action. The many essays of "Q" are permeated by an even heartier air of manliness and gusto. H. W. Garrod, professor of poetry at Oxford, formulated the prevailing academic attitude when he wrote that criticism is best when "written with the least worry of head, the least disposition to break the heart over ultimate questions." This negative, profoundly skeptical attitude toward criticism was fashionable in England and paralyzed any criticism which went beyond "the art of praise" in rambling, usually whimsical, allusive essays.

A group of writers and intellectuals known as the "Bloomsbury group" was subtler in its tastes and finer in its sensibilities, but did not achieve any break with impressionistic criticism. None of them was primarily a literary critic. Lytton Strachey (q.v.) started with a short, brilliant book, *Landmarks in French Literature* (1912), and wrote essays which show an exceptional, "un-English" taste in Racine and Pope, but often suffer from his brash wit. Virginia Woolf (q.v.) wrote sensitive, warm, evocative essays which devote attention to questions of the reading public (two collections: *The Common Reader*, 1925; and *The Second Common Reader*, 1932). Forster (q.v.) wrote a sparkling though elementary essay, *Aspects of the Novel* (1927), and collected other essays (e.g., *Abinger Harvest*, 1936). There are other English essayists (e.g., Desmond MacCarthy, F. L. Lucas [b. 1894], Connolly [q.v.]) who know how to communicate the pleasures of literature and to share their sensibility. But, in general, whatever the merits of these essayists, English criticism, before the advent of Eliot and Richards, suffered from an almost complete lack of system, method, and theory, or even coherent frame of ideas and, in its taste, propounded little more than diluted romanticism.

American criticism, about 1900, differed sharply from its English counterpart. There was hardly any academic criticism to speak of, as American professors of literature were then philologists, specializing mainly in Anglo-Saxon

or Chaucer. There was much impressionistic criticism, best represented by James Huneker (1860-1921), who brought the newest Parisian and German fashions from the Continent and described them in turgid, enthusiastic essays. In the background there loomed Henry James (q.v.), who had gone to live in England. The *Prefaces* (1907-1909) he wrote for the so-called New York edition of his novels were hardly appreciated in their time. They are the finest poetics of the novel, its point of view, its narrative techniques, its implied morality, and the most subtle, possibly oversubtle self-examination of the creative processes of a modern artist. Only Percy Lubbock (1879-1966), an English friend, in his *Craft of Fiction* (1921), gave currency to James's insights. The *Prefaces* themselves were first made available by Blackmur (q.v.) in an edition with a long analytical introduction, *The Art of the Novel* (1934).

Against the whole "genteel" tradition of American literature (q.v.), there arose early in the c. a critical movement which could be called "radical" and has obvious affinities with the rising American naturalism (q.v.). Its main spokesman was H. L. Mencken (q.v.), who was professedly a Nietzschean and "aristocrat" in his contempt for the values of a mass civilization, but as a literary critic must be described rather as a propagandist for Dreiser, Sinclair Lewis (qq.v.), and other new writers —for anybody whom he considered vigorous and alive, capable of breaking with the standards of the past. Mencken, especially as editor of the *American Mercury* (1924-33), fulfilled an important function in the self-criticism of American civilization, but as a literary critic he was a boisterous polemicist of quite erratic taste. He could extol such meretricious authors as Joseph Hergesheimer (1880-1954) or Cabell (q.v.) and had little power of characterization and analysis.

Van Wyck Brooks (1886-1963) fulfilled a similar function with his early criticism. In many books, especially *America's Coming-of-Age* (1915), Brooks deplored the plight of the artist in America and argued that "our writers who have possessed a vivid personal genius were paralyzed by the want of a social background," because a society whose end is impersonal cannot produce an ideal reflex in literature. In psychological studies of Twain ([q.v.] *The Ordeal of Mark Twain*, 1920) and James (*The Pilgrimage of Henry James*, 1925), who either surrendered to gentility or fled to Europe, Brooks pursued his ideal of a liberal, mature

America welcoming the artist and his criticism. But in recent decades Brooks has turned more and more to an uncritical and even sentimental glorification of American literary history, in a series of books beginning with *The Flowering of New England* (1936). They are little more than nostalgic chronicles. In *The Opinions of Oliver Allston* (1941), Brooks attacked all modern literature as pessimistic and recommended only "primary" writers, producing optimistic literature, "conducive to race-survival." His strange list of cheerful classics includes Tolstoi (q.v.), Dostoyevski, and Thomas Mann (q.v.).

A similar point of view was stated even more violently by De Voto (q.v.) in *The Literary Fallacy* (1944). The war changed a liberal critical movement to an uncritical, intolerant, even obscurantist "nativism." The earlier, broader social view of this critical movement was codified for literary history by Vernon Louis Parrington (1871-1928), in his *Main Currents of American Thought* (3 vols., 1927-30). Here literature is seen, in terms resembling Taine's, as an expression of national ideals, American literature as the history of Jeffersonian democracy. In Parrington much is done for a history of political ideas, but more "belletristic" writers, such as Poe, Melville, or Henry James, are slighted.

Opposed to this general trend of radicalism was the movement of the American humanists. From various sources (mainly Arnold and French neoclassicism) they drew a view of literature as a means of personal and social order. They condemned romanticism and all its forms and recommended a literature filled with a sense of balance, ethical restraint, and measure. Paul Elmer More (1864-1937) collected his essays under the title *Shelburne Essays* (11 vols., 1904-1921), to which he added a twelfth volume with the characteristic title, *The Demon of the Absolute* (1928). In the early volumes More ranged widely and showed an admirable quality of judicious sympathy which earned him comparisons with Sainte-Beuve. But More's standards became more rigid with time, and the later volumes are all devoted to an attack on aestheticism, naturalism, and modernism in the name of tradition, standards, and a philosophical dualism which rigidly upheld the necessity of an "inner check" in man against all spontaneity and caprice. Pater was no critic to More, Dos Passos' (q.v.) *Manhattan Transfer* (1925) "an explosion in a cesspool," Dreiser's

art "a miscegenation of the gutter and the psychological laboratory."

More was a learned Greek scholar who wrote in his later years a history of Christian Platonism and embraced High Anglicanism. His friend and ally, Irving Babbitt (1865-1933), differs from him sharply, though he shares his general outlook. Babbitt is a much harder, cruder writer: a violent, pungent polemist quite secular in outlook. He was a Stoic with some interest in Buddhism and Confucianism. Babbitt, a Harvard professor of French, attacked the American factualism imported from Germany in *Literature and the American College* (1908). He recommended, with many reservations, the French critics in *The Masters of Modern French Criticism* (1912), especially Ferdinand Brunetière (1849-1906). *Rousseau and Romanticism* (1919) was a powerful anti-romantic tract mercilessly ridiculing the romantic worship of genius, passion, and nature, its misconception of man as naturally good. Babbitt's books are filled with a passionate concern for ideas and ethics; they suffer from a lack of aesthetic sensibility, an obtuseness of reading, a harsh and strident manner.

More and Babbitt found several influential adherents, among whom was Norman Foerster (b. 1887). Foerster, who had written well on earlier *American Criticism* (1929), organized the statements which for a short period (1929-30) attracted wide public attention to the humanist movement. The movement failed for obvious reasons: the social conservatism of the humanists ran counter to the temper of a nation just plunged into the Depression; their rigid moralism violated the nature of literature as an art; and their hostility to the contemporary arts cut them off from literature as a living institution. Still, the humanist movement left an imprint on the American universities. It helped to emancipate literary teaching from the old factualism and spread a concern for ideas and the relation of literature to life. It influenced many critics even when they rejected the creed itself: Eliot, Francis O. Matthiessen (1902-1950), Austin Warren (b. 1899), Yvor Winters (q.v.).

But the rejuvenation of criticism came, not only in the United States but also in England, from two Americans: Pound and Eliot. Pound preached "imagism" since about 1912: a simple colloquial poetry, in rhythms close to those of spoken language, with an eye turned to the object, "austere, direct, free from emotional slither." He had violently reacted against the romantic and Victorian taste, but made, at first, little impression beyond a small following which was joined by Eliot. Eliot had begun to write criticism when at Harvard in 1909, but established a reputation as a critic only with a collection of essays *The Sacred Wood* (1920). It was secured, after the great success of *The Waste Land* (1922), with *For Lancelot Andrewes* (1928), which contained, in its preface, the famous declaration that he was "Royalist, Anglo-Catholic and classicist." In the meantime, I. A. Richards's *Principles of Literary Criticism* (1924) had made a profound impact. Richards has an entirely different intellectual background from Eliot, in positivistic psychology and in utilitarianism. Strangely and surprisingly, the doctrines of Eliot and Richards fused in many minds. Eliot and Richards influenced each other. In combination with F. R. Leavis (b. 1895) in England, and with Cleanth Brooks (b. 1906) in the United States, a body of doctrines was evolved which is the core of what is usually called the "New Criticism."

Pound, though highly important as the main instigator of the changes in taste, is himself hardly a critic. He is rather the maker of manifestoes, a man who proclaims his preferences and rankings, but never argues or analyzes as a critic should. Pound's occasional attempts at poetic theory are crude and his literary history is extremely arbitrary. He had, however, the merit of drawing attention to much poetry which was little known except to specialists: Provençal, very early Italian before Dante, and Chinese. Pound conceived as an ideal of criticism the task "to define the classic." He succeeded in construing a highly selective ancestry for his own poetry and in disparaging everything that did not fit the pattern. According to Pound, there is nothing in German poetry besides the *Minnesänger* and Heine. There is nothing in French between Villon and the symbolists. In English, Milton is "the most unpleasant poet," a "thorough-going decadent," and among the English 19th c. poets only Landor and Browning find favor in Pound's eyes. Pound was less interested in prose; he wrote in detail only on James and Joyce (q.v.). Pound had a personal interest in James's problem of the American expatriate and was one of the first fervent admirers of Joyce. He has the courage of his opinions and the boldness of a specific new taste. But his concept of poetry is very narrow and his idea of tradition is that of an agglomeration of appealing hobbies, un-

connected glimpses of most diverse civilizations and styles. He often behaves like a "barbarian in a museum" (Yvor Winters).

T. E. Hulme (1883-1917) is usually coupled with Pound as a precursor of Eliot. He may have influenced Pound in the formulation of the imagist creed. But Eliot never knew Hulme, who was killed in the war. His writings (with the exception of scattered articles) appeared only in 1924, as *Speculations*. By then Eliot's views were fully established. Hulme has been much overrated; he reflects a new taste and imports new ideas, but he had little to say which is his own. Much of his writing is straight exposition: of Bergson (q.v.) and of Worringer's *Abstraktion und Einfühlung* (1908). But Bergsonism and a worship of abstract geometrical art are contradictory and Hulme could never reconcile the two. In his most independent essay, "Romanticism and Classicism," Hulme expounds the antiromanticism of the Action Française and of Lasserre. Romanticism is to him the revolution, bourgeois liberalism, "spilt religion," a sentimental trust in human nature. Against this, Hulme pits classicism, which implies a belief in original sin. The contrast is then pinned to the Coleridgean distinction of imagination and fancy. Imagination is romantic, fancy classical. What is needed today is a fanciful, precise, visual poetry. Hulme makes a faltering attempt to claim Coleridge and Bergson for this kind of "classicism," but cannot succeed. He wants an imagist, metaphorical poetry, in free verse. But it is hard to see what all this has to do with Bergson and his romantic philosophy of flux (except the emphasis on the concrete) and how it can be brought in line with admiration for Byzantine mosaics, Egyptian sculpture, and Epstein. Apparently we have to do with different stages in the development of a young man (the writings on plastic art all date from December 1913 to July 1914) who had a long way to go toward the definition of an original point of view. But he was an important symptom.

Eliot is often similar in taste to Pound. But as a critic he is immeasurably subtler and more profound. Like Pound, Eliot reacted strongly against romanticism and Milton. He exalted Dante, the Jacobean dramatists, the metaphysical poets, and the French symbolists as the bearers of *the* tradition of great poetry. But in Eliot we are not only confronted with a change of taste. The new tradition is defended in terms of a new classicism, of a whole superstructure of ideas which appeals to the Latin and Christian tradition. It is anchored in a theory of poetry which starts with a psychology of poetic creation. Poetry is not the "overflow of powerful feelings," is not the expression of personality, but is an impersonal organization of feelings which demands a "unified sensibility," a collaboration of intellect and feeling in order to find the precise "objective correlative," the symbolic structure of a work of art. Eliot expounded a scheme of the history of English poetry which postulates a "unified sensibility" before the middle of the 17th c., especially in the metaphysical poets, and then traces its "dissociation," in the purely intellectual poetry of the 18th c. and the purely emotional poetry of the 19th. He postulated the need of reintegration, fulfilled in his own poetry (and that of other contemporaries such as Pound). It is both intellectual and emotional; it concerns the whole man, not only the heart. But while Eliot speaks of unified sensibility, of the fusion of thought and feeling, he still insists that poetry is not knowledge of any kind. The poet is no philosopher or thinker. "Neither Shakespeare nor Dante did any thinking." A poet such as Dante who has taken over the system of Thomas Aquinas is preferable, in this respect, to a poet such as Shakespeare who has picked up ideas from anywhere or to Goethe who has construed his own personal philosophy. Eliot, who had earlier defended the "integrity" and autonomy of poetry, came to the recognition of a double standard in criticism: artistic and moral-philosophical-theological. "The 'greatness' of literature," he argued, "cannot be determined solely by literary standards." More and more Eliot judged works of literature by their conformity to the tradition and to orthodoxy. The distinction between "art-ness" and "greatness," which again divorces form and content, grew out of Eliot's preoccupation with the question of "belief" in literature. The problem whether the reader should or must share the ideas of an author worried Eliot and Richards greatly.

Eliot took several often conflicting positions, at one time arguing that the reader need not agree and later coming to the conclusion that we cannot give poetic assent to anything which we consider "incoherent, immature and not founded on the facts of experience" (as the poetry of Shelley appeared to Eliot). But Eliot's criticism was at its best when he could forget about "belief" and the related problem of "sincerity" (how far has the poet to believe the ideas he expresses?) and, rather, analyze the work itself. Eliot constantly stressed the role of language in poetry, which should be "the perfection of common language." Milton's language is condemned as artificial and conventional. Poetry must not lose touch with the living language. Eliot defended what used to be called prosaic poetry such as that of Dryden or Dr. Johnson. But he could think of poetry often also as logic of the imagination, a sequence of images or even moments of emotional intensity. Sound and meter seem to him less central, as the "music" of poetry means to him much more than sound-patterns. It is the interplay of sound and meaning and of the secondary meanings. In "music" the poet touches the frontiers of consciousness: yet the poet is not a primitive man, but rather contains all history. Poets are related to their times; they cannot help expressing them, even their chaos, but, on the other hand, poetry is also timeless. There is a final hierarchy of the poets, an ultimate greater or less. There is an interplay between "Tradition and the Individual Talent" (1919). Tradition involves the historical sense and the historical sense to Eliot "involves a perception, not only of the pastness of the past, but of its presence." A poet should write "not merely with his own generation in his bones, but with a feeling that the whole literature of Europe from Homer on has a simultaneous existence and composes a simultaneous order." Tradition is the classical tradition descended from Greece and Rome. Rome (and such a poet as Virgil) is the indispensable link in the chain of tradition. Germany is sometimes excluded from this unity of European culture, defined as both Christian and classical. But in his later years Eliot welcomed Germany back again into the European fold and even recanted his earlier opinion, which excluded Goethe from the great classics, praising his "wisdom" and even his science.

Eliot thus construed the tradition very selectively. It converged on his practice as a poet: the bright visual imagination of Dante, the living speech of the later Shakespeare, of Donne and Dryden, the dramatic lyricism of Donne, Browning, and Pound, the "wit" and "unified sensibility" of the metaphysical poets, the "irony" of Laforgue, the impersonality of Mallarmé and Valéry (q.v.). Much of Eliot's impact is due to his practical criticism: to his brief, dogmatic, assertive but persuasive and subtle essays which seem often to proceed only by his quoting a few passages and making brief comparisons.

In several lectures (e.g., "The Frontiers of Criticism," 1956) Eliot slighted his own criticism, deplored the influence of some catchphrases derived from it, and detached himself from what he calls the "lemon-squeezer school of criticism." From the point of view of literary criticism, Eliot's influence declined in his later years. His interests shifted away from pure criticism, and he was apt to use literature as a document for his jeremiads on the modern world. He finally became committed to a double standard which dissolved the unity of the work of art as well as the sensibility which goes into its making and the critical act itself. But, taken in its early purity, his criticism was the most influential of the c.

Only I. A. Richards can compare with Eliot in influence. Richards differs completely in aim and method, but shares many of Eliot's tastes and, with his practical criticism, has helped to define the turn toward an analysis of verbal art which prevails in English-American criticism. But Richards is primarily interested, in theory, in the psychic effect of poetry on the mind of its reader. Richards does not recognize a world of aesthetic values and emotions. Rather, the only value of art is the psychic organization which it imposes on us, what Richards describes as "the patterning of impulses," the equilibrium of attitudes it induces. The artist is conceived almost as a mental healer and art as therapy. Richards has not, however, been able to describe this effect of art very concretely, though he thinks that it will replace religion as a social force. He has finally to admit that the desired, balanced poise can be given by "a carpet or a pot, by a gesture as by the Parthenon." It does not ultimately matter whether we like good or bad poetry, as long as we order our minds. Thus Richards' theory—which is objective and scientific in its pretensions and often appeals to future advances of neurology—ends with critical paralysis: a complete divorce between the poem as an objective structure and the reader's mind.

But fortunately Richards has eluded, in practice, the consequences of his theory and has come to grips with specific poetic texts by applying a theory of meaning first developed in *The Meaning of Meaning: A Study of the Influence of Language upon Thought* (with C. K. Ogden, 1923). In *Principles of Literary Criticism* (1924) Richards analyzed the different components of a work of art in psychological terms, into sensations, images, emotions, attitudes, and suggested standards of evaluation:

a grading of poetry in terms of complexity with a preference for a poetry of "inclusion" (a term derived from Santayana [q.v.]), a difficult poetry which would resist ironic contemplation. Richards' analysis of meaning, which distinguishes between sense, tone, feeling, and intention, emphasizes the ambiguities of language, the function of metaphor as central to poetry. Later, in *Coleridge on Imagination* (1934), Richards even restated the romantic theory of imagination as fusing and unifying, in which the most disparate elements of the world come together. The affinity with Eliot's "unified sensibility" is obvious; but in Richards, poetry is even more deliberately cut off from all knowledge and even reference. On the basis of a simple dichotomy between intellectual and emotive language, truth is assigned to science, while art can do nothing but arouse emotions which must, however, be patterned, equipoised, complex, to achieve the purpose of mental ordering. Poetry at most elaborates the myths by which men live, even though these myths may be untrue, may be mere "pseudo-statements" in the light of science.

In his later essays (the newest collection is *Speculative Instruments,* 1955) Richards has given up his earlier reliance on neurology, but the point of view has remained in substance the same. Richards is primarily a theorist and has written little on actual texts; but *Practical Criticism* (1928), a book which analyzes the papers of students who were set to discuss a series of poems given to them without the names of the authors, shows Richards' pedagogical talent in the teaching and analyzing of poetry. He distinguishes the various sources of misunderstanding: the difficulty of making out the plain sense of a poem, the lack of sensibility to meter and rhythm, the misinterpretation of figurative language, the critical pitfalls of stock-responses, of sentimentality or hardness of heart, of ideological or technical preconceptions. Richards' technique of interpretation analyzes language, but unlike the logical positivists it favors a great flexibility of vocabulary and trains in distinguishing shades of meaning.

This is the starting point of Richards' most gifted English disciple, Empson (q.v.), who, in *Seven Types of Ambiguity* (1930; revised ed., 1953) developed, in a series of brilliant interpretations of poetic passages, a scheme which allowed him to distinguish types of ambiguity, progressing in complexity, with the increasing distance from the simple statement. Empson draws out implicit meanings, defines by multiple definitions, and pursues to the farthest ends the implications, poetic and social, of difficult, witty, metaphorical poetry. He is not only an analyst but a critic who tries to justify his own taste in poetry and disparages simple romantic emotionalism or vagueness. In his later books Empson has combined this method of semantic analysis with ideas drawn from psychoanalysis and Marxism. In *Some Versions of Pastoral* (1935), a term which includes proletarian literature, *Alice in Wonderland* is psychoanalyzed, and Gray's "Elegy Written in a Country Churchyard" is interpreted as a defense of Tory conservatism. In *The Structure of Complex Words* (1950), Empson has freed himself from the emotionalism of Richards and has developed a concept of meaning which allows for knowledge and reference. He has again displayed an amazing ingenuity in verbal analysis and an acute awareness of social implications. Terms such as "wit" or "honest" are analyzed in different contexts, in Pope or Shakespeare.

But Empson often leaves the realm of literary criticism for a special kind of linguistics and has become more and more enmeshed in a private world of associations and speculations which lose contact with the text and use it only as pretext for his fireworks of wit and recondite ingenuity. Empson's recent book, *Milton's God* (1961; revised ed., 1965), is even further removed from literary criticism. It is an attack on Christianity and, in particular, on the conception of God the Father sacrificing His Son. Milton is praised for his picture of God in *Paradise Lost*, a God who seems to Empson "astonishingly like Uncle Joe Stalin." The poem has "barbaric power" because Milton could express "a downright horrible conception of God."

The impulses emanating from Eliot and Richards were most effectively combined, at least in England, in the work of F. R. Leavis and his disciples grouped around the magazine *Scrutiny* (1932-53). Leavis is a man of strong convictions and harsh polemical manners. He has in recent years sharply underlined his disagreement with the later developments of Eliot and Richards. But his starting point is there: in Eliot's taste and in Richards' technique of analysis. He differs from them mainly by a strongly Arnoldian concern for a moralistic humanism. In *New Bearings in English Poetry* (1932) he criticized Victorian and Georgian poetry, and praised and analyzed the later

Yeats (q.v.), the early Eliot, and the newly discovered Gerard Manley Hopkins (1844-89), whose poems had been published for the first time in 1918. *Revaluation* (1936) was the first consistent attempt to rewrite the history of English poetry from a 20th c. point of view. Spenser, Milton, Tennyson, and Swinburne recede into the background; Donne, Pope, Wordsworth, Keats, Hopkins, Yeats, and T. S. Eliot emerge as the carriers of the great tradition.

In contrast to Eliot, Leavis admires Pope much more than Dryden and establishes his descent from the metaphysical poets. Like Eliot, Leavis disparages Shelley "as repetitious, vaporous, monotonously self-regarding, and often emotionally cheap." But he appreciates Wordsworth for his sanity (though he does not share his philosophy) and Keats for his emotional maturity. Similarly, Leavis attempted in *The Great Tradition* (1948) to establish a new selection from the English novel. The 18th c. novelists and Scott are dismissed, as are Dickens ("a great entertainer"), Thackeray, and Meredith. Only Jane Austen, George Eliot, Henry James, Conrad (q.v.), and D. H. Lawrence (q.v.) survive. Leavis practices close reading, a training in sensibility, which has little use for literary history or theory. But "sensibility" with Leavis means also a sense for tradition, a concern for culture, for humanity. On the one hand, he rejects Marxism, and on the other, the orthodoxy of Eliot. He admires a local culture, the organic community of the English countryside.

Leavis has sharply criticized the commercialization and standardization of English literary life and has defended the need for tradition, for a social code and order, for "maturity," "sanity," and "discipline." But these terms are purely secular and include the ideals of D. H. Lawrence, whom Leavis interprets to conform to a healthy tradition (see *D. H. Lawrence, Novelist,* 1955). Leavis' emphasis on the text, and even the texture of words, is often deceptive: his observations on form, technique, and language are often haphazard and arbitrary. Actually he leaves the verbal surface very quickly in order to define the particular emotions or sentiments an author conveys. He becomes a social and moral critic, who, however, insists on the continuity between language and ethics, on the morality of form. Leavis' ultimate value criterion, "Life," remains, however, bafflingly obscure: it means anti-aestheticism, realism, optimism, or just courage

317

and devotion in turn, as, on the whole, Leavis as a resolute empiricist, leaves his premises unexamined and displays a complacent distrust of and even hatred for theory.

Leavis has managed to assemble a group of disciples, of whom many have contributed importantly to the development of English criticism. Lionel Charles Knights (b. 1906), in *Drama and Society in the Age of Jonson* (1937) and in *Explorations* (1947), is mainly concerned with the Elizabethans. Derek Traversi (b. 1912) has interpreted Shakespeare, with great sensitivity, especially in *An Approach to Shakespeare* (1938) and *Shakespeare: The Last Phase* (1954). Martin Turnell (b. 1908) has written extensively, though often loosely, on French literature (q.v.). His *The Classical Moment: Studies in Corneille, Molière, Racine* (1947), *The Novel in France* (1950), *Baudelaire* (1952), and *The Art of French Fiction* (1959), which exalts Stendhal and Proust (q.v.) at the expense of Balzac and Flaubert, are instructive but often diffuse and erratic books. Mrs. Q. D. Leavis, in *Fiction and the Reading Public* (1932), supplied the arguments for the general view of the decline of modern taste and the shrinking of a cultivated audience. Marius Bewley (b. 1918), an American adherent, has studied Hawthorne and Henry James (in *The Complex Fate*, 1952) and the 19th c. American novel (in *The Eccentric Design*, 1957). The intransigence of the group has diminished its immediate effectiveness; F. R. Leavis does not even recognize parallel efforts elsewhere. But in spite of shortcomings in sympathy, a certain provinciality and an excessive preoccupation with the pedagogy of literature, Leavis and his group have produced fine practical criticism which has established the new taste and again justified the social role of literature in a minority culture.

Side by side with what could loosely be called Eliotic criticism, a number of English critics were active who could be labeled "neoromantic." They are men who finally appeal to an inner voice, to the subconscious mind, and who think of criticism mainly as a process of self-expression and self-discovery. Still, all have learned from Eliot and would have written quite differently without him as a model.

John Middleton Murry (1889-1957) passed through bafflingly diverse stages in his development. He has written a *Life of Jesus* (1926), as well as *The Necessity of Communism* (1932). Murry, once widely admired, has been losing influence steadily, as his later books are neither good biography nor good criticism, and indulge more and more in private theosophic speculation. But it seems unfair to neglect his early criticism because of the vagaries of his search for God. His book *Dostoevsky* (1916), though often quite mistaken in its interpretations, was an early attempt to see Dostoyevksi as a kind of symbolist. *The Problem of Style* (1922) is remarkably similar in outlook to Eliot's early phase, though Eliot is not mentioned. There is the same emphasis on visual imagination, on metaphor as a mode of apprehension, on the transformation of emotion in a work of art which Murry calls "crystallization." His early collection of essays, *Aspects of Literature* (1920), and *Countries of the Mind* (1922), should also be classed with Eliotic criticism. But Murry's book *Keats and Shakespeare* (1925) shows a shift: it is a biographical interpretation (often sensitive and moving) of Keats's growth and struggle for maturity, of his "soul-making." The parallel with Shakespeare, however, remains obscure, and the tone has become fervent and often oracular. *Son of Woman, the Story of D. H. Lawrence* (1931) is a highly personal interpretation of his friend and enemy: it makes Lawrence out a weakling who willed himself into vitality. An arbitrary theosophy invaded the books *William Blake* (1933) and *Shakespeare* (1936), and there is hardly anything to be said for the dull book *Jonathan Swift* (1954).

The same fate seems to have befallen R. Wilson Knight (b. 1897). His early writings, especially *The Wheel of Fire* (1929), elaborate a technique of Shakespeare interpretation by leading images and clusters, by some kind of metaphorical organization. Knight still had contact with the text, a feeling for evidence, though the antithesis, tempest versus music, seems pressed too hard. But Knight's later books show a gradual deterioration of critical intelligence. The same method is applied indiscriminately to all writers: whether Pope or Wordsworth, Milton or Byron. All poetry is reduced to a conveyor of the same mystic message. The allegorical reading of Milton anticipating even details of World War II (with Hitler as Satan) and the interpretation of Byron as "the next Promethean man in Western history after Christ" (in *Byron: The Christian Virtues*, 1952), are so fantastic that they cease to be criticism or scholarship.

By far the best of these neoromantic critics was Sir Herbert Read (q.v.). He advocated surrealism (q.v.), psychoanalysis, and the use of the Jungian collective unconscious in literature (see Psychology and Literature), but basically kept a central critical insight into organic form. His *Wordsworth* (1930) pressed the theme of Wordsworth's supposed feeling of guilt because of his affair with Annette Vallon very far. In his *In Defence of Shelley* (1936) he attempted a psychoanalysis of Shelley which serves as a rather double-edged apology for his life. But the core of Read's writings is to be found in the *Collected Essays on Literary Criticism* (1938) and *The True Voice of Feeling* (1953), in which a theory of organic form, of spontaneity, obscurity, myth, and dream is propounded with constant appeals to the great English romantic poets, particularly Coleridge, in whom Read found anticipations of Freudianism and existentialism (q.v.). Read shows sensitivity, style, and a theoretical mind. Though he advocated surrender to the "dark unconscious," he did so sanely and clearly. His irrationalism was always tempered by a lively sense of the social role of both the arts and crafts.

RECENT AMERICAN CRITICISM

Recent American criticism is usually lumped together under the term the "New Criticism," from the title of a book, published in 1941, by J. C. Ransom (q.v.). It is a misleading term, as it suggests a far greater unity of purpose and doctrine than close examination of recent American critics will reveal. It is hard to find anything in common among all the more important American critics except a reaction against the impressionism or naturalism (q.v.) of the past and a general turn toward a closer analysis of the actual text of a work of art. But even this generalization does not hold good for many critics. It is better to distinguish, at least roughly, two main groups: those who draw on the other sciences (psychoanalysis, myth, Marxism, semantics) in order to bring their insights to an understanding of literature; and those who have focused single-mindedly on the work of art, have tried to develop techniques of analysis peculiarly suited to poetry, and have defended poetry as a way to a knowledge of concrete reality. The first group of writers tend to become general critics of civilization; the second has concentrated on a modern apology of poetry against science and has attempted to define its peculiar nature and function. Only four critics in this second group, J. C. Ransom, Allen Tate (q.v.), Cleanth

Brooks, and Robert Penn Warren (q.v.), the so-called "Southern critics," have had close personal relations and form a coherent group unified in its outlook and main preoccupations.

Possibly the best-known American critic (certainly in Europe) is Edmund Wilson (q.v.), a critic of great versatility and facility who has, in turn, applied almost every method to his texts and written on almost every subject. He began his career with *Axel's Castle* (1931), a book about the symbolist movement in Western literature, with chapters on Yeats, Valéry, Eliot, Proust, Joyce, and Gertrude Stein (qq.v.), and a conclusion which predicted the demise of symbolism (q.v.) in favor of a social collective art. Though Wilson is hostile to aestheticism and decadence, his exposition of the masters of the 20th c. is sympathetic, as, on the whole, he aims at conveying enjoyment and envisages rather vaguely a reconciliation of symbolism and naturalism, art and life, criticism and history. His later writings are not unified books (with the exception of an account of socialist and communist theories of history in *To the Finland Station,* 1940), but collections of essays ranging widely over modern literature. The influence of Marxism (always sharply distinguished from Stalinism) is often discernible and, more prominently, the method of psychoanalysis. *The Wound and the Bow* (1941) takes the Philoctetes story as a symbol of the relationship between the artist's wound, his neurosis, and his bow—his art—and shows with great finesse, in studies of Dickens and Kipling (q.v.), that psychoanalytical insight can be joined with literary taste. In all his many collections, from *The Triple Thinkers* (1938) to *The Shores of Light* (1952), Wilson shows his mastery of the form of the essay (q.v.), his tolerant taste, his skill in exposition, his brilliance of formulation, his secular common sense, and strong social concern.

But Wilson, though highly meritorious in his general effect on a wide reading public, lacks analytical power and suffers from frequent lapses into journalistic indiscriminations and personal idiosyncrasies. With the exception of some original insights into the psychic histories of some of his subjects, Wilson ultimately is a middleman, immensely readable, intelligent, and sensitive, but lacking in a personal center and theory.

L. Trilling is also rather a general critic of civilization than strictly a critic of literature. He writes excellently, with common sense and discrimination, on both Freudianism and the Kinsey Report. He began with a good though diffuse book, *Matthew Arnold* (1939), and has collected his essays in *The Liberal Imagination* (1950) and *The Opposing Self* (1955). His chief concern is the relation between literature and politics. Trilling, a convinced liberal (in the American sense), is worried about the gulf between the rationality of his political convictions and the imaginative insights of modern literature as represented by Proust, Joyce, Eliot, Kafka (q.v.), Rilke (q.v.), Gide (q.v.), etc. A man of modern sensibility with a taste for Henry James and Forster (qq.v.), to whom he devoted a small book (*E. M. Forster*, 1943; 2nd revised ed., 1965), and a dislike for naturalism (Dreiser [q.v.]), he is only able to state his problem, but cannot solve it in his own terms precisely because he believes that ideas are emotions and that politics permeates literature. He finally has to come to recognize the "fortuitous and gratuitous nature of art, how it exists beyond the reach of the will alone." His fine essay on Keats shows his increasing feeling for selves conceived in opposition to general culture, for the alienation of the artist as a necessary device of his self-realization.

A similar combination of modern literary sensibility and social concern permeates the work of Francis O. Matthiessen, except that his development went in the opposite direction from Trilling's. He began (after some academic research) with a sympathetic interpretation, *The Achievement of T. S. Eliot* (1935), and then produced *The American Renaissance* (1941), a long careful study of Emerson, Thoreau, Hawthorne, Melville, and Whitman. It combines an Eliotic concern for language and diction, for symbolism and myth, with a fervent belief in the possibilities of democracy in America. Two books on Henry James pursue the old aesthetic interests, while many articles (some collected in *The Responsibilities of the Critic,* 1952) and a book (*Theodore Dreiser,* 1951) show increasingly a change of taste in the direction of realism and an overwhelming, passionately earnest concern with the social duties of the critic, in a Marxism reconciled with Christianity.

Kenneth Burke (b. 1897) attempts the most ambitious scheme of recent American criticism: he combines the methods of Marxism, psychoanalysis, and anthropology, with semantics, in order to devise a system of human behavior and motivation which uses literature only as a starting point or illustration.

Burke is rightly admired for the uncanny quickness of his mind, his astonishing originality in making connections, his dialectical skill, and terminological inventiveness. He has influenced recent criticism by his special terms and mannerisms. But judged as literary criticism, much of his work is irrelevant, and literature, more and more, is even violated and distorted in his work to serve quite extrinsic arguments and purposes.

Burke was still primarily a literary critic in *Counter-Statement* (1931), a collection of essays which contains, for instance, a brilliant comparison of Gide and Thomas Mann (q.v.). But with *Permanence and Change* (1935) and *Attitudes toward History* (1937), he began to indulge in speculations on psychology and history and to discuss literature only in the sense that, with him, life is a poem and all men are poets. *The Philosophy of Literary Form* (1941) ostensibly returns to literature. It develops a "dialectical" or "dramatic" criticism interpreting poetry as a series of "strategies for the encompassing of situations," in practice as an act of the poet's personal purification. For example, Coleridge's *Rime of the Ancient Mariner* is elaborately interpreted as "a ritual for the redemption of his drug." Similarly, in *A Grammar of Motives* (1945), Keats's "Ode on a Grecian Urn" is read in terms of the identity of love and death, of capitalist individualism and Keats's tubercular fever, in almost complete disregard of the text. *A Grammar of Motives* is the first part of a trilogy (of which the second part, *A Rhetoric of Motives*, was pub. in 1950, but the third part, *A Symbolic of Motives*, is still in progress) in which Burke attempts to construe a whole philosophy of meaning, human behavior, and action. Five terms—act, scene, agent, agency, and purpose—are used as main categories: literary illustrations abound, but the center of the whole project is elsewhere. All distinctions between life and literature, language and action disappear in Burke's theory.

Burke has increasingly lost any sense for the integrity of a work of art, the relevance of an observation or bright idea to a text. He has become imprisoned in a private world of terms and concepts, often so weirdly in opposition to ordinary usage that his speculations seem to evolve in a void. A system which plans to embrace all life ends as a baffling phantasmagoria of "strategies," categories, "charts," and "situations."

In Burke the expansion of criticism has

reached its extreme limit. At the opposite pole is the group of "Southern critics," J. C. Ransom, Allen Tate, Cleanth Brooks, and Robert Penn Warren, who have concentrated on a close study of poetic texts and a modern apology for poetry. But it would be a mistake to think of them as aesthetes or even formalists, as their concern with poetry has social and even religious implications: they have defended Southern conservatism and have seen—as Leavis did in England—the evils of urbanization and commercialization, the need for a healthy society which alone can produce vital literature. But the Southern critics have kept their concept of culture separate from their literary criticism, since they understand that art is an autonomous realm and that poetry has its own peculiar function.

Though the theories of the Southern critics could be described as a fusion of those of Eliot and I. A. Richards, they differ from them importantly in having broken with their emotionalism. They recognize that poetry is not merely emotive language, but conveys a kind of knowledge, a particular kind of concrete presentational knowledge. Thus, the analysis of a work of art has to proceed from objectively recognizable factors of the work itself rather than from the reader's responses. Ransom, the oldest of the group, an eminent poet himself, has developed the view (in *The World's Body*, 1938) that poetry conveys a sense of the particularity of the world. "As science more and more completely reduces the world to its types and forms, art, replying, must invest it again with the body." But purely physical or imagist poetry is only a first stage. "Platonic" poetry, poetry merely disguising or allegorizing truths, is bad. True poetry is like the "metaphysical" poetry of the 17th c., a new perception of the world, a new awareness of its *Dinglichkeit*, conveyed mainly by extended metaphor and pervasive symbolism. Ransom emphasizes the "texture" of poetry, its seemingly irrelevant detail, though he upholds the need of an overall "structure" (a logical content). In practice, he is often, with his insistence on "texture," in danger of reintroducing the old dichotomy of form and content. In the *New Criticism* (1941), Ransom discussed Richards, Eliot, and Yvor Winters (q.v.) with many reservations and concluded by asking for an "ontological" critic who would treat an order of existence not created in scientific discourse. Ransom draws from Charles W. Morris (b. 1901), a logical positivist, the term "icon" to suggest the symbol

in art, and, in a later paper (in *Poems and Essays*, 1955), has used the Hegelian term, the "concrete universal," in an attempt to recognize the universalizing power of art while preserving the emphasis on the concrete, on metaphor, and its references to nature.

Allen Tate is, like Ransom, preoccupied with a defense of poetry against science. Science gives us abstraction, poetry concreteness, science partial knowledge, poetry complete knowledge. "Poetry alone gathers up the diverse departments of the intellect into a humane and living whole." Abstraction, mere idea, violates art. Good poetry proceeds from a union of intellect and feeling, or rather from a "tension," a word which Tate not only interprets in the sense of unresolved conflict between abstraction and sensation, but derives from cutting off the prefixes of the words "extension" and "intension." Tate has elaborated his concept of poetry in several collections of essays, of which *On the Limits of Poetry* (1948) and *The Man of Letters in the Modern World* (1955) are the most inclusive.

Tate consistently rejects the attempt of Richards to make poetry a kind of therapy or make it take the place of religion. He sharply attacks both the scientific and the emotionally romantic view. Scientism, positivism, includes for Tate also historicism, the preoccupation with externals of the conventional literary scholar and any purely sociological approach. But literature is not taken out of society: on the contrary, Tate is deeply worried by the decay of an organic society and a religious world view, which alone, to his mind, can support a living tradition of art. Paradoxically, Tate, however, admires poetry most when it reflects the dissolution of tradition without losing its grasp of it. His essays on Poe, Emily Dickinson, T. S. Eliot, and Yeats show how these poets found personal substitutes for the old myths and symbols, while his discussion of Hart Crane ([q.v.], a personal friend) serves to show the failure of the modern artist who has not found support in tradition.

Tate has written widely, as a reviewer, mainly on modern poetry, but his interests have broadened gradually to include, for instance, Dante. He has become a convert to Roman Catholicism, and his recent writings indicate an increasing skepticism as to the role of poetry and criticism in the modern world. Compared to the urbane, ironical, restrained Ransom, Tate is a passionate, even violent, and often polemical and personal writer.

321

Cleanth Brooks has been described as the systematizer and technician of the "New Criticism." He has, no doubt, a sweet reasonableness and a gift for pedagogy and conciliatory formulation. His textbook, written in collaboration with Robert Penn Warren ([q.v.], *Understanding Poetry,* 1938), has done more than any other single book to make the techniques of the New Criticism available in the classroom of the American colleges and universities and to present the techniques of analysis as something to be learned and imitated. But Brooks is not merely a popularizer and codifier. He has his own personal theory. He has taken the terminology of Richards, deprived it of its psychologistic presuppositions, and transformed it into a remarkably clear system. It allows him to analyze poems as structures of tensions: in practice, of paradoxes and ironies.

Paradox and irony, with Brooks, are terms used very broadly. Irony is not the opposite of an overt statement, but "a general term for the kind of qualification which the various elements in a context receive from the context." It indicates the recognition of incongruities, the ambiguity, the union of opposites which Brooks finds in all good, that is, complex poetry. Poetry must be ironic in the sense of being able to withstand ironic contemplation. The method, no doubt, works best when applied to Donne or Shakespeare, Eliot or Yeats, but in *The Well-Wrought Urn* (1947), a collection of analyses of poems, Brooks has shown that even Wordsworth and Tennyson, Gray and Pope yield to this kind of technique. The whole theory emphasizes the contextual unity of the poem, its wholeness, its organism, while it allows a close analysis of its linguistic devices.

While Brooks is usually content to confine himself to his specialty—a masterly analysis of hidden meanings and relationships in metaphors and key-words—he is also a critic as his scheme permits him definite value judgments. Poets are ranked in terms of their success in resolving patterns of tensions, and the history of English poetry is seen in a new perspective. In *Modern Poetry and the Tradition* (1939) the romantic and Victorian ages appear as periods of decline compared to the 17th c., the greatest age of English poetry, while our own century appears as one of the revival of a properly "ironical," "tough," and complex poetry, as we find it in the later Yeats or Eliot. Brooks convincingly attacked what he calls "the heresy of paraphrase," that is, all attempts to reduce a poem to its prose-content, and he has defended

critical absolutism: the need of judgment against the excesses of relativism.

In a recent book, *William Faulkner: The Yoknapatawpha Country* (1963), Brooks has changed his method strikingly: he patiently examines the social picture, the intellectual and religious implications, and the themes and characters of Faulkner's (q.v.) main novels. The "formalistic" preoccupation has disappeared, as is also obvious from a series of published lectures, *The Hidden God: Studies in Hemingway, Faulkner, Yeats, Eliot, and Warren* (1963), which announces its main topic in the title.

The fourth of the Southern critics, Robert Penn Warren, a fine novelist and poet, has published only one volume of criticism (*Selected Essays,* 1955). The essay "Pure and Impure Poetry" states the argument for inclusive, complex, difficult (though impure) poetry memorably, and his essays on Hemingway (q.v.), Faulkner, Thomas Wolfe (q.v.), and on Coleridge's *Rime of the Ancient Mariner* show his skill in symbolist interpretation which widens into a study of the imagination and its role in the modern world.

Among the critics who cannot be called Southern, Blackmur (q.v.) was nearest to the general outlook of the Southern group. He was, in contrast to them, strongly influenced by Kenneth Burke and in recent years expressed dissatisfaction with their concentration on "close reading." Blackmur himself started as an extremely subtle, refined, elusive analyst, mainly of modern American poetry and Henry James. He was closely concerned with language and words, diction, imagery, rhyme and meter, and later tried to systematize his practice in a general theory of "language as gesture." "Gesture," which for Blackmur was basic to all the arts, is a term combining symbol and expression: a "cumulus of meaning" achieved by all the devices of poetry—punning, rhyme, meter, tropes. Criticism is defined as the "formal discourse of an amateur"—amateur in the sense of lover of poetry. Sympathy, identification, is required and any external methodology—Freudianism, Marxism, semantics—were rejected.

Increasingly, Blackmur felt the narrowness of the techniques of the New Criticism and saw that literature should, after all, be judged as a moral act in society. His perspective widened to include Dostoyevski and Tolstoi (q.v.): in method, he adopted economic and psychoanalytical ideas. But in theoretical reflections he seemed not to have reached any clarity or system of his own. His essays (collected in *Language as Gesture*, 1952; and *The Lion and the Honeycomb,* 1955) often show a disconcerting loss of contact with the text and a random experimentation with new sets of terms and contraries: symbol, myth, form, "rational imagination," even behavior. Blackmur—just because of his great talent, versatility, and subtlety—illustrated the predicament of much recent American criticism: its involvement in a private world of concepts, feelings, and terms, groping toward a general philosophy of life on the occasion of literature, and a distrust of inherited and traditional methods which leads to reliance on purely personal perceptions and combinations. In some of Blackmur's essays the privacy of terms and feelings reached a stage of fuzziness: his supersubtlety stylistically reminds one of the last stage of Henry James, but has, in Blackmur, become so completely divorced from traditional procedures that it seems impossible to keep any interest in the solution of the riddles propounded.

While Blackmur moved into an opaque world of private ruminations, Yvor Winters could be called a lucid rationalist—a rationalist with a vengeance. Throughout his critical writings (collected under the titles, *In Defence of Reason*, 1947; *The Function of Criticism*, 1957; *On Modern Poets*, 1959; *Forms of Discovery,* 1967), Winters has persecuted obscurantism, irrationalism, and has bluntly stated that poetry is good only insofar as a poem makes a defensible rational statement about a given experience. Winters believes in absolute moral truths, and even in the moral content of poetry. He has acidly and often vehemently attacked obscurity in modern poetry and despises the whole of the romantic tradition of spontaneous emotional expression. Poe is to Winters a bad poet and writer. Emerson, Hawthorne, and Whitman seem to him hopelessly self-indulgent, and Eliot and Ransom are both included in *The Anatomy of Nonsense* (1943). Winters admires an obscure transcendentalist poet, Jones Very (1813-80), much more than Emerson, puts Robert Bridges (q.v.) and Sturge Moore (1870-1944) above Yeats and Eliot, and praises many minor poets. He could be easily dismissed as a crotchety doctrinaire, as a moralist similar to the new humanists.

But despite his moralism and rationalism, Winters is a "new critic," a man of modern sensibility, a fine analyst of poetry and fiction who understands that "poetic morality and poetic feelings are inseparable; feelings and technique, structure, are inseparable." Form is to him the decisive part of the moral content. He has devised elaborate classifications of poetic structures and described the effects of meter well. He has raised questions about the ontological status of poetry and has argued well against many of the theories of Eliot and Ransom. But the excessively dogmatic manner which hides a very personal and even eccentric sensibility has vitiated Winters' effectiveness, which might have been very salutary as a counterweight against the irrationalism of the time. He has remained alone on the fringes of the movement.

In recent years the main movement of the New Criticism seems to have reached a point of exhaustion. Though, externally, the movement has been very successful in penetrating into the universities and monopolizing the critical journals, a state of stagnation has set in: there are now many imitators who apply the method mechanically and unimaginatively. On some points the movement has not been able to go beyond its initial narrow circle: the selection of European writers who have attracted the attention of the critics is oddly narrow and subject to the distortion of very local and temporary perspective. On the whole, the historical perspective of most critics has remained very short. Literary history is still beyond the ken of the criticism. Also the relations to modern linguistics and aesthetics remain unexplored. Much of the study of style, diction, and meter remains strangely dilettantish; and aesthetics, while discussed in practice continuously, remains without a sure philosophical foundation. Still, there are some hopeful signs of consolidation and expansion. William K. Wimsatt (b. 1907), in his *Verbal Icon* (1953), has made an attempt to consolidate and expand the teachings of the New Criticism. He has brilliantly argued against the fallacious tendency of criticism to trust the intention of the author and has criticized Richards for his reliance on the emotion affecting the reader. In his epilogue to *Literary Criticism: A Short History* (with C. Brooks, 1957), Wimsatt has made the clearest and most persuasive statement of a theory of literature which allows him to keep all three poles of literary theory: the mimetic, the emotive, and the expressionistic. The symbol, the concrete universal, remains the center of poetic theory, but ways are found to keep the relationship of poetry to morals and society intact.

The New Criticism of the last decades, as a

movement, seems to have run its course. It has immeasurably raised the level of awareness and sophistication in American criticism. It has developed ingenious new methods of an analysis of poetry and its devices: imagery and symbol. It has defined a new taste averse to the romantic tradition. It has supplied an important apology of poetry in a world dominated by science. But it has been unable to go successfully beyond its rather narrow confines, and it has not escaped the dangers of ossification and institutionalization.

In recent years several attempts have been made to replace the New Criticism. Among these the so-called "Chicago Aristotelianism" is the most distinct and most clearly organized. A group of scholars from Chicago University, headed by Ronald S. Crane (1886-1967), published a large, 650-page volume, *Critics and Criticism* (1952), which is, in part, devoted to very learned studies in the history of criticism and in part defends a view of literature sharply critical of the basic assumptions of the New Criticism. The role of language, metaphor, and symbol is minimized and all emphasis is put on plot and structure: Aristotle's *Poetics* serves as an inspiration for the terminology and the general scheme. In *The Languages of Criticism and the Structure of Poetry* (1953), Crane has scored many polemical points against the hunters of paradoxes, symbols, and myths. But he and his followers (the most concretely critical is Elder Olson [b. 1909]) are unable to offer any positive remedies beyond the most arid classifications of hero-types, plot structures, and genres. With them, genre theory reaches more than neoclassical rigidity: for instance, Dante's *Divina Commedia* is classified as didactic and not as mimetic or symbolic. The armature of scholarship, especially imposing in the writings of the philosopher Richard McKeon (b. 1900), hides insensitivity to literary values: the professed "pluralism" and interest in the "pleasure" of literature disguises a lack of critical standards. These scholars want to arrive at them by a foolproof, mechanical way, resuscitating an Aristotelianism quite inadequate to the problems of modern literature. The whole enterprise seems an ultra-academic exercise destined to wither on the vine.

Much more successful, diverse, and stimulating was the myth criticism which, under the influence of Frazer and Jung, arose as a reaction to the New Criticism. It flourishes in England and France, but in the United States it assumed a particular vitality, as it was able to absorb many of the achievements of the New Criticism, at least with its best practitioners. Myth appealed to many because it allows the discussions of themes and types, usually considered part of the "content" and thus not quite respectable to formalist critics. Huck Finn floating down the Mississippi with Jim is a "myth," and so is any truth which is generally accepted by society. "Myth" can be simply another name for ideology, *Weltanschauung*. Richard Chase (1914-62), in *Quest for Myth* (1949), identifies all good, sublime literature with myth. But more accurately and usefully, myth means a system of archetypes recoverable in rituals and tales, or a scheme of metaphors, symbols, and gods created by a poet such as Blake or Yeats.

Among the American myth-critics we must, however, make distinctions. There are allegorizers, who find the story of redemption throughout Shakespeare or discover Swedenborgianism in the novels of Henry James. There are those who expound the private mythologies of Blake, Shelley, or Yeats as gospel truths. But there are others who are genuine literary critics. Francis Fergusson (b. 1904), in his *Idea of a Theater* (1949), uses the results of the Cambridge school to consider the theater of all ages, from Sophocles to T. S. Eliot, as ritual. Philip Wheelwright (b. 1901), in *The Burning Fountain* (1954), combines myth interest with semantics, and studies also, in a later book, *Metaphor and Reality* (1962), the sequence from literal meaning through metaphor and symbol to myth. Northrop Frye (b. 1912), in his *Anatomy of Criticism* (1957), combines, rather, myth criticism with an attempt at an all-embracing theory of literature which is mainly a theory of genres. Frye devises an intricate scheme of modes, symbols, myths, and genres for which the Jungian archetype is the basic assumption. There are four main genres: comedy, romance, tragedy, and satire, and these correspond to the four seasons: spring, summer, autumn, and winter, the rhythm of nature. The most surprising confrontations are made and the most extravagant claims for the method are put forward. Literature "imitates the total dream of man" and criticism will "reforge the links between creation and knowledge, art and science, myth and concept." Frye draws freely on the whole range of literature and interprets often sensitively and wittily (see also his *Fables of Identity, Studies in Poetic Mythology*, 1963), but he wants to discard all distinctions between good and bad works of art and ceases then to be a critic.

The newest trend of American criticism in recent years is existentialism (q.v.). It hardly can be described as dependent on Heidegger or Sartre (q.v.). It is rather a vocabulary, a mood, or it can be "phenomenology," an attempt at reconstructing the author's "consciousness," his relation to time and space, nature and society, in the manner of French critics such as Georges Poulet ([b. 1902] who was active in the United States) or Jean-Pierre Richard (b. 1922). Geoffrey Hartman (b. 1929), in his *Unmediated Vision* (1954) and *Wordsworth* (1964), traces a dialectic of perception and consciousness, and J. Hillis Miller's (b. 1928) books—*Dickens: The World of His Novels* (1959), *The Disappearance of God: Five Nineteenth Century Writers* (1963), and *Poets of Reality: Six Twentieth Century Writers* (1965) —analyze the interior landscape or the presumed personal world of each author with great subtlety. The theme of loneliness and despair informs Murray Krieger's (b. 1923) *Tragic Vision* (1960), in which the tragic hero (or rather "visionary") is the man of the "sickness unto death," the new nihilist. Krieger discusses Kafka, Camus (q.v.), Thomas Mann, Dostoyevksi, and Melville. It is in the nature of the method that the individual work of art as an aesthetic structure is ignored and that the critic aims at discovering, rather, some inner world behind the text. The method fits the concerns of our time for answers to the ultimate questions and the interest in the personal approach of great writers to the "human condition," but the traditional issues of art and criticism are slighted.

Recent criticism looks constantly elsewhere, wants to become sociology, politics, philosophy, theology, and even mystical illumination. It may be a need of the time, but the state of criticism has become precarious if it is not any more concerned with analyzing, interpreting, and judging works of art.

BIBLIOGRAPHY

(1) **Marxism:** Antowiak, A., *Sowjetische Literaturkritik* (1953); Hankin, R. M., "Postwar Soviet Ideology and Literary Scholarship," in *Through the Glass of Soviet Literature* (1953); Lukács, G., *Beiträge zur Geschichte der Ästhetik* (1954); Erlich, V., "Social and Aesthetic Criteria in Soviet Russian Criticism," in *Continuity and Change in Russian and Soviet Thought*, ed. E. J. Simmons (1955);

(2) **Psychoanalytical and Jungian:** Hoffman, F. J., *Freudianism and the Literary Mind* (1945); Trilling, L., "Freud and Literature," in *The Liberal Imagination* (1950); Fraiberg, L., *Psychoanalysis and American Literary Criticism* (1960); Philipson, M., *Outline of a Jungian Aesthetics* (1963);

(3) **Italy:** Marzot, G., "La critica e gli studi di letteratura italiana," in *Cinquant 'anni di vita intellettuale italiana 1896-1946*, ed., C. Antoni and R. Mattioli (1946); Russo, L., *La critica letteraria contemporanea*, 3 Vols., (1946-47, 1953); Borlenghi, A., "La critica letteraria dal De Sanctis ad oggi," in *Letteratura Italiana: le Correnti*, Vol. II, (1956);

(a) On Croce: Bosanquet, B., "Croce's Aesthetic," British Academy Lecture (1919); Lemerre, J., *L'Esthetique de B. Croce* (1936); Sgroi, C., *B. Croce, Svolgimento storico della sua estetica* (1947); Bergel, L., "Croce as a Critic of Goethe," in *CL*, I (1949); Wellek, R., "Benedetto Croce: Literary Critic and Historian," *CL*, V (1953); Seerveld, G. C., *Benedetto Croce's Early Aesthetic Theories and Literary Criticism* (1958); Orsini, G. N. G., *Benedetto Croce: Philosopher of Art and Literary Critic* (1961);

(b) New Trends: Cressatti, L. F. de, *Las Corrientes de Crítica e Historiografía Literarias en la Italia actual* (1955); Gorlier, C., "Contemporary Italian Literary Criticism," in *The Literary Review* (1959); Scaglione, A., "Literary Criticism in Postwar Italy," in *IQ*, IV (1960);

(4) **France:** Van Tieghem, P., *Petite Histoire des grandes doctrines littéraires en France* (1940);

(a) On Valéry: Bémol, M., *La méthode critique de Paul Valéry* (1950); Hytier, Jean, *La Poétique de Valéry* (1953); Trans. R. Howard (1966);

(b) On Thibaudet: "Hommage à A. Thibaudet," in *NRF*, XLVII (1930); Glauser, A., *Albert Thibaudet et la critique créatrice* (1951); Davies, J. C., *L'Oeuvre critique d'Albert Thibaudet* (1955);

(c) On Rivière: Turnell, M., *Jacques Rivière* (1953); Price, B. A., Introduction to *The Ideal Reader* (1960);

(d) On Du Bos: Bertocci, A. P., *Charles Du Bos and English Literature* (1949); Gouhier, M., *Charles Du Bos* (1951);

(e) Existentialism: Bonnefoy, Y., "Critics— English and French," in *Encounter*, IX (1958); Girard, R., "Existentialism and Literary Criticism," in *YFS*, XVI (1955-56) (also in *Sartre*, ed. E. Kern, [1962]);

(f) On Béguin: *Albert Béguin, 1901-57*, special number of *Esprit*, XXVI (1958); Poulet, G., "La pensée critique d'Albert Béguin," in *Cahiers du Sud*, No. 360 (1961);

(g) On Poulet: Spitzer, L., "A propos de la vie de Marianne," in *Romanische Literaturstudien* (1959); Miller, J. H., "The Literary Criticism of Georges Poulet," in *MLN*, LXXVIII (1963);

(h) On Blanchot: Hartman, G., "The Fulness and Nothingness of Literature," in *YFS*, XVI (1955-56; Picon, G., "L'Oeuvre critique de Maurice Blanchot," in *Crit*, XIV (1956);

(5) **Spain:** Jeschke, H., *Die Generation von 1898 in Spanien* (1934); Emilia de Zuleta, *Historia de la crítica española contemporánea* (1966);

(a) On Ortega and Unamuno: Weyl, H., "Ortega y Gasset," in *UTQ*, VI (1937); Villaseñor, J. S., *Ortega y Gasset Existentialist* (1948); Curtius, E. R., *Kritische Essays zur Europäischen Literatur* (1950); Livingston, L., "Ortega y Gasset's Philosophy of Art," in *PMLA*, LXVII (1952);

(6) **Russia:** Zhirmunskij, V., "Formprobleme in der russischen Literaturwissenschaft," in *Zeitschrift für slavische Philologie*, I (1925); idem, "Problems of Method in the Study of Literature in Russia," in *Slavonic Review*, VI (1927); Tomashevskij, B., "La Nouvelle École d'histoire littéraire en Russie," *RS*, VIII (1928); Voznesenskij, A. N., "Die Methodologie der russischen Literaturwissenschaft," in *Zeitschrift für slavische Philologie*, IV (1927) and V (1928); Gourfinkel, N., "Les Nouvelles Méthodes d'histoire littéraire en Russie," *Le Monde slave*, VI (1929); Kridl, M., "Russian Formalism," *The American Bookman*, I (1944); Harkins, W. E., "Slavic Formalist Theories in Literary Scholarship," *Word*, VII (1951); Erlich, V., *Russian Formalism: History—Doctrine* (1955); Pomorska, K., *Russian Formalist Theory and Its Poetic Ambiance* (1968); Ambrogio, J., *Formalismo e Avanguardia in Russia* (1968);

(7) **Czechoslovakia:** Wellek, R., "Modern Czech Criticism and Literary Scholarship," in *HSS*, II (1954); idem, "Recent Czech Literary History and Criticism," in *Essays on Czech Literature* (1963); Garvin, P. L., *A Prague School Reader on Esthetics, Literary Structure, and Style* (1964);

(8) **Germany:** Discussions of German literary scholarship of the time: Marholz, W., *Litera-*

turgeschichte und Literaturwissenschaft (1923, 1932); Benda, O., *Der gegenwärtige Stand der deutschen Literaturwissenschaft* (1928); Oppel, H., *Die Literaturwissenschaft der Gegenwart* (1939); Wehrli, M., *Allgemeine Literaturwissenschaft* (1951); Just, K. G.; "Essay," in *Deutsche Philologie im Aufriß*, II (1955);

(a) On George circle, besides Wolters listed in text: Rössner, H., *Georgekreis und Literaturwissenschaft* (1938); Salin, E., *Um Stefan George* (1954);

(b) On Gundolf: Ergänzungsheft (Gundolf-Heft) of *Euphorion* (1921); Wellek, R., "The Literary Criticism of Friedrich Gundolf," in *CL*, IX (1968);

(c) On Hofmannsthal: Naef, K. J., *Hugo von Hofmannsthals Wesen und Werk* (1938);

(d) On Borchardt: Uhde-Bernays, H., *Über Rudolf Borchardt* (1954);

(e) On Kassner: T. Wieser, *Die Einbildungskraft bei Rudolf Kassner* (1949);

(f) On Kommerell: Holthusen, H. E., "Max Kommerell und die deutsche Klassik," in *Das Schöne und das Wahre* (1958);

(g) Expressionism: There seems to be no study of expressionist theories; descriptive accounts can be found in Soergel, A., *Dichtung und Dichter der Zeit, Neue Folge* (1925);

(h) On Nazi literary history: Atkins, H. G., *German Literature through Nazi Eyes* (1941);

(i) On Heidegger: Buddeberg, E., *Heidegger und die Dichtung* (1953); Allemann, B., *Hölderlin und Heidegger* (1954);

(j) On Spitzer: Wellek, R., "Leo Spitzer, 1887-1960," in *CL*, XII (1960);

(k) On recent "interpretation": Bruford, W. H., *Literary Interpretation in Germany* (1952);

(9) **England and the United States:** Anthologies: Jones, P. M., ed., *English Critical Essays: Twentieth Century* (1933); Stallman, R. W., ed., *Critiques and Essays in Criticism, 1920-1948. Representing the Achievement of Modern British and American Critics* (1949); Ransom, J. C., ed., *The Kenyon Critics: Studies in Modern Literature from the Kenyon Review* (1951); Zabel, M. D., ed., *Literary Opinion in America* (1951); Aldridge, J. W., ed., *Critiques and Essays in Modern Fiction* (1952); West, R. B., ed., *Essays in Modern Literary Criticism* (1952); Brown, C. A., ed., *The Achievement of American Criticism* (1954); Hyman, S. E., ed., *The Critical Performance* (1956); Howe, I., ed., *Modern Literary Criticism* (1958); Goldberg, G. J., and Goldberg, N. M., eds., *The Modern Critical*

Spectrum (1962); Slote, B., ed., *Myth and Symbol: Critical Approaches and Applications* (1962); Sutton, W., and Foster, R., eds., *Modern Criticism: Theory and Practice* (1963); Grebstein, P. N., ed., *Perspectives in Contemporary Criticism* (1968);

Discussions:

(a) On English Criticism: Williams, O., *Contemporary Criticism of Literature* (1925); Watson, G., *The Literary Critics* (1962);

(b) On American Criticism: Smith, B., *Forces in American Criticism* (1939); Hyman, S. E., *The Armed Vision: A Study in the Methods of Modern Literary Criticism* (1948); O'Connor, W. V., *An Age of Criticism: 1900-1950* (1952); La Drière, J. C., *Directions in Contemporary Criticism and Literary Scholarship* (1953-55); Stovall, F., ed., *The Development of American Criticism* (1955); Krieger, M., *The New Apologists for Poetry* (1956); Pritchard, J. P., *Criticism in America* (1956); Wimsatt, W. K., and Brooks, C., *Literary Criticism: A Short History* (1957); Leary, L., *Contemporary Literary Scholarship* (1958); Lang, H., *Studien zur Entstehung der neueren amerikanischen Literaturkritik* (1961); Weimann, R., *"New Criticism" und die Entwicklung bürgerlicher Literaturwissenschaft* (1962); Sutton, W., *Modern American Criticism* (1963); Wellek, R., "Philosophy and Postwar American Criticism," in *Concepts of Criticism* (1963);

(c) On Henry James: Morris, R., *Henry James's Criticism* (1929); Edel, L., *The Prefaces of Henry James* (1931); Blackmur, R. P., Introduction to *The Art of the Novel: Critical Prefaces by Henry James* (1934); Wellek, R., "Henry James's Literary Theory and Criticism," in *AL*, XXX (1958);

(d) On the Humanist Movement: Mercier, L. J., *Le Mouvement humaniste aux États-unis* (1928); Eliot, T. S., "The Humanism of Irving Babbitt," in *Selected Essays* (1932); Shafer, R., *Paul Elmer More and American Criticism* (1935); Manchester, F., and Shepar, O., *Irving Babbitt* (1941); Dakin, A. H., *Paul Elmer More* (1960); Wellek, R., "Irving Babbitt, Paul Elmer More and Transcendentalism," in *Transcendentalism and Its Legacy*, ed. M. Simon and T. H. Parsons (1966); Duggan, F. X., *Paul Elmer More* (1966);

(e) On T. S. Eliot: Oras, A., *The Critical Ideas of T. S. Eliot* (1932); Costello, M. C., *Between Fixity and Flux: A Study of the Concept of Poetry in the Criticism of T. S. Eliot* (1937); Unger, L., ed., *T. S. Eliot: A Selected*

Critique (1948); Brombert, V., *The Criticism of T. S. Eliot* (1949); Vivas, E., "The Objective Correlative of T. S. Eliot," in *Creation and Discovery* (1955); Esch, A., "T. S. Eliot als Literaturkritiker," in *Sprache und Literatur Englands und Amerikas,* II (1956); Wellek, R., "The Criticism of T. S. Eliot," in *SR* (1956); Séan, L., *T. S. Eliot and the Idea of Tradition* (1960);

(f) On Hulme: Roberts, M., *T. E. Hulme* (1938); Krieger, M., in *The New Apologists for Poetry* (1950); Jones, A., *T. E. Hulme* (1960);

(g) On Pound: Orsini, G. N. G., "Ezra Pound, Critico letterario" in *Letterature moderne,* VII (1957); Norman, C., *Ezra Pound* (1960);

(h) On Richards: Ransom, J. C., "I. A. Richards," in *The New Criticism* (1941); Crane, R. S., "I. A. Richards on the Art of Interpretation," in *Critics and Criticism* (1952); Vivas, E., "Four Notes on I. A. Richards's Aesthetic Theory," in *Creation and Discovery* (1955); Hotopf, W. H., *Language, Thought, and Comprehension: A Case Study of the Writings of I. A. Richards* (1965); Wellek, R., "On Rereading I. A. Richards," in *Southern Review,* III, N.S. (1967);

(i) On Empson: Ransom, J. C., "Mr. Empson's Muddles," in *Southern Review,* IV (1938); Brooks, C., "Empson's Criticism," *Accent Anthology* (1946); Olson, E., "William Empson, Contemporary Criticism and Poetic Diction," in *Critics and Criticism,* ed. R. S. Crane (1952);

(j) On Leavis: Buckley, V., in *Poetry and Morality* (1959); Steiner, G., "F. R. Leavis," in *Encounter,* XVIII (1962); Wellek, R., "The Literary Criticism of F. R. Leavis," in *Literary Views,* ed. C. Camden (1963);

(k) On Burke: Warren, A., "Kenneth Burke: His Mind and Art," in *SR,* XLI (1933); Bewley, M., "Kenneth Burke as Literary Critic," in *The Complex Fate* (1952); Knox, G., *Critical Moments: Kenneth Burke's Categories and Critiques* (1957); Rueckert, W. H., *Kenneth Burke and the Drama of Human Relations* (1963);

(1) On New Criticism: Rubin, L. D., and Jacobs, R. D., eds., *Southern Renascence: The Literature of the Modern South* (1965); Bradbury, J. M., *The Fugitives: A Critical Account* (1958); Foster, R., *The New Romantics: A Reappraisal of the New Criticism* (1962); Stewart, J. L., *The Burden of Time, The Fugi-*

tives and Agrarians (1965); Karanikas, A., *Tillers of a Myth: The Southern Agrarians as Social and Literary Critics* (1966);

(m) On Tate and Ransom: Roellinger, F. X., "Two Theories of Poetry as Knowledge," in *Southern Review,* VII (1942); Winters, Y., in *The Anatomy of Nonsense* (1943); *SR,* LVI (1948); Spears, M. E., "The Criticism of Allen Tate," in *SR,* LVII (1949); Meiners, R. K., *The Last Alternatives: A Study of the Works of Allen Tate* (1963); Young, T. D., ed., *John Crowe Ransom, Critical Essays and a Bibliography* (1968);

(n) On Brooks: Crane, R. S., "The Monism of Cleanth Brooks," in *Critics and Criticism* (1952);

(o) On the Chicago Critics: Wimsatt, W. K., "The Chicago Critics: The Fallacy of the Neoclassic Species," in *The Verbal Icon* (1954)

RENÉ WELLEK

LITHUANIAN LITERATURE

The Lithuanians, an ancient people, speaking one of the oldest Indo-European languages, have nevertheless lacked, for most of their long history, a written literature of their own. Powerful neighbors, constantly pressing them from the south and the east against the Baltic Sea, have forced the Lithuanians to spend their best energies in the struggle for survival. Under those conditions, the literary genius of the nation was preserved in its rich and ancient folklore. The Lithuanian folk song (those that survived long enough to be recorded, that is) concerns itself with the lyrical expression of an intimate relationship between man and nature, and with a lucid, restrained statement of man's basically tragic situation in a world ruled by sorrow and death.

The first important work of written literature came, in the middle of the 18th c., from the pen of Kristijonas Duonelaitis (1714-80), a Protestant clergyman in East Prussia. His rural epic *Metai* describes the daily life of the Lithuanian peasant as he plods the treadmill of time toward the hoped-for eternity in which his plain country virtue is to meet its just reward. In vigorous, earthy language Duonelaitis exhorts his countrymen to resist both the oppression and the corrupt enticements coming from the alien culture of the German overlords.

The first significant writers in Lithuania proper—Simanas Daukantas (1793-1864), Sim-

anas Stanevičius (1799-1848), and Motiejus Valančius (1801-1875)—were stimulated by the winds of romantic nationalism blowing from Western Europe. Their desire was to arouse Lithuanian self-respect and to encourage allegiance to the country's indigenous cultural values.

Somewhat aloof from these stood the lonely, talented figure of Antanas Baranauskas (1835-1902), who achieved fame with his one major work—*Anykščių šilelis* (1858 f.)—a long lyrical poem in melodious syllabic verse that sung of the past glories of a pine grove near his home.

The groundswell of romantic nationalism produced intensified resistance against the russification policies of the tsarist regime, which in 1865 had gone so far as to proclaim a ban against Lithuanian books printed in the Latin alphabet. The lifting of the ban in 1904 released the creative energies of a large number of writers whose works established a solid foundation for the further growth of Lithuanian literature.

By far the best of the romantic poets was Maironis (q.v.). His emotionally intense patriotic poems raised Lithuanian poetic diction and prosody to a new dimension. Using the language firmly, he demonstrated sure handling of the syllabo-tonic meters and great sensitivity to the nuances of relationship between rhythm, emotion, and idea. In prose, the major writer of the period was Juozas Tumas-Vaižgantas (1869-1933), who wrote chatty, colorful tales about the emerging national consciousness in the life of the Lithuanian countryside.

Their works, as well as those of Marija Pečkauskaite-Šatrijos Ragana (1878-1933), Julija Žymantienė-Žemaitė (1845-1921), and Antanas Žukauskas-Vienuolis (1882-1958), spanned a period of crucial changes in Lithuanian history, extending from the Russian Revolution of 1905, through World War I, to the establishment of an independent Lithuanian state. Vienuolis, in fact, lived to see his country occupied by the Nazi Germans in 1940 and to become one of the party-controlled writers in Lithuania under Soviet rule.

Vincas Krėvė-Mickevičius (1882-1954), however, chose self-exile when the Soviet armies returned to Lithuania in 1944. A prolific and complex writer, Mickevičius distinguished himself in several genres. Nostalgia for Lithuanian antiquity inspired him to write *Dainavos šalies senų žmonių padavimai* (1912), a series of highly stylized legends dealing with heroes of times past. Present-day Lithuania led him to write realistic stories about villagers, living in close intimacy with nature, who possessed, in Krėvė's eyes, the undefinable, deep strength that had sustained his people through countless ages. This same power figures prominently in his plays *Šarūnas* (1911) and *Skirgaila* (1925), which deal with crucial moments in Lithuanian history. And in a biblical epic *Dangaus ir žemės sūnūs* (1949), Mickevičius pursued his search for the secret of human fortitude to a confrontation between man and God.

The development of poetry after Maironis went in the direction of symbolism (q.v.). Jurgis Baltrušaitis (q.v.), most of whose poetry was written in Russian, was himself a prominent member of the circle of Russian symbolists. His Lithuanian poems are distinguished for the severe clarity of vision and the ascetic restraint that he brings to the contemplation of man's relationship to Eternity.

Balys Sruoga (1896-1947), who experimented vigorously with verse forms, succeeded in combining the symbolist outlook with the imagery and diction of the Lithuanian folk song. In his verse drama Sruoga returned to classical order and clarity developing, as in the play *Milžino paunksmė* (1930), philosophical portrayals of historical figures in an atmosphere of lyrical contemplation.

Faustas Kirša (1891-1964) and Vincas Mykolaitis (q.v.) followed the Western trends of symbolism, particularly the French. They remained, however, intimately bound to the indigenous traditions, to the Lithuanian manner of translating reality into metaphor and symbol as it had developed in folklore.

Mykolaitis became widely known for his quasi-autobiographical novel *Altorių šešėly* (1933), in which he pictured the inner struggles of a young priest who comes to realize that he has misunderstood his calling and tries in vain to come to terms with an evanescent image of God. Like the young priest, Mykolaitis made a similarly unsuccessful effort to meet the requirements of socialist realism under Soviet occupation with the novel *Sukilėliai* (1957), the subject of which is the Polish-Lithuanian uprising against the Russians in 1863.

The literary traditions of Lithuania minor, begun so well with Duonelaitis, were continued by Vilius Storasta-Vydūnas (1868-1953) and by Ieva Simonaitytė (b. 1897). The most philosophical of Lithuanian authors, Vydūnas constantly sought, in his many plays and other writings, to understand the ultimate meaning of man's existence in terms of mystical images of "eternal light," which is the unending principle of life and the spark of divinity in man.

Ieva Simonaitytė, in her novel *Aukštųjų Šimonių likimas,* directed her attention toward the social and historical realities that were determining the fortunes of her people. She saw them as a diminishing ethnic entity that was being gradually swallowed up by the German colonists in East Prussia.

In the 1920's the influence of Russian futurism (q.v.) and Western European expressionism manifested itself in the "Four Winds" movement, so called after the title of a literary periodical edited by Kazys Binkis (1893-1942). The movement's manifesto contains all the brash statements that were so dear to the futurists: the worship of the machine age; the desire to forge and hammer out poetry like iron by an effort of rational will; contempt for "insipid romantics" and "starry-eyed symbolists."

Nevertheless, Binkis's own verse remained light and lyrical in essence, since Lithuania— a land of quiet lakes and green meadows—did not offer the industrial realities necessary for the development of truly dynamic futurism.

Other important members of the movement were Juozas Petrėnas-Tarulis (1889) and Teofilis Tilvytis (b. 1904).

The second important literary movement of the 1920's was called the "Third Front." Third Front writers were leftists who were interested in fighting social and economic injustice and who were committed to the budding Lithuanian proletariat and to the peasantry. The most important poet in this group was Salomėja Neris (1904-1945), although her deeply lyrical and feminine poetry, vibrant with warm personal feeling, transcended the outlines of any particular ideology. Petras Cvirka (1909-1947) wrote novels of social satire directed against the ruling Lithuanian bourgeoisie, in which he glorified the honest work of simple peasants. The literary critic Kostas Korsakas (b. 1909) and the poet Antanas Venclova (b. 1906) also played a significant role in this movement. Korsakas, Cvirka, Venclova, Neris, and Tilvytis were later to form the nucleus of those who produced the Soviet Lithuanian literature that emerged in the aftermath of World War II.

In the 1930's Lithuanian literature came of age in the sense that art itself, as an embodiment of a personal vision of reality, became the object of primary concern. Bernardas Brazdžionis (b. 1907) believed that reality was permeated and made meaningful by the hidden presence of God. The frequent biblical references in his works create a feeling not only of Christian devotion, but also of a romantic longing for some dimly perceived, intensely desired, ultimate home for the soul. He treats nature, both in broad outlines and in minute details, as a stage setting for his poetic drama of life as a holy pilgrimage toward death. This mood is especially strengthened by Brazdžionis' skillful handling of rhythm and syntax, and by his fine sensitivity to the musical qualities of words.

The poetry of Jonas Aistis (q.v.) broke new ground in the uses of poetic language. Skillfully combining plain everyday language with highly refined literary formulas, he created an intoxicating effect of a still raw, but already inspired, reality, quivering on the verge of poetic fulfillment. Having spent a good deal of time in France, Aistis reshaped the techniques of modern French poetry into a new, highly personal, but also very typical, Lithuanian verse idiom. Much of his work consists of an intense confrontation with the values and possibilities of art itself, conveyed sometimes directly in its own terms and sometimes through poetic formulations of the themes of love, patriotism, of painful human solitude, and of his closeness to the Lithuanian landscape.

Other significant poets of the time were Antanas Miškinis (b. 1905), who used the language and lyrical texture of the native folk songs to perfect a poetry of highly personal lyricism, and Kazys Boruta (1905-1965)—a poet who asserted the spirit of freedom and of individual human dignity.

The prose writers in this period were strongly influenced by impressionism, especially of the Scandinavian variety. Though Ignas Šeinius (1889-1959) was to spend much of his life in Sweden, the imprint of such authors as Hamsun (q.v.) can be seen in his best work, the novella *Kuprelis* (1913), which was written before he left Lithuania. The story tells about a gifted, physically disfigured dreamer who is doomed to vegetate in the provinces. The double psychological tension of the story consists of the desire for personal happiness and the deformity that prevents it on the one hand, and intellectual yearning versus gray reality on the other.

Antanas Vaičiulaitis (q.v.) established his reputation with the novel *Valentina*, in which delicate shades of feeling in the soul of a man possessed by love are carefully integrated into the total structure of the work, which is made up of summer light and evening shadow, cricket song and sudden storms—all of which are handled in a manner reminiscent of the French impressionist painters. Vaičiulaitis is also known for his stories of country life and for his fairy tales.

Jurgis Savickis (1890-1952) belongs among the better Lithuanian prose stylists. His outstanding qualities are brevity, precision, and a certain dry, elegant irony of understatement that he uses when describing situations fraught with possible tragic meanings. The main theme of his short stories appears to be the blindness of small men—the careerist, the bourgeois, the semi-intellectual—to the immensity of the life passing them by. Savickis spent considerable time in Western Europe, in the Lithuanian diplomatic service, and had good opportunities for observing the human comedy of petty ambitions and moral inadequacies, both at home and abroad.

Other significant prose writers are Juozas Grušas (b. 1901) and Jurgis Jankus (b. 1906), as well as Liudas Dovydėnas (b. 1906). Grušas, who still lives in Soviet-occupied Lithuania, has recently shown himself a gifted playwright. He is writing historical plays as well as plays that approach the modern concept of the theater of the absurd.

The events of World War II and their consequences for the Lithuanian people—the German occupation, the return of the Soviets in 1944—resulted in splitting the literary community into two parts. Some writers remained in Lithuania and submitted to Communist Party dictates in art, while others withdrew to the West and were confronted with the variety, and perhaps confusion, of the literary trends prevailing in Western Europe and the United States. The older writer, finding himself sometimes unable to comprehend the intellectual and artistic challenge implicit in the tragedy of his exile, often withdrew into reminiscences of home, or else allowed his bitter patriotic fervor to shape the purposes of his art.

New developments came from a generation of younger writers who, because they were only beginning to emerge by 1944, were sufficiently flexible to be able to respond to the new experiences of spiritual and artistic life that the West offered. Paradoxically, the primary source of their new inspiration must be sought still in Lithuania, in the person of Vytautas Mačernis (1920-45). He was a gifted existentialist poet whose poetic visions stimulated his friends to seek new relationships between themselves, art, and reality.

The young exiles gathered around the

periodical *Literatūros lankai,* which was started in Buenos Aires in 1952. Their guiding spirit at the beginning was the poet Juozas Kėkštas (b. 1915), who has since returned to Lithuania. Another poet, Kazys Bradūnas (b. 1917), contributed a good deal to organizing the movement, which was to call itself the "Earth" collective.

Bradūnas's early verse was permeated with direct existential pain, born of a physical sense of loss, of sudden alienation in a strange country. Later Bradūnas deepened and at the same time sublimated his sorrow by reconstructing a Lithuanian mythology of those who lived and died on Lithuanian earth through countless ages, thus performing an unending sacrifice before the living presence of God, whether He be understood in pantheistic, pagan terms, or as the Christian God of later generations.

Alfonsas Nyka-Niliūnas (b. 1920) achieved a breakthrough in Lithuanian literary criticism by demanding that the vague, impressionistic approaches of the past be replaced by informed, systematic, and lucid literary analysis. His main contribution to the literature of exile, however, is in his poetry. Niliūnas is a highly complex, searching poet, capable of transforming philosophical quest into intense lyrical emotion, of integrating his own visions with the creative efforts of all mankind by means of subtly interconnected systems of symbolic and intellectual references. His basic position is existentialist— the recognition of reality, especially for an exile, is equivalent to the understanding of alienation.

Closely connected with the "Earth" collective were also some prose writers, notably Algirdas Landsbergis (b. 1924) and Antanas Škėma (1911-61). Landsbergis's first novel, *Kelionė,* re-created the experience of war and exile on a plane on which chronological time sequence is replaced by an inner continuum of thought and feeling, as if a new mosaic were to be created from the broken pieces of reality destroyed by World War II. Landsbergis also writes short stories and plays in which his satirical intelligence is directed at the sometimes tragic inadequacies of man.

Antanas Škėma, in his novel *Balta drobulė* and in a number of short stories and plays, depicts the condition of man as that of being in exile, since the logical inevitabilities that rule the universe do not provide for the principle of life, much less for the irrational urge of creativity that constitutes the divine spark of man.

Therefore, the more perfect an organism, the greater is its suffering, and in man the supreme qualities of mind fulfill themselves in supreme agony. Škėma's works often contain cruel, even melodramatic, situations centered around the conflict between freedom and tyranny.

Other significant novelists are Aloyzas Baronas (b. 1917), a prolific writer of quixotic, paradoxical works that investigate man's basic values against the background of ashes left by the holocaust of World War II, and Vincas Ramonas (b. 1905), whose *Kryžiai* depicts the traumatic encounter between the peasants of independent Lithuania and the invading Soviet ideology, borne on the backs of tanks.

Marius Katiliškis (b. 1915), in such novels as *Miškais ateina ruduo* and *Užuovėja,* evokes Lithuania in all its elemental power and shows how the people who inhabit it must live in an indissoluble bond with the soil, as if they were mere configurations upon the surface of continuing life. Then it comes as a special shock to realize that the impossible *has* happened; that these people have actually been separated from their soil; that they have become exiles, groping in vain for some meaning to their lives.

Pulgis Andriušis (b. 1907) re-creates the atmosphere of Lithuanian countryside in lush, ornate prose, exploiting to the fullest all the resources of the language to spin a web of enchanting memory.

In drama the exile Kostas Ostrauskas (b. 1926) is writing theater-of-the-absurd plays. His main attention is focused upon death as an unimaginable, yet inevitable, final event in the life of both body and mind. Since no rational dialogue is possible between man's intelligence and the incomprehensible void facing it, absurdity must necessarily be the overwhelming presence in any drama purporting to depict the human condition. In such plays as *Pypke* and *Duobkasiai* Ostrauskas calls for defiant reassertion of life in the face of death, even if such an act remains ultimately meaningless.

Similarly, death dominates the poetry of Algimantas Mackus (1932-64). In his work, the condition of exile necessitates a reversal of all the meanings and values of conventional poetic language that are based upon the consciousness that an artist is at home in the world. Mackus was developing a systematic reconstruction of all basic metaphorical and semantic connotations in poetic imagery, assigning the meaning of death to terms that ordinarily mean life. The result is a shattering picture of reality as a visible expression of the ultimate void. In this context Mackus placed the specific events, feelings, and beliefs of the Lithuanian exiles. The result is an image of a deathbound community of lost men in a universe that cannot contain any meaning. Yet, in the very clarity of his dark vision, Mackus managed to lend a tragic dignity to the stature of man.

Perhaps the greatest, certainly the most complex and subtle Lithuanian poet, is Henrikas Radauskas (b. 1910). Although his first book of verse came out in 1935, he cannot be readily identified with any of the then-prevalent trends and movements in independent Lithuania. Neither does he belong among the younger poets, whose main theme is exile. The theme of Radauskas's poetry is ultimately art itself, whereas exile, death, nature, history, and the mythological and metaphysical aspects of man's experience constitute the component elements of an esthetic entity called a poem. Thus, the ultimate encounter is between art and all the dimensions of reality.

Art creates itself by passing through reality like some magical force, by transforming all aspects of being, by creating multiple interconnections where none existed before. In this way it constructs a universe that both mirrors and contains, violates and blends with, everything that we call reality. In all these transfigurations Radauskas is especially concerned with the perfection of language and form, with achieving the ultimate potential of the sound and meaning of words. Radauskas's best poetry, in such collections as *Žaibai ir vėjai* and *Strėlė danguje,* has been written in exile.

The literature of Soviet-occupied Lithuania was for a long time at a low point. "Inspiration" came from the desk drawer of a Communist Party bureaucrat; questions of style and technique became subordinate to the ideological requirements of socialist realism. Only in recent years, particularly after destalinization, have new talents come forward, replacing the submissive and often quite mediocre older writers.

Among the best poetic talents is Eduardas Mieželaitis (b. 1919), winner of the All-Union Lenin Prize in Literature. In his work honest attempts to convey personal experience are combined with an interest in experimenting with poetic diction and form.

Justinas Marcinkevičius (b. 1930) delves deeply into the soul of his people, searching among the ruins of sorrows long endured for the promise of the future. Especially noteworthy is his narrative poem *Kraujas ir pelenai,*

which describes the total destruction of a Lithuanian village by the Nazis during World War II.

Judita Vaičiūnaitė (b. 1937), Janina Degutytė (b. 1928), and Sigitas Geda (b. 1943) are young poets who are producing works of genuine artistic value. In their approach the official communist ideology seems rather an irrelevance. Mykolas Sluckis (b. 1929), Romualdas Lankauskas (b. 1932), and Jonas Avyžius (b. 1922) are talented writers of prose fiction. Kazys Saja (b. 1932) has been experimenting successfully with modernist devices in the theater.

BIBLIOGRAPHY: Engert, H., *Aus litauischer Dichtung* (1935); Mauclere, J., *Panorama de la litterature lithuanienne contemporaine* (1938); Jungfer, V., *Litauen, Antlitz eines Volkes* (1948); Devoto, G., *Storia della letteratura baltiche* (1957); Landsbergis, A., ed., *The Green Oak* (selected translations of Lithuanian poetry, 1962); Landsbergis, A., ed., *The Green Linden* (selected translations of Lithuanian folk songs, 1964)

RIMVYDAS SILBAJORIS

LLORÉNS TORRES, Luis

Puerto Rican poet, b. 14 May 1878, Juana Díaz; d. 16 June 1944, San Juan de Puerto Rico

L. studied in Spain, where he published his first works. In his own country he became an out-and-out representative of modernism. The periodical *Revista de las Antillas* (1913), which he created, dominated the intellectual life of Puerto Rico for a long time; it provided a vehicle by which the renewers of poetry and the opponents of the United States' annexation policy could make their views known.

L.'s work is an unusual mixture of poetry and prose, fantasy and realism, idealization and irony. It was influenced by Darío, Chocano (qq.v.), and Walt Whitman (1819-92). In addition to his "long poems" L. also wrote *jíbaros* —popular poetry in short forms.

WORKS: *Al pie de la Alhambra* (1899); *Sonetos sinfónicos* (1914); *Velas épicas* (1929); *La canción de las Antillas y otras poemas* (1929); *Alturas de América* (1940)

BIBLIOGRAPHY: Arce de Vásquez, M., "Las décimas de L. T.," in *Asomante,* XXI (1965), 37-46

* * *

LOPEZ ALBÚJAR, Enrique

Peruvian novelist and short story writer, b. 23 Nov. 1872, Piura

L. A., member of the Peruvian Academy of Letters and associate member of the Royal Spanish Academy, was by profession a lawyer who, as a judge, has spent many years in the interior of his native Peru. L. A. is one of Peru's most dynamic short story writers. His short stories are masterpieces that reveal a keen interpretation and a profound understanding of the mind and soul of the Peruvian Indians, both as individuals and as a people. These realistic (sometimes they border on the naturalistic), stories, often containing delicate auto-biographical notes, sparkle with irony. He never minimizes the tragic conditions of the Indian peoples in whose midst he has lived for many years.

The writings of L. A. are vigorous, epic tableaux, in which the author dramatizes graphically the power of *la tierra* (Mother Earth) and the powerlessness of the Indian. His protagonist is the Indian of the Peruvian Sierra as he eternally yields to Mother Nature, as he is perpetually subjugated by the forces of tradition, by ancient atavisms, and by the brutality of the white people. The Indian is an individual completely lacking "awareness of his own individuality" because he is saturated with a deterministic, pantheistic conception of life that ties him forever to nature.

Cruelty, suffering, human debasement—and a plea for justice—are the themes repeated throughout L. A.'s works. Speaking of his work, L. A. said that all of it tends to reflect what is "real and tragic, beautiful and strong in our vernacularism." He also said: "I have not wanted to create only, but to pour on the page certain aspects of the life of a race, which, if today seems to be our shame, yesterday was our glory, and tomorrow may be our salvation."

FURTHER WORKS: *Cuentos andinos* (1920); *De mi casona* (1924); *Matalaché* (1928); *Nuevos cuentos andinos* (1937); *El Hechizo de Tomai-quichua* (1943); *Las Caridades de la señora Tordoya* (1955)

BIBLIOGRAPHY: Bazán, A., *Antología del cuento peruano* (1942); Frikart, F., "The Short Stories of E. L. A. and Their Milieu," in *Hispania*, XXVII (1944), 482-88; Nemtzow, M., "Acotaciones al costumbrismo peruano," in *RI*, XV, No. 28 (1949), 45-52; Gómez Lance, B. R., "El indio y la naturaleza en los cuentos de E. L. A.," in *RI*, XXV, No. 49 (1960), 141-45; Arias-Larreta, A., "Don E. L. A.," in *Nuevo Democracia*, XLI, i (1961), 98-101

BETTY RITA GOMEZ LANCE

LOTI, Pierre

(pseud. of *Louis-Marie-Julien Viaud*), French novelist, b. 14 Jan. 1850, Rochefort, Charente-Inférieure; d. 10 June 1923, Hendaye

L., who came from a Huguenot family, joined the navy in 1867 and went to the Pacific, Japan, and Algeria. On May 21, 1891, he was elected to the French Academy. Promoted to commander in 1899, he participated in the fighting in China in 1900. L. belonged to the exotic movement, founded by the painter-poet Eugene Fromentin (1820-75). He created his novels out of his sea experiences, drawing upon his impressionistic diaries (*Journal intime 1878-85*, published by S. P. Loti, 2 vols., 1925-29). *Aziyadé* (1879) is set in Turkey; *Le Mariage de Loti-Rarahu* (1880; Rarahu, or, The Marriage of Loti, 1890) in Tahiti; *Le Roman d'un spahi* (1881; The Romance of a Spahi, 1890), in Senegal. His outstanding novel, *Pêcheur d'Islande* (1886; An Iceland Fisherman, 1887) is about simple Breton fishermen.

L.'s basic theme—man's restless search for a spiritual goal and for wisdom of his own—raises his novels far above the level of the naturalistic documentaries of exoticism. Weary of civilization and afflicted with the *mal de siècle* of Western culture, L. sought salvation in a return to the primitive, which he hoped to find in non-Western settings. The primitive and the elemental is sometimes embodied in the exotic women characters with whom his heroes, modeled on L. himself, are linked. Yet his search for the want-free, blissful primitive state ends in the realization that a 19th c. European heritage cannot be effaced.

A subsequent series of novels, among which is *Mon Frère Yves* (1883; My Brother Yves, 1887), deal with seafaring.

L. influenced Farrère, P. Benoît, Mac Orlan (qq.v.), and the colonial novel.

FURTHER WORKS: *Fleurs d'ennui* (1883); *Propos d'exil* (1887); *Madame Chrysanthème* (1887; Japan, 1915); *Japonerie d'automne* (1887); *Le Roman d'un enfant* (1890; Story of a Child, 1901); *Le Livre de la pitié et de la mort* (1891; The Book of Pity and of Death, 1892);

Fantôme d'Orient (1891); *Matelot* (1893);
Œuvres complètes (11 vols., 1894-1911); *Le
Désert* (1895; The Sahara, 1921); *Jerusalem*
(1895); *La Galilée* (1896); *Ramuntcho* (1897);
Judith Renaudin (1898); *Les Derniers Jours de
Pékin* (1901; The Last Days of Pekin, 1902);
L'Inde sans les Anglais (1903); *Vers Ispahan*
(1904); *La Troisième Jeunesse de Madame
Prune* (1905); *Les desenchantées* (1906); *Un
pèlerin d'Angkor* (1912); *Turquie agonisante*
(1913; Turkey in Agony, 1913); *Prime jeunesse*
(1919); *Suprêmes visions d'Orient* (1921); *Lettres
à Madame Juliette Adam* (1924). **Selected English trans.:** *Selections from P. L.* (1897); *Stories
from P. L.* (1933)

BIBLIOGRAPHY: Lemaître, J., *Les Con-
temporains* (1898); Giraud, V., *Les Maîtres de
l'heure* (Vol. I, 1911); Serban, N., *P. L.: sa vie
et son oeuvre* (1924); Farrère, C., *P. L.* (1929);
de Traz, R., *P. L.* (1948); Brodin, P., "Should
We Forget P. L.?," *American Society of the
Legion of Honor Magazine,* XXXIII (1962),
97-104; Gwatkin, F. A., "P. L. and Japan,"
Asian Review, LIX (1963), 164-78; Dubois, J.,
"P. L. aujourd'hui," *Revue des Sciences
Humaines,* No. 117 (1965), pp. 81-92

BRIGITTE KAHR

LOUŸS, Pierre

(pseud. of *Pierre-Felix Louis*), French poet
and novelist, b. 10 Dec. 1870, Ghent; d. 4 June
1925, Paris

L.'s admiration for Ronsard and Victor
Hugo made him decide while still young to be
a writer. He excelled precociously in music,
foreign languages, and classics. In 1890 Regnier
(q.v.) introduced him to Leconte de Lisle and
Stéphane Mallarmé. He became a friend of
Gide and Valéry (qq.v.), whom he introduced
to Mallarmé in 1891. L. was particularly
influenced by M. Barrès's (1862-1923) *Un
Homme libre,* D'Annunzio's (q.v.) aphrodisiac
works, and Wilde's (q.v.) *Salomé.* He was an
enthusiastic Wagnerian and the mentor of his
friend Claude Debussy. After 1904 L., ill and
almost blind, weary of his fame, withdrew from
literary life and devoted himself exclusively to
poetry and scholarship.

L. began as a symbolist (see symbolism)
poet but never collected these poems for publication. In a rhythmic, musical prose he
glorified sensuous beauty and the feminine
body and soul. The delicate prose poems of

Le Chansons de Bilitis (1895; The Songs of
Bilitis, 1904) describe the life of a Lesbos
courtesan.

L'Aphrodite (1896; Aphrodite, 1925) recalls
Flaubert's *Salammbô* and France's (q.v.)
Thaïs; in this Alexandrian novel L. calls
sensuality the writer's prime requirement. *La
Femme et le pantin* (1898; The Woman and
Puppet, 1930) is an outspokenly erotic novel.
Les Aventures du roi Pausole (1901; The
Adventures of King Pausole, 1932), a satire on
contemporary morals, amusingly continues the
tradition of the Voltairean short novel.

FURTHER WORKS: *Astarté* (1891); *San-
guines* (1903); *Poétique* (1916); *Le Crépuscule
des nymphes* (1925); *Journal inédit* (1926-27);
Psyché (1927); *Poésie* (1927); *Journal intime,
1882-1891* (1929); *Œuvres complètes* (8 vols.,
1929-31); *Poésies de P. L.* (2 vols., 1945);
Œuvres choisies (5 vols., 1950)

BIBLIOGRAPHY: Gaubert, E., *P. L.* (1904)
and *Le Tombeau de P. L.* (1925); Beaubourg,
M., *et al., Le Souvenir de P. L.* (1928); Franke,
K., *P. L.* (1937); Cardinne-Petit, R., *P. L. intime*
(1942) and *P. L. inconnu* (1948); Farrère, C.,
Mon ami P. L. (1953); Fleury, R., "Junot, Duc
d'Abrantès, et P. L.: Leur parenté," *Bulletin du
Bibliophile et du Bibliothequaire,* (1962), pp.
86-92

DAVID J. NIEDERAUER

LOWELL, Robert

American poet, b. 1 March 1917, Boston,
Mass.

L., descendant of New England Calvinists,
comes from one of America's most distinguished
families. In the tradition of the Lowell family
he attended St. Mark's and Harvard. Then, as
part of his rebellion against the milieu he was
born to, he transferred to Kenyon College,
where he studied literature under Ransom and
Jarrell (qq.v.) In 1940 he converted to Roman
Catholicism, but, finding no peace in this faith,
he renounced it in 1948. He married the gifted
writer Jean Stafford, but the marriage lasted
only a few years. In 1942 he refused to be drafted
and was jailed as a conscientious objector. In
1949 he married the writer Elizabeth Hardwick.
He now lives in Manhattan and teaches at
Harvard.

L.'s first book of poetry, *Land of Unlikeness*
(1944), aroused interest in literary circles. It was
soon followed by *Lord Weary's Castle* (1946),

PIERRE LOTI

ROBERT LOWELL

which won the Pulitzer Prize. In 1951 L. published *The Mills of the Kavanaughs.*

The poetry in his first three books, which is characterized by complicated rhyme patterns and symbolic language, voices bold and powerful attacks on the war and on Puritan ethics and on the failure of these ethics. In pounding rhythm and ringing rhymes he evokes the sea, the coast, the people who live and have lived there.

L.'s recent poetry is compressed and has a forceful impact. His unusually keen sense of form controls the fury in his poetry. His careful rhyme schemes, in which he avoids easy rhyming, give his poetry a gritty brilliance. In *Life Studies* (1959), L. uses facts in elegies to his friends, and in dramatic monologues about historic figures, about himself as a conscientious objector and a father, and about today's Boston.

L. has a thoroughly historical mind that has been nourished by his labors on translations and adaptations. In *Imitations* (1962) he offers versions of poems by Rilke, Pasternak (qq.v.), Homer, Sappho, Villon, Baudelaire, and others. In *Near the Ocean* (1967) his translations of Dante, Horace, and Juvenal keep very faithfully to the originals—"as faithfully as I am able or dare or can bear to be" (R.L.). The grandeur and the cruelty of Rome comes alive in "The Vanity of Human Wishes," which is a translation of Juvenal's Tenth Satire, yet his subtle use of language gives the reader the chilling sensation of here and now.

L. also tried his hand at playwriting. *The Old Glory* (1964) is made up of three short plays, each of which expresses one aspect of the American dilemma. In *Endecott and the Red Cross* the problem is religion, especially Puritanism; in *Major Molineux,* politics; and in *Benito Cereno,* the racial situation. But, essentially, *The Old Glory* is about human nature and the contradictions on which America is built. L. writes New England's epitaph, instead of singing its praise as others have done.

Stephen Spender (q.v.) calls Lowell a "pioneer extending the frontier of language, making notable conquests of material which often seems too eccentric for poetry and consolidating it in very strong and compact form ... a humanist kind of poetry, in which disparate experiences are bound up within the sensibility of a poet, who has himself an immense compassion combined with clearness and hardness."

FURTHER WORKS: *Phaedra* (1963); *Hawthorne* (1964); *For the Union Dead* (1964);

Selected Poems (1965); *The Voyage, and Other Versions of Poems by Baudelaire* (1968); *Prometheus Bound* (1968)

BIBLIOGRAPHY: Blackmuir, R. P., *Form and Value in Modern Poetry* (1946); Jarrell, R., "From the Kingdom of Necessity," in *The Nation* (18 Jan. 1968), pp. 164-174; Deutsch, B., *Poetry in Our Time* (1952); Jarrell, R., *Poetry and the Age* (1953); Mazzaro, J., *The Achievement of R. L.* (1960); Staples, H. B., *R. L., The First Twenty Years* (1962); Simon, J., "The Old Glory," in *Book Week* (20 Feb. 1966); "The Second Chance," in *Time* (2 June 1967); Davison, P., "The Difficulties of Being Major," in *The Atlantic* (Oct. 1967)

GERTRUDE C. SCHWEBELL

LOWRY, Malcolm

English novelist, b. 28 July 1909, Liverpool; d. 27 June 1957, London

L. left school to ship on a sailing vessel for China. He later traveled extensively. From 1929 to 1932 he studied philosophy at Cambridge. He wrote his first novel (*Ultramarine,* 1933) in 1932, although he considered only the fifth version (*Under the Volcano,* 1947)—which he had finished in 1944—definitive. L. called this work "a drunken Divine Comedy." L. sees man as both the Janus-faced creature of nature and history and the androgynous Adam: wholeness and unity can be found only in the rejoining through love of two sundered beings. If love is rejected, man and woman experience the gulf between the infinite and the world; their road leads to Hell.

L. mixes cabbalistic ideas with Central American Indian legends. His cryptic language identifies him as an originally creative disciple of Joyce (q.v.) and his power of words recalls Wolfe (q.v.). His novel was followed in 1955 by a collection of short stories entitled *Hear Us, O Lord, from Heaven Thy Dwelling Place.*

FURTHER WORKS: *Selected Poems* (ed. Earle Birney and Margerie Lowry; 1962); *Selected Letters* (ed. Harvey Breit and Margerie Lowry; 1965); *Dark Is the Grave Wherein My Friend Is Laid* (ed. Margerie Lowry and Douglas Day; 1968)

BIBLIOGRAPHY: Woodcock, G., "M. L.'s *Under the Volcano, MFS,* IV (1958), 151-56; Edmonds, D. H., "M. L.: A Study of His Life

LUGONES

and Work," *DA,* XXVI (1966), 7315; Aiken, C., "M. L.," *Times Literary Supplement,* 16 Feb. 1967, p. 127, and 13 April 1967, p. 317; Edmonds, D. H., "The Short Fiction of M. L.," *Tulane Studies in English,* XV (1967), 59-80; Stern, J., "M. L.—A First Impression," *Encounter,* XXIX (1967), iii, 58-68

HELMUT M. BRAEM

LUGONES, Leopoldo

Argentine poet, novelist, essayist, and historian, b. 13 June 1874, Río Seco, Córdoba; d. 19 Feb. 1938, Buenos Aires

L. was the most influential man-of-letters in Argentine public life of the twentieth century. After some youthful writing and political activity in his native province of Córdoba, L. joined the *modernista* group writing in Buenos Aires under the leadership of Darío (q.v.). Here, with Payró (q.v.) and José Ingenieros (1877-1925), he was active in the Centro Socialista de Estudios. But L.'s political thinking changed rapidly. Emotional instability and restlessness, as well as the reading of Nietzsche (q.v.) prompted his turn from socialism to nationalism.

The same restlessness rules L.'s poetic evolution. He thought of himself primarily as a poet. From his first important book, *Las montañas del oro* (1897), however, his poetry is at the service of a desire for fashionable success. From the grandiloquence of this book, influenced by Victor Hugo (1802-1885) at his most oratorical L. went to *Los crepúsculos del jardín* (1905). In these sonnets, L., influenced by the naive morbidity of Albert Samain (1858-1900) and the nervousness of the *fin de siècle,* attempts to express neurasthenias new to the River Plate region. The *Lunario sentimental* (1909) is derivative of the easy irony and dandyism of Jules Laforgue (1860-87). But L. at his best as a poet appears only when dealing with his own country, as in *Odas seculares* (1910), *El Libro fiel* (1912), and *El Libro de los paisajes* (1912). In *El Libro de los paisajes* the description of his native landscape gives his verse an authority he never equaled.

L.'s work in prose is even more diverse and uneven. His prose is at its best in *La Guerra gaucha* (1905), a book of sketches in which the courage and the glory of the *gaucho* guerrillas are set forth in a decadent luxuriousness of words. He also wrote short stories, *Cuentos fatales* (1924) and a novel, *El Ángel*

336

LYRIC POETRY

de la sombra (1926). A good deal of L.'s prose writing stems from his educational and political activities: he was the director of the library of the National Council of Education from 1914 to his death and was made the representative to the Committee on Intellectual Cooperation of the League of Nations. In 1926, L. was awarded the Premio Nacional de Literatura.

Condemned by both talent and fame to a public life for which he was not fit, L. sought release from his many commitments and entanglements in suicide.

FURTHER WORKS: *Las fuerzas extrañas* (1906); *Las horas doradas* (1922); *Romancero* (1924); *Poemas solariegos* (1928); *Romances del Río Seco* (1930); *Poesías completas* (1949); *Obras poéticas completas* (1952)

BIBLIOGRAPHY: Borges, J. L., *L.* (1955); Ara, G., *L. L.* (1958); Moreno, J. C., "Silence in the Poetry of L. L.," in *Hispania,* XLVI (1963), 760-63; Castellani, L., *L.* (1964); Scari, R. M., "La formación literaria de L.," in *DA,* XXIV (1964), 4199; Sola Gonzalez, A., "Las *Odas seculares* de L. L.," in *RI,* XXXII (1966), 23-51

BERNARD GICOVATE

LYRIC POETRY

ENGLAND AND AMERICA

The Post-symbolist Tradition, and the Alternative

For some years now it has seemed to observers both in London and the U.S. that post-symbolist principles have ceased to bear fruit in English and American poetry. Poets and critics alike have come around to the assumption that poems make rationally apprehensible statements about reality, and hence that a good poem is, at least to some degree, paraphrasable into connected prose sense. This is in the sharpest contrast to the notion that a poem is a linguistic construct, a self-contained universe, and that the better the poem the more indomitably will it resist paraphrase. Yet it is this last assumption that has governed, not just the revolutionary poetry of Eliot and Pound and William Carlos Williams (qq.v.), but also—though perhaps with less rigor—the generation of the twenties in America (Crane, Stevens,

Marianne Moore, Ransom, Tate [qq.v.]), of the thirties in England (Auden and the unjustly neglected Prince [qq.v.]), and of the forties in both countries (Dylan Thomas, Theodore Roethke [qq.v.]).

The most immediately welcome effect of this change of heart has been a revaluation of poets who either lived through the post-symbolist revolution unaffected by it (in England, Bridges and Hardy [qq.v.], in America, Frost and Edwin Arlington Robinson [qq.v.]), or else were "odd men out" in their generations (in England, Graves and Empson [qq.v.], in America, Louise Bogan and Winters [qq.v.]). Some of these (Hardy, for instance, and Frost) have never lacked for readers and have in fact reached a much wider public than the more obscure poets who attracted the avant-garde intelligentsia. Others, such as Robinson and Bridges, while never totally excluded from representative anthologies, have been and still are generally neglected, undervalued, and misunderstood.

Poetry and Paraphrase

Largely because Winters has applied himself for almost thirty years to the formulation of a scholarly and systematic poetic theory, the existence of such an alternative is more generally recognized, and in general the issues involved are clearer, to the young American poet today than to his contemporary in Britain, where alternative models are not so obviously available. This gap exists because some British poets outside the symbolist tradition have had interests and ambitions too specialized (for instance the exquisite lyricist of twilight states of consciousness, de la Mare [q.v.]), or because, like the poets of World War I—Wilfred Owen (q.v.), Isaac Rosenberg (1890-1918), and Edward Thomas (1878-1917)—they died before they had established a sufficiently large and various body of work. Other poets who appear, and even deliberately attempt, to provide a model outside the symbolist tradition, exert in fact a more ambiguous influence.

Graves, for instance, has elaborated in a prose work, *The White Goddess,* a system of occult wisdom conveyed in cryptic allegories and common, as he maintains, to ancient Mediterranean and ancient Celtic poetry and folklore. Plainly this is the wisdom he seeks to convey, and this cryptic language is his vehicle, in many of his beautifully chiseled and formally old-fashioned lyrics. Yeats [q.v.] similarly made use in his poems of an occult system and a cryptic poetic grammar of images, but Yeats, true to his early indoctrination by French symbolism (q.v.), at least sometimes allowed that the system that he elaborated in the prose work, *A Vision,* may be merely a device for the writing of poems which are intended to be meaningful (though not perhaps paraphrasable) in quite other terms than those of the system. Graves demands that his poems of this kind be understood in no other terms than those he has expounded; yet any reader who cannot give credence to Graves's system of doctrine is forced, if he is to enjoy the poems at all, to read them as if they were post-symbolist poems, in which the paraphrasable statements are only incidental to the true meaning that defies paraphrase. A similar case is that of the younger poet, Empson, who has sometimes been thought to exemplify a firmer alternative to post-symbolist practice. But it seems, on the contrary, that Empson differs from his contemporary Dylan Thomas, far more in appearance than in fact. Though the calculated ambiguity of an Empson poem can be worked out whereas Thomas's rhetoric mostly baffles analysis, Empson and Thomas are nevertheless alike in cultivating deliberate ambiguities so as to defy paraphrase.

More genuinely original than either Empson or Graves was the novelist D. H. Lawrence (q.v.). In his poems, especially in his *vers libre,* Lawrence appears to be the only British disciple of Whitman. Therefore, he has more in common with such American poets as Williams and Crane than with any of his countrymen. He differs from Crane and Williams, however, in that he is quite unconvinced by the Whitmanesque and Emersonian ideology, which he gave a clinical account of in his *Studies in Classic American Literature.* This has affected his poems, which are distinguished particularly by a vivid exactness in the registering of sense impressions, a descriptive precision that the Whitmanesque afflatus can seldom pause for. In this aspect Lawrence's poetry resembles that of his contemporaries, the imagists, but he surpasses them because his handling of sense impressions is the unforced expression of sympathy with and reverence for the natural creation as opposed to the doctrinaire position of the imagists. However, his creative energies went rather into prose fiction, and he was content to leave his poetry loose in form and to restrict himself to the expression of a relatively narrow sector of experience.

Of older English models, Hardy, while generally acknowledged as a very great poet, is idiosyncratic. This is not true of his poetic strategies in general or of his philosophical allegiances, but this is to be seen in his diction, which is at once pedantic and colloquial in a way that too often produces among his imitators only a labored pastiche of his own too distinctive style. Moreover, Hardy, as his novels indicate, is the inhabitant of a world vanished too completely for his poetic strategies to be readily acceptable to the conditions of today. Physically Hardy's world is that of peasant communities that were already anachronistic in the England of Queen Victoria in which Hardy wrote of them; they were representative of a way of life that Hardy knew to be doomed even as he was recording it. This recognition is one source of his atheistic fatalism, just as another is the intellectual world that he inhabited, the rigidly predetermined material universe of 19th c. biology and geology. Nevertheless, some poets, notably Auden and Ransom, have contrived to emulate Hardyesque techniques to good effect; and in Auden's poetry in particular this strain, no less than the Marxist interests of his earliest and best period, tends to move him out of the post-symbolist line of succession.

Less idiosyncratic is another late Victorian who survived into the 20th c., the gentleman-scholar Bridges. But Bridges finds fewer and fewer readers (though his poems continue to appear in anthologies), and in neither country and least of all his native land is Bridges studied as providing a usable alternative to post-symbolist theory and practice. What damaged Bridges's reputation grievously was the revelation that as literary executor of Gerard Manley Hopkins, the friend of his youth, he delayed for forty years the publication of Hopkins's poems. When the poems appeared in 1920 and the astonishing revolutionary genius of Hopkins stood revealed, still more when Hopkins's letters were printed and Bridges was shown to have had little sympathy with his friend's experiments, Bridges's name became a byword for frigid academicism. Nevertheless, if British poetry in the next few years is to draw upon native resources (instead of putting itself to school in America—and why should it not?), British poets will have to reread and reassess the Bridges-Hopkins correspondence.

Metrical Verse and Vers Libre

Nothing else, for instance, could so clearly direct attention to a problem that cannot await solution much longer—the state of English metrics. There is of course no necessary connection between symbolist and post-symbolist verse and the practice of *vers libre*. One poet in the symbolist tradition, Yeats, eschewed free verse throughout his career, whereas such nonsymbolist poets as Whitman in America and Hopkins in England either practiced *vers libre* or paved the way for it by their experiments. Nevertheless, it is true that Pound and Eliot, the pioneers of post-symbolist verse in English, were also pioneers of *vers libre*, and it is also true that recent poets, reacting away from post-symbolist strategies, tend to return to strict metrical and stanzaic forms. But the ravages of a period when *vers libristes,* however exacting in their own writing, seemed to be advising every poet to trust solely to his ear are not to be repaired in a day; and contemporary writing in meter too often falls into metronomic monotony.

Bridges, the last writer on traditional prosody who wrote out of his own experience, may have to be overhauled in the light of modern discoveries, and traditional metrics will have to be augmented by a rationale of free verse. Here again the American Winters has led the way, establishing that the structural principle of English *vers libre* is a ratio to be maintained between heavily stressed and more lightly stressed syllables, and again between those and syllables receiving no stress at all. Since English syllables as spoken may vary infinitely in the weight of the stress, the distribution of stress in English *vers libre* is an extremely delicate and difficult matter. Traditional English verse, which is accentual-syllabic, is governed by the number of syllables as well as by the weight of the stress. In this, the line is divided into metrical feet, and a syllable becomes stressed or unstressed only in relation to the other syllable or syllables *in the same foot*. The distribution of stresses is therefore easier in strict verse than in *vers libre,* in which the weight of the stress must be determined in relation to syllables not just in the same foot but throughout the poetic line or even throughout the whole poem. Winters finds that the best *vers libre* in English has been written by Pound, by Stevens, and by William Carlos Williams in his youth; to these names most readers would wish to add that of Eliot. Modern free verse then is only a variant of English accentual verse, which has been recognized as a legitimate method of prosody ever since the Middle Ages. The result of the era of *vers libre* supremacy is that the British poet in particular will have to relearn all the traditional expertise of variation in accentual-syllabic verse, whether the method is that of exploiting the quantitative element in the language or (a coarser device) the one of substitution, e.g. of a trisyllabic for a disyllabic foot. Among British poets currently writing, the most expert practitioner of these traditional skills is probably Robert Graves.

When Hopkins's verse was first published (long after his death), what first attracted attention was his metrical theory of "sprung rhythm," by which he attempted to combine the flexibility of spoken rhythms with systemtic formal strictness. It was Hopkins's conviction that such strictness in its own terms was an essential of poetry, and this distinguished his metrical practice from Whitman's (as he recognized himself) and from that of other *vers libristes*. But it was soon felt that the system he proposed was too cumbersome, and that by marking on his poems the stresses he wanted, Hopkins was confessing the inadequacy of his system. What survived from his metrical practice to influence later poets was a single powerful effect, which perhaps the whole system was elaborated to rationalize and control—the crowding together of as many as four heavily stressed syllables in succession. This effect can be contrived, though not without difficulty, in traditional accentual-syllabic meters, and accordingly poets such as Dylan Thomas have been able to compass this effect, of stresses crowded together, without endorsing the Hopkinsian system, which has therefore been jettisoned. Similarly, the concepts that Hopkins threw out to his correspondents—"inscape," "instress"—have resisted attempts to adopt them into the general terminology of criticism, since it seems that the poetic realities they were coined to designate are bound up too closely with the peculiar philosophical and aesthetic position of their author.

Poetic Diction

What continues, and rightly so, to excite poets and critics alike in Hopkins is his vocabulary and his syntax. These are precisely the matters that have in the present century most occupied the attention of critics writing in English. Many British critics in particular, mean to praise a poem very highly when they say that it "has the accent of living speech." Yet such an approach runs the risk of precluding altogether the whole idea of poetic diction, since that term, if properly understood, surely acknowledges that the language of poetry may or must diverge from the spoken language. This bias toward the colloquial has put too much weight on a connection that undoubtedly exists, one between modern poetry in English and certain poets of the 17th c., notably Donne (1573-1631) and Marvell (1621-78). These represent a strain of colloquial poetry in a period otherwise dominated by the very uncolloquial genius of Milton.

But if Eliot is sometimes similarly colloquial, only an eye focused on linguistic texture to the exclusion of all else could fail to note that whereas the structure of a poem by Donne is characteristically that of logical though impassioned argument, the structure of a poem by Eliot is characteristically that of progression by association among images merely juxtaposed. It is true that Eliot's and Pound's early poetry finds room for puns and other kinds of word play that are found in Shakespeare and Donne but hardly at all since Pope. Yet if the new poetry was thus unashamedly "intellectual", the intellectualism was much closer to that of Mallarmé (1842-98) than to that of Donne. Moreover, much of this criticism never thought to question the nature of the spoken language that was to be poetry's model. The language as spoken by whom, and in what circumstances? Hopkins had asked himself and had gone some way toward answering this question. But what appealed to the critics of 1920 was Hopkin's round condemnation of archaisms in poetic language, and his assertion that "the language of poetry must always be the current language heightened." Pound and Eliot seemed to be voicing the same opinion when they derided Miltonic magniloquence in the interest of the colloquial symbolism of Laforgue (1860-87) and Corbière (1845-75), at that time their masters. Moreover the fashionable poetry of the period 1900-1914 certainly employed a diction too far out of touch with spoken usage; and this was true even of the greatest poet of that generation, Yeats, who grew in stature as his language became, if not colloquial, at least more conversational in its vocabulary as well as its rhythms. But what did most to justify the demand for colloquial poetry was the example of the inspired colloquialism of Hopkins. Those critics were not wrong who gave to Hopkins's audacities in the coining of words, in syntactical ellipses, in the use of dialect expressions, the term "Shakespearean." What was Shakespearean, of course, was the success of these audacities, the effect that Hopkins always gave— which was that all his departures from standard usage, however startling, were yet in the spirit of the language as spoken. Yet Hopkins's language was Shakespearean in another way, in being inimitable; it was no model for other poets to follow. Accordingly, at a later period when Eliot (to some extent) and Pound (conspicuously) were using more elevated and elaborate language, Auden, when he wished to rise above the colloquial even slangy diction of which he was a master, adapted pre-Shakespearean forms, mediaeval and Anglo-Saxon, in order to achieve the elevated tone that his readers were by now so suspicious of. It was only in the years of World War II that the instructed British public tolerated, under the influence of Dylan Thomas, a poetry that was not colloquial; and this tolerance did not long survive the war.

Narrative and Musical Structure

In respect to diction, an interesting comparison between the two most distinguished American poets who learned little or nothing from French symbolism can be made. Frost, who from the first used an extremely bare and flat conversational language, the language of the New England farmer that he was, achieved at once and kept a greater measure of public recognition than Edwin Arlington Robinson, who favored, at least in his shorter nonnarrative poems, an extremely literary language. The peculiar and, as some have thought, not altogether wholesome effect of Frost is the combination of this homespun directness of tone and vocabulary with a notably devious and oblique conduct of poetic argument; and there is the same contrast between the rural sturdiness of his settings and overt themes, and a sophisticated almost cynical irony in his moral outlook. Frost has also experimented in longer narrative poems, but here, while the conduct of the narrative is frequently interesting, the flat plainness of the diction does nothing to offset the lack of rhythmical interest in the regular iambic blank verse. Robinson, who alone of modern poets in English has essayed really long blank verse narratives, has profited from the greater liberties he allows himself in

departing from the spoken norm. Though rather often the conduct of the narrative is excessively oblique (rather in the manner of the prose of James [q.v.]), Robinson, for instance in "Lancelot," contrives to keep his blank verse interesting by shifting tone as the level of his diction shifts, and by playing off the syntactical against the metrical units.

Another traditional narrative poem is "The Comedian as the Letter C" by Stevens. Here, as elsewhere, Stevens solves the problem of finding an elevated yet flexible diction by carrying much further a technique already used by Pound and Eliot (which they learned from the French) —the attitude towards language of *le dandy*, at once arrogant and fastidious. This stratagem colors much more in Stevens than just his diction, and it constitutes his most considerable debt to the symbolist tradition. Yet "The Comedian as the Letter C," like Stevens's greatest poem, "Sunday Morning," not only uses language in the manner of Shakespeare's sonnets (like unfashionable poets of the last century such as George Meredith [1828-1909]), but also raises explicitly, though so early in the poet's career, the problem of finding a subject. This is not in the ordinary way a problem for the symbolist poet, since a subject that would permit of definition would open the door to the paraphrase that he seeks to obstruct. Lacking a subject, Stevens never got to the point of doing without it; accordingly all his best poems are among his earliest. He never again attempted a narrative structure, and his later poems of any length take the form of poetic sequences, loosely and obscurely connected by what looks like an argument in epistemology. Despite the splendour of his diction, despite the fineness of his ear (for he has written beautiful blank verse as well as *vers libre*), Stevens's later poems cannot conceal the anomaly of an apparently didactic poetry in which *le dandysme*, persisting in the diction to cast a facile defensive irony, suggests (what is perhaps too true) that, for all his apparently didactic stance, the poet does not care about the subject he professes to expound.

To poets writing in the symbolist tradition or taking cognizance of the symbolist aesthetic, the narrative poem is barely a possibility. Eliot for instance has remained true to a central thesis of French symbolist thought, in proceeding on the assumption that a poem of any length must employ a structure analogous to the structures of music. From this point of view the musical analogy deliberately invited in the title

"Four Quartets" is all of a piece with the principles operating in his "Waste Land." This has not prevented commentators from treating "Four Quartets" as if it constituted a theological treatise with some of the argumentative links left out. Still less has it stopped them from treating "The Waste Land" as an allegorical narrative similarly complicated by ellipses. Yet it should be plain that Eliot throughout his career neither has nor could have considered narrative structure as any longer a serviceable structure for poems. Characteristically, Eliot's poems explore a situation, not a train of events, and if he explores the situation by moving through or around it, this movement is not through a sequence in recorded time, but is rather in the musical terms of theme and variations, or motif, development, restatement, countertheme.

The same principles operate in what is by any grounds the most ambitious poetic structure of our time, at least in English, the *Cantos* of Pound. The author's description of this as "plotless epic" sufficiently shows that it is written on the assumption that a narrative structure for poetry is no longer a real possibility. Yet Pound, in the earlier "Hugh Selwyn Mauberley," had come near to writing a narrative poem. This, like the *Cantos* and indeed all the work of Eliot, shows the impact of imagism.

Symbolist aesthetic certainly, but still more the example of Chinese poetry, contributed to the theory behind the imagist movement. At bottom it was a theory about poetic cognition: it maintained that whereas other sorts of knowledge were built up by comparison and classification, that is, by abstracting from two perceptions a quality common to both, poetic knowledge was attained by juxtaposing two or more particular perceptions in all their particularity, that is, by refusing to abstract a common quality from them, refusing even to see them as related in terms of this abstraction. This meant in practice that the poet refused to limit the affinity between his "ideas" or his "images" to any one logical relation of the sorts designated by such words as "although," "if," "whereas," and "because." Carried to its logical extreme, this meant the elimination of syntax from poetry, except in the extended and perhaps metaphorical sense in which one may speak of a syntax of music. Accordingly, though "Hugh Selwyn Mauberley" is narrative in that it is the imaginary biography of a fictitious man of letters (and displays, once again, some affinity with attitudes and concerns of James),

yet it resolves itself into a series of images or cinematographic "shots," juxtaposed without explicit logical connection. And it is perhaps appropriate that the work, divided as it is into short sections and written to a great extent in quatrains, should seem to answer as readily to the description "poetic sequence," as to the name of "poem." It is, however, the most intelligent and skillful attempt yet made to reconcile narrative structure with musical structure in poetry. A much less successful attempt has been made by William Carlos Williams in his *Paterson* and by Crane in "The Bridge."

Drama and Dramatic Structure

Just as these works, with "Hugh Selwyn Mauberley," represent poetic narrative transformed under the pressures of symbolist aesthetic on the one hand, and on the other, through Pound, of Oriental precedent, so the plays of Yeats show the idea of poetic drama similarly transformed—and under the same pressures. For it was the Oriental Noh play, grafted on to the symbolist poetic drama of Maeterlinck (q.v.), which produced the poetic drama of Yeats's maturity, in which all the conventions of naturalistic dramaturgy are replaced by conventions nearer to those of ritual and the dance, in which masked impersonal players punctuate the speaking of poetry with balletlike patterned movements, to the occasional accompaniment of gong or drum. This corpus of work by Yeats stands alone, and he has as yet found no successors. Eliot, for instance, having begun in "Sweeney Agonistes" and *Murder in the Cathedral* with a drama near to ritual, developed steadily toward accepting all the naturalistic conventions, his verse becoming gradually more self-effacing or self-denying in the process.

But dramatic poetry is not the same as poetry for the stage. And much lyrical poetry of the present century is, if one may believe its commentators and apologists, proud to be called "dramatic." In the first place much American poetry (that of Ransom and Tate for instance) is dramatic in that it seeks to express and heighten a state of tension between two incompatible attitudes in, or responses toward, a given situation. Like the early poetry of Auden, it does not seek to resolve the contradiction or let down the tension; and it is this which, by defying prose paraphrase, sets it in the postsymbolist tradition. But a lot of this poetry is dramatic in a less recondite sense, in that what appear to be lyrical or reflective poems (Eliot's "Lovesong of J. Alfred Prufrock," for instance, or his "Gerontion") are dramatic monologues, to be understood as spoken by the poet through an assumed character. Pound, who alone of modern poets developed the dramatic monologue straight from the Victorian master of this genre, Robert Browning (1812-89), used the word "persona" to describe the voice—not quite the poet's voice, yet significantly related to his—which is to be imagined as speaking the poems to the reader. In an ambitiously orchestrated poem such as Pound's *Cantos* or Eliot's "Waste Land," we see how the doctrine of the "persona" locks in with the imagist doctrine of communication by simple juxtaposition of images. For if the shift from image to image is accompanied by a shift in the tone of voice (intimated by changes of diction and rhythm), then the poet in juxtaposing images is juxtaposing personae, and speaking not through any one of them but in the chorus they make together. Yeats's more complicated doctrine of the mask and the antimask is clearly an elaboration of the idea of the "persona." And in the work of Amy Lowell (1874-1925) the poem as dramatic monologue is quite patently once again Browningesque.

This prevailing tendency (which incidentally satisfies the demand for the accent of living speech, while not binding the poet to any one mode of that speech) obviously has something to do with the modern poet's unsureness about his own identity—he is so far from the confidence necessary to write the nakedly didactic that he cannot define his own being but writes his poems in order to find himself. Thus to find one's self by adopting the selves of others, to attain to sincerity by a hard-won ironical detachment from one's own poses in fancy dress—this is the modern variant of the ancient paradox by which the poet is a liar who pretends what is not, but only in order to learn and to say what is.

BIBLIOGRAPHY: Eliot, T. S., *The Sacred Wood* (1920); Bridges, R., *Milton's Prosody* (1921); Hulme, T. E. *Speculations* (1924); Richards, I. A., *Principles of Literary Criticism* (1924); Winters, Y., *In Defense of Reason* (1937); Fenollosa, E., *The Chinese Written Character as a Medium for Poetry* (1946); Davie, D., *Articulate Energy* (1955); Hopkins, G. M., *Letters* (2nd ed., 1955-1956); Hopkins, G. M., *Notebooks and Papers* (1937); Moore, G., *Poetry Today* (1958); Forrest, E. W. C., *Romantic Continuity in Major 20th-century Poetry* (1959); Rosenthal, M. L., *The Modern Poets* (1960); Pearce, R. H., *The Continuity of American Poetry* (1961); Cambon, G., *Recent American Poetry* (1962); Press, J., *Rule and Energy: Trends in British Poetry Since the 2nd World War* (1963); Hamilton, I., *The Poetry of War 1939-45* (1965); Mills, R. J., *Contemporary American Poetry* (1965); Dembo, L. S., *Conceptions of Reality in Modern American Poetry* (1966); Miller. J. H., *Poets of Reality* (1966); Unger, L., ed., *Seven Modern American Poets: An Introduction* (1967)

DONALD DAVIE

FRANCE

GENERAL TENDENCIES

Post-Symbolist Poetry of Transition

A. Barre's epoch-making dissertation "Le symbolisme" appeared in 1911. Legitimized now by the Sorbonne, such problems as *verslibrisme*, sound symbolism, dissociation, and esotericism, which had still been controversial at the turn of the century, officially became academic questions. By about 1910 the breakthrough of a poetry founded on and at the same time in reaction against—Baudelaire (1821-67), Rimbaud (1854-91), Mallarmé (1842-98), Tristan Corbière (1845-75), Jules Laforgue (1860-87), and Jarry (q.v.) was complete.

This poetry accepted as a matter of course suggestion, ellipsis, syntactic freedom, *vers libre,* and the use of analogies instead of logical progression, yet it diverged in the most varied ways from the inwardness of symbolism (q.v.).

Unbridgeable as the gulf separating naturists, fantaisistes, unanimists, futurists, and cubists from each other may be, they were all concerned with the outward side of the here and now; they all tried to poeticize everyday experience and to incorporate the prosaic into poetry. In this they were logically continuing the mixtures of styles and genres introduced by the romantics. From Rousseau (1712-78) and Chateaubriand (1768-1848), through Gide and Camus (qq.v.) and on up to our time, the novel, novella, diary, and essay are pervaded by the element of lyricism. In addition, the romantics, by breaking down traditional rhythms, had already brought French verse closer to prose. A hardness that is in opposition to the fluid musical idiom of the symbolists now becomes apparent in lyric poetry.

The symbolists had striven for an unattainable "purity" of the word, which, freed from all materiality in the designated thing, would itself become the object of the poem. In the hands of the post-symbolists, language turns into film strips in the kaleidoscopic images of which odds and ends of daily life mingle with harshly illuminated fragments of inner life. Here the worlds of the real and the imagined intermingle rapidly.

This approach existed in the now outmoded, almost traditional poetry of the unanimists, extolling a modest humanitarian ideal—as found in Romains (q.v.), Charles Vildrac (b. 1882), Jacques Chennevière (b. 1886), Duhamel (q.v.), and Luc Durtain (pseud. of André Nepveu, b. 1881)—as well as in the poetry of the radical futurism (q.v.) of Emilio Marinetti (1876-1944) whose goal was to disintegrate language. Between the two schools stands the poetry of Cendrars, Salmon, and Morand (qq.v.); close to life, it shuns all musical or high-flown elements, and looks toward "modernity" in Baudelaire's sense.

Almost in the spirit of German romanticism, the fantaisistes—Tristan Klingsor (pseud. of Leon Leclère, b. 1874), Jean-Marie Bernard (1881-1915), and Tristan Derème (pseud. of Philippe Huc, 1889-1941)—introduced irony (q.v.) and the comic into poetry in emulation of Laforgue. Among the minor poets Carco and Mac Orlan (qq.v.) capture the seamy side of modern city life in poems that are often self-parodies, while Paul-Jean Toulet (1887-1920), in his posthumously published *Contrerimes* (1939), treats country themes ironically yet in rigorous imitation of erudite verse forms of the 16th c.

All these forms of poetry represent a transitional lyricism that is probably without enduring value. In part, it expresses utopian hopes; in part it accepts the present and records the common pulsebeat of man and the city, of the individual and the machine. Yet these often ephemeral lyricists have one thing in common with the century's greatest poets—a certain sobriety, an almost scientific attitude, which is also to be found in Valéry (q.v.). Great emotions are skeptically bypassed; the poetic confession is suppressed or ironically mocked. "Nonpoetry" (which Marinetti established as a principle without giving it a name) is also evident among the less revolutionary spirits. Here the poetic hero is replaced by a kind of antihero, a figure shaped by the darker side of city life, sometimes by its underworld.

Poetry of Discontinuity and Constructivism

Jacob, Cocteau, and Apollinaire (qq.v.) set the tone in the development of modern poetry. Here, as in Reverdy (q.v.), poetry and "modernity" are in direct contact. Here the present day in all its stridence, with its movies, advertising, machines of all kinds, cubist painting, atonal music, and Russian ballet, borne along on the tide of poetic rhetoric, is fused with emotions stemming from inner life into poetry laden with personal myth. At the centre of this myth stands an exoticism that stems (as for instance in Apollinaire) from an ever-fresh perception of the environment, be it Paris, the Rhine, or the front lines.

In Apollinaire's poetry the *mot juste,* purged of all preconceptions, acquires a freedom previously undreamed of. Here the most trivial everyday occurrence may reveal hidden depths that transcend reality. The unexpected in itself —which Apollinaire named *surréalité*—is exalted to the essence of poetry. The poem becomes a "construction"—and this is also true in Cocteau and Jacob. Ellipses and tensions are sharply superimposed in images that shatter all logic. Cocteau vividly jumbles scraps of inner life, opium dreams, and external reality, while at the same time stressing the literal, nonsymbolic nature of the images. The dividing line between "inner" and "outer," between dream and waking experience, between time and timelessness, is blurred. Poetry loses its subjectivity. It becomes pure optics. The poet's eye, turned now toward the outside, now inward, becomes a lens that photographs the turmoil of the headlong rush of images with sober objectivity. In Apollinaire's "Zone" and "Cortège," for instance, the motley fragmentation of his experience of the present moment, held together only by the surge of language, becomes a pure series of images.

A playful discontinuity is constructed whose variegations have their counterpart in a favorite subject of contemporary cubist painting— the Harlequin costume. Metaphors are "spontaneously" piled one upon another with no heed for organic or melodic structure. In its simultaneity of metaphors, the poem becomes a cubist Harlequin costume and thus a mask, a symbol of nature overcome by art and becoming supernature, superreality or "surreality."

If the symbolists tried, in Valéry's words, to

reconquer from music what it had taken from lyricism, it can be said of Cocteau, Jacob, Reverdy, and Apollinaire that they radically explode the differentiation established by Lessing in his *Laokoon* between poetry and the visual arts. They replace the linear succession of metaphors peculiar to poetry by a juxtaposition of metaphors without time sequence, as Lessing described it for the fine arts. Only the metaphysical unity of the poetic language—like the Harlequin costume in Picasso's painting—now holds together, within the poem, the multicolored checkerboard of perceptions of the inner and outer world, the juxtaposed shreds of the world of imagination and the world of phenomena.

For all their repudiation of symbolism, these poets continue the work of Rimbaud and Mallarmé by trying to give lyrical expression to the ineffable. At the same time, like the symbolists, they distinguish poetry from "mere literature," a word that they use in Verlaine's derogatory sense.

Angelism and the Limits of Poetry

In Baudelaire, Rimbaud, Mallarmé, and later in Valéry, the poem became an experiment and a means of grasping the unknown. Jacques Maritain (b. 1882) regards this tendency as a dangerous development of poetry in the direction of theology and a "despotic spirituality." The art of Baudelaire and Rimbaud transcends the limits of the mind. "Yet these regions are those of the greatest dangers; there the most difficult metaphysical problems attack poetry; there the good and bad angels engage in battle" (*Frontières de la poésie*, 1935, p. 28).

The artistic creator becomes godlike; his creation is for him both an attempt and a temptation. He truly becomes the real attempter (experimenter) and tempter in every sense, including the diabolical, while his work becomes for him as for the reader an attempt and a temptation to capture the free and the formless in a verbal thing. The temptation to reach the absolute, the "pure spirit" beyond matter, divesting oneself in the process of one's humanity—that is, to become *angel* (even at the peril of becoming a fallen angel) exists in Mallarmé's and Valéry's word magic and in Rimbaud's "word alchemy" as much as in the angel-obsessed poetry of Cocteau and Jacob. The experimental compulsion to force the poem beyond the limits of poetry dominates nearly all 20th c. poets with the exception of Aragon,

Éluard, Char (qq.v.), and Jean Grosjean (b. 1912).

Destruction of Reason: Futurism, Dadaism, Surrealism

In Mallarmé and Rimbaud the word had already ceased to be a rational sign. Ambiguous, divorced from its communicative function, it became a suggestive end in itself and, according to Hugo Friedrich's analysis, an expression of "purely" lyrical content bordering on silence. Emilio Marinetti continued the dissolution of grammatical connections introduced by Mallarmé—though in a different sense. The dadaism of Tzara (q.v.) breaks up sentences and words to create a kind of antipoetry out of meaningless shards of sound. Protest against academicism, against old-fashioned, sleepy wallowing in emotion and the worship of reason in a world dominated by the absurd, the irrational, and the violent reached their climax in the surrealist revolution of Breton, Artaud, Desnos, Aragon, Éluard (qq.v.), Philippe Soupault (b. 1897), René Crevel (1900-1935), Benjamin Péret (1899-1959), and others.

Aloof from "moral" or rational censorship, and despite its short reign (1924-29), surrealism (q.v) impregnated all modern poetry and art with its values. Here life was no longer poeticized: it became itself poetry, down to its unconscious depths. There was a collective effort "to express the true function of thought by means of a pure, psychic automatism, whether in writing or in other quite different ways—rules of thinking outside all censorship of reason, outside aesthetic and moral prejudices" (*Manifesto*). The aim was absolute freedom of expression as it exists before reason begins its interpretations. Though one may doubt—with Raissa Maritain (1883-1960)—the possibility of purely automatic writing, it is clear that here poets attempt for the first time to put into practice the boldest doctrines of such romantics as Novalis (1772-1801) and to follow, without reservations and without shrinking from scandals, the road of the French symbolists toward discontinuity (with the Marquis de Sade [1740-1814] and Freud [1856-1939] serving as patron saints).

Fargue, Saint-John Perse, Pierre-Jean Jouve, Supervielle (qq.v.), and Reverdy, though close to surrealism, developed outside the movement which had produced many important French poets. Only Breton still supports it.

Rhetoric and Dialectic

Despite membership in the Communist Party, Éluard and Aragon remained pure poets, even when their poetry assumes a didactic guise.

They also wrote good love poetry (which had been almost extinct since Baudelaire and Apollinaire) as well as exercises in classical and archaic meters. The energy-laden images in Char's poetry lead over into aphorisms and sentences; with deliberate economy of words they transfer the essence of an experience to the tensions of the poem.

Rhetoric, too, rejected by Verlaine, finds new champions. Avoiding personal lyricism, Audiberti (q.v.), explores the elemental poetic power of language, trying to discover new rhetorical values that reside in the nature of the word itself. He wants to bring about a further hardening of the word into an object, which turns the poem into an end in itself; at the same time Audiberti's poetry attempts to end the fragmentation of experience. While Audiberti seems to exaggerate the need for abstraction that Ortega y Gasset (q.v.) calls "the dehumanization of art," the poetry of Grosjean, with its lofty style bordering on the epic, asserts with the force of prophecy that loneliness is man's fate. His poetry, based on Biblical and Arabic rhetoric, is diametrically opposed, in its richness of imagery and abrupt juxtaposition of psychological and nature metaphors, to the almost antipoetic everyday language of the subtly ironical poems of Prévert and Queneau (qq.v.). Its tonality stands midway between that of Edmond Fleg (b. 1874) and Claudel (q.v.).

The work of Patrice de La Tour du Pin (b. 1911) and Emmanuel (q.v.) tends also toward the rhetorical; their poetry combats self-alienation in passionately dialectical metaphors. Dialectics in the strictly Hegelian sense is used by Yves Bonnefoy (b. 1923). Here, through a process of antitheses, the language of lyricism fades into silence only to be reborn out of its self-destruction.

Objectivity

The objectivity of Ponge (q.v.) makes use of dialectic in its Kafkaesque effort to achieve a synthesis of the fantastic and the natural. Trying to get nearer to nature from which man has been alienated by science, Ponge endows things such as a pebble or a shell with a voice. He tries to give "density" (*Dichtigkeit*) to the slippery, treacherous word, which, confronted with the material object, appears literally "super-fluous." *Dichten* (the writing of poetry) comes to mean, in Heidegger's sense, *Verdichten* (concentration) of language. The creation of the *Ge-dicht* (poem) is here a kind of vivisection of what is to become a poem. Ponge's poetic experimentation illustrates the aperçu of Jean Grenier (b. 1898) that in the 20th c. the sketch is more highly esteemed than the finished masterwork. Ponge's art not only opposes poetic magic, mysticism, and revelation: it destroys the very nature of the lyrical. In overcoming romanticism, symbolism, and surrealism, it overcomes poetry itself. This is done in the name of classicism, even though Ponge, in his need for clarity (despite the concentration [*Verdichtung*] of language) and his love for classical Alexandrines (which even lurk in his prose), sees himself as a successor of Condillac (1715-80) and even of Malherbe (1555-1628).

TECHNIQUE AND THEORY

Vers libéré

Twentieth c. poetry assimilates the aesthetic achievements of symbolist poetic technique. In his resistance to the neoclassicism of the Parnassians, Verlaine (1844-96) went beyond the romantic dismemberment of the Alexandrine and in 1880 introduced *vers libéré*. Its characteristics are meters that have an odd number of syllables and lines that exceed the maximum classical length found in the Alexandrine. The traditionally rejected hiatus and the enjambment legitimized by the romantics, are polemically cultivated by the practitioners of *vers libéré,* who also attempt to fix the changing values of the mute *e*. More rigorous rhythmic accentuation of syllabic meter now makes the presence of iambics and anapests evident even in "monotonous" French verse. The traditional alternation of masculine and feminine rhymes is discarded. Rhyme is retained in looser form, often parodying itself. This together with the fixed number of syllables, distinguishes *vers libéré* from *vers libre* as first used by Rimbaud in two poems in *Les Illuminations* ("Marine" and "Mouvement"), published by Verlaine in 1886.

Vers libre

Vers libre has no syllabic meter and no regularly recurring metric stress. Its rhythmic units, which change at will, derive their "pulsebeat" from the nature of the object treated by the poem. Rhyme or assonance is retained or discarded to suit the uniqueness of each poem. Gustave Kahn (1859-1936), was one of the foremost champions of *verslibrisme,* which counted among its practitioners Laforgue, Édouard Dujardin (1861-1949), Moréas (q.v.), and others. Verhaeren, Henri de Régnier, and Francis Jammes (qq.v.) also went through a *vers libristic* phase.

Prose Poem

Gaspard de la nuit (1842) by Aloysius Bertrand (1807-1841) became the prototype of this genre, which was important in the work of Baudelaire, Rimbaud, and Mallarmé, as well as in more recent poetry, where it is found alongside classicistic and archaic forms and those of *verslibrisme.*

Innovations (*Péguy, Claudel, Ponge*)

Péguy's (q.v.) poetry establishes a kind of balance between rhythm and the impact of the experience. *Rallentando* and constant repetition mark ever-renewed incantations of his poetry, and endow it with a strangely melodious mixture of mystical fervor and monotony. After attempts with *verslibrisme,* Claudel early found his individual style in the "verset," which resembles the Biblical verse and might be called "the breathing of the soul." Man takes in life in gulps and in the supreme act of exhalation gives it back as an intelligible word (*la ville*). Liberated from meter and prosody, Claudel's "verset" stands midway between prose and poetry. Although Péguy's and Claudel's innovations are used generally in epic and dramatic poetry, they deserve mention here because the work of these poets is constantly pervaded by a deeply lyrical character.

The controversy over *verslibrism* and other unorthodox versification, still virulent at the beginning of the 20th c., died out before World War I. Jacob, Cocteau, and Apollinaire fully freed French versification from traditional shackles. Apollinaire's *calligrammes* were followed by Ponge's *idéogrammes.* From now on the poet could make whatever use of traditional techniques he chose, along with the innovations introduced by the romantics and symbolists, without losing avant-garde stature.

Renewal of Rhyme by Apollinaire and Aragon

Verlaine had treated rhyme with contempt. Except for the exaggerated rhyming in the word play of Desnos, in which whole lines rhyme, the surrealists abandoned all rhyme schemes. In 1940, however, the former surrealist Aragon arrived at a new viewpoint: since all French rhymes seem to be fixed, "rhyming" had become a synonym for "plagiarizing." To the lifeless rigidity of traditional French rhyme routines, Aragon opposes the example of Apollinaire who renews rhyme schemes by changing the rules for what both classics and romantics had called "masculine" and "feminine" rhymes. Apollinaire had stated categorically that all rhymes based on a stressed consonant (and not only on the silent *e*) were to be regarded as feminine rhymes; rhymes on a vowel or nasal sound were to be called masculine. Rhymes of this kind do already exist in French folk poetry; Aragon now suggests that one must move further in the same direction.

"In 1940, in the era of radio and non-Euclidian geometries," Aragon wrote, "we must discover new rhyme schemes; in an age that has degraded man to a hitherto unknown extent, the poet must make material things sing, and the non-sensical rhyme becomes the only kind of sense. In other words, we must now win for rhyme the same freedom that in the time of symbolism was mistakenly claimed for *vers libre* and *vers libéré.*" Aragon proposes a new form of enjambment in which the rhyme itself is dissected by dividing it between the end of one line and the beginning of the next. He brings to his discussion of this subject an erudition unequaled in French prosody since the *grands rhétoriqueurs* of the late 15th c.

Analogy and Free Imagery

In Baudelaire's poetry analogies often replace logical sequences; the thought withdraws behind the image. The symbolists, the surrealists, and their successors try in various ways to escape from the logical constraint of the word. The "rational verbal view" of the cosmos is now replaced by a viewpoint in which "images spontaneously string themselves together." Their uncensored juxtaposition corresponds to the untrammeled freedom of the unconscious; thus a new "order" arises within the human universe. In accordance with the law of simultaneous impressions, metaphors that are logically independent of one another should appear simultaneously in everyday speech. Thus the image, in the meaning given it by Jean Paulhan (b. 1884), Jaloux (q.v.), and Breton, becomes inner revelation existing prior to speech of any kind.

Breton attacks "language, this most inadequate of all conventions." "We must incessantly put words to shame, even strip them of their power to mean something, and thus make their treachery impossible. . . . Surrealistic images are like opium dreams, which force themselves upon man spontaneously and despotically. One can no longer escape them. . . . Then the mind becomes convinced of the supreme reality of these metaphors and soon finds that they enrich its knowledge. In the dizzying workings of the mind metaphors seem to offer the only guide." For Breton, the truest images of surrealism are the ones that defy translation into practical language. Raissa Maritain challenges the surrealist dogma of automatic writing. For her the surrealists' mistake lies in believing that their substantial truth finds expression through this psychic automatism, and in regarding this automatism as equivalent to the actual thought process, and finally in assuming that this is all there is to it. She adds that automatism destroys the impulse to concentrate and to collect that had formerly unified life (*Situation de la poésie,* 1938). Nevertheless, the surrealists' attempt to capture, in the intuitive image, "pure" thought—before any censorship by reason intervenes—guarantees for language the freedom that the symbolists had won for versification.

POETRY, FREEDOM, AND THE ABSOLUTE

In conclusion, it may be noted that the road from symbolism to 20th c. poetry, via the liberation of versification, of rhyme, of language (in its logical, rhetorical, and dialectical relations), of the image, and of the content of the conscious mind and of the unconscious, has led to a stage of experimentation in which the poet—transcending the nature of poetry— becomes a medium of vision; in other words, he becomes a phenomenologist who sees inner and outer reality as well as the word-phenomenon turned object. He tries to capture the world of the simplest objects in their complex outer appearance. Fundamentally different as poets such as Ponge and Valéry may be, Valéry's recognition that "we possess nothing

deeper than our skins" applies to them just as much as to the most recent antipoetry.

In its quest for the absolute, modern poetry performs an ontological task. Whether it expresses the unconscious, makes statements about the cosmos as reflected in the poet's soul or in his word, or is love poetry (as in Aragon and Éluard), its content is not limited to these subjects. It is poetry and poetics; it is act of creation and reflection upon the nature of creativity; it is object and sign of the creative act, giving rise to a new image of the cosmos. It becomes again, no matter in what form, a magic incantation whose formula forces the unknown into the enchanted circle of outward appearance. Rimbaud spoke of the poet's Promethean mission—he becomes the true "thief of fire." "If what he brings back from below is shaped, he reflects its shape; if it is amorphous, he renders the formless." This metaphor contains more than a mere statement on the overcoming of form by the absolute of poetic necessity. It reveals the nature of modern poetry, whose Promethean poet, instead of ascending to the realm of the gods to steal the Olympian fire, descends to the depths of the underworld to bring man's hell out into the light of day. Here, and in the search for the unknown, lies the *romantic* heritage of 20th c. poetry.

But French poetry since Baudelaire is also pervaded by a certain *classicism,* if we apply to it Valéry's criterion. "A Classicist is that writer who harbors a critic within himself and who allows this critic to penetrate to his innermost recesses, where he may then participate in the poetic labors." As Hugo Friedrich says, confessional poetry gives way to epistemological poetry, which systematically recreates the world by means of the "densifying" (*verdichtend*) word. The decisive feature is no longer the inner experience, as it was for romanticism, but the act of naming in which the inner experience *ex-presses* itself, and, pushing outward, becomes utterance, *ex-pression,* work of art, material object, and thus a part of objective reality. This happens regardless of whether the poet uses symbolist, surrealist, or objective processes or some other means to dematerialize, by means of the word, matters of inward and outward reality, and to transform them into a "matter of language," a verbal *thing.* The final result will always be a structure of images in which man testifies to the overwhelming absurdity of the interrelationship between self and world, and to the sovereignty he derives from his power to bring nature under his spell through the linguistic creative act of naming. In this connection Ortega y Gasset's thesis of the dehumanization of art in the 20th c. might be reversed, and it might be maintained that the poet metamorphoses the realm of objective reality into the completely human world of language, which, through its characteristic feature of abstraction, creates its own object.

BIBLIOGRAPHY: Breton, A., *Manifeste du surréalisme* (1929); Aragon, L., "La rime en 1940," in *Le Crèvecœur* (1940); Paulhan, J., *Clef de la poésie* (1944); Friedrich, H., *Die Struktur der modernen Lyrik von Baudelaire bis zur Gegenwart* (1956); le Hir, Y., *Esthétique et structure du vers français d'après les théoriciens du XVIᵉ siècle à nos jours* (1956); Suberville, F. J., *Histoire et théorie de la versification française* (1956); Cornell, K., *The Post-Symbolist Period* (1958); Picon, G., "Domaine de la poésie," in *Histoire des littératures,* vol. iii (1958); Cailois, F. R., *Art poétique* (1959); Maritain, J. and R., *Situation de la poésie* (n.d.); Chiari, J., *Contemporary French Poetry* (1952); Bosquet, A., *Verbe et vertige* (1961); Bo, C., *Poesia francese del Novecento da Apollinaire a Char* (1966)

KURT WEINBERG

GERMANY

Three names mark the history of 20th c. German poetry from its beginning to its first peak: George, Hofmannsthal, and Rilke (qq.v.). The origins of these important poets reach back to the last decade of the 19th c. When Nietzsche (q.v.) died on 25 Aug. 1900, in Weimar, George was thirty-two, Hofmannsthal and Rilke twenty-six. The period of their youth was the period of industrial expansion, those decades after the war of 1870-71 when the last traces of European structure that had distinguished German literature up to the death of Friedrich Hölderlin (1770-1843) had long vanished. While there was hardly an area of science to which the Germany of the second half of the 19th c. did not make a decisive contribution, while the swift growth of industry provided bourgeois society with a life of comfort and security, intellectually this period was astonishingly sterile. What Broch (q.v.)

called this "vacuum of values in German art" needed to be filled—particularly in the field of poetry.

The first beginnings are to be found in Holz (q.v.). In the poems of his collection *Das Buch der Zeit* (1885), the modern city, the industrial environment, and working-class misery become for the first time topics of lyric poetry. But the traditional tools of poetic formalism, such as meter, rhyme and stanza, were no longer appropriate to the new subjects of this "thoroughgoing naturalism" (q.v.), for which Holz also provided the theoretical basis. Seeking new possibilities and aiming at a faithful reproduction of reality even in its most minute details, Holz developed his *Sekundenstil*—a formative principle whose theoretical premises contained from the very outset the seed of failure, at least as regards the poem. In his "Phantasus" poems Holz sought to create "a mirror of the cosmos, extending from the razor to the planetary systems"; however, "the poetic skill of Arno Holz was constantly at war with his artistic conscience, which allowed him too much leeway for deliberate experiment" (F. Martini). Holz worked on this gigantic lyrical work until 1921; its radicality for the time being precluded all possibility of further formal development but its monumentality served as a model for Däubler and Otto zur Linde (qq.v.).

The new poetic form that Holz thought he had discovered, recognizable even externally by its characteristic axial typography, seemed, in its almost total abandonment of all traditional techniques, to signify the liquidation of all poetic form. Actually, it is clear that unconsciously not only the dadaists but—paradoxically—the very founders and champions of rigorous constructivism such as Eugen Gomringer (b. 1925) and Helmut Heissenbüttel (b. 1921) went back to Holz's poetic model as one among several others. For the moment, however, his efforts had no far-reaching results.

How diverse the points of departure of those who strove in the poem for a valid formulation of a new sense of the world were, how different their intentions and tendencies, becomes evident when one realizes that not only such contrasting individualities as George, Hofmannsthal, and Rilke were simultaneously at the height of their creativity but also poets of expressionism (q.v.), such as Benn (q.v.), the founders of dadaism (q.v.), and the many independent poets such as Trakl (q.v.), Konrad Weiß, or Oskar Loerke. While Hofmannsthal and especially Rilke exercised a far more lasting influence through their poetry than George did, we are still indebted to George for having, among other things, put German poetry in touch with the forms and ideas of French symbolism (q.v.)—George met Verlaine (1844-96) and Mallarmé (1842-98) in Paris in 1889—and for having incorporated into it, through his poetry, elements of rigorous Romance formalism. It was also from the ideas of the modern French poets that George derived his autocratic, aristocratic view of art and life. The "tendency toward pretentiousness, the early-acquired adoption of the role of an exceptional being subject to laws different from those governing the common man—all these character traits are confirmed and intensified by the encounter with Mallarmé" (F. Schonauer).

Man's position in the cosmos—here lay Hofmannsthal's problem. The naturalists wanted to reproduce everything that exists; Hofmannsthal speaks of his "passionate desire to bring everything that exists into relationship" ("Der Dichter und diese Zeit," 1907). "Just as the innermost sense of all men creates around them time and space and the world of things, so it creates out of past and present, animal and man, out of the dream and the real, out of great and small, the sublime and the right, the world of relations"—this is Hofmannsthal's definition of poetry. Life, dream, and death—this triad is the keynote of his whole work. At the age of twenty-five Hofmannsthal, a born poet, decided to give up writing poetry for ever. While a decision of this kind can certainly be interpreted as a repudiation of George, it signifies primarily a decisive break with all pan-aesthetic ersatz religions on the part of Hofmannsthal, a Catholic bred in a strong tradition. Of the French anti-naturalists he said: "The modern psychological poets delve into what should be skimmed over and treat superficially what should be treated in depth." He greeted irrationalism with the statement: "Profundity must be concealed. Where? On the surface." The fundamental poetic posture expressed in poems such as "Ballade des äußeren Lebens," "Manche freilich . . .," and "Terzinen über die Vergänglichkeit," formally seems anything but revolutionary, but such poems are sustained by an insight into cosmic relationships as unerring as a sleepwalker's movements and by a melancholic musicality.

They have been analyzed by Broch in his great essay "Hofmannsthal und seine Zeit" as follows: "The characteristic thing about Hofmannsthal's poetry is its 'dreamlike scenic quality' evoked by a 'transformation' which has nothing to do with theatrical 'dramatization' or 'monologization.' In this process of 'turning inside out,' the original poetic content of the poem remains completely intact; instead, it is 'looked at from outside.' Instead of evoking a picture of an evening through the devices of poetic technique, Hofmannsthal writes his famous line 'Und dennoch sagt der viel, der "Abend" sagt.' ('And yet in saying "evening," much is said.') In this 'turning inside out,' this 'shift in point of view,' which in its 'outer-directedness' is a basic element of rigorous Latin formalism, Hofmannsthal's 'scenic poetry' introduced a new note into German literature and thence into world literature." This turn toward the scenic is, to be sure, brought to its climax by poets such as Brecht (q.v.) and Benn or, a generation later, Eich (q.v.), in very different ways. In every case, however, it is connected with a definite repudiation of experiential poetry (that of romanticism, for instance).

If one were to take up Curtius' (q.v.) statement that Hofmannsthal was "the last poet of the old Europe," one would have to add that the first poet of a new epoch in the old Europe is the poet of the *Duino Elegies* and the *Sonnets to Orpheus*. Speaking of his early poems, Rilke himself wrote to Stefan Zweig (q.v.): "It seems to me that I had such a need to say one thing and always this one thing that they were simply replaced later by a better, more mature formulation." Essentially, he says, they are no more than "surviving provisional formulations" in the face of "the definitive one."

The "one thing" is Rilke's own very personal "myth of 'Being,'" which cannot be interpreted religiously, still less 'theologically'—not even in the poems of the *Stundenbuch*—for the god that Rilke means is not the transcendent god beyond time and space but the 'numinous aspect of the multiplicity of things within the world, Being in itself as it manifests itself in a thousand different shapes in time and space,' and in this context even the *Stundenbuch* poems are by no means 'more religious' than, for example, the 'thing poems' " (H. E. Holthusen). Broch actually speaks of "a baptizing function" of lyric poetry (though not in the religious, theological sense).

For Rilke the task of the poet was to help things to realize their own nature in the poem, to cause them to become themselves. In things God is "one who is becoming." Finally the poet must achieve in his work—in his whole self— "the unity of life and death." Thus Rilke went far beyond what Hofmannsthal intended when he spoke of bringing all that exists into mutual relationship.

The "definitive formulation" that Rilke anticipated in his letter to Stefan Zweig came in his great hymnic cycles, the *Duino Elegies* and the *Sonnets to Orpheus*. Not only do these mark a climax in German literature unequalled since Hölderlin; they also rank—along with the *Charmes* of Valéry (q.v.), which appeared in the same year (1922), *The Waste Land* of Eliot (q.v.) and the *Ulysses* of Joyce (q.v.)—among the masterworks of a new world literature. Within the German-speaking world they solve for the first time the central problem with which all art and poetry of the first half of the 20th c. had been consciously or unconsciously grappling. In this shift of form from the external to internalization, from visible architecture to invisible structure, they achieve the Copernican turn in poetry.

Essentially this "shift from the external to internalization" is not just the problem of the poets of expressionism, surrealism (q.v.), and dadaism. Consciously or unconsciously it is also the problem of the representatives of a new nature poetry, such as the group around Wilhelm Lehmann and a number of independents such as Konrad Weiß (who has hardly been appreciated from this point of view). In the Lehmann group Elisabeth Langgässer (q.v.) is probably the most important representative of modern Christian poetry. Nor can a more convincing explanation be found for the simultaneous presence within the poetry of as coherent a group as the expressionists of such utterly different "content" as, for example, encounters with love in Else Lasker-Schüler (1869-1945), melancholy visions of catastrophe in Trakl, and life-nausea in Benn.

Neither is there any other plausible explanation for the fact that the expressionists make common cause with Rilke and Hofmannsthal, at least theoretically, both in their disassociation from the aestheticism of neoromanticism and in their rejection of naturalism's preoccupation with the reproduction of reality.

Another remarkable point is that poets such as Bergengruen, Carossa, Gertrud von Le Fort, Hesse, Schneider (qq.v.), and Rudolf Alexander Schröder (1878-1962)—especially when they are consciously bound to a strong Christian tradition—are almost completely unaffected by this problem of a shift in form. The more rigidly they are bound to the changeless subject matter of a deep-rooted Christianity, the less the com-

pulsion to confront it in their poetry with the realities of a new era. In other words, such a serious, not to say embittered, struggle for new artistic "means of expression" presupposes an existential crisis, a radical questioning, or even a rejection, of the traditional system of values, and thus a *tabula rasa* of commitment, a "vacuum of values," either on the part of the artist or in the existential reality of the period. In most poets of expressionism, both these factors prevailed.

Paul Klee said in his diary: "I create *pour ne pas pleurer*; that is the last and the first reason." In a letter to Lou Andreas-Salomé, Rilke calls this "making things out of fear," while according to Benn, "style [i.e., artistic form] bears within itself the proof of existence." This statement by Benn, who until his death felt himself to be the spokesman of expressionism, shows that the expressionists—and, ultimately, the writers of all lyric poetry of world stature—are concerned with more than just the artistic statement of a "new sense of the world." The word "artisticism" crops up again and again in Benn. He speaks of "the absolute poem," the "poem without belief, without hope, directed toward nobody." He interprets the term artisticism as "an attempt, within the general collapse of contents that matter, to experience oneself as a content that matters." He also interprets it as "an attempt to posit a new transcendence, against the general nihilism of values." He stresses very firmly that there is no such thing as "isolated form, form in itself" because form "is Being, is the artist's existential task."

Just as the philosophical representatives of existentialism (q.v.) are not content with scientific definition, but themselves enter into the process of finding truth in order to experience in this philosophizing the "proof of existence," so the poet seeks to realize himself in the poem. The poem becomes for the poet an existential entity; at the same time it is his answer to the "form-seeking power of nothingness." This is no longer *l'art pour l'art*; that zero mark, that "borderline situation," has already been passed and "overcome." What is now adhered to is the "fanatical moralism of artistic *réalisation*," a "rigorous monism in art ... a sanctification of productive achievement" (Holthusen). Thus the system of art values supersedes all others. "Poetology" becomes a "doctrine of salvation"—an event unprecedented in German literature, which has a definite theological side to it.

Poets such as Pound, Auden (qq.v.), Eliot, Benn, and the modern French poets are the direct or indirect models of most German poets of the younger generation such as Ingeborg Bachmann, Celan, Eich, Enzensberger, Krolow, Piontek (qq.v.), Gomringer, Heissenbüttel, Walter Höllerer (b. 1922), Hans Egon Holthusen (b. 1913). These earlier poets sought to "weave out of the totality of the human spirit the artistic tapestry of their poetry. Here history is brought to a halt; a universal time is established in which past and future appear as integral components of the present" (G. Blöcker).

Such a spacious definition of poetry admits at first glance any "form" and any "content." Similarly, a term such as surrealism carried to the extreme would be an appropriate starting point for a typology of the poem (in other languages as well as in German) at midcentury. However, the poem as an existential entity does not, as Benn repeatedly stressed, presuppose any "content" separable from the "form." Neither is there such a thing as a compelling range of *topoi* for lyrical forms. Even Benn resorts to a negative topography in describing what the midcentury poem is not like. If a poem by one of the "greats" happens to fall within the canon of his negative categories, the canon is simply bracketed out. Essentially Benn says no more than that the "exorbitant" poem uses a more disciplined language and deeper metaphors than "feuilleton" poetry.

Andreas Donath's study of *Form-Elemente der modernen Lyrik* is more informative. It explores lyrical techniques: identification instead of comparison, identification reversed and made abstract, concretization in the image of these abstractions, and the breaking of relational bonds with reality. But this study also proves that the existing tools and methods of stylistic analysis no longer adequately define the new reality of the poem. Wilhelm Emrich's study *Zur Ästhetik der modernen Dichtung* ranks with works by Walter Höllerer and S. Melchinger as one of the most fruitful attempts to identify the aesthetic categories of modern poetry. It shows that the shift from external to internal form, from visible architecture to invisible structure, probably constitutes the only reliable identifying feature we so far have in dealing with the new reality in the literature as well as in all the poetry of the first half of this century. Höllerer points out that the language of poetry today is based on quite other "experiential assumptions" than those of

the 19th c. Like Melchinger, he mentions change in perspective as a particularly characteristic feature. He speaks of a disturbing widening or narrowing of the field of vision, of the new approach to grammatical relationships, and of the tension between quite different images within the poem that encircle its center. Höllerer makes the remarkable observation that the "fine focusing of poetic language makes it impossible to translate into other languages poems that depend on such tensions."

Melchinger's great contribution lies in his warning against the erroneous belief that there exists in poetry "a progressive development toward a (utopian) goal of perfection." On the contrary, experience shows that all the "patterns" that poetry has produced over the centuries "exist side by side and are capable of inspiring creativity." What, in his view, ultimately determines the quality of a poem is not the type of pattern used but the degree of inevitability of its coming into being and the "distance the poet has succeeded in covering on his road toward the perfection of his creation."

BIBLIOGRAPHY: Curtius, E. R., *Kritische Essays zur europäischen Literatur* (1950); Eliot, T. S., *Ausgewählte Essays* (1950); Benn, G., *Probleme der Lyrik* (1951); Holthusen, H. E., *Der unbehauste Mensch* (1951); Curtius, E. R., *Französischer Geist im 20. Jahrhundert* (1952); Eliot, T. S., *Der Vers: Vier Essays* (1952); Heselhaus, C., "Deutsche Lyrik im 20. Jahrhundert," in *Deutsche Literatur im 20. Jahrhundert* (1954); Holthusen, H. E., *Ja und Nein* (1954); Emrich, W., "Zur Ästhetik der modernen Dichtung," in *Akzente* (1954); Höllerer, W., "Nach der Menschheitsdämmerung," in *Akzente* (1954); Broch, H., *Dichten und Erkennen, Essays*, vol. i, (1955); Friedrich, H., *Die Struktur der modernen Lyrik* (1956); Killy, W., *Wandlungen des lyrischen Bildes* (1956); Melchinger, S., "Vor einem Stoß neuer Lyrik-Bände: Ist moderne Lyrik modern?" in *WuWahr*, XI (1956); Blöcker, G., *Die neuen Wirklichkeiten* (1957); Donath, A., "Formelemente der modernen Lyrik," in *Texte und Zeichen*, vol. iii (1957); Wiese, B. von, ed., *Die deutsche Lyrik*, vol. ii (1957); Leonhard, K., *Silbe, Bild und Wirklichkeit* (1957; Holthusen, H. E., *Das Schöne und das Wahre* (1958); Holthusen, H. E., *Rainer Maria Rilke in Selbstzeugnissen und Bilddokumenten* (1958); Adorno, T. W., *Noten zur Literatur* (1958); Closs, A., "Die neuere deutsche Lyrik, vom Barock zur Gegenwart," in *Deutsche Philologie im Aufriß*, vol. ii

(2nd ed., 1958); Grimm, R., "Montierte Lyrik," in *Germanisch-Romanische Monatsschrift,* VIII (1958); Schonauer, F., *Stefan George in Selbstzeugnissen und Bilddokumenten* (1960); Klein, J., *Geschichte der deutschen Lyrik* (2nd ed., 1960); Heselhaus, C., *Deutsche Lyrik der Moderne, von Nietzsche bis Yvan Goll* (1960); Kayser, W., *Geschichte des deutschen Verses* (1960); Hamburger, M., and Middleton, C., eds., *Modern German Poetry 1910-1960: An Anthology with Verse Translations* (1962); Schöne, A., *Über politische Lyrik im 20. Jahrhundert* (1965); Forster, L., "German Lyric Poetry since Gottfried Benn," in *Forum for Modern Language Studies,* II (1966), 291-304; Domin, H., ed., *Doppelinterpretationen: Das deutsche zeitgenössische Gedicht zwischen Autor und Leser* (1966)

ALBERT ARNOLD SCHOLL

RUSSIA

Taking as its point of departure symbolism (q.v.), which dominated the scene at the turn of the century, Russian lyric poetry up to the mid-1920's developed considerable richness of form patterned on both Western European and native Russian models.

Symbolism puts the main stress in the poem on the musical, rhythmic element, which often becomes the dominant stylistic chord and perceptibly modifies both the logical structure and the plastic conception. Almost all technical potentialities of rhythmization and "instrumentation" (i.e., stylization through sound) are exploited. The semantic limits of individual words are transcended by an ever-new emotional —and often deliberately irrational—use of images, while the range of poetic language is enriched with far-fetched, often manneristic or affected terms.

Verse form also shows great variety. Older forms that had dropped out of use, especially those of a more formal character such as the sonnet, terzina, and triolet, are revived, while at the same time several romantic forms become vehicles for new symbolist subjects. The erotic ballad has been written by Bryusov (q.v.), the gypsy "romance" by Blok (q.v.), the verse narrative by Bryusov and Blok, the elegy by Annenski (q.v.), the lullaby and the cradle song by Sologub (q.v.).

After symbolism a particularly important factor in verse structure is the canonization of unscanned, purely accentual verse (the Russian *dol'nik*), little used hitherto, which is lightened by more frequent use of trisyllabic feet (anapests, dactyls, and amphibrachs). The number of stresses, unlike the number of syllables, generally remains constant or varies at quite regular intervals (as in Blok's *Dvenadtzat'*). Nevertheless, in Biely we already find experiments with completely free rhythms (*Khristos voskres,* 1918). Later Mayakovski (q.v.), in particular, continues the tradition of purely accentual verse, which he develops into a sophisticated technique.

Free rhyme also plays an important role in modern Russian poetry. Since 1910 this "approximative rhyme" has established itself more and more firmly alongside conservative rhyme.

Between 1913 and 1923 the acmeists—Anna Akhmatova, Gumilev, and Mandelstamm (qq.v.) —led an opposition movement against the predominantly musical and rhythmic structure of symbolist verse. On the semantic level they laid stronger emphasis on the logical and literal content of the word. The melody of their poetry —even in its phonetic aspect—is that of speech rather than song. Mandelstamm's poetry especially derives compelling forcefulness from its blending of the banal and the commonplace with melancholy, awe-inspiring images from a mythical world.

Russian futurism (q.v.) shows itself primarily in a purely experimental attitude toward the word. With the help of abstraction, which they adopted from painting and music, futurists, such as David Burlyuk (b. 1882) and Velimir Khlebnikov (q.v.), strive for a "translogical" language (*zaumnyi yazyk*), which, freely invented, turns the word into mere sound and blurs the context.

Pasternak (q.v.), who was close to the futurists, was a willful creator of astonishing yet technically precise poetic syntax and a master of an expressiveness so wonderfully vivid that it sometimes attained a metaphysical quality. The poetry of Yesenin (q.v.) also reveals an expressive world all his own. Yesenin came from a Russian village background. His characteristic language is marked by unusual idioms borrowed from popular speech along with elements of Slavic liturgical language.

Willful extremism in language and form, which remained dominant until 1925, was followed by a strong tendency toward declamatory verse coinciding with the politicization of literature. Even the most classicistic 18th c. forms, such as the fable, the epigram, and the satirical fairytale, are revived as political vehicles (in Dem'yan Bednyi [1883-1945], for instance). The same is true of the heroic verse epic as written by Bagritzki, Selvinski (qq.v.), Mayakovski, and, more recently, A. T. Tvardovski (b. 1910).

At the end of the 1950's the greatest formal subtlety in Russian poetry was to be found in translations. Samuel Marshak's (1887-1964) translations of Shakespeare's sonnets, Lozinski's version of the *Divine Comedy*, and many of Pasternak's translations are particularly outstanding.

BIBLIOGRAPHY: Zhirmunski, V., "Preodolevshiye simvolizm," in *Russkaya mysl'* (1916); Jakobson, R., *Noveishaya russkaya poeziya* (1921); Gumilev, N., *Pis'ma o russkoi poezii* (1923); Tynyanov, Y., *Arkhaisty i novatory* (1929); Markov, V., "Mysli o russkom Futurizme," in *Novyi zhurnal* (1954); Erlich, V., *Russian Formalism* (1955); Donchin, G., *The Influence of French Symbolism on Russian Poetry* (1958); Jomashevski, B., *Stikh i yazyk* (1959); Poggioli, R., *The Poets of Russia, 1890-1930* (1960); Reavey, G., ed., *The New Russian Poets, 1953-1966: An Anthology* (1966)
JOHANNES HOLTHUSEN

SPAIN

The term "contemporary Spanish lyric poetry" denotes a reality that, if carefully examined, will be found to belong more to the immediate past than to the present. This becomes particularly clear if we ask ourselves what the essential characteristic of 20 c. poetry is. From the very outset contemporary Spanish poetry bore a markedly revolutionary aspect; in fact it represents one of the greatest revolutions in the history of lyric poetry. Neither the Renaissance nor romanticism changed the structure of poetic diction so drastically as have contemporary writers.

The unseen groundwork for this revolution was provided by two forces that were in fact new only in the intensity with which they now emerged: individualism and irrationalism. Both were also fundamentals of romanticism, but their impact during that period was not felt with such intensity or in the same way. Thus the poetic art of the 20th c., while unquestionably antiromantic, inhabits the intellectual environment originally invented by the romantics but departs from it through the drastic change in direction that the irrationalistic and individualistic trend has undergone.

Romantic irrationalism did perhaps manifest itself in the poet's attitude to the poem (spontaneity, improvisation, digressions, etc.), but it did not essentially affect its verbal substance. This—apart from a very few exceptions that anticipated what was to come—retained the relatively logical character of all earlier poetic tradition. The 20th c. poet, on the other hand, has a rational attitude to the poem (sense of composition, anticipation, precision, etc.) and an irrational one where its conscious vocabulary is concerned. In many typical cases words are used rather for the sake of the involuntary, unconscious associations they can arouse than for their conceptual content. The general lack of rigor in composition, the lack of order in exposition, and the underestimation of form —which were common tendencies among the Romantics—go against the grain of the contemporary poet, who is much more conscientious and responsible, not to say overexact, in these matters. On the other hand, the romantic urge to say everything and to leave nothing, or very little, to the reader's imagination and associative powers is in complete contrast to the sensibility of our age, which takes much more pleasure in allusions and subtle suggestions than in conceptually clear, logical statement.

The 20th c. poet is rigorous in everything pertaining to the structure of his work, but he is a magician when it comes to dealing with the atmosphere that words subconsciously evoke. He is fundamentally an irrationalist since he is irrational with regard to word meaning, the foundation of every statement; he is rational as regards external things, as regards the formal or compositional surface of the work itself, which strives for a certain degree of structural perfection. Many critics have seen only the latter aspect of modern poetry and have spoken unsympathetically of the "intellectualism" of the poet of our time—a term that in itself does not adequately characterize this type of poetry and that may be confusing and misleading.

The first work of Antonio Machado (q.v.), *Soledades,* contains lines that illustrate the modern poet's ambivalent position (irrationalism as to content and intellectualism as to form) and at the same time reveal how early 20th c. poetry (Machado, Unamuno, Jiménez [qq.v.]) differs in the intensity of this phenomenon from that written between 1927 and 1940, for instance, by Guillén, Salinas, García Lorca, Aleixandre, Alberti, Diego Cendoya, Alonso, or Cernuda (qq.v.). The lines from *Soledades* are: "*Las ascuas de un crepúsculo morado/ detrás del negro cipresal humean./En la glorieta en sombra está la fuente/con su alado y desnudo Amor de piedra/que sueña mudo. En la marmórea taza/reposa el agua muerta.*" (The embers of a violet twilight/smolder behind the cypress grove./In the shadowy square stands the fountain/with its winged, naked stone Cupid/who silently dreams. In the marble basin /rests the dead water.)

The obviously logical concentration of this poem, which at first glance suggests no irrational use of words, would be deceptive if analysis did not probe more deeply. With the utmost simplicity it describes a simple landscape: twilight, a woods, a square, and a fountain with a Cupid. Yet this description, hardly melancholy in itself, pervades the reader's mind with a lasting impression of gravity and heavyheartedness. This impression is produced by the irrational aura that surrounds the solid body of each word like an invisible atmosphere. The most important words in Machado's poem, which have no gloomy connotation conceptually, nevertheless suggest the idea of the transitoriness of all objective reality.

Besides irrationalism as to content, this poem also shows the alert carefulness with which the poet fashions the structure of his work. From start to finish the writer's intuition has been guided by a responsible sense of the whole that would not countenance the least slackening in the continuous interlinking of words that enables them to serve the above-mentioned nonrational ends.

Machado's poetry still retains a strong logical framework that conceals an invisible structure irrational in nature. A further step in this direction was to be taken by such poets as Aleixandre and Cernuda in Spain and Neruda (q.v.) in Chile, who began their careers as surrealists around 1928. This step consisted in discarding all thematic accessories, the whole conceptual apparatus, and retaining exclusively —or almost exclusively—the associative aura that is more or less subconscious in origin. A series of unconnected words—unconnected in the logical sense—is enough to convey this. Thus surrealism (q.v.) is anticipated in essence in a poet so tradition-bound in appearance yet so revolutionary in substance as Antonio Machado.

Between Antonio Machado and the surrealist poets stretches a whole poetic movement, that increasingly intensifies the presence of the irrationally lyrical (Salinas, Guillén, García Lorca, Alberti, Diego Cendoya). This process is discernible not only in the strictly associative power of words but also in certain elements of some poets' vision of the world (overemphasis of the elemental in García Lorca, Neruda, and especially Aleixandre) and in a new use of the image.

In the hands of the modern poet the image is drastically reshaped. Traditionally, the metaphor was based on a physical or moral similarity or on a similarity in value between the objects compared. If we were not capable of instantly recognizing that blond hair and gold are very close in color, we would not find the expression "hair like gold" (which we so often encounter in poetry) poetic. The 20th c. irrationalistic revolution also changed the manner in which images are perceived. What now matters is not the objective resemblance between the real aspect and the aspect evoked by the metaphorical equation but the similar reaction that both aspects produce in the reader. The poet is no longer trying to reveal a distinct objective likeness—which was traditionally his objective—but that distant, vague resemblance that is indispensable in making the emotions that both essences arouse in us coincide sufficiently. A contemporary poet can write "*un pajarillo es como/un arco iris*" (a little bird is like/a rainbow) with reference to a little gray, motionless bird, if this little bird and the rainbow arouse the same loving feeling in his mind.

In the typically modern image (traditionally structured images are, of course, still being used too), the remote objective resemblance linking the two halves of the metaphorical equation— the innocence, for example, of the pure, clear colors of the rainbow and the innocence of the little bird in its appealing defenselessness —is not recognized by the intellect in the spontaneous act of reading. (The reverse is true of the traditional image.) First one feels an emotion; only after that does it become clear, through a process of analysis that the reader need not engage in unless he chooses to, that there is some slight—objective—relationship between the two bits of creation the poet has linked together.

This kind of imagery makes its first appearance—though still tentatively—in Jiménez. Not until the generation of 1925 did it achieve its full force. Then it reached its height of complexity and richness in a member of this generation, Aleixandre, especially as he gradually emerged from his early surrealism and step by step gave metaphor a place in his work.

This irrationalistic process, which was steadily intensified, from 1888—when *Azul* by the Nicaraguan poet Darío (q.v.) appeared—to 1940, has its parallel in individualism. This is not to be found in romanticism; it exists to a lesser degree as early as the Trecento in Italy and Spain, forges ahead by leaps and bounds in the Renaissance and, even more, in the post-Renaissance and the baroque, and finally dies out under the pressure of the rationalistic universalism peculiar to 18th c. neoclassicism. The individualism of romanticism, however, was stronger and more conspicuous in its literary aspect. It carried over into the compulsion—which amounted to a mania and which is not found in contemporary poetry—to flaunt the self here, there, and everywhere. It was also reflected in the belief that the poem must be born of an inner, not an outer impulse. It should have its *raison d'être* in the genius of the poet himself.

Individualism of this kind grew stronger over the years, after romanticism had become outdated. As the 19th c. drew to a close, the writer made of his life a semipublic spectacle, sometimes serious, but nearly always eccentric. The poets of this period indulged in anything that allowed them to express rampant individualism, from the fixed ideas of Unamuno, the red umbrella of Azorín (q.v.), the witty impudence of Benavente (q.v.), or the willful orthography of Jiménez, to the impenetrable virgin forest of the beard of Valle-Inclán (q.v.)—even to delivering a lecture while seated on an elephant, as Gómez de la Serna (q.v.) did in Paris.

Turn-of-the-century individualism also, of course, penetrated both world outlook and style. For the first time in the history of Spanish literature a homogeneous literary school emerged, though the concept of the world that it expressed doubtless varied from member to member. Azorín named this group the Generation of '98. Baroja y Nessi (q.v.), the novelist of the school, denied that such a school existed, basing his view on the dissimilarity of the writers' various styles without realizing that this dissimilarity was unquestionably what held the group together. Its members all shared this pronounced individualism, which produced great discrepancies not only in their interpreta-

tion of life but also in form and language. Because of their individualism, the romantics refused to "imitate," yet they all shared, more or less, the same cosmic vision. The similarity of outlook among the Generation of '98, on the other hand, consisted solely in the tenet that writers must not copy anybody else.

The generation of 1925 went even further in this direction. To be sure, the more superficial demonstrations of individualism were abandoned. The biographies of García Lorca, Alberti, Aleixandre, Cernuda, and Guillén have nothing the least bit theatrical about them. These were all such great poets that they founded the richest literary group ever assembled in Spain in so brief a period. The style of these poets—especially that of Aleixandre and Guillén—marked the highest peak of the individualistic movement. No one in the history of Spanish literature can be compared with them. Their language differs spontaneously from all others; their world is unique. Hardly a poem, hardly a line, by any one of them is understandable at first glance; the reason for this lies as much in the form as in the content, and also in the extremely individual view of the world that they present or imply.

Twentieth c. Spanish drama is relatively weak; the novel has shown no steady development, although up to 1940 it was represented by a few powerful but isolated authors. Poetry, on the contrary, shows continuity, richness, diversity, and intensity—qualities that had never all been concentrated in one epoch in Spain since the 17th c. And the Spanish 17th c. is richer only if literature is taken as a whole, not if only the poetry of the two periods is being compared. Although the contemporary period has been considerably shorter, it has produced a series of poets who may even surpass the *siglo d'oro*.

The structure of every literary epoch encourages or discourages the growth of one particular literary genre; the genre that wins out is the one that most adequately expresses the essence or the underlying idea of the *Zeitgeist*. Thus the rationalism and, later, the universalism that dominated the 18th c. made the neoclassical period a great century in criticism but an average one in poetry. Lyric poetry, on the other hand, was in keeping with 20th c. irrationalistic and individualistic currents and their particular forms. If one also bears in mind that among the European nations Spain had always been less influenced by logical criteria and more responsive—both for better and for worse—to individualistic stimuli, the great poetic development that begins in 1888 becomes completely understandable.

About 1940 the situation began to change, and by 1947 a new picture had emerged in which both irrationalism and individualism ceased to be formative influences in the evolution of poetry. The poet no longer strives to be creative in the individual or absolute sense; he even prefers not to stand out from the common mass—and prides himself upon not doing so. One of these poets writes: "*Yo, José Hierro, un/hombre/como hay muchos ...*" (I, José Hierro, a/man/like many others ...).

As never before, the awareness of one's fellow-man, of one's neighbor, becomes so intense that the self is eclipsed, at least as a majority program. What they hoped would emerge was a lyric poetry that would be concerned with everything that was happening outside the poet's own intimate life, concerned with the historical situation of the country and even with that of the rest of the world.

This drastic weakening of individualism had two important consequences. First, the extreme originality in conception and style that made the work of the previous generation so brilliant is no longer required of the poet. Again, as in the period of romanticism, poets tend to share a common view of the world. Each poet's individuality merely expresses his personal reaction to the great theme of concern for mankind.

Second, the generations no longer appear as separate entities. All poets, old and young, are today engaged in a common enterprise and are working from the same aesthetic basis. Typically, even authors who between 1925 and 1940 were producing works of an extremely individualistic character, such as Aleixandre, Guillén, and Neruda, have moved on to meta-personal themes, which now provide the point of departure of their poetry. This shows that the existence of literary generations can be meaningfully posited only for epochs that exalt the stature of the individual. The urge to be different was a concern for differing groups with differing time-spans. Thus the theory of generations applies only to a very concrete period.

The latest lyric poetry tones down the grandiose irrationalism that preceded it while admitting conceptual elements on an increasing scale. Partly for this reason, partly because of the importance attributed in modern poetry to one's fellow-man (the emphasis now focuses on the qualities that link man to others rather than on his alienating qualities—on man's less individualistic, less exceptional, and more universal aspects, that is—), poetic language comes closer to the language of speech. The use of a logical nexus, usually more compatible with prose, goes along with this. Recent poetry tends toward realism.

Fiction rather than lyric poetry is now the genre that best lends itself to the communication of the new human and literary condition. Obvious signs of this are the rise of the novel (q.v.) in recent years and also the more or less narrative trend of much contemporary poetry. Nevertheless, talented writers are still devoting themselves to the art of lyric poetry in its narrowest sense. These include Leopoldo Panero (1909-1962), Vicente Gaos (b. 1919), Rafael Morales (q.v.), Blas de Otero (b. 1916), José Hierro (b. 1922), Claudio Rodríguez (b. 1934), and José Angel Valente (b. 1929).

The momentousness of the preceding period would seem to guarantee a tradition of excellence for lyric poetry. However, the lead may pass in future to the fictional genres, which are now gaining strength.

BIBLIOGRAPHY: Salinas, P., *La poesía de Rubén Darío* (1948); Salinas, P., *Literatura española del siglo XX* (1949); Gullón, R., *La poesía de Jorge Guillén* (1949); Durán Gili, M., *El superrealismo en la poesía española contemporánea* (1950); Valverde, J. M., *Estudios sobre la palabra poética* (1952); Alonso, D., *Poetas españoles contemporáneos* (1952); Cano, J. L., *De Machado a Bousoño* (1955); Zubiría, R., *La poesía de Antonio Machado* (1955); Sainz de Robles, F. C., *Historia y antología de la poesía española* (1955); Bousoño, C., *La poesía de Vicente Aleixandre* (2nd ed., 1956); Bousoño, C., *Teoría de la expresión poética* (1956); Cernuda, L., *Estudios sobre poesía española contemporánea* (1957); Paulau de Nemes, G., *Vida y obra de Juan Ramón Jiménez* (1957); Vivanco, L. F., *Introducción a la poesía española contemporánea* (1957); Gil de Biedma, J., *La poesía de Jorge Guillén* (1960); Cano, J. L., *Poetas españoles del siglo XX* (1960); Castellet, J. M., *Veinte años de poesía española* (1960); Ley, C. D., *Spanish Poetry Since 1939* (1962); Quiñones, F., *Ultimos rumbos de la poesía española* (1966)

CARLOS BOUSOÑO

M

MACAULAY, Rose

English novelist, poet, and essayist, b. 1 Aug. 1881, Cambridge; d. 30 Oct. 1958, London

In her satires M. fought "the Philistines, the barbarians and the lackadaisical" and sought to appeal to the underprivileged minority dedicated to precise thinking. In her novels and essays she makes fun of the vulgarity of public life, the optimism of liberal and religious organizations, and Anglo-Saxon foibles. M., who belonged to the Bloomsbury group (see English literature), was considered an astute social critic of the 1920's. Her audacious satires, with plots full of coincidences, got the better of the progressivist, emotion-dominated novels of the Edwardian era. In *Told by an Idiot* (1923) she seems to parody Galsworthy's (q.v.) family saga. Her less satirical novel, *Potterism* (1920), is her most serious account of modern society; here the Potter family transforms all ideals into an opportunist "Potterism." *Going Abroad* (1934), her most amusing novel, is akin to the work of Norman Douglas (1868-1952). In the character Rome in *Told by an Idiot*—the stylish, free onlooker, smiling skeptically despite her fatal illness—M. sketched her own self-portrait. In her later works the Anglican Church emerges as a life-shaping force.

FURTHER WORKS: *Abbots Verney* (1906); *The Furnace* (1907); *The Secret River* (1909); *The Valley Captives* (1911); *Views and Vagabonds* (1912); *The Lee Shore* (1912); *The Two Blind Countries* (1914); *The Making of a Bigot* (1914); *Non-Combatants and Others* (1916); *What Not: A Prophetic Comedy* (1919); *Three Days* (1919); *Dangerous Ages* (1921); *Mystery at Geneva* (1922); *Orphan Island* (1924); *A Casual Commentary* (1925);

Catchwords and Claptrap (1926); *Crewe Train* (1926); *Twenty-Two Poems* (1927); *Keeping up Appearances* (1928; Am., Daisy and Daphne, 1928); *Staying with Relations* (1930); *Some Religious Elements in English Literature* (1931); *They Were Defeated* (1932; Am., The Shadow Flies, 1932); *Milton* (1934); *Personal Pleasures* (1935); *I Would Be Private* (1937); *The Writings of E. M. Forster* (1938); *And No Man's Wit* (1940); *Life Among the English* (1942); *They Went to Portugal* (1946); *Fabled Shore: From the Pyrenees to Portugal* (1949); *The World My Wilderness* (1950); *Pleasure of Ruins* (1953); *The Disguises of Love* (1953); *The Towers of Trebizond* (1956); *The End of Pity* (1958); *Letters to a Friend*, ed. Constance B. Smith (1961); *Last Letters to a Friend*, ed. Constance B. Smith (1962); *Letters to a Sister*, ed. Constance B. Smith (1964)

BIBLIOGRAPHY: Kuehn, R. E., "The Pleasures of R. M.: An Introduction to Her Novels," in *DA*, XXIII (1962), 2136-37; Bensen, A., "The Ironic Aesthete and the Sponsoring of Causes: A Rhetorical Quandary in Novelistic Technique," in *English Literature in Transition*, IX (1966), 39-43; Lockwood, W. J., "R. M.," in Hoyt, C. A., ed., in *Minor British Novelists* (1967), pp. 135-56; Swinnerton, F., "R. M.," in *KR*, XXIX (1967), 591-608

WERNER VORDTRIEDE

MACCAIG, Norman

Scottish poet, b. 14 Nov. 1910, Edinburgh

Since the death of Muir (q.v.), M. has generally been considered the best Scottish poet writing in English. Although he has never written in Scots, M. is thoroughly Scottish and has always participated in the Scots renaissance movement by his poems, reviews, and editing. He can read Gaelic, he spends his summers in the Highlands, the settings of his poems were until very recently the Highland county of Sutherland or Edinburgh, and he has never evinced a desire to emigrate (as many of his countrymen have). His Scottishness is also apparent from the way his poems show the distinctive Scottish qualities of worrying a metaphysical problem from a myriad of directions, the wit of wry understatement, and (like William Dunbar) technical virtuosity.

He has received two Scottish Arts Council awards, the Poetry Book Society's recommendation and their annual award, the Heinemann Award, and has had poems commissioned by B.B.C. In 1967 he was appointed the first Lecturer in Creative Writing at the University of Edinburgh.

His poems in the late thirties and forties (which he has repudiated) are surrealistic impressions without paraphrasable meaning. In 1955 (nine years had elapsed since his last volume), *Riding Lights* presented the kind of poems that were to appear in the four collections of the next ten years. All these are short lyrics of subtle and regular prosody. Except for an implied humanism—which occasionally becomes insistent—they present no general views. Many of them treat subjects such as death and love by considering the identity of the poet and the relationship between the poet and the object he observes. Alluding to M.'s practice of evoking concrete objects in plays of wit and philosophical puzzlings, MacNeice (q.v.) aptly called him a "physical metaphysical." Most of these poems are descriptions, the elements of which by witty word play become illuminating metaphors of multiple meanings.

M.'s recent poetry (e.g., *Surroundings*, 1966) shows new developments: free verse, a sense of history and social morality, a studied plainness of expression, and some Italian and American settings. M.'s poems are obviously influenced by John Donne, and they have been likened to those by Day Lewis, Muir, MacNeice, and William Empson (qq.v.). He has influenced a number of younger Scottish poets, such as Robin Fulton (b. 1937) and Iain Crichton Smith (b. 1928).

FURTHER WORKS: *Far Cry* (1943); *The Inward Eye* (1946); *The Sinai Sort* (1957); *A Common Grace* (1960); *Round of Applause*

(1962); *Measures* (1965); *Rings on a Tree* (1968)

BIBLIOGRAPHY: Smith, I. C., "The Poetry of N. M.," in *Saltire Review*, No. 19 (1959), 20-23; Fulton, R., "Selves, Myths, and Landscapes," in *New Saltire*, No. 10 (Dec. 1963), 20-23; Press, J., *Rule and Energy* (1963), pp. 172-81; *Akros*, III, No. 7 (March 1968), an issue devoted to M., with articles by H. MacDiarmid, C. Saunders, A. Scott, G. Fraser (pp. 21-47)

JOHN C. WESTON

MACDIARMID, Hugh

(pseud. of *Christopher Murray Grieve*), Scottish poet and essayist, b. 11 Aug. 1892, Langholm, Dumfriesshire

C. M. Grieve first found it necessary to write under the now common pseudonym in 1922 when he began to publish in his own monthly (*Scottish Chapbook*, 1922-23) his lyrics in Scots and his prose pieces defending the literary revival of Scots, in contradiction to his own former practice and advice. Having found his true voice, M. then published two books of remarkable Scots poems, *Sangschaw* (1925) and *Penny Wheep* (1926). These are short lyrics which use native ballad and song rhythms and forms; many were influenced by the imagists, but most succeed in combining in a highly individual way the bluntness and wry irony of colloquial Scots with a deep pathos. Frequently present is a characteristic metaphoric extension of the Scots scene to the universe. These volumes also contain four longer philosophical, mystical poems about the limits of knowledge, the unity of all things, and the nature of language.

These longer poems were a prelude to sections of his masterpiece, *A Drunk Man Looks at the Thistle* (1926). This unusual interior monologue is a sequence of comic and erotic scenes, of flyting, satire, and highly symbolic lyrics, reasonings, and prophesies, held together by the character and situation of the poet, who contemplates the thistle (the flowers and shaggy leaves representing the "Caledonian Antisyzygy"—one of M.'s favorite ideas—the twofold nature of the poet, Scotland, and the world) and has other symbolic visions after an evening in a tavern. M.'s purpose is to express, by speculations about the creative process, the social evolution as it has developed to the ideal of the complete individual freedom of self-realization, and to satirize the present world's distance from that ideal. The form with its ballad and folk rhythms is more medieval dream vision and goliardic lyric than modern; but the poem is as modern in its ideas and references as Eliot's (q.v.) *The Waste Land*.

In *To Circumjack Cencrastus* (1930) M. again attempted, less successfully, to structure a long poem of diverse modes around controlling symbols, but there are differences: more English, a new political explicitness, and a new interest in Gaelic civilization. These differences become more pronounced in his next collections of shorter pieces, *First Hymn to Lenin* (1931), *Scots Unbound* (1932), *Stony Limits* (1934), and *Second Hymn to Lenin* (1935). Almost all the poems that he has published since then were written during the thirties. There are shorter pieces, most of which are written in English, and he has also published fragments of a single gigantic composition, "Mature Art;" the largest such fragment is *In Memoriam James Joyce* (1955). "Mature Art," which M. calls "poetry of fact," has few images, many long quotations, long lists of names, arcane diction, and no prosodic regularity, and either discusses ideas with great concentration and energy from an almost bewildering multiplicity of directions—or prophesies and denounces. The closest analogue to M.'s poetry of fact is Ezra Pound's (q.v.) *Pisan Cantos*.

Besides writing original poems, he has done much journal and book editing, many verse translations (those from the Gaelic with the help of Sorley Maclean are superb) and written some short stories in Scots, biographies, and two autobiographies, and thousands of pieces of polemical prose. His main interests have been Scottish nationalism, communism, and language, all of which are viewed from a mystical vision very distinctively his own. The most important formal influences on his early Scots poetry were native: the traditional ballad, the folk song, and Jamieson's Dictionary. Other important influences at different times have been Dostoyevski, Chestov, Solov'iov, John MacLean (the Scots communist-nationalist), William Blake, Joyce (q.v.), Francis George Scott (the Scots composer), Yeats (q.v.), Doughty (q.v.), Valéry (q.v.). Alone he established a literary movement, first called by Denis Saurat the Scottish Renaissance, to produce literature in Scots as intellectual, sophisticated, international, and current as was Scotland's poetry of the 16th c. Thus the motto of the movement was, "Not Burns, Dunbar." The group

that rallied around this movement includes William Soutar (1898-1943), George Campbell Hay (b. 1915), Neil Gunn (b. 1891), Sorley Maclean (b. 1911), Alexander Scott (b. 1920), Douglas Young (b. 1913), Sydney Goodsir Smith (b. 1915), Robert Garioch (b. 1909), and Tom Scott (b. 1918).

FURTHER WORKS: *Annals of the Five Senses* (1923); *Contemporary Scottish Studies* (1926); *Albyn, or Scotland and the Future* (1927); *At the Sign of the Thistle* (1934); *Scottish Scene* (with L. G. Gibbon, 1934); *Scottish Eccentrics* (1936); *The Islands of Scotland* (1939); *Lucky Poet* (1943); *A Kist of Whistles* (1947); *Cunningham Graham* (1952); *Francis George Scott* (1955); *Three Hymns to Lenin* (1957); *The Battle Continues* (1957); *Burns Today and Tomorrow* (1959); *The Kind of Poetry I Want* (1961); *Collected Poems* (1962; revised ed., 1967); *The Company I Keep* (1966); *A Lap of Honour* (1967); *The Uncanny Scot* (ed. K. Buthlay; 1968)

BIBLIOGRAPHY: Leavis, F. R., "M.'s Second Hymn to Lenin," in *Scrutiny* (1935), p. 305; Daiches, D., "M. and Scottish Poetry," in *Poetry* (1948), pp. 202-218; Craig, D., "M.'s Poetry," in *Voice of Scotland* (April 1956), pp. 6-19; Scott, T., "Some Poets of the Scottish Renaissance," in *Poetry* (1956), pp. 43-47; Singer, B., "Scarlet Eminence," in *Encounter* (March 1957), pp. 49-62; Wittig, K., *The Scottish Tradition in Literature* (1958), pp. 281-88; Buthlay, K., *H. M.* (Writers and Critics Series, 1964); Duval, K., and Smith, S. G., eds., *H. M.: A Festschrift* (1962); Glen, D., *H. M. and the Scottish Renaissance* (1964); National Library of Scotland, *H. M., Catalogue No. 7* (1967); Smith, I. C., *The Golden Lyric* (1967); *Agenda,* double issue on M. and Scottish poetry, V: 4 and VI: 1 (1967-68)

JOHN C. WESTON

MACHADO DE ASSIS, Joaquim Maria

Brazilian poet and narrative writer, b. 21 June 1839, Rio de Janeiro; d. there 29 Sept. 1908

M. achieved his first successes as a writer of novels and stories in the 1860's. From 1881 on, when he was already committed to realism, he gradually moved toward a unique place in the cultural and literary life of Brazil. He was a cofounder of the Brazilian Academy of Literature (1897) and became its permanent president.

Of his novels, *Helena* (1876) best represents his romantic period; this is a study of complicated feminine psychology set in metropolitan Rio de Janeiro. *Memórias póstumas de Brás Cubas* (1881), a love story, is his first wholly realistic novel. Three other very successful novels show a similar trend: *Quincas Borba* (1891), the story of an unhappy provincial character who becomes involved in big-city vice and loses his money, his illusions, and his reason; *Dom Casmurro* (1899), M.'s most widely read work, which depicts a: man's painful doubts about the nature of love; and *Memorial de Aires* (1908), a novel in memoir form.

M.'s art reaches its height in his sophisticated handling of psychology, emotional paradoxes, and women. His narrative technique is simple; his humor unquestionably shows an English influence. He is the most widely read Brazilian writer and the most influential one of the 20th c., especially through his advocacy of the symbolist and neospiritual movements in his later years.

FURTHER WORKS: *Quase ministro* (1864); *Os deuses de casaca* (1866); *Phalenas* (1870); *Americanas* (1870); *Contos fluminenses* (1870); *Resurreição* (1872); *Histórias de meia noite* (1873); *A mão e a luva* (1874); *Iaiá Garcia* (1878); *Tu só, tu, puro amor* (1881); *Papéis avulsos* (1882); *Histórias sem data* (1884); *Várias histórias* (1896); *Páginas recolhidas* (1899); *Poesias completas* (1901); *Esaú e Jacó* (1904); *Relíquias de casa velha* (1906); *Obras completas* (31 vols., 1938); *Obra completa* (2 vols., 1959); *Obra completa* (3 vols., 1962)

BIBLIOGRAPHY: Pereira, L. M., *M.* (2nd ed., 1946); Galante de Sousa, J., *Bibliografia de M.* (1955); Pinto, C., *M.* (1958); Meyer, A., *M.* (1958); Grieco, A., *M.* (1959); Caldwell, H., *Brazilian Othello of M.* (1960); Pimentel, A., *M. de A. e outros estudos* (1962); Virgillo, C., "Some Themes in M. de A.'s Short Stories," in *DA,* XXV (1964), 488; Viana Filho, L., *A vida de M. de A.* (1965); Barrow, L., "Ingratitude in the Works of M. de A.," in *Hispania,* XLIX (1966), 211-17; Param, C., "M. de A. and Dostoyevsky," in *Hispania,* XLIX (1966), pp. 81-87; Virgillo, C., "Love and the 'Causa Secreta' in the Tales of M. de A.," in *Hispania,* pp. 778-86; Botrel, J. F., et al., *Etudes luso-brésiliennes* (1966)

ANTONIO SOARES AMÓRA

MACHADO Y RUIZ, Antonio

Spanish poet and dramatist, b. 26 July 1875, Seville; d. 21 Feb. 1939, Collioure, France

M., son of a famous Seville folklorist, moved to Madrid in 1883 with his family and was educated at the Institución Libre de Enseñanza, a college with liberal, anticlerical tendencies. For a time he worked as a translator in Paris. He was a friend and originally a pupil of Dario (q.v.) but soon diverged from Dario's poetry, although he never lost his great admiration for the founder of modernism. He became professor of French at the Soria Instituto in Castile, where he lived with his wife until her death in 1912.

In 1911 M. attended the lectures of Henri Bergson (q.v.) in Paris and was deeply influenced by his philosophy. From 1912 to 1919 he taught at the Baeza Instituto in Jaen, then at the Segovia Instituto, where he established an elementary school. Beginning in 1926, he and his brother Manuel M. (q.v.) collaborated on several successful plays. In 1931 he was transferred to Madrid. While he always maintained contact with the poets of his own generation (Martinez Ruíz, Jiménez, and particularly Unamuno [qq.v.]), he also witnessed the emergence of new poetic trends, which, however, never affected his work. When the Spanish Civil War broke out, he supported the liberal, republican Spain he had always championed. In 1939 he left Spain for France, but, frail and ill, died shortly afterward. M., a distinctive representative of the Generation of '98, left a body of work small in size but of unique literary value.

His first volume of poems, *Soledades* (1903), which was reissued three years later, with several poems added, under the title *Soledades, galerías y otros poemas,* marks the first phase—one of subjective, meditative poetry—of his literary career. His poetry of this period seems to be entirely evocative, arising out of memories lying beneath a veil of melancholy longing. In forms of classic simplicity and in clear, pure language reminiscent of the poetry of Gustavo Adolfo Bécquer (1836-70), he evokes impressions of childhood. Through these transparent poetic fragments shimmers a lonely soul, a resigned captive of its troubles, lost in its search for God.

The publication of *Campos de Castilla* (1912) initiated a second phase in M.'s poetry. In more expansive, rounded forms, sometimes using alexandrines, sometimes the stronger framework

JOAQUIM MACHADO DE ASSIS

ARCHIBALD MACLEISH

of the assonanced or rhymed "silva" or the traditional style of the epic romances, M. sang of the Castilian landscape, of its towns and fields. His austerity and ascetic cast of mind were better suited than any other to the landscape of Castile, with its bare plateaus, gloomy crags, sparse vegetation and cold, immense sadness. In his glorification of Castile as the center of Spain's "solar plexus," he agreed with Unamuno, Azorín, and Baroja y Nessi (qq.v.), the other great figures of the Generation of '98. Yet M. had a critical eye for Castile's stolid, weak-willed inhabitants, the incarnation of a Spain that he exhorted to change and progress. This work is, however, primarily important not for its ideas but for its powerful descriptive and analytical view of Spain and for the deep, noble, masculine timbre of its feeling and expression.

M.'s stay in the little Andalusian town of Baeza produced a temporary liking for the traditional *copla* or *cantar breve* forms, of which *Nuevas canciones* (1924) offers the best example, but his preoccupation with philosophical problems diverted him from this new departure. From 1917 on his *Poesías completas* (1917; 7th ed., 1956) grew, volume by volume. Out of the poetic exploration of the secret chambers of memory grew a wise, restrained, crystalline poetry of great originality and depth, expressed for the most part in the form of maxims or rhymed aphorisms. M. upheld the definition of poetry as "the word in time" and advocated the retention of physical background, intellectual content, and even of the anecdote as a means of poetically capturing the temporal quality of life. Where form was concerned, he recommended the retention of rhyme as expressing the temporal, and the primacy of the verb for the sake of its dynamism. These poetics, rooted in Bergsonian vitalism and Heidegger's existentialism, which rank sensitive poets, such as the medieval Jorge Manrique and the Romantic Bécquer, above representatives of the atemporal, decorative Baroque, such as Góngora or Calderón, culminated in M.'s prose work *Juan de Mairena* (1936). Here M., speaking as a professor of rhetoric and poetics, expressed his opinion in philosophical, poetological, and sometimes political aphorisms and fragments.

Most of the verse plays for the Madrid theater, on which he collaborated with his brother Manuel, treat themes from Andalusian history, though a few, such as *Las adelfas* (1928), have a contemporary setting. *La Lola*

se va a los puertos (1930) and *La Duquesa de Benameji* (1931) were particularly successful; to some extent they constitute a prologue to the great poetic theater of García Lorca (q.v.). Although M. was always admired by the majority of Spanish writers and readers, his true significance has been recognized in Spain only in the last three decades. He raised poetry to "the category of a poetic anthropology." Translated, admired, and studied by poets and critics in countless countries, the great poet of the Generation of '98, the poet of Castile, has been and is still a vigorous influence in Spain.

FURTHER WORKS: *Desdichas de la fortuna, o Julianillo Valcárcel* (1926); *Juan de Mañara* (1927); *La Prima Fernanda* (1931); *La tierra de Alvar González* (1939); *Obras completas de Manuel y A. M.* (1947, 2d ed. 1957); *Eighty Poems of A. M.* (Spanish text with translations, 1959)

BIBLIOGRAPHY: Peers, E. A., *A. M.* (1940); Serrano Plaja, A., *A. M.* (1945); *Cuadernos Hispanoamericanos,* XI-XII (1949), special A. M. volume; Serrano Poncela, S., *A. M.* (1954); Zubiría, R., *La poesía de A. M.* (1955); Gullón, R., *Las secretas galerías de A. M.* (1958); Sánchez Barbudo, A., *Estudios sobre Unamuno y M.* (1959); De Lara, T., *A. M.* (1960); Ilie, P., "A. M. and the Grotesque," in *Journal of Aesthetics and Art Criticism,* XXII (1963), 209-16; Ilie, P., "Verlaine and M . . . .," in *CL,* XIV (1963), 261-65; *Torre,* XII (1964), special A. M. volume; Gullón, R., *Relaciones entre A. M. y Juan Ramón Jiménez* (1964); Sister Katharine Elaine, "Man in the Landscape of A. M.," in Bleiberg, G., and Fox, E. I., *Spanish Thought in the Twentieth Century* (1966), pp. 272-86

GONZALO SOBEJANO

MACHADO Y RUIZ, Manuel

Spanish poet and dramatist, b. 29 Aug. 1874, Seville; d. 19 Jan. 1947, Madrid

M. received the same Madrid education as his brother Antonio and, like him, went to Paris, where he came in contact with Moréas (q.v.) and was influenced by symbolism (q.v.), especially that of Paul Verlaine (1844-96). By profession he was a librarian. He wrote poems and criticism and collaborated with his brother on plays. Unlike his brother, he sympathized with Franco in the Spanish Civil War.

His early literary activity was influenced by Darío (q.v.) but he contributed several new features to modernism. His first book *Alma* (1902) has an almost Arabic tinge of indifference and nihilism, its themes are those of the Generation of '98, and some of the poems in this collection are in a refined Parnassian style. *Caprichos* (1905) offers sketches from Bohemian life and themes akin to Verlaine's, further developed in *El mal poema* (1909) into a mixture of Parisian wickedness and gypsylike bragging. These erotic themes, which seem quite original, are in remarkable contrast to M.'s brilliant poetic "imitations" (mainly in sonnet form) of the visual arts in *Museo* (1907) and particularly in *Apolo* (1911; Rubens, Velásquez, Murillo, Titian, etc.). From the poems collected in *Cante hondo* (1912) and *Sevilla y otros poemas* (1918), the soul of Andalusia emerges, vividly and impersonally. These poems differ substantially from the folk poetry of Alberti (q.v.) or García Lorca (q.v.) but are nonetheless a step in that direction. Compared to those of García Lorca, the same is true of M.'s dramatic works (see A. Machado). The intellectual side of this instinctively serene poet is revealed in the stoic spirit of his *Ars Moriendi* (1922).

FURTHER WORKS: *Los cantares* (1907); *La guerra literaria, 1898-1914,* (1913); *Un año de teatro* (1918); *Phoenix* (1936); *Horas de oro* (1938); *Poesía* (1940 and 1942); *Antología* (1940); *Cadencia de cadencias* (1943); *Poesías escogidas* (1951)

BIBLIOGRAPHY: Pérez Ferrero, M., *Vida de Antonio Machado y M. M.* (1947); Newberry, W., "The Influence of Pirandello in Two Plays of Manuel and Antonio Machado," in *Hispania*, XLVIII (1965), 255-60; Marchesi, S., "Storia ed arte di Spagna nella poesia di M. M.," in *Studi di letteratura . . . in onore di Bruno Revel* (1965), pp. 385-92

GONZALO SOBEJANO

MACHAR, Josef Svatopluk
Czech poet, b. 29 Feb. 1864, Kolín; d. 17 March 1942, Prague

M. came of a working-class background; he did not finish his studies at law school and became a bank employee in Vienna. During World War I he joined the underground movement against the Austrian-Hungarian monarchy and worked in close association with the Czech leaders Thomas G. Masaryk and Karel Kramář. From 1916 to 1917 he was imprisoned for his political activities.

In the years following World War I, M. who for some time had been the most influential Czech poet, entered the political life of the new Czechoslovak republic. He was elected to the National Assembly and from 1919 to 1924 was Inspector General of the Czech army. In later years, he sharply opposed President Masaryk, with whom he had had a close association. This position affected adversely his acceptance as a poet.

M. is a major exponent of Czech realism. His style is sober; his poetry is free from pathos yet compelling. He was a severe, basically pessimistic critic of the political and social tendencies of the times, as is already evident in his poetic work *Confiteor* (3 vols., 1887-92; final ed., 1899-1901). *Tristium Vindobona* (1893), like the satirical epic *Boží bojovníci* (1897), is an indictment of the Austro-Hungarian social order.

Under the influence of Nietzsche (q.v.) he turned against Christianity and the Catholic church in his lyric-epic poem *Golgotha* (1901), and again in the historical verse cycle *Svědomim věků* (9 vols., 1905-1927). His autobiography, *Konfese literáta* (1902), is significant.

FURTHER WORKS: *Zde by měly kvésti růže* (1894); *Magdalena* (1894; Magdalen, 1916); *Výlet na Krym* (1900); *Satiricon* (1904); *Svědomím věků* (I., *V záři hellenského slunce* [1906]; II., *Jed z Judey* [1906]; III., *Barbaři* [1911]; IV., *Pohanské plameny* [1911]; V., *Apoštolové* [1911]; VI, *Oni* [1921]; VII, *On* [1921]; VIII, *Kručky dějin* [1926]; IX, *Kam to spěje* [1926]); *Kriminál* (1918); *Tristium Praga* (1926); *Řím* (1927); *Pět roků v kasárnách* (1927); *Sebrané spisy* (1927-49); *Zapomínaní a zapomenutí* (1929)

BIBLIOGRAPHY: Martinek, V., *J. S. M.* (1912; rev. ed., 1948); Pešata, Z., *M.* (1959)

JOHANNA WOLF

MACKENZIE, Compton
(pseud. of *Sir Edward Montagu Compton*), English novelist, critic, dramatist, and historian, b. 17 Jan. 1883, West Hartlepool

M. studied law at Oxford, practiced it briefly, but disliked it and soon devoted himself entirely to literature. Shortly before the outbreak of World War I, during a stay in Italy, he was converted to Roman Catholicism. Later he became a supporter of Scottish nationalism.

Unlike many of his contemporaries, M. eschewed experiments with form; he was interested only in character and background. Despite his romantic spirit, which sometimes shows the influence of Robert Louis Stevenson, he is a master of realism.

The novel *Carnival* (1912), deals with life in the pre-1914 London theater. This was followed by *Coral* (1925) and *Figure of Eight* (1936) on similar subjects. *Sinister Street* (Vol. 1, 1913 [Am., Youth's Encounter, 1913]; Vol. 2, 1914) is a broad-scale developmental novel to which M. owes his present literary reputation. In it M. traces the life of Michael Fanes from his early childhood, schooldays, and years at Oxford, until he goes astray in the Soho underworld. The love story, *Guy and Pauline* (1915; Am., Plasher's Mead, 1915) expresses an idyllic romanticism. M.'s voluminous later fiction (e.g., *Sylvia Scarlett* [1918, complete ed., 1927], the story of a young girl hungry for life, and his religious trilogy about the life of a young Anglican priest who is finally converted, *The Altar Steps* [1922], *The Parson's Progress* [1923], and *The Heavenly Ladder* [1924]) never attained the level of these earlier novels.

M.'s humorous novels open up a completely different world. *Vestal Fire* (1927) and *Extraordinary Women* (1928) are witty satires in the remarkable setting of an Anglo-American artists' colony on Capri, while the themes of *The Monarch of the Glen* (1941), *Whisky Galore* (1947), *Hunting the Fairies* (1949), etc., stem from the folk humor of M.'s native Scotland. His novel cycle, *Four Winds of Love* (*The East Wind*, 1937; *The South Wind*, 1937; *West to North*, 1940; *The West Wind*, 1940; *The North Wind*, 1944-45), is the fruit of a rich and unusually vigorous lifetime devotion to literature. In his tracing of the development of one character, M. illuminates the spiritual state of a whole generation.

FURTHER WORKS: *The Gentleman in Grey* (1906); *Poems* (1907); *The Passionate Elopement* (1911); *Kensington Rhymes* (1912); *Sylvia and Michael* (1919); *Poor Relations* (1919); *Columbine* (1920); *The Vanity Girl* (1920); *Rich Relatives* (1921); *The Seven Ages of Women* (with Archibald Marshall, 1923); *Gramophone Nights* (1923); *Santa Claus in Summer* (1924); *The Old Men of the Sea* (1924); *Fairy Gold* (1926); *Rogues and Vagabonds* (1927); *The Life and Adventures of Sylvia Scarlett* (complete ed., 1927); *Extremes Meet* (1928); *Gallipoli Memories* (1929); *The*

Three Couriers (1929); *April Fools* (1930); *Told* (1930); *First Athenian Memories* (1931); *Buttercups and Daisies* (1931; Am., For Sale, 1931); *Our Street* (1931); *The Lost Cause* (1931); *Greek Memories* (1932); *Unconsidered Trifles* (1932); *Prince Charlie* (1932); *Water on the Brain* (1933); *Literature in My Time* (1933); *Reaped and Bound* (1933); *The Darkening Green* (1934); *Marathon and Salamis* (1934); *Prince Charlie and His Ladies* (1934); *Catholicism and Scotland* (1936); *Pericles* (1937); *The Windsor Tapestry* (1938); *A Musical Chair* (1939); *Aegean Memories* (1940); *The Red Tapeworm* (1941); *Calvary* (1942); *Wind of Freedom* (1943); *Keep the Home Guard Turning* (1943); *Mr. Roosevelt* (1943); *Brockhouse* (1944); *Dr. Benes* (1945); *The Vital Flame* (1945); *All Over the Place* (1949); *Coalport* (1951); *Eastern Epic* (Vol. I, 1951); *I Took a Journey* (1951); *The Rival Monster* (1952); *The Queen's House* (1953); *Echoes* (1953); *Realms of Silver* (1953); *Ben Nevis Goes East* (1954); *Eastern Epic* (Vol. II, 1954); *My Record of Music* (1955); *Thin Ice* (1956); *Rockets Galore* (1957); *Sublime Tobacco* (1957); *Tatting* (1957); *The Lunatic Republic* (1959); *Tight Little Island* (1959); *Greece in My Life* (1960); *Cat's Company* (1960); *Catmint* (1961); *Mezzotint* (1961); *Our Moral Courage* (1962); *My Life and Times, Octave 1-Octave 6* (1963-67); *The Stolen Soprano* (1965); *Little Cat Lost* (1965); *Paper Lives* (1966); *Literature in My Time* (1967); *Rogues and Vagabonds* (1967)

BIBLIOGRAPHY: Robertson, L., *C. M., An Appraisal of His Literary Work* (1955); Erlansson, T. R., "A Critical Study ... of Sir C. M.: The Growth and Decline of a Critical Reputation," in *DA*, XXV (1965), 7265

GERALD HINTEREGGER

MACLEISH, Archibald

American poet, narrative writer and essayist, b. 7 May 1892, Glencoe, Ill.

A second-generation Scot, with forebears on his mother's side extending back to the Mayflower, M. was reared in a happy, upper-middle-class home by exceptional parents, both of whom had strong religious and philanthropic interests. He attended a preparatory school in Connecticut, then Yale, where he displayed extraordinary versatility, excelling in athletics as well as in literary and intellectual affairs. His circle of acquaintances included Stephen

Vincent Benét and Wilder (qq.v.). Next came Harvard Law School (at which he was influenced heavily in a liberal direction by Felix Frankfurter); this was followed by marriage, field artillery service in World War I, and the practice of law in Massachusetts.

In 1923 M. broke sharply with his past by moving his family to Paris, where he settled down to the life of a full-time poet. For six years he labored in seclusion, producing four volumes of poetry, *The Pot of Earth* (1925), *Nobodaddy* (1926), *Streets in the Moon* (1926), *The Hamlet of A. M.* (1928), all of them indebted to the works of Pound and the French symbolists (qq.v.). His poetry of this period is preoccupied with the question of man's position in the cosmos, and it lays the foundation for the humanistic views he has promoted throughout his career in letters.

His apprenticeship over, in 1928 M. returned to the United States, where he joined the staff of *Fortune* magazine. His assignments forced him to probe into the crisis conditions in American business during the Great Depression. Very soon his poetry took on a new social focus and a new style, with Sandburg (q.v.) supplying the inspiration. He won a Pulitzer Prize with *Conquistador* (1932), a narrative poem in free terza rima in which M. attempts to find in Cortez' conquest of Mexico a key to the understanding of America and its future. He moved into social satire with *Frescoes for Mr. Rockefeller's City* (1933) and then into the theater with a play entitled *Panic* (1935). Two plays for radio, *The Fall of the City* (1937) and *Air Raid* (1938), show his concern over the menace of fascism and underscore what has been one of the strongest characteristics of M.'s work—experimentalism in verse forms and techniques.

Beginning with his appointment as Librarian of Congress in 1938, M. gave the next ten years of his life to a variety of government posts, his service with UNESCO being the last. *Actfive and Other Poems* (1948) marked his return to poetry and to private life. From 1949 to 1962 M. was Boyleston Professor of Rhetoric and Oratory at Harvard, a position which left him free to write six months out of each year.

His most important work of recent years is *J. B.* (1958), a drama in verse in which he confronts, through the medium of the Job story, the problem of human suffering. Philosophically it is his most profound creation, and it was strong enough dramatically to sustain a

good run on Broadway. In *J. B.* are intertwined the two forces which have done the most to shape M.'s career—love of poetry and dedication to human betterment.

FURTHER WORKS: *Songs for a Summer's Day* (1915); *Tower of Ivory* (1917); *The Happy Marriage and Other Poems* (1924); *Einstein* (1929); *New Found Land* (1930); *Poems, 1924-1933* (1933); *Public Speech* (1936); *Land of the Free* (1938); *America Was Promises* (1939); *Union Pacific* (1939); *The Irresponsibles* (1940); *The Next Harvard* (1941); *The American Cause* (1941); *A Time to Speak* (1941); *American Opinion and the War* (1942); *A Time to Act* (1943); *Colloquy for the States* (1943); *The American Story* (1944); *Poetry and Opinion* (1950); *Freedom Is the Right to Choose* (1951); *Collected Poems, 1917-1952* (1952); *The Trojan Horse* (1952); *This Music Crept by Me upon the Waters* (1953); *Songs for Eve* (1954); *Poetry and Journalism* (1958); *The Secret of Freedom* (1959); *Poetry and Experience* (1961); *The Collected Poems of Archibald MacLeish* (1963); *The Dialogues of Archibald MacLeish and Mark Van Doren* (1964); *The Eleanor Roosevelt Story* (1965); *Heracles* (1967); *The Wild Old Wicked Man* (1968)

BIBLIOGRAPHY: Mizener, A., "The Poetry of A. M.," *Sewanee Review*, XLVI (Oct. 1938), 501-519; Brooks, C., *Modern Poetry and the Tradition* (1939); Sickels, E., "A. M. and American Democracy," *American Literature*, XV (Nov. 1943), 223-37; Raiziss, S., *The Metaphysical Passion* (1952); Lutyens, D. B., *The Creative Encounter* (1960); Falk, S. L., *A. M.* (1965); Goodwin, K. L., *The Influence of Ezra Pound* (1967)

COLIN CAMPBELL

MACNEICE, Louis

English poet, radio playwright and critic, b. 12 Sept. 1907, Belfast; d. 3 Sept. 1963, London

M. studied classical philology and philosophy at Merton College at Oxford and emerged in the 1930's, along with his Oxford fellows Auden, Day Lewis, and Spender (qq.v.), as part of a new generation of writers destined to dominate the British literary scene for a decade. With the issues of the 1930's passed, however, it is clear now that his poetry had little in common with that of the "Auden group." He showed none of his colleagues' interest in political commitment. He shared neither their leftist sympathies, their inner struggles with conflicting ideological allegiances, nor their special fondness for the social reform to be extracted from writers such as Freud and D. H. Lawrence (q.v.).

In his poetry, though it is often personal and always unpretentious, M. examines the traditional human dilemmas with the generous yet skeptical temperament of a classical scholar who sees a variety of sides to every problem. He knows all the contradictory philosophical postures assumed in the past, as well as the persisting responses of the human heart. Habitually he writes of all these with sympathy, warmth, and even affection, yet refuses allegiance to any single program, doctrine, or set of temperamental inclinations. From this detachment arises his characteristic pragmatic humanism. Very much aware of human vanity, imperfection, and transience, he insists on the value of all human experiences, however philosophically incompatible. Experiences are real and primary, the whole stuff of life; generalizations, however interesting, are no more than further illustrations of the delightful variousness of existence. Ultimately he finds life undecipherable, but meaningful and good.

M.'s special talent is to create the illusion of improvisation, the performance held together at its best by an inexhaustible stream of unpredictable and lively images that give to his elegiac, meditative poems the vitality of an exceptionally active intelligence, and to less introspective verse the excitement of sprightly leaps, even joyous headlong dashes, from image to image.

WORKS: *Blind Fireworks* (1929); *Roundabout Way* (1932); *Poems* (1935); *The Agamemnon of Aeschylus* (1936); *Letters from Iceland* (with W. H. Auden; 1937); *Out of the Picture* (1937); *The Earth Compels* (1938); *I Crossed the Minch* (1938); *Modern Poetry* (1938); *Zoo* (1938); *Autumn Journal* (1939); *The Last Ditch* (1940); *Selected Poems* (1940); *Poems, 1925-1940* (1940); *Plant and Phantom* (1941); *The Poetry of W. B. Yeats* (1941); *Meet the U.S. Army* (1943); *Christopher Columbus* (1944); *Springboard: Poems 1941-1944*; (1944); *The Dark Tower* (1947); *Holes in the Sky: Poems 1944-1947* (1948); *Collected Poems, 1925-1948* (1949); *Goethe's Faust* (abridged, 1951); *Ten Burnt Offerings* (1952); *Autumn Sequel* (1954); *The Other Wing* (1954); *Visitations* (1957); *Eighty-Five Poems* (1959); *Solstices* (1961); *The Burning Perch* (1963); *The*

Mad Islands, and the Administrator (1964); *Selected Poems*, ed. W. H. Auden (1964); *The Strings are False* (1965); *Varieties of Parable* (1965)

BIBLIOGRAPHY: Scarfe, F., *Auden and After* (1942); Curnow, A., "L. M.," in *Landfall*, XVIII (1964), 58-62; Gitzen, J. L., "The Poet as 'Educated Ordinary Man': The Poetic Theory and Practice of L. M.," in *DA*, XXVI (1965), 3337; Press, J., *L. M.* (1965; 2nd ed., 1967); Wain, J., "M. as Critic," in *Encounter*, XXVII (1966) 49-55

JUSTIN REPLOGLE

MAC ORLAN, Pierre

(pseud. of *Pierre Dumarchey* [*Dumarchais*]) French novelist and short story writer, b. 26 Feb. 1882, Péronne, Somme

M.'s early works were in a mocking vein (*La Maison du retour écoeurant,* 1912; *Le Rire jaune,* 1914). *Le Chant de l'équipage* (1918) has this same characteristic too, although here the theme of adventure is already coming to the fore, to be pursued again in *À Bord de "L'étoile matutine"* (1920; Aboard the "Morning Star," 1962) in which M. presents a colorful description of pirate life in bygone days. In his enchanting *Petit Manuel du parfait aventurier* (1920) M. presents a half-serious, half-ironic theory of the adventurer. Adventure is again the main theme of the epic-scale story *La Cavalière Elsa* (1921), which has a contemporary setting.

The fantastic also attracted M.; it plays its part in the black magic of *Le Nègre Léonard et Maître Jean Mullin* (1920), in the uncanny mysteries of *Malice* (1923), and in *Marguerite de la nuit* (1925), a modern adaptation of the Faust story. Above all, M. was fascinated by the shady characters of Montmartre and the waterfront, whom he evokes in *Aux Lumières de Paris* (1925) and *Images sur la Tamise* (1925), in the short stories in *Sous la lumière froide* (1926), and in the novels *Le quai des brumes* (1927) and *La tradition de minuit* (1930).

M. is by no means a naturalistic writer bent on faithful reproduction. He lets himself be captivated by the poetry of an enigmatic world which he transforms with his imagination. He has occasionally used poetic forms (*L'inflation sentimentale,* 1922; *Simone de Montmartre,* 1924), which show his closeness to his friends

Apollinaire and F. Carco (qq.v.) and his fondness for the folk song (*Chansons pour accordéon,* 1953).

FURTHER WORKS: *La Bête conquérante* (1914); *Les Poissons morts* (1917); *La Clique du café Brebis* (1920); *La Vénus internationale* (1923); *Les Pirates de l'Avenue du Rhum* (1925); *Rue des Charettes* (1927); *Chronique des temps désespérés* (1927); *Miamis* (1928); *Dinah Miami* (1928); *Villes* (1929); *Uranie ou l'astronomie sentimentale* (1929); *La Bandera* (1931); *Le Printemps* (1931); *La Légion étrangère* (1933); *La Nuit de Zeebrugge* (1934); *Le Tueur no. 2* (1935); *Masques sur mesure* (1937); *Lautrec le peintre* (1941); *L'ancre de miséricorde* (1941; The Anchor of Mercy, 1967); *Père Barbançon* (1946); *Montmartre* (1946); *Les dés pipés* (1952); *Poésies documentaires complètes* (1954); *Le mémorial du petit jour* (1955); *Quartier réservé* (1956); *Pig, le petit cochon savant* (1956); *Le Gros rouge* (1957); *La Pension de Mary Stuart* (1958); *Babet de Picardie* (1958); *Maurice de Vlaminck, 1876-1958* (1958; Vlaminck, 1958); *La Petite Cloche de Sorbonne* (1959); *La Sirène du Nord* (1960); *Calamity Bob, et autres histoires* (1961); *La Vérité sur Manon Lescaut* (1963); *Picardie* (1964); *Mémoires en chanson* (1965)

BIBLIOGRAPHY: Berger, P., *P. M.* (1951); Bloch, A., "P. M.'s Fantastic Vision of Modern Times," *MLQ,* XXIV (1963), 191-96

PIERRE BELLAUNAY

MADARIAGA (Y ROJO), Salvador de

Spanish writer and statesman, b. 23 July 1886, Corunna

M. studied in Paris, at the Collège Chaptal, École Polytechnique, and École Nationale Supérieure, during the period 1900-1910, was a mining engineer in Spain from 1911 to 1916, and worked as a free-lance writer in London between 1916 and 1920. In 1912 he married Constance Archibald, a Scotswoman.

M. was appointed by the Spanish government to the Secretariat of the League of Nations in 1921; was head of the disarmament section, 1922-27; was given the chair of Spanish literature, Oxford, 1927; was Spanish ambassador to the United States in 1931, and to France in 1932. He was also elected deputy to the Spanish Republican parliament and appointed Minister of Education. Staunch democrat, opposed to the extremism of both left and

right, M. left Spain in 1936 after the outbreak of the Spanish Civil War and never returned. He settled in Oxford, where he still lives.

President or board member of many international organizations, broadcaster for various European networks, associated with UNESCO until the admission of Franco Spain, tireless lecturer and traveler, M. has won countless academic and government honors, including the 1963 Prix d'Europe (50,000 Swiss francs) "to promote the idea that Europe is a cultural and political entity."

Trilingual, M. writes in Spanish, English, or French on a range of topics so vast that he has been called "one of the ten greatest intellects of the twentieth century." Among the best known of his sixty-odd books (more than one hundred books, counting his translations of his own works) are: *Englishmen, Frenchmen, Spaniards* (1928), a study in comparative national psychology; the controversial biographies, *Christopher Columbus* (1939) and *Bolívar* (1951); the history of 19th- and 20th-c. *Spain* (latest revision, 1958); and the best-selling novel *El corazón de piedra verde* (1942; The Heart of Jade, 1944). There have been many editions of these and M.'s other books. M.'s most recent work, *Los tres estudiantes de Salamanca* (1962), is a collection of three plays.

FURTHER WORKS: *Shelley and Calderón* (1920, 2d ed., 1965); *Romances de ciego* (1922); *The Genius of Spain* (1923); *La Jirafa sagrada* (1925); *El enemigo de Dios* (1926; 2d ed., 1966); *Guía del lector del Quijote* (1926); *Disarmament* (1929); *Sir Bob* (1930); *Anarquía o jerarquía* (1935); *Elysian Fields* (1937); *Theory and Practice in International Relations* (1937); *The World's Design* (1939); *Hernán Cortés* (1941; 2d ed., 1958; Eng., 1967); *Rosa de cieno y ceniza* (1942); *Victors Beware* (1945); *The Rise of the Spanish American Empire* (1947); *The Fall of the Spanish American Empire* (1947; 2d ed., 1963); *El Hamlet de Shakespeare* (1949); *El toisón de oro* (1950); *Bosquejo de Europa* (1951); *Ramo de errores* (1952); *Essays with a Purpose* (1954); *La camarada Ana* (1954); *Romances para Beatriz* (1955); *De la angustia a la libertad* (1955); *Guerra en la sangre* (1956); *Una gota de tiempo* (1958); *Presente y porvenir de Hispanoamérica* (1959); *General, márchese usted* (1959); *La que huele a romero y tomillo* (1959); *Democracy versus Liberty* (1960); *The Blowing up of the Parthenon* (1960); *De Galdós a Lorca* (1960); *El Sol, la luna y las estrellas* (1960); *El semen-*

SALVADOR DE MADARIAGA

MAURICE MAETERLINCK

tal negro (1961); *Latin America between the Eagle and the Bear* (1962); *Los Dioses sanguinarios* (1962); *Las Fantasmas* (1962); *Los Salzburgs* (1964); *Retrato de un hombre de pie* (1964; Portrait of a Man Standing, 1968); *Sanco Panco* (1964); *Satanael* (1967); *Yo-yo y yo-él* (1967)

BIBLIOGRAPHY: Del Rio, A., "S. de M.," in *Ibérica* (Nov. and Dec., 1956); "One of Ten Greatest Intellectuals," editorial in *The Milwaukee Journal* (18 May 1959); Sarmiento, J. C., "Bolivar, por M.," in *El Universal* (5 April 1959); Sedwick, F., "M., 'El enemigo de Dios,' and the Nature of Charity," in *Hispania,* XLIII (May 1960), No. 2, 169-73; Predmore, M. P., "M.'s Debt to Unamuno's *Vida de Don Quijote y Sancho*," in *Hispania,* XLVII (1964), 288-94

FRANK SEDWICK

MAETERLINCK, Maurice
(-Polydore-Marie-Bernard)

Belgian poet, dramatist, and essayist, b. 29 Aug. 1863, Ghent; d. 6 May 1949, Nice

Shortly after being called to the bar, M. turned to writing. In 1886 he became a follower of Villiers de l'Isle-Adam, Saint-Paul Roux, and others. Early symbolist poems appeared in *La Pléiade, La Wallonie,* and elsewhere, but he first made his reputation with plays produced at the symbolist theater of P. Fort (q.v.) and Lugné-Poe. Later he achieved world fame as a philosophical essayist. He traveled throughout Europe and North America, first in 1920 and again in 1940 as a refugee, and returned to France two years before his death.

A mood of melancholy and loneliness pervades his first collection of poems *Serres chaudes* (1889). His dreamy, allusive poems, full of metaphors linking material things with mental states, led M. Raymond to call him "a true precursor of postwar poetry"—that is, a surrealist. His second book of poems *Douze chansons* (1896) also derives from symbolism but strikes a less personal note.

M. achieved immediate success as a playwright with *La princesse Maleine* (1889; Princess Maleine, 1902). His early plays *L'intruse* (1890; The Intruder, 1916), *Les aveugles* (1890; The Blind, 1916), and *Intérieur* (1894; Interior, 1899) reflect his pessimism. Brooding over the approach of death, his heroes blindly succumb to fate. As a theoretician of symbolist drama, M. ascribed little importance to plot.

The mysterious Mélisande (*Pelléas et Mélisande,* 1892; Pelleas and Melisanda, 1913) dies in silence, without revealing her fateful love for the Tristan- and Hamlet-like Pelléas. Debussy's musical setting subtly enhances M.'s lyrically pure, often childlike style. In the manifold action of *Monna Vanna* (1902; Eng., 1903), his dramatic masterpiece, M. turned away from symbolist drama. This play, set in 15th c. Pisa, presents Monna's psychological conflict between duty and extramarital love. Not until *L'oiseau bleu* (1909; The Blue Bird, 1909) did M. shake off his fear of death. This fairytale-like play, which in form resembles Ibsen's *Peer Gynt,* is an allegory of M. the thinker searching for happiness; in his voluminous philosophical works this quest proves to be a search for personal happiness. In these works M. tries to pierce the mysteries of life and death, while giving poetic form to the abstract. In *Le trésor des humbles* (1896; The Treasure of the Humble, 1897) and *Le temple enseveli* (1902; The Buried Temple, 1902) he found consolation in the mysticism of Ruysbroek, Novalis, and Emerson, and strength in the stoicism of Marcus Aurelius. In his studies of insect communities, *La Vie des abeilles* (1901; The Life of the Bee, 1901), *La Vie des termites* (1926; The Life of the Termite, 1927), and *La Vie des fourmis* (1930; The Life of the Ant, 1930), observation is linked with intuition; they show how M. found a basis for his pantheism in instinct. Here, as in his later metaphysical studies *Le grand secret* (1921; The Grand Secret, 1922) and *Devant Dieu* (1937), he attained a tranquil agnosticism; for him life remained always a divine mystery.

FURTHER WORKS: *Aglavaine et Sélysette* (1896; Aglavaine and Selysette, 1903); *Ariane et Barbe-Bleue* (1901; Ariane and Barbe-Bleue, 1910); *Théâtre* (3 v., 1901); *Joyzelle* (1903; Eng., 1905); *Le Double jardin* (1904; The Double Garden, 1904); *L'Intelligence des fleurs* (1907; The Intelligence of the Flowers, 1907); *La Mort* (1913; Death, 1912); *Marie-Madeleine* (1913; Mary Magdalen, 1910); *Le Miracle de Saint-Antoine* (1919; A Miracle of Saint Anthony, 1918); *Le Bourgmestre de Stilmonde* (1919; The Burgomaster of Stilemonde, 1919); *Les Fiançailles* (1922); *Le Malheur passe* (1925); *La Puissance des morts* (1926); *Marie-Victoire* (1927); *Juda de Kérioth* (1929); *Douze chambres* (1929); *Pages choisies* (1929); *Souvenirs* (1930); *Avant le grand silence* (1934; Before the Great Silence, 1935); *La Princesse*

Isabelle (1935); *La Grande porte* (1939); *Bulles bleues, souvenirs heureux* (1948); *Jeanne d'Arc* (1948); *L'Autre monde; ou le cadran stellaire* (1942); *Théâtre inédit* (L'Abbé Sétubal; Les Trois justiciers; Le Jugement dernier; 1959)

BIBLIOGRAPHY: Bailly, A., *M.* (1931); Harry, G., *La Vie et l'œuvre de M. M.* (1932); Lecat, M., *M. M. et son œuvre* (1951); Pasquier, A., *M. M.* (1954); Compère, G., *Le Théâtre de M. M.* (1955); Vanwelkenhuysen, G., *Vocations littéraires* (1959); Andrieu, J. M., *M.* (1962); in *Marche Romane*, XII (Oct.-Dec., 1962), special M. issue; Romains, W.-P., *M. M.* (1963); Brachear, R., "M. M. and his 'Musée Grévin,'" in *FR*, XL (1966), 347-51

DAVID J. NIEDERAUER

MAILER, Norman

American novelist, essayist, and screenwriter, b. 31 Jan. 1923, Long Branch, N.J.

M. grew up in Brooklyn, graduated from Harvard as a construction engineer, and served, during World War II, in the Pacific theater of war as an aerial photograph expert and as a voluntary rifleman in a reconnaissance platoon.

The Naked and the Dead (1948), M.'s first book, which brought him world fame, has been recognized as one of the major novels to come out of World War II. M.'s book was highly praised for its authenticity, for capturing the feeling and smell of war, for its descriptions of hope and hatred and despair. But the true power of the novel stems from M.'s acute penetration into the mind of man.

The Deer Park (1955), which was promoted as a sensational sex book, is actually a complex story about Hollywood celebrities in a famous California desert-resort that involves more than shocking revelations about sex, greed, and ambition. M. is a vengeful moralist as he describes the "golden garbage heap" (*New York Herald Tribune*). An uneven, brutal book, it was criticized harshly by reviewers, though it was also praised for its powerful prose and its intensive character development.

In 1959 M. published *Advertisements for Myself,* which is an account of his experiences with drugs and liquor and sex. A collection of short stories, essays, parts of his novels, even harsh reviews of his work, connected by a self-

commentary, it has been called one of the "great works of confessional autobiography" in American literature, and is of special interest as a reflection of the postwar era. Later he was to warn young people that "marijuana opens the senses and weakens the mind. In the end you pay for what you get. There is a moral economy to one's vices."

M. has also written brilliant short stories and provocative essays and articles on mass culture, politics, beatniks, hipsters (*The White Negro,* 1957), existentialism, pornography, and homosexuality. For several years in the early 1960s he wrote a monthly column, *The Big Bite,* in *Esquire.* His reportage was excellent, his articles "edifying and annoying as one has come to expect from M." (*Saturday Review*).

In *An American Dream* (published in 1965, it had already appeared as a serialized novel), M. is writing again, with grim irony and real anger, of a world that is preparing to destroy itself. He pounds at his reader like an evangelical preacher shouting about hellfire and brimstone, as he prophesies our decline and fall with a kind of frenetic insight into the problems of our time. M.'s vision of American life in the early sixties, of the brutal, vile, often decadent forces under a surface of tranquillity and order, is disturbingly perceptive.

The Armies of the Night: History as a Novel, the Novel as History (1968) is about the Pentagon demonstration in October 1967. It might be the most valid picture in print of what is happening to us today. As brilliant an account as Whitman's diary of the Civil War, this work (which is repugnant at times) sparkles with flashes of poetry and wit and superb descriptions.

M. writes with moving concern about "the mad middle-class children with their innocence, their lust for apocalypse, their unbelievable indifference of waste: twenty generations of buried hopes perhaps engraved in their chromosomes, and now burning like faggots in the secret inquisitional fires of LSD, . . . a Devil's drug, designed to consume the love of the best and leave them, liver-wasted, weeds of the big city." Some reviewers considered this book better than *The Naked and the Dead.*

In the late sixties M. turned to the film, working as screenwriter, producer, and actor. *Beyond the Law* (1968) is a sardonic drama about the police and lawbreakers in a police precinct, where the cops seem to be fighting a losing battle for sanity. Lieutenant Francis

NORMAN MAILER

BERNARD MALAMUD

Xavier Pope (played by N. M.)—sin-ridden himself, still a loser though he seems to be winning—lightens the doom with the faint suggestion that true love may still offer some hope, even for our wretched world. *Beyond the Law* is a blazing assault on us—we are prisoners of our indifference, and M. wants to open the jail.

M. projects himself as a man wallowing in sex and sin—"sin is my jailer, my liberator, my sword, my horse." Out of anguished despair about modern life's unsolvable problems, he has made the pursuit of sexual experience into an ideology—a concrete solution for problems.

Because of his sure handling of narrative and pace, his drive to probe deeply into his characters, his lyricism, his forceful prose, his defiant and assaultive attitudes, his preacher's rage, his superb reportage, his strong personality, his bold unorthodoxy, M., who since 1948 has exerted great intellectual and literary influence, is one of the most exciting though controversial modern American writers.

FURTHER WORKS: *A Calculus at Heaven* (1944); *Barbary Shore* (1951); *Death for the Ladies, and Other Disasters: Being a Run of Poems, Short Poems, Very Short Poems, and Turns of Prose* (1962); *The Presidential Papers of N. M.* (1963); *Cannibals and Christians* (1966); *The Deer Park: A Play* (1967); *The Short Fiction of N. M.* (1967); *Why Are We in Vietnam?* (1967); *Wild 90* (film, 1968); *Miami and the Siege of Chicago: An Informal History of the Republican and Democratic Conventions of 1968* (1968)

BIBLIOGRAPHY: Aldridge, J. W., *After the Lost Generation* (1950); Downes, R. H., *A Bio-Bibliography of N. M.* (1957); "Love among the Love-Buckets," in *Time* (17 Oct. 1955); "N. M.'s Despair," in *Newsweek* (17 Oct. 1955); Malaquais, J., "Reflections on Hipsterism," in *Dissent* (1957); *"Noxious Nostrum,"* in *Newsweek* (15 March 1965); Wolfe, Tom, "Son of Crime and Punishment," in *The New York Herald Tribune* (14 March 1965); Bersani, L., "The Interpretation of Dreams," in *PR*, XXXII (1965), 603-08; Pritchard, W. H., "N. M.'s Extravagances," in *Massachusetts Review*, VIII (1967), 562-68; "M.'s America," in *Time* (11 Oct. 1968)

GERTRUDE C. SCHWEBELL

MAIRONIS

(pseud. of *Jonas Mačiulevičius-Mačiulis*), Lithuanian writer, b. 2 Nov. 1862, Pasandravis; d. 28 June 1932, Kaunas

M. was a Catholic priest. From 1909 on he headed the seminary of Kaunas University, and from 1922 on was professor of moral theology at that university.

As a writer he brought 19th c. Lithuanian national romanticism to its height, while his poetry prepared the way for modern Lithuanian literature. The principal themes of his poetry are idealization of his country and its early times and love of its landscape, language, and folkways. His verse is characterized by flawless rhyme, linguistic simplicity, and austerity of line and stanza structure. M. first introduced accented meter into Lithuanian poetry, which superseded the old meters based on the number of syllables.

His epic works also have a lyrical quality and deal with Lithuanian life during the country's transition to independence. M.'s dramas depict the era of Vytautas the Great, such as *Kestučio mirtis, Vytautas pas kryžuočius, Vytautas karalius,* (1922-29).

FURTHER WORKS: *Pavasario balsai* (1895); *Tarp skausmu i garbe* (1895); *Jaunoji Lietuva* (1908); *Raseiniu Magde* (1909); *Mūsu vargai* (1920)

BIBLIOGRAPHY: Tumas, J., *M.* (1926); Vaičiulaitis, A., ed., *M.* (1963)

ANTANAS MACEINA

MALAGASY LITERATURE

Before European missionaries introduced the printing press in the 19th c., Madagascar possessed highly developed forms of oral art: the most widely practiced genres were the proverbs (*ohabolana*), public oratory (*kabary*), the folk tale (*angano*), and the fashionable poetic competitions known as *hain-teny*; also popular were dramatic rituals and festivities in which dancing and music by professional performers called *mpilalao* were as important as plot and the spoken word.

In 1818 King Radama I (1792-1828) allowed the London Missionary Society to settle on the island. The first printing press was built in 1827, and in 1835 the Bible was the first book to be printed; the first vernacular newspaper,

Teny Soa, came out in 1866. Since then journalistic life in Madagascar has always been uncommonly lively: no other area of the French empire could boast as large a number of vernacular newspapers and little magazines, which fostered the promotion of literature; indeed, most Malagasy novels were first printed in serial form.

Imaginative writing in Malagasy can be said to begin in the late 19th c. with *Fanoharana,* a free adaptation of La Fontaine's *Fables* by a French-educated Jesuit priest, Basilide Rahidy (d. 1883), and with the tales and *hain-teny* of an L.M.S.-educated Protestant minister, Ingahibe Rainitovo (1852-?).

Apart from the edifying sentimental novels of Rev. Rabary (1864-1947), the next generation was remarkable chiefly for its theatrical achievements. Its best representatives were exceptionally versatile, being journalists, novelists, poets, and musical composers as well as playwrights. But the chief contribution of Alexis Rakotobe (?—?), Justin Rainizanabololona (1861-1938), and Tselatra Rajaonah (1863-1931) at the turn of the c. was the creation of Malagasy musical comedy, which fused the native tradition of the *mpilalao* and the influence of the French operetta; their favorite theme is love, but the plays usually end on a moralizing note. Further, they gave teaching and encouragement to such younger dramatists as Dondavitra (1880-1936), whose best-known play, *Peratra Mahavariana,* was performed in 1906; Wast Ravelomoria (1886-1951), who wrote comedies of manners; Romain Andrianjafy (1888-1917), who directed his own company, "Tananarive-Theatre"; Jasmina Ratsimiseta (1890-1946), who imitated the French *théâtre de boulevard*; Naka Rabemanantsoa (1892-1943) and Justin Rajoro (1893-1949), the founders of the first Malagasy acting company "Telonohrefy." Most of the early 20th c. plays never reached print.

Madagascar became a French protectorate in 1895 and a French colony in 1905. All teaching was henceforth done in French; no native could be appointed to an official position if he did not know French. Although a number of writers were imprisoned in 1915 during the severe repression of a plot engineered by the cultural association "Vy Vato Sakelika," the colonial regime did not put an immediate end to the ebullient literary activity of the Malagasy people. Together with Justin Rainizanabololona, Edouard Andrianjafintrimo (b. 1881) experimented with rhyme and new metrical schemes based on French and Latin prosody.

Rev. Maurice Rasamuel (1886-1954), chiefly known for his historical and oratorical works, wrote his novel *Tao Manjakadoria* (1942). Madagascar's first woman novelist, Charlotte Razafiniaina (b. 1894), who wrote plays, poems, and *hain-teny* as well, produced several social novels dealing with the problems of acculturation. This was also the generation of the greatest lyric poet in the Malagasy language, Ramanantoanina (1891-1940); his nostalgic work was studied by the first notable Malagasy critic, Charles Rajoelisolo (b. 1896), who was also a historian and a gifted short story writer. Another prominent representative of this generation was Rodlish (b. 1897), the author of serious dramas such as *Ranomody* (1926) and *Sangy mahery* (1936), which deal with the theme of frustrated love and offer a critique of the native caste system; he also published in cooperation with Jean Narivony (b. 1898), two anthologies of Malagasy poetry, *Amboara voafantina* (1926) and *Kolokalo tatsinana* (1929).

Among the writers born after Madagascar came under French authority, there has been a noticeable estrangement from the use of the vernacular language for literary purpose. On the other hand, there arose a gifted school of French-writing poets whose eldest representative is M. E. Robinary (b. 1892). Although many popular novelettes were printed in Tananarive, there has been a steady decline in the number of legitimate writers. Apart from the short stories of Elie Raharolahy (b. 1901), the bulk of later Malagasy creative writing consists of the lyric poetry of Fredy Rajaofera (b. 1902) and especially J. V. S. Razakandrainy (b. 1913), better known under the pseudonym of Dox. Madagascar shares with the Cape Verde Islands and northern Nigeria the peculiarity of having bilingual poets, such as Fidelis-Justin Rabestimanandranto (b. 1907) and Régis Rajemisa-Raolison (b. 1913), who handle their mother tongue and the European language with equal ease.

ALBERT S. GÉRARD

MALAMUD, Bernard

American novelist and short story writer, b. 26 April 1914, Brooklyn, N.Y.

M. has oscillated between the forms of the novel and the short story, between the devices of realism and surrealism, between the strategies of broad satire and lyric impressionism.

His first novel, *The Natural* (1952), is a surrealistic baseball story, deft and compelling in spite of its uncertainty of tone. *The Assistant* (1957), more naturalistic in its presentation, records the bleak milieu of the urban Jewish immigrant in America with some few fine touches of surrealism and grim humor. M.'s most satisfying volume, *The Magic Barrel* (1958), fuses his variegated talents within the confining restrictions of Yiddish humor and the short-story form. The effect of these stories is one of bittersweet grotesquerie—they are at the same time poignant, comic, and warmly humane. *A New Life* (1961) is an oversprawled novel of academic life that lacks the economical bite and grotesque vision of M.'s best work.

M.'s mastery of the Jewish-American idiom and his unerring sense of the pathetically humorous incongruity emerge most successfully in the shorter literary forms where scene and image and style can fuse in a poetic suspension. When he employs longer forms M. tends to flatten both his style and his content into ineffectual satire and dull reportage.

FURTHER WORKS: *Noonday* (1961); *Idiots First* (1963); *The Fixer* (1966); *A Malamud Reader* (1967)

BIBLIOGRAPHY: Rovit, Earl H., "B. M. and the Jewish Literary Tradition," in *Critique*, III:2 (Winter-Spring, 1960), 3-10; Hassan, Ihab, *Radical Innocence* (1961); *Critique*, VII (1965), ii, special M. issue; Richman, S., *B. M.* (1966)

EARL ROVIT

MALAPARTE, Curzio

(pseud. of *Kurt Erich Suckert*), Italian novelist, essayist, poet, scenarist, and playwright, b. 9 June 1898, Prato; d. 19 July 1957, Rome

M.'s politics and literary production were marked by diverse influences. Following World War I, in which he served as a volunteer, M. became a fascist, but he was eventually expelled from the party, imprisoned, and ultimately he served the American Army in World War II. The associations of his last days included people of varying opinions like Tambroni and Togliatti, Secchia, and Fanfani.

In 1924 in Rome M. founded the fortnightly *La Conquista dello Stato*. From 1928 to 1931 he was coeditor of the *Fiera letteraria*, and, between 1929-31, was editor of *La Stampa* in Turin. He founded the literary magazine *Prospettive*, which appeared during 1937-43.

There is evidence that, in M.'s early journalistic career, fascism probably appealed to him because of its strong nationalistic emphasis. In 1926 in Rome M. founded with Bontempelli the magazine *900*, a quarterly with articles in French, whose pan-European character was manifest in an international editorial board, including Joyce and Ehrenburg (qq.v.). Significantly within a short time M. abandoned the *900* to join the "Strapaese" group in 1927, which opposed the internationalism of the *900* and expressed its nationalistic ideas in such publications as *Il Selvaggio* and *L'Italiano*. During the period 1932-43 M. wrote for the *Corriere della sera,* under the name "Candido," and for *Il Tempo* in a column titled "Battibecco."

The three works that have most contributed to making M. an international figure are *Don Camalèo* (1946; first appeared in *La Chiosa* in 1928); *Kaputt* (1945; Eng., 1946), and *La Pelle* (1949; The Skin, 1952; first published in French as *La Peau,* 1948). The latter two novels evoked a world-wide but mixed reaction. In these novels, M.'s style, sometimes scabrous and often swelling with lengthy enumeration, but always arresting, aims at presenting critically the reality of war and its consequences. He creates a striking picture of reality, which has been described on the one hand as unprejudiced and on the other as distorted. As a whole his work suggests affinities with a wide variety of writers from D'Annunzio to Papini (qq.v.) in Italy, as well as with many foreign writers.

FURTHER WORKS: *Le nozze degli eunuchi* (1921); *La rivolta dei santi maledetti* (1921); *L'Europa vivente* (1923); *Italia barbara* (1925); *Avventure di un capitano di sventura* (1927); *L'arcitaliano* (1928); *Intelligenza di Lenin* (1930); *Le Technique du coup d'état* (in French, 1931; in Italian, *Tecnica del colpo di stato,* 1948; Coup d'État: The Technique of Revolution, 1932); *I custodi del disordine* (1931); *Sodoma e Gomorra* (1931); *Fughe in prigione* (1936); *Sangue* (1937); *Viaggio in interno* (1938); *Donna come me* (1940); *Il Volga nasce in Europa* (1943; The Volga Rises in Europe, 1957); *Il sole è cieco* (1947); *Il battibecco* (1949); *La storia di domani* (1949); *Opere complete* (1954); *Maledetti toscani* (1956; Those Cursed Tuscans, 1964); *Io in Russia e in Cina* (1958); *Mamma marcia* (1959); *L'Inglese in paradiso* (1960); *Benedetti italiani* (1961); *Lenin buonamina* (1962); *Don Camalèo, e altri scritti satirici* (1963); *Diario di uno straniero a Parigi* (1966)

BIBLIOGRAPHY: Vegliani, F., *M.: A Biography* (1957); Cione, E., *Napoli e M.* (1950)

JOHN VAN EERDE

MALÈGUE, Joseph

French novelist, b. 8 Dec. 1876, Latour d'Auvergne, Puy-de-Dôme; d. 30 Dec. 1940, Nantes

M. was a teacher, but in 1936 retired to a family estate near Nantes. His novel *Augustin ou Le maître est là* (1929) places him as a modern French Catholic writer, though closer to the psychological novels of Estaunié (q.v.) than to Mauriac or Bernanos (qq.v.). *Augustin* is a novel of spiritual development dominated by the conflict between belief and disbelief. M.'s skill in the analysis of mental and emotional life led Jacques Madaule to call him "a Catholic Marcel Proust."

The religious content of M.'s novels is very closely related to Pascal's *Pensées*. A second, unfinished novel appeared posthumously (*Pierres noires*, 1958). Its hero is a man defeated by life, and in it M. describes France at the end of the 19th c., especially the social and religious progress of country people.

FURTHER WORKS: *De l'annonciation à la nativité* (1935); *Petite suite liturgique* (1938); *Pénombres* (1939); *Sous la meule de Dieu* (1948)

BIBLIOGRAPHY: Michael, E., *M.* (1957); Pitou, S., "M. and Positivism," in *Renascence,* XVI (1964), 146-48; Pitou, S., "M., Posthumously," in *Renascence,* pp. 214-18

* * *

MALLEA, Eduardo

Argentine novelist and essayist, b. 14 Aug. 1903, Bahía Blanca

M. studied law at Buenos Aires University. For several years he edited the literary supplement of the newspaper *La Nación* and later became a diplomat.

His very personal style sets him apart from other writers of his generation. The volume of essays, *Historia de una pasión argentina* (1935), and the novel *La Bahía de silencio* (1940) are particularly characteristic. They deal with Argentina's individuality and destiny, and, as in *Las Águilas* (1943) and *La Torre* (1951), M. attacks the property-owning classes and im-

plies that the country's salvation lies in a return to the simple, strict standards of the old landed aristocracy.

In *Fiesta en noviembre* (1938) and *Los Enemigos del alma* (1950) M. treats contemporary social conflict in its more general aspects. As literature, M.'s best novel is *Todo verdor perecerá* (1941). Set in provincial Argentina, it is an account of a woman who is broken by the narrowness of life in the Argentine province.

FURTHER WORKS: *Cuentos para una inglesa desesperada* (1926); *Nocturno europeo* (1935); *La Cuidad junto al rio inmóvil* (1936); *El Sayal y la púrpura* (1941); *Rodeada está de sueño; El Vínculo* (1946); *Chaves* (1951); *Notas de un novelista* (1954); *El Simbad* (1956); *Poesión* (1958)

BIBLIOGRAPHY: Morsella, A., *E. M.* (1957); Petersen, F., "The Relationship of Narrative Technique to Theme in E. M.'s *Poesión,*" in *BA,* XXXVIII (1964), 361-66; Shaw, D. L., "Narrative Technique in M.'s *La bahía de silencio,*" *Symposium,* XX (1966), 50-55; Armstrong, A. Q., "E. M. y la búsqueda de la argentinidad," *DA,* XXVII (1966), 1811A; Belloni, M., "The Inner Silence of E. M.," *Américas,* 19 Oct. 1967, 20-27; Flint, J. M. "The Expression of Isolation: Notes on M.'s Stylistic Techniques," *BHS,* XLIV (1967), 203-209

FERNANDO ALEGRIA

MALMBERG, Bertil (Frans Harald)

Swedish poet and writer, b. 13 Aug. 1889, Härnösand; d. 11 Feb. 1958, Stockholm

M. came of the humanistically oriented bourgeoisie and was chiefly influenced by German writers—George, Rilke, and the later Mann (qq.v.), as well as Schiller and Hölderlin. His work ranged from aesthetic immoralism to an ethically conceived artistic creed. In his later works, however, he abandoned his previous strict regard for form in favor of surrealism (q.v.). A period in Munich (1917-26) was of great importance to M., who occasionally wrote in German.

Although he began to publish in 1908, M. was not recognized until 1935, with *Dikter vid gränsen,* a volume of poetry of apocalyptic moods and heroic pessimism. The attraction of Frank Buchman's Oxford movement is reflected in the confessional poems in *Sångerna om samvetet och ödet* (1938), but his subsequent collections *Flöjter ur ödsligheten* (1941) and *Under månens fallande båge* (1947) mark his return to an archaic, mystical, hymnlike poetry.

M.'s late work shows a lapidary pathos and a belief in the power of poetic works of art to conquer the transitoriness of life.

FURTHER WORKS: *Bränder* (1908); *Uppgörelse och löfte* (1911); *Dåd och dröm* (1912); *Atlantis* (1916); *En blödande jord* (1917); *Fiskebyn* (1919); *Orfika* (1923); *Åke och hans värld* (1924; Åke and His World, 1940); *Slöjan* (1927); *Vinden* (1929); *Illusionernas träd* (1932); *Tyska intryck* (1936); *Värderingar* (1937); *Dikter i urval* (1939); *Excellensen* (1942); *Men bortom marterpålarna* (1948); *Samlade dikter* (1949); *Staden i regnet* (1949); *Utan resolution* (1949); *Ett stycke väg* (1950); *Med cyclopöga* (1950); *Ett författarliv* (1952); *Lek med belysningar* (1953); *Gustaf Hellström* (1953); *Dikter* (2 vols., 1954); *Klaviatur* (1955); *Edvard Backström* (1955); *Förklädda memoarer* (1956)

BIBLIOGRAPHY: Ahlberg, A., *B. M.* (1939); Allwood, M. S., *Twentieth Century Scandinavian Poetry* (1951); Holm, I., and Platen, M. v., *La littérature suédoise* (1957); Bergman, E., *Diktens värld och politikens: B. M. och Tyskland 1908-28* (with German resumé; 1967)

ERNST ALKER

MALRAUX, André

(pseud. of *A. Berger*), French novelist, b. 3 Nov. 1901, Paris

After completing his archeological and oriental studies, M. lived in the Far East (China and Indochina) from 1923 to 1927. Later he devoted himself to literature, occasionally engaging in politics. In 1936, for instance, he organized a Pilots' Foreign Legion for the Spanish Republican government. In 1940 he was wounded and taken prisoner, but later escaped and joined the French Resistance. In 1944, with the rank of colonel, he commanded the Alsace-Lorraine Brigade. From 1945 to 1946 he was Minister of Information in the government of General de Gaulle, and when de Gaulle returned to power in 1958, M. was made Minister of Cultural Affairs. The intervening years he had devoted mainly to history and aesthetics.

M.'s novel *Les Conquérants* (1928; The Conquerors, 1929) established him not only as an outstanding writer of his generation but also as one of the first great exponents of *littérature engagée*. This book, like his later *La Condition humaine* (1933; Man's Fate, 1934), was directly inspired by the Chinese Revolution. Several contemporary critics labeled the author of these novels and of *La Voie royale* (1930; The Royal Way, 1935), with their Chinese and Indochinese settings, a novelist of the "exotic"; others took them as documentary reports of the Chinese Revolution. But none of these novels is a "documentary" or a "piece of journalism" any more than are *Le temps du mépris* (1935; Days of Wrath, 1936) and *L'Espoir* (1937; Man's Hope, 1938), despite the fact that they feature Nazism and the Spanish Civil War.

The problems of M.'s characters have little to do with the place or circumstances furnishing the background of the story, and the central action in *Les Conquérants* or *La Condition humaine,* for instance, might just as well have occurred during the Russian Revolution of 1917 as a few years later in China.

The Chinese Revolution gave M. the opportunity of comparing his ideas on man and action with reality. Later he transposed his experiences to a fictional plane without aiming at exoticism but following the principle (formulated later in *L'espoir*) that dominates both his life and his writing: "The best thing a man can do with his life is to transform widest experience into awareness." The true heroes of these novels are not Chinese but Europeans, who think and feel as Europeans: there is no more effective way of stressing that they remain "outside" the historic event in which they participate and which to them is merely a kind of "unveiling." Above all, each of the characters embodies the eternal dialogue between the man of action and the man who strives primarily for the self-perfection that will give meaning to his existence. This is particularly evident in *La Voie royale* where, deep in the heart of Asia, the two leading characters have an adventure that has lost all "social" context and occurs on a purely inward plane. The real theme of this work is the inner adventure of modern man. This adventure may sometimes coincide with historical events or be determined by them, but it is by no means always, or necessarily, dependent on them. M.'s concept of man is not grounded in "engagement."

M.'s trail-blazing novel *Les Conquérants* first posed the problem of the relationship between the revolutionary and the revolution itself. The action takes place in Canton, the seat of the Kuomintang government, which is fighting British imperialism. The characters comprise three types, apart from the Chinese people: the terrorists—the "romantics" of the revolution (Hong, Rebecci); the Bolsheviks—the "experts" for whom the end justifies the means (Borodin, Nicolaieff); and finally the conquerors themselves (Garine), for whom action is an expression of passion and a desire for fulfillment rather than a striving for power. There is a basic conflict in the position of this latter group: holding that society is absurd, it should side with the terrorists on emotional grounds; on the other hand, it is attracted by the "activism" of the Bolsheviks.

La Condition humaine is about the revolution in Shanghai and the subsequent bloody suppression of the communists, who would not surrender the city to Chiang Kai-shek. Moscow supports Chiang because to the Communist International the ends (however distant) justify the means (however terrible) and human individuals do not count. This political and human tragedy is enacted by the same revolutionary types found in the earlier novels.

These heroes appear once more in *La Voie royale,* though here man is no longer in conflict with his fellows, with society and history, but solely with himself; he is delivered over to his tragic fate, a thrall to his own compulsions. As a novel, *La Voie royale* is perhaps less rich and complex than *Les Conquérants, La Condition humaine,* or *L'Espoir,* but in no other work has M. given such penetrating expression to the tragedy within man's mind or emphasized so poignantly that this is a tragedy of the individual man. M.'s heroes are completely alone, even in love; they know only that form of love that offers no deliverance from loneliness—the sensual.

On account of the tragic note pervading all M.'s novels, his work has sometimes been called sadistic. But according to M. it is the tragedy of existence that transforms man and forces him to reveal himself—even if only to himself. Using or suffering violence, tortured, tormented, in the face of death he discovers his most secret, fascinating countenance. It is always the countenance of a solitary man. The greatness of the tragic hero as M. portrays him lies in clear-sightedly and resolutely resisting utter hopelessness to the very last through the effort of the human spirit to give meaning to the meaningless.

The constant recurrence of themes, human types, and dramatic settings is of no less significance in M.'s work than his artistic "manner." After the Chinese Revolution and the Spanish Civil War, amid the turmoil of the years between 1939 and 1945, M. was confronted once more by his eternal temptation: the deed or action that forces man to fulfill himself. But it is noteworthy that the novel that resulted from the impact of this new experience is not a witness to "something undergone," in the manner of *L'Espoir,* but a work that deliberately turns its back on all "actuality"— namely, *Noyers de l'Altenburg* (1948; The Walnut Trees of Altenburg, 1952) in which M. attacks metaphysical questions. Having started out with man, he returns to man, once again rejecting incidental political "engagement" as a formative force. This is the primary message of *Noyers de l'Altenburg,* which was continued and elaborated in M.'s great works on art which appeared over more than a decade: *La Psychologie de l'art* (3 vols., 1947-50; The Psychology of Art, 1949-50); *Saturne* (1950; Saturn: An Essay on Goya, 1957); *Les Voix du silence* (1951; The Voices of Silence, 1953); *Le Musée imaginaire de la sculpture mondiale* (2 vols., 1952-54; Museum Without Walls, 1967).

M. believes that only in his artistic creations does man reveal his true greatness—his eternal passionate wish to find a meaning for existence. Art is a constant rebellion against nothingness and senselessness—"art is a counterfate." It has been said of M. that he "entered art as he might have entered a religious order." His aim in doing so is that of his total work: "to try to make men aware of the greatness of which they know nothing."

FURTHER WORKS: *Lunes en papier* (1921); *La Tentation de l'Occident* (1926); *D'une jeunesse européenne* (1926); *Ecrits* (1927); *Royaume Farfelu* (1928); *La Lutte avec l'ange* (1943); *Esquisse d'une psychologie du cinéma* (1947); *Goya* (1947); *La Création artistique* (1948); *La Monnaie de l'absolu* (1950); *La Métamorphose des dieux* (1957; Metamorphosis of the Gods, 1960); *Antimémoires* (1967; Antimemoirs, 1968)

BIBLIOGRAPHY: Picon, G., *M. par lui-même* (1953); Boisdeffre, P. de, *M.* (4th ed., 1957); Sigaux, G., *M.* (1959); Hartmann, G., *M.* (1960); Blumenthal, G., *A. M.* (1961); Frank, J., "M.'s Metaphysics of Art," in *SR,* LXX (1962), 620-50; Blend, C. D., *A. M., Tragic Humanist,*

ANDRÉ MALRAUX

HEINRICH MANN

(1963); Sonnenfeld, A., "M. and the Tyranny of Time," in *Romantic Review,* LIV (1963), 198-212; Hoffman, J., *L'Humanisme de M.* (1963); Fitch, B. T., *Les Deux Univers romanesques de M.* (1964); Langlois, W. G., *A. M.: The Indo-China Adventure* (1966); Grosjean, J., "Les *Antimémoires* de A. M.," in *NRF* (15 Oct. 1967), 658-66

CLAUDE ELSEN

MANDELSTAMM, Ossip Emiliyevich

Russian poet, b. 15 Jan. 1891, Warsaw; d. 27 Dec. 1938, near Vladivostok

M., one of the leaders of acmeism (see Russian literature), was the son of a Jewish merchant; he spent his childhood in Saint Petersburg and Pavlovsk. After a visit to Paris in 1907, and after he had become enthusiastically acquainted with modern French poetry, M. started, in 1909, to publish his own poems in the magazine *Apollo.* In 1910 he studied Old French in Heidelberg, and in 1911 he became a student of philology at the University of Saint Petersburg. Soon he was to meet Gumilev (q.v.) and to join his poets' guild, becoming a militant acmeist.

During the revolution and civil war, M. changed residence, living for a time in the south and then settling in Moscow. After the revolution he continued to write—as always, his output was limited—but remained outside the main current of Soviet literature. After 1932 M.'s name disappeared from the pages of Soviet periodicals. Verbal reports, contradicting in details, agree that following the publication of an epigram he wrote on Stalin in 1934, he was arrested and exiled, that he returned from exile, that he was again arrested in 1938. He died the same year in a camp in which temporary prisoners were secured.

M.'s first book of verse, *Kamen'* (1913), contains his most acmeistic poems. The theme of gravity predominates, and frequent topics are architecture, music, and literature. In his treatment of history, M. manages to combine a detached bird's-eye view with deep subjective penetration. In these poems archaisms are intermingled skillfully with everyday expressions in sonorous lines that move at a majestic pace.

In the critical essay *"Utro akmeizma"* (1919), M. makes an interesting attempt to broaden the commonly held theory of acmeism and postulates "the word as such" to be the only reality in poetry while he assigns to the "logos" a lesser role—that of being simply a component of form. In his later theoretical writings M. speaks of words that do not denote an object but "freely select, as if for a home, this or that object's meaning...a dear body."

In his next book of poems, *Tristia* (1922), M. continues to pursue his neoclassical interests by the use of motifs of ancient Greece and Rome, of 17th-c. France, and of the Russian empire, and introduces Crimean poems. These poems show some lightening of structure and more emphasis on the purely verbal aspects of verse. Here M. seems almost to be tending toward a loosening of semantics. The tragic note that permeates the book sounds especially strongly in the poems of the death of prerevolutionary Petersburg.

Shum vremeni (1925), a book of autobiographical essays, recreates the atmosphere of the poet's childhood and his stay in the Crimea in 1920. They evidence M.'s inherent feeling for history and a detached, almost impersonal touch. *Yegipetskaya marka* (1928), in which M. experiments with prose, is a surrealistic tale with a Saint Petersburg background. M.'s late poems have a highly complex texture approaching futurism (q.v.). Some of them seem to be written in a private code. Their prevalent theme is the poet's dialogue with his time. The poems that M. wrote in jail and exile, which were published in New York many years later (fifty-seven poems, in *Vozdushnyye Puti,* II, 1961), can be ranked among the high points of Russian tragic poetry.

Though M. wrote little, and though his popularity with the average reader suffers because of the classical restraint of his lines and his propensity to see everything *sub specie aeternitatis,* his originality, mastery of technique, broad culture, and the sustained quality of his poems have earned him a prominent place among Russian poets of this century.

FURTHER WORKS: *O poezii. Sbornik statei* (1928); *Stikhotvoreniya* (1928); *Sobraniye sochinenii* (1955). **Selected English trans.:** *The Prose of O. M.* (1965)

BIBLIOGRAPHY: Struve, G., "O. E. M.: Opyt biografii i kriticheskovo kommentariya," in M.'s *Sobraniye sochinenii* (1955); Poggioli, R., "Commento a M.," in *Pietre di paragone* (1939); Strakhovski, L., *Craftsmen of the Word: Three Poets of Modern Russia* (1949); pp. 83-100; Makovski, S., "O. M.," in *Portrety sovremennikov*

VLADIMIR MARKOV

MANN, Heinrich

German novelist, dramatist, and essayist, b. 27 March 1871, Lübeck; d. 12 March 1950, Santa Monica, Calif.

In 1931 M., a brother of Thomas M. (q.v.), was appointed president of the Prussian Academy of Arts, Division of Literature. In 1933 he emigrated to France, in 1940 to the U.S.A. In 1949 the (East) German Democratic Republic awarded him its first national prize. He was offered the presidency of the Germany Academy of Arts, but died before he could assume it.

His first novel, *In einer Familie* (1894), already marks him as a critic of his time, which he saw as a time of the decline of the middle class but also of the rise of democracy, advancing under the socialist banner. Originally his criticism of the social class that controlled public life at that time was partly modeled on the 19th c. French social critics. He later gave it sharper, satirical form in the novels *Im Schlaraffenland* (1900; In the Land of Cockaigne, 1925), and *Professor Unrat* (1905; Eng., The Blue Angel, 1932; Am., Small Town Tyrant, 1944). In contrast to these works of contemporary political significance, around 1900 M. wrote several novels and novellas describing ecstatically living, decadent, exceptional characters; these include the trilogy *Die Göttinnen oder Die drei Romane der Herzogin von Assy: Diana, Minerva, Venus* (1902-1903; The Golden, 1918; Diana, 1929) and the novella *Pippo Spano* (1904-1905). They show the influence of Nietzsche and D'Annunzio (qq.v.), intensified by the impact Italy made upon M. during several long visits. These books represent a first climax in M.'s work.

In the next few years he was more concerned with political questions. The trilogy *Der Untertan* (1914; Am., The Patrioteer, 1921, Eng., Man of Straw, 1947), *Die Armen* (1917; The Poor, 1917), and *Der Kopf* (1925; The Chief, 1925) makes an extremely acute, caustic criticism of society in the Germany of Wilhelm II; M. later indicted the Weimar Republic—and finally National Socialism—with the same impatient bitterness. The presentation is often grotesque and overdone, the tone intransigent. Nearly all of M.'s dramatic work and many of his essays (*Zola*, 1915) appeared during the years from 1911 to 1932.

While he was a refugee in France, a country to which he felt strong spiritual ties, M. wrote, as a counterpart to the *Untertan* series, the novels *Die Jugend des Königs Henri Quatre* (1935; Young Henry of Navarre, 1937) and *Die Vollendung des Königs Henri Quatre* (1937; Henry, King of France, 1939). This return to history gave him another opportunity to voice his social criticism and advocate his program of "humanistic socialism." This concern with contemporary political questions was even more explicitly stated in numerous essays and pamphlets.

At the center of M.'s view of the world stands man. He is to be led to inner-worldly "happiness" through a social order based on "reason" and "humanity." M. accepted the doctrine of socialism at a very early stage; later he came closer to communism, though he never adopted the Marxist position. Toward the end of his life the aggressive acerbity of his words was tempered by a patient skepticism.

FURTHER WORKS: *Das Wunderbare* (1897); *Die Jagd nach Liebe* (1903-1904); *Flöten und Dolche* (1905); *Eine Freundschaft* (1905); *Mnais und Ginevra* (1906); *Stürmische Morgen* (1906); *Zwischen den Rassen* (1907); *Die Bösen* (1908); *Die kleine Stadt* (1909; The Little Town, 1931); *Die Rückkehr vom Hades* (1911); *Die Schauspielerin* (1911); *Die große Liebe* (1912); *Madame Legros* (1913); *Brabach* (1917); *Bunte Gesellschaft* (1917); *Drei Akte* (1918); *Der Weg zur Macht* (1919); *Die Ehrgeizige* (1920); *Macht und Mensch* (1920); *Die Tote* (1921); *Diktatur der Vernunft* (1923); *Der Jüngling* (1924); *Abrechnungen* (1924); *Das gastliche Haus* (1924); *Kobes* (1925); *Liliane und Paul* (1926); *Mutter Marie* (1927; Mother Mary, 1928); *Eugenie* (1928; The Royal Woman, 1930); *Sieben Jahre* (1929); *Sie sind jung* (1929); *Die große Sache* (1930); *Geist und Tat* (1931); *Ein ernstes Leben* (1932); *Die Welt der Herzen* (1932); *Es kommt der Tag* (1936); *Lidice* (1943); *Ein Zeitalter wird besichtigt* (1946); *Der Atem* (1949); *Empfang bei der Welt* (1950); *Eine Liebesgeschichte* (1953); *Unser natürlicher Freund* (1957); *Traurige Geschichte von Friedrich dem Großen* (1960); *Friedrich der Große* (1961); *Thomas Mann— H. M. Briefwechsel 1900-1949* (1965)

BIBLIOGRAPHY: Schröder, W., *H. M.* (1931); Sinsheimer, H., *H. M.'s Werk* (1931); Lemke, H., *H. M.* (1946); Ihering, H., *H. M.* (1951); Specht, G., *Das Problem der Macht bei H. M.* (1954); Kantorowicz, A., *Heinrich und Thomas M.* (1956); Weisstein, U., *H. M.* (1962); Piana, T., *H. M.* (1964); Yuill, W. E., "H. M.," in Natan, A., ed., *German Men of*

Letters, II (1964), 199-224; Banuls, A., *H. M.* (1966); Linn, R. N., *H. M.* (1967)

GEORG SPECHT

MANN, Klaus (Heinrich Thomas)

German-American novelist, dramatist, and essayist, b. 18 Nov. 1906, Munich; d. 22 May 1949, Cannes

M. was the eldest son of Thomas M. (q.v.), and his sister Erika M. (b. 1905) is also a writer and journalist. The high standard of culture in his family background—a rare combination of patriarchic awareness of traditionalism and receptivity toward any kind of progress—was almost unconsciously absorbed by the precocious boy. Decisively influenced in his education and development by the markedly individualistic atmosphere of the Odenwald School, he began to write at the age of sixteen. A series of stories and plays, reflecting the restlessness of the times and alternating between coquettish self-revelation and an ethic of universal brotherhood, appeared between 1925 and 1930; it included the novel *Der fromme Tanz* (1926) from which one segment of the young upper-middle-class intellectuals of the Weimar Republic derived its nickname "the K.M. generation."

After 1933 M. emigrated; together with Gide, Huxley, and his uncle H. Mann (qq.v.), he founded the German refugee periodical *Die Sammlung*. After several years of restless traveling he wrote a series of important books, including the Tchaikovsky novel *Symphonie Pathétique* (1935; Pathetic Symphony, 1938), the refugee novel *Der Vulkan* (1939), and the report of his own life *The Turning Point* (1942), which in its expanded German version, *Der Wendepunkt* (1952), deals particularly with old Europe revisited.

M.'s work is to a great extent a personal testimony. Nevertheless he was more variously and closely in touch with the world than almost anyone else of his generation; his friends included leading political and intellectual figures in all countries. M.'s personal testimony becomes a valid documentation of the times, not least through the strong element of self-criticism which characterized it from the beginning. At 43 he took his life.

FURTHER WORKS: *Vor dem Leben* (1925); *Anja und Esther* (1925); *Kindernovelle* (1926; The Fifth Child); *Revue zu Vieren* (1926); *Heute und Morgen* (1927); *Rundherum*

(1929); *Abenteuer* (1929); *Gegenüber von China* (1929); *Alexander, Roman der Utopie* (1930; Alexander, a Novel of Utopia, 1930); *Geschwister* (1939); *Auf der Suche nach einem Weg* (1931); *Kind dieser Zeit* (1932); *Treffpunkt im Unendlichen* (1932); *Flucht in den Norden* (1934; Journey into Freedom, 1936); *Mephisto* (1936); *Vergittertes Fenster* (1937); *Escape to Life* (1939); *The Other Germany* (1940); *Heart of Europe* (1943); *André Gide and the Crisis of Modern Thought* (1943)

BIBLIOGRAPHY: *K. M. zum Gedächtnis* (tributes from friends, 1950); Strich, F., *Kunst und Leben* (1960); Baden, H. J., *Literatur und Selbstmord: Cesare Pavese, K. M., Ernest Hemingway* (1965)

CAROL PETERSEN

MANN, Thomas

German novelist and critic, b. 6 June 1875, Lübeck; d. 12 Aug. 1955, Kilchberg am Zürichsee, Switzerland

The history of the German novel culminates in M.'s work. He restored to German prose literature the international status which it had not enjoyed since the time of Jean Paul and the Romantics. His name belongs with those of Proust and Joyce (qq.v.) in any discussion of the modern novel. The intellectual features of his age are clearly recognizable in his writing, which represents that moment in the development of European realism when its basic humanistic assumptions were called into question. Yet whereas his great contemporaries, like Proust or Joyce, reflected this predicament through the form of their writing, M. preserved the outward conventions of realistic fiction but charged them with a new irony. From the outset both the content and form of his work are governed by his sense that art is suspect. In the early writings, such as *Buddenbrooks* (1901; Eng., 1924), *Tonio Kröger* (1903; Eng., in *Stories of Three Decades*, 1914; also in *Stories of a Lifetime*, 1961), *Der Tod in Venedig* (1911; Death in Venice, 1925), it is apparently only from the standpoint of a middle-class social morality that art is criticized; but the "impossibility" of art in the modern world became finally the very center, the tragic and ironical substance, of *Doktor Faustus* (1947; Eng., 1949). The essence of M.'s artistic irony lies in his daring attempt to make the historically inevitable inappropriateness of traditional forms for conveying the content of modern ex-

377

perience into the very material of a new work of art. And since this irony (q.v.) mirrors the fate of a civilization which can only take itself seriously by the aid of much ironical reflection, M.'s fiction tells more of the story of modern Europe's spiritual history than that of almost any other writer. Because he is narrating still in the style of his less problematic literary ancestors, it is natural and necessary for him to interweave his narrative with commentary, reflection, and thought, while essay writing itself forms an important aspect of his work, closely allied to his fiction.

M. came of a prosperous business family which played a prominent part in the social life of the old Hanseatic town of Lübeck. His mother was of Brazilian origin, however, and M. liked to attribute the conflicts he experienced between his "burgher" morality and his "artistic" temperament to this southern and exotic strain. After his father's death (1891) the family moved to Munich, and M. followed two years later after he had finished his schooling at the Lübeck Gymnasium. In Munich he at first took a job with an insurance company, then enrolled as a student at the university; soon afterward he went with his brother Heinrich M. (q.v.) to Italy, where he lived for about two years (mainly in Rome and Palestrina). It was here that he began the story of the decline of a northern family, the Buddenbrooks, which was completed on his return to Munich and published in 1901. Its appearance was the most important event in M.'s life. For its success, remarkable in the annals of modern literature because for once the popular verdict agreed with that of the most exclusive critics, established his career as that of a great writer; from now on to talk of his biography is to talk of his writing, for life acquired meaning only through his writing.

In 1905 M. married Katja Pringsheim, daughter of a Munich family of bankers and scholars. The stabilizing effect of his marriage is reflected in the humorous novel *Königliche Hoheit* (1909; Royal Highness, 1916). The collapse of "conservative" values, in a spiritual rather than party-political sense, which M. saw in World War I and its likely aftermath, inspired his polemical "intellectual autobiography," *Die Betrachtungen eines Unpolitischen* (1919), and his masterful parody of the genre that is called the *Bildungsroman* in German—*Der Zauberberg* (1924; The Magic Mountain, 1927). The confusions of postwar politics, the happiness and cares of domesticity,

his tenderness as a father (of six children), the deep anxiety caused by the Fascist conspiracy against humanity—these are the themes of *Herr und Hund* (1918; Bashan and I, 1923); *Gesang vom Kindchen* (1919); *Unordnung und frühes Leid* (1926; Early Sorrow, 1929; Disorder and Early Sorrow, 1929); *Mario und der Zauberer* (1930; Mario and the Magician, 1930). The fate of the *émigré,* which took him first in 1933 to Switzerland and led finally to Princeton and California, is anticipated in the imaginative "flight" from modernity back to the "wellsprings" of myth in the tetralogy *Joseph und seine Brüder* (1933-42; Joseph and His Brothers, 1934-44), of which the first two volumes, *Die Geschichten Jakobs* (1933; Eng., The Tales of Jacob, 1934; Am., Joseph and His Brothers, 1934) and *Der junge Joseph* (1935; The Young Joseph, 1935), appeared in Germany, while Volumes III and IV, *Joseph in Ägypten* (1936; Joseph in Egypt, 1938) and *Joseph der Ernährer* (1943; Joseph the Provider, 1945), had to be published abroad. M. had now also forfeited any political rights in his homeland, and wrote a classic rejection of National Socialism in his letter to the University of Bonn.

He gave vent to his political anger in radio broadcasts to the German people; at the same time his imagination conceived in the figure of Joseph in Egypt a reconciliation of humanitarian idealism with the realities of power, of the exile with his people. In *Lotte in Weimar* (1939; The Beloved Returns, 1940) he evoked the figure of Goethe—an unexpected spiritual relation of Joseph—and in a style of affectionate ironical intimacy showed the always recurring and always fruitful trouble which a creative spirit encounters in a world so little disposed to accommodate his creative desires. And while Germany foundered in the abyss of war, this author who had renounced his homeland wrote the novel which in its style and theme most confesses his nationality, the all but untranslatable *Doktor Faustus* (1947; Eng., 1948), where the old quarrel between the artistic spirit and society reaches its evil conclusion: the damnation both of the socially nihilistic artist and of his spiritually nihilistic society. After the publication of this novel M.'s visits to Europe became more and more frequent, until he finally settled on Lake Zürich in 1952. Here at the age of almost eighty he finished the first (and only) volume of a work begun in 1911: *Die Bekenntnisse des Hochstaplers Felix Krull* (1922; enlarged ed., 1936; new

THOMAS MANN

version, 1954; Confessions of Felix Krull, Confidence Man, 1955), in which art takes its revenge for all that it has had to suffer: this time with profound gaiety and scandalous insolence, at the expense of a world which genius may at least deceive, even if it can teach it nothing. After this masterly extravagance he devoted his last words to the memory of Friedrich Schiller (*Versuch über Schiller* [1955; On Schiller, 1958]), the poet to whom literature meant nothing except as a verbal act of concern for the spiritual fate of mankind.

Neither M.'s unmistakable style nor his literary method bears the marks of any decisive "influence." At the time of writing *Buddenbrooks* he felt himself to be indebted to the realistic and naturalistic tradition of the Russian and French novelists, above all Turgenev, the brothers Goncourt, and Zola (q.v.). The only German influence was perhaps Theodor Fontane; not until late in life did he come to admire the art of Adalbert Stifter and Gottfried Keller. A profounder source of inspiration for his work may be discovered, however, in German philosophy and music, in Arthur Schopenhauer, Nietzsche (q.v.), and Richard Wagner. The intellectual irony in *Buddenbrooks,* more fundamental than may at first appear beneath the serene epic tone of the narrative, represents the author's moral reservations toward those great voices of extreme (and contradictory) spiritual aspirations in the 19th c. which so entirely fascinated him. This novel is an ironical critique both of Schopenhauer's metaphysical pessimism and of Nietzsche's antimetaphysical affirmation of life; and while M.'s love of Wagner is reflected in its very structure, it is morally denied by the content of the story, which shows this same music as the audible spirit of decadence. That the increase in spiritual distinction from one generation of the Buddenbrooks to the next should be at the expense of a disastrous decrease in their vital fitness to survive, is an ironic variation of Schopenhauer's doctrine. But it is Nietzsche's philosophy which prompts the scene where the last head of the firm, Thomas Buddenbrook, at a moment of crisis in his life dreamily consoles himself by imagining another meaning to emerge from the page of Schopenhauer before him: a dithyrambic assurance of life's undying vigor, surviving all individual decline. No matter if his sickly son is possessed body and soul by music and by death, he himself will live again in all those

stronger generations of men to come who will master life better than he has done.

That man's spiritual gifts are a form of illness, that life is the enemy of spirit, remain the persistent, underlying theme of M.'s work, as he discovers ever new variations, and shifts the accent of moral approval or denial now toward this extreme, now toward that. For Tonio Kröger (hero of the novella by that name), a most painful sense of exclusion from life is the penalty he must pay for being an artist, yet he is a good artist just because of his deep desire for life, which is inspired by love. This again is fundamentally Nietzsche's view, expressed though it is in the language of a sentimental idyll. But in *Der Tod in Venedig* it is Schopenhauer's pessimistic conception of love and art which informs the portrait of the writer in all his classic detachment from life and the analysis of the final breakdown of his longing for life into a fatally sick passion. In each case, however, the style of these stories conveys the author's ironic doubts as to the validity of any final pronouncement.

This same ironic attitude provides him next with a key to the understanding of German culture itself, whose "musical-pessimistic" characteristics he defends in *Die Betrachtungen eines Unpolitischen* as a profound awareness of life's irreducible polarity—so different in this from the trite single-mindedness of the spokesman of progress (Mann coined the word *Zivilisationsliterat* for this kind of, as he thought, typically West European writer), whose superficial notion of life as a progressive cause is seen as a betrayal of all tragic irony, of the wisdom that confronts life always with the knowledge of death. Yet immediately afterward in *Der Zauberberg,* the novel set in the sanatorium of a sick Europe, the hero's dream, when he comes closest to dying, ends with the commandment: "For the sake of goodness and love, man shall let death have no sovereignty over his thoughts." But here the final irony comes when the hero does at last leave behind him the demonic inspiration of love and death: for he returns to the "life" of a soldier in 1914, disappearing, as he serves his newfound ideal, into the mud of Flanders.

The Joseph tetralogy develops, through the mediating figure of its biblical hero, the possibility of a new state (and health) of mind, freeing itself from the mythical Hebrew religion on the one hand and the death cult of the Egyptians on the other to achieve true

379

knowledge, nourished on dreams yet refined with most civilized irony, in the service of man. And the Goethe novel plays a variation on this theme by making Lotte, the symbol of Werther's delirium of love and death, also the witness to the classic genius's later mastery of life. It might appear that the basically pessimistic irony of the earlier work had indeed entered a new phase of ironical affirmation. But what follows is *Doktor Faustus,* the vision of a most fateful aberration of both life and mind. This "German tragedy," which is at the same time also a diagnosis of European culture, would not have touched so profound a level of despair, had the tragedy constituted simply the content of the book.' It in fact, however, constitutes also its form. M.'s elaborately intricate style had reflected doubtlessly from the beginning his awareness of how impossibly various are the objections which can be raised against every possible formulation of the truth. Now even this precarious possibility collapsed. His inveterate tendency to parody pronounces a death sentence on art as a medium: the artist capable of speaking *any* adequate truth about the Nazi disaster does not and cannot exist. He has to be invented. Where life itself becomes literally unspeakable, then anything that is still said about it is no better than a parody of the truth. The story can only be told by a fictitious narrator, who is allowed just to succeed because he, Serenus Zeitblom, the fictitious biographer of Faust–Adrian Leverkühn, is not a writer at all, but a naïve man, so naïve that he can still tell of aberrations too terrible for any literary convention to contain.

Among the many honors bestowed on M. were the Nobel Prize in 1929 and the Goethe Prize in 1949.

FURTHER WORKS: *Der kleine Herr Friedemann* (1898); *Wälsungenblut* (1921); *Erzählungen* (2 vols., 1922; includes "Enttäuschung," 1896; "Der Bajazzo," 1897; "Der Weg zum Friedhof," 1901; "Gladius Dei," 1902; "Das Wunderkind," 1903; "Ein Glück," 1904; "Beim Propheten," 1904; "Schwere Stunde," 1905; "Das Eisenbahnunglück," 1907; "Fiorenza," 1916); *Gesammelte Werke* (15 vols., 1922-1935); *Rede und Antwort* (1922); *Bemühungen* (1925); *Pariser Rechenschaft* (1926); *Die Forderung des Tages* (1930; Order of the Day, 1942); *Leiden und Größe der Meister* (1935; Freud, Goethe, Wagner, 1937); *Ein Briefwechsel* (1937); *Dieser Friede* (1938); *Achtung, Europa!* (1938); *Deutsche Hörer!* (1945); *Aus-*

gewählte Erzählungen (1945; including now "Die vertauschten Köpfe," 1944 [The Transposed Heads, 1941] and "Das Gesetz," 1944); *Adel des Geistes: Sechzehn Versuche zum Problem der Humanität* (1945); *Leiden an Deutschland* (1946); *Neue Studien* (1948); *Die Enstehung des Doktor Faustus: Roman eines Romans* (1949; The Genesis of a Novel, 1961); *Der Erwählte* (1951; The Holy Sinner, 1952); *Altes und Neues* (1953; Essays of Three Decades, 1947); *Die Betrogene* (1953); *Nachlese Prosa 1951-1955* (1956); *Briefe an Paul Amann, 1915-1952* (1959); *T. M. an Ernst Bertram, 1910-1955* (1960); *T. M.—Karl Kerényi, Gespräch in Briefen* (1960); *Gesammelte Werke* (12 vols., 1960); *Briefe* (ed. Erika Mann; 3 vols., 1961-1965; *T. M.—Robert Faesi: Briefwechsel* (1962); *T. M.—Heinrich Mann: Briefwechsel, 1900-1945* (ed. Klaus Mann; 1965); *Das essayistische Werk* (ed. Hans Bürgin; 8 vols., 1968)

BIBLIOGRAPHY: Eloesser, A., *T. M.: Sein Leben und sein Werk* (1925); Mittner, L., *L'opera di T. M.* (1936); *Neue Rundschau,* 1945 (special issue for M.'s 70th birthday); Hamburger, K., *M.'s Roman "Joseph und seine Brüder"* (1945); Cassirer, E., "T. M.'s Goethebild, eine Studie über "Lotte in Weimar," *GR,* XX (1945); Perl, W. H., *T. M., 1933-1945: Vom deutschen Humanisten zum amerikanischen Weltbürger* (1945); Kerényi, K., *Romandichtung und Mythologie: Ein Briefwechsel mit T. M.* (1945); Bauer, A., *T. M. und die Krise der bürgerlichen Kultur* (1946); Neider, C., ed., *The Stature of T. M.* (1947); Fougère, J., *T. M. ou La Seduction de la mort* (1947); Mann, V., *Wir waren Fünf, Bildnis der Familie M.* (1949); Alegría, F., *Ensayo sobre cinco temas de T. M.* (1949); Mayer, H., *T. M.: Sein Leben und Werk* (1950); Hatfield, H., *T. M.* (1951); *Wendepunkt. Ein Lebensbericht* (1952); Thieberger, R., *Der Begriff der Zeit bei T. M.* (1952); Lesser, J., *T. M. in der Epoche seiner Vollendung* (1952); Wolffheim, H., "Das Interesse als Geist der Erzählung, ein Beitrag zur Stilphysiognomie T. M.'s," *Euphorion,* XLVII (1953); Eichner, H., *T. M. Eine Einführung in sein Werk* (1953); Heller, E., *Enterbter Geist* (1954); Leibrich, L., *T. M.* (1954); Lindsay, J. M., *T. M.* (1954); Lervile, K., ed., *Andsmenneskets Ansvar,* Nordiske Akademikeres Festskrift for T. M.'s 80th birthday (1955); Jonas, K. W., *Fifty Years of T. M. Studies* (1955); Stresau, H., *T. M. und sein Werk* (1955); Lion, F., *T. M.* (1955); Flinker,

M., ed., *Hommage de la France à T. M.* (1955);
Faesi, R., *T. M.* (1955); Thomas, R. H., *T. M.
The Meditation of Art* (1956); Mann, E., *Das
letzte Jahr* (1956); Mann, M., *Vergangenes und
Gegenwärtiges. Erinnerungen* (1956); Mayer,
H., *Leiden und Größe T. M.'s* (1956); Kantoro-
wicz, A., *Heinrich u. T. M.* (1956); Tecchi, B.,
T. M. (1956); Kaufmann, F., *T. M. The World
as Will and Representation* (1957); Lukács, G.,
T. M. (1957); Wolff, H. M., *T. M.: Werk und
Bekenntnis* (1957); Heller, E., *The Ironic Ger-
man. A Study of T. M.* (1958); Mann, J., *Aus
Dodos Kindheit* (1958); Bürgin, H., *Das Werk
T. M.'s* (1959); Flinker, M., *T. M.'s politische
Betrachtungen im Lichte der heutigen Zeit*
(1959); Bauer, A., *T. M.* (1960); Strich, F.,
Kunst und Leben (1960); Hellersberg-Wen-
driner, A., *Mystik der Gottesferne* (1960);
Altenberg, P., *Die Romane T. M.'s* (1961)

ERICH HELLER

This turn-of-the-century Bohemian did not, at
some time or other, *become* a profoundly ethical
character: he had always been one.... In this world,
irony takes the place of grace: it objectivates,
lightens, liberates, even when it assumes the tragic
mask of an inexorable force of nature.... His
original existence, purely aesthetic (or so it seemed),
was aided by ... his "citizen's love for the human,
the living, and the ordinary"—one might also say
for what is wholesomely commonplace, with which
his inmost nature thus maintained a relation of
ironic gratitude....

Schneider, R., "Kurzer Nachruf auf T. M.,"
in *Die Neue Rundschau*, 67 (1956), 521 ff.

T. M. is a realist who is remarkably faithful to
reality—indeed worshipful toward it. Even though
his details and, still more, his plots, his ideas and
concepts, by no means stop at the surface of everyday life, even though his literary form is a far cry
from any naturalism, the substance of his creation,
in the end, never goes beyond reality. What we find
in T. M.'s work is middle-class Germany (supple-
mented by its genesis, by an exploration of the paths
that have led up to it), and a penetrating grasp of
its inner problems. The dialectic of these problems,
by its very nature, points beyond itself, but never
does it become a utopian perspective of the future,
realistically animated, and magically imputed to the
present.... T. M. is an extreme example of the type
of writer whose greatness lies in being "a mirror of
the world."

Lukács, G., *T. M.* (1953), p. 9 ff.

T. M.'s way could not be that of a restorer, but it
could not be that of a skeptic either. Irony was
certainly needed, and there was no ironist like T. M.

This irony, though, was not to be romantic irony,
through whose fingers the world slips away, but
pedagogical irony, of which Goethe was the great
master and Mephistopheles his most sublime
creation. It had to be joined—and this T. M.
recognized and fulfilled—by human kindness and
confidence in man's future.

Mayer, H., *Leiden und Größe T. M.'s* (1956), p. 46

Perhaps every man possesses a multiplicity of
selves. T. M.'s originality lies in the acuity with
which he perceives the gradients between them. An
event or an experience is not just registered: it
expands in range and density like a sound thrown
back by an echo.... Thus his art is not direct; it
is never naturalism merely reproducing nature;
neither is it mere mirroring, as in aestheticism.
Instead, the natural world is registered by the
citizen [in M.], then perhaps communicated to the
poet, who tosses it back into nature. Finally, however, the artist seizes it and lifts it to a completely
different sphere.

Lion, F., *T. M., Leben und Werk* (1955), p. 50 f.

... Both brothers are sharp psychologists and
strive for utmost psychological penetration for the
sake of truth. To be sure, the indomitable urge for
truth led Heinrich Mann to extreme compression,
to the aphoristic style and aphoristic thinking of the
great French moralists. It led T. M. to an epic
vastness of scale, to extreme detail and dialectic
multiplied to the hundredth degree. What mattered
to both of them was truth alone. But stylistically
Heinrich Mann seems to speak the most succinct
truth and to leave it at that, indifferent to the
possibility of being misunderstood, while T. M.
seeks effectiveness.... Of the two brothers it is, in
fact, T. M. who shows dilettante characteristics—a
most artistic and skillful dilettante, of course, who
through a tremendous effort has transformed,
though not entirely eradicated, these characteristics.
Precisely for this reason he never slips into clumsi-
ness, and in all his quite extraordinary epic experiments always maintains his very own manner. This
is why he had relatively few failures.... Nevertheless
he, the lifelong conservative, was much more
extreme than his brother Heinrich, the lifelong rebel.
He was much more complicated, and in many
instances the result of excessive complication is a
certain naiveté. He was much more out for admiration than his brother, much more vulnerable, more
ambitious, more endangered and more dangerous,
in all innocence.

Kesten, H. *Der Geist der Unruhe* (1959), p. 315 ff.

... From his lofty eminence the teleologizing and
theologizing writer can thumb his nose at the
theologian. For the writer has surpassed the man
of God in what is normally the latter's prerogative—
the symbolic interpretation, both prospective and
retrospective, of prophetic and half-prophetic words

from the Old and New Testaments. He does this by making his whole old-new, remote-fresh patriarchal tale, with all its decisive turns and events, into a symbol of divine promise, telling this story too as the story of the stone "which the builders refused."

Schröder, R. A., Die Aufsätze und Reden I
(1952), p. 1025

This pervading temper is related to the irony of Nietzsche's ultimate men inasmuch as in both cases the wealth of historical experiences (in the widest sense, which includes the mythical) seems to have been stamped out into a convenient functional coinage. Mythical repetition in the hands of T. M. corresponds exactly, with regard to language, to the style repetition of parody. Thus all that Joseph does is fundamentally myth-parody—which need not as such imply any impious intention. While Nietzsche clearly saw the danger of barrenness and deathly rigidity despite outwardly extreme mobility and colorfulness, T. M.'s Joseph interprets the ironical game he plays as a particular kind of prudence before God and a higher form of obedience. Here we detect that vestige of the eighteenth century, of the enlightenment's reckless optimism, which is discernible throughout T. M.'s work, despite the fact that he is also one of the most successful portrayers of decadence. . . . But where is the deep wellspring of the past, of which the prologue to the Joseph tetralogy speaks so evocatively? Closer examination shows that it has evaporated into the typical, which is timeless, and its evocation remains clever, ironical shifting of theater sets. As the myth has dwindled to a mythological schema, so the historical threatens to dwindle to a schematic repetition of outworn models. Life is reduced to the imitation and parody of lived life.

Allemann, B., Ironie und Dichtung
(1956), p. 151 f., p. 167

Nietzsche's significance lies in his having clearly demonstrated the problem of nihilism in his time, M.'s in the proof that even the nihilist, the man who realizes the senselessness of a life bound to suffering, need not despair, for precisely in the spirit, which Nietzsche reveres so highly and brought so low, M. sees a means of transcending the painfullness of all being. He who can meet life ironically, smiling, without bitterness, overcomes nihilism and shares in the miracle of free and easy unconcern regained.

Wolff, H. M., T. M. (1957), p. 142 f.

Joseph, like The Magic Mountain before it, is a novel of education. . . .
The Magic Mountain, too, teaches nothing but living. To teach living is the purpose of literature, theology, and medicine. From one book to the next, a man endowed with imagination must soberly study all three of these, and a few other disciplines besides, in order to be able to "invent". . . .
A man educates himself as he writes, encompassing

more of life in each book, attaining, by way of knowledge that expands each time, the wisdom that is his goal. What has that to do with Germany?
. . . He had believed Germany to be morally secure. This explains [his] implacable anger.

Mann, H., Ein Zeitalter wird besichtigt
(1947), p. 214 f.

A German work: by virtue of the hallucinatory method put to the service of fact, by virtue of the quest for magical wisdom, whose whispered or half-heard secrets float between the lines, destined, it seems, to remain deliberately as inconspicuous as possible, by virtue of the presence of those great entities that haunt Germanic meditation—the Earth Spirit, the Mothers, and Death, a death more active, more virulent than elsewhere, mysteriously fused with life itself and sometimes endowed with the attributes of love. Finally, this work is German by virtue of its solid symphonic structure, of the contrapuntal character of its parts elaborated over more than half a century. But in this Germanic dough, as in Germany itself, foreign yeasts have been at work. It is to the Greece of the Mysteries that the heroes of Death in Venice and The Magic Mountain owe their supreme revelation. Jewish and Talmudic—even more than biblical—thought impregnate the learned circumlocutions of Joseph— and this in a period when the German state was decreeing the destruction of Israel. In The Magic Mountain a fatidic Asia stammers through the lips of Mynheer Peppercorn.
In the work of T. M. these last books occupy a position more or less comparable to that of A Winter's Tale or Cymbeline in Shakespeare's. The notions of pessimism and optimism have been definitely left behind. The world of fixed forms and the world of moving forms, order and disorder, life-in-death and death-in-life, have become various aspects of a mysterium magnum in which the old alchemist will from now on be quite at home. The notion of the game gradually replaces the notion of danger.

Yourcenar, M., "Humanisme de T. M.," in
Hommage de la France à T. M. (1955), p. 23 ff.

MANSFIELD, Katherine

(pseud. of Kathleen Beauchamp-Murry), English short story writer, b. 14 Oct. 1888, Wellington, New Zealand; d. 9 Jan. 1923, Fontainebleau, France

M. was the daughter of Harold Beauchamp, an English banker who lived in New Zealand. She spent her childhood in Karori, near Wellington, and in 1903 went to London to study music at Queen's College. She also wrote her first poems at this time, having published her first short story at the age of nine. In 1906 she returned to New Zealand, but she could not readjust to her former country and two years later went back to Europe. In 1909 she married the musician George Bowden. In 1911 she met the writer John Middleton Murry (1889-1957), whom she married seven years later. Years of restless existence followed; M. had suffered from tuberculosis since 1917 and lived alternately in England and on the continent. Among her friends were D. H. Lawrence, and Huxley (qq.v.). In the last year of her life she joined the communal group and brotherhood founded by the Russian philosopher Gurdjieff at Le Prieure, near Fontainebleau.

M.'s fame rests on her novellas and short stories in which she "re-created her country, though this country was not New Zealand but a timeless country of innocence and purity" (J. M. Murry).

Most of her stories grow out of personal recollections. "Her imagination was the freely running imagination of childhood and dreams, which disregards limits; it was made even more vivid by an exceptional talent for observation. She looked upon every happening with the devoted concern of one who wants to grasp the essence of things" (F. Braun). Her principal literary model was Chekhov (q.v.). Maurois (q.v.) called her work "genuinely feminine impressionism."

M. had, as she once said herself, "four loves: nature, people, secrets, and a fourth that nobody is allowed to mention." She succeeded in combining the realistic with the soulful, the cruel (and sometimes the cynical) with the nostalgic, the demonic with the tender.

She also reviewed many books for the magazines *Rhythm, The Blue Review, The New Age,* and *Athenaeum.*

FURTHER WORKS: *In a German Pension* (1911); *Prelude* (1918); *Je Ne Parle Pas Français* (1918); *Bliss* (1920); *The Garden Party* (1922); *The Dove's Nest* (1923); *Poems* (1923); *Something Childish* (1924; Am., The Little Girl, 1924); *Journal of Katherine Mansfield,* ed. J. Middleton Murray (1927; enlarged 1954); *The Letters of Katherine Mansfield,* ed. J. Middleton Murry (1928); *The Aloe* (1930); *Novels and Novelists,* ed. J. Middleton Murry (1930); *Stories: A Selection,* ed. J. Middleton Murry (1930); *The Scrapbook of Katherine Mansfield,* ed. J. Middleton Murry (1938); *Collected Stories* (1945); *Letters to J. Middleton Murry, 1913-22,* ed. J. Middleton Murry (1951)

BIBLIOGRAPHY: Mantz, R. E., *The Critical Bibliography of K. M.* (1931); Mantz, R. E., and Murry, J. M., *The Life of K. M.* (1933); Carco, F., *Souvenirs sur K. M.* (1934); Friis, A., *Life and Stories of K. M.* (1946); Berkmann, S., *K. M.* (1951); Alpers, A. *K. M.* (1954); Murry, J. M., *K. M. and Other Literary Studies* (1959); Kleine, D. W., "Method and Meaning in the Stories of K. M.," in *DA,* XXII (1962), 2397; Hagopian, J. T., "Capturing M's 'Fly,'" in *MFS,* IX (1964), 385-90; Kominaes, S. B., "K. M.: The Way to Fontainebleau," in *DA,* XXVII (1966), 1370; Yen, Y., "K. M.'s Use of Point of View," in *DA,* XXVIII (1967), 647a-648a

PAUL WIMMER

MARAGALL I GORINA, Joan

Spanish poet (Catalan language), b. 10 Oct. 1860, Barcelona; d. there, 20 Dec. 1911

Defying the tradition of his industrialist family, M. devoted himself entirely to literature and journalism. He was a supporter of the Catalan nationalist party but declined all offers of political office and lived a withdrawn life in the country. He was in touch with the "Generation of '98", especially with Unamuno (q.v.). Although M. wrote many of his articles in Spanish, he belongs primarily to Catalan literature (q.v.), for his works represent the point of departure of modern Catalan poetry. He also translated Goethe and other writers into Catalan.

His poetry is concerned with direct reality. The *Poesies* (1895) are love poems, while the poem "Cant espiritual" is a hymn to nature in its earthly form. This serenely tranquil poetry is also profoundly Christian in content. *Visions i cants* (1900) recounts Catalan legends.

FURTHER WORKS: *Les disperses* (1904); *Enllà* (1906); *Nausica* (1910); *Visions y seqüències* (1911); *Obres completas,* 25 v. (1929-1955)

BIBLIOGRAPHY: Reig, C., *El mundo poético de M.* (1944); D'Ors, E., *Estilos del pensar...J. M.* (1945); Fuster, J., "Frente a frente: Unamuno, M.," in *Indice,* XVII (1964), No. 192, pp. 22-24

ALONSO ZAMORA VICENTE

MARCEL, Gabriel

French dramatist, critic, and philosopher, b. 7 Dec. 1889, Paris

M. has long been considered the leading exponent of "Christian existentialism," although he deplores the label and calls himself "neo-Socratic," i.e., Christian-Socratic. After the Lycée Carnot he attended the Sorbonne and obtained his *agrégation de philosophie* in 1910. Professor at the lycées of Vendôme, Condorcet, and Sens, he left teaching in 1923 (except for a brief return during World War II as substitute teacher) and became reader for two publishers, Grasset and Plon. In 1926 he created for Plon the collection "Feux Croisés" devoted to foreign authors. He became drama critic for *L'Europe Nouvelle* and contributed many articles to the *Nouvelle Revue française*. Since World War II he has been drama critic of *Nouvelles Littéraires*. He received the Grand Prix de Littérature de l'Académie Française in 1949. The following year he presented himself unsuccessfully to the Academy, but in 1952 he was elected a member of the Académie des Sciences Morales et Politiques. The University of Hamburg awarded him the Goethe Hanseatic Prize in 1956, and two years later he obtained the Grand Prix National des Lettres. He is an officer of the Legion of Honor and Commander of the Ordre des Arts et Lettres.

After a childhood largely influenced by an agnostic father and a very liberal aunt, he met Charles Du Bos (1882-1939) and Mauriac (q.v.) and in 1929 converted to Catholicism. Prior to this conversion M. had become interested in the writings of Jaspers (q.v.), and it is M. who as early as 1925 introduced Kierkegaard (q.v.) and the term "existential" to France.

The existentialism of M., like that of Sartre (q.v.), demands a positive act; but unlike Sartre, M. maintains that this "engagement" is basically a matter of religious choice which must strive to find God. According to M., the modern age, which he calls a "technocracy" in *Le Déclin de la sagesse* (1954; The Decline of Wisdom, 1954), has imposed upon us a responsibility which we may not shed, but against which we must fight with spiritual weapons. In this technocratic world M. pictures the philosopher as the guide who will lead humanity back to saner values and a stronger faith by which it can live. In the analysis of the individual M. stresses the body—not in the abstract, but the Christian *flesh*—as the root of all human shortcomings, desires, and sins. However, one should not think of this as a pessimistic philosophy, for man, above all, must strive to be, not to have. To do this he must wrench himself free from the possessiveness of our technocratic age and open his heart to love.

Most of the philosophic writings of M. are either collections of talks and articles or rambling "journal" type jottings. As a result they have not enjoyed great literary success. The drama of M. is merely another expression of the philosopher. Except for *Rome n'est plus dans Rome* (1951), whose timeliness gave it a slight measure of success, the theater of M. has not been able to captivate French audiences. This drama, which its author calls a theater of the soul in exile, shows the tragedy of all forms of alienation. In spite of the denials of the author, his entire dramatic production is very much *à thèse*. The main theme seems to be the sterility of passions and the efforts of man to free himself from them.

M. has always felt the need to bring his philosophy to the public, and so it is not surprising that the dramatic production parallels the philosophic output. *Le Seuil invisible* (1914) and *Trois pièces* (Le regard neuf, Le Mort de demain, La Chapelle ardente) (1931), two collections of plays written as early as 1911, illustrate the awakening of the author of *Journal métaphysique* (1927; Metaphysical Journal, 1952). *Le Fanal* (1936), *Le Chemin de Crête* (1936), and *Le Dard* (1936) show up the fundamentally ambiguous position of man as seen in *Être et avoir* (1935; Being and Having, 1949). *La Dimension Florestan* (1952), *Mon Temps n'est pas le vôtre* (1953), and *Croissez et multipliez* (1955) show an old man at odds with the times. At all times, however, M. accentuates the transcendence of the individual over everything else. The plays are deep, intellectual, and difficult, but unfortunately undramatic. In them M. presents the problems that have concerned him all his life and to which he has yet to find solutions.

FURTHER WORKS: *La Grâce* (1911); *Le Palais du sable* (1913); *Le Coeur des autres* (1921); *L'Iconoclaste* (1923); *La Chapelle ardente* (1925); *Un Homme de Dieu* (1925; A Man of God, 1952); *Le Quatuor en fa dièse* (1925); *Le Monde cassé* (1933); *Position et approches concrètes du mystère ontologique* (1933); *La Soif* (1938); *Du Refus à l'invocation* (1940); *L'Horizon* (1945); *La Métaphysique de Royce* (1945; Royce's Metaphysics, 1956);

Homo viator (1945; Eng., 1951); *Théâtre comique* (1947); *Vers un autre royaume* (1949); *La Fin des temps* (1950); *Le Mystère de l'être* (1951; Mystery of Being, 1950-51); *Les Hommes contre l'humain* (1951: Man Against Mass Society, 1952); *Théâtre et religion* (1959); *L'Heure théâtrale de Giraudoux à Jean-Paul Sartre* (1959); *Fragments philosophiques, 1909-1914* (1962)

BIBLIOGRAPHY: Chénu, J., *Le Théâtre de G. M. et sa signification métaphysique* (1948); Troisfontaines, R., *De L'Existence à l'être: La Philosophie de G. M.* (1953); Sottiaux, E., *G. M.* (1956); Dary, M., *G. M.* (1959); Cain, S., *G. M.* (1963); Miceli, V. P., "M.: The Drama of Transcendence," in *Thought,* XL (1965), 193-224; Cooper, N. R., "A Study of the Poetry of G. M.," in *DA,* XXVI (1966), 7313; Hughes, H. S., "M., Maritain and the Secular World," in *American Scholar,* XXXV (1966), 728-49

CLAUDE K. ABRAHAM

MAROTTA, Giuseppe

Italian novelist and short story writer, b. 5 April 1902, Naples; d. 10 Oct. 1963, Naples.

M. is one of those Italian narrative writers whose humanity makes them internationally understood, even though they write mainly about their own native provinces. After a successful debut with *Divorziamo, per piacere?* (1934), followed by *Questa volta mi sposo* (1940), and *Nulla sul serio* (1946), he found his own style in *L'oro di Napoli* (1947; Return to Naples, 1951). Out of a mosaic of scenes and anecdotes narrated in very realistic language, which leans toward the grotesque, emerges a picture of the city of Naples and its social problems and of the way its inhabitants face their lot with a brilliant mixture of cunning, good nature, and "animal spirits." Of his later fiction the short stories *San Gennaro non dice mai no* (1948; San Gennaro Never Says No, 1950) and *A Milano non fa freddo* and the novels *Mezzo miliardo* (1951) and *Le madri* (1952) deserve mention.

FURTHER WORKS: *Pietre e nuvole* (1950); *Gli alumni del sole* (1952); *Corraggio, guardiamo* (1954); *Salute a noi* (1955); *Questo buffo cinema* (1956); *Marotta ciak* (1958); *Il vento in Gabbia* (1961); *Visti e perduti* (1961); *Di riffe o di raffi, Articoli di cinema, 1962-1963* (1965)

BIBLIOGRAPHY: Bruno, F., "Profilo di G. M.," *Baretti,* IV (1963), 42-48; Colombo, A., "G. M., ironia e pietá di un patetico scrittore," *Letture,* XIX (1964), 243-256; Vigo, D., "Rapporto fra espressione e ispirazione in G. M.," *Vita e Pensiero,* XLIX (1966), 328-339

HORST RÜDIGER

MARQUAND, John Phillips

American novelist, b. 10 Nov. 1893, Wilmington, Del.; d. 16 July 1960, Newbury, Mass.

After graduating from Harvard University in 1915, M. worked briefly on *The Boston Transcript* before becoming a first lieutenant of artillery in World War I. After the war he returned to journalism and began to write fiction. His "Mr. Moto" adventure stories in *The Saturday Evening Post* made him famous as a master of popular writing; his reputation as a serious novelist of American manners was established with *The Late George Apley* (1937), which won a Pulitzer Prize in 1938.

M. wrote novels of social comedy in the tradition of Jane Austen (1775-1817), William Makepeace Thackeray (1811-63), Anthony Trollope (1815-82), William Dean Howells (1837-1920), and Edith Wharton (q.v.). His subject is the behavior of the middle and upper-middle classes in America, and his point of view is both ironic and sympathetic. As a social historian he was greatly concerned with time and change: his favorite narrative technique was the flashback, setting his protagonist in the double context of past and present.

The Late George Apley initiated a series of novels which make up an American *comédie humaine.* Like *Wickford Point* (1939) and *H. M. Pulham, Esq.* (1941), it is a gently satirical study of the pressures exerted by tradition and caste in upper-class Boston society. *So Little Time* (1943) sets a middle-aged playwright's sense of the passage of time against the background of New York and Hollywood on the brink of World War II. *Point of No Return* (1949), the story of a young banker's uncertain search for success, is a penetrating treatment of the competitive motive in American life. *Melville Goodman, U.S.A.* (1951) treats the special world of the middle and high army brass, and *Sincerely, Willis Wade* (1955) looks at the smug, self-made American industrialist.

FURTHER WORKS: *Prince and Boatswain* (1915); *The Unspeakable Gentleman* (1922);

Four of a Kind (1923); *Lord Timothy Dexter of Newburyport, Massachusetts* (1925); *Black Cargo* (1925); *Warning Hill* (1930); *Haven's End* (1933); *No Hero* (1935); *Ming Yellow* (1935); *Think Fast, Mr. Moto* (1937); *Mr. Moto Is So Sorry* (1938); *Last Laugh, Mr. Moto* (1942); *Repent in Haste* (1945); *B. F.'s Daughter* (1946); *Thirty Years* (1954); *Life at Happy Knoll* (1957); *Stopover: Tokyo* (1957); *Women and Thomas Harrow* (1958); *Timothy Dexter Revisited* (1960)

BIBLIOGRAPHY: Brady, C. A., "J. P. M.," in Gardner, H. C., ed., *Fifty Years of the American Novel, 1900-1950* (1952); Kazin, A., "J. P. M. and the American Failure," in *The Atlantic* (Nov. 1958); Holman, C. H., *J. P. M.* (1965)

DONALD EMERSON

MARQUINA, Eduardo

Spanish dramatist, poet, and narrative writer, b. 21 Jan. 1879, Barcelona; d. 21 Nov. 1946, New York

M.'s family came from Aragon. He ranks among the foremost exponents of poetic drama, which he, like the brothers Machado y Ruiz (qq.v.), tried to revitalize. His work is inspired by love of imperial Spain and the "golden age." M.'s plays usually deal with epic subjects; *Las hijas del Cid* (1908), for instance, is an adaptation of the ancient story of the Cid. *El pavo real* (1922) and *Era una vez in Bagdad* (1932) show a modernistically elaborate treatment of background. In the "cloak and dagger" play Don Luis Mejía (1925), written in collaboration with Alfonso Hernández Catá (1885-1940), M. attempts the Don Juan theme. *La ermita, la fuente y el río* (1925) is a highly poetic comedy, *Cuando florezcan los rosales* (1910) a sentimental one.

FURTHER WORKS: *Odas* (1900); *Las vendimias* (1901); *Elegías* (1905); *La caravana* (1907); *Almas anónimas* (1908); *Doña Maria la Brava* (1909); *En Flandes se ha puesto el sol* (1909); *Vendimión* (1909); *Canciones del momento* (1910); *Las flores de Aragon* (1914); *Tierras de España* (1914); *El gran capitán* (1916); *Maternidad* (1917); *Don Luis Mejía* (1925); *El camino de la felicidad* (1929); *Fuente escondida* (1931); *Santa Teresa de Jesús* (1932); *El estudiante endiablado* (1942)

BIBLIOGRAPHY: Snyder, I., "A Twentieth

Century Adaptation of Lope's 'La Dorotea,'" *Hispania*, XLII (1959), 320-29; Fernández-Santos, A., "En Flandes se ha puesto el sol," *Indice*, XV (1961), 23; Montero Alonso, J., *Vida de E. M.* (1965)

ALONSO ZAMORA VICENTE

MARSMAN, Hendrik

Dutch poet, essayist, and narrative writer, b. 30 Sept. 1899, Zeist; d. 21 June 1940, en route from France to England

In the 1920's M. was regarded as the exponent of the ecstatic life, of "vitalism," expressed in poetic critiques and dazzlingly shrill poems (*Verzen*, 1923). Nevertheless his work also showed negative impulses: hatred and fear of death. Death is the central problem of his poetry, from the despair of *Paradise Regained* (1927) and *Porta nigra* (1934) to the acceptance of his late poems. The expressionism (q.v.) of *Verzen* survives to some extent in his later work, though here it is countered by a southern, Mediterranean spirit which introduces clarity and objectivity. The strongly autobiographical poem *Tempel en kruis* (1940), his formal masterwork, is a proclamation of southern paganism, implying a rejection of the Christian tradition and its concept of sin. M. was strongly influenced by Nietzsche (q.v.).

FURTHER WORKS: *Penthesilena* (1925); *De anatomische les* (1926); *De vliegende Hollander* (1927); *De lamp van Diogenes* (1928); *De vijf vingers* (1929); *Witte vrouwen* (1930); *Voorpost* (1931); *Kort geding* (1931); *De dood van Angèle Degroux* (1933); *Heden ik, morgen gij* (with S. Vestdijk; 1936); *H. Gorter* (1937); *Verzameld werk* (4 vols., 1938-47); *Menno ter Braak* (1939); *Verzamelde gedichten* (1941)

BIBLIOGRAPHY: Van der Ree, A. P., *Interpretatie van M...* (1956); Lehning, A., *M.* (1959); Verbeeck, R., *De dichter H. M.* (1959); Brandt Corstius, J. C., "Tekst en context van M.'s *De Zee*," *Forum der Letteren* (1961), pp. 126-37; Schulte Nordholt, J. W., "M. en Achterberg i een Jeugdherinnering," *Maatstaf*, XI (1964), 714-719

KAREL REIJNDERS

MARTIN DU GARD, Roger

French novelist and playwright, b. 23 March 1881, Neuilly-sur-Seine; d. 23 Aug. 1958, Bellême, Orne

M. studied archaeology but later turned to literature. His novels constitute a social history of the times. *Jean Barois* (1913) dealt with the Dreyfus Affair and with the relationship between religion and science. Like his first book, *Devenir!* (1909), his masterwork, the eight-part novel *Les Thibault* (1922-40; The World of the Thibauts, 1939-41), exemplified his theory of human development through the gradual decline of a family. Antoine and Jacques Thibault come of a very devout family, but both lose their faith as their inner estrangement from the bourgeois world becomes complete. Jacques joins the revolutionary movement—there is a description of socialism's failure in the great crisis of Summer 1914—and sacrifices himself in the cause of pacifism. Antoine, gassed during the war, slowly wastes away, fully conscious that he is rapidly approaching death. Yet, in spite of everything, Antoine's notebooks, intended for the next generation, hold out hope of human progress.

M.'s work influenced many younger writers, including Camus, Curtis, and Gary (qq.v.). He himself has acknowledged how much he owes to Tolstoi (q.v.). Although he was no great supporter of naturalism (q.v.), his fundamental ideas, especially his pessimistic *Weltanschauung* sometimes coincide with Émile Zola's (q.v.). Despite his inner sympathy for his characters, M., the narrator, often seems indifferent and cold, so that his novels occasionally have the objective tone of a historical record. Artistically M. was one of the most fastidious French writers since Flaubert (1821-80). He destroyed two completely finished works ("L'Une de nous," 1910; "L'Appareillage," 1913) because they did not meet his standards. In 1937 he received the Nobel Prize for Literature.

FURTHER WORKS: *Le Cahier gris* (1922); *Le pénitencier* (1922); *La Belle saison* (1923); *La Consultation* (1928); *La Sorellina* (1928); *La Mort du père* (1929); *Été 1914* (1936; Summer 1914, 1941); *Épilogue* (1940); *Le Testament du père Leleu* (1923; Papa Leleu's Will, 1921); *La Gonfle* (1928); *La Confidence africaine* (1930); *Un Taciturne* (1931); *Vieille France* (1933; The Postman, 1954); *Notes sur A. Gide* (1951; Recollections of André Gide, 1953)

BIBLIOGRAPHY: Lalou, R., *R. M.* (1937); Borgal, C., *R. M.* (1957); Daix, P., *Réflexions sur la méthode de R. M.* (1957); Brenner, J., *R. M. du G.* (1961); Gibson, R., *R. M.* (1961);

Robidoux, R., *R. M. et la réligion* (1964); Schalk, D. L., *R. M.: The Novelist and History* (1967)

KONRAD BIEBER

MARTINSON, Harry Edmund

Swedish novelist, poet, and essayist, b. 6 May 1904, Jämshög, Blekinge

M. had a hard childhood and went to sea at fourteen. A few years after his return he became known through a contribution to the anthology *Fem unga* (1929) notable for its lack of political tendentiousness, modern form, and vital, primitive attitude to life. Four subsequent prose works made up an entity: *Resor utan mål* (1932) and *Kap Farväl* (1933; Cape Farewell, 1934) are travel stories; in *Nässlorna Blomma* (1935) and *Vägen ut* (1936) M. recreates his childhood hardships without the least bitterness and with liberating humor. *Vägen till Klockrike* (1948; The Road, 1955), his most important novel so far, goes on from here; this harks back to his experiences and is pervaded by a romantic nature mysticism for which his earlier "nature studies" *Svärmare och harkrank* (1937), *Midsommardalen* (1938), and *Det enkla och det svåra* (1939) prepared the way.

M.'s prose is naïvely spontaneous and at the same time artistically sophisticated. It is distinguished by visual plasticity, linguistic inventiveness, and an often bizarrely exotic imagination. His later volumes of poems, *Passad* (1945), *Cikada* (1953), *Aniara* (1956; Aniara; A Review of Man in Time and Space, 1963); *Gräsen i Thule* (1958), and *Vagnen* (1960), show increased virtuosity of language; here he combines bold originality with a cosmic attitude and presents the disorientation of modern man in a harmonious form. *Cikada* and *Aniara* especially are rich in unusual symbolism and represent a unique contribution to poetic science fiction.

FURTHER WORKS: *Spökskepp* (1929); *Nomad* (1931); *Natur* (1934); *Wildbuketten* (1935); *Verklighet till döds* (1940); *Den förlorade jaguaren* (1941); *Dikter* (1952); *Lotsen från Moluckas* (1954); *Utsikt från en grastuva* (1963); *Vinden på marken* (1964)

BIBLIOGRAPHY: Kristensen, T., *H. M.* (1941); Oldberg, R., *Den unge H. M.* (1954); Holm, I., *H. M.* (1960); Bergmann, S. A., "H. M. and Science," in *Proceedings of the*

Fifth International Study Conference on Scandinavian Literature (1966), pp. 99-120

JORIS TAELS

MASEFIELD, John

English poet and novelist, b. 1 June 1878, Ledbury, Herefordshire; d. 12 Dec. 1967, Boar's Hill

At thirteen M. became a cadet on the *Conway,* a training sailing ship. After adventurous years on the high seas and in America he returned to England in 1897, sure of his literary vocation. In 1902 he scored a notable success with *Salt Water Ballads,* a volume of poems modeled on Kipling (q.v.). This, like M.'s later works, is inspired by his familiarity with all the romance and all the brutality of seafaring life. The vigorous swing of "Sea Fever," "Cargoes," and others of the most successful poems from this collection and from the subsequent widely ranging *Ballads and Poems* (1910) won them lasting popularity. M.'s rich inventiveness and his dexterity with language and rhythm led him to write somewhat too easily and spontaneously, so that his work lacks rigor of form and depth of content.

M. made his most decisive impact on contemporary English life with *The Everlasting Mercy* (1911), the first of his many stories in verse. In forceful language, in the form of rhymed couplets, an itinerant preacher tells of his conversion, while the specifically Christian element required by the theme soon dissolves into an ethically heightened nature-pantheism and ecstaticism typical of M. Here as elsewhere in his best work M. shows himself to be an important representative of naturalism (q.v.). However, his innate optimism and English gentleman's equanimity soon recover from the assaults of berserk naturalism. The powerful impact of *The Everlasting Mercy* was not entirely the result of its poetic worth; to some extent it came from the belief that here M. had finally vanquished romantic, Victorian linguistic usage and rhythm and had thus enabled other poets, too, to break through into a world of truly modern poetic style. It turned out, however, to be no more than a personal breakthrough within established tradition and to be incapable of further development. When English poetry actually did acquire a new basis during the following decade, chiefly through the experiments of Eliot (q.v.), it became clear that M. belonged to the old guard rather than

the avant-garde. This was confirmed when he was made Poet Laureate in 1930.

That M. was never a wholehearted naturalist is clear from the slight case of Pre-Raphaelite worship of beauty that he developed at an early stage. It was quite in keeping that he should have been a friend of Synge and Yeats (qq.v.) and should have allowed them to influence his poetry and plays, which have a strong tendency to vagueness.

M. set forth his confession of faith in the long poem-cycle *Lollingdon Downs* (1917). Never has the world of ideas of Goethe's time, with the modifications it underwent up to 1914, been so unproblematically summarized and popularized as in this pleasant poetry spiced now and again with naturalistic forcefulness. Thanks largely to the magical term "beauty," an optimistic emotional mysticism goes comfortably hand in hand with the positivistic world view of natural science.

FURTHER WORKS: *Ballads* (1903; rev., 1910); *A Mainsail Haul* (1905; rev., 1913, 1954); *Sea Life in Nelson's Time* (1905); *On the Spanish Main* (1906); *A Tarpaulin Muster* (1907); *Captain Margaret* (1908); *Multitude and Solitude* (1909); *The Tragedy of Nan* (1909); *The Tragedy of Pompey the Great* (1910); *Martin Hyde: the Duke's Messenger* (1910); *A Book of Discoveries* (1910); *Lost Endeavour* (1910); *William Shakespeare* (1911; rev., 1954); *The Street of Today* (1911); *Jim Davis* (1911); *The Story of a Roadhouse* (1912); *The Widow in the Bye Street* (1912; Am., *The Everlasting Mercy and The Widow in the Bye Street,* 1912); *Dauber* (1913); *The Daffodil Fields* (1913); *Philip the King* (1914); *The Faithful: a Tragedy in Three Acts* (1915); *The Locked Chest; The Sweeps of Ninety-Eight* (1916); *John M. Synge* (1915); *Sonnets and Poems* (1916); *Good Friday* (1916); *Poems* (1917); *A Poem and Two Plays* (1918); *Collected Poems and Plays* (1919); *Reynard the Fox, or The Ghost Heath Run* (1919); *Enslaved* (1920); *Right Royal* (1920); *King Cole* (1921); *Jean Racine's Berenice* (1922; Am., *Esther and Berenice,* 1922); *Melloney Hotspur* (1922); *Selected Poems* (1922); *Leather Pocket Edition of Masefield's Work* (8 vols., 1922); *The Dream* (1922); *A King's Daughter: A Tragedy in Verse* (1923); *The Taking of Helen* (1923); *Collected Poems* (1923; rev., 1932, 1938, 1946); *Recent Prose* (1924; rev., 1932); *Sard Harker* (1924); *Shakespeare and Spiritual Life* (1924); *The Trial of Jesus* (1925); *Collected*

Works (4 vols., 1925); *Odtaa* (1926); *Tristan and Isolt* (1927); *The Midnight Folk* (1927); *The Coming of Christ* (1928); *Midsummer Night* (1928); *Poems* (1929); *The Hawbucks* (1929); *Easter* (1929); *The Wanderer of Liverpool* (1930); *Chaucer* (1931); *Minnie Maylow's Story* (1931); *A Tale of Troy* (1932); *The Conway from Her Foundation to the Present Day* (1933); *End and Beginning* (1933); *The Bird of Dawning* (1933); *The Taking of the Gry* (1934); *The Box of Delights* (1935); *Victorious Troy, or The Hurrying Angel* (1935); *The Collected Works* (5 vols., 1935); *Eggs and Baker* (1936); *A Letter from Pontus* (1936); *The Square Peg, or The Gun Fella* (1937); *The Country Scene* (1937); *Dead Ned* (with Edward Seago, 1938); *Tribute to Ballet* (1938); *Live and Kicking Ned* (1939); *Basilissa: A Tale of The Empress Theodora* (1940); *Some Memories of W. B. Yeats* (1940); *Gautama, the Enlightened* (1941); *In the Mill* (1941); *Conquer: A Tale of the Nika Rebellion in Byzantium* (1941); *A Generation Risen* (1942); *Land Workers* (1942); *Wanderings Between One and Six Years* (1943); *New Chum* (1944); *A Macbeth Production* (1945); *Thanks Before Going* (1946); *A Book of Both Sorts* (1947); *Badon Parchments* (1947); *A Play of St. George* (1948); *On the Hill* (1949); *In Praise of Nurses* (1950); *St. Katherine of Ledbury and Other Ledbury Papers* (1951); *So Long to Learn* (1952); *Poems: Complete Edition* (1953); *The Bluebells* (1961); *Old Raiger* (1964); *Grace before Ploughing* (1966)

BIBLIOGRAPHY: Thomas, G. O., *M.* (1932); Strong, L. A. G., *J. M.* (1952); Spark, M., *J. M.* (1953); Handley-Taylor, G., ed., *J. M. . . . Bibliography* (1960); Graves, R., "Robert Graves on J. M.," *TLS*, 22 June 1967, p. 568

EUDO C. MASON

MASTERS, Edgar Lee

American poet, dramatist, and prose writer, b. 23 Aug. 1868, Garnett, Kan.; d. 5 March 1950, Philadelphia

Born in Kansas, M. lived almost all his first fifty-five years in Illinois, home of his father and paternal grandparents. His boyhood was spent mainly in Petersburg and Lewistown, and his young manhood in Chicago, where he was a successful lawyer as a partner of Clarence Darrow and later in independent practice. From 1923 until his death his main city of residence was New York.

M. is known principally for his *Spoon River Anthology* (1915), some of the poems in which were first published in 1914 in William Marion Reedy's St. Louis *Mirror*. The book was an extraordinarily influential and popular volume of short poems, largely in free verse, each supposedly spoken by an inhabitant of the Spoon River (Illinois) cemetery. Often the speakers tell in death what they might not or could not have told in life; the result is a candid picture of small-town life, a forerunner of such books as *Winesburg, Ohio* by S. Anderson (q.v.). At the time of publication, reviewers argued over whether the epitaphs, most of them in free verse, were poetry. Today most critics recognize that many of them are stripped, evocative poetry of much merit.

M. also wrote political and literary essays, plays, volumes of narrative, dramatic, and lyric poetry, novels, biography, autobiography, and history. Consistently present as motifs in his books are a political Jeffersonianism, agrarianism, idealization of his Illinois grandparents and father, love of Illinois but viewed critically, curiosity about all experience, extreme freedom toward sex. Particularly notable among his prose works are his extraordinarily frank autobiography, *Across Spoon River* (1936), his biography *Lincoln: The Man* (1931), an iconoclastic study of the mind and nature of Lincoln, and his sympathetic biography *Vachel Lindsay* (1935). Especially notable among the other volumes of verse are *Domesday Book* (1920) and *The New Spoon River* (1924).

Before 1915 M. published four volumes of conventional and imitative poetry, seven undistinguished plays, and a book of essays. Between 1915 and 1950 he published, in addition to seven novels and eight books of autobiography, biography, and history, twenty-four books of poetry. Fourteen are collections of miscellaneous verse; four are book-length narratives; six are volumes of dramatic poems. Among the thousands of lines of conventional verse in these volumes are many lines deserving to be called poetry. Although the wrote much that was inferior to the best of which he was capable, and although he is largely known for *Spoon River Anthology*, M. was an extraordinarily prolific and versatile writer.

FURTHER WORKS: *A Book of Verses* (1898); *Maximilian, A Play in Five Acts* (1902); *The New Star Chamber and Other Essays* (1904); *The Blood of the Prophets*

(1905); *Althea, A Play in Four Acts* (1907); *The Trifler, A Play* (1908); *The Leaves of the Tree, A Play* (1909); *Eileen, A Play in Three Acts* (1910); *The Locket, A Play in Three Acts* (1910); *Songs & Sonnets* (1910); *The Bread of Idleness, A Play in Four Acts* (1911); *Songs & Sonnets, Second Series* (1912); *The Great Valley* (1916); *Songs and Satires* (1916); *Toward the Gulf* (1918); *Starved Rock* (1919); *Mitch Miller* (1920); *The Open Sea* (1921); *Children of the Market Place* (1922); *Skeeters Kirby* (1923); *The Nuptial Flight* (1923); *Mirage* (1924); *Selected Poems* (1925); *Lee, A Dramatic Poem* (1926); *Kit O'Brien* (1927); *Levy Mayer and the New Industrial Era* (1927); *Jack Kelso, A Dramatic Poem* (1928); *The Fate of the Jury, An Epilogue to Domesday Book* (1929); *Gettysburg, Manila, Acoma* (1930); *Lichee Nuts* (1930); *Godbey, A Dramatic Poem* (1931); *The Serpent in the Wilderness* (1933); *The Tale of Chicago* (1933); *Dramatic Duologues, Four Short Plays in Verse* (1934); *Richmond, A Dramatic Poem* (1934); *Invisible Landscapes* (1935); *The Golden Fleece of California* (1936); *Poems of People* (1936); *The New World* (1937); *The Tide of Time* (1937); *Whitman* (1937); *Mark Twain, A Portrait* (1938); *More People* (1939); *Illinois Poems* (1941); *Along the Illinois* (1942); *The Sangamon* (1942)

BIBLIOGRAPHY: Flaccus, K., *E. L. M.: A Biographical and Critical Study* (1955); Hartley, L., "E. L. M., Biographer and Historian," *Journal of the Illinois State Historical Society*, LIV (Spring 1961), 56-83; Hartley, L., *Spoon River Revisited*, Ball State Monograph No. 1 (1963); Hartley, L., "The Early Plays of E. L. M.," *Ball State University Forum*, VII (1966), ii, 26-38

LOIS HARTLEY

MATOŠ, Antun Gustav

Croatian poet, critic, and fiction writer, b. 13 June 1873, Tovarnik; d. 17 March 1914, Zagreb

M. studied in Vienna, lived for several years in Geneva and Paris, and became a teacher in Zagreb. He began to publish novellas in 1892. His first works, which conform to the earlier realistic tradition in form, treat specifically Croatian themes and criticize the *bourgeoisie* and political conditions during the Khuen period (*Iverje*, 1899). Later, under the influence of Poe and E. T. A. Hoffmann, he presented

bizarre, terror- and horror-stricken characters in tragicomic situations (*Novo iverje*, 1900; *Umorne priče*, 1909).

M. introduced in Croatia impressionistic literary criticism concentrating on formal analysis (*Ogledi, Priče i impresije*, 1905; *Vidici i putovi*, 1907; *Pečalba*, 1913). As an excellent essayist no less than as a poet (*Pjesme*, 1923) he had an important influence on the development of Croatian and Serbian literature.

FURTHER WORKS: *Naši ljudi i krajevi* (1910); *Sabrana djela* (14 vols., 1954 ff.)

BIBLIOGRAPHY: Gesemann, B., *Die serbokroatische Literatur* (1930); Čolak, T., ed., *A. G. M.* (1965)

EMIL ŠTAMPAR

MAUGHAM, William Somerset
English writer, b. 25 Jan. 1874, Paris; d. 16 Dec. 1965, Antibes, France

M. was educated in France, England and Germany; and since 1929 he made his home at Cap Ferrat, French Riviera.

The richest and most popular author throughout the world, prolific but rarely content to exploit a success, M.'s writings are characterized by variety and professional competency. Never considered a major author, he has a loyal following among critics who admire his broad interests, his impeccable style, and his masterful combination of the shocking and humorous, the callous and sentimental.

A young physician, M. began as a naturalist (*see* naturalism) depicting a London slum girl crushed by forces beyond her control (*Liza of Lambeth*, 1897). His next novel, *The Making of a Saint* (1898), a not very successful experiment resumed triumphantly in old age with *Then and Now* (1946) and *Catalina* (1948), described the *risorgimento*. M. was particularly happy in analyzing women, and *Mrs. Craddock* (1902; rev. 1955), the short novel *Rain* (1921; pub. as *Sadie Thompson*, 1928), *The Painted Veil* (1925), and *Theatre* (1937) are outstanding examples of this ability. M.'s greatest novel, a semiautobiographical novel of 250,000 words in which he packed his complete philosophy, the observations of forty years, is undoubtedly *Of Human Bondage* (1915), originally entitled "The Artistic Temperament of Stephen Carey."

Finer but slighter are other novels of the artist: *The Moon and Sixpence* (1919), based on the life of Gauguin; *Cakes and Ale, or the Skeleton in the Cupboard* (1930), a marvelous integration jauntily picturing many aspects of artists' life, not intended as an attack upon Hardy (q.v.) and only incidentally upon Walpole; and *Christmas Holiday* (1939). His constant concern with spiritual values illumines the satirical *Bishop's Apron* (1906; dramatized as *Loaves and Fishes,* 1911); *The Narrow Corner* (1932); *The Razor's Edge* (1944), which has many splendid scenes and characters but a disappointing young American pilgrim hero; *Catalina* (1948); and *The Unknown* (1920), a discussion drama. He even attempted science fiction with *The Magician* (1908).

From 1902 to 1933 M. returned to his first love, the theater, writing thirty-one dramas—three are adapted translations—and a screenplay, "The Verger," in 1950. Beginning with farce and the heavily naturalistic and cynical *A Man of Honour* (1903), by 1908 M. had four plays running at once in London. Of his eight farces, *Home and Beauty* (1919) is a perfect howl, and *Penelope* (1912) and *The Unattainable* (1916) are not far below. High comedy was his forte. Especially *Our Betters* (1917) and *The Circle* (1921), *The Constant Wife* (1926), and the more astringent *The Breadwinner* (1930) will long be landmarks in this difficult form. *The Letter* (1927), *The Sacred Flame* (1928), attempting semipoetic dialogue, and *For Services Rendered* (1932) are first-rate melodramas. Many of M.'s plays are serious examinations of society: *Smith* (1909), *Landed Gentry* (1910), *The Land of Promise* (1914) set in Canada; his most beautiful is *Sheppey* (1933), a modern morality. *Caesar's Wife* (1919), set in Egypt, and the panoramic *East of Suez* (1922), set in China, are romantic.

M. made the world his home and knew Spain and Oceania inside out. His travel books—*The Land of the Blessed Virgin* (1905; pub. as *Andalusia,* 1920), *On a Chinese Screen* (1922), *The Gentleman in the Parlour* (1930), and *Don Fernando, or Variations on Some Spanish Themes* (1935; rev. 1950)—are among his most amusing and attractive.

Often admired (and often denounced) as a writer of short fiction, "the English Maupassant" has published nine volumes of this but left some uncollected. Those set in Oceania, melodramas like "Mackintosh," "Red," "The Pool," "The Outstation," "The Book Bag," "Neil MacAdam," and the fairy tale "Princess September," are the best known; but, like Kipling and Conrad (qq.v.), whom he much resembles, those nearer home, like "Before the Party," "The Round Dozen," "The Alien Corn," "The Three Fat Women of Antibes," "An Official Position," "The Facts of Life," "Winter Cruise," "The Kite," are often better. *Ashenden, or The British Agent* (1928) graphically describes M.'s life as a secret agent during World War I; and *Cosmopolitans* (1936), a book of short-short stories, has gems such as "The Luncheon," "Mr. Know-All," "The Judgment Seat," and "The Bum." "Faith" from the early *Orientations* (1899) should be reprinted.

M. ably discussed the writer's craft and after 1947 was a popular critic. In numerous prefaces to his and others' works, in his delightful autobiographies *The Summing Up* (1938) and *Strictly Personal* (1942), in *Great Novelists and Their Novels* (1948); Eng., Ten Novels and Their Authors; rev. ed. pub. as *The Art of Fiction,* 1955), in *A Writer's Notebook* (1949), in many asides throughout his works, and even in his introductory remarks in his filmed short stories, he stressed compression, clarity, euphony, the importance of regular working hours, of centering on plot and character rather than mood or technical virtuosity, and of transmitting an author's personality through his work, thus obtaining release from troubling memories. The remarkably readable M. liked to chat with his audience about art, religion, philosophy, and life in general. He revived the *First Person Singular* (1931), title of a short-story collection. He sold or gave away his remarkable collection of paintings, and left his millions to aid promising young authors.

FURTHER WORKS: *The Hero* (1901); *Mademoiselle Zampa* (1903); *The Merry-go-round* (1904); *Lady Frederick* (1907); *Jack Straw* (1908); *The Explorer* (1908); *Mrs. Dot* (1908); *The Noble Spaniard* (1909, 1953); *The Tenth Man* (1910); *The Perfect Gentleman* (1913); *Love in a Cottage* (1918); *The Trembling of a Leaf* (1921); *The Camel's Back* (1924); *The Casuarina Tree* (1926); *Dramatic Works* (Vols. I-VI, 1931-34); *The Book Bag* (1932); *The Mask and the Face* (1933); *Ah King* (1933); *Altogether* (1934; Am., East and West, 1934); *Non-Dramatic Works* (1934-51); *The Collected Works* (1936-38); *My South Sea Island* (1936); *The Favourite Short Stories* (1937); *The Round Dozen* (1939); *Princess September and the Nightingale* (1939); *The Mixture as Before* (1940); *France at War* (1940); *Books and You* (1940); *Up at the Villa* (1941); *The Hour Before the Dawn* (1942); *The Unconquered* (1944);

Creatures of Circumstance (1947); *Quartet* (1948); *Trio* (1950); *The Complete Short Stories* (1951); *The Writer's Point of View* (1951); *Encore* (1952); *The Vagrant Mood* (1952); *The Collected Plays* (1952); *The Selected Novels* (1953); *The Partial View* (contains *The Summing Up* and *A Writer's Notebook*, with new preface, 1954); *The Travel Books of W. S. M.* (1955); *Points of View* (1958); *Purely for My Pleasure* (1962); *Looking Back* (1962); *Selected Prefaces and Introductions of S. M.*, ed. George Shively (1964); *The Wit and Wisdom of S. M.*, ed. Cecil Hewetson (1966); *A M. Twelve*, ed. Angus Wilson (1966)

BIBLIOGRAPHY: Aldington, R., *W. S. M.* (1939); Tonas, K. W., *Bibliography of the Writings of W. S. M.* (1950); Brophy, J., *S. M.* (1952); Papajewski, H., *W. S. M.* (1952); Stott, R. T., *The Writings of W. S. M.* (1956); Pfeiffer, K. G., *S. M.* (1959); Maugham, R., *Somerset and All the Maughams* (1966); Kanin, G., *Remembering Mr. M.* (1966); Nichols, B., *A Case of Human Bondage* (1966)

ALLEN B. BROWN

MAURIAC, Claude
French novelist, b. 25 April 1914, Paris

M., son of F. M. (q.v.), wrote volumes of critical essays for twenty years before publishing his first novel, *Toutes les femmes sont fatales* (1957; All Women are Fatal, 1964), a work of otherwise minor importance. With the publication in 1959 of his second novel, *Le Dîner en ville* (Eng., Dinner in Town, 1963; Am., The Dinner Party, 1960), however, M.'s international reputation as one of the leading members of the "new novel" school in France was firmly established. *Le Dîner en ville* and the novel which followed, *La Marquise sortît à cinq heures* (1961; The Marquise Went Out at Five, 1962), are abstract attempts to present to the reader the simultaneity of the perception and the thought processes of the characters, to present the whole of the relationships between the characters and the world they inhabit. Although his novels could certainly not be called complete successes, M. does seem to approach the limit of the power of words to depict people and their environment during a certain time to an uninvolved intellect. His critical works are extremely valuable in any study of what the "new novelists" are trying to do and of why and how their school came into being.

FURTHER WORKS: *Introduction à une mystique de l'enfer* (1938); *La Corporation dans l'état* (1941); *Aimer Balzac* (1945); *Jean Cocteau* (1945); *La Trahison d'un clerc* (1945); *Malraux ou le mal du héros* (1946); *André Breton* (1949); *Conversations avec André Gide* (1951; Conversations with André Gide, 1965); *M. Proust* (1953); *Hommes et idées d'aujourd'hui* (1953); *L'Amour du cinéma* (1954); *Petite littérature du cinéma* (1957); *La Littérature contemporaine* (1958; The New Literature, 1959), *L'Agrandissement* (1963); *La Conversation* (1964)

BIBLIOGRAPHY: Johnston, S. L., "Structure in the Novels of C. M.," in *FR*, XXXVIII (1965), 451-58; Mercier, V., "The Immobilization of Time," in *Nation* (1 Feb. 1965), pp. 119-21

DONALD SANFORD PETREY, JR.

MAURIAC, François
French poet and novelist, b. 11 Oct. 1885, Bordeaux

M., who is best known as a Catholic writer, came from a home divided in religious background. His father, a freethinker, died when M. was not yet two years old. His mother, a devout Catholic influenced by Jansenist thought, gave M. a distinctly pious education. His attendance from the age of five at the Catholic College of Grand-Lebrun, taught by the Marist Fathers, turned him toward introspective self-analysis and scrupulosity. Yet the mature writer has never ceased to acknowledge his grateful recognition of this early tutelage and the preservation from evil it afforded him.

M. likewise is ambivalent in his attitude toward his childhood surroundings. He has always loved Malagar, the family estate bought by his great-grandfather whose formula was "order, work, economy." M.'s novels are filled with the atmosphere of the Landes, the land of marsh and pine near Bordeaux. This fact has led some critics to name M. a regionalist writer. Yet one of M.'s chief themes is his rebellion against the bourgeois farmers, his bitter criticism of their tenaciousness of material goods and their avaricious spirit. In politics he is likewise severe toward middle-class conservatism.

M.'s early literary influences are many. Often they reflect his personal relationship and debt to the writers rather than a detached objective judgment on his part. *Mes Grands Hommes*

W. SOMERSET MAUGHAM

FRANÇOIS MAURIAC

(1950, Men I Hold Great, 1952) has as chapter headings the names of Pascal, Molière, Voltaire, Rousseau, Chateaubriand, Maurice and Eugénie de Guérin, Balzac, Flaubert, Barrès, Gide (q.v.), G. Greene (q.v.), and others. M. has also done studies on Racine, Proust (q.v.), and Lafon. The French names predominating in such a list are indicative of his nationalistic orientation. The variety and number of the types represented suggest the rich complexity of M.'s mind.

Of all these writers, Pascal seems foremost in his influence. A sensitive Christian intellectual, deeply conscious primarily of his direct relationship with a personal God, Pascal is a type attractive to M., whose spiritual ordeal has similar characteristics. Of Bazin, M. writes: "Let us above all admire the way he introduces God into the most human drama." This same constant absorbing consciousness of God's presence and the concomitant anxiety about the conscious conflict between nature and grace are Pascal's heritage to M.

To this must be added M.'s admiration for Proust and for the subtle psychological explorations which mark the latter's work. When critics name M. as the chief French novelist since Proust, they are no doubt allying the two in their poetic style, their reliance on remembrance of things past, and their use of interior monologue (q.v.). Yet Proust's interior world never revolves about a personal God. Further, M. is more surely in the tradition of Bloy and Bernanos (qq.v.) in his passionate awareness of the supernatural, though for M. the drama is more subtle and intimate than apocalyptic and symbolic.

Poetry, which M. claims as characteristic of his work, was the form in which he published first in 1909, when Les Mains jointes appeared. Weak as literature, tentative as first works often are, the volume was yet a determining force in M.'s choice of vocation as a writer.

But the novels, the genre in which he was to achieve fame, came soon after. In 1913 appeared the first, L'Enfant chargé de chaînes (1913; Young Man in Chains, 1963), La Robe prétexte (1914; The Stuff of Youth, 1960), Le Chair et le sang (1920; Flesh and Blood, 1955), Le Fleuve de feu (1923; The River of Fire, 1954). The sentimental tone of the first novel gave way in later books to profound reflection on the struggle of piety against the world around it. Often this conflict is illustrated through the characters of adolescents experiencing the first pangs of fleshly desire. In these novels, too, adolescent rebellion sometimes is pictured against the clichés of bourgeois society.

Although characterization and plot grow in strength with the craftsman's practice, M. from the first showed a native talent for creating atmosphere. In Journal II (1937), published much later, he says of himself: "I am a metaphysician working on the concrete. Owing to a certain gift of atmosphere, I try to make the Catholic universe of evil perceptible, tangible, odorous. The theologians give us an abstract idea of the sinner; I give him flesh and blood."

In 1922 Le Baiser au lépreux (A Kiss for the Leper, 1950), the first of the better-known novels, appeared. Here the theme which has become closely identified with M., that of distrust of human love, first made a notable appearance. For M. each person is marked by isolation; the novelist seems deeply convinced of the futility of human love in its attempt at communion with another. Ultimately, as many of M.'s novels demonstrate, the human heart finds its solace in confrontation with the "Other," with God alone.

Le Baiser au lépreux puts forth both negative and positive aspects of this theme. M. portrays Jean Péloueyre, seemingly repulsive in appearance and clumsy in action, although gentle. Jean is married to Noémie, a young and beautiful woman, whose disgust for her husband she cannot hide. Separation is only temporary, for Noémie has a religious sense of duty. She tries valiantly to disguise her returning distaste. But Jean knows the truth and happily places himself in physical danger caring for a consumptive, anxious as he is that death put an end to the agony of his hurt. Noémie prepares to dedicate the rest of her life to his memory. Throughout, there is the implication of the fear one has of a loved person, fear "because of what he takes out of us, because he takes advantage for his own use, of a part of us, and because of the limits which he imposes upon us."

"Those who love us form us," M. reflects in Le Jeune Homme (1926; The Weakling and The Enemy, 1952). These restraints that love puts upon us sometimes result in rebellion.

The same theme in a different context, family love, is seen at its epitome in Genetrix (1923; Eng., 1950). Here M. explores the fiendishly selfish love of Mme Cazenave for Fernand, her son. The latter, his marriage having ended by the tragic death of his wife, finds his only pure love in his mother.

M. once wrote, "The Desert of Love might

serve as the title for my entire work." With the work bearing this title in 1925 began the publication of M.'s three greatest novels. *Le Désert de l'amour* (The Desert of Love, 1929) was followed in 1927 by *Thérèse Desqueyroux* (1927; Thérèse, 1928) 2d. ed., 1963 and in 1932 by *Le Noeud de vipères* (1932; Viper's Tangle, 1933).

The themes of isolation of the human person, the conviction that human love is powerless ever to communicate fully to another, the essential impenetrability of the human heart, except to God alone—all these are clearly set forth in *Le Désert de l'amour.* This novel opens with the meeting, after seventeen years, of Raymond Courrèges, a burned-out roué of thirty-five, and Maria Cross, the now fortyish woman who initiated his career by her scorn of him. As a spoiled, indolent widow of twenty-seven, Maria, mistress of the wealthy Victor Larousselle, had deliberately attracted her physician, Dr. Courrèges. Tiring of him, she then pursues Raymond, his grubby, adolescent son. Flattered by her attentions and her half-serious show of affection, Raymond makes passionate advances toward Maria, who disgusted and sickened by his youthful brutality, repels him. Maria, frightened and shamed by the episode, comes face to face with herself and her pathetic, restless quest for love; but Raymond's frustration vents itself in a life of revenge on women.

Love, in the experience of Maria Cross, Raymond Courrèges, and his father, Doctor Courrèges, is a barren thing; it is a desert with all of the accompanying connotations. Love for this trio is a place of solitude and utter desolation, a place of temporary oasis which eventually and inevitably becomes a mirage. It is a place where one may become desiccated and devitalized, as does Dr. Courrèges, maddened in the heat of passion, as does Raymond, or brought to one's knees, as is Maria Cross in the loneliness where only God and oneself exist.

Thérèse Desqueyroux uses a more subtle dilemma as its starting point. The inviolability of the human person and the futility of human passion as a source of knowledge are the background of the book. Thérèse, a young, strong woman of the provinces, finds her marriage to Bernard, a coarse and complacent landowner, to be unbearable, and she becomes his would-be murderess. M. succeeds admirably here in sustaining an atmosphere of mystery around

Thérèse. He forgoes his characteristic use of sudden and artistically unwarranted intervention of divine grace to bring about instant conversion. But the Preface carries his own dissatisfaction with the lack of resolution: "I could have wished, Thérèse, that sorrow might have turned your heart to God.... But had I shown you thus redeemed there would have been no lack of readers to raise a cry of sacrilege, even though they may hold as an article of Faith the Fall and Ransom of our torn and twisted natures."

Before M. wrote the third novel of this distinguished trio, he seemed to have resolved the tragic struggle between passion and conscience which had marked his earlier writing, where nature herself seems allied with pagan sensuality against God. No reconciliation had appeared possible for M. when he wrote *Souffrances du pécheur* (1928). In this essay M. expresses the Jansenist paradox in his opening sentence: "Christianity makes no provision for the flesh. It suppresses it."

However, the retraction of this extreme statement, *Bonheur du chrétién* (1929), was hailed by Charles du Bos as the record of a conversion, a peaceful treaty achieved within M. himself. In *Bonheur* M. acknowledges the *Souffrances* as the rebellious outpourings of a man who "accuses the Author of life of failing to make provision for the flesh and the Author of life takes vengeance by overwhelming this soul and this body in his love to the point that he confesses the law of the spirit to be, indeed, the law of the flesh."

It may be that M.'s newly achieved serenity of spirit provided the creative stimulus for *Viper's Tangle,* which is probably his greatest work. *Thérèse* is artistically admirable because of M.'s restraint in introducing the intervention of the supernatural. Yet in this later novel the master stroke of the novelist's judgment appears in his choice of the miserly Louis, whose heart is a "viper's tangle," as his narrator. Here at last M., through a series of entries in Louis's diary, can easily and credibly reveal the intimate workings of grace within the sordid world of greedy men, within the shrunken heart of the loveless old man himself. The novelist here brings the reader to assent to Louis's change of heart without benefit of his own commentary or persuasion.

Viper's Tangle also serves as a synthesis of characteristic M. themes: the bourgeois family as an institution, the mediocrity of innumerable

Christians, the disillusionment seemingly inevitable in human love, the isolation of the individual.

Several novels written later, *Galigaï* (1952; The Loved and the Unloved, 1952), *Les Anges noirs* (1936; The Mask of Innocence, 1953), and *L'Agneau* (1954; The Lamb, 1955), demonstrate the theme of isolation, but only once in the remainder of his writing does M. show comparable achievement. This was in his *La Pharisienne* (1941); The Woman of the Pharisees, 1946), which uses the device of a narrator. Here his theme is the subtlety of a complacent Christian's hypocritical self-delusion resulting in the spiritual wreckage of the "woman," Brigitte Pian. The novel is powerful, though perhaps less moving than *Viper's Tangle*.

The fictional world M. creates is acknowledged to be sharply limited; it exists only in the particular atmosphere he creates. His style is highly poetic—rhythmic, economic, full of suggestion. Of the poetry of the novel, M. says: "There is little danger in the novel's invading the rest of literature. I believe that only poetry counts and that only through the poetical elements enclosed in a work of art of any genre whatever does that work deserve to last. A great novelist is first of all a great poet. Both Proust and Tolstoy were because their power of suggestion was boundless."

M. has written some drama; his *Asmodée* (1938; Asmodée The Intruder, 1939) was the first play by a living author to be produced by the Comédie-Française. But here his talents are not seen to best advantage.

His religious writings are searching, at times anguished, always highly relevant to the troubled times in which he has lived. Best among them is probably *Le Fils de l'homme* (1958; The Son of Man, 1960), a meditation on the life of Christ. It is less controversial than his *Vie de Jésus* (1936; Life of Jesus, 1937), which emphasizes the human qualities of Christ.

As a journalist he made his mark in the columns of *Figaro* and in *La Table Ronde*. Three volumes of collected articles, *Journal* I (1934) and succeeding volumes in 1937 and 1940, included some of the best of M.'s prose.

The highest tribute to M.'s art came with his winning of the Nobel Prize for Literature in 1952. He is held by many to be the greatest living French novelist.

FURTHER WORKS: *L'Adieu à l'adolescence*

(1911); *Préséances* (1921; Questions of Precedence, 1958); *Le Mal* (1924); *La Vie et la mort d'un poète* (1924); *Orages* (1925); *Le Jeune homme* (1926); *Bordeaux* (1926); *Proust* (1926); *La Province* (1926); *La Rencontre avec Pascal* (1926); *Le Tourment de Jacques Rivière* (1926); *Destins* (1928; Destinies, 1929); *Le Roman* (1928); *Dieu et Mammon* (1929; God and Mammon, 1930); *Voltaire contre Pascal* (1930); *Trois grands hommes devant Dieu* (1930); *Ce qui était perdu* (1930); *Souffrances et bonheur du chrétien* (1931; Anguish and Joy of the Christian Life, 1964); *Le Jeudi Saint* (1931; The Eucharist, 1944); *L'Affaire Favre-Bulle* (1931); *Blaise Pascal et sa soeur Jacqueline* (1931); *René Bazin* (1931); *Commencements d'une vie* (1932); *Pélerins de Lourdes* (1932); *Le Romancier et ses personnages* (1933); *Le Drôle* (1933; The Holy Terror, 1964); *La Fin de la nuit* (1935); *Les Maisons fugitives* (1939); *Les Chemins de la mer* (1939; The Unknown Sea, 1948); *Ne pas renier ...* (1944); *La Rencontre avec Barrès* (1945); *Sainte Marguerite de Cortone* (1945; Saint Margaret of Cortona, 1948); *Les Mal aimés* (1945; The Egoists, 1959); *Le Bâillon dénoué* (1945); *Du côté de chez Proust* (1947; Proust's Way, 1947); *Journal d'un homme de trente ans* (1948); *Terres franciscaines ...* (1950); *Le Sagouin* (1951; The Little Misery, 1952); *La Pierre d'achoppement* (1951; The Stumbling Block, 1952); *Paroles catholiques* (1954; Words of Faith, 1955); *Bloc-notes, 1952-1957* (1958); *Mémoirs intérieurs* (1959; Eng., 1960); *Le Mystère Frontenac* (1961; The Frontenacs, 1961); *Le Nouveau bloc-notes, 1958-1960* (1961); *La Vie de Racine* (1962); *Ce que je crois* (1962; What I Believe, 1963); *De Gaulle* (1964; Eng., 1966); *Nouveaux mémoirs intérieurs* (1965); *D'autres et moi* (1966)

BIBLIOGRAPHY: Du Bois, C., *F. M. et le problème du romancier catholique* (1933); Schwarzenbach, J., *Der Dichter des zwiespältigen Lebens F. M.* (1938); Sartre, J.-P., "F. M. et la liberté," in *NRF* (1 Feb. 1939); Hourdin, G., *M., romancier chrétien* (1945); Rideau, E., *Comment lire F. M.* (1945); Heppenstall, R., *The Double Image* (1947); North, R. G., *Le Catholicisme dans l'œuvre de F. M.* (1950); Cormeau, N., *L'Art de F. M.* (1951); O'Donnell, D., *Maria Cross: Imaginative Patterns in a Group of Modern Catholic Writers* (1952); Simon, P.-H., *M. par lui-même* (1953); Robichon, J., *F. M.* (1953); Jarrett-Kerr, M., *F. M.* (1954); Peyre, H., *Contemporary French Novel*

(1955); Seelmann-Eggebert, U., "F. M.," in *Christliche Dichter der Gegenwart* (1955); Vandromme, P., *La Politique littéraire de F. M.* (1957); Maurois, A., *Grands Écrivains du demi-siècle* (1957); Moloney, M. F., *F. M.: A Critical Study* (1958); Prévost, J.-L., *Le Roman catholique* (1958); Grall, X., *M., journaliste* (1960); Alyn, M., *F. M.* (1960); Biordan, S. F. E., *The Concept of Love in the French Catholic Literary Revival* (1962); Griffiths, R., *The Reactionary Revolution: The Catholic Revival in French Literature* (1965); Engler, W., *The French Novel from the Nineteenth Century to the Present* (1968)

SISTER MARIA HUMILIATA, I.S.M.

M. did not write several different novels; he wrote one single novel, a great monumental work dealing with man, with the drama of man, who having fallen through sin strives for liberation through grace. . . .

. . . He maintains that for the Christian there can be no happiness but only tragedy, and if we try to compare his Christian faith with that of other contemporary thinkers we are always reminded of Dostoyevsky's or Unamuno's gloominess. Spanish starkness and sadness, the tragedy of Spanish crucifixes, the ghastly distortion of Goya's paintings —all this is somehow reflected in M. M. is more Spanish than French.

Schwarzenbach, J., *F.M.* (1938), pp. 7, 214

A Catholic sensibility struggling against sensuality—this is what characterizes M.'s Christianity. A deep need for love and forgiveness—this is the essence of his faith.

. . . Is it overstepping the rights of criticism to point out that Cybele and Christ go shares in his work? M. the novelist has nothing much to do with Christianity (except perhaps in *Le baiser au lépreux*); M. the essayist and critic, on the other hand, is a Catholic writer.

Boisdeffre, P. de, *Métamorphose de la Littérature*, I (1953), pp. 206, 245

In a modern way, in the novel as well as in the drama, M.'s whole work revives the utmost tragic intensity in a setting of the utmost economy, the purity of line and the beautiful austerity of dramatic structure to which *Phèdre* and *Bérénice* owe their immortal greatness.

M. is a writer for whom the visible world has not ceased to exist, whose characters have the solidity and importance of men with souls to save or lose, and a writer who claims the traditional and essential right of a novelist, to comment, to express his views.

The vents of M.'s novels are used not to change characters but to reveal characters—reveal them gradually with an incomparable subtlety. . . .

This modern novelist, who allows himself the freedom to comment, comments, whether through his characters or in his own "I", again and again in the very accents of Pascal. . . .

If Pascal had been a novelist, this is the method and the tone he would have used.

Greene, G., *The Lost Childhood and Other Essays* (1951), pp. 70ff

Thus the structure of his art is tragic in essence or, if you prefer, the aesthetic category from which it derives is the tragic—and sometimes the sublime. . . . Passion is indeed the fundamental key in M.'s work. His admirable psychology of love that, with lucid sureness and an overwhelming emotional tone of heartrending truth, continually reveals the most elusive nuances, the most hidden actions, laying bare the conflicts and the most tragic suffering—this infallible knowledge of the human heart transformed into miraculous artistry is the unmistakable sign of this primacy.

Cormeau, N., *L'Art de F.M.* (1951), pp. 167, 253

What M. has put before us, in some of the most painful as well as the most beautiful books of the interwar period is, then, these simple, eternal problems that perpetually overwhelm us— this unique problem of authentic contact with another human being. All this is said with splendid lyricism by a writer who is a great artist, but it is clear from the outset that perhaps nothing stands between M. and Monsieur Sartre except a misunderstanding, since this problem, the problem of the other one, of the relationship with someone else, is also the central problem of many existential departures. Paradoxically, it is in M. that experience is lived most vigorously, felt with most intensity; it is in him that it acquires its full value for our existence. If it does not end in despair, it is because in our writer it is completed by a second experience of love: that of divine love.

Kanters, R., *Des écrivains et des hommes* (1952), p. 144

But dark as his image of man may be and as unlimited the truths that he proclaims, this does not make him anything more than the greatest average writer France can claim today.

. . . M. is always average, even where his artistry sets him above his time. Prominent rather than outstanding, he possesses all good qualities but not too much of any one of them. He was in the Resistance yet dissociated himself from the excesses of its reprisals; he is nonpolitical yet conservative; he is Catholic without being a missionary, ascetic and yet a great portrayer of the sins of the flesh; he is a fanatical provincial and at the same time a superior metropolitan journalist; he gives property its due yet repudiates its misuse; he is a pious recluse who is nonetheless often to be seen in Paris salons; in brief, his nature is so complete in itself that it precludes everything offensive as well as all banality. What you might call a magnificent specimen of civilization—but flickering with glimmers of Hell.

Sieburg, F., *Nur für Leser* (1955), p. 227

MAURIŅA, Zenta

German-Latvian novelist and essayist, b. 15 Dec. 1897, Lejasciems

Paralyzed since childhood, Zenta M., daughter of a physician, studied in Riga and Heidelberg (under Friedrich Gundolf (1880-1931) and Curtius [q.v.]) and later in Florence and Paris. In 1944 she was forced to flee to Germany and since 1946 has lived in Uppsala, Sweden, and West Germany. Since then she has written mostly in German.

Her work embraces the Eastern and Western cultural heritage, Christianity, classical antiquity, and the oriental search for God. Her principal theme is the conquest of pain and hatred through the power of the spirit and of love. In her essays in particular she has created an individual form, a ritually accented, suggestive style.

WORKS: *Dostojevsky* (1925; A Prophet of the Soul; Fyodor Dostoevsky, 1940); *Daži pamata motīvi Raina mākslā* (1928); *Janis Poruks un romantisms* (1929); *Baltais celš* (1935); *Dzīves apliecinātāji* (1936); *Saules meklētāje* (1938); *Frica bardas pasaules uzskats* (1938); *Kopoti raksti* (2 vols., 1939); *Dzīves vilcienā* (1941); *Prometeja gaismā* (1942); *Trīs brāļi* (1946); *Mosaik des Herzens* (1947); *Gestalten und Schicksale* (1949); *Die weite Fahrt* (1951); *Denn das Wagnis ist schön* (1953); *Um des Menschen willen* (1955); *Begegnung mit E. Ney* (1956); *Die eisernen Riegel zerbrechen* (1957); *Sieben Gäste* (1957); *Auf der Schwelle zweier Welten* (1959); *Über Liebe und Tod* (1960); *Welteinheit und die Aufgabe des Einzelnen* (1963); *Die Langeweile und der gehetzte Mensch* (1965); *Die Aufgabe der Dichterin in unserer Zeit* (1965); *Jahre der Befreiung, schwedische Tagebücher, 1951-1958* (1965); *Verfremdung und Freundschaft* (1966); *Buch der Freundschaft* (1967)

BIBLIOGRAPHY: Ermanis, P., *Z. M., Leben und Werk* (1939); Dietrich, M., *Ein Leben aus abendländischem Geist* (1953); Schempp, O., *Das Herz hat Flügel* (1957); Šilbajoris, R.,

"Ausserhalb der Heimat entstandene litauische Literatur," *Acta Baltica,* VI (1967), 221-35

* * *

MAUROIS, André

(pseud. of *Emile [Salomon Wilhelm] Herzog*), French biographer and novelist, b. 26 July 1885, Elbeuf, Normandy; d. 9 Oct. 1967, Neuilly

The Herzog family came from Alsace, in 1871 transferring their textile factory to Elbeuf, near Rouen, where M. came under the decisive influence of Alain (q.v.), then a teacher at the *lycée* and later a famous critic. M. entered the family business as a textile salesman.

During World War I, when he served as an interpreter at British headquarters, he wrote *Les Silences du Colonel Bramble* (1918; The Silence of Colonel Bramble, 1919), in which he describes with vivid characterization the clash of French and English mentalities under the impact of war. *Le Général Bramble* (1918; General Bramble, 1921; rev. ed. pub. as *Les Discours du Docteur O'Grady*, 1922) continued this theme.

With his biography *Ariel ou La Vie de Shelley* (1923; Eng., Ariel, A Shelley Romance, 1924; Am., Ariel, The Life of Shelley, 1924), M. founded the literary genre of the *biographie romancée*, a designation he introduced into the history of literary forms in the preface to *Ariel* but which he later dropped as a "misleading term." Much of M.'s work is in the form of fictionalized biography. Among those written in a rather popular style are *Tourguéniev* (1931), *Voltaire* (1932; Engl., 1932), *Frédéric Chopin* (1942; Eng., 1942), and *Robert et Elizabeth Browning* (1955).

In other works, M. adheres more closely to biographical documents and utilizes secondary sources. *La Vie de Disraëli* (1927; Disraeli: A Picture of the Victorian Age, 1927) was followed by *Don Juan ou La Vie de Byron* (1930; Byron, 1930), which introduced unpublished letters discovered by M. Then came *Lyautey* (1931; Eng., Marshal Lyautey, 1931; Am., Lyautey, 1931), *Edouard VII et son temps* (1933; Engl., King Edward VII and His Times, 1933; Am., The Edwardian Era, 1933), *Chateaubriand* (1938; Chateaubriand, Poet, Statesman, Lover, 1938), *Lélia ou La Vie de George Sand* (1952; Lélia, The Life of George Sand, 1953), *Olympio ou La Vie de Victor Hugo* (1954; Olympio, The Life of Victor Hugo, 1956)—which overstressed erotic gossip

—and *Les Trois Dumas* (1957; The Titans, A Three Generation Biography of the Dumas, 1957).

À la Recherche de Marcel Proust (1949; Eng., The Quest for Proust, 1950; Am., Proust, The Portrait of a Genius, 1950) is based on M.'s personal memories. This kind of biography achieved international success and was widely imitated. Many works by Zweig (q.v.) and Giles Lytton Strachey (1880-1932) treat the same periods in German- and English-speaking countries in a similar type of biographical essay written with keen awareness of history.

In the field of the novel M. himself named Stendhal (1783-1842) and Kipling (q.v.) as his models. He finds his subjects in upper-middle-class and industrial milieus. *Bernard Quesnay* (1926; Eng., 1927; rev. ed., 1928), *Climats* (1928; Eng., Whatever Gods May Be, 1929; Am., Atmosphere of Love, 1929), *Le Cercle de famille* (1932; The Family Circle, 1932), and *Terre promise* (1945) deserve mention here. M. has also written several volumes of short stories —*Meïpe ou La Délivrance* (1926; Mape: The World of Illusion, 1926; enlarged edition published as *Les Mondes imaginaires,* 1929) and *Le Peseur d'âmes* (1931; The Weigher of Souls, 1931)—and children's books.

M. emerges from his work as a cultural ambassador of France and an essentially bourgeois novelist of marriage and the family. He is admired for his lucid mind, formed by his Jewish family tradition, on the one hand, and his engaging common sense on the other. He owes his success to his unobtrusive technique, his balance and *bon sens,* and to his fluid, clear, understandable style. In the novels he is both moralist and rationalist. Since he avoided all extremes, reconciled passions instead of fomenting them, and was a wise, smiling, judiciously analytical advocate of the existing order, a wide reading public took him as its spokesman and he was officially honored (member of the Académie Française since 1938). His influence in France and abroad is, however, restricted to nonliterary circles.

FURTHER WORKS: *Ni Ange ni Bête* (1919); *Les Bourgeois de Witzheim* (1920); *Dialogues sur le commandement* (1924; Three Dialogues on Leadership, 1925); *Arabesques* (1925); *Les Anglais* (1926); *Bernard Quesnay* (1926; Eng., 1927; pub. in a shorter form as "La Hausse et la Baisse" in 1922; rev. ed., 1928); *Conseils à un jeune Français partant pour l'Angleterre* (1927); *La Conversation* (1927; Conversation,

1930); *Petite Histoire de l'Espèce Humaine* (1927); *Un Essai sur Dickens* (1927; Dickens, 1935); *Études Anglaises* (1927); *Le Chapitre Suivant* (1927; The Next Chapter: The War Against the Moon, 1927); *Rouen* (1927); *Aspects de la Biographie* (1928; Aspects of Biography, 1928); *Voyage au pays des Articoles* (1928; A Voyage to the Island of the Articoles, Eng., 1928, Am. 1929); *Contact* (1928); *Le Pays des trente-six mille volontés* (1928; The Country of Thirty-six Thousand Wishes, 1930); *Fragments d'un journal de vacances* (1929); *Le Côté de Chelsea* (1929; Chelsea Way, 1930); *Relativisme* (1930); *Patapoufs et Filifers* (1930; Fattypuffs and Thinifers, 1940); *Sur le Vif— L'exposition coloniale de Paris* (1931); *L'Amérique Inattendue* (1931); *Proust et Ruskin* (1932); *L'Anglaise et d'autres femmes* (1932; Ricochets: Miniature Tales of Human Life, 1935); *Mes Songes que voici* (1933); *Introduction à la Méthode de Paul Valéry* (1933); *Chantiers américains* (1933); *L'Instinct du bonheur* (1934); *Sentiments et coutumes* (1934); *Magiciens et logiciens* (1935; Prophets and Poets, 1937; enlarged ed. pub. as Points of View, 1968); *Premiers contes* (1935); *Histoire d'Angleterre* (1937; The Miracle of England, 1937; later titled, A History of England); *La Machine à lire les pensées* (1937; The Thought-Reading Machine, 1938); *Un Art de vivre* (1939; the Art of Living, 1940); *Discours de réception à l'Académie Française* (1939); *Etats-Unis 39: Journal d'un voyage en Amérique* (1939); *Les Origines de la guerre de 1939* (1939); *Tragédie en France* (1940; Eng., Why France Fell, 1941; Am., Tragedy in France, 1940); *Études littéraires* (2 vols., 1941-44); *Mémoires* (1942; Eng., Call No Man Happy, 1943; Am., I Remember, I Remember, 1942); *Seven Faces of Love* (1944; Sept visages de l'amour, 1946; rev. ed. of Cinq visages de l'amour, 1942); *Histoire des Etats-Unis* (1943; The Miracle of America, 1944); *Toujours l'inattendu arrive* (1943); *Eisenhower* (1945; Eisenhower, the Liberator, 1945); *Franklin, la Vie d'un Optimiste* (1945; Franklin, The Life of an Optimist, 1945); *Espoirs et Souvenirs* (1945); *Études américaines* (1945); *Washington* (1946; Washington, The Life of a Patriot, 1946); *Etats-Unis 46* (1946; From My Journal, 1948); *Journal d'un tour en Suisse* (1946); *Conseils à un jeune Français partant pour les Etats-Unis* (1947); *Retour en France* (1947); *Histoire de la France* (1947); The Miracle of France, 1948; later titled A History

of France); *Les Mondes impossibles* (1947);
Quand la France s'enrichissait (1947); *Rouen
dévasté* (1947); *Journal d'un tour en Amérique
Latine* (1948; My Latin-American Diary, 1953);
Alain (1950); *Les Nouveaux discours du
Docteur O'Grady* (1950; The Return of Doctor
O'Grady, 1951); *Le Dîner sous les marronniers*
(1951); *Cours de bonheur conjugal* (1951; The
Art of Being Happily Married, 1953); *Ce que
je crois* (1951); *Destins exemplaires* (1952);
Lettres à l'Inconnue (1953; To an Unknown
Lady, 1957); *Portrait de la France et des
français* (1955); *Aux Innocents les mains
pleines* (1955); *Hollande* (1955); *Périgord*
(1955); *Discours prononcé à l'Académie Fran-
çaise pour la réception de Jean Cocteau* (1955);
Louis XIV à Versailles (1955); *Les Roses de
Septembre* (1956; September Roses, 1958); *La
France change de visage* (1956); *Lecture mon
doux plasir* (1957; The Art of Writing, 1960);
Dialogue des vivants (1957); *Portrait d'un ami
qui s'appelait moi* (1959); *La Vie de Sir Alexander Fleming* (1959; The Life of Sir Alexander
Fleming, Discoverer of Penicillin, 1959); *Pour
Piano seul: Toutes les Nouvelles de André
Maurois* (1960); *Adrienne ou la Vie de
Madame de La Fayette* (1960; Adrienne, The
Life of the Marquis de La Fayette); *Histoire
parallèle: Histoire des États-Unis de 1917 à
1961* (with Louis Aragon, 4 vols, 1962; also
pub. as *Les Deux Géants: Histoire des Etats-
Unis et de l'URSS de 1917 à nos jours*, 1962-
64); *De Proust à Camus* (1963; From Proust
to Camus; Profiles of French Writers, 1966);
Choses nues (1963); *Napoléon* (1964), *Promé-
thée ou la Vie de Balzac* (1965; Prometheus,
The Life of Balzac, 1966); *De Gide à Sartre*
(1965); *Lettre ouverte à un jeune homme sur la
conduite de la vie* (1965); *Au Commencement
ètait l'action* (1966). **Selected English trans.:**
Collected Stories of A. M. (1967)

BIBLIOGRAPHY: Fillon, A., *A. M.: Romancier* (1937); Sauvenier, J., *A. M.* (1939); Suffel,
J., *A. M.* (1963); Kolbert, J., "The Worlds of
A. M.," *Susquehanna University Studies*, VII
(1965), 215-30; Kolbert, J., "A Few Notes on
the Short Fiction of A. M.," in *Studies in Short
Fiction*, III (1966), 104-16; Kolbert, J., "A. M.'s
Esthetics of Biography," in *Bulletin of the
Rocky Mountain Language Association*, XXI
(1967), 45-51; Lemaitre, G., *M.: The Writer
and His Work* (1968)

BRUNO BERGER

MAURRAS, Charles-Marie-Photius

(pseuds.: *Léon Rameau, Pierre Garnier,
Xénophon XIII, Octave Martin*), French writer,
b. 20 April 1868, Martigues, near Marseille;
d. 16 Nov. 1952, Tours

M. came of the politically conservative
Catholic middle class of southern France. He
began his literary career with stories and essays,
that fervently imitated the classical style, and
with very philosophical poems. Even before he
knew of Nietzsche (q.v.), he explored the
dichotomy between the Dionysiac and
Apollonian senses of life, using the ideas of
the 18th c. traditionalists to support his notions
(de Bonald, de Maistre, Balzac, Comte). From
this emerged a systematic philosophy and theory
of art and politics—a *Weltanschauung* that in
acknowledgment to Comte he named *positiv-
isme organisateur*. The contrast between the
"aesthetic of harmony" as the basis of all culture and the "aesthetic of character" as an
individualistic, culture-destroying principle is
developed chiefly in *Le Chemin du paradis*
(1894), early "stories" to be interpreted sometimes mythically, sometimes allegorically, but
never purely as fiction; in the travel memoirs
Anthinéa, d'Athènes à Florence (1901); and in
La Musique intérieure, a collection of poems
first published in 1925, M.'s antiromantic
position was particularly clearly defined in the
ironic *Les Amants de Venise, George Sand et
Musset* (1902). *Le Conseil de Dante* (1920) and
La Sagesse de Mistral (1926) display political
ideas derived from aesthetics, while the romantic and traditional concepts of order are very
strikingly contrasted in *Trois Idées politiques,
Chateaubriand, Michelet, Sainte-Beuve* (1898).

In the 1890's M., together with Moréas (q.v.),
founded the École Romane, a rallying point for
all champions of classicism. In 1896 he finally
committed himself to the doctrine of monarchy.
The *Enquête sur la monarchie 1900-1909* (1909;
final ed., 1937) became the basis of reactionary
"integral nationalism." In 1898 M. intervened
in the Dreyfus Affair and with Henri Vaugeois
and Pujo founded the review *L'Action française*, which a decade later (March 21, 1908)
became the daily newspaper that was to
influence public opinion significantly, especially
among students, civil servants, and the army.

After his excommunication and the condemnation of his books by the Catholic Church
in 1926, and particularly after the condemnation
of his ideological "doctrinairism" by the surviving legitimate heir to the throne, M.'s

authority declined. In 1938 he became a member of the Académie Française (expelled in 1945 after his trial). In 1940 he justified his ideological collaboration with the Vichy government on the grounds of its decentralized, patriotic position, but in 1945 he was sentenced to life imprisonment for "collaboration."

WORKS: *L'avenir de l'intelligence* (1905); *Le Dilemme de Marc Sangnier, essai sur la démocratie religieuse* (1906); *Si le coup de force est possible ...* (1910); *L'étang de Berre* (1915); *L'allée des Philosophes* (1924); *Le Mystère d'Ulysse* (1923); *Anatole France, politique et poète* (1924); *Essai sur la critique* (1925); *Un débat sur le Romanticisme* (1929); *Principes* (1931); *Mes idées politiques* (1937); *Devant l'Allemagne éternelle* (1937); *La Seule France* (1941); *La Balance intérieure* (1952); *Pascal puni* (1953); *Lettres de prison* (1958)

BIBLIOGRAPHY: Thibaudet, A., *Les Idées de M.* (1920; 2nd ed., 1931); Maritain, J., *Une Opinion sur C. M.* (1926); Daudet, L., *M. et son temps* (1928); Bernanos, G., *Scandale de la vérité* (1939) and *Nous autres français* (1939); Massis, H., *M. et notre temps* (2 vols., 1951-52); Joseph, R., and Forges, J., *Biblio-iconographie de C. M.* (1953-54); Curtis, M., *Three Against the Third Republic* (1959); Joseph, R., *Le Poète C. M.* (1962); Vandromme, P., *M., L'Église de l'ordre* (1965); Fabrègues, J. de, *C. M. et son "Action française"* (1966)

SIGRID VON MASSENBACH

MAYAKOVSKI, Vladimir Vladimirovich

Russian poet and dramatist, b. 19 July 1893, Bagdády (now Mayakovski), Georgia; d. 14 April 1930, Moscow

M., the leading figure of Soviet poetry, was born into a forest ranger's family. After his father's death the family moved to Moscow, where M. continued to attend school, though he did not graduate. After eleven months in jail for revolutionary activities (1906), he was released because he was still a minor. He enrolled in the School of Painting, Sculpture, and Architecture in 1910, but was expelled for the modernism of his work. His meeting with D. Burlyuk in 1912 brought out his interest in poetry, and soon M. became the doyen among Russian futurist (see futurism) poets, contributing to their publications and appearing in sensational tours across Russia.

His first book of verse, *Prostoye kak mychaniye,* appeared in 1916. The Russian Revolution of 1917 was greeted by M. with enthusiasm. From then on he tried to serve it in his works and to identify himself with it, either by making propaganda posters for the central press agency, *Rosta,* or by writing political verse for the paper *Komsomol'skaya Pravda.* Between 1923 and 1925 M. edited *Lef,* the magazine of futurists then campaigning for utilitarian art (in 1927 it reappeared as *Novyi Lef*). He also traveled extensively, in France, Germany, Poland, Mexico, the United States, and elsewhere.

Criticized by orthodox literary circles for individualism and "formalism," M. abandoned *Lef* and joined the officially recognized organization, the Association of Proletarian Writers (R.A.P.P.).

Soon after, M. committed suicide. Some saw reasons for M.'s death in his love life; others, in the constant Marxist criticism of his works; still others think he felt out of tune with his time. Whatever the reason, careful reading discloses that the motif of suicide pervades his poems from the very beginning. In 1935 Stalin established M.'s posthumous reputation by saying that "M. was and still remains the most talented poet of our Soviet epoch, and an indifferent attitude toward his memory is a crime." That pronouncement started a cult of M. in the U.S.S.R., a cult that has continued ever since.

M.'s first important work was his futuristic drama, *Vladimir Mayakovski* (1914), in which he characterizes himself as a symbolic poet and a defender of all who are unhappy. In *Oblako v shtanakh* (1915), a long poem, M. defies the accepted forms of art, state, love, and religion, and prophesies the coming revolution. It was followed by *Fleita-pozvonochnik* (1915) and *Chelovek* (1916), in both of which M. continued his ever-recurring theme of tragic love. *Voina i mir* (1916), another long poem, is a passionate attack on war. *Misteriya-buff* (1918; revised edition, 1921) is an Aristophanes-like play in verse, written for huge crowds, full of satire and revolutionary cosmism; it parodies the story of Noah's Ark and the style of a medieval morality play.

In *150.000.000* (1921), also a long poem, M. personifies the capitalistic West and the new Soviet Russia in the gigantic images of Wilson and Ivan. *Pro éto* (1923), M.'s last great poem of unrequited love, reflects his preoccupation with ideas of the physical resurrection of the

ANDRÉ MAUROIS

VLADIMIR MAYAKOVSKI

dead, similar to those of Fedorov. *Vladimir Il'ich Lenin* (1925) is probably M.'s only artistically convincing poem on this subject.

In the essay "Kat delat' Stikhi" (1926), M. gives an interesting glimpse into his creative process. In the well-known short poem "Sergeyu Yeseninu" (1926), he judges the suicide of the famous poet Yesenin (q.v.) as a moral mistake. In the long poem *Khorosho!* (1927), M. describes the Russian Revolution and the Russian Civil War and gives an optimistic picture of Soviet life and its future. But M.'s two plays in prose—*Klop* (1928; in *The Bedbug and Selected Poetry*, 1960) and *Banya* (1929) —both produced but later banned, are bitter satires on Soviet bureaucracy and the smugness of the new middle class; they express the horror with which M. reacted to the vulgarity of post-revolutionary life. An introduction to the poem *Vo ves' golos* (published posthumously in 1930) states M.'s credo of political poetry; in it he attempts to define his place in Soviet literature.

M.'s loneliness and emotional conflict can be seen both in his life and in his work. In spite of his sincere attempts to become a collectivist poet, he could not overcome his innate individualism; the result is the tragic undercurrent that appears so frequently in his poems. The virility of his loud, extroverted works is sometimes accompanied by a tinge of childish helplessness.

M.'s poetry is of great originality in style and content. After the early futuristic poems he worked out a simpler, but still a modern, idiom that combined the language of the streets with that of the podium. Although he strove for "depoetization," fought against refinement, and approached his themes in an often primitive, direct way, his verse shows great mastery of his craft, strong rhythmical foundations, virtuosic use of elaborate metaphors (with a predilection for hyperboles), complex use of rhyme, ingenious word creation, and daring syntactical inversions. He was the first Russian poet to write his poems consistently in accentual verse.

M. has been compared variously with Béranger, Heinrich Heine, Freiligrath, and Nekrasov for his social and political tendencies, with Walt Whitman for his egotism and rhythmic innovations, with Rimbaud for his rebelliousness, and with Verhaeren (q.v.) for his urbanism. He influenced Aseyev, Bagritzki, Selvinski, Tikhonov, Yevtushenko (qq.v.) and a score of secondary Soviet poets. Among non-

Russians, his influence can be seen in the work of Aragon, Neruda, and Becher (qq.v.).

FURTHER WORKS: *V. M.* (10 vols., 1928-33); *Polnoye sobraniye sochinenii* (12 vols., 1939-49). **Selected English trans.:** *M. and His Poetry* (1945)

BIBLIOGRAPHY: Jacobson, R., "O pokolenii, rastrativshem svoikh poetov," in *Smert' V. Mayakovskovo* (1931); Trenin, V., *V "masterskoi stikha" Mayakovskovo* (1937); Kamenski, V., *Zhizn' s Mayakovskim* (1940); Shklovski, V., *O Mayakovskom* (1940); *V. M.: Sbornik.* Vol. 1. (1940); *M.: materialy i issledovaniya* (1940); *M. 1930-1940: stat'i i materialy* (1940); Triolet, E., *M., poète russe,* ed. P. Seghers (1945); Katanyan, V., *M. Literaturnaya khronika* (1948); Pertzov, V., *M. Zhizn' i tvorchestvo: Do Velikoi Oktyabr' skoi Revolyutzii* (1950); Bachtin, N., "M.," in Oxford Slavonic Papers (1951); Blake, P., "The Two Deaths of V. M.," in M.'s *The Bedbug and Selected Poetry* (1960)

VLADIMIR MARKOV

McCARTHY, Mary

American novelist, essayist, and critic, b. 21 June 1912, Seattle, Wash.

Orphaned by the influenza epidemic of 1918, Mary M. spent her formative years under the influence of Roman Catholic, Protestant, and Jewish relatives. She attended Catholic and Episcopal schools, as well as Vassar College, from which she was graduated in 1933. After college she worked in a publishing house and as an editor and theater critic for *Partisan Review*; she taught English for a brief time at two women's colleges. She has been married four times; her second husband was Edmund Wilson (q.v.), by whom she had her only child. All of these experiences have been used by her as source material for her novels and short stories.

Consistently described as witty, clever, sophisticated, honest, and savagely satiric, Mary M.'s approach to writing fiction is distinguished by a relentlessly frank analysis of such forces as sexuality, the appeal of communism, the social pretense found in the artist or intellectual and to a lesser extent the claims of the modern world on persons raised in middle-class economic, religious, artistic, and political environments, who find such values disappearing as their social status rises. Her first book, *The*

Company She Keeps (1942), is a collection of loosely linked stories concerning a woman closely resembling Mary M. herself (some are admittedly autobiographical), who decides for fashionable reasons on a divorce, joins a fashionable literary-political crowd after the divorce, and goes through psychoanalysis. The disillusionment with communism felt by liberals in the 1930's is especially fully developed in this book, as it is in her next, *The Oasis* (Eng., Source of Embarrassment, 1949), a short novel concerning a utopian society of artists and intellectuals that collapses from the sheer incompetence of the well-meaning but utterly ineffective idealists in the society.

The Groves of Academe (1952), as the title suggests, concerns a college not unlike those at which Mary M. taught. An incompetent liberal professor, to avoid dismissal, implies that he had once been a communist and that the threat of dismissal is a witch hunt—a particularly clever idea in the era of Senator Joseph McCarthy, when the book appeared. Immediately supported by the many other faculty liberals, the professor is rehired at the book's end and the well-meaning, freedom-defending college president is forced to resign. This satiric inversion of justice and freedom raises again the question of the value of the liberals' integrity and intellectualism.

A Charmed Life (1955) is set in a New England artists' colony to which the central character returns with a new husband, is seduced by her previous husband, and dies en route to an abortionist. With scarcely any plot and with completely stereotyped characters, this book not only contains endless digressions on art and literature but also more systematically and ruthlessly dissects character than do the previous books. *The Group* (1963), the most famous of Mary M.'s novels, concerns eight Vassar graduates of her own graduating class, who discover most of the by now familiar facts about sex, politics, art, etc. As with *A Charmed Life,* this novel has little plot, but it differs not only in having a larger set of characters but also in having less vitriolic satiric thrust.

Since all Mary M.'s fiction deals with the same character types and the same basic themes it can profitably be examined as a unit. As such, it will be seen at once that she is frequently less able to handle the demands of the novel than she can those of the short story; endings are contrived, for instance, and even some "novels" (e.g., *The Company She Keeps*) are really series of stories, at which the author

excels. But the autobiographical quality is most pervasive and obvious. It is no surprise, then, that *Memories of a Catholic Girlhood* (1957) is her finest book, distinguished as it is by sensitive, warm, and revealing comments about many of the same matters developed in her fiction. This book, which incorporates much of *Cast a Cold Eye* (1950), a collection of both stories and brief autobiographical pieces, has little of the forced or digressive polemicizing found in the longer fiction; it shows Mary M.'s vigor, intelligence, and wit—her major fictional virtues—better than do most of her novels.

FURTHER WORKS: *Venice Observed* (1956); *Sights and Spectacles 1937-1956* (1956); *The Stones of Florence* (1959); *On the Contrary: Articles of Belief, 1946-1961* (1961); *Theatre Chronicles 1937-1962* (1963; incorporates most of *Sights and Spectacles 1937-1956*); *The Humanist in the Bathtub* (1964; includes selections from *On the Contrary* and *Theatre Chronicles*); *Vietnam* (1967); *Hanoi* (1968)

BIBLIOGRAPHY: Chamberlain, J., "The Conservative Miss M.," in *National Review,* XV (22 Oct. 1963), xvi, 353-55; Eisinger, C., *Fiction of the Forties* (1963), pp. 128-35; Ohmann, C., and R. M., "Classnotes from Vassar," in *Commonweal,* LXXIX (27 Sept. 1963), i, 12-15; Cook, B., "M. M.: One of Ours?," in *Cath. W.,* CXCIX (April 1964), 34-42; Schlueter, P., "The Dissections of Mary M.," in Moore, H. T., ed., *Contemporary American Novelists* (1964), pp. 54-64; Auchincloss, L., *Pioneers and Caretakers* (1965); McKenzie, B., *M. M.* (1966); Grumbach, D., *The Company She Kept* (1967)

PAUL SCHLUETER

McCULLERS, Carson

American novelist and short-story writer, b. 19 Feb. 1917, Columbus, Ga.; d. 29 Sept. 1967

Originally a music student, Carson M. enjoyed early success as a novelist with *The Heart is a Lonely Hunter* (1940), *Reflections in a Golden Eye* (1941), and *The Member of the Wedding* (1946). Interested in drama, she rewrote *The Member of the Wedding* for the stage (1951). Another play would follow, but it was her long story, *The Ballad of the Sad Café* (first published in *Harper's Bazaar* in 1943), that kept critical attention on her.

Possibly her finest work, *The Ballad of the Sad Café* (1951) dramatizes Carson M.'s con-

MARY McCARTHY

H. L. MENCKEN

stant theme of isolation. Cousin Lyman and Amelia are grotesques in the S. Anderson (q.v.) tradition. Their enormities of passion, their physical and sexual deformities, reflect the terrible loneliness of human life. Though only love can assuage this "malady," humans tend to vest their love in unobtainable love objects. Tragically, the lover pursues, thoughtless of what pain he might inflict, while the beloved fears and hates the lover.

In *Clock Without Hands* (1961) Carson M. traces America's racial dilemma to this same loneliness and to the fear of death. Isolated through his refusal to face death honestly, the protagonist (dying of cancer) hates Jews and Negroes. When he learns that death, though certain, has no claim on the time of life, he frees himself from prejudice and isolation.

FURTHER WORKS: *The Square Root of Wonderful* (1958)

BIBLIOGRAPHY: Smith, S. M., "C. McC.: A Critical Introduction," *DA*, XXV (1964), 3583-84; Evans, O. W., *C. McC.: Her Life and Work* (1965; Am., *The Ballad of C. McC., A Biography*)

STANLEY STUART

MEDEK, Rudolf
Czech novelist, poet, and playwright, b. 8 Jan. 1890, Königgrätz; d. 22 Sept. 1940, Prague

At the beginning of his writing career, M. was identified with symbolism (q.v.) and decadence, from which, however, he soon turned away to write poetry and novels in the spirit of nationalism. His war poems, *Lví srdce* (1919) and his war novels, *Veliké dny* (1923) and *Anabase* (1927)—which described the fate of the Czech Legion in Russia, in which he served as a high-ranking officer—established him as the leading representative of Czech nationalist literature in the 1930's. He received the National Prize for his play *Plukovník Švec* (1928).

FURTHER WORKS: *Půlnoc bohů* (1912); *Ohnivý drak* (1921); *Živý kruh* (1923); *Ostrov v bouři* (1925); *Láska a smrt* (1925); *Mohutný sen* (1926); *Vinný keř* (1928); *Srdce a válka* (1930); *Jiří Poděbradský* (1934)

BIBLIOGRAPHY: Novák, A., *Die tschechische Literatur* (1931); Meriggi, B., *Storie della letteratura ceccha e slovacca* (1958)

JOHANNA WOLF

MEERSCH, Maxence van der
(pseud. of *Josef Cardijn*), French narrative writer of Flemish descent, b. 4 May 1907, Roubaix; d. 14 Jan. 1951, Le Touquet

After studying literature and law, M. became a lawyer and editor in Lille. He made his reputation with the novel *L'Empreinte du Dieu* (1936; ... Hath Not the Potter, 1937), which received the Prix Goncourt. Nearly all his very realistic novels and short stories (which tend to neglect form and language in favor of plot) are set in the Franco-Belgian border country or in Flanders. The life of working people in industrial centers and big city slums shocked M. deeply. His early works are radically Marxist; later he advocated an active, socially-oriented Christianity.

FURTHER WORKS: *La Maison dans la dune* (1932); *Quand les sirènes se taisent* (1933; When the Looms Are Silent, 1934); *Invasion 14* (1935; Invasion, 1937); *L'élu* (1937); *Les Pêcheurs d'hommes* (1940; Fishers of Men, 1947); *Le Péché du monde* (1941); *Corps et âmes* (1943; Bodies and Souls, 1948); *La Petite Sainte Thérèse* (1947); *La Fille pauvre* (1948); *Maria, fille de Flandre* (1948; *Le Coeur pur* (1948); *Vincent* (1948); The Bellringer's Wife, 1951); *La Compagne* (1955; The Hour of Love, 1957); *Masque de chair* (1958)

BIBLIOGRAPHY: Reus, R., *Portrait morpho-psychologique de M.* (1952)

PAUL WIMMER

MEHRING, Walter
German narrative and political writer, b. 29 April 1896, Berlin

After publishing some expressionist poetry in the periodical *Der Sturm*, M. made his debut in political cabaret and revived the art of the *chansonnier*. His play *Der Kaufmann von Berlin* (1929), staged by Piscator, presented a deliberately shocking picture of the inflation period. After 1923 M. lived mainly in Paris (*Algier*, 1927; *Paris in Brand*, 1927), where he also wrote the novel *Müller. Die Chronik einer deutschen Sippe* (1935), the story of a family persecuted by National Socialist laws. After coming to the U.S.A. he wrote *The Lost Library* (1951), the "autobiography of a culture," a unique account of two generations of Germany's past, as reflected in the contents and fate of his father's library.

FURTHER WORKS: *Die Frühe der Städte* (1916); *Das politische Kabaret* (1920); *Das Ketzerbrevier* (1921); *Europäische Nächte* (1924); *Lieder, Gedichte und Chansons des W. M.* (1929); *Arche Noah S.O.S. Neues trostreiches Liederbuch* (1931); *Die höllische Komödie* (1932); *... und Euch zum Trotz* (1934); *Die Nacht der Tyrannen* (1937); *Timoshenko, Marshal of the Red Army* (1942); *No Road Back* (1944); *Verrufene Malerei* (1958); *Berlin-Dada* (1959); *Morgenlied eines Gepäckträgers* (1959); *Neues Ketzerbrevier* (1962)

BIBLIOGRAPHY: Verkeuf, W., *Dada* (Ger., 1957; Eng., 1961); Geerdts, H. J., *Deutsche Literaturgeschichte in einem Band* (1965), pp. 563-65

BRUNO BERGER

MEIRELES, Cecília
Brazilian poet, b. 7 Nov. 1901, Rio de Janeiro; d. there, 9 Nov. 1964

Orphaned at an early age, Cecília M. grew up in her grandmother's house in Rio. She described her childhood as one of "silence and solitude," but she also claimed that these were positive factors in her development. She was graduated from normal school in 1917 and began a career in teaching. In 1922 she married the painter Fernando Correia Dias. Three daughters were born of the marriage, including the actress Maria Fernanda.

Cecília M. published her first book of verse, *Espectros,* in 1919, and continued to write from then on along with her professional and domestic duties. At various times she was education editor of the *Diário de Notícias* of Rio and professor of Portuguese and Brazilian literature at the University of the Federal District. She was an enthusiastic traveler, and much of her work was the result of her numerous trips abroad. She visited India (in preparation for which she learned Hindi and Sanskrit), Israel, Europe, and the Azores. She was also a translator of works by Maeterlinck, García Lorca, Anouilh, Ibsen, Tagore, Rilke, Virginia Woolf (qq.v.), and Pushkin.

Cecília M. cannot really be grouped with the modernist poets who revolutionized Brazilian poetry in 1922; she is more a continuer of the line of the symbolist poets active at the turn of the c. Her poetry is extremely personal, much of it a search for herself within the environment she saw about her. Three predominant themes are space, sea, and solitude,

handled stylistically by variations of form, sound, and color. In her work there is a pervasive lyricism, characteristic of much Luso-Brazilian poetry; and she sometimes felt drawn to Portuguese medieval poets, with the result that some of her verse has the tone of troubadoresque poetry.

Critics have praised her style as a high expression of lyricism but have shown dissatisfaction with her tendency to make the poetic moment too explicit. In this she strayed from the path of her symbolist antecedents and was at a distance from her modernist contemporaries. Her predilection for the short, clear, definitive line, deceptively simple, places her close to Jiménez (q.v.), although her work is without the nuances found in the Spanish poet. Cecília M. was always preoccupied with being understood, which might have come from the fact that she was also the author of several children's books.

Her best-regarded work is a collection of poems based on the story of the abortive movement for Brazilian independence in the late 18th c., *Romanceiro da Inconfidência* (1953). Her poetry has appeared in English in various reviews, and there is a selection of her work in *Modern Brazilian Poetry,* edited by John Nist (1962).

FURTHER WORKS: *Nunca Mais e Poema dos Poemas* (1923); *Baladas para El-Rei* (1925); *Viagem* (1939); *Vaga Música* (1942); *Mar Absoluto* (1945); *Retrato Natural* (1949); *Amor em Leonoreta* (1952); *O Aeronauta* (1952); *Pequeno Oratório de Santa Clara* (1955); *Pistóia, Cemitério Militar Brasileiro* (1955); *Canções* (1956); *Giroflé, Giroflá* (1956); *Romance de Santa Cecília* (1957); *Obra Poética* (1958); *Problemas de Literatura Infantil* (1959); *Metal Rosicler* (1960); *Poemas Escritos na India* (1962); *Antologia Poética* (1963); *Ou Isto ou Aquilo* (1963); *Poesia* (1967)

BIBLIOGRAPHY: Introduction and studies by various critics in the definitive anthology of her work, *Obra Poética*; Perez, R., *Escritores Brasileiros Contemporâneos,* 2nd series (1964)

GREGORY RABASSA

MELL, Max
Austrian poet, narrative writer, dramatist, poet, and essayist, b. 10 Nov. 1882, Marburg, Drau

M., the son of a teacher, studied philology

in Vienna, where he lives. His works, with the Christian faith as their subject matter, confront the assault on chaos, and are written in a highly disciplined language.

M.'s early work was influenced by Hofmannsthal, Rilke (qq.v.), and the humanistic ideal of culture, as his *Lateinische Erzählungen* (1904), set in humanistic Italy, and his volume of novellas *Die drei Grazien des Traums* (1906) show. In 1910 he turned to a new thematic area: the immediate present and the people of his own region. The novella *Barbara Naderers Viehstand* (1914) describes peasant types. *Die Osterfeier* (1921) shows M.'s love of legend; in order to replace the broken figures in a wayside Station of the Cross, three young men undertake to "represent" the saints on Easter Day. *Das Apostelspiel* (1923; Apostle Play, 1934) tells, in simple rhymed couplets, the story of two robbers who break into a lonely mountain hut and are converted by the childish faith of a little girl. In *Das Nachfolge-Christi-Spiel* (1927) a band of robbers crucify a count; after his rescue, in a pure spirit of sacrifice he enters upon the Imitation of Christ as expressed in love for his enemies. In the play *Die Sieben gegen Theben* (1932) M. turned to a classical theme, while in *Der Nibelunge Not* (2 parts, 1944-51) he attempts to combine the heroic saga and Christian ideas. In the drama *Jeanne d'Arc* (1956), which depicts the final phase of the Rouen trial, he successfully achieves "a dramatic presentation of the way salvation carries across a specific time and space" (B. von Heiseler).

The core of all M.'s works is understanding —and therefore forgiving—love, together with faith in the conquest of evil through awareness of the divine in man. His poems, which are heartfelt, close to nature, and musical, also reflect this spiritual attitude.

M. is by no means a regionalist. His work, which stands outside the great literary currents, seeks to bring into synthesis, in the tradition of Grillparzer and Raimund, closeness to nature, the Christian heritage, a classical intention in style, a baroque manner, and the Austrian spirit.

FURTHER WORKS: *Jägerhaussage* (1910); *Das bekränzte Jahr* (1911); *Gedichte* (1919); *Das Wiener Kripperl von 1919* (1921); *Das Schutzengelspiel* (1923); *Ein altes deutsches Weihnachtsspiel* (1924); *Morgenwege* (1924); *Das Spiel von den deutschen Ahnen* (1935); *Steirischer Lobgesang* (1938); *Das Donauweib-* chen (1938); *Mein Bruder und ich* (1938); *Adalbert Stifter* (1939); *Verheißungen* (1943); *Gabe und Dank* (1949); *Das Vergelt's Gott* (1950); *Aufblick zum Genius* (1955); *Prosa, Dramen, Verse* (4 vols., 1962)

BIBLIOGRAPHY: Emich, I., *M. M., Der Dichter und sein Werk* (1957); Hill, F. J., "M. M., Dramatist," *DA*, XIX (1959), 2952-53
PAUL WIMMER

MENCKEN, Henry Louis

American journalist, editor, essayist, and philologist; b. 12 Sep. 1880, Baltimore; d. there, 29 Jan. 1956

M. started his writing career in 1899 as a reporter on the Baltimore *Morning Herald,* later becoming its editor; in 1906 he began his long association with the Baltimore *Sun.* Two years later he joined the *Smart Set* as literary critic; from 1914 to 1923 with George Jean Nathan he was co-editor of the magazine. In 1924 M. launched the *American Mercury* with a denunciation of the South as the "Sahara of the Bozart," a judgment which he supported with his scoffing of the fundamentalist position at the Scopes "monkey trial." He also attacked Boston censorship by selling banned copies of the *Mercury* and winning his court case with the Watch and Ward Society. Until his retirement from the editorship in 1933 M. made the *Mercury* the center of controversy with his debunking of religion, journalism, genteel traditionalism, and politics. His attacks upon puritanism, hypocrisy, and stupidity were widely applauded by young intellectuals of the 1920's.

His first serious books, *George Bernard Shaw: His Plays* (1905) and *The Philosophy of Friedrich Nietzsche* (1908), reveal his clever, satiric, iconoclastic criticism of "booboisie" manners and morals. His vexations and vituperations continued through six volumes of *Prejudices* (1919, 1920, 1922, 1924, 1926, 1927). M. a skillful manipulator of words, had, in addition, a scholarly curiosity about the nature of his native tongue which resulted in his exhaustive, fully documented study *The American Language* (1919; 4th revision, 1936) and *Supplement One* (1945) and *Supplement Two* (1948) to this work. In these volumes M. perceptively analyzed the historical development, pronunciation, spelling, grammar, slang, proper names, and foreign borrowings of American English. In 1942 he brought out a

New Dictionary of Quotations, a compendium gleaned from a half century of extensive reading. M. summed up his career in three entertaining autobiographical volumes, *Happy Days* (1940), *Newspaper Days* (1941), and *Heathen Days* (1943). Throughout his life M. kept up his war against human folly and weakness with his humorous, though always serious, attacks with a "style flexible, fancy-free, ribald, and always beautifully lucid: a native product unlike any other style in the language" (Alistair Cooke).

FURTHER WORKS: *Ventures into Verse* (1903); *What You Ought to Know About Your Baby* (with L. K. Hirschberg; 1910); *Men Versus the Man* (with R. R. La Monte; 1910); *The Artist* (1912); *Europe after 8:15* (with G. J. Nathan and W. H. Wright; 1914); *A Little Book in C Major* (1916); *A Book of Burlesques* (1916); *A Book of Prefaces* (1917); *Ireland and Her Books* (1917); *Damn! A Book of Calumny* (1918); *In the Defense of Women* (1918); *The Literary Capital of the United States* (1920); *Heliogabalus* (1920); *The American Credo* (with G. J. Nathan; 1920); *Notes on Democracy* (1926); *James Branch Cabell* (1927); *Treatise on the Gods* (1930); *Making a President* (1932); *Treatise on Right and Wrong* (1934); *A Christmas Story* (1946); *Minority Report* (1956); *A Carnival of Buncombe* (1956); *The Bathtub Hoax* (1958); *The Letters of H. L. M.,* ed. Guy J. Forgue (1961); *H. L. M.'s "Smart Set" Criticism* (ed. W. H. Nolte; 1968)

BIBLIOGRAPHY: Boyd, E., *H. L. M.* (1925); Goldberg, I., *The Man M.* (1925); Kemler, E., *The Irreverent Mr. M.* (1950); Manchester, W., *Disturber of the Peace* (1951); Angoff, C., *H. L. M.: Portrait from Memory* (1956); Singleton, M. K., *H. L. M. and the American Mercury Adventure* (1962), *Menckeniana,* No. 10 (1964), Issue on M. as literary figure; Wagner, P., *H. L. M.* (1966)

RALPH M. ADERMAN

MENEN, Aubrey

(pseud. of *Salvator Aubrey Clarence Menon*), Anglo-Indian writer, b. 22 April 1912, London

Briefly a drama critic for *The Bookman* (1934) and director at the Experimental Theatre in London (1935-36), then for several years a director of motion pictures (including service for the government of India), M. published in

1947 *The Prevalence of Witches,* the first and best of a series of brightly satirical novels, ironically descriptive of British personality types as they react in wittily exaggerated exotic situations. Attacking the shallow stereotypes of patriotism, justice, business, sex, M. provides only shallow characterization; the dialogue, however, is always lively and sophisticated.

Menen's *Dead Men in the Silver Market* (1953) is a short autobiographical and anecdotal discussion of false and true patriotism, particularly the English and Indian varieties. Like his novels, it is surprisingly light in touch for its didactic seriousness.

Since 1955, M. has been a prolific writer of travel articles for the magazine *Holiday.* He has published two books about Italy, where he now lives: *Rome For Ourselves* (1961; Eng., *Rome Revealed,* 1960) and *Speaking the Language Like a Native* (1963).

FURTHER WORKS: *The Stumbling Stone* (1949); *The Backward Bride* (1950); *The Duke of Gallodoro* (1952); *The Ramayana Retold* (1954); *The Abode of Love* (1957); *Angelina* (1958); *The Fig Tree* (1959); *SheLa: A Satire* (1962); *A Conspiracy of Women* (1965)

BIBLIOGRAPHY: McLeod, A. L., ed., *The Commonwealth Pen* (1961); Srinivasa Iyengar, K. R., *Indian Writing in English* (1962); Alphonso, J. B., "Indo-English Fiction," *Literature East and West,* VIII (1964), 6-14

HERBERT MCARTHUR

MEYRINK, Gustav

Austrian novelist, b. 19 Jan. 1868, Vienna; d. 4 Dec. 1932, Starnberg

When the naturalistic novel was at its height in Vienna, M. introduced a romantically oriented trend, which, like the work of Kafka (q.v.), is deeply rooted in the mysterious, occult atmosphere of old Prague. In his first and most successful novel, *Der Golem* (1915; The Golem, 1928), M. expressed Prague's impact upon him in dreamlike visions showing the weird figure of the Golem, which according to legend inhabits an inaccessible room in the Prague ghetto, gaining fateful domination over the characters. In his later novels, *Das grüne Gesicht* (1916), *Walpurgisnacht* (1917), and *Der Engel vom westlichen Fenster* (1927), M. again explored the possibilities of transforming dream images and waking dreams into scenes with every appearance of reality. He thus came to be considered a precursor of Kafka and of modern dream-poetry.

M. combined a fondness for the gruesome and uncanny (like E. T. A. Hoffman and Poe) with an acute, colorful sense of humor which reached the pitch of satire in *Des deutschen Spießers Wunderhorn* (1913), short stories attacking hypocritical philistinism and bureaucratic nonsense. M. ranked with Polgar, Čapek, and Tucholsky (qq.v.) as one of the leading social-critical *feuilletonists* of the first three decades of the 20th c. His pessimistic social criticism was later intensified into an apocalyptic vision of a doomed Europe.

FURTHER WORKS: *Der heiße Soldat* (1903); *Orchideen* (1904); *Das Wachsfigurenkabinett* (1907); *Fledermäuse* (1916); *Der weiße Dominikaner* (1921); *An der Schwelle des Jenseits* (1923)

BIBLIOGRAPHY: Sperber, H., *Motiv und Wort bei M.* (1918); Frank, E., *G. M.: Werk und Wirkung* (1957); Buskirk, W. R. van, "The Bases of Satire in G. M.'s Work," *DA,* XIX (1958), 141-42

HERBERT FRENZEL

MICHAËLIS, Karin

(pseud. of *Katharina Stangeland*), Danish novelist, b. 20 March 1872, Randers, Jutland; d. 11 Jan. 1950, Copenhagen

From 1895 to 1911 Karin M. was married to S. Michaelis (q.v.). From 1898 on she wrote many novels (sometimes two or three a year). From 1903 to 1913 and from 1920 to 1925 she traveled in the U.S.A. and Central Europe on lecture tours. She spent her last years on Thurø (near Fünen), where after 1933 she took in refugees from the Nazis.

Karin M.'s greatest success was *Den farlige alder* (1910; The Dangerous Age, 1911), a short novel about physical and psychic crises in a woman of forty. In other novels she used the interior monologue as a medium for the unhindered flow of personal memories. Her work is dominated by wishful dreams. Her most valuable book is *Pigen med glasskårene* (1924), the first volume of an autobiographical series in which the relatively sober description of reality prevails over the fantastic and the sentimental. *Bibi-Bøgerne* (1929-38), six volumes of stories for young girls, was also an international success.

FURTHER WORKS: *Højt Spil* (1898); *Barnet* (1902; Andrea, the Tribulations of a Child, 1904); *Lillemor* (1902); *Betty Rosa* (1908); *Elsie Lindtner* (1911; Eng., 1912); *Bogen om kaerlighed* (1912); *Grev Sylvains haevn* (1913); *Krigens ofre* (1916); *Don Juan after døden* (1919); *Lille unge kone* (1921); *Mette Trap og hendes unger* (1922); *Syv søstre sad* (1923); *Traeet på godt og ondt* (1924-30); *Lille løgnerske* (1925); *Hemmeligheden* (1926); *Synd og sorg og fare* (1928); *Følgerne* (1930); *Pigen der smilede* (1929); *Hjertets vagabond* (1930); *Mor* (1935); *Little Troll* (1947); *Vidunderlige verden* (1948-51); *Farlige Famlen* (1949); *Lys og Skygge* (1950)

BIBLIOGRAPHY: Kjaergaard, H., *Die dänische Literatur der neuesten Zeit* (1934); Mitchell, P. M., *A History of Danish Literature* (1957); Møller-Kristensen, S., *Dansk Litteratur 1918-1952* (5th ed., 1959) and "Die dänische Literatur nach 1900," *Schweizer Monatshefte,* XLV (1965), 461-472

EMIL FREDERIKSEN

MICHAËLIS, Sophus

Danish poet, novelist, and dramatist, b. 14 May 1865, Odense (Fünen Island); d. 28 Jan. 1932, Copenhagen

M. studied Romance and German philology and art history. He was a skilled translator, especially from German, French, and Portuguese. As a poet he tried to translate the language of visual form into the language of words in the spirit of Théophile Gautier and was a supporter of aestheticism (*Livets Fest,* 1900, in particular). In his early realistic novels he revealed himself as the most radical Nietzschean of his generation. In 1895 and 1901 he published neoromantic novels, then in 1914 *Hellener og Barbar,* a glorification of the superman and of Hellenism. His late poetry tends to be rhetorical and pathetic. His plays, the most famous of which is *Revolutionsbryllup* (1906), are influenced by Ibsen and Maeterlinck (qq.v.). M. typified the period of 1890-1914 and was a member of the Georg Brandes group, but he ended in obscurity.

FURTHER WORKS: *Digte* (1889); *Solblomster* (1893); *Æbelø* (1895); *Sirener* (1898); *Giovanna* (1901); *Palmerne* (1904); *Den evige søvn, 1812* (1912); *Blåregn* (1913); *Samlede romaner,* (3 vols., 1919); *Romersk forår* (1921); *Abailard og Héloïse* (1926)

BIBLIOGRAPHY: See bibliography for Karin
Michaëlis

EMIL FREDERIKSEN

MICHAUX, Henri

French poet, narrative writer, and essayist of
Belgian descent, b. 24 May 1899, Namur

M. comes of a respected middle-class family.
His interest was first captured by the mystics
Ruysbroek, Pascal, and Hello; he wanted to
live the life of a saint. However at eighteen he
broke off his medical studies and went to sea,
visiting England, America, and Brazil. Reading
Lautréamont at the age of twenty-five won
him over to literature. He was encouraged in
his first attempts by Supervielle (q.v.) and
Franz Hellens (b. 1891), who published his
first poems in Le Disque Vert. In 1926 Paulhan
(q.v.) persuaded him to contribute to the
Nouvelle Revue française and Commerce, the
journal of avant-garde literature. M. continued
to travel: to equatorial America (Ecuador,
1929), India and China (Un Barbare en Asie,
1933; A Barbarian in Asia, 1949). From 1937
to 1939, together with Bernard Groethuysen
and Rolland de Renéville, he edited Hermes,
which was to provide a common forum for
philosophy, poetry, and mysticism. He spent
the war years in the south of France, where
he wrote his great poems Epreuves, exorcismes,
1940-1944 (1945). His travels were now over,
except for journeys to imaginary lands; these
inner experiences were set down in Voyage en
Grande Garabagne (1936), Au Pays de la
Magie (1942), and Ici, Poddéma (1946). Here
M. builds a world in which all that man usually
represses into the bottommost depths of his own
being is made objective—a world of anxieties,
fear, and complexes. The more fantastic the
creatures that inhabit this world, the more
"realistically" and precisely they are described.

M.'s world is a dangerous, aggressive one
which keeps man, constantly in peril, always
on the alert. The psychical attrition and moral
collapse threatening the individual in modern
society are represented by corresponding
phenomena from the physical world and thereby
exorcised, though M. does not use allegory or
formal symbolism. Constant watchfulness is
necessary lest one simply slip out of existence;
weariness follows and, ultimately, the peace of
resignation, expressed in clear, purely lyrical
poems. M. knows one other escape from this
fate: humor—another form of exorcism. And

so he invents the Chaplinesque figure of Monsieur Plume, totally bewildered by his
adventures, which are improbable, often bloody
yet always authentic.

Recently M. has concerned himself with the
problem of hallucination and the extension of
consciousness through drugs, especially mescalin. He wanted to explore new paths of
experience; ecstasy and the visions of drug-
induced rapture might lead man's consciousness
up to the infinite, right to the "gates of awareness." Ailleurs—"elsewhere"—the keyword to
M.'s thought and life, is here asserted to the
utmost, leading him to the furthest limit, where
madness and reason collide and the human
personality dissolves. Like Huxley (q.v.), M.
experimented on himself and wrote factual,
poetically intense accounts of his experiences in
Misérable Miracle, la mescaline (1956), L'Infini
turbulent (1957), and Connaissance par les
gouffres (1961; Light Through Darkness, 1963),
a modified form of the moral and physiological
self-study so common in modern French
literature.

FURTHER WORKS: Fable des origines
(1923); La Nuit remue (1925); Qui je fus
(1927); Mes propriétés (1929); Un Certain
Plume (1931); Prosa (1932); Entre centre et
absence (1936); Plume, précédé de lointain intérieur (1938); Sifflets dans le temple (1938);
Peintures (1939); Le Lobe des monstres (1944);
Labyrinthes (1944); Apparitions (1946);
L'Espace du dedans (1944; The Space Within,
1950); Liberté d'action (1945); Meidosems
(1948); Nous deux encore (1948); La Vie dans
les plis (1949); Poésie pour pouvoir (1949);
Passages (1951); Nouvelles de l'étranger
(1952); Face aux verrous (1954); Paix dans
les brisements (1959); Vents et poussières,
1955-1962 (1962); Vers la complétude (1966)

BIBLIOGRAPHY: Gide, A., Découvrons
H. M. (1941); Poulet, R., La laterne magique
(1956); Bertelé, R., H. M. (1957); Mauriac, C.,
La Littérature contemporaine (1958); Bréchon,
R., M. (1959); Bellour, R., H. M. (1965);
Broome, P., "M. and the Exorcism of God,"
Australian Journal of French Studies, II (1965),
191-220; Murat, N., M. (1967)

MICHEL EUVRARD

MIEGEL, Agnes

German poet and narrative writer, b. 9 March
1879, Königsberg; d. 26 Oct. 1964, Salzurflen

M., who originally wanted to be a teacher,

HENRI MICHAUX

EDNA ST. VINCENT MILLAY

worked on the Königsberg *Ostpreußische Zeitung* from 1920 to 1926. After 1926 she devoted herself to writing lyric poetry and novellas.

Like the characteristic spiritual climate of her native East Prussia, M.'s poetry is severe yet pervaded by a proud awareness of mission. This mission is eloquently expressed in her ballads, the earliest of which were published by Münchhausen (q.v.) in his *Göttinger Musenalmanach* of 1898. All M.'s poems deal with her native country, which has conferred many honors upon her. An often tragic feeling for the constant shift from love to warfare, from joy of living to melancholy, is the keynote of her fiction, in which plot and characters are, indeed, often of minor importance.

FURTHER WORKS: *Gedichte* (1901); *Balladen und Lieder* (1907); *Gedichte und Spiele* (1920); *Geschichten aus Altpreußen* (1926); *Die schöne Malone* (1926); *Spiele* (1927); *Gesammelte Gedichte* (1927); *Kinderland* (1930); *Dorothee, Heimgekehrt* (1931); *Der Vater* (1932); *Herbstgesang* (1932); *Kirchen im Ordensland* (1933); *Gang in die Dämmerung* (1934); *Unter hellem Himmel* (1936); *Das Bernsteinherz* (1937); *Katrinchen kommt nach Hause* (1937); *Frühe Gedichte* (1939); *Wunderliches Weben* (1940); *Ostland* (1940); *Im Ostwind* (1940); *Ordensdome* (1940-41); *Mein Bernsteinland und meine Stadt* (1944); *Flüchtlingsgedichte* (1949); *Gesammelte Gedichte* (1949); *Die Blume der Götter* (1950); *Die Meinen* (1951); *Der Federball* (1951); *Truso* (1958); *Mein Weihnachtsbuch* (1959); *Heimkehr* (1962); *Gesammelte Werke* (6 vols., 1952-56)

BIBLIOGRAPHY: Meidinger-Geise, I., *A. M. und Ostpreußen* (1955); Krieger, E., *A. M.* (1959); Wagner, R. M., ed., *Leben war ich dir gut: A. M. zum Gedächtnis* (1965)

JOSEF FUCHS

MILLAY, Edna St. Vincent

American poet, b. 22 Feb. 1892, Rockland, Maine; d. 19 Oct. 1950, Steepletop (near Austerlitz), N.Y.

M. wrote poetry long before she went to college, and won several prizes from *St. Nicholas Magazine*. A solid education at Barnard and Vassar colleges prepared her for the world. "Renascence," her first major poem, she wrote when only a nineteen-year-old girl, in the same year that the magazine *Poetry* was launched by Harriet Monroe. Simple diction masked her wonderment and love of "The How and Why of all things, past, and present, and forevermore"; the poem, published in *The Lyric Year,* made her famous. Subsequent volumes of poetry preached hedonism, anger that death should be so powerful, and love of the arts ("On Hearing a Symphony by Beethoven"). Her tone was that of a young girl new to a big city who was shocked by its evil, and had decided to master its tempo. Despite their bravura, her lyrics communicated a girlish innocence that won her large audiences.

M. admired classical poets like Catullus, but observed nature closely. Her work with the Provincetown Players and her experiments with verse drama (notably *Aria Da Capo,* 1920) made her a Greenwich Village celebrity. Her libretto for *The King's Henchman* (music by Deems Taylor, produced in 1927) was a serious contribution to American opera. She won the Pulitzer Prize in 1922 for *The Harp-Weaver and Other Poems*; married Eugen Jan Boissevain the following year; and moved in 1925 to the farm in the Berkshires.

During the 1920's M. was tremendously excited by the Sacco-Vanzetti case, wrote several poems on the subject, and pleaded with the government of Massachusetts to commute the death sentence. What began as a concern with social injustice broadened, with the appearance of *Conversation at Midnight* (1937), into a consideration of international problems. Much of her later poetry was censured by critics as didactic and journalistic, and she agreed that she had not learned how to convert the ideals of a beleaguered democratic world to poetry of the first order. Her final years were spent fighting illness, personal disappointment, and a declining reputation. Nevertheless, she was the most exciting woman poet since Emily Dickinson and a distinguished contributor to both the lyric and the sonnet traditions.

FURTHER WORKS: *Renascence* (1917); *A Few Figs from Thistles* (1920); *The Lamp and the Bell* (1921); *Second April* (1921); *Two Slatterns and a King* (1921); *Poems* (1923); *Distressing Dialogues* (1924); *The Buck in the Snow and Other Poems* (1928); *Poems Selected for Young People* (1929); *Fatal Interview* (1931); *The Princess Marries the Page* (1932); *Wine from These Grapes* (with George Dillon; 1934); *Flowers of Evil* (trans. of Baudelaire, 1936); *Huntsman, What Quarry?* (1939); *Make*

Bright the Arrows (1940); *Collected Sonnets* (1941); *The Murder of Lidice* (1942); *Letters of E. St. V. M.*, ed. A. R. Macdougall (1952); *Mine the Harvest* (1954); *Collected Poems* (1956)

BIBLIOGRAPHY: Sheean, V., *The Indigo Bunting: A Memoir of E. St. V. M.* (1951); Britton, N. A., *E. St. V. M.* (1967); Gray, J., *E. St. V. M.* (1967)

HAROLD OREL

MILLER, Arthur

American playwright, novelist, and essayist, b. 17 Oct. 1915, New York

Son of a New York textile manufacturer impoverished by the great depression, M. worked his way through the University of Michigan, was associated with federal theater projects in the late thirties, and served in the U.S. Marines during World War II. In 1945, M. began work as a scriptwriter in Hollywood, an occupation he has since intermittently pursued. Since the production of *All My Sons* (1947), M.'s writing for the theater has enjoyed great success. In 1965 M. was elected President of the International P.E.N. Club. Of his three marriages, the one to film actress Marilyn Monroe (1926-1962) enjoyed wide publicity. M. wrote *The Misfits* (1961), a filmscript for a psychologizing Western, especially for her.

Misfits and *After the Fall* (1964), a play incorporating large parts of the Monroe scenario, are exceptions in M.'s *œuvre* by not being primarily concerned with social criticism. M.'s best-known work has consistently dealt with mid-20th-c. political and social problems—anti-Semitism, fascism, political persecution, and the fate of the underdog in large, urban-technological societies. His point of view is more that of a moralist in the Judeo-Christian tradition than that of a Marxist. To him anti-Semitism is the great social evil. M. firmly condemns it in both its American (*Focus*, 1945) and National Socialist (*Incident at Vichy*, 1964) varieties.

In M.'s other social plays, individual excesses rather than environmental problems are castigated. The fall of the central characters both in *All My Sons* and in *Death of a Salesman* (1949) is precipitated by their roles as fathers in conflict with their sons. In *All My Sons,* a war profiteer attempts to justify his actions to his sons. In *Death of a Salesman,* Willy Loman is undone more because his sons act out the false values he has taught them than by the brutal

treatment he receives at the hands of the firm he has served.

The Crucible (1953) indirectly criticizes Senator Joseph McCarthy's antidemocratic excesses by recalling the Salem witch trials of 1692 to a modern theatrical audience. Not all virtue here, however, lies on the side of the "witches."

A highly skilled writer for the stage, M. cannot be called a theatrical innovator. Ibsen, Chekhov, and O'Neill (qq.v.) are his models for such dramatic experimenting as occurs, e.g., in *Death of a Salesman* and *A View from the Bridge*. With Tennessee Williams, MacLeish, and Wilder (qq.v.), M. belongs to a mid-20th-c. generation of American dramatists who have successfully adapted earlier theatrical innovations to the requirements of the Broadway stage. M.'s central social concerns are very much rooted in the historical events he witnessed as a young man—economic depression and the growing threat of totalitarianism, especially that of National Socialism. For that reason, his work seems to be more meaningful to members of his own generation than to younger theatrical audiences.

FURTHER WORKS: *Situation Normal* (1944); *The Man Who Had All the Luck* (1944); *A Memory of Two Mondays* (1955); *Collected Plays* (1957); *I Don't Need You Any More* (1967); *The Price* (1968)

BIBLIOGRAPHY: Welland, D., *A. M.* (1961); Huftel, S., *A. M.: The Burning Glass* (1965); Moss, L., *A. M.* (1967); Murray, E., *A. M.: Dramatist* (1967)

W.B.F.

MILLER, Henry

American narrative writer, dramatist, and essayist, b. 26 Dec. 1891, New York

M.'s parents came of simple German stock. He had a modest education and tried various occupations before devoting himself finally to writing. From 1930 to 1939 he lived in France, chiefly in Paris. After a long stay in Greece (for a time with Durrell [q.v.]), he returned to the U.S.A. in 1940. Since 1942 he has lived in California, since 1947 at Big Sur (Partington Ridge).

M.'s work belongs to the early 20th c. literary revolt against the bourgeois world and the technological mechanization of existence. He took his standards for the critique of culture largely from Nietzsche (q.v.) and Oswald Spengler; the spirit of revolt links him consciously with Rimbaud and Breton (q.v.); Joyce and Céline (qq.v.) influenced his concept of human reality; his confidence in life stems from the optimism of the American pioneers; his sexualism was corroborated by D. H. Lawrence (q.v.). In style he acknowledges as his masters the great Russians, Laurence Sterne, Rabelais, Stendhal, and Balzac, and among his contemporaries Cendrars (q.v.) and others.

M.'s artistic medium is a blatant naturalism shifting abruptly into dreamlike, visionary prose poetry which for almost inexplicable imaginative imagery and knowledge of the subconscious surpasses Apollinaire and Éluard (qq.v.). He occasionally adopts the French Surrealists' technique of "automatic writing" and claims to have heard and transcribed "dictation." His books lack artistic form; they reveal an explosive talent incapable of and disinclined for self-discipline. His total work is a single monstrous self-portrait—the pair of novels *Tropic of Cancer* (1934) and *Tropic of Capricorn* (1939) and the short stories *Black Spring* (1936) no less than the admittedly autobiographical trilogy *The Rosy Crucifixion*: *Sexus* (1949), *Plexus* (French, 1952; Eng., 1953), and *Nexus* (1960); and the minor works in his own defense: *The World of Sex* (1940) and *Obscenity and the Law of Reflection* (1944). Even his verdict on contemporary culture, *Max and the White Phagocytes* (1938), *The Wisdom of the Heart* (1941), *The Air-Conditioned Nightmare* (1945), and analyses of other writers such as Rimbaud and Lawrence serve as vehicles of self-interpretation. He uses the first person almost exclusively. This self-obsession is not free from pathological elements split personality, a superiority complex, paranoid delusions, hatred of the mother. Despite his thoroughgoing, naïvely experienced egocentricity, M. achieves masterful portrayals of other individuals; the people who interest him are mainly asocial, wayward misfits (he once called himself "the *minnesingerv* of the *lumpenproletariat*"). This has to do with his rejection of the way of life of domesticated Western man; in his earlier works M. even calls for total destruction and glorifies chaos.

Confronted with the "machinery of death" of civilization, especially in its American form, M. remained an "anarchist"; in his late books his nihilistic impulses seem to have been overcome. In *Big Sur and the Oranges of Hieronymus Bosch* (1955) peace, love, compassion, and mercy are the guiding principles of a new order, though according to *The Colossus of Maroussi* (1941), M.'s egocentric travel book about Greece, this new order can only be attained after passing through impending unprecedented catastrophes. M. is totally uninterested in social reform and current politics.

His (extremely nonerotic) sexuality has nothing pseudo-mystical or cultic about it. The shocking obscenities in many of his books, like the appalling blasphemies, are designed to jolt the reader out of his apathetic acceptance of established misorder. The defiant exhibition of sexuality is meant as a protest against the coercion of civilization; it also represents a violent escape from the machine world back to the natural and the primitive, though M. undeniably also takes a coarse delight in it for its own sake.

In M.'s development religious traits have emerged more and more clearly. He is a professed non-Christian without any hostility toward Christ. To him God is "full reality," nature, cosmos, and man forming a whole inspired by a lawful universal intelligence. Religiousness is belief and confidence in life. His acceptance of life also unconditionally embraces the ugly, ill, repulsive, and negative. Nevertheless M. is disturbed by the problem of evil—he even speaks of "sojourns in Hell" and has ghastly visions of annihilation, chaos, and the sovereignty of Satan—but evil necessarily remains insoluble for him. With the maturity of age—and to some extent through the influence of oriental mysticism and wisdom— the gnostic-theosophic elements in his thinking have grown stronger. God is in man; He is the truly human man; after the catastrophes there will dawn an era of higher humaneness which will hold things in control through metatechnical powers.

M.'s work, with its power of imagery and passion for words, which make nonsense of all aesthetic categories, is more a natural phenomenon than art, more a contemporary historical document than poetic fiction. Although it may be confused with the antihumane *littérature noire* in external appearance, its function is to champion man against technocracy. Thus it marks a turning point in the sense of life.

FURTHER WORKS: *Lawrence Durrell and*

H. M.: A Private Correspondence (1963); *H. M. on Writing* (ed. T. H. Moore; 1964); *Stand Still like the Hummingbird* (1964); *Greece* (1964); *Letters to Anaïs Nin* (ed. G. Stuhlmann; 1965); *Selected Prose* (1965)

BIBLIOGRAPHY: Moore, N., *H. M.* (1943); Perlès, A., *My Friend H. M.* (1955); Omarr, S., *H. M.* (1960); Schmiehle, W., *H. M.* (1961); White, E., ed., *H. M., Between Heaven and Hell* (1961); Haan, J. de, *Milleriana* (1963); Wickes, G., ed., *H. M. and the Critics* (1963); Widmer, K., *H. M.* (1963); Wickes, G., *H. M.* (1966); Gordon, W. A., *The Mind and Art of H. M.* (1967)

ANTON BÖHM

MILLIN, Sarah Gertrude

South African novelist, biographer, essayist, and diarist, b. 19 March 1889, Barkly (near Kimberley)

A fearless and uncompromising mind, a sharp, staccato style, and powerful, thought-provoking themes—these are the attributes which have established M. as the foremost South African writer. The people of her books are South African in the true sense, but their experiences are universal.

Although as a novelist M. is famous for her works on race—*God's Stepchildren* (1924), *The Coming of the Lord* (1928), *The Herr Witchdoctor* (1941), *King of the Bastards* (1950), *The Burning Man* (1952)—her range is so wide and her thought so penetrating that no particular social group can be singled out as her special field of interest. She has with equal facility dealt with religion, art, history, class, and psychology in her novels.

In nonfiction her achievement is as versatile. Her biographies *Rhodes* (1933) and *Smuts* (1936) are still authoritative, while her books on South Africa, *The South Africans* (1926) and *The People of South Africa* (1951), are standard works. One of her major achievements is a comprehensive diary of World War II in six volumes (*War Diary*, 1944-48).

FURTHER WORKS: *The Dark River* (1919); *Middle-Class* (1921); *Adam's Rest* (1922); *The Jordans* (1923); *Mary Glenn* (1925); *An Artist in the Family* (1927); *The Fiddler* (1929); *Men on Voyage* (1930); *The Sons of Mrs. Aab* (1931); *Three Men Die* (1934); *What Hath a Man?* (1938); *The Night Is Long* (1941); *World Blackout* (1944); *The Measure of My*

Days (1955); *The Wizard Bird* (1962); *White Africans Are Also People* (1966)

BIBLIOGRAPHY: Snyman, J. P. L., *Works of S. M.* (1955)

J. P. L. SNYMAN

MIŁOSZ, Czesław

Polish poet, narrative writer, and essayist, b. 30 June 1911, in Lithuania

From 1946 to 1950 M. was in the diplomatic service. In 1951 he left his native Poland and now lives in Paris.

He writes an exquisite style and his work abounds in bold images. His major poetic works are *Trzy zimy* (1936), *Ocalenie* (1945), and *Światło dzienne* (1953). His novel *La Prise du pouvoir* (1953; Polish, *Zdobycie władzy*, 1953; Seizure of Power, 1953) was awarded the Prix Littéraire Européen. *Dolina Issy* (1955) is a developmental novel with a Polish-Lithuanian setting; it contains mythical elements.

The treatise *Zniewolony umysł* (1952; Fr. *La Pensée captive*, 1953; Captive Mind, 1953) which was translated into several languages (Karl Jaspers wrote the preface to the German edition), is an analysis of intellectual enslavement and the conduct of the intelligentsia under the Communist regime. All M.'s works reveal a humanistic attitude arising from an awareness of the dangers threatening modern man.

M. has translated many works by American, English, and French authors into Polish (Shakespeare, Whitman, Eliot [q.v.], Baudelaire).

FURTHER WORKS: *Poemat o czasie zastyglym* (1933); *Kontynenty* (1958); *Rodzinna Europa* (1959); *Król Popiel* (1962); *Wiersze: London* (1967)

BIBLIOGRAPHY: Heyst, A., "Polish Literature in Exile," *Wiseman Review*, CCXXXV (1961), 177-81; Kuncewicz, M., ed., *The Modern Polish Mind* (1962)

* * *

MIŁOSZ (Lithuanian, *Milasius*), Oscar (Vladislas de Lubicz)

Lithuanian poet (French language), b. 28 May 1877, Čeréja; d. 2 March 1939, Fontainebleau

M. was descended from an old Lithuanian

noble family. In 1889 his parents moved to Paris, where he pursued classical and oriental studies. He frequented the Parisian literary coterie that included Moréas, Fort, and G. Moore (qq.v.). In 1918 he lost his property in Lithuania. After the peace treaty he became Lithuanian minister in Paris and in 1931 acquired French citizenship. In his later years he grew increasingly solitary and turned in a Franciscan mood to nature; toward the end of his life he devoted himself almost entirely to biblical exegesis, particularly of the Apocalypse.

M.'s early poems are written in regular, classical forms and are strongly influenced by Baudelaire, while the typical poetry of his mature period is generally in free, long lines and blends sadness and a premonition of death with nostalgia for youth and a yearning for the utmost love and knowledge. His novel *L'Amoureuse Initiation* (1910) is also intensely poetic; it is set in 18th c. Venice and describes the love of an eccentric old nobleman for a youthful beauty. The transformation of sensual love into love of God is the theme of the play *Miguel Mañara* (1912; Eng., 1918) about the historical Don Juan, who died in the odor of sanctity. In contrast, the play *Méphiboseth* (1914) deals with the lame son of Jonathan and his warnings to David; mystical observations on love, sin, and David's mission in the Christian event of salvation form its crux. M.'s later works are distinctly esoteric; in the tradition of Swedenborg, Saint Martin, and the Apocalypse, they strive for direct insight into the secrets of the earthly and the eternal.

M. also translated poetic works in the Nordic languages (*Chefs-d'oeuvre lyriques du Nord*, 1912) and the first part of Goethe's *Faust* into French and published a collection of Lithuanian folk tales (*Contes et fabliaux de la vieille Lithuanie*, 1930; *Contes lithuaniens de ma Mère L'Oye*, 1934). His poetic personality made so deep an impression in France that Fort called him "the French Goethe" and "Europe's most precious gift to France."

FURTHER WORKS: *Le Poème des décadences* (1899); *Les Sept solitudes* (1904); *Scènes de Don Juan* (1906); *Les Éléments* (1910); *Epître à Storge* (1917); *La Confession de Lemuel* (1922); *Ars magna* (1925); *Le Poème des Arcanes* (1927); *Le Cantique de la connaissance* (1927); *Poèmes 1895-1927* (1930); *La Clef de l'Apocalypse* (1938); *L'Apocalypse de Saint Jean déchiffrée* (1938); *Œuvres complètes* (8 vols., 1945-48); *Textes inédits* (1959). **Selected English trans.:** *Fourteen Poems by O. V. de L. M.* (1952)

BIBLIOGRAPHY: Miomandre, F. de, *Le Pavillon du mandarin* (1921) and *M., hommages et documents inédits* (1944); Rousselot, J., *O. V. de L. M.* (1950); Cassou, J., *Trois poètes: Rilke, M., Machado* (1954); Richter, A., *M.* (1965)

HANS GROSSRIEDER

MINULESCU, Ion

Rumanian poet, narrative writer, and dramatist, b. 7 Jan. 1881, Bucharest; d. there, 20 July 1944

M. is the most typical exponent of the Rumanian symbolist school. Influenced by Villiers de l'Isle Adam (1838-89), he began in 1908 with the short stories *Casa cu geamurile portocalii* and made his reputation as a poet with *Romanţe pentru mai târziu* (1908), *De vorbă cu mine însumi* (1941) and *Nu sunt ce par a fi* (1936). His symbolism (q.v.) is external; he was a popularizer of this movement. A more characteristic trait is his inexhaustible talent for invention. His verses are musical, his rhetoric declamatory, his humor baroque. Yet behind his poetry is a genuine unquietness; he was quite at home with melancholy and the idea of death, and treated everything, especially the experiences of love and death, with a touch of wit and irony. His prose and plays show the same verve and imagination, though an exaggeratedly burlesque humor often interrupts the development and mood of the plot.

FURTHER WORKS: *Lulu Popescu* (1920); *Masti de bronz şi lampioane de porţelan* (1920); *Pleacă berzele* (1920); *Rosu galben şi albastru* (1924); *Manechinul sentimental* (1926); *Spovedanii* (1927); *Allegro ma non troppo* (1927); *Strofe pentru toată lumea* (1930); *Citiţi-le noaptea* (1930); *Bărbierul regelui Midas* (1931); *Nevasta lui Mos Zaharia* (1937); *Versuri* (1939); *Cine-i autorul acestui roman sensaţional* (1943)

BIBLIOGRAPHY: Dragomirescu, M., *M.* (1924); Munteanu, B., *Geschichte der neueren rumänischen Literatur* (1943)

VIRGIL IERUNCA

MIRBEAU, Octave

French novelist and dramatist, b. 16 Feb. 1850, Trévières; d. 16 Feb. 1917, Paris

Son of a Norman doctor, like Flaubert, M. was a lifelong satirist whose bitterness was directed against human stupidity. He defended the Impressionists (paradoxically, in reactionary newspapers), fought social injustice, and as an antimilitarist sided with Captain Dreyfus. His unhappy childhood and youth led him to revolt against a society devoid of all ideals and to a deep hatred of the contemporary clergy; this is reflected in his autobiographical novels *Le Calvaire* (1886); (Calvary, 1922), *L'Abbé Jules* (1888), and *Sébastien Roch* (1890). He owes his choice of themes largely to the Goncourt brothers and Huysmans (q.v.). His impetuous style reflects an often sadistically tinged eroticism. *Le Jardin des supplices* (1899; Torture Garden, 1931) describes orgies, opium dreams, and terrible scenes of torture; the risqué *Journal d'une femme de chambre* (1900; Célestine, Being the Diary of a Chambermaid, 1933) attacks the degradation of domestic service. His novels are episodic and written in the first person; they defend the anarchic freedom of the individual against social prejudice. This theme also dominates his last novel, *Dingo* (1913), whose hero is a German shepherd dog.

M.'s first play, the gripping proletarian drama *Les Mauvais Bergers* (1898), was written under the influence of G. Hauptmann's (q.v.) *Weber*. His masterpiece, *Les Affaires sont les affaires* (1903; Business Is Business, 1905), is a comedy of character castigating the inhuman selfishness of the modern financier.

M. belonged to the Académie Goncourt. After an eventful career in journalism he retired to his estate, Cheverchemont.

FURTHER WORKS: *Lettres de ma chaumière* (1885); *Les Vingt et un jours d'un neurasthénique* (1902); *Forces et moralités* (1903); *La 628-E 8* (1908); *Le Foyer* (1909); *La Pipe de cidre* (1918); *La Vache tachetée* (1918); *Chez l'illustre écrivain* (1919); *Un Gentilhomme* (1920); *Les Grimaces et quelques autres chroniques* (1928); *Oeuvres* (9 vols., 1934-36)

BIBLIOGRAPHY: Revon, M., *O. M., son œuvre* (1934); Schwarz, M., *O. M., vie et œuvre* (1966)

KURT WEINBERG

MIRÓ, Gabriel

Spanish novelist and essayist, b. 28 July 1879, Alicante; d. 27 May 1930, Madrid

M. began his studies at the Jesuit college in Orihuela, Alicante, a town whose circumscribed, church-dominated atmosphere became the setting for several of his novels. He studied law in Valencia and Granada, and was already well known in literary circles when in 1920 he moved to Madrid, where he held modest office positions and devoted his spare time to literature. M.'s art—indeed, his whole being—is rooted in his native province, the luminous garden-landscape of the Mediterranean coast of Spain.

He became known through his short novels such as *Nómada* (1908) and *La palma rota* (1909), which immediately revealed his narrative and stylistic talent and brilliant powers of observation and expression. In his book *Del vivir* (1904) and his novel *Las cerezas del cementerio* (1910) he treated themes from his home province: the life of outcasts, supersuperstition, and fatalism. The Spanish Mediterranean coast also inspired his description of the atmosphere of the Holy Land in *Figuras de la pasión del Señor* (1916); here in strong, vivid language he tells the story of Christ's Passion, stressing the human element more than the divine. The *Libro de Sigüenza* (1917), in which Sigüenza, the author's alter ego, roams through the villages and towns of Alicante, and *El humo dormido* (1919), in which M. concentrates on customs and traditions rather than his subjective experiences, are poetic prose works intended merely to bring to life landscapes, people, and impressions; they cannot be called novels and cannot really be classified. M. next wrote two longer novels, *Nuestro Padre San Daniel* (1921) and *El Obispo leproso* (1926), in which the narrative element is more forceful. Both are set in the old town of Oleza (actually Orihuela), where the atmosphere is a heady mixture of religion and eroticism, liturgy and sensuality. The plots are lengthy; the minute description of provincial life recalls Flaubert; the static, hesitant way the action develops suggests Proust (q.v.). In these novels M., a devout Christian who enthusiastically admired actions of generous Christian charity, presents characters typical of a narrower, naïve concept of religion. His aesthetic creed, a passion for pure art and beauty in any concrete form whatever, is reflected in a brilliant style which reached its utmost perfection in his last book, *Años y leguas* (1928), in which M. wrote perhaps the most beautiful Spanish prose of the 20th c.

M. stands between literary modernism and the "Generation of '98" (see Spanish literature); both trends affected him, modernism of course more strongly, since it provided the point of departure for his work and aesthetic ideas.

FURTHER WORKS: *La novela de mi amigo* (1908); *Dentro del cercado* (1912); *El abuelo del Rey* (1915); *El ángel, el molino y el caracol del faro* (1921); *Niño y grande* (1922); *Obras completas* (12 vols., 1931-36); *Obras completas* (1 vol., 1942)

BIBLIOGRAPHY: Lizón, A., *G. M. y los de su tiempo* (1944); Ramos, V., *Vida y obra de G. M.* (1955); Van Praag-Chantraine, J., *G. M.* (1959); Sánchez, J. C., *G. M. y su obra* (1960); King, E. L., "G. M. Introduced to the French," *Hispanic Review,* XXIX (1961), 324-32; Ramos, V., *El mundo de G. M.* (1964); Vidal, R., *G. M.: Le style, les moyens d'expression* (1964); O'Sullivan, S., "Watches, Lemons and Spectacles: Recurrent Images in the Works of G. M.," *BHS,* XLIV (1967), 107-21

GONZALO SOBEJANO

MISTRAL, Gabriela

(pseud. of *Lucila Godoy Alcayaga*), Chilean poet, b. 7 April 1889, Vicuña; d. 10 Jan. 1957, Hempstead, N.Y.

For seventeen years M. was a country school-teacher and thus got to know Chile, from its farthest south (Punta Arenas) to the saltpeter deserts of Antofogasta, as well as the hard life of the Chilean workers and peasants. She expressed her reaction to her fiancé's suicide in poems full of rebellion and execration but tinged with a forlorn helplessness. Gradually she tried to possess herself in Christian submission and identified the image of the dead man with that of Christ sacrificing Himself. Her poems abounded in biblical echoes; mercy, forgiveness, and charity superseded youthful passion.

In 1914 M. won a literary contest with her *Sonetos de la muerte.*

In 1922 she went to Mexico to participate in a school reform. The publication of the volume of poetry *Desolación* in New York in 1922 brought her fame; it was followed by

Ternura (1924) and *Tala* (1938). She represented her country as consul in Madrid, Lisbon, Nice, Brazil, and the U.S.A.

To the Spanish-American world M. represents the living incarnation of the ideals she stood for: protection of the exploited and the persecuted, social emancipation of women, children's welfare, justice for the oppressed races, and the Indian's right to decent social integration. However her poetic work is not confined to purely philanthropic subjects. Her themes are the emotions of futility, disillusionment and sin, the pain of erotic passion, motherhood, children, social and psychological problems. Her language, especially in *Tala,* is realistic, direct, and vigorous, with a slight tendency to the archaic. She seemed to be familiar with the Spanish mystics and was imbued with the primitive wisdom of the Chilean and Spanish peasants. The spiritual basis of her poetry is Catholicism; the rich symbol-structure of *Tala* rests on the heritage of the Old Testament.

M.'s work produced several disciples in South America, the most famous being Ibarbourou (q.v.). As "queen of the rich literature of Latin America" M. received the Nobel Prize in 1945 and the Chilean national prize in 1951.

FURTHER WORKS: *Lecturas para mujeres* (1923); *Rondas para niños* (1930); *Nubes blancas* (1930); *La Oración de la maestra* (1930); *Antología* (1941); *Poemas de las madres* (1950); *Poesías completas* (1958); *Motivas de San Francisco* (1965); *Antología de G. M.* (1967). **Selected English trans.:** *Selected Poems of G. M.* (1957)

BIBLIOGRAPHY: Pinilla, N., *Biografía de G. M.* (1946); Iglesias, A., *G. M.* (1950); Arce de Vásquez, *G. M.* (1958); Pomés, M., *G. M.* (1964); Preston, M. C. A., *A Study of Significant Variants in the Poetry of G. M.* (1964); García Prada, C., *Letras hispanoamericanas: Ensayos de simpatía* (1965)

FERNANDO ALEGRIA

MOBERG, Carl Arthur Vilhelm

Swedish novelist and dramatist, b. 20 Aug. 1898, Algutsboda, Småland

M., who belonged to a poor family, was originally a craftsman but, after taking university extension courses, became a journalist. His early works (pre-1911) are psychologically realistic regional novels with a social slant and often a strong erotic element. The trilogy about the character Knut Toring (*Sänkt sedebetyg*, 1935; *Sömnlös*, 1937; *Giv oss jorden*, 1939; complete Eng. translation, The Earth Is Ours, 1940), who turns his back on city life to return to his native province, is partly auto-biographical. The historical novel *Rid i natt!* (1941; Ride This Night!, 1943) about Sweden's struggle against foreign domination was success-ful as a topical allegory. It was followed by a tetralogy about Swedish emigrants to America in 1850 (*Utvandrarna*, 1949; The Emigrants, 1951), their first encounter with the New World (*Invandrarna*, 1952; Unto a Good Land, 1954), and their social progress (*Nybyggarna*, 1956; *Sista brevet till Sverige* [The Last Letter Home, 1961] 1959). M.'s realistic narrative technique was an important factor in the great success of this work. His dramas and satirical comedies treat themes similar to those of the novels. Among the best are *Hustrun, Bröllopssalut* (1929), *Marknadsafton* (1930), *Våld* (1933); *Änkeman Jarl* (1940), and *Vår ofödde son* (1945).

FURTHER WORKS: *Kassabrist* (1926); *Raskens* (1927); *Långt från landsvägen* (1929); *A. P. Rosell, bankdirektör* (1932); *Soldat med brutet gevär* (1934; When I was a Child, 1956); *Mans kvinna* (1936); *Jungfrukammare* (1938); *En löskekarl* (1940); *Brudarnas källa* (1946); *Gudens hustru* (1946); *Den okända släkten* (1950); *Det gamla riket* (1953); *Lea och Rakel* (1954); *Därför är jag republikan* (1955); *Därför är jag monarkist* (1955); *Domaren* (1957); *Sagoprinsen* (1960); *Nattkyparen* (1961); *Din stund på jorden* (1963; A Time on Earth, 1965); *Werke* (14 vols., 1946 ff.); *Lustspel och enaktare, kvinnodramer, äktenskapdramer* (1957)

BIBLIOGRAPHY: Gustafson, A., "A Dream Worth Dying For," in *American-Scandinavian Review*, XXX (1942), 296-307; Ollén, G., *V. M.* (1945); Mårtensson, S., *En bok om V. M.* (1953); Winther, S. K., "M. and A New Genre for the Emigrant Novel," in SS, XXXIV (1962), 170-82; Alexis, G. J., "M.'s Immigrant Trilogy: A Dubious Conclusion," in SS, XXXVIII (1966), 20-25; Alexis, G. J., "Sweden to Minne-sota: V. M.'s Fictional Reconstruction," in *AQ*, XVIII (1966), 81-94

JORIS TAELS

MOLNÁR, Ferenc

Hungarian playwright and novelist, b. 12 Jan. 1878, Budapest; d. 1 April 1952, New York

Son of a physician, M. studied law in Geneva and Budapest but soon addressed himself to writing short stories and novels. In 1896 he be-came editor of the newspaper *Budapesti Napló*. His first success as a playwright was won with his comedy *Az ördög* (1907; The Devil, 1908). In 1910 he participated in the first literary cabaret of Budapest, and he has been called "the wittiest Hungarian emcee ever." During World War I he was a war correspondent.

With his first drama, *Liliom* (1909; Eng., 1927), M. was thrust into world fame. This play combined an unusual mixture of naturalism (which M. used in developing his characters) and the supernatural. Liliom, an unscrupulous barker at an amusement park, married the honest girl he loved. Failing in his efforts to steal and kill—his chosen ways of making a living—he finally committed suicide. At the heavenly court, he was condemned to sixteen years of purgatory, but—so that he could gain salvation by doing one good deed for his wife (whom he had treated brutally) or his daughter—he was permitted to return to earth for one day in the guise of a beggar in the custody of two heavenly guardians. When he met his wife and his daughter, he behaved so outrageously, deriding the dead Liliom, whom his wife Julie still loved, even striking his frightened daughter, that his guardians were forced to take him back to hell as unredeem-able. It was effective theater. After *Liliom* the world thronged to see M.'s numerous plays, bestowing fame and fortune on him.

With the advent of Hitler, M. came to America in 1940. The world he had lovingly chronicled had disappeared. The arrogant and decadent Hungarian aristocracy as well as the impudent, irresponsible, common man, the era of Franz Josef, emperor of Austria-Hungary, the life that M. had delighted in observing—all of it was gone forever.

M.'s work was well received on the American stage. A great triumph was *Carousel* (1946), the outstandingly successful musical comedy by Rodgers and Hammerstein that was based on *Liliom*. The Play's the Thing (based on *Játék a kastélyban*, 1926) was adapted by P. G. Wodehouse in 1948. *The Spa: A Play after F. M.* (based on *Riviera*, 1926) was adapted by Edward Chodorov in 1957.

An innate sense of good theater, a taste for

HENRY MILLER

GABRIELA MISTRAL

CARL MOBERG

worldly wisdom, cynicism, erotic piquancies, romantic sentimentality, and melancholy, an ability to write witty, frivolous, smart dialogue —M. brought these and other faculties to the task of re-creating on the stage Budapest life at the turn of the century. Unconcerned with morality or politics, he pleased the sophisticated as well as the petty bourgeois and became the most successful Hungarian playwright of the century.

FURTHER WORKS: *Magdolna és egyéb elbeszélések* (1897); *A csókok ejszakája és egyéb elbeszélések* (1898); *Az éhes város* (1900); *Egy gazdátlan csónak története* (1901); *Józsi és egyéb kis komédiák* (1902); *A doktor ur* (1902; The Lawyer, 1937); *Éva* (1903; Eng., 1952); *Józsi* (1904); *Rabok* (1907; Prisoners, 1925); *A Pál utcai fiuk* (1907; The Paul Street Boys, 1928); *Muzsika* (1908); *Ketten beszélnek* (1909); *A testőr* (1910; The Guardsman, 1937); *A farkas* (1912; The Tale of the Wolf, 1937); *Kis hármaskönyv* (1914); *A fehér felhő* (1916; The White Cloud); *Farsang* (1916); *Uri divat* (1917; Fashions for Men, 1927); *Az aruvimi erdö titka* (1917); *Szentolvajok* (1918); *Marshall* (1919; Marshal, 1919); *Andor* (1918); *A hattyú* (1920; The Swan, 1927); *Shinház* (1921; The Good Fairy, 1952); *Égi és földi szerelem* (1922; Heavenly Earthly Love, 1937); *A vörös malom* (1922; The Red Mill, 1937); *As üvegcipő* (1924; The Glass Slipper, 1937); *Csendélet* (1925; Still Life, 1937); *A gőzoszlop* (1926; The Captain of St. Margaret's, 1945); *Összes munkai* (20 vols., 1928); *Olympia* (1928, Eng., 1928); *Egy, kettő, három* (1929); *A jo tündér* (1930); *Valaki* (1932); *Harmónia* (1932); *A zenélő angyal* (1933; Angel Making Music, 1934); *Az ismeretlen leány* (1934); *Nagy szerelem* (1935); *Csoda a hegyek közt* (1936; Miracle in the Mountains, 1941); *A zöld huszár* (1937); *Delila* (1938); *Öszi utazás* (1939; Autumn Journey, 1942); *Arthur* (1943; Eng., 1952); *Panoptikum* (1944; Waxworks, 1952); *Szivdobogas* (1947; Game of Hearts, 1952); *Companions in Exile: Notes for an Autobiography* (1950; translated from the unpublished Hungarian ms.). **Selected English trans.:** *Plays of M.* (1927); *The Plays of F. M.* (1929; reprinted as *All the Plays of M.*, 1937); *Romantic Comedies: Eight Plays* (1952)

BIBLIOGRAPHY: Hernadi, P., "Ungarische Dichtung im 20. Jahrhundert," *WZ*, IX (1963), xii, 3-9; Remenyi, J., *Hungarian Writers and Literature* (Molnar, A. J., ed., 1964); Tezla, A., *An Introductory Bibliography to the Study of Hungarian Literature* (1964); Vécsei, I., *M. F.* (1966)

GERTRUDE C. SCHWEBELL

MOLO, Walter von

German novelist and essayist, b. 14 June 1880, Sternberg, Moravia; d. 27 Oct. 1958, near Murnau

As a young man M. adopted Vienna as his home; he attended technical college there and worked for ten years as an engineer. From 1915 to 1932 he was a writer in Berlin, and from 1928 to 1930 he was president of the poetry division of the Preußische Akademie der Künste. After that he lived on his farm at Murnau, Upper Bavaria.

M.'s world is an idealistic one; he believed in the precedence of the superior man over the inferior and in the determining power of genius. He therefore specialized in depicting great historical figures. Of his earliest works he later acknowledged only four small-scale novels written between 1907 and 1911, which he collected under the title *Liebessymphonie* (1924). His *Schiller-Roman* (4 parts, 1912-16) shows his skill at transforming phases of life into action and movement. It was followed by a trilogy about the heroic history of Prussia; *Fridericus* (1918), *Luise* (1919), *Das Volk wacht auf* (1922); collected under the title *Ein Volk wacht auf* (1922). *Bobenmatz* (1925; reissued, 1947 as *Der Menschenfreund*) is the story of a modern social apostle.

M.'s Christian heritage is particularly apparent in *Die Legende vom Herrn* (1927; reissued 1951) and in the memoir *Zum neuen Tag* (1950).

FURTHER WORKS: *Als ich die bunte Mütze trug* (1904); *Wie sie das Leben zwangen* (1906); *Klaus Tiedemann, der Kaufmann* (1908); *Mensch Luther* (1928; Brother Luther, 1929); *Zwischen Tag und Traum* (1930); *Ein Deutscher ohne Deutschland* (1931); *Holunder in Polen* (1933); *Der kleine Held* (1934); *Eugenio von Savoy* (1936); *Geschichte einer Seele* (1938; Ein Stern fiel in den Staub, 1958); *Das kluge Mädchen* (1940); *Loblied des Leides* (1947); *Die Affen Gottes* (1950); *So wunderbar ist das Leben* (1957); *Wo ich Frieden fand* (1959)

BIBLIOGRAPHY: Munk, F. C., *W. v. M.* (1924); Anon., *W. v. M.: Erinnerunger, Würdigungen, Wünsche* (1950)

WILHELM GRENZMANN

MOMBERT, Alfred

German poet, b. 6 Feb. 1872, Karlsruhe; d. 8 April 1942, Winterthur, Switzerland

M. went to the universities in Heidelberg, Leipzig, Munich, and Berlin. From 1899 to 1906 he lived as a lawyer in Heidelberg, after which he turned to writing. In 1940 he was sent to the concentration camp of Gurs in southern France, but friends in Switzerland succeeded in getting permission to take the aging poet to their home, where he died soon afterward.

As a poet M. began with a collection called *Tag und Nacht* (1894), which reflects the current naturalism (q.v.) mixed with decadence and sentimentality. *Der Glühende* (1896) shows the influence of early art nouveau in Germany, especially in its abundance of plant imagery. By *Die Schöpfung* (1897), where he confines the art nouveau elements to the sphere of earthbound eroticism, and uses for the sphere of pure intellectualism the language of Nietzsche's (q.v.) *Zarathustra,* he had evolved his personal style. These sharp contrasts are slightly lessened in the following collections—*Der Denker* (1901) and *Die Blüte des Chaos* (1905)—where the two seemingly unconnected worlds of *Die Schöpfung* are placed in a dialectical relationship, reflecting the masculine and feminine elements of human feeling as manifestations of spirit and soul, but elevated into a sphere of a highly symbolical world of primeval situations.

A further step in this direction is M.'s *Der himmlische Zecher* (1909), in which he tries to combine the orgiastic and the intellectual in the figure of a heavenly reveler, symbolizing the *élan vital* of Bergson's (q.v.) intuitionism and the German "philosophy of life." M. is working in a similar vein in his dramatic trilogy *Aeon, der Weltgesuchte, Aeon zwischen den Frauen,* and *Aeon vor Syrakus* (1907-1911). His *Held der Erde* (1919), influenced by the experience of World War I, celebrates the archaic outburst of power as a "dance of weapons," that leads to an imperialism of the soul; this reveals the impact on M. of the expressionist (q.v.) ecstasy and messianism.

In his dramas *Aiglas Herabkunft* (1929) and *Aiglas Tempel* (1931) the expressionist elements are replaced by a more realistic picture of the world, although the visionary elements are not completely lacking. They even appear in his last cycle of poems, *Sfaira der Alte* (1936-42), in which he goes back to his beginnings. In this he writes about the aspects of harmony that he loved as well as about his last bitter experiences with National Socialism and his final deportation to a concentration camp.

M. did not belong to a certain school or group of writers, but he may well be compared with such authors as Däubler, Linde (qq.v.), or Rudolf Pannwitz (b. 1881), who tried like him to renew old mythical concepts in a rather syncretistic manner. He thought of himself not as a simple lyric poet but as an elevated prophet or visionary of the inner landscape of human existence. In his poetry, therefore, which is mainly symbolistic (q.v.) and full of Nietzschean imagery, baroque metaphors, and impressionistic splendor, he experiments with many 20th c. literary techniques.

FURTHER WORKS: *Der Sonne Geist* (1905); *Einführung in sein Werk und Auswahl,* ed. by H. Hennecke (1952); *Briefe an Richard und Ida Dehmel* (1956)

BIBLIOGRAPHY: Strobl, K. H., *A. M.* (1906); Benndorf, F. K., *M.s Geist und Werk* (1913); Benz, R., *Der Dichter A. M.* (1947); Hermand, J., "Der Prozeß des mythischen 'Bilderns' bei M.," *Monatshefte* (1961)

JOST HERMAND

MONNIER, Thyde (actually *Mathilde*)

French novelist and poet, b. 22 July 1887, Marseille

M. received a prize for her volume of short stories *Mon Bel Été* (1926). She then began a series of novel cycles in the documentary tradition, the best-known of which, *Les Desmichels* (7 vols., 1937 ff.), describes, partly through flashback technique, the fate and passions of several generations of a Provençal peasant family; it is notable for its abundance of characteristic figures and for its colorful depiction of landscape. A Zolaesque naturalism (q.v.) is softened by tact and feminine delicacy. Indifferent to religion, M. links her characters to the metaphysical world through belief in fate and affinity with nature (*Grand Cap,* 1937; *Le Pain des pauvres,* 1937; *Nans le berger,* 1942; *La Demoiselle,* 1944; *Travaux,* 1946; *Le Figuier stérile,* 1947; *Les Forces vives,* 1948). She also wrote other cycles (*Petites Destinées,* 3 vols., 1937 ff.; *Pierre Pacaud,* 4 vols., 1942 ff.; *Franches-Montagnes,* 5 vols., 1949 ff.; *Moi,* 4 vols., 1949 ff.) and several novels about life in the ports and countryside of southern France.

FURTHER WORKS: *La Rue courte* (1937); *Annonciata* (1939); *Fleuve* (1942); *Le Vin et le sang* (1946); *Amour de la vie* (1949); *La Combe* (1950); *Coeur* (1951); *L'Huile vierge* (1952); *Le Déjeuner sur l'herbe* (1953); *Retour aux îles* (1954); *Jetée aux bêtes* (1955); *La Désirade* (1956); *Madame Roman* (1957); *Je ne suis pas des vôtres* (1958); *Les Cinq doigts de la main* (1959); *Le Jour vert* (1960); *La Graine* (1962); *La Ferme des quatre reines* (1963); *J'ai joué le jeu* (1963)

* * *

MONTALE, Eugenio
Italian poet, b. 12 Oct. 1896, Genoa

M. first became known among Italy's modern poets as a landscape lyricist. In his first major collection of poems, *Ossi di seppia* (1925), the individual quality of the Ligurian coast is presented through various thematic cycles whereby M. seeks to contrast the originally "austere" aspect of the landscape with the modern Riviera paradise. There are extensive descriptions of the sea, which M. sees as a manifold symbol of eternity, infinity, and purity of soul. He was inspired here by the "Cimetière marin" of Valéry (q.v.) and more generally by the thematically similar sea poetry of French symbolism (q.v.). Formal emulation of symbolism is also discernible in M.'s often obscure manner of expression—conjuring with words, association, analogy, and "suggestive writing." In M., however, as in Ungaretti (q.v.), these techniques serve the ideal of succinct, crucial statement (essentialism) and thus produce that type of difficult poetry that Italian critics have named "hermeticism." With Ungaretti, M. is now considered the founder of this movement and thus of the most notable branch of modern Italian poetry (*see* Italian Literature).

In the next few years M. developed the style of darkly subjective emotional symbolism to the last consequences of poetic autonomy. In the volume of poems *Le occasioni* (1939) he almost entirely renounces the possibility of being logically understood by concealing the "subjects" (*occasioni*) of his poems or appending them playfully in a commentary on himself.

The poems in *La bufera e altro* (1956) show a successful combination of this technique with a return to a warmer human tone. The gentler humaneness of this work may be attributable, as in Quasimodo (q.v.), to the horrors

of war. In his testament "Piccolo Testamento", contained in this volume, M. reaffirms his belief in the inevitability of his poetic journey.

FURTHER WORKS: *La casa dei doganieri e altri versi* (1932); *Finisterre* (1943); *Quaderno di traduzioni* (1948); *Farfalla di Dinard* (1956); *Il colpevole, con tre disegni di Ottone Rosai* (1966). **Selected English trans.:** *The Promised Land and Other Poems* (1957); *Poems* (1959); *Selected Poems* (1965)

BIBLIOGRAPHY: Lunardi, R., *E. M. e la nuova poesia* (1948); Beall, C., "E. M.'s *Sarcofaghi*," in Crisafulli, A., ed., *Linguistic and Literary Studies in Honor of Helmut A. Hatzfeld* (1965), pp. 65-78; Almansí, G., "Earth and Water in M.'s Poetry," in *Forum for Modern Language Studies*, II (1966), 377-85; Ramat, S., *M.* (1966); Cambon, G., "E. M.'s 'Motets': The Occasions of Epiphany," in *PMLA*, LXXXII (1967), 471-82; Pipa, A., "Memory and Fidelity in M.," *IQ*, XXXIX-XL (1967), 62-79; Pipa, A., *M. and Dante* (1968)

HERBERT FRENZEL

MONTHERLANT, Henry Millon de
French novelist and dramatist, b. 1 April 1896, Paris

M. belongs, on his father's side, to an old Catalan family, and he explains by this origin the strong Jansenist current which runs through many of his works as well as his steadfast attachment to Spain. In 1911 he entered the Catholic college of Sainte-Croix de Neuilly, from which he was expelled for insubordination; this incident was the subject of his play *La Ville dont le prince est un enfant* (1951).

He joined the army in 1916 and was severely wounded on the battlefield in 1918; but he found in the army, as later in sports, a school of energy and discipline. M.'s first book, a collection of essays, *La Relève du matin* (1920), drew its inspiration from his college and war experiences.

His first novel, *Le Songe* (1922; The Dream, 1962), relates the adventures and loves of Alban de Bricoule, an obvious personification of M. himself, as regards war and a passion for sports. War again inspired the lyrical *Chant funèbre pour les morts de Verdun* (1924). *Les Bestiaires* (1926; The Bullfighters, 1927), a novel in which Alban de Bricoule reappears, and the essay *Les Olympiques* (1924) are both paeans to sport, especially to bullfighting, which M. had witnessed and admired on his many trips and sojourns in Spain. An essay, *Aux Fontaines du désir* (1927), reassesses the author's philosophical and moral positions, as well as his present detachment from Maurice Barrès (1862-1923), who had previously been one of his masters.

A libertine current, the other facet of M.'s complicated personality, dominates the series *Les Jeunes filles* (1936), *Pitié pour les femmes* (1936; Pity for Women, 1938, contains Young Girls and Pity for Women), *Le Démon du bien* (1937), and *Les Lépreuses* (1939; translations of these latter two are published as The Lepers, Eng., 1940, and as Costals & the Hippogriff, Am., 1940). The hero of these four novels is Costals (the very antithesis of Alban de Bricoule), a cynical, bitter, disillusioned character who despises the women who have fallen in love with him.

M. was scarcely more indulgent to men in the novel *Les Célibataires* (1934; Am., Perish in Their Pride, 1936; Eng., The Bachelors. 1960). M.'s novels are lively, spirited, eloquent, and even forceful, but they are too often marred by lyrical outbursts or violent denunciations, excesses of rhetoric, and the frequent intrusion of the author's own remarks and reflections in the thread of the story.

Since World War I, M. has devoted his talent exclusively to the stage, and his successes in the drama have been outstanding. There again two opposite veins, Christian and pagan, divide his plays. Four of these have their setting in Spain. *La Reine morte* (1942; Queen after Death, or How to Kill Women, 1951), inspired by a play of Luis Vélez de Guevara, was performed at the Comédie Française in 1942, during the German occupation of France. M. reaches the height of mystic exaltation in *Le Maître de Santiago* (1947; Master of Santiago, 1951) with the common sacrifice of Don Alvaro and his daughter Mariana, and in *Port-Royal* (1954; Eng., 1962), which presents a single day in August 1664 in the troubled history of the nuns when Mother Agnès dares resist the orders of the archbishop of Paris. *Le Cardinal d'Espagne* (1960) puts on the stage Don Cisneros, regent and prime minister of Spain, pitiless in the time of his triumph and crushed by his unexpected disgrace.

An entirely different tone reigns in *Malatesta* (1946; Eng., 1951)—whose title character during the Italian Renaissance is at the same time a poet, a scholar, a warrior, a libertine, and an assassin, yet fundamentally a religious man who

is deeply in love with his wife—and in *Don Juan* (1958), an unsuccessful attempt to write yet another comedy on a famous topic.

M.'s plays are almost entirely psychological, and external happenings are few and of little importance. He has sought to explore in depth complicated and contradictory characters; Ferrante and Inez in *La Reine morte,* Don Alvaro, Cardinal Cisneros, Mother Agnès, and Sister Angélique in *Port-Royal.* His style is clear, rapid, incisive, and admirably suited to the exigencies of the stage and of dramatic dialogue. The *Carnets* (1957) and the numerous *notes de théâtre,* prefaces, and postfaces which M. has appended to many editions of his plays provide valuable information about their origins and geneses as well as on M.'s aims and dramatic technique.

M. was elected to the French Academy in March 1960 without having been a candidate. After a long interruption he has written another novel: *Le Chaos et la nuit* (1963; Chaos and Night, 1964).

FURTHER WORKS: *Le Paradis à l'ombre des épées* (1924); *Les Onze devant la porte dorée* (1924); *La Petite Infante de Castille* (1929); *L'Exil* (1929); *Mors et vita* (1932); *Encore un instant de bonheur* (1934); *Service inutile* (1935); *L'Equinoxe de septembre* (1939); *Le Solstice de juin* (1941); *Sur les femmes* (1942); *Fils de personne* (1944; No Man's Son, or More Than Blood, 1951); *Demain il fera jour* (1949; Tomorrow the Dawn, 1951); *Celle qu'on prend dans ses bras* (1950); *Le Fichier parisien* (1952); *L'Histoire d'amour de la rose de sable* (1955; Desert Love, 1957); *Les Auligny* (1956); *Brocéliande* (1956); *La Guerre civile* (1965). **Selected English trans.:** *The Master of Santiago, and Four Other Plays* (1951); *Port Royal, and Other Plays* (1962)

BIBLIOGRAPHY: Faure-Biguet, J. N., *Les Enfances de M.* (1948); Saint-Pierre, M. de, *M., bourreau de soi-même* (1949); Laprade, J. de, *Le Théâtre de M.* (1950); Perruchot, H., *M.* (1959); *La Table Ronde,* special M. issue (April 1960)

FERNAND VIAL

MOORE, George Augustus
Anglo-Irish poet, novelist, dramatist, and essayist, b. 24 Feb. 1852, Moore Hall, County Mayo; d. 20 Jan. 1933, London

After a haphazard education, considerable

HENRY DE MONTHERLANT

MARIANNE MOORE

freedom to do as he pleased, and equipped with a lively imagination and a sound knowledge of the racing stables, M. was left at eighteen with an adequate income and no profession. In 1873, after spending a few years in London, M. went to Paris to study painting and soon found himself on the periphery of the group of French impressionists whom he continued to admire much of his life. Most of his fiction shows signs of his interest in painting and his considerable knowledge of the art. The practical result of these studies and friendships was *Modern Painting* (1893), mainly essays he had contributed to *The Speaker*. Having no talent for painting and having been introduced between 1877 and 1880 to some of the French writers associated with the naturalist movement in prose fiction and the symbolist movement in poetry, M. turned his hand to writing. *Flowers of Passion* (1878) and *Pagan Poems* (1881), in the main poor imitations of Baudelaire, showed M. he had no great talent in this genre. However, the painters and the decadent and symbolist poets helped M. to discover new subjects for fiction and a new way of seeing. Zola (q.v.), the Goncourts, Turgenev, and perhaps Huysmans (q.v.) helped him to discover the form best suited to his talents. He wrote *A Modern Lover* (1883) in imitation of Zola, and there followed such volumes as *A Mummer's Wife* (1885), *A Drama in Muslin* (1886), and *Spring Days* (1888), each in various ways a modification of Zola's manner.

Even in these early years of his career M. was dissatisfied with what he considered the surface psychological portraiture in the French novel and in the work of, among other English writers, Fielding. He was already searching for a way of expressing states of mind and emotions more subtly and penetratingly. *Esther Waters* (1894), his greatest success, in his use of the impressionistic painter's techniques, his counterpointing of tones, already showed a marked shift away from the naturalistic manner. Some of his early short stories, as in *Celibates* (1895), are in a sense exercises in subtle psychological portraiture.

In mid-career, with *Evelyn Innes* (1898) and *Sister Teresa* (1901), M. carried the search for a new technique still further by adapting Wagner's experiments in music to fiction, very likely with some hints drawn from d'Annunzio's (q.v.) novels and with the aid of technical knowledge garnered from Edward Martyn (1859-1923), Edouard Dujardin (1861-1949), and the musical circle which gathered around Arnold Dolmetsch. His subject more often became the private inner life in conflict with the public outer-directed life. His techniques increasingly borrowed from painting and music. The effects of these experiments on his fictions are next seen in *The Untilled Field* (1903) and *The Lake* (1905), written during the ten-year period of his return to Ireland. This period is recorded in his novelistic autobiography, *Hail and Farewell* (1911, 1912, 1914), which has something of the manner of a Wagnerian opera cast in a comic vein. As this work reveals, M. clashed with other leaders of the Irish literary renaissance, and he soon realized that the Irish movement could no longer serve his interests and talents.

From about 1915 to 1933 M. turned his back on the larger public and published most of his work in expensive limited editions. His later work, that of the "melodic line," is thus little known. The complex, flowing style, which often has the ring of a long recitative, is perhaps best illustrated by his brilliant *The Brook Kerith* (1916) and in his prose epic *Héloïse and Abélard* (1921).

Even if one accepts only *A Mummer's Wife*, *Esther Waters*, *The Untilled Field*, *The Lake*, *The Brook Kerith*, *Confessions of a Young Man* (1886), *Modern Painting*, and *Hail and Farewell* as thoroughly noteworthy work, M. was a considerable artist of varied talents. He wrote or had a hand in a number of quite competent plays in various manners, e.g., *The Bending of the Bough* (1900), *The Strike at Arlingford* (1893), *The Apostle* (1911), and *Diarmuid and Grania* (produced, 1901), a play written in collaboration with Yeats (q.v.). He also played an important role in freeing the artist from the stranglehold of the lending libraries (*Literature at Nurse*, 1885), in introducing French literature to the English (*Impressions and Opinions*, 1891; *Confessions of a Young Man*), in stimulating the Irish literary movement (*Hail and Farewell*), and in publicizing the French impressionist painters. However, M. will undoubtedly be longest remembered for his novels, his essays, and his imaginative autobiographical writings.

FURTHER WORKS: *A Mere Accident* (1887); *Parnell and His Island* (1887); *Vain Fortune* (1892); *Memoirs of My Dead Life* (1906); *A Story-Teller's Holiday* (1918); *Avowals* (1919); *The Coming of Gabrielle* (1920); *In Single Strictness* (1922; revised as *Celibate Lives*, 1927); *Conversations in Ebury*

Street (1924); *The Pastoral Loves of Daphnis and Chloe* (1924); *Ulick and Soracha* (1926); *Letters to Edouard Dujardin, 1886-1922* (1929); *Aphrodite in Aulis* (1930); *A Communication to My Friends* (1933); *Letters to John Eglinton* (1942); *Letters to Lady Cunard* (1957); "Letters to Edmund Gosse, W. B. Yeats, Mary Hutchinson, R. I. Best, and Nancy Cunard" (diss. by Charles Burkhart, Univ. of Maryland, 1957); " 'Evelyn Innes and Sister Teresa' by George Moore: A Variorum Edition" (diss. by John Denny Fisher, Univ. of Illinois, 1959)

BIBLIOGRAPHY: Freeman, J., *A Portrait of G. M.* (1922; with a bibliography by Henry Danielson); Morgan, C., *Epitaph for G. M.* (1935); Hone, J. M., *The Life of G. M.* (1936); Nejdefors-Frisk, S., *G. M.'s Naturalistic Prose* (1952); Brown, M., *G. M.: A Reconsideration* (1955); Cunard, N., *G. M.* (1956); Collet, G.-P., *G. M. et la France* (1957); Gerber, H. E., "An Annotated Bibliography of Writings about George Moore," *English Fiction in Transition,* II:2 (2 pts., 1959), 1-91, III:2 (1960), 34-46, IV:2 (1961), 30-42, and supplementary items in various issues thereafter; Gilcher, E., "Bibliography of the Works of G. M." (unpublished)

HELMUT E. GERBER

MOORE, Marianne (Craig)

American poet, translator, and essayist, b. 15 Nov. 1887, St. Louis

In a lifetime of association with literature Marianne M. has established herself as a poet of individual style, which is the result of a scrupulous attention to all the minor details of rhyme, line length, and rhythm and is above all adapted to the necessity for representing objects in vivid, sharp, concrete images.

Much of Marianne M.'s youth was spent in Pennsylvania, where she received her education: first at the Metzger Institute, in Carlisle (1896-1905), then at Bryn Mawr College, from which she was graduated in 1909. From 1911 to 1915 she taught stenography in the government Indian school at Carlisle, a post she assumed after a period of travel in England and France in 1911.

Marianne M.'s career as a poet began with the publication of some poems in an English magazine, the *Egoist*. In 1921 a group of her friends published a collection of her poems in England (*Poems,* the Egoist Press), though without her knowledge. Her career at this time included a four-year term as an assistant in a branch of the New York Public Library (1920-24). At the end of that period an edition of her poems was published in New York as *Observations* (1924). For this volume she received the Dial Award. She left her library position in 1925 to become acting editor of the *Dial* magazine in New York until it ceased publication in 1929.

Most of Marianne M.'s qualities as a poet are already revealed in the poems of the first two volumes. The title of the second most aptly defines them: they are shrewd, precise "observations," often concerning the minutiae of the human character and disposition; many of them comment wryly upon the eccentricities of the literary mind—its extravagances as well as its excellences. In the volumes that followed that of 1924, she expanded upon its style as well as worked over individual poems to enlarge them and to make their discourse more elaborate.

Selected Poems (1935), introduced by Eliot's (q.v.) most perceptive essay, in some cases shows remarkable changes in the texts of the early poems. There followed two slender volumes, *What Are Years* (1941) and *Nevertheless* (1944). In 1952 the *Collected Poems* appeared, and in 1954 she completed her translations of *Selected Fables of La Fontaine*. A year later she published a collection of critical prose, *Predilections*; these essays, all of them written in her special style, generously studded with pertinent quotations, are a prose extension of many of her poetic commentaries. Some of the essays date from the years of her association with the *Dial*; others were from recent studies and appreciations. In all cases, prose and poetry, she demonstrated a keen sense of poetic values and a discriminating and wise "editorial" sense. Two volumes of poems succeeded the *Collected Poems*: *Like a Bulwark* (1956) and *O To Be a Dragon* (1959). She has also been active in recent years giving lectures and readings at universities and poetry centers. Two of these, the Ewing lectures at the University of California, Los Angeles, were published in 1958.

In an interview for the *Paris Review* (Summer-Fall 1961), Marianne M. stated that "what I write ... could only be called poetry because there is no other category in which to put it. ..." She went on to describe her manner of composing: a "felicitous phrase springs to mind" together with "some thought or object of equal attraction;" from there the poetry develops along fairly strict structural and syllabic lines, though the rhymes are often light and unusual in the way they force the pronunciation of the rhyming words (e.g., *sun* and *legion*). The stanza is a unit carefully and even rigidly held to, in terms of identical syllable counts and rhyme patterns. She has spoken of her great indebtedness to the prose masters, specifying Doctor Johnson, Sir Thomas Browne Sir Francis Bacon, and some others. Her quotations, which are woven into her stanzaic patterns, are largely from prose stylists, though Shakespeare and Dante are pre-eminent as poets and overshadow the prose artists she mentioned. As for her special kind of poetic line, she said, "I am governed by the pull of the sentence as the pull of a fabric is governed by gravity. . . ."

These and other frank and revealing admissions suggest the distinctive nature of Marianne M.'s poetry; it can scarcely be said to have derived from any specific source, nor is it an imitation of previous modes. If anything, her poetry is part of the "new poetry" of 1910-25 usually called "Imagism." But she is like the Imagists only in her insistence upon precision of language, the importance of the image as poetic center, and her independence of traditional forms. In her poems the stanzas are worked out in terms of what she calls the "pull and tug" of sentences, yielding both to idea (or image) and syntax. The stanzas are usually exactly measured and balanced; the lines vary radically but are knitted together and carefully balanced in the stanzaic counterpoint; the titles are frequently, rhythmically and topically, a part of the poems (they lead directly into the poems and may often be called syllabically a part of them). Her manner is often that of wry observation, in which the ostensible object (a scene, a gesture, an animal, an *objet d'art*) serves the purpose of the fabulist. She looks at the human condition often in the manner of the conscientious observer, drawing inferences of ironic similarity between animal and human gestures. In this sense her poems remain shrewd, witty, precise commentary on generalized manners; occasionally, and especially in the later poems, her observations are not unmixed with an emotional commitment to direct moral judgment (as in the poem "In Distrust of Merits"), and in these cases the tone differs considerably from her characteristic manner.

FURTHER WORKS: *The Pangolin and Other Verse* (1936); *Nevertheless* (1944); *Idiosyncrasy and Technique* (1958); *A M. M. Reader* (1961); *The Absentee* (1962); *Tell Me, Tell Me* (1966); *The Complete Poems* (1967)

BIBLIOGRAPHY: Blackmur, R. P., *The Double Agent* (1935), pp. 141-71; Eliot, T. S., "Introduction," in M. M.'s *Selected Poems* (1935), pp. vii-xiv; *Quarterly Review of Literature,* IV (1948), special M. M. issue; Zabel, M. D., *Literary Opinion in America* (1951), pp. 385-92; Fowlie, W., in *SR* LX (1952), 537-47; Hoffman, F. J., in *Poetry,* LXXXII (Dec. 1953); Snodgrass, W. D., in *Western Review,* XIX (Autumn 1954), 57-64; "Interview," in *Paris Review,* XXIV (Summer-Fall 1961), 56-66

FREDERICK J. HOFFMAN

MORALES, Rafael

Spanish poet, b. 31 July 1919, Talavera de la Reina, Toledo

M. has led an active literary life in which he has lectured, given poetry readings, and contributed to magazines. The Premio Nacional de Literatura, which he received for *Canción sobre el asfalto* (1954), and the grant from the Fundación Juan March, which made possible the publication of *La máscara y los dientes* (1964), are indicative of the recognition that his poetry has received.

M.'s first book, *Poemas del toro* (1943), is a collection of sonnets about the primitive and blindly instinctive force of the bull and the mysterious tragedy that surrounds him. The predominating themes of *El corazón y la tierra* (1945) are the presence or absence of life and love. In *Los desterrados* (1947), M. writes about misfortune in its many forms. The invocation to God that closes the book seems outweighed by the tragedies of all the lepers, the blind, the idiots, the sick and lonely exiled beings who exist without hope or love. *Canción sobre el asfalto* is pervaded by tenderness and pity. M. insistently observes the most humble and forgotten things—his abandoned jacket, a ragpicker's sack, a garbage can, or an acacia tree in the city. In *La máscara y los dientes,* M.'s sense of the bitterness and hopelessness of man's solitary life has become intensified. Opportunely the long "lirodrama" commences with a quotation from the Prophet Jeremiah: "they have taught their tongues to speak lies and weary themselves to commit iniquity."

423

M. observes the drama of his subjects with pity while he emphasizes the tragedy of their having lost what he considers essential to them: the bull loses its strength; man, love and illusion; a jacket, its functional value. These themes, expressed in simple repetitive language, are written in traditional verse forms among which the sonnet is preferred.

FURTHER WORKS: *Poemas del toro y otros versos* (1949); *Antología y pequeña historia de mis versos* (1958); *Granadeño, toro bravo* (1964)

BIBLIOGRAPHY: Alarcos Llorach, E., "Canción sobre el asfalto", *Pliego Crítico* (1955); Cano, J. L. *Nueva poesía española* (1958); *Poesía española del siglo XX* (1960)
RAYMOND S. SAYERS

MORALES, Tomás

Spanish poet, b. 10 Oct. 1884, Moya, Canary Islands; d. 15 Aug. 1921, Las Palmas

In 1900, M. left the Canary Islands to study medicine in Cádiz and Madrid. He returned to his native land ten years later to practice medicine and to continue writing.

M. belongs to the final phase of the Spanish modernist school. In Madrid he had become friendly with the modernists Villaespesa (q.v.), and Enrique Díez-Canedo (1879-1944). His first compositions, published in 1908 as *Poemas de la Gloria, del Amor y del Mar* and incorporated in 1922 into *Las Rosas de Hércules,* appeared originally in the *Revista Latina,* managed by Villaespesa.

Most of M.'s poems have been collected into three books, each of which is entitled *Las Rosas de Hércules.* The early poems appear in *Las Rosas de Hércules* of 1922. After opening with "Canto inaugural," it is divided into three sections. "Vacaciones sentimentales," (Part I) which contains colorful poems that evoke the poet's past, is, significantly, dedicated to Antonio Machado (q.v.). "Poemas de asuntos varios" (Part II), the poems of which were inspired by the modernists, evokes enamored couples, the fragrance of jasmine, a distant violin in a garden, a nymph and a shepherd on the banks of the Tagus. It also includes erotic and exquisitely sensual poems. "Poemas del mar" (Part III) was directly inspired by the screeching pulleys of an old frigate, the monotony of a seaman's song, a worm-eaten tender, or the moan of a foghorn.

The *Las Rosas de Hércules* of 1919, the only one published during M.'s lifetime, opens with "Prelude." "Los himnos fervorosos," (Part I) includes poems exalting the power of the allies and Don Juan of Austria's victory at Lepanto, and the "Oda al Atlántico," a brilliant hymn to the ocean and to man's conquest of it. It is followed by (Part II) "Alegorías," which contains a triumphal dithyramb to Darío (q.v.). "Epístolas, elogios, elogios fúnebres" (Part III) is composed of poems of circumstance, written to commemorate the centenary of a sculptor of religious images, the death of a friend, the visit of Salvador Rueda Santos (1857-1933) to the Canary Islands, the painter Nestor. "Poemas de la cuidad comercial" (Part IV) were inspired by direct observation of life in Las Palmas; the commercial Triana Street, the Turkish bazaars, the proud arrival of a squadron, or the peace and quiet of the picturesque Vegueta district. This volume concludes with a poem to the poet's wife, Leanor Ramos.

The last *Las Rosas de Hércules,* which begins with "Himno al volcán" and includes some unfinished poems, is a book projected by the poet but not published until 1956 in an edition of the three *Las Rosas de Hércules.*

Those poems expressive of the emotion inspired by direct observation of his native island and of natural phenomena, such as the ocean and the volcano Teide, make a more original contribution to Spanish poetry than that made by his work based on literary models, either symbolist (q.v.) as in "Poemas de asuntos varios" or familiar and sentimental as in "Vacaciones sentimentales". M.'s accent is heroic and orchestral; his vocabulary, often sensuous, rich, and expressive; his verse extensive, brilliant, and sonorous.

FURTHER WORKS: Drama: *La Cena de Bethania* (1955)

BIBLIOGRAPHY: Díez-Canedo, E., Prologue to *Las Rosas de Hércules* (1922); Diaz Plaja G., *La poesía lírica española* (1937); Valbuena Prat, A., *Historia de la poesía canaria* (1937); Nuez Caballero, S., *T. M.* (1956)
RAYMOND S. SAYERS

MORAND, Paul

French novelist, poet, short story writer, and essayist, b. 13 March 1888, Paris

M. studied at Oxford, became a diplomat,

and after World War II lived for a time in exile. He began with two volumes of poetry, *Lampes à arc* (1919) and *Feuilles de tempéra-ture* (1920), whose daring modernism is related to that of Apollinaire and Cendrars (qq.v.). The short stories *Tendres stocks* (1921; preface by Proust [q.v.]; Green Shoots, 1923) are remarkable for a style full of surprises and unusual images, which recalls Giraudoux (q.v.). However, M. later toned down his style, though it continued to be dominated by his talent for acute observation which flinches from nothing and by curiosity, aloofness, and sometimes irony. All these qualities can be found in the feverishly high-pitched stories in two symmetri-cally coordinated volumes, *Ouvert la nuit* (1922; Open All Night, 1923) and *Fermé la nuit* (1923; Closed All Night, 1924); in the novel *Lewis et Irène* (1924, Lewis and Irene, 1925) in which woman's new position plays havoc with established order and emotional patterns; as well as in *Chronique du XXe siecle: L'Europe galante* (1926; Europe at Love, Eng., 1926, Am., 1927), a faintly satirical sketch of erotic behavior in postwar Europe; *Bouddha vivant* (1927; The Living Buddha, Eng., 1927, Am., 1928), about Europe as the opposite of Asia; *Magie noire* (1928; Black Magic, 1929), a description of the Negro people of Africa and America; and *Champions du Monde* (1930; World Champions, 1931), the story of four young Americans. M.'s most successful works are the city-sketches *New York* (1929; New York, 1931) and *Londres* (1933; Frenchman's London, 1934).

In his later work M. has drawn still closer to the traditional psychological novel and novella, as can be seen in his powerful, brutal portraits in *Les extravagants* (1936), *Hécate et ses chiens* (1954), and *La folle amoureuse* (1956).

FURTHER WORKS: *Rien que la terre* (1926; Nothing But the Earth, 1927); *Le Voyage* (1927); *Paris-Timbouctou* (1928); *Hiver caraïbe* (1929); *Flèche d'Orient* (1931; Orient Air Express, 1932); *Air indien* (1932; Indian Air, 1933); *France la douce* (1934; The Epic-Makers, 1935); *L'Homme pressé* (1941); *Journal d'un attaché d'ambassade* (1948); *Girau-doux* (1948); *Marcel Proust, Souvenirs ...* (1949); *Le Flagellant de Séville* (1951); *Fin de siècle* (1957); *Le Lion écarlate* (1959)

BIBLIOGRAPHY: Garnier, C., *P. M.* (1955); Guitard-Auviste, G., *P. M.* (1956); Beck, T. T., "A Study of Style and Imagery in the Early Prose Works of P. M.," *DA*, XXII (1962), 2394-95; Knowlton, E. C., "Chinese Elements in P. M.'s *Mr. U.*," *Chinese Culture*, V (1964), iii, 34-41; Delvaille, B., *P. M.* (1966)

PIERRE BELLAUNAY

MORAVIA, Alberto

(pseud, of *Alberto Pincherle*), Italian novel-ist, short story writer, dramatist, and essayist, b. 28 Nov. 1907, Rome

The best-known of contemporary Italian novelists was born into a middle-class family. Because of severe osteomyelitis, much of his adolescence was spent in various sanatoriums in northern Italy. The experience of living far away from his family, without any close friends or playmates, hastened his maturity. Forced to interrupt his schooling at an early age, M. educated himself by reading with intensity and pleasure the great classics of continental Euro-pean fiction and drama—Boccaccio (1313-75), Ariosto (1474-1533), Shakespeare, and Molière (1622-73), among others. He drew on the experi-ence of these lonely sanitorium years some years later to write one of his most perceptive short stories, "Hiverno di un ragazzo malato" (A Sick Boy's Winter), which is a story about a timid hospitalized youngster who is tormented, because of his sexual awkwardness, by his roommate, an aggressive traveling salesman.

While in Bressanone in 1925, M. began writ-ing what was to be his first published novel, brought out at his own expense by Alpes of Milan—*Gli Indifferenti* (1929; The Time of Indifference, 1953). The book might well have gone unnoticed, had it not caught the interest of Borgese (q.v.), then the literary critic of the influential Milanese daily *Il Corriere della sera*. Borgese's favorable review turned the book into an immediate best seller, and into one of the most discussed books of the first half of this century. The novel, written in a terse and gray style, has as its dominant themes the deca-dence and estrangement of the *bourgeoisie* as revealed through the false and shallow love affairs of three people—an aging mother and her two children, Carla and Michele, the latter a law student and the real hero of the story. Beyond the literal story itself, however, the novel is permeated with a profound awareness of a world left on the brink of total disillu-sionment, hanging on to shabby values, acting as though it were perennially on a stage, manipulated by the invisible hand of mechanical instincts.

After the appearance of the novel M. undertook several assignments for newspapers and magazines, and as a roving reporter he visited Switzerland, France, England, Mexico, and the United States.

M.'s second novel, a long, turgid, and on the whole unsatisfactory book, *Le Ambizioni sbagliate* (1935; Mistaken Ambitions, 1955), may be classified as an attempt to write an Italian version of a Dostoyevskian novel. Two years later M. produced *L'Imbroglio,* a collection of five excellent long short stories that revealed him to be a master of the genre and a superb observer of the immense frailties and pretensions of a vast gallery of human beings. Once again he treated the familiar themes of sex, power, and money, adding this time a new ingredient: the human incapacity to achieve either true love or a measure of happiness in a world torn by moral confusion and a debasement of values.

After an interlude of some years—during which M. published an amusing novel, *La Mascherata* (1941; The Fancy Dress Party, 1952), in which he satirized the ridiculous nature of totalitarian governments, and a collection of short stories, *L'Epidemia* (1944), written in a surrealistic vein—he completed *Agostino* (1944; Two Adolescents, 1950). Possibly his finest work to date, this novella is a sensitive and poignant study of the awkwardness and difficulties of an adolescent, trying desperately to enter the adult world through a much desired sexual affair.

M. began to secure a reputation outside of Italy some years after the end of World War II, when his novel *La Romana* (1947; The Woman of Rome, 1949) was translated into English. This novel depicts the life of a lowly but compassionate Roman whore and her numerous encounters with intellectuals, would-be revolutionaries, secret police officials, thugs, and murderers.

The postwar years have proved to be very fruitful and prolific for M. In 1949 he wrote *L'Amore coniugale* (Conjugal Love, 1951), the story of a would-be writer who decides to abstain from relations with his wife in order to devote his energies to his novel—only to discover that his wife is betraying him with a disgusting man, the town barber. *Il Disprezzo* (1954; A Ghost at Noon, 1955) tells about the contempt developed by a woman for her husband when she becomes aware that he does

not hesitate to allow his boss, an important movie producer, to make advances to her so long as it will further his career and security.

La Ciociara (1957; Two Women, 1958), perhaps M.'s most realistic and believable novel, is a story about two women and their escape to the hills of the Roman countryside when the war has reached the gates of the city. The novel obviously derives from M.'s similar experience when, in the closing months of the war, he and his wife, the novelist, Elsa Morante (they are no longer married to each other) fled to Fondi, a town in the Ciociara region, where they spent several months in a pigsty waiting for the arrival of the Allied troops.

Among M.'s more recent works are *La Noia* (1960; The Empty Canvas, 1962) and *L'Automa* (1962). *La Noia* is an ambitious attempt to give Italy a *nouveau roman sui generis*. Here M. dissects the meaning, essence, and consequences of that familiar and universal disease known as "ennui" as it is experienced by a would-be painter, who has given up painting when he realizes he has nothing to say on his canvas, and who is having a love affair with a beautiful model named Cecilia. *L'Automa* is a collection of forty-one short stories that dramatizes the mechanical, robotlike behavior of people who have forgotten how to feel about things and the estrangement of modern man from his environment and himself.

An intelligent and skillful narrator, M. has brought much distinction to the literature of his country. Neither a stylistic nor a structural innovator, he has tried, using old techniques, to tell new truths about human nature, thereby creating a gallery of engrossing, strange, and yet strangely believable human beings. He has endeavored to explore, frequently with depth and force, some of the important problems and preoccupations of modern man, and has succeeded in illuminating the character of existence in our century.

FURTHER WORKS: *La Bella vita* (1935); *I Sogni del pigro* (1940); *L'Amante infelice* (1943); *La Speranza* (1944); *La Disubbidienza* (1948); *Il Conformista* (1951; The Conformist, 1951); *l Racconti* (1952); *Racconti romani* (1954; Roman Tales, 1957); *Teatro* (1958); *Un Mese in URSS* (1958); *Nuovi racconti romani* (1959; More Roman Tales, 1963); *Un'Idea dell'India* (1962); *Cortigiana stanza* (1965); *Racconti romani, a cura di Oreste del Buono* (1965); *Una cosa è una cosa* (1967); *La revolutione culturale in Cina* (1967; The Red

Book and the Great Wall, 1968); *Racconti di Alberto Moravia* (1968)

BIBLIOGRAPHY: De Michelis, E., *Introduzione a M.* (1954); Baldanza, F., "The Classicism of A. M.," in *MFS*, III (1958, 309-320; Lewis, R. W. B., "Eros and Existence", in *The Picaresque Saint* (1959); Pacifici, S., *A Guide to Contemporary Italian Literature: From Neorealism to Futurism* (1962), pp. 29-56

SERGIO PACIFICI

MORÉAS, Jean

(pseud. of *Iannis Papadiamantopoulos*), Greek poet, dramatist, short story writer, and essayist, b. 15 April 1856, Athens; d. 30 March 1910, Paris

M., the son of Greek parents, settled in Paris and wrote in French. His early poems were influenced by symbolism (q.v.), but he was later drawn to neoclassicism. In 1891, with Maurras and others, he founded the École Romane, the members of which looked to the poets of the Pléiade as models. His best poetry appears in *Les Stances* (6 vols., 1898-1901; Vol. 7, 1920), in which he tried to bring classical elegance into harmony with his melancholic sense of life. *Iphigénie à Aulide* (1903) is considered to be the most important neoclassic drama.

FURTHER WORKS: *Les Syrtes* (1885); *Les Cantilènes* (1886); *Les premières armes du symbolisme* (1889); *Eriphyle* (1894); *Contes de la vieille France* (1904); *Iphigénie* (1904); *Poèmes et Sylves* (1907); *Variations sur la vie et les livres* (1910); *Oeuvres* (2 vols., 1923-27); *Oeuvre en prose, morceaux choisis* (1927)

BIBLIOGRAPHY: Niklaus, R., *J. M.* (1936); Thomas, L., *Souvenirs sur M.* (1941); Embiricos, A., *Les Étapes de J. M.* (1948); Ménard, J., *De Corneille à Saint-Denys-Garneau* (1957); Bo, C., *Poesia francese del Novecento da Apollinaire a Char* (1966)

ALDO TAGLIAFERRI

MORETTI, Marino

Italian poet and fiction writer, b. 18 July 1885, Cesenatico, Romagna

As a poet M. can be considered a successor of the "Crepuscolari" (*see* Italian Literature). As a fiction writer he is notable for unhurried,

affectionate observation of provincial backgrounds, quiet awareness of people and their modes of conduct, and attention to little things. These determine the theme and psychological treatment of *La voce di Dio* (1920, reissued 1931) and also the tone of nostalgic reminiscence of his autobiographical novel *Mia madre* (1924). *Il romanzo della mamma* (1924) and *Il tempo felice* (1929) are sequels to the latter work. *I puri di cuore* (1923, reissued 1938) is a passionate apology for the weak; *Il trono dei poveri* (1928) has been called a worldly paraphrase of the New Testament parable of Mary and Martha.

FURTHER WORKS: *L'autumno della vergine* (1903); *Fraternità* (1906); *Poesie scritte col lapis* (1910); *Poesie di tutti i giorni* (1911); *Poesie* (1919); *I lestofanti* (1909); *I pesci fuori d'acqua* (1914); *L'isola dell'amore* (1920); *I due fanciulli* (1922); *Il sole del sabato* (1916); *Libro dei sorprendenti vent'anni* (1931); *L'Andreana* (1935); *Anna degli elefanti* (1937); *Scrivere non è necessario* (1938); *Pane in desco* (1940); *La vedova Fioravanti* (1941); *I coniugi Allori* (1946); *Il fiocco verde* (1948); *Il pudore* (1950); *Il ciuchino* (1953); *Il tempo migliore* (1953); *50 novelle* (1954); *Uomini soli* (1954); *La casa del Santo Sangue* (1957); *La camera degli sposi* (1958); *Tutte le novelle* (1959); *Cento novelle* (1959); *Il libro de miei amici* (1960); *Romanzi della mia terra* (1961)

BIBLIOGRAPHY: Casuati, F., *M. M.* (1952); Viviani, A., *M. M.* (1960); Cinti, J., *M. M.* (1966)

GIORGIO DOLFINI

MORGENSTERN, Christian

German poet and prose writer, b. 6 May 1871, Munich; d. 31 March 1914, Merano (now in Italy)

M. was the son and grandson of landscape painters. He first studied economics and law, then philosophy and art history. When he fell ill in 1893, the friendship of Friedrich Kayssler (1874-1945) and the encouragement of the Hart brothers (see naturalism) had a decisive influence on "Zarathustra's lark," as he thought of himself under the spell of Nietzsche's (q.v.) books. His first volume of verse, *In Phantas Schloß* (1895), is part hymnic, part playful; not merely in title does it suggest Holz (q.v.). The early *Galgenlieder* (1905; Eng., Christian Morgenstern's Galgenlieder: A Selection; translated and with an Introduction by Max Knight, 1964), on the other hand, have an individual tone. Between 1897 and 1905 M. wrote four volumes of serious poems, the volume *Palmström* (1910), and also made translations (including Ibsen's [q.v.] *Brand* and *Peer Gynt*). An inner crisis, reflected in *Melancholie* (1906), ended his "worldly period" and led him beyond Nietzsche to Kierkegaard, Meister Eckhart, and the Gospel of St. John (*Einkehr*, 1910). In 1908 his spiritual conflict was allayed when he met his future wife, Margareta, whom he married in 1910 (*Ich und Du*, 1911). On his mystical "inward way," M. sought not merely faith but a knowledge of God. He believed he had found the clarity he sought in Rudolf Steiner's anthroposophy, and as a personal disciple dedicated his last volume of poetry, *Wir fanden einen Pfad* (1914), to Steiner.

M. shared with contemporaries such as Hofmannsthal and Rilke (qq.v.) the consciousness of a lost universal unity and the attempt to regain it through introversion. When his hope that art would offer access to being failed him, he turned to Steiner and made art subservient to his mystical *Geisteswissenschaft* (spiritual science). As a result his serious poetry became not merely increasingly intellectual but actually "philosophy in verse" (B. F. Martin). Despite its undeniable musicality, much of it is "stated rather than created" (J. Pfeiffer). M.'s strength lies in the epigram; this is proved by the volume of aphorisms *Stufen* (1918)—"a spiritual diary" (E. Lissauer). An attitude of human goodness and universal responsibility linked M. to the Expressionists. His mastery of the surprising insight also underlies his grotesque poetry. Its humor comes not so much from the comic element in everyday things as from expressively setting this element off against an intellectually and linguistically conceived reality.

FURTHER WORKS: *Horatius travestitus* (1897); *Und aber ründet sich ein Kranz* (1902); *Der Gingganz* (1913); *Epigramme und Sprüche* (1920); *Mensch Wanderer* (1927); *Meine Liebe ist groß* ... (1936); *Das aufgeklärte Mondschaf* (1941); *Egon und Emilie* (1950); *Quellen des Lebens* ... (1951); *Ein Leben in Briefen* (1952)

BIBLIOGRAPHY: Sperber, H., and Spitzer, L., *Motiv und Wort* (1918); Martin, B. F., *M.'s Dichtungen* (1931); Bauer, M., *C. M.* (1933; 2nd ed., 1954); Steiner, R., *M.* (1935); Hiebel, E., *C. M.* (1957); Hubel, M., *C. M.* (1957); Ray, A., "C. M., Poet of the *Galgenlieder*," *American-German Review*, XXVII (1961), 4-7; Forster, L., "C. M.," in Natan, A., ed., *German Men of Letters* II (1964), 79-99; Walter, J., *Sprache und Spiel in C. M.'s "Galgenliedern"* (1966)

HELLMUTH HIMMEL

MÓRICZ, Zsigmond

Hungarian novelist, short story writer, and dramatist, b. 30 June 1879, Tiszacsécse; d. 4 Sept. 1942, Budapest

M., the son of a peasant and a clergyman's daughter, was educated in fine Calvinist schools. After studying theology and law, he became a reporter for the Budapest *Az Ujság*. In 1909, at the publication of his first short story in *Nyugat*, the radical publication that was the spearhead of the new Hungarian literature, he became a leading writer in the new literary movement. In the last years of his life he founded *Kelet Népe*, an important periodical. In 1938, troubled by expanding fascism and World War II, he retired to his country home at Leányfalu, where he died shortly after finishing his novel *Rózsa Sándor* (1940-42). Throughout a lifetime of uninterrupted work, he published the novels, short stories, plays, reportage, and essays that have earned him his recognition as the major Hungarian prose writer of the 20th c.

In the tradition of Zola's (q.v.) naturalism (q.v.), M. wrote honestly, realistically, occasionally even crudely, about the peasant and the petit bourgeois in the provinces. His picture is that of a stifling and bleak society doomed by the dominance of sex, greed, and hatred. This world can be seen in *Sárarany* (1910). M. has made himself so powerfully felt that his observation of provincial life has become the standard interpretation to the modern Hungarian.

Among M.'s most significant works is *Erdély* (1922-35), a trilogy. in which he turns from the contemporary to recreate the story of two princes—the fevered, inordinate man versus the sober level-headed man. The background is the Hungarian Principality of Transylvania in the 17th c.

Another respected work is *Életem regénye* (1939). In this concrete, factual, though introspective autobiography, M. scrutinizes the events at the turn of the century.

FURTHER WORKS: *Sári bíró* (1909); *Az isten háta mögött* (1911); *Kerek Ferkó* (1913);

ALBERTO MORAVIA

KAI MUNK

Árvalányok (1914); *A fáklya* (1917; The Torch, 1931); *Szegeńy emberek* (1918); *Légy jó mind-halálig* (1922; Be Faithful unto Death, 1962); *Búzakalász* (1924); *Az asszony közbeszól* (1924); *A pillangó* (1924); *Kovilágos virradatig* (1926); *Rokonok* (1933); *A boldog ember* (1935); *Forr a bor* (1936); *Rab orozlán* (1936); *Összes művei* (1935, 1954 ff.)

BIBLIOGRAPHY: Féja, G., *Z. M.* (1939); Urbán, E., *M. Z.* (1947); Móricz, M., *M. Z. indúlasa* (1959); Sivirsky, A., *De Hongaarse letterkunde van onze tijd* (1960); Móricz, M., *M. Z. érkénese* (1966); Móricz, V., ed., *M. Z.* (1967)

LINA MAINIERO

MORRIS, Wright

American novelist, b. 6 Jan. 1910, Central City, Neb.

M. studied in Chicago and at Pomona College, in southern California. After extensive travel in America and Europe—a long stay in Paris proved very influential—he settled in California.

Beginning with his first book, *My Uncle Dudley* (1942), M. has established himself as one of the outstanding American writers of the 1940's and 1950's. For all his originality and discreet experimentation, his novels stand squarely in the American tradition; thematically his work is dominated by what America has meant to him, especially his own region of America—the vast western plains (although he is not to be classified as a regionalist). The tension between small town and big city, between city slickers and hicks, is seen as an essential factor in American life. M.'s characterization shows subtle insight; his main characters especially are prey to restlessness and disorientation but also to passivity and a sense of transitoriness and decay. To M. things become signs, revealing the people who make use of them. In two books, *The Inhabitants* (1946) and *The Home Place* (1948), photography (chiefly pictures of objects, houses, and rooms) is on an equal footing with the literary text: things are supposed to speak for themselves. *The Deep Sleep* (1953) sketches a family and a house through the events of a single day. *The Huge Season* (1954) paints a disillusioned picture of the generation of the 1920's; here, as in *Ceremony in Lone Tree* (1960), past and present are contrasted.

Stylistically M. took Hemingway (q.v.) as his master; he tries to achieve "maximum effect with the minimum of words."

FURTHER WORKS: *The Man Who Was There* (1945); *The World in the Attic* (1949); *Man and Boy* (1951); *The Works of Love* (1951); *The Field of Vision* (1956); *Love Among the Cannibals* (1957); *The Territory Ahead* (1958); *What a Way to Go* (1962); *Cause for Wonder* (1963); *One Day* (1965); *In Orbit* (1967)

BIBLIOGRAPHY: *Critique*, IV (1962), no. 4, M. issue; Morris, W., "The Origin of a Species, 1942-1957," *Massachusetts Review*, VII (1966), 121-35; Shetty, M. N., "The Fiction of W. M.," *DA*, XXVII (1967), 3471

GERD VAN BEBBER

MUIR, Edwin

Scottish novelist, poet, critic, essayist, and translator, b. 15 May 1887, Deerness, Orkney Islands; d. 3 Jan. 1959, Cambridge, England

M. had no formal education after the age of fourteen, when his family moved to Glasgow. His awakening as a serious writer followed closely his marriage to Willa Anderson in 1919, a period of psychoanalysis in London (1920-21), and residence in Prague, Dresden, and Austria (1921-25); his first volume of serious criticism, *Latitudes* (1924), *First Poems* (1925), and his first novel, *The Marionette* (1928) stem from the time when he and his wife also began translating continental works into English (they later introduced to English readers major works by Kafka and Broch [qq.v.]). *Transition, Essays on Contemporary Literature* (1926), *The Structure of the Novel* (1928), and *The Present Age, from 1914* (1939) contain criticism of originality and power.

M.'s importance as a poet was recognized in England with the publication of *Journeys and Places* (1937), *The Narrow Place* (1943), *The Voyage and Other Poems* (1946), *The Labyrinth* (1949), and his remarkable volume of autobiography *The Story and the Fable* (1940). M. was director of the British Institute in Prague from 1945 to 1948 and in Rome from 1948 to 1949. With *Essays on Literature and Society* (1949; rev. 1965), *Collected Poems: 1921-1951* (1952), and *One Foot in Eden* (1956) he received international recognition as one of the most significant voices in modern English literature. From 1950 to 1955 he was warden of Newbattle Abbey College, near Edinburgh, and in 1955-56 Norton Professor at Harvard University in Cambridge, Mass. In his last years M. was writing poetry (*Collected Poems: 1921-1958*, 1960) preparing his Norton lectures for publication (*The Estate of Poetry*, 1962), and working on a book concerning the Scottish ballad (posthumously completed by Willa M.).

As poet, critic, and journalist M. was chiefly concerned with authentic individual imagination; he opposed anything which crippled it or threatened it. Whether his immediate materials were dreams, myths, memories of his childhood in the Orkneys, or responses to the contemporary world, his poems embody an individual vision of the life of man.

FURTHER WORKS: *We Moderns: Enigmas and Guesses* (1918); *Chorus of the Newly Dead* (1926); *John Knox—Portrait of a Calvinist* (1929); *The Three Brothers* (1931); *Poor Tom* (1932); *Variations on a Time Theme* (1934); *Scottish Journey* (1935); *Social Credit and the Labour Party* (1935); *Scott and Scotland: The Predicament of the Scottish Writer* (1936); *The Scots and their Country* (1946); *Prometheus* (1954); *Selected Poems*, ed. T. S. Eliot (1965)

BIBLIOGRAPHY: Hall, J. C., *E. M.* (1956); Blackmur, R. P., "E. M.: Between the Tiger's Paws," in *KR*, XXI (1959), 419-36; Hamburger, M., "E. M., in *Encounter*, LXXXVII (1960), 46-53; Gardner, H., *E. M.* (1961); Holloway, J., "The Poetry of E. M.," in *HudR*, XIII (1961), 550-67; Summers, J. H., "The Achievement of E. M.," in *Massachusetts Review*, II (1961), 240-60; Butter, P. H., *E. M.* (1962); Mellown, E. W., *Bibliography of the Writings of E. M.* (1965; augmented London ed., 1966); Butter, P. H., *E. M.: Man and Poet* (1966)

JOSEPH H. SUMMERS

MÜNCHHAUSEN, Börries von

German poet and prose writer, b. 20 March 1874, Hildesheim; d. 16 March 1945, Altenburg

M. was descended from a famous family. After studying law and serving in World War I, he entered the Ministry of Foreign Affairs and later lived on his estates. His ambition was to encompass life within the form of the ballad, "the prince of German poetry." Partly in emulation of his models Moritz von Strachwitz and Theodor Fontane, he took his themes from history, the Bible, legends, and old chronicles

and from his own imagination. Sound dominates all these ballads, which are characterized by onomatopoeic effects. As in Agnes Miegel (q.v.), the transcendental is unimportant; the happenings are purely of an earthly nature and are often given a harsh interpretation. M.'s humor often has a somewhat "Prussian" tinge. M. also wrote popular "songs" and, notably, articles on ballad theory. As the end of World War II approached, he committed suicide.

FURTHER WORKS: *Gedichte* (1897); *Juda* (1900); *Balladen* (1901); *Ritterliches Liederbuch* (1903); *Herz im Harnisch* (1911); *Die Standarte* (1916); *Fröhliche Woche mit Freunden* (1922); *Das Balladenbuch* (1924; enlarged ed. 1950); *Liederbuch* (1928); *Die Garbe* (1933); *Idyllen* (1933; enlarged ed. 1953); *Geschichten aus der Geschichte* (1934)

BIBLIOGRAPHY: Kaiser, W., *Geschichte der deutschen Ballade* (1936), pp. 275-82, 284-89; Seidel, I., "B. v. M.," in *Westermanns Monatshefte* XI (1950-51)

INGO SEIDLER

MUNK, Kai (Harald Leininger)

Danish dramatist, poet, and prose writer, b. 13 Jan. 1898, Maribo, Lolland Island; d. 4 or 5 Jan. 1944

M. (born Petersen) lost both parents in early childhood and was adopted by the M. family, members of a popular Pietist sect. From 1924 on he was pastor of the little community of Vedersø in western Jutland. He wrote about sixty plays (of which only a third were performed and not more than five have any contemporary significance) and numerous essays and sermons that aroused interest when they appeared. *En Idealist* (1928; Herod the King, 1953), a play about Herod, was originally a failure; but in 1931 M. scored a success with his play *Cant* (Eng. 1953) which presents Henry VIII as a despot and eroticist who cleverly disguises his desires as divine commands. *Ordet* (1932; The Word, 1953) the most frequently performed Scandinavian drama, deals with characters from Jutland; it is a miracle play yet remains close to reality. *De Udvalgte* (1933), another biblical drama, is about sin and faith, weakness and good will in King David. In 1935 M. published *Kaerlighed*, the drama of an unbelieving pastor and his love for a married woman; dramatically weak but poetically vital, this play expresses M.'s own wishful dreams. The same is true of *I Braendingen* (1937), which describes a writer and anti-Christian prophet of freedom (modeled on Brandes [q.v.] who comes to grief when his son deserts him and his followers fail to comprehend him.

In 1938 the Herod play was given a second, successful production, of which only the English-language version survives in print. Herod, striving for absolute power yet incapable of murdering Jesus and feeling that God has beaten him, dies in despair. Its construction and style link this play with German expressionism (q.v.). M.'s dramatic work reached its peak in *Han sidder ved Smeltediglen* (1938; He Sits at the Melting Pot, 1953). This play is politically engaged; it represents a Christian protest against the National Socialist persecution of the Jews. It is true that since his youth M. had admired dictatorship and rejected democracy; a man of absolute will and power seemed to him a reflection of God. Yet here a weak man grows into a courageous man of faith who defies a regime of injustice. This play ranks with *Ordet* as a moving proclamation of M.'s belief in miracles.

During the German occupation of Denmark M. wrote his last religious play, *Egelykke* (1940; Eng., 1954) about the crisis and vocation of the national prophet Grundtvigs. His historical play *Niels Ebbesen* (1942), dealing with German-Danish antagonism in the Middle Ages, with present-day parallels, was read by the Danish people in secret, along with his curtain raiser *Før Cannae* (1943; Before Cannae, 1953) in which Hannibal becomes a Hitler figure, while Fabius represents the Danish resistance. Through these plays and even more through sermons and poems disseminated both openly and clandestinely M. became a growing symbol of national revolt against the occupying power. Gestapo agents arrested and murdered him.

FURTHER WORKS: *Os bærer den himmelske glæde* (1934); *Vedersø Jerusalem retur* (1934); *Sejren* (1936); *Knaldperler* (1936); *10 Oxford-Snapshots* (1936); *Pilatus* (1937); *Diktatorinden* (1938); *Dette dødsens legeme* (1938); *Tempelvers* (1939); *Fugl Fønix* (1939); *Navigare Necesse* (1941); *Sværg det, Drenge* (1941); *Ved Babylons floder* (1941); *Det unge Nord* (1942); *Med ordets svaerd* (1942); *Med Sol og megen Glaede* (1942); *Foråret så sagte kommer* (1942); *Så fast en borg* (1942); *Tre praedikaener* (1943); *Jesus historier* (1943); *Ewalds død* (1943); *Den blå anemone* (1943); *8 nye dikte* (1944); *Den skæbne ej til os* (1944); *Four Sermons* (1944); *Saml dig, Norden* (1945); *Et norsk digt om Norge* (1946); *Døden* (1946); *I Guds bismer* (1946); *Ansigter* (1947); *Alverdens-Urostifterne* (1947); *Mindeudgave* (9 vols., 1948-49)

BIBLIOGRAPHY: Larsen, J. K., *K. M. som Dramatiker* (1941); Gustafson, A., Introduction to *Scandinavian Plays of the Twentieth Century* (2nd series, 1944); Henriques, A., *K. M.* (1945); Nøjgaard, N., *K. M.* (1958); Jakobsen, G., *K. M.* (1960); Svendsen, H.-M. and W., *Geschichte der dänischen Literatur* (1964); Vosmar, J., ed., *Modernismen i dansk litteratur* (1967)

EMIL FREDERIKSEN

MURDOCH, Iris

English novelist and essayist, b. 15 July 1919, Dublin, Eire

Born of Anglo-Irish parents, Iris M. grew up in London and attended the Badminton School, Bristol. At Somerville College, Oxford, she gained high honors, taking her degree in 1942. The next five years she spent working for the British Treasury and (1944-46) for UNRRA, mostly in Belgium and Austria. In 1947 she returned to Oxford as a tutor and fellow in philosophy at St. Anne's College. She is married to John Bayley, novelist and critic.

Iris M.'s first writings were in philosophy. She contributed an essay, "Metaphysics and Ethics," to the volume *The Nature of Metaphysics* (1957); before this she published a brief introductory volume, *Sartre: Romantic Rationalist* (1953) in the series called "Studies in Modern European Literature and Thought." Even in this volume her preoccupation with certain definitions concerning the novel is evident; so that it may be said that the emphasis upon Sartre (q.v.) as novelist (she barely mentions the plays) was an anticipation of herself as novelist. She does not resemble Sartre, except in very minor particulars; but it is clear from her statements in the study of the French existentialist that she regards the novel as a crucial center of social and moral representation.

Iris M. distinguishes between what she has called the "crystalline" and the "journalistic" styles in the modern novel: the two aims (to produce a closely-coiled, carefully constructed object of art and "to describe the world around one in a fairly loose and cheerful way") are rarely combined and tend to fly apart. The ideal fiction is one in which there is formal control but in which the form is not *sui generis* or inclined to serve as an excuse for failure to bring characters to life.

Her own novels, she said, are begun each time in the hope that "a lot of people who are not me are going to come into existence in some wonderful way." The real moral challenge is to create characters and to allow them a separate, independent existence. Iris M.'s novels have seemed to "oscillate between attempts to portray a lot of people and giving in to a powerful plot or story."

Under the Net (1954), her first novel, seems a play upon the conflict between conceptualizing and intuitive personalities; its end result appears to be something of a stalemate, though the hero's survival and the protection of his special individuality would suggest the important view that the individual triumphs over intellectual conceptions of him held by his friends and by himself.

In *The Flight from the Enchanter* (1956) the conflict is overtly dramatized in a series of attempts to resist the authoritarian impositions of a character called Mischa Fox, who tries to dominate all people about him, succeeds in some but not in all cases. In the crucial event Rosa Keepe, daughter of a pioneer feminist and sponsor of liberal causes, eventually breaks the spell, to flee from the "enchanter." The novel is a quite successful attempt to balance "myth" and fact. *The Sandcastle* (1957) is in part an attempt to present a minor 20th c. version of *Middlemarch,* a novel which she admired as "that brilliant study of being-for-others"; it is also a study of the effect of emotional distraction upon the work of art itself. On the surface it is a commonplace story of the temptations of adulterous love in a school community; but it is the effect of emotional stress and strain upon the forms of art and upon the grasp it has upon reality that enables the novel to transcend its occasion.

The Bell (1958) is perhaps Iris M.'s best demonstration of what she defines as the most responsible act of the novelist: to create individuals and then to give them a separate imaginary existence so that they may join human society and significantly help to define it. A variety of types are allowed existence, and—in the religious community that is the setting—the formal properties of myth help to substantiate and to lend form to the represen-

tation. In *A Severed Head* (1961) the novelist's ingenuity runs away with the work, and the characters emerge less real than ludicrous actors in symbolic charades. *An Unofficial Rose* (1962) shows that Iris M. has recovered her powers of representation: there are many people in this novel, and their relationships are convincingly given within a richly inhabited world. In *The Unicorn* (1963) she risks combining myth with human plot and action. At times this strangely plotted novel, with its suggestions of Gothic tracery and its extremes of human types, seems to lose its relation to the reality its author has always insisted is the central challenge of the novel form. The novel concludes satisfactorily, though not before it has suffered many strange vicissitudes of plot.

Iris M., who began as a philosopher is now considered to be one of the greatest literary talents of contemporary England.

FURTHER WORKS: *The Italian Girl* (1964); dramatization of *A Severed Head* (with J. B. Priestley, 1964); *The Red and the Green* (1965); *Time of the Angels* (1966); *The Nice and the Good* (1968); *Bruno's Dream* (1968)

BIBLIOGRAPHY: Karl, F., *The Contemporary English Novel* (1962), pp. 260-65; Gindin, J., *Postwar British Fiction* (1962), pp. 178-95; O'Connor, W. V., *The New University Wits* (1963), pp. 54-74; Kermode, F., "Interview with I. M.," in *PR* (Spring 1963); Byatt, A. S., *Degrees of Freedom: The Novels of I. M.* (1966); Wolfe, P., *The Disciplined Heart: I. M. and Her Novels* (1966)

FREDERICK J. HOFFMAN

MUSIL, Robert (Edler von)

Austrian novelist, dramatist, and essayist, b. 6 Nov. 1880, Klagenfurt; d. 15 April 1942, Geneva, Switzerland

The son of a professor of engineering, M. was educated at military schools 1892-97. He turned to engineering after a stint as an officer, but changed to philosophy and experimental psychology and obtained his doctorate with a dissertation on Ernst Mach in Berlin in 1908. From 1911-14 M. was librarian at the Technische Hochschule in Vienna, he also was briefly an editor of *Die Neue Rundschau*. He served as an officer in the Austrian army during World War I and in various Austrian Ministries in the immediate postwar period. From 1923 M. lived in Vienna and Berlin supporting him-

IRIS MURDOCH

ROBERT MUSIL

self as a writer. He emigrated to Switzerland in 1938, where he died in poverty and virtually unknown.

From the time of the publication of his first novel *Die Verwirrungen des Zöglings Törleß* (1906; Young Törless, 1921), which portrays the fears and emotional insufficiencies of an adolescent against the somber background of a military school, M.'s chief concern focused on the problem of achieving an emotional equilibrium within his characters as well as in relation to their fellow human beings. His early two short stories *Vereinigungen* (1911), however, were extreme in their setting as well as in their prose. In *Die Vollendung der Liebe* and *Die Versuchung der stillen Veronika* an insufferable reality is transformed by an excessive inflation of the imagination. The resulting intensification of the emotions causes a spiritual, nonphysical union with the beloved. The two plays *Die Schwärmer* (1921) and *Vinzenz und die Freundin bedeutender Männer* (1924) are stepping stones towards a more tangible achievement of the equilibrium. In them M. suggests a fusion of reality and the imagination. In states of strong emotional intensity, borders and limits vanish, and a short integration with one's fellow men can be achieved. The rational, modern intellectual, however, must resort to an artificial intensification, he must consciously transform reality through adoption of a scientifically bold morality. Somewhat more traditional in form are the three short stories *Drei Frauen* (1921-24). The problems and imbalances created by the rational, logical, but emotionally limited male in his relationship with the emotionally more complex female are in each case resolved.

M.'s early works are all in some sense preparatory to the great novel *Der Mann ohne Eigenschaften* (3 vols., 1930-43; partially translated as The Man Without Qualities, 1965), on which he worked for almost twenty years. It was left unfinished at his death. Ulrich, the hero of the novel, the secretary of a celebration of the Austro-Hungarian Empire planned for 1918 in 1913 (with the basic irony implied that the empire will have collapsed by the time of the celebration) is the man without qualities, hence the man with an unimpaired potential, who like his creator has been an officer, engineer, and mathematician. Ulrich takes a year's leave from life to find its meaning. His scientific training helps him to reject preconceived notions in favor of new possibilities and to look at life as a laboratory.

In addition, he stipulates emotional intensity as the only meaningful basis of morality. He rejects traditional notions of good and evil and replaces them with a new, mobile morality based on faith and intensity. In order to achieve this new morality, Ulrich scrutinizes his own character with utmost precision. His life has been characterized by a preponderance of the "relentless passions," the active and appetitive traits. His emotional equilibrium can be recovered if he fosters the passive and affective emotions which have been surpressed. The term *"Erdensekretariat der Genauigkeit und Seele"* expresses Ulrich's attempt at resolution of his emotional difficulties. It fuses the two most obvious polarities of the human spirit, reason and imagination, truth and metaphor. This term applies now to an inner balance, the proper self-love, *philautia*, the love of the lower drives of the body for the higher ones. Ulrich has been lacking this self-love, he has correspondingly never been able to love other people, his relationships with women have been sexual only. Equilibrium and balance are approached by Ulrich after he meets his sister Agathe, the sister who is like himself, and not like himself, who embodies the fusion of likeness and unlikeness, the conditions of the metaphor. In the relationship of brother and sister in which they analyze their emotional life, they experience the *"andere Zustand"*, a state of mystical intensity upon a rational basis, the highest degree of feeling. Yet Musil was unable to project this highly personal solution into a social plan. His novel remains a torso, both physically and intellectually.

FURTHER WORKS: *Rede zur Rilke Feier* (1927); *Nachlaß zu Lebzeiten* (1936); *Über die Dummheit* (1937)

BIBLIOGRAPHY: Arntzen, H., *Satirischer Stil in R. M.'s Der Mann ohne Eigenschaften* (1960); Pike, B., *R. M.: An Introduction to His Work* (1961); Kaiser, E. and Wilkins, E., *R. M., Eine Einführung in das Werk* (1962); Baumann, G., *R. M., Zur Erkenntnis der Dichtung* (1965); Karthaus, U., *Der andere Zustand, Zeitstrukturen im Werke R. M.'s* (1965)

WILHELM BRAUN

MYERS, Leopold Hamilton

English novelist, b. 6 Sept. 1881, Cambridge; d. 8 April 1944, London

Born of distinguished parents, educated at

Eton and Cambridge University, M. lived a life of increasing unhappiness that culminated in suicide. He came to repudiate what he felt to be the moral disintegration and false, nonpersonal values of an acquisitive capitalist society; by 1940 he was a communist.

Soon after the publication of his first novel, *The Orissers* (1922), M. was drawn into the Bloomsbury circle. He reacted bitterly against it: "to personal distaste was joined intellectual and moral disagreement" (Bantock). The decisive influence on his work was exercised by the great psychologists Freud, Jung, and Adler.

The Near and the Far (1943), the tetralogy of novels set in an imaginary 16th c. India, constitutes M.'s claim to being one of the few really important English novelists writing between the world wars (Walter Allen, in *The English Novel*). The tetralogy includes the novels *The Near and the Far* (1929), *Prince Jali* (1931), *Rajah Amar* (1935; all together as a trilogy, *The Root and the Flower*, 1935), and *The Pool of Vishnu* (1940). Reviewing the whole sequence, Richard Church (b. 1893) termed it "the conscious voice of the spiritual state of Europe today."

M.'s place in English literature is at present undefined: his novels are not widely read, but they are passionately admired in influential circles. *The Near and the Far*, in any serious critical view, is a noble achievement: "M.'s masterpiece ... superior to the works of Virginia Woolf and Forster [qq.v.] in seriousness of moral intent and depth of spiritual insight" (Bantock). This may not be too much to claim. The tetralogy is an inquiry into the nature of civilization and the problems of personal responsibility, of personality itself and of the quality of human experience.

"Instead of being an expression of problems and beliefs, M.'s best novels are rather a means in themselves of defining the problems and clarifying the beliefs" (D. W. Harding, in *Scrutiny*).

FURTHER WORKS: *Arvat, A Dramatic Poem* (1908); *The Clio* (1925); *Strange Glory* (1936)

BIBLIOGRAPHY: Harding, D. W., "The Novels of L. H. M.," *Scrutiny*, III (1934); Leavis, F. R., "L. H. M.," *Scrutiny*, XVI (1949); Rudd, M., "L. H. M. and *The Near and the Far*," *Mandrake*, No. 9 (1953); Bantock, G. H., *L. H. M.: A Critical Study* (1956)

DOUGLAS BROWN

MYKOLAITIS, Vincas

(pseud.: *Putinas*), Lithuanian poet, narrative writer, and dramatist, b. 5 Jan. 1893, Pilotiškiai

M. first studied Catholic theology, then, in Munich and Freiburg on the Unstrut, literature and art history. He became a literary scholar in Lithuania.

He is Lithuania's greatest and most influential poet. He developed from "national romanticism" via symbolism (q.v.) to realism. His main theme is the conflict between man and God. For him this was based on personal experience, for in 1932 M., who had been a priest, broke with the Catholic church. His autobiographical novel *Altorių šešėly* (1933), famous in Lithuania, describes this process. The demand for freedom from the ties of the Church, but also resignation and pessimism, are the keynotes of his poetry. In his plays woman becomes the vessel of man's resentment of God. His last short story *1863 metų sukilimas* (1956) conforms to Communist aesthetic theory.

FURTHER WORKS: *Raudoni žiedai* (1916); *Raštai* (2 vols., 1921); *Žiedas ir moteris* (1926); *Sukileliai* (1927); *Nuvainikuota vaidilute* (1927); *Tarp dvieju aušru* (1927); *Valdovas Keliai ir kryžkeliai* (1936); *Krize* (1938); *Sveikinu žeme* (1950); *Adomas Mickevičius ir lietuviu literatura* (1955)

BIBLIOGRAPHY: Grinius, J., *Putino lyrika* (1932); Sietynas, A., "The Condition of a Free Prisoner: Poetry and Prose of V. M.-P.," in *Lituanus*, XI (1965), i, 48-69

ANTANAS MACEINA

MYRIVILIS, Stratis

(pseud. of *Stratis Stamatopoulos*), Greek novelist and short story writer, b. 30 June 1892, Island of Lesbos

After studying literature and law at the University of Athens, M. was for many years a journalist. He was long director of the Greek Parliament Library and general program director of the Greek National Broadcasting Institute (1936-51). In 1958, M. was elected to the Greek National Academy, and he has been president of the Greek National Writers' Society four times.

M.'s realistic works are characterized by his love of lyrical expression and his ability to portray character. A number of M.'s works have been translated into German, French, and English. Outside of Greece he is best known for his *I Zoï en tapho* (1930; Life in the Tomb, 1932), the theme of which is the need to share all suffering and joy with others.

M. belongs to the inner circle of those authors whose works have shaped modern Greek literature.

FURTHER WORKS: *He daskala me la chrysa matia* (1933); *Ta pagana* (1946); *Ho Pan* (1947); *He Panagia he gorgona* (1950)

BIBLIOGRAPHY: Mirambel, A., *La Littéra-ture grecque moderne* (1953); Lavagnini, B., *Storia della letteratura neoellenica* (1955)

ISIDORA ROSENTHAL-KAMARINEA

N

NABOKOV, Vladimir Vladimirovich

(pseud. until 1940: *V. Sirin*), Russian-American writer, b. 23 April 1899, Saint Petersburg

Son of an eminent liberal statesman, N. emigrated to England in 1919, where he studied Russian and French literature at Cambridge University. From 1922 to 1937 he lived in Berlin; from 1937 to 1940, in Paris. During this period he published (in Russian) poems, plays, short stories, and novels, four of which have so far been translated into English: *Camera obscura* (1934; Laughter in the Dark, 1938), *Otchayaniye* (1936; Despair, 1937), *Priglasheniye na kazn'* (1938; Invitation to a Beheading, 1952), *Dar* (1937-38, 1952; The Gift, 1963). *Emigré* critics, presumably referring to his lack of concern for "human interest," intellectual playfulness, conscious brilliance of style, and attention to form, found in his work "non-Russian" qualities. This may be true if N. is compared with the great but diffuse Russian novelists of the 19th c. However, his imagination is essentially a poet's; it is probably more appropriate to applaud his rediscovery of the epigrammatic precision and rhythmic balance of Pushkin.

Since coming to the United States in 1940, N. has written in English. From 1948 to 1958 he was professor of Russian literature at Cornell University. His best-known novel, *Lolita* (Paris, 1955; U.S., 1958), was the despair of commentators; some found the story of the liaison between a forty-year-old man and a twelve-year-old girl funny; others found it tragic. The great majority considered it significant and profound even as they quarreled over its meaning.

Critics have busied themselves with categorizing N., labeling him a symbolist (see symbolism), an allegorist, a decadent, a surrealist (see surrealism), greeting his fiction variously as the *coup de grâce* and the renaissance of the novel. The student ought not to bother much about these terms. More significant, too, than "influences" is the recurring theme of the works themselves: the autonomy of the poetic imagination. The creative act is most obviously central in *The Real Life of Sebastian Knight* (1941), *Pale Fire* (1962), and *The Gift,* which turn on the shifting relationships among an author, the world he inhabits, and the worlds he invents. Imagination in its obsessive, self-destructive phase dominates *Laughter in the Dark* and *Lolita. Invitation to a Beheading* and *Bend Sinister* (1947) develop yet another aspect, the "antisocial" but inviolable nature of creativity. N.'s allied concept of creative memory provides the wry victory in *Pnin* (1957). This concept becomes clear upon comparison of incidents from his memoir *Conclusive Evidence* (1951; *Drugiye berega,* 1954)—which also shows his interest in lepidoptery, painting, and chess—with their uses in various of his novels; the memoir is as "fictional" an account —at times more so (see "Mlle. I," in *Nabokov's Dozen* [1958]).

For N. reality is subjective, deepening with the gradual accumulation of knowledge. The fugitive perceptions of any given character are played against those created by the reader's further knowledge and against the author's seemingly final understanding. N. manipulates his readers as if they were his characters. One of his techniques (see the imaginary confrontations of Godunov-Cherdyntsev and Koncheyev in *The Gift*) is to create as reality a character's

VLADIMIR NABOKOV

OGDEN NASH

experience, then undercut it in terms of a more objective reality—which only enriches the first. N. frequently uses the device of the doppelgänger to provide complementary realities for both reader and characters: prisoner and executioner in *Invitation to a Beheading,* the two poets of *The Gift,* the artist and the critic of *Pale Fire.* Similarly, "sensitive" Humber Humbert and Lolita have "gross" images in Quilty and Charlotte Haze. The biographer-narrator of *The Real Life of Sebastian Knight* eventually proclaims his identity with his subject, a paradox understood by him in one sense, in two others by the reader; thus N. adds a helical twist to multiplicity while insisting on "the oneness of human perception."

Finally, on the level at which life mimics art, N.'s works in English seem to be reproducing, one by one, those in Russian. This can be seen when one compares the subject and style of *Invitation to a Beheading* and *Bend Sinister, Laughter in the Dark* and *Lolita, The Gift* and *Pale Fire.* The biographical techniques of chapter four in *The Gift* reappear in *Nikolai Gogol* (1944).

"The essence of N.'s singular art [lies] in its linking of an unusually audacious vision of the world with an uncommonly sensuous language" (G. Struve). He restores to the novel direct, loving percipience of the precise weight and texture of things; the reader discovers how complex their relationships are. He gives, not a view of life, but ways of viewing life, confident that taken together, the possibilities will fuse to a living whole. By his own definition (*Nikolai Gogol,* p. 55), this fusion is poetry: "The mysteries of the irrational as perceived through rational words. True poetry of this kind provokes—not laughter and not tears—but a radiant smile of perfect satisfaction, a purr of beatitude." It is this joy that N.'s writing characteristically engenders.

FURTHER WORKS: *Grozd', Gornyi put'* (1923); *Mashenka* (1926); *Korol', dama, valet* (1928); *Zashchita Luzhina, Vozvrashcheniye Khorba* (1930); *Soglyadatai; Podvig* (1932); *Nine Stories* (1947); *Stikhotvoreniya* (1952); *Vesna v Fial'te i drugiye rasskazy* (1956); *Poems* (1959); *The Defense* (1964); *The Eye* (1965); *Notes on Prosody* (1965); *The Waltz Invention* (1966); *Quartet* (An Affair of Honor, Lik, The Vane Sisters, The Visit to the Museum; 1966); *Speak, Memory* (1966; rev. ed. of *Conclusive Evidence,* 1951); *King, Queen, Knave* (1968). **Translations:** *Three Russian Poets* (1943); *The Song of Igor's Campaign* (1960); *Eugene Onegin* (1964)

BIBLIOGRAPHY: Struve, G., "V. S. (N.)," in *Slavonic Review,* XII (1933-34), 436-44; Aldridge, A. O., "*Lolita* and *Les Liaisons Dangereuses,*" in *WSCL,* II (1960), iii, 20-26; Ivask, I., "The World of V. N.," in *RussR,* XX (1961), 134-42; Pryce-Jones, A., "The Fabulist's Worlds: V. N.," in Balakian, N., and Simmons, C., eds., *The Creative Present* (1963), pp. 65-78; Green, M., "The Morality of *Lolita,*" in *KR,* XXVIII (1966), 352-77; Stegner, S. P., *Escape into Aesthetics: The Art of V. N.* (1966); Field, A., *N.: His Life and Art* (1967); *WSCL,* VIII (1967), ii: special N. issue, also published as Dembo, L. S., ed., *N.* (1967)

ALLAN DANZIG

NASH, (Frederic) Ogden
American humorist, b. 19 Aug. 1902, Rye, N.Y.

N. is primarily a writer of humorous verse whose originality depends on a combination of satire, wit, nonsense, and technical skill in the handling of rhythm and rhyme. Since 1929 he has been a prolific contributor of short verses to periodicals. He has published collections of his poems, verse librettos, and anthologies of humor, and has written or edited books for children. As a satirist he pictures the foibles of the upper middle class in an urban East Coast milieu. Though genial and urbane, he is penetrating in his treatment of the hypocritical and pretentious, the provincial and platitudinous. His animal portraits are memorable. In his verse, effects of wit and nonsense are gained by use of parody and burlesque, of intentionally tangled American syntax, and a constant, imaginative play on words and sounds, including multilingual puns ("Who's afreud of the big bad dream?"). N. has great virtuosity in metrics and is a master of the gnomic epigram, the limerick, and the closed couplet, both long and short. His marked originality depends chiefly on two devices: extraordinarily long rhythmic lines simulating speech patterns, often yoked with short rhyming lines, and, above all, paranomia in rhyme. Unexpected (often recondite or polysyllabic) rhymes and deliberately inexact rhymes produce humorous couplets that join a play of wit with pun and, on occasion, symbol.

WORKS: *Hard Lines* (1931); *Free Wheeling* (1931); *Happy Days* (1933); *Four Prominent So and So's* (1934); *The Primrose Path* (1935); *The Bad Parents' Garden of Verse* (1936); *I'm a Stranger Here Myself* (1938); *The Face is Familiar* (1940); *Good Intentions* (1942); *One Touch of Venus* (1944, musical comedy with S. J. Perelman); *Many Long Years Ago* (1945); *Selected Verse* (1946); *Musical Zoo* (1947); *Versus* (1949); *Family Reunion* (1950); *Parents Keep Out* (1951); *The Private Dining Room* (1953); *You Can't Get There from Here* (1957); *The Christmas That Almost Wasn't* (1957, with Kurt Weill and S. J. Perelman); *Verses from 1929 on* (1959); *A Boy Is a Boy* (1960); *The New Nutcracker Suite and Other Innocent Verses* (1962); *Everyone but Thee and Me* (1962); *Girls Are Silly* (1962); *A Boy And His Room* (1963); *The Adventures of Isabel* (1963); *Marriage Lines; Notes of a Student Husband* (1964); *The Untold Adventures of Santa Claus* (1964); *The Animal Garden* (1965); *The Cruise of the Aardvark* (1967); *Santa Go Home* (1967); *The Mysterious Ouphe* (1967)

BIBLIOGRAPHY: Sewell, E., *The Field of Nonsense* (1952)

FLORENCE L. WALZL

NATSUME Soseki

(pseud. of *Kinnosuke Natsume*), Japanese novelist, b. 7 Feb. 1867, Tokyo; d. there, 9 Dec. 1916

S. graduated from the University of Tokyo in 1890, where he specialized in English literature. In 1903 he became lecturer in English at the same university. In 1907 he resigned from his teaching post to take up writing as a career.

Between 1905, when S. began publishing in serial form his first full-length novel—*Wagahai Wa Neko De Aru* (1905-1906; I Am a Cat, 1906-1909)—and the time of his death, he published more than a dozen novels, most of which are still read widely. *Wagahai Wa Neko De Aru* and *Botchan* (1906; Young Master, 1918) are comic novels, in which the author satirizes various kinds of philistines and intellectual mountebanks of his day. Despite their great success, S. was not content to be a comic novelist. His next novel *Kusamakura* (1906; The Grass Pillow; 1927) is a lyrical tour-de-force in which he describes a painter's sojourn in a

438

remote mountain village. S. called it, quite aptly, "a haiku-like novel."

S.'s representative later works—*Mon* (1910; "The Gate"), *Kojin* (1912-13; The Wayfarer, 1967), *Kokoro* (1914; The Heart, 1927), and *Michikusa* (1915; The Wayfarer, 1967)—are brooding psychological novels, all concerned with the theme of isolation. Their protagonists are middle-class, well-educated, modern Japanese, who lead desperately lonely lives. They have either betrayed or have been betrayed by someone close, and are made bitter and lonely through guilt or disillusionment. There is no solution to their problems, except, perhaps, death. The protagonist of *Mon* seeks his escape in religion, but fails; in *Kojin* he is left at the end of the novel on the verge of madness; and in *Kokoro*, considered by many Japanese critics to be S.'s most successful work, he kills himself.

Despite the distinction of premodern Japanese fiction, S. claimed that he owed little to his Japanese predecessors. Yet for all their modern problems, his characters seem utterly Japanese and move against backgrounds that are described with a delicacy uniquely Japanese.

S. was the first Japanese novelist to describe articulately and to dramatize persuasively the plight of the alienated modern Japanese, and his lasting popularity in Japan seems to be due to the fact that he was able to combine his close examination of complex, modern personalities with his native talent for lyricism.

FURTHER WORKS: *Gubijinsō* (1907); *Sanshirō* (1908); *Sore kara* (1909); *Garasudo no naka* (1915); *Meian* (1916); *S. zenshū* (1935-37)

BIBLIOGRAPHY: McClellan, E., "An Introduction to S.," *Harvard Journal of Asiatic Studies,* XXII, 150-208; Keene, D., *Japanese Literature* (1953); Matsui, S., "East and West in N. S.: The Formation of a Modern Japanese Novelist," in *Meanjin,* XXVI (1967), 282-94

EDWIN MCCLELLAN

NATURALISM

Naturalism, as a literary movement, grew out of 19th c. realism. It wanted to tell the whole truth about life and faithfully to represent contemporary reality. Reality, in turn, was tested by the application of the scientific method to the mental and social world of man. The resulting bias of the naturalist, to see the everyday life of the common people against the background of constant historical movement, decisively influenced the conventions of the novel, the drama, and, to a lesser degree, lyric poetry.

The chief impetus for naturalism came from the deterministic philosophical theories of the 19th c. which dominated both the natural and social sciences. Malthus (1766-1834), Comte (1798-1857), Lyell (1797-1875), Darwin (1809-1882), T. H. Huxley (1825-95), and Spencer (1820-1903) had, through their writings, revolutionized science. The concept of reality as an evolutionary process toward ideal and perfect ends was replaced by evolutionary theories which saw process as the result of blind and purposeless forces in nature.

Accordingly man and his actions were now viewed as products of the internal and external pressures of heredity and environment. Even his selfishness was no longer judged as a perversion of his inner nature but was assumed to arise from external situations which could not be controlled by freedom and intelligence.

The dominant forces in this new world were soon identified with sexual impulses or economic conditions. Long before Freud, Schopenhauer, in *The World as Will and Idea* (1818), had asserted that sex "is really the invisible central point of all action and conduct ... the sexual passion is the kernel of the will to live. ... Indeed, one may say man is concrete sexual desire." Marx disagreed by associating man's deepest motives with historic economic conditions: "Consciousness must rather be explained from the contradictions of material life, from the existing conflict between the social forces of production and the relations of production" (*Contribution to the Critique of Political Economy*, 1859).

For literary criticism the turning point came with Taine's *History of English Literature* (1865). By applying anatomical principles to literary studies, Taine isolated three different sources as contributing to elementary psychological states: race (man's permanent impulse), surroundings (man's physical and social circumstances), and the epoch (man's acquired momentum). Taine showed all three to be operative in the work of Stendhal, whom he called a naturalist because the latter had "introduced scientific processes into the history of the heart."

Novelists likewise appropriated the methods of science in programmatic fashion. The brothers Goncourt, for instance, had justified *Germinie Lacerteux* (1864) with an appeal to methods of experimental biology. But there is evidence (Edmond de Goncourt's diary, Dec. 3, 1871) that the brothers were less concerned with science than with common people as an exotic stimulant for refined tastes.

Émile Zola (q.v.) was the first novelist to go to the heart of the social problem. Under the influence of Claude Bernard ("Introduction à la médecine expérimentale," 1865) and Prosper Lucas ("Traité philosophique et physiologique de l'hérédité naturelle," 1847-50), Zola transferred the experimental method from physiology to writing by turning the writer into an observer of natural facts and into an experimenter consciously modifying circumstances for purposes of interpretation and hypothesis.

In the preface to *Thérèse Raquin* (1867) Zola had compared the novel to a test tube in which the "mechanism of passion" would be studied. *The Experimental Novel* (1880) constitutes a more precisely formulated theory of the writer as the experimental moralist. That Zola meant what he said can be seen from the title of his novel cycle: *Les Rougon-Macquart, histoire naturelle et sociale d'une famille sous le Second Empire* (1871-92). In twenty novels Zola deals with the offspring of the alcoholic Macquart and the degenerate Adelaide Fouqué and probes the depth of social disease and the violence afflicting the rich and poor alike.

Although Zola had few direct disciples—at the beginning of their careers both Maupassant and Huysmans (q.v.) contributed to his anthology, *Soirées de Médéan* (1881)—his polemics forced modern writers to treat the novel as a mature art form which not only reflected social reality but also mirrored the moral problems involved in this reality. The close relation between artistic and ethical responsibilities could no longer be ignored, and the necessity of narrowing the gap between fact and fiction in the process of selecting material was obvious to all who had seen the sordidness in the underside of life. The novel seemed to be the ideal instrument for social reform.

This affected deeply the techniques then in use. Plots became as sprawling as life itself; themes concentrated on the typical in experience; and characters, despite their seeming individualism in speech and behavior, represented standard types. Yet the wealth of life documented by detailed enumeration and painstaking rendition of the *procès verbal* manifests a high degree of seriousness on the part of naturalist writers.

When these new techniques merged with the

439

vital traditions and passionate convictions of other national and regional writers, powerful works came into being. This is particularly true for the social criticism of the Germans —Max Kretzer (1854-1941), Hermann Sudermann (1857-1928), Clara Viebig (1860-1952), and G. Hauptmann (q.v.); and of the searching analysis of the bourgeois habitat and lower-class ideals in the Anglo-Saxon countries— G. Moore, Bennett, Galsworthy (qq.v.), and George R. Gissing (1857-1903).

It is more difficult to trace the influence of naturalism on writers in the southwest and south of Europe; nevertheless it seems to have been powerful. Italian regionalism relies heavily on the milieu of worker, peasant, and lower middle class—Verga, Grazia Deledda (qq.v.), Luigi Capuana (1839-1915) and Matilda Serao (1856-1927)—while the Spanish often combine the historical with the social in their portrayal of burghers, peasants and fishermen—Pérez Galdos, Palacio Valdés, Blasco-Ibáñez (qq.v.), José María de Pereda y Sánchez de Porría (1833-1905), Clarín (1852-1901), and Bazan (1852-1921). Portugal also contributed to naturalism in the works of José Maria de Eça de Queiroz (1843-1900). But the humor, satire, and mysticism of the latter soon transcended naturalist canons.

Naturalism flourished best in America, at first as a response to a darkening social outlook: the harsh futility of life in nature (Jack London, 1876-1916), on the farm (Hamlin Garland, 1860-1940), or in the city (Stephen Crane, 1871-1900). The second phase put a sociological emphasis on heredity and environment. Dreiser's *Sister Carrie* (1901), S. Anderson's *Winesburg, Ohio* (1919), and S. Lewis's (qq.v.) *Main Street* (1920) all established the interrelationship of sexual and economic appetites as controlling factors in the lives of human beings.

The political implications of economic forces were also recognized. Frank Norris (1870-1902) wrote the two volumes of his projected trilogy *The Epic of Wheat* (1901, 1903), and Upton Sinclair (q.v.) applied the theories of Henry George to big business: *The Jungle* (1906), *King Coal* (1917), and *Oil* (1927). Their revolutionary energy spills over into the works of the next generation which systematically utilizes the teachings of Freud and Marx—Dos Passos, a trilogy: *U.S.A.* (1930-36); Farrell, a trilogy: *Studs Lonigan* (1932-35); and Caldwell (qq.v.), *Tobacco Road* (1932).

With Steinbeck (q.v.), who has been called the archetype of the naturalist writer, attention shifts gradually from the external world to the inner life of man. There is tenderness and sensitivity in his brutalized derelicts (*Of Mice And Men,* 1937) and displaced farmworkers (*The Grapes of Wrath,* 1939). But his consciousness of crisis and the demands for just social action do not prevent him from abandoning the conventions of sociological naturalism and employing other styles.

In spite of the numerical strength of the naturalist novelists, few of them can rival those great dramatists who, at least in their beginnings, were even more deeply rooted in naturalism: Henrik Ibsen (q.v.) in Norway, Strindberg (q.v.) in Sweden, G. Hauptmann (q.v.) in Germany, G. B. Shaw (q.v.) in England, Chekhov (q.v.) in Russia, Benavente (q.v.) in Spain, Antona-Traversi (1857-1934) in Italy, and O'Neill (q.v.) in America. Ever since Dumas *fils*'s advocacy of the *drame à thèse* and *théâtre utile* and the adaptation and performance of Zola's *Thérèse Raquin* in 1873, the stage has been the ideal arena for displaying social problems. The conflict of the individual with society and the loneliness and suffering of man have been presented in scenes of contemporary life and the idiom of the day.

Ibsen, often called the father of modern drama, is the dominant figure. Eschewing the "lie of life" of romance, he turned typical social problems into plays with a strongly antisocial flavor: the falsity of conventional marriage (*A Doll's House,* 1879), the destructive consequences of a man's heredity (*Ghosts,* 1881), the pressure of society on the individual (*An Enemy of the People,* 1882), and the inner compulsions of personality (*Hedda Gabler,* 1890). Like Hauptmann and Shaw after him —Shaw late in his life repudiated naturalism and extolled Shakespeare, Mozart, and Wagner as his models—Ibsen turned away from naturalism in his later works.

As could be expected, naturalism soon encountered strong opposition, especially in the drama. To neutralize the aversion to naturalism and to make naturalistic plays available to a large audience, André Antoine founded the Théâtre Libre in Paris in 1887, and Otto Brahm opened the Freie Bühne in Berlin in 1889. Antoine produced plays by H. F. Becque (1837-1899), P.-E. Hervieu (1857-1915), and Eugène Brieux (1858-1933); Brahm, plays by Ibsen, Strindberg, Hauptmann, Halbe (q.v.), and Sudermann.

For lyric poetry, naturalism with its pragmatic bias had little to offer. The American E. L. Masters (*Spoon River Anthology*, 1915) and the Italian Ada Negri (1870-1945; *Tempeste*, 1894) were two of the few who seriously attempted to deal with their age in a more truthful and direct way than had been customary. Only in Germany did naturalism succeed in shaping new theories of lyricism.

This was due primarily to the influence of Holz (q.v.), who improved on Zola by establishing the thesis that art is nature seen through a window. Reduced to an equation this reads: art=nature−x. The unknown quality is man's dependency on language. In his fight to create a rhythmical poetry without rhyme and to extend the range of themes and subject matter, Holz was supported by Johannes Schlaf (1862-1941) and K. F. Henckell (1864-1929). But their theories had little impact outside Germany.

There can be no doubt that naturalism, by making accessible a wealth of new themes and materials, by encouraging flexibility in the selection and treatment of subjects, and by fostering a persistent bias toward biological evolution, has helped modern literature come to maturity. It had, as Willard Thorp maintains, "put man and his experience squarely into nature over against which he had hitherto been set." It had courageously battled romance by picturing the day-by-day actualities and by substituting "a slice of life" for facile idealizing.

But its virtues cannot hide its defects. Relying too often on literal fact and precisely documented circumstance, the naturalist's material is often so flat and external as to inhibit the search for value and meaning (Rahv, *Image and Idea*). This severely limits the variety of creative means at the disposal of the artist. Zola himself is at his best when unknowingly he writes as a symbolist, while barely escaping melodrama when rigorously practicing his thesis.

Furthermore the concept of reality with which 19th c. science operated is no longer in use. Consequently human personality and experience seen in terms of the broadly typical cannot answer the perplexity of postmodern man. In any event we can no longer accept the claim of the naturalists that they alone dealt truthfully with reality simply by having created the illusion that its methods were more real than others. Like many styles before and after it, naturalism can only be viewed as one of several powerful conventions which have left their mark on contemporary literature.

BIBLIOGRAPHY: Parrington, V. L., *Main Currents in American Thought* (1930); Beach, J. W., *The Twentieth Century Novel* (1932); Comfort, A., *The Novel and Our Time* (1948); Rahv, P., "Notes on the Decline of Naturalism," *Image and Idea* (1949); Wellek, R., and Warren, A., *Theory of Literature* (1949); Jokes, A. E., Jr., "Darwinism and its Relationship to Realism and Naturalism in American Fiction, 1860-1900," *The Drew University Bulletin*, No. 38 (December 1950); Cowley, M., "A Natural History of American Naturalism," in *Critiques and Essays on Modern Fiction 1920-1951*, ed. J. W. Aldrich (1952); Fergusson, F., "Ghosts and the Theater of Modern Realism," in *Essays in Modern Literary Criticism*, ed. R. B. West (1952); Auerbach, E., *Mimesis: The Representation of Reality in Western Literature* (1953); Gardiner, H. C., *Norms for the Novel* (1953); Friederich, W. P., *Outline of Comparative Literature* (1954); Walcutt, C. C., *American Literary Naturalism, A Divided Stream* (1956); Stone, E., ed., *What Was Naturalism?* (1959); Thorp, W., "The Persistence of Naturalism in the Novel," *American Writing in the Twentieth Century* (1960)

FRANZ K. SCHNEIDER

NAZOR, Vladimir

Croatian poet and narrative writer, b. 30 May 1876, Postire, Brač; d. 19 June 1949, Zagreb

N. studied natural science in Graz and Zagreb and became a teacher. In 1942 he joined the Partisans. After the war he became president of the praesidium of Croatia.

He began at the end of the 19th c. as a poet, but developed independently and held aloof from the conflict between the "young" and "old" writers (see Yugoslavian literature). His poems and stories, with themes drawn from the past (*Slavenske legende*, 1900; *Hrvatski kraljevi*, 1912) are full of love of nature and joy of living. The ballads and novellas in *Krvava košulja* (1905) and *Veli Jože* (1908) strengthened nationalist feeling among the oppressed Croats of Istria, while the poems in *Lirika* (1910) and *Nove pjesme* (1913) identified him as the poet of revolutionary youth. *Medved Brundo* (1915) is the most important of his animal epics. Periodically, however, N. withdrew into the realm of subjective problems (*Intima*, 1915); his later poems also show a tendency to mysticism. He described youthful experiences in realistic novellas. *Pastir Loda* (1938), a fantasy novel, re-creates his country's history from antiquity to the present. His Zagreb novellas, *Zagrebačke novele* (1942), have a distinct social slant. Using themes drawn from the Partisan experience during World War II, he published the epic *Ahasver* (1945), expressing his search for understanding. A master of language and particularly of richly variegated verse form, N. also wrote technical treatises on meter and translated works of Shakespeare, Heine, Goethe, Baudelaire, Leopardi, Carducci, and Pascali.

FURTHER WORKS: *Istarske priče* (1913); *Pjesni ljuvene* (1915); *Utva zlatokrila* (1916); *Priče iz djetinjstva* (1924); *Djela* (16 vols., 1946-50)

BIBLIOGRAPHY: Barac, A., *V. N.* (1918); Marjanovic, M., "V. N.," in *Carmen Vitae* (1924); Raditsa, B., "Notes on the Croatian and Serbian Literatures," in *Journal of Croatian Studies,* III-IV (1962-63), 65-89; Vučetić, Š., "V. N.," in *Republika* (Zagreb), XXI (1966), 421-27

EMIL ŠTAMPAR

NEO-AFRICAN LITERATURE

There have existed, in the Antilles, since the beginning of the nineteenth century, Negro novelists and poets writing in the French language. These writers were the product of colonial assimilation, and as good students they modeled their prose and verse on the French masters—Flaubert (1821-80), Balzac (1799-1850), Leconte de Lisle (1818-94), Sully-Prudhomme (1839-1907), and particularly Lamartine (1790-1869) and Victor Hugo (1802-1885).

The Guyane poet, Léon Damas, was one of the first to revolt against this cultural alienation of the Negro. He said his fellow Negro writers were "reproduction poets" whose sole aim was to write a "touristic literature, exotic enough to please the French reading public."

In 1923 a group of Negro and mulatto students in Martinique founded the ephemeral review, *Légitime Défense* (the local government banned its first and only issue) in order to protest against the mediocrity and artificiality of the literary works that Negroes were and had been writing. They demanded that the Negro intellectual cease to negate his own racial

past. Etienne Lero denounced the poet who "makes it a point of honor that a white may read his books without guessing the pigmentation of the author." It is significant that a few years later, in 1937, Damas should entitle his first volume of verses *Pigments*.

If *Légitime Défense* failed as a review, its influence was to reach Paris and stimulate Negro intellectuals. A group composed of Léopold Sédar Senghor (Sénégal), Aimé Césaire (q.v.) (Martinique), and Léon Damas founded the review *L'Étudiant Noir* in 1935. This very unpretentious review served as a platform from which Negro intellectuals—of either Antillese or African origin—could begin to formulate and analyze the various problems that confronted them. These problems were not limited to geography but involved the entire Negro race. The major contribution of *L'Étudiant Noir* was its stubborn opposition to any attempt by the French at cultural assimilation.

With World War II the group disbanded. Césaire returned to his native Martinique, where he continued his militant activities for the liberation of the Negro. He directed the review *Tropiques*, which emphasized the cultural values of the Negro, Antillese folklore, and the basic dignity of the Negro race. He incited his people to struggle to reconquer a liberty that had been lost three centuries earlier.

Above all, it is with the founding of the review *Présence Africaine* (which was also to become the largest publishing house of African matters) by Alioune Diop in 1948 that the first phase of the Negro cultural revolt was completed. *Présence Africaine,* this "window upon the world," opened its pages to "all contributors of goodwill (white, yellow, or black) who might be able to help define African originality and to hasten its introduction into the modern world." The review served also as a *prise de conscience* for the Negro himself, for, as Alioune Diop pointed out, the Negro intellectual after World War II was "unable to return to his original roots, yet he had not assessed what his role should be in the future family of nations."

At the onset the orientation of *Présence Africaine* was predominantly cultural. Soon, however, it became apparent that considerations of culture involved inevitably a political point of view. The group of contributors to the review included writers who, by the nature of things, had also become political leaders in their now independent countries. The necessity of the coexistence of two domains, the cultural and the political, was brilliantly argued for by Sékou Touré at the Second Congress of Negro Writers and Artists in Rome (1959). Henceforth, the publications of *Présence Africaine* included beside the poetic texts of Senghor, David Diop, and others, the cultural and political essays of Sékou Touré, Césaire, Rabemananjara, Mamadou Dia, and even the contributions (in translations) of English-speaking writers such as Nkrumah.

Out of the group of *Présence Africaine* emerged the concept of *négritude*. Césaire was responsible for the invention of this neologism, which he used for the first time in his long poem, *Cahier d'un retour au pays natal* in 1939. By *négritude*, Césaire understood the "simple recognition of the fact of being a Negro and the acceptance of this fact and of its cultural and historical consequences." Complementary to Césaire's definition, Senghor was to state, a few years later, that *négritude* was "the sum total of all the cultural values of Africa."

With time *négritude* has come to mean not only the characteristics of past African culture but also the psychological behavior of the Negro as he reacts to all aspects of that culture, to the problems of slavery, segregation, colonialism, and to the social and moral problems emerging in the modern world. Sartre (q.v.) in his challenging preface to the first anthology of Senghor, which he entitled *Orphée Noire,* stated that *négritude* was the "being-in-the-world" of the Negro. In other words, it is the particular manner in which the Negro feels the world and defines himself in relation to it. *Négritude* then is the *Weltanschauung* of the Negro.

Négritude has been confused with Negro revolt and with antiwhite aggressiveness. Such an interpretation is based upon a limited understanding of Negro thinking. In the concept of *négritude,* the Negro revolt is only a stage, one during which the Negro refuses to accept any longer the anathema cast at his race. This first phase is initial; it corresponds to an emergence of Negro self-awareness that is necessary if the way is to be paved to a more constructive revolt. *Négritude* is what differentiates the African Negro from other men, what individualizes his behavior, what underlines his sociopolitical structures, his history, his religions, and his artistic achievements as distinct from those of other races. It is a cultural *specificity* that can be called by many other terms (as is being done in recent times), such as "African origi-nality," "African personality," or simply "Africanity."

Négritude became the name of the literary movement that became conscious of and reflected this African *specificity*. Henceforth, the Negro writer was to claim for himself the right and obligation to express his *négritude* as it is manifested both in his culture and in his temperament.

The principal themes that *négritude* concerned itself with were new to universal literature: the slave trade, exile and nostalgia for Africa, the evocation of the sufferings of the Negroes everywhere in the world. The writers focused sharply upon specific areas in which Negroes had been wronged, such as segregation, lynching, prejudices, and humiliations, and the ills of colonialism in the form of forced labor, destruction of indigenous cultures, and assimilation of personality. Altogether the literature of *négritude* can be considered as the Passion of the Negro, in a religious sense. Sartre said that *négritude* was the proclamation of the Good Tidings.

Another cluster of themes centers around the evocation of the geographic *milieu* of the African Negro, and around the daily social realities: savannas and forests, the simple, slow-flowing lives of the people in the villages, their societies, the varied and sometimes complex systems of values, the ancestral as well as the modern concepts of the African, indeed all the ways by which, according to Senghor, the African is able to shed "the dust of Occidental civilization" and to return to his sources and to his original *négritude*.

It must be said that the English-language African writers appear reticent about the concept of *négritude*. They have even expressed, at times, a marked hostility to it. The many reasons for this attitude on their part stem from the particular realities (cultural and political) that have faced the English-speaking Africans since their independence or while still in search of that independence. The language barrier between French-speaking and English-speaking Africans, which so often causes misunderstandings, is another factor. Nonetheless, while acknowledging the English-speaking African's opposition to the concept of *négritude* (and respecting it), we would like to point out that in their literary works—whether in the poems of Gabriel Okara, John Pepper Clark, or Christopher Okigbo, or in the plays of Wole Soyinka, or in the novels of Amos Tutuola—these

African writers illustrate sensitively certain aspects of *négritude,* as defined by the French-speaking theoreticians.

In the fifteen years preceding the various moments of independence for African countries, the movement of *négritude* produced a Pleiade of poets, novelists, and essayists, who were all of different origins. Antillese, Americans, Africans (both French- and English-speaking) and Portuguese (among whom is the most eminent Angola poet Mario de Andrade) found they had a common bond in *négritude.* The *Présence Africaine* group influenced the whole Negro world by the foundation of the *Société Africaine de Culture* (SAC), which in turn formed smaller organizations designed to promote aspects of Negro culture. SAC organized two major congresses—the Congress of Negro Writers and Artists of 1956 in Paris and the aforementioned one—1959 in Rome—where Negro intellectuals of the world met and exchanged views.

In literature proper, we should mention first the poets featured in the *Anthologie de la nouvelle poésie nègre et malgache* of 1948. Among this first wave of poets were Rabearivelo, Rabemananjara, Rainaivo, Birago Diop, David Diop, Guy Tirolien, Paul Niger, and others. This anthology also included the work of the leaders—Léopold Sédar Senghor, Aimé Césaire, Damas, Jacques Roumain, J. F. Brière, and Gilbert Gratiant.

Between the years 1950 and 1960 there was an active development in the field of the novel. Among the French-writing novelists were Mongo Beti, Camara Laye, Bernard Dadié, Benjamin Matip, Olympe Bhely-Quénum, Ferdinand Oyono, Abdoulaye Sadji, and Sembene Ousmane. Among the English-language novelists—to mention only a few—were Peter Abrahams, Wright (q.v.), and Ezekiel Mphahlele. In the Caribbean region, the major novelists were Stephen Alexis, Edouard Glissant, Georges Lamming, Raphaël Tardon, and Joseph Zobel.

Young poets, among whom were René Depestre, Georges Desportes, Lamine Dhiakaté, Paulin Joachim, and Epanya Yondo, began to explore, in newer forms, the now classical themes of *négritude.*

There was also a growing interest in the essay form, which permitted the Negro intellectual to discuss his culture. The African essay ranges widely in subject matter—from sculpture to economy, from linguistics to politics. The major essayists were Hampaté Ba, Aimé

Césaire, Mamadou Dia, Alioune Diop, David Diop, Cheik Anta Diop, Frantz Fanon, Nkrumah, Kenyatta, Léopold Sédar Senghor, and Sékou Touré.

The period of the 1960's was the period of independence for many African countries. The Negro world, once unified by a common striving for liberty, found itself suffering from fragmentation now that its goal was achieved. Although the pan-African dream was not abandoned, each independent nation turned first to the problems raised by its new sovereignty. This was to have serious cultural consequences.

The present African literature seeks new directions. This transitional stage is characterized by a slowing-down of literary production as well as a greater variety of objectives, themes, and genres.

Many authors who had written the first literature of *négritude* ceased to write once the goal of independence was achieved. Some are involved so strenuously in the affairs of their own state that they find it difficult to extricate themselves from politics to pursue literature. Others who were no more than circumstantial writers nourished poetically by the political crisis have ceased to write.

Meanwhile, there are still writers in Negro America, in the Antilles, in South Africa and Angola, who continue to raise cries of revolt; their works express the passion and despair felt by the first writers of *négritude* which is even magnified in those writers of today by their present isolation.

The majority of African writers now turn to domestic problems. In Mali the novels of Seydou Badian Kouyaté and of Gologo study the confrontation of generations and the coexistence of traditional and modern societies. In Sénégal, Cheik Amidou Kane, in perhaps the major modern novel in French-language Africa, *L'Aventure Ambiguë,* raises the same question at the philosophical level,. How, he asks, can the educated African integrate Cartesian thought with African mysticism? He also examines the problem of decolonization, and how classes in societies and individuals are affected by it. Also in Sénégal, Sembene Ousmane, in the tradition of "social-realism," proceeds to a clinical and often very powerful investigation of social problems involving the African proletariat, in such novels as *Les Bouts De Bois De Dieu* and *L'Harmattan.*

The desire to identify with and to translate faithfully the realities of African life, both modern and ancestral, has contributed to the development of two new genres since the period of independence: the play and the novella.

In Cameroun (and in Nigeria) we find the flowering of a *théatre de moeurs,* which is both a lyrical and dramatic theater. Often the themes are treated in the form of parodies, which, while poking fun at human frailty, serve as concrete analyses of many problems of modern Africa: alcoholism, unemployment, the dowry, the contractual marriage, the corruption of civil servants; conflicts between generations (sons and elders), between the chiefdom in the villages and the modern government representations, between European medicine and traditional sorceries. In general, all these plays reflect the impact created by two civilizations meeting and the inevitable processes of acculturation resulting from it.

The attitudes of the writers confronted with these problems depend upon their backgrounds, and the particular conditions existing in their country. Some authors appear to favor the retaining of traditional values; others are more "modern" in their solutions. This variation of attitudes reflects the hesitations of the African intellectual who faces conflicting values.

The most worthy theatrical achievements in Cameroun are those of Guillaume Oyono, Jacques Mariel Nzouankeu, Etienne Yanou, and Stanislas Owona. In English the Nigerian authors John Pepper Clark and Wole Soyinka have written brilliant plays that treat of similar problems.

The *novella,* in the hands of Sembene Ousmane (*Voltaique*), Bernard Dadié (*Le Pagne noir*), and many others, deals frankly with modern problems. It is a form particularly suitable to the African personality. In its brevity and in its often colloquial tone it may resemble closely the tale (*conte*) or even the fable, which are favorite traditional forms of entertainment for all Africans. That is perhaps why it is difficult to attempt to distinguish between an African *novella* and a *conte*; African storytellers spin their yarns and do not worry much about the form.

Jacques Nzouankeu and Matip, Ibrahim Said and Jean Malonga, Abdou Anta Ka and Camara Laye continue in the tradition of Birago Diop, Ousmane Soce, and Bernard Dadié. They recapture in lively and saucy vignettes the fantastic and humorous world of the village night vigils around small fires when an old uncle or aunt told stories everyone knew but whose versions always varied according to the circumstances or the teller.

When a story is treated on a wider scope, the *novella* may attain the dimensions of an epic novel. This is true of the *Soundjata* of Djibril Tamsir Niane or the *Savane Rouge* of Fily Dabo Sissoko. We may even include in these diverse manifestations of the African *novella* such extensions as a lyrical drama (as in *La Mort de Chaka*) a verse-ballet (as in the *Poèmes africains* of Keita Fodeba), or even a mythical poem (as in *Le Conte de l'araignée* or *Le Passage de la sanaga*). Both of these poems are recited in the oral tradition of the Mvet (in Beti) in which the elements of poetry, dance, and music are interwoven into a single fabric and in which the audience is called upon to participate, during the rendition of these poems, by asking questions, making remarks, or even joining in the dancing.

The writers who draw their inspiration for the oral tradition act as translators, adapters, and re-creators of culture and poetry. They preserve thus a cultural continuity that is threatened with disappearance amidst the growing modern world of Africa. They also suggest a possible creative formula that might prove very fruitful for the development of a vigorous and indigenous modern African literature.

Recently we have witnessed the regression of two genres, the purely autobiographical novel and the militant anticolonial type of poetry, both of which served a decisive function during the preindependence period. Anticolonial poetry has not entirely disappeared; some aspects of it—and not the most vital—have been translated into a recent type of poetry that could be termed "political." This is the poetry of social-realism found particularly in Mali and Guinée and in general in all of French-speaking Africa. It includes many odes to rulers, expressions of political doctrines, fervent assertions of loyalty, and the like. Such poems are often published in the daily local newspapers. This type of poetry is perhaps too closely associated with propaganda and political directions, and too many of these poems evidence neglect or scorn for aesthetic and critical criteria, to survive the test of time. Meanwhile, they may serve as interesting and pertinent documents on political tempers in this phase of African development.

But there are also poets who, seeking new means of literary expression, are willing to experiment and to question both their subject matter and their form. They even try to innovate by returning in inspiration to the oral tradition. The Camerounian Charles Ngandé is one of these. And then there are the younger poets, such as Ernest Alima, Blaise Diagne, Lamine Niang, Okala Alene, and Epanya Yondo, who attempt to free themselves of all influences in order to cultivate a more personal and individual mode of expression.

The future of African poetry in French is bright if only because of the recent appearance of two young poets who by their amazing imagination and their technical maturity appear to continue in the enlightened tradition of the first poets of *négritude*. They are the Congolese Gérald Felix Tchikoya u' Tamsi and the Mauritian Edouard Maunick. Neither political nor traditionalist in spirit, their poetry transcends racial and national problems. Each in his own elaborate idiom dramatizes the more universal themes of love, justice, fraternity, modern man's alienation and the dilemma of language.

Modern African poetry will surely be the result of diverse influences: the rediscovery of traditional poetry, and the integration of forms of thought of the modern world, both African and Occidental. The new forms that will probably emerge will have gained vigor from the contribution of the vernacular and the elaboration of individualist modes. Altogether, there exists now in the French language a literature worthy of an autonomous designation and demanding a separate study. The African poets and the prose writers are defining by their works a mode of life that is typically African; they are also expressing their own essence as Negroes and the sense of their presence in the world.

BIBLIOGRAPHY: Moore, G., *Seven African Writers* (1962); Kesteloot, L., *Les écrivains noirs de langue française: naissance d'une littérature* (1963); Moore, G., and Beier, U., *Modern Poetry from Africa* (1963); Snyder, E., "The Problem of *Négritude* in Modern French Poetry," *Comparative Literature Studies,* special advance issue (1963), 101-114

LILYAN KESTELOOT-LAGNEAU
EMILE SNYDER

NERUDA, Pablo

(pseud. of *Neftalí Reyes Basualto*), Chilean poet, b. 12 July 1904, Parral

N. is considered Latin America's leading contemporary poet; his work constitutes a valid South American contribution to present-day culture.

He attended high school in Temuco and studied French for three years at the Universidad de Chile. At an early age he had two volumes of poetry in print (*Crepusculario,* 1923; *Veinte poemas de amor y una canción desesperada,* 1924) and another finished (*El hondero entusiasta,* not published until 1933). Before going to Burma as Chilean consul in 1926, he published two new works, *Tentativo del hombre infinito* (1925) and *El habitante y su esperanza.* In Burma he drafted one of his major works, *Residencia en la tierra* (3 vols., 1931-37). In Madrid he founded the poetry magazine *El caballo verde.*

When the Spanish Civil War broke out, he immediately volunteered his services to the Republican government. At the end of the war he returned to Chile and joined the Communist party. He was elected to the senate, but lost his seat in parliament for slandering the president. Wanted by the authorities, he first hid in the interior of the country, then left Chile for Europe. The Soviet Union awarded him the Stalin Prize for Literature and the Lenin Peace Prize. In 1952 he returned to Chile.

Even in his early work N. almost instinctively discarded the forms of *modernismo* and strove for a happy medium between romanticism and French symbolism (q.v.). The main themes of these poems are sensual love and metaphysical doubt; their tone is always melancholy; their topics are anecdotal. In *Crepusculario* the note of political protest found in his later works is already perceptible.

Tentativo del hombre infinito initiates an entirely new period in his work. N. no longer seems to be on solid ground; fearfully he listens for the realities crowding in upon him, inflicting blow after blow. His language is rich in images, but they are piled one upon another without logical connection, not dominated by any political or philosophical doctrine. Here N. first ventures into the realm of the unconscious, in verses in which the cold beauty of *creacionismo* gives way all too abruptly to a surrealist exuberance of symbols.

Residencia en la tierra bears all the hallmarks of N.'s surrealist style: the "chaotic stocktaking" of the reality which surrounds the poet; the veiled autobiographical allusions; the profound analysis of the time concept; fear of transience and death; the mythologizing animation of lifeless things by way of strange thought associations, metaphors, or epithets; the attempt to apply to descriptive and narrative writing the techniques invented by cubist and

PABLO NERUDA

surrealist painters (*see* surrealism); and lastly, like an everflowing underground current, an intense sexual tension, often expressed in anxiety, a sense of annihilation, and *Weltschmerz.* "The unique poetic quality of *Residencia en la tierra* lies in its great intensity of feeling, in the sharpness of man's confrontation with the fundamental facts of his existence, and formally in the somberness of poetic expression" (A. Alonso).

The surrealist manner predominates in Volume III of *Residencia en la tierra,* too, although the poem "Reunion bajo las nuevas banderas" already shows an ideological shift which changes the inmost nature of N.'s poetry; from now on his work is to be entirely at the service of the Communist cause.

In 1950 N. published the collection *El canto general;* here the poetic images still retain their baroque complexity. The intuitive capturing and crystallizing of the spirit of individual Latin American nations through their landscape and history was unanimously praised by the critics. In 1954 he wrote *Las uvas y el viento,* which is purely political, and *Odas elementales* (Elementary Odes, 1961), in which he tried to express some of his political ideas in artistic form.

FURTHER WORKS: *Alturas de Machu Pichu* (1954; The Heights of Machu Pichu, 1966); *Las uvas y el viento* (1954); *Oda a la tipografía* (1956); *Tercer libro de las odas* (1957); *Estravagario* (1958); *Todo lleva tu nombre* (1959); *Navegaciones y regresos* (1959); *Canción de gesta* (1960); *Cien sonetos de amor* (1960); *Las piedras de Chile* (1960); *Cantos ceremoniales* (1961); *Los primeros versos de amor* (1961); *Plenos poderes* (1962); *La insepulta de Paita* (1962); *Nuevas odas elementales* (1963); *Todo el amor* (1964); *Los versos del capitán, poemas de amor* (1964); *Memoria de isla negra* (5 vols.: *Donde nace la lluvia; La luna en el laberinto; El fuego cruel; El cazador de raíces; Sonata crítica;* 1964); *Una casa de arena* (1966); *La barcarola* (1967). **Selected English trans.:** *Selected Poems* (1961); *We Are Many* (1967)

BIBLIOGRAPHY: Alonso, A., *Poesía y estilo de P. N.* (1940); Jorge de Lellis, M., *P. N.* (1957); Solama, R., *Para una crítica a P. N.* (1957); Marcenac, J., *P. N.* (1959); Aguirre, M., *Genio y figura de P. N.* (1964); Silva Castro, R., *P. N.* (1964); Loyola, H., *Ser y morir en P. N.* (1967)

FERNANDO ALEGRÍA

NEUMANN, Alfred

German novelist and playwright, b. 15 Oct. 1895, Lautenburg, West Prussia; d. 3 Oct. 1952, Lugano, Switzerland

N. spent his youth in Berlin and was a reader for a publishing house and for a time a director at the Munich Kammerspiele before deciding to make writing his career. A storyteller with a gift for cogent intellectual analysis and imaginative psychology, he depicts man's mistakes and confusion through historical examples. His most important and best-known work is the rationalistic novel *Der Teufel* (1926; Am., The Devil, 1929; Eng., The Deuce, 1929), a portrait of lust for power and political fanaticism based on the life of Louis XI of France and Oliver Necker, the king's confidant and *éminence grise.* The theme of political destiny recurs in most of N.'s other socially critical novels and short stories, which expose the fanaticism of the politically ambitious and the satanic element in power and in the lust for it. This is seen again in "Der Patriot" (1925; Am., The Patriot, 1928; Eng., Such Men Are Dangerous, 1928), which was adapted for the stage, and in the novel *Der Held* (1930), about the political assassination of Walter Rathenau. This theme reappears in the novel trilogy about Napoleon III: *Neuer Cäsar* (1934; Am., Another Caesar, 1935; Eng., The New Caesar, 1935); *Kaiserreich* (1936; Am., The Gaudy Empire, 1937; Eng., Man of December, 1937); and *Die Volksfreunde* (1941; The Friends of the People, 1951). N. also wrote plays, poems, and adaptations from French, English, and Italian.

FURTHER WORKS: *König Haber* (1926; King Haber and Other Stories, 1930); *Rebellen* (1927; The Rebels, 1929); *Guerra* (1928; Eng., 1930); *Narrenspiegel* (1932; The Mirror of Fools, 1933); *Der Pakt* (1949; Eng., Look Upon This Man; Am., Strange Conquest, 1954); *Königin Christine von Schweden* (1936; The Life of Christina of Sweden, 1936); *Es waren ihrer sechs* (1944; Six of Them, 1945)

BIBLIOGRAPHY: Anon., *Stimmen der Freunde: Der Romancier A. N. und sein Werk* (1957); Dietze, W., ed., *Die respektlose Muse* (1968)

PAUL WIMMER

NEVEUX, Georges

French playwright, b. 25 Aug. 1900, Poltava, Ukraine

Son of a Russian mother and a French army officer temporarily stationed in the Ukraine, N. began a legal career in France. He pleaded a few cases near Nice; but in 1922, on army service in the Rhineland, he started to compose dramas. Like Adamov and Ionesco (qq.v.) he was a friend of surrealist poets in Paris during the late 1920's; his first poems and plays reflect latent tendencies of surrealism (q.v.). An ingenious *opéra-chanson*, *Contrebande* (1928), was his debut as playwright. *La Beauté du diable* (1929) contained weird but limpid poems.

As Jouvet's (q.v.) secretary N. became immersed in Parisian theatrical affairs. His own play, *Juliette ou la clef des songes* (1930), staged by Falconetti, incited fisticuffs and controversy when some of the French public denounced its dream-world fantasies. Disappointed, N. gave up writing for the theater for thirteen years, turning to film scenarios and journalism. *Le Voyage de Thésée* (1943) was a masterful return to the theater. This hypnotic drama whirls the spectator dizzily amid metaphorical overtones suggested by the mythical combat between Theseus and the Minotaur. With its simultaneous outer and inner fabrics of mystery, woven in a tenuous poetic style, *Le Voyage de Thésée* embodies N.'s subtle artistry at its best.

Plainte contre inconnu (1946) featured a collective lawsuit attacking God, the "unknown" artisan of human anguish. This play prefigured the agonies and metaphysical malaise of the theater of the absurd which marked the 1950's. A curious drama merging burlesque and quasi-tragic views of destiny, *Zamore* (1953) was one of N.'s most successful combinations of the real and the unreal, of sadness and light-hearted whimsy. N., probably influenced by Chekhov and Giraudoux (qq.v.), believed in the basic doubling of human personality and that of life itself on two levels: the pathos of physical reality and the balm of spiritual illusion. *Le Système deux* (1955) dramatized this duplicity.

With *La Voleuse de Londres* (1960) N. won wider recognition on the boulevards of Paris. This bantering comedy portraying London's 19th c. underworld is enlivened by a tongue-in-cheek irony, gayer and less sociological than Brecht's (q.v.) in *The Threepenny Opera*.

N. was also a skillful translator and critic of foreign plays. His adaptations of dramas by Shakespeare, Chekhov, Lope de Vega, and others were staged by the Comédie-Française and Jean-Louis Barrault.

A crucial enigma traverses N.'s plays. How is contemporary man to reconcile the two embattled halves of his being, his material contingency and his powers of spirituality? The theater of N. offers no ready answer. N.'s importance, as an independent, original, and evocative dramatist unclassifiable by doctrine or school, may be considerable when more sensational and more ephemeral modes of modern theater disappear.

FURTHER WORKS: *Ma Chance et ma chanson* (1943); *J'ai un beau château* (1948); *Proverbiales* (1950); *Les Filles de la Rochelle* (1953); *Le Loup et la rose* (1953); *Théâtre dans une bouteille: Le Canari, Les Nuits de Chicago, Les quatre opérations* (1954); *Monsieur Il* (1960), *La Voleuse de Londres* (1960); *La Roulette et le souterrain* (1967)

BIBLIOGRAPHY: Brée, G., "N.: A Theatre of Adventure," *YFS*, XIV (Winter 1954-55), 65-70; Pronko, L. C. "G. N.: The Theatrical Voyage," *DramaS*, III: 2 (Fall 1963), 244-52

KENNETH S. WHITE

NEW ZEALAND LITERATURE

It is now evident that harshly negative judgments of New Zealand literature, long fashionable both from within the country and from overseas, can no longer be justly made. During the postwar years new poets, novelists, and story writers have appeared in numbers sufficient, not only to encourage each other in what is still a remote situation, but to attract notice elsewhere. Unlike Katherine Mansfield (q.v.), whose literary ambitions drove her into expatriation, the New Zealander of the 1950's and early 1960's could depend upon a growing acceptance of his work, if still limited by the smallness of the total population and by a lingering smallness of mind among some of the local audience.

Thus the work of poets like Allen Curnow (b. 1911), James K. Baxter (b. 1926), or Denis Glover (b. 1912) may be said to fulfill the promise of earlier figures like William Pember Reeves (1857-1932), who was also a notable interpreter of New Zealand social and political life, Jessie Mackay (1864-1938), or Ursula Bethell (1874-1945). By now, the fiction of Frank Sargeson (b. 1903) already lends itself to interpretation as a notable link between numerous but undistinguished chronicles of settlement or adventure and the psychological studies of Janet Frame (b. 1924), Ian Cross (b. 1925), and several others. Sargeson's achievements include the successful introduction of a colloquial language appropriate to the plain people of his works, which recall depression-born novels by John A. Lee (b. 1891) and Robin Hyde (pseud. of Iris Guiver Wilkinson, 1906-1939). The most significant predecessors of these moderns (Mansfield excepted) were William Satchell (1859-1952) and Jane Mander (1871-1949).

The land itself interested Samuel Butler (1835-1902), who recalled it vividly in *Erewhon* (1872) and *Erewhon Revisited* (1901), and his contemporary F. E. Maning (1811-93), who (unlike Butler) remained in the country. Maning's *Old New Zealand* (1863) concerned itself with an account of early contact with the Maoris, whimsically and delightfully presented. Herbert Guthrie-Smith (1861-1940), on the other hand, took antipodean nature as his theme and produced in *Tutira* (1921) a unique chronicle of a North Island sheep station through forty years of rapid transformation. A tradition of interblended literary and social criticism has been fostered through the writings of E. H. McCormick (b. 1906) and M. H. Holcroft (b. 1902) and, since 1946, in the periodical *Landfall*.

To come to terms with a difficult environment, resisting the blandishments of complacency in isolation and persevering against neglect, has been the task of the New Zealand intellectual for several generations. The extent to which he has succeeded may be measured in such retrospective collections as Curnow's and Brasch's anthologies. These bear scars from the struggle but suggest also a clear note of victory. Unless signs fail, New Zealand's claims to an increasingly mature, self-confident self-expression will continue to be pressed by capable advocates.

BIBLIOGRAPHY: Holcroft, M. H., *Discovered Isles: A Trilogy* (1950); Davin, D., *New Zealand Short Stories* (1953); McCormick, E. H., *New Zealand Literature: A Survey* (1959); Curnow, A., *The Penguin Book of New Zealand Verse* (1960); Stevens, J., *The New Zealand Novel* (1961); Brasch, C., *Landfall Country: Work from Landfall 1947-61* (1962); see also issues of the magazine *Landfall*

JOSEPH JONES

NEZVAL, Vítězslav

Czech poet, b. 26 May 1900, Biskupovice, Southwest Moravia; d. 6 April 1958, Prague

N.'s lasting significance lies in his pre-World War II volumes of poems, which opened new directions to Czech poetry. Like Jiří Wolker (1900-1924), who died young, N. belongs to a generation deeply impressed in its youth by the Communist revolution. Committed to the left politically, they felt bound also to accept the radical principles then dominating art in France and the Soviet Union. N., a sophisticated improviser, quickly and effortlessly mastered a variety of forms. His hallmark is the loose stringing together of ideas, not logically but by daring association. Metaphor points the way to the unconscious; a breath of sensual joy of living pervades the poems. In the collection *Edison* (1928) the apotheosis of civilization is linked with the cult of night, but in the important volume of poems *Básně noci* (1930) grief, nostalgia, and fear of life and death prevail. This work and even more *Žena v množném čísle* (1934) and *Praha s prsty deště* (1936) reveal N.'s tendency to surrealism (q.v.).

Stalin (1949), a volume of poetry written under the Communist regime, is propagandistic. However, poems expressing N.'s love for his country (*Z domoviny*, 1950; *Chrpy a města*, 1955) show undiminished poetic strength.

FURTHER WORKS: *Pantomima* (1924); *Židovský hřbitov* (1928); *Hra v kostky* (1929); *Básně noci* (1930); *Pět prstů* (1932); *Skleněný havelok* (1932); *Milenci z kiosku* (1932); *Zpáteční lístek* (1933); *Řetěz štěstí* (1936); *Sbohem a šáteček* (1934); *Historický obraz* (1939; enlarged ed., 1945); *Pět minut za městem* (1940); *Veliký orloj* (1949); *Zpěv míru* (1950; Song of Peace, 1951); *Dílo* (35 vols, 1950 ff.); *Z domoviny* (1950); *Křídla* (1952)

BIBLIOGRAPHY: Novak, A., *Die tschechische Literatur* (1931); Kratochvil, L., *Wolker a N.* (1936); Rechcigl, M., ed., *The Czechoslovak Contribution to World Culture* (1964); Svoboda, J., *Přítel V. N.* (1966)

OTTO TUREČEK

NIETZSCHE, Friedrich

German philosopher and poet, b. 15 Oct. 1844, Röcken bei Lützen; d. 25 Aug. 1900, Weimar

N.'s father, a Protestant pastor, died prematurely, and the boy was reared by his mother, grandmother, and two aunts. At an early age N. showed musical as well as literary aptitude, and he soon became an accomplished pianist, improvising brilliantly; some of his compositions, although amateurish, reveal unique harmonies (*Ermanarich, Manfredmeditationen*). After completing preparatory studies at the eminent Gymnasium, Schulpforta, N. attended the universities of Bonn and Leipzig, where he studied classical philology under F. Ritschl. His mentor's enthusiastic recommendation won N. a post at the University of Basel in 1869, and he was appointed full professor the following year. In the war of 1870 he served briefly as a medical orderly until incapacitated by dysentery and diphtheria. During his academic career N. was plagued by poor health—migraine headaches, violent retching, and periods of near-blindness, presumably the result of venereal infection contracted at Leipzig—which led to extended leaves after 1876 and retirement in 1879.

His association in these years with the historian Jacob Burckhardt and the composer Richard Wagner no doubt shaped his thinking significantly. N. had met Wagner in 1868 and was enamored with his music. Discovery of a mutual regard for Schopenhauer's pessimism resulted in warm friendship. Basic differences in musical and philosophical outlook, however, eventually led to estrangement. N. devoted the next decade to formulating his philosophical ideas. His was a lonely existence in rented rooms, the winters usually being spent on the Italian Riviera and the summers in the Swiss Engadine. In 1882 he unsuccessfully proposed marriage to Lou Salomé, later paramour of the poet Rilke (q.v.). While in Turin in 1889 N. went hopelessly insane. He was cared for in Naumburg until his mother's death in 1897, and then taken by his sister, Elisabeth, to Weimar, where she had established a N. Archive. Elisabeth published N.'s works and literary remains. However, her desire to create a N. legend—even forging letters to make it appear that she had been her brother's confidante—heightened the confusion concerning N.'s views. For years Elisabeth's N. Archive feuded with the German N. Society until, under the Nazis, the former adopted the party line and the latter was disbanded.

Three main periods may be discerned in N.'s writings: (1) indebtedness to Schopenhauer and, to a lesser extent, Wagner; (2) the break with metaphysical tradition; (3) N.'s own dionysiac world view.

N.'s first important essay, *Die Geburt der Tragödie* (1872; The Birth of Tragedy, 1910), is concerned with cultural regeneration. N. believed that pre-Socratic Greek tragedy contained an apollonian or mythical element and a dionysiac or orgiastic element. The former gave rise to an exalted mood experienced in breaking the painful bond of individuation. The latter, a mirage of beautiful deities, lured Greek man back from the "buddhistic" otherworldliness engendered by the dionysiac mood. Just as Greek tragedy had helped produce the highest type of Greek man, a new German tragedy based on German music since Bach and Beethoven and on the rich store of German myth, could serve to stay the cultural decline since 1870.

When conservative scholars assailed the work as unsound—N.'s views on Greek tragedy are widely held today—N. attacked directly what he felt to be the smug optimism and shallow rationalism of the times. *Unzeitgemäße Betrachtungen* (1873-76; Thoughts out of Season, 1909-1913) respectively castigates David F. Strauss as a cultural philistine, denounces superficial and conservative historicity, and lauds Schopenhauer and Wagner—casting the two last-named in the role of "heroic" pessimists!

With *Menschliches, Allzumenschliches* (1878-80; Human, All-too-human, 1909-1911), a disillusioned N. switched his allegiance from Schopenhauer to the 17th c. French moralists, rejected metaphysics, and espoused the freethinker. Re-examining human knowledge in historical psychological perspective, N. concluded that the world was a meaningless chaos, man devoid of free will, and human motivation traceable to desire or fear. Pity he abhorred above all as culturally enervating. *Morgenröte* (1881; Dawn of Day, 1903) and *Fröhliche Wissenschaft* (1882; Joyful Wisdom, 1910) ruminates further on moral preconceptions. The latter also shows a transition, both in style and content, to N.'s mature attitude; the scholarly style yields in the second half to paradoxical epigrams and symbolic poems; contextually, increased emphasis is placed on masculinity, barbarism, war, and health as means to restore lost vitality.

N.'s poetic masterpiece, *Also sprach Zarathustra* (1883-85; Thus Spake Zarathustra, 1909), written in free verse parodying the psalmodic tone of the Bible, proclaims the superman who, hopefully, will one day inherit the earth. Free from conventional moral restraints and heeding only his own "will to power," the superman nevertheless embodies utmost self-discipline. He is a heroic and tragic figure, affirming life although aware that it is devoid of meaning except for the eternity and immortality posited in "eternal recurrence." He is a creative genius, as in creation alone lies redemption from suffering. Despite his strong will, he is close kin to N.'s earlier freethinker and to the sage Zarathustra; will to power is less political than metaphysical. N. later justified "eternal recurrence," the central theme in *Also sprach Zarathustra* and the key notion of his mature outlook, scientifically in terms of a finite world in infinite time, but basically "eternal recurrence," as does "will to power," reflects his conception of being as "endless becoming."

Jenseits von Gut and Böse (1886; Beyond Good and Evil, 1907), returning to the aphoristic form, continues the supramoral evaluation and, together with its sequel, *Zur Genealogie der Moral* (1887; Genealogy of Morals, 1896), discusses the presumed historical origin of morality. The semantic shift in words such as "noble" led N. to conclude that in prehistoric time whatever the strong had done was considered "good." Hence codes stressing humility and altruism were later "slave moralities" foisted by the weak on the strong as an expression of their resentment and hidden "will to power." The weak Judaic-Christians had triumphed in this fashion over the strong Romans. Whereas N. hitherto had praised "bad" as synonymous with "new," he now expressed admiration for such things as "beast-of-prey," "blond beast," "Aryan master race," furnishing ammunition for fascist and Nazi propaganda.

The works of the last years are even more extreme. *Der Antichrist* (1888) and much of *Götzendämmerung* (1889; Twilight of the Idols, 1896) accentuate the attack on Christianity, and the literary autobiography *Ecce Homo* (written 1889, pub. 1908) parodies Christ's martyrdom. *Der Fall Wagner* (1888; The Case of Wagner, 1896) and *N. contra Wagner* (1889) assail Wagner as decadent. *Wille zur Macht* (1901, expanded 1906; Will to Power) is an arbitrary collection of N.'s aphorisms posthumously compiled by Elisabeth. This alleged magnum opus led for a time to the widespread belief (A. Bäumler) that "will to power" as political force was N.'s final doctrine. In 1956 K. Schlechta bitterly assailed *Wille zur Macht* on the basis of manuscript chronology, but the work is still considered by several eminent scholars to contain the quintessence of N.'s metaphysics.

Indeed, widespread disagreement prevails as to N.'s mature views. The psychologist W. Lange-Eichbaum contends that N.'s mind after 1880 was distorted by progressive paralysis. The existentialist K. Jaspers maintains that N. had no system and juxtaposed contradictory views to stimulate his readers to independent thinking. K. Schlechta holds that N. was a nihilist who posited wishful hypotheses. K. Löwith, M. Heidegger, E. Fink, and E. Heftrich argue that N. had a consistent system grounded in the notion of "eternal recurrence."

Ignored during his lifetime, N. became known around 1890 as a result of his insanity and lectures on him by the Danish critic Brandes (q.v.). N.'s fame spread like wildfire after his death. During World War I millions of German soldiers carried *Also sprach Zarathustra* in their packs. Hitler presented Mussolini on his sixtieth birthday with a gold-bound edition of N.'s works. After 1945 many German intellectuals publicly disowned N. as irresponsible, but elsewhere numerous studies on him have continued to appear. During 1947-53 a fifteen-volume Spanish edition of N.'s works came out in Madrid and Buenos Aires. Most of them were translated into Japanese from 1950 to 1953. Over four thousand books and articles in twenty-eight languages have been written on N.

Investigation of N.'s enormous influence as prose stylist, impressionist and expressionist poet, and revolutionary thinker has only begun; comprehensive studies are available for Scandinavia and the Hispanic world. An astonishing number of Germany's most eminent authors owe a debt to N. Traceable in part to him are Hesse's (q.v.) concept of *Amor fati*, T. Mann's (q.v.) essayistic style, "life" concept, and basic motifs in *Der Zauberberg* and *Doktor Faustus*, the erotic vitalism of Wedekind, Dehmel, H. Mann, and Edschmid (qq.v.), the supermen of Ernst (q.v.), the life-spirit dualism and later immoral heroes of Kaiser (q.v.), the racist views of Benn, Rilke, and Hofmannsthal (qq.v.), the heroic pose and aphoristic style of E. Jünger (q.v.), the decay of values (*Wertzerfall*) of Broch (q.v.).

FURTHER WORKS: *N.'s Werke* (16 vols., 1895-1904); *Werke* (20 vols., 1905 ff.); *Werke und Briefe* (9 vols., 1933 ff.); *Werke des Zusammenbruchs* (ed. E. Podach; 1961); *Gesammelte Briefe* (5 vols., 1904-1909). **Selected English trans.:** *Complete Works* (18 vols., 1909-1913); *The Portable N.* (ed. W. Kaufmann; 2 vols., 1959)

BIBLIOGRAPHY: Andreas-Salomé, L., *N. in seinen Werken* (1894, 1924); Förster-N., E., *Das Leben F. N.'s* (1895-1904); Salter, W. M., *N. the Thinker,* (1917); Bertram, E., *N.* (1918; 7th ed. 1929); Andler, C., *N., Sa vie et sa pensée* (6 vols., 1920-31; 2nd ed. 1958); Klages, L., *Die psychologischen Errungenschaften N.'s* (1926); Bianquis, G., *N. en France* (1929); Löwith, K., *N.'s Philosophie der ewigen Wiederkehr des Gleichen* (1935); Klein, J., *Die Dichtung N.s* (1936); Jaspers, K., *N.* (1936; 3rd ed. 1950); Martin, A. v., *N. und Burckhardt* (4th ed. 1947); Mann, T., "N. in the Light of Modern Experience," *Commentary* (1948); Reyburn, H., *N.: The Story of a Human Philosopher* (1948); Lange-Eichbaum, W., *N.: Krankheit und Wirkung* (1948); Kaufmann, W., *N.: Philosopher, Psychologist, Antichrist* (1950); Blunk, R., *F. N.: Kindheit und Jugend* (1953); Wolf, H., *F. N.: Der Weg zum Nichts* (1956); Borland, H., *N.'s Influence on Swedish Literature* (1956); Lea, F., *The Tragic Philosopher* (1957); Schlechta, K., *Der Fall N.* (2nd ed. 1959); Reichert, H., *N. Literature in the Postwar Era* (1959); Reichert, H., and Schlechta, K., eds., *International N. Bibliography* (1960); Fink, E., *N.'s Philosophie* (1960); Heidegger, M., *N.* (2 vols., 1961); Heftrich, E., *N.'s Philosophie* (1962); Rukser, U., *N. in der Hispania* (1962); Love, F., *Young N. and the Wagnerian Experience* (1963); Reichert, H., *N. and Georg Kaiser* (1964)

HERBERT REICHERT

NIN, Anaïs

American novelist, critic, and diarist, b. 1914, Paris

Daughter of the Spanish pianist and composer Joaquin Nin, Anaïs N. came at age eleven with her Danish mother to the U.S. In 1929 she settled in Paris, where she was active in literary and artistic circles, associating with Henry Miller, Artaud (qq.v.), and Otto Rank among others. She encouraged Miller, backed the publication of *The Tropic of Cancer* financially, and wrote the preface to the first edition. Her first book, published in 1932, was a critical study of D. H. Lawrence (q.v.), whose ideas were strongly to influence her own fiction. *House of Incest* (1936) is a prose poem composed largely of dreams surrealistically presented. Obscure in places, the book is important as the cornerstone of a long effort to convey the significance of recurrent dreams, fantasies, and myths without destroying them by explication. *House of Incest, Winter of Artifice* (1939), and the fiction that has followed, draw heavily on the vivid and richly detailed diary that N. began as a child and that now extends to more than a hundred volumes. The diary attempts to capture the present and record it—especially at moments of intense emotion, which N. believes are most self-revealing—and to bind individual experiences together so as to yield the pattern of a total personality. It provides an anchor in one level of reality for the mythic novels, which often flow cinematically.

In 1940 N. returned to New York, where she was a lay analyst under the supervision of Rank; her absorption with psychoanalysis, which had begun a decade before, has had a formative influence on all of her writing. The first book published after her return was a collection of potently evocative short stories, *Under a Glass Bell* (1944), which was followed over a number of years by what are in reality parts of an extended novel: *Ladders to Fire* (1946), *Children of the Albatross* (1947), *The Four Chambered Heart* (1950), *A Spy in the House of Love* (1954), and *Solar Barque* (1958). Her most recent novels are *The Seduction of the Minotaur* (1961) and *Collages* (1964); the last title well describes the book's structure.

N.'s fiction is mostly written in the third person, and though there are a number of resemblances to Joyce and Virginia Woolf (qq.v.), she differs from them in not structuring novels so clearly in time, even warped time. Nor, despite dependence upon her diary, are her novels autobiographical in the sense that Miller's are. Furthermore, they are remarkably free of detail, seeming almost pallid to an age that hankers for documentary reality; the pallor of detail and the amorphousness in time vary from book to book and are less marked in the more recent *Seduction of the Minotaur*. But the central preoccupation that accounts for these traits remains unchanged: the life of the mind (which is reality to N.) communicated mythically.

The dimensions of what N. is trying to do have become clear only in recent years and are set forth in the title under which the parts of her long novel were published in 1959—*Cities of the Interior*. She is striving for the delineation of a complex interior world, one so vast that it will, she feels, counterpoise external reality.

N.'s writing is almost always moving, but it puzzles the reader who is not able to hold in check for a while his appetite for immediate meaning, and since the incidental attractions of the novels were not sufficient to win easy recognition for such a subject matter treated in such a manner, she herself published some of the early books. By the time that Henry Miller's letters to her were published in 1965, the importance of her work was becoming more and more widely recognized, and all of the earlier books had been republished.

The Diary of Anaïs Nin (Vol. I, 1966; Vol. II, 1968), which covers the period from 1931 to 1939, is shorter than the section of the original upon which it is based because some of the people involved did not wish to appear in the published version, but it throws new light on N.'s fiction, illuminates literary and artistic life of Paris in the 1930's, and is most significant as a work of art in its own right—a work which, for all its detail, has the same fundamental concerns as N.'s other writings.

FURTHER WORKS: *Realism and Reality* (1946); *On Writing* (1947); *The Novel of the Future* (1968)

BIBLIOGRAPHY: Evans, O., *A. N.* (1968)

ROBERT B. VOITLE

NOAILLES, Anna-Elisabeth de

French poet and narrative writer, b. 15 Nov. 1876, Paris; d. there, 30 April 1933

Born a Brancovan, N. came of a princely Walachian-Rumanian and Greek line and married into the ancient aristocratic N. family. As a poet she brings to ultimate perfection the romantic forms and subjects that took shape under the influence of Paul Verlaine and especially Jammes (q.v.). Jammes's bucolic spiritualization of nature pervades her lyrical poetry; for this "muse of the garden" the world of plants has even greater significance. Her delicate, decadent sensibility enables her to combine nature mysticism, the dream, the seen and the unseen, body and heart.

After some early poems, "Litanies," in the *Revue de Paris,* she published her first volume *Le Coeur innombrable* (1901), followed by eight more volumes of poems that show no significant thematic or formal expansion. *Les Éblouissements* (1907) includes landscape sketches of Asia Minor and Greece; here nostalgia for childhood begins to play a larger role. N. did not always escape the danger of rhetoric and sentimentalism. The main theme of *Les* *Vivants et les morts* (1913) is the search for religious ties; in *Le Poème de l'amour* (1924) Bergson (q.v.) noted "a metaphysics of the world of emotion"; *L'Honneur de souffrir* (1927) deals with the problem of death.

N.'s prose works are marred by excessive lyricism and sentiment. The novel *Le Visage émerveillé* (1904), the love diary of a nun, provoked a scandal. A novel "Octave" and her "Journal" remained unfinished. N. was universally recognized, except for a few literary opponents, and during her lifetime was considered France's greatest woman poet.

FURTHER WORKS: *L'Ombre des jours* (1902); *La Nouvelle Espérance* (1903); *La Domination* (1905); *De la Rive d'Europe à la rive d'Asie* (1913); *Les Forces éternelles* (1920); *Conte triste, avec une moralité* (1921); *A. R. Kipling* (1921); *Les Innocentes ou La Sagesse des femmes* (1923); *Discours* (1924); *Quatre témoignages sur Anatole France* (1924); *Passions et vanités* (1926); *Mes poèmes d'enfance* (1928); *Exactitudes* (1930); *Choix de poésies* (1930); *Le Livre de ma vie* (1932); *Derniers vers et poèmes d'enfance* (1934)

BIBLIOGRAPHY: Larnac, J., *Comtesse de N.* (1931); Fargue, L.-P., *A. de N.* (1947); DuBos, C., *La Comtesse de N. et le climat du génie* (1949); Cocteau, J., *Reines de France* (1952); De la Rochefoucauld, É., *A. de N.* (1956); Cocteau, J., *La Comtesse de N., oui ou non* (1963); Perche, L., *A. de N.* (1964); Aragon, L., "Chez A. de N.," in *NRF* (15 Oct. 1967), pp. 725-27; Sutton, H., "Two Poets of Childhood," in *BA,* XLI (1967), 261-66

VIRGIL IERUNCA

NORTH AFRICAN LITERATURE: French Language

Around 1930, after a century of colonization, all literature drawing its inspiration from the North African area was dominated by the exotic and the picturesque. To French writers, this neighboring yet totally foreign world offered merely novel feelings and sights. During World War II, however, Algiers became the capital of fighting France, and Frenchmen temporarily quartered there no longer saw North Africa through tourists' eyes. In the eyes of the native population, France lost much of her former prestige. About 1950, after maturing for several years in silence, the first works of North African writers in the French language appeared, revealing to the mother country and to the world a truly vital North Africa expressing its own personality. Simultaneously, in the works of Camus (q.v.), Gabriel Audisio (b. 1900; *Jeunesse de la Méditerranée*, 2 vols., 1935-36; *Feuilles de Fresnes*, 1945), Roblès (q.v.), and others, the French population of North Africa became articulate.

The first books by native authors writing in French were in striking contrast to earlier works of French literature on North African themes. The serious, bitter tone soon became accusatory. One of the earliest, largely autobiographical works might furnish a generic title for them all—Mouloud Deraoun's *Le Fils du pauvre* (1954). Whether the writer be Arab like Dib (q.v.), Berber like Feraoun and Mouloud Mammeri (b. 1917 in Haute Kabylie; *La colline oubliée*, 1952; *Le sommeil du juste*, 1955), or Jew like Albert Memmi (b. 1922 in Tunis; *La statue de sel*, 1953; *Agar*, 1955; *Portrait du colonisé*, 1957), his first compulsion is to describe his hard childhood. The childhood of the natives was often dominated by hunger; even children could not escape seeing that this condition did not exist in the lives of the colonists. Although North Africa never knew the official discrimination of South Africa, the writers, usually sons of poor families, had realized that the biggest estates and most businesses belonged to the French. Their image of France included ominous figures forming the background of daily life: the gendarme, the government official, the *colon*—all hostile powers. Thus all these novels testify to the estrangement of two ethnic groups as the root cause of race hatred.

This hatred would be sterile except for the growing nationalism. Even though the mountain Berbers and the plains Arabs are traditionally enemies—because of historical events and differences of language and customs—they felt themselves allied against the French.

In none of the fictional characters is awareness of Algerian nationality based on religious faith; in fact, some of them are convinced atheists. While the Kabyle writers tend to lament the collapse of their ancestral moral code, the young Arab intellectuals, in the latest works of Dib and Kateb Yacine (b. 1928), are impatiently eager to shake off Islam's oppressive yoke.

Thus hunger, misery, despair, humiliation, alienation, and a rising nationalism that already feels strong enough to criticize Islam from within are the recurring themes of North African literature. Essentially, however, the literature expresses an indictment of France. This indictment is contradictory in that its arguments are drawn from French 18th c. philosophy rather than from Karl Marx, and that it values purity of language far more highly than the French colonists do themselves. These classicist tendencies are particularly noticeable in Dib, though his careful style does not preclude certain archaisms. Whatever the individual writer's personal style (naturalism [q.v.] in Feraoun, Orientalism in Ahmed Sefrioui [*Le chapelet d'ambre*, 1946-48; *La boîte a merveille*, 1954], a percussive style in Driss Chraibis [*L'âne*, 1956], baroque Faulknerian lyricism in Kateb Yacine's *Nedjma* [1956]), they are all vitally concerned with good linguistic form. They also seek to appeal primarily to Parisian literary circles.

BIBLIOGRAPHY: *Actes du Colloque sur la littérature africaine d'expression française, Dakar . . . 1963* (1965); Doob, L. W., ed., *Ants Will Not Eat Your Fingers: A Selection of Traditional African Poems* (1966); Beier, U., ed., *Introduction to African Literature* (1967); Brench, A. C., *The Novelist's Inheritance in French Africa* (1967); Tucker, M., *Africa in Modern Literature* (1967)

MARCEL MOUSSY

NORWEGIAN LITERATURE

The dissolution of the union with Sweden in 1905, World War I, the victory of Fascism, World War II, and the German occupation—these are the decisive historical events that left their mark on Norway's intellectual and literary life. In their late work all four of the 19th c. "great men," Henrik Ibsen (q.v.), Bjørnstjerne Bjørnson (1832-1916), Alexander Kielland (1849-1906), and Jonas Lie (1833-1908), anticipated one central problem of the 20th c.: the rise of materialism and the bitter struggle of the individual against anonymous forces. In the naturalistic movement of the 1880's the pendulum swung briefly in the opposite direction, and a tide of materialistic thinking swept into art. The result was the "tired souls" (*Trætte mænd*, 1891) of Arne Garborg (1851-1924) and the novels of Amalia Skram ([1837-1905] *Forraadt*, 1892; *Hellemyrsfolket*,

4 vols., 1887-1900), whose point of departure was Ibsen's social dramas. The unfathomable, homeless drifter Sigbjørn Obstfelder (1866-1900), too, is one of those will-o'-the-wisp, *fin de siècle* spirits whose Danish counterparts Bang (q.v.) and Jens Peter Jacobsen (1847-85) had such a lasting influence on contemporary German literature. In Heiberg (q.v.) turn-of-the-century pessimism was transformed into optimistic acceptance of life; he was already the poet of the 1890's, pushing onward, like the other writers of this period, beyond the philosophic and aesthetic bounds of naturalism (q.v.). Their outstanding representative was undoubtedly Hamsun (q.v.), whose radically individualistic writing, with its hostility to civilization and proclamation of an entirely new communion with nature, must be viewed against the background of the neoromantic tendencies of the time. The intensity of his characterization and his melodious language lift him as an artist onto an unassailable level, while his bias, whenever it broke through, aroused the most violent opposition. His hatred of the Western democracies associates humiliating personal experiences in America with rather vague reformist ideas, seeking to renew existence at the fountainhead of life.

Though Marxist and Darwinian theories were not widely disseminated until just before World War I, the leaders of the intelligentsia were profoundly skeptical of the dogmas of materialism. The far-reaching social upheavals caused by extraordinarily sudden industrialization were unmistakable. At first Norway experienced a boom, which, in conjunction with dissolution of the union with Sweden, led to rapid financial and economic growth. Falkberget (q.v.), Kristoffer Uppdal (b. 1878), and Hamsun were alert observers of the social shifts of this period. Hamsun poured scorn on the class-conscious proletariat and castigated the materialistic "new Norway." Aukrust (q.v.), the sensitive lyric poet, cursed the machine age. In his ten-volume novel *Dansen gjennom skuggeheimen* (1911-24) Uppdal presents a whole gallery of "new men," from the asocial tramp to the responsible labor delegate. Johan Bojer (1872-1959) took a positive attitude to this social development (*Sigurd Braa,* 1916), while Tore Ørjasæter (b. 1886) wanted to reconcile the opposing forces. The later works of several poets of the older generation such as Egge (q.v.) and Hans E. Kinck ([1865-1926], *Emigranter,* 1904; *Sneskavlen brast,* 3 vols., 1918-19) reflect the new social tensions.

The year 1914 was the second turning point in the intellectual life of Norway. The prewar period had promised a golden age, and its proud confidence lasted several years beyond 1914; after all, the international conflict was very far away. The historian Ludvig Daae (1834-1910), Nils Kjær (1870-1924), Sigurd Ibsen (1859-1930), and several other critical minds recognized the futility of belief in progress. The retrospective analysis of the prewar intellectual climate made by Kristian Elster (1881-1947) in *Den skjønne ungdom* (1922) appears sharply satirical. It seemed almost impossible to hold aloof from the beautiful illusion; Sigrid Undset (q.v.) herself acknowledged how difficult it was to live as man "among men who believe in man's perfectibility." In her novels *Gymnadenia* (1929; The Wild Orchid, 1931) and *Den brændende busk* (1930; The Burning Bush, 1932) she painted a masterful picture of the changing aspects of the prewar, war, and postwar periods.

War and its events per se left remarkably few traces on Norwegian literature. "Undisturbed, Norwegian authors went on writing about eroticism and the joys of motherhood," said one critic in 1919. Nevertheless, horror at the European Armageddon throbs unmistakably in the poems of Aukrust ("Norrønasong"), in Ørjasæter's *Manns kvævde* (1915), and in the poems of Uppdal. The more deeply probing analyses (most of them in epic forms)—notably *Menneskenes lodd* (1945) by Christiansen (q.v.); *Erik* (1931) by Fangen (q.v.); and *Syvstjernen* (1924) by Hoel (q.v.)—did not appear until later. Conflict is apparent in the very titles of the play *Vår ære og vår makt* (1935) by Grieg (q.v.) and of Paul Gjesdahl's (b. 1893) *Tilskuere* (1931). *Under skråtaket* (1927) by Nini Roll Anker (1873-1942) sharply contrasts European misery with Norwegian prosperity.

The generation that came of age in the postwar years and the 1920's had acquired its formative ideas in the progressivist prewar period. It still regarded the world war, not as an apocalyptic event, but as an interlude, a regression on the part of humanity that must be reversed. It was aware of established values: home, marriage, family (consistently repudiated by antibourgeois neoromanticism), country, faith, tradition. The re-creation of the past gives its work depth. The 1920's are often referred to as another golden age in Norwegian literature. Their writers inherited the naturalists' gift for acute observation and skill in characterization, but the realistic style gains depth from their confident faith and genuine humanism. The "Norgeskantate" of N. C. Vogt (1864-1937) is the forerunner of the regional poetry of the 1920's. Uppdal's characters are late successors of the saga heroes. Barbara Ring (1870-1955), Gabriel Scott (1874-1958), and Mikkjel Fønhus (b. 1894), the writer of wilderness and animal stories, should be mentioned in this connection. Three writers, however, achieved European stature: Duun (q.v.), whose "Juvikfolke" have been called the last powerful descendants of the heroic sagas; Sigrid Undset, whose *Kristin Lavransdatter* (1920-22) goes back to the 14th c. in order to make visible the formative powers of northern man; and Falkberget.

The so-called "Hoel-Christiansen generation" is slightly younger. It emerged under quite different circumstances from the Duun-Undset group. It had just entered maturity when it felt the shock of the outbreak of war, and it never found the strength to bridge this deep cleft between two eras and to reach the past again. For this generation the gods were dead; faith in man was destroyed. *The Waste Land* by Eliot (q.v.) became its symbol. The Russian revolution seemed to promise a way out, and for a time Communism found fertile soil among Norwegian radicals. In 1931 the Communist International was founded, and immediately afterward the Clarté movement of Barbusse (q.v.) spread to Norway. Its guiding personality was Erling Falk (1887-1940). Hoel was attracted to the movement; he and Falk edited the periodical *Mot Dag*, in whose pages some of the most dynamic minds spoke out: Vogt, Cora Sandel (b. 1880), and the eminent poet Bull (q.v.). Although it left no deep mark on practical life, the movement exerted a powerful influence, which might be traced in Hoel, Helge Krog (b. 1889), and Øverland (q.v.). It has been said of Øverland, who is perhaps the most significant and versatile Norwegian poet of the 20th c., that he immunized young Norwegians against the Hamsun bacillus, against the playful turn-of-the-century yearning for beauty, against individualism and aestheticism. In the prewar era Øverland had been one of the most carefree advocates of aesthetic individualism; now even he expressed the conviction that poetry had a function in society.

In complete contrast to the Duun-Undset generation, these writers rejected convention and tradition and took a hostile attitude toward church, Christianity, and family. But they also rejected class-war slogans and stood for intellectualistic individualism. The poets of the 1920's are "disillusioned"; their weapons are irony, sarcasm, and caustic criticism. And this had one remarkable consequence: the supporters of Falk lost contact with the working class, and thus no autonomous proletarian poetry developed in Norway, as it did in Sweden. The one major exception was R. W. Nilsen (1901-1929), a poet of fascinating power.

The journal *Vor Verden*, under the enterprising editorship of Fangen, attacked the disillusioned radicals and Communism. The leader of this new movement, which emerged about 1925, maintained a liberal-conservative position with strong religious accents. The definitely religious cast of the 1920's can be seen in Aukrust, Ørjasæter, Uppdal, Falkberget, Scott, and Bojer. Christiansen, too, treats religious problems; and Nini Roll Anker and Sigrid Undset, pursuing Catholic and neo-Thomist ideas, take their place beside European figures such as Claudel and Chesterton (qq.v.).

During the 1920's the influence of Sigmund Freud was powerful and fruitful in literature; the pioneering works were Nini Anker's *Fru Castrups datter* (1918) and Hoel's *Veien vi går* (1922).

On the other hand, the assimilation of modern poetic forms took place very gradually. While modern trends were already apparent in the 1920's in Sweden, Finland, and Denmark, the more conservative Norwegians were utterly opposed to formal experiments. What was required of the Norwegian writer—and what he required of himself—were clear ideas, clear form, clear articulation. The Nordic saga was still, as it always had been, the revered model for great art. Among more recent writers, Dostoyevski, France (q.v.), and the Swede H. E. F. Söderberg (1869-1941), whose anti-Christian, individualistic tone captivated Hoel, Øverland, Krog, and others, gained a following. The monologue technique of Joyce (q.v.) was adopted as a modern medium for psychological analysis. A surprisingly early contact with Kafka (q.v.) deserves mention. Hoel, author of the novel *Syvstjernen,* claimed to be Kafka's first disciple in world literature, and indeed he did recognize Kafka's significance as a mirror of the modern consciousness before he was accepted in Germany. Common to all the trends of the 1920's is an impulse to retreat, a tendency to withdraw, to take refuge in the only certainty remaining: the self. Only in the next decade does the will to break out of isolation meet with success.

In retrospect the transition to the 1930's looks like a brief breathing space between crises and wars. Hoel's *Syndere i Sommersol* (1927) and Krog's *På solsiden* (1927) typify this, as do the extraordinarily popular novels of Trygve Gulbranssen (1894-1962).

Early in the 1930's the world economic crisis began to be felt in Norway. Stock market crashes, unemployment, and new social conflict were the results. However, attention was soon diverted to political events in Europe. The intellectual fight against Fascism was led by the Swedish writer Lagerkvist (q.v.), whose *Bödeln* (1933) had a telling success.

In the journal *Fritt Ord*, edited by Kristian Schjelderup (b. 1894), who himself wrote an acute analysis of the period in his *På vei mot hedenskapet* (1935), writers such as Hoel, Øverland, and Undset spoke out. Undset published anti-Fascist pamphlets in German which attracted wide attention. On the other side stood Hamsun—almost alone. He came under fire when he attacked the German pacifist Carl von Ossietzky in 1935. Grieg, who returned from a stay in Russia in 1936, remained in the Communist camp. For a time it seemed that Communism and anti-Fascism were making common cause in the so-called popular front, but this collapsed under the impact of reports from Stalinist Russia, and Grieg was the only ranking Norwegian writer to remain loyal to Stalin's ideology.

Only now did the influence of psychoanalysis begin to be widely felt. In 1934 Wilhelm Reich's *Massenpsychologie des Faschismus* appeared in Copenhagen, and shortly afterward Reich settled in Norway. The outstanding representatives of this trend are Harald Schjelderup (b. 1895), Kristian Schjelderup, Ola Raknes (b. 1887), Øverland, and Hoel. The new psychological theories provided young men eager for emancipation with fresh ammunition against the puritan-pietistic tradition. *I sommer* (1932) by Gunnar Larsen (1900-1958) blazed the trail, and Oskar Alexander Braaten (1881-1939), Rolf Stenersen (b. 1899), Hans Backer Fürst (b. 1887), and Lars Berg (b. 1901) should also be mentioned here. It must be noted, however, that the "antipuritan revolt" never went as far among the more reserved, shy Norwegians as it did in Sweden; the extremist return to primitivism, for instance, never became popular. Thus the conflict between generations as a

literary theme is encountered more rarely in Norway than elsewhere.

Ideological controversy also extended to religion. In 1932 Einar Molland (b. 1908) introduced Karl Barth's philosophy to Norway. The struggle against the church became particularly intense in 1933.

In 1926 Hoel had insisted in *Nordisk Tidsskrift* that the Norwegians drew mainly from their own sources. Besides, there was a lack of translations, of curiosity, and of receptivity toward what was going on abroad. Conversely, the work of Norway's intelligentsia rarely penetrated beyond the frontiers of Scandinavia. In 1930 the famous "Gule serie" began to appear; within ten years it grew to fifty volumes of modern world literature. Suddenly the Norwegians were more up-to-date than even the Swedes and Danes. Names such as Faulkner, Sinclair Lewis, Dos Passos, and Hemingway (qq.v.) made their appearance. For the first time America—which Hamsun never seemed to tire of deriding—was discovered as a land of progress, democracy, and individualism. The spirit of this newly assimilated literature was politically radical, socially critical, often strongly satirical, antibourgeois, and antipuritan The first reactions may be seen in Sandemose (q.v.), Arthur Omre (b. 1887), and Nils Johan Rud (b. 1908). Stylistic influences are so obvious that critics even spoke of the "Hemingway style" of many young Norwegians. The similarity of this style to that of the sagas is striking. It strives for objectivity and produces an emotionally cold—even inhibited—effect; at the same time it has an urge toward action. Another trend led in the direction of journalism. Some of the major writers of this generation, such as G. Larsen and Borgen (q.v.) were originally journalists. The direct result of all these influences was the flowering of the Norwegian novel.

Other influences from abroad were effective too: principally D. H. Lawrence, G. Greene, Malraux, Fallada (qq.v.), and again Kafka, whose *Der Prozeß* (1925), for instance, inspired Larsen's *Weekend i evigheten* (1934). On the other hand, the influence of Joyce was negligible. As one of the few Norwegian exponents of the proletarian novel with political aspirations that reached such a high level in Sweden in the 1930's, Hjalmar Waage (1892-1939) deserves mention.

A. H. Winsnes has drawn attention to a recurrent key theme of the interwar period: the individual's dialogue with his environment.

A deep commitment to self-knowledge and self-accusation pervades the literature of this decade. It first becomes perceptible in the Duun-Undset generation, dominates the Fangen-Christiansen generation, and reaches full pitch in the leading figures of the 1930's (Hoel and Sandel). However, as Winsnes shows, Ibsen had already encountered and crystallized this problem. His work is more timely than ever; his indictment is a modern one, directed against selfishness, pride, and arrogance, and against the one-sided rule of the male. A mood of ruthless self-analysis marks the literature of this period.

As soon as the German occupation began, censorship went to work. Fangen and Øverland were arrested. Of Norway's approximately two hundred writers, six or seven sided with the occupying power, the most illustrious among them being Hamsun. Those who went on writing turned to historical themes or camouflaged burning contemporary problems in other ways: *Kimen* (1940) by Vesaas (q.v.), Christiansen's *Mannen fra bensinstasjonen* (1941), Falkberget's *An-Magritt* (1940), *Under himmelteiknet* (1911) by Inge Krokann (b. 1893). Øverland and Eiliy Skard (b. 1898) invented a sophisticated technique of veiled allusion. Sigrid Undset, Hoel, Krog, and Grieg had emigrated.

After the war, diaries were published, such as *Fra dag til dag* (1946) by Odd Nansen (b. 1901), in the one camp, and Hamsun's *På gjengrodde stier* (1949), in the other. Writers tried to explain the catastrophe that had descended upon Norway and mankind: among others, Hoel, Krog, Johan Borgen (*Ingen sommar*, 1944), Sigurd Evensmo ([b. 1912], *Englandsfarere*, 1945), Fangen, Vesaas (*Huset i mørket*, 1945), Sandemose, Gunnar Helweg-Larsen ([b. 1887], *Stormfulde døn*, 1945) Nils Johan Rud (novel trilogy, *Fredens sønner*, 1946; *Kvinner i advent*, 1948; *Vi var jordens elskere*, 1949), Synnøve Christensen (pseud. of Mai Brøgger [b. 1919], *Det kimmar dagar efter dessa*, 1943), and Sandel.

During the occupation the Norwegian people were sustained by fighting spirit, the will to survive, and a longing for freedom. In the postwar years faith and hope gave way to insecurity, perplexity, and fear. In the late 1940's and early 1950's a tendency to discard traditional forms of language became obvious. Bull, Ørjasæter, and H. T. Wildenvey (b. 1886), who invented original, unexpected forms of expression, broke new ground in poetry. Modernist tendencies appear in the 1930's in Emil Boy-

son (b. 1897) and in the 1940's in C. D. Gill (b. 1910) and Gunnar Reiss-Andersen ([b. 1896], *Prinsen av Isola*, 1949). J. I. Bjørneboe (b. 1920), who prefers strict forms, shows classical influences, while J. A. Bjerke (q.v.) pursues similar ends in a more playful vein. The highly talented Vesaas developed an extremely personal, richly symbolic style, which characterizes his collection of poems *Lykka fori ferdesmenn* (1949). Kåre Holt ([b. 1917], *Det store veiskillet,* 1949; *Demring,* 1946) is a notable but isolated exponent of Norwegian existentialism.

On the whole, a return to *poésie pure* seems to be in the making. Neoromanticism and nature mysticism, a preference for the symbolic novel, the revival of myth, dream, and vision, mark the most recent developments. In this connection Nils Johan Rud's rejection of analytics in art and of the problem novel is noteworthy. Holt, Bjørneboe, Finn Carling ([b. 1925], *Piken og fuglen,* 1952), and Solveig Christov ([b. 1918], *Torso,* 1952) have boldly pioneered in these new directions. In the field of drama Ørjasæter (*Christophorus,* 1948), Vesaas, Aslaug Vaa (b. 1889), Tormod Skagestad (b. 1920), and Inger Hagerup (b. 1905; radio plays) have followed the lines of Ibsen, Strindberg, García Lorca, and Wilder (qq.v.).

BIBLIOGRAPHY: Jorgenson, T., *History of Norwegian Literature* (1933); Bach, G., *The History of Scandinavian Literatures* (1938); Christiansen, H., *Norwegische Literaturgeschichte* (1953); Houm, P., *Norsk Litteraturhistorie* (1955); Dale, J., *Norsk Litteraturhistorie* (1962); Downs, B. W., *Modern Norwegian Literature, 1860-1918* (1966); Heiberg, J., *Norwegian Literature, Anno 1965* (1967)

OTTO OBERHOLZER

NOSSACK, Hans Erich

German novelist, essayist, and dramatist, b. 30 Jan. 1901, Hamburg

Son of a Hamburg merchant, N. studied philosophy and law and worked as a factory worker, traveling salesman, and journalist before joining his father's business.

An important and independent writer to whom recognition was denied until relatively late in his career, N.'s first work was not published until 1947. Proscribed from publishing by the Nazis because of former left-wing affiliations, N. continued to write clandestinely, but lost all his manuscripts during the Allied raids on Hamburg in 1943. The ensuing physical and emotional devastation marked the turning point in N.'s life, for by associating Hamburg's fate with his own, he effectively freed himself from the coils of the past. The situation is graphically and soberly recorded in "Der Untergang," a piece from *Interview mit dem Tode* (1948; retitled *Dorothea* in 1950), in which N. recognizes and welcomes the chance offered to make a complete break with a bankrupt society.

It is this theme of the total rejection of the past, of release from societies inimical to the real development of man, and the implications of this for the whole question of personal identity, that forms the nucleus of his work. N. believes one must push out to the very limits of experience, into the unknown, or *"das Unversicherbare"* as he calls it. In *Spätestens im November* (1955), protest against the conventional and the norm is seen as the first step toward self-fulfillment even though the outcome ends in disaster. The very fact that a stale and meaningless pattern of existence has been recognized as such and questioned is sufficient for N. The important factor is to have the courage to be oneself, to be an individual.

The brilliant *Unmögliche Beweisaufnahme* (1959; The Impossible Proof, 1968) deals with the problem of trying to live by two different realities: what man really is, and the image society has of man. The "account" takes the form of a trial in which communication between a judge and a defendant is reduced to a minimum, in a witty and often ironic dialogue, as the two realities are explored. This failure of understanding that occurs between these two men is seen by N. as a consequence of the increasing bureaucratization and institutionalization of society against which he believes it is his duty to warn—and he does so repeatedly.

The relationship between what is real and unreal has become increasingly tenuous for N., and his characters tend to move in mysterious and strange settings that are at one and the same time recognizable and yet also vaguely unfamiliar. This precarious focal point has been cleverly expanded in *Der jüngere Bruder* (1958) to examine not only the main protagonist's own nebulous identity and relationship to others but also to juxtapose a physically recognizable Europe with disturbingly out-of-focus elements. The ever-present tendency to fuse the real and unreal in surrealistic or mythical forms reaches its climax in *Nach dem letzten Aufstand* (1961), which comprises an often bewilderingly

rich mixture of complex time and space elements welded to create an alliance between this world and another more mysterious one, in which there is a highly stylized reflection of postwar Germany's dilemmas.

In cool, restrained prose, N. portrays with striking forcefulness man's condition, precarious and threatened, his inner loneliness and basic unrelatedness. N.'s works are all in the first person yet are not strictly autobiographical despite their very personal tone.

A clearer understanding of N.'s artistic purpose and *Weltanschauung* is obtained by reading his essays, the most important collection of which is entitled *Die schwache Position der Literatur* (1966). In this book N.'s special moralistic stance (akin to Camus's [q.v.]) is well defined.

N. has been a percipient and relentless critic of his society who, through reasoned and always quiet argument, has never wavered from his firm conviction that the solution to man's problems lies within man himself and that all he, as a writer, can do is "to render an account."

FURTHER WORKS: *Gedichte* (1947); *Nekyia. Bericht eines Überlebenden* (1947); *Die Rotte Kain* (1949); *Publikum und Dichter* (1949-50); *Die dichterische Substanz im Menschen* (1954); *Der Neugierige* (1955); *Spirale. Roman einer schlaflosen Nacht* (1956); *Die Hauptprobe* (1956); *Über den Einsatz* (1956); *Der Weg ins Verschweigen* (1957); *Freizeitliteratur. Eine Fastenpredigt* (1959); *Begegnung im Vorraum* (1963); *Ein Sonderfall* (1963); *Das kennt man* (1964); *Sechs Etüden* (1964); *Das Testament des Lucius Eurinus* (1965); *Dies lebenlose Leben* (1967)

BIBLIOGRAPHY: Biser, E., "Der Wegbereiter. Zur Gestalt des Engels im Werk H. E. N.s," in *Deutsch Unterricht*, XVI, 5 (1964), 22-33; Boelich, W., "Nachwort" to *Der Untergang* (1963), 55-60; Jahnn, H. H., "Kleine Rede auf H. E. N.", in *Sinn und Form*, 2 (1955), 213-19; Kasack, H., "Rede auf den Preisträger", in *Jahrbuch der deutschen Akademie für Sprache und Dichtung*, (1961), 79-89; Keith-Smith, B., "H. E. N.," in *Essays on Contemporary German Literature*, (1966), 63-85; Prochnik, P., "Controlling Thoughts in the Work of H. E. N.", in *German Life and Letters*, XIX, 1 (1965), 68-75

PETER PROCHNIK

NOUVEAU, Germain (Marie-Bernard)

French poet, b. 31 July 1851, Pourrières; d. there, 4 April 1920

At first N. lived an artist's life in Paris, attracted as much to painting as to literature. He was strongly influenced by Rimbaud, with whom he went to London in 1874. On his return he got to know Verlaine. In order to earn a living N. took a modest position in the Ministry of Education, but gave this up in 1883. He became a teacher of drawing, but after a crisis in 1891 he tried to live entirely according to the example of Jesus Christ. Until 1911 he led an unsettled, wandering life in France, Italy, Spain, and Algeria, painting portraits for board and lodging and begging outside churches. He then returned to his native village and lived in emulation of St. Benoît Labre in complete isolation in a lonely hut.

N.'s first poems still show the strong influence of Rimbaud. Verlaine's influence prevails in the early religious poems he collected under the title "La doctrine de l'amour." These were published in 1904 (without N.'s consent) as *Savoir aimer* and later, between 1910 and 1925, as *Poèmes d'humilis.* In *Les Valentines,* written in 1885 and published in 1922, N. arrived at his own tone and personal manner of statement. This erotic work contains the cycle "Baisers"—passionate, often extremely profane love poems. Toward the end of his life N. reverted to a simple, popular tone and wrote the naïve, touchingly religious poems "Ave Maris Stella."

N. did not publish a single work during his lifetime; only *Les dixains réalistes* and *Ave Maris Stella* appeared in magazines with his consent. His *Oeuvres poétiques* were published only between 1953 and 1955.

N.'s life and work impressed the supporters of surrealism (q.v.). For Aragon and Breton (qq.v.) he ranked with Rimbaud.

BIBLIOGRAPHY: Lopez, A., *La Vie étrange d'Humilis* (1928); Saillet, M., *Sur la route de Narcisse* (1958)

JACQUES BRENNER

NOVEL

Judging by the size of printings, it would appear that contemporary literature reaches its widest audiences through the novel. However, novels of literary importance account for only a relatively small proportion of this mass popularity. It is hardly surprising, therefore, that critics are unable to agree whether the novel of recent decades has been heading toward a golden age or a crisis.

In 1670 P. D. Huet, one of the earliest theoreticians of the novel, defined this genre as an imaginary story of adventures in love, written in studied prose with the object of entertaining and edifying the reader. It is a remarkable feature of the history of the novel that after several centuries this definition still holds good for the popular light novel, the class which includes nearly all best sellers, while it has become almost meaningless in connection with the modern novel of literary rank. Obviously the segment of the world and the range of experiences dealt with in the modern novel are no longer confined to the erotic. No less important thematically are the social, philosophical, and psychological areas that the novel has taken over in the course of its development. Moreover, the modern author is not content simply to tell an invented story. The relationship of fiction to reality has itself become a subject for the novel, and the playing with illusion on the borderline between fiction and reality offers the novelist a unique opportunity of philosophizing without writing an essay. Finally, the distinction between the entertaining and the edifying that used to be accepted as a matter of course has become quite irrelevant to modern aesthetics (see literary criticism and literary aesthetics) and literary theory.

The dawn of a new era in the history of the novel, which had long been approaching, was seen most strikingly after the turn of the century in the novels of Proust and Joyce (qq.v.). In totally different ways *À La Recherche du temps perdu* (1913-27) and *Ulysses* (1922) demonstrate the break with the great tradition of storytelling established by such writers as Cervantes, Fielding, La Fayette, Wieland, Scott, Balzac, and Raabe. The innovators, too, have their precursors, as, for instance, Dostoyevski, Flaubert, and James (q.v.), although in the works of these writers modernity and tradition are closely interlocked. Of the many essential distinguishing features of the modern novel three are particularly characteristic: first, deemphasis of the exterior world of material things and happenings except when these can be symbolically heighted, rendered transparent to reveal an idea, or used as a setting for processes taking place in the consciousness; second, the novelist's preoccupation with the theme of time (*see* Time and Literature); third, experimentation with narrative technique and procedure.

From its beginnings the novel had of course shown an affinity for the private, intimate world of the individual; but the inner world, the consciousness and its substance and processes, became an immediate, acute representational problem only under the impact of the psychologies of William James, Bergson (q.v.), and Freud. Newly discovered insights into the autonomy of the consciousness made the traditional method of depicting mental processes, established in such works as *Clarissa* (by Samuel Richardson, 1747-48) and *Werther* (by Goethe, 1774) and long accepted as exemplary, seem insufficiently authentic to produce the illusion of direct insight into the drama within the consciousness of a fictional character. New forms were therefore developed for depicting consciousness, designed to make the narrative word a mirror, as it were, of the substance of consciousness. They range from traditional accounts of thought, in which inner happenings are "reported" in the same way as outer ones, through the extremely subtle form of *erlebte Rede* and interior monologue (q.v.) to the apparently realistic reproduction of the "stream of consciousness." Most authors limit their representation of the substance of consciousness to suggestive stylization; a few carry experimentation with language so far that in the end not only syntactical structure but even word forms lose their contours and merge with one another. These authors believe that in this way they can portray the streams of images, concepts, and ideas—what Virginia Woolf called the "ceaseless rain of thousands of fragmentary impressions"—within the consciousness. Techniques of this kind were developed and tried out by Edouard Dujardin (1861-1941), Beer-Hofmann, Proust, Schnitzler, Joyce, Virginia Woolf, Faulkner, Broch (qq.v.), and others. Any critique of this experiment in storytelling that takes the realistic plausibility of such portrayals of consciousness as sole touchstone misses its essential point. In the representation of consciousness, as in the literary representation of any other area of our perceived reality, reality can only be stylized and suggested, never authentically reproduced. Thus the literary criterion for the evaluation of such experiments can only be the degree of the illusion of reality the writer succeeds in producing.

In the novel of consciousness the external world shrinks to a skeleton of relatively trivial mundane objects and events. Everything that in the earlier novel formed the focus of interest —the colorful world with its abundance of things, the bustling activity of its inhabitants, dramatic situations, and so on, which, however, even in earlier works were never an end in themselves but usually served to reveal "the culture in the light of the exciting action" (Petsch)—here recedes into the background. A few phases of an utterly unexceptional happening generally suffice to set up the constellation of characters which will produce the thoughts and moods that here form the real content of the novel. External action in Virginia Woolf's *To the Lighthouse* (1927) or in *La Modification* (1957) by Butor (q.v.) is so reduced that it could be exhaustively summarized in a few sentences.

This minimization of external events is accompanied by de-emphasis of the great, crucial events in the life of man—the catastrophes, the major scenes and "set pieces" that are such an intrinsic part of the baroque novel. Events of this kind no longer represent life's true dividing lines or pivotal points; these are now sought in more prolonged states of consciousness within which changes are very slowly brewing. Even where the external world has not yet been ousted from the picture by the rampant proliferation of consciousness, that world undergoes a remarkable transformation. It becomes quite transparent, so that the reader is forced to look right through it and focus, so to speak, on a *weltanschaulich* or philosophical problem, as for instance in *La Nausée* (1938) by Sartre (q.v.). Alternatively, it may be loaded with symbolic meaning, as in the novels of Kafka (q.v.), which are to be taken as symbols, almost as allegories, and therefore as typical, exemplary experiential situations rather than scenes from one private, individual life history.

The role of time in the novel is twofold: as a theme (the experience of time) and as a structural element (the novel as the art of presenting time). The two are closely related, since a description of the structure of time can suggest the nature of the experience of time. Moreover, the experience of time is part of the general intellectual and cultural climate of a period and changes with that climate. Thus the mathematical, mechanical concept of time that was still appropriate to 16th and 17th c. classical cosmology has today become questionable.

Proust, Virginia Woolf, and T. Mann (q.v.) made time and the experiencing and conveying of it the most urgent problem in contem-

461

porary literature. The reasons for this, however, lie further back. Flaubert wanted to make time the real subject of his *roman sans sujet*. Moreover, Flaubert was one of the first to realize that the novel in its traditional form can at most discuss time but can never convey it as an experience. Thus experiments in broadening the range of what the novel form can convey were imperative here, too. T. Mann poses the question anew for our time in *Der Zauberberg* (1924): "Can one narrate time —time itself, as such, in itself?" His own answer is more skeptical than the ones given by Proust in *À La Recherche du temps perdu*, by Joyce in *Ulysses,* and by Virginia Woolf in *To the Lighthouse*. These and similar works in fact attempt to overcome the "single track" nature of time in fiction, with its strict pattern of "now" and "and then." The new dimensions consist in breadth of time (simultaneity of various events), in its depth ("duration," the pressure of the past on the present moment), and in the direction of the flow of time (reversibility or suspension of chronology).

In older fictional tradition simultaneity could be rendered only sequentially. The consecutive mode of language makes it almost impossible to convey simultaneity. For the novel the solution lay once again in creating an illusion through suggestion. Thus two or more lines of action are cut up into short segments which then alternate rapidly and kaleidoscopically, that is, almost simultaneously. An even closer approximation of simultaneity in two streams of action is achieved by constantly introducing into the account of one stream verbal motifs that refer back to the other, simultaneous one. Joyce makes notable use of this technique in the Ormond Hotel chapter of *Ulysses*. With Proust's *À La Recherche du temps perdu* the concept of "duration" became an immediate problem of artistic communication: how to reveal the pressure of countless past moments upon every present moment; how to convey the experiential identity of happenings which have their historical place on entirely different levels of time. Proust's path was smoothed by the conventions, generally accepted since the time of Laurence Sterne (1713-68), of stratification of time and time shift—the constant shift of the story from present time to various time levels of past events. The recollected event then often becomes visible at the depth of several different strata of time upon which the narrative has just touched. Time shift and time stratification are not tied to any particular narrative

situation. In *À La Recherche du temps perdu* they are used in a first-person form; in *Die Strudlhofstiege* (1951) by Doderer (q.v.) with a specific third-person narrator; in Huxley's (q.v.) *Eyeless in Gaza* (1936) in an abstract ("narratorless") composition. Time shift reveals the depth of time. A comparable process is the illumination of space in all its breadth by a cross section of several simultaneous streams of action. *Manhattan Transfer* (1925) and *U.S.A.* (3 vols., 1927-36) by Dos Passos, (q.v.), *Les Hommes de bonne volonté* (28 vols., 1932-56) by Romains, (q.v.), *Berlin Alexanderplatz* (1929) by Döblin (q.v.), and the last volume of Broch's (q.v.) *Die Schlafwandler* (3 vols., 1931) use this technique.

Time shift, time stratification, cross-section panorama, and the breaking up of the story line into segments considerably diminish the importance of the original chronological order of an action sequence as the basis of structural form. Ulrich, the "man without qualities" in *Der Mann ohne Eigenschaften* (3 vols., 1930-43) by Musil (q.v.), deplores the loss of an order of life which had its counterpart in the narrative formula: "After that had happened, this occurred." Ulrich's experience is a symptom of the times which recurs again and again in the contemporary novel. The leisurely epic overview of the chronological course of an action sequence construes an untrue image of real experiencing, which everywhere breaks out of the order of chronology, often far more intent on the circumstantial than on the consecutive aspect of fast-moving events. The straight chronological life story, which, thanks largely to the *roman fleuve* of the "grand tradition," had become the prototype for depicting human life, has now become suspect as a structural form to many writers. They therefore substitute for straight chronology a sequence of events such as might exist within the memory of a narrator or in the consciousness of one of the characters. Thus, for example, the hero and the many characters of Doderer's *Die Strudlhofstiege* are introduced to the reader not in chronologically arranged scenes but in episodes which the "narrating consciousness" (Thomas Mann) recalls in a seemingly associative sequence pointing far more vigorously toward the horizontal (simultaneous) than toward the vertical (sequential) dimension of time. Similarly in Faulkner's *Absalom, Absalom!* (1936) the action is dredged up in nonchronological sequence from the depths of the "narrating consciousness."

Thus experimentation with the narrative process and the search for new narrative forms are closely connected with the desire of many modern writers to find a way of representing the substance of consciousness and the experience of time. But the reasons for this experimentation lie further back. The traditional narrative method, which relied on a narrator endowed with the authority of superior insight and with unimpeachable judgment, became useless as the system of values on which that authority was based collapsed or became questionable. There were two ways around this: an ironical treatment of the narrator and the authority he represents or, alternatively, minimization of the narrator, his commentaries on events, and his personal testimony. The elimination of the individual narrator was particularly appropriate to the novel of consciousness and to any work concerned primarily with the subjectivity of a character's experience presented with a minimum of commentary, from the viewpoint of the character concerned.

This development, too, extends back at least to the middle of the last century. Flaubert imposed such precision and restraint upon his narrative style that material objects and people in the story seem to speak directly to the reader. Since then for a writer to side overtly with or against his characters has come to seem provincial, moralistic, and Victorian, and many writers have rejected it. James in his later novels written about the turn of the century introduced the strict "point of view" technique, which clearly establishes and consistently conforms to the viewpoint from which a given segment of fictional reality is seen. In this narrative method the narrator's interventions are generally confined to short, quite impersonal "stage directions" concerning the action. In *The Ambassadors* (1903) the focal center of all that is observed and experienced—the center from which the reader, too, believes himself to be perceiving events—is, throughout, one and the same character: Lambert Strether, one of those exceedingly intelligent and sensitive natures that triumphantly come into their own in novels of this kind, although they would appear somewhat colorless and passive in a more conventional novel. In novels of this type all matter has become experience; happenings are communicated to the reader only to the extent that they are capable of provoking a reaction in the consciousness of some character. The modern reader's demand for the illusion of representational objectivity finds its maximum gratification in the apparently unedited subjectivity of a fictional character's experience and consciousness.

The structure of earlier novels was largely determined by the course of the principal character's life, traced by the narrator in chronological order of events. Structural accentuation was provided through the alternation of broad storytelling and tightly compressed action. In the novel of consciousness this gives way to a structure of story elements and episodes ultimately rooted in the associations of one of the characters. The structure demonstrates to the reader, so to speak, how the consciousness of a particular character imposes a subjective order upon the course of events—an order which conveys the connection between the story elements existing, not in reality, but within the consciousness of the character. Here, indeed, the novel of consciousness is merely logically continuing something already very skillfully done in earlier novels such as Sterne's *Tristram Shandy* and Wilhelm Raabe's (1831-1910) *Stopfkuchen,* where an individual narrator apparently allows his thoughts and memories free play as they skip from one subject to another.

Natural or "storytelling" structural forms may be completely jettisoned when a novelist resorts to an abstract mode of composition. In this case he very often incorporates structural elements drawn from music (fugal or leitmotif technique), from the film (montage), or even from experimental painting (collage).

The principal structural unit of such novels is not the lengthy action sequence but the segment, a relatively shorter action passage generally abruptly introduced and equally abruptly concluded. Since there are no explanatory transitional passages between segments, the normal method of linking the narrative passages by "and then," "because," or "therefore" no longer works. Nevertheless the segments, which are often set off from one another by lines, dots, or other typographical marks, also provide a recognizable sense structure. The contrast produced by the immediate juxtaposition of segments may be used to obtain indirect effects of commentary: irony (q.v.), for instance, as in Huxley's (q.v.) *Brave New World* (1932), or the suggestion of pathos, criticism, etc. Döblin in *Berlin Alexanderplatz* and Dos Passos in *Manhattan Transfer* and *U.S.A.* use segmentation to present cross sections of life in the cities they describe. Between segments of narrated action Dos Passos intersperses documentary material: headlines, snatches of songs, advertising slogans, and brief profiles of contemporary personalities. In general, segmentation makes it easier to introduce digressions, essays, documentary reports, panoramic sketches of the times, etc. Thus in the last volume of Broch's *Die Schlafwandler* a series of essayistic social commentaries on the contemporary "collapse of values" and an episodic "story of the Salvation Army girl in Berlin" quite unrelated to the plot are inserted between segments dealing with the main action. Another use of segmentation is found in *Les Faux-monnayeurs* (1925) by Gide (q.v.) and in Huxley's *Point Counter Point* (1928), where the order of segments is backed up by an implied analogy with musical compositions. The verbal leitmotif as an "alerting" connecting link between individual segments is used in the segment novels of Gide, Huxley, Virginia Woolf, and Dos Passos; it also plays a role in the novels of Proust and T. Mann.

Even in 1932 J. W. Beach still regarded the elimination of the personal narrator as the essential characteristic of the modern novel. Certainly the "narratorless" novel has become very common since the beginning of the 20th c. Today however, especially in German literature, where the narratorless novel never established itself as firmly as it did in English and American literature, a revival of the personally narrated novel is evident. The hallmark of this new personal narrative method is the relationship of tension (depicted in a great variety of ways) between the personal narrator and the world of fictional characters he describes. W. Kayser sees the beginning of the modern novel in the works of Fielding and Wieland because these writers first succeeded in presenting the narrator in a narrative posture that reveals a clearly defined personal attitude to characters and plot. The new novel with a personal narrator derives from this fruitful tradition but tends to go beyond 18th and 19th c. models in two respects: individualization of the narrator and the attention paid to the handling of the narrative process itself.

Almost simultaneously literary criticism begins to realize that the magisterial narrator is to be regarded as a fictitious character and not simply as a portrait of the author. This vitally affects the interpretation of many classic novels. Thus in the modern novel the mental profile of the fictitious narrator is frequently very clearly outlined, and the author's own autobiographical traits are quite often deliber-

ately suppressed. The narrator's attitude to the fictional reality emphasizes the individual nature of his narrator's role; the narrator's digressions and commentaries readily give a touch of what Musil calls "constructive irony" to his story. This narrative attitude is clearly demonstrated in T. Mann's *Der Zauberberg,* Musil's *Der Mann ohne Eigenschaften*, and Doderer's *Die Strudlhofstiege*. Mann and Musil again incorporate into the novelistic structure the essay, which in Fielding already formed a part—though a still incompletely integrated part—of the novel. This, too, tends to shift the focus of the imaginary action away from the characters and toward the narrator. At the same time the reader's interest is diverted from the story to the storyteller by the sometimes very detailed treatment of the narrative process. Occasionally the narration actually becomes the main theme, as, for instance, when the narrative process is fixed in time and the narrator's "here and now" carefully described, and when problems of narrative technique are discussed with the reader. In these novels the narrator's guiding function is everywhere in evidence, though it is sometimes camouflaged by the apparent predominance of association in determining the course of the story or by a certain readiness on the part of the "narrating consciousness" to let itself be diverted by sudden notions, to skip apparently willfully from one line of action to another, and so on.

The first-person novel has undergone most of the changes outlined here in a form consistent with its narrative posture. Leaving aside *Tristram Shandy,* which was far ahead of its time, its power of presentation as a novel of consciousness first became obvious in *À La Recherche du temps perdu*. Here Proust makes use, in virtually all possible variations, of retrospection on the part of the first-person narrator and of confrontation of the narrating and the experiencing self—two chronologically separate strata of the narrator's consciousness. In still another way, the "I" of *To Be a Pilgrim* (1942) by Cary (q.v.) gropes his way back to earlier phases of his consciousness. In T. Mann's first-person novel *Felix Krull* (1922, 1936, 1954), however, as in his other novels, we are aware of an irony which everywhere seems to revoke the personal narrator's claim to stand above the events and things represented. In this work play with illusion and reality, which had become practically impossible in the narratorless novel, re-enters the modern novel. The "I" of *Justine* (1957) and *Balthazar* (1958) by Durrell (q.v.) is more interested in creating the broadest possible simultaneous panorama of happenings in the fictitious world than in penetrating the temporal depth of experience. Camus (q.v.) offers still another variation: the "I" of *L'Étranger* (1942) speaks as through a marble mask of impersonality and apparent detachment, especially at the very moments when he is most personally involved. Here the outwardly stoical attitude of many of the heroes of Hemingway (q.v.) probably set the pattern.

In *La Jalousie* (1957) by Robbe-Grillet (q.v.) the depersonalization of the first-person narrator—if this term still applies at all—is carried even further. As with the panning of a motion picture camera, our only clues to the reactions of the "I-character" to what is going on now come from the choice of objects registered and from occasional adjustments in depth of focus. Thus the boundary leading to the objective novel has been crossed. Moreover, in Robbe-Grillet's novels all the material trappings of the exterior world are restored to their hereditary rights; sometimes, indeed, the author's deliberate overstressing of them makes their role more important than that of the characters.

Do these and other similar observations indicate the end of an evolutionary phase or a return to the great tradition of the novel? Will the next phase be a period of modification to suit the times, of fresh interpretation of traditional forms, rather than experimentation and breaks with tradition? The answer must be left to the future, as must the decision as to which of the forms, structures, and narrative methods brought to the novel by writers since 1900, with their delight in experimentation, will be permanently incorporated into the genre. Whatever the novel of the future may be like, it will enjoy a literary prestige which this genre —stigmatized until the 19th c. as mere entertainment, a "stepbrother" of serious drama and epic poetry—owes almost entirely to the ambitious and difficult novels of our time.

BIBLIOGRAPHY: Spielhagen, F., *Beiträge zur Theorie und Technik des Romans* (1883); Spielhagen, F., *Neue Beiträge zur Theorie und Technik der Epik und Dramatik* (1898); Friedemann, K., *Die Rolle des Erzählers in der Epik* (1910); Lukács, G., *Die Theorie des Romans* (1920); Lorck, E., *Die 'erlebte Rede'* (1921); Hirt, E., *Das Formgesetz der epischen, dramatischen und lyrischen Dichtung* (1923); Woolf, V., "Modern Fiction," in *The Common Reader* (1925); Walzel, O., *Das Wortkunstwerk* (1926); Forster, E. M., *Aspects of the Novel* (1927); Lewis, W., *Time and Western Man* (1927); Duhamel, G., *Essai sur le roman* (1928); Curtius, E. R., *James Joyce und sein "Ulysses"* (1929); Mauriac, F., *Le Romancier et ses personnages* (1930); Dujardin, É., *Le Monologue intérieur* (1931); Lubbock, P., *The Craft of Fiction* (1931); Beach, J. W., *The Twentieth Century Novel* (1932); Muir, E., *The Structure of the Novel* (1932); Petsch, R., *Wesen und Formen der Erzählkunst* (1934); Koskimies, R., *Theorie des Romans* (1935); Groethuysen, B., "De Quelques Aspects due temps," in *Recherches philosophiques* (vol. V; 1935-1936); Fox, R. W. *The Novel and the People* (1937); Thibaudet, A., *Réflexion sur le roman* (1938); Staiger, E., *Die Zeit als Einbildungskraft des Dichters* (1939); Pouillon, J., *Temps et roman* (1946); Liddell, R., *A Treatise on the Novel* (1947); Magny, C. E., *L'Âge du roman américain* (1948); O'Connor, W. V., ed., *Forms of Modern Fiction* (1948); Müller, G., "Erzählzeit und erzählte Zeit," in Kluckhohn-Schneider Festschrift (1948); Sartre, J.-P., *Qu'est-ce que la Littérature* (1948); James, H., *The Art of the Novel* (1950); Meyer, H., *Zum Problem der epischen Integration,* in *Trivium,* VIII (1950); Poulet, G., *Études sur le temps humain* (1950); Olbrich, W., and Beer, J., eds., *Der Romanführer* (12 vols., 1950-1961); Mendilow, A. A., *Time and the Novel* (1952); Humphrey, R., *Stream of Consciousness in the Modern Novel* (1954); Lämmert, E., *Bauformen des Erzählens* (1955); Stanzel, F., *Die typischen Erzählsituationen im Roman* (1955); Friedman, M., *Stream of Consciousness* (1955); Edel, L., *The Psychological Novel, 1900-1950* (1955); Jauß, H. R., *Zeit und Erinnerungen in Marcel Prousts À la Recherche . . .* (1955); Kayser, W., *Entstehung und Krise des modernen Romans* (1955); Meyerhoff, H., *Time in Literature* (1955); Robbe-Grillet, A., "Une Voie pour le roman futur," in *Nouvelle Revue française* (July 1956); Sarraute, N., *L'Ère du soupçon* (1956); McCormick, J., *Catastrophe and Imagination: An Interpretation of the Recent English and American Novel* (1957); Meyer, K. R., *Zur erlebten Rede im englischen Roman des 20. Jahrhunderts* (1957); Allen, W., *The Novel Today* (1958); Mauriac, C., *La Littérature contemporaine* (1958); Pérez de Ayala, R., *Principios y finales de la novela* (1958); Fricker, R., *Der moderne englische Roman* (1958); Kayser, W., *Die Vortragsreise* (1958); Von Doderer, H., *Grundlagen und Funktion des Romans* (1959); Blanchot, M., *Le Livre à venir* (1959); Kreuder, E., *Das Unbeantwortbare, Aufgaben des mo-

dernen Romans (1959); Allott, M., *Novelists on the Novel* (1959); Brooks, C., and Warren, R. P., *Understanding Fiction* (1959); Mueller, W. R., "The Prophetic Voice," in *Modern Fiction* (1959); Zeltner-Neukomm, G., *Das Wagnis des französischen Gegenwartsromans* (1960); Horst, K. A., *Das Spektrum des modernen Romans* (1960); Bassermann, D., *Der andere Roman* (1961); Daiches, D., *The Novel and the Modern World* (1961); Booth, W. C., *The Rhetoric of Fiction* (1961); Wescott, G., *Images of Truth* (1962); Goldmann, L., *et al., Problèmes d'une sociologie du roman: Revue de l'Institut de Sociologie* (1963), ii; Brennan, J. G., *Three Philosophical Novelists: James Joyce, André Gide, Thomas Mann* (1964); Church, M., *Time and Reality: Studies in Contemporary Fiction* (1964); Mizener, A., *The Sense of Life in the Modern Novel* (1964); Stanzel, F., *Typische Formen des Romans* (1964); Axthelm, P. M., *The Modern Confessional Novel* (1967)

FRANZ K. STANZEL

NOVELLA

The novella, which caters to unexpected twists, to irony and paradox, has itself a history full of these traits. Though fed by ancient Oriental, Arabic, Greek, Latin, Provençal, French, and Italian story materials, it did not reach directive norms until Boccaccio's *Decamerone* (1348-53), still considered a near-perfect prototype of the genre. A characteristic product of *Romania* (*Cent Nouvelles Nouvelles,* 1440; Marguerite de Navarre's *Heptaméron,* 1558; Cervantes's *Novelas Ejemplares,* 1613), combining Romanic love of living and of dramatic action with an acute sense of form, it has become, since Cervantes, with such stellar novellistic authors as Basile, Gozzi, Verga (q.v.), and Pirandello (q.v.) of Italy, Mérimée and Maupassant of France notwithstanding, a very secondary art form in its native habitat.

Its finest sustained flowering since its early Italian debut occurred in the cultural areas of Europe that used German as the literary language in the 19th c. (Kleist, Gotthelf, Stifter, Keller, Storm, G. Hauptmann [q.v.]). In English-speaking areas "novella" usually means, nowadays, no more than a short novel, though specific stories may be excellent samples of the continental genre (e.g., James Purdy's (b. 1923) *63: Dream Palace,* 1957). But for

all its auspicious beginnings with Chaucer and its vogue in 16th c. England, the art form has been domesticated neither there nor in America, where Poe channeled the best efforts of briefer prose into the short story (q.v.), nor in Russia, though she produced one of the impressionist novella-writers most influential in the 20th c.: Chekhov (q.v.).

In German-writing areas structure and function of the *Novelle* intrigued practitioners (Wieland, Goethe, Tieck, Grillparzer, Hebbel, Storm, Heyse) and critics (Lessing, A. W. and F. Schlegel, Laube, Mundt, and Hettner) of the highest distinction from its naturalization in the late 1700's through the 1800's. While little theoretical consensus had been reached by 1900, the *Novelle* had emerged, next to the lyric poem, as the most distinguished German contribution to Western literature. Not until the 1950's was there a massive breakthrough in Germanic scholarship on the *Novelle,* at the very moment when the genre has been superseded, if not replaced, by the short story and overshadowed by the drama, the radio play (*Hörspiel*), the novel, and lyric poetry.

Even though the theory of the novella has never attained the coherence and general acceptance of the structure of two literary forms closely related to it, the drama (q.v.) and the ballad, its individual ingredients, though weighted very differently, have long been identified: above all, the "unheard-of occurrence that has actually happened" (Goethe), its sharp profile (Heyse's "silhouette" and "falcon"), and its reversal (Tieck's "Wendepunkt") closely related to the "peripeteia" of the drama.

What a novella relates must be unique, or at least very striking, but realistic; it must be dramatic not only in creating tension but also in the objectivity of its presentation. Here the novella comes close to the journalistic news story, and it is by no means accidental that two of the finest German novellas, Kleist's *Marquise von O.* (1810-11; The Marquise von O., 1929) and Keller's *Romeo und Julia auf dem Dorfe* (1856; A Village Romeo and Juliet, 1897), as well as one of the most successful ones, Zweig's (q.v.) *Amokläufer* (1922; Amok, 1931), are (in fact or allegedly) based on newspaper stories. The decline of the novella in the 20th c. is, in part, attributable to the usurpation by newspapers of human-interest stories.

The novella is, then, originally a news item (genuine or doctored or invented) designed to divert a mixed, refined audience temporarily displaced and disturbed by ill fate (e.g., the plague in the *Decamerone,* war in Goethe's *Unterhaltungen*). The tales are told by various tellers who constitute the frame of the work. This is still the structure of Goethe's *Unterhaltungen deutscher Ausgewanderten* (1794-95; Recreations of German Emigrants, 1854); with some modifications, of C. F. Meyer's *Hochzeit des Mönchs* (1884; The Monk's Wedding, 1887), which has reduced story and teller to one but preserved the aristocratic nature of the audience; and Theodor Storm's *Schimmelreiter* (1888; The Ride of the White Horse, 1913-15), which is likewise content with one teller, has subjected the auditors to a bourgeois metamorphosis but preserved, like Meyer, Goethe, and Boccaccio before him, the original purpose of distracting them from ominous happenings. The purpose of the storytelling, the mixed character of the gourmet audience, the social obligation not to monopolize the "conversation" nor to intrude with personal feelings bound to embarrass the company, have determined, far beyond the "frame" and the originally assumed conditions of novella-telling, lasting features of the genre: a fluent, cultivated manner of relating; avoidance of extremes, whether melodramatic or vulgar, likely to make the mixed audience uncomfortable; stress on diversion of a sophisticated nature, not excluding the risqué but ennobling it by smooth presentation; relative brevity so as not to bore the listeners; stress on events rather than on subjective interpretation or preaching; perfection of vocabulary and style; tautness and limpidity of organization; and the discharge of audience tension through a *pointe,* the crowning last sentence of the novella, often with an ironic twist, derived from the usually witty *pointe* of the anecdote, mother of the novella.

How has this entrenched novellistic tradition fared in the 20th c.? The "frame" has survived in many variations, but is no longer central to the structure of the novella and, indeed, has not been so since Kleist. It still serves a purpose, if a perfunctory one, in G. Hauptmann's (q.v.) *Der Ketzer von Soana* (1918; The Heretic of Soana, 1923), where it is a moat protecting the author (alias editor) of a shocking story from possible recriminations of the public, or, more usefully, in Zweig's *Amokläufer,* where it helps in bridging the gap between an eerie story and the reader and becomes artistically significant in its own right, as it had done in the *Schimmelreiter* and as it will do,

more emphatically still, in Zweig's *Schachnovelle* (1942; The Royal Game, 1944). On a far higher level of existential, artistic, and novellistic import, Musil (q.v.) uses the realistic and politically tinged frame of the *Amsel* (1928) to bring out the mystic message of the three experiences related (see Wiese [1962], pp. 299-318).

In *Der Ketzer von Soana, Amokläufer,* and *Schachnovelle* the frame has changed from the third person singular to the first; in T. Mann's (q.v.) *Mario und der Zauberer* (1930; Mario and the Magician, 1930), to the half-objective, half-subjective first person plural. The change to the "I" occurs in a good many 20th c. novellas with or without frames; Hofmannsthal's (q.v.) version of the *Erlebnis des Marschalls von Bassompierre* (1900; An Episode in the Life of the Marshal de Bassompierre, 1952), Hesse's (q.v.) novelistic tale *Die Marmorsäge* (1907), Kafka's (q.v.) *Ein Landarzt* (1919; A Country Doctor, 1940), Schnitzler's (q.v.) *Fräulein Else* (1924; Eng., 1925), and Musil's *Amsel.* The turn to the "I" in the age of impressionism and introspection is not surprising, but has not necessarily resulted in the loss of distance between teller and tale essential to the novella. The "I" form has also aided in preserving, while modifying, the oral tinge of the novella, its "registering aloud," its fresh immediacy, a kind of apparent disorderedness and incoherence (amazingly coherent, however, by hindsight) which maintains the rigorous obligation of the novella to tell what "happened" whether the teller understands it or not. *Mario und der Zauberer* offers a particularly sophisticated example of studied improvisation on the part of an author, or rather "reporter," who is still "confused" by a jarring occurrence. "If I knew the meaning, I would not need to tell you the story," says Musil in the next to the last sentence of *Amsel.* And he concludes: "But it is as if you heard a whisper or merely a rustling without being able to differentiate between the two." In an age of fragmentation and atomization, centripetal symbolism dissolves into centrifugality and allegorism. The symbol becomes a token, a signal (v. Wiese, pp. 21 ff., 299 ff.). Dream and reality are interchangeable (ibid., pp. 307-8). The novella seems to move back in the direction of the fairy tale (Kafka, Musil), with which it had long entertained largely unexplored links (Boccaccio, Wieland, Goethe, Tieck, Brentano, Chamisso, Keller).

Psychological depth-probing, the possibility,

even probability, that everything points to every-thing (v. Wiese, p. 310), is dangerous if not fatal to the novella unless accompanied by the puritanic control of language of a Kafka, the exceptional literary finesse of a T. Mann, or the somnabulent artistic tact of a Schnitz-ler and a Musil. Certain elements of 20th c. existence—its cult of violence, the potential absurdity of life—have, to be sure, provided *novella* writers with new or intensified media of expression revitalizing the novella though artistically dangerous to a strict form. Among these are exacerbated irony, grotesque playful-ness, dogged limitation to a small symptomatic segment of experience, the shrinking of symbols, open-endedness of experience and form, and layers of camouflage over the point of the story (see v. Wiese [1963], p. 75). All these features, however, lend themselves as well, and prob-ably better, to the short story. The "unheard-of" of the novella has become very usual in our cataclysmic age (Erné, p. 109); the short story derives some of its most telling effects from surviving shreds of the usual (e.g., a kitchen clock) emphasizing the chaos, the brokenness of postwar life (Borchert [q.v.]). "Moreover, the degree of identification which a modern short story demands is incomparably greater than any demand of the sort among the stories of the *Decameron*" (Valency, [1960], p. 20).

What remains, in the 1960's, vital in the structure of the novella? The basic require-ment of an "unheard-of actual happening" told with self-control, finesse, and objectivity per-sists, but the adventure tends to be more of an inward one. The unity formerly supplied by profiled action (silhouette, falcon) or, more ex-ternally, by a frame can now, in part, be ex-pressed by a unity of mood, of style. The exper-ience must be complete, not fragmentary as in the short story. The (particularly German) novella must continue to guard against moral-izing (except in the frame), theorizing, melo-dramatic wallowing in sentiment, and lyric ex-pansionism, against wordiness, excess of learnedness, and psychological implausibilities present in such highly heralded works as *Der Ketzer von Soana, Amokläufer,* Strauss's *Der Schleier* (1920), Wiechert's *Hirtennovelle* (1935), and Andres's (qq.v.) *Wir sind Utopia* (1943; We Are Utopia, 1955). Attempts to return to classic patterns of the novella (Ernst's *Der Weg zur Form* [1906], Binding, R. Huch, von LeFort, Schäfer, Scholz [qq.v.]) have been wholly (*Der*

Schleier) or partly (Bergengruen [q.v.], *Die drei Falken,* 1937) unsuccessful.

Musil's definition of the *Novelle* (1914) main-tains continuity with the novellistic tradition while adapting it to 20th c. existence: "A sudden, self-contained stimulation of the mind results in the *Novelle*" in which the writer should describe "something that befalls him, that shakes him up; nothing that was in you from birth, but a dispensation of destiny. In this one experience the world is suddenly plumbed, or his eyes turn inward; in this one example he believes he can see how everything is really: that is the experience [*Erlebnis*] of the *Novelle*" (*Tagebücher* [1955], p. 684). The more hopeless the struggle of the individual against demonic forces (Kunz, ca. 1834), the more admirable the artistic triumph of the author as the last and only remaining token of victory of order over chaos. The future of the novella, if there is to be one, lies in the direction of Kafka and Musil.

BIBLIOGRAPHY: Mitchell, R., *Heyse and his Predecessors in the Theory of the Novelle* (1915); Pongs, H., *Das Bild in der Dichtung,* Vol. II (1939); Papst, W., "Die Theorie der Novelle in Deutschland (1920-1940)," *Roma-nistisches Jahrbuch,* II (1949), 81-124; Lange, V., Introduction to *Great German Short Stories and Novels* (1952); Papst, W., *Novellentheorie und Novellendichtung. Zur Geschichte ihrer Antinomie in den romanischen Literaturen* (1953); Arx, B. v., *Novellistisches Dasein. Spielraum einer Gattung in der Goethezeit* (1953); Kunz, J., "Geschichte der deutschen Novelle vom 18. Jahrhundert bis auf die Gegen-wart," *Deutsche Philologie im Aufriß,* Vol. II (1954; 2nd ed., 1960); Silz, W., *Realism and Reality: Studies in the German Novelle of Poetic Realism* (1954); Wiese, B. v., *Die deutsche Novelle von Goethe bis Kafka,* Vol. I (1956; 7th ed., 1963); Lockemann, F., *Gestalt und Wandlungen der deutschen Novelle. Geschichte einer literarischen Gattung im neunzehnten und zwanzigsten Jahrhundert* (1957); Stein-hauer, H., Introduction to *Die deutsche Novelle* (1958); Koskimies, R., "Die Theorie der Novelle," *Orbis Litterarum,* XIV (1959) 65-88; Valency, M., Introduction to *The Palace of Pleasure* (1960); Klein, J., *Geschichte der deutschen Novelle von Goethe bis zur Gegen-wart* (4th ed., 1960); Martini, F., "Die deutsche Novelle im 'bürgerlichen Realismus,'" *Wirken-des Wort,* X (1960); 257-78; Bennett, E., and

Waidson, H., *A History of the German Novelle* (2nd ed., 1961); Doderer, K., "Novelle," in *Lexikon der Weltliteratur,* Vol. II (1961); Erné, N., *Kunst der Novelle* (2nd ed., 1961); Wiese, B. v., *Die deutsche Novelle von Goethe bis Kafka,* Vol. II (1962); Himmel, H., *Die Novelle im Zeitalter der Massenschicksale* (1963); Wiese, B. v., *Novelle* (1963)

HENRY H. H. REMAK

NUŠIČ, Branislav

Serbian dramatist and essayist, b. 8 Oct. 1864, Belgrade; d. there, 19 Jan. 1938

N. studied law, was a consular official for ten years, and then stage director. Familiar with the world of the theater since his youth, N. paid his tribute to contemporary taste with plays in the style of Ibsen (q.v.) and Hermann Sudermann (1857-1928): among others, *Pučina* (1901). He also wrote historical dramas and patriotic travel books in the exalted spirit of the national revolution (*Knez Ivo od Semberije,* 1900; *Nahod,* 1923). However, his talent had full play only in his socially critical

comedies, humorous sketches, political satires, and *feuilletons,* which for several decades made him the most popular Serbian writer. N. drew his material from Belgrade, with its colorfully jumbled society caught in an abrupt transition from the narrowness of village life to the bustle of European civilization.

FURTHER WORKS: *Pripovetke jedne kaplara* (1886); *Sumnjivo lice* (1888); *Protekcija* (1889); *Listici* (1889); *Narodni poslanik* (1896); *Tako je moralo biti* (1900); *Običan čovek* (1900); *Pučina* (1901); *Kosovo* (2 vols., 1902 ff.); *Opštinsko dete* (1902); *Svet* (1906); *Ben-Akiba* (1907); *Hadži Loja* (1908); *Put oko sveta* (1910); *Autobiografija* (1924); *Gospodja ministarka* (1929); *Hadzi loja* (1908); *Ožalošćena porodica* (1934); *Analfabeta* (1935); *Sabrana dela* (25 vols., 1935-38); *Dr.-Doktor* (1936); *Pokojnik* (1937); *Odabrana pozorišna dela* (2 vols., 1951)

BIBLIOGRAPHY: Kadić, A., *Contemporary Serbian Literature* (1964); Nikolić, M., "Die Entstehung des serbischen Nationaltheaters im 19. Jahrhundert," in *Maske und Kothurn,* XII (1966), 203-209

STANISLAUS HAFNER

Date Due
